lonely planet

Southeastern
Europe

Slovenia
p485

Croatia
p171

Bosnia &
Hercegovina
p69

Serbia
p457

Romania
p395

Montenegro
p367

Kosovo p325

Bulgaria
p113

Albania
p36

Macedonia
p337

Turkey
p525

Greece
p235

THIS EDITION WRITTEN AND RESEARCHED BY

Marika McAdam,

Alexis Averbuck, James Bainbridge, Mark Baker,

Chris Deliso, Peter Dragicevich, Mark Elliott, Tom Masters,

Craig McLachlan, Anja Mutić, Tamara Sheward

914.304
504

BRIAN HAGIWARA/GETTY IMAGES ©

GREEK CUISINE P316

JEAN-PIERRE LESCOURRET/GETTY IMAGES ©

AYA SOFYA, İSTANBUL,
TURKEY P531

ON THE ROAD

Contents

ON THE ROAD

Contents

SURVIVAL GUIDE

welcome to Southeastern Europe

Ripe for Adventure

Your timing couldn't be better. Countries that were once hard going have oiled the infrastructure and rolled out the welcome mat. Cities that once made headlines for all the wrong reasons are now impressing with their diversity and authenticity. Landmarks that were all but obliterated in the 1990s – such as Mostar's iconic 16th century stone bridge and Dubrovnik's Old Town walls – have been painstakingly resurrected. Beyond the sights to be seen though, it's the unabashed hospitality that makes each day spent in Southeastern Europe surprising. A quiet lunch by yourself can quickly morph into dinner by the seaside with enthusiastic locals who won't hear of you not trying everything on the menu. This is a region brimming with fresh adventures, more accessible than ever before.

Great Outdoors

Rocky mountains and terracotta towns plunge spectacularly into the Adriatic Sea along the Croatian and Albanian Riviera. Greece and Turkey make the most of Aegean islands, which boast the perfect marriage of azure waters and blinding white buildings. Parts of Southeastern Europe have been luring outdoor adventurers for centuries, but some pockets are only now being added to adrenalin junkies' do-before-you-die lists. Dramatic

JEAN-PIERRE LESCOURRET/GETTY IMAGES ©

Cobblestone streets, fairy tale forests, wine regions, medieval towns, sandy beaches, ancient ruins, cosmopolitan capitals, spice bazaars, haunted castles and a couple of thousand islands. Adventure, anyone?

(left) St Stephen's Square (p212), Hvar Island, Croatia
(below) Church detail, Sofia (p116), Bulgaria

DOUG MCKINLAY/GETTY IMAGES ©

mountains like Romania's Bucegi, Bulgaria's Rodopi and Albania's ominous 'Accursed Mountains' are made for hiking and biking, while there are wild rivers to raft in Bosnia and Hercegovina as well as Slovenia. For those who would rather just absorb the great outdoors than set out to conquer it, some of the ferry rides in Southeastern Europe glide you past idyllic scenery incomparable to any in the world.

Home to History

Though change is coming on quickly, timeless traditions and cultural customs aren't falling by the wayside. Blood feuds in some parts aren't as ancient as they ought to be and pastoral scenes are still as home grown as they ever were. It's a region where you can barely keep up with the nightlife, but will still get stuck behind a horse and cart. Urban landscapes are a pop-up book of ancient architecture on a grand scale, and winding Ottoman streets are punctuated by Austro-Hungarian villas and the occasional communist concrete block. Throw in Gothic castles, Roman ruins and Venetian facades, then wrap it all in a medieval wall and plonk it by the sea. History isn't just ancient in Southeastern Europe, it's epic. This was the home of the Spartans, the birthplace of Zeus, and the battle ground of the Byzantine and Ottoman Empires; a stroll through town can evoke the rise and fall of civilisations.

❯Southeastern Europe

BERLIN ❂

GERMANY

❂ **WARSAW**

POLAND

Transylvania, Romania
Medieval and possibly
haunted castles (p408)

CZECH REPUBLIC

PRAGUE ❂

Pristina, Kosovo
Southeastern Europe's
newest capital (p328)

Mostar, Bosnia & Hercegovina
Newly restored old
bridge (p86)

SLOVAKIA

CARPATHIAN MOUNTAINS

Suceava ◉

Mt Triglav, Slovenia
Majestic views from
Slovenia's highest peak (p505)

VIENNA ❂ ❂**BRATISLAVA**

Kiskorei-vistarolp

Bistrita ◉

Iaşi ◉

BUDAPEST ❂

Cluj-Napoca ◉ **ROMANIA**

HUNGARY **TRANSYLVANIA**

Szeged ◉

Timişoara ◉ **Sibiu** ◉ ◉ **Braşov**

AUSTRIA

Mt Triglav ▲**LJUBLJANA**

Pécs ◉

ZAGREB

Sava

SERBIA

Novi Sad ◉

BUCHAREST ❂

Trieste ◉

◉**Rijeka**

BOSNIA & HERCEGOVINA

BELGRADE ❂

Craiova ◉

Pula ◖

SAN MARINO ❂

Zadar ◖

CROATIA

SARAJEVO ❂

Niš ◉ **SOFIA** ❂ **STARAPLANINA**

Montana ◉ *Danube* **BULGARIA**

Adriatic Islands, Croatia
Cloud nine just off
the coast (p212)

Split ◉ ◖ **Mostar**

Brač
Hvar

KOSOVO

Kârdzhali ◉

Rodopi Mountains

Dubrovnik ◉ Kotor ◖ **PRISTINA** ❂

PODGORICA ❂

MONTENEGRO ◉ Shkodra

SKOPJE ❂

MACEDONIA

❂**ROME**

Adriatic Sea

TIRANA ❂

◉**Ohrid**

Dubrovnik, Croatia
Views of city and sea from
Dubrovnik's formidable
city walls (p218)

Berat ◉ ◉**Korça**

ITALY

ALBANIA

Aegean Sea

◉ **Meteora**

Corfu ◖

Tyrrhenian Sea

GREECE

ATHENS ❂

Bay of Kotor, Montenegro
Rock ramparts defend
Montenegro's pièce
de résistance (p370)

Ionian Sea

Cyclades Islands

Berat, Albania
The 'town of a thousand
windows' (p51)

Ionian Islands

Cret

Meteora, Greece
Monasteries perched on
rocky pinnacles (p263)

Ohrid, Macedonia
Holy lake and picture-
perfect church (p349)

MEDITERRANEAN SE

20°E

0 | 400 km
0 | 200 miles

UKRAINE

Black Sea Beaches, Bulgaria
White sands on the Black Sea (p149)

CHIȘINĂU

MOLDOVA

Crimea

GEORGIA

Tulcea

Danube Delta

Constanța

Black Sea

40°E

Varna

Burgas

İstanbul, Turkey
East and West fall in love (p527)

Fırat

Murat

Istanbul

Sea of Marmara

★ANKARA

TURKEY

Ephesus

Euphrates

SYRIA

✪NICOSIA

LEBANON

Dodecanese Islands

CYPRUS

30°E

JORDAN

ISRAEL & THE PALESTINIAN TERRITORIES

14 TOP EXPERIENCES

Ancient Landmarks, Greece

1 From Athens' renowned Acropolis to the skeletal remains of Knossos, Greece (p235) offer some of Europe's most impressive historical sights. There's the oracular Temple of Apollo at Delphi, perched above the Gulf of Corinth; Olympia, home to the first Olympic Games; Epidavros acoustically perfect theatre; and the mystical Sanctuary of Asclepius. Olive and orange groves surround the vast ruins of Mystras, a one-time part of the Byzantine Empire. Start with the Acropolis and follow the path of history all over Greece's landscape. The Parthenon, Athens

İstanbul, Turkey

2 Straddling Europe and Asia, İstanbul (p527) is one of the world's greatest cities. Once the capital of the Byzantine and Ottoman Empires, its heritage can still be seen in the buildings which cluster around Sultanahmet, including the Aya Sofya, Blue Mosque, Topkapı Palace and Grand Bazaar. After marvelling at their glittering interiors, it's time to experience this 13-million-strong metropolis' vibrant contemporary life. Cross the Galata Bridge, passing ferries and fish kebap stands, to Beyoğlu, full of chic rooftop bar and rowdy taverns. Nightlife in Beyoğlu

RICARDO DE MATTOS/GETTY IMAGES ©

Bay of Kotor, Montenegro

3 There's a sense of secrecy and mystery to the Bay of Kotor (p370). Grey mountain walls rise steeply from steely blue waters, getting higher and higher as you progress through their folds to the hidden reaches of the inner bay. There, ancient stone settlements hug the shoreline, with Kotor's ancient alleyways concealed in its innermost reaches, behind hefty stone walls. Talk about drama! But you wouldn't expect anything else of the Balkans, where life is exuberantly Mediterranean, lived full of passion on these ancient streets.

Meteora, Greece

4 Meteora's (p263) towering rock spires are a stunning natural sight in their own right, but even more incredible are the elaborate 14th-century monasteries built on top of them. There were originally 24 monasteries (one for each pinnacle) though nowadays only six remain, accessible by stairs cut into the rock. Make the ascent and you're rewarded with breathtaking views of the surrounding landscape and, on quiet days, a sense of almost otherworldly serenity. For a completely different experience, Meteora's vertical peaks provide superb rock climbing. Monastery of Agias Varvaras Rousanou

JEAN-PIERRE LESCOURRET/GETTY IMAGES ©

ERIC NATHAN/ALAMY ©

DANITA DELIMONT/GETTY IMAGES ©

Pristina, Kosovo

5 Kosovo hasn't yet found its way onto the travel trail in Europe. Until recently it was shrouded in a veil of controversy, the smell of conflict lingering in the air and burnt out buildings hovering like a bad conscience. Nowadays Pristina (p328) is a who's who of European and international organisations. The cosmopolitan population bustles between the bars and restaurants, while the 'New Born' statue in the midst of it all still stands tall, resolutely symbolising the forward-facing momentum of the country.

Walking the Old City Walls, Dubrovnik, Croatia

6 Get up close and personal with the city by walking Dubrovnik's spectacular city walls (p218). No visit is complete without a leisurely stroll along these ramparts, the finest in the world and Dubrovnik's main claim to fame. Built between the 13th and 16th centuries, they are still remarkably intact today and the vistas over the terracotta rooftops and the Adriatic Sea are sublime, especially at dusk when the sundown turns the hues dramatic and the panoramas unforgettable.

TRAVELER1116/GETTY IMAGES ©

Island Hopping in the Adriatic, Croatia

7 From short jaunts between islands to overnight rides along the length of the Croatian coast, travelling by sea is a great and inexpensive way to see the Croatian side of the Adriatic (p201). Take in the scenery of this stunning coastline as you whiz past some of Croatia's 1244 islands – if you have cash to splash, take it up a couple of notches and charter a sailboat to see the islands in style, propelled by winds and sea currents.
Korčula Island (p215)

Berat, Albania

8 This wine-producing region's town (p51) reigns supreme in terms of Ottoman-style wonder and magic. From the river, look up at the multi-windowed white and black Unesco-listed houses, then wander up the cobblestone paths to take a closer look. Meander through the living and breathing castle area – complete with a museum filled with stunning iconography by Onufri. Stay in Berat's Ottoman-style hostel or one of the two traditional-homes-turned-hotels and go for an evening walk along the promenade for a truly enlivening experience.

Ohrid, Macedonia

9 Whether on the way down from Ohrid's stoic medieval castle, coming up through the Old Town's stone laneways, or gazing at the restored Plaošnik, every visitor pauses at Sveti Jovan at Kaneo, a church set high on a bluff overlooking the lake. From this prime spot for absorbing Ohrid (p349), one can gaze upon sublime architecture, idling sunbathers and distant fishing skiffs – all framed by the rippling green of Mt Galičica to the southeast and the endless expanse of lake stretching out everywhere else. Church of Sveti Jovan at Kaneo

Dragačevo Trumpet Assembly, Guča, Serbia

10 Otherwise a typical Serbian village, each August the hamlet of Guča morphs into an orgiastic den of cacophonous revelry for the Dragačevo Trumpet Assembly (p476), where musicians play brass instruments in a frenetic fashion unlike anywhere else on earth. Hundreds of orchestras descend on Guča to show off their skills; appreciative crowds dance through the streets and plaster money on the musicians' sweaty foreheads. This is Serbia personified: uninhibited, joyful, wild... and very, very loud.

10

Castles & Mountains of Transylvania, Romania

11 The region that inspired Bram Stoker to create Dracula is bound to have some seriously spooky castles, and Transylvania (p408) certainly doesn't disappoint. Monumental Bran Castle, south of Braşov, is suitably vampiric, but our favourite haunt has to be the 13th century Râşnov fortress not far down the road. The castles are nestled high amid the Carpathians, a relatively under-explored mountain range that is ideal for outdoor activities, including hiking, mountain biking and skiing. Bran Castle (p416)

Mt Triglav & Vršič Pass, Slovenia

12 For such a small country, Slovenia has got it all: charming towns, great wines, a Venetian-inspired seashore and, most of all, mountains. The highest peak, Mt Triglav (p505), stands particularly tall in local lore. Indeed, the saying goes that you're not really Slovene until you've climbed to the top. If time is an issue and you're driving, head for the high-altitude Vršič Pass, which crosses the Julian Alps and leads down to the sunny coastal region in one hair-raising, spine-tingling hour.

JOSE FUSTE RAGA/GETTY IMAGES ©

Black Sea Beaches, Bulgaria

13 Sun, sand and sea might not be what you associate with Southeastern Europe, but Bulgaria's Black Sea coast (p149) has plenty of great beaches. The pristine sands of resorts like Sunny Beach and Golden Sands attract international tourists with nightlife and water sports, while the resort towns of Varna and Burgas have long stretches of beach on their doorstep. If you want to escape the crowds, head south to elegant Tsarevo, or far north for remote sandy beaches. Kiten beach (p160), south of Sozopol

Mostar, Bosnia & Hercegovina

14 If the 1993 bombardment of Mostar's (p86) iconic 16th century stone bridge underlined the heartbreak of Yugoslavia's brutal civil war, its painstaking reconstruction has come to symbolise a peaceful post-conflict era. The charming Ottoman quarter has been especially convincingly rebuilt and is once again a delightful patchwork of stone mosques, souvenir peddlers and inviting cafes, besieged by tourists in summer. You can still find bombed out buildings, but these seem to have become an almost organic part of the townscape. Stari Most (Old Bridge)

need to know

Buses

» Not always luxurious but mostly reliable, even in remote areas. Offer glimpses of stunning scenery in mountainous areas.

Trains

» Some epic overnight train journeys await in this region. Major cities are well connected but services are patchy in regional areas.

When to Go

Dry climate
Warm to hot summers, mild winters
Mild to hot summers, cold winters
Cold climate

Sarajevo
GO May–Jun

Belgrade
• GO May–Aug

Bucharest
GO May–Sep

İstanbul
GO Apr–May

Dubrovnik
GO May–Sep

Sofia
GO Mar–Sep

Athens
• GO Apr–Jun

Your Daily Budget

Budget less than
€40

» Hostel beds for as little as €10

» Self-catering is easy everywhere

» Save by sleeping in private rooms and campsites

Midrange
€40–150

» Midrange hotels average about €50 per night

» Standard restaurant meals for about €10

» Comfortable train travel in 'soft' sleepers

Top end over
€150

» Upwards of €100 for top end, prime-view hotel

» Prime dishes in a fine restaurant about €25

» Hire cars about €30 per day

High Season
(Jun–Aug)

» High temperatures and balmy evenings.

» Hotels will be more expensive; book in advance, particularly by the beach.

» Big draws like Dubrovnik, Croatian and Greek Islands, Athens and İstanbul will be crowded.

Shoulder
(Apr–Jun & Sep–Oct)

» Prices drop and crowds dwindle.

» The weather remains mild and warm.

» All up, the best time to travel in Southeastern Europe.

Low Season
(Nov–Apr)

» Hotel prices drop to their lowest.

» Days can be dark and cold.

» Many attractions and coastal towns all but close.

» Time to hit the ski slopes!

Driving

» Outside Albania, Bosnia and Hercegovina and Kosovo roads are generally good, though drivers aren't always. Note where hire cars can't be taken. Drive on the right.

Ferries

» Sometimes over-crowded people movers between islands, sometimes highlights in their own right. Be early and patient in high season. Book ahead on popular routes.

Bicycles

» Some magnificent routes to ride, but long-distance cyclists are still a novelty in parts. Motorists aren't yet as cycle-cautious as they should be.

Planes

» Competitive fares for connections between hubs throughout the region and with Western Europe. Internal flights aren't as common, nor as necessary.

Websites

» **Lonely Planet** (www.lonelyplanet.com/europe) Destination information, hotel bookings, traveller forum and more.

» **Hostels.com** (www.hostels.com) Budget accommodation in a couple of clicks.

» **Visit Europe** (www.visiteurope.com) Practice advice and useful links.

» **Southeast European Times** (www.setimes.com) Region-specific economics and politics.

» **BBC News** (www.bbc.co.uk/news/world/europe) Find out what's going on before you arrive.

Money

» The euro is used in Greece, Kosovo, Montenegro and Slovenia.

» Countries that don't use the euro are Albania (lekë), Bosnia and Hercegovina (convertible mark), Bulgaria (lev), Croatia (kuna), Macedonia (Macedonian denar), Romania (Romanian lei), Serbian (Serbian dinar) and Turkey (Turkish lira).

» Euro, US dollars and British pounds are easiest to exchange.

» ATMs are widespread, with some rural exceptions. See individual country chapters for more information.

Visas

» Citizens of many countries (including Australia, Canada, UK, USA, New Zealand and Japan) generally don't require a visa for stays of up to 90 days in Albania, BiH, Croatia, Greece, Kosovo, Macedonia, Montenegro, Romania, Serbia and Slovenia. Other nationals should contact embassies or consulates.

» Australian, Canadian, UK and US citizens do need a visa for Turkey – buy it on arrival.

Arriving

Many travellers arrive in Southeastern Europe by train, bus or car. Air hubs include:

» **İstanbul, Ataturk International Airport** Half-hourly buses 4am to 1am; frequent metro and tram services

» **Belgrade, Nikola Tesla airport** Half-hourly buses 4am to 12am

» **Athens, Eleftherios Venizelos International Airport** Frequent 24hr buses; metro 5.30am to 11.30pm

» **Zagreb, Zagreb Airport** Hourly Croatia Airlines bus

What to Take

» **Travel insurance** covering all the activities you're planning and some you're not

» **GPS devices** with the right maps, particularly for drivers and cyclists

» **Classic travel literature** for epic overland journeys

» **Swiss army knife** (not in your hand luggage) for slicing cheese and popping corks

» **European plug adapter** for your gadgets

» **Unlocked mobile phone** keep costs low with local SIM cards (don't forget the charger)

» **Set of smart clothes** for visiting monasteries, as well as for the odd evening out

» **A decent-sized shawl or sarong** to cover your shoulders in the sun and your head in Orthodox Churches and mosques. Also doubles as an emergency towel, sheet or blanket

» **Enough SD cards** for your camera to allow for unbridled snap happiness

if you like...

Sun, Sand & Sea

Many people don't associate Southeastern Europe with beaches, but this region boasts coasts along the Adriatic, Ionian, Aegean, Mediterranean and Black Seas. Blue waters lap up to medieval towns, and there are still some secluded sandy spots to be found.

Island hopping, Croatia 1244 islands clutter up the clear waters of the Adriatic Sea; flit between them on a yacht (p171)

Greek islands Blinding white buildings against startlingly blue waters, these floating patches of paradise look airbrushed and are neatly linked with ferries (p235)

Drymades Beach, Albania This white sandy beach is the backpacker's holy grail and the place to go on an otherwise built-up coastline (p55)

Black Sea Coast, Bulgaria There are beautiful beaches along the Black Sea Coast; skip the resort towns and head to Sozopol or Tsarevo and the quiet coves between (p149)

Turquoise Coast, Turkey This aptly-named coast shines with transparent waters, hidden coves and ancient ruins to explore (p564)

Outdoor Action

The relative affordability of adventures mean that Southeastern Europe is a playground for thrill seekers and outdoor aficionados. The region is as good for strapping on safety gear as it is for just kicking back and soaking up the great outdoors.

Bovec & Bled, Slovenia Happening hubs of extreme sports, from canyoning to paragliding (p500)

Lake Koman, Albania A memorable ferry in Albania's remote mountainous north (p49)

Great value skiing Increasingly serviceable and affordable, try Bjelašnica, Jahorina and Vlašić in Bosnia and Hercegovina (BiH) or Durmitor in Montenegro (p388)

Rafting & kayaking Paddle the Vrbas Canyons in BiH (p103) or Montenegro's Tara River (p388)

Bridge diving, BiH After some training (and at your peril), leap from Mostar's Stari Most (p86)

Shipwreck diving, Croatia A calcified 3rd century Roman ship is submerged off Croatia's Mljet Island (p216)

Plitvice Lakes National Park, Croatia Turquoise water, lush forest and waterfalls (p188)

Danube Delta, Romania Sprawling wetlands slathered with birdlife, where the Danube meets the Black Sea (p439)

Old Towns

You won't find slippery marble stones, cobbled squares, tangled back streets and crumbling walls quite like this anywhere but Southeastern Europe. Time spent lost in an Old Town is time well spent.

Dubrovnik, Croatia Marble-paved streets and glorious ocean views can be admired from Dubrovnik's resplendent city walls (p218)

Kotor, Montenegro Walled Kotor is dramatically wedged between the sea and the steeply rising grey mountainside (p372)

Rhodes, Greece This World Heritage–listed Old Town has 12m-thick medieval walls and vividly ancient atmosphere (bar the throngs of visitors) (p293)

Sarajevo, BiH Enjoy a Turkish coffee in the bustling old Turkish quarter of town (p72)

Antalya, Turkey Antalya's Roman-Ottoman old quarter, Kaleiçi, is a gateway to the Turquoise Coast and Turkish Riviera (p573)

Berat, Albania This meandering town with its Unesco-listed black and white houses is so consistently old that even the hostels are Ottoman-style (p51)

» Mykonos, Greece (p271)

Monasteries

Nothing screams Southeastern Europe like a medieval monastery perched on a cliff-top. Guarding centuries of history, monastic life goes on behind their ancient exteriors much as it ever did. Monastery-made produce for sale makes for special souvenirs.

Meteora, Greece Six 14th century monasteries spectacularly crown foreboding towers of rock. The mind boggles at the thought that there were once 24 (p263)

Ostrog Monastery, Montenegro Otherworldly Ostrog is built into a cliff-face 900m above the Zeta valley (p385)

Zrze Monastery, Macedonia This serene cliff-top monastery offers sweeping views of the Pelagonian Plain and is home to priceless Byzantine artwork (p358)

Southern Bucovina, Romania The intricately painted churches of Southern Bucovina are artistic and cultural monuments (p436)

Fruška Gora, Serbia The few visitors to the serene monasteries in Fruška Gora national park make for authentic exploration (p475)

Rila Monastery, Bulgaria Artistic and religious treasures are tucked in a forest valley a day trip from Sofia (p126)

Wining & Dining

The spread of culinary and liquid treats on offer is astounding, from freshly made local produce, to delicacies plucked from the ocean. Wines will also surprise for the low price tag relative to high palatability by any standard.

Istrian delights, Croatia Top eateries serve up truffles, wild asparagus and fresh seafood, with *rakija* (brandy) to start (p228)

Kebap, Turkey A Turkish staple, kebap can mean a classic *döner* or a more sophisticated *İskender*. Eat them all and become a kebap connoisseur (p598)

Seafood, Greece Swig on ouzo while snacking on grilled octopus; not a bad way to pack away some calories (p316)

Wine regions Have a glass or four of vino in Hercegovina (p95), the Bulgarian wine town of Melnik (p127), the Tikveš region of Macedonia (p358), and the Nemea region of Greece (p257)

Nightlife

Whatever your party pace, you'll find it here. This is a region where the sound spectrum spans from grungy urban dens to Balkan turbofolk, and from smooth bar tunes and smoky jazz clubs to beach parties.

Belgrade, Serbia One of the nightlife capitals of the world, Belgrade's eclectic party scene is limited only by imagination and the number of hours in the day (p468)

Ios & Mykonos, Greece There are party pockets dotted throughout the Greek islands; summer revellers flock to the bars and clubs of Ios (p279) and Mykonos (p271)

Hvar Town, Croatia It's incredible that Hvar island hasn't sunk with all the jumping up and down. There are also sublime beaches to recover on (p214)

Athens, Greece Things get going after midnight in Athens at bars, dance clubs and beachfront venues (p249)

Cluj-Napoca, Romania Cluj's historic back streets are crawling with friendly student party animals who will recruit you into their revels (p421)

month by month

January

As folk recover from Christmas and New Year celebrations, the winter cold sets in. If you can't beat it, better to embrace it by hitting the snow-covered mountains for white days and cosy nights.

Great-Value Skiing

Fresh snowfall means excellent conditions for skiing and snowboarding. After the first week of January most hotels offer their lowest annual rates, making skiing affordable for all. Try the Bosnian slopes at Bjelašnica and Jahorina, or Bulgaria's Mt Vitosha range or Bansko.

Küstendorf Film & Music Festival

Created and curated by Serbian director Emir Kusturica, this international indie-fest in the town of Drvengrad, near Zlatibor in Serbia, eschews traditional red-carpet glitz for oddball inclusions vying for the 'Golden Egg' prize.

February

The cold continues and towns can still be quiet, unless Carnival is being celebrated. Carnival can happen anywhere between late January and early March, depending on when Easter falls. Book accommodation in advance (particularly in Rijeka, Croatia).

Croatian Carnivals

Carnival is a big deal in parts of Croatia, with the Rijeka Carnival the most salubrious of them all. There are two weeks of pageants, street dances, concerts, masked balls, exhibitions and parades.

Strumica Carnival, Macedonia

Drawing several thousand visitors from Macedonia and elsewhere, the carnival involves five days of drinking, debauchery and costumed merry-making. It's a well-organised event with a masked ball, a special children's day, door-to-door parading and cash prizes for sophisticated costumes and floats.

March

Spring brings flowers and warmer weather to the Balkans, but there's still some unpredictable rainfall. Further north in Slovenia, the ski season kicks off with thrilling competitions on the ski slopes.

Ski Sports, Slovenia

Those who enjoy watching thrilling acrobatics on the ski slopes will enjoy the Vitranc Cup (www.pokal-vitranc.com) slalom competition in Kranjska Gora. Also consider the record-setting Ski-Jumping World Championships (www.planica.si) in Planica on the third weekend in March.

Kooky Kukeri, Bulgaria

Kooky by name and quirky by nature, this festival (also known as Pesponedelnik) features fearsome masked dancers dressed in shaggy fur outfits and bells who parade around Shiroka Lâka to ward off evil spirits.

April

Spring has arrived bringing mild temperatures and sunshine. Things can be busy at Easter; anticipate crowds and price hikes, and some memorable celebrations (particularly in Greece). Outside of the Easter period, hotel prices remain low.

Music Biennale Zagreb

Held over 10 days every odd-numbered year, Zagreb's Music Biennale (www.mbz.hr/eng) is Croatia's headline musical festival. Since it was established in 1961, it has grown in reputation and now attracts world-class performers from a range of musical persuasions.

May

Beautiful sunny weather makes this a wonderful time to visit the region. Life on the coast is starting up as hotels begin to open for the season and the festival calendar moves into top gear.

Druga Godba, Slovenia

Ljubljana's flamboyant festival of alternative and world music features everything from new jazz to contemporary folk music. Alongside a rich concert program, there are also film screenings, workshops, debates and seminars to attend.

Relive Bulgarian History

Military history fans should not miss the spectacular annual re-enactment of the 1876 April Uprising against the Turks in the charming mountain town of Koprivshtitsa, bizarrely held on the 1st or 2nd of May.

Rafting in Bosnia & Hercegovina

After the spring rains, May is the time for experienced rafters to head to the fast-flowing river gorges of Bosnia & Hercegovina (BiH), but if you're a beginner, stay away until summer when conditions are calmer.

June

Summer has arrived and with it comes hot, sunny weather and a full festival schedule. This is a great time for sunning yourself on the beach before the holiday hordes descend and prices soar.

Hartera Festival, Rijeka

Experience some of the best young rock bands and top indie acts from around Europe at this three-day underground festival in an abandoned paper factory in Rijeka, which has become the highlight of some peoples' year. The festival is sometimes held in July.

İstanbul Music Festival, Turkey

Catch a classical concert in a sultan's palace or jazz in a 4th-century church during İstanbul's month-long music fest. Hundreds of notable ensembles appear each year including the likes of the Vienna Philharmonic Orchestra.

Hellenic Festival, Greece

The ancient theatre in Epidavros and the Theatre of Herodes Atticus are the headline venues of Athens' annual cultural shindig. The festival (www.greekfestival.gr), which runs from mid-June to August, features music, dance, theatre and much more besides.

Oil-Wrestling Championships, Turkey

Huge crowds gather in Edirne in late June or early July to cheer greased-up wrestlers as they slap each other around during the Kirkpinar wrestling festival (www.kirkpinar.com), the world's oldest wrestling event.

July

Stake your claim early to get in on the action during July. Temperatures and crowds peak particularly in coastal resorts at the end of the month as school breaks up for the long summer vacation.

EXIT Festival, Serbia

Thousands of revellers enter the state of EXIT each July within the walls of the Petrovaradin Fortress in Novi Sad (www.exitfest.org). Book early for tickets, as international headlining acts draw music lovers from all over the continent.

Summer Festivals

Thousands flock to summer festivals throughout the region. Cultural events are held all over towns like

Zagreb, Ohrid, Ljubljana and Dubrovnik, to celebrate the best music, art, dance, theatre and literature on a backdrop of high spirits and balmy weather.

☆ Mostar Bridge Diving Competition, Bosnia & Hercegovina

Crowds throng the rocky banks of the Neretva River to watch daredevil divers leap off Mostar's iconic old bridge, Stari Most, and plunge into the green waters 21m below.

August

This is the hot height of summer, with many of the region's resorts packed out with holidaymakers and coast-bound roads jammed with traffic. Cities inland are quieter.

★ Sarajevo Film Festival

Since it grew out of the ruins of the '90s civil war, the Sarajevo Film Festival (www. sff.ba) has become one of the largest film festivals in Europe. Commercial and art-house flicks are showcased, mostly with English subtitles. Held in July or August.

☆ Dragačevo Trumpet Assembly, Guča, Serbia

One of the most exciting and bizarre events in all of Southeastern Europe, August sees hundreds of thousands of revellers descend on the tiny town of Guča to damage their eardrums, livers and sanity over four cacophonous days of revelry (www.guca.rs).

★ Terraneo Festival, Croatia

Croatia's newest festival has quickly become a summer highlight. This big five-day dance party, located in an old army barracks in Šibenik, draws in Croatian hipsters for its amazing line-up of international and local performers.

September

September is a lovely month to be beside the seaside. The summer crowds have gone back to work and taken peak prices with them, but it's still hot enough for swimming and hiking.

★ Dance with Slovenian Cows

Really. This mid-September salubrious weekend of folk dancing, music, eating, drinking and general merry-making in Bohinj marks the return of the cows from their high pastures to the valleys in ebullient Slovenian style.

🏃 Adventure Race, Montenegro

Montenegro's gruelling Adventure Race (www.adventuremacemontenegro.com) is not the only way to enjoy the Bay of Kotor's dramatic beauty, but it's certainly the toughest. Held in late September or early October, it involves an entire day of kayaking, mountain biking, trekking and orienteering.

November

November is a quiet time with not a whole lot going on. On the plus side, accommodation is cheap and readily available. Head south for a chance of sunshine or enjoy indoor attractions.

★ Martinje, Zagreb

The Feast of St Martin is an annual wine festival held in Zagreb to celebrate the end of the grape harvest as Croatian wineries begin the crushing process. Expect lots of wine, good food and high spirits.

★ Sarajevo International Jazz Festival, BiH

Reminding you that 'the best jazz is where you least expect it', this well-known and well-organised jazz festival (www.jazzfest.ba) packs out venues around Sarajevo in early November, as it showcases the best of local and international jazz talent.

December

The build up to Christmas is a jolly time, often marked by gift-giving, family get-togethers and midnight mass on the 24th of December. In the mountains, the ski season kicks off mid-month.

★ Tirana International Film Festival, Albania

Each December Tirana holds its annual film festival (www.tiranafilmfest.com), the only one of its kind in Albania. It brings together everything from feature films to short films, animated films and documentaries from Albania and abroad.

itineraries

Whether you've got 10 days or two months, these itineraries provide a starting point for the trip of a lifetime. Want more inspiration? Head online to lonelyplanet. com/thorntree to chat with other travellers.

Ten Days
Highlights in a Hurry

> For a taste of the Adriatic coast, base yourself in **Dubrovnik** for a few days. Spend a day in the Old Town enjoying resplendent views from the meticulously restored city walls. Get an early start on your second day for a day or overnight trip to **Mostar**, in Bosnia and Hercegovina, for a glimpse of the iconic Balkan bridge and to explore resurrected Ottoman, Orthodox and Austro-Hungarian architectural gems shining like new again. Next, head to nearby Montenegro for an overnight stay at the sublime **Bay of Kotor** with its majestic rock ramparts.

From Dubrovnik, fly to the thriving metropolis of **Athens**. After a couple of days exploring the ancient Acropolis and museums, move on to **Meteora** to boggle at 14th century monasteries perched on rocky cliff tops. Continue overland to lively **Thessaloniki**, with its Byzantine cultural treasures. Finally, take a bus or fly to the minaret-studded skyline of **İstanbul**, one of the greatest cities in the world. With the polished glamour of Europe and the exotic energy of Asia, İstanbul is the place to end your Southeastern Europe sojourn with thoughts of starting on the spice trail into the Middle East.

Southeastern Europe from A to T

> This ambitious overland odyssey takes in all twelve countries of the region from Albania to Turkey.

Start in **İstanbul**, at the juncture of East and West, before heading to **Antalya** on the 'Turkish Riviera'. Continue along the coast to the ancient Roman City of **Ephesus (Efes)**. Work your way through ruins along the coast, past the legendary town of **Troy** with a side trip to the WWI pilgrimage site of **Gallipoli**.

Back in İstanbul, cross into Bulgaria and enjoy the Black Sea, first at laid-back **Sozopol** and then further north at more dynamic **Varna**. After traipsing through **Rusenski Lom Nature Park**, make your way to the Romanian capital of **Bucharest** for a couple of days of city sightseeing. Explore mountains and castles from the Gothic town of **Braşov**, then via the Saxon town of **Sibiu**, keep moving to Serbia's heady capital, **Belgrade**.

If your timing is right, head north to the EXIT music festival in **Novi Sad**, and explore the mellow monasteries of nearby **Fruška Gora**. Make the overland journey across inland Croatia to **Zagreb**. From there, take a relaxing detour to Slovenia's capital **Ljubljana** and the nearby town of **Bled**. Now plunge directly south to **Rijeka** back into Croatia. Wind your way down the Dalmatian coast to **Zadar** and then **Split**, from where you can enjoy some island hopping.

From the walled city of **Dubrovnik**, detour into Bosnia and Hercegovina for the historic old town of **Mostar** and its rebuilt old bridge. Immerse yourself in the fascinating cultural fusions of **Sarajevo** before returning to the sea, this time at Montenegro's **Bay of Kotor**. Head inland to visit the awesome **Ostrog Monastery** then further north to the primeval forests of **Biogradska Gora National Park**. Now head to Kosovo and explore the tiny country's monasteries from **Pristina** before continuing to the historic Macedonian capital of **Skopje**, with its Ottoman and Byzantine architecture. Continuing southeast, explore the wineries of the **Tikveš region**. Via old world **Bitola**, go to **Ohrid** to see the other-worldly Church of Sveti Jovan at Kaneo, perched above the lake.

Moving on into Albania, take in the wild colours of **Tirana** before travelling south via the Unesco World Heritage–listed cities of **Berat** and **Gjirokastra**. Finally, take the ferry in **Saranda** to **Corfu** in Greece. Relax. You've earned it.

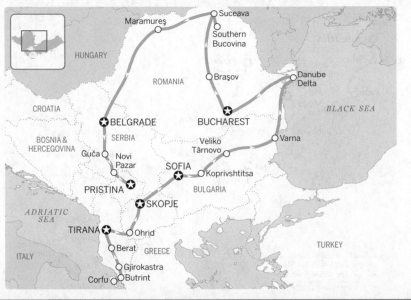

Six Weeks
Remote Ramblings

> One of the delights of Southeastern Europe is the fact that there are still remote regions to explore. This ramble through some of the more off-beat pockets of Southeastern Europe takes in bustling cities, rural towns and some waterside respite. This is the journey to embark on if you really want to get to know the region and its people.

After charging your batteries on the Greek beach of **Corfu**, take a ferry to Albania. Spend a couple of days exploring the ruins of **Butrint** and **Gjirokastra**, before continuing on to the picturesque Unesco-listed town of **Berat**. Move north into to the colourful Albanian capital of **Tirana** to soak up the cultural assets of the city.

Leaving Albania, head east into the mountains of Macedonia. Spend at least a couple of days in beautiful **Ohrid** for its picture-perfect monastery and some swimming in its eponymous lake. Make your way to the Macedonian capital of **Skopje** where Ottoman and Byzantine architecture meet in the streets.

From here, move overland to Bulgaria where your first obvious stop is **Sofia**, an underrated and accessible urban gem that offers access to the museum town of **Koprivshtitsa**. It gets even better east in **Veliko Târnovo**, the ancient capital dramatically set on a rapid river. From here, it's a cinch to get to the beach town of **Varna** on the Black Sea coast.

Continue up along the coast into Romania to experience its lush **Danube Delta**. When you crave company again, plunge into the urban eclecticism of **Bucharest**. Once you have had your fill of city life, base yourself for a couple of days in **Braşov** to take in the famed haunts of Transylvania. Head deeper into the rural heartland of Romania; using **Suceava** as a base, explore the peculiarly painted churches of **Southern Bucovina** and the last thriving peasant society of Europe in **Maramureş**.

Continue across the country towards Serbia, and return to the throngs of people in **Belgrade** to explore innumerable museums by day and clubs by night. Head south, and if your timing is right, experience the Dragačevo Trumpet Assembly of **Guča**. Continue down to **Novi Pazar** with its bizarre Turkish tones. If all is well at the border, cross into Kosovo and explore its monasteries from **Pristina**.

City to City via Sea
The Whole Shebalkan

Three Weeks
From City to City via Sea

Starting and ending in two of the great cities of the world, this delightful odyssey begins in **İstanbul**, which straddles East and West. Highlights of the city include Topkapı Palace, Aya Sofya and the Blue Mosque. Further along the Aegean coast, **Çanakkale** is a popular base for visiting **Gallipoli** – site of horrific loses during WWI – and the legendary town of **Troy**. Follow the coast to **Ephesus (Efes)** near Selçuk, which is home to the remains of the Temple of Artemis, one of the Seven Wonders of the Ancient World. From nearby Kuşadası, take a ferry 3km to the Greek island of **Samos**, a hub of Hellenic culture.

Now that you've hit the Greek Islands, start hopping! Sail south to **Naxos**, the largest and greenest of the Cyclades islands, on your way to **Santorini**, an Aegean gem with volcanic cliffs sheering up from the limpid blue sea. Stop at laid-back **Paros** and the popular beaches of Antiparos on your way north to much-visited **Mykonos**. Now jump on a ferry to **Piraeus** on the mainland, a 30-minute metro ride from **Athens**. Conclude your journey with a visit to the Acropolis, one of the most significant and iconic monuments in Europe.

Six Weeks
The Whole Shebalkan

Ease yourself into the Balkans with a laid-back start in the Slovenian capital of **Ljubljana**. After a side trip to picturesque **Bled**, plunge south for sea breezes on Croatia's dramatic Dalmatian Coast.

Starting in **Rijeka**, continue along the coast to marble-coated **Zadar**, then on to **Split** and architecturally awesome **Dubrovnik**. Detour into Bosnia and Hercegovina for the iconic Old Bridge of **Mostar** and the captivating capital city of **Sarajevo**. Plunge back to the beach, this time to Montenegro's **Bay of Kotor**. Continue south into Albania, and spend a couple of days in hectic **Tirana**; consider an excursion to **Berat**, the 'town of a thousand windows'. From Tirana, make your way overland via bus into Macedonia, for the holy lake of **Ohrid** and onwards to the Macedonian capital of **Skopje**. After soaking up the sights of Skopje, head to new kid on the block, Kosovo. Base yourself for a couple of days in **Pristina** to explore Kosovo's monasteries. After checking on the border situation to determine which routes into Serbia are currently the best, pick up the pace in **Belgrade**, a hub of history, culture and late-night hedonism.

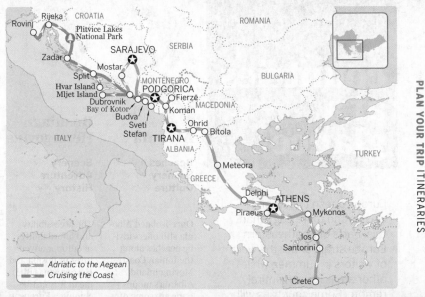

Adriatic to the Aegean
Cruising the Coast

Three Weeks
Adriatic to the Aegean

Two Weeks
Cruising the Coast

Embark on offbeat adventures between the Adriatic and Aegean Seas. First, walk along the magnificent walls of **Dubrovnik** and trip out to nearby islands. Then head into Bosnia and Hercegovina, stopping at **Mostar** on your way to **Sarajevo**. After enjoying the Turkish and Austrian stylings of the town, plunge south into Montenegro, visiting the **Bay of Kotor** on your way to **Podgorica**. In Albania, take the stunning Lake Koman ferry between the villages of **Koman** and **Fierzë**. Stop off in **Tirana** to experience the culture of the capital, before continuing on into Macedonia and the majestic monastery on **Lake Ohrid**. After pausing in the old world town of **Bitola** continue on into Greece.

Climb russet rock pinnacles to the exquisite monasteries of **Meteora**. Stop at the ruins of **Delphi** as you make your way down to the thriving metropolis of **Athens**. Spend two or three days taking in the unfathomably ancient Acropolis and visiting archaeological treasures of the town. Then, use the ferry hub of **Piraeus** as a gateway to access the islands of the Aegean. Consider heading to gay-mecca **Mykonos**, party island **Ios**, quintessential **Santorini**, or world-unto-itself **Crete**.

Take it easy along the Dalmatian Coast for a couple of weeks. Start in the cobblestoned fishing village of **Rovinj**, then take in the landscapes of cape Rt Kamenjak, near Pula, on your way to **Rijeka**. From here, detour to **Plitvice Lakes National Park** for its famed falls, then plunge down to **Zadar**, to wander through the slippery marble streets of the Old Town.

Keep cruising the coast to **Split**, home to the Diocletian's Palace and gateway to **Hvar Island**. After a few days on Hvar, continue down to **Dubrovnik**, with foreboding walls that are a crowning glory of the coast. From here, take a side trip to forest-covered **Mljet Island**.

If you still have time and can't get enough of the coast, leave Croatia and explore tiny but tantalising Montenegro, where historic towns line the limestone cliffs of the **Bay of Kotor**. Further along the Adriatic coast, you will find **Budva**, with its atmospheric Old Town and numerous beaches. Five kilometres south is the cherry on the coast, **Sveti Stefan**, with iconic terracotta roofs and views you could stare at all day.

countries at a glance

Europe doesn't get more classic and more edgy than this. Parts of Southeastern Europe strain under the weight of visitors in summer, while other areas remain entirely remote. Some countries will project you back to the birth of ancient civilisations, while in others you will bear witness to new nations finding their feet. It's impossible to generalise about a region as diverse as this one, with crumbling monasteries teetering on clifftops, upbeat urban capitals, otherworldly landscapes, decadent dining, world class wine, rugged mountains and rushing rivers all wrapped in ribbons of majestic coastline, sprinkled with thousands of paradisaical islands, and packed with memorable people who can't wait to welcome you.

Albania

Beaches ✓✓
Scenery ✓✓✓
Culture ✓✓

Once-isolated Albania still offers idyllic beaches along the Ionian Coast. Moving inland, Albania's mountains are some of Europe's most spectacular; the Koman ferry is possibly its most beautiful boat ride. Tucked away in far-flung landscapes, village life is still governed by traditions that have long been forgotten elsewhere; you may encounter sworn virgins and shepherds in these parts. Meanwhile, in Tirana, hip cafe culture rules the day and club culture takes hold of the night.

p36

Bosnia & Hercegovina

Scenery ✓✓
Adventure ✓✓✓
History ✓✓

The accessibility and affordability of outdoor adventures in Bosnia and Hercegovina (BiH) mean it is fast becoming a European hub for kayaking, skiing, hiking and mountain biking. Its mixed Muslim and Christian heritage is reflected in the food, culture and architecture. Rebuilt historical centres showcase its history; scars of recent horrors still show in parts, Socialist eyesores taint rural landscapes, Ottoman and Austro-Hungarian buildings loom in urban centres, and charming medieval castles are dotted around elsewhere.

p69

Bulgaria

Hiking ✓✓✓
Architecture ✓✓
Beaches ✓✓

The seaside towns of the Black Sea coast cater to varied tastes, offering both secluded retreats and thumping resorts. Away from the coast, Bulgaria's six mountain ranges make for spectacular and diverse hiking, not to mention cycling, mountaineering, wildlife watching and skiing. Picturesque country towns host churches and monasteries full of ancient icons and air dense with incense, and the crumbling remnants of ancient history are well showcased in the museums and galleries of the cities.

p113

Croatia

Coastline ✓✓✓
Food ✓✓
Scenery ✓✓✓

The Old Towns of Zagreb, Zadar, Split and Dubrovnik are full of fans, but take your time getting between them. The 1778km coastline of Croatia is lined with fantastical ancient towns, sleepy fishing villages, glitzy beaches and seafood restaurants. Off the coast, 1244 islands cater for almost anyone's idea of idyllic; eurochic yacht life sails past backpacker beach party ghettos. Istria's food and wine are decadent, while eight national parks showcase Croatia's extraordinary scenery.

p171

Greece

Monuments ✓✓✓
Islands ✓✓✓
Food ✓✓

There are many reasons that Greece is a do-before-you-die destination. Azure blue waters frame blinding white buildings on beguiling islands. Ferries glide between soft sandy beaches. Hearty tavernas serve seafood so fresh it's still flapping. People greet you and live life with gusto. As if this weren't enough, there's also the Acropolis, still stoically presiding over pulsating Athens, a stalwart icon of ancient civilisation and the life-source of Western culture.

p235

Kosovo

Architecture ✓
Monasteries ✓✓
Scenery ✓

Things aren't simple in Europe's newest country. International expats bustle around cosmopolitan Pristina with its mix of modern shops and Ottoman-style bazaars. Beyond the capital, Kosovo's Serbian monasteries have outstanding frescoes, age-old atmosphere and forbidding walls that have withstood the turbulence of times past. The hills around Peja are ideal for scenic hiking and skiing. A visit to Kosovo is not only fascinating, but also contributes to the country's emergence onto the European travel scene.

p325

Macedonia

Scenery ✓✓
Monasteries ✓✓
Adventure ✓

A Balkan-Mediterranean hybrid, Macedonia offers hassle-free travel through a spectrum of experiences. Lake Ohrid is rimmed by spectacular towns and swimming spots. Macedonia's Byzantine churches house important medieval art, while its monasteries are all about location, perched on cliff ridges or even built into cliff faces. Hikers, climbers and mountain bikers can enjoy panoramas over untouched mountain landscapes, while wine connoisseurs can savour a drop of vino with laidback locals among the seemingly endless vineyards.

p337

Montenegro

Scenery ✓✓✓
Bays ✓✓✓
Adventure ✓✓

Size isn't everything. Montenegro crams a lot into a small space, including resplendent sandy beaches, luxury retreats, extreme sports, jagged mountain peaks, dramatic gorges and charming old towns wrapped in a Mediterranean climate. The cherry on top is the Bay of Kotor, where rugged mountains and orange-roofed ancient towns emerge dramatically from the sea. Hikers gravitate to Montenegro's impressive national parks, while rafters paddle their way through the sheer walls of the Tara Canyon.

p367

Romania

Mountains ✓✓✓
Villages ✓✓
Monasteries ✓✓

Rural Romania is home to village life and peasant societies that endure here like nowhere else. The Carpathian Mountains offer some of Europe's finest (and least crowded) hiking; Southern Transylvania's Saxon villages are guardians of ancient churches; and the painted monasteries of Southern Bucovina are among the region's most outstanding artistic achievements. Added to this are Gothic medieval castles and citadels, and in-your-face bustling Bucharest, which makes for an entirely unique and utterly fascinating travel destination.

p395

Serbia

Culture ✓✓
Contrasts ✓✓
Parties ✓✓✓

The sounds emanating from the clubs of Belgrade, the all-out edgy EXIT festival, and the Dragačevo Trumpet Assembly in Guča are reinventing Serbia's old image as the bad boy of the Balkans. Serbians don't do things by halves; the hospitality is palpable and the diversity is unexpected. With art nouveau architecture up north, Turkish-toned Novi Pazar down south, Roma communities dotted between and Serbian Orthodoxy throughout, Serbia is a place to unlearn what you think you know.

p457

Slovenia

Scenery ✓✓✓
Outdoor Sports ✓✓
Architecture ✓✓

More than half of Slovenia is covered in forest, making it an outdoor playground for energetic grown ups who head to Bovec and Bled to ski, hike, climb and canyon. There are a multitude of ways to experience the Slovenian Alps and the scenic prizes it awards. Architectural offerings are surprisingly eclectic too; Gothic churches, baroque palaces and art nouveau buildings are in pristine condition in Ljubljana, a charming gateway from Western to Southeastern Europe.

p485

Turkey

History ✓✓✓
Ruins ✓✓✓
Beaches ✓✓✓

From the evocative ruins of Ephesus to the sumptuous beaches on the Turquoise Coast, Turkey is a seductive mix of Mediterranean charm and Eastern promise. See-it-to-believe-it Cappadocia seems like a piece of another planet, and places like Mt Nemrut and Olympos fantastically fuse natural splendour and ancient achievement. Europe and Asia fuse in İstanbul, a veritable capital of cosmopolitanism, where sky-high bars and minarets tower over chic cafes and bustling bazaars.

p525

> Every listing is recommended by our authors, and their favourite places are listed first

> Look out for these icons:

 TOP CHOICE Our author's top recommendation

A green or sustainable option

FREE No payment required

See the Index for a full list of destinations covered in this book.

On the Road

Albania

Why Go?

Albania has natural beauty in such abundance that you might wonder why it's taken 20 years for the country to take off as a tourist destination since the end of a particularly brutal strain of communism in 1991. So backward was Albania when it emerged blinking into the bright light of freedom that it needed two decades just to catch up with the rest of Eastern Europe. Now that it arguably has done so, Albania offers a remarkable array of unique attractions, not least due to this very isolation: ancient mountain codes of behaviour, forgotten archaeological sites and villages where time seems to have stood still are all on the menu. With its stunning mountain scenery, a thriving capital in Tirana and beaches to rival any elsewhere in the Mediterranean, Albania has become the sleeper hit of the Balkans. But hurry here, as word is well and truly out.

Best Places to Eat

- » Kujtimi (p60)
- » Era (p43)
- » Tradita G&T (p47)
- » Oda (p43)

Best Places to Stay

- » Tradita G&T (p47)
- » Hotel Rilindja (p48)
- » Hotel Mangalemi (p53)
- » Hotel Kalemi (p59)

When to Go
Tirana

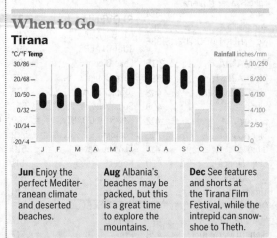

Jun Enjoy the perfect Mediterranean climate and deserted beaches.

Aug Albania's beaches may be packed, but this is a great time to explore the mountains.

Dec See features and shorts at the Tirana Film Festival, while the intrepid can snowshoe to Theth.

Connections

Albania has excellent connections in all directions: daily buses go to Kosovo, Montenegro, Macedonia and Greece. The southern seaport of Saranda is a short ferry trip from Greece's Corfu, while in summer ferries also connect Himara and Vlora to Corfu. Durrës has regular ferries to Italy. Travellers heading south from Croatia can pass through Montenegro to Shkodra (via Ulcinj), and loop through Albania before heading into Macedonia via Pogradec or Kosovo via the Lake Koman Ferry or new super-fast Albania–Kosovo highway. There are, however, no international train routes from Albania.

ITINERARIES

One Week

Spend a day in busy Tirana, checking out the various museums as well as the Blloku bars and nightclubs. On day two, head up the Dajti Express cable car and then make the two-hour trip to the Ottoman-era town of Berat. Spend a few nights in Berat, before continuing down the coast for a couple of days on the beach in Himara or Drymades. Loop around for one last night in charming Gjirokastra before returning to Tirana.

Two Weeks

Follow the first week itinerary and then head north into Albania's incredible 'Accursed Mountains'. Start in Shkodra, from where you can get transport to Koman for the stunning morning ferry ride to Fierzë. Continue the same day to the charming mountain village of Valbonë for a couple of nights, before trekking to Theth and spending your last couple of nights in the beautiful Theth National Park.

Essential Food & Drink

» **Byrek** Pastry with cheese or meat.
» **Fergesë** Baked peppers, egg and cheese, and occasionally meat.
» **Midhje** Wild or farmed mussels, often served fried.
» **Paçë koke** Sheep's head soup, usually served for breakfast.
» **Qofta** Flat or cylindrical minced-meat rissoles.
» **Sufllaqë** Doner kebab.
» **Tavë** Meat baked with cheese and egg.
» **Konjak** Local brandy.
» **Raki** Popular spirit made from grapes.
» **Raki mani** Spirit made from mulberries.

AT A GLANCE

» **Currency** lekë
» **Language** Albanian
» **Money** ATMs in most towns
» **Visas** Most visitors don't need one – a 90-day stamp is issued at the border

Fast Facts

» **Area** 28,748 sq km
» **Capital** Tirana
» **Country code** ☎355
» **Emergency** Ambulance ☎127, fire ☎128, police ☎129

Exchange Rates

Australia	A$1	114.59 lekë
Canada	C$1	107.95 lekë
Euro Zone	€1	140.19 lekë
Japan	¥100	116.24 lekë
New Zealand	NZ$1	91.85 lekë
UK	UK£1	165.99 lekë
USA	US$1	109.70 lekë

Set Your Budget

» **Budget hotel** €10–15 per person
» **Two-course meal** €8
» **Museum entrance** €1–3
» **Beer** €1.50
» **City transport ticket** 30 lekë

Resources

» **Albania-Hotel** (www.albania-hotel.com)
» **Balkanology** (www.balkanology.com/albania)
» **Journey to Valbona** (www.journeytovalbona.com)

Albania Highlights

1 Catch the **Lake Koman Ferry** (p49) through stunning mountain scenery, then continue to **Valbonë** and trek the 'Accursed Mountains'.

2 Explore the Unesco World Heritage–listed museum towns of dramatic **Berat** (p51), the so-called 'city of a thousand windows'.

3 Catch some sun at **Drymades** (p55), just one of the many beaches on the south's dramatic Ionian Coast.

4 Travel back in time to the ruins of **Butrint** (p58), hidden in the depths of a forest in a serene lakeside setting.

5 Feast your eyes on the wild colour schemes and experience the hip Blloku cafe culture in **Tirana** (p39).

6 Take a trip into the traditional Southern Albanian mountain town of **Gjirokastra** (p59), with is spectacular Ottoman-era mansions and impressive hilltop fortress.

TIRANA

♪04 / POP 764,000

Lively, colourful Tirana is the beating heart of Albania, where this tiny nation's hopes and dreams coalesce into a vibrant whirl of traffic, brash consumerism and unfettered fun. Having undergone a transformation of extraordinary proportions since it awoke from its communist slumber in the early 1990s, Tirana is now unrecognisable, with its buildings painted in horizontal primary colours, and public squares and pedestrianised streets a pleasure to wander.

Trendy Blloku buzzes with well-dressed *nouvelle bourgeoisie* hanging out in bars or zipping between boutiques, while the city's grand boulevards are lined with fascinating relics of its Ottoman, Italian and communist past – from delicate minarets to loud socialist murals. Tirana's traffic does daily battle with both itself and pedestrians in a constant scene of unmitigated chaos. Loud, crazy, colourful and dusty – Tirana is never dull.

◉ Sights

The centre of Tirana is Skanderbeg Sq, a large traffic island with an equestrian statue of the Albanian national hero at its centre. Running through the square is Tirana's main avenue, Blvd Zogu I, which becomes Blvd Dëshmorët e Kombit (Martyrs of the Nation Blvd) south of the square. At the street's northern end is Tirana's train station; head to the other end and you're at the small Tirana University building.

NORTH OF THE RIVER

Sheshi Skënderbej SQUARE
(Skanderbeg Sq) Skanderbeg Sq is the best place to start witnessing Tirana's daily goings-on. Until it was pulled down by an angry mob in 1991, a 10m-high bronze statue of Enver Hoxha stood here, watching over a mainly car-free square. Now only the **equestrian statue of Skanderbeg** remains, deaf to the cacophony of screeching horns as cars four lanes deep try to shove their way through the battlefield below.

TOP CHOICE **National History Museum** MUSEUM
(Muzeu Historik Kombëtar; Sheshi Skënderbej; adult/student 200/60 lekë; ⊙10am-5pm Tue-Sat, to 2pm Sun) The largest museum in Albania holds most of the country's archaeological treasures and a replica of Skanderbeg's massive sword (how he held it, rode his horse and fought at the same time is a mystery). The mosaic mural entitled *Albania* adorning the museum's facade shows Albanians victorious and proud from Illyrian times through to WWII. The collection is almost entirely signed in English and takes you chronologically from ancient Illyria to the postcommunist era. The highlight of the museum is a terrific exhibition of icons by Onufri, a renowned 16th-century Albanian master of colour. A disturbing and very important gallery devoted to those who suffered persecution under the communist regime is the most recent addition to the collection, though frustratingly almost none of this display is in English.

National Art Gallery GALLERY
(Galeria Kombëtare e Arteve; www.gka.al; Blvd Dëshmorët e Kombit; admission 200 lekë; ⊙10am-6pm Mon-Sat) Tracing the relatively brief history of Albanian painting from the early 19th century to the present day, this beautiful space also has temporary exhibits that are worth a look. Downstairs there's a small but interesting collection of 19th-century paintings depicting scenes from daily Albanian life, while upstairs the art takes on a political dimension with some truly fabulous examples of Albanian socialist realism.

Et'hem Bey Mosque MOSQUE
(Sheshi Skënderbej; ⊙8am-11am) To one side of Skanderbeg Sq, the 1789–1823 Et'hem

BUNKER LOVE

On the hillsides, beaches and generally most surfaces in Albania, you will notice small concrete domes (often in groups of three) with rectangular slits. Meet the bunkers: Enver Hoxha's concrete legacy, built from 1950 to 1985. Weighing in at 5 tonnes of concrete and iron, these little mushrooms are almost impossible to destroy. They were built to repel an invasion and can resist full tank assault – a fact proved by their chief engineer, who vouched for his creation's strength by standing inside one while it was bombarded by a tank. The shell-shocked engineer emerged unscathed, and tens of thousands were built. Today, some are creatively painted, one houses a tattoo artist, and some even house makeshift hostels.

Tirana

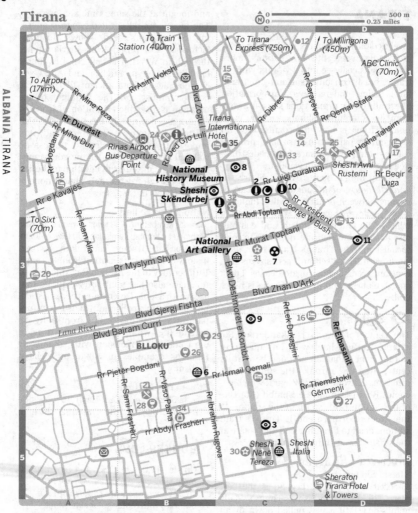

Bey Mosque was spared destruction during the atheism campaign of the late 1960s because of its status as a cultural monument. Small and elegant, it's one of the oldest buildings left in the city. Take your shoes off to look inside at the beautifully painted dome.

Clock Tower TOWER
(Kulla e Sahatit; Rr Luigj Gurakuqi; admission 100 lekë; ⊙9am-1pm Mon, 9am-1pm & 4-6pm Thu; 🛜) Behind the mosque is the tall clock tower, which you can climb for impressive views of the square. Further on up the street, look for

the socialist realist **statue of the Unknown Partisan.**

Palace of Culture NOTABLE BUILDING
(Pallate Kulturës; Sheshi Skënderbej) To the east of Sheshi Skënderbej is the white stone Palace of Culture, which has a theatre, shops and art galleries. Construction of the palace began as a gift from the Soviet people in 1960 and was completed in 1966, years after the 1961 Soviet–Albanian split.

Fortress of Justinian RUINS
(Rr Murat Toptani) If you turn up Rr Murat Toptani, behind the National Art Gallery,

Tirana

◉ **Top Sights**

National Art Gallery C3
National History Museum B2
Sheshi Skënderbej B2

◉ **Sights**

1 Archaeological Museum C5
2 Clock Tower C2
3 Congress Building C5
4 Equestrian Statue of Skanderbeg C2
5 Et'hem Bey Mosque C2
6 Former Residence of Enver
  Hoxha B4
7 Fortress of Justinian C3
8 Palace of Culture C2
9 Pyramid C4
10 Statue of the Unknown Partisan C2
11 Tanners' Bridge D3

◉ **Activities, Courses & Tours**

12 Outdoor Albania C1

◉ **Sleeping**

13 Brilant Antik D3
14 Capital Tirana Hotel C2
15 Freddy's Hostel C1
16 Green House C4
17 Hostel Albania D2
18 Hotel Serenity A2
19 Rogner Hotel Europapark Tirana C4

20 Tirana Backpacker Hostel A3

◉ **Eating**

21 Era B4
   Green House .... (see 16)
22 Oda D2
23 Patisserie Française B4
24 Piazza B2
25 Stephen Centre D2

◉ **Drinking**

26 Charl's B4
27 Kaon Beer Garden D4
28 Radio B4
29 Sky Club Bar B4

◉ **Entertainment**

30 Academy of Arts C5
   Folie .... (see 31)
31 Kinema Millennium 2 .... C3
32 Theatre of Opera & Ballet C2

◉ **Shopping**

Adrion International Bookshop ..... (see 8)
33 Market C2
34 Natyral & Organik B5

ⓘ **Transport**

Avis .... (see 19)
35 Hertz C2

you'll pass the 6m-high walls of the Fortress of Justinian, the last remnants of a
Byzantine-era castle. These days half a cin-
ema/nightclub overflows over the top. East
from here, on the corner of Rr Presidenti
George W Bush and the Lana River, is **Tanners' Bridge**, a small 19th-century slippery-
when-wet stone bridge.

SOUTH OF THE RIVER

Pyramid   NOTABLE BUILDING
(Blvd Dëshmorët e Kombit) Designed by En-
ver Hoxha's daughter and son-in-law and
completed in 1988, this monstrously un-
attractive building was formerly the Enver Hoxha Museum, and more recently a
convention centre and nightclub. Today,
covered in graffiti and surrounded by the
encampments of Tirana's homeless, its
once white marble walls are now crumbling but no decision on whether to demol-
ish or restore it appears to have yet been
reached.

Congress Building   NOTABLE BUILDING
(Blvd Dëshmorët e Kombit) Another creation of
the former dictator's daughter and son-in-
law is the square Congress Building, just a
little down the boulevard from the Pyramid.
Follow Rr Ismail Qemali two streets north
of the Congress Building and enter the once
totally forbidden but now totally trendy
Blloku area. This former Communist Party
elite hang-out was opened to the general
public for the first time in 1991. Security
still guards the **former residence of Enver
Hoxha** (cnr Rr Dëshmorët e 4 Shkurtit & Rr Ismail
Qemali).

Archaeological Museum   MUSEUM
(Muzeu Arkeologik; Sheshi Nënë Tereza; admission
100 lekë; ☺10.30am-2.30pm Mon-Fri) The collection here is comprehensive and impressive in parts, but there's no labelling in any
language, nor tours in English offered, so
unless this is your field, you may find yourself a little at a loss to get much out of the

museum. A total renovation is on the cards, but as one staff member pointed out to us, they've been waiting for this since 1985, so don't hold your breath.

Martyrs' Cemetery   CEMETERY

At the top of Rr Elbasanit is the Martyrs' Cemetery, where some 900 partisans who died in WWII are buried. The views over the city and surrounding mountains (including Mt Dajti to the east) are excellent, as is the sight of the immense, beautiful and strangely androgynous Mother Albania statue (1972). Hoxha was buried here in 1985 but in 1992 he was exhumed and interred in an ordinary graveyard elsewhere. Catch a municipal bus heading up Rr Elbasanit; the grand driveway is on your left.

☞ Tours

Get off the beaten track or discover Albania's tourist attractions with a Tirana-based tour company.

Albanian Experience   TOURS

(☑2272 055; www.albania-experience.al; Sheshi Italia, Sheraton Tirana Hotel) Organises tours of Albania with knowledgeable guides.

Outdoor Albania   TOURS

(☑2227 121; www.outdooralbania.com; Rr Sami Frasheri, Pallati Metropol) Excellent trailblazing adventure tour agency offering hiking, rafting, snowshoeing, sea and white-water kayaking and, in summer, hikes through the Alps.

✸ Festivals & Events

Tirana International Film Festival CINEMA
(www.tiranafilmfest.com) This festival is held each late November/early December and features both short and feature films from its international competition winners, as well as new cinematic work from Albanian filmmakers.

⌁ Sleeping

TOP CHOICE Brilant Antik   HOTEL €€
(☑2251 166; www.hotelbrilant.com; Rr Jeronim de Rada 79; s/d €50/60; ✳☎) This charming house-cum-hotel has plenty of character, a central location and welcoming English-speaking staff to ease you into Tirana life. Rooms are spacious, decently furnished with the odd antique, and breakfast downstairs is a veritable feast each morning.

Rogner Hotel Europapark Tirana   HOTEL €€€
(☑2235 035; www.hotel-europapark.com; Blvd Dëshmorët e Kombit; s €150-180, d €170-210, ste €240-290; ✳@☎✺) With an unbeatable location in the heart of the city, the Rogner is a peaceful oasis with a huge garden, tennis court and facilities such as banks, travel and car-rental agencies. The rooms are spacious, extremely comfortable and come with flat-screen TVs.

Green House   BOUTIQUE HOTEL €€€

(☑068 2072 262, 4521 015; www.greenhouse.al; Rr Jul Variboba 6; s/d €80/90; ✳☎) In a cool spot in Tirana sits this modern 10-room hotel with downlit, stylish rooms that might be the city's coolest. Its sprawling downstairs terrace restaurant is a friendly expat hang-out with a varied menu and a long wine list. It looks up at one of Tirana's quirkiest buildings.

TOP CHOICE Tirana Backpacker Hostel   HOSTEL €
(☑068 3133 451, 068 4682 353; www.tiranahostel.com; Rr Myslym Shyri, Vila 7, behind Alpet petrol station; dm €13, d €40, without bathroom €28; ✳☎) Albania's first ever hostel now boasts very smart new premises in the centre of town, and looks more like a fancy restaurant than a hostel at first glance. There are three six-bed dorms, all with their own facilities, and several comfortable doubles, including one with a great balcony. All rooms are equipped with air-con, but you'll need to pay €3 extra per room per night to turn it on. The place is very social, with a busy bar-restaurant downstairs and plenty of atmosphere.

Capital Tirana Hotel   HOTEL €€

(☑2258 575, 069 2080 931; www.capitaltiranahotel.com; Rr Qemal Stafa; s/d €40/65; P✳☎) Opened in 2012, this thoroughly modern 29-room hotel just a stone's throw from Skanderbeg Sq is a welcome addition to Tirana's accommodation scene. It may be a little sterile and businesslike, but the rooms are of good quality with flat-screen TVs and minibars, staff are very helpful and the location on a busy shopping street is great.

Hostel Albania   HOSTEL €

(☑067 2783 798; www.hostel-albania.com; Rr Beqir Luga 56; dm €11-12, d €30; @☎) This hostel has small four- and six-person dorms, though the basement's 14-bed dorm (€11) is the coolest spot in summer and dividers hide the fact that there are so many bunks down there. Zen space is in the outdoor shoes-off oriental lounge, and a filling breakfast with filter coffee is included. The artist owners provide great information about the local art scene, and the location is central.

Freddy's Hostel
HOTEL €

(☎2266 077, 068 2035 261; www.freddyshostel. com; Rr Bardhok Biba 75; dm €12, r €32-56; ❋ ❀) Freddy's is run by a friendly family whose knowledge of the city is second to none. The clean, basic bunk-free rooms have lockers and come in different configurations. Breakfast isn't included with the cheapest dorm places, but the central location is hard to beat. The owners can also arrange long-term apartment rentals.

Hotel Serenity
HOTEL €€

(☎2267 152; Rr Bogdani 4; s/d €25/40; ❋@❀) This villa-style hotel in a side street in central Tirana has a semi-boutique feel with stylish rooms and contemporary fittings. Despite the busy main road nearby, this is a quiet location. Rooms have tiled floors, minibars and TVs, and offer excellent value. Breakfast is not included.

Milingona
HOSTEL €

(☎069 2070 076, 069 2049 836; www.milingona-hostel.com; Rr Risa Cerova 197/2, off Rr Dibres; tent €7, dm €11-12, d €30; @❀) Now in a new location a 15-minute walk from Skanderbeg Sq, 'the Ant' takes up a large house in a residential district and is cared for by multilingual sisters Zhujeta and Rozana. There are large dorms (sleeping six and eight people), each of which shares facilities with another dorm on the same floor. There's a large shared kitchen, a living room, a roof terrace and a garden. To get here from the centre, walk up Rr Dibres, and when it splits, bear right after the Medresa, and Rr Risa Cerova is the first street on the right.

✖ Eating

Most of Tirana's best eating is in and around Blloku, a square of some 10 blocks of shops, restaurants, cafes and hotels situated one block west of Dëshmorët and along the Lana River in south Tirana.

TOP CHOICE Era
ALBANIAN, ITALIAN €€

(☎2266 662; www.era.al; Rr Ismail Qemali; mains 300-700 lekë; ◷11am-midnight; ✐) This local institution serves traditional Albanian and Italian fare in the heart of Blloku. The inventive menu includes oven-baked veal and eggs, stuffed eggplant, pizza, and pilau with chicken and pine nuts. Be warned: it's sometimes quite hard to get a seat as it's fearsomely popular, so you may have to wait. Delivery and takeaway are both available.

TOP CHOICE Oda
ALBANIAN €€

(Rr Luigj Gurakuqi; mains 350-550 lekë; ◷noon-11pm) Bright flashing lights will guide you to this endearing little restaurant down a lane where you can choose from two brightly lit dining rooms or an atmospheric terrace. The place is stuffed full of traditional Albanian arts and crafts, and while its popularity with travellers means you won't feel like you've discovered a truly authentic slice of the country, the delicious menu and pleasant atmosphere make it well worth a visit.

Piazza
ITALIAN €€

(Rr Ded Gjo Luli; mains 400-700 lekë; ◷noon-11pm) Behind the national museum, this restaurant consistently gets rave reviews from visitors who enjoy the formal service, the stylish interior and the fine Italian cuisine. The fish is the speciality here, and it's cooked to perfection, while the wine list has some excellent local vintages.

Green House
ITALIAN €€

(Rr Jul Variboba 6; mains 400-800 lekë) Downstairs from the small eponymous hotel, the Green House boasts an enviable terrace that hums with the buzz of the local Blloku crowds day and night. The menu is strongly Italian leaning, but there are Albanian and other international dishes too.

Patisserie Française
BAKERY €

(Rr Dëshmorët e 4 Shkurtit 1; pastries from 150 lekë; ◷8am-10pm; ❀) This popular Blloku cafe has has an array of sweet pastries, macaroons and sandwiches plus good coffee to boot. It's a good breakfast option.

Stephen Centre
CAFE €€

(Rr Hoxha Tahsim 1; mains 400-700 lekë; ◷8am-8pm Mon-Sat; ❀) If you like your fries thin, your wi-fi free and the spirit Christian, here's the cafe for you. A veritable institution in Tirana, the Stephen Centre also offers accommodation upstairs in single-bed configurations (single/double €35/50).

🍷 Drinking

Most of Tirana's nightspots are concentrated in the Blloku neighbourhood, and most will have you partying on to the wee hours.

Radio
BAR

(Rr Ismail Qemali 29/1) Set back from the street is this very cool yet understated and friendly bar. Check out the owner's collection of antique Albania-made radios while sipping cocktails with groovy locals.

Charl's
BAR

(Rr Pjetër Bogdani 36) Charl's is a consistently popular bar with Tirana's students because of its ever-varying live music on the weekends, and disco/dance crowd-pleasers the rest of the time. The relaxed vibe is enhanced by the bar's open-air garden.

Kaon Beer Garden
BEER HALL

(Rr Asim Zeneli; ⊙noon-1am) For those who hate the hassle of ordering beer after beer, here's Kaon. Its popular 'keg-on-the-table' approach means it can be hard to get a table in the evening (queuing is normal), but once you get in, it's a pleasant outdoor bar and restaurant in the fancy villa-filled part of town. You won't go hungry; Albanian meals start from 200 lekë. Locally brewed beer comes in standard glasses, or tabletop 2- and 3-litre 'roxys'.

Sky Club Bar
BAR

(Rr Dëshmorët e 4 Shkurtit, Sky Tower) Start your night here for spectacular city views from the revolving bar on top of one of the highest buildings in town.

☆ Entertainment

There is a good choice of entertainment options in Tirana, in the form of bars, clubs, cinema, performances, exhibitions and even 10-pin bowling. For the low-down on events and exhibitions, check posters around town. For alternative events, ask at Milingona hostel and Hostel Albania.

TOP CHOICE Tirana Express
GALLERY, MUSIC

(www.tiranaekspres.wordpress.com; Rr Karl Gega) This fantastic nonprofit arts project has converted a warehouse behind Tirana's semi-derelict train station into an arts space that hosts revolving temporary exhibits, concerts, installations and other events that appeal to Tirana's arty, alternative crowd. Go along and see what's on during your visit. Opening hours vary depending on what's on.

Folie
CLUB

(Rr Murat Toptani) This is where the big-name DJs come to play, and though the crowd can be a little more concerned with being seen than actually enjoying themselves, it's a great outdoor venue for a loud night out.

Kinema Millennium 2
CINEMA

(Rr Murat Toptani; tickets 300-500 lekë) Current-release movies that are cheaper the earlier in the day you go. At night it's a nightclub.

Theatre of Opera & Ballet
THEATRE

(☑2224 753; www.tkob.al; Sheshi Skënderbej; tickets from 350 lekë; ⊙performances from 7pm, from 6pm winter) Check the listings and posters outside the theatre for performances.

Academy of Arts
THEATRE

(☑2257 237; www.artacademy.al; Sheshi Nënë Tereza) Classical music and other performances take place throughout the year in either the large indoor theatre or the small open-air faux-classical amphitheatre; both are part of the university. Prices vary according to the program.

🛍 Shopping

Souvenir shops on Rr Durrësit and Blvd Zogu I sell red Albanian flags, red T-shirts, red lighters, bunker ashtrays and lively traditional textiles.

🍃 Natyral & Organik
FOOD & DRINK

(Rr Vaso Pasha) This tiny store in Blloku not only supports small village producers by stocking their organic olive oil, honey, herbs, tea, eggs, spices, raki and cognac (these make great gifts, but be aware of customs regulations in the countries you're travelling through), it's also a centre for environmental activism.

Market
FOOD & DRINK

(Sheshi Avni Rustemi) Buy fruit, vegetables and deli produce here; nearby Rr Qemal Stafa has secondhand stalls selling everything from bicycles to bedheads.

Adrion International Bookshop
BOOKS

(Sheshi Skënderbej, Palace of Culture; ⊙9am-9pm Mon-Sat) The place to head for maps, guides and English-language books.

ⓘ Information

Tirana has plenty of ATMs linked to international networks.

ABC Clinic (☑2234 105; www.abchealth.org; Rr Qemal Stafa 260; ⊙9am-1pm Mon, Wed & Fri, to 5pm Tue & Thu) Has English-speaking Christian doctors and a range of services, including brief (600 lekë) and normal (1200 lekë) consultations.

Hygeia Hospital Tirana (☑2390 000; www. hygeia.al; Tirana-Durrës Hwy) This new Greek-owned private hospital has a 24-hour emergency department.

Post Office (Rr Çameria; ☺8am-8pm) A shiny and clean oasis in a street jutting west from Sheshi Skënderbej. Smaller offices operate around the city.

Tirana in Your Pocket (www.inyourpocket. com) Has a local team of writers providing up-to-date coverage of Tirana. It can be downloaded free or bought at bookshops, hotels and some of the larger kiosks for 500 lekë.

Tirana Tourist Information Centre (☑2223 313; www.tirana.gov.al; Rr Ded Gjo Luli; ☺9am-5pm Mon-Fri, to 2pm Sat) Friendly staff make getting information easy at this government-run initiative just off Skanderbeg Sq.

❶ Getting There & Around

There's now a good network of city buses running around Tirana costing 30 lekë per journey (payable to the conductor), although most of the sights can be covered easily on foot.

Air

The modern **Nënë Tereza International Airport** (Mother Teresa Airport; ☑2381 800; www. tirana-airport.com.al) is at Rinas, 17km northwest of Tirana. The Rinas Express airport bus operates an hourly (8am to 7pm) service from Rr Mine Peza on the western side of the National History Museum for 250 lekë one way. The going taxi rate is 2000 to 2500 lekë. The airport is about 20 minutes' drive away, but plan for possible traffic jams.

Bicycle

This was the main form of transport for Albanians until the early 1990s, and it's having a comeback (cyclists seem to make more headway in Tirana's regular traffic snarls). Bike hire is available from several hostels.

Bus

You have the option of buses or *furgons* (minibuses). There is no official bus station in Tirana, though there's a makeshift bus station beside the train station where some buses drop passengers off and depart from. Confusingly, other buses and *furgons* depart from ever-changing places in and around the city, so check locally for the latest departure points. You can almost guarantee that taxi drivers will be in the know; however, you may have to dissuade them from taking you the whole way.

Furgons are usually slightly more expensive than buses and leave when full. Buses for Pristina in Kosovo (€20, five hours, three daily) leave from beside the museum on Blvd Zogu 1. To Macedonia, there are buses via Struga (€15, five hours) to Tetovo (€20, seven to eight hours) and Skopje (€20, eight hours) from the same spot. Buses to Ulcinj (€20) and Budva (€30) in Montenegro depart from 6am in front of the tourist information centre. If you're heading to Athens (€35, 15 hours), buses leave at around either 8am or 7pm from outside the travel agencies on Blvd Zogu 1. Most bus services are fairly casual; you turn up and pay the driver.

Car

Lumani Enterprise (☑04-2235 021; www. lumani-enterprise.com) is a local car-hire company. International companies in Tirana include the following (each also has an outlet at the airport):

Avis (☑2235 011; www.avis.al; Blvd Dëshmorët e Kombit, Rogner Hotel Europapark)

DOMESTIC BUSES FROM TIRANA

DESTINATION	PRICE (LEKË)	DURATION	DISTANCE (KM)
Berat	400	2½hr	122
Durrës	150	1hr	38
Elbasan	300	1½hr	54
Fier	400	2hr	113
Gjirokastra	800	7hr	232
Korça	600	4hr	181
Kruja	150	30min	32
Pogradec	500	3½hr	150
Saranda	1200	7hr	284
Shkodra	300	2hr	116
Vlora	500	4hr	147

Europcar (☑2227 888; www.europcar.com; Rr Durrësit 61)

Hertz (☑2262 511; www.hertzalbania.com; Sheshi Skënderbej, Tirana Hotel International)

Sixt (☑068 2068 500, 2259 020; Rr e Kavajës 116)

Taxi

Taxi stands dot the city, and taxis charge 300 to 400 lekë for a ride inside Tirana and 600 lekë at night and to destinations outside the city centre. Reach agreement on price with the driver before setting off. **Radio Taxi** (☑224 4444), with 24-hour service, is particularly reliable.

Train

The rundown train station is at the northern end of Blvd Zogu I. Albania's trains range from sort of OK to very decrepit, and as a result Albanians only tend to travel by train if they can't afford the bus. Seven trains daily go to Durrës (70 lekë, one hour). Trains also depart for Elbasan (190 lekë, four hours, 2.10pm), Pogradec (2km out of town; 295 lekë, eight hours, 5.30am), Shkodra (145 lekë, 3½ hours, 1.15pm) and Vlora (250 lekë, 5¾ hours, 4.25pm). Check timetables at the station the day before travelling. Purchase tickets before hopping on the train.

AROUND TIRANA

Just 25km east of Tirana is **Mt Dajti National Park** (1611m). It is the most accessible mountain in the country, and many Tiranans go there to escape the city rush and have a spit-roast lamb lunch. A sky-high, Austrian-made cable car, **Dajti Express** (www.dajtiekspres.com; return 700 lekë; ☉9am-9pm Tue-Sun), takes 15 minutes to rise to (almost) the top. It's a scenic trip over bunkers, forest, farms and hilltops. Once there, you can avoid all the touts and their minibuses and take the opportunity to stroll through lovely, shady beech and pine forests. There are grassy picnic spots along the road to the right, but if you didn't pack a picnic, try the lamb roast and spectacular views from the wide terrace of the **Panorama Restaurant** (mains 500 lekë).

To get to the Dajti Express departure point, take the public bus from outside Tirana's clock tower to 'Porcelain' (30 lekë). From here, it's a 1.5km walk uphill, or you can wait for a free bus transfer. Taxis seem to charge what they want to the Dajti Express drop-off point, but the trip from Tirana should only cost 600 lekë. It's also possible to drive or cycle to the top.

NORTHERN ALBANIA

Northern Albania is a scenic wonderland where the incredible landscape of the 'Accursed Mountains' dominates and the rich and independent mountain culture strongly flavours all journeys. The north also boasts rich wildlife around beautiful Lake Shkodra, not to mention the ancient city of the same name. This may be the Albania of blood feuds, but anyone visiting northern Albania will be amazed by how friendly and welcoming locals are.

Shkodra

☑022 / POP 95,000

Shkodra (Shkodër), the traditional centre of the Gheg cultural region, is one of the oldest cities in Europe. The ancient Rozafa Fortress has stunning views over the nearby lake, while a concerted effort to renovate the buildings in the Old Town has made wandering through Shkodra a treat for the eyes. Many travellers pass through here between Tirana and Montenegro, or en route to the Lake Koman Ferry and the villages of Theth and Valbonë, but it's worth spending a night to soak up this pleasant and welcoming place.

As the Ottoman Empire declined in the late 18th century, Shkodra became the centre of a semi-independent *pashalik* (region governed by a pasha, an Ottoman high official), which led to a blossoming of commerce and crafts. In 1913 Montenegro attempted to annex Shkodra (it succeeded in taking Ulcinj), a move not approved of by the international community, and the town changed hands often during WWI. Badly damaged by an earthquake in 1979, Shkodra was subsequently repaired and is Albania's fifth-largest town. The communist-era Hotel Rozafa in the town centre does little to welcome guests, but it makes a good landmark: restaurants, the information centre and most of the town's sights are close by.

◉ Sights

Rozafa Fortress   CASTLE

(admission 200 lekë; ☉8am-10pm) Three kilometres southwest of Shkodra, near the southern end of Lake Shkodra, the Rozafa Fortress was founded by the Illyrians in antiquity and rebuilt much later by the Venetians and then the Turks. The fortress derives its name from a woman named

Rozafa, who was allegedly walled into the ramparts as an offering to the gods so that the construction would stand. The story goes that Rozafa asked that two holes be left in the stonework so that she could continue to breastfeed her baby. There's a spectacular wall sculpture of her near the entrance of the castle's museum (admission 150 lekë; ⊙8am-7pm). Some nursing women come to the fortress to smear their breasts with the milky water that seeps from the wall during some months of the year. Municipal buses (30 lekë) stop near the turn-off to the castle, and it's a short walk up from there.

**Marubi Permanent
Photo Exhibition** GALLERY
(Rr Muhamet Gjollesha; admission 100 lekë; ⊙8am-4pm Mon-Fri) Hidden behind a block of shops and flats, the Marubi Permanent Photo Exhibition has fantastic photography by the Marubi 'dynasty', Albania's first and foremost photographers. The first-ever photograph taken in Albania is here, taken by Pjetër Marubi in 1858. The exhibition shows fascinating portraits, places and events. Not only is this a rare insight into what things looked like in old Albania, it is also a small collection of mighty fine photographs. To get here, go northeast of the clock tower to Rr Çlirimi; Rr Muhamet Gjollesha darts off to the right. The exhibition is on the left in an unmarked building, but locals will help you find it if you ask.

🛏 Sleeping & Eating

TOP CHOICE **Tradita G&T** BOUTIQUE HOTEL €€
(✆2240 537, 068 2086 056; www.traditagt.com; Rr Edith Durham; s/d/tr €35/50/55; P🤛) By far the best choice in town, this innovative, well-managed guesthouse is a delight. Housed in a painstakingly restored 17th-century mansion that once belonged to a famous Shkodran writer, the Tradita heaves with Albanian arts and crafts and has traditional yet very comfortable rooms with terracotta-roofed bathrooms and locally woven bed linen. A homemade, homegrown breakfast awaits guests in the morning and the restaurant serves excellent fish dishes in an ethnographic museum atmosphere. If you're heading Lake Koman way, the owner can arrange for the bus to pick you up from the hotel, and very happily shares a great deal of local knowledge with guests.

Hotel Kaduku HOTEL €€
(HK; ✆069 2551 230, 42 216; www.hotel-kaduku.com; Sheshi 5 Heronjtë; s/d/tr/ste €23/32/48/50; ❄🤛) This popular, modern hotel is behind Raiffeisen Bank on the roundabout near Hotel Rozafa. Its two wings have been renovated, but rooms are a little on the small side, and the bathrooms even more so. It's clean and friendly though, and the staff are able to provide information about getting to and from Theth.

Çoçja ITALIAN €€
(Rr Hazan Riza; mains 300-800 lekë; ⊙10am-11pm) This classy place on a pleasant piazza a block north of the pedestrianised Rr Kolë Idromeno is all gleaming white tablecloths, timber floors and a refreshing lack of kitsch in the design choices. The menu encompasses great pizza as well as more exciting fare such as veal ribs and chicken fillet with mushrooms and cream. There's also a great little courtyard garden that's perfect for summer drinks.

Piazza Park PIZZA €€
(Bul Skënderbeg; mains 300-900 lekë) Where the locals return to, night after night, day after day for people-watching and overload music. The pizza is good though, and you've the choice of eating indoors in a smart dining room, or outside on the busy summer terrace. It's right next to the Mother Teresa monument on the main drag.

ℹ Information

The information office (a stand-alone booth) at the intersection of Bul Skënderbeg and Rr Kolë Idromeno is open daily, and until 9pm in summer.

ℹ Getting There & Away

BUS There are hourly *furgons* and buses to and from Tirana (300 lekë, two hours, 6am to 4pm). From Shkodra, *furgons* depart from outside Radio Shkodra near Hotel Rozafa. *Furgons* to Ulcinj in Montenegro leave at 9am and 4pm (600 lekë, two hours) from the other side of the park abutting Grand Hotel Europa. They fill quickly. From Ulcinj, buses leave for Shkodra at 6am and 12.30pm. Catch the 7am bus to Lake Koman (800 lekë, two hours) in time for the wonderful ferry trip along the lake to Fierzë near Kosovo. *Furgons* depart for Theth daily at 7am (700 lekë).
TAXI It costs between €40 and €45 for the trip from Shkodra to Uncinj in Montenegro, depending on your haggling skills.
TRAIN Trains depart Tirana daily at 1.15pm (145 lekë), and arrive in Shkodra at 4.50pm, but you'll

need to be up early to catch the 5.40am train back. *Furgons* meet arriving trains.

Theth & Valbonë

These small villages deep in the 'Accursed Mountains' are all but deserted in winter (Theth locals head south to live in Shkodra), but come summer they're a magnet for those seeking beauty, isolation, mystery and adventure. From Theth, three circular hikes are very clearly marked out with red and white markers. It's possible to hike in the region without a guide, but they're helpful and charge between 3000 and 4000 lekë per day. Official guides charge €50.

The main hike is from Theth to Valbonë (or vice versa) and takes roughly six to seven hours. It takes around three hours to trek from Theth's centre (742m) to Valbonë pass (1812m), then a further two hours to the houses of Rragam and 1½ hours along a riverbed to near Bajram Curri. It's a spectacular hike and many visitors' highlight of Albania. If possible, combine it with the Koman Ferry for the ultimate Albanian mountain experience, though you're far better doing the circuit anticlockwise (ie going from Valbonë to Theth) if you choose to include the ferry.

◉ Sights

Kulla   HISTORIC BUILDING
(Theth; admission €1) Visit this fascinating 'lock-in tower' in central Theth where men waited, protected, during a blood feud.

⌂ Sleeping & Eating

Many of Theth's traditional homes have become B&Bs (complete with Western-style bathrooms with hot showers), while in less developed Valbonë, hotels tend to be new builds specifically designed for the needs of travellers. Due to the absence of restaurants in both villages, hotels often include breakfast, lunch and dinner in the deal.

TOP CHOICE Hotel Rilindja   GUESTHOUSE €€
(Valbonë; ☎067 3014 638; www.journeytovalbona.com; per tent €6, r €30-34) Pioneering tourism in Valbonë since 2005, the Albanian-American run Rilindja is a real treat and garners rave reviews from travellers who love the comfortable accommodation and excellent food. A new 12-room building was due to open in 2013 1km up the road from the original building, which is located at the entrance to Valbonë. The five rooms in the old

building share a bathroom, except for one that has private facilities. With fluent English spoken, the helpful owners can organise hikes, picnics and transport.

Çarku Guesthouse   GUESTHOUSE €€
(Theth; ☎069 3164 211; www.guesthouse-thethi-carku.com; per person €25; ☺Apr-Oct) Book in advance for a bed in this charming family home with thick stone walls, timber floors, a garden and farm. Food is all grown locally and meals are delicious. It's well signposted as you enter the village.

Guesthouse Tërthorja   GUESTHOUSE €€
(Theth; ☎069 3840 990; www.terthorja-guesthouse-tethi.com; per person incl full board €25) This renovated guesthouse has whitewashed walls, a sports field, sports equipment and a resident cow. Accommodation is in rooms sleeping up to five people and there are stunning views of the mountains all around.

Hotel & Camping Tradita   CHALET €€
(Valbonë; ☎067 301 4567, 067 383 800 14; s/d €25/50) This collection of five newly built chalets has a fantastic location in the middle of the village with extraordinary views in all directions. The pine cabins each come with hot water and private facilities, and the owner, Isa, also offers six further rooms in his adjacent stone house. There's a good restaurant on-site too.

❶ Getting There & Around

BUS Though Theth is only 70km from Shkodra, expect the occasionally hair-raising *furgon* trip to take four hours. The *furgon* leaves from Shkodra at 7am, and most hotels in town will be able to call ahead the night before and book you a seat on the bus, and sometimes, to have the bus pick you up from the hotel.

FERRY A popular route is to take the 7am *furgon* from Shkodra to the Koman Ferry, travel by ferry (two hours) then jump on a *furgon* from the ferry to Valbonë. If you're heading into Kosovo, it takes roughly 50 minutes to the border by car from the ferry terminal, but check that the car ferry is still running.

TAXI To get to Theth from Shkodra by taxi, expect to pay €100.

CENTRAL ALBANIA

Central Albania crams it all in. Travel an hour or two from Tirana and you can be Ottoman house-hopping in brilliant Berat, musing over ancient ruins in deserted Apol-

DON'T MISS

THE LAKE KOMAN FERRY

One of Albania's undisputed highlights is this superb three-hour ferry ride through the vast Lake Koman, connecting the towns of Koman and Fierzë. Lake Koman was created in 1978 when the River Drin was dammed, with the result that you can cruise through spectacular mountain scenery where many incredibly hardy peasants still live as they have for centuries, tucked away in tiny mountain villages.

The ferry is not set up for tourism, which makes the entire trip feel like a great adventure. The best way to experience the ride is to make a loop beginning and ending in Shkodra, and taking in Koman, Fierzë, Valbonë and Theth. Normally there are two ferries daily in the summer months – a passenger ferry that leaves Koman at 9am and a car ferry that leaves Koman at 10am. However, the car ferry didn't run in 2012 due to declining demand, and so it's likely that in future only the passenger ferry will run. Check www.journeytovalbona.com for the latest information.

The passenger ferry (500 lekë per person) arrives in Fierzë at around 1pm and is met by *furgons* that will take you to either Bajram Curri (200 lekë) or to Valbonë (400 lekë). There's no real reason to stay in Bajram Curri though, unless you plan to head to Kosovo. Hikers will want to head straight for Valbonë, where you can stay for a night or two before doing the stunning day hike to Theth, where you can stay for another night or two before taking a *furgon* back to Shkodra.

lonia or haggling for antiques in an Ottoman bazaar in Kruja.

Kruja

📞 0511 / POP 20,000

Kruja is Skanderbeg's town. Yes, Albania's hero was born here, and although it was over 500 years ago, there's still a great deal of pride in the fact that he and his forces defended Kruja from the Ottomans until his death. As soon as you get off the *furgon,* you're face to knee with a statue of Skanderbeg wielding his mighty sword with one hand, and it just gets more Skanderdelic after that.

From the road below, Kruja's houses appear to sit in the lap of a mountain. An ancient castle juts out to one side, and the massive Skanderbeg Museum juts out of the castle itself. The local plaster industry is going strong so expect visibility-reducing plumes of smoke to cloud views of the Adriatic Sea. Kruja's sights can be covered in a few hours, making this an ideal town to visit en route to Tirana's airport.

◉ Sights

Castle CASTLE
(⌚24hr) Inside Kruja's sprawling castle grounds are Albania flag sellers, pizza restaurants and an array of mildly interesting sights, though few actually castle-related.

National Ethnographic Museum MUSEUM
(admission 300 lekë; ⌚9am-1pm & 4-7pm Tue-Sun) This traditional home in the castle complex below the Skanderbeg Museum is one of the best in the country. Set in an original 19th-century Ottoman house that belonged to the affluent Toptani family, this museum shows the level of luxury and self-sufficiency the household maintained by producing its own food, drink, leather and weapons. They even had their very own mini *hammam* (Turkish bath) and watermill. The walls are lined with original frescos from 1764. The English-speaking guide's detailed explanations are excellent; offer a tip if you can.

Skanderbeg Museum MUSEUM
(admission 200 lekë; ⌚9am-1pm & 4-7pm Tue-Sun) Designed by Enver Hoxha's daughter and son-in-law, this museum opened in 1982, and its spacious seven-level interior displays replicas of armour and paintings depicting Skanderbeg's struggle against the Ottomans. The museum is something of a secular shrine, and takes itself very seriously indeed, with giant statues and dramatic battle murals.

Teqe MOSQUE
A short scramble down the cobblestone lane are the remains of a small *hammam* as well as a functioning *teqe* – a small place of worship for those practising the Bektashi branch of Islam. This beautifully decorated *teqe* has been maintained by

KRUJA: ENTERING SKANDERBEG'S TOWN

At a young age, Gjergj Kastrioti, the son of an Albanian prince, was handed over as a hostage to the Turks, who converted him to Islam and gave him a military education at Edirne in Turkey. There he became known as Iskander (after Alexander the Great) and Sultan Murat II promoted him to the rank of bey (governor), thus the name Skanderbeg.

In 1443 the Turks suffered a defeat at the hands of the Hungarians at Niš in present-day Serbia, and nationally minded Skanderbeg took the opportunity to abandon the Ottoman army and Islam and rally his fellow Albanians against the Turks. Skanderbeg made Kruja his seat of government between 1443 and 1468. Among the 13 Turkish invasions he subsequently repulsed was that led by his former commander, Murat II. Pope Calixtus III named Skanderbeg the 'captain general of the Holy See' and Venice formed an alliance with him. The Turks besieged Kruja four times. Though beaten back in 1450, 1466 and 1467, they finally took control of Kruja in 1478 (after Skanderbeg's death).

successive generations of the Dollma family since 1789. Skanderbeg himself reputedly planted the knotted olive tree at the front.

Bazaar
MARKET

This Ottoman-style bazaar is the country's best place for souvenir shopping and has WWII medical kits, antique gems and quality traditional ware, including beautifully embroidered tablecloths, copper coffee pots and plates. You can watch women using looms to make *kilims* (rugs) and purchase the results.

❶ Getting There & Away

Kruja is 32km from Tirana. Make sure your *furgon* from Tirana (150 lekë, 30 minutes) is going to Kruja, not just Fush Kruja, the modern town below. It is very easy to reach the airport (150 lekë, 15 minutes) by *furgon* or taxi from here, and it's en route to Shkodra, though you'll need to pull over a bus on the busy Tirana–Shkodra highway as they don't drive up the mountain into the town itself.

Durrës

☎ 052

Durrës was once – albeit briefly – Albania's capital. It's now virtually an extension of Tirana, joined to the capital by a ceaseless urban corridor full of hypermarkets and car dealerships. Blessed with a decent 10km stretch of beach, Durrës is sadly a lesson in unplanned development; hundreds of hotels stand side by side, and it's terribly crowded in the summer months. Despite this, there's an interesting amphitheatre

to see, although the famous archaeological museum on the seafront has been demolished and a new one is currently being built on the same site.

◉ Sights

Amphitheatre of Durrës
RUINS

(Rr e Kalasë; admission 300 lekë; ⊙9am-7pm) The Amphitheatre of Durrës was built on the hillside inside the city walls in the early 2nd century AD. In its prime it had the capacity to seat 15,000 to 20,000 spectators, but these days a few inhabited houses occupy the stage, a reminder of its recent rediscovery (in 1966) and excavation. The Byzantine chapel in the amphitheatre has several beautiful mosaics. There are knowledgable English-speaking guides on site daily until 3pm; they work on a tipping basis.

🛏 Sleeping

Hotel Ani
HOTEL €€

(☎224 228; anihoteldurres@yahoo.it; 1 Shëtitorja Taulantia; r from €60; Ⓟᙇ🌐) This very smart property faces the site of the new archaeological museum and backs onto the seafront. The smart and classy lobby gives way to spacious and comfortable rooms, and service is friendly and efficient.

Nais Hotel
HOTEL €€

(☎230 375, 052 224 940; hotelnais@hotmail.com; Rr Lagja 1, off Bul Epidamni; r €25-40; ᙇ🌐) Just a short wander from the amphitheatre in the centre of town, this friendly family-run place is a comfortable midrange option. Rooms are clean and modern, with a good breakfast served downstairs and the beachfront just moments away.

✕ Eating & Drinking

Palma ITALIAN €€

(Rr Taulantia; mains 400-1000 lekë) One of the better bets on the busy and commercial seafront, this smart place has a large menu of pizza, grills and fish dishes, and is a great spot to soak up the passing crowds.

Bar Torra BAR

(Sheshi Mujo Ulqinaku) This Venetian tower was opened by a team of local artists and was one of the first private cafes in Albania. There are art displays (and cosy nooks) downstairs, and in summer you can gaze around Durrës from the top of the tower.

❶ Getting There & Away

BOAT Agencies around the train station sell tickets for the many ferry lines plying the Durrës–Bari route (single deck €40, eight hours). **Venezia Lines** (☑052 383 83; www.venezialines.com) has the fastest boat to Bari (€60, 3½ hours). Ferries also depart Durrës for Ancona most days in summer (€65, 17 hours) and at least three days a week throughout the year.

BUS & FURGON *Furgons* (200 lekë, one hour) and buses (150 lekë, one hour) to Tirana leave from beside the train station when they're full. Buses leave for Shkodra at 7.30am and 1.30pm (400 lekë, three hours). In summer, long-distance buses and *furgons* going to and from Saranda, Gjirokastra, Fier and Berat (400 lekë, 1½ hours) bypass this station, picking up and dropping off passengers at the end of Plazhi i Durrësi, east of the harbour, which can be reached by the 'Plepa' orange municipal bus (30 lekë, 10 minutes). In July and August many buses connect Durrës with Pristina in Kosovo (€15, five hours).

TRAIN Seven trains a day head to Tirana (70 lekë, one hour, 6.15am, 8.45am, 9.20am, 1.05pm, 3.12pm, 4.45pm and 8.05pm). Trains also depart for Shkodra (1.05pm), Pogradec (6.45am), Elbasan (6.45am, 3.25pm) and Vlore (5.35pm). Check at the station for changes in departure times.

Apollonia

The ruined city of ancient **Apollonia** (admission 700 lekë; ⊙9am-5pm) is 12km west of Fier, which is 90km south of Durrës. Set on rolling hills among olive groves, with impressive views all around, Apollonia (named after the god Apollo) was founded by Greeks from Corinth and Corfu in 588 BC and quickly grew into an important city-state, which minted its own currency and benefited from a robust slave trade. Under the Romans (from 229 BC), the city became a great cultural centre with a famous school of philosophy.

Julius Caesar rewarded Apollonia with the title 'free city' for supporting him against Gnaeus Pompeius Magnus (Pompey the Great) during the civil war in the 1st century BC, and sent his nephew Octavius, the future Emperor Augustus, to complete his studies here.

After a series of military and natural disasters (including an earthquake in the 3rd century AD that turned the river into a malarial swamp), the population moved southward into present-day Vlora, and by the 5th century only a small village with its own bishop remained at Apollonia.

There is far less to see at Apollonia than there is at Butrint, but there are some picturesque ruins within the 4km of city walls, including a small original theatre and the elegant pillars on the restored facade of the city's 2nd-century-AD administrative centre. You may be able to see the 3rd-century-BC **House of Mosaics** from a distance, though they're often covered up with sand for protection from the elements. Inside the **Museum of Apollonia** complex is the Byzantine monastery and Church of St Mary, which has gargoyles on the outside pillars. Much of the site remains to be excavated, but recent discoveries include a necropolis outside the castle walls with graves from the Bronze and Iron ages.

❶ Getting There & Away

Apollonia is best visited on a day trip from Tirana, Durrës, Vlora or Berat.

Furgons depart for the site (50 lekë) from Fier's '24th August Bar' (ask locals for directions). From Fier, *furgons* head to Durrës (200 lekë, 1½ hours), Tirana (400 lekë, two hours), Berat (300 lekë, one hour) and Vlora (200 lekë, 45 minutes).

If you'd prefer not to wait for the *furgon*, a taxi will charge approximately 500 lekë one way from Fier.

Berat

☑032 / POP 71,000

A highlight of any trip to Albania is a visit to beautiful Berat. Its most striking feature is the collection of white Ottoman houses climbing up the hill to its castle, earning it the title of 'town of a thousand windows' and helping it join Gjirokastra on the list of Unesco World Heritage sites in 2008. Its rugged mountain setting is particularly evocative when the clouds swirl around the tops of the minarets, or break up to show the icy top of Mt Tomorri.

The old quarters are lovely ensembles of whitewashed walls, tiled roofs and cobblestone roads. Surrounding the town, olive and cherry trees decorate the gentler slopes, while pine woods stand on the steeper inclines. The modern town is dominated by the huge dome of the brand-new Berat University, while elsewhere the bridges over the Osumi River to the charmingly unchanged Gorics side include a 1780 seven-arched stone footbridge.

In the 3rd century BC an Illyrian fortress called Antipatrea was built here on the site of an earlier settlement. The Byzantines strengthened the hilltop fortifications in the 5th and 6th centuries, as did the Bulgarians 400 years later. The Serbs, who occupied the citadel in 1345, renamed it Beligrad, or 'White City'. In 1450 the Ottoman Turks took the town. After a period of decline, in the 18th and 19th centuries the town began to thrive as a crafts centre specialising in woodcarving. Berat today is now a big centre for tourism in Albania, though it has managed to retain its easygoing charm and friendly atmosphere.

◎ Sights

TOP CHOICE **Kalasa** CASTLE
(admission 100 lekë; audio guide 500 lekë; ⊘24hr) The neighbourhood inside the castle's walls still lives and breathes; if you walk around this busy, residential neighbourhood for long enough you'll invariably stumble into someone's courtyard thinking it's a church or ruin (no one seems to mind, though). In spring and summer the fragrance of chamomile is in the air (and underfoot), and wildflowers burst from every gap between the stones. The highest point is occupied by the Inner Fortress, where ruined stairs lead to a Tolkienesque water reservoir. Views are spectacular in all directions.

TOP CHOICE **Onufri Museum** GALLERY
(admission 200 lekë; ⊘9am-1pm & 4-7pm May-Sep, 9am-4pm Oct-Apr, closed Mon) Kala was traditionally a Christian neighbourhood, but fewer than a dozen of the 20 churches remain. The quarter's biggest church, **Church of the Dormition of St Mary** (Kisha Fjetja e Shën Mërisë), is the site of the

Onufri Museum. The church itself dates from 1797 and was built on the foundations of a 10th-century church. Onufri's spectacular 16th-century artworks are displayed on the ground level along with a beautifully gilded iconostasis.

Churches & Chapels CHURCHES
Ask at the Onufri Museum if you can see the other churches and tiny chapels in Kala, including **St Theodore** (Shën Todher), close to the citadel gates; the substantial and picturesque **Church of the Holy Trinity** (Kisha Shën Triades), below the upper fortress; and the little chapels of **St Mary Blachernae** (Shën Mëri Vllaherna) and **St Nicholas** (Shënkolli). Some of the churches date back to the 13th century. Also keep an eye out for the **Red Mosque**, by the southern Kala walls, which was the first in Berat and dates back to the 15th century.

Chapel of St Michael CHURCH
Perched on a cliff ledge below the citadel is the artfully positioned little chapel of St Michael (Shën Mihell), best viewed from the Gorica quarter.

Ethnographic Museum MUSEUM
(admission 200 lekë; ⊘9am-1pm & 4-7pm May-Sep, 9am-4pm Oct-Apr, closed Mon) Down from the castle, this museum is in an 18th-century Ottoman house that's as interesting as the exhibits. The ground floor has displays of traditional clothes and the tools used by silversmiths and weavers, while the upper storey has kitchens, bedrooms and guest rooms decked out in traditional style. Check out the *mafil*, a kind of mezzanine looking into the lounge where the women of the house could keep an eye on male guests (and see when their cups needed to be filled). There are information sheets in Italian, French and English.

Mangalem Quarter NEIGHBOURHOOD
Down in the traditionally Muslim Mangalem quarter, there are three grand mosques. The 16th-century **Sultan's Mosque** (Xhamia e Mbretit) is one of the oldest in Albania. The **Helveti teqe** behind the mosque has a beautiful carved ceiling and was specially designed with acoustic holes to improve the quality of sound during meetings. The Helveti, like the Bektashi, are a dervish order, or brotherhood, of Muslim mystics. The big mosque on the town square is the 16th-century **Lead Mosque** (Xhamia e Plumbit), so named because of the lead coating its

sphere-shaped domes. The 19th-century **Bachelors' Mosque** (Xhamia e Beqarëvet) is down by the Osumi River; look for the enchanting paintings on its external walls. This mosque was built for unmarried shop assistants and junior craftsmen, and is perched between some fine Ottoman-era shopfronts along the river.

🏃 Activities

Bogove Waterfall   HIKING
Catch the 8am or 9am *furgon* to Bogove via Skrappar, or a later bus to Polican then transfer to a *furgon* to Bogove. Lunch at Taverna Dafinat above the bus stop, then follow the path along the river (starting on the Berat side) to this icy waterfall.

Çobo Winery   WINE TASTING
(📞122 088; www.cobowineryonline.com; 🔾) The Çobo family winery is the best known in Albania, and it's worth checking out. Try its Shesh i Bardhe, Trebiano, Shesh i Izi and Kashmer wines, and, of course, its Raki me Arra. Any bus/*furgon* heading to Tirana can drop you off at the winery for 100 lekë.

Albania Rafting Group   TOURS
(📞2006 621; www.albrafting.com) This pioneering group runs rafting tours for all levels to some stunning gorges around Berat and Permet. Everyone from children to pensioners is welcome, and the various tours start at around €20 to €65 per person per day.

🛏 Sleeping & Eating

🅃🅞🅟 Hotel Mangalemi   HOTEL €€
(📞068 2323 238, 232 093; www.mangalemihotel.com; Rr Mihail Komneno; r from €35; 🄿🔾) This hotel is housed in two sprawling Ottoman houses where all the rooms are beautifully furnished in traditional Berati style and balconies give superb views. Its terrace restaurant has great Albanian food with bonus views of Mt Tomorri. It's on the left side of the cobblestone road leading to the castle, just a short wander from the town centre.

🅃🅞🅟 Berat Backpackers   HOSTEL €
(📞069 474 8060, 069 3064 429; www.beratbackpackers.com; Gorica; tent/dm/r €7/12/28; 🕘Apr-Nov; @🔾) Albania's best hostel is the brainchild of Englishman Scott; he's transformed a traditional house in the Gorica quarter (across the river from Mangalem)

into a vine-clad hostel with a basement bar, alfresco drinking area and a cheery, relaxed atmosphere that money can't buy. There's a shaded camping area on the terrace, cheap laundry available, two airy dorms with original ceilings, and one excellent-value double room that shares the bathroom facilities with the dorms.

Hotel Muzaka   HOTEL €€
(📞231 999; www.hotelmuzaka.com; Gorica; s/d from €40/50; 🄿❄🔾) This superb new addition to Berat's hotel scene is a careful restoration of an old stone mansion on the riverfront in Gorica, just over the footbridge from the centre of town. Wooden floorboards, gorgeous bathrooms and beautifully chosen pieces of furniture in the 10 spacious rooms make this a good option for those looking for some style as well as tradition in their accommodation.

White House   ITALIAN €€
(Rr Santa Lucia; mains 200-1000 lekë; 🕘8am-11pm) On the main road that runs north of the river, this smart place has a superb roof terrace with sweeping views over Berat, and serves up a mean pizza to boot. There's also a classier dining room downstairs with air-conditioning, perfect for a blowout meal.

Antigoni   ALBANIAN €€
(mains 600 lekë) This bustling restaurant may have an unusual style of service (some call it ignoring), but the Mangalem and Osumi River views from its upper levels are outstanding, and the food and local wine are both good.

ℹ Information

The town's **information centre** (www.bashkia-berat.com) is located in the council building, parallel to the Osumi River in new Berat.

ℹ Getting There & Away

Buses and *furgons* run between Tirana and Berat (400/500 lekë, 2½ hours) half-hourly until 3pm. From Tirana, buses leave from the 'Kombinati' station (catch the municipal bus from Sheshi Skënderbej to Kombinati for 30 lekë). In Berat, buses depart from and arrive in Sheshi Teodor Muzaka next to the Lead Mosque in the centre of town. There are buses to Vlora (350 lekë, 2½ hours, hourly until 2pm), Durrës (300 lekë, 1½ hours, five per day) and Saranda (1200 lekë, six hours, two daily at 8am and 2pm) via Gjirokastra (1000 lekë, four hours).

SOUTHERN COAST

With rough mountains falling head-first into bright blue seas, this area is wild and ready for exploration. The coastal drive between Vlora and Saranda is easily one of the most spectacular in Eastern Europe and shouldn't missed by any visitor to Albania. While beaches can be jam-packed in August, there's plenty of space, peace and happy-to-see-you faces in the low season. Sadly, the poorly planned development in the past decade has rather blighted many of the once-charming coastal villages, but there's still plenty of untouched beauty to be found here.

Vlora

📳 033 / POP 184,000

It's here in sunny Vlora (the ancient Aulon) that the Adriatic Sea meets the Ionian, but the beaches are muddy and grubby, and the port town has really outgrown itself and is now a morass of overdevelopment. History buffs will still enjoy the museums and historic buildings, while beach lovers should hold out for the villages of Dhërmi, Drymades or Jal, all further south.

👁 Sights

Sheshi i Flamurit   SQUARE

At Sheshi i Flamurit (Flag Sq), near the top of Sadik Zotaj, a magnificent socialist-realist **Independence Monument** stands proud against the sky with the flag bearer hoisting the double-headed eagle into the blue. Near the base of the monument lies the grave of local Ismail Qemali, the country's first prime minister.

Ethnographic Museum   MUSEUM

(Sheshi i Flamurit; admission 100 lekë; ⊘9am-noon Mon-Sat) This ethnographic museum is jam-packed with relics of Albanian life. It's hidden behind an inconspicuous metal fence.

Muzeu Historik   MUSEUM

(Rr Ismail Qemali; ⊘8am-2pm daily, 5-8pm Tue-Thu in summer.) This antiquities museum opposite the ethnographic museum and just off Vlora's main square, Sheshi i Flamurit, has been renovated and has a good collection of ancient artefacts including Bronze Age relics and items from the Roman era. Labelling is spotty, however.

Muradi Mosque   MOSQUE

The 16th-century Muradi Mosque is a small elegant structure made of red and white stone, with a modest minaret; its exquisite design is attributed to one of the greatest Ottoman architects, Albanian-born Sinan Pasha.

National Museum of Independence   MUSEUM

(admission 100 lekë; ⊘9am-1pm & 5-8pm Tue-Sun) Down by the harbour, the National Museum of Independence is housed in the villa that became the headquarters of Albania's first government in 1912. The preserved offices, historic photographs and famous balcony make it an interesting place to learn about Albania's short-lived, but long-remembered, 1912 independence.

🛈 Getting There & Away

BUS & FURGON Buses (500 lekë, four hours) and *furgons* (600 lekë, three hours) to Tirana and Durrës (500 lekë, 2½ hours) whiz back and forth from 4am until 7pm. Buses to Saranda (900 lekë, six hours) and on to Gjirokastra (1000 lekë, seven hours) leave at 7am and 12.30pm. There are nine buses a day to Berat (300 lekë, two hours). Buses leave from Rr Rakip Malilaj; departures to Athens (€25) and cities in Italy (from €70) depart from Muradi Mosque.

FERRY Vlora to Brindisi in Italy takes around six hours. From Monday to Saturday there are

---

LLOGARAJA PASS NATIONAL PARK

Reaching the pine-tree-clad Llogaraja Pass National Park (1025m) is a highlight of travels in Albania. If you've been soaking up the sun on the southern coast's beaches, it seems impossible that after a steep hairpin-bend climb you'll be up in the mountains tucking into spit-roasted lamb and homemade wine. There's great scenery up here, including the *pisha flamur* (flag pine) – a tree resembling the eagle design on the Albanian flag. Watch clouds descending onto the mountain, shepherds on the plains guiding their herds, and thick forests where deer, wild boar and wolves roam. Check out the resident deer at the Tourist Village before heading across the road to the cute family-run cabins at **Hotel Andoni** (📳068 240 0929; cabins 4000 lekë). The family does a wonderful lamb roast lunch (800 lekë) here.

departures from Brindisi at 11pm and Vlora at noon (deck €35). There are also ferries to Corfu during the summer months with Finikas Lines.

TRAIN The daily train departs Tirana for Vlora at 4.30pm and Vlora for Tirana at 4.30am (250 lekë, five hours).

Drymades

As you zigzag down the mountain from the Llogaraja Pass National Park, the white crescent-shape beaches and azure waters lure you from below. The first beach before the alluvial fan is Palasa, and it's one of the last bar/restaurant/hotel-free beaches around.

The next beach along is Drymades beach. Turn right just after the beginning of the walk down to Dhërmi beach and you'll be on the sealed road that twists through olive groves. After a 20-minute walk you'll be on its rocky white beach.

🛏 Sleeping & Eating

TOP CHOICE Sea Turtle CAMPGROUND €
(☑069 4016 057; per person incl half-board from 1000 lekë; ⊙Jun-Sep) This great little set-up is run by two brothers. Each summer they turn the family orange orchard into a vibrant tent city, and the price includes the tent (with mattresses, sheets and pillows), breakfast and a family-cooked dinner (served up in true camp style). Hot showers are under the shade of old fig trees.

Drymades Inn Resort CABINS €€
(☑069 2074 004, 069 2074 000; www.drymades-inn.al; s/d €40/60; 🅿❄️🛜🌊) This attractive constellation of blue-painted timber cabins under the shade of pine trees is just a step away from the blue sea and the glorious beach. There's a bar, restaurant and shaded playground, plus a classic beach bar with a straw roof. Prices halve off-peak, which is by far the best time to come, as in high summer it's rammed.

Dhërmi

Dhërmi beach is well and truly under the tourist trance in summer: expect booked-out accommodation and an almost unbearable rubbish problem. Despite this, there is fun to be had, and, if techno isn't your style, there's peace and quiet to be had, too. It's made up of lovely rocky outcrops, Mediterranean-blue water and tiny coves.

The beach is 1.5km below the Vlora–Saranda road, so ask the driver to stop at the turn-off on the Llogaraja side of the village. From here it's an easy 10-minute walk downhill.

🛏 Sleeping & Eating

Blu Blu CABINS €€
(☑068 6090 485; r from €80; ⊙May-Oct; ❄️🛜) Hello? Whose stroke of genius is this? Turn left at the bottom of the road to Dhërmi, and follow the road almost to its end. Here you'll find one of the best 'no disco' beachside spots in Albania. Little white cabins with sea views sit among banana trees, and the bar/restaurant serves great food. Rooms start at €30 in May.

Hotel Greccia HOTEL €€
(☑069 6848 858, 069 5302 850; joanna_nino@hotmail.com; r from €60; 🅿❄️🛜) This smart five-floor place is on the hillside just above the village on the road down from the coastal highway. It's well set up for a comfortable stay, with balconies giving great views over the sea or back towards the mountains, and sleekly minimalist rooms that are kept spotlessly clean.

Hotel Luciano RESTAURANT €€
(mains 400-700 lekë) Sure, the mosaic on the wall of this waterfront pizza and pasta joint says 'no', but it's a resounding 'yes' to its wood-fired pizzas. It's the first place you'll find after walking down the hill from the main road.

Himara

☑0393 / POP 4500

This sleepy town has fine beaches, a couple of pleasant Greek seafood tavernas, some smart modern hotels and an interesting Old Town high on the hill. Most of the ethnic Greek population left in the 1990s, but many have returned – Greek remains the mother tongue of its people. The lower town comprises three easily accessible rocky beaches and the town's hotels and restaurants. The main Vlora–Saranda road passes the entrance to the hilltop castle, which, like Berat's, still houses many people. A taxi to the castle from Himara costs 300 lekë.

🛏 Sleeping

Rapo's Resort LUXURY HOTEL €€€
(☑22 856; www.raporesorthotel.com; s & d €120-130; ❄️🛜🌊) This top-end resort has smart

interior design, sparkling bathrooms and great service. It's near the beach, and also houses a massive swimming pool. For €9 anyone can relax by the pool for the day. Annoyingly at these high prices, wireless is limited to the lobby.

Kamping Himare   CAMPGROUND €
(☎068 5298 940; www.himaracamping.com; tent per person 800 lekë; ☺Jun-Sep) Midnight movies in an open-air cinema add to the appeal of this camping ground across the road from the beach in an olive and orange grove. Tent rate includes mattresses, sheets and pillows. Try the restaurant's sublime pancakes (100 lekë) for breakfast.

Manolo   BOUTIQUE HOTEL €€
(☎22 375; d €50) Right by the main beach in the centre of the village, Manolo is a cool bar downstairs with four contemporary and comfortable rooms that show good attention to detail and have sea views.

❶ Getting There & Away

Buses to Saranda and Vlora pass through Himara in the early morning; check with locals exactly when, as schedules change all the time.

Vuno & Jal

Less than 10 minutes' drive from Himara is Vuno, a tiny hillside village above a picturesque beach (Jal, pronounced Yal). Outdoor Albania renovated Vuno's primary school, and each summer its classrooms are filled with blow-up beds and it becomes **Shkolla Hostel** (☎068 4682 353, 068 3133 451; www.tiranahostel.com; tent/dm €4/7; ☺late Jun-Aug). What it lacks in infrastructure and privacy it makes up for with its goat-bell soundtrack and evening campfire. From Vuno, walk over the bridge and follow the rocky path to your right past the cemetery.

It's a challenging 40-minute signed walk through olive groves to picturesque Jal, or a 5km walk along the main beach road. Jal was a victim of the permit police a few years ago, and since then new structures have taken on a temporary tone. Jal has two beaches; one has free camping while the other has a **camping ground** (including tent 2000 lekë) set back from the sea. Fresh seafood is bountiful in Jal and there are plenty of beachside restaurants in summer.

Saranda

☎0852 / POP 37,700

Saranda has grown rapidly in the past decade; skeletal high-rises crowd around its horseshoe shape and hundreds more are being built in the outlying region. Saranda is bustling in summer – buses are crowded with people carrying swimming paraphernalia and the weather means it's almost obligatory to go for a swim. A daily stream of Corfu holidaymakers take the 45-minute ferry trip to Albania, add the Albanian stamp to their passports and hit Butrint or the Blue Eye Spring before heading back.

The town's name comes from Ayii Saranda, an early monastery dedicated to 40 saints; its bombed remains (including some preserved frescos) are still high on the hill above the town. The town was called Porto Edda for a period in the 1940s, after Mussolini's daughter.

Saranda's stony beaches are quite decent and there are plenty of sights in and around town, including the mesmerising ancient archaeological site of Butrint and the hypnotic Blue Eye Spring. Between Saranda and Butrint, the lovely beaches and islands of Ksamil are perfect for a dip after a day of exploring.

Four main streets arc around Saranda's bay, including the waterfront promenade that becomes prime *xhiro* (evening walk) territory in the evening.

◉ Sights

Synagogue   RUINS
(Rr Skënderbeu; ☺24hr) This 5th-century synagogue is centrally located and is evidence of one of the earliest Balkan-Jewish communities.

Museum of Archaeology   MUSEUM
(Rr Flamurit; ☺9am-2pm & 4-9pm) This office-like building houses a well-preserved 6th-century mosaic floor in its basement and has an interesting display about nearby Butrint. It's one block behind the harbour.

Castle of Lëkurësit   CASTLE
This former castle is now a restaurant with superb views over Saranda and Butrint lagoon, especially at sunset. A taxi there costs about 1000 lekë return; arrange a time for the driver to pick you up, or it's a 15-minute walk up from the Saranda–Tirana road.

🛏 Sleeping

Hotel Porto Eda   HOTEL €€
(www.portoeda.com; Rr Jonianët; r €50; P✳🌐) Referencing the temporary name given to Saranda during the fascist occupation, this hotel is nevertheless a charming place and about as central as you can get, overlooking the harbour. The 24 rooms are comfortably and stylishly laid out, most with balconies, and the welcome is warm.

SR Backpackers   HOSTEL €
(📱069 4345 426; www.backpackerssr.hostel.com; Rr Mitat Hoxha 10; dm €11; @🌐) The hostel with the most central location in Saranda, this is also the cheapest option. Housed in an apartment and hosted by the gregarious English-speaking Tomi, the 14 beds here are spread over three dorms, each with its own balcony. There's one shared bathroom, a communal kitchen and a friendly atmosphere.

Hairy Lemon   HOSTEL €
(📱069 3559 317; www.hairylemonhostel.com; cnr Mitat Hoxha & E Arberit; dm €12; 🌐) With a prime 8th-floor location, a clean beach at its base and a friendly, helpful atmosphere, this Irish-run backpacker hostel is a good place to chill out. There's an open-plan kitchen and lounge, and two dorm rooms with fans and sea breezes. Follow the port road for around 10 minutes and continue when it becomes dirt; it's the orange-and-yellow apartment block on your right.

Hotel Palma   HOTEL €€
(📱22 929; Rr Mitat Hoxha; r from €30; ✳🎦) Right next to the port, this hotel is good value and an easy walk into the town. Some rooms have great views with large balconies and all are super-clean. If you're up for it, guests get free entry into the on-site summer disco.

🍴 Eating

Veliani   ALBANIAN €€
(Bul Hasan Tahsini; mains 450-1100 lekë) Right in the heart of town, this upmarket place right on the waterfront isn't cheap, but does an excellent selection of Albanian dishes, including its signature octopus in red wine – a true local speciality.

Pizza Limani   PIZZA €€
(Bul Hasan Tahsini; pizza 400-800 lekë) The best pizza in town can be found on the seafront at this reliable and buzzing place with a giant terrace with superb harbour view and an excellent variety of tasty toppings on wood-fired oven-cooked dough.

Tani   SEAFOOD €
(mains 250-550 lekë) This portside seafood restaurant is run by chef Tani, who prides himself on serving dishes he's invented himself. The oven-baked filled mussels are a cheesy delight, and it's in a cool vine-draped location.

Dropulli   TRADITIONAL €
(cnr Rr Skënderbeu & Rr Mitro Dhmertika; mains 350 lekë) A local restaurant that has Albanian holidaymakers returning to it day after day has to be good, and vegetarians will love the melt-in-your-mouth stuffed peppers with tasty rice; ask for it to be served with potatoes.

🛈 Information

Banks with ATMs line the sea road (Rr 1 Maji) and the next street inland (Rr Skënderbeu).

Saranda's **ZIT information centre** (Rr Skënderbeu; ⊙8am-4pm Mon-Fri, 9am-2pm & 4-9pm Sat & Sun Oct-Jun, 8.30am-2pm & 4-10pm Jul-Sep) is the most established in Albania and provides information about transport and local sights. The newer, bigger tourist information centre on the promenade sells travel guides, souvenirs, Ismail Kadare novels and maps.

🛈 Getting There & Away

The ZIT information centre opposite the synagogue ruins has up-to-date bus timetables.

BUS The main bus station is uphill from the ruins on Rr Vangjel Pando. Municipal buses go to Butrint via Ksamil on the hour from 7am to 5pm (100 lekë, 30 minutes), leaving from the roundabout near the port and opposite ZIT. Buses to Tirana (1300 lekë, eight hours) via Gjirokastra (350 lekë) leave at 5am, 6.30am, 8.30am, 9.30am, 10.30am, 2pm and 10pm. The 5.30am and 9pm Tirana bus takes the coastal route (1300 lekë, eight hours) via Vlora (900 lekë). There are two buses and *furgons* an hour to Gjirokastra's new town (350 lekë, 1½ hours) – they all pass the turn-off to the Blue Eye Spring. Buses to Himara (400 lekë, two hours) leave around four times a day. Buses to the Greek border near Konispoli leave Saranda at 8am and 11am (200 lekë); otherwise you can reach the Greek border via Gjirokastra.

FERRY Finikas (📱067 2022 004, 260 57; www.finikas-lines.com; Rr Mithat Hoxha) at the port sells ferry tickets for Corfu with a daily departure at 10.30am (€19, 45 minutes). A slower boat departs daily at 4.30pm (€19, 90 minutes) and in summer a third ferry departs

Saranda at 4.30pm Thursdays, Saturdays and Sundays. From Corfu there are three ferries: one daily at 9am, one daily at 6.30pm and one at 9.15am Thursdays, Saturdays and Sundays. Note that Greek time is one hour ahead of Albanian time.

TAXI Taxis wait for customers at the bus stop and opposite Central Park on Rr Skënderbeu. A taxi to the Greek border at Kakavija costs 4000 lekë.

Around Saranda

BUTRINT

The ancient ruins of Butrint (www.butrint.org; admission 700 lekë; ⊙8am-dusk), 18km south of Saranda, are renowned for their size, beauty and tranquillity. They're in a fantastic natural setting and are part of a 29-sq-km national park. Set aside at least two hours to explore this fascinating place.

Although the site had been inhabited long before, Greeks from Corfu settled on the hill in Butrint (Buthrotum) in the 6th century BC. Within a century Butrint had become a fortified trading city with an acropolis. The lower town began to develop in the 3rd century BC, and many large stone buildings had already been built by the time the Romans took over in 167 BC. Butrint's prosperity continued throughout the Roman period, and the Byzantines made it an ecclesiastical centre. The city then went into a long decline and was abandoned until 1927, when Italian archaeologists arrived. These days Lord Rothschild's UK-based Butrint Foundation helps maintain the site.

As you enter the site the path leads to the right, to Butrint's 3rd-century-BC Greek theatre, secluded in the forest below the acropolis. Also in use during the Roman period, the theatre could seat about 2500 people. Close by are the small public baths, where geometric mosaics are buried under a layer of mesh and sand to protect them from the elements.

Deeper in the forest is a wall covered with crisp Greek inscriptions, and the 6th-century palaeo-Christian baptistry decorated with colourful mosaics of animals and birds, again under the sand. Beyond are the impressive arches of the 6th-century basilica, built over many years. A massive Cyclopean wall dating back to the 4th century BC is further on. Over one gate is a relief of a lion killing a bull, symbolic of a protective force vanquishing assailants.

The top of the hill is where the acropolis once was. There's now a castle here, housing an informative museum (⊙8am-4pm). The views from the museum's courtyard give you a good idea of the city's layout, and you can see the Vivari Channel connecting Lake Butrint to the Straits of Corfu. There are community-run stalls inside the gates where you can buy locally produced souvenirs.

❶ Getting There & Away

The municipal bus from Saranda to Butrint costs 100 lekë and leaves hourly from 7am to 5pm. It passes through Ksamil.

KSAMIL

Ksamil, 17km south of Saranda, has three small, dreamy islands within swimming distance and dozens of beachside bars and restaurants that open in the summer. The public Saranda–Butrint bus stops twice in the town (100 lekë; leaves hourly 1am to 5pm); either stop will get you to the pristine waters, though if you look closely you'll realise that the sand is trucked in.

Twenty-two kilometres east of Saranda, the Blue Eye Spring (Syri i Kaltër; per person/car 50/200 lekë) is a hypnotic pool of deep blue water surrounded by electric-blue edges like the iris of an eye. Bring your swimming gear and a towel, as it's a great spot for a dive into the cold water on a summer's day. It feeds the Bistrica River and its depth is unknown. It's a pleasant spot; blue dragonflies dash around the water, and the surrounding shady oak trees make a pleasant picnic spot, though it's often crowded in the summer months. There's a restaurant and cabins nearby. If you don't mind a 2km walk, any bus travelling between Saranda and Gjirokastra can drop you off at the spring's turn-off.

Hotel Joni (☎069 2091 554; s/d €20/25; 🛜) is a clean hotel near the roundabout. There are plenty of 'rooms to rent' (averaging €20 per night) in private homes closer to the water, and seafood restaurants perch along the beachfront in summer.

EASTERN ALBANIA

Close to the Greek border and accessible from the Tirana–Saranda bus route is the Unesco World Heritage–listed town of Gjirokastra, surely one of Albania's most magical places and birthplace to two of its most famous sons. Expect bunker-covered mountains, winter-time snowfields and plenty of roads leading to Greece.

Gjirokastra

☎084 / POP 43,000

Defined by its castle, roads paved with chunky limestone and shale, imposing slate-roofed houses and views out to the Drina Valley, Gjirokastra is an intriguing hillside town described beautifully by Albania's most famous literary export and local-born author, Ismail Kadare (b 1936), in *Chronicles of Stone*. Archaeological evidence suggests there's been a settlement here for 2500 years, though these days it's the 600 'monumental' houses in town that attract visitors. Some of these magnificent houses, a blend of Ottoman and local architectural influence, have caved in on themselves, and Unesco funding is being spent to maintain them. Gjirokastra-born former dictator Enver Hoxha made sure his hometown was listed as a museum city, but after the fall of the communist regime the houses fell into disrepair.

◉ Sights

Gjirokastra Castle   CASTLE

(admission 200 lekë; ☉8am-8pm) The town's moody castle hosts an eerie collection of armoury and is the setting for Gjirokastra's folk festival (held every four or five years). There's been a fortress here since the 12th century, although much of what can be seen today dates to the early 19th century. It's definitely worth the steep walk up from the Old Town, as well as an extra 200 lekë to visit its interior Museum Kombetar and see prison cells and more armoury. One of the more quirky sights on display is that of a recovered US Air Force jet that was shot down during the communist era.

TOP CHOICE Zekate House   HISTORIC BUILDING

(admission 200 lekë; ☉9am-6pm) This incredible three-storey house dates from 1811 and has twin towers and a double-arched facade. It's fascinating to nose around the almost totally unchanged interiors of an Ottoman-era home, especially the upstairs galleries, which are the most impressive. The owners live next door and collect the payments; to get here, follow the signs past the Hotel Kalemi and keep zigzagging up the hill.

Skenduli House   HISTORIC BUILDING

(Rr Ismail Kadare; admission 200 lekë; ☉9am-7pm) The latest Ottoman-era mansion to receive a (partial) renovation, the Skenduli House

is well worth a visit and desperately needs contributions to pay for the remaining restoration work. You'll most likely be shown around by Mr Skenduli himself, who speaks Italian and some basic French, but no English. The house dates from 1700 and has many fascinating features.

Ethnographic Museum   MUSEUM

(admission 200 lekë; ☉9am-6pm) This museum houses local homewares and was built on the site of Enver Hoxha's former house. Its collection is interesting if you're a fan of local arts and crafts, but don't come expecting anything about Hoxha himself.

Bazaar   HISTORIC SITE

The 'Neck of the Bazaar' makes up the centre of the Old Town and contains artisan shops that support masters of the local stone- and wood-carving industries.

🛌 Sleeping

Definitely stay in the scenic Old Town, though there are accommodation options in the new town if you can't find a room.

TOP CHOICE Hotel Kalemi   HOTEL €€

(☎068 2234 373, 263 724; draguak@yahoo.com; Lagjia Palorto Gjirokastra; r €35; P🌸❄@🛜) This delightful, large Ottoman-style hotel has spacious rooms adorned with carved ceilings, antique furnishings and large communal areas, including a broad verandah with Drina Valley views. Some rooms even have fireplaces, though bathrooms can be on the cramped side. Breakfast (juice, tea, a boiled egg and bread with delicious fig jam) is an all-local affair.

Kotoni B&B   B&B €

(☎263 526, 069 2366 846; www.kotonihouse.com; Rr Bashkim Kokona 8; s/d from €20/25; P❄🛜) Hosts Haxhi and Vita look after you in true Albanian style here: they love Gjirokastra and are happy to pass on information, as well as pack picnics for guests' day trips. The fact that these rooms are 220 years old makes up for their small size, while the astonishing views and friendly cats further sweeten the deal. Laundry is available, and fishing trips and hikes can be arranged.

Hotel Çajupi   HOTEL €€

(☎269 010; www.cajupi.com; Sheshi Çerçiz Topulli; s/d/tr €30/40/55; ❄) Aside from its relatively gargantuan size, it's hard to tell that this breezy and friendly place was once the default communist-era hotel for foreigners. Rooms are spacious, clean and pleasant. The hotel is located on the main square of the Old Town, perfectly situated for exploration. Breakfast is a fairly lame affair, but the rooftop restaurant affords great views.

Hotel Sopoti HOSTEL €
(☑069 399 8922; Sheshi Çerçiz Topulli; per person 1000 lekë) The shared bathrooms here are extremely basic, but if you can get past that, this budget place is a steal. It boasts a great location in the heart of the Old Town, as well as clean rooms, many of which have gorgeous traditional floor tiles and balconies with superb valley views. If there's nobody at reception, go into the next-door cafe, where the owner works. Breakfast isn't included.

✕ Eating

TOP CHOICE Kujtimi ALBANIAN €
(mains 200-600 lekë; ☉11am-11pm) On the left-hand side of the path to Fantazia Restaurant is this wonderfully laid-back outdoor restaurant, run by the Dumi family. Try the delicious *trofte* (fried trout; 400 lekë), the *midhje* (fried mussels; 350 lekë) and *qifqi* (rice balls fried in herbs and egg, a local speciality). The terrace here is the perfect place to absorb the charms of the Old Town, and while it's popular with travellers, on a typical night it's still bustling with locals too.

Fantasia Restaurant ALBANIAN €€
(mains 200-750 lekë; ☉noon-11pm) This modern place doesn't exactly overflow with local colour or traditional charm, but it has a large menu ranging from pizza to Albanian dishes, pastas and meat grills that keeps tour groups happy. It's located by a viewpoint with great views across the valley.

❶ Information

The new town (no slate roofs here) is on the main Saranda–Tirana road, and a taxi up to or back from the Old Town is 300 lekë.
Information Centre (☉8am-4pm Mon-Fri, 9am-2pm & 4-9pm Sat & Sun Oct-Jun, 8.30am-2pm & 4-10pm Jul-Sep) Opposite Çajupi Hotel behind the statue of the partisans.

❶ Getting There & Away

Buses pass through the new town on their way to Tirana and Saranda, and *furgons* also go to Saranda (300 lekë, one hour). It takes about an hour to get to the Blue Eye Spring from Gjirokastra; buses to and from Saranda pass by its entrance, which is 2km from the spring itself. Buses to Tirana (1200 lekë, seven hours) leave on the hour from 5am – the last one passes through after 11pm. There are also irregular *furgons* to Berat (1000 lekë, four hours). From the bottom of the hill leading from the Old Town, turn left and walk 800m to find the ad hoc bus station just after the Eida petrol station.

UNDERSTAND ALBANIA

Albania Today

Albania managed to manoeuvre itself around the crippling economic crisis that gripped other European countries in 2008, and economic growth has continued. Despite this, infrastucture deficiencies still plague the country. Albania joined NATO in 2009 and may well become an official EU membership candidate in 2013, if elections to be held then are deemed fair.

History

Albanians call their country Shqipëria, and trace their roots to the ancient Illyrian tribes. Their language is descended from Illyrian, making it a rare survivor of the Roman and Slavic influxes and a European linguistic oddity on a par with Basque. The Illyrians occupied the western Balkans during the 2nd millennium BC. They built substantial fortified cities, mastered silver and copper mining, and became adept at sailing the Mediterranean. The Greeks arrived in the 7th century BC to establish self-governing colonies at Epidamnos (now Durrës), Apollonia and Butrint. They traded peacefully with the Illyrians, who formed tribal states in the 4th century BC.

Roman, Byzantine & Ottoman Rule

Inevitably the expanding Illyrian kingdom of the Ardiaei, based at Shkodra, came into conflict with Rome, which sent a fleet of 200 vessels against Queen Teuta in 229 BC. A long war resulted in the extension of Roman control over the entire Balkan area by 167 BC.

Under the Romans, Illyria enjoyed peace and prosperity, though large agricultural estates were worked by slaves. The Illyrians preserved their own language and traditions despite Roman rule. Over time the populace slowly replaced their old gods with the new Christian faith championed by Emperor Constantine. The main trade route between Rome and Constantinople, the Via Egnatia, ran from the port at Durrës.

When the Roman Empire was divided in AD 395, Illyria fell within the Eastern Empire, later known as the Byzantine Empire. Three early Byzantine emperors (Anastasius I, Justin I and Justinian I) were of Illyrian origin. Invasions by migrating peoples (Visigoths, Huns, Ostrogoths and Slavs) continued through the 5th and 6th centuries.

In 1344 Albania was annexed by Serbia, but after the defeat of Serbia by the Turks in 1389 the whole region was open to Ottoman attack. The Venetians occupied some coastal towns, and from 1443 to 1468 the national hero Skanderbeg (Gjergj Kastrioti) led Albanian resistance to the Turks from his castle at Kruja. Skanderbeg won all 25 battles he fought against the Turks, and even Sultan Mehmet-Fatih, the conqueror of Constantinople, could not take Kruja. After Skanderbeg's death the Ottomans overwhelmed Albanian resistance, taking control of the country in 1479, 26 years after Constantinople fell.

Ottoman rule lasted 400 years. Muslim citizens were favoured and were exempted from the janissary system, whereby Christian households had to give up one of their sons to convert to Islam and serve in the army. Consequently, many Albanians embraced the new faith.

Independent Albania

In 1878 the Albanian League at Prizren (in present-day Kosovo) began a struggle for autonomy that the Turkish army put down in 1881. Further uprisings between 1910 and 1912 culminated in a proclamation of independence and the formation of a provisional government led by Ismail Qemali at Vlora in 1912. These achievements were severely compromised when Kosovo, roughly one-third of Albania, was ceded to Serbia in 1913. The Great Powers tried to install a young German prince, Wilhelm of Wied, as ruler, but he wasn't accepted and returned home after six months. With the outbreak of WWI, Albania was occupied in succession by the armies of Greece, Serbia, France, Italy and Austria-Hungary.

In 1920 the capital city was moved from Durrës to less vulnerable Tirana. A republican government under the Orthodox priest Fan Noli helped to stabilise the country, but in 1924 it was overthrown by the interior minister, Ahmed Bey Zogu. A northern warlord, he declared himself King Zogu I in 1928, but his close collaboration with Italy backfired in April 1939 when Mussolini ordered an invasion of Albania. Zogu fled to Britain with his young wife, Geraldine, and newborn son, Leka, and used gold looted from the Albanian treasury to rent a floor at London's Ritz Hotel.

On 8 November 1941 the Albanian Communist Party was founded with Enver Hoxha as first secretary, a position he held until his death in April 1985. The communists led

---

FAMILY FEUD WITH BLOOD AS THE PRIZE

The *Kanun* (Code) was formalised in the 15th century by powerful northern chieftain Lekë Dukagjin. It consists of 1262 articles covering every aspect of daily life: work, marriage, family, property, hospitality, economy and so on. Though the *Kanun* was suppressed by the communists, there has been a revival of its strict precepts in northern Albania.

According to the *Kanun,* the most important things in life are honour and hospitality. If a member of a family (or one of their guests) is murdered, it becomes the duty of the male members of that clan to claim their blood debt by murdering a male member of the murderer's clan. This sparks an endless cycle of killing that doesn't end until either all the male members of one of the families are dead, or reconciliation is brokered through respected village elders.

Hospitality is so important in these parts of Albania that the guest takes on a godlike status. There are 38 articles giving instructions on how to treat a guest – an abundance of food, drink and comfort is at his or her disposal, and it is also the host's duty to avenge the murder of his guest, should this happen during their visit. It's worth reading *Broken April*, by Ismail Kadare, a brilliant exploration of people living under the *Kanun*.

the resistance against the Italians and, after 1943, against the Germans.

Communist Albania

In January 1946 the People's Republic of Albania was proclaimed, with Hoxha as president and 'Supreme Comrade'.

In September 1948 Albania broke off relations with Yugoslavia, which had hoped to incorporate the country into the Yugoslav Federation. Instead, it allied itself with Stalin's USSR and put into effect a series of Soviet-style economic plans – raising the ire of the USA and Britain, which made an ill-fated attempt to overthrow the government.

Albania collaborated closely with the USSR until 1960, despite Krushchev's denunciation of Stalin in his 1954 'secret speech'. However, when a heavy-handed Khrushchev demanded that a submarine base be set up at Vlora in 1961, Albania broke off diplomatic relations with the USSR and reoriented itself towards Maoist China.

From 1966 to 1967 Albania experienced a Chinese-style cultural revolution. Administrative workers were suddenly transferred to remote areas and younger cadres were placed in leading positions. The collectivisation of agriculture was completed and organised religion was completely banned.

Following the Soviet invasion of Czechoslovakia in 1968, Albania left the Warsaw Pact and embarked on a self-reliant defence policy. Some 60,000 igloo-shaped concrete bunkers were built at this time, the crumbling remains of which can still be seen all over the country today. Under the communists, some malarial swamps were drained, hydroelectric schemes and railway lines were built, and the literacy level was raised. Albania's people, however, lived in fear of the Sigurimi (secret police) and were not permitted to leave the country. Many were tortured, jailed or murdered for misdemeanours such as listening to foreign radio stations.

With the death of Mao Zedong in 1976 and the changes that followed in China after 1978, Albania's unique relationship with China also came to an end, and the country was left totally isolated and without allies. The economy was devastated and food shortages became more common.

Post-Hoxha

Hoxha died in April 1985 and his associate Ramiz Alia took over the leadership. Restrictions loosened (Albania was opened up to tourists in organised groups) but people no longer bothered to work on the collective farms, leading to food shortages in the cities. Industries began to fail and Tirana's population tripled as people took advantage of being able to freely move to the city.

In June 1990, inspired by the changes that were occurring elsewhere in Eastern Europe, around 4500 Albanians took refuge in Western embassies in Tirana. After a brief confrontation with the police and the Sigurimi, these people were allowed to board ships for Brindisi in Italy, where they were granted political asylum.

Following student demonstrations in December 1990, the government agreed to allow opposition parties, and the Democratic Party, led by heart surgeon Sali Berisha, was formed.

The March 1992 elections ended 47 years of communist rule, with parliament electing Sali Berisha president. Former president Alia was later placed under house arrest for writing articles critical of the Democratic government, and the leader of the Socialist Party, Fatos Nano, was also arrested on corruption charges.

During this time Albania switched from a tightly controlled communist regime to a rambunctious free-market free-for-all. A huge smuggling racket sprang up in which stolen Mercedes-Benz cars were brought into the country, and the port of Vlora became a major crossing point for illegal immigrants from Asia and the Middle East into Italy.

In 1996, 70% of Albanians lost their savings when private pyramid-investment schemes, believed to have been supported by the government, collapsed. Riots ensued, elections were called, and the victorious Socialist Party under Nano – who had been freed from prison by a rampaging mob – was able to restore some degree of security and investor confidence.

In 1999 a different type of crisis struck when 465,000 Kosovars fled to Albania as a result of a Serbian ethnic-cleansing campaign. The influx had a positive effect on Albania's economy, and strengthened the relationship between Albania and Kosovo.

For the past decade Albania has found itself in a kind of mini-boom, with a lot of money being poured into construction projects and infrastructure renewal. The general election of 2005 saw a return of Berisha's Democratic Party to government, and in 2009 they narrowly won again, forming a coalition with the Socialist Movement for Intergration (LSI).

People

Albania's population is made up of approximately 95% Albanians, 3% Greeks and 2% 'other' – comprising Vlachs, Roma, Serbs, Macedonians and Bulgarians. The majority of young people speak some English, but speaking a few words of Albanian (or Italian, and, on the south coast, Greek) will be useful. Like most Balkan people, Albanians shake their heads sideways to say yes *(po)* and usually nod and 'tsk' to say no *(jo* – pronounced 'yo'*)*. Albanians familiar with foreigners often take on the nod-for-yes way, which increases confusion.

The Ghegs in the north and the Tosks in the south have different dialects, music, dress and the usual jokes about each other's weaknesses.

Albanians are nominally 70% Muslim, 20% Christian Orthodox and 10% Catholic, but more realistic statistics estimate that up to 75% of Albanians are nonreligious. Religion was ruthlessly stamped out by the 1967 cultural revolution, when all mosques and churches were taken over by the state. By 1990 only about 5% of Albania's religious buildings were left intact. The rest had been turned into cinemas or army stores, or were destroyed. Albania remains a very secular society.

The Muslim faith has a branch called Bektashism, similar to Sufism, and its world headquarters were in Albania from 1925 to 1945. Bektashi followers go to *teqe* (temple-like buildings without a minaret), which are found on hilltops in towns where those of the faith fled persecution. Most Bektashis live in the southern half of the country.

Arts

Literature

One Albanian writer who is widely read outside Albania is Ismail Kadare (b 1936). In 2005 he won the inaugural Man Booker International Prize for his body of work. His books are a great source of information on Albanian traditions, history and social events, and exquisitely capture the atmosphere of the country's towns, as in the lyrical descriptions of Kadare's birthplace, Gjirokastra, in *Chronicle in Stone* (1971). *Broken April* (1990), set in the northern highlands before the 1939 Italian invasion, describes the life of a village boy who is next in line in a desperate cycle of blood vendettas.

Cinema

During Albania's isolationist years the only Western actor approved by Hoxha was UK actor Sir Norman Wisdom (he became quite a cult hero). However, with so few international movies to choose from, the local film industry had a captive audience. While much of its output was propagandist, by the 1980s this little country was turning out an extraordinary 14 films a year. Despite a general lack of funds, two movies have gone on to win awards at international film festivals. Gjergj Xhuvani's comedy *Slogans* (2001) is a warm and touching account of life during communist times. This was followed in 2002 by *Tirana Year Zero,* Fatmir Koci's bleak look at the pressures on the young to emigrate. *Lorna's Silence* (2008), a film about Albanians living in Belgium, was awarded in the 2008 Cannes Film Festival.

Music

Blaring from cars, bars, restaurants and mobile phones – music is something you get plenty of in Albania. Most modern Albanian music has clarinet threaded through it and a goat-skin drum beat behind it. Polyphony, the blending of several independent vocal or instrumental parts, dates from ancient Illyrian times, and can still be heard, particularly in the south.

Visual Arts

One of the first signs of the Albanian arts scene are the multicoloured buildings of Tirana, a project organised by the capital's former mayor, Edi Rama, himself an artist. The building's residents don't get a say in the colour or design, and come home to find their homes daubed in spots, paintings of trees, or even paintings of laundry drying under their windowsills.

One of the most delicious Albanian art treats is to be found in Berat's Onufri Museum. Onufri was the most outstanding Albanian icon painter of the 16th and 17th centuries, and his work is noted for its unique intensity of colour, derived from natural dyes that are as fresh now as the day he painted with them.

Environment

Albania consists of 30% vast interior plains, 362km of coast and a mountainous spine that runs its length. Mt Korab, at 2764m, is Albania's highest peak.

The country's large and beautiful lakes include the Balkans' biggest, Lake Shkodra, which borders Montenegro in the north, and the ancient Lake Ohrid in the east (one-third Albanian, two-thirds Macedonian). Albania's longest river is the Drin (280km), which originates in Kosovo and is fed by melting snow from mountains in Albania's north and east. Hydroelectricity has changed Albania's landscape: Lake Koman was once a river, and the blue water from the Blue Eye Spring near Saranda travels to the coast in open concrete channels via a hydroelectricity plant. Agriculture makes up a small percentage of land use, and citrus and olive trees spice up the coastal plains. Most rural householders grow their own food.

National Parks & Wildlife

The number of national parks in Albania has risen from six to 15 since 1966 and include Dajti, Llogara, Tomorri, Butrint, Valbonë and Theth. Most are protected only by their remoteness, and tree-felling and hunting still take place. Hiking maps of the national parks are available, though they can be hard to find (try *Wanderkarte Nordalbanien* for Theth).

Albania's Alps have become a 'must-do' for hikers, and they're home to brown bear, wolf, otter, marten, wild cat, wild boar and deer. Falcons and grouse are also Alpine favourites, and birdwatchers can also flock to wetlands at Lake Butrint, Karavasta Lagoon and Lake Shkodra (though the wetlands aren't pristine).

Lake Ohrid's trout is endangered (but still eaten), and endangered loggerhead turtles nest on the Ionian coast and on the Karaburun Peninsula, where there have also been sightings of critically endangered Mediterranean monk seals.

Environmental Issues

During communism, there were around 2000 cars in the country. Now it seems everyone has one, with many of Albania's older cars being diesel Mercedes-Benzes stolen from Western Europe. As a consequence of the explosion, air-pollution levels in Tirana are five to 10 times higher than in Western European countries.

Illegal logging and fishing reached epidemic proportions during the 1990s, and there are signs of it today; fishing for the endangered *koran* trout in Lake Ohrid continues, as does fishing with dynamite along the coast.

Albania was practically litter-free until the early 1990s, as everything was reused or recycled, but today there's literally rubbish everywhere. Walk around the perimeter of a hotel in a picturesque location and you'll come across its very unpicturesque dumping ground. Some Albanians are doing their bit to improve these conditions, and a 'raising awareness' campaign against litter was started by well-known Albanians in 2010.

Food & Drink

In coastal areas the calamari, mussels and fish will knock your socks off, while high-altitude areas such as Llogaraja have roast lamb worth climbing a mountain for.

Offal is popular; *fërgesë Tiranë* is a traditional Tirana dish of offal, eggs and tomatoes cooked in an earthenware pot.

Italian influences mean vegetarians will probably become vegitalians, and many restaurants serve pizza, pasta or grilled and stuffed vegetables.

Local Drinks

Raki is very popular. The two main types are grape raki (the most common) and *mani* (mulberry) raki. Ask for homemade if possible *(raki ë bërë në shtëpi)*. If wine is more your cup of tea, seek out the Çobo winery near Berat and its Shesh i Bardhe white. Local beers include Tirana, Norga (from Vlora) and Korça. Coffee remains the standard drink of choice at any time of day.

SURVIVAL GUIDE

Directory A–Z
Accommodation

With almost every house, bar and petrol station doubling as a hotel, you might think you'll never have trouble finding a bed in Albania, and you're right, though seaside towns are often booked out in August.

Homestays abound in Theth, while the number of camping grounds is increasing; you'll find them at Himare, Livadhi, Dhërmi and Drymades (from €4 per person). Most have hot showers, on-site restaurants and entertainment.

All but the most basic places have free wireless internet for guests.

The following price categories for the cost of a double room in high season are used in the listings in this chapter.

€ less than €30

€€ €30 to €80

€€€ more than €80

Activities

Hiking and adventure sports are gaining popularity in Albania, and **Outdoor Albania** (☑2227 121; www.outdooralbania.com; Rr Sami Frasheri, Pallati Metropol) is an excellent organisation at the forefront of the industry. Smaller operatives are starting up: **Albania Rafting** (☑2006 621; www.albrafting.com) runs rafting tours of the Osumi River and canyons in Berat. Hiking in the Alps, particularly around Theth and Valbonë, is popular (with and without guides), as is mountain biking around the country.

Business Hours

Banks 9am to 3.30pm Monday to Friday

Cafes & Bars 8am to midnight

Offices 8am to 5pm Monday to Friday

Restaurants 8am to midnight

Shops 8am to 7pm; siesta time can be any time between noon and 4pm

Embassies & Consulates

There is no Australian, Canadian, New Zealand or Irish embassy in Albania. The following embassies and consulates are in Tirana:

French Embassy (☑04-238 9700; www.ambafrance-al.org; Rr Skënderbej 14)

German Embassy (☑04-2274 505; www.tirana.diplo.de; Rr Skënderbej 8)

Netherlands Embassy (☑04-2240 828; www.albanie.nlambassade.org; Rr Asim Zeneli 10)

UK Embassy (☑04-2234 973; www.ukinalbania.fco.gov.uk; Rr Skënderbej 12)

US Embassy (☑04-2247 285; http://tirana.usembassy.gov; Rr Elbasanit 103)

Food

The following price categories for the cost of a main course are used in the listings in this chapter.

€ less than 200 lekë

€€ 200 lekë to 500 lekë

€€€ more than 500 lekë

Gay & Lesbian Travellers

Extensive antidiscrimination legislation became law in 2010, but did not extend to legalising same-sex marriage. Gay and lesbian life in Albania is alive and well but is not yet organised into clubs or organisations. Gaydar will serve gay and lesbian visitors well here: you'll have to ask on the street or online where the parties are. The alternative music and party scene in Tirana is queer-friendly.

Internet Access

If you've brought your own smartphone or laptop you can access free wi-fi in most hotels and many restaurants around the country. Internet cafes (increasingly rare) cost around 100 lekë per hour.

Money

The lekë is the official currency, though the euro is widely accepted; you'll get a better rate in general if you use lekë. Accommodation is generally quoted in euros but can be paid in either currency. ATMs (found in most of Albania's towns, bar remote villages) usually offer to dispense cash in either currency.

Albanian banknotes come in denominations of 100, 200, 500, 1000, 2000 and 5000 lekë. There are five, 10, 20, 50 and 100 lekë coins.

Albanian lekë can't be exchanged outside the country, so exchange them or spend them before you leave.

Credit cards are accepted only in the larger hotels, shops and travel agencies, and few of these are outside Tirana.

It's polite to leave your change as a tip.

Post

The postal system is fairly rudimentary – there are no postcodes, for example – and it certainly does not enjoy a reputation for efficiency.

Public Holidays

New Year's Day 1 January
Summer Day 16 March
Nevruz 23 March
Catholic Easter March or April
Orthodox Easter March or April
May Day 1 May
Mother Teresa Day 19 October
Independence Day 28 November
Liberation Day 29 November
Christmas Day 25 December

Telephone

Albania's country phone code is ☎355 (dial ☎+ or ☎00 first from a mobile phone).

Three established mobile-phone providers are Vodafone, AMC and Eagle, and a fourth licence has been promised. Don't expect isolated areas to have coverage (though most do, including Theth). Prepaid SIM cards cost around 1000 lekë and include credit. Mobile numbers begin with ☎06. To call an Albanian mobile number from abroad, dial ☎+355 then either ☎67, ☎68 or ☎69 (ie drop the 0).

Tourist Information

Tourist information offices with some English-speaking staff operate in Tirana, Shkodra, Saranda, Gjirokastra (www.gjirokastra.org) and Berat (www.bashkia-berat.net).

Travellers with Disabilities

High footpaths and unannounced potholes make life difficult for mobility-impaired travellers. Tirana's top hotels do cater to people with disabilities, and some smaller hotels are making an effort to be more accessible. The roads and castle entrances in Gjirokastra, Berat and Kruja are cobblestone, although taxis can get reasonably close.

Visas

Visas are not required for citizens of EU countries or nationals of Australia, Canada, New Zealand, Japan, South Korea, Norway, South Africa or the USA. Travellers from other countries should check www.mfa.gov.al. Passports are stamped for a 90-day stay.

A €10 entry and exit fee was abolished some years ago; do not be conned into paying this by taxi drivers at border crossings.

Women Travellers

Albania is a safe country for women travellers, but outside Tirana it is mainly men who go out and sit in bars and cafes in the evenings. You may tire of being asked why you're travelling alone.

Getting There & Away
Air

Nënë Tereza International Airport is 17km northwest of Tirana and is a modern, well-run terminal. There are no domestic flights within Albania. The following airlines fly to and from Albania:

Adria Airways (☎04-2272 666; www.adria.si) Flies to Ljubljana.

Air One (☎04-2230 023; www.flyairone.it) Flies to Milan, Pisa and Venice.

Alitalia (☎04-2230 023; www.alitalia.com) Flies to Rome, Verona, Turin, Naples, Florence, Genoa, Milan, Catania and Venice.

Austrian Airlines (☎04-2235 029; www.austrian.com) Flies to Vienna.

BelleAir (☎04-2240 175; www.belleair.it) Flies to Pristina, Ancona, Rimini, Forli, Bari, Pescara, Naples, Trieste, Perugia, Milan, Treviso, Turin, Palma, Bologna, Pisa, Florence, Rome, Geneva, London, Prague, Brussels and Vienna.

British Airways (☎04-2381 991; www.britishairways.com) Flies to London.

Lufthansa (☎04-2258 010; www.lufthansa.com) Flies to Vienna and Munich.

Olympic Air (☎04-2228 960; www.olympicair.com) Flies to Athens.

Turkish Airlines (☎04-2258 459; www.turkishairlines.com) Flies to İstanbul.

Land
BORDER CROSSINGS

There are no passenger trains into Albania, so your border-crossing options are buses, *furgons,* taxis or walking to a border and picking up transport on the other side.

Montenegro The main crossings link Shkodra to Ulcinj (Muriqan) and to Podgorica (Hani i Hotit).

Kosovo The closest border crossing to the Koman Ferry terminal is Morina, and further south is Qafë Prush. Near Kukës use Morinë for the highway to Tirana.

Macedonia Use Blato to get to Debar, quiet Qafë e Thanës to the north of Lake Ohrid, or Sveti Naum, near Pogradec, to its south. There's also a crossing at Stenje.

Greece The main border crossing to and from Greece is Kakavija on the road from Athens to Tirana. It's about half an hour from Gjirokastra and 250km west of Tirana, and can take up to three hours to pass through during summer. Kapshtica (near Korça) also gets long lines in summer. Konispoli is near Butrint in Albania's south.

BUS

From Tirana, regular buses head to Pristina, Kosovo; to Struga, Tetovo and Skopje in Macedonia; to Budva and Ulcinj in Montenegro; and to Athens and Thessaloniki in Greece. *Furgons* and buses leave Shkodra for Montenegro, and buses head to Kosovo from Durrës. Buses travel to Greece from Albanian towns on the southern coast and buses to Italy leave from Vlora.

CAR & MOTORCYCLE

To enter, you'll need a Green Card (proof of third-party insurance, issued by your insurer); check that your insurance covers Albania.

TAXI

Heading to Macedonia, taxis from Pogradec will drop you off just before the border at Tushëmisht/Sveti Naum. Alternatively, it's an easy 4km walk to the border from Pogradec. It's possible to organise a taxi (or, more usually, a person with a car) from where the Koman Ferry stops in Fierzë to Gjakove in Kosovo. Taxis commonly charge €40 from Shkodra to Ulcinj in Montenegro.

Sea

Two or three ferries per day ply the route between Saranda and Corfu, in Greece, and there are plenty of ferry companies making the journey to Italy from Vlora and Durrës, as well as additional ferries from Vlora to Corfu.

Getting Around

Bicycle

Cycling in Albania is tough but certainly feasible. Expect lousy road conditions including open drains, some abysmal driving from fellow road users and roads that barely qualify for the title. Organised groups head north for mountain biking, and cyclists are even spotted cycling the long and tough Korça–Gjirokastra road. Shkodra, Durrës and Tirana are towns where you'll see locals embracing the bike, and Tirana even has bike lanes.

Bus

The first bus/*furgon* departure is often at 5am and things slow down around lunchtime. There are many buses catering for the crowds along the coast in July and August. Fares are low, and you either pay the conductor on board or when you hop off.

Municipal buses operate in Tirana, Durrës, Shkodra and Vlora, and trips cost 30 lekë.

Car & Motorcycle

Albania's drivers are not the best in the world, mostly due to the communist era, when car ownership required a permit from the government, and only two were issued to nonparty members. As a result, the government didn't invest in new roads, and most Albanians were inexperienced motorists. Nowadays the road infrastructure is improving; there's an excellent highway from Tirana to Kosovo, and the coastal route from the Montenegro border to Butrint, near Saranda, is in good condition.

Tourists are driving cars, motorbikes and mobile homes into the country in greater numbers, and, apart from bad roads and bad drivers, it's generally hassle-free.

Off the main routes a 4WD is a good idea. Driving at night is particularly hazardous; follow another car on the road as there's rarely any road markings or street lighting.

DRIVING LICENCE

Foreign driving licences are all that's required to drive a car in Albania.

CAR HIRE

There are lots of car-hire companies operating out of Tirana, including all the major international agencies. Hiring a small car costs from €35 per day.

ROAD RULES

Drinking and driving is forbidden, and there is zero tolerance for blood-alcohol readings. Both motorcyclists and passengers must wear helmets. Speed limits are as low as 30km/h in built-up areas and 35km/h on the edges, and there are plenty of speed cameras monitoring the roads. Keep your car's papers with you, as police are active checkers.

Hitching

Though never entirely safe, hitchhiking is quite a common way for travellers to get around – though it's rare to see locals doing it.

Train

Albanians prefer bus and *furgon* travel, and when you see the speed and the state of the (barely) existing trains, you'll know why. However, the trains are dirt cheap and travelling on them is an adventure. Daily passenger trains leave Tirana for Durrës, Shkodra, Fier, Vlora, Elbasan and a few kilometres out of Pogradec. Check timetables at the station in person, and buy your ticket 10 minutes before departure. Albania is not connected to neighbouring countries by train.

Bosnia & Hercegovina

Includes »

Why Go?

This craggily beautiful land retains some lingering scars from the heartbreaking civil war in the 1990s. But today visitors will more likely remember Bosnia and Hercegovina (BiH) for its deep, unassuming human warmth and for the intriguing East-meets-West atmosphere born of fascinatingly blended Ottoman and Austro-Hungarian histories.

Major drawcards are the reincarnated antique centres of Sarajevo and Mostar, where rebuilt historical buildings counterpoint fashionable bars and wi-fi–equipped cafes. Elsewhere Socialist-era architectural monstrosities are surprisingly rare blots on predominantly rural landscapes. Many Bosnian towns are lovably small, wrapped around medieval castles and surrounded by mountain ridges or cascading river canyons. Few places in Europe offer better rafting or such accessible, inexpensive skiing.

Best Places to Eat

» Mala Kuhinja (p79)

» Bridge-view restaurants, Mostar (p92)

» Riverside restaurants on the Una (p105)

» Vinoteka Vukuje (p96)

Best Places to Stay

» Muslibegović House (p90)

» Hotel Platani (p96)

» Želenkovac (p104)

» Kostelski Buk (p105)

When to Go

Sarajevo

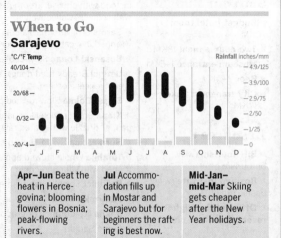

Apr–Jun Beat the heat in Hercegovina; blooming flowers in Bosnia; peak-flowing rivers.

Jul Accommodation fills up in Mostar and Sarajevo but for beginners the rafting is best now.

Mid-Jan–mid-Mar Skiing gets cheaper after the New Year holidays.

AT A GLANCE

» **Currency** Convertible mark (KM, BAM)

» **Language** Bosnian, Croatian, Serbian

» **Money** ATMs widely available in towns

» **Visas** Not required for most visitors

Fast Facts

» **Area** 51,129 sq km

» **Capital** Sarajevo

» **Country code** ☑387

» **Emergency** Ambulance ☑124, fire ☑123, police ☑122

Exchange Rates

Australia	A$1	1.59KM
Canada	C$1	1.51KM
Euro Zone	€1	1.96KM
Japan	¥100	1.62KM
New Zealand	NZ$1	1.28KM
UK	UK£1	2.32KM
USA	US$1	1.53KM

Set Your Budget

» **Budget hotel room** 70KM

» **Two-course meal** 18KM

» **Museum entrance** 1–5KM

» **Beer** 2–4KM

» **City transport ticket** 1.80KM

Resources

» **BiH Tourism** (www.bhtourism.ba)

» **Bosnian Institute** (www.bosnia.org.uk)

» **Office of the High Representative** (www.ohr.int)

Connections

Regular buses link the Croatian coast to Mostar and Sarajevo plus there's a little-publicised Trebinje–Dubrovnik service. Trains link Sarajevo to Zagreb, Belgrade and Budapest-Keleti, the only direct overland link to Hungary. There are numerous bus connections to Serbia and Montenegro from Sarajevo, Višegrad and Trebinje.

ITINERARIES

Six Days

Arriving from Dubrovnik (coastal Croatia), roam Mostar's Old Town and join a day tour visiting Počitelj, Blagaj and the Kravice waterfalls. After two days in Sarajevo head for Jajce then bus down to Split (Croatia). Or visit Višegrad en route to Mokra Gora and Belgrade (Serbia).

Two Weeks

Add Trebinje and (if driving) historic Stolac between Dubrovnik and Mostar. Ski or go cycling around Bjelašnica, visit the controversial Visoko pyramid and old-town Travnik en route to Jajce, and consider adding in some high-adrenaline rafting from Banja Luka, Bihać or Foča.

Essential Food & Drink

» **Ćevapi (Ćevapčići)** Minced meat formed into cylindrical pellets and served in fresh bread with melting *kajmak* (thick semi-soured cream).

» **Pljeskavica** Patty-shaped Ćevapi.

» **Burek** Bosnian *burek* are cylindrical lengths of filo-pastry filled with minced meat, often wound into spirals. *Buredici* is the same served with *kajmak* and garlic, *sirnica* is filled instead with cheese, *krompiruša* with potato and *zeljanica* with spinach. Collectively these pies are called *pita*.

» **Sarma** Small *dolma*-parcels of rice and minced meat wrapped in a cabbage or other green leaf.

» **Bosanski Lonac** Slow-cooked meat-and-veg hotpot.

» **Uštipci** Bready fried dough-balls often eaten with sour cream, cheese or jam.

» **Sogan Dolma** Slow roasted onions filled with minced meat.

» **Klepe** Small ravioli-like triangles served in a butter-pepper drizzle with grated raw garlic.

» **Hurmastica** Syrup-soaked sponge fingers.

» **Tufahija** Whole stewed apple with walnut-filling and topped with whipped cream.

» **Ražnijići** Shish kebab (ie meat barbequed on skewers).

» **Pastrmka** Trout.

» **Rakija** Fruit brandy or grappa.

» **Ligne** Squid.

Bosnia & Hercegovina Highlights

❶ Nose about Mostar's atmospheric Old Town and admire the magnificently rebuilt **Stari Most** (p86).

❷ Raft down one of BiH's fast-flowing rivers – whether from **Foča** (p97) **Bihać** (p105) or **Banja Luka** (p101).

❸ Ski the 1984 Olympic pistes at **Jahorina** (p84) or **Bjelašnica** (p85) or explore the wild uplands behind them.

❹ Potter around the timeless pedestrian lanes of **Sarajevo** (p72), and sample its fashionable cafes and eclectic nightlife.

❺ Gaze through willow fronds at the Unesco-listed 16th-century bridge in **Višegrad** (p97) that inspired a Nobel Prize–winning novel.

❻ Wine and dine in historic little **Trebinje** (p96) and wander the low-key, stone-flagged Old Town.

❼ Tune in to the mystical energy of **Visoko** (p98), asking yourself if you're really climbing the world's biggest pyramid.

SARAJEVO

☑033 / 436,000

In the 1990s Sarajevo was on the edge of annihilation. Today it's a vibrant yet very human city, notable for its attractive contours and East-meets-West ambience.

Beyond the stone-flagged alleys of central Baščaršija, 'Turkish Town', steep valley sides are fuzzed with red-roofed Bosnian houses and prickled with uncountable minarets, climbing towards green-topped mountain ridges. Westward, Sarajevo sprawls for over 10km through Novo Sarajevo and dreary Dobrijna past dismal ranks of bullet-scarred apartment blocks. At the westernmost end of the tramway spine, affluent Ilidža gives the city a final parkland flourish. In winter, Bjelašnica and Jahorina offer some of Europe's best-value skiing, barely 30km away.

History

Romans had bathed at Ilidža's sulphur springs a millennium earlier, but Sarajevo was officially 'founded' by 15th-century Turks. It rapidly grew wealthy as a silk-importing entrepôt and developed considerably during the 1530s when Ottoman governor Gazi-Husrevbey lavished the city with mosques and covered bazaars. In 1697 the city was burnt by Eugene of Savoy's Austrian army. When rebuilt, Sarajevo cautiously enclosed its upper flank in a large, fortified citadel, the remnants of which still dominate the Vratnik area.

The Austro-Hungarians were back more permanently in 1878 and erected many imposing central-European-style buildings. However, their rule was put on notice by Gavrilo Princip's fatal 1914 pistol shot that

killed Archduke Franz Ferdinand, plunging the world into WWI.

Less than a decade after hosting the 1984 Winter Olympics, Sarajevo endured an infamous siege that horrified the world. Between 1992 and 1995, Sarajevo's heritage of six centuries was pounded into rubble and its only access to the outside world was via a metre-wide, 800m-long tunnel under the airport. Bosnian Serb shelling and sniper fire killed over 10,500 Sarajevans and wounded 50,000 more. Uncountable white-stoned graves on Kovači and up near Koševo Stadium are a moving testimony to those terrible years.

⊙ Sights & Activities

The best way to really 'feel' the city is to stroll Old Sarajevo's pedestrian lanes and grand avenues and climb the gently picturesque slopes of Bjelave and Vratnik for sweeping views. Seeking out key museums is likely to take you into much more modern, businesslike Novo Sarajevo and on to park-filled Ilidža at the distant western end of the tram network.

OLD SARAJEVO

Baščaršija, the bustling old Turkish quarter is a warren of marble-flagged pedestrian courtyards and lanes full of mosques, copper workshops, jewellery shops and inviting restaurants. The riverbanks and avenues Ferhadija and Maršala Tita are well endowed with Austro-Hungarian architecture. And attesting to Sarajevo's traditional religious tolerance, you'll find within a couple of blocks several mosques, a synagogue, the artfully floodlit 1872 **Orthodox Cathedral** (Saborna Crkva Presvete Bogordice; Map p76; Trg Oslobođenja) and the **Catholic Cathedral** (Katedrala Srca Isusova; Map p76; Trg Fra Grge Martića 2; ⊙9am-4pm) where Pope John Paul II served mass in 1997. The area's charms are best discovered by wandering between the many street cafes.

Pigeon Square NEIGHBOURHOOD
(Map p76) Nicknamed Pigeon Sq for all the birds, Baščaršija's central open space centres on the **Sebilj**, an ornate 1891 drinking fountain. It leads past the lively (if tourist-centric) coppersmith alley, **Kazandžiluk**, leading down to the garden-wrapped 16th-century **Baščaršija Džamija** (Baščaršija mosque; Map p76; Baščaršija 37).

Bursa Bezistan MUSEUM
(Map p76; www.muzejsarajeva.ba; Abadžiluk 10; admission 3KM; ⊙10am-6pm Mon-Fri, 10am-3pm Sat) The six-domed 1551 Bursa Bezistan was

BOSNIA & HERCEGOVINA SARAJEVO

SARAJEVO IN TWO DAYS

Plunge into the pedestrianised 'Turkish' lanes of **Baščaršija** and the street cafes of **Ferhadija**. From the spot where a 1914 assassination kicked off WWI, cross the cute **Latin Bridge** for a beer at **Pivnica HS** or dinner overlooking the city rooftops at **Biban**.

Next day ponder the horrors of the 1990s siege era at the moving **History Museum** and unique **Tunnel Museum**. Recover with a drink at eccentrically Gothic **Zlatna Ribica** and a feisty gig at **Underground**.

originally a silk-trading bazaar. Today it's a small museum with bite-sized overviews of the city's history and a compelling model of Sarajevo as it looked in 1878.

Gazi-Husrevbey Mosque   MOSQUE
(Map p76; www.vakuf-gazi.ba; Saraći 18; admission 2KM; ☺9am-noon, 2.30-3.30pm & 5-6.15pm May-Sep, closed Ramadan) Ottoman governor Gazi-Husrevbey funded a series of splendid 16th-century buildings of which this mosque forms the greatest centrepiece. Its cylindrical minaret contrasts photogenically with the elegant stone clock tower off Mudželeti Veliki alley. The associated madrassa (Religious School; Saraći 33-49) across Saraći is used for occasional exhibitions and book sales, its time-worn stonework contrasting conspicuously with the brand new library next door.

Vijećnica   ARCHITECTURE
(Map p76) With its storybook neo-Moorish facades, the 1892 Vijećnica is Sarajevo's most beautiful Austro-Hungarian era building. Originally the City Hall, Franz Ferdinand was on the way back from here when shot by Princip in 1914. It later became the Bosnian National Library. However, during the 1990s siege it was deliberately hit by a Serb incendiary shell. Around 90% of its irreplaceable collection of manuscripts and Bosnian books was destroyed and for nearly two decades the building remained a sorry skeleton. Reconstruction is finally advancing and due for completion in April 2014.

Sarajevo 1878–1918   HISTORICAL MUSEUM
(Map p76; Zelenih Beretki 2; admission 2KM; ☺10am-6pm Mon-Fri, 10am-3pm Sat) This one-room exhibition examines the city's Austro-Hungarian–era history and the infamous 1914 assassination of Franz Ferdinand that happened right outside, ultimately triggering WWI.

Jewish Museum   MEDIEVAL SYNAGOGUE
(Muzej Jevreja BiH; Map p76; Mula Mustafe Bašeskije 40; admission 2KM; ☺10am-6pm Mon-Fri, 10am-1pm Sun) More religiously open-minded than most of Western Europe in its day, the 15th-century Ottoman Empire offered refuge to the Sephardic Jews who had been evicted en masse from Spain in 1492. While conditions varied, Bosnian Jews mostly prospered, until WWII that is, when most of the 14,000-strong community fled or were murdered by Nazis. The community's story is well told in this 1581 Sephardic synagogue that still sees active worship during Rosh Hashana (Jewish New Year).

Academy of Arts   ARCHITECTURE
(Likovna Akademija; Map p76; www.alu.unsa.ba; Obala Maka Dizdara 3) Originally built in 1899 as an evangelical church, the Gothic Revival–style Academy of Arts looks like a mini version of Budapest's magnificent national parliament building. Since August 2012 it has been fronted by Festina Lente ('Hurry Slowly'), an Escheresque new footbridge that 'loops-the-loop'.

BJELAVE & VRATNIK

TOP CHOICE Svrzo House   HOUSE MUSEUM
(Svrzina Kuća; Map p76; ✆535264; Glođina 8; admission 3KM; ☺10am-6pm Mon-Fri, 10am-3pm Sat) An oasis of white-washed walls, cobbled courtyards and partly vine-draped dark timbers, this 18th-century house museum is brilliantly restored and appropriately furnished, helping visitors imagine Sarajevo life in eras past. Notice the čekme dolaf (food hatch), designed to prevent inter-sex fratenization.

Izetbegović Museum   MUSEUM
(Map p74; www.muzejalijaizetbegovica.ba; Ploča bb; admission 2KM; ☺10am-6pm Mon-Fri, 10am-3pm Sat) Above the Kovaći cemetery where he's buried, there's a small but fascinating museum to Alija Izetbegović. Even if you're not interested in BiH's first president, the setting (in the historic Kula Ploče Tower) is interesting and the visit lets you walk along a last surviving section of city wall emerging at the Kula Širokac Tower.

Vratnik   NEIGHBOURHOOD
The once-vast Vratnik Citadel was built in the 1720s and reinforced in 1816. Not much remains but there are superb views from the grassy-topped Yellow Bastion (Žuta Tabija; Map p74; Jekovac bb). Minibus 55 gets you reasonably close.

NOVO SARAJEVO

During the 1992–95 siege, the wide road from the airport (Zmaja od Bosne) was dubbed 'sniper alley' because Serb gunmen in surrounding hills could pick off civilians as they tried to cross it. The distinctive, pudding-and-custard coloured Holiday Inn (Map p74; www.holidaysarajevo.com; Zmaja Od Bosne 4) famously housed most of the embattled journalists covering that conflict.

Greater Sarajevo

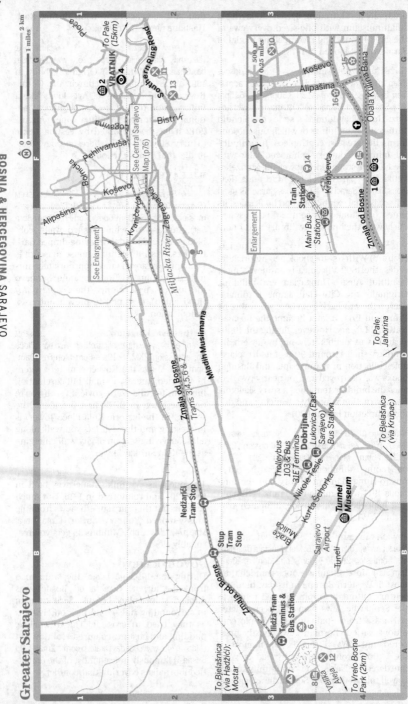

To Pale (15km)

Ploča

VRATNIK 4

Southern Ring Road

Logavina

13

Pehlivanuša

Bistrik

See Central Sarajevo Map (p76)

Bolnička

Koševo

Alipašina

Kranjčevća

See Enlargment

Miljacka River Zagrebačka

Zmaja od Bosne

Trams 3,4,5,6 & 7

Mladih Muslimana

5

To Pale: Jahorina

Nedžarići Tram Stop

Stup Tram Stop

Zmaja od Bosne

To Bjelašnica (via Krupac)

Dobrinja

Lukovica (East Sarajevo) Bus Station

Trolleybus 103 & Bus 31E Terminus

Nikole Tesle

Kurta Schorka

Braće Mulića

Sarajevo Airport

Tunel

Tunnel Museum

To Bjelašnica (via Hadžići); Mostar

Ilidža Tram Terminus & Bus Station

6

7

8

Velika Aleja

12

To Vrelo Bosne Park (2km)

Enlargement

10

Koševo

15

Alipašina

16

Obala Kulina Bana

Train Station

14

Kranjčevća

9

1

3

Main Bus Station

Zmaja od Bosne

2 km
1 miles

500 m
0.25 miles

N

Greater Sarajevo

◎ Top Sights

◎ Sights

✪ Activities, Courses & Tours

🛏 Sleeping

✖ Eating

◉ Drinking

✪ Entertainment

BOSNIA & HERCEGOVINA SARAJEVO

National Museum MUSEUM

(Zemaljski Muzej Bosne-i-Hercegovine; Map p74; www.zemaljskimuzej.ba; Zmaja od Bosne 3; ◷temporarily closed) Bosnia's biggest and best endowed museum closed in October 2012 due to persistent funding problems. Ironically it had been a rare institution to have remained at least partly functioning throughout the siege era, and its impressive 1913 quadrangle of neo-classical 1913 buildings survived reasonably intact. Assuming it reopens, the greatest highlights are its Illyrian and Roman carvings and especially the world-famous **Sarajevo Haggadah**, a 14th-century Jewish codex said to be worth a billion US dollars. Geraldine Brooks' 2007 historical novel *People of the Book* is a part-fictionalised account of how the Nazis failed to grab it during WWII.

Outside at the front are some exceptional medieval *stećci* (carved grave slabs).

History Museum MUSEUM

(Map p74; Zmaja od Bosne 5; admission 4KM; ◷9am-7pm Mon-Fri, 10am-2pm Sat-Sun) More than half of the small but engrossing History Museum 'non-ideologically' charts the course of the 1990s conflict. Affecting personal exhibits include examples of food aid, DIY guns, stacks of Monopoly-style 1990s dinars and a makeshift siege-time 'home'. The effect is emphasised by the building's miserable and still partly war-damaged 1970s architecture. Directly behind, the amusingly tongue-in-cheek **Tito Cafe** (www.caffetito.ba; ◷24hr) has stormtrooper-helmet lampshades and garden seating surrounded by WWII artillery pieces.

ILIDŽA & BUTMIR

TOP ᴄʜᴏɪᴄᴇ **Tunnel Museum** WAR MUSEUM

(Tunel Spasa; Map p74; www.tunelspasa.ba; Tuneli bb 1; admission 5KM; ◷9.15am-5pm, last entry 4.30pm) For much of the 1990s war, Sarajevo was virtually surrounded by hostile Serb forces. Butmir was the last Bosniak-held part of the city still linked to the outside world. However, between Butmir and Sarajevo lies the airport runway. Although it was supposedly neutral and under tenuous UN control, crossing it would have been suicidal during the conflict. The solution was a hand-dug 800m tunnel beneath the runway. That was just enough to keep Sarajevo supplied with arms and food during the three-year siege. Most of the tunnel has since collapsed, but this museum retains a 20m section and gives visitors a glimpse of its hopes and horrors. Photos are displayed around the shell-pounded house that hides the tunnel entrance and there's a 20-minute video showing footage of the city bombardment and the wartime tunnel experience.

Joining a city tour that includes a visit here can often prove cheaper than coming by taxi and your guide can add a lot of useful insight. Alternatively take tram 3 to Ilidža (35 minutes, 11km from Baščaršija), then switch to Kotorac-bound bus 32 (10 minutes, twice hourly, 3km). Get off at the last stop, walk across the bridge, then turn immediately left down Tuneli for 500m.

Vrelo Bosne Park PARK

The focus of this extensive park is a patchwork of lush mini-islands at the cliff-mouth source of the Bosna River. While it's not worth a special trip from central Sarajevo, if you're staying in Ilidža the park makes

Central Sarajevo

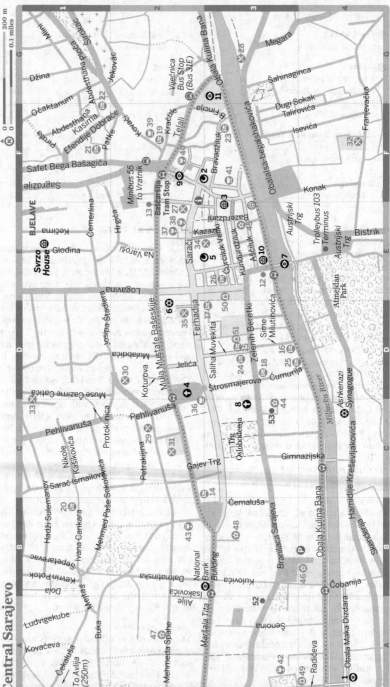

Central Sarajevo

a pleasant outing accessible by horse-cart or on foot along Velika Aleja, an elegantly tree-lined pedestrian avenue stretching 3km from Ilidža's main hotel area.

Termalna Rivijera   SWIMMING
(Map p74; www.terme-ilidza.ba/en; Butmirska Cesta 18; adult/child Mon-Fri 13/10KM, Sat & Sun 15/12KM; ⊙9am-10pm Sun-Fri, 9am-2am Sat) A complex of indoor and outdoor swimming pools 600m east of Ilidža tram terminus.

☞ Tours

Insider   TOUR
(Map p76; ☎061-190591; www.sarajevoinsider.com; Zelenih Beretki 30; ⊙9am-6pm Mon-Fri, 9.30am-2pm Sat-Sun) Wide range of tours in and be-

yond Sarajevo. Popular daily offerings include the two-hour Tunnel Tour (€15, 2pm) and excellent three-hour 'Times of Misfortune' (€27, 11am), visiting sites related to the 1990s conflict. Tour customers get free entrance to Insider's two-room Siege 'museum' (otherwise 3KM), 17 photo-text panels explaining the Yugoslav conflict from Tito's death to Dayton.

Sarajevo Funky Tours   TOUR
(Map p76; ☎062-910546; www.sarajevofunkytours. com; Besarina Čikma 5) A similar range of tours to Insider.

Sarajevo Free Tour   TOUR
Impressive 90-minute city walking tour starting 3pm from the tourist office or

4.30pm from Insider. Runs most days in summer. Pay through tips.

Green Visions
TOUR
(Map p74; ☑717290; www.greenvisions.ba; opposite Radnićka 66; ⊙9am-5pm Mon-Fri) Ecotourism specialist Green Visions offers a wide range of weekend and tailor-made hiking trips into the Bosnian mountains and villages with some fixed-day departures.

🎉 Festivals & Events

Baščaršijske Noći
ARTS
(Baščaršija Nights; www.bascarsijskenoci.ba) Wide-ranging arts fest lasting all July.

Jazz Festival
MUSIC
(www.jazzfest.ba) Local and international jazz in early November.

Sarajevo Film Festival
FILM
(www.sff.ba) Globally acclaimed with commercial and art-house movies, most with English subtitles. Held in August or late July.

🛏 Sleeping

If you arrive without anywhere booked and everything seems full, there's still a chance of finding a bed through one of the three agencies on the north side of Mula Mustafe Bašeskije at Baščaršija tram stop.

CITY CENTRE

Hotel Michele
BOUTIQUE HOTEL €€€
(Map p76; ☑560310; www.hotelmichele.ba; Ivana Cankara 27; r €75-105, apt €120-150; ❀🔊) Behind the exterior of an oversized contemporary townhouse, this offbeat guesthouse welcomes you into a lobby-lounge full of portraits, pinned butterflies and elegant fittings. Age-effect elements are in evidence in the 12 new standard rooms but what draws celebrity guests including Morgan Freeman and Kevin Spacey are the vast, indulgently furnished apartments with antique (if sometimes mismatching) furniture.

TOP CHOICE Villa Wien
GUESTHOUSE €€
(Map p76; Ćurčiluk Veliki 3; s/d 143/186KM; ❀🔊) Six well-equipped rooms decorated in opulent pseudo–belle époque style are hidden away above the Wiener Café. They are relatively good value perhaps because there's no reception – you have to check in a few blocks away at the less impressive yet more expensive Hotel Art (Map p76; ☑232855; www.hotelart.ba; Ferhadija 30a; s/d/ste 183/236/306KM; P❀@🔊).

Hotel Central
HOTEL €€€
(Map p76; ☑033-561800; www.hotelcentral.ba; Cumurija 8; s/d/ste 200/240/300KM; ❀🔊🔊) Behind a grand Austro-Hungarian facade, most of this newly renovated 'hotel' is in fact an amazing three-floor gym complex with professional-standard weight rooms, saunas and big indoor pool manned by qualified sports training staff. The 15 huge, fashionably appointed guest rooms lead off corridors painted lugubriously deep purple.

TOP CHOICE Hostel Old City
HOSTEL €
(Map p76; ☑555355; www.hosteloldcity.ba; Sime Milutinovića 1; dm €15; ❀@🔊) One floor of a regal 1908 townhouse has been given a very impressive makeover in keeping with its heritage. Features include big lockers, well-constructed beds and a lounge with Latin Bridge balcony views.

Hotel Kovači
HOTEL €€
(Map p76; ☑573700; www.hotelkovaci.com; Kovači 12; s/d/tr/apt €50/70/90/100; ❀🔊) This wonderfully central family hotel blends a chic, understated modernism with a traditional design that incorporates overhanging ('doksat') windows. Its fresh white rooms are softened with photos of 19th-century Sarajevo on protruding panels.

City Boutique Hotel
BOUTIQUE HOTEL €€
(Map p76; ☑566850; www.cityhotel.ba; Mula Mustafe Bašekije 2; r Fri-Sat €76-91, Sun-Thu €94-114; ❀🔊) Contemporary, designer rooms in rectilinear modernist style feature striking colours and backlit ceiling panels. There's a 6th-floor self-serve lounge-cafe and rooftop terrace with limited views. Reception 24 hours.

Residence Rooms
HOSTEL €
(Map p76; ☑200157; www.residencerooms.ba; 1st fl, Saliha Muvekita 1; dm/s/d/tr €15/25/40/45; @🔊) High ceilings, ample common areas and widely spaced beds in the dorms all make for a convivial hostel experience. The lively bars directly outside can be a blessing or curse depending on your party plans.

HCC Sarajevo Hostel
HOSTEL €
(Map p76; ☑062-993330; www.hcc.ba; 3rd fl, Saliha Muvekita 2; dm €12-16, s €20-25, d €28-35; ❀@🔊) This sociable hostel has big lockers (padlock rental €1), a stylishly decorated kitchen/dining area and a bright lounge/lobby with DVDs to watch and a guitar to strum.

Pansion Divan
PENSION €

(Map p76; 061420254; www.facebook.com/pansion.divansarajevo; Brandžiluk 38; s €20-30, tw €30-35;) Above an Ali Baba's cave of a restaurant, these 10 neat, unfussy rooms with private bathrooms don't have reception or common room but at such bargain prices one can't complain. Wi-fi in five rooms.

Hotel Safir
HOTEL €€

(Map p76; 475040; www.hotelsafir.ba; Jagodića 3; s/d €50/72;) Off stairways featuring vibrantly colour-suffused flower photos, rooms come with little mirror 'windows', conical basins and beam-me-up-Scotty shower booths. Six out of eight have a kitchenette.

Travellers Home
HOSTEL €

(Map p76; 70 242 400; www.myhostel.ba; Ćumurija 4, 1st fl; dm 25-38KM, d 62-92KM; 24hr;) One of Sarajevo's many high-ceilinged house-hostels, Travellers Home has outstandingly helpful, informative staff and a central yet peaceful locaton. Lockers are backpack-sized and power-points are accessible from each bunk.

Hotel Telal
HOTEL €

(Map p76; 525125; www.hotel-telal.ba; Abdesthana 4; s/d/tr/apt €30/40/45/60;) Reception feels a little claustrophobic and the walls are thin but the en suite rooms are comparatively smart and well tended for the rock-bottom price.

ILIDŽA & AIRPORT AREA

Several indulgent yet well-priced hotels lie in green, pleasant Ilidža. Parking is easier here than downtown but it's a 35-minute tram ride from Sarajevo's old centre.

TOP CHOICE Casa Grande
HOTEL €€

(Map p74; 639280; www.casagrande-bih.com; Velika Aleja 2; s/d/tr/q 68/113/138/165KM;) Designed like an aristocratic 1920s villa, the Casa Grande sits amid the plane trees right at the start of Ilidža's classic avenue, Velika Aleja. Rooms range from spacious to huge and are remarkably luxurious for the price. Expect satellite TV, leather-padded doors, 30-nozzle full-body shower pods and framed imitations of 'classic' art.

AutoKamp Oaza
CAMPING GROUND €

(Map p74; 636140; oaza@hoteliilidza.ba; per person 10KM, plus per tent/car/campervan 7/10/15KM, bungalows 60-105KM) Tree-shaded camping and caravan hook-ups (electricity 3KM extra)

tucked behind the Hotel Imzit, 1.5km west of Ilidža tram terminus.

✘ Eating

For inexpensive snack meals look along Bradžiluk or Kundurdžiluk: Bosna is a good place for cheap, fresh *burek*. Locals argue whether Hadžić, Mrkva or Željo is the best *ćevabdžinica* (ćevapi servery).

CITY CENTRE

Mala Kuhinja
FUSION €€

(Map p76; 061 144741; www.malakuhinja.ba; Josipa Štadlera 6; meals 20-25KM; noon-4pm Mon-Sat) There's no menu at this tiny, fusion-food gem where the chefs simply ask you what you do/don't like and then set about making culinary magic. Sit at the three-seat 'bar' to watch the show in all its glory. Reservations advisable.

Dveri
EUROPEAN €€

(Map p76; 537020; www.dveri.co.ba; Prote Bakovića 12; meals 11-18KM; 8am-11pm;) This tourist-friendly 'country cottage' eatery is densely hung with loops of garlic, corn cobs and gingham-curtained 'windows'. Classic European meat-based dishes are supplemented by inky risottos, vegie-stuffed eggplant and garlic-wine squid. There's a well-chosen wine list including some excellent Hercegovinian Blatinas.

To Be or Not to Be
INTERNATIONAL €€

(Map p76; 233265; Čizmedžiluk 5; meals 10-22KM; 11am-11pm;) Arched metal shutters creak open to reveal a tiny two-table room lovably decorated in traditional Bosnian style. Try the daring, tongue-tickling steak in chilli chocolate (22KM). The restaurant's name, with 'or Not' crossed out as a message of positivity, was originally a poster slogan for the 1994 Sarajevo Winter Festival, held against all odds during the siege.

Sushi San
SUSHI €€

(Map p76; 833034; www.sarajevosushi.com; Muse Ćazima Ćatića 33 ; 2-piece sushi 5-6KM; 11am-8pm Mon-Sat;) The sushi master at this tiny six-stool box restaurant learned his trade in San Fransisco and manages to produce salmon nigiri that will impress even salmon-haters. Caters to various embassies.

Pivnica HS
INTERNATIONAL €€

(Map p76; sarajevska-pivara.ba/restaurant; Franjevačka 15; pasta 8-10KM, mains 13-25KM; 10am-1am;) If Willy Wonka built a beer hall it might look like this – a giant festival of Las

Vegas vaudeville. Meals are well presented and satisfying and this is the only place you can be sure of finding Sarajevskaya full range of tap beers (brewed next door).

Karuzo
SEAFOOD €€

(Map p76; ✆444647; www.karuzorestaurant.com; Dženetića Čikma 2; pasta 13-18KM; mains 15-35KM; ⏰noon-3pm Mon-Fri, 6-11pm Mon-Sat; ⚡📖) This friendly little meat-free restaurant is styled vaguely like a yacht's interior. Along with fish dishes and sushi there are some imaginative vegetarian options including chard pockets with smoked tofu and basil sauce. The owner is both waiter and chef so don't be in a hurry.

Inat Kuća
BOSNIAN €€

(Spite House; Map p76; ✆447867; www.inatkuca. ba; Velika Alifakovac 1; mains 12-20KM, snacks 10KM; ⏰10am-10pm; 📖) This Sarajevo institution occupies a classic Ottoman-era house that's a veritable museum piece with central fire-flue, antique decor and a great little riverside terrace. The menu tells the story of its odd name but some of the typical Bosnian fare (stews, *dolme*) can be slightly lacklustre.

Vegehana
VEGETARIAN €

(Map p76; www.vegehana.ba/; Ferhadija 39; mains 5-10KM; ⏰10am-9pm Mon-Fri, noon-9pm Sat; ⚡📖) The first fully vegetarian, organic eatery in Sarajevo uses plenty of Tahina, quinoa, tofu and seitan meat-substitute.

Markale
MARKET

(Map p76; Mula Mustafe Bašeskije; ⏰7am-5pm Mon-Sat, 7am-2pm Sun) Markale is an unassuming huddle of vegetable stalls. The massacre of marketgoers here in a 1995 Serb mortar attack proved a 'last straw', triggering NATO air strikes against the forces besieging Sarajevo.

GREATER SARAJEVO

Biban
BOSNIAN €€

(Map p74; ✆033-232026; Hošin Brijeg 95a; mains 7-16KM; ⏰10am-10pm Mon-Fri, 10am-9pm Sun; 📖) Encompassing the whole Sarajevo Valley, Biban's panoramic city views trump even those of better-known Park Prinčeva, but the food is cheaper (and simpler) including typical meat dishes, squid and trout. The 10KM plates of *uštipci* (fist-size fried doughballs served with sour cream) are big enough to feed three people. Walk 600m uphill from Park Prinčeva, turning left after Nalina 15a.

Park Prinčeva
BALKAN, EUROPEAN €€€

(Map p74; ✆222708; www.parkprinceva.ba; Iza Hidra 7; meals 16-32KM; ⏰9am-11pm; 📖) Like

Bono and Bill Clinton before you, gaze down across the city, the old city hall beautifully framed between rooftops, mosques and twinkling lights. Minibus 56 from Latin Bridge passes outside. Try the chicken in cherry sauce.

Avlija
BISTRO €€

(Map p74; ✆444 483; Sumbula Avde 2, opposite 53 Čekaluša; 9-20KM; ⏰8am-11pm; 📖) Locals and in-the-know expats cosy up at painted wooden benches in this unpretentious covered yard, dangling with trailing potplants, strings of peppers and little witches. Generous portions of Central European pub food wash down merrily with local draft beers.

Ildžis 1968
ITALIAN €

(Map p74; Velika Aleja 3; mains 6-10KM, beer 2.50KM) Staying in Ilidža? Then consider drinking or dining at this rustic-effect wooden house filled with guitars, spinning wheels and giant model ships. At night it's very moodily lit and the woodland location is just as romantic by day. Pastas are copious, beautifully presented and served with oodles of Parmesan. It is two-minute stroll north of Casa Grande along tree-lined Velika Aleja.

🍷 Drinking

As chilly April melts into sunny May, terraces blossom and central Sarajevo becomes one giant street cafe.

Bars

TOP CHOICE Zlatna Ribica
BAR

(Map p76; Kaptol 5; ⏰10am-2am) This inspiring little cafe-bar is loaded with eccentricities, including drink menus hidden away in old books that dangle from lampshades. Music swerves unpredictably between jazz, Parisian croons, opera, reggae and The Muppets. Wine might arrive with a free scallop-shell of grapes. And the uniquely stocked toilet will have you laughing out loud.

Pravda
COCKTAIL BAR

(Map p76; www.pravda.ba; Radićeva 4c; ⏰8am-midnight) Choose from marigold-patterned chill-out sofas or white-enamel perch-stools, then strike your pose amid Sarajevo's gilded youth. Oh no, don't say they've all gone next door to Cafe Nivea?! Or decamped to Dekanter?

Caffe 35
BAR

(Map p74; Avaz Twist Tower, 35th fl; coffee/cake/ beer 2/3/4KM, sandwiches 3-5KM; ⏰9am-11pm) If you're waiting for a train, what better place to do so than admiring a full city panorama from the 35th floor of 'The Balkans' Tallest Tower'. Upstairs for 1KM you can see the same views in the open air with bars instead of windows. The glass elevator coming back down feels like it's freefalling.

Barhana
BAR

(Map p76; Đugalina 8; beer/rakija 2/3KM, mains 6-20KM; ⊘10am-midnight) Sample a selection of flavoured local shots in a hidden courtyard behind the equally enticing Babylon bar. A wide range of fair value meals is served.

Cafes

Kuća Sevdaha
CAFE

(Map p76; www.artkucasevdaha.ba/en/; Halači 5; ⊘9am-11pm) Sip Bosnian coffee, juniper sherbet or rose water while nibbling local sweets and listening to the lilting wails of *sevdah*, traditional Bosnian music. The ancient building that surrounds the cafe's glassed-in fountain courtyard is now used as a museum celebrating great 20th-century *sevdah* performers (admission 3KM, open 10am to 6pm Tuesday to Sunday).

Caffe Divan
CARAVANSERAI

(Map p76; Morića Han, Saraći 77; ⊘8am-midnight) Relax in wicker chairs beneath the wooden beams of a gorgeous, historic caravanserai courtyard whose stables now contain an alluring Iranian carpet shop. The restaurant section (kitchen till 10pm) serves good *klepe* (a kind of garlic ravioli).

Čajdžinica Džirlo
TEAHOUSE

(Map p76; www.facebook.com/CajdzinicaDzirlo; Kovači 16; ⊘8am-10pm) Miniscule but brimming with character, Džirlo offers 45 types of tea (per pot 4KM), many of them made from distinctive Bosnian herbs. Good coffee and local sherbets are also available. It's on a steeply sloping stretch of Kovači amid old workshops including metal beaters and a coffee roaster.

Dibek
BAR

(Map p76; Laledžina 3; ⊘8am-11pm) Smoking a hookah (*nargile* or water pipe; 5KM) is back in fashion as you'll see in this DJ-led bar that spreads colourful low stools beneath a central tree on a tiny Old Town square. Excellent coffee too.

Alfonso
CAFE

(Map p76; Trg Fra Grge Martica 4; ⊘8am-11pm) Great espressos served at open-air pavement seating that sprawls around the Catholic cathedral, or inside where a hip interior includes a catwalk between cushioned sunken seat spaces.

☆ Entertainment
Nightclubs & Live Music

Within the old city, there are two small but ever-lively areas of late night music bars: around the Hacienda, and beneath HCC Sarajevo Hostel. Other clubs tend to be further west.

Underground
LIVE MUSIC

(Map p76; www.underground.ba; Maršala Tita 56; ⊘7pm-5am) Especially on Friday and Saturday nights, talented bands give classic rock songs a romping rework in this medium-sized basement venue. Free entry, tap beers 2.50KM.

FIS Kultura
LIVE MUSIC

(Bock; Map p74; Musala bb; ⊘6pm-2am) There's no sign so just follow the bass-beat to locate this tiny basement venue. Musical styles range wildly from grunge to punk to 'urban' party. Some nights private parties take over. It's on Musala, a north–south lane two blocks west of Radićeva.

Rooms Club & Restaurant
DJS, LIVE MUSIC

(Map p74; www.facebook.com/roomsclubsarajevo; Maršala Tita 7; ⊘9.30pm-4am Wed, Fri & Sat) This subterranean trio of stone cavern rooms includes a restaurant that serves till 3am, a sofa-dotted lounge and a contrastingly boistrous bar-performance area with live gigs that pull in crowds after midnight, especially on Wednesdays. The 5KM cover includes one drink.

Club Jež
CLUB

(Map p76; http://jez.nash.ba/v2; Zelenih Beretki 14b; ⊘9pm-late) This intimate stone-vaulted cavern club heaves with young local revellers overdosing on turbofolk. Cover charges (around 5KM) include one drink.

Sloga
CLUB

(Map p76; www.cinemas.ba; Seljo, Mehmeda Spahe 20; ⊘8pm-3am) This cavernous, blood-red club-disco-dance hall caters to an excitable, predominantly student crowd but dancing is oddly impeded by rows of tables. Cover charge 5KM at weekends. Occasional concerts.

Hacienda
DJ

(Map p76; Bazerdžani 3; ⊘10am-very late) The not-quite-Mexican food could be spicier. Not so the ambience, which by 2am has

BOSNIA & HERCEGOVINA SARAJEVO

often morphed this cane-ceilinged cantina into one of the Old Town's most happening night spots. If it's quiet, try nearby alternatives Pirates Pub and Caffe Red.

Performing Arts

National Theatre   PERFORMING ARTS
(Narodno Pozorište; Map p76; ☑221682; www.nps. ba; Obala Kulina Bana 9; tickets from 10KM; ☺box office 9am-noon & 4-7.30pm) Classically adorned with fiddly gilt mouldings, this proscenium-arched theatre hosts a ballet, opera, play or philharmonic concert virtually every night from mid-September to mid-June.

🛍 Shopping

Baščaršija's pedestrian lanes are full of jewellery stalls and wooden-shuttered souvenir shops flogging slippers, Bosnian flags, carpets, archetypal copperware and wooden spoons, though if you're heading to Mostar, you might find prices better there.

Some Sarajevo bookshops still stock the darkly humorous *Sarajevo Survival Guide*, originally published during the 1992–93 siege, as well as guidebooks, magazines and English-language books on ex-Yugoslavia.

Dugi Bezistan   COVERED BAZAAR
(Map p76; www.vakuf-gazi.ba; ☺8am-8pm Mon-Fri, 9am-2pm Sat) Another of Gazi-Husrevbey's 16th-century architectural legacies, the stone-vaulted covered bazaar is little more than 100m long, but squint and you could be in Istanbul. Many of its 52 shops sell inexpensive souvenirs, cheap handbags and sunglasses (from 5KM).

BuyBook   BOOKSHOP
(Map p76; ☑716450; www.buybook.ba; Radićeva 4; ☺9am-8pm Mon-Fri, 10am-6pm Sat)

Šahinpašić   BOOKSHOP
(Map p76; ☑667210; www.btcsahinpasic.com; Vladislava Skarića 8; ☺9am-9pm Mon-Sat)

ℹ Information

ATMs are outside the bus station, inside the airport and sprinkled all over the city.

For currency exchanges, there's an airport post-counter (☺9am-5pm Mon-Fri), Postbank (☺8am-4pm Mon-Fri) branch hidden around the west side of the train station building and many banks along Ferhadija. At weekends try the Hotel Europe.

City.Ba (www.city.ba/en) Reviews of clubs, pubs, restaurants and more

Internet Caffe Baščaršija (Aščiluk bb; per hr 2KM; ☺8am-midnight)

Klinički Centar Univerziteta Sarajevo (☑445522; www.kcus.ba; 1st fl, DIP Bldg, Stepana Tomića bb/Bolnička 25 ; ☺8am-2pm Mon-Fri) English-speaking 'VIP Clinic' within the vast Koševo Hospital complex. Take bus 14 from Dom Armije to Hotel Belvedere and then walk 300m northwest.

Lonely Planet (www.lonelyplanet.com/bosnia-and-hercegovina/sarajevo)

Sarajevo Navigator Useful free maps and monthly guide pamphlets. Widely available.

Sonar (www.sonar.ba) Listings and information.

Tourist Office (Map p76; www.sarajevo-tourism.com; Sarači 58; ☺9am-8pm Mon-Fri, 10am-6pm Sat-Sun)

ℹ Getting There & Away

Air

An hour is ample for check-in at Sarajevo's modern but very compact international airport (☑234841; www.sarajevo-airport.ba; Kurta Schorka 36; ☺5am-11pm), about 12km southwest of Baščaršija.

Bus

Sarajevo's main bus station (Map p74; ☑213100; Put Života 8) primarily serves locations in the Federation, Croatia and Western Europe. Most services to the Republik Srpska (RS) and Serbia leave from Lukovica (East Sarajevo) Bus Station (Map p74; ☑057-317377; Nikole Tesle bb). The latter lies way out in the suburb of Dobrijna, 400m beyond the western terminus stop of trolleybus 103 and bus 31E. To some destinations, buses leave from both stations. For Jajce, take Banja Luka buses.

Train

From the train station (☑655330; Put Života 2) useful services include the following:
Belgrade (51.20KM, eight hours) Departs 11.49am.
Budapest (1st/2nd class 122.40KM, 11¼ hours) Departs 6.55am, routed via Osijek (Croatia, 55.40KM). Returns from Budapest-Keleti at 9.56am.
Mostar (9.90KM, 2¼ hours) Departs 7.05am, 8.05am and 6.18pm.
Zagreb (74.30KM, 9¼ hours) Trains depart 10.54am and 9.27am. No couchette service.

ℹ Getting Around

To/From the Airport

Trolleybus 103 and bus 31E both run to the centre, picking up around 700m from the terminal. To find the stop turn right out of the airport following black-backed 'Hotel' signs. Take the first left, shimmy right-left-right past Hotel Octagon, then turn third right at the Panda car wash (Brače

BUSES FROM SARAJEVO

DESTINATION	DEPARTURE POINT	PRICE (KM)	DURATION	FREQUENCY
Banja Luka	Main bus station	32.90	5hr	5am, 7.45am, 9.15am, 2.30pm, 3.30pm, 4.30pm, 6.30pm
Banja Luka	East Sarajevo bus station	31	5hr	9.30am, 11.30am
Bihać	Main bus station	42	6½hr	7.30am, 1.30pm, 10pm
Belgrade (Serbia)	Main bus station	47	7½hr	6am
Belgrade (Serbia)	East Sarajevo bus station	40-55	8-11hr	8am, 9.45am, 12.30pm, 3pm, 10pm
Dubrovnik (Croatia)	Main bus station	47	7hr	7.15am, 10am, plus 2.30pm, 10.15pm summer
Foča	East Sarajevo bus station	9	1½hr	11.15am, 6.15pm, plus Trebinje, Podgorica & Herceg Novi services
Herceg Novi	East Sarajevo bus station	46	7½	9am plus summer specials
Jajce	Main bus station, East Sarajevo bus station	23.50	3½hr	Take Banja Luka buses
Ljubljana (Slovenia)	Main bus station	92	8½hr	8.40pm Tue, Fri, Sun
Mostar	Main bus station	18	2½hr	15 daily, 6.50am-7.55pm
Munich (Germany)	Main bus station	140	19hr	8am
Niš	East Sarajevo bus station	46	11hr	8.40am, 6pm
Novi Pazar	Main bus station	32	7-8hr	3pm, 9pm, 10pm
Pale	East Sarajevo bus station	3.50	40min	14 daily Mon-Fri, 6 on Sat & Sun
Pale	Main bus station	5.70	25min	7am, 10am, 2pm
Podgorica (Montenegro)	East Sarajevo bus station	36	6hr	8.15am, 2pm, 8pm, 10.30pm
Split (Croatia), via Mostar	Main bus station	53.50	7½hr	10am, 9pm, plus 7am in summer
Split (Croatia), via Livno	Main bus station	53.50	7¼hr	6am
Travnik	Main bus station	17	2hr	9 daily
Trebinje via Sutjeska National Park	East Sarajevo bus station	26	5hr	7.45am, 1pm, 4.05pm
Tuzla	Main bus station	21	3¼hr	9 daily
Visoko	Main bus station	6.30	50min	at least hourly by Kakanj bus
Vienna (Austria)	Main bus station	100	14½hr	11.15am
Zagreb (Croatia)	Main bus station	54	9½hr	6.30am, 12.30pm, 10pm
Zagreb (Croatia) via Bosanski Brod	Main bus station	54	8½hr	9.30am

Mulića 17). Before the Mercator Hypermarket (Mimar Sinana 1) cross the road and take the bus-trolleybus going back the way you've just come.

Metered taxis charge around 7KM to Ilidža, 16KM to Baščaršija. The airport closes 11pm to 5am.

Bicycle Rental

Gir (Map p76; ☑350 523; www.gir.ba; Zelenih Berekti 14a; city bike per hr/day/5-days 3/15/25KM, mountain bike 4/20/35KM; ◎10am-6pm) This cycle shop is 'hidden' within the commercial passageway that leads to Club Jež.

Car

Central Sarajevo isn't driver-friendly and hotel parking is very limited but a car makes it much easier to reach the surrounding mountain areas.

Public Transport

You can find timetables on www.gras.co.ba/hodnik.htm. Click 'Redove Voznje' then select mode of transport.

Single-ride tickets are 1.60/1.80KM from kiosks/drivers and must be stamped once aboard. Day tickets (5.60KM) are only sold from kiosks. They cover all trams and trolleybuses plus most buses (but not 31E).

Useful routes include the following. All service frequency reduces on Sunday.

Tram 3 (every four to seven minutes) From Ilidža passes the Holiday Inn then loops one way (anticlockwise) around Baščaršija. Last tram back to Ilidža departs Baščaršija at 12.10am.

Tram 1 (every 12 to 25 minutes) Starts at the train station then does the same loop as Tram 3. From the train station you could alternatively walk to the nearest Tram 3 stop in about seven minutes.

Trolleybus 103 (every six minutes till 11pm) Runs along the southern side of the city from Austrijski Trg passing near Green Visions en route to Dobrijna (35 minutes). Handy for Lukovica (East Sarajevo) bus station and the airport.

Bus 31E (three per hour, 6.30am to 10pm) Vijećnica to Dobrijna (for Lukovica bus station).

Taxi

Taxis from the central ranks (Latin Bridge, Hotel Kovači, etc) often want to fix a set fee. For reliable on-the-metre fares (2KM plus about 1KM per kilometre) call **Paja Taxis** (☑412555) .

AROUND SARAJEVO

Mountains rise directly behind the city, offering convenient access to winter skiing or summer rambles. Landmine dangers remain in some areas so stick to well-used paths especially in forests.

Jahorina
☑057

Of BiH's Olympic ski resorts, multi-piste **Jahorina** (www.oc-jahorina.com; ski pass per day/week 33/160KM, ski-set rentals per day 25-40KM) has by far the widest range of hotels, each within 300m of one of Jahorina's seven main ski lifts. In summer, Termag Hotel (p84) rents mountain bikes (per half-/full day 7/10KM) and quads (per hour for one/two people 50/70KM). There's an (over)heated indoor pool at **Hotel Board** (www.hotelboard-jahorina.com; guests/non-guests free/20KM; ◎10am-10pm year-round).

🛏 Sleeping & Eating

Hotels are strung out for 2.5km, starting from a small seasonal shopping 'village' where you'll find the cheaper *pansions* – all close out of season except Hotel Kristal. The Termag Hotel is 300m above, the Board is a little further then the road divides, passing the aging **Bistrica** one way, Dva Javora the other. Past the still-ruined Hotel Jahorina, the road tunnels beneath Rajska Vrata before dead-ending at the top of the Skočine Lift. Quoted ski-season rates are for mid-January to March with half-board; summer rates include breakfast only.

Termag Hotel　　　　　　HOTEL €€€
(☑270422; www.termaghotel.com; s/d/ste 115/152/200KM, new block 55-100KM, ski season d/ste from 240/300KM, new block 65-110KM; **P**☎🏊) Within an oversized mansion built in Scooby Doo Gothic style, the Termag is a beautifully designed fashion statement where traditional ideas and open fireplaces are given a stylish, modernist twist. Note that guests booking the new, less exclusive rooms in a 2013 humbacked extension will not enjoy free access to the sauna, pool and underground parking.

Rajska Vrata　　　　　　　　LODGE €€
(☑065 142244; www.jahorina-rajskavrata.com; d/tr €50/75; ☎) Beside the longest piste in town, this perfect alpine ski-in cafe-restaurant has rustic sheepskin benches around a centrally flued real fire. The cosy pine-walled bedrooms are only available March to November.

Hotel Dva Javora　　　　　　HOTEL €€
(☑270481; www.hoteldvajavora.com; per person B&B 40KM, ski season 65-90KM; ☎) Upstairs above a row of seasonal sports shops, the

modern lobby bar has an attractive, open feel. Rooms are fairly plain but with new pine beds and clean checkerboard bathrooms. Wi-fi in the bar.

Pansion Sport LODGE €€
(☑270333; www.pansion-sport.com; d Sun-Fri 54-80KM, Sat 84-124KM; ☻mid-Dec–early Apr) Pleasant Swiss chalet–style guesthouse in the resort's 'village area'. There's a spacious glass-fronted bar full of big wicker chairs.

ℹ Getting There & Away

Jahorina is 6.5km off the newly improved road leading between Istochno Sarajevo (27km) and Pale (13km). Buses run in ski season only, departing from Pale (3KM, 25 minutes) at 7am, 3pm and 11.30pm, returning from Hotel Bistrica.

Bjelašnica

☑033

BiH's second Olympic ski field rises above the two-hotel resort of Bjelašnica (www. bjelasnica.ba; ski pass per day/night/week 27/15/180KM), around 30km south of Sarajevo. An attraction here is the floodlit night skiing (6pm to 9pm) and, in summer, the possibilities of exploring the magical mountain villages (p85) behind. You can rent bicycles (per hour/day 5/30KM) and quads (per hour 60KM to 100KM) from the excellent new Hotel Han (☑584150; www.hotelhan. ba; s/d summer 56.50/95KM, d mid-Dec–Mar 155-185KM; ☜), a stylish yet reasonably priced

construction directly facing the main piste. Fronted by what looks like a giant Plexiglas pencil, the friendly but older Hotel Maršal (☑584129, 584100; www.hotel-marsal.ba; s/d summer 71.50/96KM, Christmas-early Mar d 116-136KM; ☜) rents skis, boots and poles (guests/non-guests per day 15/20KM) in season and has a nightclub.

Aimed at cross-country enthusiasts (it's away 5km from the downhill pistes), the great-value Hostel Feri (☑775555; www.feri. ba; Veliko Polje; per person summer/winter/New Year 74.20/94.20/114.20KM, s 54.60-84.60KM; ☜) charges the same per person whether you're in a double or six-bedded room. It's luxurious for a 'hostel', with flat-screen TVs, gym and ski-season-only sauna included.

On weekends in season bus 44 runs from Sarajevo's National Museum at 9am, returning at 3.30pm from Hotel Maršal. In summer you'll need wheels.

HERCEGOVINA

Hercegovina is the part of BiH that no one in the West ever mentions, if only because they can't pronounce it. The arid, Mediterranean landscape has a distinctive beauty punctuated with barren mountain ridges and photogenic river valleys. Famed for its fine wines and sun-packed fruits, Hercegovina is sparsely populated, but it has some intriguing historic towns and the Adriatic coast is just a skip away.

BJELAŠNICA'S MOUNTAIN VILLAGES

If you're driving, don't miss exploring the web of rural lanes tucked away in the uplands above Bjelašnica. Most famous is timeless Lukomir, 19km by a manageable unpaved road starting to the right of Aurora 97 snack-shack near Bjelašnica's Hotel Maršal. From a knoll that's less than five minutes' obvious climb beyond the road end in Lukomir village, a 360-degree panorama is one of the best in Bosnia encompassing the layered stone hamlet, sloping stony sheep pastures behind and a plunging gorge backed by a far horizon of rocky-knobbed peaks. There's a seasonal house-cafe in Lukomir but for a little more 'civilisation' head for Umoljani. Tucked into a partly wooded cwm, 16km from Bjelašnica, Umoljani has three little restaurant-cafes and two *pansions*. The Restoran Studeno Vrelo (☑061 709540; coffee/snack 1.50/5KM), the only one to open year-round, charges just 20KM per person to sleep in the cute three-bedroom log house behind. Koliba seasonal cafe displays excellent hiking maps on its exterior wall. Pansion Umoljani (☑061 228142) has a big-view terrace. The asphalted approach road to Umoljani is beautiful and there are *stećci* just above the road around 2.5km before the village. There's a hiking trail from Lukomir down to Umoljani but by road you need to backtrack 8km then descend via Milišići (which has its own appeal and some further great views) and turn right at the sharp junction 1.2km from Šabiči. Green Visions (p78) and other agencies organise a range of summer activities to get you to and around this lovely area.

Mostar

♪036 / POP 111,600

At dusk the lights of numerous millhouse restaurants twinkle across gushing streamlets. Narrow Kujundžiluk 'gold alley' bustles joyously with trinket sellers. And in between, the Balkans' most celebrated bridge forms a majestic stone arc between reincarnated medieval towers. It's an enchanting scene. Do stay into the evening to see it without the summer hoards of day trippers. Indeed stay longer to enjoy memorable attractions in the surrounding area as well as pondering the city's darker side – still vivid scars of the 1990s conflict that remain visible beyond the cobbled lanes of the attractively restored Ottoman quarter. Be aware that between November and April most tourist facilities will be in wholescale hibernation.

History

Mostar means 'bridge-keeper', and the crossing of the Neretva River here has always been its raison d'être. In the mid-16th century, Mostar boomed as a key transport gateway within the powerful, expanding Ottoman Empire. Some 30 *esnafi* (craft guilds) included tanners (for whom the Tabhana was built), and goldsmiths (hence Kujundžiluk, 'gold alley'). In 1557, Suleyman the Magnificent ordered a swooping stone arch to replace the suspension bridge whose wobbling had previously terrified tradesmen as they gingerly crossed the fast-flowing Neretva River. The beautiful Stari Most (Old Bridge) that resulted was finished in 1566 and came to be appreciated as one of the era's engineering marvels. It survived the Italian occupation of WWII, but after standing for 427 years the bridge was destroyed in November 1993 by Bosnian Croat artillery in one of the most poignant and depressingly pointless moments of the whole Yugoslav civil war.

Ironically Muslims and Croats had initially fought together against Serb and Montenegrin forces that had started bombarding Mostar in April 1992. However, on 9 May 1993, a bitter conflict erupted between the former allies. A de facto frontline emerged north–south along the Bulvar and Aleksi Šantiće street with Croats to the west, Bosniaks to the east. For two years both sides swapped artillery fire and by 1995 Mostar resembled Dresden after WWII, with all its bridges destroyed and all but one of its 27 Ottoman-era mosques utterly ruined. Vast international assistance efforts rebuilt almost all of the Unesco-listed old city core, including the classic bridge, painstakingly reconstructed using 16th-century-style building techniques and stone from the original quarry. However, nearly two decades after the conflict, significant numbers of shattered buildings remain as ghostlike reminders. The psychological scars will take generations to heal and the city remains oddly schizophrenic, with two bus stations and two postal systems – one Bosniak and the other Croat.

◉ Sights

Stari Most   BRIDGE

The world-famous Stari Most (Old Bridge) is the indisputable visual focus that gives Mostar its special magic. The medieval bridge's pale stone magnificently throws back the golden glow of sunset or the tasteful night-time floodlighting. Numerous well-positioned cafes and restaurants, notably behind the Tabhana (an Ottoman-era enclosed courtyard), tempt you to sit and savour the scene. If you wait long enough you are likely to see someone jump 21m off the parapet into the icy Neretva below. This is not an attempt at suicide but an age-old tradition maintained by an elite group of young men. There's even an annual bridge-diving competition (July). At other times, however, divers will only generally jump once their hustlers have collected enough photo money from onlookers. If you want to jump yourself (from €25), ask at the Bridge-Divers' Clubhouse beside the bridge's western end. They can organise a wetsuit, basic training and two divers who await beside the river below in case of emergencies.

At the bridge's eastern side, the Old Bridge Museum (adult/student 5/3KM; ◷10am-6pm summer, 11am-2pm winter, closed Mon) has two parts, both offering relatively sparse exhibits. First you climb up a five-storey stone defence tower for partial views and interesting but limited displays about Stari Most's context and construction. Climb back down to walk through the bridge's archaeological bowels, and you'll emerge on Kujundžiluk.

Crooked Bridge   BRIDGE

(Kriva Ćuprija) Resembling Stari Most but in miniature, the pint-sized Crooked Bridge crosses the tiny Rabobolja creek amid a layered series of millhouse restaurants. The original bridge, weakened by wartime as-

IMAGES OF MOSTAR

At least four compelling videos of Mostar's demise and rebirth are on show around town. Each is subtly different but all include tragic footage of the moment the old bridge was blown apart. A decent free choice is within the **Old Hamam** (beside Tabhana; ⊙10am-4pm May-Oct) where an exhibition looks building-by-building at Mostar's destruction and reconstruction. Bookshop **Galerija Old Bridge** (Stari Most; ⊙9am-10pm), a former mosque right on the bridge's southwest parapet, plays and sells a similar DVD (€10). A 10-minute version concentrating more on bridge-diving is screened in a comfy cinema-style room at the Museum of Hercegovina. And there's a slow-moving 15-minute video shown at the Old Bridge Museum.

An **exhibition** (Helebija Kula, Stari Most; 6KM; ⊙9am-8.30pm Apr-Nov) of around 50 black-and-white still photos depicting city life during wartime is shown within the semi-circular Helebija Kula, a former gunpowder tower directly behind the Bridge Divers' Clubhouse. They're powerful images but there's no video and entry fees seem steep.

saults, was washed away by floods of 2000, but rebuilt a year later.

Koski Mehmed Paša Mosque   MOSQUE
(Mala Tepa 16; mosque/mosque & minaret 4/8KM; ⊙8am-8pm Apr-Sep, 9am-5pm Oct, closed Nov-Mar) Entered from a gated courtyard, the rebuilt 1618 Koski Mehmed Paša Mosque lacks a certain finess in its interior but climbing the claustrophobic minaret allows you to enjoy sweeping town views. The most attractive part of the mosque complex is the small courtyard outside with its fountain taps and garden area (access free).

Bišćevića Ćošak   HOUSE
(Turkish House; Bišćevića 13; admission 4KM; ⊙8.30am-6.30pm mid-Apr–Oct, closed winter except by tour) Bišćevića Ćošak is a slightly ramshackle 350-year-old Ottoman-Bosnian home with a colourfully furnished interior sporting a selection of traditional metalwork and carved wooden furniture. For interesting comparisons also visit the grander **Muslibegović House** (admission 4KM; ⊙10am-6pm mid-Apr–mid-Oct), which now doubles as a boutique hotel (p90).

Former Front Line   HISTORIC AREA
Nearly two decades after the conflict, many buildings remain as bullet-pocked skeletal wrecks, especially along Mostar's former 'front line'. Every year more are restored but you'll still see several tragic ruins around Spanski Trg, including the triangular nine-storey tower that was once **Ljubljanska Banka** (Kralja Zvonimira bb). Meanwhile Trg Musala, once the heart of Austro-Hungarian Mostar, is still scarred by the stumpy war-ruined shell of the once splendid **Hotel Neretva** (Trg Musala).

Museum of Hercegovina   MUSEUM
(http://muzejhercegovine.com; Bajatova 4; admission 5KM; ⊙8am-4pm Mon-Fri, 8am-1pm Sat) This small museum with archaeological and ethnographic sections, occupies the former house of Džemal Bijedić, former head of the Yugoslav government who died in mysterious circumstances in 1978. The unexplained plane wheels recall Mostar's Yugo-era aero-industry. Anton Zimlo's pre-WWI photos include a view of the Old Bridge carpet-decked for Austrian Emperor Franz Josef's 1910 visit.

Karađozbeg Mosque   MOSQUE
(Braće Fejića bb; mosque/mosque & minaret 4/8KM; ⊙times vary, closed during prayers) Mostar's most important mosque, built in 1557 but heavily damaged during the war, is now completely renovated with distinctive lead-roofed wooden verandah and four-domed madrassa annexe now used as a clinic.

Roznamedži Ibrahimefendi Mosque   MOSQUE
(Braće Fejića bb) This early-17th-century mosque was the only one to survive the 1993–35 shelling relatively unscathed. Its associated **madrassa**, demolished in 1960, has now also been rebuilt, the reincarnation hosting shops and a cafe.

☞ Tours

Some homestays and hostels, including Majdas, Nina and **Miran's** (☎062 115333; www.hostelmiran-mostar.com; Pere Lažetića 13), offer walking tours around town and/or great-value full-day trips visiting Blagaj, Međugorje, Počitelj and the Kravice waterfalls for around 70KM. **Almira Travel** (☎551873; www.almira-travel.ba; Mala Tepa 9) offers alternative regional

BOSNIA & HERCEGOVINA MOSTAR

Mostar

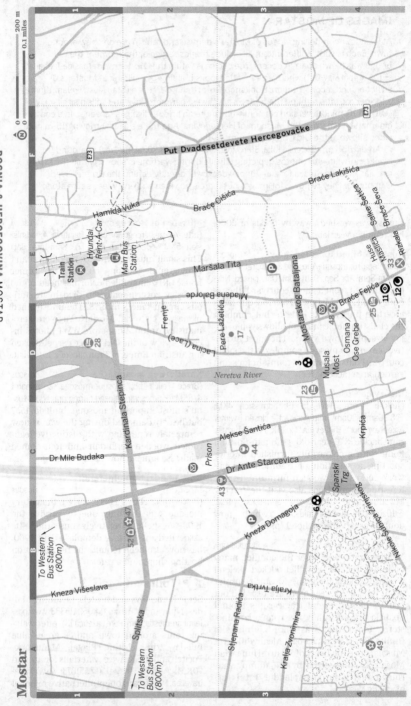

0
0
200 m
0.1 miles

Put Dvadesetdevete Hercegovačke

E73

Braće Lakišića

Braće Ćišića

Hamida Vuka

Train Station

Hyundai Rent-A-Car

Main Bus Station

Maršala Tita

Mladena Balorde

Frenje

Lacina (Lace)

Pere Lažetića

17

28

Mostarskog Bataliona

Braće Fejića

48

25

Osmana Ose Grebe

Huse Maslića

Salke Šetića

Braće Ševa

33

Rizkala

11

12

Musala Most

3

Neretva River

23

Kardinala Stepinca

Dr Mile Budaka

Prison

Alekse Šantića

44

Dr Ante Starcevica

43

Spanski Trg

6

52

47

To Western Bus Station (800m)

Kneza Višeslava

Splitska

To Western Bus Station (800m)

Kneza Domagoja

P

Kralja Tvrtka

Stjepana Radića

Kralja Zvonimira

Nikole Šubića Zrinskog

49

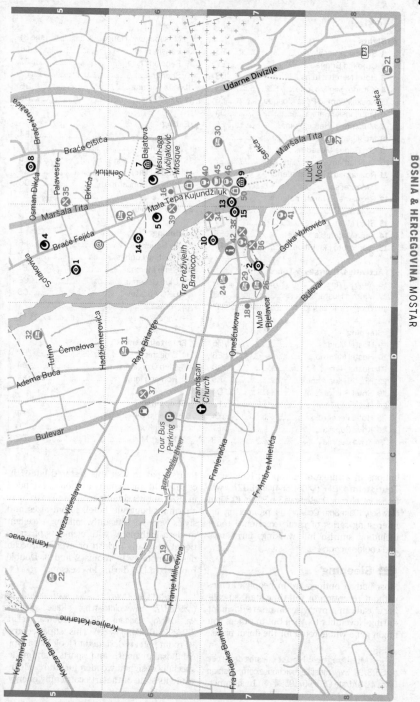

Mostar

◎ Sights

⊙ Activities, Courses & Tours

◉ Sleeping

⊗ Eating

◉ Drinking

◉ Entertainment

◉ Shopping

options in a range of European languages. **Tourist Info BH** (☏061 564146 561127; www.tourist-infobh.com; Onešćukova 39; ☸8am-10.30pm May-Sep, 10am-8pm Oct-Apr) is pioneering an interesting series of rural experience tours including sunrise hill walking, farm-stays and cooking courses.

🛏 Sleeping

Most budget options are in people's homes without reception or full-time staff, so calling ahead can prove wise. Some are dormant during November to April but in others you might get a whole room for the dorm price.

TOP CHOICE **Muslibegović House** HISTORIC HOTEL €€
(☏551379; www.muslibegovichouse.com; Osman Đikća 41; s/d/ste €60/90/105; ✳🛜) In summer, tourists pay to visit this restored late-17th-century Ottoman courtyard house, extended in 1871. But it's simultaneously an extremely charming boutique hotel. Room sizes and styles vary significantly, mixing excellent modern bathrooms with elements of traditional Bosnian, Turkish or even Moroccan design, notably in rooms 2 and 3. Double rooms cost €75 during low season.

🛏 **Hotel Old Town** BOUTIQUE HOTEL €€
(☏558877; www.oldtown.ba; Rade Bitange 9a; d/tr/q standard 180/250/300KM, deluxe 210/290/400KM; ℙ✳🛜) This super-central 10-room hotel is designed to look like a typical Bosnian house and sports handmade, specially designed wooden furniture. Meanwhile its state-of-the-art ecofriendly energy-

saving systems include waste-burning furnaces for water heating and air circulation to save on air-con wastage. Standard rooms are tucked into sloping roof eaves.

Kriva Ćuprija
MILLHOUSE €€
(☑550953; www.motel-mostar.ba; r 70-130KM, apt 100-180KM; ✳🖥) Set above the famous little Crooked Bridge, this delightful central getaway enjoys the soothing sounds of gushing streams and charming mill-styled stone architecture. Idyllic views from the suites' semi-private terraces cram together old rooftops, minarets and a mountain-ridge backdrop. Rooms are impeccably clean if not necessarily large. Co-owned **Kriva Ćuprija 2** (Maršala Tita 186) is more stylishly appointed and has two hot-tubs on a rear deck but lacks the quaint location of the original.

Shangri-La
B&B €€
(☑551819; www.shangrila.com.ba; Kalhanska 10; d €49-59; 🅿✳🖥) Quiet yet central, a pseudo-19th-century facade hides rooms that are contemporary and better appointed than those of many Mostar hotels. The rooftop views are hard to beat and the English-speaking hosts are faultlessly welcoming without being intrusive.

Hostel Majdas
HOSTEL €
(☑062 265324, 061 382940; www.hostelmajdas. com; 1st fl, Franje Milicevica 39; dm/d without bathroom €12/27; ⊙closed Oct-Mar; ✳@🖥) By sheer force of personality, and a very human awareness of traveller needs, the host family has transformed this once dreary tower-block apartment into Mostar's cult hostel. Space is tight in the colour-coordinated bunk dorms and little communal areas, but it's a great place to meet fellow travellers; there are lockers, FAQ and cultural-tip sheets, inexpensive laundry, a book exchange and a taxi sign-up sheet. Sharp-witted Bata runs popular full-day regional tours several times weekly.

Hotel Pellegrino
HOTEL €€
(☑062 969000; www.hotel-pellegrino.ba; Faladžića 1c; s €50-80, d €80-120; ✳🖥) The big pluses here are the oversized, elegantly appointed studio rooms (many with kitchenette) and excellent anti-allergenic bedding. But there is no reception, just a door-bell, and despite the five floors there are neither views nor a lift.

Hotel Bristol
BUSINESS HOTEL €€
(☑500100; www.bristol.ba; Mostarskog Bataljona; s/d from €50.50/81.50; ✳🖥) Classier than you'd guess from the rectilinear concrete ex-

terior, there's an expansive piano bar, riverside terrace and a lift accessing the typical business-style rooms. There are desks even in the poky little singles.

Villa Fortuna
B&B €€
(☑551888; www.villafortuna.ba; Rade Bitange 34; s/d/tr/apt €30/40/60/80, incl breakfast €35/50/70/100; 🅿✳🖥) Behind the bland travel-agency facade, fresh if compact air-con rooms lead off a hallway with a museum-like collection of local tools and metalwork. Behind is a sweet little private courtyard area in mock farmhouse style.

Villa Mike
HOMESTAY €€
(☑062 661535, 580929; www.villamike-mostar. com; Tutina 15; s/d without bathroom €30/50; ✳🖥🏊) Villa Mike is a private house offering four sparklingly clean, brand new homestay rooms sharing two bathrooms. The obliging owner speaks good English, but most remarkably there's an excellent private swimming pool in the walled backyard.

Hostel Nina
HOSTEL €
(☑061 382743; www.hostelnina.ba; Čelebica 18; dm/d without bathroom €11/22; ✳@) Popular homestay-hostel run by an obliging English-speaking lady whose husband, a war survivor and former bridge jumper, runs regional tours that often end up over bargain beers at his bar in the Tabhana. Sometimes when the main hostel has been full, guests have been relocated to an **annex** that lacks much charm and is far less central.

Pansion Aldi
HOSTEL €
(☑061 273457, 552185; www.pansion-aldi.com; Laćina 69a; dm €10; 🅿✳@🖥) Handy for the bus station, 17 beds in five large, simple rooms share a kitchenette and three small toilet-shower cubicles. It's slightly austere but there's a river-facing terrace garden.

Pansion Oscar
PENSION €
(☑580237, 061 823649; Onešćukova 33; s/d €30/40/45, s/d/tr/q without bathroom €20/30/50/60; ✳🖥) Oskar is essentially a pair of family homes above a summer-only cocktail/shisha garden-bar slap bang in the historic centre. Standards vary somewhat between the nine rooms, with the best in the eaves of the newer back house. They're not bookable through hostel websites so this is a good punt if you're arriving without reservations.

Hostel Miturno
HOSTEL €
(☑552408; www.hostel-miturno.ba; Braće Felića 67; dm/d €10/20; ⊙closed Jan & Feb; 😊✳🖥) Run

by a youthful, music-loving crew, this central mini-hostel has a handful of rooms and small dorms above a main-street shop. The TV room-lobby is cramped but social and has a colourful graffiti-chic. Free coffee.

✖ Eating

Cafes and restaurants with divine views of the river cluster along the riverbank near Stari Most. Although unapologetically tourist-oriented, their meal prices are only a *maraka* or two more than any ordinary dive. Along Mala Tepa and Braće Fejića you'll find a morning **vegetable market** (◷6.30am-2pm), supermarkets and several inexpensive places for *ćevapi* and other Bosnian snacks.

Babilon   BALKAN €€
(Tabhana; mains 8-20KM; 🖪) Along with restaurants Bella Vista, Mlinica and Teatr next door, the Babilon has stupendous terrace views across the river to the Old Town and Stari Most. The food might be less impressive than the views, but some of the set 'tourist menus' are excellent value. Unlike several of its fellows, Babilon remains open in winter.

Hindin Han   BALKAN €€
(Jusovina bb; mains 7-20KM; ◷11am-11pm; 🛜🖪) Hindin Han is a rebuilt historic building with several layers of summer terrace perched pleasantly above a side stream. Locals rate its food as better than most other equivalent tourist restaurants, and the stuffed squid certainly passes muster. The highly quaffable house wine costs 3.75KM per glass.

Šadrvan   BALKAN €€
(Jusovina 11; mains 7-23KM; ◷closed Jan; 🖪) On a vine- and tree-shaded corner where the pedestrian lane from Stari Most divides, this tourist favourite has tables set around a trickling fountain made of old Turkish-style metalwork. The menu covers all bases and takes a stab at some vegetarian options. Meat-free *đuveč* (KM7) tastes like ratatouille on rice.

ABC   ITALIAN €
(🖉061 194656; Braće Fejića 45; pizza & pasta 6-10KM, mains 13-17KM; ◷9am-10.30pm Mon-Fri, noon-10.30pm Sat & Sun; 🖪) Above a popular cakeshop-cafe, this relaxed pastel-toned Italian restaurant is decorated with photos of old Mostar and dotted with aspidistras. Pizzas are bready but the pastas come with an extra bucketful of parmesan. Try plate-lickingly creamy Aurora tortellini (9KM).

Urban Grill   BOSNIAN €
(Mala Tepa 26; mains 5-17KM; ◷8am-11pm Mon-Sat, 9am-11pm Sun) No longer limiting itself to *ćevapi*, this brightly modern take on Bosnian-rustic now serves a wider variety of local specialities but the secret trump card remains its little lower terrace with an unexpectedly excellent Old Bridge view.

Konoba Boncampo   BOSNIAN €€
(Husne Rebca 15 Bulevar; mains 8-18KM; ◷8am-10.30pm) You'll wonder why on earth we've sent you to this hard-to-find, visually ordinary locals' eatery at the base of a residential tower block. But try their *mučkalica* ('everything' dish) and shots of Bosnia's best *slivovice* (plum brandy from Goražde) and you might understand.

Eko-Eli   BOSNIAN €
(Maršala Tita 115; mains 2.50-3.50KM; ◷7am-11pm) Escape the tourists and watch typical Bosnian *pita* snacks (including *krompirača*, *sirnica*, *burek* and *zeljanica*) being baked over hot coals. Take away, eat at the communal table, or dine in the almost comically uninspired bar next door.

🍷 Drinking

Ali Baba   BAR
(Kujundžiluk; ◷24hr Jun-Sep, 7am-7pm Oct, closed winter) Take a gaping cavern in the raw rock, add colourful low lighting, fat beats and Fashion TV and hey presto, you've got this one-off party bar. A dripping tunnel leads out to a second entrance on Maršala Tita.

OKC Abrašević   BAR
(🖉561107; www.okcabrasevic.org; Alekse Šantića 25) This understatedly intellectual smoky box of a bar offers Mostar's most vibrantly alternative scene and has an attached venue for offbeat gigs. It's hidden away in an unsigned courtyard on the former front line. Draft beer from 2KM. Hours vary.

Terasa   CAFE
(Maršala Tita bb; ◷weather dependent) This spectacular open-air perch-terrace surveys Stari Most and the old city towers from altogether new angles. Enter through the little roof-garden of art studio Atelje Novalić.

Club Calamus   COCKTAIL BAR
(Integra Bldg, 5th fl, Dr Ante Starčevića bb; ◷10am-2am) DJs spin trancy beats after 10pm in this top-floor cocktail bar whose summer rooftop

section affords fascinating if poignant views over some of Mostar's worst war ruins.

Caffe Marshall
BAR

(Oneščukova bb; ⊘8am-1am) This minuscule box bar has a ceiling draped with musical instruments and is often the latest to be active in the Old Bridge area.

Wine & More
WINE BAR

(Mala Tepa; ⊘9am-11pm; 🔊) Play Bacchus, sampling Trebinje's famous Tvrdoš Monastery wines (per glass 5KM) at barrel tables on the Old Town's time-polished stone stairways.

Blasting Lounge
BAR

(Riverside; cocktails 5-10KM; ⊘10am-late, closed mid-Nov–mid-May) Sip cocktails and fresh juice (no coffee machine) on a parasol-shaded bank of outdoor bag-cushions while gazing back at Stari Most.

☆ Entertainment

OKC Abrašević (p92) hosts occasional concerts and Ali Baba (p92) fills its summer cave with contemporary dance sounds, particularly on weekend party nights. There are several DJ cafes and nightclubs around the Rondo. Website www.bhclubbing.com gives upcoming listings.

Romana Inn
DISCO

(www.romanainn.com; ⊘10.30pm-5am Thu-Sat) Large, somewhat generic weekend disco.

Club Oxygen
NIGHTCLUB

(www.biosphere.ba/biosfere-stranice-oxigen-en. html; Braće Fejića bb; ⊘variable) Oxygen has DJ-parties and occasional live gigs.

Dom Herceg Stjepan Kosača CULTURAL CENTRE

(http://kosaca-mostar.com/; Rondo; 🔊) Diverse shows and concerts include occasional touring operas, ballets and theatre from Croatia.

Cinestar
CINEMA

(www.blitz-cinestar-bh.ba) Multiplex in the big new Mepas Mall (www.mepas-mall.com; Kardinala Stepinca bb).

🛍 Shopping

The stone-roofed shop-houses of Kujundžiluk throw open metal shutters to sell colourfully inexpensive Turkish and Indian souvenirs including glittery velveteen slippers, pashmina-style wraps, fezzes, *boncuk* (evil-eye) pendants and Russian-style nested dolls. You can still find pens fashioned from old bullets and shell casings hammered into works of art. However, as supplies of war debris are finally being exhausted, artisans such as coppersmith Ismet Kurt (Kujundžiluk 5; ⊘9am-8pm) are increasingly using old cutlery and trays instead as starting materials.

ℹ Information

While no longer technically legal, in fact most businesses readily accept euros and Croatian

BOSNIA & HERCEGOVINA MOSTAR

BUSES FROM MOSTAR (MAIN BUS STATION)

DESTINATION	PRICE (KM)	DURATION	FREQUENCY
Banja Luka via Jajce	25	6hr	1.30pm
Belgrade (Serbia)	58	11 hr	7.30pm, 9pm
Čapljina	6	40min	11.15am, 1pm, 3.25pm
Dubrovnik (Croatia)	32	3-4hr	7am, 10am, 12.30pm
Herceg Novi via Kotor	71	4½hr	7am (plus 2.30pm Fridays)
Sarajevo	20	2½hr	6am, 6.30am, 7am, 9am, 10am, 11am, 3pm, 4pm, 5pm, 6.15pm
Split (Croatia)	33	4½hr	6.15am, 7am, 11.15am, 12.50pm
Stolac	6	1hr	roughly hourly
Trebinje via Nevesinje	21	3hr	6.15am Mon-Sat, 3.30pm, 5.30pm
Vienna (Austria) via Maribor	110	12hr	8.30am
Zagreb (Croatia)	43-52	9½hr	7am, 9am, 8.15pm

kuna as well as marakas. Braće Fejića, the main commercial street, has banks, ATMs, a pharmacy, supermarkets and an internet cafe. Mostar websites include **Grad Mostar** (www.turizam. mostar.ba), the **Hercegovina Tourist Board** (www.hercegovina.ba) and **Visit Mostar** (www. visitmostar.org).

Bosniak Post Office (Braće Fejića bb; ☺8am-8pm Mon-Fri, 8am-6pm Sat)

Croat Post Office (Dr Ante Starčevića bb; ☺7am-7pm Mon-Sat, 9am-noon Sun)

Tourist Information Centre (☑397350; Trg Preživjelih Branioco; ☺9am-9pm Jun-Sep, closed Oct-May) See also Tourist Info BH (p90).

ⓘ Getting There & Around

AIR Mostar airport (OMO; ☑350992; www. mostar-airport.ba), 6km south of town off the Čapljina road, has no scheduled flights.

BICYCLE The souvenir stall beside the tourist info centre rents bicycles (per half-/full day €10/15) during the tourist season.

BUS Most long-distance buses use the **main bus station** (☑552025; Trg Ivana Krndelja) beside the train station. However, Renner buses to Stolac, a 4.30pm bus to Split (25KM) and seven weekday services to Međugorje (4KM, 45 minutes) start from the inconveniently located **western bus station** (☑348680; Autobusni Kolodvor; Vukovarska bb). It's around 800m from Mepas Mall, following Splitska west then the turning right at the third major junction. Yellow **Mostar Bus** (☑552250; www.mostarbus. ba/linije.asp) services to Blagaj start from opposite the train station and pick up passengers at Lučki Most stop.

CAR Hyundai Rent-A-Car (☑552404; www. hyundai.ba; main bus station; per day/week from 75/390KM; ☺8am-11am & noon-4pm Mon-Fri, 9am-3pm Sat) offers good-value car hire including full insurance without deductible. Add 17% tax.

TRAIN Trains to Sarajevo (9.90KM, 2¼ hours) depart at 8.02am, 2.10pm and 6.43pm daily.

Around Mostar

By joining a tour or hiring a car you could visit Blagaj, Počitelj, Međugorje and the Kravice waterfalls all in one busy day.

BLAGAJ

☑036 / POP 4000

The signature sight in pretty Blagaj village is the half-timbered **Tekija** (Dervish House; www.fidantours.ba/tekke; ☺8am-10pm summer, 8am-7pm winter) standing beside the surreally blue-green Buna River where it gushes out

of a cliff cave. Upstairs the Tekija's wobbly wooden interior entombs two 15th-century Tajik dervishes and attracts pious pilgrims. The best views are from across the river on a footpath leading behind the attractive riverside **Vrelo Restaurant** (☑572556; mains 8-27KM; ☺9am-10pm).

Walking to the Tekija takes 10 minutes from the seasonal **tourist information booth** (☺variable, closed Oct-Mar). En route you'll pass the **Ottoman Villa** (☑061 273459; www.velagomed.ba; Velagicevina bb; admission 2KM; ☺10am-7pm, closed mid-Oct–Apr), an 18th-century Ottoman homestead with a unique set of island mill-meadow gardens. Out of hours the house's traditionally furnished little lounge transforms into the 'Oriental Nights' homestay room (€20 per person), by far the best of four guest rooms that share a single bathroom. There's a 'hanging garden' eating area outside and the French-speaking owner plans 'fair trade' tours. Alternatively, for accommodation try the friendly **Kayan Pansion** (☑061 241136, 572299; nevresakajan@yahoo.com; per person €10; ✷), offering 11 beds in seven interconnected rooms above an ultra-friendly family home with sizeable gym. It's unmarked, set back across a side road from the octagonal 1892 **Sultan Sulejman Mosque**.

Mostar Bus (www.mostarbus.ba/linije.asp) routes 10, 11 and 12 from Mostar all run to (or very near) Blagaj (2.10KM, 30 minutes), with 16 services on weekdays but only a handful at weekends (last return 8pm).

MEĐUGORJE

☑036 / POP 4300

On 24 June 1981 a vision appeared to six local teenagers in Međugorje (www.med-jugorje.hr). What they believe they saw was a manifestation of the Holy Virgin. As a result, this formerly poor wine-making backwater has been utterly transformed into a bustling Catholic pilgrimage centre and continues to grow even though Rome has not officially acknowledged the visions' legitimacy. Today Međugorje has a blend of honest faith and cash-in tackiness that is reminiscent of Lourdes (France) or Fatima (Portugal) but there's little of beauty here and nonpilgrims generally find a one-hour visit ample to get the idea. The town's focus is double-towered 1969 **St James' Church** (Župna Crkva). In a garden 200m behind that, the mesmerising **Resurrected Saviour** (Uskrsli Spasitej) is a masterpiece of contemporary sculpture showing a 5m-tall metallic

Christ standing crucified yet cross-less, his manhood wrapped in scripture. At times the statue's right knee 'miraculously' weeps a colourless liquid that pilgrims queue to dab onto specially inscribed pads.

A 3km (5KM) taxi ride away at **Podbrdo** village, streams of the faithful climb **Brdo Ukazanja** (Apparition Hill) on red-earth paths studded with sharp stones. They're headed for a white statue of the Virgin Mary marking the site of the original 1981 visions. If you're fit you could nip up and back in 20 minutes but pilgrims spend an hour or more contemplating and praying at way stations, a few walking barefoot in deliberately painful acts of penitence.

For satelite mapped points of interest see www.medjugorjemap.com

POČITELJ
☑ 036 / POP 350

The stepped Ottoman-era fortress village of Počitelj is one of the most picture-perfect architectural ensembles in BiH. Cupped in a steep rocky amphitheatre, it's a warren of stairways climbing between ramshackle stone-roofed houses and pomegranate bushes. The large 1563 **Hadži Alijna Mosque** has been fully restored since the 1990s' destructions while the 16m **clock tower** (Sahat Kula) remains bell-less as it has been since 1917. The most iconic building is the climbable octagonal **Gavrakapetan Tower** in the still part-ruined **Utvrda** (Fort). But for even better panoramas climb to the uppermost rampart bastions. Breathtaking!

Accommodation is limited. Two new pine-walled **apartments** (d/tr €40/60; ☀) need to be pre-booked through English-speaking **Mediha Oruč** (☑ 062 481844), generally summer only. Year-round, simple **homestay rooms** (☑ 062 230023, 826468; per person €10) are rented by Razira Kajtaz who is often to be found hawking souvenirs at the gate-tower at the entrace to the Old Town. Three cafe-restaurants serve drinks and limited grill-meals.

Počitelj is right beside the main Split–Mostar road, 4km north of Čapljina. Mostar–Split, Mostar–Čapljina and some Mostar–Stolac buses pass by. By car, try to arrive an hour before sunset for perfect light and fewer Croatian tour groups.

KRAVICE WATERFALLS
In spring this stunning mini-Niagara of 25m **cascades** pounds itself into a dramatic, steamy fury. In summer the falls themselves are less impressive but surrounding pools

---

WINE DIVINE

Hercegovina's home-grown wines are a revelation. Local *živalka* grapes yield dry yet fruit-filled whites while suitably aged *blatina* and *vranac* reds can be velvety and complex. In restaurants, ordering *domaći* ('house') wine by the carafe (ie 'open') costs from just 15KM per litre. That's far less than by the bottle and ensures that you're drinking a really local drop. It's possible to visit a selection of rural wineries (see www.wineroute.ba) but it often pays to phone ahead.

---

become shallow enough for swimming. The site is 15 minutes' walk from a car park that's 4km down a dead-end road turning off the M6 (Čapljina–Ljubuški road). Turn at km42.5. There's no public transport.

Stolac
☑ 036 / POP 12,000

The attractive castle town of Stolac was the site of Roman Diluntum (3rd century AD) and became a prominent citadel from the 15th century. Stolac suffered serious conflict in 1993. The displaced population has long since returned and the town's greatest historical buildings have been painstakingly reconstructed. However, Stolac still hasn't fully recovered, war damage remains painfully evident and the only hotel has closed.

At the central junction, the large, mural-fronted 1519 **Čaršija Mosque** has been splendidly rebuilt. Following the Brevaga River upstream for 900m from here you'll pass the cute cubic **Ćuprija Mosque**, little stone-arched **Inat Ćuprija** (bridge) and three picturesque, if derelict, 17th-century stone **mill-races** before reaching unpretentious **Nota** (Kukovac bb; coffee/beer 1/2KM, pizza 4-7KM; ☺ 8am-11pm) cafe-pizzeria. It's unmarked but obvious with a terrace on stilts above the lip of a clogged horseshoe of waterfall.

Downstream from Čaršija Mosque, the tree-lined main street (Hrvatske-Brante, aka Ada) passes a diagonal switchback track that leads up to the hefty **castle ruins**. Around 300m further along Hrvatske-Brante is another group of historic buildings, some rebuilt. Across the bridges, views of the castle site are most memorable from near the Auro petrol station, 50m south of the graffiti-covered bus station.

Beside the Mostar road 3km west of Stolac is **Radimlja Necropolis** (admission free). At first glimpse it looks like a quarryman's yard. But on closer inspection the group of around 110 blocks prove to include some of Bosnia's most important *stećci* (carved grave-markers). Entry is free if you ignore the book-bearing beggar.

Buses run Mostar–Stolac (6KM) approximately hourly. There's no Stolac–Trebinje bus whatsoever but you might persuade locals to act as taxi and take you to Ljubinje (20km, 40KM), from where a 4.15pm minibus runs daily to Trebinje (8KM, one hour). The Stolac–Ljubinje road crosses a former wartime no-man's-land passing the still bombed-out hilltop hamlet of Žegulja at km33.2.

EASTERN BOSNIA & HERCEGOVINA

To get quickly yet relatively easily off the main tourist trail, try linking Sarajevo or Mostar to Dubrovnik via Trebinje, or head to Belgrade via Višegrad. Both journeys take you through the semi-autonomous Republika Srpska.

Trebinje

☎059 / POP 36,000

It's just 28km from Dubrovnik (28km), but in tourist terms a whole world away. Trebinje's small, walled **Old Town** (Stari Grad) is attractive but very much 'lived in', its unpretentious cafes offering a fascinating opportunity to meet friendly local residents and hear Serb viewpoints on divisive recent history. The Old Town ramparts back onto the riverside near a 19th-century former Austro-Hungarian barracks which now houses the **Hercegovina Museum** (www. muzejhercegovine.org; Stari Grad 59; admission 2KM; ☉8am-2pm Mon-Fri, 10am-2pm Sat).

Trebinje's 1574 **Arslanagić Bridge** (Perovića Most), 700m northeast of Hotel Leotar, is a unique double-backed structure but it's sadly let down by the unexotic suburban location to which it was moved in the 1970s.

For phenomenal views, take the 2km winding lane leading east behind the hospital to hilltop Hercegovacka Gracanica. The compact but eye-catching **Presvete Bogorodice Church** (Hercegovačka Gračanica) was

erected here in 2000 to re-house the bones of local hero Jovan Dučić. Its design is based on the 1321 Gračanica monastery in Kosovo, a building that's symbolically sacred to many Serbs. The brand new **Arhangel Mihailo Church** on a second hilltop across town provides a certain sense of urban symmetry.

Siniša Kunić (☎065 645224; www.walkwith-me.ba) offers small-group forest, hiking and pilgrimage trips.

🛏 Sleeping & Eating

Trebinje has half a dozen hotels including three motels across the river near the hospital. Within the Old Town, pizza windows sell slices for 1.50KM and there are many local-oriented cafe-bars including two at the river bank hidden behind the museum.

Hotel Platani BOUTIQUE HOTEL €€
(TOP CHOICE) (http://hotel-platani-trebinje.com; Trg Svobode; s/d/tr Platani-1 63/85/100KM, Platani-2 72/104/128KM; ❋🗐) The Platani's two stone buildings both have distinctly Gallic-looking glass/wrought-iron overhangs and overlook the prettiest central square, shaded with chestnut and plane trees. Platini-1 is perfectly adequate but choose Platini-2 for its stylish contemporary rooms with virginal white sheets and Klimt-esque art. Some back rooms suffer road noise but it's fabulous value for money. So too is the excellent terrace restaurant where you can sip generous glasses of velvety Tvrdoš Vranac red wine for just 4KM.

Vinoteka Vukoje 1982 WINE & CUISINE €€
(TOP CHOICE) (☎270370; www.podrum-vukoje.com; Mirna 28; mains 8-20KM; 🗐) Come for the free wine tasting (including Vukuje's irresistible Vranac Reserve) then stay for their imaginative cuisine employing a range of local herbs and meats. The two stylishly appointed new dining rooms have pale decor and sepia photos of the vineyards. From Hotel Platani it's 1.2km towards Bileća, 200m beyond the Niščić turn.

❶ Information

Tourist Office (☎273410; www.trebinjeturizam. com; Jovan Dučića bb; ☉8am-8pm Mon-Fri, 8am-3pm Sat May-Oct, 8am-4pm Mon-Fri, 9am-2pm Sat Nov-Apr) Diagonally opposite Hotel Platani-1 near the Old Town's western gate.

❶ Getting There & Away

The **bus station** (Autobusko Stajalište; Vojvode Stepe Stepanovića) is simply a shelter within a parking area, 200m west of the old town.

BUSES FROM TREBINJE

There are no buses to Stolac.

DESTINATION	PRICE (KM)	DURATION	FREQUENCY
Belgrade (Serbia) via Višegrad	52	11 hr	8am, 9.45pm
Dubrovnik (Croatia)	10	45min	10am Mon-Sat (returns at 1.30pm)
Foča	16	2½hr	take Belgrade, Novi Sad, Pale or Sarajevo buses
Ljubinje	8	1hr	3.05pm Mon-Fri, 7pm daily
Mostar via Nevesinje	24	3hr	6.15am, 10am, 2.30pm
Novi Sad	53	12hr	5.30pm
Pale	28.50	4½hr	5am
Podgorica via Nikšič	33	3½hr	8.30am, 3pm, 4.30pm
Sarajevo	26	4hr	5am, 7.30am, 11am

Trebinje To Višegrad

Trebinje–Belgrade and Trebinje–Sarajevo buses pass through the glorious **Sutjeska National Park** (www.npsutjeska.srbinje.net). Magnificent tree-dappled grey rock crags flank the Sutjeska canyon like scenes from classical Chinese paintings. A few kilometres further north the canyon opens out near an impressively vast concrete **Partizans' Memorial** commemorating the classic WWII battle of Tjentište. Mountaineers and hikers can explore more of the national park's scenic wonders with extreme-sports outfit **Encijan** (☑058-211150, 058-211220; www.pkencijan.com; Kraljapetra-I 1; ☺9am-5pm Mon-Sat), based in Foča (25km further north). Encijan also organises world-class rafting on the Tara River that cascades out of Europe's deepest canyon (across the Montenegrin border) then thunders over 21 rapids (class III to class IV in summer, class IV to class V in April).

Višegrad

☑058 / POP 20,000

A convenient stop between Sarajevo and Belgrade, Višegrad's main attraction is its 10-arch **Mehmet Paša Sokolović Bridge**. Built in 1571 it was immortalised in Ivo Andrić's Nobel Prize–winning classic *Bridge on the Drina*. To build on the connection, Višegrad is constructing **Andrićgrad** (www.andricgrad.com), a stone-walled mini 'old'

town that's due to open in 2014 as a historical fantasy cum cultural museum. Višegrad is otherwise architecturally unexciting but it's set between a series of impressive river canyons. On summer weekends there are usually **boat trips** (Sonja; ☑065-142742; per person incl lunch from 30KM) to explore them. Check booking details with the helpful **tourist office** (☑620950; www.visegradturizam.com; ul Kozachka; ☺8am-4pm Mon-Fri, 8am-3pm Sat) near the southern end of the old bridge. Their website has a town map.

A recently reconstructed narrow-gauge railway runs from Višegrad's decrepit station to Mokra Gora (Serbia), linking up with the popular Šargan 8 tourist train (p479). In 2012 the service departed Višegrad weekends only at 3pm (adult/child 800/400 Serbian Dinars) but frequency should increase. The train makes a sightseeing stop at the historic, if almost totally reconstructed, **Dobrun Monastery** (km11.5, Višegrad–Belgrade road), a resonant site for Serbs as Karađorđe hid here immediately before launching the 1804 Serb uprising.

🛌 Sleeping & Eating

Hotel Višegrad   HOTEL €€

(☑620710; www.hotel.visegrad24.info; Trg Palih Boraca; s/d/tr 49/83/123KM; ☺7am-11pm; ☎) The facade is sickly yellow concrete, showers are feeble and decor's hardly stylish but friendly receptionists manage some English and the location is perfect, right at the riverside at the end of the historic bridge. The blandly

BUSES FROM VIŠEGRAD

DESTINATION	DEPARTURE POINT	PRICE (KM)	DURATION	FREQUENCY
Banja Luka	Hotel Višegrad	46	9hr	8am via Sarajevo
Belgrade (Serbia)	Hotel Višegrad	27	5½hr	5.15am
Belgrade (Serbia)	North side	27	5½hr	3.15am, 9.50am, 1.30pm
Foča	Hotel Višegrad	10	80min	7.15am, 9.30am
Mostar	North side	32	6hr	3.10am
Niš	North side	30	7hr	11.15am & alternate days 9.10pm
Sarajevo Lukavic	North side	19	3hr	12.45pm
Trebinje	North side	29	5hr	Overnight at 11.15pm
Užice	Hotel Višegrad	10	90min	11.30am, 6pm via Dobrun & Mokra Gora

boxlike restaurant (mains 6KM to 14KM) pumps out loud Europop, but its terrace frames bridge views between willow, pine and plane trees. And the inexpensive local fare is surprisingly well cooked. Wi-fi in restaurant only.

ⓘ Getting There & Away

Buses depart from outside the Hotel Višegrad as well as the north side of the old bridge and/or at Motel Okuka (1km northeast of the centre).

CENTRAL & WESTERN BOSNIA

West of Sarajevo lies a series of mildly interesting historic towns, green wooded hills, river canyons and rocky crags. The area offers ample opportunities for exploration and adrenaline-rush activities.

Visoko

📞 032 / POP 17,000

Once the capital of medieval Bosnia and the spiritual centre of the controversial Bosnian Church, this unremarkable leather-tanning town had been largely forgotten during the 20th century. Then Bosnian archaeologist Semir Osmanagic hatched a bold theory that Visoko's 250m-high Visočica Hill is in fact the World's Greatest Pyramid (Piramida Sunca; www.piramidasunca.ba), built approximately 12,000 years ago by a long-disappeared superculture.

The mainly forested 'Sun Pyramid' does indeed have a seemingly perfect pyramidal shape when viewed from some angles (despite a long ridge at the back) and plates of bafflingly hard ancient 'concrete' found here are cited as having once covered the hill, creating an artificially smoothed surface. Visits to the archaeological excavations (without/with guide 3/5KM) start with a stiff 20-minute climb from a car park and info point-ticket booth near Bistro Vidikovac. To get there from Visoko bus station takes around 15 minutes' walk starting by crossing the river towards the Motel Piramida-Sunca. However, imediately across the bridge turn left down Visoko's patchily attractive main street, Alije Izetbegovića, at the start of which is an information office (Alije Izetbegovića 53; ⊙8am-4pm Mon-Fri). Renamed Čaršijska, the street then curves to point directly towards the pyramid summit. After the bazaar veer left into Tvrtka/Mule Hodžić then turn right up the narrow asphalt lane directly beyond the church to find Bistro Vidikovac.

Other nearby hills are mooted to be lesser pyramids and archaeologists are busily investigating prehistoric subterranean labyrinths, notably the Tunnel Ravne (📞062 730299; admission 5KM; ⊙call ahead), of which more is excavated every year. Guided hard-hat tours leave fairly regularly from an information booth outside (open 9am to 7pm) but you might have to wait a while. To find the site head 2km towards Kakanj from the Motel Piramida-Sunce. Turn left after the

Bingo Hypermarket and climb 500m up a tiny asphalt lane.

Young people come from across Europe to volunteer with the pyramids project and to soak up what many of them consider to be a potently spiritual earth energy that the valley exudes.

ℹ Getting There & Away

Visoko is a stop for buses between Sarajevo (6.30KM, 50 minutes) and Kakanj (5KM, 35 minutes) running 18 times daily (seven times Sundays), last return to Sarajevo at 9.20pm. For Travnik and Jajce, direct buses depart Visoko at 8.10am, 9.50am, 2.10pm and 4.10pm or change in Zenica (14 buses on weekdays).

Travnik

✍ 030 / POP 27,500

Once the seat of Bosnia's Turkish viziers (Ottoman governors), Travnik is now best known for its sheep cheese – and as the birthplace of Nobel prize–winning author Ivo Andrić, who set his classic *Bosnian Chronicle* here. It's a pleasant place to spend a couple of hours when travelling between Sarajevo and Jajce.

For a basic walking tour exit the bus station to the south (down steps), cross a partly tree-shaded car park and turn left along Bosanska, Travnik's patchily interesting main street. You'll pass the distinctive **Sahat Kula** stone clocktower and 19th-century **Haji Alibey Mosque** before reaching the dreary Yugoslav-area **Hotel Lipa** (☎511604; Lažajeva 116/Bosanska 91; s/d/tr 52/84/111KM) in front of which the **Viziers' Turbe** is a pair of dome-sheltered collectons of Ottoman-era tombstones. At Bosanska's eastern end is Travnik's celebrated **Many Coloured Mosque** (Šasend Džamija; Bosanska 203) first built in 1757. Its fa-

mous murals have faded but it retains a little *bezistan* (mini-bazaar) built into the arches beneath its main prayer house.

Behind the mosque, take the pedestrian underpass beneath the M5 highway and follow Varoš steeply uphill to **Stari Grad** (☎518140; adult/student 2/1.50KM; ⊙8am-8pm Apr-Oct, by appointment Nov-Mar), Travnik's medieval grey-stone castle. Behind its extensively restored ramparts the multi-sided keep houses a modest museum of local history and costumes. Returning from the fortress, turn left on Musala beside the R&M store (Varoš 42) and immediately left again down the Hendek stairway. You'll emerge on Šumeća near Motel Aba. Turn left here to find Plava Voda (p100), a gaggle of restaurants flanking a merrily gurgling stream, criss-crossed by small bridges. Tucked behind here is the Moorish-styled **Elči-Ibrahimpaša Madrassa**.

🛏 Sleeping & Eating

Central hotels suffer from road rumble as do half a dozen other motels strung 10km along the eastbound M5. Travnik's better (but mostly winter-only) hotels are 27km northwest in the three-lift ski-resort of Vlašić (www.babanovac.net) above Babanovac village.

Motel Aba　　　　　　　　　　HOTEL €
(☎511462; www.aba.ba; Šumeća 166a; s 35-40KM, d/tr/q 50/70/80KM; 🛜) Handily near to Plava Voda, Aba provides highly acceptable, unfussy en suite rooms at unbelievably reasonable prices. The stairs and road noise are minor niggles, wi-fi works well and there's limited free parking. Breakfast costs 10KM extra.

Blanca　　　　　　　RESORT & SPA €€€
(☎519900; www.blancaresort.com; s €52-165, d €74-242, tr €132-273; 🏊) If you don't mind driving

---

ANDRIĆ'S TRAVNIK

Readers who enjoyed *Bosnian Chronicle* can add several Andrić-related sites to their Travnik explorations. All are on or near Bosanska. An alien-eyed bust of the author sits in the churchyard of the **Sv Ivana Krstitelja Church** (Bosanska 93). The vine-covered old building now containing the banal **Caffe Consul** (Bosanska 135; coffee 1KM; ⊙8am-11pm) was indeed the *Chronicle's* setting for the consul's house. Between Bosanska 171 and 169 head a short block north to find a traditionally styled Bosnian house designed to look like Andrić's birthplace and now containing a two-room **Andrić Museum** (☎518140; Zenjak 13; adult/student 2/1.50KM; ⊙9.30am-5pm Apr-Oct, 8am-4pm Mon-Fri, 10am-2pm Sat & Sun Nov-Mar). And across the stream from the Konoba Plava Voda (p100), is a moorish-styled cafe now called **Lutvina Kahva** (Plava Voda; ćevapi 2.50-9KM, mains 9-11KM; ⊙7am-10pm) that also featured in the book.

BUSES FROM TRAVNIK

DESTINATION	PRICE (KM)	DURATION	FREQUENCY
Babanovac	4	45min	10am, 3.10pm
Bihać	35.20	6hr	9.30am, 3.30pm, 4.20pm, 11.30pm
Jajce	8-12.70	1½hr	7.45am, 9.30am, 3pm, 4.20pm, 5.10pm, 5.30pm, 11.30pm
Sarajevo	15.50-17	2hr	6.50am, 8.05am, 9am, 10.40am, 12.15pm 3.40pm, 6.30pm, 7.30pm
Split (Croatia) via Bugojno	23-31	4½hr	6.50am, 8.20am, 11.10am, noon, 5.50pm
Zenica	5-7	1hr	25 daily

to Vlašić, the 2010 Blanca is a luxurious mountain getaway. Right at the base of the ski-jump, this complex uses wooden chalet elements to soften an overall sense of poised designer cool. Guests get free use of four different saunas, the indoor swimming pool has recliner chairs at view windows and unlike virtually every other Vlašić hotel it's open year-round. 'Classic' rooms have no view whatsoever while 'superior' rooms are huge. 'Premium' rooms strike the best balance.

Konoba Plava Voda   BOSNIAN €€
(Šumeće bb; meals 4.50-20KM; ⊘7am-10pm; 🛜)
This attractive warren of rooms is decked out like an ethnographic museum and has a tempting summer terrace in the attractive Plava Voda springs area. The menu is in English, portions generous and the kitchen stays open relatively late even off season.

Travnički Sir   CHEESE SHOP
(Bosanska 157; ⊘8am-6pm Mon-Sat, 8am-3pm Sun) This small shop, overflowing with wooden churns, specialises in Travnik's trademark white cheese.

ℹ Getting There & Away

Travnik's **bus station** (☑792761) is off Sehida (the M5 highway) around 500m west of centre. Its ticket office has keys for a left-luggage room (*garderob*).

Jajce

☑030 / POP 30,000
Above an impressive urban waterfall, Jajce's fortified Old Town climbs a steep rocky knoll to the powerful, ruined castle where Bosnia's medieval kings were once crowned.

The surrounding array of mountains, lakes and canyons make Jajce a potentially useful exploration base.

⊙ Sights

Individually, none of old Jajce's attractions are major drawcards but together they make for an interesting two-hour exploration. Add in the surrounding lakes and canyons and you might want to stay for days.

For a quick visit, exit the bus station and walk anticlockwise around the bluff for views of the classic **waterfalls**. Before crossing the footbridge into town, you can visit the **AVNOJ Museum** (admission 2KM; ⊘9am-5pm) for five minutes to contemplate a gilded polystyrene statue of Tito in the hall where Yugoslavia's postwar socialist constitution was formulated in 1943. Across the river, past several cafes burrowed into the rock-face and through the city wall via the **Travnik Gate** (Sadije Softića 1; ⊘7am-11pm), you'll find Jajce's main shopping street. From the likeable Hotel Stari Grad you can escape the banal 20th-century architecture by climbing Svetog Luke past the new, if limited, **Ethno Museum** (Zavičajna Etno Zbinca; Svetog Luke bb; 1KM; ⊘8am-4pm Mon-Fri, 9am-4pm Sat & Sun) and a 15th-century **campanile tower**. Peep into the **Catacombs** (Svetog Luke bb; admission 1KM; ⊘9am-7pm May-Oct, 9am-5pm Nov-Apr), a small but imaginatively lit 15th-century crypt whose rough-carved sun-moon-cross centrepiece is a rare surviving memorial to the once independent Bosnian church. Up a stairway-street past the tiny, boxlike **Dizdar Džamija** (Women's Mosque) is the sturdy main **fortress** (adult/child 1/0.50KM; ⊘8am-7pm). Inside is mostly bald grass but there are sweeping views from the ramparts.

To return, backtrack to the Dizdar Džamija, turn left along Stari Grad and descend a section of the citadel wall to the **Midway Tower** (Mala Tabija) before retrieving the lane to the Hotel Stari Grad.

Just outside the old city, one block north then west of the conspicuous hypermarket and boxy **Hotel Turist** (☎658151; www.hotel-turist98.com; Kraljice Katerine bb; s/d/tr/q 58/86/109/138KM; ✻) you'll find the **Mithraeum** (Mitrasova 12), a unique 4th-century sculpture featuring a bullfighting Mithras (the pre-Zoroastrian Persian sun god 'rediscovered' by mystical Romans). It's in a glass-sided enclosure at the end of Mitrasova.

The road on the south side of Hotel Turist, just before the bridge, leads west passing the good value Jajce Youth Hostel after 400m. Here guests can rent bicycles (per hour/day 4/10KM) and continue another 4km to the lovely **Pliva Lakes** (Plivsko Jezero) where wooded mountains reflect idyllically in calm, clear waters. Between the two main lakes, a collection of 17 **miniature watermills** form one of Bosnia's most photographed scenes. And 800m beyond, passing the well-organised **Autokamp** (☎647210; campsite per person 8KM; bungalow from s/d 38/56KM; ☉Apr–mid-Oct), you'll find two lakeside hotels including the bargain-priced Plaža Motel at the jetty where pleasure boats are rented in summer.

🛏 Sleeping & Eating

Hotel Stari Grad CENTRAL HOTEL €€
(☎654006; www.jajcetours.com; Svetog Luke 3; s/d 57/84KM, apt 82-154KM; ✻✻☏) Although it's not actually old, beams, wood panelling and a heraldic fireplace give this comfortable little hotel a look of suavely modernised antiquity. Beneath the part-glass floor of the appealing lobby-restaurant (mains 10KM to 14KM) are the excavations of an Ottoman-era *hammam* (Turkish bath).

Jajce Youth Hostel HOSTEL €
(☎063 262168; www.jajce-youth-hostel.com; S Tomaševića 11; dm/d/tr 8/20/24KM; ℗@☏) Offering some of the cheapest formal accommodation in rural Bosnia, rooms are neater than you'd guess from the slightly unkempt public spaces and all have en suite bathrooms.

Plaža Motel LAKESIDE MOTEL €
(☎647200; www.motel-plaza.com; M5 (Bihać hwy) km91; s/d/tr/q 40/70/99/120KM, pizza 7-11KM, mains 9-14KM) Simple, inexpensive rooms above a large lakeside restaurant whose summer dining terrace serves trout, pizza or *ćevapi* right at the waterfront. Jezero-bound buses pass by.

Banja Luka

☏051 / POP 232,000
Since 1998 Banja Luka has been what's probably Europe's least-known 'capital' (of the Republika Srpska). The city is lively

BUSES FROM JAJCE

DESTINATION	PRICE (KM)	DURATION	FREQUENCY
Banja Luka	8.50-12.80	1½hr	7.30am, 9.30am, 12.50pm, 4.20pm, 5.30pm, 6.50pm
Bihać	19-27.20	3½hr	7.30am, 11.30am, 12.30pm, 5.30pm
Jezero	2	15min	7.30am, 9.15am, 11.30am, 12.30pm, 4.40pm, 6.50pm
Mostar	18-18.50	5hr	1.25pm, 2.20pm
Sarajevo	23.50-27	3½hr	7.10am, 8.50am, 9.10am, 10.25am, 5.25pm, 12.30am
Split (Croatia)	31	4½hr	6am (from Split departs at 12.30pm)
Travnik	8-12.70	1¼hr	Take Zenica or Sarajevo buses
Zagreb (Croatia)	31-38	6½hr	7.30am, 8am, 10am, 11.15am, 12.30pm, 4pm, 6pm, 12.30am
Zenica	13.50-15	2¼hr	8.15am, 8.50am, 1.40pm, 3.15pm

more than lovely but it's a useful transport hub if you're planning rafting, canyoning or other adventure sports in the surrounding countryside. To organise any of the above contact Guideline (☑466411; www.guidelinebl. com; Kralja Petra 7; ⊗8am-8pm Mon-Fri, 9am-2pm Sat, cafe 8am-10pm daily) whose brand new information centre doubles as a traveller cafe with free internet (not just wi-fi). Alternatively discuss things with the enthusiastic tourist office (☑490308; www.banjaluka-tourism.com; Kralja Petra 87; ⊗8am-6pm Mon-Fri, 9am-2pm Sat). Both are conveniently found along the city's lengthy main drag, Kralja Petra.

Historic Banja Luka was ravaged by a 1969 earthquake then, late in the civil war, was flooded by Serb refugees from Croatia who dynamited over a dozen historic mosques. The most famous of these, the Ferhadija Džamija (Kralja Petra 42), is now being painstakingly reconstructed using traditional masonry techniques. On the riverside directly southeast, enclosing an area parkland, are the two-storey, 16th-century fortress walls of Kastel Banja Luka. Summer festivities held here include the famous Demofest (www.demofest.org; ⊗late July), a play-off competition between up-and-coming raw garage bands.

Otherwise, only two central city blocks offer much architectural appeal. These surround the memorable Orthodox Cathedral of Christ Saviour (Saborni Hram Hrista Spasitelja; www.hhsbl.org; Trg Srpskih Vladara 3), rebuilt between 2004 and 2009 using alternate layers of crab-pink and mustard-yellow stone. Its domes are eye-catchingly gilded and its brick belltower looks like a Moroccan minaret on Viagra.

The Republic Srpska's sizeable 'national' museum (www.muzejrs.com; Đure Daničića 1; admission 1KM; ⊗8am-7pm Mon-Fri, 10am-2pm Sat & Sun) has a scattering of stuffed birds but mainly walks visitors through the region's history from archaeological digs to horse worship to the horrors of the Ustashi concentration camps of WWII – which is a major culminating focus. Much is in English. The museum is entered from the east side of the large library/theatre building, a block east of the distinctive 1933 Hotel Palas (Kralja Petra 60).

🛏 Sleeping & Eating

Running parallel to Kralja Petra, there are cheap snack bars in courtyards off Veselina Maslaše and many street cafes on its northern extension, Bana Milosavlevica. Close to the canoe club on Save Kovačevića, some 800m east of Ho(s)tel Hertz, are several characterful yet relatively inexpensive bars with tree-shaded riverside frontage: try Monnet (Save Kovačevića 42), Deda Luka (Save Kovačevića 32; beer/pizza from 1.20/3KM; ⊗7am-midnight) or Castra (Save Kovačevića 46).

Vila Vrbas   BOUTIQUE HOTEL €€
(☑433840; Brace Potkonjaka 1; s/d/ste 80/110/130KM; P❀☎) Polished, excellent-value guest rooms are available above this relatively upmarket restaurant with a spacious terrace shaded by plane trees. From here there are glimpses of the castle ramparts across the river.

Hotel Talija   BOUTIQUE HOTEL €€
(☑327460; www.hoteltalija.com; Srpska 9; s/d/apt standard 123.50/157/147KM, superior 143.50/177/247KM; ❀☎) Above a classy pizzeria-cafe, the standard rooms are nothing exceptional but the brand new superior rooms are a whole level above with very elegant coffee-and-

BUSES FROM BANJA LUKA

DESTINATION	PRICE (KM)	DURATION (HR)	FREQUENCY
Belgrade (Serbia)	41.5	5¾-7½	many 5am-5pm plus 9pm & 11.30pm
Bihać	20	3	5.30am, 7.30am, 1pm, 2pm
Jajce	11.50	1½	6.40am, 7.45am, 1pm, 2pm, 4pm
Sarajevo	31	5	6.30am, 7.45am, 2.30pm, 4pm, 5pm, 12.30pm
Zagreb (Croatia)	31	7	3.15am, 6.30am, 8.45am, 9.10am, 11.30am, 4pm, 5.30pm

cream decor. Apartments give it all they've got with lashings of gilt and bold cubist-style artworks. It's 150m east of the cathedral on the road that passes MacTire (www.facebook.com/MacTire.Pub) Irish pub-restaurant.

Hotel Atina BUSINESS HOTEL €€
(☎334800; www.atinahotel.com; Slobodana Kokanovica 5; 92/124/144KM; P✳⊛☎) Smart without undue extravagance; the main features are stylish rectilinear fittings and a helpfully central yet quiet location just east of the castle.

City Smile Hostel HOSTEL €
(☎214187; www.citysmilehostel.com; Skendera Kulenovića 16; dm/d 22/54KM; ☎) A large house turned into a friendly family-style hostel with a kitchen and small sitting area. Though officially on Skendera Kulenovića (the southwestern extension of Kralja Petra), the entrance is on Duška Koščige.

Ho(s)tel Herz HOSTEL €
(☎066 617627; www.hostelherz.com; Milana Rakića 22; dm/d/tr 22/70/100KM) One of several new hostels, this bright, tailor-made place has tight-packed dorms but their four private rooms are hotelstandard en suite affairs. Triples add a fold-out sofa. Breakfast 5KM. It's 300m east of Hotel Atina.

❶ Getting There & Away

AIR The **airport** (☎535210; www.banjaluka-airport.com) is 22km north. The only commercial flight is a stop-off on BH Airlines' thrice-weekly Sarajevo–Zürich run.

BICYCLE Mountain bikes can be rented from **Cycling Shop** (www.cyclingshop-banjaluka.com; Gundulićeva 104; per hr/day 2/15KM), 1.3km northeast of central Banja Luka.

BUS The **main bus** and **train stations** (☎922000; Prote N Kostića 38) are together, 3km north. Access by buses 6, 8 or 10 from near Hotel Palas (opposite the tourist office).

TRAIN Destinations include Zagreb (27KM, 4¼ hours) at 3.49pm and 2.10am and Sarajevo (25KM, five hours) at 1.17pm and 1.49am.

Around Banja Luka

VRBAS CANYONS

Between Jajce and Banja Luka the Vrbas River descends through a series of lakes and gorges that together form one of BiH's foremost adventure-sport playgrounds. At Karanovac, 11km from Banja Luka by bus 8A, **Rafting Centar Kanjon** (☎065 882085;

WORTH A TRIP

CASTLE CAPERS

Dotted between the faceless post-industrial towns of utterly untouristed northeastern Bosnia are several very photogenic medieval castle ruins.

Srebrenik Truly dramatic crag-top setting 6km east of Srebrenik town.

Tešanj Powerful ruins rise above a loveable Old Town square.

Vranduk Small ruins set in BiH's most idyllic castle village, around 10km north of Zenica.

Gradačac Gradačac town centre is dominated by a partly reconstructed castle with a restaurant on top.

Doboj The city is a drab railway junction but the castle hosts costumed festivals and there's a great little cafe-tower.

www.guidelinebl.com; Karanovac; ☺Apr-Oct) is a reliable, well-organised extreme-sports outfit offering guided canyoning (€25 including lunch), quad biking, hiking and especially top-class rafting. Rafting requires groups of at least four people but joining others is usually easy enough at short notice in summer. Some weekends there's a rare opportunity for floodlit night-rafting (with a week's advance reservation). Kanjon is building budget cottage accommodation and with its hypnotic river views, their splendid **Pastir Restaurant** (mains 7.50-15KM, uštipci 5KM) is one of the region's better dining spots.

Another decent stopping point if you're driving by is **Krupa na Vrbasu** (25km from Banja Luka). Set 700m off the main road here is a dainty set of cascades tumbling down between little wooden mill-huts. The tiny car park is overlooked by house-cafe **Krupski Slapovi** (coffee 1KM; ☺8am-10pm).

The Jajce road winds steeply on past two dams. The higher one is overlooked by the stubby rock ruins of what was once **Bočac Citadel**.

Bihać

☎037 / POP 80,000
In central Bihać, a closely clumped **church tower**, **turbe** (tomb) and 16th-century stone **tower-museum** (☎223214; admission 2KM;

WORTH A TRIP

ŽELENKOVAC

Lost in relatively remote forests, the eccentric 'eco-village' of Želenkovac (☎030-278649; www.zelenkovac.org; John Lenon Sq; bed per person 10-25KM) is an inspirationally alternative retreat based around a ramshackle former watermill transformed into a gallery-bar-cafe. Half a dozen Tolkeinesque wooden cottages offer rustic accommodation, some with open fireplaces and indoor bathrooms. International voluntary camps meet here, and there's a July artist colony week. Hiking possibilities abound though many visitors simply hang out and strum guitars with like-minded locals. To find Želenkovac turn off the Jajce–Bihać road at Podbrdo's Eco petrol station, head 7km south towards Baraći, then 500m (left) into the forest.

⊙call ahead) look very photogenic viewed through the trees across gushing rapids. But that's about all there is to see here apart from nearby **Fethija Mosque**, converted from a rose-windowed medieval church in 1595. Bihać could make a staging post for reaching Croatia's marvellous **Plitvice Lakes** (www.np-plitvicka-jezera.hr) just 30km away (p188). Otherwise visit the **Una National Park information office** (www.nationalpark-una.ba; Bosanska 1; ⊙8am-4.30pm Mon-Fri, 11am-3pm Sat, 11am-1pm Sun, closed weekends Nov-Apr) then head for the lovely Una Valley, preferably on a raft!

🛏 Sleeping & Eating

Opal Exclusive   RIVERSIDE HOTEL €€
(☎228586, 224182; www.hotelopalexclusive.net; Krupska bb; s/d/apt 89/138/196KM; P❄🐕🛜) Hidden away but only 300m north of the centre, the Opal's spacious rooms vary considerably in attractiveness but the best are appealing with paintings in gilt frames and lovely views over the river rapids. Similar views are shared by the tree-shaded terrace restaurant (mains 7KM to 25KM) and the top-floor fitness room.

Villa Una   GUEST HOUSE €€
(☎311393; villa.una@bih.net.ha; Bihaćkih Branilaca 20; s/d/tr 52/74/96KM, superior s/d 62/84KM; ⊙7-11am & 6-10pm; P❄🛜) In this very friend-ly *pansion*, homey standard rooms suffer some road noise but are every bit as comfortable as the rear 'superior' versions. It's very handy for the bus station with a front-age painted to look half-timbered.

ℹ Getting There & Away

Disguised as a mini-casino, Bihać's **bus station** (☎311939) is 1km west of the centre, just off Bihaćkih Branilaća towards Sarajevo. Destinations include the following:

Banja Luka (22KM, three hours) Departs 5.30am, 7.30am, 1pm and 3pm via Bosanska Krupa and Otoka Bosanska.

Ostražac (4.50KM, 25 minutes) via **Kostela** (2.50KM, 10 minutes) Use Cazin-bound buses, 10 times daily on weekdays, 8.50am, 11.30am and 3.30pm Saturday, 3.30pm only Sunday.

Plitvice Jezero The 4.45pm Zagreb bus passes Plitvice (8KM). Otherwise change at Grabovac (11KM, 45 minutes).

Sarajevo (46KM, six to seven hours) Departs 12.45am, 7.30am, 2.30pm and 10pm, via Travnik.

Zagreb (25KM, three hours) Departs 4.45am, 10.20am, 2pm and 4.45pm.

Around Bihać

UNA RIVER VALLEY

The adorable Una River goes through varying moods. In the lush green gorges northwest of Bihać, some sections are as calm as mirrored opal while others gush over widely fanned rapids. There are lovely **watermill restaurants** at Bosanska Krupa and near Otoka Bosanska. And up 4km of hairpins above the valley, spookily Gothic **Ostrožac Fortress** (☎061 236641; www.ostrozac.com) is the most inspiring of several castle ruins.

Southwest of Bihać there's a complex of cascades at **Martin Brod** while the river's single most dramatic falls are at glorious **Štrbački Buk** (5KM; ⊙8am-7pm May-Oct), which forms the centrepiece of the new **Una National Park** (www.nationalpark-una.ba). The easiest access is 8km along a good, largely flat unpaved lane from Orašac on the Kulen Vakuf road via National Park Gate 3. In dry conditions you can alternatively start from Gate 1 (Gorevac, 200m off the Bihać–Sarajevo road, 16km from Bihać) but that route uses 14km of woodland lanes that are rolling, very narrow and somewhat rocky (keep right then left at the only two turns en route).

The festive Una Regatta in late July sees hundreds of kayaks and rafts following a three-day course from Kulen-Vakuf to Bosanska Krupa via Bihać.

🏃 Activities

Various companies offer rafting (€25 to €55, six-person minimum), kayaking and a range of adventure sports. Each has its own campsite and provides transfers from Bihać since all are rurally based. Choices include the following:

Una Kiro Rafting   RAFTING
(☎037-361110; www.una-kiro-rafting.com) A big multisport outfit with extensive if over-manicured facilities at the southeast edge of greater Bihać.

Bjeli Una Rafting   RAFTING
(☎061 138853, 037-380222; www.una-rafting.ba; Klokot) At Klokot west of Bihać.

Una-Aqua   RAFTING
(☎061 604313; www.una-aqua.com; Račić) Across the river from Neron at Račić.

🍽️ Sleeping & Eating

TOP CHOICE **Kostelski Buk**   RIVERSIDE HOTEL €€
(☎037-302340; www.kostelski-buk.com; M14, Kostela; s/d €40/59, superior €44/70.50; P❄️🛜) The Louis XVI chairs and leather-padded doors might be a little glitzy for some tastes but rooms are superbly equipped, amply sized and come with luxurious mattresses worthy of a five-star hotel. Superior rooms have river views surveying a set of waterfall rapids. The view is shared by the terrace seating of the very reliable lower restaurant (mains 8KM to 30KM) whose excellent seafood platters (40KM for two people) wash down well with the Hercegovinian Riesling (per litre 20KM). It's 9km from Bihać towards Banja Luka.

Neron Turistički Centar   RIVERSIDE ROOMS €
(☎061 142585; www.neronraft.com; Lohovo; per person without/with private bathroom 25/30KM; ☺May-Sep) Perched by the river at Lohovo where the Una's most testing rafting route ends (13km from Bihać, 5km southeast of Ripac), this museum-like cottage-restaurant (mains 7KM to 18KM)) and hotel is one of the most characterful dining/sleeping options on the Una. The three best rooms sleep three and come with kitchenette and views of the rapids.

Motel Estrada   FAMILY HOTEL €
(☎070-218933; Ostrožac; per person 20KM) Homestay-style en suite rooms in the fifth unmarked house on the left up the Pročići road; 300m southwest of Ostrožac castle.

UNDERSTAND BOSNIA & HERCEGOVINA

Bosnia & Hercegovina Today

Under EU and American pressure BiH has centralised considerably over the last decade in a movement away from the original Dayton 'separate powers' concept. BiH now has a unified army, common passports and a single currency though there remain three separate postal systems. Many, but by no means all, refugees have returned and rebuilt their prewar homes. Politicians running the RS are less radically nationalist these days though during the October 2012 elections the spectre of eventual RS independence was publically raised. Meanwhile in the Federation, the relative complexity of the canton system has proved unwieldy leading to funding-log-jams, most notably for the National Gallery and National Museum. While deep post-conflict scars remain, today economics, job security and corruption are the greatest concern for most Bosnians. Non-payment of wages is a growing worry for those working in the 'grey' private economy while getting certain decent government jobs is rumoured to cost applicants a hefty bribe. When reports suggested that political parties were paying 50KM for votes in the 2012 election, one harried working mother told us 'I wish they'd asked me! I'd have taken 40KM'.

History

Be aware that much of BiH's history remains highly controversial and is seen very differently according to one's ethno-religious viewpoint.

In AD 9 ancient Illyrian Bosnia was conquered by the Romans. Slavs arrived from the late 6th century and were dominant by 1180, when Bosnia first emerged as an independent entity under former Byzantine governor Ban Kulina. BiH had a patchy golden age between 1180 and 1463, peaking in the

Entities of BiH

late 1370s when Bosnia's King Tvtko gained Hum (future Hercegovina) and controlled much of Dalmatia.

Blurring the borderline between Europe's Catholic west and Orthodox east, medieval Bosnia had its own independent church. This remains the source of many historical myths, but the long-popular idea that it was 'infected' by the Bulgarian Bogomil heresy is now largely discounted.

Turkish Ascendancy

Turkish raids whittled away at the country throughout the 15th century and by the 1460s most of Bosnia was under Ottoman control. Within a few generations, easy-going Sufi-inspired Islam became dominant among townspeople and landowners, many Bosnians converting as much to gain civil privileges as for spiritual enlightenment. However, a sizeable proportion of the serfs *(rayah)* remained Christian. Bosnians also became particularly prized soldiers in the Ottoman army, many rising eventually to high rank within the imperial court. The early Ottoman era also produced great advances in infrastructure, with fine mosques and bridges built by charitable bequests. Later, however, the Ottomans failed to follow the West's industrial revolution. By the 19th century the empire's economy was archaic, and all attempts to modernise the feudal system in BiH were strenuously resisted by the entrenched Bosnian-Muslim elite. In 1873 İstanbul's banking system collapsed under the weight of the high-living sultan's debts. To pay these debts the sultan demanded added taxes. But in 1874 BiH's

harvests failed, so paying those taxes would have meant starving. With nothing left to lose the mostly Christian Bosnian peasants revolted, leading eventually to a messy tangle of pan-Balkan wars.

Austro-Hungarian Rule

These wars ended with the farcical 1878 Congress of Berlin, at which the Western powers carved up the western Ottoman lands. Austria-Hungary was 'invited' to occupy BiH, which was treated like a colony even though it theoretically remained under Ottoman sovereignty. An unprecedented period of development followed. Roads, railways and bridges were built. Coal mining and forestry became booming industries. Education encouraged a new generation of Bosnians to look towards Vienna. But new nationalist feelings were simmering: Bosnian Catholics increasingly identified with neighbouring Croatia (itself within Austria-Hungary) while Orthodox Bosnians sympathised with recently independent Serbia's dreams of a greater Serbian homeland. In between lay Bosnia's Muslims (40%), who belatedly started to develop a distinct Bosniak consciousness.

While Turkey was busy with the 1908 Young Turk revolution Austria-Hungary annexed BiH, undermining the aspirations of those who had dreamed of a pan-Slavic or greater Serbian future. The resultant scramble for the last remainders of Ottoman Europe kicked off the Balkan Wars of 1912 and 1913. No sooner had these been (unsatisfactorily) resolved than the heir to the Austrian throne was shot dead while visiting Sarajevo. One month later Austria declared war on Serbia and WWI swiftly followed.

BiH in Yugoslavia

WWI killed an astonishing 15% of the Bosnian population. It also brought down both the Turkish and Austro-Hungarian empires, leaving BiH to be absorbed into proto-Yugoslavia.

During WWII, BiH was occupied partly by Italy and partly by Germany, then absorbed into the newly created fascist state of Croatia. Croatia's Ustaše decimated Bosnia's Jewish population, and they also persecuted Serbs and Muslims. Meanwhile a pro-Nazi group of Bosnian Muslims committed their own atrocities against Bosnian Serbs while Serb Četniks and Tito's Communist Partizans put up some stalwart resistance to the Germans (as well as fighting each other). The BiH mountains proved ideal territory for Tito's flexible guerrilla army, whose greatest victories are still locally commemorated with vast memorials. In 1943, Tito's antifascist council meeting at Jajce famously formulated a constitution for an inclusive postwar, socialist Yugoslavia. BiH was granted republic status within that Yugoslavia but up until 1971 (when *Muslim* was defined as a Yugoslav 'ethnic group'), Bosniaks were not considered a distinct community and in censuses had to register as Croat, Serb or 'Other/Yugoslav'. Despite considerable mining in the northeast and the boost of the 1984 Sarajevo Winter Olympics, BiH's economy remained relatively underdeveloped.

The 1990s Conflict

In the post-Tito era, as Yugoslavia imploded, religio-linguistic (often dubbed 'ethnic') tensions were ratcheted up by the ultra-nationalist Serb leader Slobodan Milošević and equally radical Croatian leader Franjo Tuđman. Although these two were at war by spring 1991, they reputedly came up with a de facto agreement in which they planned to divide BiH between breakaway Croatia and rump Yugoslavia.

Under president Alija Izetbegović, BiH declared independence from Yugoslavia on 15 October 1991. Bosnian Serb parliamentarians wanted none of this and withdrew to set up their own government at Pale, 20km east of Sarajevo. BiH was recognised internationally as an independent state on 6 April 1992 but Sarajevo was already under siege both by Serb paramilitaries and by parts of the Yugoslav army (JNA).

Over the next three years a brutal and extraordinarily complex civil war raged. Best known is the campaign of 'ethnic' cleansing in northern and eastern BiH creating the 300km 'pure'-Serb Republika Srpska (RS). But locals of each religion will readily admit that 'there were terrible criminals on our side too'. In western Hercegovina the Croat population armed itself with the help of neighbouring Croatia, eventually ejecting Serbs from their villages in a less reported but similarly brutal war.

Perhaps unaware of the secret Tuđman–Milošević understanding, Izetbegović had signed a formal military alliance with Croatia in June 1992. But by early 1993 fighting had broken out between Muslims and Croats, creating another war front. Croats attacked Muslims in Stolac and Mostar, bombarding their historic monuments and blasting Mostar's famous medieval bridge into the river. Muslim troops, including a small foreign *mujahedin* force, desecrated churches and attacked Croat villages, notably around Travnik.

UN Involvement

With atrocities on all sides, the West's reaction was confused and erratic. In August 1992, pictures of concentration-camp and rape-camp victims (mostly Muslim) found in northern Bosnia spurred the UN to create Unprofor, a protection force of 7500 peacekeeping troops. Unprofor secured the neutrality of Sarajevo airport well enough to allow the delivery of humanitarian aid, but overall proved notoriously impotent.

Ethnic cleansing of Muslims from Foča and Višegrad led the UN to declare 'safe zones' around the Muslim-majority towns of Srebrenica, Župa and Goražde. But rarely has the term 'safe' been so misused. When NATO belatedly authorised air strikes to protect these areas, the Serbs responded by capturing 300 Unprofor peacekeepers and chaining them to potential targets to keep the planes away.

BOSNIA & HERCEGOVINA HISTORY

WHAT'S IN A NAME?

Geographically Bosnia and Hercegovina (BiH) comprises Bosnia (in the north) and Hercegovina (Her-tse-GO-vina in the south), although the term 'Bosnian' refers to anyone from BiH, not just from Bosnia proper. Politically, BiH is divided into two entirely different entities. Southwest and central BiH falls mostly within the Federation of Bosnia and Hercegovina, usually shortened to 'the Federation'. Meanwhile most areas bordering Serbia, Montenegro and the northern arm of Croatia are within the Serb-dominated Republika Srpska (abbreviated RS). A few minor practicalities (stamps, phonecards) appear in different versions and the Cyrillic alphabet is more prominent in the RS, but these days casual visitors are unlikely to notice much immediately visible difference between the entities.

In July 1995 Dutch peacekeepers watched as the starving, supposedly 'safe' area of Srebrenica fell to a Bosnian Serb force led by the infamous Ratko Mladić. An estimated 8000 Muslim men were slaughtered in Europe's worst mass killings since WWII. Battered Goražde held out thanks to sporadically available UN food supplies. By this stage, Croatia had renewed its own internal offensive, expelling Serbs from the Krajina region of Croatia in August 1995. At least 150,000 of these dispossessed people then moved to the Serb-held areas of northern Bosnia.

Finally, another murderous Serb mortar attack on Sarajevo's main market (Markale) kick-started a shift in UN and NATO politics. An ultimatum to end the Serbs' siege of Sarajevo was made more persuasive through two weeks of NATO air strikes in September 1995. US president Bill Clinton's proposal for a peace conference in Dayton, Ohio, was accepted soon after.

The Dayton Agreement

While maintaining BiH's prewar external boundaries, Dayton divided the country into today's pair of roughly equally sized 'entities', each with limited autonomy. Finalising the border required considerable political and cartographic creativity and was only completed in 1999 when the last sticking point, Brčko, was belatedly given a self-governing status all of its own. Meanwhile BiH's curious rotating tripartite presidency has been kept in check by the EU's powerful High Representative (www.ohr.int).

For refugees (1.2 million abroad, and a million displaced within BiH), the Dayton Agreement emphasised the right to return to (or to sell) their prewar homes. International agencies donated very considerable funding to restore BiH's infrastructure, housing stock and historical monuments.

BOOKS

Bosnia: A Short History by Noel Malcolm is a very readable introduction to the complexities of Bosnian history. In *Not My Turn To Die,* by Savo Heleta, the memoirs of a besieged family at Goražde give insights into the strange mixture of terror, boredom and resignation of the 1990s conflict.

BuyBook (www.buybook.ba) produces several regional guidebooks.

People

Bosniaks (Bosnian Muslims, 48% of the population), Bosnian Serbs (Orthodox Christians, 37%) and Bosnian Croats (Catholics, 14%) differ by religion but are all Southern Slavs. Physically they are indistinguishable so the term 'ethnic cleansing', applied so often during the war, should more accurately have been called 'religio-linguistic forced expulsions'. The prewar population was mixed, with intermarriage common in the cities. Stronger divisions have inevitably appeared since the civil war of the 1990s which resulted in massive population shifts, changing the size and linguistic balance of many cities. Bosniaks now predominate in Sarajevo and central BiH, Bosnian Croats in western and southern Hercegovina, and Bosnian Serbs in the RS, which includes Istochno (East) Sarajevo and Banja Luka. Today social contact between members of the three groups remains somewhat limited. Religion is taken seriously as a badge of 'ethnicity' but spiritually most people are fairly secular.

Arts
Crafts

BiH crafts from *kilims* (woollen flat-weaves) to copperware and decoratively repurposed bullet casings are widely sold in Mostar's Kujundžiluk and Sarajevo's Baščaršija.

Stećci (singular *stećak*) are archetypal Bosnian forms of oversized medieval gravestones, best known at Radimlja near Stolac.

Literature

Bosnia's best-known writer, Ivo Andrić (1892–1975), won the 1961 Nobel Prize for Literature. With extraordinary psychological agility, his epic novel, the classic *Bridge on the Drina,* retells 350 years of Bosnian history as seen through the eyes of unsophisticated townsfolk in Višegrad. His *Travnik Chronicles* (aka *Bosnian Chronicle*) is also rich with human insight, portraying Bosnia through the eyes of jaded 19th-century foreign consuls in Travnik.

Many thought-provoking essays, short stories and poems explore the prickly subject of the 1990s conflict, often contrasting horrors against the victims' enduring humanity. Quality varies greatly but recommended collections include Miljenko

Jergović's *Sarajevo Marlboro* and Semezdin Mehmedinović's *Sarajevo Blues*.

Movies

The relationship between two soldiers, one Muslim and one Serb, caught alone in the same trench during the Sarajevo siege was the theme for Danis Tanović's Oscar-winning 2002 film *No Man's Land*. The movie *Go West* takes on the deep taboo of homosexuality as a wartime Serb-Bosniak gay couple become a latter-day Romeo and Juliet. *Gori Vatra* (aka *Fuse*) is an irony-packed dark comedy set in the Bosnian castle town of Tešanj just after the war, parodying efforts to hide corruption and create a facade of ethnic reintegration for the sake of a proposed visit by US president Bill Clinton.

Music

Sevdah (traditional Bosnian music) typically uses heart-wrenching vocals to recount tales of unhappy amours, though singing it was once used as a subtle courting technique. Sarajevo has an annual **Jazz festival** (November) and a new October **Punkfest**. The post-industrial salt-mining city of Tuzla has vibrant rap and metal scenes.

Environment

BiH is predominantly mountainous. The mostly arid south (Hercegovina) dips one tiny toe of land into the Adriatic Sea at Neum then rises swiftly into bare limestone uplands carved with deep grey canyons. The central mountain core has some 30 peaks rising between 1700m and 2386m. Further north and east the landscape becomes increasingly forested with waterfalls and alpine valleys, most famously in the magnificent Sutjeska National Park. In the far northeast the peaks subside into rolling bucolic hills flattening out altogether in the far north.

SURVIVAL GUIDE

Directory A–Z

Accommodation

Except in hostels, quoted room prices assume a private bathroom and breakfast unless otherwise indicated.

High season means June to September generally but late December to early March in ski resorts. In Mostar and Sarajevo summer prices rise 20% to 50% and touts appear at the bus stations. Our price ranges for a double room:

€ less than 80KM/€40

€€ 80KM/€40 to 190KM/€100

€€€ more than 190KM/€100

ACCOMMODATION TYPES

Hostels Usually bunk rooms in a semi-converted private home. Few have reception desks. Essentially Mostar, Sarajevo and Banja Luka only.

Hotels Anything from re-vamped Tito-era concrete monsters to elegantly restored Austro-Hungarian gems via modernist boxes and over-sized *pansions*.

Motels Generally new and suburban and ideal for those with cars. However, occasionally the term simply implies a lower midrange hotel so don't automatically assume there's much parking.

Pansions Anything from a glorified homestay to a little boutique hotel.

Ski hotels From Christmas to mid-January availability is stretched and prices rise up to 50%. Most close during April to November.

Activities

Skiing Inexpensive yet high quality at Jahorina, Bjelašnica or Vlašić.

Rafting Reaches terrifyingly difficult class V in April/May but is more suitable for beginners in summer. Top spots are around Foča, Bihać and Banja Luka.

Hiking and mountain biking Many upland areas and national parks have mine-safe, marked trails.

Business Hours

Office hours 8am to 4pm Monday to Friday.

Banks 8am to 6pm Monday to Friday, 8.30am to 1.30pm Saturday.

Shops 8am to 6pm daily.

Restaurants 11.30am to 10.30pm, often later in summer. Restaurant closing time depends on customer demand more than fixed schedules.

Embassies & Consulates

You can find a list of foreign embassies and consulates in Sarajevo on http://www.bosnia.org.uk/bosnia/viewtype.cfm?typeID=229.

Food

Average costs for restaurant main courses:

€ less than 10KM

€€ 10KM to 25KM

€€€ more than 25KM

Gay & Lesbian Travellers

Although homosexuality was decriminalised per se in 1998 (2000 in the RS), attitudes remain very conservative. Association Q (www.queer.ba) nonetheless attempts to empower the self-reliance of the gay community in BiH. Gay Romeo (www.gayromeo.com) chat site reportedly has several hundred Sarajevo members.

Internet Access

Most hotels and some cafes offer free wi-fi.

Money

» ATMs accepting Visa and MasterCard are ubiquitous.

» Bosnia's convertible mark (KM or BAM) is pronounced *kai-em* or *maraka* and divided into 100 fenig. It's tied to the euro at approximately €1=1.96KM. Though no longer officially sanctioned, many businesses still unblinkingly accept euros, for minor purchases using a slightly cutomer-favourable 1:2 rate. Exchanging euros is markedly better than changing other currencies as there's no rate-split.

» Exchanging travellers cheques usually requires the original purchase receipt.

Post

BiH fascinates philatelists by having three parallel postal organisations, each issuing their own stamps: BH Pošta (www.posta.ba; Federation), Pošte Srpske (www.postesrpske.com; RS) and HP Post (www.post.ba; Croat areas, western Mostar).

Public Holidays

NATIONWIDE HOLIDAYS

New Year's Day 1 January

Independence Day 1 March

May Day 1 May

National Statehood Day 25 November

ADDITIONAL HOLIDAYS IN THE FEDERATION

Kurban Bajram (Islamic Feast of Sacrifice)

Ramazanski Bajram (end of Ramadan)

Gregorian Easter March/April

Gregorian Christmas 25 December

ADDITIONAL HOLIDAYS IN THE RS

Orthodox Easter April/May

Orthodox Christmas 6 January

Safe Travel

Landmines and unexploded ordnance still affect 2.8% of BiH's area. There were six mine-deaths in 2010. BHMAC (www.bhmac.org) clears more every year but total clearance isn't envisaged before 2019. Stick to asphalt/concrete surfaces or well-worn paths in affected areas, avoiding war-damaged buildings.

Telephone

Mobile-phone companies BH Mobile (☎061- and ☎062-), HT/EroNet (☎063-) and M-Tel (☎065-) all have virtually nationwide coverage.

Country code ☎+387

International operator ☎1201

Local directory information ☎1188

Travellers with Disabilities

Bosnia's steep townscapes are full of stairways and rough streets that can prove very awkward if you're disabled. A few places have wheelchair ramps in response to all the war wounded, but smaller hotels won't have lifts and disabled toilets remain extremely rare.

Visas

Stays of under 90 days require no visa for citizens of most Europeans countries and Australia, Brunei, Canada, Japan, Malaysia, New Zealand, Singapore, South Korea, Turkey and the USA. Other nationals should see www.mfa.ba for visa details and where to apply: several of those nationalities can get a visa on arrival at Sarajevo airport. You might require a letter of invitation or a tourist-agency voucher. Visitors without 150KM per day's intended stay could technically be refused entry, though checks are very rare.

Getting There & Away

Air

All flights use Sarajevo airport, though BH Airlines Zurich flights stop at Banja Luka. Alternatively consider flying to Dubrovnik, Split or Zagreb (Croatia) and connecting to BiH by bus or train.

The following airlines fly to Bosnia & Hercegovina:

Adria (www.adria.si) Via Ljubljana

Austrian (www.austrian.com) Via Vienna.

BH Airlines (Map p76; ☎768335, 033-550125; www.bhairlines.ba; Branilaca Sarajeva 15; ⊗9am-5pm Mon-Fri, 9am-2pm Sat) Pronounced 'Bay-Ha', the national carrier flies a few time weekly from Sarajevo to Copenhagen, İstanbul and Zürich via Banja Luka.

Croatia Airlines (www.croatiaairlines.com) Via Zagreb.

Germanwings (www.germanwings.com) Köln-Bonn.

JAT (www.jat.com) Belgrade.

Lufthansa (www.lufthansa.com) Via Munich.

Norwegian (www.norwegian.no) Twice weekly to Stockholm and Oslo.

Turkish Airlines (www.thy.com) Via İstanbul.

Land

BUS

Buses to Zagreb and/or Split (Croatia) run at least daily from most towns in the Federation and to Serbia and/or Montenegro from many RS towns. Buses to Vienna and Germany run several times weekly from bigger BiH cities.

CAR & MOTORCYCLE

Drivers need Green Card insurance and an EU or International Driving Permit. Transiting Neum in a Croatian hire car is usually hassle-free.

TRAIN

The modest international network links Sarajevo to Belgrade, Zagreb (via Banja Luka), Budapest (via Osijek, Croatia) and to Ploče (coastal Croatia via Mostar).

Getting Around

Bicycle

Cyclists who can handle the hills will find BiH's secondary routes helpfully calm. There are off-road trails for mountain bikers but beware of straying from them in areas where landmines remain a danger.

Bus

Bus stations pre-sell tickets. Between towns it's normally easy enough to wave down any bus en route. Advance reservations are sometimes necessary for overnight routes or at peak holiday times. The biggest company, Centrotrans, has online timetables (click 'Red Vožnje').

Frequency drops drastically at weekends. Some shorter-hop routes stop altogether on Sundays.

Fares are around 7KM per hour travelled. Return tickets are often cheaper than two singles but are limited to one specific company. Expect to pay 2KM extra per stowed bag. Some bus-station ticket offices have a *garderob* for left luggage (from 2KM).

Car & Motorcycle

There's minimal public transport to BiH's most spectacular remote areas so having wheels can really transform your trip. Bosnia's winding roads are lightly trafficked and a delight for driving if you aren't in a hurry. **BIHAMK** (☎033 222210; www.bihamk.ba; Skenderija 23; annual membership 25KM; ⊗8am-4.30pm Mon-Fri, 9am-noon Sat) offers road assistance and towing services (call ☎1282 or ☎1288).

HIRE

International chains are represented while smaller local outfits are often based at hotels. Most companies add 17% VAT. A good deal is Hyundai.ba; its standard rates include full insurance, theft protection and CDW. Pick-up/drop-off is possible at Mostar train station, Novo Sarajevo or Sarajevo airport without extra charge for open-jaws. Prices drop October to April.

ROAD RULES

Drive on the right. First-aid kit, warning triangle, reflective vest and spare bulb kits are compulsory.

» The blood-alcohol limit is 0.03%.
» Headlights must be kept on day and night.
» LPG availability is very limited.
» Parking is awkward in Mostar, central Trebinje and Sarajevo, but contrastingly easy elsewhere. In town centres expect to pay 1KM per hour (attendant or meter) when marked *parking naplatu*.
» Petrol is typically around 2% cheaper in RS than Federation.

» Seat belts are compulsory.
» Snow chains are compulsory on some mountain roads (November to April) and wherever snow is over 5cm deep.
» Speed limits vary: 130km/h (Kakanj–Sarajevo motorway), 100km/h (other dual carriageways), 80km/h (rural), 60km/h or less (in town). Absurdly slow limits are often posted with no obvious logic but police spot-checks are common.
» Winter tyres are compulsory mid-November to mid-April.

Train

Trains are slower and less frequent than buses but generally around 30% cheaper. RS Railways (www.zrs-rs.com/red_voznje.php) has full, up-to-date rail timetables.

Bulgaria

Includes »

Best Places to Eat

» Manastirska Magernitsa (p121)
» Mehana Mencheva Kâshta (p128)
» Han Hadji Nikoli (p142)
» Di Wine (p152)

Best Places to Stay

» Hotel Niky (p117)
» Hotel Bolyarka (p128)
» Hotel Renaissance (p131)
» Hotel Bolyarski (p141)
» Hotel Tony (p155)

Why Go?

Bulgaria (България) may be best known for its long, sandy Black Sea beaches, but there's much more to see than that. Bulgaria boasts no fewer than seven mountain ranges and varied landscapes ideal for hiking, cycling, climbing and wildlife-watching. The country has some of Europe's most modern ski resorts as well. You'll find churches and monasteries full of vibrant icons, picturesque villages of timber-framed houses and cobbled lanes, and dramatic reminders of the country's ancient heritage, from Thracian tombs and Roman ruins to medieval fortresses, Ottoman mosques and communist monuments slowly crumbling away into history. Bulgaria's cities, too, reward visitors, with treasure-filled museums and galleries, and parks sprinkled with cafes and restaurants. Getting around is easy and still remarkably cheap so brush up on your Cyrillic, buy a bus ticket and get ready to explore.

When to Go
Sofia

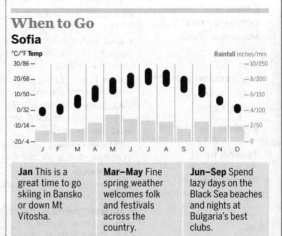

Jan This is a great time to go skiing in Bansko or down Mt Vitosha.

Mar–May Fine spring weather welcomes folk and festivals across the country.

Jun–Sep Spend lazy days on the Black Sea beaches and nights at Bulgaria's best clubs.

AT A GLANCE

» **Currency** Lev (lv)
» **Language** Bulgarian
» **Money** ATMs are everywhere
» **Visas** Not required for citizens of the EU, UK, USA, Canada, Australia and New Zealand

Fast Facts

» **Area** 110,910 sq km
» **Capital** Sofia
» **Country code** ☑359
» **Emergency** ☑112

Exchange Rates

Australia	A$1	1.60 lv
Canada	C$1	1.51 lv
Euro Zone	€1	1.96 lv
Japan	¥100	1.63 lv
New Zealand	NZ$1	1.28 lv
UK	UK£1	2.32 lv
USA	US$1	1.53 lv

Set Your Budget

» **Budget hotel room** 50 lv
» **Two-course meal** 10 lv
» **Museum entrance** 4–10 lv
» **Beer** 2 lv
» **City transport ticket** 1 lv

Resources

» **BG Maps** (www.bgmaps.com)
» **Bulgaria Travel** (www.bulgariatravel.com)
» **Beach Bulgaria** (www.beachbulgaria.com)

Connections

Although Sofia has international bus and train connections, it's not necessary to backtrack to the capital if you're heading to Bucharest or İstanbul. From central Veliko Târnovo, for example, there are daily trains both ways – and much of the country offers overnight buses to İstanbul. Heading to Greece or Belgrade by train means going through Sofia; for Skopje, you'll need to catch a bus from there, too.

ITINERARIES

One Week

Start with a day in Sofia, visiting the Archaeological Museum and Borisova Gradina, then take the bus to Veliko Târnovo for a few days of sightseeing and hiking. Next, head to Varna for some sea and sand. More adventurous travellers may want to head further south along the coast to prettier resorts closer to the Turkish border.

Two Weeks

After a couple of days in Sofia, catch a bus to Plovdiv and wander the cobbled lanes of the Old Town. From there, take a day trip to visit the Bachkovo Monastery. After a few days in Plovdiv, make for the coast, staying a couple of nights in ancient Sozopol. Head north to overnight in Varna then get a connection to Ruse for a glimpse of the Danube and some fine museums. Finish in Veliko Târnovo.

Essential Food & Drink

» **Banitsa** Flaky cheese pasty, often served fresh and hot.
» **Kebabche** Thin, grilled pork sausage, a staple of every *mehana* (tavern) in the country.
» **Tarator** On a hot day there's nothing better than this delicious chilled cucumber and yoghurt soup, served with garlic, dill and crushed walnuts.
» **Beer** You're never far from a cold beer in Bulgaria. Zagorka, Kamenitza and Shumensko are the most popular nationwide brands.
» **Wine** They've been producing wine here since Thracian times and there are some excellent varieties to try.
» **Kavarma** This 'claypot meal', or meat stew, is normally made with either chicken or pork and is one of the country's most popular dishes.
» **Shkembe chorba** Traditional stomach soup is one of the more adventurous and offbeat highlights of Bulgarian cuisine.
» **Shishcheta** This shish kebab, consisting of chunks of chicken or pork on wooden skewers with mushrooms and peppers, is widely available.
» **Musaka** Admittedly, Bulgarian moussaka bears more than a passing resemblance to its Greek cousin but it's a delicious staple of cheap cafeteria meals.

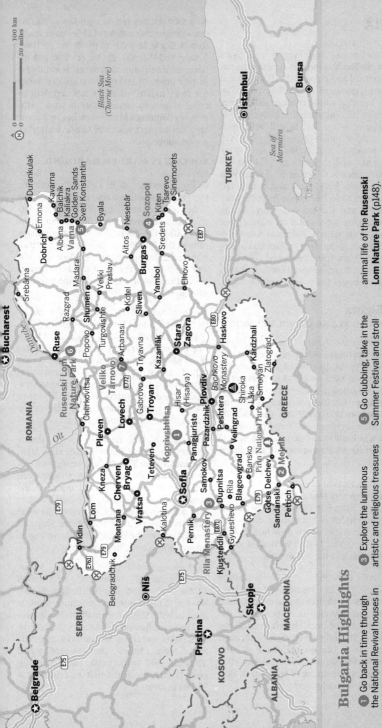

Bulgaria Highlights

1 Go back in time through the National Revival houses in **Koprivshtitsa** (p137).

2 Sip a glass or two of refreshing Bulgarian vino in the wine town of **Melnik** (p127).

3 Explore the luminous artistic and religious treasures of Bulgaria's revered **Rila Monastery** (p127).

4 Relax on the sands of the Black Sea at **Sozopol** (p158).

5 Go clubbing, take in the Summer Festival and stroll through Primorski Park in cosmopolitan **Varna** (p149).

6 Discover the wild landscapes and rich bird and animal life of the **Rusenski Lom Nature Park** (p148).

7 Visit the tsars' medieval stronghold in **Veliko Târnovo** (p139).

SOFIA

♪02 / POP 1.3 MILLION

Bulgaria's capital and biggest city, Sofia (София; *So*-fia) is at the very heart of the nation's political and cultural life. It's no grand metropolis, true, and it's usually bypassed by tourists heading to the coast or ski resorts, but they're missing something special. The old east-meets-west feel is still here, with a scattering of onion-domed churches, Ottoman mosques and stubborn Red Army monuments, and the city's grey, blocky architecture adds a lingering Soviet tinge to the place. Vast, leafy parks and manicured gardens offer welcome respite from the busy city streets and the ski slopes and hiking trails of mighty Mt Vitosha are right on the doorstep. With many of Bulgaria's finest museums and art galleries to explore and plenty of excellent bars, restaurants and entertainment venues, you might well end up sticking around for longer than you imagined.

◉ Sights

PLOSHTAD ALEKSANDER NEVSKI

FREE **Aleksander Nevski Church**   CHURCH
(pl Aleksander Nevski; ⊙7am-7pm) One of *the* symbols of Sofia, this massive church was built between 1882 and 1912 in memory of the 200,000 Russian soldiers who died fighting for Bulgaria's independence during the Russo-Turkish War (1877–78). Designed by the Russian architect AN Pomerantsev, the church was built in the neo-Byzantine style and adorned with mosaics and gold-laden domes.

Aleksander Nevski Crypt   GALLERY
(Museum of Icons; pl Aleksander Nevski; adult/student 6/3 lv; ⊙10am-6pm Tue-Sun; ▣1) To the left of the church's main entrance, a door leads down to the crypt, which now houses Bulgaria's biggest and best collection of icons, stretching back to the 5th century.

Sveta Sofia Church   CHURCH
(ul Parizh; ⊙7am-7pm summer, to 6pm winter; ▣9) Sveta Sofia Church is the capital's oldest, and gave the city its name. Inside the much-restored red-brick church, you can see evidence of its earlier incarnations through glass panels in the floor. Outside are the Tomb of the Unknown Soldier and an eternal flame, and the grave of Ivan Vazov, Bulgaria's most revered writer.

National Gallery for Foreign Art   GALLERY
(www.foreignartmuseum.bg; ul 19 Fevruari 1; adult/student 6/3 lv, last Mon of month free; ⊙11am-6.30pm Wed-Mon; ▣1, 2) An eclectic assemblage of international artwork is exhibited in this huge, squeaky-floored gallery, ranging from Indian woodcarvings and African tribal masks to countless 19th- and 20th-century paintings. Minor sketches by Renoir and Matisse and works by Gustave Courbet are on show too.

SOFIA CITY GARDEN & AROUND

Royal Palace   PALACE
(ul Tsar Osvoboditel; ▣20) Originally built for the Ottoman police force, it was here that Bulgaria's national hero, Vasil Levski, was tried and tortured before his execution in 1873. After the liberation, the building was remodelled in 1887 as the home of Prince Alexander Battenberg and became the official residence of the royal family. It houses the National Art Gallery and Ethnographical Museum.

National Art Gallery   GALLERY
(pl Battenberg, Royal Palace; adult/student 6/3 lv; ⊙10am-6pm Tue-Sun; ▣20) This gallery holds one of the country's most important collections of Bulgarian art, with several rooms full of mainly 19th- and 20th-century paintings. All the big names are represented, including the ubiquitous Vladimir Dimitrov, whose orange, Madonna-like *Harvester* hangs in the former music room.

Ethnographical Museum   MUSEUM
(pl Battenberg, Royal Palace; adult/student 3/1 lv; ⊙10am-4pm Tue-Sun; ▣20) Displays on regional costumes, crafts and folklore are spread over two floors, and many of the rooms, with their marble fireplaces, mirrors and ornate plasterwork, are worth pausing over themselves; note the lobster, fish and dead duck on the ceiling of what was once presumably a royal dining room.

Archaeological Museum   MUSEUM
(www.naim.bg; pl Nezavisimost; adult/student 10/2 lv; ⊙10am-6pm May-Oct, to 5pm Tue-Sun Nov-Apr; ▣10) Housed in a former mosque built in 1496, this museum displays a wealth of Thracian, Roman and medieval artefacts. Highlights include a mosaic floor from the Sveta Sofia Church, the 4th-century BC Thracian gold burial mask, and a magnificent bronze head, thought to represent a Thracian king.

President's Building
NOTABLE BUILDING

(pl Nezavisimost; 🚇10) The Bulgarian president's office isn't open to the public, but the **changing of the guard** ceremony (on the hour) is a spectacle not to be missed, as soldiers in raffish Ruritanian uniforms stomp their way to their sentry boxes outside.

Party House
NOTABLE BUILDING

(pl Nezavisimost; 🚇20) This domineering Stalinist monolith, built in 1953, was once headquarters of the Bulgarian Communist Party. It is now used as government offices. The red star that perched on top of the building is in the **Museum of Socialist Art** (ul Lachezar Stanchev 7, Iztok; admission 6 lv; ⊘10am-5.30pm Tue-Sun; Ⓜ GM Dimitrov).

PLOSHTAD SVETA NEDELYA & AROUND

Sveta Nedelya Cathedral
CHURCH

(pl Sveta Nedelya; Ⓜ Serdika) Completed in 1863, this magnificent domed church is one of the city's major landmarks, noted for its rich, Byzantine-style murals. It was blown up by communists on 16 April 1925 in an attempt to assassinate Tsar Boris III. Over 120 people were killed in the attack, but Boris escaped unharmed.

Sveta Petka Samardzhiiska Church
CHURCH

(bul Maria Luisa; Ⓜ Serdika) Closed due to surrounding excavations at the time of research, this tiny church was built during the early years of Ottoman rule (late 14th century), which explains its sunken profile and inconspicuous exterior. Inside are some 16th-century murals. It's rumoured that the Bulgarian national hero Vasil Levski is buried here.

BULEVARD VITOSHA & PLOSHTAD BULGARIA

Bulevard Vitosha
NEIGHBOURHOOD

Extending south of pl Sveta Nedelya, towards its towering namesake, Mt Vitosha, this central section of bul Vitosha is now a car-free strip with Sofia's ritziest shops, along with a few trendy coffee bars. After a kilometre it reaches **Ploshtad Bulgaria**, an elongated tree-lined plaza.

Monument to the Bulgarian State
MONUMENT

At the northern end of Ploshtad Bulgaria is the Monument to the Bulgarian State. Now fenced off, the socialist-era eyesore was erected in 1981 to celebrate the 1300th anniversary of the Bulgarian Empire, but it has been slowly falling apart for years.

BORISOVA GRADINA & AROUND

Monument to the Soviet Army
MONUMENT

(Ⓜ Kliment Ohridski) Near the entrance to Borisova Gradina, this gigantic monument was built in 1954 and is a prime example of the forceful socialist-realism of the period. The place of honour goes to a Red Army soldier atop a column, surrounded by animated cast-iron sculptural groups depicting determined, gun-waving soldiers and grateful, child-caressing members of the proletariat.

Red House
GALLERY

(www.redhouse-sofia.bg; ul Lyuben Karavelov 15) The Red House is a lively cultural centre, with a busy program covering everything from heavyweight political debates and lectures to film screenings, concerts and dance performances. The house once belonged to the sculptor Andrey Nikolov (1878–1959) and some of his works are displayed in the **Nikolov Hall** (admission free; ⊘3-7pm Tue-Sat) here.

🛏 Sleeping

Accommodation in Sofia tends to be more expensive than anywhere else in Bulgaria, with prices comparable to those in Western European cities. Good-quality budget hotels are a rarity, and cheaper places that do exist are often either squalid dives or in awkward-to-reach locations; hostels are a better deal.

TOP CHOICE Hotel Niky
HOTEL €€

(📞953 0110; www.hotel-niky.com; ul Neofit Rilski 16; r/ste from 80/120 lv; P⊜❄☎📶; 🚇1) Offering excellent value and a good central location, Niky has comfortable rooms and gleaming bathrooms, while the smart suites have kitchenettes with microwave ovens, fridges, and coffee and tea. It's a popular place and frequently full. Advance reservations are recommended.

Residence Oborishte
BOUTIQUE HOTEL €€€

(📞0885 006 810; www.residence-oborishte.com; ul Oborishte 63; s/d/ste from 180/200/220 lv; ⊜❄☎; 🚇9, 72) A salmon-pink '30s-era home with its own bistro, the Residence has nine rooms and sumptuous suites with cherry-wood flooring, antique-style furnishings and lots of space. The penthouse (260 lv) has a view over the Aleksander Nevski Church. Prices drop by 20% at weekends.

Sofia

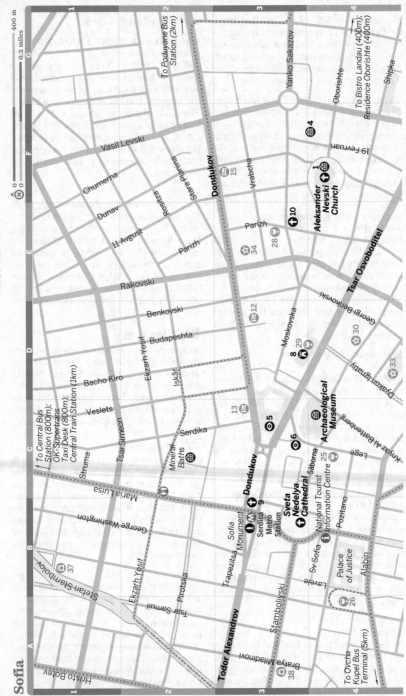

400 m
0.2 miles

To Poduyane Bus Station (2km)

To Central Bus Station (800m); OK-Supertrans Taxi Desk (800m); Central Train Station (1km)

Hristo Botev

Stefan Stambolov

Ekzarh Yosif

Tsar Samuil

Pirotska

Trapezitsa

George Washington

Maria Luisa

Struma

Tsar Simeon

Bacho Kiro

Veslets

Serdika

Iskar

Ekzarh Yosif

Budapeshta

Benkovski

Rakovski

Parizh

11 Avgust

Dunav

Chumerna

Vasil Levski

Rositza

Stara Planina

Dondukov

Vrabcha

Parizh

Parizh

Yanko Sakazov

Oborishte

To Bistro Landau (400m); Residence Oborishte (400m)

Shipka

19 Fevruari

Aleksander Nevski Church

Tsar Osvoboditel

Georgi Benkovski

Moskovska

Dyakon Ignatiy

Knjaz Al Batenberg

Lege

Archaeological Museum

Saborna

National Tourist Information Centre

Sveta Nedelya Cathedral

Dondukov

Serdika Metro Station

Sofia Monument

Mineral Baths

Stamboliyski

Braця Miladinovi

Todor Alexandrov

Alabin

Lavele

Sv Sofia

Palace of Justice

Pozitano

Pozitano

To Ovcha Kupel Bus Terminal (5km)

15

4

1

10

28

34

12

30

33

8

29

5

13

6

25

9

M

26

38

37

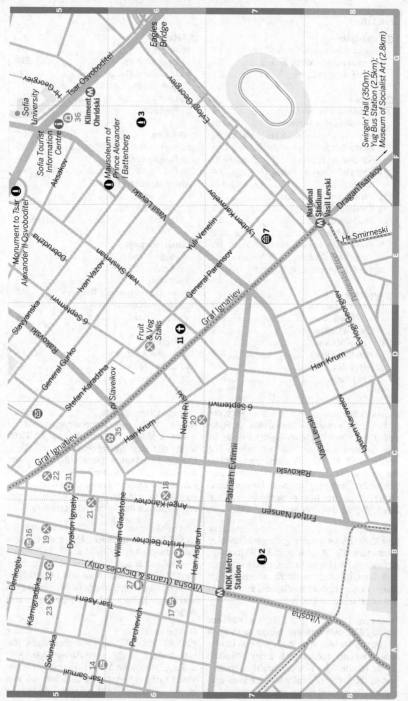

BULGARIA SOFIA

Swingin' Hall (350m);
Yug Bus Station (2.5km);
Museum of Socialist Art (2.8km)

Sofia

Arena di Serdica
LUXURY HOTEL €€€
(☑819 9191; www.arenadiserdica.com; ul Budapeshta 2-4; r from 220 lv; P⊕✳➲) Rooms in this modern five-star hotel are plush but understated. The hotel's name comes from the remains of the 4th-century Roman amphitheatre that were uncovered during construction and are now preserved below the foyer. There's also a 'Roman-style' spa.

Arte Hotel
HOTEL €€
(☑402 7100; www.artehotelbg.com; bul Dondukov 5; r/ste from 110/220 lv; ✳➲; ➲20) Welcoming city-centre hotel with bright, modern rooms and contemporary artwork adorning the walls. Prices drop at weekends, and breakfast is an additional 20 lv.

Hotel Les Fleurs
BOUTIQUE HOTEL €€€
(☑810 0800; www.lesfleurshotel.com; bul Vitosha 21; r from 270 lv; P⊕✳➲; ➲10) You can hardly miss this central hotel, with gigantic blooms on its facade. The flowery motif is continued in the large, carefully styled rooms and there's a very good restaurant on-site.

Canapé Connection
HOSTEL €
(☑441 6373; www.canapeconnection.com; ul William Gladstone 12a; dm/s/d from 20/46/60 lv; @; ➲1) Run by three young travellers, Canapé is a homey place with eight- and four-bed dorms featuring smart wooden bunks and wooden floors, as well as private rooms. Homemade *banitsa*, pancakes and croissants are on the breakfast menu.

Hostel Gulliver
HOSTEL €
(☑987 5210; www.gulliver1947-bg.com; bul Dondukov 48; dm/s/d 18/38/48 lv; ➲; ➲20) Just a couple of blocks north of pl Aleksander Nevski, Gulliver is a clean and brightly furnished place with a couple of five-bed dorms and three doubles. All rooms have TVs and fridges.

Hostel Mostel
HOSTEL €
(☑0889 223 296; www.hostelmostel.com; bul Makedoniya 2; dm/s/d from 20/50/60 lv; P➲; ➲6, 9, 12) Popular Mostel occupies a renovated 19th-century house, and has six- and eight-bed dorms, either with shared or

private bathrooms, as well as a single and a couple of doubles. Guests have use of a kitchen and cosy lounge.

Red House   B&B €€

(☑988 8188; www.redbandb.com; ul Lyuben Karavelov 15; s/d from 50/80 lv; @; MVasil Levski, 🚌10) Attached to the Red House cultural centre, in an unusual Italianate building designed for the sculptor Andrei Nikolov. All rooms are individually decorated, though none have private bathrooms and some are a bit basic.

✗ Eating

Compared with the rest of Bulgaria, Sofia is gourmet heaven, with an unrivalled range of international cuisine and new, quality restaurants springing up all the time. It also has countless snack bars, fast-food outlets and cafes dotted across town. If you're on a budget, there are plenty of kiosks where you can buy fast food such as *banitsa* and *palachinki* (pancakes).

TOP CHOICE Manastirska Magernitsa   BULGARIAN €€

(☑980 3883; www.magernitsa.com; ul Han Asparuh 67; mains 5-10 lv; ⓢ11am-2am; ☻) This traditional *mehana* is among the best places in Sofia to sample authentic cuisine. The enormous menu features recipes collected from monasteries across the country, with dishes such as 'drunken rabbit' stewed in wine, as well as salads, fish, pork and game.

Pastorant   ITALIAN €€€

(☑981 4482; www.pastorant.eu; ul Tsar Assen 16; mains 11-26 lv; ⓢnoon-10.30pm; ☻🖉) This charming pea-green restaurant provides an intimate setting for high-quality Italian cuisine, including some inventive pasta and risotto dishes, and traditional favourites such as saltimbocca and pesto chicken.

Annette   MOROCCAN €€

(☑0885 139 676; www.annette.bg; ul Angel Kânchev 27; mains 8-18 lv; 🕿) With its cushion-filled couches, glowing candles, lanterns and spicy aromas, this is a great place for authentic Moroccan cooking, including a big selection of *mezze*, and tagine meals such as lamb with figs and apricots, and chicken in wine sauce.

Olive Garden   MEDITERRANEAN €€

(☑481 1214; www.olivegardensofia.com; ul Angel Kânchev 18; mains 10-22 lv; ⓢ11am-11pm; 🕿🖉) Expertly cooked roast lamb, trout, salmon, pasta and risotto are served here. There's a

smart indoor dining room or you can sit in the little garden with its mulberry tree. A cheaper lunch menu is also offered.

Bistro Landau   BISTRO €€€

(☑814 4888; www.bistrolandau.com; ul Oborishte 63; mains 12-30 lv; ⓢ7am-10.30pm; ☻🕿; 🚌9, 72) Attached to the Residence Oborishte (p117), this romantic bistro offers an eclectic menu of interesting dishes such as beef entrecote, breaded tilapia, trout and sausages in curry sauce.

Before & After   CAFE €€

(☑981 6088; ul Hristo Belchev 12; mains 5-15 lv; ⓢ10am-midnight; ☻🕿; 🚌8) With its stylish art nouveau interior, this is an agreeable spot for light meals and drinks. Pasta, risotto, fish and steaks feature on the menu.

Olive's   INTERNATIONAL €€

(ul Graf Ignatiev 12; mains 7-18lv; ☻🖉🖐; 🚌10) Walls splashed with vintage advertising posters and mock newspapers for menus give Olive's a quirky twist, and the international cuisine is excellent, featuring dishes such as chicken skewers, pasta, steaks and burgers.

🍷 Drinking

There's a seemingly inexhaustible supply of watering holes all over Sofia. The cheapest places to grab a beer are the kiosks in the city's parks; if you're looking for more sophisticated ambience, the city centre has plenty of swish new bars.

Pri Kmeta   PUB

(At the Mayor's; www.prikmeta.com; ul Parizh 2; ⓢnoon-4am; 🕿; 🚌20) Microbrewery serving its own Kmetsko beer. There are seats at ground level, but the cellar beer hall, with its gleaming copper vats, is more atmospheric, and hosts regular live-music events.

Ale House   BEER HALL

(www.alehouse.bg; ul Hristo Belchev 42; ⓢ11am-midnight; 🚌9) No need to queue at the bar at this convivial beer hall – the tables have their own

---

SELF-CATERING

An abundance of fresh fruit and veg can be yours at the Ladies' Market (p123) and the stalls along ul Graf Ignatiev, outside the **Sveti Sedmochislenitsi Church** (Church of the Seven Saints; ul Graf Ignatiev; ⓢ7am-7pm; 🚌10).

BULGARIA SOFIA

beer taps. Food is also served, and there's live music on Fridays and Saturdays.

Lavazza Espression
CAFE

(bul Vitosha 44; ⊙8am-10pm; ☎) This trendy little cafe brings a touch of Italian style to the city centre, with a long list of coffees to choose from, and a brief menu of light meals and sandwiches.

Toba & Co
COCKTAIL BAR

(ul Moskovska 6; ⊙8.30am-6am) Ensconced in what was once Tsar Ferdinand's butterfly house, in the gardens at the rear of the Royal Palace, this discreet cafe is a charming spot to indulge in a cocktail or two, as well as ice cream and cakes.

Upstairs
COCKTAIL BAR

(bul Vitosha 18; ⊙10am-2am) Join the in crowd with a cocktail on the 1st-floor terrace stools, looking down on the shoppers and trams of bul Vitosha, or lounge on the sofas inside.

Buddha Bar
LOUNGE

(ul Lege 15a; ⊙24hr; ☎; 🖳10) Very hip, very trendy and very crowded, this Buddha-bedecked drinking spot also serves food, and has a nightly disco from around 9pm.

Exit
GAY

(☑0887 965 026; ul Lavele 16; ⊙8am-2am; ☎; 🖳8) This modern and fashionable bar/diner is a popular gay venue, with a DJ party every evening.

☆ Entertainment

If you read Bulgarian, or at least can decipher Cyrillic, *Programata* is the most comprehensive source of entertainment listings; otherwise check out its excellent English-language website, www.programata.bg. You can book tickets online at www.ticketpro.bg.

Nightclubs

Some clubs charge a cover of anywhere between 2 lv and 15 lv, mostly on weekends when live bands are playing.

Swingin' Hall
LIVE MUSIC

(☑963 0059; bul Dragan Tsankov 8; ⊙9pm-4am; 🖳10) Huge club offering an eclectic program of live music each night, ranging from jazz and blues to rock and folk pop.

Social Jazz Club
JAZZ

(☑0884 622 220; pl Slaveikov 4; ⊙10pm-4am Mon-Sat; 🖳10) The place to go to catch some quality live jazz, with leading international acts.

Escape
CLUB

(ul Angel Kânchev 1; cover 10 lv; ⊙10pm-late Thu-Sun) Sofia's favourite central disco, Escape has various theme nights including Britpop parties, hip-hop and drum'n'bass night.

Avenue
CLUB

(☑0898 553 085; ul Atanas Manchev 1a, Studentski Grad; ⊙24hr; 🖳94) One of the more popular student joints, Avenue plays both Western songs and Bulgarian *chalga* (folk pop) music.

ID Club
GAY

(www.idclub.bg; ul Kârnigradska 19b; ⊙9pm-5am Tue-Sat; ☎) ID is a big, glittering gay club with three bars, theme nights, cabaret and a playlist including everything from house to *chalga*.

Performing Arts

Ticket prices vary. For the Opera House or National Theatre, they may cost anything from 10 lv to 30 lv; shows at the National Palace of Culture can be much more expensive, with tickets running to 70 lv for international acts.

National Opera House
OPERA

(☑987 1366; www.operasofia.com; bul Dondukov 30, entrance on ul Vrabcha; ⊙ticket office 9am-2pm & 2.30-7pm Mon-Fri, 11am-7pm Sat, 11am-4pm Sun; 🖳9, 🖳20) Opened in 1953, this monumental edifice is the venue for grand opera and ballet performances, as well as concerts.

National Palace of Culture
CONCERT VENUE

(NDK; ☑916 6368; www.ndk.bg; pl Bulgaria; ⊙ticket office 9am-7pm; ☎; MNDK) The NDK (as it's usually called) has 15 halls and is the country's largest cultural complex. It maintains a regular program of events throughout the year, ranging from film screenings and trade shows to big-name international music acts.

Bulgaria Hall
CLASSICAL MUSIC

(☑987 7656; ul Aksakov 1; ⊙ticket office 9am-6pm; 🖳9) The home of the excellent Sofia Philharmonic Orchestra, this is the place for classical music concerts.

Ivan Vazov National Theatre
THEATRE

(☑811 9219; www.nationaltheatre.bg; ul Dyakon Ignatiy 5; ⊙ticket office 9.30am-7.30pm Mon-Fri, 11.30am-7.30pm Sat-Sun; 🖳9) One of Sofia's most elegant buildings, the Viennese-style National Theatre opened in 1907, and is the city's main stage for Bulgarian drama.

🛍 Shopping

Bulevard Vitosha is Sofia's main shopping street, mostly featuring international brand-name boutiques interspersed with restaurants. More shops cluster along ul Graf Ignatiev, while ul Pirotska is a central pedestrian mall lined with cheaper shops selling clothes, shoes and household goods.

Knizharnitsa   BOOKS
(Sofia University underpass; ⊙8.30am-8.30pm Mon-Fri, 9am-8.30pm Sat, 10am-8.30pm Sun; MKliment Ohridski) One of the better selections of English, French and German-language novels, with a little cafe on-site.

Ladies' Market   MARKET
(ul Stefan Stambolov; ⊙dawn-dusk; 🚌20) Stretching several blocks between ul Ekzarh Yosif and bul Slivnitsa, this is Sofia's biggest fresh-produce market. Fruit and vegetables, cheap clothes, shoes, car parts, kitchen utensils and pretty much anything else you can think of can be bought here. It does get very crowded, so watch your belongings.

Stenata   OUTDOOR EQUIPMENT
(🖉980 5491; www.stenata.com; ul Bratia Miladinovi 5; ⊙10am-8pm Mon-Fri, 10am-6pm Sat, 11am-6pm Sun; 🚌4) The best place in town to buy hiking, climbing and camping equipment, including backpacks, tents and sleeping bags.

ℹ Information

Dangers & Annoyances

The main danger you are likely to face comes from the dreadful traffic; pedestrian crossings and traffic lights don't mean much to many drivers, so be extra careful when crossing. Note that traffic lanes and pedestrian areas are marked only by faintly painted lines on the cobbles around pl Aleksander Nevski and pl Narodno Sabranie, and although a large section of bul Vitosha is now off-limits to private cars, you should still watch out for trams and for vehicles zipping out of the side streets.

Sofia has a large population of stray dogs – it is estimated that as many as 10,000 animals roam the city's streets, and there have been instances of people being attacked, seriously injured and even killed. You are unlikely to encounter packs of dogs in the centre, but exercise caution and do not approach feral dogs.

Medical Services

Neomed Pharmacy (🖉951 5539; bul General Totleben 2b; ⊙24hr; 🚌4)

Pirogov Hospital (www.pirogov.bg; bul General Totleben 21; 🚌4)

Tokuda Hospital (🖉403 4000; www.tokudabolnica.bg; bul Nikola Vaptsarov 51b; ⊙24hr; 🚌88) Modern, Japanese-run private hospital with English-speaking staff.

Money

Unicredit Bulbank (cnr ul Lavele & ul Todor Alexandrov)

Post

Central Post Office (ul General Gurko 6; ⊙7.30am-8.30pm)

Tourist Information

National Tourist Information Centre (🖉987 9778; www.bulgariatravel.org; ul Sveta Sofia; ⊙9am-5pm Mon-Fri; 🚌5) Helpful, English-speaking staff and glossy brochures for destinations around Bulgaria.

Sofia Tourist Information Centre (🖉491 8345; Sofia University underpass; ⊙8am-8pm Mon-Fri, 10am-6pm Sat & Sun; MKliment Ohridski) Lots of free leaflets and maps, and helpful English-speaking staff.

Websites

Programata (www.programata.bg) Comprehensive eating, drinking and clubbing information.

Sofia (www.sofia.bg) Official municipal website, with business information.

Sofia Life (www.sofia-life.com) Bar and restaurant reviews, as well as practical advice.

Sofia Traffic (www.sofiatraffic.bg) Information on public transport.

ℹ Getting There & Away

Air

The only domestic flights within Bulgaria are between Sofia and the Black Sea. Bulgaria Air flies daily to Varna, with two or three daily flights between July and September. Bulgaria Air also flies between the capital and Burgas.

Bus

Sofia's **Central Bus Station** (Tsentralna Avtogara; www.centralnaavtogara.bg; bul Maria Luisa 100; 24hr; 🚌7), right beside the train station, handles services to most big towns in Bulgaria as well as international destinations. There are dozens of counters for individual private companies, as well as an information desk and an **OK-Supertrans taxi desk** (⊙6am-10pm). Departures are less frequent between November and April.

From the far smaller **Ovcha Kupel bus station** (🖉955 5362; bul Tsar Boris III, Zapad; 🚌5) – sometimes called Zapad (West) station – a few buses head south to Bansko, Blagoevgrad and Sandanski.

From tiny **Yug bus station** (🖉872 2345; bul Dragan Tsankov 23; 🚌413, MJoliot-Curie),

TRANSPORT FROM SOFIA

Bus

DESTINATION	PRICE (LV)	DURATION (HR)	FREQUENCY (SUMMER)
Albena	36	8	4-5 daily
Bansko	16	3	5-6 daily
Burgas	30	7-8	6-10 daily
Kazanlâk	16	3½	4-5 daily
Nesebâr	37	7	5-10 daily
Plovdiv	14	2½	several hourly
Ruse	29	5	hourly
Shumen	31	6	7 daily
Sliven	24	5	8 daily
Smolyan	25	3½	6-7 daily
Sozopol	32	7	6-8 daily
Varna	33	7-8	every 30-45min
Veliko Târnovo	22	4	hourly
Vidin	20	5	6-7 daily

Train

DESTINATION	PRICE (LV) 1ST-/2ND-CLASS FARE	DURATION (HR)	FREQUENCY (DAILY)
Burgas	23.60/18.90 (fast), 28.80/23.10 (express)	7-8	4 fast & 2 express
Gorna Oryakhovitsa	18.30/14.60 (fast), 21.40/17.20 (express)	4-4½	6 fast & 2 express (for Veliko Târnovo)
Plovdiv	11.30/9 (fast), 14.30/11.50 (express)	2½-3	6 fast, 3 express & 4 slow
Ruse	23.60/18.90	6	3 fast
Varna	29.50/23.60 (fast), 36.90/29.60 (express)	7½-9	5 fast & 1 express
Vidin	17.30/13.30 (fast)	5	3 fast

buses and minibuses leave for Samokov (6 lv, one hour, every 30 minutes).

From the ramshackle **Poduyane bus station** (☎847 4262; ul Todorini Kukli; 🚌79) – aka Iztok (East) station – buses leave infrequently for small towns in central Bulgaria, such as Troyan (15 lv, three hours, two daily).

Train

The **central train station** (bul Maria Luisa; 🚇1, 7) is a massive, rather cheerless concrete hive, built in the 'Brutalist' style in the '70s.

Destinations for all domestic and international services are listed on timetables in Cyrillic, but departures (for the following two hours) and arrivals (for the previous two hours) are listed

in English on a large screen on the ground floor. Other facilities include a post office, **left-luggage office** (per bag per day 2 lv; ⏰6am-11pm), cafes, a supermarket and accommodation agencies.

Same-day tickets are sold at counters on the ground floor, while advance tickets are sold in the gloomy basement, accessed via an unsigned flight of stairs obscured by another set of stairs that heads up to some snack bars. Counters are open 24 hours, but normally only a few are staffed and queues are long. Don't turn up at the last moment to purchase your ticket, and allow extra time to work out the confusing system of platforms, indicated with Roman numerals, and tracks.

❶ Getting Around

To/From the Airport

Sofia airport (✆937 2211; www.sofia-airport.bg; off bul Brussels; minibus 30) is located 12km east of the city centre. Minibus 30 shuttles between the airport and pl Nezavisimost for a flat fare of 1.50 lv; you can catch it outside the Sheraton Hotel. Bus 84 from Terminal 1 and bus 284 from Terminal 2 (which handles the bulk of international flights) both take a slow and meandering route before depositing you opposite Sofia University.

When you emerge into the arrivals hall you will immediately be greeted by taxi drivers offering you a ride into town, at often ridiculously inflated rates; bypass these and instead head to the reputable OK-Supertrans taxi office counter, where you can book an official, meter-equipped taxi. They will give you a slip of paper with the three-digit code of your cab, which will normally be immediately available. A taxi (using the meter) from the airport to the city centre should cost no more than 15 lv.

Car & Motorcycle

Frequent public transport, cheap taxis and horrendous traffic all provide little or no incentive to drive a private or rented car around Sofia. If you wish to explore further afield, though, a car will come in handy.

Avis (✆945 9224; www.avis.bg; Sofia airport, Terminal 2; ◷9am-9pm)

Hertz (✆439 0222; www.hertz.bg; bul Nikola Vaptsarov 53; ◷9am-5.30pm Mon-Fri, 10am-2pm Sat; ◻88)

Sixt (✆945 9276; www.tsrentacar.com; Sofia Airport, Terminal 2; ◷8am-11pm)

Public Transport

Public transport – trams, buses, minibuses and trolleybuses, as well as the underground metro – run from 5.30am to 11pm every day.

Many buses, trams and trolleybuses are fitted with on-board ticket machines; tickets within Sofia cost 1 lv. However, it's far easier and quicker, especially during peak times, to buy tickets from kiosks at stops along the route before boarding.

If you plan to use public transport frequently, buy a one-day/five-day/one-month transit card (4/15/50 lv), which is valid for all trams, buses and trolleybuses (but not the metro). All tickets must be validated by inserting them in the small machine on-board; once punched, tickets are nontransferable. Inspectors will issue on-the-spot fines (10 lv) if you don't have a ticket; unwary foreigners are a favourite target.

Sofia's metro system (www.metropolitan.bg) is expanding and at the time of research much of the centre was being dug up for new lines. Tickets cost 1 lv but cannot be used on other forms of public transport. Useful central stations include Serdika, near pl Sveta Nedelya, Kliment Ohridski, close to Sofia University, and NDK, at the southern end of bulevard Vitosha.

Taxi

By law, taxis must use meters, but those that wait around the airport, luxury hotels and within 100m of pl Sveta Nedelya will often try to negotiate an unmetered fare – which, of course, will be considerably more. All official taxis are yellow, have fares per kilometre displayed in the window, and have obvious taxi signs (in English or Bulgarian) on top.

In the unlikely event you can't find a taxi, you can order one by ringing **OK-Supertrans** (✆973 2121; www.oktaxi.net) or **Yellow Taxi** (✆911 19). You will usually need to speak Bulgarian.

AROUND SOFIA

Boyana
Бояна
✆02

Boyana is a peaceful and prosperous suburb of Sofia, 8km south of the city centre. Once a favourite retreat for communist leaders and apparatchiks, these days it's home to Sofia's wealthy elite and two of the capital's major attractions.

◉ Sights

National Museum of History　MUSEUM
(www.historymuseum.org; ul Vitoshko Lale 16; admission 10 lv, with Boyana Church 12 lv; ◷9.30am-6pm; minibus 21) Housed in the former communist presidential palace, this museum occupies a stunning, if inconvenient, setting; unless a coach party turns up, you may have the place to yourself. The exhaustive collection includes Thracian gold treasures, Roman statuary, folk costumes, weaponry and icons, while outside you can see some Russian MiG fighters.

Boyana Church　CHURCH
(www.boyanachurch.org; ul Boyansko Ezero 3; adult/student 10/1 lv, combined ticket with National Historical Museum 12 lv, guide 10 lv; ◷9.30am-5.30pm Apr-Oct, 9am-5pm Nov-Mar; ◻64, minibus 21) The tiny, 13th-century Boyana Church is around 2km south of the museum. It's on Unesco's World Heritage list – its 90 murals are rare survivors from the 13th century and are among the very finest examples of Bulgarian medieval artwork. They include the oldest known portrait of St John of Rila,

along with representations of King Konstantin Asen and Queen Irina.

ⓘ Getting There & Away

Minibus 21 runs to Boyana from the city centre (pick it up on bul Vasil Levski). It will drop you right outside the gates of the museum and connects the museum with Boyana Church. You can also take bus 63 from pl Ruski Pametnik, or bus 64 from the Hladilnika terminal. Signs advertising the museum line the motorway, but it's not easy to spot the building, which is set back from the road behind a screen of trees. A taxi (about 8 lv one way) from the city centre to the museum is probably the easiest option of all; for the museum, ask for the 'Residentsia Boyana'.

Vitosha Nature Park

📷 02

The Mt Vitosha range, 23km long and 13km wide, lies just south of the city. It's sometimes referred to as the 'lungs of Sofia' for the refreshing breezes it deflects onto the often-polluted capital. The mountain is part of the 227 sq km Vitosha Nature Park (www.park-vitosha.org), the oldest of its kind in Bulgaria (created in 1934). The highest point is Mt Cherni Vrâh (Black Peak; 2290m), the fourth-highest peak in Bulgaria, where temperatures in January can fall to -8°C.

As well as being a popular ski resort in winter, the nature park is popular with hikers, picnickers and sightseers on summer weekends, and receives 1.5 million visitors a year. There are dozens of clearly marked hiking trails, a few hotels, cafes and restaurants, and numerous huts and chalets that can be booked through the Bulgarian Tourist Union.

🏃 Activities

The mountain has dozens of well-marked hiking trails. It's worth paying 5 lv for the Cyrillic trail map Vitosha Turisticheska Karta (1:50,000), available in Sofia. Popular trails include the steep 90-minute trip up Mt Cherni Vrâh (2290m) from Aleko; a three-hour trek east of Mt Sredets (1969m) from Aleko past Goli Vrâh (1837m) to Zlatni Mostove; and a three-hour hike from Boyana Church past a waterfall to Zlatni Mostove.

The skiing, from mid-December to April, covers 29km of the mountain; it's generally cheaper here than ski resorts (about 30 lv for a lift ticket) and you can ski higher (the peak is 1800m). Rental equipment is available; try to avoid busy weekends.

Most people reach the mountain by chairlift. Dragalevtsi has two chairlifts, located a few kilometres up from the village bus stop (walk via the creekside) – one lift goes to Bai Krâstyo, the second to Goli Vrâh (1837m). The other option is the six-person gondola at Simeonovo, which runs from Friday to Sunday (closed in April), and goes to Aleko, a popular hike/ski hub. It's possible to go up either Dragalevtsi or Simeonovo, hike 30 minutes, and return down the other.

ⓘ Getting There & Away

To Aleko, bus 66 departs from Sofia's Hladilnika terminal 10 times a day between 8am and 7.45pm on weekends, and four times a day on weekdays. Minibus 41 runs from Sofia city centre to Simeonovo (1.50 lv).

RILA & PIRIN MOUNTAINS

These two mountain chains snuggle up to the Greek border south of Sofia, and are made of serious Alps-like rocky-topped peaks full of rewarding hikes. It's here that one of Bulgaria's most famous sites, Rila Monastery, stands guarded by mountains, while Melnik is a favourite spot for wining weekends. For hiking, the monastery is a possible starting point, with several trails meeting others higher up. Pirin hikes are generally tougher than Rila ones, with more abrupt slopes. In summer it's better to end by walking down to Melnik.

Rila Monastery
Рилски Манастир

📷 07054

Bulgaria's largest and most renowned monastery emerges abruptly out of a forested valley in the Rila Mountains. It's a major attraction for both Bulgarian pilgrims and foreign tourists. On summer weekends the monastery is especially busy, though at other times it provides more solitude. Stay at a nearby hotel or camping ground, or even at the monastery itself to experience Rila's photogenic early mornings and late evenings. You can also hike the surrounding mountains.

Rila Monastery was founded in AD 927 by hermit monk Ivan Rilski. Originally built 3km to the northeast, it got its current location in 1335. By the 14th century's end, it had become a powerful feudal fiefdom. While plundered early in the 15th century, the monastery was restored in 1469, when Rilski's relics were returned from Veliko Tărnovo. Rila Monastery was vital to the preservation of Bulgarian culture and religion under the Ottomans, who destroyed it several times.

An accident, however, caused Rila's greatest modern catastrophe: an 1833 fire nearly engulfed all monastic buildings. The inundation of funds from Bulgarian and foreign donors allowed reconstruction to commence within a year. In 1961 the Communist regime proclaimed Rila a national museum and 22 years later it became a Unesco World Heritage site.

⊙ Sights

FREE **Rila Monastery** MONASTERY
(⊘6am-9pm) Bulgaria's most famous monastery is set in a towering forested valley. The 300 monk cells span four levels of colourful balconies, overlooking a large misshapen courtyard, while the Nativity Church, built in the 1830s, contains 1200 magnificent murals.

Museum MUSEUM
(Rila Monastery; 8 lv; ⊘8am-5pm) The monastery's museum, in the compound's southeastern corner, contains 18th- and 19th-century ecclesiastical paraphernalia, prints and Bibles. The centrepiece is the astonishing Rila Cross – a double-sided crucifix carved by a certain Brother Raphael between 1790 and 1802. It's incised in miniature with 140 biblical scenes and inscriptions, and about 650 human figures.

Ethnographic Museum MUSEUM
(8 lv; ⊘8am-5pm) Beside the Samokov gate in the northeast of the monastic compound, this museum displays regional folk costumes, textiles and crafts.

Church of Rozhdestvo Bogorodichno CHURCH
(Church of the Nativity; Rila Monastery) This is Bulgaria's grandest monastery church. Built between 1834 and 1837, the structure is crowned by three domes. Its outside walls are covered with frescos both vivid and harrowing (or humorous, depending on your disposition).

They depict hell, where demons with whips, chains and pitchforks torture sinners in various states of woe and undress. The happier paintings depict the virtuous, accompanied by angels and saints.

🛏 Sleeping & Eating

Hotel Tsarev Vrah HOTEL €
(☏2280; www.tzarevvrah.com; s/d/tr 35/45/60 lv) On monastery-owned lands, the renovated Tsarev Vrah has clean, though not terribly well-lit rooms. Most balconies offer forest views, but you can request a monastery-view room. The hotel cooks decent renditions of Bulgarian cuisine (mains 6 lv to 11 lv), and the leafy garden tables are popular for a summer repast. It's signposted about 150m from Samokov gate.

Rila Monastery's Rooms MONASTERY €
(☏0896 872 010; www.rilamonastery.pmg-blg.com; r 30-60 lv) Rila Monastery offers older, dorm-style rooms (communal facilities have toilets, but no showers), and some nicer en suite rooms. In summer, the latter can be booked up by midday, so call ahead or arrive early. The reception office (in the southern wing) handles bookings.

Rila Restaurant BULGARIAN €
(mains 7-12 lv; ⊘8am-midnight) This restaurant, specialising in Bulgarian grills and local fish, is the area's most atmospheric, set in a traditionally decorated 19th-century building.

❶ Getting There & Away

Most travellers visit Rila Monastery from Sofia or Blagoevgrad. From Sofia's Ovcha Kupel bus station there is one daily morning bus (17 lv, 2½ hours) which returns in the afternoon. However, the monastery gets five daily buses from Rila village (4 lv), making the latter a better transport hub.

For monastery day trips by bus from Sofia you need to leave before 8am for Dupnitsa (1½ hours) from the central bus station or Ovcha Kupel bus station. Then grab the next bus to Rila village or monastery and repeat the process back to Dupnitsa, which also has train connections to Sofia.

Melnik   Мелник

☏07437 / POP 385
Officially Bulgaria's smallest town, tiny Melnik – hidden by jutting pyramid-style claysand mountains at the dramatic southwest end of the Pirins – is one of the country's most famous wine centres, and also has great day hikes. Family-run *mehanas* (taverns) boast their own barrels of blood-red Melnik, the unique local varietal, which is sold in plastic jugs on the dirt streets. A century ago, Melnik was home to 20,000

MELNIK'S RUINS

Of Melnik's original 70 churches only 40, mostly ruins, survive. The 10th-century **Bol-yaskata Kâshta**, one of Bulgaria's oldest homes, is in ruin except for some partially standing walls. You can peer in and enjoy great views too. Nearby is the ruin of the 19th-century **Sveti Antoni Church** (also not signposted).

A signposted path leads to the **Sveti Nikolai Church** (1756), and to the Despot Slav's ruined **Slavova Krepost Fortress**. Both are visible from the Bolyaskata Kâshta ruins, or from near the Lumparova Kâshta Hotel. The trail veers east along the ridge about 300m to the **Sveta Zona Chapel**.

The **Turkish Baths** are difficult to recognise, standing just before the Mehana Mencheva Kâshta tavern. **Sveti Petâr and Pavel Church** (1840) is down from the Hotel Melnik's car park. Just below the Kordopulov House, the 15th-century **Sveta Varvara Church** has retained its walls and floor, and displays icons where visitors light candles. The caretaker at Sveti Nikolai Church can open the closed churches.

people – mostly Greeks – until much of it burned down during the 1912–13 Balkan Wars. The population never recovered and you can still see the ruins of many old family homes on the village outskirts. From the bus stop, roads run on either side of a largely dry creek into town.

◉ Sights

The major sights here, unsurprisingly, are wineries. Melnik's wines, celebrated for more than 600 years, include the signature dark red, *Shiroka Mehichka Loza*. Shops and stands dot Melnik's cobblestone paths, with reds and whites for 3 lv to 4 lv and up. Try to sample first and buy from the refrigerator; avoid bottles displayed in the sun all day.

Mitko Manolev Winery   WINERY
(incl tasting 2 lv; ⏰9am-dusk) For the most atmospheric adventure in *degustatsia* (wine tasting), clamber up the slippery cobblestones to Mitko Manolev Winery. It's basically a cellar dug into the rocks, and a hut with tables and chairs outside, with both reds and whites available. It's along the hillside trail between the Bolyaskata Kâshta ruins and the Kordopulov House.

Kordopulov House   MUSEUM
(☏265; admission 2 lv; ⏰8am-8pm) Built in 1754 and a former home of one of Melnik's foremost wine merchants, this is a truly impressive structure. The lovely sitting rooms have been carefully restored, and boast 19th-century murals, stained-glass windows and exquisite carved wooden ceilings, plus couches along the walls, bedecked with colourful pillows.

🛏 Sleeping

Private rooms (15 lv to 20 lv per person) usually come with shared bathrooms. Look for the 'Rooms to Sleep' signs.

TOP CHOICE Hotel Bolyarka   HOTEL €€
(☏2383; www.bolyarka.hit.bg; s/d/apt incl breakfast 40/60/130 lv; P🌀🐕) The spiffy Bolyarka has elegant and well-decorated rooms, and apartments with fireplaces. Sauna and massage treatments are available, but the authentic Ottoman-era *hammam* (Turkish bath) is for viewing only. The on-site restaurant is excellent. Bolyarka is about 300m straight down the main street on the right-hand side.

Hotel Bulgari   HOTEL €
(☏2215; www.hotelbulgari.net; s/d 30/50 lv; 🐕) This imposing new hotel, located after the square on the left, seems out of place. But the rooms are shiny, spacious and surprisingly good value. The cavernous restaurant is more suited to banquets than intimate dining, though.

🍴 Eating

Melnik's best eats are at hotel/pension restaurants, though other worthy spots abound. Aside from the local wine, try the traditional *banitsa*, a local speciality, and the mountain river trout.

TOP CHOICE Mehana Mencheva Kâshta   BULGARIAN €
(☏339; mains 6-11 lv; ⏰10am-11.30pm) This tiny tavern, down towards the end of the village, has an atmospheric upper porch overlooking the main street. It's popular with locals and does the full run of Bulgarian dishes.

Chinarite Restaurant   BULGARIAN €€
(☎0887 992 191; mains 5-8 lv; 🛜) Chinarite and **Loznitsite Tavern** (☎283; mains 5-8 lv) are next door midway up the main road, by the bridge. The former also serves homemade Melnik *banitsa* and has a small wine cellar for tasting, while the latter has an inviting, vine-covered outdoor setting and good Bulgarian fare.

❶ Getting There & Away

One daily direct bus connects Melnik with Sofia (17 lv, four hours) though times vary. One daily direct bus serves Blagoevgrad (9 lv, two hours). Three daily minibuses go from Sandanski to Melnik, continuing to Rozhen.

Bansko   Банско

☎0749 / POP 8562

Bansko is the big daddy of Bulgarian ski resorts. With trails from 900m to 2600m high, and with more than 100 hotels and pensions, the once-quiet village has more beds than permanent residents. In winter, Brits, Russians, Bulgarians and others come to ski (and party) in this sunny yet snow-filled resort. In summer things are quieter (except for an August jazz festival), and the action shifts to the leafy central square.

◎ Sights

**House Museum of
Nikola Vaptsarov**   MUSEUM
(☎8304; pl Nikola Vaptsarov; admission 3 lv; ☺8am-noon & 2-5.30pm) This house museum was the birthplace of Nikola Vaptsarov (1909–42), a respected antifascist poet and activist. Influenced by communist ideology while a student, his populist writings caused his arrest and torture by the wartime fascist government; he wrote his most famous poem while awaiting execution. Period decor, plus photographs, documents and Vaptsarov's personal belongings are exhibited.

Velyanov's House   MUSEUM
(☎4181; ul Velyan Ognev 5; admission 3 lv; ☺9am-noon & 2-5pm Mon-Fri) Velyanov's House features elaborately painted scenes and woodcarvings from the 'Bansko School' of carving, icon and fresco painting.

Sveta Troitsa Church   CHURCH
(pl Vǎzhrazhdane; ☺7am-7pm) Sveta Troitsa Church (1835) is surrounded by a 1m-thick and 4m-high stone wall, and features magnificent wooden floors and faded murals.

It also hosts Bansko's major landmark: the 30m-high **clock tower** (1850). Until Sofia's Alexander Nevsky Cathedral was completed in 1912, it was Bulgaria's largest church.

🏃 Activities

Bansko boasts Bulgaria's most reliable skiing conditions. The snow, often 2m thick between mid-December and mid-April, sometimes lasts until mid-May. Lifts and slopes are modern and well-maintained, while snow-making equipment works during above-freezing temperatures.

Bansko also boasts a state-of-the-art gondola (carrying eight people). The trip lasts 20 minutes and takes skiers directly from town and onto the slopes at **Baderishka Polyana**, with pubs, restaurants and ski schools. At time of research, a second gondola was expected to open here in 2013. From Baderishka Polyana, another chairlift accesses more trails at Shiligarnika, which has four chairlifts and five draglifts. Bansko has 10 chairlifts and 16 draglifts.

Chalin Vrag I and II are the most famous of Bansko's 15 (and counting) ski runs, which total 67km, along with 8km of cross-country trails. The total trail coverage comprises 35% for beginners, 40% for intermediates, and 25% advanced.

An all-day Bansko lift pass costs 70 lv, though prices rise yearly.

Pirin Sport (☎8537; ul Gen St Kovachev 8) rents ski equipment (from about 55 lv per day) and snowboarding gear, and provides instructors for both sports. Similar services are provided by **Intersport** (☎4876), and some hotels near the gondola. Intersport rents mountain bikes in summer.

🛏 Sleeping

Bansko accommodation ranges from simple private rooms to five-star luxury hotels. Discreet camping is possible in the Pirin National Park. Most foreigners come on package tours, but independent bookings are possible; the Bansko Tourist Information Center recommends rooms for all budgets. Book ahead for ski season, when rates are 25% higher.

Hotel Avalon   HOTEL €€
(☎88 399; www.avalonhotel-bulgaria.com; ul Eltepe 4; s/d/tr/ste €20/30/40/55; 🅿@) A friendly, British-run place popular with budget travellers, the Avalon has airy rooms, some with spas, plus a restaurant serving French and Italian fare. The owners also organise local

excursions. It's in the backstreets before the centre, to the left if coming from the bus/ train stations (a five-minute walk).

Hadzhiradonova Kâshta PENSION €

(☎8276; ul Buirov 7; s/d from 25/30 lv) An atmospheric house with large, traditionally furnished rooms with sheepskin bedspreads and spotless bathrooms. It overlooks a pretty courtyard, east of pl Vazrazhdane.

✕ Eating

Bansko's traditional *mehanas* offer regional delicacies and excellent local wine. Some close in summer.

Mehana Pri Dedo BULGARIAN €€

(pl Nikola Vaptsarov; mains 6-9 lv; ⊙8am-midnight; ☞) This main-square *mehana* serves good international and Bulgarian fare at prices half those of the bigger restaurants (rates don't increase in winter, either). There's an airy deck in summer and, in winter a cosy interior where a live guitarist croons pop classics. The laid-back owner will drive guests to their hotel for free if they've had too much to drink.

Mehana Tumbeva Kâshta BULGARIAN €€

(☎0899 888 993; ul Pirin 7; mains 5-11 lv; ⊙8am-midnight) This small and friendly bar-and-grill rests in a secluded garden (the cosy interior functions in winter) between the two central squares. It offers meat specialities and lighter fare.

ℹ Information

Bansko Tourist Information Center (☎88 580; infocenter@bansko.bg; pl Nikola Vaptsarov 1; ⊙9am-5pm) This centrally located tourist centre has friendly and informed staff who can advise on accommodation, cultural and outdoor activities, and upcoming events. They sell Bansko town maps (4 lv), with hotels, restaurants and banks listed on the front, and the Pirin National Park map on back; the similarly priced winter map features Bansko's ski trails, gondola and lifts too.

Pirin National Park Office (www.pirin-np. com; ul Bulgaria 4) Informs about long Pirin Mountain treks.

ℹ Getting There & Away

Fifteen daily buses serve Bansko from Sofia (17 lv, three hours), most via Blagoevgrad. Buses from Blagoevgrad cost 6 lv. Several more buses travelling to Gotse Delchev stop at Bansko.

From Bansko, four or five daily buses serve Blagoevgrad (two hours). Two morning buses serve Plovdiv (16 lv, 3½ hours). Between mid-

June and mid-September, three daily minibuses (4 lv) serve Hizha Banderitsa.

The coolest route to Bansko, however, is by narrow-gauge railway. This is the last such route in Bulgaria, from Bansko to Septemvri station in five hours (5 lv, four daily), from where you continue west to Sofia or east to Plovdiv and beyond.

Three daily trains depart Bansko for Septemvri. The ticket office only sells tickets 10 minutes before departure time, so ascertain these times ahead.

THRACIAN PLAIN & THE RODOPIS

Sitting in the wide-open Thracian plain, Plovdiv lies just within the cusp of the thickly forested Rodopi Mountains rising to the south. Like the Pirin and Rila, the Rodopis have good hikes and offer culturally rich villages. Smolyan is a key Rodopi hub from where you can travel further into the Rodopi range or east to out-of-the-way Kârdzhali to see the Thracian remains of Perperikon.

Plovdiv Пловдив

☑032 / POP 338,184

With its art galleries, winding cobbled streets and bohemian cafes, Plovdiv (*Plovdiv*) equals Sofia in culture and is a determined rival in nightlife as well. Being a smaller and less stressful city, Plovdiv is also great for walking. As a major university town, Plovdiv has a lively, exuberant spirit.

Plovdiv's appeal derives from its lovely Old Town, largely restored to its mid-19th-century appearance and marked by winding cobblestone streets. It's literally packed with atmospheric house museums and art galleries and – unlike many other cities with 'Old Towns' – has eminent artists still living and working within its tranquil confines. The neighbourhood boasts Thracian, Roman, Byzantine and Bulgarian antiquities, most impressive being the Roman amphitheatres – the best preserved in the Balkans and still used for performances.

◉ Sights

Revival-era wooden-shuttered homes lean over narrow cobbled lanes in this hilly neighbourhood and about a dozen renovated *kâshta* (traditional homes) are now kept as museums. Also here are several art galleries, a couple of museums and some of Plovdiv's most interesting churches.

Roman Amphitheatre
HISTORIC SITE

(ul Hemus; 3 lv; ⊙8am-6pm) Plovdiv's magnificent 2nd-century AD Amphitheatre, built by Emperor Trajan was only uncovered during a freak landslide in 1972. It once held about 6000 spectators. Now largely restored, it again hosts large-scale special events and concerts. Visitors can admire the amphitheatre from several lookouts along ul Hemus, or from the cafes situated above.

Roman Stadium
HISTORIC STADIUM

This once huge stadium is mostly hidden under the pedestrian mall. However, in 2012 the subterranean southern back end was renovated and stairways from different sides now allow entrance into the gleaming rows. A small shop below provides some info and souvenirs.

Ethnographical Museum
MUSEUM

(☑625 654; ul Dr Chomakov 2; adult/student 5/1 lv; ⊙9am-noon & 2-5.30pm Tue-Thu, Sat & Sun, 2-5.30pm Fri) This intriguing museum houses 40,000 exhibits, including folk costumes, musical instruments, jewellery and traditional crafts such as weaving, metalworking, winemaking and beekeeping. Tools displayed range from grape-crushers and wine-measures to apparatus used for distilling attar of roses.

Historical Museum
MUSEUM

(☑623 378; ul Lavrenov 1; 2 lv; ⊙9am-noon & 1-5.30pm Mon-Sat) The Historical Museum concentrates on the 1876 April Uprising and the massacre of Bulgarians at Batak, which directly led to Russia declaring war on Turkey the next year. Built in 1848 by Dimitâr Georgiadi, it's also called the *Georgiadi Kâshta*.

Archaeological Museum
MUSEUM

(☑624 339; pl Saedinenie 1; adult/child under 7yr 5 lv/free) Thracian and Roman pottery and jewellery, and ecclesiastical artefacts, icons and liturgical paraphernalia are on display here, along with a collection of 60,000 archaeological items.

Permanent Exhibition of Dimitar Kirov
GALLERY

(☑635 381; Kiril Nektariev 17; adult/student 5/1 lv; ⊙9am-5pm Mon-Fri) This special place, housed in a grand Old Town mansion where Plovdiv's budding artists worked in the 1960s, celebrates the life and works of Dimitar Kirov, who died in 2008 at the age of 73. Arguably Plovdiv's most original artist, Kirov's works are marked by bold and vivid uses of colour, from mosaics to abstracts.

Church of Sveti Konstantin & Elena
CHURCH

(ul Sâborna 24; ⊙8am-7pm) Plovdiv's oldest church, this was built over a late Roman church. It's dedicated to Constantine the Great, the 4th-century emperor who made Orthodox Christianity the state religion, and his mother, Sveta Helena. The current church, however, dates to 1832. The wonderful iconostasis was painted by Zahari Zograf between 1836 and 1840. The covered portico features sumptuous frescoes.

Dzhumaya Mosque
MOSQUE

(pl Dzhumaya; ⊙6am-11pm) The largely renovated Dzhumaya Mosque, one of the Balkans' oldest, dates from the mid-15th century. With a 23m-high minaret, it was the largest of Plovdiv's more than 50 Ottoman-era mosques, though its thunder has slightly been stolen by the renovated Roman Stadium remains opposite.

🛏 Sleeping

TOP CHOICE Hotel Renaissance
BOUTIQUE HOTEL €€

(☑266 966; www.renaissance-bg.com; pl Vâzhrazhdane 1; s/d incl breakfast from 115/145 lv; P❋@🛜) This lovely boutique hotel between the Old Town and the main shopping streets aims to recreate a National Revival–era home through its intricate Plovdiv-style floral wall and ceiling paintings. Each room is unique, with handsome wood floors. Some boast period furniture. (Note the Arabic-language property document from 1878). Friendly, English-speaking owner Dimitar Vassilev is a fount of local knowledge.

Hikers Hostel
HOSTEL €

(☑0896 764 854; www.hikers-hostel.org; ul Sâborna 53; incl breakfast tent/dm/s/d without bathroom 12/20/43/48 lv; @🛜) The ideal place for independent travellers to chill in Plovdiv's Old Town, Hikers has comfy couches, outside tables, and sleeping choices ranging from tents and dorms to lofts and private rooms. There's free wi-fi, a computer, lockers for luggage, and laundry service (5 lv). If full, they offer (less appealing) private rooms and dorms near Dzhumaya Mosque.

Hebros Hotel
BOUTIQUE HOTEL €€€

(☑260 180; www.hebros-hotel.com; ul K Stoilov 51; s/apt incl breakfast 200/240 lv; ❋🛜) This two-century-old mansion in the Old Town has a subdued elegance in its 10 well-furnished, spacious rooms – it's a bit pricier than others, but tremendously atmospheric. There's

Plovdiv

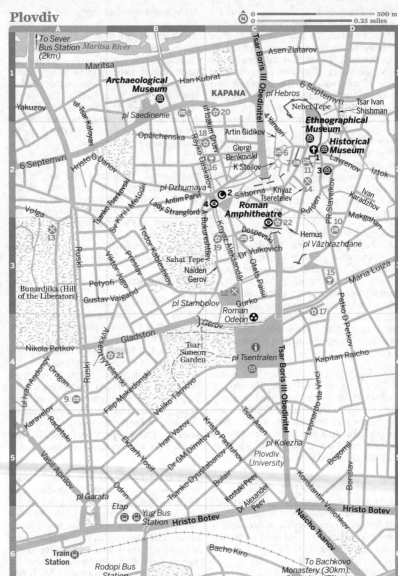

a back courtyard, spa and sauna (25 lv extra), plus a great restaurant.

Dali Art Hotel BOUTIQUE HOTEL €€€
(☎621 530; ul Otets Paisii 11; d/ste/apt incl breakfast 100/130/150 lv; ❄☎) This intimate hotel off the mall has eight airy rooms, including two apartments, with appropriately minimalist decor. However, it's most distinguished by its friendly and relaxed staff – not to mention original works by Dali.

Plovdiv

Hotel Leipzig   HOTEL €€
(☏654 000; www.leipzig.bg; bul Ruski 70; s/d/apt from 82/100/124 lv; ℙ❋🐾) This sharply renovated old fixture has more than 60 appealing modern rooms and apartments designed with eclectic, colourful decor uncommon in a place that doubles as a business hotel and wedding banquet venue. Some rooms have great views of the Hill of the Liberators, and there's a restaurant, bar and casino.

Plovdiv Guest House   HOSTEL €
(☏622 432; www.plovdivguest.com; ul Sâborna 20; dm/s/d/q €9/25/30/45; ❋@🐾) Another backpacker option on Sâborna, this offers clean

and bright dorms with 10, eight and four beds, and there's one spacious attic double. Dorms feature their own self-contained and modern bathroom/shower. There's an outdoor cafe out the back, above the ancient Roman wall.

Hotel Elite   HOTEL €€
(☏624 537; ul Rayko Daskalov 53; d/ste 60/100 lv; ❋) The modern and reasonably priced hotel is on the corner of bul 6 Septemvri, just west of the Kapana bar district. Rooms are insulated from road noise, and it's clean and comfortable. The suites, however, are really glorified doubles.

✕ Eating

Puldin Restaurant   INTERNATIONAL €€€
(☏631 720; ul Knyaz Tseretelev 8; mains 8-15 lv; ⊙9am-midnight; 🐾) The magical Puldin is one of Plovdiv's most atmospheric restaurants. In one dining room, the famous whirling dervishes of the Ottoman Empire once whirled themselves into ecstatic exhaustion, while in the cellar hall Byzantine-era walls and Roman artefacts predominate.

Hebros Hotel Restaurant   BULGARIAN €€€
(☏625 929; ul K Stoilov 51; mains 11-22 lv; 🐾) The upscale restaurant of the eponymous hotel enjoys a secluded garden setting and does excellent and innovative Bulgarian cuisine, such as rabbit with plums, braised trout, and pork with blue cheese.

Restaurant Renaissance   INTERNATIONAL €€
(pl Vâzhrazhdane 1; mains 9-17 lv; ⊙10am-10:30pm Tue-Sun) The restaurant of the Hotel Renaissance cooks up a wide range of inventive appetisers (duck lung stuffed with apple, anyone?), plus grills, risottos, and fresh fish from the Aegean. The local wine list is particularly strong, and the service is friendly and attentive.

Malâk Bunardzhik   BULGARIAN €€
(☏446 140; ul Volga 1; mains 5-10 lv; 🐾) Quality Bulgarian cuisine is served at this popular place with garden dining and live music most nights.

🍷 Drinking

Several good places occupy the district called Kapana, meaning 'the trap', referring to its tight streets (north of pl Dzhumaya, between ul Rayko Daskalov to the west and bul Tsar Boris Obedinitel to the east).

TOP CHOICE Naylona
BAR

(☎0889 496 750; ul Giorgi Benkovski 8, Kapana; ◷noon-4am; 🖥) They say the owners of this Kapana dive bar purposely didn't fix the roof so that the rain would trickle in; whatever the story, this damp, bare-bones place usually playing classic (and other) rock remains the unwashed, long-haired antithesis of Plovdiv style.

Art Bar Maria Luiza
BAR

(bul Maria Luiza 15; ◷8am-4am; 🖥) Too pretty to be just a dive bar, the Maria Luisa has dedicated owners who keep adapting the decor to suit their whims. The colourful downstairs is particularly stylish, vaguely reminiscent of 1920s Paris.

Dreams
CAFE €

(☎627 142; pl Stambolov; sandwiches around 2 lv; ◷9am-11pm; 🖥) This excellent and popular cafe is the perfect place to relax; sit before the giant, gushing fountain on a balmy summer's day. It serves good cakes, along with numerous alcoholic and nonalcoholic drinks.

☆ Entertainment

Much of the nightlife lingers around the Kapana district, around ul Benkovski north of Dzhumaya mosque.

Nightclubs

Petnoto
CLUB

(☎0898 542 787; ul Ioakim Gruev 36, Kapana; ◷8am-6am; 🖥) The pinstriped Petnoto combines a bar, small restaurant and a stage where Bulgarian bands and DJs perform.

City Place
CLUB

(☎0888 715 657; bul Maria Luiza 43; ◷11pm-6am; 🖥) Plovdiv's longest-running nightclub was formerly called Paparazzi. In its current incarnation it has seen some slick renovations though the DJ-driven house music, *chalga* (Bulgarian pop music) and hip-hop playlist remain the same.

Infinity
CLUB

(☎0888 281 431; Bratya Pulievi 4, Kapana; ◷10am-late; 🖥) Varied music, from pop to dance, is played at this club in Kapana favoured by students.

TRANSPORT FROM PLOVDIV

Bus

DESTINATION	PRICE (LV)	DURATION (HR)	FREQUENCY
Bansko	14	3½	2 daily
Blagoevgrad	13-15	3	3 daily
Burgas (private)	19	4	2 daily
Hisar	2.20	1	12 daily
Karlovo	8	1½	half-hourly
Ruse (private)	19	6	1 daily
Sliven	14	3	5 daily
Sofia	9	2½	half-hourly
Varna	22	7	2 daily
Veliko Tărnovo (private)	17	4½	3 daily

Train

DESTINATION	PRICE (LV)	DURATION (HR)	FREQUENCY
Burgas	14.60	6	6 daily
Karlovo	3.90	2	5 daily
Sofia	1st-/2nd-class 9/7 (express)	2½	14 daily

Theatre & Opera

Plovdiv Opera House   OPERA
(632 231; opera@thracia.net; ul Avksentiy Veleshki)
Classic and modern European operas are performed in Bulgarian at this venerable hall.

**Nikolai Masalitinov
Dramatic Theatre**   THEATRE
(224 867; ul Knyaz Aleksandâr 38) One of Bulgaria's top theatres, it features everything from Shakespeare to Ibsen (usually, in Bulgarian).

Roman Amphitheatre   THEATRE
(ul Hemus) The amphitheatre hosts Plovdiv's annual Verdi Festival (June), plus other summertime opera, ballet and music performances.

ℹ Information

Exchange offices line ul Knyaz Aleksandâr and ul Ivan Vazov. Most close on Sunday. ATMs are widespread, including around pl Dzhumaya and ul Knyaz Aleksandâr, though not in the Old Town's upper reaches.

Internet Café Speed (2nd fl, bul Maria Luiza 1)
Main Post Office (pl Tsentralen; ⊙7am-7pm Mon-Sat, to 11am Sun) Has several computers with online access.

Patrick Penov Personal Trips & Tours (0887 364 171; www.guide-bg.com) Licensed tour guide Svetlomir 'Patrick' Penov has two decades of experience leading individual and small group tours all over Bulgaria, covering everything from gastronomy and wine to churches and culture.

Tourist Information Centre (tic@plovdiv.bg; pl Tsentralen 1; ⊙9am-7pm) This helpful centre by the post office provides maps, finds local accommodation and more.

ℹ Getting There & Away

Bus

Plovdiv's main station is **Yug bus station** (626 937), with public and private buses operating. Yug is diagonally opposite the train station and a 15-minute walk from the centre (a taxi costs 5 lv to 7 lv). Alternatively, local buses (80 stotinki) stop across the main street outside the station, on bul Hristo Botev.

The **Sever bus station** (953 011), in the northern suburbs, has one daily bus to Pleven (23 lv), Ruse (12 lv), Koprivshtitsa (6 lv) and Veliko Târnovo (20 lv).

Etap (632 082; Yug bus station) sells bus tickets to İstanbul (40 lv), Athens (140 lv) and more.

Train

Plovdiv sits on the major Sofia–Burgas line and has many trains. Plovdiv's **train station** (bul

Hristo Botev) is well organised, though the staff don't speak English. Computer screens at the station entrance and in the underpass leading to the platforms list recent arrivals and upcoming departures. The luggage storage (2 lv per bag for 24 hours) office is always open.

Smolyan   Смолян

⌀0301 / POP 30,283

The longest (10km) and highest town in Bulgaria (1010m), Smolyan is actually an amalgamation of four villages, and the southern Rodopi Mountains' administrative centre. The steep and forested mountains rise abruptly on its southern flank, lending a lovely backdrop to a town that's otherwise rather gritty. As in most of the Rodopi region, there's a notable Pomak Muslim population here. It's an alternative place to stay for skiing Pamporovo and Chepelare, though certainly not the most beautiful one. Smolyan is also a base for exploring the seven Smolyan Lakes, the caves of Golubovitsa, partially underwater, and Uhlovitsa, with its bizarre rock formations.

◎ Sights

Planetarium   PLANETARIUM
(83 074; bul Bulgaria 20; 5 lv) Bulgaria's biggest planetarium, about 200m west of Hotel Smolyan, offers a spectacular show (35 to 40 minutes) with commentary in English, French or German at 2pm Monday to Saturday, and in Bulgarian at other times. The foreign-language shows are for groups of five or more; otherwise, you'll pay 25 lv for a solo viewing.

Historical Museum   MUSEUM
(62 727; Dicho Petrov 3; 5 lv; ⊙9am-noon & 1-5pm Mon-Sat) Behind the civic centre, this museum's exhibits include Palaeolithic artefacts, Thracian armour and weaponry, Rodopi weaving and woodcarving, plus numerous traditional musical instruments and folk costumes (most notably the fantastical Kuker outfits worn at New Year celebrations). Upstairs has photos and models of traditional buildings.

🛏 Sleeping

The tourist office arranges private accommodation (about 20 lv per person). Ask about camping in the hills outside town.

Hotel Kiparis A   HOTEL €€
(64 040; www.hotelkiparis.eu; bul Bulgaria 3a; s/d/apt incl breakfast 50/75/110 lv; ❄🐾📶) This

WORTH A TRIP

BACHKOVO MONASTERY

About 30km south of Plovdiv, the magnificent **Bachkovo Monastery** (Bachkovo; admission free; ⊗6am-10pm) was founded in 1083 by Georgian brothers Gregory and Abasius Bakuriani, aristocrats in Byzantine military service. The monastery flourished during the Second Bulgarian Empire (1185–1396), but was ransacked by Turks in the 15th and 16th centuries. Major reconstructions began in the mid-17th century. Bachkovo's now Bulgaria's second-largest monastery, after Rila.

In the courtyard, the **Church of Sveta Bogoroditsa** (1604) contains frescos by Zahari Zograf from the early 1850s. Other highlights include the 17th-century iconostasis, more 19th-century murals and a much-cherished icon of the Virgin, allegedly painted by St Luke, though actually dating from the 14th century. Pilgrims regularly pray before the silver-encased icon.

The monastery's southern side houses the former **refectory** (1601). The walls are filled with stunning frescos relating the monastery's history. A gate beside the refectory leads to a (rarely open) courtyard; this leads to the **Church of Sveti Nikolai** (1836). During the 1840s, Zograf painted the superb *Last Judgment* inside the chapel; note the condemned, nervous-looking Turks on the right and Zograf's self-portrait (no beard) in the upper-left corner.

Around 50m from the monastery entrance, the restored **Ossuary** features wonderful medieval murals, but remains closed.

A prominent explanation board provides monastic history (in English, French and German), and a map of **hiking trails** to nearby villages. A helpful guidebook (15 lv) is available too.

To get here, take any bus (3 lv) to Smolyan from Plovdiv's **Rodopi bus station** (⊘657 828), disembark at the turn-off about 1.2km south of Bachkovo village and walk about 500m uphill. There are also direct buses half-hourly.

---

comfortable hotel with an excellent spa centre has plush and light-toned rooms, plus all the mod cons.

Three Fir Trees House　　　　PENSION €
(⊘81 028; www.trieli.hit.bg; ul Srednogorets 1; s/d/apt without bathroom 30/40/80 lv; @🛜) Some 200m east of the main bus station, this relaxed family-run place has well-maintained rooms. It's signposted, down the steps from bul Bulgaria. Bathrooms are shared. There's an excellent, varied breakfast (5 lv), and the helpful, multilingual owner arranges tours and rental cars, plus a cheap laundry service.

✖ Eating

Rodopski Kat　　　　　　　BULGARIAN €€
(bul Bulgaria 3; mains 5-8 lv; ⊗7am-2am) This nice restaurant, wedged between hotels in the centre, is excellent for traditional Rodopean fare.

Riben Dar　　　　　　　　SEAFOOD €€
(⊘63 220; ul Snezhanka 16; mains 6-12 lv) In the western neighbourhood of Nevyasta, this is great for delicious fresh fish, such as Rodopi Mountain trout. Take a taxi (3 lv to 5 lv).

ℹ Getting There & Away

Most buses to/from Smolyan use the **main bus station** (⊘63 104; bul Bulgaria) at Smolyan's western end. Four daily buses serve Sofia (28 lv, 3½ hours) and hourly buses serve Plovdiv (17 lv, 2½ to three hours), via Chepelare (6 lv, one hour) and Pamporovo (4 lv, 30 minutes).

From near the station, local buses 2 and 3 (80 stotinki, every 20 minutes) serve the centre. Walk left out of the station and turn left up a double set of stairs; after 50m, you'll see the stop on the left. The taxi rank is further down the street. By taxi, it's around 3 lv to the tourist information centre.

CENTRAL BULGARIA

Bulgaria's central heartland is vital to the national consciousness for its role in the 18th- and 19th-century National Revival; this legacy lingers in the period architecture of Koprivshtitsa, and at battle sites such as the forested Shipka Pass. Central Bulgaria is ideal for hiking, climbing, caving, horseback riding and other outdoor activities in the Stara Planina mountains. The lowlands are famous too for the Valley of Roses, near Kazanlâk, an important producer of rose oil.

Most impressive, however, is Veliko Târnovo, once capital of the Bulgarian tsars. Built into steep hills and bisected by a river, its fortress is among Europe's most impressive.

Koprivshtitsa
Копривщица

📞 07184 / POP 2900

This unique museum village, nestled between Karlovo and Sofia, is a perfectly preserved hamlet filled with Bulgarian National Revival–period architecture, cobblestone streets, and bridges that arc gently over a lovely brook. Nearly 400 buildings of architectural and historical significance are protected by government decree, some of them restored churches and house museums containing fascinating collections of decor and implements from yesteryear. Some of the traditional homes function as guesthouses or restaurants, most loaded with traditional ambience, making Koprivshtitsa a romantic getaway, too.

⊙ Sights

Koprivshtitsa boasts six house museums. Some are closed either on Monday or Tuesday. To buy a combined ticket for all (adults/students 5/3 lv) visit the souvenir shop **Kupchinitsa**, near the Tourist Information Centre.

Oslekov House   HISTORIC BUILDING
(ul Gereniloto 4; ⊙closed Mon) Built between 1853 and 1856 by Oslekov, a rich merchant killed in the line of duty during the 1876 April Uprising, this is arguably the best example of Bulgarian National Revival–period architecture in Koprivshtitsa. It has a triple-arched entrance, spacious interior, stylish furniture and brightly coloured walls.

Kableshkov House   HISTORIC BUILDING
(ul Todor Kableshkov 8; ⊙closed Mon) A well-travelled wealthy local, Todor Kableshkov (1851–76) is revered as having (probably) been the person who fired the first shot in the 1876 uprising against the Turks. This, his glorious former home, dates back to 1845 and has exhibits about the April Uprising.

🛏 Sleeping

The tourist information centre can help arrange private rooms (40 lv to 50 lv).

Hotel Trayanov Kâshta   GUESTHOUSE €
(📞3750; ul Gereniloto 5; d/tr/apt 40/50/60 lv) Perhaps the most atmospheric place in

town, this house with a garden inside an enclosed courtyard has only a few rooms, all traditionally furnished and colourful. The upstairs balcony overlooking the back lawn is a great place for an evening drink.

Bonchova House   GUESTHOUSE €
(📞2614; ul Tumangelova Cheta 26; d/apt 30/50 lv) Close to the Kalachev Bridge, this cosy place has two bright, modern rooms and an apartment; the common room is relaxing and has a working fireplace. Breakfast is 5 lv extra.

✕ Eating

Traditional *kâshtas* can be found on side streets. They serve meaty meals, but some keep seasonal hours.

Dyado Liben   BULGARIAN €
(📞2109; ul Hadzhi Nencho Palaveev 47; mains 4-9 lv; ⊙11am-midnight; 🛜) Astonishingly big, this traditional restaurant housed in a mansion dating from 1852 is a wonderfully atmospheric place for an evening meal. Management says it can seat 100 people, all in a warren of halls graced with ornately painted walls. Find it just across the bridge leading from the main square inside the facing courtyard.

ℹ Information

There are ATMs and a post office/telephone centre inside the village centre.

Tourist Information Centre (www.koprivshtitsa.info; pl 20 April; ⊙10am-1pm & 2-7pm) This very helpful and friendly centre, in a small maroon building on the main square, provides local information and can organise private accommodation from 25 lv per person.

ℹ Getting There & Away

Getting to Koprivshtitsa is a bit of a challenge. Being 9km north of the village, the train station requires a shuttle bus (2 lv, 15 minutes), which isn't always timed to meet incoming trains. Trains do come from Sofia (11 lv, 2½ hours, four daily) and connections can be made for Plovdiv and other points, such as Burgas, which gets a daily train (18 lv, five hours). Alternatively, Koprivshtitsa's bus stop is central and has more frequent connections, including five daily buses to Sofia (13 lv, two hours) and one to Plovdiv (12 lv, two hours).

Kazanlâk   Казанлък

📞 0431 / POP 46.990

A bit rough around the edges, Kazanlâk is nevertheless a fascinating town where Bulgaria's various ethnic and religious groups commingle amicably. Life revolves around the loud central square, pl Sevtopolis. Most famous, however, are the archaeological remains from the area's ancient Thracian civilisation.

Kazanlâk is also the jumping-off point for journeys across the Valley of Roses (Rozovata Dolina), a wide plain blooming with roses, responsible for more than 60% of the world's supply of fragrant rose oil. Crossing the plain, one ascends to Shipka village and Shipka Pass, site of a decisive showdown in the 1877–78 Russo-Turkish War.

◎ Sights

Thracian Tomb of Kazanlâk   MUSEUM

(Tyulbe Park; admission 20 lv; ⊙10am-5pm) In hilly Tyulbe Park is a very large and very locked tomb. Built in the 4th century BC for a Thracian ruler, it was discovered in 1944 during a bomb shelter construction, and is now a Unesco World Heritage site. Along the dromos (vaulted entry corridor), a double frieze depicts battle scenes. The burial chamber is 12m in diameter and covered by a beehive dome typical of Thracian design in the 3rd to 5th centuries BC. The dome's murals depict events such as a funeral feast and chariot race. The tomb is a 15-minute walk northeast of the central square, across the small Stara Reka (Old River).

Museum   MUSEUM

(☑64 750; Tyulbe Park; admission 2 lv; ⊙10am-6pm) This museum has a full-scale Thracian Tomb replica. Most visitors choose not to spend the 20 lv required to see the real thing as the replica basically gives you the same experience. The staff guiding you around the faux tomb are friendly and speak good English.

Iskra Museum & Art Gallery   MUSEUM

(☑23 741; ul Sv Kiril i Metodii; adult/student 2/1 lv; ⊙9am-6pm Mon-Fri) This gallery displays extensive archaeological finds including pottery, jewellery and tools from excavations of Thracian tombs such as the one at Tyulbe Park. All explanations are in Bulgarian, so the brochure (2 lv) in English, French or German is helpful. Upstairs, numerous paintings are displayed, including some by renowned local artists such as Ivan Milev and Vasil Barakov. Purchase the printed catalogue (in English and French; 3 lv).

Kulata Ethnological Complex   MUSEUM

(☑621 733; ul Knyaz Mirski; admission 3 lv, with rose-liquor tasting 4 lv; ⊙8am-noon & 1-6pm) Just down from Tyulbe Park and the Thracian Tomb, you'll find the appealing Kulata (Tower) district, site of the Kulata Ethnological Complex. A replica of a one-storey peasant's home and wooden sheds with agricultural implements and carts are among the rustic exhibits.

A courtyard leads to the two-storey House of Hadzhi Eno, built by a wealthy rose merchant in Bulgarian National Revival–period style. Some explanations in German and English are given, and you may be invited by the caretaker to sample some rose tea, liquor or jam.

FREE Museum of the Roses   MUSEUM

(☑23 741; ul Osvobozhdenie; ⊙9am-5pm summer) The grandly named Research Institute for Roses, Aromatic and Medicinal Plants houses this tiny museum. It's 3km north of centre up ul Osvobozhdenie; take a taxi (3 lv, one way), or bus 3 from Kazanlâk's main square. The photos and displays explain (in Bulgarian only) the 300-year-old method of cultivating the roses, picking their petals and processing the oil.

🛌 Sleeping & Eating

Hotel Palas   HOTEL €€

(☑62 311; www.hotel-palas.com; ul Petko Stajnov 9; s/d/ste incl breakfast 82/96/120 lv; P🗷🛜) This posh place opposite the post office and near the main square offers spacious, classy rooms. The suites are enticing and great value (prices can be negotiable for multinight stays). The restaurant is respectable though service is slow when busy. The buffet breakfast is better-than-average, though the 'spa centre' is only opened on request.

Hadzhi Eminova Kâshta   GUESTHOUSE €

(☑62 595; bul Nikola Petkov 22; s/d/apt 20/30/40 lv) This established guesthouse offers big, traditionally furnished rooms featuring woollen quilts and overlooking an authentic 19th-century walled compound. The one apartment is huge and worth booking ahead. All rooms feature bathrooms, though they tend to be small, and the restaurant is excellent.

Roza Hotel   HOTEL €€

(☑50 105; www.hotelrozabg.com; ul Rozova Dolina 2; s/d from 50/70 lv; 🗷@🛜) Set atop an office complex opposite the square, the Roza has a small collection of rooms and a giant, astroturfed terrace with panoramic views. The rooms on the hall's right-hand side are smaller, with beds jammed in lengthways, whereas the slightly larger ones on the left are more normal (and slightly pricier).

New York Bar & Grill INTERNATIONAL €€
(pl Sevtopolis; mains 5-10 lv; 🛜) When in Kazanlâk... This eternally popular restaurant-pub on the square has a big menu (with pictures), serving everything from pizza to fish and grills. It's not gourmet, but the locals love it.

ℹ️ Information

Internet Centre (ul Otets Paisii; per hour 1 lv; ⊙9am-11pm)

Post Office (ul 23 Pehoten Shipchenski Polk)

Tourist Information Centre (🖉62 817; ul Iskra 4; ⊙8am-1pm & 2-6pm Mon-Fri) Assists with hotels, excursions and general information about the town.

ℹ️ Getting There & Away

From the bus and train stations, it's a 10-minute walk (or 2 lv cab ride) northwards to the square. Kazanlâk's **bus station** (🖉62 383; ul Kenali) has connections to Sofia (18 lv, 2½ hours, six daily), Veliko Târnovo (17 lv, 2½ hours), and Plovdiv (13 lv, two hours).

The Kazanlâk **train station** (🖉662 012; ul Sofronii) serves Sofia (21 lv, 3½ hours, three daily) and Burgas (19 lv, three hours, four daily), via Karlovo (5 lv, one hour, six daily). Trains to or from Plovdiv often involve changing at the Tulovo station, just before Kazanlâk station.

Veliko Târnovo
Велико Търново

🖉062 / POP 68,735

The evocative capital of the medieval Bulgarian tsars, sublime Veliko Târnovo is dramatically set amid an amphitheatre of forested hills, divided by the ribboning Yantra River. Commanding pride of place is the magisterial Tsarevets Fortress, citadel of the Second Bulgarian Empire. It's complemented by scores of churches and other ruins, many still being unearthed. As the site of Bulgaria's most prestigious university, Veliko Târnovo also boasts a revved-up nightlife that many larger towns would envy. There's great food and drink, too, in restaurants offering commanding views of the river and castle, or located in the Varosha quarter, with its terracotta rooftops and lounging cats.

◉ Sights

Tsarevets Fortress FORTRESS
(adult/student 6/2 lv, scenic elevator 2 lv; ⊙8am-7pm Apr-Sep, 9am-5pm Oct-Mar) This reconstructed fortress dominates the skyline and is one of Bulgaria's most beloved monuments. It features remains of more than 400 houses, 18 churches and numerous monasteries, dwellings, shops, gates and towers.

The fortress has a long history. Thracians and Romans used it as a defensive position, and the Byzantines built the first significant bulwark here between the 5th and 7th centuries. The fortress was rebuilt and fortified by the Slavs and Bulgars between the 8th and 10th centuries, and again by the Byzantines in the early 12th century. When Târnovgrad became the Second Bulgarian Empire's capital, the fortress was truly magnificent, but with the Turkish invasion in 1393, it was sacked and destroyed.

The Patriarch's Complex and Baldwin Tower have received the most restoration, and considerable random rubble is lying about. Not much English-language information is provided, but guided English-language tours (10 lv) can be arranged by the Tourist Information Centre.

Sarafkina Kâshta MUSEUM
(ul General Gurko 88; adult/student 6/2 lv; ⊙9am-6pm Mon-Fri) Built in 1861 by a rich Turkish merchant, this fine five-storey National Revival–style house museum displays antique ceramics, metalwork, woodcarvings and jewellery, and has some fascinating exhibits about traditional costumes and bread-making. Revival-period furniture fills the upper floor, along with vintage family photos.

**Museum of National Revival
& Constituent Assembly** MUSEUM
(ul Ivan Vazov; adult/student 6/2 lv; ⊙9am-6pm Wed-Mon) This museum, in a former Turkish town hall built in 1872, was where Bulgaria's first National Assembly was held to write the country's first constitution in 1879. The ground floor contains costumes, books and photos about Veliko Târnovo's history. The former assembly hall upstairs displays portraits of local personalities. The basement has classic old-town photos and some valuable icons.

**Veliko Târnovo Archaeological
Museum** MUSEUM
(ul Ivan Vazov; adult/student 6/2 lv; ⊙9am-6pm Tue-Sun) Housed in a grand old building

Veliko Târnovo

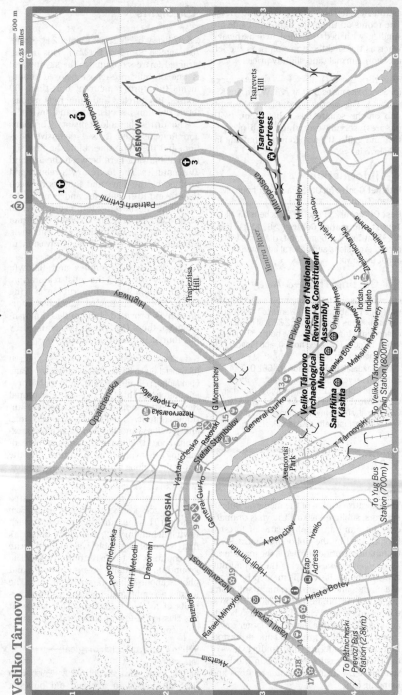

500 m
0.25 miles

Tsarevets Hill

Tsarevets Fortress

ASENOVA

Mitropolska

Patriarh Evtimii

Yantra River

Highway

Trapezitsa Hill

Opalchenska

Rezervoarska

P Tipografov

Vastanicheska

Stefan Rakovski

Stefan Stambolov

G Momarchev

General Gurko

General Gurko

N Pikolo

Museum of National Revival & Constituent Assembly

Veliko Târnovo Archaeological Museum

Ivanka Boteva

Sarafkina Kâshta

Chitalishhta

Sheynovo

Iordan Indjeto

Maksim Raykovich

To Veliko Târnovo Train Station (800m)

T Târnovski

Asenovtsi Park

VAROSHA

Poborhicheska

Kiril i Metodii

Dragoman

Buzludja

Nezavisimost

Hadji Dimitar

Rafael Mihaylov

Akatsia

Vasil Levski

A Penchev

Ivailo

Etap

Adress

Hristo Botev

To Yug Bus Station (700m)

To Pâtnicheski Prevoz Bus Station (2.8km)

M Kefalov

Hristo Ivanov

Zelenchadska

Kraljbexnza

Veliko Târnovo

with a colonnaded terrace and courtyard full of Roman sculptures, the archaeological museum contains Roman artefacts from Nikopolis-ad-Istrum, and more Roman pottery and statues from elsewhere. Medieval Bulgarian exhibits include huge murals of the tsars, while there's also some ancient gold from nearby Neolithic settlements.

Forty Martyrs Church   CHURCH
(ul Mitropolska; adult/student 5/1 lv; ⊕9am-5.30pm) This church, in the old Asenova quarter, was built in 1230 to celebrate Tsar Asen II's victory over the Byzantines. It was used as a royal mausoleum and then as a mosque by the Turks.

Church of Sveti Dimitâr   CHURCH
(ul Patriarh Evtimii) Across the river, enclosed by a high wall, is Târnovo's oldest church.

During its 1185 consecration, Tsars Asen and Petâr proclaimed an uprising against Byzantine rule, which would create the Second Bulgarian Empire (1185–1396).

Church of Sveti Petr & Pavel   CHURCH
(Church of St Peter & St Paul; ul Mitropolska; adult/student 4/2 lv; ⊕9am-6pm) Located just past the bridge, this church contains fragments of murals from the 14th to 17th centuries.

🏃 Activities

Numerous local operators offer hiking, mountain biking, horse riding and caving; ask the Tourist Information Centre (p143) for hiking maps and contacts. The centre also offers the useful *Climbing Guide,* for serious rock climbers.

🛏 Sleeping

At time of writing, Veliko Târnovo's once-plentiful accommodation scene had been hit hard by the global economic crisis, with fewer tourists venturing to Bulgaria. This is not necessarily bad for travellers, however, as surviving hotels have stepped up services while keeping prices competitive.

The Tourist Information Centre (p143) finds private rooms (25 lv to 35 lv for a single/double). For atmosphere, stay near the Samovodska Charshiya Complex in the Varosha district, along the lower (southeastern) end of ul Gurko, or near Tsarevets Fortress.

TOP CHOICE Hotel Bolyarski   HOTEL €€
(☎613 200; www.bolyarski.com; ul Stefan Stambolov 53a; s/d incl breakfast from 80/130 lv; 🅿❄🛜❄) One of the town's best hotels, the Bolyarski has a phenomenal location on the bluff on ul Stambolov, with magical views of the town and river from its long cafe patio and rooms, and close proximity to all the local restaurants and bars. Its modern, well-kept rooms are pitched at business travellers.

Hikers Hostel   HOSTEL €
(☎0889 691 661; www.hikers-hostel.org; ul Rezevoarska 91; campsites/dm/d incl breakfast 14/20/52 lv; @🛜) Still Târnovo's most laid-back hostel, Hikers has an unassuming location high in Varosha's old quarter (a 10-minute walk from downtown). Charismatic owner Toshe Hristov does free bus/train station pick-ups and also runs trips. The two dorms (one with four beds, the other with 10) are spartan but clean, and there's one double room, a kitchen and two shared bathrooms.

WORTH A TRIP

ARBANASI

Arbanasi is a historic village known for its monasteries and activities, such as horseback riding and hiking. Nearly 90 of the village's churches, homes and monasteries are state-protected cultural monuments. During the 16th century and after, it flourished under the Ottomans who, rather unusually, encouraged church-building here.

Arbanasi's three major sites, two churches and one house museum, are all covered by the same ticket (5 lv). Each opens 9.30am to 6pm daily, though they're usually closed between 1 October and 31 March.

The oldest surviving church here is the **Nativity Church** (adult/student 6/2 lv). It features a kaleidoscopic frescoed interior, with paintings (1632–49) covering its five chambers and a magnificent hand-carved central iconostasis. The 16th-century **Church of Sveti Arhangeli Mikhail and Gavril**, built over a ruined medieval church, also contains impressive frescoes.

The 17th-century **Konstantsalieva House** (admission 5 lv) was later rebuilt in National Revival style. It contains period furniture (and a souvenir shop). Arbanasi also hosts three 17th-century working monasteries: Sveti Georgi Church, the **Sveta Bogoroditsa Monastery** (☏620 322) and the **Sveti Nikolai Monastery** (☏650 345).

For equestrians, the **Arbanasi Horse Base** (☏623 668; Arbanasi), on the village's eastern edge, provides guided horseback-riding trips in the lush hills around Arbanasi. Phone for programs and prices, or consult Veliko Târnovo's Tourist Information Centre (p143).

There's no need to linger after seeing the sights, but should you seek some pampering the **Hotel Arbanassi Palace** (☏630 176; www.arbanassipalace.bg; s/d/ste from 90/125/170 lv; P❋@☎≋) is the most venerable of several clifftop resorts. This grandly ageing structure (once Todor Zhivkov's local residence) has great views over the valley towards Veliko Târnovo from the restaurant balcony and from many of the rooms.

For humbler but still decent digs, the central **Rooms Mehana Arbat** (☏631 811; s/d incl breakfast 35/50 lv) offers doubles with weathered wood floors and traditional furnishings. Bathrooms are simple but modern. It's just above the similarly named **Mehana Arbat** (☏631 811; mains 6-12 lv), which does great Bulgarian fare at reasonable prices.

Arbanasi has always attracted moneyed visitors to its clifftop 'resort' hotels, but today it's mostly visited by tour buses on day trips. If based in Veliko Târnovo (4km away), it's easy to visit the main attractions, take in the views and have lunch, and still be back in town for dinner, whether you drive (taxis are 5 lv) or even hike (90 minutes).

Slavyanska Dusha GUESTHOUSE €

(☏625 182; www.slavianska-dusha.com; ul Nikola Zlatarski 21; s/d/tr/apt from 25/35/45/60 lv; ❋☎) Very affordable and clean, this cheery guesthouse is run by a local couple who grow their own veg for the on-site restaurant. The place offers simple but nice rooms decked out in traditional decor.

Hostel Mostel HOSTEL €

(☏0897 859 359; www.hostelmostel.com; ul Iordan Indjeto 10; campsites/dm/s/d incl breakfast 18/20/46/60 lv; @☎) The famous Sofia-based Hostel Mostel has become Târnovo's biggest, with clean, modern dorm rooms and doubles with sparkling bathrooms. It's just 150m from Tsarevets Fortress – good for exploring there, but a long walk from downtown (free bus/train pick-up is possible).

Hotel-Mehana Gurko HOTEL €€

(☏627 838; www.hotel-gurko.com; ul General Gurko 33; s/d/apt 80/110/135 lv; ❋@☎) The Gurko is one of the best places to sleep (and eat) in town, located under the Old Town. Rooms are spacious and soothing, each individually decorated and with great views. There aren't any extras, but service is friendly.

✗ Eating

TOP CHOICE Han Hadji Nikoli INTERNATIONAL €€€

(☏651 291; www.hanhadjinikoli.com; ul GS Rakovski 19; mains 25-30 lv; ☎) Without doubt Veliko Târnovo's finest restaurant. Start with escargots bourguignon, move on to roast chicken with cranberry and rose wine sauce, and finish with chocolate mousse flecked with raspberries and Cointreau.

Oh, and by the way, these are just from the 'regular' menu (there's also a discreet 'gourmet room' in the back, which has its own menu).

Shtastlivetsa   BULGARIAN €€
(☎600 656; ul Stefan Stambolov 79; mains 7-14 lv; ☺11am-1am; 🖥) A local institution, the 'Lucky Man' (as the impossible-to-pronounce name means in Bulgarian) has an ideal location overlooking the river's bend and a great menu of inventive meat dishes, baked-pot specials, nourishing pizzas and (at lunchtime) delicious soups.

Ego Pizza & Grill   PIZZA €€
(☎601 804; ul Nezavisimost 17; mains 5-12 lv; ☺9am-midnight; 🖥) Probably Tårnovo's best pizza, Ego has a new location overlooking the river's bend. It's a spacious restaurant with outdoor and indoor seating with excellent views. Service can be hit-or-miss.

🍷 Drinking

Dada Bar   BAR
(ul Velcho Dzhamdzhiyata 12; ☺10pm-4am) This funky place has a subterranean bar and outdoor enclosed courtyard beyond. Good prices, good music, and gets busy after midnight – just watch your head when going down the (rather low and steep) stairway.

Geronimo Bar   BAR
(ul Vasil Levski 1; ☺7am-2am) Coffee bar by day, drinks and cocktails by night, this stylish, popular place along the main road has a vaguely American-Southwest decor.

Tequila Bar   BAR
(ul Stefan Stambolov 30; ☺12pm-3am) Overlooking the main street and near the Samovodska Charshiya Compex, Tequila Bar is a festively painted student bar with good cocktails and cheap beer.

City Pub   PUB
(ul Hristo Botev 15; ☺noon-1am) This popular British-style pub near the post officee is somewhat gimmicky, but still a hit with local students and expats.

☆ Entertainment

Veliko Tårnovo's nightlife is buzzing year-round; in summer, backpackers and other foreign travellers pass through, while September summons back the town's 20,000 university students.

Konstantin Kisimov Dramatic Theatre   THEATRE
(☎623 526; ul Vasil Levski) This theatre has regular performances from the international pantheon and Bulgarian plays. Ask the Tourist Information Centre (p143) what's on.

Melon Live Music Club   CLUB
(☎0895 424 427; bul Nezavistnost 21; ☺6pm-4am) This great spot for live music (ranging from rock to R&B and Latin jazz) is tucked halfway up the main street.

Jack   CLUB
(☎0887 203 016; ul Magistraka 5; entry 3 lv; ☺10pm-4am) This pumping student club is especially popular on weekends with house music and dancing.

Bally   CLUB
(☎0885 565 666; ul Hristo Botev 2; ☺10pm-5am Mon-Sat) This two-part club has rooms for Bulgarian folk-pop and more international pop fare. Monday is student night with special offers.

ℹ Information

Hospital Stefan Cherkezov (☎626 841; ul Nish 1)
I-Net Internet Centre (off ul Hristo Botev; per hour 1.50 lv)
Main Post Office (ul Nezavisimost)
Tourist Information Centre (☎622 148; www.velikoturnovo.info; ul Hristo Botev 5; ☺9am-6pm Mon-Fri, Mon-Sat summer) Helpful English-speaking staff can help book accommodation and rent cars.

ℹ Getting There & Away
Bus

Two (non-central) bus stations serve Veliko Tårnovo. **Pâtnicheski Prevozi bus station** (Zapad Bus Station; ☎640 908; ul Nikola Gabrovski 74), about 4km from centre, is the main intercity one. Local buses 10, 12, 14, 70 and 110 go there, along ul Vasil Levski. There's also a left-luggage office. From here, buses serve Kazanlåk (9 lv, 2½ hours, five daily), Ruse (8 lv, two hours, eight daily), Burgas (18 lv, four hours, four daily) and Plovdiv (19 lv, four hours, four daily).

The more central **Yug bus station** (☎620 014; ul Hristo Botev) has many daily buses to Sofia (21 lv, four hours), Varna (19 lv, four hours) and Burgas (23 lv, 3½ hours). From here, several daily buses also serve Shumen (13 lv, three hours) and Ruse (11 lv, two hours).

Etap Adress (☎630 564; ul Ivailo 2, Hotel Etår) has hourly buses to Sofia (22 lv, 3½ hours)

BULGARIA VELIKO TÅRNOVO

and Varna (18 lv, four hours), plus two daily buses to Dobrich (20 lv, four hours), one to Kavarna (21 lv, 4½ hours) via Albena and Balchik and one to Shumen (13 lv, two hours).

Train

The remarkably unhelpful **Veliko Târnovo train station** (☑620 065), 1.5km west of town, has been known to ask for a 'fee' to provide train information. Three daily trains serve Plovdiv (21 lv, five hours). Trains also serve Burgas (21 lv, five hours, three daily), Varna (20 lv, five hours, three daily) and Sofia (21 lv, 4½ hours, six daily). Regular trains serve Târnovo's other train station, at Gorna Oryakhovitsa. From the Veliko Târnovo station, buses 10, 12, 14, 70 and 110 go to the centre. Alternatively, take a taxi (3 lv to 6 lv).

Gorna Oryakhovitsa train station (☑826 118), 8.5km from town, is along the Sofia–Varna line. It has daily services to/from Sofia, via Pleven (18 lv, five hours, eight daily) and Varna (17 lv, four hours, three daily) and 11 trains to Ruse (9 lv, two hours).

Shumen   Шумен

☑054 / POP 80,510

There's an awful lot of concrete in Shumen, but it does make its own beer, the popular Shumensko. This somewhat faded but friendly industrial city full of communist memorials is crowned by a striking medieval fortress, and has tasty eateries and fun drinking spots. The town's offerings include several museums and a lengthy pedestrian mall, bul Slavyanski, which stretches from the city park to the main square, pl Osvobozhdenie.

◉ Sights

Shumen Fortress   FORTRESS

(adult/student 3/1 lv; ☺9am-5pm Mon-Fri) Towering over the city from a steep hillside, the Shumen Fortress dates to the early Iron Age. It was reinforced by the Thracians (5th century BC). Between the 2nd and 4th centuries AD, the Romans added towers and walls. It was refortified later by the Byzantines, who made it an important garrison.

During the Second Bulgarian Empire (1185–1396), the fortress was one of northeastern Bulgaria's most significant settlements, renowned for its pottery and metalwork. However, invading Ottomans in the late 14th century burnt and looted it. Placards are dotted around the site and a yellowing information booklet (2 lv) is available at the gate.

Creators of the Bulgarian State Monument   MONUMENT

This massive Soviet-era hilltop monument was built in 1981 to commemorate the First Bulgarian Empire's 1300th anniversary. Climb the staircase behind the **History Museum** (☑857 487; bul Slavyanski 17; admission 2 lv; ☺9am-5pm Mon-Fri) for the 3km path leading from the equally communist **Partisan's Monument**. The circuitous 5km road there starts along ul Sv Karel Shkorpil at the History Museum. Go by taxi (5 lv one way) and then just walk back down the steps to the centre.

The **Information Centre** (☑852 598; admission 3 lv; ☺8.30am-5pm winter, 8am-7pm summer), about 300m from the monument, has information about the structure and surrounding flora. A 3km path passes the Information Centre and car park, finishing at Shumen Fortress.

Tombul Mosque   MOSQUE

(☑802 875; ul Rakovski 21; admission 2 lv; ☺9am-6pm) Arguably Bulgaria's most beautiful mosque and definitely the largest still used, this 1744 mosque is also called the Sherif Halili Pasha Mosque. Its Turkish nickname, *tombul* (plump) refers to its 25m-high dome. The 40m-high minaret has 99 steps. Local Muslim belief says that the courtyard fountain gushes sacred water.

⊨ Sleeping

Hotel-Restaurant Minaliat Vek   HOTEL €€

(☑801 615; www.minaliatvek.com; bul Simeon Veliki 81; s/d/apt 58/70/95 lv; ❄🎧) This hotel in the western part of town is remarkably popular with foreign travellers and represents good value. Rooms are clean and spacious (though not as terrific as the on-site restaurant). Staff are friendly and helpful.

Nirvana Art Hotel   HOTEL €€

(☑800 127; www.hotelnirvana.bg; ul Nezavisimost 25; s/d/apt from 75/85/130 lv; ❄🎧🎧) This relatively recent addition is set in a dusty residential part of south Shumen and boasts the city's most unique rooms. Each is painted in various soothing tones and with minimalist decor and the occasional canopy bed. Sauna, spa and massage (from 25 lv) are offered, and its gourmet restaurant (p145) is very good.

Hotel Zamaka   HOTEL €€

(☑800 409; www.zamakbg.eu; ul Vasil Levski 17; s/d/apt 40/60/85 lv; ❄🎧) This lovely hotel in

MADARA

Off the main highway between Shumen and Varna, Madara (Мадара) is a simple village that's home to the original, endlessly reproduced horseman figure that appears on Bulgaria's stotinki coins. The enigmatic 23m bas-relief on a sheer rock wall at the **Madara National Historical and Archaeological Reserve** (4 lv; ⊘8am-7.30pm summer, to 5pm winter) depicts a horseman spearing a lion. It's believed to date from the 8th century, though some argue it's much older. Afterwards follow a trail north and up 378 steps to a mountaintop fortress.

Public transport to Madara is limited, and the horseman is 3km up a steep road from the village. Several daily Shumen–Varna trains stop at Madara, but Shumen–Madara buses are infrequent; better to catch the bus from Shumen to Kaspichan (five daily), and then a minibus to Madara from there. A taxi from Shumen costs 30 lv return, including waiting time. Madara has no taxis.

a quiet residential neighbourhood just west of the main square has friendly staff and cosy rooms. It's set around a garden courtyard with a traditional restaurant.

✖ Eating

Minaliat Vek Restaurant BULGARIAN €€€
(☑801 615; bul Simeon Veliki 81; mains 9-17 lv; 🛜) This local favourite, part of the Minaliat Vek hotel, seeks to recreate the 'old time' tastes its name suggests. There's a long (and colourfully described) list of Bulgarian specialities plus numerous Bulgarian wines.

Katmi PANCAKES €
(pl Osvobozhdenie 12; pancakes 2 lv; ⊘7.30am-8pm) This local takeaway institution, off a side entrance on the square, offers delicious *palachinki* (pancakes) – much better than the usual Balkan crepe – with a choice of 122 different combinations. Our favourite is the all-natural blueberry and strawberry jam filling.

Nirvana Gourmet Restaurant INTERNATIONAL €€€
(☑300 127; ul Nezavisinost 25; mains 11-23 lv; 🛜) For those seeking relatively elegant international dining, it's worth the 10-minute drive or cab ride to this gourmet restaurant, with grills and Italian fare more than a notch above the average for Shumen. There's a long wine list.

❶ Getting There & Away

The bus and train stations are adjacent at Shumen's eastern end (3 lv to 5 lv by taxi). From the **bus station** (☑830 890; ul Rilski Pohod), buses serve Burgas (14 lv, three hours, four daily), Ruse (11 lv, two hours, three daily), Veliko Târnovo (11 lv, two hours, several daily), Madara (2 lv, 20 minutes, five daily), Sofia (31 lv, six hours, hourly) and Varna (11 lv, 1½ hours, nine daily). Private buses, such as those operated by **Etap Adress** (☑830 670), also stop in Shumen on the Sofia–Varna route.

From the **train station** (☑860 155; pl Garov) daily trains (including one express) serve Varna (7 lv, two hours, nine daily), and fast trains reach Sofia (19 lv, four to seven hours, two daily). Trains serve Ruse (12 lv, three hours, daily) and Plovdiv (18 lv, six hours, daily). Two trains stop at Madara. The station has a left-luggage office.

Ruse Русе

☑082 / POP 182,500

One of Bulgaria's most elegant cities, Ruse (*roo*-seh), sometimes written 'Rousse', has more than a touch of *mitteleuropa* grandness not seen elsewhere in the country. It's a city of imposing belle époque architecture and neatly trimmed leafy squares, as if a little chunk of Vienna had broken off and floated down the Danube. Its past is abundantly displayed in several museums and in its ruined Roman fortress, standing guard high over the Danube. Ruse is also a base for visiting the nearby rock monasteries and other attractions at Rusenski Lom Nature Park.

◉ Sights

Ruse Regional Museum of History MUSEUM
(www.museumruse.com; pl Aleksandar Battenberg 3; adult/student 4/1 lv; ⊘9am-6pm) The 5th-century-BC **Borovo Treasure**, consisting of silver cups and jugs adorned with Greek gods, is one of the highlights of Ruse's interesting museum. Other artefacts on display include Thracian helmets, Roman statues and 19th-century costumes.

Ruse

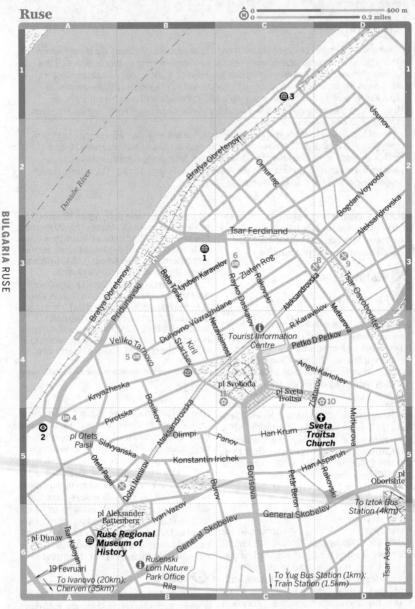

N 0 0 400 m
0 0.2 miles

FREE Sveta Troitsa Church   CHURCH
(ul Zlatarov; ⊙7am-6pm) Built in 1632 below ground level – according to the Turkish stipulation that churches should be as unobtrusive as possible – Sveta Troitsa has a fine gilt wood iconostasis and wooden pillars painted to look like marble, as well as some well-preserved icons.

**Roman Fortress of
Sexaginta Prista**   ARCHEOLOGICAL SITE
(ul Tsar Kaloyan 2; adult/student 2/1 lv; ⊙9am-noon & 12.30-5.30pm Tue-Sat) Closed for renovation

Ruse

at the time of research, little remains today of what was once a mighty Roman fort, completed in 70 AD and housing some 600 soldiers at its peak. You can still see some barracks walls and columns, and the enthusiastic custodian will show you around and bring it all to life.

Transportation Museum MUSEUM
(ul Bratya Obretenovi 5; outside/indoor displays 4/2 lv; ⊙10am-noon & 2-5pm Mon-Fri) Exhibits vintage locomotives from the late-19th and early-20th centuries, as well as carriages that once belonged to Tsar Boris III, Tsar Ferdinand and Turkish Sultan Abdul Aziz.

**Museum of the Urban
Lifestyle in Ruse** MUSEUM
(ul Tsar Ferdinand 36; adult/student 4/1 lv; ⊙9am-noon & 12.30-5.30pm) Built in 1866, this elegant townhouse features some re-created period rooms, with 19th-century furniture, paintings and chandeliers upstairs. Downstairs there are changing exhibitions on social themes.

🛏 **Sleeping**

TOP
CHOICE **City Art Hotel** BOUTIQUE HOTEL €€
(☎519 848; www.cityarthotel.com; ul Veliko Tărnovo 5; s/d 68/90 lv; ❋🛈) Offers 19 artfully styled rooms with trendy colour schemes, giant

headboards and upbeat philosophical quotations stencilled on the walls. The building is a renovated 19th-century hatmaker's shop on a quiet street near the centre, and guests receive a 10% discount at the Chinese restaurant in the back courtyard.

Anna Palace HOTEL €€
(☎825 005; www.annapalace.com; ul Knyazheska 4; s/d from 80/100 lv; P❋@) In a bright yellow, neoclassical mansion by the river terminal, the luxurious Anna Palace has large, slightly chintzy rooms. There are smaller, discounted attic singles.

English Guest House B&B €
(☎875 577; vysachko@abv.bg; ul Rayko Daskalov 34; s/d/tr from 40/60/70 lv; P❋@) A few blocks north of pl Svoboda, this British-run guesthouse has a selection of rooms in a renovated townhouse, including pricier en suite rooms. It's a sociable place where guests can mingle over some free tea in the garden.

🍴 **Eating**

TOP
CHOICE **Chiflika** BULGARIAN €€
(☎828 222; ul Otets Paisii 2; mains 6-25 lv; ⊙11am-2am Mon-Sat, noon-1am Sun) Set in several rooms following an old-world *mehana* theme, with wooden benches, rugs, fleeces on the walls and waiters in pantaloons, Chiflika is the best place in town for hearty traditional food. On the big menu are clay-pot meals, including an excellent chicken *gyuvetch* (cooked in a clay-pot), soups, grills and more adventurous options such as stewed lamb intestines (10.90 lv).

Ostankino BULGARIAN €
(ul Aleksandrovska 76; mains 3-8 lv; ⊙8.30am-midnight) Typical cheap and tasty Bulgarian food including sausages, grills, chicken steaks and fish are served at this busy cafe with outdoor tables. It's a good place to enjoy a couple of cold beers, too.

Hlebozavod Ruse FAST FOOD €
(ul Aleksandrovska; banitsa 70 stotinki; ⊙6.30am-7pm Mon-Fri, to 2pm Sat) Ruse's best takeaway snack shop draws locals all day, who come for the hot, freshly baked *banitsa*.

☆ **Entertainment**

Ruse Opera House (☎825 037; pl Sveta Troitsa), open since about 1890 and one of the town's finest buildings, and the **Sava Ognyanov Drama Theatre** (pl Svoboda), are both well known for their quality productions.

Buy tickets at the box offices, or through the Tourist Information Centre.

ℹ️ Information

There are numerous banks with ATMs and foreign exchange offices along ul Aleksandrovska and pl Svoboda, including **Unicredit Bulbank** (cnr ul Alexandrovska & pl Svoboda) and **Banka DSK** (pl Sveta Troitsa).

Polyclinic (☎834 200; ul Nezavisimost 2)

Post Office (pl Svoboda)

Rusenski Lom Nature Park Office (☎872 397; www.lomea.org; ul General Skobelev 7; ⊙9am-5pm Mon-Fri) Provides camping and hiking information and maps; can arrange trips to the Ivanovo Rock Monastery.

Tourist Information Centre (☎824 704; www.tic.rousse.bg; ul Aleksandrovska 61; ⊙9am-6pm Mon-Fri, 9.30am-6pm Sat & Sun) The helpful office hands out free city maps and leaflets.

ℹ️ Getting There & Away

Bus

The **Yug bus station** (☎828 151; ul Pristanishtna) has regular buses to Sofia (28 lv, five hours), Veliko Târnovo (10 lv, two hours), Shumen (6 lv, two hours), Burgas (27 lv, 4½ hours) and Varna (15 lv, four hours). To get to the station, take trolleybus 25 or bus 11 or 12 from ul Borisova. A taxi will cost about 4 lv.

The **Iztok bus station** (☎844 064; ul Ivan Vedur 10), 4km east of the centre, has buses to nearby destinations such as Ivanovo and Cherven in the Rusenski Lom Nature Park. Take a taxi or city bus 2 or 13, which leave from ul Gen Skobelev, near the roundabout four blocks east of ul Borisova.

Ruse-based company **Ovonesovi** (☎872 000) runs two daily minibuses to Bucharest, leaving from the Yug bus station and dropping you off in central Bucharest near the Piața Unirii metro station. Tickets are 20 lv one way or 30 lv return. Private taxis (90 lv one way) from Yug bus station also make the trip.

Train

From Ruse's grand **train station** (☎820 222; ul Pristanishtna) there are seven daily trains to Sofia (18.90 lv, six to seven hours) and two to Varna (12.20 lv, four hours).

For Romania, three daily trains serve Bucharest (25 lv, 3½ hours). Show up at least 30 minutes before the train departure time for customs and passport checks.

In the station, the **Rila Bureau** (☎828 016; ⊙9am-5.30pm) sells international train tickets. It's best to buy a Bucharest ticket on the day of travel as there are sometimes delays. The train station's **left-luggage office** (⊙6am-1.30pm & 2-8.30pm) is past the main buildings and in a smaller one up the hill. There's another branch of the **Rila Bureau** (☎834 860; ul Knyazheska 33; ⊙9am-noon & 1-5.30pm Mon-Fri) in the city centre.

Rusenski Lom Nature Park   Природен Парк Русенски Лом

This 32.6-sq-km nature park, sprawling south of Ruse around the Rusenski Lom, Beli Lom and Malki Lom Rivers, is a superb spot for birdwatching; 172 species are recorded here, including Egyptian vultures, lesser kestrels and eagle owls. It's also home to 67 species of mammals and 24 types of bats.

Most visitors are drawn first to the park's cliff churches. While around 40 medieval rock churches exist in and around some 300 local caves, only a handful are accessible, the most famous being those of Basarbovo and Ivanovo. The park also contains the second-longest cave in Bulgaria, the Orlova Chuka Peshtera (Eagle Peak Cave), between Tabachka and Pepelina villages. Thracian and Roman ruins have also been found here.

◉ Sights

Basarbovo Rock Monastery   MONASTERY
(☎082-800 765) Basarbovo is 8km south of Ruse near the Rusenski Lom River, on the road to the Ivanovo Monastery. Established sometime before the 15th century, the complex has been much restored and extended since. Visitors can see a rock-carved church with colourful icons and a little museum.

Ivanovo Rock Monastery   MONASTERY
(☎0889 370 006; Sveti Archangel Michael; adult/student 4/1 lv; ⊙9am-noon & 1-6pm) Around 4km east of Ivanovo, this Unesco World Heritage–listed monastery is built inside a cave 38m above ground. It's about a 10-minute walk on a good trail through a forest to get here. Built during the 13th century, it houses 14th-century murals regarded as some of the finest in Bulgaria, including a Last Supper scene.

Cherven Fortress   FORTRESS
(4 lv; ⊙9am-noon & 1-6pm) Just outside the village of Cherven, 15km south of Ivanovo, are the remains of a remarkably intact 6th-century citadel. Several streets, towers and churches have also been discovered, and there are great views of the river valleys and hills from the top.

🛏 Sleeping

The nature park office in Ruse and Ivanovo's **information centre** (☎081-162 203; Ivanovo town hall) provide information on accommodation, such as private rooms in Cherven, Pisanets, Nisovo and Koshov (20 lv per person) as well as small village guesthouses (from 40 lv per person).

❶ Getting There & Away

From the Iztok bus station in Ruse, two or three buses leave daily for Cherven, via Ivanovo and Koshov, from Monday to Friday (3 lv, 40 minutes). The best way to get to Ivanovo, however, is by train (every 30 minutes), as there are only three daily buses to Ivanovo in summer and fewer in winter.

Ask at the Ruse Tourist Information Centre for details on getting to Basarbovo via local bus directly from the city centre. In summer, hourly buses go to Basarbovo, though in winter they are less frequent.

BLACK SEA COAST

The Black Sea coast is the country's summertime playground, attracting tourists from across Europe and beyond, as well as Bulgarians themselves. The big, purpose-built resorts here are serious rivals to Spain and Greece, while independent travellers will find plenty to explore away from the parasols and jet skis. Sparsely populated sandy beaches to the far south and north, the bird-filled Burgas Lakes and picturesque ancient towns such as Nesebâr and Sozopol are rewarding destinations, while the 'maritime capital' of Varna is one of Bulgaria's most vibrant cities,

Varna Варна

☎052 / POP 335,000

Bulgaria's third city and maritime capital, Varna is by far the most interesting and cosmopolitan town on the Black Sea coast. A combination of port city, naval base and seaside resort, it's an appealing place to while away a few days, packed with history yet thoroughly modern, with an enormous park to amble around and a lengthy beach to lounge on. In the city centre you'll find Bulgaria's largest Roman baths complex and its finest archaeological museum, as well as a lively cultural and restaurant scene.

Dangers & Annoyances

Like elsewhere along the coast, some taxi drivers are prone to ripping off foreign visitors at the bus and train stations, so check the tariffs before getting in or, better still, pick up a cab on streets away from these places. Varna appears to be the last refuge in Bulgaria for black-market money changers, who lurk around pl Nezavisimost. Needless to say, it's illegal to change money on the street and you're sure to end up out of pocket.

◉ Sights

Archaeological Museum   MUSEUM

(ul Maria Luisa 41; adult/student 10/2 lv; ⊙10am-5pm Tue-Sun Apr-Sep, Tue-Sat Oct-Mar; ➌3, 9, 109) Exhibits at this vast museum, the best of its kind in Bulgaria, include 6500-year-old bangles, necklaces and earrings (said to be the oldest worked gold found anywhere in the world), Roman surgical implements, Hellenistic tombstones and touching oddities such as a marble plaque listing, in Greek, the names of the city's school graduates for AD 221.

Roman Thermae   RUINS

(cnr ul Han Krum & ul San Stefano; adult/student 4/2 lv; ⊙10am-5pm Tue-Sun May-Oct, Tue-Sat Nov-Apr) The well-preserved ruins of Varna's 2nd-century-AD Roman Thermae are the largest in Bulgaria, although only a small part of the original complex still stands. You can just about make out individual bathing areas and the furnaces, where slaves kept the whole thing going.

History Museum   MUSEUM

(ul 8 Noemvri 3; adult/child 4/2 lv; ⊙10am-5pm Tue-Sun May-Oct, Mon-Fri Nov-Apr; ➋20) Varna's ivy-covered History Museum is dedicated to city history between 1878 and 1939, with mock-ups of long-gone 1920s shops and offices, collections of photographs and postcards, and paraphernalia from local trades such as brewing and printing.

National Naval Museum   MUSEUM

(bul Primorski 2; 5 lv; ⊙10am-6pm Wed-Sun) The National Naval Museum hosts several galleries of model ships and uniforms. Anchors, artillery and helicopters can be seen rusting quietly in the grounds at the back, while the revered warship *Druzki,* which torpedoed a Turkish cruiser during the First Balkan War in 1912, is embedded in concrete outside.

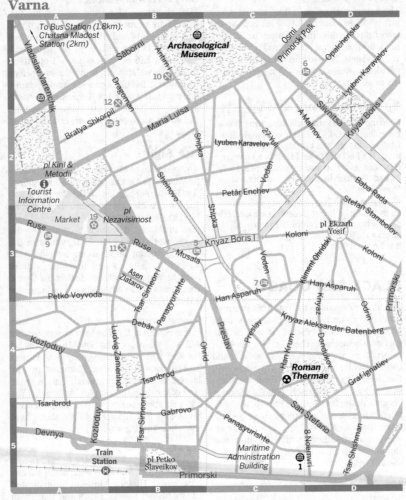

🏃 Activities

The main activity here is **swimming** and the Varna **city beach** is 8km long. The **south beach** (with its pool complex, water slides and cafes) has a popular stretch. The central beach has thinner sand patches and is dominated by clubs. Beyond to the north is a rocky area lined with restaurants, and further north there are some wider and more attractive areas of sand, as well as an outdoor **thermal pool** with year-round hot water where locals take a daily dip.

The blue-flag **Bunite Beach** north of here is one of the better places to stretch out, al-though there's a big private section, with a beach bar and tacky plastic coconut trees, where you can get a sunbed for 7 lv, a double bed for 20 lv or a 'VIP pavilion' (a canvas tent) for 50 lv. Elsewhere, beach bars rent loungers and umbrellas for about 5 lv. Just in from the beach is **Primorski Park**, a vast expanse of greenery dotted with statues, open-air cafes and popcorn vendors.

🛏 Sleeping

Varna certainly has no shortage of accom-modation, although the better (or at least,

BULGARIA VARNA

in 1912. Rooms are spacious and elegantly furnished, if a little chintzy, and the restaurant is especially good.

Modus Hotel　　　　　　　LUXURY HOTEL €€€
(☎660 910; www.modushotel.com; ul Stefan Stambolov 46; s/d from 180/200 lv; P😊❄🛜; 🚗20) Just across the road from Primorski Park, Modus is a chic boutique with suitably stylish rooms and all the facilities you'd expect. Various discounts and package deals are offered, and there's also a gym, sauna and bistro.

Hotel Hi　　　　　　　　　　HOTEL €€
(☎657 777; www.hotel-hi.com; ul Han Asparuh 11; s/d 80/112 lv; P😊❄🛜) In a quiet neighbourhood south of the main thoroughfare, Hi is a friendly place featuring stylish, cosy rooms – some very small – with TVs and minibars.

Graffit Gallery Hotel　　BOUTIQUE HOTEL €€€
(☎989 900; www.graffithotel.com; bul Knyaz Boris I 65; s/d/ste from 180/200/360 lv; P😊❄🛜😊; 🚗9) With its own art gallery, this modern designer hotel is one of Varna's more colourful

the more central) places get busy during the summer months.

Private rooms are plentiful in Varna, and pensioners with spare rooms wait around the train station to greet new arrivals. Prices tend to be around 12 lv per person, but make sure you don't end up in some out-of-the-way suburb.

TOP CHOICE Grand Hotel London　LUXURY HOTEL €€€
(☎664 100; www.londonhotel.bg; ul Musala 3; s/d Mon-Thu from 170/210 lv, Fri-Sun from 150/190 lv; P😊❄🛜) Varna's grandest hotel is this five-star establishment, which originally opened

options. The large rooms on each of the four floors follow a different theme, and there's a spa and gym too.

Hotel Astra
HOTEL €€

(☑630 524; www.hotelastravarna.com; ul Opalchenska 9; s/d 50/60 lv; ❋ 🖥; 🖵9) A real bargain by Varna standards, this central, family-run hotel has 10 spacious and comfortable rooms, all with terraces, and basic but good-sized bathrooms.

Flag Hostel
HOSTEL €

(☑0897 408 115; www.varnahostel.com; ul Bratya Shkorpil 13a; dm incl breakfast 22 lv; P 😊 🖥; 🖵3, 9) The Flag is a long-established, sociable place with a young, international party atmosphere and three dorms with single beds only (no bunks), and breakfast included. Free pick-ups from the bus and train stations are offered.

Yo Ho Hostel
HOSTEL €

(☑0886 382 905; www.yohohostel.com; ul Ruse 23; dm/s/d incl breakfast from 14/30/40 lv; @; 🖵109) Shiver your timbers at this pirate-themed place found just down the street from the Varna Opera House, with four- and 11-bed dorm rooms, two doubles and one single room. Free breakfast and pick-ups are offered, and staff also organise camping and rafting trips.

Eating

Di Wine
MODERN EUROPEAN €€€

TOP CHOICE

(☑606 050; www.diwine.bg; ul Bratya Shkorpil 2; mains 12-30 lv; 🖵9) This formal but friendly restaurant is Varna's best fine-dining spot, with a big menu of tempting dishes including a rack of lamb, T-bone steaks, guinea fowl, salmon and trout as well as cheaper barbecue dishes. There are plenty of good wines to try, too.

Tanasi
GREEK €€

(☑601 138; ul Bratya Shkorpil 16; mains 5-15 lv; 🖵9) This welcoming Greek restaurant has fresh white linen indoors, plus less formal outdoor seating. Featured dishes include stuffed aubergines, roast lamb, rabbit and various fish, and they also offer an excellent value three-course set lunch for 5 lv.

Morsko Konche
PIZZERIA €€

(pl Nezavisimost; pizzas 5-10 lv; 🖥🅿) The 'Seahorse' is a cheap and cheerful pizza place with a big menu featuring all the standard varieties, as well as some inventive creations of its own: the 'exotic' pizza comes with bananas and blueberries.

Drinking

Varna's trendiest bars are found along the beach on Kraybrezhna aleya, although many have only a brief existence in the summer sunshine. Popular hang-outs to sip seafront margaritas include **Pench's Cocktails** (Kraybrezhna aleya) and **Punta Cana** (Kraybrezhna aleya; ⊙6am-4am), while there are several coffee and cocktail bars along bul Slivnitsa.

Entertainment

Exit (⊙10pm-6am), **4aspik** (☑0885 800 297; ⊙10pm-4am), specialising in Bulgarian folk-pop, and **Copacabana** (⊙10pm-5am), with a fondness for '70s and '80s music, are just a few of the many summertime clubs along Kraybrezhna aleya.

Varna Opera House
OPERA

(☑650 555; www.operavarna.bg; pl Nezavisimost 1; ⊙ticket office 11am-1pm & 2-7pm Mon-Fri, 11am-6pm Sat) Bulgaria's second-most important opera house (after Sofia) hosts performances by the Varna Opera and Philharmonic Orchestra all year except July and August.

Open-Air Theatre
THEATRE

(Summer Theatre; ☑228 385; Primorski Park) Complete with mock ivy-covered Roman arches, this theatre hosts everything from ballet to rock concerts. Details are available at the adjoining ticket office.

Information

Internet Doom (ul 27 Yuli 13; per hour 1.60 lv; ⊙24hr) The most central of several branches around town, just behind the St Nikolai Church.

Main Post Office (ul Sâborni 36)

Tourist Information Centre (☑0887 703 242, 820 689; www.varnainfo.bg; pl Kiril & Metodii; ⊙9am-7pm; 🖵3) Plenty of free brochures and maps, and helpful multilingual staff.

Unicredit Bulbank (bul Slivnitsa)

Getting There & Away

AIR Varna's international **airport** (☑573 323; www.varna-airport.bg; 🖵409) has scheduled and charter flights from all over Europe, as well as regular flights to and from Sofia. From the centre, bus 409 goes to the airport.

BUS Varna has two bus stations – the scruffy **central bus station** (bul Vladislav Varenchik 158; 🖵148) is about 2km northwest of the city centre. There are basic cafes and a **left-luggage office** (per hour 80 stotinki; ⊙7am-7pm).

The **Chatsna Mladost Station** (☑500 039) is about 200m along a road that starts almost opposite the central bus station. From here,

BULGARIA VARNA

TRANSPORT FROM VARNA

Bus

DESTINATION	PRICE (LV)	DURATION	FREQUENCY
Albena	5	45min	several daily
Balchik	5	1hr	16 daily
Burgas	14	2hr	4 daily
İstanbul	60	10hr	2 daily
Plovdiv	27	6hr	2 daily
Ruse	15	4hr	5 daily
Shumen	8	1½hr	3 daily
Sofia	32	7hr	20 daily
Veliko Târnovo	18	4hr	20 daily

Train

DESTINATION	PRICE (LV)	DURATION (HR)	FREQUENCY
Plovdiv	24.20	7	3 daily
Ruse	12.20	4	2 daily
Shumen	6.50	1½	10 daily
Sofia	23.60	7-8	7 daily

frequent minibuses go to destinations such as Balchik and Burgas. Ticket prices are the same as from the central bus station.

TRAIN Facilities at Varna's **train station** (☑630 414; pl Slaveikov) include a **left-luggage office** (☺7.30am-8pm) and cafe.

The **Rila Bureau** (☑632 348; ul Preslav 13; ☺8.30am-5.30pm Mon-Fri, 8am-3.30pm Sat) sells tickets for international services and advance tickets for domestic trains.

North Coast

BALCHIK БАЛЧИК
☑0579 / POP 12,100

After the artificial resorts further down the coast, Balchik is a breath of fresh air. A pretty town and fishing port huddled below white-chalk cliffs, it's a low-key holiday spot that feels a world away from the likes of Albena, whose lights can be seen winking across the bay at night. The main attraction here is the Summer Palace of Romanian Queen Marie, with its lovely botanical gardens.

◉ Sights

Summer Palace of Queen Marie & Botanical Gardens   HISTORIC BUILDING, GARDENS
(Dvorets; 10 lv; ☺8am-8pm May–mid-Oct, 8.30am-6.30pm mid-Oct–Apr) At the western end of the seafront, this little palace was completed in 1926 by King Ferdinand of Romania for his English wife, Queen Marie (Balchik was then part of Romania). It was rumoured that Marie entertained her much younger Turkish lover here. Size-wise, it's a relatively modest seaside villa, although the architecture – a blend of Bulgarian, Gothic and Islamic styles topped with a minaret – is unique. The half-dozen or so rooms on show contain original furnishings, including paintings by Marie, and several photographs of the queen striking dramatic poses in the grounds. Also here is a curious collection of local archaeological finds, including Roman pottery and mammoth bones.

Behind the palace are the extensive botanical gardens. Around 600 different species of flora are featured throughout a series of themed gardens, including an impressive collection of cacti. Also within the complex are a watermill, a classical-style nymphaeum, the tiny Chapel of Sveta Bogoroditsa and even a winery.

City Historical Museum   MUSEUM
(ul Vitosha 3; 2 lv; ☺9am-noon & 1-5pm Mon-Fri) The diverse collection here includes Roman statuary, medieval pottery and vintage photographs of the town from the early 1900s.

SVETI KONSTANTIN, GOLDEN SANDS & ALBENA

North of Varna you'll find a succession of popular seaside resorts, starting with sedate Sveti Konstantin, famous for its spa treatments, before you hit the big beasts of Golden Sands and Albena, better known for their clubs, pubs and water sports.

The quiet beach resort **Sveti Konstantin** is about 9km northeast of Varna, with hotels attractively spaced out amid parkland. Established in 1946 under the name of Druzhba (Friendship), it's less commercial than other resorts and has long been popular with older holidaymakers. Indeed, it still has a number of 'rest homes' for retired civil servants and trade-union members. There are several new resort hotels geared towards young families, but this isn't the place for water sports or raucous nightlife

About 18km north of Varna, **Golden Sands** (Zlatni Pyasâtsi) was Bulgaria's original purpose-built resort, with the first hotel opening here in 1957. Today it's Bulgaria's second-largest coastal resort, with a 4km stretch of beach, and some of the best nightlife on the coast. Virtually everyone staying in the resort will be on a prebooked package, and it's not particularly friendly for walk-ins, but it's still a pretty beach for a day trip out to the coast.

Further up the road, **Albena** has a lovely, 4km-long beach and shallow water ideal for water sports. The downside are the high prices charged for just about everything and the fact that it's a package resort and not particularly user-friendly for independent travellers. That said, it's ideal to drop in for the day and swim and relax. Note that entry to the resort by private car costs 3 lv.

Ethnographic Museum MUSEUM
(ul Vitosha; 1 lv; ⊙9am-5pm Mon-Fri) Opposite the Historical Museum, this museum features folk costumes and displays relating to traditional trades and crafts such as fishing, barrel making and woodcarving.

🛏 Sleeping

Hotel Mistral HOTEL €€
(☑71 130; www.hotelmistralbg.com; ul Primorska 8b; s/d 92/112 lv; ⊛❄🔊) One of the best waterfront hotels, the four-star Mistral is an upmarket place with large rooms, all with sea-facing balconies. Prices drop by up to half outside the summer season.

Hotel Regina Maria Spa LUXURY HOTEL €€€
(☑460 065; www.reginamariaspa.com; r/ste 160/250 lv; P❄🔊⛱) Near the palace, the four-star Regina Maria offers smart rooms in a variety of styles, all with sea views. Golfing packages and fishing trips can be arranged.

Hotel Helios HOTEL €€
(☑76 970; www.heliosbg.com; d/apt 94/134 lv; P❄@⛱🐾) Helios is a modern, resort-style hotel and all rooms have balconies, many with superb sea views. Prices drop by up to 50% out of high season.

🍴 Eating

TOP CHOICE Tihoto Gnezdo CAFE €
(mains from 3 lv; ⊙9am-11pm; ☑) On the shore near the palace, this simple cafe serves light dishes such as salads and omelettes (from 3.50 lv) as well as fish. Prices are more reasonable than most seafront restaurants.

Francis Drake SEAFOOD €€€
(mains 10-30 lv; ⊙8am-midnight; 🔊) The restaurant of the Hotel Mistral is the place for some classier cuisine. Fried turbot, smoked salmon, and locally caught fish are among the offerings.

ℹ Information

The post office and telephone centre are on the main square, pl Nezavisimost. You can change money at **SG Expressbank** (ul Cherno More).

ℹ Getting There & Away

Balchik's **bus station** (☑74 069) is at the top of ul Cherno More, a steep 1km walk from the port. Minibuses travel from Balchik to Albena (3 lv, 20 minutes, every 30 minutes), Varna (5 lv, one hour, hourly) and Sofia (36 lv, 10 hours). Rather more conveniently, minibuses to Albena also call at the bus stop on ul Primorska, outside the supermarket.

Central Coast

Dominating the coastal strip between Varna and Burgas – often a mountainous ride, generally inland away from the water – is the huge, clubland resort of Sunny Beach (Slânchev Bryag) and its ancient, church-filled neighbour, Nesebâr. A few surprises can be found via out-of-the-way rough roads too.

VARNA TO BURGAS

Byala, about 54km south of Varna, is a basic town of 2100 people, set on the rising hills above the beach. Some 4km north – on a dirt road past rolling hills of vineyards – is the more attractive **Karadere beach**. Varna–Burgas buses pass by Byala.

About 13km south (past the small beach town of Ozbor, where buses stop), a road heads east a couple of kilometres towards the largely untouched **Irakli beach**, with a guesthouse and a couple of bungalows.

For the best views, a rough road rambles from Irakli for 8km up to hillside **Emona**. The trans-Bulgarian Mt Kom–Emine Cape hike (E3) ends here, and a very rough dirt road leads down to a small beach. The road curves inland, bypassing Sunny Beach and Nesebâr, and continues on 31km into Burgas.

NESEBÂR   НЕСЕБЪР
☑0554 / POP 10,300

On a small, rocky outcrop 37km northeast of Burgas, connected to the mainland by a narrow, artificial isthmus, pretty-as-a-postcard Nesebâr (Ne-*se*-bar) is famous for its surprisingly numerous, albeit mostly ruined, medieval churches. It has, inevitably, become heavily commercialised, and transforms into one huge, open-air souvenir market during the high season; outside summer, it's a ghost town. With Sunny Beach just across the bay, you have every conceivable water sport on hand. The New Town on the other side of the isthmus has the newest and biggest hotels and the main beach, but the sights are all in the Old Town.

◉ Sights & Activities

Nesebâr was once home to about 80 churches, but most are now in ruins. Characteristic of the Nesebâr style are the horizontal strips of white stone and red brick, and facades decorated with green ceramic discs.

Around 1.5km west of the Old Town is **South Beach**. All the usual water sports are available, including **jet skiing** and **waterskiing**. The longer sandy shores of Sunny Beach (Slânchev Bryag), just a few kilometres up the coast, are an alternative option.

Archaeological Museum   MUSEUM
(www.ancient-nessebar.org; ul Mesembria 2; adult/child 5/3 lv; ⊙9am-8pm Mon-Fri, 9.30am-1.30pm & 2-7pm Sat & Sun Jul & Aug) Greek and Roman pottery, statues and tombstones, as well as Thracian gold jewellery and ancient anchors are displayed here. There's also a collection of icons recovered from Nesebâr's numerous churches.

Sveti Stefan Church   CHURCH
(ul Ribarska; adult/student 5/2 lv; ⊙9am-7pm Mon-Fri, 9am-1pm & 1.30-6pm Sat & Sun) Built in the 11th century and reconstructed 500 years later, this is the best preserved church in town, renowned for its beautiful 16th- to 18th-century murals, which cover virtually the entire interior. Try to come early, as it's popular with tour groups.

FREE **Sveta Sofia Church**   CHURCH
(Old Metropolitan Church; ul Mitropolitska; ⊙dawn-dusk) At the centre of town, the vast and impressive shell of this church is surrounded by cafes and artists' stalls.

FREE **St John Aliturgetos Church**   CHURCH
(ul Mena; ⊙dawn-dusk) Overlooking the harbour to the south, this earthquake-battered building is set on a cliff and provides a picturesque setting for summertime concerts.

FREE **Christ Pantokrator Church**   CHURCH
(ul Mesembria; ⊙dawn-dusk) This church has been converted into a commercial art gallery, selling the works of local painters, mainly seascapes and views of the Old Town.

⌂ Sleeping

In summer, you'll need to book accommodation in advance. Private rooms are the best option for budget travellers. Locals offering rooms often meet tourists off the bus.

TOP CHOICE **Hotel Tony**   GUESTHOUSE €
(☑0889 268 004, 42 403; ul Kraybrezhna 20; r from 40 lv; ⊙Jun-Sep; ☒) In a great spot overlooking the sea, Hotel Tony is reasonably priced and is regularly full in summer. Rooms are simple but clean and the chatty host is very helpful.

Hotel Trinity Sea Residence   HOTEL €€
(☑46 600; www.trinity-nessebar.com; ul Venera 8; s/d/apt from 82/92/152 lv; P☒☏ꙮ) This pretty National Revival–style wooden villa has spacious rooms and apartments, many with stunning sea views, and half- and full-board deals are available. Children under eight stay free, and video games and baby cribs are available.

BULGARIA CENTRAL COAST

Prince Cyril Hotel
HOTEL €

(☑42 220; hotelprincecyril@gmail.com; ul Slavyanska 9; d from 50 lv; ❋🛜) Located on a quiet, cobbled, souvenir-stall-free lane, this is a friendly place with a variety of rooms, all with TV and fridge, but not all with air-con; check a few out first and try to avoid the cramped, top-floor fan-only rooms.

✗ Eating

All restaurants in Nesebâr are geared towards the passing tourist trade and prices are roughly twice what you'll pay away from the coastal resorts. Try to avoid those that employ touts.

Pri Shopite
BULGARIAN €€

(ul Neptun 12; mains 7-15 lv; ☑) Set in a traditional, tavern-style courtyard around a twisted, 300-year-old fig tree, this is a welcoming place with great food, including freshly caught fish, grills, steaks and vegetarian options.

Old Nesebâr
SEAFOOD €€

(☑42 070; ul Ivan Alexander 11; mains 8-15 lv) With two tiers of seating offering great sea views, this is a popular place for barbecues, grills and fish dishes, as well as salads and lighter meals.

Zlatnoto Runo
BULGARIAN €€€

(☑45 602; ul Rusalka 6; mains 8-20 lv) Overlooking the sea on the southeastern end of the peninsula, the 'Golden Fleece' serves a varied menu, including roast lamb and rabbit plus some inventive seafood dishes, such as octopus with blueberry sauce.

❶ Information

Post Office (ul Mesembria; ⊘8am-8pm Tue-Sat)

Tourist Information Centre (☑42 611; www.visitnessebar.org; ul Mesembria 10; ⊘9am-5.30pm May-Oct)

Unicredit Bulbank (ul Mesembria; ⊘8.30am-5pm Mon-Fri)

❶ Getting There & Away

Nesebâr is well connected to coastal destinations by public transport, and the town's bus station is on the small square just outside the city walls. The stop before this on the mainland is for the New Town. From the bus station, there are buses to nearby Sunny Beach (1 lv, 10 minutes, every 15 minutes), Burgas (6 lv, 40 minutes, every 30 minutes), Varna (15 lv, two hours, seven daily) and Sofia (30 lv, seven hours, several daily).

Fast Ferry (www.fastferry.bg) operates a summer-only high-speed hydrofoil service to Sozopol (one way/return from 27/54 lv, 30 minutes, three to four daily).

Burgas   Бургас

☑056 / POP 229,000

For most visitors, the port city of Burgas (sometimes written as 'Bourgas') is no more than a transit point for the more obviously appealing resorts and historic towns further up and down the coast. If you do decide to stop over, you'll find a lively, well-kept city with a neat, pedestrianised centre, a long, uncrowded beach and some interesting museums. A clutch of reasonably priced hotels, as well as some decent restaurants, makes it a practical base for exploring the southern coast.

◉ Sights & Activities

Archaeological Museum
MUSEUM

(bul Aleko Bogoridi 21; adult/student 4/2 lv; ⊘10am-6pm Mon-Sat) This small museum houses a diverting collection of local finds, including neolithic flint tools, a wooden canoe from the 5th century BC, Greek statuary and the remarkably well-preserved wooden coffin of a Thracian chieftain.

Natural History Museum
MUSEUM

(ul Konstantin Fotinov 20; adult/student 4/2 lv; ⊘10am-6pm Mon-Sat) Old-fashioned but informative displays on local flora, fauna and geology are on view here. Exhibits of rocks, seashells, butterflies and beetles occupy the ground floor, while upstairs there's a collection of stuffed birds and animals.

Ethnographical Museum
MUSEUM

(ul Slavyanska 69; adult/student 4/2 lv; ⊘10am-6pm Mon-Sat) Regional folk costumes, jewellery and furniture are on show at this museum, as well as displays covering the local weaving and fishing industries. Everything is labelled in Bulgarian.

Soviet Army Monument
MONUMENT

(pl Troikata) Standing sentinel over pl Troikata is this towering Red Army memorial, comprising a column surmounted by a saluting Russian soldier and figurative panels. It is a major city focal point.

Beach
BEACH

(🖵8, 12) Although it can't compare with beaches at the nearby resorts, Burgas beach still attracts plenty of locals on a hot summer day. It's a bit grubby at the southern end, with its long concrete pier, used as a diving platform by teenage boys and a fishing station by old men, but further on there are beach bars and restaurants.

🛏 Sleeping

TOP CHOICE Hotel California
BOUTIQUE HOTEL €€

(☎531 000; www.burgashotel.com; ul Lyuben Karavelov 36; s/d 60/70 lv; P❄❀📶; 🖥4) This appealing boutique hotel on a quiet side street about five minutes' walk west of the centre is a winner, with large rooms featuring colourful wall prints and especially soft mattresses. Guests get a 20% reduction in the excellent restaurant.

Hotel Chiplakoff
BOUTIQUE HOTEL €€

(☎829 325; www.chiplakoff.com; ul Ferdinandova 88; s/d 50/60 lv; P❀@) A 10-minute walk west of the centre, this hotel occupies an attractively restored mansion, designed by the same architect who built the city's grand train station. Rooms are large and contemporary in style, and the original spiral staircases have been retained; there's no lift, however. There's a popular pizza restaurant downstairs.

Grand Hotel Primoretz
LUXURY HOTEL €€€

(☎812 345; www.hotelprimoretz.bg; ul Knyaz Al Battenberg 2; s/d/ste from 216/236/296 lv; P❄❀📶; 🖥12) This huge, five-star complex at the southern end of the city beach looks out of scale in Burgas, but excellent facilities include a spa and indoor and outdoor pools. Sea views cost a little extra, as does the wi-fi and parking, which seems a bit cheeky at these prices.

Fotinov Guest House
HOTEL €€

(☎0878 974 703; www.hotelfotinov.com; ul Konstantin Fotinov 22; s/d 72/82 lv; ❀📶) Conveniently located right in the city centre, with a selection of brightly coloured rooms, featuring fridges, kettles and cable TV. The multilingual staff are friendly and helpful, and there's even a small sauna.

Burgas Hostel
HOSTEL €

(☎825 854; hostelburgas@gmail.com; ul Slavyanska 14; dm incl breakfast 20 lv; @; 🖥12) The only hostel in town didn't bother with a fancy name. It sports five- and eight-bed dorms, plus a small lounge and kitchen.

🍴 Eating & Drinking

Outlets along bul Aleko Bogoridi sell pizza, kebabs and ice cream, while there are several summertime bars along the beach, most of which also serve food.

Roma
ITALIAN €€

(☎825 467; bul Aleko Bogoridi 60; mains 6-20 lv; 🖥8) This trendy Italian place has a wide menu ranging from simple pasta and risotto dishes (5 lv to 6 lv) to pricier options such as grilled sea bass (20 lv). Steaks, grills and various fish dishes are available. Reservations are advisable in the evenings.

Vodenitsata
BULGARIAN €

(Water Mill; ☎0899 174 715; mains from 3 lv; ◷10am-2am; 🖥12) Standing on the seafront overlooking the beach, this is a traditional wood-cabin affair, which is always packed out with locals. Specialities include grilled fish, barbecues, steaks and salads.

London Pub & Restaurant
BRITISH €€

(ul Tsar Simeon 4a; mains 8-20 lv; ◷10am-1am; 📶; 🖥12) Catering to homesick British expats and visitors, come here for all-day English breakfasts, as well as mixed grills and steak-and-onion pie. The kitchen closes at 9pm, but drinks are served until 1am.

TOP CHOICE China Tea House
TEAHOUSE

(pl Troikata 4; tea from 2 lv; ◷8.30am-10pm Mon-Fri, 11am-10pm Sat; 📶) Oil paintings by local artists decorate this chilled-out teahouse, which offers a big menu of black, green and herbal teas, as well as a few freshly prepared vegetarian dishes.

Samba Lounge
BAR

(◷8am-midnight) One of the more attractive beach bars, set on decking over the sand and surrounded by potted flowers. It's a pleasant spot to relax with a beer (2 lv) and they also serve light meals such as salads and soups throughout the day.

☆ Entertainment

In summer, nightclubs and bars materialise between the trees of Maritime Park; among the more reliable is **Alibi** (☎0897 962 262; Maritime Park; ◷11pm-late), offering 'retro nights', dance and Latino music. Live music, dance and drama performances often take place at the Summer Theatre, while the **Sea Casino Cultural Centre** (Maritime Park) hosts a varied program of concerts and exhibitions.

For something more sophisticated, find out what's on offer at the **Adriana Boudevska Drama Theatre** (☎842 266; ul Tsar Asen

TRANSPORT FROM BURGAS

Bus

DESTINATION	PRICE (LV)	DURATION	FREQUENCY
Sozopol	4.50	40min	every 30min
Nesebâr	6	40min	every 30-40min
Sunny Beach (Slânchev Bryag)	6	45min	every 30-40min
Primorsko	7	1hr	every 30min
Sofia	30	7-8hr	several daily
Plovdiv	17	4hr	several daily
Varna	14	2hr	every 30-40min

Train

DESTINATION	PRICE (LV)	DURATION (HR)	FREQUENCY
Sofia	23.10	7-8	6 daily
Plovdiv	19	5-6	7 daily
Kazanlâk	14.40	3	2 daily

l 36a) or the Burgas Opera House (☑840 762; www.operabourgas.com; ul Sv Kliment Ohridski 2).

ℹ Information

Numerous banks with ATMs can be found along ul Aleksandrovska and ul Aleko Bogorid, including Unicredit Bulbank (ul Aleksandrovska), Central Cooperative Bank (ul Aleksandrovska) and Raffeisen Bank (ul Ferdinandova).

Post Office (ul Tsar Petâr 2)

Tourist Information Centre (☑825 772; www.tic.burgas.bg; ul Hristo Botev; ☺8.30am-5.30pm Mon-Fri; ☐12) At the entrance to the underpass below ul Hristo Botev, the city's tourist office has English-speaking staff and plenty of brochures.

ℹ Getting There & Away

AIR Bulgaria Air links Burgas Airport (☑870 248; www.bourgas-airport.com; ☐15), 10km northeast of town, with Sofia three times a day (April to October). In summer, WizzAir (www.wizzair.com) connects Burgas with London Luton, Budapest, Prague and Warsaw. Other carriers fly to destinations in Germany and Russia.

BUS Yug bus station (cnr ul Aleksandrovska & ul Bulair), outside the train station at the southern end of ul Aleksandrovska, is where most travellers arrive or leave. There are regular buses to coastal destinations. Departures are less frequent outside summer.

A number of agencies around Yug bus station, including Union-Ivkoni (☑840 986), run coaches to İstanbul each day (55 lv, seven hours). Nışıklı Turızm (☑841 261; ul Bulair) has several daily departures (55 lv to 60 lv) from outside its office. Union-Ivkoni also runs daily buses to destinations in Greece, including Thessaloniki (80 lv, 13 hours).

TRAIN The historic train station (ul Ivan Vazov) was built in 1902. Through the ticket windows (☺8am-6pm) on the right, you can buy advance tickets for domestic and international services, while same-day tickets can be bought at the windows (☺24hr) on the left. The left-luggage office (☺6am-10.45pm) is outside the station.

International tickets are also available at the Rila Bureau (☺8am-5.30pm Mon-Thu, to 4pm Fri, to 3.30pm Sat) inside the station.

South Coast

The finest sandy beaches dot the coast south from Sozopol to the Turkish border, though some come with less-appealing modern beach resorts. It helps to have wheels, but you can reach many rewarding spots by bus, too.

SOZOPOL   СОЗОПОЛ
☑0550 / POP 5000

Ancient Sozopol, with its charming Old Town of meandering cobbled streets and pretty wooden houses huddled together on a narrow peninsula, is one of the coast's real highlights. With two superb beaches, genial atmosphere, plentiful accommodation and good transport links, it has long been a popular seaside resort and makes an excellent base for exploring the area. Although not quite as crowded as Nesebâr, it is becoming ever more popular with international visitors. There's a lively cultural scene, too, with plenty of free concerts and other events in summer.

◉ Sights & Activities

The town's two beaches are attractive, though waves can be quite high. The 1km-long **Harmanite Beach** is wide and clean and offers a water slide, paddle boats, volleyball nets and beach bars. At the southern end, incongruously, archaeological excavations have uncovered stone sarcophagi on the site of the ancient **Apollonia necropolis**.

The **Town Beach** (or Northern Beach) is another pleasant curve of sand, but it's smaller, gets *very* crowded, and doesn't offer the same number of beachside cafes, restaurants and bars.

Archaeological Museum · MUSEUM
(ul Han Krum 2; 4 lv; ⊙9am-6pm, closed Sat & Sun winter) Housed in a drab concrete box near the port, this museum has a small collection of local finds. The high-quality Hellenic ceramics, dating from the 5th century BC, give an indication of the wealth and sophistication of early citizens, and there are lots of anchors and amphorae dredged up from ancient shipwrecks.

Southern Fortress Wall & Tower Museum · RUINS, MUSEUM
(ul Milet 40; adult/student 4/3 lv; ⊙9.30am-8pm Jul & Aug, to 5pm May, Jun, Sep & Oct) The reconstructed walls and walkways along the rocky coastline, and a 4th-century-BC well that was once part of a temple to Aphrodite here are free to explore – the few, mostly empty, rooms you get to see for your 4 lv are something of an anticlimax.

Church of Sveta Bogoroditsa · CHURCH
(ul Anaksimandâr 13; 1 lv; ⊙10am-1pm & 2-6pm) This 15th-century church was built below street level, as required at the time by the Ottoman rulers. Set in a courtyard with a giant fig tree, it is one of the most picturesque in town, with an exquisite wooden iconostasis and a pulpit carved with bunches of grapes.

Church of Sveti Georgi · CHURCH
(ul Apolonia; ⊙9am-1pm & 3-8pm Mon-Sat, 7am-1pm & 3-8pm Sun) This is another attractive church, with a fine painting of St George and the Dragon over the entrance and an impressive 19th-century iconostasis. The custodians here are rather keen to enforce the dress code (no shorts).

⌁ Sleeping

Sozopol has countless private homes offering rooms. Look for signs along Republikanska in the New Town and pretty much anywhere in the Old Town.

TOP CHOICE Art Hotel · HOTEL €€
(☑24 081; www.arthotel-sbh.com; ul Kiril & Metodii 72; d Jul-Sep 75 lv, Oct-Jun from 40 lv; ❋⊗) This peaceful Old Town house, belonging to the Union of Bulgarian Artists, is located within a walled courtyard towards the tip of the peninsula, away from the crowds. It has a small selection of bright and comfortable rooms with balconies, most with sea views, and breakfast is served on the terraces directly over the sea.

Hotel Villa List · HOTEL €€
(☑22 235; www.hotellist-bg.com; ul Yani Popov 5; s/d from 65/92 lv; ❋@⊗⊛) With a superb setting just off the town beach, big rooms with balconies and an outdoor pool with a view over the sea, Villa List is very popular and frequently fully booked in summer. There's even a 'nude terrace' for that all-over tan.

Hotel Diamanti · HOTEL €€
(☑22 640; www.hoteldiamanti.com; ul Morski Skali; d/apt 80/120 lv; ⊖❋⊗⊛) Another Old Town hotel, Diamanti has a variety of rooms, some with sea views, including apartments with kitchenettes. Larger apartments are available in a second building nearby. There's also a terrace restaurant with live music in summer.

Sasha Khristov's Private Rooms · PENSION €
(☑23 434; ul Venets 17; s/d 20/30 lv) This lovely family home in the Old Town faces the art gallery at the end of the Sozopol peninsula. It comprises good-sized rooms and a large apartment. Book ahead in summer.

✕ Eating

Fish, naturally enough, is the local speciality, and several reasonably priced restaurants are strung out along the port area. The best restaurants in town are on ul Morski Skali, and are large and traditional affairs with some spectacular views. The pedestrianised section of ul Ropotamo, alongside Harmanite Beach, is packed with cafes, restaurants and bars. They're all pretty much the same.

TOP CHOICE **Panorama**   SEAFOOD €€€

(ul Morski Skali 21; mains 8-20 lv) As the name suggests, this place has an open terrace with a fantastic view towards Sveti Ivan island. Fresh, locally caught fish is a mainstay of the menu, and service is quick and friendly.

Bizhou   SEAFOOD €€

(ul Kraybrezhna; mains 4-9 lv) This simple harbourside restaurant is good value, specialising in a variety of fresh fish dishes. Bulgarian staples such as *kebabcheta* (grilled minced meat with spices) and salads are also available.

❶ Information

Many banks with ATMs can be found along the Old Town's main streets and around the New Town's main square.

Post Office (ul Apolonia; ⊙7am-8.30pm)

Unicredit Bulbank (ul Lazuren Bryag)

❶ Getting There & Away

The small public **bus station** (ul Han Krum) is just south of the Old Town walls. Buses leave for Burgas (4.50 lv, 40 minutes) about every 30 minutes between 6am and 9pm in summer, and about once an hour in the low season.

In summer, hourly buses go to Primorsko (4.50 lv, 35 minutes). Public buses leave up to three times a day for Sofia.

Fast Ferry (⊘0877 908 004; www.fastferry. bg; Fishing Harbour) runs ferries at least four days a week to Nesebâr (single/return from 27/54 lv, 30 minutes) between June and September.

SOZOPOL TO TSAREVO

Just south of Sozopol, an inland road rambles past undeveloped Stork Beach (Alepu), a protected beach backed by marsh that sees thousands of storks in August. The bustling resort towns of Primorsko (22km south of Sozopol) and Kiten (5km further south) attract mostly Bulgarian holidaymakers; neither is that atmospheric, but both have fine beaches and plenty of midrange hotels.

TSAREVO   ЦАРЕВО

⊘0590 / POP 5800

Spread lazily over two small peninsulas jutting out into the Black Sea, Tsarevo is a quiet, elegant little town, once a popular holiday spot for the Bulgarian royal family. Called Vasiliko until 1934, it was renamed Tsarevo ('royal place') in honour of Tsar Boris III; the communists then renamed it Michurin (after a Soviet botanist) in 1950, and it reverted once again in 1991. The centre, on the northern peninsula, has a calm, affluent atmosphere and feels more like a real town than some of Tsarevo's resort neighbours.

◉ Sights

Overlooking the rocky headland at the end of the main road, ul Han Asparuh, are the peaceful Sea Gardens, offering dramatic panoramic views across the Black Sea. Other sights of interest include the Church of Sveti Tsar Boris-Mikhail, dedicated to the former king, and the tiny Church of the Holy Trinity, built in 1810 above the beach, accessed by steps on the northern side of the headland. It's a small but picturesque scrap of sand with a couple of bars.

Across the wide bay, the southern peninsula is of less interest, dominated by modern apartments and holiday homes, although the headland, reached by scrambling over rocks, has Tsarevo's best beach. Sadly, this is no secret cove, as it's also occupied by the giant Serenity Bay hotel.

⬛ Sleeping & Eating

Hotel Zebra   HOTEL €€

(⊘55 111; www.hotel-zebra.com; ul Han Asparuh 10; s/d Jul & Aug 60/76 lv, s/d Sep-Jun from 46/56 lv; ⓟ✳@☀) Near the Sea Gardens, this modern complex offers superb value. The large, comfortable rooms all have balconies and sparkling bathrooms, and there's an outdoor pool and restaurant.

Hotel Chaika   HOTEL €

(⊘0888 249 125; www.chaika.in; ul Han Asparuh 21; d 25-40 lv) In the centre of town, the Chaika is an older hotel which has been renovated. Most of the brightly painted rooms have balconies with sea views and are great value for this price.

Ribarska Sreshta   SEAFOOD €€

(mains 5-12 lv; ⊙7am-midnight; ☎) Fresh fish is on the menu at this harbourside restaurant, in a hotel of the same name.

❶ Getting There & Away

Tsarevo's bus station is at the top of ul Mikhail Gerdzhikov, about 2km west of the centre. Minibuses to Burgas (9 lv, 50 minutes) run roughly every 30 minutes to one hour between 6am and 8pm via Kiten and Primorsko, and there are two daily buses to Sofia (37 lv, eight hours).

NORTHWEST BULGARIA

Bulgaria's little horn – jutting up between Romania and Serbia – is a bit of a backwater that's way off the usual tourist trail. Curved to the northeast by the Danube, it has seen plenty of military struggles, and prehistoric forces have forged stunning rock formations and gorges that make for great hiking and rock climbing. The train from Sofia goes past impressive Iskâr Gorge, south of Mezdra.

Vidin   Видин

♪094 / POP 48,000

Resting on a bend in the Danube in the far northwest of Bulgaria, Vidin feels a long way from anywhere, and unless you're crossing into Romania, there's little obvious reason for you to make your way up here. The population has shrunk dramatically over the last decade or so, and it can appear forlorn and eerily deserted. Having said all that, Vidin does enjoy some fine riverside views and its one major attraction, the majestic Baba Vida fortress, is one of the best preserved in the country.

◎ Sights

Baba Vida Museum-Fortress   FORTRESS
(adult/student 4/2 lv, combined ticket with Archaeological Museum 5 lv; ⊗8.30am-5pm Mon-Fri, 9.30am-5pm Sat & Sun) About 1km north of the centre, the marvellously intact Baba Vida Museum-Fortress is largely a 17th-century Turkish upgrade of 10th-century Bulgarian fortifications, which in turn were built upon the ruins of the 3rd-century Roman fort of Bononia. There's little to see inside, but it's an atmospheric place. Watch out for uncovered holes and the sheer drops from the top.

Archaeological Museum   MUSEUM
(ul Tsar Simeon Veliki 12; adult/student 4/2 lv, combined ticket with Baba-Vida Fortress 5 lv; ⊗9am-noon & 1.30-5.30pm Tue-Sat) Inside the former Turkish prison, this little museum holds a scrappy collection of neolithic flints, Roman statue fragments, medieval swords and 19th-century rifles. There's no English labelling and it's only worth a quick look.

🛏 Sleeping

Anna-Kristina Hotel   HOTEL €€
(☑606 038; www.annakristinahotel.com; ul Baba Vida 2; d from 84 lv; P❈@≋) Housed inside a century-old Turkish bathhouse set back from the river, the Anna-Kristina is a wel-

coming, if slightly formal, place with spacious rooms and smart modern bathrooms. There's a summer-only outdoor pool (10 lv extra) and a restaurant.

Old Town Hotel   BOUTIQUE HOTEL €€
(Hotel Staryat Grad; ☑600 023; www.oldtownhotel. dir.bg; ul Knyaz Boris I 2; s/d/tr 60/80/100 lv; ❈🤖) Centrally located near the Old Town *Stambol Kapia* gateway, this charming boutique hotel has just eight rooms inside a renovated townhouse, fitted with antique-style furnishings and original works by local artists.

Hotel Bononia   HOTEL €
(☑606 031; www.hotelbononia.net; ul Bdin 2; s/d 36/39 lv; ❈) Just around the corner from the riverside park, the Bononia is an old-style hotel, though it offers acceptable rooms that are good value. It also has a decent restaurant.

✗ Eating & Drinking

Vidin has a few good restaurants and some cafes, though they're fairly subdued. The most popular are off the south side of the square before the Danube. There are no river views from most restaurants or cafes, thanks to the high river wall.

Classic Pizzeria   PIZZERIA €
(ul Aleksandar II 25; mains 5-15 lv) Opposite the Port Authority building on the riverbank, this is one of the better places in town, with a big menu of pizzas and pasta dishes, as well as locally caught fish.

❶ Information

Foreign exchange offices, banks and several ATMs line ul Tsar Simeon Veliki and pl Bdintsi.

❶ Getting There & Away

From Vidin's public **bus station** (ul Zhelezhnicharska) there are two or three daily buses to Belogradchik (5 lv, 1½ hours). Nearby is the private Alexiev bus station, from where there are several daily buses to Sofia (20 lv, four hours) via Vratsa (10 lv).

Three fast trains travel daily to Sofia (13.80 lv, five hours) via Vratsa (8 lv, three hours).

Belogradchik Белоградчик

♪0936 / POP 5150

The crisp mountain air and the weird and wonderful rock formations rising from a lonely hill are what draw visitors to little Belogradchik, on the eastern edge of the Stara Planina mountain range. Although rather remote, Belogradchik's charms are starting to attract more visitors.

👁 Sights

Belogradchik Rocks   OUTDOORS

The massive Belogradchik limestone rock formations cover an area of around 90 sq km and tower over the town. They are accessible by road, about 2km west of town. The tall, oddly shaped and variously hued rocks have inspired many local legends.

Kaleto Fortress   FORTRESS

(admission 4 lv; ⊙9am-6pm Jun-Sep, to 5pm Oct-May) Almost blending in with the surrounding rocks is the Kaleto Fortress, originally built by the Romans and later expanded by the Byzantines, Bulgarians and Turks. Most of what you see today was completed in the 1830s. You can wander round three courtyards and explore the defensive bunkers, while accessing the highest rocks involves a precarious climb up steep ladders.

History Museum   MUSEUM

(pl 1850 Leto; 1 lv; ⊙9am-noon & 2-5pm Mon-Fri) The history museum, housed in a National Revival–era building built in 1810, displays folk costumes, jewellery and traditional local crafts such as woodcarving and pottery.

🛏 Sleeping & Eating

Hotel Madona   GUESTHOUSE €

(📞65 546; www.madonainn-bg.com; ul Hristo Botev 26; s 20-30 lv, d 40-60 lv; 🛜) This cosy guesthouse has six traditional-style rooms, 600m up from the main square (it's signposted). The restaurant is one of the best in town, and guests can hire mountain bikes for 7 lv per day.

Hotel Castle Cottage   GUESTHOUSE €€

(📞0898 623 727; www.castlecottage.eu; ul Tsolo Todorov 36; s/d 35/70 lv; 🅿🛜) Standing not far from the fortress entrance, Castle Cottage is built in solid wood-and-stone traditional style. It offers one comfortable bedroom and two maisonettes, each individually designed, a log fire in winter and outdoor hot-tubs in summer.

Restaurant Elit   BULGARIAN €

(📞64 558; ul Yuri Gagarin 2; mains 4-6 lv; ⊙9am-midnight) Elit is one of a handful of restaurants in town, offering a variety of traditional Bulgarian dishes. It's an uphill walk (600m) up steep ul Vasil Levski and then off to the left.

ℹ Information

Tourist Information Centre (📞64 294; milena-tourist_centre@abv.bg; ul Poruchik Dvoryanov 5; ⊙9am-5pm Mon-Fri) Can help with accommodation and gives out maps.

ℹ Getting There & Away

From the **bus station** (📞63 427), three or four daily buses serve Vidin (5 lv, 1½ hours). A 6am bus serves Sofia (16 lv, four hours). The three daily buses that serve the train station, 9km away at Gara Oreshets (2 lv, 20 minutes), are timed to meet the Sofia-bound train. Several daily trains from Gara Oreshets serve Vidin (5 lv, 30 minutes), Vratsa (7 lv, 20 minutes) and Sofia (10 lv, three hours, 30 minutes).

A taxi from Belogradchik to Gara Oreshets train station costs 5 lv. For very early morning trains, taxis wait in front of the bus depot.

UNDERSTAND BULGARIA

History

Becoming Bulgaria

Thracians moved into the area of modern Bulgaria in around 5000 BC and Greek colonists from the south began settling cities on the Black Sea coast from the 7th century BC. By AD 100 Bulgaria was part of the Roman Empire. The first Slavs migrated here from the north in the 5th century AD and the first Bulgarian state was formed in AD 681.

The fierce Bulgars first reached these areas from their expansive territories between the Caspian and Black Seas. By the time the Byzantine Empire conquered Bulgaria in 1014, the first state had created a language, the Cyrillic alphabet and a national church. Bulgaria gained independence from Constantinople in 1185, and this second kingdom, based in Veliko Târnovo, lasted until the Ottomans took control in 1396.

Under the Ottomans

The next 500 years were spent living 'under the yoke' of Ottoman rule. The Orthodox Church persevered by quietly holing up in monasteries. Higher taxes for Christians saw many convert to Islam.

During the 18th and 19th centuries, many 'awakeners' are credited with reviving Bulgarian culture. By the 1860s several revolutionaries (including Vasil Levski and Hristo Botev) organised *cheti* (rebel) bands for the unsuccessful April Uprising of 1876. With Russia stepping in, the Turks were defeated in 1878, and Bulgaria regained its independence.

War & Communism

With eyes on lost Macedonia, following a series of painful Balkan Wars (including WWI), Bulgaria aligned with Nazi Germany in WWII with hopes to expand its borders. Famously, however, Tsar Boris III said 'no' to Hitler, refusing to send Bulgaria's Jewish population to concentration camps, sparing up to 50,000 lives.

Towards the end of the war, the communist Fatherland Front gained control of Bulgaria, and Georgi Dimitrov became the first leader of the People's Republic in 1946. The royal family was exiled. A program of rapid industrialisation and collectivisation followed and under Todor Zhivkov, the country's leader from 1954–89, Bulgaria became one of the most repressive of the Eastern Bloc regimes, and the most loyal of Russia's client states, even proposing to join the USSR in 1973.

Modern Bulgaria

The communists were finally ousted in 1989, although reforming as the Socialist Party, they were re-elected into office the following year. In 2001, history was made when the former king, Simeon II, was elected as Bulgaria's prime minister; the first former monarch to return to power in Eastern Europe. Bulgaria joined NATO in 2004 and the EU in 2007, but low wages, organised crime and corruption are sources of continual complaint and anguish. That anguish came to a head in 2013, when the government of Prime Minister Boyko Borisov was forced to resign in the face of economic stagnation and rising energy prices.

People

The population of Bulgaria is about 7.3 million, and continues to shrink – it has been estimated that 1.4 million people have left the country over the last 20 years. Bulgarians and Slavs constitute roughly 85% of the population, with the largest minorities being Turks (9%) and Roma (4.5%).

There are around 200,000 Pomaks – Muslims of Slavic origin – in the villages of the Rodopi Mountains, although many consider themselves to be ethnic Turks and others claim to be descended from ancient Balkan tribes converted by Arab missionaries a thousand years ago, but nobody knows for sure. There's also a small Jewish population of about 5000, mostly living in Sofia. During the communist era Bulgaria was officially atheist. These days, about 83% of the population are Orthodox Christian and 12% are Muslim (almost all of these are Sunni).

Arts

Music
FOLK MUSIC

The vaguely oriental sounds of Bulgarian folk music offer an evocative aural impression of the country. Traditional instruments include the *gaida* (bagpipes), *gadulka* (a bowed stringed instrument) and *kaval* (flute). As in many peasant cultures, Bulgarian women were not given access to musical instruments, so they usually performed the vocal parts. Bulgarian female singing is polyphonic, featuring many voices and shifting melodies, and women from villages in the Pirin Mountains are renowned for their unique singing style. Regular folk music and

---

VASIL LEVSKI

It's a name you'll see on street signs and public buildings in every Bulgarian town, and the matinee idol looks will soon become familiar from the countless moustachioed, gazing-into-the-distance statues across the country; a bit like Che Guevara but with neater hair. It's Vasil Levski, the 'Apostle of Freedom' and Bulgaria's undisputed national hero.

Born Vasil Ivanov Kunchev in Karlovo in 1837, Levski (a nickname meaning 'Lion') originally trained as a monk, but in 1862 fled to Belgrade to join the revolutionary fight against the Turks, led by Georgi Rakovski. A few years later he was back, travelling incognito around Bulgaria, setting up a network of revolutionary committees. Levski, who believed in the ideals of the French Revolution, was a charismatic and able leader of the independence movement, but he was captured in Lovech in December 1872 and hanged in Sofia in February 1873; the Levski Monument marks the spot where he died.

dance festivals are held around Bulgaria, and are great opportunities to experience the culture.

CONTEMPORARY SOUNDS

The most distinctive sound in Bulgarian contemporary music is the spirited, warbling, pop-folk idiom known as *chalga*. Influenced by Balkan, Turkish, Arabic and even flamenco rhythms, this is sexy, sweaty, repetitive dance music and is looked down on by many Bulgarians who consider it vulgar. Bands often feature a scantily clad female lead vocalist and play jazzed-up traditional Balkan tunes on instruments such as the electric guitar, clarinet and synthesiser. It's loud, brash and often self-consciously cheesy, and isn't to everyone's tastes, but there are plenty of clubs around Bulgaria that play little else, and it's hard to avoid on TV or radio. One of the biggest names in contemporary *chalga* is Azis, a gay, white-bearded, transvestite Roma.

Architecture

The most obvious product of the prodigious and creative Bulgarian National Revival era is the unique architectural style of homes seen throughout the country. These were either built side-by-side along narrow cobblestone streets, as in Plovdiv, or surrounded by pretty gardens, as in Arbanasi.

The wood-and-stone homes were usually painted brown and white (though some were more colourful), and featured bay windows and tiled roofs. Ceilings were often intricately carved and/or painted with bright murals and rooms would have several small fireplaces and low doors.

Architectural designs and styles of furniture differed from one region to another. The colour, shape and size of the typical home in Melnik contrasts significantly with those found in Arbanasi. Some of the most stunning examples of National Revival–period homes can also be appreciated in traditional villages such as Koprivshtitsa, Tryavna and Shiroka Lŭka. There are also examples among the Old Towns of Plovdiv and Veliko Tărnovo, and at the re-created Etâr Ethnographic Village Museum near Gabrovo.

Visual Arts

Most of Bulgaria's earliest artists painted on the walls of homes, churches and monasteries. The works of these anonymous masters are considered national treasures, and rare surviving examples can be seen in churches and museums across the country, including the lovely Boyana Church, near Sofia.

Throughout the Ottoman occupation, the tradition of icon painting endured as a symbol of national culture and identity. The highpoint for Bulgarian icon painting came during the National Revival period, and the most famous artist of the time was Zahari Zograf (1810–53), who painted magnificent murals in the monasteries at Rila, Troyan and Bachkovo.

Environment

Bulgaria lies in the heart of the Balkan peninsula, stretching 502km from the Serbian border to the 378km-long Black Sea coast.

Bulgaria is one-third mountains. The Stara Planina (also known as the Balkan Mountains) stretch across central Bulgaria. In the southwest are three higher ranges: the Rila Mountains, south of Sofia (home to the country's highest point, Mt Musala, 2925m); the Pirin Mountains, just south towards Greece; and the Rodopi Mountains to the east.

Although Bulgaria has some 56,000 kinds of living creature – including 400 bird species and one of Europe's largest bear populations –

CHANTS & CHURCH MUSIC

Bulgarian ecclesiastic music dates back to the 9th century and conveys the mysticism of chronicles, fables and legends. To hear Orthodox chants sung by a choir of up to 100 people is a moving experience. Dobri Hristov (1875–1941) was one of Bulgaria's most celebrated composers of church and choral music, and wrote his major choral work, *Liturgy No 1*, for the Seven Saints ensemble, Bulgaria's best-known sacred-music vocal group, based in Sofia's Sveti Sedmochislenitsi Church.

The Sofia Boys' Choir, formed in 1968, brings together boys from various schools in the capital, aged eight to 15, and has performed around the world to great acclaim. As well as their traditional Easter and Christmas concerts, they are known for their Orthodox choral music and folk songs.

THE INIMITABLE CHRISTO

The most famous living Bulgarian artist is Christo Javacheff, known simply as Christo. Born in Gabrovo in 1935, he studied at Sofia's Fine Arts Academy in the 1950s and met his French-born wife, Jeanne-Claude, in Paris in 1958.

They have worked in collaboration since 1961, when they created their first outdoor temporary installation, *Stacked Oil Barrels*, at Cologne Harbour. Since then, the couple, who moved to New York in 1964, have made a name for themselves with their (usually) temporary, large-scale architectural artworks, often involving wrapping famous buildings in fabric or polypropylene sheeting to highlight their basic forms.

In 1985 they created *The Pont Neuf Wrapped*, covering the Parisian landmark in golden fabric for 14 days, while in 1995 the *Reichstag* in Berlin was covered entirely with silver fabric, and in 2005, *The Gates* was unveiled in New York's Central Park; an impressive installation consisting of 7503 vinyl gates spread over 32km of walkways.

Christo and Jeanne-Claude are still working on major projects around the world, and current schemes still in the planning stage include *The Mastaba,* a gigantic stack of 410,000 multicoloured oil barrels – first conceived in 1977 – to be built in the desert in Abu Dhabi. For the latest, see www.christojeanneclaude.net.

BULGARIA FOOD & DRINK

most visitors see little wildlife, unless venturing deep into the thickets and mountains. Popular birdwatching spots near the Black Sea include Burgas Lakes, west of Burgas, and Durankulak Lake, near the Romanian border.

Bulgaria has three national parks (Rila, Pirin and Central Balkan) and 10 nature parks, all of which offer some protection to the environment (and have tourist potential). The EU has funded a number of projects to offer more protection, particularly along the Black Sea Coast and the Rodopi Mountains. Also see www.bulgariannationalparks.org.

Food & Drink

Fresh fruit, vegetables, dairy produce and grilled meat form the basis of Bulgarian cuisine, which has been heavily influenced by Greek and Turkish cookery. Pork and chicken are the most popular meats, while tripe also features heavily on traditional menus. You will also find recipes including duck, rabbit and venison, and fish is plentiful along the Black Sea coast, but less common elsewhere.

Staples & Specialities

Skara (grilled meats) especially pork, are among the most popular dishes served in Bulgarian restaurants, *mehana*s and snack bars. You can't escape the omnipresent *kebabche* (grilled spicy pork sausages) and *kyufte* (a round and flat pork burger), which are tasty, filling and cheap staples of Bulgarian menus, usually served with chips/fried potatoes *(pârzheni kartofi)* or salad. The *kyufte tatarsko,* a seasoned pork burger filled with melted cheese, is another variant. The Greek-influenced *musaka* (moussaka), made with minced pork or veal and topped with potatoes, is a quick lunchtime staple of cafeterias.

Shishcheta (shish kebabs), consisting of chunks of chicken or pork on wooden skewers with mushrooms and peppers, and various steaks, fillets and chops are widely available.

Meat stews and 'claypot meals' (hot, sizzling stews served in clay bowls) are traditional favourites. *Kavarma,* normally made with either chicken or pork, is one of the most popular dishes. Exact recipes vary from one region to the next, but the meat is cooked in a pot with vegetables, cheese and sometimes egg, and is brought sizzling to your table.

Drinks

Coffee is the beverage of choice for most Bulgarians, though tea is also popular. Most common are the herbal *(bilkov)* and fruit *(plodov)* variety; if you want real, black tea, ask for *cheren chai* and if you'd like milk, ask for *chai s'mlyako.*

The national spirit is *rakia* (a clear and potent kind of brandy, usually made from grapes), and there are countless brands available. It's drunk as an aperitif, and served with ice in restaurants and bars, which often devote a whole page on their menus to list regional *rakia*s on offer.

Bulgaria's excellent wines are a product of its varied climate zones, rich soil and proud tradition. Foreign interest and investment in recent years have made Bulgarian wines increasingly known and appreciated abroad. Wine-loving travellers can sample them at rustic wineries, in gourmet urban restaurants, and even at roadside stands.

SURVIVAL GUIDE

Directory A–Z

Accommodation

Bulgaria offers pretty much every kind of accommodation option you can think of, from spartan mountain huts to the most opulent five-star hotels. Accommodation is most expensive in Sofia and other big cities, notably Plovdiv and Varna. Elsewhere, prices are relatively cheap by Western European standards. If you're travelling independently around the country, one indispensable publication is the *Bulgaria B&B and Adventure Guidebook* (13.50 lv) published by the Bulgarian Association for Alternative Tourism (☏02-980 7685; www.baatbg.org; bul Stambolyiiski 20 B, Sofia), which lists sustainable, family-run guesthouses all over Bulgaria. You can buy it at Zig Zag Holidays (☏02-980 5102; www.zigzagbg. com; bul Stamboliyski 20-V; ☺9.30am-6.30pm Mon-Fri) in Sofia.

As you would expect, prices are highest in the coastal resorts between July and August, and in the skiing resorts from December to March. Outside high season, many resort hotels close down. So if you're thinking of staying in, for example, Pamporovo in September or Nesebâr in February, phone ahead to see what the situation is.

Several useful websites offer acccomodation information or online booking facilities.

BgStay (www.bgstay.com)

BG Globe (www.bgglobe.net)

Bulgaria Hotels (www.bulgaria-hotels.com)

Hotels in Bulgaria (www.hotels.bg)

Sofia Hotels (www.sofiahotels.net)

PRICE RANGES

The following price ranges refer to a double room with bathroom in high season. Unless otherwise stated, breakfast is included in the price.

$ less than 60 lv

$$ 60 lv to 120 lv (200 lv in Sofia)

$$$ more than 120 lv (200 lv in Sofia)

CAMPING & HUTS

Camping grounds normally consist of wooden cabins in a patch of forest and are usually quite simple, but cheap. Camping outside camping grounds is technically illegal and potentially dangerous.

Hizhas (mountain huts) dot the high country and range in quality – they are shown on most Bulgaria maps. Most are basic places intended only for a one-night stopover. Many are now privately run (and cost about 10 lv to 30 lv per person); some more remote ones are free. In July and August, you may wish to reserve ahead at an agency.

PRIVATE ROOMS

Travellers on a budget can rent *stai pod naem* (private rooms), often offered by agencies or private individuals at train and bus stations. Rates range from 10 lv or 15 lv per person in smaller towns, to 35 lv or more in places such as Sofia, Plovdiv and Varna. Cheaper places tend to be far from the city centre.

Activities

All kinds of outdoor activities are catered for in Bulgaria, with hiking, biking, mountaineering, rock climbing, diving and skiing being just some of the sports available. The country is promoted as a growing ski destination, with new resorts in the Pirin mountains, while the country's unspoilt, mountainous terrain makes it ideal for trekking and hiking, with numerous well-marked trails and a system of mountain huts, or *hizhas,* for hikers to sleep in. Water sports are popular on the Black Sea coast, although these tend to be confined to the big package-holiday resorts. Windsurfing, paragliding, scuba diving and a host of other watery activities can be arranged during summer.

Cycling Bulgaria (www.cycling.bg) Multiday mountain-bike tours.

Hiking in Bulgaria (www.bghike.com) Guided hiking trips.

Neophron (www.birdwatchingbulgaria.net) Runs 10- to 14-day guided birdwatching trips across the country, which can be combined with botany and bearwatching tours.

Business Hours

Banks 9am to 4pm Monday to Friday

Bars 11am to midnight (or later)

Government offices 9am to 5pm Monday to Friday

Post offices 8am to 6pm Monday to Friday

Restaurants 11am to 11pm

Shops 9am to 6pm

Discount Cards

International Student (ISIC, www.isic.org), Youth (IYTC) and Teacher (ITIC) discount cards can be used in Bulgaria, offering a range of discounts on transport, accommodation, restaurants, shopping, entertainment venues and tourist attractions. Cards may be bought in Bulgaria at branches of the Usit Colours travel agency (www.usit-colours.bg). Check online for current details and for participating companies.

Embassies & Consulates

New Zealanders can turn to the British embassy for assistance or contact their consulate general in Athens. Embassies are located in Sofia.

Australian Embassy (☏02-946 1334; austcon@mail.orbitel.bg; ul Trakia 37; ☐78)

Canadian Embassy (☏02-969 9710; general@canada-bg.org; ul Moskovska 9; ☐20)

French Embassy (☏02-965 1100; www.ambafrance-bg.org; ul Oborishte 27-29; ☐1)

German Embassy (☏02-918 380; www.sofia.diplo.de; ul Frederic Joliot-Curie 25; Ⓜ Joliot-Curie)

Irish Embassy (☏02-985 3425; www.embassyofireland.bg; ul Bacho Kiro 26-30; ☐20)

Netherlands Embassy (☏02-816 0300; http://bulgaria.nlembassy.org; ul Oborishte 15; 20)

Turkish Embassy (☏02-935 5500; www.sofia.emb.mfa.gov.tr; bul Vasil Levski 80; ☐94)

UK Embassy (☏02-933 9222; www.ukinbulgaria.fco.gov.uk; ul Moskovksa 9; ☐20)

US Embassy (☏02-937 5100; http://bulgaria.usembassy.gov; ul Kozyak 16; ☐88)

Food

Eating out in Bulgaria is remarkably cheap, and even if you're on a tight budget, you'll have no problem eating well. In this book, we've used the following price ranges (price of a typical main course):

€ less than 5 lv

€€ 5 lv to 10 lv

€€€ more than 10 lv

Gay & Lesbian Travellers

Homosexuality is legal in Bulgaria, though same-sex relationships have no legal recognition.

Bulgaria is conservative and opinion polls suggest a majority of Bulgarians have a negative opinion of homosexuality. Attitudes among younger people are slowly changing, and there are a few gay clubs and bars in Sofia and in other major cities.

Bulgayria (www.gay.bg)

Gay Bulgaria Ultimate Gay Guide (www.gay-bulgaria.info)

Gay Guide Bulgaria (www.gayguidebg.org)

Sofia Pride (www.sofiapride.info)

Internet Access

Wi-fi access is common in towns and cities, and is often free in hotels and restaurants. Hostels often have computers for guest use. Internet cafes have become less common in recent years, but most big towns will have at least one.

Legal Matters

Bulgaria is a member of the EU and follows the same legal system as the rest of Europe. You need to be 21 years old to rent a car and 18 or over to drink alcohol.

Money

The currency is the lev (plural: leva), comprised of 100 stotinki. It is usually abbreviated as lv. The lev is a stable currency. For major purchases such as organised tours, airfares, car rental, and midrange and top-end hotels, prices are often quoted in euros, though payment is usually made in leva. Bulgaria has no immediate plans to adopt the euro.

CASH

Bulgarian banknotes come in denominations of 2, 5, 10, 20, 50 and 100 leva. Coins come in 1, 2, 5, 10, 20 and 50 stotinki, and 1 lev.

CHANGING MONEY

Foreign-exchange offices can be found in all larger towns and current rates are always displayed prominently. Charging commission is no longer allowed, but that doesn't stop some from trying; always check the final amount you will be offered before handing over your cash. Avoid exchange offices at train stations, airports or tourist resorts as rates tend to be poor.

The best currencies to take to Bulgaria are euros, pounds sterling and US dollars. You may have trouble changing less-familiar currencies, such as Australian or Canadian dollars.

It's also easy to exchange cash at most of the larger banks in cities and major towns; the exchange rates listed on the electronic boards in bank windows may offer slightly higher rates than foreign exchange offices, but they may charge a commission.

CREDIT CARDS

Credit cards are commonly accepted in hotels, restaurants and shops in big cities, towns and tourist resorts, but acceptance is less widespread in rural areas. Some places, particularly the more expensive hotels, will add a 5% surcharge to your bill if you use a credit card.

TIPPING

In restaurants, round bills up to the nearest whole lev or tip 10% of the bill to reward good service. The same applies to taxi drivers.

Public Holidays

New Year's Day 1 January

Liberation Day (National Day) 3 March

Orthodox Easter Sunday & Monday March/April; one week after Catholic/Protestant Easter

May Day 1 May

St George's Day 6 May

Cyrillic Alphabet Day 24 May

Unification Day (National Day) 6 September

Bulgarian Independence Day 22 September

National Revival Day 1 November

Christmas 25 and 26 December

Safe Travel

You're unlikely to face major problems in Bulgaria. Pickpocketing or beach grab-and-runs can happen in summer, particularly on Varna's beach. There are plenty of rogue taxi drivers waiting to rip off foreigners; always use a reputable firm and if possible ask your hotel to call your cab.

Telephone

To call Bulgaria from abroad, dial the international access code, add ☎359 (the country code for Bulgaria), the area code (minus the first zero) and then the number.

MOBILE PHONES

Bulgarian mobile phones use the GSM 900/1800 network, the standard throughout Europe as well as in Australia and New Zealand, but not compatible with most mobile phones in North America or Japan. One possibility is to bring or buy an unlocked handset operating on this GSM band and purchase a local SIM card. Bulgaria has three mobile service providers which cover most of the country: **Globul** (www.globul.bg), **M-Tel** (www.mtel.bg) and **Vivacom** (www.vivacom.bg).

Mobile phone numbers can be identified by the prefixes ☎087, ☎088 or ☎089.

PHONECARDS

Prepaid phonecards for use in public telephones are available from newspaper kiosks and some shops in denominations ranging from 5 lv to 25 lv.

Travellers with Disabilities

Bulgaria is not an easy destination for travellers with disabilities. Uneven and broken footpaths are common in towns and wheelchair-accessible toilets and ramps are rare outside the more expensive hotels.

Visas

Citizens of other EU countries, as well as Australia, Canada, New Zealand, the USA and many other countries do not need a visa for stays of up to 90 days. Other nationals should contact the Bulgarian embassy in their home countries for current visa requirements.

Getting There & Away

Bulgaria is well connected by air, rail and road. Flights, tours and rail tickets can be booked online at lonelyplanet.com/bookings.

Entering the Country

Bulgaria is a member of the EU, though (as of this writing) not yet a member of the EU's common border and customs Schengen Zone. In practice, this means all border crossings, even with EU-member Romania, are subject to passport and customs inspection.

Air

AIRPORTS

The Bulgarian national carrier is **Bulgaria Air** (www.air.bg). It operates flights to destinations across Europe and the Middle East as well as domestic routes to the Black Sea coast.

Sofia Airport (☎02-937 2211; www.sofia-air-port.bg) Main point of entry to the country.

Varna Airport (www.varna-airport.bg; ☎409) Domestic flights and seasonal flights to/from European destinations.

Burgas Airport (☎870 248; www.bourgas-airport.com; ☎15) Summer charter flights.

AIRLINES

Aegean Airlines (www.aegeanair.com)

Aeroflot (☎943 4489; www.aeroflot.ru)

Aerosvit (☎980 7880; www.aerosvit.com)

Air Berlin (www.airberlin.com)

Air France (☎939 7010; www.airfrance.com)

Alitalia (☎981 6702; www.alitalia.it)

British Airways (☎954 7000; www.britishair-ways.com)

Cyprus Airways (www.cyprusair.com)

easyJet (www.easyjet.com)

Lufthansa Airlines (☎930 4242; www.lufthansa.com)

Tarom (www.tarom.ro)

Turkish Airlines (☎988 3596; www.turkishair-lines.com)

Wizz Air (☎960 3888; www.wizzair.com)

Land

BUS

Most international buses arrive in Sofia. You will have to get off the bus at the border and walk through customs to present your passport. When travelling out of Bulgaria by bus, the cost of entry visas for the countries concerned are not included in the prices of the bus tickets.

CAR & MOTORCYCLE

» In order to drive on Bulgarian roads, you will need to purchase a vignette, sold at all border crossings into Bulgaria, petrol stations and post offices. For a car, this costs 10/25 lv for one week/month.

» Your home driving licence is valid in Bulgaria for short-term stays.

» Petrol stations and car-repair shops are common around border crossing areas and along main roads.

TRAIN

There are a number of international trains from Bulgaria, including services to Roma-nia, Greece and Turkey. Sofia is the main hub, although trains stop at other towns. The daily *TransBalkan,* running between Budapest and Thessaloniki, stops at Ruse, Gorna Oryakhovitsa (near Veliko Tărnovo) and Sofia. The *Balkan Express* normally goes daily between Belgrade and İstanbul, with stops in Sofia and Plovdiv. The *Bulgaria Express* to Bucharest leaves from Sofia.

Tickets for international trains can be bought at any government-run **Rila Bureau** (www.bdz-rila.com; ⊗closed most Sun) or at some dedicated ticket offices (most open daily) at larger stations with international connections.

River & Sea

International sea travel to/from Bulgaria is limited to commercial cargo vessels. The **UKR Shipping Company** (www.ukrferry.com) runs cargo ships between Varna and Ilyichevsk in Ukraine, and also accepts individual passengers. Check the website for current arrangements and prices. There are car-ferry crossings to Romania at Vidin, Oryahovo and Nikopol.

Getting Around
Air

The only scheduled domestic flights within Bulgaria are between Sofia and Varna and Sofia and Burgas. Both routes are operated by **Bulgaria Air** (www.air.bg).

Bicycle

» Many roads are in poor condition; some major roads are always choked with traffic and bikes aren't allowed on highways.
» Many trains will carry your bike for an extra 2 lv.
» Cycling is a more attractive option in the Black Sea resorts, where there are plenty of places renting out bikes. Spare parts are available in cities and major towns, but it's better to bring your own.

Bus

Buses link all cities and major towns and connect villages with the nearest transport hub. There are several private companies operating frequent modern, comfortable buses between the larger towns, while older, often cramped minibuses also run on routes between smaller towns.

DECODING YOUR TRAIN TICKET

All tickets are printed in Cyrillic. Other than the place of departure and destination, tickets also contain other important details:

» Клас *klas* – '1' (1st class) or '2' (2nd class)

» Категория *kategoriya* – type of train, ie T (express), 255 (fast) or G (slow passenger)

» Влак *vlak* – train number

» Час *chas* – departure time

» Дата *data* – date of departure

» Вагон *vagon* – carriage number

» Място *myasto* – seat number

Union-Ivkoni (☎02-989 0000; www.union-ivkoni.bg) Links most major towns and many smaller ones.

Biomet (☎02-868 8961; www.biomet.bg) Runs between Sofia and Veliko Tärnovo, Varna and Burgas.

Etap-Grup (☎02-813 3100; www.etapgroup.com) Buses between Sofia, Burgas, Varna, Ruse and Veliko Tärnovo, as well as routes between Sofia and Sozopol, Primorsko and Tsarevo.

Car & Motorcycle

Bulgaria's roads are among the most dangerous in Europe and the level of fatalities each year is high. The worst time is the holiday season (July to September), with drink-driving, speeding and poor road conditions contributing to accidents.

The **Union of Bulgarian Motorists** (☎02-935 7935, road assistance 02-980 3308; www.uab.org; pl Positano 3, Sofia) offers 24-hour road assistance and has some helpful basic information on its website.

ROAD RULES

» Drive on the right.

» Drivers and passengers in the front must wear seat belts; motorcyclists must wear helmets.

» Blood-alcohol limit is 0.05%.

» Children under 12 are not allowed to sit in front.

» From November to March, headlights must be on at all times.

» Speed limits are 50km/h in built-up areas, 90km/h on main roads and 120km/h om motorways.

CAR HIRE

To rent a car in Bulgaria you must be at least 21 years of age and have had a licence for at least one year. Rental outlets can be found all over Bulgaria, especially in the bigger cities, airports and Black Sea resorts. Prices start at around 50 lv to 60 lv per day. You'll need a valid credit card.

Train

Bălgarski Dârzhavni Zheleznitsi – the **Bulgarian State Railways** (BDZh; www.bdz.bg) – boasts an impressive 4278km of track across the country, linking most towns and cities.

Most trains tend to be antiquated and not especially comfortable, and journey times slower than buses. On the plus side you'll have more room in a train compartment and the scenery is likely to be more rewarding.

Trains are classified as *ekspresen* (express), *bârz* (fast) or *pâtnicheski* (slow passenger). Unless you absolutely thrive on train travel or want to visit a more remote town, use a fast or express train.

Two of the most spectacular train trips are along Iskâr Gorge, from Sofia to Mezdra, and on the narrow-gauge track between Septemvri and Bansko.

Croatia

Why Go?

Croatia has been touted as the 'new this' and the 'new that' for years since its re-emergence on the tourism scene, but it's now clear that it's a unique destination that holds its own and then some: this is a country with a glorious 1778km-long coast and a staggering 1244 islands. The Adriatic coast is a knockout: its sapphire waters draw visitors to remote islands, hidden coves and traditional fishing villages, all while touting the glitzy beach and yacht scene. Istria captivates with its gastronomic delights and wines, and the bars, clubs and festivals of Zagreb, Zadar and Split remain little-explored gems. Eight national parks showcase primeval beauty with their forests, mountains, rivers, lakes and waterfalls. and you can finish up in dazzling Dubrovnik in the south – just the right finale. Best of all, Croatia hasn't given in to mass tourism: there are pockets of unique culture and plenty to discover off the grid.

Best Places to Eat

» Vinodol (p182)
» Konoba Batelina (p190)
» Foša (p203)
» Bajamonti (p209)

Best Places to Stay

» Studio Kairos (p181)
» Goli + Bosi (p208)
» Art Hotel Kalelarga (p203)
» Lešić Dimitri Palace (p215)

When to Go

Zagreb

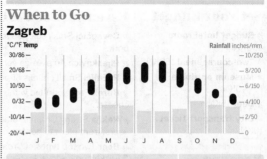

May & Sep Good weather, few tourists, full local events calendar, great for hiking	Jun Best time to visit: good weather, fewer people, lower prices and lots of festivals.	Jul–Aug Lots of sunshine, warm sea and summer festivals; many tourists and highest prices.

AT A GLANCE

» **Currency** Kuna (KN)

» **Language** Croatian

» **Money** ATMs available; credit cards accepted in most hotels and many restaurants

» **Visas** None for up to 90 days; South Africans and some other nationalities need them

Fast Facts

» **Area** 56,538 sq km

» **Capital** Zagreb

» **Country code** ☏385

» **Emergency** Ambulance ☏194, fire ☏193, police ☏192

Exchange Rates

Australia	A$1	6.21KN
Canada	C$1	5.85KN
Euro Zone	€1	7.60KN
Japan	¥100	6.30KN
New Zealand	NZ$1	4.97KN
UK	UK£1	8.99KN
USA	US$1	5.94KN

Set Your Budget

» **Budget hotel room** 450KN

» **Two-course meal** 150KN

» **Museum entrance** 10–40KN

» **Beer** 15KN

» **City transport ticket** 10KN

Resources

» **Adriatica.net** (www.adriatica.net)

» **Croatian National Tourist Board** (www.croatia.hr)

Connections

Croatia is a convenient transport hub for southeastern Europe and the Adriatic. Zagreb is connected by train and/or bus to Venice, Budapest, Belgrade, Ljubljana and Sarajevo in Bosnia and Hercegovina (BiH). Down south there are easy bus connections from Dubrovnik to Mostar and Sarajevo, and to Kotor (Montenegro). There are a number of ferries linking Croatia with Italy, including routes from Dubrovnik to Bari, and Split to Ancona.

ITINERARIES

One Week

After a day in dynamic Zagreb, delving into its simmering nightlife, fine restaurants and choice museums, head down to Split for a day and night at Diocletian's Palace, a living part of this exuberant seafront city. Then hop over to chic Hvar for a spot of partying and swimming off Pakleni Otoci. Next take it easy down the winding coastal road to magnificent Dubrovnik and take a day trip to Mljet for the final two days.

Two Weeks

After two days in Zagreb, head to Istria for a three-day stay, with Rovinj as the base, and day trips to Pula and Poreč. Go southeast next to the World Heritage–listed Plitvice Lakes National Park, a verdant maze of turquoise lakes and cascading waterfalls. After a quick visit, move on to Zadar, a real find of a city: historic, modern, active and packed with attractions. Then go on south to Split for a day or two. From here, take ferries to Hvar and then Korčula, spending a day or more on each island before ending with three days in Dubrovnik and an outing to Mljet.

Essential Food & Drink

» **Ćevapčići** Small spicy sausages of minced beef, lamb or pork.

» **Pljeskavica** An ex-Yugo version of a hamburger.

» **Ražnjići** Small chunks of pork grilled on a skewer.

» **Burek** Pastry stuffed with ground meat, spinach or cheese.

» **Rakija** Strong Croatian brandy comes in different flavours, from plum to honey.

» **Beer** Two top types of Croatian *pivo* (beer) are Zagreb's Ožujsko and Karlovačko from Karlovac.

ZAGREB

01 / POP 792,900

Everyone knows about Croatia's coast and islands, but a mention of the country's capital still draws the confused question: 'Is it worth visiting?' Here is the answer: Zagreb is a great destination, with lots of culture, arts, music, architecture, gastronomy and all the other things that make a quality capital.

Visually, Zagreb is a mixture of straight-laced Austro-Hungarian architecture and rough-around-the-edges socialist structures, its character a sometimes uneasy combination of these two elements. This mini metropolis is made for strolling the streets, drinking coffee in the permanently full cafes, popping into museums and galleries, and enjoying the theatres, concerts and cinema. It's a year-round outdoor city: in spring and summer everyone scurries to Jarun Lake in the southwest to swim, boat or dance the night away at lakeside discos, while in autumn and winter Zagrebians go skiing at Mt Medvednica, only a tram ride away, or hiking in nearby Samobor.

History

Zagreb's known history begins in medieval times with two hill settlements: Kaptol, now the site of Zagreb's cathedral, and Gradec. When the two merged in 1850, Zagreb was officially born.

The space now known as Trg Josipa Jelačića became the site of Zagreb's lucrative trade fairs, spurring construction around its edges. In the 19th century the economy expanded and cultural life blossomed with the development of a prosperous clothing trade and a rail link connecting Zagreb with Vienna and Budapest.

Between the two world wars, working-class neighbourhoods emerged in Zagreb between the railway and the Sava River, and new residential quarters were built on the southern slopes of Mt Medvednica. In April 1941, the Germans invaded Yugoslavia and entered Zagreb without resistance. Ante Pavelić and the Ustaše moved quickly to proclaim the establishment of the Independent State of Croatia (Nezavisna Država Hrvatska), with Zagreb as its capital.

In postwar Yugoslavia, Zagreb (to its chagrin) took second place to Belgrade but continued to expand. Zagreb was made the capital of Croatia in 1991, the same year that the country became independent.

Sights

As the oldest part of Zagreb, the Upper Town (Gornji Grad) offers landmark buildings and churches from the earlier centuries of Zagreb's history. The Lower Town (Donji Grad) has the city's most interesting art museums and fine examples of 19th- and 20th-century architecture.

UPPER TOWN

Museum of Broken Relationships   MUSEUM
(http://brokenships.com; Ćirilometodska 2; adult/concession 25/20KN; ⊙9am-10.30pm Jun–mid-Oct, 9am-9pm mid-Oct–May) Explore mementos that remain after a relationship ends at Zagreb's quirkiest museum. On display are donations from around the globe, in a string of all-white rooms with vaulted ceilings. Exhibits hit on a range of emotions, from a can of love incense from Indiana that 'doesn't work' to an iron from Norway once used to straighten a wedding suit. Check out the adjacent store and the cosy cafe with sidewalk tables.

Dolac Market   MARKET
(⊙7am-3pm Mon-Fri, to 2pm Sat, to 1pm Sun) Zagreb's colourful Dolac is just north of Trg Josipa Jelačića. This buzzing centre of Zagreb's daily activity since the 1930s draws in traders from all over Croatia who flog their products here. The main part of the market is on an elevated square; the street level has indoor stalls selling meat and dairy products and, towards the square, flower stands.

Cathedral of the Assumption
of the Blessed Virgin Mary   CATHEDRAL
(Katedrala Marijina Uznešenja; Kaptol; ⊙10am-5pm Mon-Sat, 1-5pm Sun) Kaptol Sq is dominated by the twin neo-Gothic spires of this 1899 cathedral, formerly known as St Stephen's. Elements of an earlier medieval cathedral, destroyed by an earthquake in 1880, can be seen inside, including 13th-century frescoes, Renaissance pews, marble altars and a baroque pulpit. Note that you might be turned away if you're not dressed appropriately: no bare legs or shoulders.

Lotrščak Tower   HISTORICAL BUILDING
(Kula Lotrščak; Strossmayerovo Šetalište 9; adult/concession 10/5KN; ⊙9am-9pm) From Radićeva 5, off Trg Jelačića, a pedestrian walkway called Zakmardijeve Stube leads to this medieval tower, which can be climbed for a sweeping 360-degree view of the city.

Croatia Highlights

1 Gape at the Old Town wall of **Dubrovnik** (p218), which surrounds luminous marble streets and finely ornamented buildings.

2 Admire the Venetian architecture and vibrant nightlife of **Hvar Town** (p212).

3 Indulge in the lively and historic delights of **Diocletian's Palace** (p204) in Split.

4 Explore the lakes, coves and island monastery of **Mljet** (p216).

5 Stroll the cobbled streets and unspoiled fishing port of **Rovinj** (p191).

6 Take in the wild landscapes of **Rt Kamenjak** (p189) cape near Pula.

7 Marvel at the turquoise lakes and waterfalls in **Plitvice Lakes National Park** (p188).

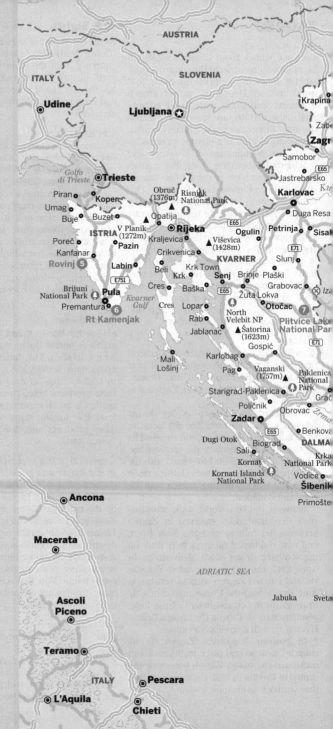

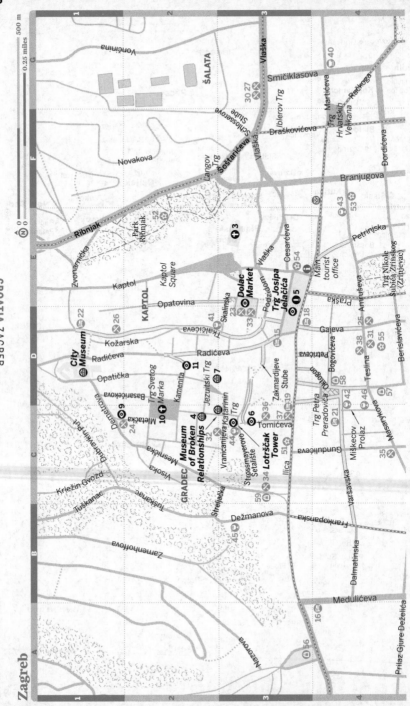

Zagreb

CROATIA ZAGREB

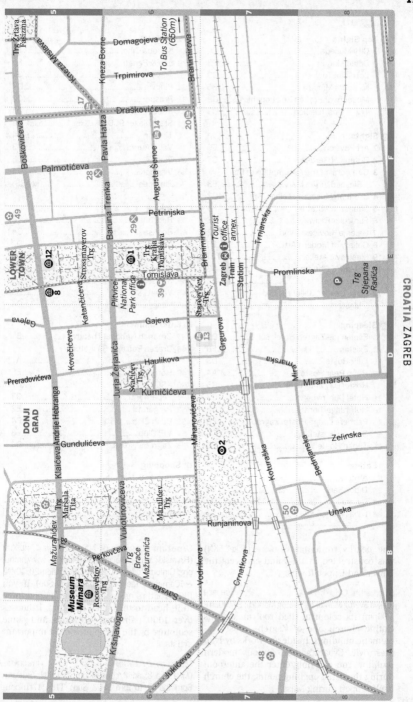

CROATIA ZAGREB

Zagreb

◉ Top Sights

City Museum	D1
Dolac Market	E3
Lotrščak Tower	C3
Museum Mimara	B5
Museum of Broken Relationships	C2
Trg Josipa Jelačića	D3

◉ Sights

1	Art Pavilion	E6
2	Botanical Garden	C7
3	Cathedral of the Assumption of the Blessed Virgin Mary	E3
4	Croatian Museum of Naïve Art	C2
5	Equestrian Statue	E3
6	Funicular Railway	C3
7	Galerija Klovićevi Dvori	D2
8	Gallery of Modern Art	E5
9	Meštrović Atelier	C1
10	St Mark's Church	C2
11	Stone Gate	D2
12	Strossmayer Gallery of Old Masters	E5

◉ Sleeping

13	Esplanade Zagreb Hotel	D6
14	Evistas	F6
15	Fulir Hostel	D3
16	Hobo Bear Hostel	A4
17	Hostel Day and Night	G5
18	Hotel Dubrovnik	D3
19	Hotel Jägerhorn	C3
20	Palmers Lodge Hostel Zagreb	F6
21	Shappy Hostel	C4
22	Taban Hostel	D1

◉ Eating

23	Amfora	D3
24	Didov San	C1
25	Dinara	D4
26	Ivica i Marica	D1
27	Karijola	G3
28	Konoba Čiho	F5
29	Lari & Penati	E6
30	Mali Bar	G3
31	Pingvin	D4
32	Prasac	C2
33	Rubelj	D3
34	Stari Fijaker 900	C3
35	Tip Top	C4
36	Vallis Aurea	C3
37	Vincek	C3
38	Vinodol	D4
	Zinfandel's	(see 13)

◉ Drinking

39	Bacchus	E6
40	Booksa	G4
41	Cica	D2
42	Kino Europa	D4
43	Kolaž	E4
44	Stross	C3
45	Velvet	B3
46	Vimpi	C4

◉ Entertainment

47	Croatian National Theatre	B5
48	Dražen Petrović Basketball Centre	A7
49	Hotpot	E5
50	KSET	B7
51	Pepermint	C3
52	Purgeraj	E2
53	Rush Club	F4
54	VIP Club	E3
55	Zagrebačko Kazalište Mladih	D4

◉ Shopping

56	Antiques Market	A3
57	Natura Croatica	D4
58	Profil Megastore	D4
59	Prostor	C3

The nearby **funicular railway** (ticket 5KN) was constructed in 1888 and connects the Lower and Upper Towns.

St Mark's Church CHURCH
(Crkva Svetog Marka; Trg Svetog Marka 5; ⏰7.30am-6.30pm) Its colourful tiled roof makes this Gothic church one of Zagreb's most emblematic buildings. Inside are works by Ivan Meštrović, Croatia's most famous modern sculptor. You can only enter the anteroom during the listed opening hours; the church itself is open during Mass.

Croatian Museum of Naïve Art MUSEUM
(Hrvatski Muzej Naivne Umjetnosti; www.hmnu.org; Ćirilometodska 3; adult/concession 20/10KN; ⏰10am-6pm Tue-Fri, to 1pm Sat & Sun) If you like Croatia's naïve art or want a good intro to it, head to this small museum. It houses over 1000 paintings, drawings and some sculpture by the discipline's most important artists.

Meštrović Atelier ARTS CENTRE
(Mletačka 8; adult/concession 30/15KN; ⏰10am-6pm Tue-Fri, to 1pm Sat & Sun) This 17th-cen-

tury building, the former home of Croatia's most recognised artist, Ivan Meštrović, now houses an excellent collection of some 100 sculptures, drawings, lithographs and pieces of furniture created by the artist.

City Museum MUSEUM
(Muzej Grada Zagreba; www.mgz.hr; Opatička 20; adult/concession 30/20KN; ☺10am-6pm Tue-Fri, 11am-7pm Sat, 10am-2pm Sun; ⊞) Check out the scale model of old Gradec, atmospheric background music and interactive exhibits that fascinate kids. There are summaries in English in each room of the museum, which is in the former Convent of St Claire (1650).

Galerija Klovićevi Dvori ART GALLERY
(www.galerijaklovic.hr; Jezuitski trg 4; adult/concession 30/20KN; ☺11am-7pm Tue-Sun) Housed in a former Jesuit monastery, this is the city's most prestigious space for exhibiting modern Croatian and international art. Note that the gallery closes in summer months.

Stone Gate LANDMARK
Make sure you take a peek at this eastern gate to medieval Gradec Town, now a shrine. According to legend, a great fire in 1731 destroyed every part of the wooden gate except for the painting of the *Virgin and Child* by an unknown 17th-century artist.

LOWER TOWN

Trg Josipa Jelačića SQUARE
Zagreb's main orientation point and the geographic heart of the city is Trg Josipa Jelačića. It has an **equestrian statue** of Jelačić, the 19th-century *ban* (viceroy or governor) who led Croatian troops into an unsuccessful battle with Hungary in the hope of winning more autonomy for his peo-

ple. The square is Zagreb's principal meeting point; sit in one of the cafes for quality people-watching.

Museum Mimara MUSEUM
(Muzej Mimara; www.mimara.hr; Rooseveltov trg 5; adult/concession 40/30KN; ☺10am-7pm Tue-Fri, to 5pm Sat, to 2pm Sun Jul-Sep, 10am-5pm Tue-Wed & Fri-Sat, to 7pm Thu, to 2pm Sun Oct-Jun) Ante Topić Mimara donated his diverse collection to Croatia. Housed in a neo-Renaissance palace, it includes icons, glassware, sculpture, Oriental art and works by renowned painters such as Rembrandt, Velázquez, Raphael and Degas.

Strossmayer Gallery of Old Masters MUSEUM
(Strossmayerova Galerija Starih Majstora; Trg Nikole Šubića Zrinskog 11; adult/concession 30/10KN; ☺10am-7pm Tue, to 4pm Wed-Fri, to 1pm Sat & Sun) Inside the neo-Renaissance Croatian Academy of Arts and Sciences, this gallery showcases the impressive fine-art collection donated to Zagreb by Bishop Strossmayer in 1884. The interior courtyard has the **Baška Slab** (1102) from Krk Island, one of the oldest inscriptions in the Croatian language.

Art Pavilion ART GALLERY
(Umjetnički Paviljon; www.umjetnicki-paviljon.hr; Trg Kralja Tomislava 22; adult/concession 30/15KN; ☺11am-7pm Tue-Sat, 10am-1pm Sun Sep–mid-Jul) The yellow Art Pavilion in a stunning 1897 art nouveau building presents changing exhibitions of contemporary art.

Gallery of Modern Art ART GALLERY
(Moderna Galerija; www.moderna-galerija.hr; Andrije Hebranga 1; adult/concession 40/20KN; ☺11am-6pm Tue-Fri, to 1pm Sat & Sun) With a glorious

CROATIA ZAGREB

ZAGREB IN TWO DAYS

Start your day with a stroll through Strossmayerov trg, Zagreb's oasis of greenery. Take a look at the **Strossmayer Gallery of Old Masters** and then walk to **Trg Josipa Jelačića**, the city's centre.

Head up to Kaptol Square for a look at the **Cathedral**, the centre of Zagreb's religious life. While in the Upper Town, pick up some fruit at **Dolac market** or have lunch at **Amfora**. Then get to know the work of Croatia's best sculptor at **Meštrović Atelier** and see his naïve-art legacy at the **Croatian Museum of Naïve Art**, followed by a visit to the quirky **Museum of Broken Relationships**. See the lay of the city from the top of **Lotrščak Tower**, then spend the evening bar-crawling along Tkalčićeva.

On the second day, tour the Lower Town museums, reserving an hour for the **Museum Mimara** and as long for the **Museum of Contemporary Art**. Lunch at **Vinodol** and digest in the **Botanical Garden**. Early evening is best at Preradovićev trg before dining and sampling some of Zagreb's nightlife.

display of Croatian artists of the last 200 years, this gallery offers an excellent overview of Croatia's vibrant arts scene.

Botanical Garden
GARDENS

(Botanički Vrt; Mihanovićeva bb; ☺9am-2.30pm Mon & Tue, 9am-7pm Wed-Sun Apr-Oct) Laid out in 1890, the garden has 10,000 plant species, including 1800 tropical flora specimens. The landscaping has created restful corners and paths that seem a world away from bustling Zagreb.

OUTSIDE THE CENTRE

Museum of Contemporary Art
MUSEUM

(Muzej Suvremene Umjetnosti; www.msu.hr; Avenija Dubrovnik 17; adult/concession 30/15KN, 1st Wed of month free; ☺11am-6pm Tue-Fri & Sun, to 8pm Sat) Housed in a dazzling new city icon designed by local starchitect Igor Franić, this swanky museum in Novi Zagreb, across the Sava River, puts on solo and thematic group shows by Croatian and international artists. The year-round schedule is packed with film, theatre, concerts and performance art.

Mirogoj
CEMETERY

(☺6am-8pm Apr-Sep, 7am-6pm Oct-Mar) A 10-minute ride north of the city centre on bus 106 from the cathedral (or a half-hour walk through leafy streets) takes you to one of Europe's most beautiful cemeteries, a verdant resting place designed in 1876. The sculpted and artfully designed tombs lie beyond a majestic arcade topped by a string of cupolas.

FREE THRILLS

Though you'll have to pay to get into most of Zagreb's galleries and museums, there are some gorgeous parks and markets to be enjoyed for nowt – and there's always window shopping!

» Taste bits of food for free at Dolac (p173) – but don't be too cheeky!

» Smell the herbs at the Botanical Garden (p180).

» Enjoy the long walks around Maksimir Park (p180).

» See the magnificent Mirogoj cemetery (p180).

» Pop inside the ever-renovated cathedral (p173).

Maksimir Park
PARK

(www.park-maksimir.hr; Maksimirska bb; ☺park 9am-dusk, info centre 10am-4pm Tue-Fri, to 6pm Sat & Sun mid-Apr–mid-Oct, 10am-4pm Tue-Fri, 8am-4pm Sat & Sun mid-Oct–mid-Apr) Another green delight is Maksimir Park, a peaceful wooded enclave covering 18 hectares; it is easily accessible by trams 11 and 12 from Trg Josipa Jelačića. Opened to the public in 1794, it was the first public promenade in southeastern Europe. There's also a modest zoo (www.zoo.hr; adult/children 30/20KN; ☺9am-8pm) here.

Dražen Petrović Memorial Museum
MUSEUM

(☏48 43 146; Savska 30; tickets 10-20KN) Pay homage to Cibona's most famous player at this museum located south along Savska, on a small square just to the west.

☞ Tours

ZET
BUS TOUR

(www.zet.hr) Zagreb's public transportation network operates open-deck tour buses (70KN) departing from Kaptol on a hop-on, hop-off basis from April through September.

Funky Zagreb
GUIDED TOUR

(www.funky-zagreb.com) Personalised tours that range in theme from wine tasting (200KN for three hours) to hiking in Zagreb's surroundings (from 635KN per person).

Blue Bike Tours
CYCLING

(www.zagrebbybike.com) Has two-hour tours (170KN) departing daily. Reserve ahead.

Zagreb Talks
WALKING TOUR

(www.zagrebtalks.com) Tours include Do You Speak Croatian? on Saturday mornings, which teaches you basic language skills (95KN; 75KN for students). From May through September only; otherwise by appointment.

✹ Festivals & Events

For a complete listing of Zagreb events, see www.zagreb-touristinfo.hr.

Music Biennale Zagreb
MUSIC

(www.mbz.hr) Croatia's most important contemporary music event is held in April during odd-numbered years.

Subversive Festival
CULTURAL

(www.subversivefestival.com) Europe's activists and philosophers descend on Zagreb in droves for film screenings and lectures over two weeks in May.

INmusic Festival
MUSIC
(www.inmusicfestival.com) A three-day extravaganza every June, this is Zagreb's highest-profile music festival, with multiple stages by the Jarun Lake.

World Festival of Animated Film
FILM
(www.animafest.hr) This prestigious festival has been held in Zagreb annually in June since 1972.

Cest is D'Best
CULTURAL
(www.cestisdbest.com) In early June, it features five stages around the city centre, around 200 international performers and acts that include music, dance, theatre, art and sports.

Ljeto na Strossu
CULTURAL
(www.ljetonastrosu.com) From late May through late September, leafy Strossmayer Šetalište comes alive with free outdoor film screenings, concerts, art workshops and best-in-show mongrel dog competitions.

Eurokaz
THEATRE
(www.eurokaz.hr) Showcasing innovative theatre troupes and cutting-edge performances from all over the world in late June/early July.

Zagreb Summer Evenings
MUSIC
A cycle of concerts in the Upper Town each July, with the atrium of Galerija Klovićevi Dvori and the Gradec stage used for the performances of classical music, jazz, blues and world tunes.

World Theatre Festival
THEATRE
(www.zagrebtheatrefestival.hr) High-quality, contemporary theatre comes to Zagreb for a couple of weeks each September, often extending into early October.

🛏 Sleeping

Zagreb's accommodation scene has been undergoing a noticeable change, with many more budget options. Prices usually stay the same in all seasons, but be prepared for a 20% surcharge if you arrive during a festival or major event, in particular the autumn fair.

If you intend to stay in a private house or apartment – a good option if you want more privacy and a homey feel – try not to arrive on Sunday because most of the agencies will be closed, unless you've made prior arrangements. Prices for doubles run from about 300KN and studio apartments start at 400KN per night. There's usually a surcharge for staying only one night. Recommended agencies include **Evistas** (🗷48 39 554; www.evistas.hr; Augusta Šenoe 28; s/d/apt from 240/290/340KN) and **InZagreb** (🗷65 23 201; www.inzagreb.com; Remetinečka 13; apt 490-665KN).

⬛ Studio Kairos
B&B €€
(🗷46 40 680; www.studio-kairos.com; Vlaška 92; s 380-440KN, d 560-660KN; 🌐🛜) This adorable B&B has four well-appointed rooms in a street-level apartment. Rooms are decked out by theme and there's a cosy common space where breakfast is served. The main square (Trg Josipa Jelačića) is a 15-minute stroll away, a five-minute tram ride (take 11 or 12) or a five-minute bike ride (bikes are available for rent).

Esplanade Zagreb Hotel
HISTORIC HOTEL €€€
(🗷45 66 666; www.esplanade.hr; Mihanovićeva 1; s/d 1385/1500KN; 🅿🌀🗙@🛜) Drenched in history, this six-storey hotel was built next to the train station in 1924 to welcome the *Orient Express* crowd in grand style. The art-deco masterpiece is replete with walls of swirling marble, immense staircases and wood-panelled lifts. Take a peek at the magnificent Emerald Ballroom and have a meal at superb **Zinfandel's restaurant** (Mihanovićeva 1; mains from 170KN).

Hotel Dubrovnik
HOTEL €€
(🗷48 63 555; www.hotel-dubrovnik.hr; Gajeva 1; s/d from 740/885KN; 🅿🌀🛜) Smack on the main square, this glass city landmark has 245 elegant units with old-school classic style and, from some, great views of the square. Check out the great specials and packages.

Hobo Bear Hostel
HOSTEL €
(🗷48 46 636; www.hobobearhostel.com; Medulićeva 4; dm 135-175KN, d from 400KN; 🌀@🛜) Inside a duplex apartment, this sparkling five-dorm hostel has exposed brick walls, hardwood floors, free lockers, a kitchen with free tea and coffee, a common room and book exchange. Take tram 1, 6 or 11 from Jelačića. The three doubles are across the street.

Hotel Jägerhorn
HOTEL €€
(🗷48 33 877; www.jaegerhorn.hr; Ilica 14; s/d/apt 598/749/1052KN; 🅿🌀@🛜) A charming little hotel that sits right underneath Lotrščak Tower (p173), the 'Hunter's Horn' has friend-

ly service and 18 spacious, classic rooms with good views (gaze over leafy Gradec from the top-floor attic rooms).

TOP CHOICE **Funk Lounge Hostel** HOSTEL € (☎55 52 707; www.funkhostel.hr; Rendićeva 28b; dm 135-165KN, d 420KN; @⚂) Located steps from Maksimir Park, this new outpost of the original Funk Hostel (southwest of the centre) has friendly staff, neat rooms and a range of freebies, including breakfast and a shot of *rakija* in the on-site restaurant and bar.

The budget end of the market has picked up greatly and various hostel options now abound. The following hostels are worth checking out: **Shappy Hostel** (☎48 30 179; www.hostel-shappy.com; Varšavska 8; dm 128-170, d from 420KN; P⚹@⚂), **Palmers Lodge Hostel Zagreb** (☎88 92 686; www.palmerslodge.com.hr; Branimirova 25; dm 120-150KN; @⚂), **Chillout Hostel Zagreb Downtown** (☎48 49 605; www.chillout-hostel-zagreb.com; Kačićeva 3b; dm 135-180KN; ⚹@⚂), **Fulir Hostel** (☎48 30 882; www.fulir-hostel.com; Radićeva 3a; ⚹@⚂), **Hostel Day and Night** (www.hosteldayandnight.com; Kneza Mislava 1), **Buzz Hostel** (☎23 20 267; www.buzzbackpackers.com; Babukićeva 1b; ⚹@⚂) and **Taban Hostel** (www.tabanzagreb.com; Tkalčićeva 82).

🍴 Eating

You'll have to love Croatian and Italian food to enjoy Zagreb's restaurants, but new places are branching out to include Japanese and other world cuisines. The biggest move is towards elegantly presented haute cuisine at haute prices.

You can pick up excellent fresh produce at Dolac market. The city centre's main streets, including Ilica, Teslina, Gajeva and Preradovićeva, are lined with fast-food joints and inexpensive snack bars.

Note that many restaurants close in August for their summer holiday, which typically lasts anywhere from two weeks to a month.

TOP CHOICE **Vinodol** CROATIAN €€ (Teslina 10; mains from 57KN) Well-prepared Central European fare much loved by local and overseas patrons. On warm days, eat on the covered patio entered through an ivy-clad passageway off Teslina. Highlights include the succulent lamb or veal and potatoes under *peka* (baked in a coal oven), as well as local mushrooms called *bukovače*.

Lari & Penati MODERN CROATIAN € (Petrinjska 42a; mains from 40KN; ⊘lunch & dinner Mon-Fri, lunch Sat) Small stylish bistro that serves up innovative lunch and dinner specials that change daily according to what's market fresh. The food is fab, the music cool and the few sidewalk tables lovely in warm weather. Closed for two weeks in August.

Tip Top SEAFOOD € (Gundulićeva 18; mains from 55KN; ⊘Mon-Sat) The excellent Dalmatian food is served by waitstaff sporting old socialist uniforms. Every day has its own set menu of mainstays.

Mali Bar TAPAS €€ (☎55 31 014; Vlaška 63; mains from 60KN; ⊘closed Sun) This new spot by star chef Ana Ugarković shares the terraced space with Karijola (p182), hidden away in a *veža* (Zagreb alleyway). The cosy interior is earthtone colourful and the food is focused on globally inspired tapas-style dishes. Book ahead.

Didov San DALMATIAN €€ (☎48 51 154; Mletačka 11; mains from 60KN) This Upper Town tavern features a rustic wooden interior with ceiling beams and tables on the streetside deck. Traditional fare hails from the Neretva River delta in Dalmatia's hinterland; try grilled frogs wrapped in proscuitto. Reserve ahead.

TOP CHOICE **Karijola** PIZZERIA € (Vlaška 63; pizzas from 42KN; ⊘Mon-Sat) Locals swear by the crispy thin-crust pizza churned out of a clay oven at this new location of Zagreb's best pizza joint. Expect high-quality toppings, such as smoked ham, olive oil, rich mozzarella, rocket and shiitake mushrooms.

Amfora SEAFOOD € (Dolac 2; mains from 40KN; ⊘lunch) This locals' lunch favourite serves super-fresh seafood straight from the market next door, paired with off-the-stalls veggies. This hole-in-the-wall has a few tables outside and an upstairs gallery with a nice market view.

Prasac MEDITERRANEAN €€ (☎48 51 411; Vranicanijeva 6; mains from 87KN; ⊘Mon-Sat; 🌿) Creative Mediterranean fare is conjured up by the Croatian-Sicilian chef at this intimate place with wooden beamed ceilings and a few alfresco tables. The market-fresh food is superb, but the service is slow and the portions small. Reserve ahead.

Stari Fijaker 900 TRADITIONAL CROATIAN €
(Mesnička 6; mains from 50KN) Tradition reigns
in the kitchen of this restaurant–beer hall
with a decor of banquettes and white linen,
so try the homemade sausages, bean stews
and *štrukli* (dumplings filled with cottage
cheese), or one of the cheaper daily dishes.

Ivica i Marica TRADITIONAL CROATIAN €€
(Tkalčićeva 70; mains from 70KN) Based on the
Brothers Grimm story *Hansel and Gretel*,
this restaurant–cake shop is made to look
like the gingerbread house from the tale,
with waiters clad in traditional costumes. It
has veggie and fish dishes plus meatier fare.
The cakes and *štrukli* are great.

Konoba Čiho SEAFOOD €€
(Pavla Hatza 15; mains from 80KN) An old-school
Dalmatian *konoba* (simple family-run establishment), where, downstairs, you can
get fish (by the kilo) and seafood grilled or
stewed. Try the wide range of *rakija* and
house wines.

Vallis Aurea TRADITIONAL CROATIAN €
(Tomićeva 4; mains from 37KN; ⊘Mon-Sat) This
true local eatery has some of the best home
cooking you'll find in town, so it's no wonder that it's chock-a-block at lunchtime for
its *gableci* (traditional lunches). Right by the
lower end of the funicular.

Pingvin SANDWICH SHOP €
(Teslina 7; ⊘9am-4am Mon-Sat, 6pm-2am Sun)
This quick-bite institution, around since
1987, offers tasty designer sandwiches and
salads which locals savour perched on a couple of bar stools.

Rubelj FAST FOOD €
(Dolac 2; mains from 25KN) One of the many
Rubeljs across town, this Dolac branch is a
great place for a quick portion of *ćevapčići*
(small spicy sausage of minced beef, lamb or
pork).

Vincek PASTRIES, CAKES €
(Ilica 18) This institution of a *slastičarna*
(pastry shop) serves some of Zagreb's cream-
iest cakes. They recently got some serious
competition, however, with **Torte i To** (Nova
Ves 11, 2nd fl, Kaptol Centar).

Dinara BAKERY €
(Gajeva 8) The best bakery in town churns
out an impressive variety of baked goodies.
Try the *bučnica* (filo pie with pumpkin).
It also has branches at Ilica (Ilica 71) and
Preradovićeva (Preradovićeva 1).

🍷 Drinking

In the Upper Town, chic Tkalčićeva is throbbing with bars and cafes. In the Lower Town,
there's bar-lined Bogovićeva and Trg Petra
Preradovića (known locally as Cvjetni trg),
the most popular spot in the Lower Town for
street performers and occasional bands.

One of the nicest ways to see Zagreb is to
join in on the *špica* – Saturday-morning pre-
lunch coffee drinking on the terraces along
Bogovićeva, Preradovićeva and Tkalčićeva.

TOP CHOICE Cica BAR
(Tkalčićeva 18) This tiny storefront bar is as
underground as it gets on Tkalčićeva. Sample one or – if you dare – all of the 25 kinds
of *rakija* that the place is famous for.

Booksa CAFE
(www.booksa.hr; Martićeva 14d; ⊘11am-8pm Tue-
Sun; 🛜) Bookworms, poets and oddballs all
come to chat and drink coffee, browse the
library, surf with free wireless and hear
readings at this book-themed cafe. There are
English-language readings here, too. It's a
10-minute stroll east of the main square. It's
closed for three weeks from late July.

Stross OUTDOOR BAR
(Strossmayerovo Šetalište; ⊘Jun-Sep) From June
to September, a makeshift bar is set up at
the Strossmayer promenade in the Upper
Town, with cheap drinks and live music
most nights. Come for the mixed-bag crowd,
great city views and leafy ambience.

Bacchus BAR
(Trg Kralja Tomislava 16; ⊘closed Sun) You'll be
lucky if you score a table at Zagreb's funki-
est courtyard garden – lush and hidden in
a passageway. After 10pm the action moves
inside the artsy subterranean space, which
hosts poetry readings and oldies' nights.

Kino Europa CAFE-BAR
(www.kinoeuropa.hr; Varšavska 3; ⊘Mon-Sat; 🛜🖥)
Zagreb's oldest cinema, from the 1920s, now
houses a glass-enclosed cafe, wine bar and
grapperia, with an outdoor terrace and free
wireless. The cinema hosts daily film screenings and occasional dance parties.

Velvet CAFE-BAR
(Dežmanova 9; ⊘8am-10pm Mon-Fri, to 3pm Sat, to
2pm Sun) Stylish spot for a good, but pricey,
cup of java and a quick bite amid the min-
imalist-chic interior decked out by owner
Saša Šekoranja, Zagreb's hippest florist.

GAY & LESBIAN ZAGREB

The gay and lesbian scene in Zagreb is finally becoming more open than it has previously been, although freewheeling it isn't.

For more information, browse www.zagrebgayguide.com.

Kolaž (Amruševa 11) This basement speakeasy-style bar behind an unmarked door caters to a primarily gay crowd.

Rush Club (Amruševa 10) A younger gay and lesbian crowd mixes at this fun club in the city centre, with themed nights such as karaoke.

Hotpot (Petrinjska 31) This new club in town has quickly become one of the favourites.

Vimpi (Miškecov Prolaz 3) Gathering spot for Zagreb's lady-loving ladies.

Velvet Gallery next door, known as 'Black Velvet', stays open till 11pm (except Sunday).

☆ Entertainment

Zagreb doesn't register high on the nightlife Richter scale, but it does have an ever-developing art and music scene. Its theatres and concert halls present a variety of programs throughout the year. Many are listed in the monthly brochure *Zagreb Events & Performances,* which is available from the main tourist office

Clubs

Club entry ranges from 20KN to 100KN. Clubs open around 10pm but most people show up around midnight. Most clubs open only from Thursday to Saturday.

VIP Club   CLUB
(www.vip-club.hr; Trg Josipa Jelačića 9; ☺closed summer) This newcomer on the nightlife scene quickly became a favourite. A swank basement place on the main square, it offers a varied programme, from jazz to Balkan beats.

Tvornica   LIVE MUSIC
(www.tvornicakulture.com; Šubićeva 2) Excellent multimedia venue 20 minutes to the east of Trg Josipa Jelačića, showcasing live music performances, from Bosnian *sevdah* (Bosnian blues) to alternative punk rock. Check out the website to see what's on.

Aquarius   CLUB
(www.aquarius.hr; Jarun Lake) Past its heyday but still a fun lakeside club with a series of rooms that opens onto a huge terrace. House and techno are the standard fare but there are also hip-hop and R&B nights. During summer, Aquarius sets up shop at Zrće on Pag (p196).

Pepermint   CLUB
(www.pepermint-zagreb.com; Ilica 24) Small and chic city-centre club clad in white wood, with two levels and a well-to-do older crowd. Programs change weekly but the vintage rockabilly, twist and swing night on Wednesday is a definite hit.

Močvara   CLUB
(www.mochvara.hr; Trnjanski Nasip bb) In a former factory on the banks of the Sava River, 'Swamp' is one of Zagreb's best venues for the cream of alternative music and attractively dingy charm. Live acts range from dub and dancehall to world music and heavy metal.

KSET   CLUB
(www.kset.org; Unska 3) Zagreb's top music venue, with anyone who's anyone performing here – from ethno to hip-hop sounds. Saturday nights are dedicated to DJ music, when youngsters dance till late. You'll find gigs and events to suit most tastes.

Jabuka   CLUB
(Jabukovac 28) 'Apple' is an old-time fave, with 1980s hits played to a 30-something crowd that reminisces about the good old days when they were young and alternative. It's a taxi ride or a walk through the woods, set away in a posh area.

Medika   CLUB
(www.pierottijeva11.org; Pierottijeva 11) This artsy venue in an old pharmaceutical factory calls itself an 'autonomous cultural centre'. It's the city's first legalised squat with a program of concerts, art exhibits and parties fuelled by cheap beer and *rakija.*

Purgeraj   CLUB
(www.purgeraj.hr; Park Ribnjak 1) Live rock, blues and avant-garde jazz are on the music menu at this funky space that attracts a pretty young crowd. The brand-new Park just

merged with Purgeraj at the time of writing and started drawing in big-name bands.

Sport
Basketball is popular in Zagreb, home to the Cibona basketball team. There's a museum (p180) dedicated to Cibona star Dražen Petrović. Games take place frequently at the **Dražen Petrović Basketball Centre** (⌨48 43 333; Savska 30; tickets from HRK35); tickets can be purchased at the door or online at www.cibona.com.

Performing Arts
Make the rounds of the theatres in person to check their programs. Tickets are usually available for even the best shows.

Zagrebačko Kazalište Mladih　　THEATRE
(⌨48 72 554; www.zekaem.hr; Teslina 7) Zagreb Youth Theatre, better known as ZKM, is considered the cradle of Croatia's contemporary theatre. It hosts several festivals.

Croatian National Theatre　　THEATRE
(⌨48 88 418; www.hnk.hr; Trg Maršala Tita 15) This neo-baroque theatre, established in 1895, stages opera and ballet performances.

Shopping
Ilica is Zagreb's main shopping street.

Prostor　　FASHION
(www.multiracionalnakompanija.com; Mesnička 5; ⏱noon-8pm Mon-Fri, 10am-3pm Sat) A fantastic little art gallery and clothes shop, featuring some of the city's best independent artists and young designers. In a courtyard off Mesnička.

Natura Croatica　　FOOD
(www.naturacroatica.com; Preradovićeva 8) Over 300 Croatian products and souvenirs are sold at this shop – from *rakija*, wines and chocolates to jams, spices and truffle spreads. A perfect pitstop for gifts.

Profil Megastore　　BOOKSTORE
(Bogovićeva 7) Inside an entryway, this most atmospheric of Zagreb bookstores has a great selection of books (many in English) and a nice cafe on the gallery.

❶ Information

Discount Cards
Zagreb Card (www.zagrebcard.fivestars.hr; 24/72hr 60/90KN) Provides free travel on all public transport, a 50% discount on museum and gallery entries, plus discounts in some bars and restaurants, and on car rental. The card is sold at the main tourist office and many hostels, hotels, bars and shops.

Emergency
Police Station (⌨45 63 311; Petrinjska 30)

Internet Access
Several cafes around town offer free wi-fi, including Booksa.

Sublink (⌨48 19 993; www.sublink.hr; Teslina 12; per hr 15KN; ⏱9am-10pm Mon-Sat, 3-10pm Sun) The city's first cybercafe, still going strong.

Medical Services
Dental Emergency (⌨48 28 488; Perkovčeva 3; ⏱10pm-6am)
KBC Rebro (⌨23 88 888; Kišpatićeva 12; ⏱24hr) East of the city, provides emergency aid.
Pharmacy (⌨48 16 198; Trg Josipa Jelačića 3; ⏱24hr)

Money
There are ATMs at the bus and train stations, the airport, and at numerous locations around town. Some banks in the train and bus stations accept travellers cheques. Exchange offices can be found in many locations around town.

MARKET DAYS

The Sunday **antiques market** (Britanski Trg; ⏱9am-2pm Sun) is one of central Zagreb's joys, but to see a flea market that's unmatched in the whole of Croatia, you have to head to **Hrelić** (⏱7am-3pm Wed & Sun). This huge open space is packed with anything – from car parts, cars and antique furniture to clothes, records, kitchenware, you name it. Shopping aside, it's also a great place to experience the truly Balkan part and chaotic fun of Zagreb – Roma music, bartering, grilled-meat smoke and general gusto. If you're going in the summer months, take a hat and slap on sunscreen – there's no shade.

By tram, take number 6 in the direction of Sopot, get off near the bridge and walk 15 minutes along the Sava to get to Hrelić; or take tram 14, get off at the last stop in Zapruđe and do the 15-minute walk from there.

Post

Post Office (☑66 26 453; Jurišićeva 13; ⊘7am-8pm Mon-Fri, to 1pm Sat) Has a telephone centre.

Tourist Information

Main Tourist Office (☑info line 800 53 53, office 48 14 051; www.zagreb-touristinfo.hr; Trg Josipa Jelačića 11; ⊘8.30am-9pm Mon-Fri, 9am-6pm Sat & Sun) Distributes free city maps and leaflets, and sells the Zagreb Card (p185).

Plitvice National Park Office (☑46 13 586; Trg Kralja Tomislava 19; ⊘8am-4pm Mon-Fri) Has details and brochures mainly on Plitvice and Velebit but also on Croatia's other national parks.

Tourist Office Airport (☑62 65 091; ⊘8.30am-9pm Mon-Fri, 9am-6pm Sat & Sun Jun-Sep) Handy for airport arrivals.

Tourist Office Annex (train station; ⊘8.30am-9pm Mon-Fri, 9am-6pm Sat & Sun Jun-Sep, 8.30am-8pm Mon-Fri, 12.30-6.30pm Sat & Sun Oct-May) Same services as the main tourist office.

Travel Agencies

Atlas Travel Agency (☑48 07 300; www.atlas-croatia.com; Zrinjevac 17) Tours around Croatia.

Croatia Express (☑49 22 237; Trg Kralja Tomislava 17) Train reservations, car rental, air and ferry tickets, hotell bookings and a daily trip to the beach from June to September.

Zdenac Života (☑48 16 200; www.zdenac-zivota.hr; 2nd fl, Vlaška 40) Thematic sightseeing tours of Zagreb plus active day trips from the capital and multiday adventures around Croatia.

Websites

Lonely Planet (www.lonelyplanet.com/croatia/zagreb)

Getting There & Away

AIR **Zagreb Airport** (☑45 62 222; www.zagreb-airport.hr) Located 17km southeast of Zagreb, this is Croatia's major airport, offering a range of international and domestic services.

BUS Zagreb's **bus station** (☑060 313 333; www.akz.hr; Avenija M Držića 4) is 1km east of the train station. Trams 2, 3 and 6 run from the bus station to the train station. Tram 6 goes to Trg Josipa Jelačića. There's a **garderoba** (left-luggage office; 1st 4hr 20KN, then per hr 2.50KN; ⊘24hr) at the bus station.

Before buying your ticket, ask about the arrival time – some of the buses take local roads and stop in every town en route. Note that listed schedules are somewhat reduced outside high season.

TRAIN The **train station** (☑060 333 444; www.hznet.hr; Trg Kralja Tomislava 12) is in the southern part of the city. As you come out of it, you'll see a series of parks and pavilions directly in front of you, which lead into the town centre. It's advisable to book train tickets in advance because of limited seating. There's a **garderoba** (Train station; lockers per 24hr 15KN; ⊘24hr) left-luggage office at the station.

Getting Around

Zagreb is a fairly easy city to navigate. Traffic is bearable and the efficient tram system should be a model for other polluted, traffic-clogged European capitals.

To/From the Airport

The Croatia Airlines bus to the airport (30KN) leaves from the bus station every half-hour or hour from about 5am to 8pm, and returns from the airport on the same schedule. Taxis cost between 110KN and 300KN.

Car

Zagreb is a fairly easy city to navigate by car (boulevards are wide and parking in the city centre, although scarce, costs 10KN per hour). Watch out for trams buzzing around.

Motorists can call **Hrvatski Autoklub** (HAK, Croatian Auto Club; ☑46 40 800; www.hak.hr; Avenija Dubrovnik 44) at ☑1987 for help on the road.

International car-hire companies include **Budget Rent-a-Car** (☑46 73 603; www.budget.hr; Oreškovićeva 27) and **Hertz** (☑48 46 777; www.hertz.hr; Vukotinovićeva 4). Local companies usually have lower rates; try **Oryx** (☑61 15 800; www.oryx-rent.hr; Grada Vukovara 74), which has a desk at the airport.

Public Transport

Public transport is based on an efficient network of trams, although the city centre is compact enough to make them unnecessary. Buy tickets at newspaper kiosks for 12KN. Tickets can be used for transfers within 90 minutes, but only in one direction.

A *dnevna karta* (day ticket), valid on all public transport until 4am the next morning, is available for 40KN at most newspaper kiosks.

Make sure you validate your ticket when you get on the tram by inserting it in the yellow box.

Taxi

Until recently, Zagreb had only one taxi company which charged astronomical fees for even the shortest ride. That changed when other companies joined the fray; all have meters now and competitive rates. **Radio Taxi** (☑060 800 800, 1777) charges 10KN for a start and 5KN per kilometre; waiting time is 40KN per hour.

TRANSPORT FROM ZAGREB

Domestic Bus

DESTINATION	PRICE (KN)	DURATION (HR)	FREQUENCY (DAILY)
Dubrovnik	205-250	9½-11	9-12
Korčula	264	11	1
Krk	113-219	3-4½	8-10
Mali Lošinj	287-312	5-6	3
Plitvice	92-106	2-3	11-15
Poreč	156-232	4-4½	11
Pula	105-196	3½-5½	17-20
Rijeka	91-155	2½-4	20-25
Rovinj	150-195	4-6	9-11
Split	115-205	5-8½	32-34
Zadar	105-139	3½-5	31

International Bus

DESTINATION	PRICE (KN)	DURATION (HR)	FREQUENCY (DAILY)
Belgrade (Serbia)	220	6	5
Munich (Germany)	375	9½	2
Sarajevo (Bosnia & Hercegovina)	160-210	7-8	4-5
Vienna (Austria)	250	5-6	3

Domestic Train

DESTINATION	PRICE (KN)	DURATION (HR)	FREQUENCY (DAILY)
Rijeka	97	4-6	6
Split	189	5-7	3

International Train

DESTINATION	PRICE (KN)	DURATION (HR)	FREQUENCY (DAILY)
Banja Luka (Bosnia & Hercegovina)	105	4½-5	2
Belgrade (Serbia)	169	6½	4
Budapest (Hungary)	230	6-7	2
Ljubljana (Slovenia)	130	2½	6
Mostar (Bosnia & Hercegovina)	292	11½	1
Munich (Germany)	674	8½-9	3
Ploče (Italy)	320	13½	1
Sarajevo (Bosnia & Hercegovina)	231	8-9½	2
Venice (Italy)	450	11½	2
Vienna (Austria)	465	6-7	2

PLITVICE LAKES NATIONAL PARK

Between Zagreb and Zadar, **Plitvice Lakes National Park** (☎751 015; www.np-plitvicka-jezera.hr; adult/concession Apr-Oct 110/80KN, Nov-Mar 80/60KN; ☉7am-8pm) comprises 19.5 hectares of wooded hills and 16 lakes, all connected by a series of waterfalls and cascades. The mineral-rich waters carve new paths through the rock, depositing tufa (new porous rock) in continually changing formations. Wooden footbridges follow the lakes and streams over, under and across the rumbling water for an exhilaratingly damp 18km. Swimming is not allowed. Your park admission also includes the boats and bus-trains you need to use to see the lakes. There is hotel accommodation onsite, and private accommodation just outside the park. Check the options with the Plitvice National Park Office (p186) in Zagreb.

Not all Zagreb–Zadar buses stop here as the quicker ones use the motorway, so check before boarding. You can check the schedules at www.akz.hr. The journey takes three hours from Zadar (95KN to 108KN) and 2½ hours from Zagreb (93KN to 106KN); there are 10 daily services.

Luggage can be left at the tourist information centre at the park's main entrance.

You'll have no trouble finding idle taxis, usually at blue-marked taxi signs; note that these are Radio Taxi stands.

For short city rides, **Taxi Cammeo** (☎060 71 00, 1212) is typically the cheapest, as the 15KN start fare includes the first two kilometres (it's 6KN for every subsequent kilometre).

ISTRIA

☎052

Continental Croatia meets the Adriatic in Istria (Istra to Croats), the heart-shaped 3600-sq-km peninsula just south of Trieste in Italy. While the bucolic interior of rolling hills and fertile plains attracts artsy visitors to its hilltop villages, rural hotels and farmhouse restaurants, the verdant indented coastline is enormously popular with the sun 'n sea set. Vast hotel complexes line much of the coast and its rocky beaches are not Croatia's best, but the facilities are wide-ranging, the sea is clean and secluded spots are still plentiful.

The coast, or 'Blue Istria', as the tourist board calls it, gets flooded with tourists in summer, but you can still feel alone in 'Green Istria' (the interior), even in mid-August. Add acclaimed gastronomy (starring fresh seafood, prime white truffles, wild asparagus, top-rated olive oils and award-winning wines), sprinkle it with historical charm and you have a little slice of heaven.

Pula

POP 57,800

The wealth of Roman architecture makes the otherwise workaday Pula (ancient Polensium) a standout among Croatia's larger cities. The star of the Roman show is the remarkably well-preserved Roman amphitheatre, which dominates the streetscape and doubles as a venue for summer concerts and festivals.

Historical attractions aside, Pula is a busy commercial city on the sea that has managed to retain a friendly small-town appeal. Just a short bus ride away, a series of beaches awaits at the resorts that occupy the Verudela Peninsula to the south. Although marred by residential and holiday developments, the coast is dotted with fragrant pine groves, seaside cafes and a clutch of fantastic restaurants. Further south along the indented shoreline, the Premantura Peninsula hides a spectacular nature park, the protected cape of Kamenjak.

☉ Sights

THE CITY

The oldest part of the city follows the ancient Roman plan of streets circling the central citadel. Most shops, agencies and businesses are clustered in and around the Old Town as well as on Giardini, Carrarina, Istarska and Riva, which runs along the harbour. The new Riva is currently being renovated, which makes the harbourfront one big construction site; the work is expected to finish in late 2013.

Roman Amphitheatre   HISTORIC BUILDING
(Arena; Flavijevska bb; adult/concession 40/20KN; ☉8am-midnight Jul & Aug, around 8am-7pm Sep-Jun) Pula's most famous and imposing sight is this 1st-century amphitheatre, overlooking the harbour northeast of the Old Town. Built entirely from local limestone, the am-

phitheatre, known locally as the Arena, was designed to host gladiatorial contests, with seating for up to 20,000 spectators. In the chambers downstairs is a small **museum** with a display of ancient olive-oil equipment. **Pula Film Festival** (www.pulafilmfestival.hr) is held here every summer, as are pop and classical concerts.

Temple of Augustus
HISTORIC BUILDING

(Forum; adult/concession 20/10KN; ☺9am-8pm Mon-Fri, to 3pm Sat & Sun Apr-Oct) This is the only visible remnant from the Roman era on the Forum, Pula's central meeting place from antiquity through the Middle Ages. This temple, erected from 2 BC to AD 14, now houses a small historical **museum** with captions in English.

Archaeological Museum
MUSEUM

(Arheološki Muzej; Carrarina 3; adult/concession 20/10KN; ☺8am-8pm Mon-Fri, 9am-3pm Sat & Sun May-Sep, 9am-2pm Mon-Fri Oct-Apr) This museum presents archaeological finds from all over Istria. Even if you don't enter the museum, be sure to visit the large **sculpture garden** around it, and the **Roman theatre** behind. The garden, entered through 2nd-century twin gates, is the site of concerts in summer.

Zerostrasse
HISTORICAL SITE

(adult/concession 15/5KN; ☺10am-10pm Jun-mid-Sep) This underground system of tunnels was built before and during WWI to shelter the city's population and serve as storage for ammunition. Now you can walk through several of its sections, which all lead to the middle, where a photo exhibit shows early aviation in Pula. There are three entrances – inquire at the tourism office.

Triumphal Arch of Sergius
RUINS

Along Carrarina are Roman walls, which mark the eastern boundary of old Pula. Follow these walls south and continue down Giardini to this majestic arch erected in 27 BC to commemorate three members of the Sergius family who achieved distinction in Pula.

THE COAST

Pula is surrounded by a half-circle of rocky beaches, each one with its own fan club. The most tourist-packed are undoubtedly those surrounding the hotel complex on the **Verudela Peninsula**, although some locals will dare to be seen at the small turquoise-coloured **Hawaii Beach** near the Hotel Park.

Rt Kamenjak
NATURE PARK

(www.kamenjak.hr; pedestrians & cyclists free, per car/scooter 25/20KN; ☺7am-10pm) For seclusion, head out to the wild Rt Kamenjak on the Premantura Peninsula, 10km south of town. Istria's southernmost point, this gorgeous, entirely uninhabited cape has wildflowers (including 30 species of orchid), 30km of virgin beaches and coves, and a delightful beach bar, **Safari** (snacks 25-50KN; ☺Apr-Sep), half-hidden in the bushes near the beach, about 3.5km from the entrance to the park. For the wildest and least-discovered stretch of the cape, head to Gornji Kamenjak, which lies between the village of Volme and Premantura. Watch out for strong currents if swimming off the southern cape. **Windsurf Bar** (☎091 512 3646; www.windsurfing.hr; windsurfing equipment/courses per hr from 70/200KN) in Premantura rents bikes and windsurfing equipment and offers kayaking excursions. Take city bus 26 from Pula to Premantura (15KN), then rent a bike to get inside the park.

🏃 Activities

At the **Orca Diving Center** (☎098 409 850; www.orcadiving.hr; Hotel Histria) on the Verudela Peninsula, you can arrange boat and wreck dives. In addition to windsurfing, Windsurf Bar (p189) in Premantura offers cycling (250KN) and kayaking (300KN) excursions.

An easy 41km **cycling trail** from Pula to Medulin follows the path of Roman gladiators. Check out **Istria Bike** (www.istria-bike.com), a tourist board–run website outlining trails, packages and agencies that offer cycling trips.

🛏 Sleeping

Pula's peak tourist season runs from the second week of July to late August. During this period it's wise to make advance reservations. The tip of the Verudela Peninsula, 4km southwest of the city centre, has been turned into a vast tourist complex replete with hotels and apartments.

Any travel agency can give you information and book you into one of the hotels, or you can contact **Arenaturist** (☎529 400; www.arenaturist.hr; Splitska 1a).

The travel agencies in Pula can find you private accommodation, but there is little available in the town centre. Count on paying from 250KN to 490KN for a double room and from 300KN to 535KN for a two-person apartment. You can also browse the list of private accommodation at www.pulainfo.hr.

Hotel Amfiteatar
HOTEL €€

(☎375 600; www.hotelamfiteatar.com; Amfiteatarska 6; s/d 475/658KN; P❋@☎) The swankiest spot in town, right by the amphitheatre, is a new hotel with contemporary rooms with upscale trimmings such as flat-screen TVs. The restaurant is one of Pula's best. There's a surcharge for stays of less than two nights.

Hostel Pipištrelo
HOSTEL €

(☎393 568; www.hostel-pipistrelo.com; Flaciusova 6; dm/s/d 124/148/296KN; ❋@☎) With its colourful facade, this recent addition to Pula's hostel scene sits right across the harbour. Its quirky thematic rooms were done up by young Pula designers. It is cash-only and closed Sundays, so call ahead.

Hotel Scaletta
HOTEL €€

(☎541 025; www.hotel-scaletta.com; Flavijevska 26; s/d 505/732KN; P❋☎) There's a friendly family vibe at this cosy hotel. The rooms have tasteful decor and a bagful of trimmings (such as minibars). Plus it's just a hop and a skip from town, and a short walk from the Arena and the waterfront.

Riviera Guest House
HOTEL €€

(☎525 400; www.arenaturist.hr; Splitska 1; s/d 360/590KN; ☎) This once-grand property in a Neo-Baroque 19th-century building is in dire need of a thorough overhaul. The saving grace: it's in the centre and the front rooms have water views.

Camping Stoja
CAMPING GROUND €

(☎387 144; www.arenacamps.com; Stoja 37; campsites per person/tent 58/37KN; ☺Apr-Oct) The closest camping ground to Pula, 3km southwest of the centre, has lots of space on the shady promontory, with a restaurant and a diving centre. Take bus 1 to Stoja.

✗ Eating

The centre of Pula is full of tourist traps, so for the best food and good value you'll have to head out of town. For cheap bites, browse around the central market, where you'll find excellent sandwiches at Garfield (Narodni Trg 9; sandwiches from 25KN; ☺9am-3pm Mon-Fri, to 2pm Sat) on the 1st floor. For a reliably good meal, head to the alfresco restaurant of Hotel Amfiteatar.

Vodnjanka
ISTRIAN €

(Vitezića 4; mains from 40KN; ☺closed Sat dinner & Sun winter) Locals swear by the real-deal home cooking at this no-frills spot. It's cheap, casual, cash-only and has a small menu that concentrates on simple Istrian dishes. To get here, walk south on Radićeva to Vitezića.

TOP CHOICE Konoba Batelina
SEAFOOD €€

(☎573 767; Čimulje 25, Banjole; mains from 85KN; ☺dinner) The superb food that awaits at this family-run tavern is worth a trek to Banjole village 3km east of Pula. The owner, fisherman and chef David Skoko, dishes out seafood that's some of the best and most creative you'll find in Istria. Reserve ahead.

Milan
MEDITERRANEAN €€

(www.milanpula.com; Stoja 4; mains from 85KN) An exclusive vibe, seasonal specialties, four sommeliers and an olive-oil expert on staff all create one of the city's best dining experiences. The five-course fish menu is well worth it.

Kantina
INTERNATIONAL €€

(Flanatička 16; mains from 70KN; ☺Mon-Sat; 🖥) The beamed stone cellar of this Habsburg building has been redone in a modern style. The ownership and culinary helm changed recently so the food quality is hit and miss.

♟ Drinking & Entertainment

Try to catch a concert in the spectacular amphitheatre (p188); the tourist office has schedules. Although most of the nightlife is out of the town centre, in mild weather the cafes on the Forum and along the pedestrian streets Kandlerova, Flanatička and Sergijevaca are lively people-watching spots. For beach-bar action, head to Verudela or Medulin.

TOP CHOICE Cabahia
BAR

(Širolina 4) This artsy hideaway in Veruda has a cosy wood-beamed interior, eclectic decor of old objects, dim lighting, South American flair and a great garden terrace out the back. It hosts concerts and gets packed on weekends. If it's too full, try the more laid-back Bass (Širolina 3), just across the street.

Cvajner
CAFE

(Forum 2) Snag a prime alfresco table at this artsy cafe right on the buzzing Forum and check out rotating exhibits in the funky interior, which showcases works by up-and-coming local artists.

Rojc
CULTURAL CENTRE

(www.rojcnet.pula.org; Gajeva 3) For an arty underground experience, check the program at Rojc, a converted army barracks that houses a multimedia art centre and studios with occasional concerts, exhibitions and other events.

DOMESTIC BUSES FROM PULA

DESTINATION	PRICE (KN)	DURATION (HR)	FREQUENCY (DAILY)
Dubrovnik	580	15	1
Poreč	72	1	5
Rovinj	38	¾	12
Split	392	10	2
Zadar	255	7	3
Zagreb	190	4	12

Zeppelin   BEACH BAR
(Saccorgiana Bay) Après-beach fun is on the menu at this new beach bar in Saccorgiana bay on Verudela, but it also does night parties ranging in theme from vodka to reggae and karaoke to martini.

ℹ Information

Active Travel Istra (☎215 497; www.activa-istra.com; Scalierova 1) Excursions around Istria, adventure trips and concert tickets.

Hospital (☎376 548; Zagrebačka 34)

IstrAction (☎383 369; www.istraction.com; Prilaz Monte Cappelletta 3) Offers fun half-day tours to Kamenjak and around Pula's fortifications, as well as medieval-themed full-day excursions around Istria.

Main post office (Danteov trg 4; ☉7am-8pm Mon-Fri, to 1pm Sat) You can make long-distance calls here. Check out the cool staircase inside.

MMC Luka (Istarska 30; per hr 25KN; ☉8am-midnight Mon-Fri, to 3pm Sat) Internet access. There's also free wi-fi all around town; inquire at the tourism office about specific locations.

Tourist Ambulance (Flanatička 27; ☉8am-9.30pm Mon-Fri Jul & Aug) Medical clinic.

Tourist Information Centre (☎212 987; www.pulainfo.hr; Forum 3; ☉8am-9pm Mon-Fri, 9am-9pm Sat & Sun summer, around 8am-7pm rest of yr) Knowledgeable and friendly staff provide maps, brochures and schedules of events in Pula and around Istria. Pick up two useful booklets: *Domus Bonus*, which lists the best-quality private accommodation in Istria, and *Istra Gourmet*, with a list of all restaurants.

ℹ Getting There & Away

BOAT Pula's harbour is located west of the bus station. **Jadroagent** (☎210 431; www.jadroagent.hr; Riva 14; ☉7am-3pm Mon-Fri) has schedules and tickets for boats connecting Istria with the islands and south of Croatia.

Commodore Cruises (☎211 631; www.commodore-travel.hr; Riva 14) sells tickets for a catamaran between Pula and Zadar (100KN, five hours), which runs five times weekly from July through early September and twice weekly in June and the rest of September. There's a Wednesday boat service to Venice (430KN, 3½ hours) between June and September.

BUS From the Pula **bus station** (☎060 304 091; Šijanska 4), located 500m northeast of the town centre, there are buses heading to Rijeka (97KN, 1½hr) almost hourly. In summer, reserve a seat a day in advance. There's also a **garderoba** (left-luggage office; per hr 2.50KN; ☉24hr) here.

There are weekly buses to Frankfurt and twice-weekly buses to Munich.

TRAIN Less than 1km north of town, the train station is near the sea along Kolodvorska. There is one direct train daily to Ljubljana (144KN, 4½ hours) and three to Zagreb (140KN, nine hours), but you must board a bus for part of the trip, from Lupoglav to Rijeka.

ℹ Getting Around

The city buses of use to visitors are 1, which runs to Camping Stoja, and 2A and 3A to Verudela. The frequency varies from every 15 minutes to every half hour (from 5am to 11.30pm). Tickets are sold at *tisak* (news stands) for 6KN, or from the driver for 11KN.

Rovinj

POP 14,400

Rovinj (Rovigno in Italian) is coastal Istria's star attraction. It can get overrun with tourists in the summer months and residents are developing a sharp eye for maximising their profits (by upgrading hotels and restaurants to four-star status), but it remains one of the last true Mediterranean fishing ports. Fishermen haul their catch into the harbour in the early morning, followed by a horde of squawking gulls, and mend their nets before lunch.

The massive Church of St Euphemia, with its 60m-high tower, punctuates the peninsula.

CROATIA ROVINJ

Wooded hills and low-rise hotels surround the Old Town, which is webbed by steep, cobbled streets and piazzas. The 13 green, offshore islands of the Rovinj archipelago make for a pleasant afternoon away.

⊙ Sights

The Old Town of Rovinj is contained within an egg-shaped peninsula. There are two harbours – the northern open harbour and the small, protected harbour to the south. About 1.5km south is the Punta Corrente Forest Park and the wooded cape of Zlatni Rt (Golden Cape).

Church of St Euphemia   CHURCH
(Sveta Eufemija; Petra Stankovića; ⊙10am-6pm Jun-Sep, 10am-4pm May, 10am-2pm Apr, by appointment Oct-Mar) The town's showcase is this imposing church, which dominates the Old Town from its hilltop location in the middle of the peninsula. Built in 1736, it's the largest baroque building in Istria, reflecting the period during the 18th century when Rovinj was its most populous town, an important fishing centre and the bulwark of the Venetian fleet.

Inside the church behind the right-hand altar, look for the marble tomb of St Euphemia, Rovinj's patron saint martyred in AD 304, whose body appeared in Rovinj one dark stormy night according to legend. The mighty 60m bell tower is topped by a copper statue of St Euphemia, which shows the direction of the wind by turning on a spindle. You can climb the tower (to the left of the altar) for 15KN.

Batana House   MUSEUM
(Pina Budicina 2; adult/child 10/5KN, with guide 15KN; ⊙10am-2pm & 7-11pm Jun-Sep, 10am-2pm & 4-6pm Tue-Sun Oct-Jan & Mar-May) On the harbour, Batana House is a museum dedicated to the *batana*, a flat-bottomed fishing boat that stands as a symbol of Rovinj's seafaring and fishing traditions.

Grisia   STREET
(🏛) Lined with galleries where local artists sell their work, this cobbled street leads uphill from behind the elaborate 1679 Balbi Arch to St Euphemia. The winding narrow backstreets that spread around Grisia are an attraction in themselves. Windows, balconies, portals and squares are a pleasant confusion of styles – Gothic, Renaissance, baroque and neoclassical. On the second Sunday in August each year, Grisia becomes an open-air art exhibition, with anyone from children to professional painters displaying their work.

Punta Corrente Forest Park   PARK
Follow the waterfront on foot or by bike past Hotel Park to this verdant area, locally known as Zlatni Rat, about 1.5km south. It's covered in oak and pine groves and boasts 10 species of cypress. You can swim off the rocks or just sit and admire the offshore islands.

🏃 Activities

Most people hop aboard a boat for swimming, snorkelling and sunbathing. A trip to Crveni Otok or Sveta Katarina is easily arranged. In summer, there are hourly boats from 5.30am till midnight to the islands of Sveta Katarina (return 30KN, 10 minutes) and Crveni Otok (return 40KN, 15 minutes). They leave from just opposite Hotel Adriatic and also from the Delfin ferry dock near Hotel Park.

Nadi Scuba Diving Centar (☎813 290; www.scuba.hr) and Petra (☎812 880; www.divingpetra.hr) offer daily boat dives. The main attraction is the Baron Gautsch wreck, an Austrian passenger steamer sunk in 1914 by a sea mine in 40m of water.

Cycling around Rovinj and the Punta Corrente Forest Park is a superb way to spend an afternoon. You can rent bicycles at many agencies around town, for around 20KN per hour or 70KN per day.

There are other exciting options, such as kayaking; book a trip through Adistra (☎095 838 3797; Carera 69). Nine-kilometre jaunts around the Rovinj archipelago cost 270KN; a 14km outing to the Limska Draga Fjord is 290KN.

☞ Tours

Most travel agencies in Rovinj sell day trips to Venice (390KN to 520KN), Plitvice (500KN to 600KN) and Brijuni (380KN to 470KN). There are also fish picnics (250KN), panoramic cruises (100KN) and boat outings to Limska Draga Fjord (150KN). These can be slightly cheaper if booked through one of the independent operators that line the waterfront; Delfin (☎848 265) is reliable.

🛌 Sleeping

Rovinj has become Istria's destination of choice for hordes of summertime tourists, so reserving in advance is strongly recommended. Prices have been rising steadily and probably will continue to do so, as the city gears up to reach elite status.

If you want to stay in private accommodation, there is little available in the Old Town, where there's also no free parking and accommodation costs are higher. Double rooms start at 220KN in the high season, with a small discount for single occupancy; two-person apartments start at 330KN. Out of season, prices go down considerably.

The surcharge for a stay of less than three nights is up to 50%, and guests who stay only one night are sometimes punished with a 100% surcharge. Outside summer months, you should be able to bargain the surcharge away. You can book through one of the travel agencies.

Except for a few private options, most hotels and camping grounds in the area are managed by **Maistra** (www.maistra.com).

TOP CHOICE **Hotel Lone** DESIGN HOTEL €€€
(✆632 000; www.lonehotel.com; Luje Adamovića 31; s/d 1478/1847KN; 🅿❋@🛜) Croatia's first design hotel, this 248-room powerhouse of style is a creation of Croatia's starchitects 3LHD. Rising over Lone bay, a 10-minute stroll from the Old Town, it has light-flooded rooms with private terraces, a restaurant and an extensive spa. Guests can use the pools at the next-door Monte Mulini.

Villa Valdibora HOTEL €€€
(✆845 040; www.valdibora.com; Silvano Chiurco 8; s/d 1080/1440KN; ❋🛜) The 11 rooms, suites and apartments in this historic building come with cool stone floors and upscale trimmings such as hydromassage showers. There's a fitness room, massages and bikes for rent.

Villa Baron Gautsch GUESTHOUSE €€
(✆840 538; www.baron-gautsch.com; IM Ronjgova 7; s/d 293/586KN; ❋🛜) This German-owned *pansion* (guesthouse), up the leafy street leading from Hotel Park, has 17 spick-and-span rooms, some with terraces and lovely views of the sea and the Old Town. It's cash (kuna) only.

Hotel Adriatic HOTEL €€€
(✆800 250; www.maistra.com; Pina Budicina bb; s/d 747/933KN; 🅿❋🛜) The location of this hotel, right on the harbour, is excellent and the rooms are well-equipped, albeit in need of renovation and on the kitschy side. The pricier sea-view rooms have more space and newer fittings.

Porton Biondi CAMPING GROUND €
(✆813 557; www.portonbiondi.hr; Aleja Porton Biondi 1; campsites per person/tent 42/26KN; ☉mid-Mar–Oct; 🐕) This beachside camping ground, which sleeps 1200, is about 700m from the Old Town.

✖ Eating

Picnickers can get supplies at the supermarket next to the bus station or at one of the Konzum stores around town.

Most of the restaurants that line the harbour offer the standard fish and meat mainstays at similar prices. For a more gourmet experience, you'll need to bypass the water vistas. Note that many restaurants shut their doors between lunch and dinner.

TOP CHOICE **Male Madlene** TAPAS €
(Križa 28; snacks from 30KN; ☉11am-2pm & 7-11pm May-Sep) Adorable spot in the owner's tiny living room hanging over the sea, where she serves up creative tapas with market-fresh ingredients, based on old Italian recipes, plus great Istrian wines by the glass.

Monte MEDITERRANEAN €€€
(✆830 203; Montalbano 75; mains from 190KN) Rovinj's top restaurant, right below St Euphemia Church, is worth the hefty cost for the pure enjoyment of its beautifully presented dishes served on the elegant glassed-in terrace. Reserve ahead in high season.

Da Sergio PIZZERIA €
(Grisia 11; pizzas 28-71KN) It's worth waiting in line to get a table at this old-fashioned two-floor pizzeria that dishes out Rovinj's best thin-crust pizza. The best is Gogo, with fresh tomato and arugula (rocket) and prosciutto.

Kantinon SEAFOOD €
(Alda Rismonda 18; mains from 30KN) A fishing theme runs through this high-ceilinged canteen, which specialises in fresh seafood at low prices. The Batana fish plate for two is great value, as are the set menus.

Ulika MEDITERRANEAN €€
(Porečka 6; mains from 100KN; 🍴) Tucked away in an alleyway, this small, pretty tavern with streetside seating excludes the staples of Adriatic food kitsch (pizza, calamari) and instead features well-prepared, if pricey, Mediterranean fare.

Veli Jože FISH €
(Križa 3; mains from 50KN) Graze on good Istrian standards, either in the eclectic interior

BUSES FROM ROVINJ

DESTINATION	PRICE (KN)	DURATION	FREQUENCY (DAILY)
Dubrovnik	628	16hr	1
Labin	80	2hr	2
Poreč	35-50	50min	15
Pula	35-45	50min	20
Rijeka	93-127	1½-3hr	5
Split	444	11hr	1
Trieste (Italy)	100-120	1½hr	2
Zagreb	150-200	4-6hr	10

crammed with knick-knacks or at the clutch of outdoor tables with water views.

🍷 Drinking

Limbo CAFE-BAR
(Casale 22b; 🛜) Cosy cafe-bar with small candlelit tables and cushions laid out on the stairs leading to the Old Town's hilltop. It serves tasty snacks and good Prosecco.

Piassa Granda WINE BAR
(Veli trg 1) This stylish little wine bar with red walls and wood-beamed ceilings has 150 wine labels, mainly Istrian, 20 *rakija* varieties and delicious snacks.

Valentino COCKTAIL BAR
(Križa 28) Premium cocktail prices at this high-end spot include fantastic sunset views from cushions scattered on the water's edge.

Havana COCKTAIL BAR
(Aldo Negri bb) Tropical cocktails, Cuban cigars, straw parasols and the shade of tall pine trees make this open-air bar a popular spot.

ℹ️ Information

There are ATMs and banks all around town. Most travel agencies will change money.

Globtour (☎814 130; www.globtour-turizam.hr; Alda Rismonda 2) Excursions and private accommodation.

Medical Centre (☎813 004; Istarska bb)

Planet (☎840 494; www.planetrovinj.com; Križa 1) Good bargains on private accommodation. Doubles as an internet cafe (6KN per 10 minutes) and has a printer.

Main post office (Matteo Benussi 4; ⊙8am-9pm Mon-Sat summer, 8am-7pm Mon-Fri, to 1pm Sat winter) You can make phone calls here.

Tourist office (☎811 566; www.tzgrovinj.hr; Pina Budicina 12; ⊙8am-10pm Jun-Sep, 8am-

3pm Mon-Fri, to 1pm Sat Oct-May) Has plenty of brochures and maps. Just off Trg Maršala Tita.

ℹ️ Getting There & Around

The bus station is just to the southeast of the Old Town. There's a **garderoba** (left-luggage office; per day 10KN; ⊙6.30am-8pm).

Poreč

POP 20,600

Poreč (Parenzo in Italian) sits on a low, narrow peninsula halfway down the western coast of Istria. The ancient Roman town is the centrepiece of a vast system of resorts that stretch north and south, entirely devoted to summer tourism. While this is not the place for a quiet getaway (unless you come out of season), there is a World Heritage–listed basilica, a medley of Gothic, Romanesque and baroque buildings, well-developed tourist infrastructure and the pristine Istrian interior within easy reach.

👁 Sights

The compact Old Town, called Parentium by the Romans, is based on a rectangular street plan. The ancient Decumanus with its polished stones is the main street running through the peninsula's middle, lined with shops and restaurants. Hotels, travel agencies and excursion boats are on the quayside Obala Maršala Tita, which runs from the small-boat harbour to the tip of the peninsula.

Euphrasian Basilica BASILICA
(Eufrazijeva bb; adult/concession 30/15KN; ⊙9am-6pm Mon-Sat, 2-6pm Sun Apr-Sep) The main reason to visit Poreč is to see the 6th-century Euphrasian Basilica, a World Heritage Site

and one of Europe's finest intact examples of Byzantine art. Built on the site of a 4th-century oratory, the sacral complex includes a church, an atrium and a baptistery. What packs in the crowds are the glittering wall mosaics in the apse, 6th-century masterpieces featuring biblical scenes, archangels and Istrian martyrs. The belfry affords an invigorating view of the Old Town.

Make sure to pop into the adjacent **Bishop's Palace**, which contains a display of ancient stone sculptures, religious paintings and 4th-century mosaics from the original oratory.

Sveti Nikola   ISLAND
There are pebble and concrete beaches to choose from here, as well as rocky breakwaters, shady pine forests and great views of the town across the way. From May to October there are passenger boats every 30 minutes (from 6.45am to 1am) from the wharf on Obala Maršala Tita.

🏃 Activities

Many recreational activities are to be found outside the town in either Plava Laguna or Zelena Laguna. For details, pick up the yearly *Poreč Info & Events* booklet from the tourist office.

From April to October, a **tourist train** operates regularly from Šetalište Antona Štifaniča by the marina to Plava Laguna (20KN) and Zelena Laguna (20KN). There's a **passenger boat** (15KN) that makes the same run from the ferry landing every hour from 9am till just before midnight.

The gentle rolling hills of the interior and the well-marked paths make **cycling** and **hiking** prime ways to explore the region. The tourist office issues a free map of roads and trails. You can rent a bike at many agencies around town for 80KN per day.

There is good diving in and around shoals and sandbanks in the area, as well as at the nearby Coriolanus, a British Royal Navy warship that sank in 1945. At **Diving Centre Poreč** (☏433 606; www.divingcenter-porec.com), boat dives start at 135KN (more for caves or wrecks) it's 355KN with full equipment rental.

🛏 Sleeping

Accommodation in Poreč is plentiful but gets booked ahead of time, so advance reservations are essential if you come in July or August.

Many travel agencies can help you find private accommodation. Expect to pay between 200KN and 250KN for a double room with private bathroom in the high season, plus a 30% surcharge for stays shorter than three nights. There is a limited number of rooms available in the Old Town, which has no parking. Look for the *Domus Bonus* certificate of quality in private accommodation.

Valamar Riviera Hotel   HOTEL €€€
(☏400 800; www.valamar.com; Maršala Tita 15; s/d 1230/1455KN; P❄@🛜) Rather swanky four-star incarnation right on the harbourfront, with a private beach on Sveti Nikola. Look out for online specials and packages.

Hotel Poreč   HOTEL €€
(☏451 811; www.hotelporec.com; Rade Končara 1; s/d 496/760KN; P❄🛜) While the rooms inside this concrete box have uninspiring views over the bus station and the construction site for the shopping centre opposite, they're acceptable. They have balconies and it's an easy walk from the Old Town.

Camping Zelena Laguna   CAMPING GROUND €
(☏410 102; www.lagunaporec.com; Zelena Laguna; campsite per adult/site 62/117KN; ⏾mid-Apr–Sep; ❄@🛜♿) Well-equipped for sports, this camping ground 5km from the Old Town can house up to 2700 people. It has access to many beaches, including a naturist one.

🍴 Eating

Gourmet   ITALIAN €€
(Eufrazijeva 26; mains from 60KN) Comforting Italian concoctions come in all shapes and forms here – penne, tagliatelle, fusilli, gnocchi and so on. There are also pizzas from a wood-fired oven as well as meat and seafood dishes. Tables spill out on the square.

TOP CHOICE Konoba Daniela   ISTRIAN €€
(☏460 519; Veleniki; mains from 65KN) In the sweet little village of Veleniki, 4.5km northeast of town, this rustic family-run tavern in an 1880s house is known for its steak tartare and seasonal Istrian mainstays. Taxis charge 80KN to 100KN one way.

Buffet Horizont   FAST FOOD €
(Eufrazijeva 8; mains from 30KN) For cheap and tasty seafood snacks such as sardines, shrimp and calamari, look out for this yellow house with wooden benches outside.

Drinking & Entertainment

In the last couple of years, Poreč has turned into Istria's party capital, with nightlife hawks coming from all parts of Europe to let loose in its late-night clubs.

Rakijarnica   BAR
(Trg Marafor 10) Funky bar that specialises in *rakija*, serving up no less than 50 varieties. The vibe is boho and there are occasional live bands and DJs.

Torre Rotonda   CAFE-BAR
(Narodni trg 3a) Take the steep stairs to the top of the historic Round Tower and grab a table at the open-air cafe to watch the action on the quays.

Byblos   CLUB
(www.byblos.hr; Zelena Laguna 1) On weekends, celeb guest DJs such as David Morales crank out electro house tunes at this humongous open-air club, one of Croatia's hottest places to party.

❶ Information

You can change money at any of the many travel agencies or banks. There are ATMs all around town. There's free wi-fi on Trg Slobode and along the seafront.

Cold Fusion (K Huguesa 2; per hr 30KN; ⊙9am-10pm) A computer centre at the bus station.

Main post office (Trg Slobode 14; ⊙8am-8pm Mon-Sat) Has a telephone centre.

Poreč Medical Centre (☑426 400; Maura Gioseffija 2)

Sunny Way (☑452 021; sunnyway@pu.t-com. hr; Negrija 1) Specialises in boat tickets and excursions to Italy and around Croatia.

Tourist office (☑451 293; www.to-porec.com; Zagrebačka 9; ⊙8am-9pm Mon-Sat, 9am-1pm & 5-9pm Sun May-Sep, 8am-4pm Mon-Fri, 9am-1pm Sat Oct-Apr) Gives out lots of brochures and useful info.

❶ Getting There & Away

The **bus station** (☑060 333 111; K Huguesa 2) is just outside the Old Town, behind Rade Končara, with a **garderoba** (left luggage; per hr 10KN; ⊙6am-9pm). There are buses to Rovinj (42KN, 45 minutes, five daily), Zagreb (226KN, 4½ hours, five daily), Rijeka (89KN, 1½ hours, seven daily) and Pula (63KN, one to 1½ hours, five daily).

Ustica Line (www.usticalines.it) runs catamarans to Trieste every Saturday during the season (210KN, 1½ hours). There are four fast catamarans to Venice daily in high season (one way 250KN to 440KN, return 390KN to 880KN,

two hours), operated by **Venezia Lines** (www. venezialines.com) and **Commodore Cruises** (www.commodore-cruises.hr).

KVARNER REGION

☑051

The Kvarner Gulf (Quarnero in Italian) covers 3300 sq km between Rijeka and Pag Island in the south, protected by the Velebit Range in the southeast, the Gorski Kotar in the east and the Učka massif in the northwest. Covered with luxuriant forests, lined with beaches and dotted with islands, the region has a mild gentle climate and a wealth of vegetation.

From the gateway city of Rijeka, Croatia's third-largest, you can easily connect to the foodie enclave of Volosko and the hiking trails inside the nature parks of Učka. The islands of Krk, Rab, Lošinj and Cres all have highly atmospheric old ports, and stretches of pristine coastline dotted with remote coves for superb swimming.

Rijeka

POP 128,700

Rijeka, Croatia's third-largest city, is an intriguing blend of gritty port and Hapsburg grandeur. Most people rush through en route to the islands or Dalmatia, but those who pause will discover charm and culture. Blend in with the coffee-sipping locals on the bustling Korzo pedestrian strip, take in the city museums and visit the imposing hilltop fortress of Trsat. Rijeka also boasts a good nightlife, intriguing festivals and Croatia's most colourful carnival.

Despite some regrettable architectural ventures in the outskirts, much of the centre is replete with ornate Austro-Hungarian–style buildings. It's a surprisingly verdant city once you've left its concrete core, which contains Croatia's largest port, with ships, cargo and cranes lining the waterfront.

Rijeka is a vital transport hub, but as there's no real beach in the city (and hotel options are few) most people base themselves in nearby Opatija.

⊙ Sights

Trsat Castle   CASTLE
(adult/concession 15/5KN; ⊙9am-8pm May-Oct, to 5pm Nov-Apr) High on a hill above the city is this semi-ruined, 13th-century fortress that houses two galleries and has great vistas from the open-air cafe.

Church of Our Lady of Trsat   CHURCH
(Crkva Gospe Trsatske; Frankopanski Trg; ⊘8am-5pm) Along with Trsat Castle, the other hill highlight is the Church of Our Lady of Trsat, a centuries-old magnet for believers that showcases an apparently miraculous icon of Virgin Mary.

City Monuments   MONUMENTS
(Trg Ivana Koblera) One of the few buildings to have survived the earthquake, the distinctive yellow **City Tower** (Gradski Toranj; Korzo) was originally a gate from the seafront to the city. The still-functioning clock was mounted in 1873.

Pass under the City Tower to the **Roman Gate** (Stara Vrata), which marks the former entrance to Praetorium, an ancient military complex; you can see the remains in a small excavation area.

Maritime & History Museum   MUSEUM
(Pomorski i Povijesni Muzej Hrvatskog Primorja; www.ppmhp.hr; Muzejski trg 1; adult/concession 10/5KN; ⊘9am-4pm Tue-Fri, to 1pm Sat) Housed in the Governor's Palace, this museum gives a vivid picture of life among seafarers, with model ships, sea charts, navigation instruments and portraits of captains.

Astronomical Centre   OBSERVATORY
(Astronomski Centar; www.rijekasport.hr; Sveti Križ 33; ⊘8am-11pm Tue-Sat) High on a hill in the east of the city, Croatia's first astronomical centre is a striking modern complex encompassing an observatory, planetarium and study centre. To get here, catch bus 7A from the centre.

✨ Festivals & Events

Rijeka Carnival   CARNIVAL
(www.ri-karneval.com.hr) This is the largest carnival in Croatia, with two weeks of pageants, street dances, concerts, masked balls, exhibitions and parades. It occurs between late January and early March, depending on when Easter falls.

Hartera   MUSIC
(www.hartera.com) Hartera is an annual electronic music festival with DJs and artists from across Europe. It's held in a former paper factory on the banks of the Rječina River over three days in mid-June.

🛏 Sleeping

Prices in Rijeka hotels generally stay the same year-round, except at popular carnival time, when you can expect to pay a surcharge. There are few private rooms in Rijeka itself; the tourist office (p198) lists these on its website. Nearby Opatija has a lot more accommodation.

Grand Hotel Bonavia   HOTEL €€€
(⌨357 100; www.bonavia.hr; Dolac 4; s/d from 800/977KN; P✳@🛜) Right in the heart of town, this striking glass-fronted modernist building is Rijeka's top hotel. The rooms are well-equipped and comfort levels are high. There's a well-regarded restaurant, a spa and a stylish pavement cafe.

Best Western Hotel Jadran   HOTEL €€€
(⌨216 600; www.jadran-hoteli.hr; Šetalište XIII Divizije 46; s/d from 706/833KN; P✳@🛜) Located 2km east of the centre, this attractive four-star hotel has seaview rooms where you can revel in the tremendous Adriatic vistas from your balcony right above the water. There's a tiny beach below.

Hotel Neboder   HOTEL €€
(⌨373 538; www.jadran-hoteli.hr; Strossmayerova 1; s/d from 462/578KN; P✳@) An iconic design, this modernist tower block offers small, neat and modish rooms, most with balconies and amazing views; however, only the superior rooms have air-conditioning.

Youth Hostel   HOSTEL €
(⌨406 420; www.hfhs.hr; Šetalište XIII Divizije 23; dm/s/d 130/236/314KN; @🛜) In the leafy residential area of Pečine, 2km east of the centre, this renovated 19th-century villa has clean, spacious (if plain) rooms and a communal TV area. Reserve ahead.

🍴 Eating

There's very little choice on Sundays, when most places are closed. Many cafes on Korzo serve light meals.

Foodies should consider heading to nearby Volosko, 2km east of Opatija, where there's a strip of really high-quality restaurants.

[TOP CHOICE] Na Kantunu   SEAFOOD €€
(Demetrova 2; mains from 45KN) If you're lucky enough to grab a table at this tiny lunchtime spot on an industrial stretch of the port, you'll be treated to the superlative daily catch.

Kukuriku   CROATIAN €€€
(⌨691 519; www.kukuriku.hr; Trg Matka Laginje 1a, Kastav; 6-course meals 380-550KN; ⊘closed Mon Nov-Easter) This opulent yet modern hotel-restaurant is owned by slow-food pioneer

Nenad Kukurin, who has a reputation for his innovative take on traditional Croatian recipes. Located in historic Kastav, Rijeka's hilltop suburb, it's worth the splurge. Take bus 18 from Rijeka (33 and 37 from Opatija).

Restaurant Spagho   ITALIAN €
(Ivana Zajca 24a; mains from 40KN) A stylish, modern Italian place with exposed brick-work, art and hip seating that offers delicious and filling portions of pasta, pizza, salads, and meat and fish dishes.

Zlatna Školjka   SEAFOOD €€
(Kružna 12; mains from 65KN) Savour the superbly prepared seafood and choice Croatian wines at this formal maritime-themed restaurant. The adjacent Bracera (Kružna 12; mains from 60KN), by the same owners, serves crusty pizza, even on a Sunday.

Mlinar   BAKERY €
(Frana Supila; items from 13KN; ⊙6am-8pm Mon-Fri, 6.30am-3pm Sat, 7am-1pm Sun) The best bakery in town, with delicious filled baguettes, wholemeal bread, croissants and *burek*.

▼ Drinking
The main drags of Riva and Korzo are the best bet for a drink, with everything from lounge bars to no-nonsense pubs.

TOP⁄CHOICE Gradena   CAFE
(www.bascinskiglasi.hr; Trsat; 🕾) Set in the grounds of Trsat Castle, this happening cafe-bar with chillout music and friendly service would rate anywhere.

Filodrammatica Bookshop Cafe   CAFE
(☎498 141; www.vbz.hr; Korzo 28) A cafe and bar with luxurious decor and a VBZ (Croatia's biggest publisher) bookshop at the back, Filodrammatica also prides itself on specialist coffees and fresh, single-source beans.

Caffe Jazz Tunel   BAR
(☎327 116; www.jazztunel.com; Školjić 12; ⊙9am-2am Mon-Fri, 5pm-2am Sat) One of the city's most popular bars, it's crowded all week long, but full to bursting on Friday and Saturday nights when you can find live music or DJs rocking the night.

❶ Information
There are ATMs and exchange offices along Korzo and at the train station.

Hospital (☎658 111; Krešimirova 42)

Main post office (Korzo 13; ⊙7am-8pm Mon-Fri, to 2pm Sat) Has a telephone centre and an exchange office.

Tourist Information Centre (☎335 882; www.tz-rijeka.hr; Korzo 33a; ⊙8am-8pm Mon-Sat Apr-Sep, 8am-8pm Mon-Fri, to 2pm Sat Oct-Mar) Has good colour city maps, lots of brochures and private accommodation lists, though the staff can be aloof.

❶ Getting There & Away
BOAT Jadroagent (☎211 626; www.jadroagent.hr; Trg Ivana Koblera 2) Has information on all boats around Croatia.

Jadrolinija (☎211 444; www.jadrolinija.hr; Riječki Lukobran bb; ⊙8am-8pm Mon-Fri, 9am-5pm Sat & Sun) Sells tickets for the large coastal ferries that run all year between Rijeka and Dubrovnik on their way to Bari in Italy, via Split, Hvar, Korčula and Mljet. Check Jadrolinija's website for up-to-date schedules and prices. All ferries depart from the new ferry terminal.

BUS The **intercity bus station** (Trg Žabica) is west of the centre, at the western edge of Riva. The bus-station **garderoba** (left-luggage office; per day 15KN; ⊙5.30am-10.30pm) is at the cafe next door to the ticket office.

If you fly into Zagreb, there is a Croatia Airlines van that goes directly from Zagreb airport to Rijeka daily (160KN, two hours, 3.30pm). It goes back to Zagreb from Rijeka at 5am. There are three daily buses to Trieste (60KN, 2½ hours)

DOMESTIC BUSES FROM RIJEKA

DESTINATION	PRICE (KN)	DURATION (HR)	FREQUENCY (DAILY)
Dubrovnik	362-503	12-13	3-4
Krk	59	1-2	14
Pula	97	2¼	8
Rovinj	90	1-2	4
Split	253-330	8	6-7
Zadar	161-210	4-5	6-7
Zagreb	137-160	2¼-3	13-15

and one daily bus to Ljubljana (175KN, five hours). To get to Plitvice (142KN, four hours), you have to change in Otočac.

CAR AMC (☑338 800; www.amcrentacar.hr; Lukobran 4) Based in the new ferry terminal building, has cars starting from 250KN per day.

TRAIN The **train station** (☑213 333; Krešimirova 5) is a 10-minute walk east of the city centre; ther's a **garderoba** (left-luggage office; per day 15KN; ☺4.30am-10.30pm). Seven daily trains run to Zagreb (100KN, four to five hours). There's one daily connection to Split (170KN, eight hours), though it involves a change at Ogulin. Two direct daily services head to Ljubljana (98KN, three hours) and one daily train goes to Vienna (319KN to 525KN, nine hours).

❶ Getting Around

Taxis are very reasonable in Rijeka (if you use the right firm). **Cammeo** (☑313 313) cabs are modern, inexpensive, have meters and are highly recommended; a ride in the central area costs 20KN.

Opatija

POP 7870

Opatija stretches along the coast, just 15km west of Rijeka, its forested hills sloping down to the sparkling sea. It was this breathtaking location and the agreeable all-year climate that made Opatija the most fashionable seaside resort for the Viennese elite during the days of the Austro-Hungarian empire. The grand residences of the wealthy have since been revamped and turned into upscale hotels, with a particular accent on spa and health holidays. Foodies have been flocking from afar too, for the clutch of terrific restaurants in the nearby fishing village of Volosko.

Opatija sits on a narrow strip of land sandwiched between the sea and the foothills of Mt Učka. Ulica Maršala Tita is the main road that runs through town; it's lined with travel agencies, ATMs, restaurants, shops and hotels.

◉ Sights & Activities

Lungomare PROMENADE
The pretty Lungomare is the region's showcase. Lined with plush villas and ample gardens, this shady promenade winds along the sea for 12km from Volosko to Lovran. Along the way are innumerable rocky outcrops – a better option than Opatija's concrete beach.

Villa Angiolina HISTORICAL BUILDING
(Park Angiolina 1; ☺9am-1pm & 4.30-9.30pm Tue-Sun summer, shorter hours rest of year) The restored Villa Angiolina houses the **Croatian Museum of Tourism**, a grand title for a modest collection of old photographs, postcards, brochures and posters tracing the history of travel. Don't miss a stroll around the verdant gardens that surround the villa, replete with gingko trees, sequoias, holm oaks and Japanese camellia (Opatija's symbol).

Učka Nature Park NATURE RESERVE
Opatija and the surrounding region offer some wonderful opportunities for hiking and biking around the Učka mountain range; the **tourist office** (☑293 753; www.pp-ucka.hr; Liganj 42; ☺8am-4.30pm Mon-Fri) has maps and information.

🛏 Sleeping & Eating

There are no real budget hotels in Opatija, but there's plenty of value in the midrange and top end. Private rooms are abundant but a little more expensive than in other areas; expect to pay around 170KN to 240KN per person.

Maršala Tita is lined with serviceable restaurants that offer pizza, grilled meat and fish, but don't expect anything outstanding. Head to nearby Volosko for fine dining and regional specialties.

Villa Ariston HISTORIC HOTEL €€
(☑271 379; www.villa-ariston.com; Ulica Maršala Tita 179; s/d 600/800KN; P❋@☎) With a gorgeous location beside a rocky cove, this historic hotel has period charm and celeb cachet in spades (Coco Chanel and the Kennedys are former guests).

Hotel Opatija HOTEL €€
(☑271 388; www.hotel-opatija.hr; Trg Vladimira Gortana 2/1; r from 486KN; P❋@☎) The setting in a Habsburg-era mansion is the forte of this large hilltop three-star hotel with comfortable rooms, an amazing terrace, a small indoor seawater pool and lovely gardens.

Medveja CAMPING GROUND €
(☑291 191; medveja@liburnia.hr; campsites per adult/tent 44/32KN; ☺Easter–mid-Oct) On a pretty pebble cove 10km south of Opatija, this camping ground has apartments and mobile homes for rent too.

Istranka ISTRIAN €
(Bože Milanovića 2; mains from 55KN) Graze on flavourful Istrian mainstays like *maneštra* (vegetable and bean soup) at this rustic-themed tavern in a small street just up from Maršala Tita.

WORTH A TRIP

VOLOSKO

Volosko is one of the prettiest places on this coastline, a fishing village that has also become something of a restaurant mecca in recent years. This is not a tourist resort, and whether you're passing through for a drink or having a gourmet meal you'll enjoy the local ambience and wonderful setting.

Rijeka and Volosko are connected by bus, or you can walk along the coastal promenade from Opatija, a 30-minute stroll past bay trees, palms, figs and oaks and magnificent villas.

Tramerka (Andrije Mohorovičića 15; mains from 65KN; ⊙Tue-Sun) It doesn't have sea views but this wonderful place scores on every other level. Chef-patron Andrej Barbieri will expertly guide you through the short menu, chosen from the freshest available seafood (the *gregada* fish stew is just stupendous) and locally sourced meats.

Skalinada (www.skalinada.org; Put Uz Dol 17; meals from 80KN) An intimate, highly atmospheric little bistro-style place with sensitive lighting, exposed stone walls and a creative menu of Croatian food (small dishes or mains) using seasonal and local ingredients.

Drinking & Entertainment

Opatija is a pretty sedate place. Its Viennese-style coffee houses and hotel terraces are popular with the mature clientele, though there are a few stylish bars. Check out the slightly bohemian **Tantra** (Lido), which juts out into the Kvarner Gulf, and **Hemingway** (Zert 2), the original venue of what is now a nationwide chain of sleek cocktail bars.

Information

Da Riva (☑272 990; www.da-riva.hr; Ulica Maršala Tita 170) A good source for private accommodation, and runs excursions around Croatia.

Linea Verde (☑701 107; www.lineaverde-croatia.com; Andrije Štangera 42, Volosko) Specialist agency with trips to Risnjak and Učka Nature Park and gourmet tours around Istria.

Tourist office (☑271 310; www.opatija-tourism.hr; Ulica Maršala Tita 128; ⊙8am-10pm Mon-Sat, 5-9pm Sun Jul & Aug, shorter hours rest of year) This office has knowledgeable staff and lots of maps, leaflets and brochures.

Getting There & Away

Bus 32 runs through the centre of Rijeka along Adamićeva to the Opatija Riviera (20KN, 15km) as far as Lovran, every 20 minutes daily until late in the evening.

Krk Island

POP 16,400

Croatia's largest island, 409-sq-km Krk (Veglia in Italian) is also one of the busiest in the summer. It may not be the most beautiful or lush island in Croatia – in fact, it's overdeveloped – but its decades of experience in tourism make it an easy place to visit, with good transport connections and well-organised infrastructure.

Getting There & Around

The Krk toll bridge links the northern part of the island with the mainland, and a regular car ferry links Valbiska with Merag on Cres (passenger/car 18KN/115KN, 30 minutes) in summer.

Krk is also home to **Rijeka airport** (www.rijeka-airport.hr), the main hub for flights to the Kvarner region, which consist mostly of low-cost and charter flights during summer.

Rijeka and Krk Town are connected by nine to 13 daily bus services (56KN, one to two hours). Services are reduced on weekends.

Six daily buses run from Zagreb to Krk Town (179KN to 194KN, three to four hours). Note that some bus lines are more direct than others, which will stop in every village en route. **Autotrans** (www.autotrans.hr) has two quick daily buses.

KRK TOWN

POP 3370

The picturesque Krk Town makes a good base for exploring the island. It encompasses a medieval walled centre and, spreading out into the surrounding coves and hills, a modern development that includes a port, beaches, camping grounds and hotels.

Sights

Highlights include the Romanesque **Cathedral of the Assumption** (Katedrala Uznešenja; Trg Svetog Kvirina; ⊙morning & evening Mass) and the fortified **Kaštel** (Trg Kamplin) facing the seafront on the northern edge of the Old

Town. The narrow cobbled streets that make up the pretty old quarter are worth a wander, although they're typically packed.

Sleeping & Eating

The Old Town only has one hotel; all the others are located in a large complex east of the centre and are very family orientated. Consult travel agencies for private accommodation. Note that the only hostel in town is pretty rundown.

TOP CHOICE Hotel Marina   BOUTIQUE HOTEL €€€
(☑221 357; www.hotelikrk.hr; Obala Hrvatske Mornarice 6; d 1460KN; P❄@☎) The only hotel in the Old Town enjoys a prime waterfront location and has 10 deluxe contemporary units.

Bor   HOTEL €€
(☑220 200; www.hotelbor.hr; Šetalište Dražica 5; s/d from 480/960KN; ☺Apr-Oct; P☎) The 22 rooms are modest and without trimmings at this low-key hotel, but the seafront location amid mature pines makes it a worthwhile place to stay.

Autocamp Ježevac   CAMPING GROUND €
(☑221 081; camping@valamar.com; Plavnička bb; campsite per adult/site 50/62KN; ☺mid-Apr–mid-Oct) Beachfront camping ground with shady pitches located on old farming terraces, with good swimming sites. It's a 10-minute walk southwest of town.

Konoba Nono   CROATIAN €
(Krčkih Iseljenika 8; mains from 40KN) Savour local specialties like *šurlice sa junećim* (pasta topped with goulash), just a hop and a skip from the Old Town.

Galija   PIZZERIA €
(www.galija-krk.com; Frankopanska 38; mains from 45KN) Munch your *margarita* or *vagabondo* pizza, grilled meat or fresh fish under beamed ceilings of this convivial part-*konoba*, part-pizzeria.

ℹ Information

The **main tourist office** (☑220 226; Vela Placa 1; ☺8am-3pm Mon-Fri) and **seasonal tourist office** (☑220 226; www.tz-krk.hr; Obala Hrvatske Mornarice bb; ☺8am-8pm Mon-Sat, 8am-2pm Sun Jun-Oct & Easter-May) distribute brochures and materials, including a map of hiking paths, and advice in many languages.

You can change money at any travel agency and there are numerous ATMs around town.

The bus from Rijeka stops at the station (no left-luggage office) by the harbour, a few minutes' walk from the Old Town.

DALMATIA

Roman ruins, spectacular beaches, old fishing ports, medieval architecture and unspoilt offshore islands make a trip to Dalmatia (Dalmacija) unforgettable. Occupying the central 375km of Croatia's Adriatic

---

LOŠINJ & CRES ISLANDS

Separated by an 11m-wide canal (with a bridge), these two highly scenic islands in the Kvarner archipelago are often treated as a single entity. On Lošinj, the more populated of the two, the pretty ports of Mali Lošinj and Veli Lošinj, ringed by pine forests and lush vegetation, attract plenty of summertime tourists. Consequently, there are varied sleeping and eating options. The waters around Lošinj are the first protected marine area for dolphins in the entire Mediterranean, watched over by the Mali Lošinj–based **Blue World** (www.blue-world.org) NGO.

Wilder, more barren Cres has a natural allure that's intoxicating and inspiring. Sparsely populated, it's covered in dense primeval forests and lined with a craggy coastline of soaring cliffs, hidden coves and ancient hilltop towns. The northern half of Cres, known as Tramuntana, is prime cruising terrain for the protected griffon vulture; see these giant birds at **Eco-Centre Caput Insulae** (☑840 525; www.supovi.hr; Beli 4; adult/concession 50/25KN; ☺9am-8pm, closed Nov-Mar), an excellent visitor centre in Beli on the eastern coast. The main seaside settlements lie on the western shore of Cres, while the highlands showcase the astounding medieval town of Lubenice.

The main maritime port of entry for the islands is Mali Lošinj, which is connected to Rijeka, Pula, Zadar and Venice in the summer. A variety of car ferries and catamaran boats are run by **Jadrolinija** (www.jadrolinija.hr), **Split Tours** (www.splittours.hr) and **Venezia Lines** (www.venezialines.com).

coast, Dalmatia offers a matchless combination of hedonism and historical discovery. The jagged coast is speckled with lush offshore islands and dotted with historic cities.

Split is the largest city in the region and a hub for bus and boat connections along the Adriatic, as well as home to the late-Roman Diocletian's Palace. Nearby are the early Roman ruins in Solin (Salona). Zadar has yet more Roman ruins and a wealth of churches. The architecture of Hvar and Korčula recalls the days when these islands were outposts of the Venetian empire. None can rival majestic Dubrovnik, a cultural and aesthetic jewel, while magical Mljet features isolated island beauty.

Zadar

📲 023 / POP 73,400

Boasting a historic Old Town of Roman ruins and medieval churches, cosmopolitan cafes and quality museums, Zadar is an excellent city. It's not too crowded, it's not overrun with tourists and its two unique attractions – the sound-and-light spectacles of the Sea Organ and the Sun Salutation – need to be seen and heard to be believed.

It's not a picture-postcard kind of place, but the mix of beautiful Roman architecture, Hapsburg elegance, a wonderful seafront and some unsightly ordinary office blocks is what gives Zadar so much character – it's no Dubrovnik, but it's not a museum town either; this is a living, vibrant city, enjoyed by its residents and visitors alike.

The centre of town is not well blessed with hotels, though a few new places are springing up each year. Most visitors stay in the leafy resort area of Borik nearby. Zadar is a key transport hub with superb ferry connections to Croatia's Adriatic islands, Kvarner, southern Dalmatia and Italy.

◎ Sights

Sea Organ   MONUMENT
Zadar's incredible Sea Organ, designed by architect Nikola Bašić, has a hypnotic effect. Set within the perforated stone stairs that descend into the sea is a system of pipes and whistles that exudes wistful sighs when the movement of the sea pushes air through it.

Sun Salutation   MONUMENT
(🔊) Right next to the Sea Organ is the Sun Salutation, another wacky and wonderful Bašić creation. It's a 22m circle cut into the pavement, filled with 300 multilayered glass

plates that collect the sun's energy during the day, and, together with the wave energy that makes the Sea Organ's sound, produce a trippy light show from sunset to sunrise that's meant to simulate the solar system.

Church of St Donat   CHURCH
(Crkva Svetog Donata; Šimuna Kožičića Benje; admission 15KN; ⊙9am-9pm May-Sep, to 4pm Oct-Apr) This circular 9th-century Byzantine structure was built over the Roman forum. A few architectural fragments are preserved inside. Notice the Latin inscriptions on the remains of the Roman sacrificial altars. Outside the church on the northwestern side is a pillar from the Roman era that served in the Middle Ages as a shame post, where wrongdoers were chained and publicly humiliated.

Museum of Ancient Glass   MUSEUM
(www.mas-zadar.hr; Poljana Zemaljskog Odbora 1; adult/concession 30/10KN; ⊙9am-9pm May-Sep, to 7pm Mon-Sat Oct-Apr) This is an impressive museum: its layout is superb, with giant lightboxes and ethereal music to make the experience special. The history and invention of glass is explained, through thousands of pieces on display: goblets, jars and vials; jewellery, rings and amulets.

Beaches   BEACHES
You can swim from the steps off the promenade and listen to the sound of the Sea Organ. There's a swimming area with diving boards, a small park and a cafe on the coastal promenade off Zvonimira. Bordered by pine trees and parks, the promenade takes you to a beach in front of Hotel Kolovare and then winds on for about a kilometre up the coast.

♈ Tours

Travel agencies offer boat cruises to Telašćica Bay and the beautiful Kornati Islands, which include lunch and a swim in the sea or a salt lake. Aquarius Travel Agency (p204) charges 250–300KN per person for a full-day trip, or ask around on Liburnska Obala (where the excursion boats are moored).

Organised trips to the national parks of Paklenica, Krka and Plitvice Lakes are also popular.

✨ Festivals & Events

Between July and September, the Zadar region showcases some of the globe's most celebrated electronic artists, bands and DJs. The ringmaster for these festivals is the Zadar-based Garden (p203) bar, but the festivals are held in a gorgeous new location, in the small village of Tisno, 45km south of Zadar. The original event, the **Garden Festival** (www.thegardenfestival.eu), has been running every July since 2006. By 2010, four other festivals (Soundwave, Suncebeat, Electric Elephant and Stop Making Sense) had joined the party between July and September.

🛏 Sleeping

Most visitors stay in the 'tourist settlement' of Borik, which isn't as bad as it sounds as it has good swimming, a nice promenade and lots of greenery. Most hotels in Borik date from Yugo days (or before) and there's also a hostel, camping ground and *sobe* (rooms) here too. Many hotels are managed by the Austria-based **Falkensteiner** (www.falkensteiner.com) group.

Contact travel agencies for private accommodation; very little is available in the Old Town, though.

ZADAR

TOP CHOICE **Art Hotel Kalelarga** BOUTIQUE HOTEL **€€€**
(📞233 000; www.arthotel-kalelarga.com; Široka 23; s/d/ste 1225/1430/2300KN; 🅿❄️🛜) Right in the heart of Zadar's Old Town, this 10-room boutique hotel is an understated beauty with a stylish cafe and spacious rooms in hues of sand and stone, with grand beds, elaborate lighting and cool lines. There is also a restaurant, which has tables on the main square.

Villa Hrešć HOTEL **€€**
(📞337 570; www.villa-hresc.hr; Obala Kneza Trpimira 28; s/d 670/850KN; 🅿❄️🛜🏊🍴) This condostyle villa is about a 20-minute walk from Zadar's historic sights. There's a coastal garden with an Old Town vista, and good-value rooms and apartments benefit from subtle colours and attractive decor. Some have massive terraces.

Hotel Venera GUESTHOUSE **€€**
(📞214 098; www.hotel-venera-zd.hr; Šime Ljubića 4a; d 460KN) A modest guesthouse that has two things going for it: a good location on a quiet street in the Old Town and the friendly family owners. Breakfast not included.

Student Hostel HOSTEL **€**
(📞224 840; Obala Kneza Branimira bb; dm 153KN; ⏱Jul & Aug) This student dormitory turns into a hostel in July and August. It's centrally located – right across the footbridge – and has no-frills three-bed rooms.

BORIK

Autocamp Borik CAMPING GROUND **€**
(📞332 074; per adult 56KN, per campsite 94-146KN; ⏱May-Oct) A good option for those who want easy access to Zadar, this camping ground is steps away from the shore at Borik. Pitches are shaded by tall pines.

🍴 Eating

Dining options in Zadar are eclectic and generally good value. You'll find elegant restaurants specialising in Dalmatian cuisine and no-nonsense canteen-style places offering filling grub.

Zadar's **market** (⏱6am-3pm), off Jurja Barakovica, is one of Croatia's best.

TOP CHOICE **Foša** MEDITERRANEAN **€€**
(www.fosa.hr; Kralja Dmitra Zvonimira 2; mains from 85KN) A classy place with a sleek interior and a gorgeous terrace that juts out into the harbour. Start by tasting the olive oils, and move on to a grilled Adriatic fish of your choice, though red-meat eaters won't be disappointed either.

Na po ure DALMATIAN **€**
(Špire Brusine 8; mains from 40KN) This unpretentious family-run *konoba* is the place to sate that appetite, with from-the-heart Dalmatian cooking: grilled lamb, calf's liver and fresh fish served with potatoes and vegetables.

Zalogajnica Ljepotica DALMATIAN **€**
(Obala Kneza Branimira 4b; mains from 35KN) The cheapest place in town prepares three to four dishes a day (think risotto, pasta and grilled meat) at knockout prices in a no-frills setting.

🍷 Drinking

Zadar has pavement cafes, lounge bars, boho bars and everything in between. Head to the district of Varoš on the southwest side of the Old Town for interesting little dive bars popular with students and arty types.

TOP CHOICE **Garden** BAR, RESTAURANT
(www.thegardenzadar.com; Bedemi Zadarskih Pobuna; ⏱late May-Oct) If anywhere can claim to have put Zadar on the map it's this remarkable bar-club-garden-restaurant perched on top of the old city walls with jaw-dropping harbour views. It's very Ibiza-esque, with cushion mattresses, secluded alcoves, vast sail-like sunshades, purple-and-white decor and contemporary electronic music.

Arsenal   BAR, RESTAURANT
(www.arsenalzadar.com; Trg Tri Bunara 1) A huge
renovated shipping warehouse that now
contains a lounge bar, a restaurant, a gallery
and a cultural centre and has a cool, cultured vibe. There are musical events, good
food and even a tourist-info desk (which
may or may not be staffed).

Caffe Bar Lovre   CAFE
(Narodni trg 1) With a huge terrace on Narodni
Trg, gorgeous Lovre has plenty of atmos-
phere and a heart-of-the-city vibe.

ⓘ Information

Aquarius Travel Agency (☑212 919; www.
juresko.hr; Nova Vrata bb) Books accommoda-
tion and excursions.
Geris.net (Federica Grisogona 81; per hr 25KN)
The city's best cybercafe.
Hospital (☑315 677; Bože Peričića 5)
Miatours (☑/fax 212 788; www.miatours.hr;
Vrata Svetog Krševana) Arranges excursions
and accommodation.
Post office (Poljana Pape Aleksandra III;
⊘7.30am-9pm Mon-Sat, to 2pm Sun) You can
make phone calls here and it has an ATM.
Tourist office (☑316 166; www.tzzadar.hr;
Mihe Klaića 5; ⊘8am-10pm Mon-Fri, to 9pm
Sat & Sun Jun-Sep, to 8pm daily Oct-May)
Publishes a good colour map and the free *Zadar
City Guide*.

ⓘ Getting There & Away

AIR Zadar's airport, 12km east of the city, is
served by **Croatia Airlines** (☑250 101; www.
croatiaairlines.hr; Poljana Natka Nodila 7) and
Ryanair (www.ryanair.com). A Croatia Airlines bus
meets all flights and costs 23KN. For a taxi, call
the very efficient and cheap **Lulić** (☑494 494).
BOAT On the harbour, **Jadrolinija** (☑254 800;
www.jadrolinija.hr; Liburnska Obala 7) has
tickets for all local ferries. Buy international
tickets from **Jadroagent** (☑211 447; jadroagent-
zadar@zd.t-com.hr; Poljana Natka Nodila 4), just
inside the city walls.
BUS The **bus station** (☑211 035; www.liburnija-
zadar.hr) is about 2km east of the Old Town and
has daily buses to Zagreb (97KN to 147KN, 3½ to
seven hours, every 30 minutes). Buses marked
'Poluotok' run from the bus station to the harbour and those marked 'Puntamika' (5 and 8) run
to Borik every 20 minutes (hourly on Sunday).
Tickets cost 10KN (15KN for two from a *tisak*).
TRAIN The **train station** (☑212 555; www.
hznet.hr; Ante Starčevića 3) is adjacent to the
bus station. There are six daily trains to Zagreb,
but the journey time is very slow indeed; the
fastest take over eight hours.

Split

☑021 / POP 178,200
The second-largest city in Croatia, Split
(Spalato in Italian) is a great place to see
Dalmatian life as it's really lived. Always
buzzing, this exuberant city has just the right
balance of tradition and modernity. Step
inside Diocletian's Palace (a Unesco World
Heritage site and one of the world's most impressive Roman monuments) and you'll see
dozens of bars, restaurants and shops thriving amid the atmospheric old walls where
Split life has been going on for thousands of
years. To top it off, Split has a unique setting. Its dramatic coastal mountains act as
the perfect backdrop to the turquoise waters
of the Adriatic. You'll get a chance to appreciate this gorgeous cityscape when making a
ferry journey to or from the city.

The Old Town is a vast open-air museum
and the new information signs at the important sights explain a great deal of Split's
history. The seafront promenade, Obala Hrvatskog Narodnog Preporoda, better known
as Riva, is the best central reference point.

History

Split achieved fame when Roman emperor Diocletian (AD 245–313) had his retirement palace built here from 295 to 305. After his death
the great stone palace continued to be used as
a retreat by Roman rulers. When the neighbouring colony of Salona was abandoned in
the 7th century, many of the Romanised inhabitants fled to Split and barricaded themselves behind the palace walls, where their
descendants continue to live to this day.

⊙ Sights

DIOCLETIAN'S PALACE
Facing the harbour, **Diocletian's Palace** is
one of the most imposing Roman ruins in
existence. Don't expect a palace though, nor
a museum – this is the living heart of the
city, its labyrinthine streets packed with people, bars, shops and restaurants.

It was built as a military fortress, imperial residence and fortified town, with walls
reinforced by square corner towers.

Each wall has a gate named after a metal:
at the northern end is the **Golden Gate**
(Zlatna Vrata), while the southern end has the
Bronze Gate; the eastern gate is the **Silver
Gate** and to the west is the **Iron Gate**. Be-
tween the eastern and western gates there's
a straight road (Krešimirova; also known as
Decumanus), which separates the imperial

residence on the southern side. The Bronze Gate, in the southern wall, led from the living quarters to the sea.

There are 220 buildings within the palace boundaries, home to about 3000 people.

Town Museum
MUSEUM

(Muzej Grada Splita; www.mgst.net; Papalićeva 1; adult/concession 10/5KN; ☺9am-9pm Tue-Fri, to 4pm Sat-Mon Jun-Sep, 10am-5pm Tue-Fri, to 1pm Sat-Mon Oct-May) Built for one of the many noblemen who lived within the palace in the Middle Ages, the Papalić Palace that houses the museum is considered a fine example of late-Gothic style. Its three floors showcase a collection of drawings, coats of arms, 17th-century weaponry and fine furniture. Captions are in Croatian.

FREE Cathedral of St Domnius
CATHEDRAL

(Katedrala Svetog Duje; Svetog Duje 5; cathedral/treasury/belfry 15/15/10KN; ☺8am-7pm Mon-Sat, 12.30-6.30pm Sun Jun-Sep, sporadic hours Oct-May) On the eastern side of the Peristil, Split's cathedral was built as Diocletian's mausoleum. The oldest remnants inside are the remarkable 13th-century scenes from the life of Christ carved on the wooden entrance doors. The choir is furnished with 13th-century Romanesque seats that are the oldest in Dalmatia. The treasury is rich in reliquaries, icons, church robes and illuminated manuscripts. You can climb the Romanesque belfry.

Note that admission to the cathedral also gets you free access to the Temple of Jupiter and its crypt. For 35KN, you can get a ticket that includes access to the cathedral, treasury and belfry.

Temple of Jupiter
TEMPLE

(temple/crypt 5/5KN; ☺8am-7pm Mon-Sat, 12.30-6.30pm Sun May-Sep) The headless sphinx in black granite guarding the entrance to the temple was imported from Egypt at the time of the temple's construction in the 5th century. Take a look at the barrel-vaulted ceiling and a decorative frieze on the walls. You can also pop into the crypt.

Ethnographic Museum
MUSEUM

(Etnografski Muzej; www.etnografski-muzej-split.hr; Severova 1; adult/concession 10/5KN; ☺9am-7pm Mon-Fri, to 1pm Sat Jun-Sep, 9am-4pm Mon-Fri, to 1pm Sat Oct-May) This mildly interesting museum has a collection of photos of old Split, traditional costumes and memorabilia of important citizens. For great Old Town views, make sure you climb the staircase that leads to the Renaissance terrace on the southern edge of the vestibule. These views are reason enough to visit.

CROATIA SPLIT

WORTH A TRIP

SOLIN (SALONA)

The ruin of the ancient city of Solin (known as Salona by the Romans), among the vineyards at the foot of mountains just northeast of Split, is the most interesting archaeological site in Croatia. Salona was the capital of the Roman province of Dalmatia from the time Julius Caesar elevated it to the status of colony. It held out against the barbarians and was only evacuated in AD 614 when the inhabitants fled to Split and neighbouring islands in the face of Avar and Slav attacks.

Begin your visit at the main entrance near Caffe Bar Salona, where you'll see an info-map of the complex. Tusculum Museum (admission 20KN; ☺7am-7pm Mon-Fri, 8am-7pm Sat, 9am-1pm Sun Apr-Sep, shorter hours rest of year) is where you pay admission for the entire archaeological reserve (you'll get a brochure with a map) as well as for the small museum with interesting sculpture embedded in the walls and in the garden. Some of the highlights inside the complex include Manastirine, the fenced area behind the car park, a burial place for early Christian martyrs prior to the legalisation of Christianity; the excavated remains of Kapljuč Basilica – one of the early Christian cemeteries in Salona – and the 5th-century Kapjinc Basilica that sits inside it. Also look out for the covered aqueduct from the 1st century AD; the 5th-century cathedral with an octagonal baptistery; and the huge 2nd-century amphitheatre.

The ruins are easily accessible on Split city bus 1 (13KN), which goes all the way to the parking lot for Salona every half-hour from Trg Gaje Bulata. From Solin you can continue on to Trogir by catching westbound bus 37 (17KN) from the Širine crossroad. Take city bus 1 back to Širine and then walk for five minutes on the same road to get to the stop for bus 37 on the adjacent highway.

Central Split

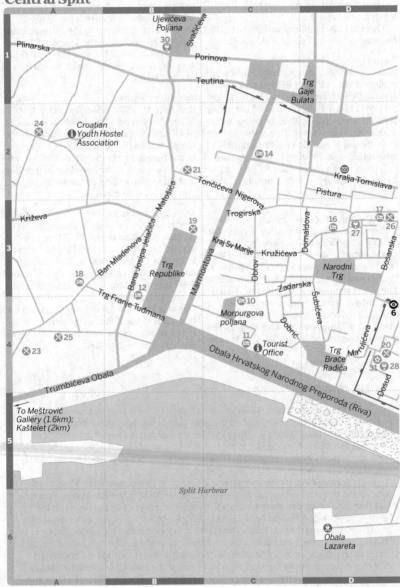

Plinarska
Ujevićeva Poljana
30
Svačićeva
Porinova
Teutina
Trg Gaje Bulata
24
Croatian Youth Hostel Association
21
Tončićeva Nigerova
Kralja Tomislava
Pistura
Matošića
Trogirska
17
Križeva
19
Kraj Sv Marije
Domaldova
16
26
27
Ban Mladenova Jelačića
Bana Josipa Jelačića
Kružićeva
Obrov
Narodni Trg
Bosanska
Trg Republike
Marmontova
18
12
Zadarska
Trg Franje Tudmana
10
Šubićeva
6
Morpurgova poljana
Dobrić
25
11
Tourist Office
Trg Braće Radića
Matulićeva
20
23
Obala Hrvatskog Narodnog Preporoda (Riva)
31
28
Dosud

Trumbićeva Obala

To Meštrović Gallery (1.6km); Kaštelet (2km)

Split Harbour

Obala Lazareta

CROATIA SPLIT

Peristil SQUARE
This picturesque colonnaded square, with a neo-Romanesque cathedral tower rising above, is a great place for a break in the sun. The **vestibule**, an open dome above the ground-floor passageway at the southern end of the Peristil, is overpoweringly grand and cavernous.

Basement Halls HISTORIC SITE
(adult/concession 35/15KN; ⊘9am-9pm daily Jun-Sep, 9am-8pm Mon-Sat, to 6pm Sun Apr, May &

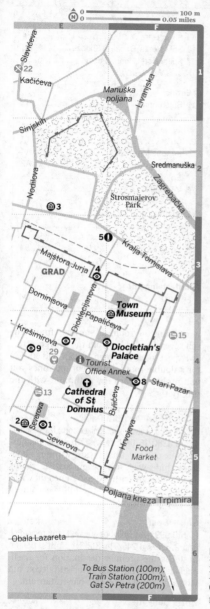

OUTSIDE THE PALACE WALLS

Gregorius of Nin   MONUMENT
(Grgur Ninski) This 10th-century statue is of the Croatian bishop who fought for the right to use old Croatian in liturgical services. Notice that his left big toe has been polished to a shine – it's said that rubbing the toe brings good luck.

Gallery of Fine Arts   GALLERY
(Galerija Umjetnina Split; www.galum.hr; Kralja Tomislava 15; adult/concession 20/10KN; ⊙11am-4pm Mon, to 7pm Tue-Fri, to 3pm Sat May-Sep, 9am-2pm Mon, to 5pm Tue-Fri, to 1pm Sat Oct-Apr) This gallery housed in a former hospital exhibits nearly 400 works of art spanning almost 700 years. Upstairs is the permanent collection; temporary exhibits downstairs change every few months. The pleasant cafe has a terrace overlooking the palace.

OUTSIDE CENTRAL SPLIT

Meštrović Gallery   GALLERY
(Galerija Meštrović; Šetalište Ivana Meštrovića 46; adult/concession 30/15KN; ⊙9am-7pm Tue-Sun May-Sep, shorter hours rest of year) At this stellar art museum, below Marjan to the west of the city centre, you'll see a comprehensive, nicely arranged collection of works by Ivan Meštrović, Croatia's premier modern sculptor. Don't miss the nearby Kaštelet (Šetalište Ivana Meštrovića 39; admission by Meštrović Gallery ticket; ⊙9am-7pm Tue-Sat, 10am-7pm Sun May-Sep, shorter hours rest of year), a fortress that Meštrović bought and restored to house his powerful Life of Christ wood reliefs.

Bačvice   BEACH
The most popular city beach is on the eponymous inlet. This biggish pebbly beach has good swimming, a lively ambience, a great cafe-bar and plenty of water games. There are showers and changing rooms at both ends of the beach.

🏃 Activities

Marjan   WALKING TRAIL
For an afternoon away from the city buzz, Marjan (178m) is the perfect destination. Considered the lungs of the city, this hilly nature reserve offers trails through fragrant pine forests, scenic lookouts and ancient chapels. There are different ways of reaching Marjan. Start from the stairway (Marjanske Skale) in Varoš, right behind the Church of Sveti Frane. It's a mild incline along old stone stairs and a scenic 10-minute trek to get to Vidilica (p210) cafe

Oct, shorter hours rest of year) Although mostly empty, save an exhibit or two, the rooms and corridors underneath the Diocletian's Palace exude a haunting timelessness that is well worth the price of a ticket.

Central Split

◎ Top Sights
Cathedral of St Domnius E4
Diocletian's Palace F4
Town Museum...F4

◎ Sights
1 Basement Halls.....................................E5
Bronze Gate................................ (see 1)
2 Ethnographic Museum.........................E5
3 Gallery of Fine Arts E2
4 Golden Gate..E3
5 Gregorius of Nin...................................F3
6 Iron Gate..D4
7 Peristil...E4
8 Silver Gate F4
9 Temple of Jupiter..................................E4

⊜ Sleeping
10 Goli + Bosi...C4
11 Hotel Adriana..C4
12 Hotel Bellevue B3
13 Hotel Vestibul Palace E4
14 Silver Central Hostel C2

15 Silver Gate F4
16 Split Hostel Booze & Snooze D3
17 Split Hostel Fiesta Siesta D3
18 Villa Varoš...A3

⊗ Eating
19 Bajamonti B3
20 Figa..D4
21 Galija..B2
22 Gušt...E1
23 Konoba Matejuška A4
24 Makrovega...A2
25 Šperun...A4
26 Villa Spiza D3

◎ Drinking
27 Bifora...D3
28 Ghetto Club D4
29 Luxor..E4
30 Paradox..B1

◎ Entertainment
31 Fluid...D4

at the top. From here, right by the old Jewish cemetery, you can follow the marked trail, stopping en route to see the chapels, all the way to **Kašjuni cove**, a quieter beach option than the buzzing Bačvice.

✯ Festivals & Events

Carnival   CULTURAL
This traditional February event sees locals dressing up and dancing in the streets for two very fun days.

Feast of St Duje   RELIGIOUS
Otherwise known as Split Day, this 7 May feast involves much singing and dancing all around the city.

Split Summer Festival   ARTS
(www.splitsko-ljeto.hr) From mid-July to mid-August, it features opera, drama, ballet and concerts on open-air stages.

🛏 Sleeping

Good budget accommodation has become more available in Split in the last couple of years but it's mostly comprised of hostels. Private accommodation is a great option and in summer you may be deluged at the bus station by women offering *sobe* (rooms available). You can also contact travel agencies. Make sure you are clear about the exact

location of the room or you may find yourself several bus rides from the town centre.

Expect to pay between 300KN and 500KN for a double room; in the cheaper ones you will probably share the bathroom with the proprietor.

TOP CHOICE Hotel Vestibul Palace   HOTEL €€€
(☏329 329; www.vestibulpalace.com; Iza Vestibula 4; s/d 1380/1670KN; ▣❉@☎) The poshest in the palace, this award-winning boutique hideaway has seven stylish rooms and suites, all with exposed ancient walls, leather and wood, and the full spectrum of upscale amenities.

Goli + Bosi   HOSTEL €€
(☏510 999; www.gollybossy.com; Morpurgova Poljana 2; dm/s/d 245/714/818KN) Split's design hostel is the premier destination for flashpackers, with its sleek futuristic decor, hip vibe and a cool lobby cafe-bar-restaurant.

Hotel Bellevue   HOTEL €€
(☏345 644; www.hotel-bellevue-split.hr; Bana Josipa Jelačića 2; s/d 620/865KN; ▣@) This atmospheric old classic has sure seen better days but it remains one of the more dreamy hotels in town, with regal-patterned wallpaper, art-deco elements, gauzy curtains and faded but well-kept rooms.

Villa Varoš
GUESTHOUSE €€

(📋483 469; www.villavaros.hr; Miljenka Smoje 1; d/ste 600/900KN; ❋🖧) Owned by a New Yorker Croat, Villa Varoš is central, the rooms are simple, bright and airy, and the apartment has a Jacuzzi and a small terrace.

Hotel Adriana
HOTEL €€€

(📋340 000; www.hotel-adriana.com; Hrvatskog Narodnog Preporoda 8; s/d 750/1100KN; ❋🖧) Good value, excellent location smack in the middle of the Riva. The rooms are not massively exciting, with navy curtains and beige furniture, but some have sea views.

CroParadise Split Hostels
HOSTEL €

(📋091 444 4194; www.croparadise.com; Čulića Dvori 29; dm 180KN, d 400-500KN, apt from 500KN; ❋@🖧) A great collection of three hostels – Blue, Green and Pink – inside converted apartments in the neighbourhood of Manuš. Five apartments are also available.

Silver Central Hostel
HOSTEL €

(📋490 805; www.silvercentralhostel.com; Kralja Tomislava 1; dm 167-190KN; ❋@🖧) In an upstairs apartment, this light-yellow-coloured boutique hostel has four dorm rooms and a pleasant lounge. It has a two-person apartment nearby and another hostel, **Silver Gate** (📋322 857; www.silvergatehostel.com; Hrvojeva 6; dm per person 167KN), near the food market.

Split Hostel Booze & Snooze
HOSTEL €

(📋342 787; www.splithostel.com; Narodni trg 8; dm 200-215KN; ❋@🖧) Run by a pair of Aussie Croat women, this party place at the heart of town has four dorms, a terrace, a book swap and boat trips. Its newer outpost, **Split Hostel Fiesta Siesta** (Kružićeva 5; dm 200-215KN, d 560KN; ❋@🖧) has five sparkling dorms and one double above the popular Charlie's Backpacker Bar.

Eating

Šperun
SEAFOOD €

(Šperun 3; mains from 65KN; 🍴) A sweet little restaurant decked out with rustic details and exposed stone walls, this favourite among the foreigners churns out decent Dalmatian classics. **Šperun Deva**, a corner bistro across the street with a few tables outside, offers breakfasts, lighter summer fare and a great daily menu.

TOP CHOICE Figa
INTERNATIONAL €

(Buvinina 1; mains from 50KN) Split's coolest little restaurant and bar, with a funky interior and tables on the stairs outside, Figa serves nice breakfasts, innovative dishes and a wide range of salads. There's live music some nights and the kitchen stays open late.

Konoba Matejuška
DALMATIAN €

(Tomića Stine 3; mains from 50KN) Cosy, rustic tavern in an alleyway minutes from the seafront, it specialises in well-prepared seafood that also happens to be well priced.

Bajamonti
INTERNATIONAL €€

(Trg Republike 1; mains from 75KN) Sleek restaurant and cafe on Trg Republike (Prokurative square), right off the Riva, with classic decor and excellent international fare. Grab a table on the square or on the mezzanine level inside.

TOP CHOICE Villa Spiza
DALMATIAN €

(Kružićeva 3; mains from 40KN; ⊘Mon-Sat) A locals' favourite within the palace walls, this low-key joint offers Dalmatian mainstays that change daily – think calamari, risotto, stuffed peppers – at low prices, served at the bar inside or at a couple of benches outside.

Makrovega
VEGETARIAN €

(Leština 2; mains from 50KN; ⊘9am-8pm Mon-Fri, to 5pm Sat) A meat-free haven with a stylish, spacious interio, a delicious buffet and à la carte food that alternates between macrobiotic and vegetarian.

Galija
PIZZERIA €

(Tončićeva 12; pizzas from 38KN) The go-to place for pizza for several decades now, Galija is the sort of joint where locals take you for a good, simple meal. Die-hard pizza fans have recently turned to the new favorite in town, **Gušt** (Slavićeva 1; pizzas from 32KN).

🍷 Drinking & Entertainment

Split is great for nightlife, especially in the spring and summer months. The palace walls are generally throbbing with loud music on Friday and Saturday nights.

Žbirac
CAFE

(Bačvice bb) This beachfront cafe is like the locals' open-air living room, a cult hang-out with great sea views, swimming day and night and occasional concerts.

Bifora
CAFE-BAR

(Bernardinova 5) A quirky crowd of locals frequents this artsy spot on a lovely little square, much loved for its intimate low-key vibe.

Ghetto Club   BAR
(Dosud 10) Split's most bohemian bar, in an intimate courtyard amid flowerbeds and a trickling fountain, with great music and a friendly atmosphere.

Luxor   CAFE-BAR
(Sveti Ivana 11) Touristy, yes, but it's great to have coffee and their delicious cake in the courtyard of the cathedral: cushions are laid out on the steps so you can watch the locals go about their business.

Vidilica   CAFE-BAR
(Nazorov Prilaz 1) Worth the climb up the stone stairs through the ancient Varoš quarter for a sunset drink at this hilltop cafe with amazing city and harbour views.

Paradox   WINE BAR
(Poljana Tina Ujevića 2) Stylish new wine bar with cool wine-glass chandeliers inside, alfresco tables and a great selection of well-priced Croatian wines and local cheeses.

Fluid   CLUB
(Dosud 1) This chic little spot is a jazzy party venue, pretty low-key and cool. Great for people-watching.

ⓘ Information

Internet Access
Several cafes around town, including Luxor offer free wi-fi access.

Backpackers Cafe (☑338 548; Kneza Domagoja bb; internet 30N; ☺7am-9pm) Also sells used books, offers luggage storage and provides information for backpackers. There's happy hour for internet use between 3pm and 5pm, when it's 50% off.

Medical Services
KBC Firule (☑556 111; Spinčićeva 1) Hospital.

Money
You can change money at travel agencies or the post office. There are ATMs around the bus and train stations and throughout the city.

Post
Main post office (Kralja Tomislava 9; ☺7.30am-7pm Mon-Fri, to 2.30pm Sat)

Tourist Information
Croatian Youth Hostel Association (☑396 031; www.hfhs.hr; Domilijina 8; ☺8am-4pm Mon-Fri) Sells HI cards and has information about youth hostels all over Croatia.

Tourist Office (☑360 066; www.visitsplit.com; Hrvatskog Narodnog Preporoda 9; ☺8am-9pm Mon-Sat, to 1pm Sun Apr–mid-Oct, 8am-8pm Mon-Fri, to 1pm Sat mid-Oct–Mar) Has Split info and sells the Split Card (35KN), which offers free and reduced prices to attractions and discounts on car rental, restaurants, shops and hotels.

Tourist Office Annex (☑345 606; www.visitsplit.com; Peristil bb; ☺9am-4pm Mon-Sat, 8am-1pm Sun Apr–mid-Oct, shorter hours rest of year) This tourist office annex on Peristil has shorter hours.

Travel Agencies
Daluma Travel (☑338 424; www.dalumatravel.hr; Kneza Domagoja 1) Arranges private accommodation, excursions and car rental.

Maestral (☑470 944; www.maestral.hr; Boškovića 13/15) Monastery stays, horse-riding excursions, lighthouse holidays, trekking, sea kayaking and more.

Turist Biro (☑347 100; www.turistbiro-split.hr; Hrvatskog Narodnog Preporoda 12) Its forte is private accommodation and excursions.

ⓘ Getting There & Away

Air
Split airport (www.split-airport.hr) is 20km west of town, just 6km before Trogir. **Croatia Airlines** (☑362 997; www.croatiaairlines.com; Hrvatskog Narodnog Preporoda 9; ☺8am-4pm Mon-Fri) operates one-hour flights to Zagreb several times a day and a weekly flight to Dubrovnik (during summer only).

A couple of low-cost airlines fly to Split, including **Easyjet** (www.easyjet.com), **germanwings** (www.germanwings.com) and **Norwegian** (www.norwegian.com).

Boat
Jadrolinija (☑338 333; www.jadrolinija.hr; Gat Sv Duje bb) handles most of the coastal ferry lines and catamarans that operate between Split and the islands. There is also a twice-weekly ferry service between Rijeka and Split (147KN, 7.30pm Thursday and Sunday, arriving at 6am). Three times weekly a car ferry goes from Split to Ancona in Italy (435KN, nine to 11 hours).

In addition to Jadrolinija's boats, there is a fast passenger boat, the **Krilo** (www.krilo.hr), that goes to Hvar Town (45KN, one hour) daily and on to Korčula (65KN, 2¾ hours).

SNAV (☑322 252; www.snav.it) has daily ferries to Ancona (Italy) from June through mid-September (660KN; five hours) and to Pescara (Italy) from late July through August (6½ hours). Also departing to Ancona from Split are **BlueLine** (www.blueline-ferries.com) car ferries (from 480KN per person, 540KN per car, 10 to 12 hours), on some days via Hvar Town and Vis.

Car ferries and passenger lines depart from separate docks; the passenger lines leave from Obala Lazareta and car ferries from Gat Sv Duje. You can buy tickets from either the main Jadro-

BUSES FROM SPLIT

DESTINATION	PRICE (KN)	DURATION (HR)	FREQUENCY
Dubrovnik	115-145	4½	25 daily
Ljubljana (Slovenia)	320	10	1 daily
Međugorje (Bosnia & Hercegovina)	100	3-4	4 daily
Mostar (Bosnia & Hercegovina)	105-128	3½-4½	9 daily
Pula	423	10-11	3 daily
Rijeka	330	8-8½	11 daily
Sarajevo (Bosnia & Hercegovina)	220	6½-8	4 daily
Triesta (Italy)	284	10½	2 daily
Vienna (Austria)	57	11½	2 weekly
Zadar	99-128	3-4	27 daily
Zagreb	114-204	5-8	40 daily

linija office in the large ferry terminal opposite the bus station, or at one of the two stalls near the docks. In summer it's necessary to reserve at least a day in advance for a car ferry and you are asked to appear several hours before departure.

Bus

Advance bus tickets with seat reservations are recommended. Most buses leave from the main **bus station** (☑060 327 777; www.ak-split.hr) beside the harbour, where there's a **garderoba** (left-luggage office; 1st hr 5KN, then 1.50KN per hr; ☺6am-10pm).

Bus 37 goes to Split airport and Trogir (21KN, every 20 minutes), also stopping at Solin; it leaves from a local bus station on Domovinskog Rata, 1km northeast of the city centre, but it's faster and more convenient to take an intercity bus heading north to Zadar or Rijeka.

Note that Split–Dubrovnik buses pass briefly through Bosnian territory, so keep your passport handy for border-crossing points.

Train

There are five daily trains between Split **train station** (☑338 525; www.hznet.hr; Kneza Domagoja 9) and Zagreb (189KN, six to eight hours), two of which are overnight. There are also two trains a day from Split to Zadar (111KN, five hours) via Knin. The station is just behind the bus station and there's a **garderoba** (left-luggage office; per day 15KN; ☺6am-10pm).

ⓘ Getting Around

Buses by **Pleso Prijevoz** (www.plesoprijevoz.hr) and **Promet Žele** (www.split-airport.com.hr) depart to Split airport (30KN) from Obala Lazareta several times daily. You can also take bus 37 from the local bus station on Domovinskog Rata (21KN, 50 minutes).

Buses run about every 15 minutes from 5.30am to 11.30pm. A one-zone ticket costs 11KN for one trip in central Split; it's 21KN to the surrounding districts.

Trogir
☑021 / POP 13,000

Gorgeous and tiny Trogir (formerly Trau) is beautifully set within medieval walls, its streets knotted and maze-like. It's fronted by a wide seaside promenade lined with bars and cafes and luxurious yachts docking in the summer. Trogir is unique among Dalmatian towns for its profuse collection of Romanesque and Renaissance architecture (which flourished under Venetian rule), and this, along with its magnificent cathedral, earned it World Heritage status in 1997.

Trogir is an easy day trip from Split and a relaxing place to spend a few days, taking a trip or two to nearby islands.

◉ Sights

The heart of the Old Town, which occupies a tiny island in the narrow channel between Čiovo Island and the mainland, is a few minutes' walk from the bus station. After crossing the small bridge near the station, go through the north gate. Most sights can be seen on a 15-minute walk around this island.

Cathedral of St Lovro   CATHEDRAL
(Katedrala Svetog Lovre; Trg Ivana Pavla II; admission 25KN; ☺8am-8pm Mon-Sat, 2-6pm Sun Jun-Sep, shorter hours rest of year) The showcase of Trogir is this three-naved Venetian cathedral built from the 13th to 15th centuries. Its glory is

the **Romanesque portal** (1240) by Master Radovan, the earliest example of the nude in Dalmatian sculpture. Enter the building through an obscure back door to see the richly decorated Renaissance **Chapel of St Ivan**, choir stalls, pulpit and **treasury**, which contains an ivory triptych. You can even climb the 47m cathedral **tower** for a delightful view.

Kamerlengo Fortress
FORTRESS

(Tvrđava Kamerlengo; admission 20KN; ⊘9am-11pm May-Oct) Once connected to the city walls, the fortress was built around the 15th century. Today it hosts concerts during the **Trogir Summer** festival, which typically begins in mid-June and lasts through to late August.

Town Museum
MUSEUM

(Gradski Muzej; Gradska Vrata 4; admission 15KN; ⊘10am-5pm Jun-Sep, 9am-2pm Mon-Fri, to noon Sat Oct-May) Housed in the former Garagnin-Fanfogna palace, the museum has five rooms that exhibit books, documents, drawings and period costumes from Trogir's long history.

ℹ️ Information

Atlas Trogir (✆881 374; www.atlas-trogir.hr; Kralja Zvonimira 10) This travel agency arranges private accommodation and runs excursions.

Portal Trogir (✆885 016; www.portal-trogir. com; Bana Berislavića 3) Private accommodation; bike, scooter and kayak rental; excursions, including quad safaris, rafting and canyoning; and internet. The agency runs runs a 90-minute walking tour of the Old Town twice a day from May to October, departing from outside the agency. It also rents out two-person kayaks for 250KN per day, which you can use to kayak around the island and to Pantan beach.

ℹ️ Getting There & Away

Southbound intercity buses from Zadar (130km) and northbound buses from Split (28km) will drop you off in Trogir. Getting buses from Trogir to Zadar can be more difficult, as they often arrive full from Split.

City bus 37 from Split leaves every 20 minutes throughout the day, with a stop at Split airport en route to Trogir. You can buy the four-zone ticket (21KN) from the driver in either direction.

There are boats to and from Split four times daily (24KN) from Čiovo (150m to the left of the bridge).

Hvar Island

✆021 / POP 10,948

Hvar Island is the number-one carrier of Croatia's superlatives: it's the most luxurious island, the sunniest place in the country and, along with Dubrovnik, the most popular tourist destination. Hvar is also famed for its verdancy and its lavender fields, as well as other aromatic herbs such as rosemary.

The island's hub and busiest destination is Hvar Town. Visitors wander along the main square, explore the sights on the winding stone streets, swim on the numerous beaches or pop off to get into their birthday suits on the Pakleni Islands, but most of all they party at night. There are several good restaurants and a number of top hotels, as well as a couple of hostels.

Stari Grad (Old Town), on the island's north coast, is a more quiet, cultured and altogether sober affair than its stylish and stunning sister. If you're not after pulsating nightlife and thousands of people crushing each other along the streets in the high season, head for Stari Grad and enjoy Hvar at a more leisurely pace.

The interior of the island hides abandoned ancient hamlets, towering peaks and verdant, largely uncharted landscapes. It's worth exploring on a day trip, as is the southern end of the island, which has some of Hvar's most beautiful and isolated coves.

🅾️ Sights

St Stephen's Square
SQUARE

(Trg Svetog Stjepana) The centre of town is this rectangular square, which was formed by filling in an inlet that once stretched out from the bay. Notice the 1520 **well** at the square's northern end, which has a wrought-iron grill dating from 1780.

Franciscan Monastery & Museum
MONASTERY

(admission 25KN; ⊘9am-1pm & 5-7pm Mon-Sat) At the southeastern end of Hvar Town you'll find this 15th-century Renaissance monastery, with a wonderful collection of Venetian paintings in the adjoining church and a cloister garden with a cypress tree said to be more than 300 years old.

Fortica
FORTRESS

(admission 25KN; ⊘8am-10pm Jun-Sep) On the hill high above Hvar Town, this Venetian fortress (1551) is worth the climb up to appreciate the sweeping panoramic views. The fort was built to defend Hvar from the Turks, who sacked it in 1539 and 1571. There's a lovely cafe at the top.

Arsenal
HISTORIC BUILDING

(Trg Svetog Stjepana; arsenal & theatre 20KN; ⊙9am-9pm) Smack in the middle of Hvar Town is the imposing Gothic arsenal, and upstairs is Hvar's prize, the **Renaissance theatre** (Trg Svetog Stjepana; admission 10KN; ⊙9am-9pm) built in 1612 – reported to be the first theatre in Europe open to plebs and aristocrats alike.

👉 Tours

Secret Hvar
GUIDED TOURS

(✆717 615; www.secrethvar.com; Trg Svetog Stjepana 4a) Don't miss the great off-road tours, which take in hidden beauties of the island's interior. It's worth every lipa of 600KN, which includes lunch in a traditional tavern and a stop on the beach.

🛏 Sleeping

As Hvar is one of the Adriatic's most popular destinations, don't expect many bargains. Most Hvar hotels are managed by **Sunčani Hvar Hotels** (www.suncanihvar.com). Accommodation in Hvar is extremely tight in July and August; try the travel agencies for help. Expect to pay anywhere from 150KN to 300KN per person for a room with a private bathroom in the town centre.

Family-run, private-apartment options are so many in Hvar that the choice can be overwhelming. Here are a few reliable, good-value apartments: **Apartments Ukić** (www.hvar-apartments-center.com), **Apartments Komazin** (www.croatia-hvar-apartments.com) and **Apartments Bracanović** (www.hvar-jagoda.com).

Hotel Riva
HOTEL €€€

(✆750 100; www.suncanihvar.com; Riva bb; s/d 1390/2617KN; ❄@) The luxury veteran on Hvar's hotel scene, this 100-year-old hotel has 54 smallish contemporary rooms and a great location right on the harbourfront, perfect for watching the yachts glide up and away.

🔝 Hotel Croatia
HOTEL €€€

(✆742 400; www.hotelcroatia.net; Majerovica bb; s/d 832/1110KN; P❄@❟) Only a few steps from the sea, this medium-sized, rambling 1930s building sits among gorgeous, peaceful gardens. The rooms are simple and old-fashioned, many with balconies overlooking the gardens and the sea.

Hostel Marinero
HOSTEL €

(✆091 174 1601; Put Sv Marka 7; dm 200-240KN; ❄❟) The location is the highlight at this six-dorm hostel right off the seafront. Dorms are basic but clean, and the restaurant downstairs is a good place to hang out. Be ready for some noise, as Kiva Bar is right next door.

Hvar Out Hostel
HOSTEL €

(✆717 375; hvarouthostel@gmail.com; Burak 23; dm 200-250KN; ❄@❟) By the same owners as Split Hostel Booze & Snooze, this party place, steps from the harbour in the maze of the Old Town, has seven well-equipped dorms, a small shared kitchen and a terrace on the top floor.

Camping Vira
CAMPING GROUND €

(✆741 803; www.campingvira.com; campsite per adult/site 60/97KN; ⊙May–mid-Oct; P@❟) This four-star camping ground on a beautiful wooded bay 4km from town is one of the best in Dalmatia. There's a gorgeous beach, a cafe and restaurant, and a volleyball pitch.

🍴 Eating

Hvar's eating scene is good and relatively varied, though, as with the hotels, restaurants often target affluent diners. Note that many restaurants close between lunch and dinner.

WORTH A TRIP

PAKLENI ISLANDS

Most visitors to Hvar Town head to the Pakleni Islands (Pakleni Otoci), which got their name – 'Hell's Islands' in Croatian – from *paklina*, the resin that once coated boats and ships. This gorgeous chain of 21 wooded isles has crystal-clear seas, hidden beaches and deserted lagoons. Taxi boats leave regularly during the high season from in front of the Arsenal to the islands of **Jerolim** and **Stipanska** (35KN, 10 to 15 minutes), which are popular naturist islands (although nudity is not mandatory). They continue on to **Ždrilca** and **Mlini** (40KN) and, further out, **Palmižana** (60KN), which has a pebble beach and the **Meneghello Place** (www.palmizana.hr), a beautiful boutique complex of villas and bungalows scattered among lush tropical gardens. Run by the artsy Meneghello family, the estate holds music recitals, and features two excellent restaurants and an art gallery. Also on Palmižana are two top restaurant-cum-hang-out spots, Toto and Laganini.

Self-caterers can head to the supermarket next to the bus station, or pick up fresh supplies at the vegetable market next door.

Konoba Menego   DALMATIAN €€
(www.menego.hr; Groda bb; mains from 60KN) At this rustic old house, everything is decked out in Hvar antiques and the staff wear traditional outfits. Try the marinated meats, cheeses and vegetables, prepared the old-fashioned Dalmatian way.

Divino   MEDITERRANEAN €€€
(☑717 541; www.divino.com.hr; Put Križa 1 ; mains from 130KN; ☺dinner only) The fabulous location and the island's best wine list are reason enough to splurge at this swank restaurant. Add innovative food and dazzling views of the Pakleni Islands and there's a winning formula for a special night out.

Konoba Luviji   DALMATIAN €€
(☑091 519 8444; Jurja Novaka 6; mains from 50KN; ☺dinner) Food brought out of the wood oven at this tavern is simple, unfussy and tasty. Downstairs is the *konoba* where Dalmatian-style tapas are served; the upstairs restaurant has Old Town views.

Nonica   PASTRIES, CAKES €
(Burak 23; ☺8am-2pm & 5-11pm Mon-Sat, 8am-2pm Sun) Savour the best cakes in town, at this tiny storefront cafe right behind the Arsenal. Try the old-fashioned local biscuits such as *rafioli* and *forski koloc*.

Zlatna Školjka   MEDITERRANEAN €€€
(☑098 16 88 797; Petra Hektorovića 8; mains from 100KN; ☺dinner Sat & Sun) This slow-food, family-tun hideaway stands out for its creative fare conjured up by a local celebrity chef. Try the unbeatable *gregada* (fish stew) with lobster and sea snails; order in advance.

🍷 Drinking & Entertainment

Hvar has some of the best nightlife on the Adriatic coast.

Falko   BEACH BAR
(☺8am-10pm mid-May–mid-Sep) A 20-minute walk west from the town centre, past Hula-Hula and Hotel Amfora, brings you to this adorable hideaway in a pine forest just above the beach. Think low-key artsy vibe, homemade *rakija*, hammocks and a local crowd.

Carpe Diem   LOUNGE BAR
(www.carpe-diem-hvar.com; Riva) This swanky harbourfront spot is the mother of Croatia's coastal clubs, with house music spun nightly

by resident DJs. The Carpe Diem Beach (www.carpe-diem-beach.com) on the island of Stipanska is the hottest place to party (from June to September), with daytime beach fun and all-night parties.

Hula-Hula   BEACH BAR
(www.hulahulahvar.com) *The* spot to catch the sunset to the sound of techno and house music, Hula-Hula is known for its après-beach party (4pm to 9pm), where all of young trendy Hvar seems to descend for cocktails. To find it, head west along the seafront.

Kiva Bar   BAR
(www.kivabarhvar.com; Fabrika bb) This happening alleyway spot is packed to the rafters most nights, with a DJ spinning old dance, pop and rock classics that really get the crowd going.

Veneranda   CLUB
(admission 100-150KN; ☺10pm-4am) A former fortress on the slope above the seafront, Veneranda is Hvar's only real club, with a great sound system and late-night parties fulled by famous DJs.

ℹ Information

Atlas Hvar (☑741 911; www.atlas-croatia.com) On the western side of the harbour, this travel agency finds private accommodation, rents bikes and boats, and books excursions to Vis, Bol and Dubrovnik.

Clinic (☑717 099; Biskupa Jurja Dubokovića 3) Medical clinic about 700m from the town centre, best for emergencies.

Del Primi (☑091 583 7864; www.delprimi-hvar.com; Burak 23) Travel agency specialising in private accommodation. Also rents jet skis.

Francesco (Burak bb; per hr 30KN; ☺8.30am-midnight) Internet cafe and call centre right behind the post office. Left luggage for 35KN per day and laundry service for 50KN per load.

Hvar Adventure (☑717 813; www.hvar-adventure.com; Obala bb) Adventure activities such as sailing, sea kayaking, cycling, hiking and rock climbing.

Pelegrini Tours (☑742 743; www.pelegrini-hvar.hr; Riva bb) Private accommodation, boat tickets to Italy with Blue Line, excursions (its daily trips to Pakleni Otoci are popular) and bike, scooter and boat rental.

Tourist office (☑741 059; www.tzhvar.hr; ☺8am-2pm & 3-9pm Jul & Aug, shorter hours rest of year) Right on Trg Svetog Stjepana.

ℹ Getting There & Away

The local Jadrolinija (p210) car ferry from Split calls at Stari Grad (47KN, two hours) six times a day in summer. Jadrolinija also has three to five catamarans daily to Hvar Town (47KN, one hour). Krilo (p210), the fast passenger boat, travels once a day between Split and Hvar Town (45KN, one hour) in summer; it also goes on to Korčula (50KN, 1½ hours). You can buy tickets at Pelegrini Tours.

Connections to Italy are available in the summer season. Two Jadrolinija ferries a week (on Saturday and Sunday night) go from Stari Grad to Ancona in Italy. Blue Line (p232) also runs regular boats to Ancona from Hvar Town. Pelegrini Tours sells these tickets.

ℹ Getting Around

Buses meet most ferries that dock at Stari Grad and go to Hvar Town (27KN, 20 minutes). There are 10 buses a day between Stari Grad and Hvar Town in summer, but services are reduced on Sunday and in the low season.

A taxi costs from 300KN to 350KN. **Radio Taxi Tihi** (☏098 338 824) is cheaper if there are a number of passengers to fill up the minivan.

Korčula Island

☏020 / POP 16,438

Rich in vineyards and olive trees, the island of Korčula was named Korkyra Melaina (Black Korčula) by the original Greek settlers because of its dense woods and plant life. As the largest island in an archipelago of 48, it provides plenty of opportunities for scenic drives, particularly along the southern coast.

Swimming opportunities abound in the many quiet coves and secluded beaches, while the interior produces some of Croatia's finest wine, especially dessert wines made from the *grk* grape cultivated around Lumbarda. Local olive oil is another product worth seeking out.

On a hilly peninsula jutting into the Adriatic sits Korčula Town, a striking walled town of round defensive towers and red-roofed houses. Resembling a miniature Dubrovnik, the gated, walled Old Town is crisscrossed by narrow stone streets designed to protect its inhabitants from the winds swirling around the peninsula.

◉ Sights

Other than the circuit of the city walls or walking along the shore, sightseeing in Korčula centres on Trg Sv Marka (St Mark's Sq).

St Mark's Cathedral CATHEDRAL
(Katedrala Svetog Marka; Statuta 1214; ◎9am-9pm Jul & Aug, Mass only Sep-Jun) Dominating Trg Sve-

tog Marka, the 15th-century Gothic-Renaissance cathedral features works by Tintoretto (*Three Saints* and *The Annunciation*). Check out the modern sculptures in the baptistery too, including a *pietà* by Ivan Meštrović.

Town Museum MUSEUM
(Gradski Muze; Statuta 1214; admission 25KN; ◎9am-9pm daily Jun-Aug, 9am-1pm Mon-Sat Sep-May) The 16th-century Gabriellis Palace opposite the cathedral houses the museum, with a stone-carving collection, prehistoric objects, and Korčulan traditional, and art, furniture, textiles and portraits.

Marco Polo Museum MUSEUM
(De Polo; admission 20KN; ◎9am-7pm Jun-Sep, 10am-4pm May & Oct) It's said that Marco Polo was born in Korčula in 1254; you can visit what is believed to be his birthplace and climb the very steep steps for an eagle's-eye vista over the Korčula Peninsula and Adriatic.

☞ Tours

Travel agencies, like Atlas Travel Agency and Kantun Tours (p216), can set you up on an island tour or a day trip to Mljet and offer mountain biking, and sea-kayaking and snorkelling trips. In the summer season water taxis offer trips to Badija Island, which features a 15th-century Franciscan monastery and a naturist beach, and the nearby village of Lumbarda, both of which have sandy beaches.

🛏 Sleeping & Eating

Korčula's hotel scene is on the bulky and resort side. If you don't fancy staying in any of the big hotels, a more personal option is a guesthouse. Atlas Travel Agency (p216) and **Marko Polo Tours** (☏715 400; www.korcula.com; Biline 5; ◎9am-9pm Mon-Fri, to 6pm Sat & Sun) arrange private rooms (from 250KN in high season).

TOP CHOICE Lešić Dimitri Palace APARTMENTS €€€
(☏715 560; www.lesic-dimitri.com; Don Pavla Poše 1-6; apt 3363-9752KN; ✽🛜) Exceptional in every way (including its rates). Spread over several town mansions, the six 'residences' have been finished to an impeccable standard, while keeping original details. The restaurant is the best in town, too.

Villa DePolo APARTMENT, RENTAL ROOMS €
(☏711 621; tereza.depolo@du.t-com.hr; Svetog Nikole bb; d 350KN; ✽🛜) These small, simple but attractive modern rooms (and apartment) come

WORTH A TRIP

OREBIĆ

Orebić, on the southern coast of the Pelješac Peninsula, has the best beaches in southern Dalmatia – sandy coves bordered by groves of tamarisk and pine. Only 2.5km across the water from Korčula Town, it makes a perfect day trip or an alternative base. After lazing on the beach, you can take advantage of some excellent hiking up and around Mt Ilija (961m) or poke around a couple of churches and museums. The best beach in Orebić is Trstenica cove, a 15-minute walk east along the shore from the port.

In Orebić the ferry terminal and the bus station are adjacent to each other. Korčula buses to Dubrovnik, Zagreb and Sarajevo stop at Orebić (on the harbourfront by the ferry port).

with comfortable beds; one has a terrace with amazing views. The location is excellent, a short walk from the Old Town.

Hotel Bon Repos   RESORT €€
(☎726 800; www.korcula-hotels.com; d 596KN; P@☎❋) On the road to Lumbarda, this huge hotel has manicured grounds, a large pool overlooking a small beach and a water-taxi service to Korčula Town.

TOP CHOICE **LD**   MODERN MEDITERRANEAN €€
(☎715 560; www.lesic-dimitri.com; Don Pavla Poše 1-6; mains from 75KN) Korčula's finest restaurant, with tables right above the water, offers delectable combinations of Med ingredients and many wonderful Croatian choices.

TOP CHOICE **Konoba Komin**   DALMATIAN €
(☎716 508; Don Iva Matijace; mains from 45KN) This family-run *konoba* looks almost medieval, with its *komin* (roaring fire), roasting meat, ancient stone walls and solid wooden tables. The menu is simple and delicious and the space tight, so book ahead.

☆ Entertainment

Between June and September there's Moreška sword dancing (tickets 100KN; 9pm Monday and Thursday) by the Old Town gate. The clash of swords and the graceful movements of the dancers/fighters make an exciting show. Travel agencies sell tickets.

ℹ Information

There are several ATMs around town, including one at HVB Splitska Banka. You can also change money at the post office or at any of the travel agencies.

Atlas Travel Agency (☎711 231; atlas-korcula@du.htnet.hr; Plokata 19 Travnja bb) Represents American Express, runs excursions and finds private accommodation.

Hospital (☎711 137; Kalac bb) About 1km past Hotel Marko Polo.

Kantun Tours (☎715 622; www.kantun-tours.com; Plokata 19 Travnja bb) Private accommodation, lots of excursions, car hire and boat tickets, plus internet access (25KN per hour) and luggage storage.

Tourist office (☎715 701; www.korcula.net; Obala Franje Tuđmana 4; ☺8am-3pm & 5-8pm Mon-Sat, 9am-1pm Sun Jul & Aug, 8am-2pm Mon-Sat Sep-Jun) On the west harbour; an excellent source of information.

ℹ Getting There & Around

There are buses to Dubrovnik (95KN, three hours, one to three daily) and one to Zagreb (245KN, 11 hours). Book ahead in summer.

The island has two major entry ports – Korčula Town and Vela Luka. All the **Jadrolinija** (☎715 410) ferries between Split and Dubrovnik stop in Korčula Town. If you're travelling between Split and Korčula you have several options.

There's a daily fast boat, the **Krilo** (www.krilo.hr), which runs from Split to Korčula (65KN, 2¾ hours) all year round, stopping at Hvar en route. Jadrolinija runs a passenger catamaran daily from June to September from Split to Vela Luka (70KN, two hours), stopping at Hvar and continuing on to Lastavo. There's also a regular afternoon car ferry between Split and Vela Luka (60KN, three hours) that stops at Hvar most days (although cars may not disembark at Hvar).

From the Pelješac Peninsula you'll find very regular boats link Orebić and Korčula. Passenger launches (20KN, 10 minutes, 13 daily June to September, at least five daily the rest of year) sail to the heart of Korčula Town. Car ferries (22KN, 15 minutes, at least 14 daily all year round) also run this route, but use the deeper port of Dominče, 3km from Korčula Town.

Scooters (320KN for 24 hours) and boats (610KN per day) are available from **Rent a Đir** (☎711 908; www.korcula-rent.net; Biline 5).

Mljet Island

☎020 / POP 1232
Of all the Adriatic islands, Mljet (Meleda in Italian) may be the most seductive. Much of the island is covered by forests and the rest

is dotted with fields, vineyards and villages. The northwestern half of the island forms **Mljet National Park** (www.mljet.hr; adult/ concession 100/50KN), where lush vegetation, pine forests and two saltwater lakes offer a scenic hideaway. It's an unspoiled oasis of tranquility that, according to legend, captivated Odysseus for seven years.

The island is 37km long, and has an average width of about 3km. The main points of entry are Pomena and Polače, two tiny towns about 5km apart.

Most people visit the island on excursions from Korčula or Dubrovnik (around 390KN and 245KN respectively), but it is possible to take a passenger boat from Dubrovnik or come on the regular ferry from Dubrovnik and stay a few days for hiking, cycling and boating.

Sights & Activities

The highlights of the island are **Malo Jezero** and **Veliko Jezero**, the two lakes on the island's western end connected by a channel. In the middle of Veliko Jezero is an islet with a 12th-century **Benedictine monastery**, which contains a pricey but atmospheric restaurant.

There's a boat from Mali Most (about 1.5km from Pomena) on Malo Jezero that leaves for the island monastery every hour at 10 minutes past the hour. It's not possible to walk right around the larger lake as there's no bridge over the channel connecting the lakes to the sea. If you decide to swim it, keep in mind that the current can be strong.

Renting a **bicycle** (25/110KN per hour/ day) is an excellent way to explore the national park. Several places including **Hotel Odisej** (744 022; www.hotelodisej.hr) in Pomena have bikes. Be aware that Pomena and Polače are separated by a steep hill. The bike path along the lake is an easier and very scenic pedal, but it doesn't link the two towns. You can rent a paddleboat and row over to the monastery but you'll need stamina.

The island offers some unusual opportunities for **diving**. There's a 3rd-century Roman wreck in relatively shallow water. The remains of the ship, including amphorae, have calcified over the centuries and this has protected them from pillaging. There's also a German torpedo boat from WWII and several walls to dive. Contact **Kronmar Diving** (744 022; Hotel Odisej).

Sleeping & Eating

The Polače tourist office arranges private accommodation (from around 250KN per double), but it's essential to make arrangements before peak season. You'll find more *sobe* signs around Pomena than Polače, and practically none at all in Sobra. Restaurants rent out rooms too.

TOP CHOICE **Stermasi** APARTMENTS €€

(098 93 90 362; www.stermasi.hr; Saplunara; apt 368-625KN; P ※) On the 'other' side of Mljet, these apartments are ideal if you want to enjoy the simple life and natural beauty of the island. Well-presented and bright, the nine modern units have terraces or private balconies. Sandy beaches are on your doorstep and guests get a 20% discount on meals at the amazing restaurant.

Soline 6 HOTEL €€

(744 024; www.soline6.com; Soline; d 598KN) This very green place is the only accommodation within the national park, with everything built from recycled products. Organic waste is composted, toilets are waterless and there's no electricity. The four studios are modern and equipped with private bathrooms, balconies and kitchens.

Camping Mungos CAMPING GROUND €

(745 300; Babino Polje; campsite per person 54KN; May-Sep) Close to the beach and the lovely grotto of Odysseus, this camping ground has a restaurant, currency exchange and a minimart.

Melita CROATIAN €€

(www.mljet-restoranmelita.com; St Mary's Island, Veliko Jezero; mains from 60KN) A more romantic spot can't be found on the island – this is the restaurant attached to the church on the little island in the middle of the big lake.

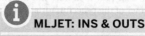

MLJET: INS & OUTS

Sightseeing boats from Korčula and the Dubrovnik catamarans arrive at Polače wharf in high season; Jadrolinija ferries use the Sobra port close to the centre of the island. The entry point for Mljet National Park is between Pomena and Polače. Your ticket includes bus and boat transfer to the Benedictine monastery. If you stay overnight on the island you only pay the park admission once.

ℹ️ Information

The **tourist office** (☑744 186; www.mljet.hr; ⊙8am-1pm & 5-7pm Mon-Sat, 9am-noon Sun Jun-Sep, 8am-1pm Mon-Fri Oct-May) is in Polače and there's an ATM next door (and another at Hotel Odisej in Pomena). There are free brochures and a good walking map for sale. There's another ATM at the Hotel Odisej in Pomena.

Babino Polje, 18km east of Polače, is the island capital. It's home to another **tourist office** (☑745 125; www.mljet.hr; ⊙9am-5pm Mon-Fri) and a post office.

ℹ️ Getting There & Away

Jadrolinija (p232) ferries stop only at Sobra (30KN, two hours) but the **G&V Line** (☑313 119; www.gv-line.hr) catamaran goes to Sobra (40KN, one hour) and Polače (54KN, 1½ hours) in the summer months, leaving Dubrovnik's Gruž harbour twice daily (9.15am and 7.10pm) and returning daily from Polače at 4.55pm, and twice daily from Sobra (6.15am and 5.35pm). You cannot reserve tickets in advance for this service; get to the harbour ticket office well in advance in high season to secure a seat (bicycles are not usually permitted either). In winter there's one daily catamaran. Tour boats from Korčula also run to Polače harbour in high season. Infrequent buses connect Sobra and Polače.

Dubrovnik

☑020 / POP 29.995

No matter whether you are visiting Dubrovnik for the first time or if you're returning again and again to this marvellous city, the sense of awe and beauty when you set eyes on the Stradun (the Old Town's main street) never fades. It's hard to imagine anyone, even the city's inhabitants, becoming jaded by its marble streets and baroque buildings, or failing to be inspired by a walk along the ancient city walls that protected a civilised, sophisticated republic for five centuries and that now look out onto the endless shimmer of the peaceful Adriatic.

History

Founded 1300 years ago by refugees from Epidaurus in Greece, medieval Dubrovnik (Ragusa until 1918) shook off Venetian control in the 14th century, becoming an independent republic and one of Venice's more important maritime rivals, trading with Egypt, Syria, Sicily, Spain, France and later Turkey. The double blow of an earthquake in 1667 and the opening of new trade routes to the east sent Ragusa into a slow decline, ending with Napoleon's conquest of the town in 1808.

The deliberate shelling of Dubrovnik by the Yugoslav army in 1991 sent shockwaves through the international community but, when the smoke cleared in 1992, traumatised residents cleared the rubble and set about repairing the damage. Reconstruction has been extraordinarily skilful. All of the damaged buildings have now been restored.

After a steep postwar decline in tourism, Dubrovnik has bounced back. Today it is the most prosperous, elegant and expensive city in Croatia and a real tourism magnet.

◉ Sights

All the sights are in the Old Town, which is entirely closed to cars. Looming above the city is Mt Srđ, which is connected by cable car to Dubrovnik. Pile Gate is the main entrance to the Old Town; the main street is Placa (better known as Stradun).

OLD TOWN

TOP CHOICE City Walls & Forts   CITY WALLS

(Gradske Zidine; adult/concession 70/30KN; ⊙9am-6.30pm Apr-Oct, 10am-3pm Nov-Mar) No visit to Dubrovnik would be complete without a walk around the city walls, the finest in the world and Dubrovnik's main claim to fame. Built between the 13th and 16th centuries, they enclose the entire city in a protective veil more than 2km long and up to 25m high, with two round and 14 square towers, two corner fortifications and a large fortress. The views over the town and sea are great – this walk could be the highlight of your visit. The main entrance and ticket office to the walls is by the 1537 Pile Gate. You can also enter at the Ploče Gate in the east (wise at really busy times). The walls can only be walked clockwise.

TOP CHOICE War Photo

Limited   PHOTOGRAPHIC GALLERY

(☑326 166; www.warphotoltd.com; Antuninska 6; admission 30KN; ⊙9am-9pm daily Jun-Sep, to 3pm Tue-Sat & to 1pm Sun May & Oct) A powerful experience, this state-of-the-art photographic gallery has beautifully displayed and reproduced exhibitions curated by the gallery owner and former photojournalist Wade Goddard, who worked in the Balkans in the 1990s. In addition to temporary shows, there's a permanent exhibition devoted to the war in Yugoslavia. It closes from November to April.

**Franciscan Monastery
& Museum**   MONASTERY

(Muzej Franjevačkog Samostana; Placa 2; adult/concession 30/15KN; ⊙9am-6pm) Inside this monastery complex is a mid-14th-century **cloister**, one of the most beautiful late-Romanesque structures in Dalmatia. Further inside you'll find the third-oldest functioning **pharmacy** in Europe, in business since 1391. The small monastery **museum** has a collection of relics, liturgical objects including chalices, paintings and gold jewellery and pharmacy items.

Dominican Monastery & Museum
MONASTERY

(Muzej Dominikanskog Samostana; off Ulica Svetog Dominika 4; adult/concession 20/10KN; ☺9am-6pm May-Oct, to 5pm Nov-Apr) This imposing 14th-century structure in the northeastern corner of the city is a real architectural highlight, with a forbidding fortress-like exterior that shelters a rich trove of paintings from Dubrovnik's finest 15th- and 16th-century artists.

Rector's Palace
PALACE

(Pred Dvorom 3; adult/concession 35/15KN; audioguide 30KN; ☺9am-6pm May-Oct, to 4pm Nov-Apr) This Gothic-Renaissance Rector's Palace built in the late 15th century houses a museum with artfully restored rooms, portraits, coats-of-arms and coins, evoking the glorious history of Dubrovnik. Today the atrium is often used for concerts during the Summer Festival (p221).

Cathedral of the Assumption of the Virgin
CATHEDRAL

(Stolna Crkva Velike Gospe; Poljana M Držića; ☺morning & late-afternoon Mass) Completed in 1713 in a baroque style, the cathedral is notable for its fine altars. The cathedral **treasury** (Riznica; adult/concession 10/5KN; ☺8am-5.30pm Mon-Sat, 11am-5.30pm Sun May-Oct, 10am-noon & 3-5pm Nov-Apr) contains relics of St Blaise as well as 138 gold and silver reliquaries largely made in the workshops of Dubrovnik's goldsmiths between the 11th and 17th centuries.

Sponza Palace
PALACE

(Placa) The 16th-century Sponza Palace was originally a customs house, then a minting house, a state treasury and a bank. Now it houses the **State Archives** (Državni Arhiv u Dubrovniku; admission 20KN; ☺8am-3pm Mon-Fri, to 1pm Sat) and the **Memorial Room of the Defenders of Dubrovnik** (☺10am-10pm Mon-Fri, 8am-1pm Sat), a heartbreaking collection of portraits of young people who perished between 1991 and 1995.

Onofrio Fountain
FOUNTAIN

One of Dubrovnik's most famous landmarks, Onofrio Fountain was built in 1438 as part of a water-supply system that involved bringing water from a well 12km away.

Serbian Orthodox Church & Museum
CHURCH, MUSEUM

(Muzej Pravoslavne Crkve; Od Puča 8; adult/concession 10/5KN; ☺9am-2pm Mon-Sat) This 1877 Orthodox church has a fascinating collection of icons dating from the 15th to 19th centuries.

Synagogue
SYNAGOGUE

(Sinagoga; Žudioska 5; admission 20KN; ☺10am-8pm Mon-Fri May-Oct, to 3pm Nov-Apr) The oldest Sephardic and second-oldest synagogue in the Balkans, dating back to the 15th century, has a small museum inside.

Orlando Column
MONUMENT

(Luža Sq) This popular meeting place used to be the spot where edicts, festivities and public verdicts were announced.

EAST OF THE OLD TOWN

★ Cable Car
CABLE CAR

(www.dubrovnikcablecar.com; Petra Krešimira IV; adult/concession 87/50KN; ☺9am-10pm Tue-Sun May-Oct, shorter hours rest of year) Dubrovnik's cable car whisks you from just north of the city walls up to Mt Srđ in under four minutes, for a stupendous perspective of the city from a lofty 405m, down to the terracotta-tiled rooftops of the Old Town and the island of Lokrum, with the Adriatic and distant Elafiti Islands filling the horizon.

Homeland War Museum
MUSEUM

(www.tzdubrovnik.hr; admission 20KN; ☺8am-6pm Apr-Oct, 9am-4pm Nov-Mar) Dedicated to the 'Homeland War' – as the 1990s war is dubbed in Croatia – this place inside a Napoleonic Fort, just above where the cable car drops you off, is interesting for those who want to learn more about Dubrovnik's wartime history.

THE COAST

The nicest beach that's walkable from the Old Town is below **Hotel Bellevue** (Petra Čingrije 7). In the Old Town, you can also swim below the two Buža bars.

Banje Beach
BEACH

(Outside Ploče Gate) Banje Beach is the most popular city beach, though it's even more crowded now that a section has been roped off for the exclusive EastWest Club (p223). Just southeast of here is **Sveti Jakov**, a good local beach that doesn't get rowdy and has showers, a bar and a restaurant. Buses 5 and 8 will get you there.

Dubrovnik

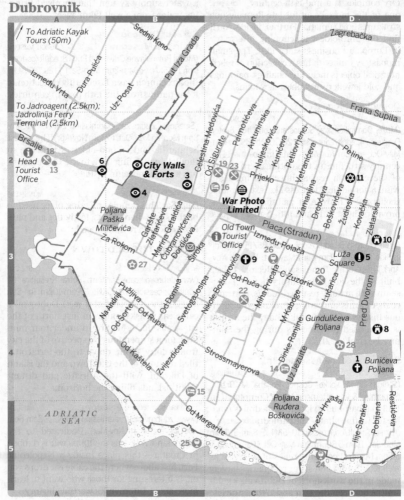

Lapad Bay BEACH
Lapad Bay is brimming with hotel beaches that you can use without a problem; try the bay by Hotel Kompas. A little further on is the good shallow **Copacabana Beach** on Babin Kuk Peninsula. If you're a naturist, head down to **Cava**, signposted near Copacabana Beach. In the Old Town, you can also swim below the two Buža bars.

Lokrum Island ISLAND
A better option than the mainland beaches is to take the **ferry** (return 40KN; ☉last return boat 6pm) that shuttles roughly hourly in summer to lush Lokrum Island, a national park with a rocky nudist beach (marked FKK), a botanical garden, the ruins of a medieval Benedictine monastery and an attractive cafe-restaurant.

🏃 Activities

Navis Underwater Explorers DIVING
(☎099 35 02 773; www.navisdubrovnik.com; Copacabana Beach; ⊛) Recreational dives (including the wreck of the *Taranto*) and courses.

**Adriatic Kayak
Tours** KAYAKING, WHITE-WATER RAFTING
(☎091 72 20 413; www.adriatickayaktours.com; Zrinsko Frankopanska 6) Kayak excursions (from a half-day paddle to a week-long trip);

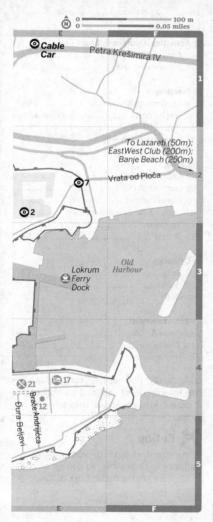

Cable Car

Petra Krešimira IV

E · F

1

To Lazareti (50m);
EastWest Club (200m);
Banje Beach (250m)

2

7

Vrata od Ploča

2

Lokrum
Ferry
Dock

Old
Harbour

3

4

21

17

12

Braće Andrijića

Dura Beljevi

5

E · F

it also offers white-water rafting on the Tara River in Montenegro.

Tours

Dubrovnik Walks WALKING
(☎095 80 64 526; www.dubrovnikwalks.com) Excellent guided walks in English. One-hour Old Town tours (90KN) run twice daily. The meeting place is the Fuego club just west of the Pile Gate. No reservation is necessary.

Adriatic Explore BUS, BOAT
(☎323 400; www.adriatic-explore.com; Bandureva 4) Day trips to Mostar and Montenegro (both

360KN) are very popular. Excursions to Korčula and Pelješac (390KN) are offered, too.

Festivals & Events

The **Feast of St Blaise** is held on 3 February, and **Carnival** is also held in February.

Dubrovnik Summer Festival CULTURAL
(☎326 100; www.dubrovnik-festival.hr; tickets 50-300KN) A major cultural event over five weeks in July and August, with theatre, music and dance performances at different venues in the Old Town.

Sleeping

Private accommodation is generally the best option in Dubrovnik, which is the most expensive destination in Croatia. Beware the scramble of private owners at the bus station and ferry terminal: some provide what they say they offer while others are scamming. Expect to pay from 300KN for a double room, and from 500KN for an apartment in high season.

OLD TOWN

TOP CHOICE Karmen Apartments APARTMENTS €€
(☎098 619 282, 323 433; www.karmendu.com; Bandureva 1; apt 450-1200KN; ✱⊕) Run by an Englishman who has lived in Dubrovnik for decades, these four inviting apartments with plenty of character enjoy a great location a stone's throw from Ploče harbour. Book well ahead.

TOP CHOICE Fresh Sheets HOSTEL €
(☎091 79 92 086; www.igotfresh.com; Sv Šimuna 15; dm/d 210/554KN; @⊕) The only hostel in the Old Town is a warm place right by the city walls, with clean and simple dorms and a double with a sea view. It's run by a hospitable crew who organise imaginative outings, international dinners and other fun stuff.

Apartments Amoret APARTMENTS €€
(☎091 53 04 910; www.dubrovnik-amoret.com; Dinke Ranjine 5; apt 755-1423KN; ✱⊕) Spread over three historic buildings in the heart of the Old Town, Amoret offers 11 high-quality renovated studio apartments, all with bathrooms, a dash of art and parquetry flooring, and kitchenette-style cooking facilities.

Hotel Stari Grad BOUTIQUE HOTEL €€€
(☎322 244; www.hotelstarigrad.com; Od Sigurate 4; s/d 1350/1800KN; ✱⊕) This Old Town hotel is all about location – it's very close to the Pile Gate and just off the Stradun. Its eight

Dubrovnik

rooms are smallish but neat and attractive. Staff are sweet and views from the rooftop terrace dramatic.

OUTSIDE THE OLD TOWN

Begović Boarding House PRIVATE ACCOMMODATION €
(☏435 191; www.begovic-boarding-house.com; Primorska 17; dm/r/apt 150/320/385KN; P@) A steep walk uphill from Lapad harbourfront, this welcoming family-run place has smallish but clean pine-trimmed rooms, some opening out onto a communal garden with amazing views. There's free pick-up from the bus or ferry, free internet, a kitchen and excursions.

Hotel Ivka HOTEL €€
(☏362 600; www.hotel-ivka.com; Put Sv Mihajla 21; s/d 593/785KN; P🌢@🛜) Modern three-star hotel with pleasant, spacious rooms that have wooden floors (and most have a balcony). Comfort levels are high given the prices. It's closer to Lapad and the ferry terminal than the Old Town, but on a regular bus route.

Dubrovnik Backpackers Club HOSTEL €
(☏435 375; www.dubackpackers.com; Mostarska 2d; dm 120-170KN; @🛜) Run by a very hospi-table family, this sociable backpackers has free internet, local calls and tea/coffee, plus a guests' kitchen and a balcony with bay views.

✗ Eating

There are a number of very average restaurants in Dubrovnik, so choose carefully. Prices here are the highest in Croatia.

TOP CHOICE **Oyster & Sushi Bar Bota Šare** SUSHI €€
(☏324 034; www.bota-sare.hr; Od Pustijerne bb; oysters/sushi per piece from 12/15KN) Fresh Ston oysters and the best sushi this side of Dalmatia, plus an absolutely divine setting, with views of the cathedral from its terrace tables.

Lucin Kantun CROATIAN €€
(☏321 003; Od Sigurate bb; mains from 80KN) A modest-looking place with shabby-chic decor, a few pavement tables and some of the most creative food in Dubrovnik. Virtually everything on the short meze-style menu is freshly cooked from an open kitchen so you may have to wait a while at busy times.

Taj Mahal BOSNIAN, INTERNATIONAL €
(www.tajmahaldubrovnik.com; Nikole Gučetićeva 2; mains from 40KN) It's like an Aladdin's cave, with an interior loaded with Ottoman decorations and subdued lighting, and great Bosnian food. There are also three pavement tables.

Oliva Gourmet MEDITERRANEAN €€
(☎324 076; www.pizza-oliva.com; Cvijete Zuzorić 2 ; mains from 100KN; ⌨) A lovely little place with a terrace on a tiny street and a cute interior with vintage pieces, dishing out simple and local food. The Oliva Pizzeria, next door, has good pizza.

Wanda ITALIAN €€
(☎098 94 49 317; www.wandarestaurant.com; Prijeko 8; mains from 70KN) This is a very classy Italian, with good Croatian wines and dishes such as osso buco with saffron risotto and beautifully crafted pastas.

Dubravka 1836 INTERNATIONAL €
(www.dubravka1836.hr; Brsalje 1; mains from 49KN) This place has arguably Dubrovnik's best dining terrace, with stunning wall and sea views. Though it draws quite a touristy clientele, locals still rate the fresh fish, risotto and salads, pizza and pasta.

🍷 Drinking

TOP CHOICE Buža BAR
(Ilije Sarake) Finding this isolated bar-on-a-cliff feels like a real discovery as you duck and dive around the city walls and finally see the entrance tunnel. It showcases tasteful music and a mellow crowd soaking up the vibes, views and sunshine.

Buža II BAR
(Crijevićeva 9) Just a notch more upmarket than the original, this one is lower on the rocks and has a shaded terrace where you can snack on crisps, peanuts or sandwiches.

EastWest Club COCKTAIL BAR
(www.ew-dubrovnik.com; Frana Supila bb) By day this upmarket outfit on Banje Beach rents out sun loungers and umbrellas and serves drinks to the bathers. When the rays lengthen, the cocktail bar opens.

Gaffe IRISH PUB
(Miha Pracata bb) The busiest place in town, this huge pub has a homely interior and a long, covered side terrace.

☆ Entertainment

TOP CHOICE Lazareti CULTURAL CENTRE
(☎324 633; www.lazareti.com; Frana Supila 8) Dubrovnik's best cultural centre, Lazareti hosts cinema nights, club nights, live music, gigs and pretty much all the best things in town.

Troubadur LIVE MUSIC
(☎412 154; Bunićeva Poljana 2) Come to this corner bar, a legendary Dubrovnik venue, for live jazz concerts in the summer.

Open-Air Cinema CINEMA
(Kumičića, Lapad) In two locations, it's open nightly in July and August with screenings starting after sundown. Also in the Old Town (Za Rokom).

ℹ Information

There are numerous ATMs in town, in Lapad and at the ferry terminal and bus station. Travel agencies and post offices will also exchange cash.

Atlas Travel Agency (www.atlas-croatia.com) With offices in Gruž Harbour (☎418 001; Obala Papa Ivana Pavla II 1, Gruž Harbour) and Pile Gate (☎442 574; Sv Đurđa 1, Pile Gate), this outfit organises excursions within Croatia and to Mostar and Montenegro. It also finds private accommodation.

Hospital (☎431 777; Dr Roka Mišetića) A kilometre south of Lapad Bay.

Lonely Planet (www.lonelyplanet.com/croatia/dubrovnik)

Main Post Office (cnr Široka & Od Puča)

Netcafé (www.netcafe.hr; Prijeko 21; per hr 30KN) A place to chill even if you're not surfing; has fast connections, CD burning, good drinks and coffee.

Tourist Office (www.tzdubrovnik.hr; ⊙8am-8pm daily Jun-Sep, 8am-3pm Mon-Fri & 9am-2pm Sat Oct-May) Maps, information and the indispensable *Dubrovnik Riviera* guide. The smart new head office (☎020 312 011; Brsalje 5) that's under construction just west of the Pile Gate should open by the time you read this. There are also offices at Gruž Harbour (☎417 983; Obala Stjepana Radića 27), the bus station (☎417 581; Obala Pape Ivana Pavla II 44a), Lapad (☎437 460; Šetalište Kralja Zvonimira 25) and at Široka (☎323 587; www.tzdubrovnik.hr; Široka 1; ⊙8am-8pm daily Jun-Sep, 8am-3pm Mon-Fri, 9am-2pm Sat Oct-May) in the Old Town.

ℹ Getting There & Away

Air

Daily flights to/from Zagreb are operated by **Croatia Airlines** (☎01 66 76 555; www.croatiaairlines.hr). Fares vary between 270KN

BUSES FROM DUBROVNIK

DESTINATION	PRICE (KN)	DURATION (HR)	FREQUENCY (DAILY)
Korčula	105	3	2
Kotor	130	2½	2-3
Mostar	130	3	3
Orebić	95	2½	2
Plitvice	350	10	1
Rijeka	370-510	13	4-5
Sarajevo	230	5	2
Split	140	4½	19
Zadar	190-230	8	8
Zagreb	270	11	7-8

for promo fares and around 760KN for flexi fares. The trip takes about an hour. Croatia Airlines also operate nonstop flights to Frankfurt and seasonal routes to cities such as Rome, Paris and Amsterdam.

Dubrovnik airport is served by over 20 other airlines from across Europe.

Boat

The **Jadrolinija ferry terminal** (☎418 000; www.jadrolinija.hr; Gruž Harbour) and the bus station are next to each other at Gruž, several kilometres northwest of the Old Town.

A twice-weekly Jadrolinija coastal ferry heads north to Korčula, Hvar, Split, Zadar and Rijeka. There's a local ferry that leaves Dubrovnik for Sobra and Polače on Mljet (60KN, 2½ hours) twice a week throughout the year; in summer there are also catamarans, which have a daily service to both Sobra and Polače (150KN, 1½ hours). Several daily ferries run year-round to the outlying Elafiti Islands of Koločep, Lopud and Šipan.

Ferries also go from Dubrovnik to Bari, in southern Italy; there are six a week in the summer season (300KN to 450KN, nine hours) and two in the winter months.

Jadroagent (☎419 000; Obala Stjepana Radića 32) books ferry tickets and has info.

Bus

Buses out of Dubrovnik **bus station** (☎060 305 070; Obala Pape Ivana Pavla II 44a) can be crowded, so book tickets ahead in summer. There's a **garderoba** (left-luggage office; 1st hr 7KN, then per hr 2KN; ⊙4.30am-10pm) at the station.

Split–Dubrovnik buses pass briefly through Bosnian territory, so keep your passport handy for border-crossing points.

All bus schedules are detailed at www.libertas dubrovnik.hr.

ⓘ Getting Around

Čilipi international airport (www.airport-dubrovnik.hr) is 24km southeast of Dubrovnik. Atlas buses (35KN) leave from the main bus station irregularly, supposedly two hours before Croatia Airlines domestic flights, but it's best to check the latest schedule at the Atlas Travel Agency (p223) by the Pile Gate. These airport buses stop in Dubrovnik at Zagrebačka cesta, just north of the old town, en route out of the city (but not at the Pile Gate). Buses leave the airport for Dubrovnik bus station (via the Pile Gate in this direction) several times a day and are timed to coincide with arrivals; if your flight is late there's usually still one waiting.

Dubrovnik's buses run frequently and generally on time. The key tourist routes run until after 2am in summer, so if you're staying in Lapad there's no need to rush home.The fare is 15KN if you buy from the driver but only 12KN if you buy it at a kiosk.

UNDERSTAND CROATIA

Croatia Today

Croatia harbours a love-hate relationship with its own politicians, its political arena fuelled by constant drama. The pinnacle occurred in 2009, with the surprise resignation of then prime minister Ivo Sanader. In 2010 Sanader was arrested in Austria, in 2011 he was extradited to Croatia and later that year he was put on trial in Zagreb. The Sanader scandal remains the talk of the town; a fifth indictment on corruption charges was filed in September 2012.

Kukuriku Coalition

Croatian politics took a major turn in the 2011 parliamentary election, when the SDP joined three other centre-left parties to create the so-named Kukuriku coalition, an opposition bloc headed up by Zoran Milanović. Kukuriku won with an absolute majority, ousting Hrvatska Demokratska Zajednica (HDZ, Croatian Democratic Union), which had been in government for 16 of the 20 years since Croatia became independent in 1991.

Milanović took office as Croatia's prime minister in December 2011. But the slightly uplifted spirits quickly descended back into general discontent with politics, mainly due to the European debt crisis and the unpopular austerity measures that ensued.

EU Accession

In January 2012, about 44% of Croats turned up to vote in the referendum on European Union (EU) accession and supported the joining by a margin of two to one. But attitudes towards EU accession remain divided, in no small part due to the crisis. The divide aside, Croatia is slated to become the EU's 28th member state, which – on paper at least – will catapult it out of the Balkans and place it firmly in Central Europe. But the accession is no big bang; Croatia's inner strife remains.

Economic Woes

Croatia's economy has been in a shambles for several years, and the global downturn plus the EU crisis aren't helping. Unemployment is high, people's salaries are often months overdue, longstanding national companies are going bankrupt, pensions are ridiculously low and unemployment compensation isn't much better. Needless to say, from the point of view of the average Croat, life is tough and the global financial crisis has made itself clearly known. *Kriza* (crisis) is among the most uttered words in Croatia today; you'll hear it everywhere, all the time, like a mantra. Despite the double-dip recession, Croatia stands as a promising emerging market. It is compensating for the drastic drop in foreign investments by rapid growth in tourism revenue. It has, in fact, become the fastest-growing tourism market in the entire Mediterranean.

History

Since time immemorial, people have come and gone, invading, trading and settling. For long periods, the Croats have been ruled by and have fought off others – Venetians, Ottomans, Hungarians, Habsburgs, the French and the Germans. The creation of Yugoslavia after WWII brought some semblance of unity to the south Slavic nations. Yet it didn't last long. After the death of Yugoslav leader Tito in 1980, Yugoslavia slowly disintegrated, and a brutal civil war ensued.

Controversial Constituition

With political changes sweeping Eastern Europe, many Croats felt the time had come to separate from Yugoslavia, and the elections of April 1990 saw the victory of Franjo Tuđman's HDZ. On 22 December 1990, a new Croatian constitution changed the status of Serbs in Croatia from that of a 'constituent nation' to a national minority.

The constitution's failure to guarantee minority rights and mass dismissals of Serbs from the public service stimulated the 600,000-strong ethnic Serb community within Croatia to demand autonomy. In early 1991 Serb extremists within Croatia staged provocations designed to force federal military intervention. A May 1991 referendum (boycotted by the Serbs) produced a 93% vote in favour of independence, but when Croatia declared independence on 25 June 1991, the Serbian enclave of Krajina proclaimed its independence from Croatia.

War

Under pressure from the EC (now the EU), Croatia declared a three-month moratorium on its independence, but heavy fighting broke out in Krajina, Baranja (the area north of the Drava River opposite Osijek) and Slavonia. This initiated what Croats refer to as the Homeland War. The Serb-dominated Yugoslav People's Army intervened in support of Serbian irregulars, under the pretext of halting ethnic violence.

When the Croatian government ordered a shutdown of 32 federal military installations in the republic, the Yugoslav navy blockaded the Adriatic coast and laid siege to the strategic town of Vukovar on the Danube. During the summer of 1991, a quarter of Croatia fell to Serbian militias and the Yugoslav People's Army.

In late 1991, the federal army and the Montenegrin militia moved against Dubrovnik, and the presidential palace in Zagreb was hit by rockets from Yugoslav jets in an apparent assassination attempt on President Tuđman. When the three-month moratorium ended, Croatia declared full independence. Soon after, Vukovar finally fell when the Yugoslav army moved in, in one of the more bloodthirsty acts in all of the Yugoslav wars. During six months of fighting in Croatia, 10,000 people died, hundreds of thousands fled and tens of thousands of homes were destroyed.

Dayton Accord

Beginning on 3 January 1992, a UN-brokered ceasefire generally held. At the same time, the EU, succumbing to pressure from Germany, recognised Croatia. This was followed by US recognition, and in May 1992 Croatia was admitted to the UN.

The fighting continued until the Dayton Accord, signed in Paris in December 1995, recognised Croatia's traditional borders and provided for the return of eastern Slavonia. It was effected in January 1998. The transition proceeded relatively smoothly, but the two populations still regard each other with suspicion.

Postwar Politics

Franjo Tuđman's combination of authoritarianism and media control, and tendency to be influenced by the far right, no longer appealed to the postwar Croatian populace. By 1999 opposition parties united to work against Tuđman and the HDZ. Tuđman was hospitalised and died suddenly in late 1999, and planned elections were postponed until January 2000. Still, voters turned out in favour of a centre-left coalition, ousting the HDZ and voting in the centrist Stipe Mesić, who held the presidential throne for 10 years.

People

According to the 2011 census, Croatia has a population of roughly 4.3 million people, a decline from the prewar population of nearly five million. A discouraging economic outlook is largely responsible for a steady decline in Croatia's population, as educated young people leave in search of greater opportunities abroad. Then there was the still-recent war of the 1990s, during which about 50% of the Serbian population departed; less than half have returned. The post-independence economic crunch that followed sparked a mass exodus of Croats; some 120,000 emigrated. That was balanced out by the roughly equal number of ethnic Croat refugees who arrived from BiH and some 30,000 who came from the Vojvodina region of Serbia. These days, the recession-powered brain drain continues. It's not surprising: Croatia is right behind Spain and Greece when it comes to unemployment rates of young educated under-30s.

Religion

According to the most recent census, 87.8% of the population identifies as Catholic, 4.4% Orthodox, 1.3% Muslim, 0.3% Protestant and 6.2% other and unknown. Croats are overwhelmingly Roman Catholic, while Serbs belong to the Eastern Orthodox Church, a division that has its roots in the fall of the Roman Empire.

It would be difficult to overstate the extent to which Catholicism shapes the Croatian national identity. The Church is the most trusted institution in Croatia, rivalled only by the military. Religious holidays are celebrated with fervour and Sunday Mass is strongly attended.

Arts

Literature

Croatia's towering literary figure is 20th-century novelist and playwright Miroslav Krleža (1893–1981). His most popular novel is *The Return of Philip Latinovicz* (1932), which has been translated into English.

BOOKS

Lonely Planet's *Croatia* is a comprehensive guide to the country.

Interesting reads about Croatia include Rebecca West's *Black Lamb and Grey Falcon*, a classic travel book which recounts the writer's journeys through Croatia, Serbia, Bosnia, Macedonia and Montenegro in 1941. British writer Tony White retraced West's journey in *Another Fool in the Balkans* (2006), juxtaposing modern life in Serbia and Croatia with the region's political history. *Croatia: Travels in Undiscovered Country* (2003), by Tony Fabijančić, recounts the life of rural folks in a new Croatia. *Plum Brandy: Croatian Journeys* by Josip Novakovich is a sensitive exploration of his family's Croatian background.

Some contemporary writers worth reading include expat writer Dubravka Ugrešić, best known for her novels *The Culture of Lies* and *The Ministry of Pain*. Slavenka Drakulić's *Café Europa – Life After Communism* is an excellent read, while Miljenko Jergović's *Sarajevo Marlboro* and *Mama Leone* powerfully conjure up the atmosphere of life in pre-war Yugoslavia.

Music

Although Croatia has produced many fine classical musicians and composers, its most original musical contribution lies in its rich tradition of folk music. The instrument most often used in Croatian folk music is the *tamburica*, a three- or five-string mandolin that is plucked or strummed. Translated as 'group of people', *klapa* is an outgrowth of church-choir singing. The form is most popular in rural Dalmatia and can involve up to 10 voices singing in harmony.

There's a wealth of homegrown talent on Croatia's pop and rock music scene. Some of the most prominent pop, fusion and hip-hop bands are Hladno Pivo (Cold Beer), Pips Chips & Videoclips, TBF, Edo Maajka, Vještice (The Witches), Gustafi and the deliciously insane Let 3.

Visual Arts

Vlaho Bukovac (1855–1922) was the most notable Croatian painter in the late 19th century. Important early-20th-century painters include Miroslav Kraljević (1885–1913) and Josip Račić (1885–1908). Post-WWII artists experimented with abstract expressionism but this period is best remembered for the naive art that was typified by Ivan Generalić (1914–92). Recent trends have included minimalism, conceptual art and pop art. Contemporary Croatian artists worth checking out include Lovro Artuković, Sanja Iveković, Dalibor Martinis, Andreja Kulunčić, Sandra Sterle and Renata Poljak.

Environment

Croatia is shaped like a boomerang: from the Pannonian plains of Slavonia between the Sava, Drava and Danube Rivers, across hilly central Croatia to the Istrian peninsula, then south through Dalmatia along the rugged Adriatic coast.

The narrow Croatian coastal belt at the foot of the Dinaric Alps is only about 600km long as the crow flies, but it's so indented that the actual length is 1778km. If the 4012km of coastline around the offshore islands is added to the total, the length becomes 5790km. Most of the 'beaches' along this jagged coast consist of slabs of rock sprinkled with naturists. Don't come expecting to find sand, but the waters are sparkling clean, even around large towns.

Croatia's offshore islands are every bit as beautiful as those off the coast of Greece. There are 1244 islands and islets along the tectonically submerged Adriatic coastline, 50 of them inhabited. The largest are Cres, Krk, Mali Lošinj, Pag and Rab in the north; Dugi Otok in the middle; and Brač, Hvar, Korčula, Mljet and Vis in the south.

Wildlife

Deer are plentiful in the dense forests of Risnjak National Park, as are brown bears, wild cats and *ris* (lynx), from which the park gets its name. Occasionally a wolf or wild boar may appear but only rarely. Plitvice Lakes National Park, however, is an important refuge for wolves. The rare sea otter is also protected in Plitvice, as well as in Krka National Park. Two venomous snakes are endemic in Paklenica – the nose-horned viper and the European adder.

The griffon vulture, with a wingspan of 2.6m, has a permanent colony on Cres, and Paklenica National Park is rich in peregrine falcons, goshawks, sparrow hawks, buzzards and owls. Krka National Park is an important migration route and winter habitat for marsh birds as well as rare golden eagles and short-toed eagles. Kopački Rit Nature Park, near Osijek in eastern Croatia, is an extremely important bird refuge.

National Parks

When the Yugoslav federation collapsed, eight of its finest national parks ended up in Croatia. These have a total area of 96,135 sq km, of which 74,260 sq km is land and 21,875 sq km is water. Around 8% of Croatia is given over to its protected areas.

The dramatically formed karstic gorges and cliffs make Paklenica National Park along the coast a rock-climbing favourite. More rugged is the mountainous Northern Velebit National Park, a stunning patchwork of forests, peaks, ravines and ridges that backs northern Dalmatia and the Šibenik-Knin region. The abundant plant and animal life, including bears, wolves and deer, in the Plitvice Lakes National Park between Zagreb and Zadar has warranted its inclusion on Unesco's list of World Natural Heritage sites. Both Plitvice Lakes and Krka National Parks (near Šibenik) feature a dramatic series of cascades and incredible turquoise lakes.

The Kornati Islands consist of 140 sparsely inhabited and vegetated islands, islets and reefs scattered over 300 sq km – an Adriatic showpiece easily accessible on an organised tour from Zadar. The northwestern half of the island of Mljet has been named a national park due to its two highly indented saltwater lakes surrounded by lush vegetation. The Brijuni Islands near Pula are the most cultivated national park since they were developed as a tourist resort in the late 19th century and were the getaway paradise for Tito.

Environmental Issues

The lack of heavy industry in Croatia has had the happy effect of leaving its forests, coasts, rivers and air generally fresh and unpolluted, but, as ever, an increase in investment and development brings forth problems and threats to the environment.

With the tourist boom, the demand for fresh fish and shellfish has risen exponentially. The production of farmed sea bass, sea bream and tuna (for export) is rising substantially, resulting in environmental pressure along the coast. Croatian tuna farms capture the young fish for fattening before they have a chance to reproduce and replenish the wild-fish population.

Coastal and island forests face particular problems. The dry summers and brisk *maestrals* (strong, steady westerly winds) also pose substantial fire hazards along the coast. In the last 20 years, fires have destroyed 7% of Croatia's forests.

Food & Drink

Croatian food is a savoury smorgasbord of taste, echoing the varied cultures that have influenced the country over the course of its history. You'll find a sharp divide between the Italian-style cuisine along the coast and the flavours of Hungary, Austria and Turkey in the continental parts.

Staples & Specialities

Zagreb and northwestern Croatia favour the kind of hearty meat dishes you might find in Vienna. Juicy spit-roasted and baked meat features *janjetina* (lamb), *svinjetina* (pork) and *patka* (duck), often accompanied by *mlinci* (baked noodles) or *pečeni krumpir* (roast potatoes).

Coastal cuisine is typically Mediterranean, using a lot of olive oil, garlic, fresh fish and shellfish, and herbs. Along the coast, look for lightly breaded and fried *lignje* (squid) as a main course. For a special appetiser, try *paški sir*, a pungent, hard cheese from the island of Pag. Dalmatian *brodet* (stewed mixed fish served with polenta) is another regional treat.

Istrian cuisine has been attracting international foodies for its long gastronomic tradition, fresh foodstuffs and unique specialities. Typical dishes include *maneštra*, a thick vegetable-and-bean soup, *fuži*, hand-rolled pasta often served with truffles or game meat, and *fritaja* (omelette often served with seasonal veggies). Istrian wines and olive oil are highly rated.

Drinks

It's customary to have a small glass of brandy before a meal and to accompany the food with one of Croatia's many wines. Today winemaking is undergoing a renaissance in the hands of a new generation of winemakers with a focus on preserving indigenous varieties and revitalizing ancestral estates. Quality is rising, exports are increasing and the wines are garnering global awards and winning the affections of worldly wine lovers thirsty for authentic stories and unique terroirs. Croatians often mix their wine with water, calling it *bevanda*. *Rakija* (brandy) comes in different flavours. The most commonly drunk are *loza* (grape brandy), *šljivovica* (plum brandy) and *travarica* (herbal brandy).

The two top types of Croatian *pivo* (beer) are Zagreb's Ožujsko and Karlovačko from Karlovac. The small-distribution Velebitsko has a loyal following among in-the-know beer drinkers. You'll probably want to practise saying *živjeli!* (cheers!).

Where to Eat & Drink

Most restaurants cluster in the middle of the price spectrum – few are unbelievably cheap and few are exorbitantly expensive. A restaurant *(restoran)* is at the top of the food chain, generally presenting a more formal dining experience. A *gostionica* or *konoba* is usually a traditional family-run tavern. A *pivnica* is more like a pub, with a wide choice of beer. A *kavana* is a cafe. Self-service cafeterias are quick, easy and inexpensive, though the quality of the food tends to vary.

Restaurants are open long hours, often noon to 11pm (some midnight), but many close on Sunday out of peak season.

Vegetarians & Vegans

Outside of major cities like Zagreb, Rijeka, Split and Dubrovnik, vegetarian restaurants are few but Croatia's vegetables are usually locally grown and quite tasty. *Blitva* (swiss chard) is a nutritious side dish often served with potatoes. The hearty *štrukli* (baked cheese dumplings) are a good alternative too.

SURVIVAL GUIDE

Directory A–Z

Accommodation

Private accommodation is a lot more affordable in Croatia; it's very often great value if you don't mind foregoing hotel facilities.

Note that many establishments add a 30% charge for less than three-night stays and include 'residence tax', which is around 7KN per person per day. Prices quoted in this chapter do not include the residence tax.

The following price categories for the cost of double room with bathroom are used in the listings in this chapter.

€ less than 500KM

€€ 500KN to 900KN

€€€ more than 900KN

Breakfast is included in the prices for all hotels.

CAMPING

Nearly 100 camping grounds are scattered along the Croatian coast. Most operate from mid-April to mid-September, give or take a few weeks. The exact times change from year to year, so it's wise to call in advance if you're arriving at either end of the season.

Nudist camping grounds (marked FKK) are among the best, as their secluded locations ensure peace and quiet. Bear in mind that freelance camping is officially prohibited. A good site for camping information is www.camping.hr.

HOSTELS

The Croatian YHA (☑01-48 29 291; www.hfhs. hr; Savska 5/1, Zagreb) operates youth hostels in Rijeka, Dubrovnik, Zadar, Zagreb and Pula. Nonmembers pay an additional 10KN per person per day for a stamp on a welcome card; six stamps entitle you to membership. The Croatian YHA can also provide information about private youth hostels in Zadar, Dubrovnik and Zagreb.

HOTELS

Hotels are ranked from one to five stars with most in the two- and three-star range. In August, some hotels may demand a surcharge for stays of less than three or four nights, but this is usually waived during the rest of the year, when prices drop steeply. In Zagreb prices are the same all year.

PRIVATE ROOMS

The best value for money in Croatia is a private room or apartment, often within or attached to a local home – the equivalent of small private guesthouses in other countries. Book private accommodation through travel agencies, by dealing directly with proprietors who meet you at the local bus or ferry station, or by knocking on the doors of houses with *sobe* or *zimmer* (rooms available) signs.

Whether you deal with the owner directly or book through an agency, you'll pay a 30% surcharge for stays of less than four or three nights and sometimes 50% or even 100% more for a one-night stay, although you may be able to get them to waive the surcharge if you arrive in the low season. Some will even insist on a seven-night minimum stay in the high season.

If you land in a room or apartment without a blue *sobe* or *apartmani* sign outside, the proprietor is renting to you illegally (ie not paying residence tax). They will probably be reluctant to provide their full name or phone number and you'll have absolutely no recourse in case of a problem.

Activities

There are numerous outdoorsy activities in Croatia.

Cycling Croatia has become a popular destination for cycle enthusiasts. See www.bicikl.hr and www.pedala.com.hr.

Diving Most coastal and island resorts have dive shops. For more info see the Croatian Association of Diving Tourism (www.croprodive.info), Croatian Diving Federation (www.diving-hrs.hr) and Pro Diving Croatia (www.diving.hr).

Hiking For information about hiking in Croatia, see the Croatian Mountaineering Association (www.plsavez.hr).

Kayaking and rafting Zagreb-based Huck Finn (www.huck-finn.hr) is a good contact for sea and river kayaking packages as well as rafting.

Rock climbing and caving For details, contact the Croatian Mountaineering Association or check its speleological department website at www.speleologija.hr.

Windsurfing For info about windsurfing in Croatia, see the Croatian Windsurfing Association (www.hukjd.hr) or www.wind-surfing.hr.

Yachting A good source of information is the Association of Nautical Tourism (Udruženje Nautičkog Turizma; 051 209 147; www.croatiacharter.com; Bulevar Oslobođenja 23, Rijeka), which represents all Croatian marinas, and Adriatic Croatia International Club (www.aci-club.hr).

Business Hours

Hours can vary across the year.

Banks 9am to 7pm Monday to Friday, 8am to 1pm or 9am to 2pm Saturday

Bars and cafes 8am to midnight

Offices 8am to 4pm or 9am to 5pm Monday to Friday, 8am to 1pm or 9am to 2pm Saturday

Restaurants noon to 11pm or midnight, closed Sunday out of peak season

Shops 8am to 8pm Monday to Friday, to 2pm or 3pm Saturday

Embassies & Consulates

The following are all in Zagreb.

Albanian Embassy (01-48 10 679; Jurišićeva 2a)

Australian Embassy (01-48 91 200; Nova Ves 11, Kaptol Centar)

Bosnia & Hercegovina Embassy (01-45 01 070; Torbarova 9)

Bulgarian Embassy (01-46 46 609; Nike Grškovića 31)

Canadian Embassy (01-48 81 200; Prilaz Gjure Deželića 4)

Czech Embassy (01-61 77 246; Radnička Cesta 47/6)

French Embassy (01-48 93 600; Andrije Hebranga 2)

German Embassy (01-61 58 100; Ulica Grada Vukovara 64)

Hungarian Embassy (01-48 90 900; Pantovčak 257)

Irish Embassy (01-63 10 025; Miramarska 23)

Netherlands Embassy (01-46 42 200; Medvešćak 56)

New Zealand Embassy (01-46 12 060; Vlaška 50a)

Polish Embassy (01-48 99 444; Krležin Gvozd 3)

Romanian Embassy (01-46 77 550; Mlinarska 43)

Serbian Embassy (01-45 79 067; Pantovčak 245)

Slovakian Embassy (01-48 77 070; Prilaz Gjure Deželića 10)

Slovenian Embassy (01-63 11 000; Savska cesta 41/annex)

UK Embassy (01-60 09 100; I Lučića 4)

US Embassy (01-66 12 200; Thomas Jefferson 2)

Food

Prices in this chapter are based on a main course.

€ less than 80KN

€€ 80KN to 150KN

€€€ more than 150KN

Gay & Lesbian Travellers

Homosexuality has been legal in Croatia since 1977 and is tolerated, but not welcomed with open arms. Public displays of affection between same-sex couples may be met with hostility, especially beyond the major cities.

Exclusively gay clubs are a rarity outside Zagreb, but many of the large discos attract a mixed crowd. On the coast, gay men gravitate to Rovinj, Hvar, Split and Dubrovnik, and tend to frequent naturist beaches.

In Zagreb, the last Saturday in June is Gay Pride Zagreb day.

Most Croatian websites devoted to the gay scene are in Croatian only, but a good starting point is www.travel.gay.hr.

Money

CREDIT CARDS

Amex, MasterCard, Visa and Diners Club cards are widely accepted in large hotels, stores and many restaurants, but don't count on cards to pay for private accommodation or meals in small restaurants. You'll find ATMs accepting MasterCard, Maestro, Cirrus, Plus and Visa in most bus and train stations, airports, all major cities and most small towns.

CURRENCY

Croatia uses the kuna (KN). Commonly circulated banknotes come in denominations of 500, 200, 100, 50, 20, 10 and five kuna. Each kuna is divided into 100 lipa. You'll find silver-coloured 50- and 20-lipa coins, and bronze-coloured 10-lipa coins.

TAX

Travellers who spend more than 740KN in one shop are entitled to a refund of the value-added tax (VAT), which is equivalent to 22% of the purchase price. In order to claim the refund, the merchant must fill out the Tax Cheque (required form), which you must present to the customs office upon leaving the country. Mail a stamped copy to the shop within six months, which will then credit your credit card with the appropriate sum.

TIPPING

If you're served well at a restaurant, you should round up the bill, but a service charge is always included. Bar bills and taxi fares can also be rounded up. Tour guides on day excursions expect to be tipped.

Public Holidays

New Year's Day 1 January

Epiphany 6 January

Easter Monday March/April

Labour Day 1 May

Corpus Christi 10 June

Day of Antifascist Resistance 22 June; marks the outbreak of resistance in 1941

Statehood Day 25 June

Homeland Thanksgiving Day 5 August

Feast of the Assumption 15 August

Independence Day 8 October

All Saints' Day 1 November

Christmas 25 and 26 December

Telephone

MOBILE PHONES

If you have an unlocked 3G phone, you can buy a SIM card for about 50KN. You can choose from four network providers: VIP (www.vip.hr), T-Mobile (www.t-mobile.hr), Tomato (www.tomato.com.hr) and Tele2 (www.tele2.hr).

PHONE CODES

To call Croatia from abroad, dial your international access code, then ☎385 (the country code for Croatia), then the area code (without the initial ☎0) and the local number.

To call from region to region within Croatia, start with the area code (with the initial ☎0); drop it when dialling within the same code.

Phone numbers with the prefix ☎060 are either free or charged at a premium rate, so watch the small print. Phone numbers that begin with ☎09 are mobile phone numbers.

PHONECARDS

To make a phone call from Croatia, go to the town's main post office. You'll need a phone card to use public telephones. Phonecards are sold according to *impulsi* (units), and you can buy cards of 25 (15KN), 50 (30KN), 100 (50KN) and 200 (100KN) units. These can be purchased at any post office and most tobacco shops and newspaper kiosks.

Tourist Information

The Croatian National Tourist Board (www.croatia.hr) is a good source of info. There are regional tourist offices that supervise tourist development, and municipal tourist offices that have free brochures and information.

Travellers with Disabilities

Due to the number of wounded war veterans, more attention is being paid to the needs of disabled travellers in Croatia. Public toilets at bus stations, train stations, airports and large public venues are usually wheelchair accessible. Large hotels are wheelchair accessible, but very little private accommodation is. Bus and train stations in Zagreb, Zadar, Rijeka, Split and Dubrovnik are wheelchair accessible, but the local Jadrolinija ferries are not. For further information, get in touch with Hrvatski Savez Udruga Tjelesnih Invalida (☎01-48 12 004; www.hsuti.hr; Šoštarićeva 8, Zagreb), the Croatian union of associations for physically disabled persons.

Visas

Citizens of the EU, USA, Canada, Australia, New Zealand, Israel, Ireland, Singapore and the UK do not need a visa for stays of up to

90 days. South Africans must apply for a 90-day visa in Pretoria. Contact any Croatian embassy, consulate or travel agency abroad for information.

Getting There & Away

Getting to Croatia is becoming ever easier, especially if you're arriving in summer. Low-cost carriers are finally establishing routes to Croatia, and a plethora of bus and ferry routes shepherd holidaymakers to the coast.

Air

There are direct flights to Croatia from a number of European cities; however, there are no nonstop flights from North America to Croatia.

There are several major airports in Croatia.

Dubrovnik Airport (www.airport-dubrovnik.hr) Nonstop flights from Brussels, Cologne, Frankfurt, Hanover, London (Gatwick and Stansted), Manchester, Munich and Stuttgart.

Pula Airport (www.airport-pula.com) Nonstop flights from London (Gatwick) and Manchester.

Rijeka (www.rijeka-airport.hr) Nonstop flights from Cologne and Stuttgart.

Split Airport (www.split-airport.hr) Nonstop flights from Cologne, Frankfurt, London, Munich, Prague and Rome.

Zadar (www.zadar-airport.hr) Nonstop flights from Bari, Brussels, Dublin, London, Munich and more.

Zagreb Airport (www.zagreb-airport.hr) Direct flights from all European capitals, plus Cologne, Hamburg and Stuttgart.

Land

Croatia has border crossings with Hungary, Slovenia, BiH, Serbia and Montenegro.

Buses run to destinations throughout Europe.

From Austria, **Eurolines** (www.eurolines.com) operates buses from Vienna to several destinations in Croatia.

Bus services between Germany and Croatia are good, and fares are cheaper than the train. All buses are handled by **Deutsche Touring GmbH** (www.deutsche-touring.de); there are no Deutsche Touring offices in Croatia, but numerous travel agencies and bus stations sell its tickets.

Sea

Regular boats from the following companies connect Croatia with Italy:

Blue Line (www.blueline-ferries.com)

Commodore Cruises (www.commodore-cruises.hr)

Emilia Romagna Lines (www.emiliaromagnalines.it)

Jadrolinija (www.jadrolinija.hr)

Split Tours (www.splittours.hr)

SNAV (www.snav.com)

Termoli Jet (www.termolijet.it)

Ustica Lines (www.usticalines.it)

Venezia Lines (www.venezialines.com)

Getting Around

Air

Croatia Airlines (☎01-66 76 555; www.croatiaairlines.hr) Croatia Airlines is the only carrier for flights within Croatia. There are daily flights between Zagreb and Dubrovnik, Pula, Split and Zadar.

Bicycle

Cycling can be a great way to explore the islands. Relatively flat islands such as Pag and Mali Lošinj offer the most relaxed biking, but the winding, hilly roads on other islands offer spectacular views. Bicycles are easy to rent along the coast and on the islands. Some tourist offices, especially in the Kvarner and Istria regions, have maps of routes and can refer you to local bike-rental agencies. Even though it's not fully translated into English yet, www.pedala.hr is a great reference for cycling routes around Croatia.

Boat

JADROLINIJA FERRIES

Jadrolinija (www.jadrolinija.hr) operates an extensive network of car ferries and catamarans along the Adriatic coast. Ferries are a lot more comfortable than buses, though somewhat more expensive.

Services operate year-round, though they are less frequent in winter. Cabins should be booked a week ahead. Deck space is usually available on all sailings. You must buy tickets in advance at an agency or a Jadrolinija office. Tickets are not sold on board. In summer months, you need to check in two hours in advance if you bring a car.

Somewhat mediocre fixed-price menus in onboard restaurants cost about 100KN; the cafeteria only offers ham-and-cheese sandwiches for 30KN. Do as the Croats do: bring some food and drink with you.

LOCAL FERRIES

Local ferries connect the bigger offshore islands with each other and with the mainland, but you'll find many more ferries going from the mainland to the islands than from island to island.

On most lines, service is less frequent between October and April. Extra passenger boats are added in the summer; these are usually faster, more comfortable and more expensive. On some shorter routes, ferries run nonstop in summer and advance reservation is unnecessary.

Buy tickets at a Jadrolinija office or at a stall near the ferry (usually open 30 minutes prior to departure). There are no ticket sales on board. In summer, arrive one to two hours prior to departure, even if you've already bought your ticket.

Cars incur a charge; calculated according to the size of car and often very pricey. Reserve as far in advance as possible. Check in several hours in advance. Bicycles incur a small charge.

There is no meal service; you can buy drinks and snacks on board. Most locals bring their own food.

Bus

Bus services are excellent and relatively inexpensive. There are often a number of different companies handling each route so prices can vary substantially. Luggage stowed in the baggage compartment under the bus costs extra (7KN a piece, including insurance).

BUS COMPANIES

The companies listed here are among the largest.

Autotrans (☎060 30 20 10; www.autotrans. hr) Based in Rijeka. Connections to Istria, Zagreb, Varaždin and Kvarner.

Brioni Pula (☎052-535 155; www.brioni. hr) Based in Pula. Connections to Istria, Padua, Split, Trieste and Zagreb.

Contus (☎023-317 062) Based in Zadar. Connections to Split and Zagreb.

Croatiabus (☎01-61 13 073; www.croatiabus.hr) Connecting Zagreb with towns in Zagorje and Istria.

Samoborček (☎01-48 19 180; www. samoborcek.hr) Connecting Zagreb with towns in Dalmatia.

TICKETS & SCHEDULES

At large stations, bus tickets must be purchased at the office, not from drivers. Try to book ahead to be sure of a seat, especially in the summer.

Departure lists above the various windows at bus stations tell you which window sells tickets for your bus. On Croatian bus schedules, *vozi svaki dan* means 'every day' and *ne vozi nedjeljom i blagdanom* means 'no service Sunday and holidays'.

Some buses travel overnight, saving you a night's accommodation. Don't expect to get much sleep, though, as the inside lights will be on and music will be blasting the whole night. Take care not to be left behind at meal or rest stops, which usually occur about every two hours.

Car & Motorcycle

Croatia's motorway connecting Zagreb with Split is only a few years old and makes some routes much faster. Zagreb and Rijeka are now connected by motorway, and an Istrian motorway has shortened the travel time to Italy considerably.

Although the new roads are in excellent condition, there are stretches where service stations and facilities are few and far between. You can reach roadside assistance on ☎1987.

CAR HIRE

In order to rent a car you must be 21 or over, with a valid driving licence and a valid credit card.

Independent local companies are often much cheaper than the international chains, but the big companies offer one-way rentals. Sometimes you can get a lower car-rental rate by booking the car from abroad, or by booking a fly-drive package.

CAR INSURANCE

Third-party public liability insurance is included by law with car rentals, but make sure your quoted price includes full collision insurance, known as a collision damage waiver (CDW). Otherwise, your responsibility for damage done to the vehicle is usually determined as a percentage of the car's value, beginning at around 2000KN.

If you rent a car in Italy, many insurance companies will not insure you for a trip into Croatia. Border officials know this and may refuse you entry unless permission to drive into Croatia is clearly marked on the insurance documents.

Most car-rental companies in Trieste and Venice are familiar with this requirement and will furnish you with the correct stamp. Otherwise, you must make specific inquiries.

DRIVING LICENCE

Any valid driving licence is sufficient to drive legally and rent a car; an international driving licence is not necessary.

The **Hrvatski Autoklub** (HAK, Croatian Auto Club; ☎46 40 800; www.hak.hr; Avenija Dubrovnik 44) offers help and advice. For help on the road, you can contact the nationwide **HAK road assistance** (Vučna Služba; ☎987).

ON THE ROAD

Petrol stations are generally open from 7am to 7pm and often until 10pm in summer. Petrol is Eurosuper 95, Super 98, normal or diesel. See www.ina.hr for up-to-date fuel prices.

You have to pay tolls on all motorways, to use the Učka tunnel between Rijeka and Istria, to use the bridge to Krk Island, and on the road from Rijeka to Delnice.

For general news on Croatia's motorways and tolls, see www.hak.hr. The radio station HR2 broadcasts traffic reports in English every hour on the hour from July to early September.

ROAD RULES

In Croatia you drive on the right, and the use of seatbelts is mandatory. Unless otherwise posted, the speed limits for cars and motorcycles are 50km/h in built-up areas, 100km/h on main highways and 130km/h on motorways.

On two-lane highways, it's illegal to pass long military convoys or a line of cars caught behind a slow-moving truck.

It's illegal to drive with a blood alcohol content higher than 0.5%.

You are required to drive with your headlights on even during the day.

Local Transport

The main form of local transport is bus (although Zagreb and Osijek also have well-developed tram systems).

Buses in major cities such as Dubrovnik, Rijeka, Split and Zadar run about once every 20 minutes, less on Sunday. A ride is usually around 10KN, with a small discount if you buy tickets at a *tisak* (news stand).

Small medieval towns along the coast are generally closed to traffic and have infrequent links to outlying suburbs.

Bus transport within the islands is infrequent since most people have their own cars.

Train

Trains are less frequent than buses but more comfortable. For information about schedules, prices and services, contact **Croatian Railways** (Hrvatske Željeznice; ☎060 333 444; www.hznet.hr).

Zagreb is the hub for Croatia's less-than-extensive train system. No trains run along the coast and only a few coastal cities are connected with Zagreb. For travellers, the main lines of interest are the following:

Zagreb–Rijeka–Pula Via Lupoglava, where passengers switch to a bus.

Zagreb–Osijek

Zagreb–Split

Domestic trains are either 'express' or 'passenger' (local). Express trains have 1st- and 2nd-class cars, plus smoking and nonsmoking areas. A reservation is advisable for express trains.

Express trains are more expensive than passenger trains; any prices quoted in this chapter are for unreserved 2nd-class seating.

There are no couchettes on domestic services. There are sleeping cars on overnight trains between Zagreb and Split.

Baggage is free on trains; most stations have left-luggage services charging around 15KN a piece per day.

EU residents who hold an InterRail pass can use it in Croatia for free travel, but you're unlikely to take enough trains to justify the cost.

Greece Ελλάδα

Includes »

Best Places to Eat

- » Marco Polo Café (p294)
- » Alaloum (p258)
- » Café Avyssinia (p247)
- » Spondi (p249)
- » Taverna Lava (p282)

Best Places to Stay

- » 1700 (p269)
- » Amfitriti Pension (p257)
- » Francesco's (p280)
- » Pension Sofi (p278)
- » Hotel Afendoulis (p296)

Why Go?

Don't let headline-grabbing financial woes put you off going to Greece. The alluring combination of history and hedonism, which has made Greece one of the most popular destinations on the planet, continues to beckon, and now is as good a time as ever to turn up for some fun in the sun. Within easy reach of magnificent archaeological sites are breathtaking beaches and relaxed tavernas serving everything from ouzo to octopus. Wanderers can island-hop to their heart's content, while party types can enjoy pulsating nightlife in Greece's vibrant modern cities and on islands such as Mykonos, Ios and Santorini. Add welcoming locals with an enticing culture to the mix and it's easy to see why most visitors head home vowing to come back. Travellers to Greece inevitably end up with a favourite site they long to return to – get out there and find yours.

When to Go
Athens

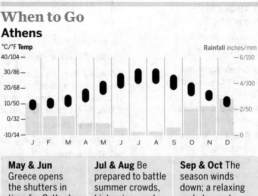

May & Jun Greece opens the shutters in time for Orthodox Easter; the best months to visit.

Jul & Aug Be prepared to battle summer crowds, high prices and soaring temperatures.

Sep & Oct The season winds down; a relaxing and pleasant time to head to Greece.

AT A GLANCE

» **Currency** euro (€)
» **Language** Greek
» **Money** ATMs all over; banks open Mon-Fri
» **Visas** Schengen rules apply

Fast Facts

» **Area** 131,944 sq km
» **Capital** Athens
» **Country code** ☑30
» **Emergency** ☑112

Exchange Rates

Australia	A$1	€0.82
Canada	C$1	€0.77
Japan	¥100	€0.83
New Zealand	NZ$1	€0.65
UK	UK£1	€1.18
USA	US$1	€0.78

Set Your Budget

» **Budget hotel room** €50
» **Two-course meal** €20
» **Museum entrance** €5
» **Beer** €2.50
» **Athens metro ticket** €1.40

Resources

» **Greek National Tourist Organisation** (www.gnto.gr)
» **Virtual Greece** (www.greecevirtual.gr)
» **Ancient Greece** (www.ancientgreece.com)
» **Greek Ferries** (www.openseas.gr)

Connections

For those visiting Greece as part of a trip around Europe, there are various exciting options for reaching onward destinations overland or by sea.

There are regular ferry connections between Greece and the Italian ports of Ancona, Bari, Brindisi and Venice. Similarly, there are ferries operating between the Greek islands of Rhodes, Kos, Samos, Chios and Lesvos and the Aegean coast of Turkey. Island-hopping doesn't have to take you back to Athens.

Overland, it's possible to reach Albania, Bulgaria, the Former Yugoslav Republic of Macedonia (FYROM) and Turkey from Greece. If you've got your own wheels, you can drive through border crossings with these four countries. There are train and bus connections with Greece's neighbours, but check ahead, as these have been affected by the financial crisis. At the time of writing, no international train services from Greece were running.

ITINERARIES

One Week

Explore Athens' museums and ancient sites on day one before spending a couple of days in the Peloponnese visiting Nafplio, Mycenae and Olympia; ferry to the Cyclades and enjoy Mykonos and spectacular Santorini.

One Month

Give yourself some more time in Athens and the Peloponnese, then visit the Ionian Islands for a few days. Explore the villages of Zagorohoria before travelling back to Athens via Meteora and Delphi. Take a ferry from Piraeus south to Mykonos, then island-hop via Santorini to Crete. After exploring Crete, take the ferry east to Rhodes, then north to Symi, Kos and Samos. Carry on north to Chios, then head to Lesvos. Take the ferry back to Piraeus when you're out of time or money.

Essential Food & Drink

» **Gyros Pitta** The ultimate in cheap eats. Pork or chicken shaved from a revolving stack of sizzling meat is wrapped in pitta bread with tomato, onion, fried potatoes and lashings of tzatziki (yoghurt, cucumber and garlic). Costs €2 to €3.
» **Souvlaki** Skewered meat, usually pork.
» **Greek salad** Tomatoes, cucumber, onion, feta and olives.
» **Grilled octopus** All the better with a glass of ouzo.
» **Ouzo** Sipped slowly, this legendary aniseed-flavoured tipple turns a cloudy white when ice and water are added.
» **Raki** Cretan fire water produced from grape skins.
» **Greek coffee** A legacy of Ottoman rule, Greek coffee should be tried at least once.

ATHENS ΑΘΗΝΑ

POP 3.8 MILLION

Ancient and modern, with equal measures of grunge and grace, bustling Athens is a heady mix of history and edginess. Iconic monuments mingle with first-rate muse- ums, lively cafes and alfresco dining, and it's downright fun. With Greece's financial dif- ficulties Athens has revealed its more restive aspect, but take the time to look beneath the surface and you'll discover a complex me- tropolis full of vibrant subcultures.

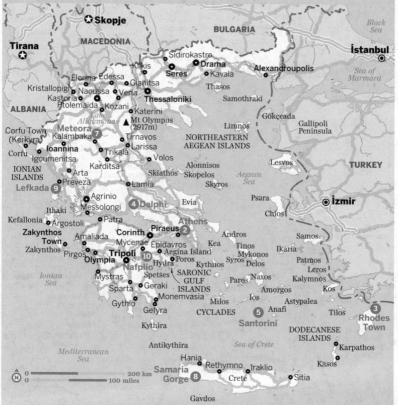

Greece Highlights

1 **Island-hop** (p322) at your own pace under the Aegean sun

2 In **Athens** (p237), trace the ancient to the modern from the Acropolis to booming nightclubs

3 Lose yourself within the medieval walls of **Rhodes Old Town** (p293)

4 Search for the oracle amidst the dazzling ruins of **Delphi** (p262)

5 Stare dumbfounded at the dramatic volcanic caldera of incomparable **Santorini** (p280)

6 Sip **ouzo** (p316) while munching on grilled octopus

7 Climb russet rock pinnacles to the exquisite monasteries of **Meteora** (p263)

8 Hike through Crete's stupendous **Samaria Gorge** (p288)

9 Let your cares float away from the pristine west-coast beaches of **Lefkada** (p308)

10 Use quaint **Nafplio** (p257) as a base for exploring the back roads and ruins of the Peloponnese

Central Athens

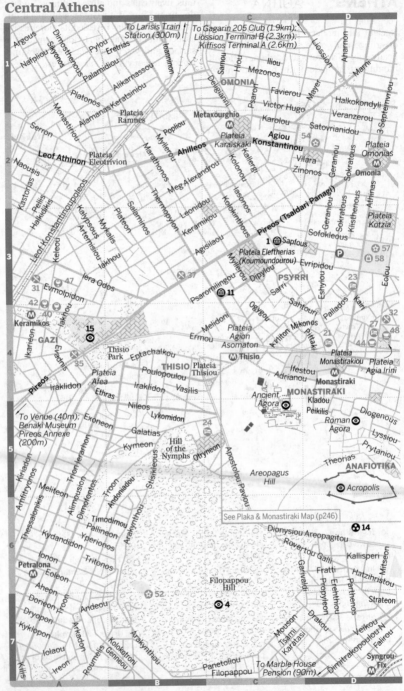

To Larisis Train Station (300m)

To Gagarin 205 Club (1.9km); Liossion Terminal B (2.3km); Kiffisos Terminal A (2.6km)

OMONIA

Metaxourghio

Plateia Karaiskaki

Agiou Konstantinou

Ahilleos

Plateia Ramnes

Leof Athinon

Plateia Eleotrivion

Pireos (Tsaldari Panagi)

1 Sapfous

Plateia Eleftherias (Koumoundourou)

Plateia Omonias

Omonia

Plateia Kotzia

PSYRRI

11

Keramikos

GAZI

15

Thisio Park

THISIO

Plateia Thisiou

Thisio

Plateia Afea

Plateia Monastirakiou

Plateia Agia Irini

Ancient Agora

MONASTIRAKI

Monastiraki

Roman Agora

ANAFIOTIKA

Hill of the Nymphs

Areopagus Hill

Acropolis

See Plaka & Monastiraki Map (p246)

14

To Venue (40m); Benaki Museum Pireos Annexe (200m)

Petralona

Filopappou Hill

52

4

To Marble House Pension (90m)

Syngrou Fix

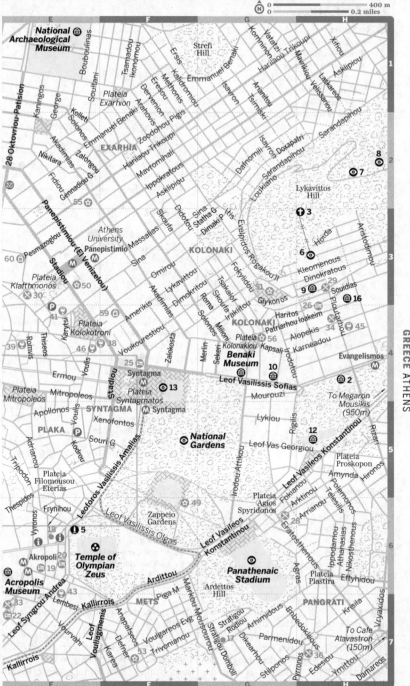

Central Athens

History

The early history of the city of Athens, named after the goddess of wisdom Athena, is inextricably interwoven with mythology, making it impossible to disentangle fact from fiction. What is known is that the hilltop site of the Acropolis, with two abun-dant springs, drew some of Greece's earliest Neolithic settlers.

Athens' golden age, the pinnacle of the classical era under Pericles (r 461–429 BC), came after the Persian Empire was repulsed at the battles of Salamis and Plataea (480–479 BC). The city has passed through many hands and cast off myriad invaders, from Sparta to Philip II of Macedon, the Roman and Byzantine Empires, and, most recently, the Ottoman Empire. In 1834 Athens superseded Nafplio as the capital of independent Greece.

◎ Sights

TOP CHOICE **Acropolis**   HISTORIC SITE
(Map p246; ☎210 321 0219; http://odysseus.culture.gr; adult/child €12/6; ⊙8am-8pm Mon-Fri, to 3pm Sat & Sun; ⋈Akropoli) Arguably the most important ancient monument in the Western world, the Acropolis attracts multitudes of visitors, so head there in the early morning or late afternoon.

The site was inhabited in Neolithic times and the first temples were built during the Mycenaean era in homage to the goddess Athena. People lived on the Acropolis until the late 6th century BC, but in 510 BC the Delphic oracle declared that the Acropolis should be the province of the gods. When all of the buildings were reduced to ashes by the Persians on the eve of the Battle of Salamis (480 BC), Pericles set about rebuilding a city purely of temples.

Enter near the **Beule Gate,** a Roman arch added in the 3rd century AD. Beyond this lies the **Propylaea,** the enormous columned gate that was the city's entrance in ancient times. Damaged in the 17th century when lightning set off a Turkish gunpowder cache, it's since been restored. South of the Propylaea, the small, beautiful **Temple of Athena Nike** has been recently restored.

It's the **Parthenon,** however, that epitomises the glory of ancient Greece. Completed in 438 BC, it's unsurpassed in grace and harmony. To achieve the appearance of perfect form, columns become narrower towards the top and the bases curve upward slightly towards the ends – effects that make them look straight. The remains of its metopes, pediments and frieze can be seen at the Acropolis Museum.

The Parthenon was built to house the great statue of Athena commissioned by Pericles, and to serve as the new treasury. In AD 426 the gold-plated 12m-high statue was taken to Constantinople, where it disappeared.

To the north, lies the **Erechtheion** and its much-photographed caryatids, the six maidens who support its southern portico. These are plaster casts – the originals are in the Acropolis Museum (and one is in London).

ATHENS IN TWO DAYS

Walk the deserted morning streets of the charming Plaka district to reach the **Acropolis** and **Ancient Agora**, beating the crowds. Dig in to *mezedhes* at **Tzitzikas & Mermingas** before spending the afternoon at the **Acropolis Museum** and the **National Archaeological Museum**. Enjoy Parthenon views over dinner at **Café Avyssinia** or sup on gyros at **Thanasis**.

On day two, watch the changing of the guard at **Plateia Syntagmatos** (Syntagma Sq) before crossing the **National Gardens** to the **Panathenaic Stadium** and the **Temple of Olympian Zeus**. Visit the wonderful **Benaki Museum**, **Byzantine & Christian Museum** or the **Museum of Cycladic Art**, then rest up for a night out in **Gazi**.

On the southern slope of the Acropolis, the importance of theatre in the everyday lives of ancient Athenians is made manifest in the enormous **Theatre of Dionysos** (☎210 322 4625; Dionysiou Areopagitou; admission €2, free with Acropolis Pass; ⊙8am-8pm Mon-Fri, 8am-3pm Sat & Sun; underground rail Akropoli). Built between 340 and 330 BC on the site of an earlier theatre dating to the 6th century BC, it held 17,000 people. The **Stoa of Eumenes** (Map p238), built as a shelter and promenade for theatre audiences, runs west to the **Odeon of Herodes Atticus** (☎210 324 1807; www.hellenicfestival.gr; Dionysiou Areopagitou; underground rail Akropoli), built in Roman times (and open only for performances).

Acropolis Museum   MUSEUM
(Map p238; ☎210 900 0901; www.theacropolismuseum.gr; Dionysiou Areopagitou 15, Makrygianni; admission €5; ⊙8am-8pm Tue-Sun, to 10pm Fri; ⋈Akropoli) Don't miss this superb museum on the southern base of the hill, and magnificently reflecting the Parthenon on its glass facade; it houses the surviving treasures of the Acropolis.

Bathed in natural light, the 1st-floor **Archaic Gallery** is a forest of statues, including stunning examples of 6th-century *kore* (maidens). Finds from temples pre-dating the Parthenon include sculptures such as Heracles slaying the Lernaian Hydra, and a lioness devouring a bull.

UNCERTAIN TIMES

» Due to the financial difficulties in Greece, which became acute starting in 2010, opening hours, prices and even the existence of some establishments have fluctuated much more than usual.

» At the time of writing the government was running many archaeological sites on their shorter winter hours (closing around 3pm). This could change.

» If in doubt, call ahead.

The museum's crowning glory is the top-floor **Parthenon Gallery**, a glass hall built in alignment with the Parthenon, which is visible through the windows. It showcases the temple's metopes and 160m frieze shown in sequence for the first time in over 200 years. Interspersed between the golden-hued originals, white plaster replicates the controversial Parthenon Marbles removed by Lord Elgin in 1801 and later sold to the British Museum.

Other highlights include five **caryatids**, the maiden columns that held up the Erechtheion (the sixth is in the British Museum), a giant floral acroterion and a movie illustrating the history of the Acropolis.

The surprisingly good-value restaurant has superb views; there's also a fine museum shop.

Ancient Agora   HISTORIC SITE
(Map p246; ☎210 321 0185; http://odysseus.culture.gr; Adrianou; adult/child €4/2, free with Acropolis pass; ☻8am-3pm, museum closed 8-11am Mon; ⓂMonastiraki) The Ancient Agora was the marketplace of early Athens and the focal point of civic and social life; Socrates spent time here expounding his philosophy. The main monuments of the Agora are the well-preserved **Temple of Hephaestus** (Monastiraki), the 11th-century **Church of the Holy Apostles** (Monastiraki) and the reconstructed **Stoa of Attalos**, which houses the site's excellent **museum**.

Roman Agora   HISTORIC SITE
(Map p246; ☎210 324 5220; cnr Pelopida & Eolou, Monastiraki; adult/child €2/1, free with Acropolis pass; ☻8.30am-3pm; ⓂMonastiraki) The Romans built their agora just east of the ancient Athenian Agora. The wonderful **Tower of the Winds** was built in the 1st century

BC by Syrian astronomer Andronicus. Each side represents a point of the compass and has a relief carving depicting the associated wind.

TOP CHOICE **National Archaeological Museum**   MUSEUM
(Map p238; ☎210 821 7717; www.namuseum.gr; 28 Oktovriou-Patision 44, Exarhia; adult/child €7/free; ☻1-8pm Mon, 8am-3pm Tue-Sun; ⓂViktoria, ⓑ2, 4, 5, 9 or 11 Polytechnio stop) One of the world's great museums, the National Archaeological Museum contains significant finds from major archaeological sites throughout Greece. The vast collections of Greek art masterpieces include exquisite **Mycenaean gold artefacts**, **Minoan frescos** from Santorini and stunning, enormous statues.

Temple of Olympian Zeus   RUIN
(Map p238; ☎210 922 6330; adult/child €2/free, free with Acropolis pass; ☻8am-3pm; ⓂSyntagma, Akropoli) Begun in the 6th century BC, Greece's largest temple is impressive for the sheer size of its Corinthian columns: 17m high with a base diameter of 1.7m. It took more than 700 years to build, with Emperor Hadrian overseeing its completion in AD 131, and sits behind **Hadrian's Arch** (Map p238; cnr Leoforos Vasilissis Olgas & Leoforos Vasilissis Amalias; ⓂSyntagma).

Panathenaic Stadium   HISTORIC SITE
(Map p238; Leoforos Vasileos Konstantinou, Pangrati; adult/child €3/1.50; ☻8am-7pm; ⓂAkropoli) The Panathenaic Stadium, built in the 4th century BC as a venue for the Panathenaic athletic contests, was restored (including seats of Pentelic marble for 70,000 spectators) and hosted the first modern Olympic Games in 1896, as well as some events of the 2004 Olympics.

Benaki Museum   MUSEUM
(Map p238; ☎210 367 1000; www.benaki.gr; Koumbari 1, cnr Leoforos Vasilissis Sofias, Kolonaki; adult/child €7/free, free Thu; ☻9am-5pm Wed, Fri & Sat, to midnight Thu, to 3pm Sun; ⓂSyntagma, Evangelismos) This superb museum houses an extravagant collection, including ancient sculpture, Persian, Byzantine and Coptic objects, Chinese ceramics, icons, El Greco paintings and fabulous traditional costumes. The museum's annexes around the city: **Museum of Islamic Art** (Map p238; ☎210 325 1311; Agion Asomaton 22 & Dipylou 12, Keramikos; adult/child €7/free; ☻9am-5pm Thu-Sun; ⓂThisio) and **Benaki Museum**

Pireos Annexe (☎210 345 3111; www.benaki.
gr; Pireos 138, cnr Andronikou, Rouf; admission €5;
⊙10am-6pm Wed, Thu & Sun, to 10pm Fri & Sat,
closed Aug; Ⓜ Keramikos).

Museum of Cycladic Art
MUSEUM

(Map p238; ☎210 722 8321; www.cycladic.gr;
Neofytou Douka 4, cnr Leoforos Vasilissis Sofias,
Kolonaki; adult/child €7/free; ⊙10am-5pm Mon,
Wed, Fri & Sat, 10am-8pm Thu, 11am-5pm Sun; Ⓜ E-
vangelismos) This wonderful private museum
was custom-built to display its extraordinary collection of Cycladic art, with an emphasis on the early Bronze Age. It's easy to
see how the graceful marble statues, some
dating from 3000 BC to 2000 BC, influenced
the art of Modigliani and Picasso.

TOP
CHOICE Byzantine &
Christian Museum
MUSEUM

(Map p238; ☎210 721 1027; www.byzantinemuse-
um.gr; Leoforos Vasilissis Sofias 22, Kolonaki; adult/
child €4/free; ⊙9am-4pm Tue-Sun; Ⓜ Evangelismos) This outstanding museum presents a
priceless collection of Christian art, dating
from the 3rd to 20th centuries, exceptionally
presented in expansive multilevel galleries
in a restored villa. Artefacts include icons,
frescoes, sculptures, textiles, manuscripts,
vestments and mosaics.

FREE Parliament &
Changing of the Guard
CEREMONY

(Map p238; Plateia Syntagmatos; Ⓜ Syntagma) In
front of the parliament building on Plateia
Syntagmatos, the traditionally costumed
evzones (guards) of the Tomb of the Unknown Soldier change every hour on the
hour. On Sunday at 11am, a whole platoon
marches down Vasilissis Sofias to the tomb,
accompanied by a band.

FREE Filopappou Hill
LANDMARK, PARK

(Map p238; Ⓜ Akropoli) Also called the Hill of
the Muses, Filopappou is identifiable southwest of the Acropolis by the Monument of
Filopappos at its summit. Built between
AD 114 and 116, it honours Julius Antio-
chus Filopappos, a prominent Roman consul. The hill's pine-clad slopes offer superb
views, with some of the best vantage points
for photographing the Acropolis. Small
paths weave all over the hill, but the paved
path to the top starts near the *periptero*
(kiosk) on Dionysiou Areopagitou. After
250m, the path passes the Church of Agios

Dimitrios Loumbardiaris, which contains
fine frescoes.

FREE Lykavittos Hill
LANDMARK

(Map p238; Ⓜ Evangelismos) Pine-covered
Lykavittos is the highest of the eight hills dotting Athens. Climb to the summit for stunning views of the city, the Attic basin and the
islands of Salamis and Aegina (pollution per-
mitting). Little Chapel of Agios Giorgios
is floodlit at night and open-air Lykavittos
Theatre hosts concerts in summer.

The main path up starts at the top of Lou-
kianou, or take the funicular railway from
the top of Ploutarhou.

FREE National Gardens
GARDENS

(Map p238; entrance on Leoforos Vasilissis Sofias
& Leoforos Vasilissis Amalias, Syntagma; ⊙7am-
dusk; Ⓜ Syntagma) A delightful, shady refuge
during summer, these gardens contain a
large playground, a duck pond and a tranquil cafe.

☞ Tours

The usual city tours exist like open-bus Cit-
ySightseeing Athens (Map p246; ☎210 922
0604; www.city-sightseeing.com; Plateia Syntagmatos, Syntagma; adult/child €15/6.50; ⊙every 30min
9am-8pm; Ⓜ Syntagma), Athens Segway
Tours (Map p238; ☎210 322 2500; www.athens
segwaytours.com; Eschinou 9, Plaka; 2hr tour €59;
Ⓜ Akropoli) or the volunteer This is My Athens (www.thisisathens.org). Get out of town
on the cheap with Athens: Adventures
(☎210 922 4044; www.athensadventures.gr).
Hike or kayak with Trekking Hellas (☎210
331 0323; www.trekking.gr; Saripolou 10, Exarhia;
Ⓜ Viktoria).

CONTEMPORARY ART

Athens is not all about ancient art. For a taste of the contemporary, visit:

Taf (The Art Foundation; Map p246; www.theartfoundation.gr; Normanou 5, Monastiraki; ☉1pm-midnight; Ⓜ Monastiraki) Eclectic art and music gallery.

Onassis Cultural Centre (www.sgt.gr; Leoforos Syngrou 109, Neos Kosmos; Ⓜ Syngrou-Fix) Multimillion-euro visual and performing arts centre.

National Museum of Contemporary Art (Map p238; www.emst.gr; Leoforos Vas Georgiou B 17-19, enter from Rigilis; adult/child €3/free; ☉11am-7pm Tue, Wed & Fri-Sun, to 10pm Thu; Ⓜ Evangelismos) Will be moving to the old Fix brewery on Leoforos Syngrou.

Xippas Gallery (Map p238; Patriarhou Ioakeim 53, Kolonaki; ☉Tue-Sat; Ⓜ Evangelismos)

Medusa Art Gallery (Map p238; www.medusaartgallery.com; Xenokratous 7, Kolonaki; Ⓜ Evangelismos)

Andreas Melas & Helena Papadopoulos Gallery (Map p238; http://melaspapadopoulos.com; Epikourou 26, cnr Korinis, Psyrri; ☉noon-6pm Tue-Fri, noon-4pm Sat; Ⓜ Omonia)

Technopolis (Map p238; ☎210 346 7322; Pireos 100, Gazi; Ⓜ Keramikos) Former gasworks turned cultural centre.

Festivals include:

Art-Athina (www.art-athina.gr) International art in May.

Athens Biennial (www.athensbiennial.org) Every two years from June to October.

ReMap (www.remap.org) Parallel event to the Biennial, exhibiting in abandoned buildings.

✱ Festivals

Hellenic Festival PERFORMING ARTS
(www.greekfestival.gr; ☉late May-Oct) Top line-up of local and international music, dance and theatre in venues across Athens and Epidavros' ancient theatre.

🛌 Sleeping

Discounts apply in low season, for longer stays and online. Book well ahead for July and August.

Plaka

Central Hotel BOUTIQUE HOTEL €€
(Map p246; ☎210 323 4357; www.centralhotel.gr; Apollonos 21, Plaka; s/d incl breakfast from €80/100; ❋@; Ⓜ Syntagma) Pass through the sleek lobby and by the attentive staff to spacious white rooms hung with original art and decked out with all the mod cons. Some balconies have Acropolis views, as does the rooftop, where you can sunbake and relax in the Jacuzzi.

New BOUTIQUE HOTEL €€€
(Map p246; ☎210 628 4565; www.yeshotels.gr; Filellinon 16, Plaka; s/d incl breakfast from €170/185; Ⓟ❋; Ⓜ Syntagma) Smart New is the latest entry on the high-end Athens scene. Wheth-

er you dig the groovy, designer furniture or the pillow menu (tell 'em how you like it!), you'll find some sort of decadent treat to tickle your fancy.

Hotel Adonis HOTEL €
(Map p246; ☎210 324 9737; www.hotel-adonis.gr; 3 Kodrou St, Plaka; s/d/tr incl breakfast €45/55/75; ❋@; Ⓜ Syntagma) Comfortable rooms, newly renovated bathrooms, conscientious staff and Acropolis views from the breakfast room/bar keep folks coming back.

Niki Hotel HOTEL €€
(Map p246; ☎210 322 0913; www.nikihotel.gr; Nikis 27, Syntagma; s/d/tr incl breakfast €55/65/118; ❋@; Ⓜ Syntagma) This small hotel bordering Plaka with contemporary furnishings has well-appointed rooms and a two-level suite for families (€145), with Acropolis-view balconies.

Plaka Hotel HOTEL €€
(Map p246; ☎210 322 2096; www.plakahotel.gr; Kapnikareas 7, cnr Mitropoleos, Plaka; s/d/tr incl breakfast from €90/110/125; ❋; Ⓜ Monastiraki) Folks come here not for the tidy, bland rooms but for the excellent Acropolis views from the rooftop garden and top-floor digs.

Hotel Acropolis House
PENSION €€

(Map p246; ☎210 322 2344; www.acropolishouse. gr; Kodrou 6-8, Plaka; s €65, d €65-82, tr from €113, q from €136, all incl breakfast; ❄️🛜; ⓜSyntagma) This well-situated hotel in a 19th-century house feels more pension than hotel, with a comfy sitting room and hospitable management. Guests chat amicably over breakfast.

Student & Travellers' Inn
HOSTEL €

(Map p246; ☎210 324 4808; www.studenttravel-lersinn.com; Kydathineon 16, Plaka; dm €20-22, s/d/tr €45/55/65, without bathroom €30/50/60; ❄️@🛜; ⓜSyntagma) The mixed-sex dorms may be spartan and housekeeping a bit lean, but extras (laundry, left luggage) make up for it.

Monastiraki

TOP CHOICE Magna Grecia
BOUTIQUE HOTEL €€

(Map p246; ☎210 324 0314; www.magnagreciaho-tel.com; Mitropoleos 54, Monastiraki; d incl breakfast €95-135; ❄️🛜; ⓜMonastiraki) Enjoy Acropolis views from the front rooms and rooftop terrace in a historic building opposite the cathedral. Imaginatve, luxe rooms sport comfortable mattresses.

Hotel Cecil
HOTEL €€

(Map p238; ☎210 321 7079; www.cecil.gr; Athinas 39, Monastiraki; s/d/tr incl breakfast from €55/70/85; ❄️@🛜; ⓜMonastiraki) Aromatic spices waft into the lobby from nearby Asian markets, but double-pane windows keep the high-ceilinged rooms in this classical building quiet.

Tempi Hotel
HOTEL €

(Map p238; ☎210 321 3175; www.tempihotel.gr; Eolou 29, Monastiraki; d/tr €57/67, s/d without bathroom €35/47; ❄️🛜; ⓜMonastiraki) No-frills rooms may be tiny, but some have balconies overlooking Plateia Agia Irini. A communal kitchen and nearby markets make it ideal for self-caterers.

Syntagma

Hotel Grande Bretagne
LUXURY HOTEL €€€

(Map p238; ☎210 333 0000; www.grandebre-tagne.gr; Vasileos Georgiou 1, Syntagma; r/ste from €275/960; ℗❄️@🛜; ⓜSyntagma) Dripping with elegance and old-world charm, *the* place to stay in Athens has always been these deluxe digs. Built in 1862 to accommodate visiting heads of state, it ranks among the great hotels of the world. From the decadent, chandeliered lobby, to the exquisite guestrooms, divine spa and rooftop restaurant, this place is built for pampering.

Makrygianni & Koukaki

TOP CHOICE Athens Backpackers
HOSTEL, APARTMENT €

(Map p238; ☎210 922 4044; www.backpackers. gr; Makri 12, Makrygianni; dm incl breakfast €23-28, 2-/4-/6-person apt €90/120/150; ❄️@🛜; ⓜAkropoli) This excellent, popular hostel also has great apartments and boasts a rooftop party bar with Acropolis views, kitchen, daily movies, and the friendly Aussie management hosts (free!) barbecues. Breakfast and nonalcoholic drinks are included; long-term storage, laundry and airport pick-up available.

TOP CHOICE Athens Gate
BUSINESS HOTEL €€

(Map p238; ☎210 923 8302; www.athensgate.gr; Leoforos Syngrou Andrea 10, Makrygianni; s/d incl breakfast from €120/130; ❄️@🛜; ⓜAkropoli) With stunning views over the Temple of Olympian Zeus from the spacious front rooms, and a central (if busy) location, this totally refurbished hotel is a great find. Stylish, immaculate rooms have all the mod cons, staff are friendly and breakfast is served on the superb rooftop terrace with 360-degree Athens views.

Hera Hotel
BOUTIQUE HOTEL €€

(Map p238; ☎210 923 6682; www.herahotel.gr; Falirou 9, Makrygianni; s/d from €75/90, ste from €180; ❄️@🛜; ⓜAkropoli) The ornate interior complements the hotel's lovely neoclassical facade. The rooftop garden, restaurant and bar boast spectacular views and it is a short walk to the Acropolis and Plaka.

Marble House Pension
PENSION €

(☎210 923 4058; www.marblehouse.gr; Zini 35a, Koukaki; s/d/tr €35/45/55, d/tr/q without bathroom €40/50/65; ❄️🛜; ⓜSyngrou-Fix) This long-standing Athens favourite is on a quiet cul-de-sac 10 minutes' walk from Plaka. Step through the garden to quiet, spotless rooms. For air-con add €9.

Psyrri & Thisio

Athens Style
HOSTEL, APARTMENT €

(Map p238; ☎210 322 5010; www.athensstyle. com; Agias Theklas 10, Psyrri; dm €20-28, s/d/tr €51/80/96, apt from €90; ❄️@; ⓜMonastiraki) This bright, arty hostel, the newest in town, has dorm beds and well-equipped apartments. The cool basement lounge holds art exhibitions, a pool table and home cinema; the rooftop bar has Acropolis views.

Plaka & Monastiraki

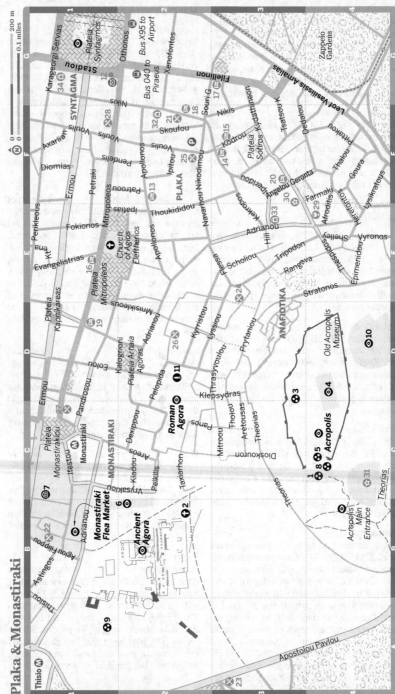

0   200 m
0   0.1 miles

Plaka & Monastiraki

Hotel Erechthion
HOTEL €

(Map p238; ☑210 345 9606; www.hotelerechthion.gr; Flammarion 8, cnr Agias Marinas, Thisio; s/d/tr €40/60/70; ❂☏; ⓂThisio) Simple, clean rooms with TVs, refrigerators, veneer furniture and basic bathrooms are not the highlights here. Much more impressive are the fantastic Acropolis views from the balconies, the low price and the homey neighbourhood.

Kolonaki

TOP CHOICE Periscope
BOUTIQUE HOTEL €€

(Map p238; ☑210 729 7200; www.periscope.gr; Haritos 22, Kolonaki; d incl breakfast from €145; ❂☏; ⓂEvangelismos) A hip hotel with a cool, edgy look, this place has comfortable minimalist rooms with all the mod cons and a quiet location.

✗ Eating

In addition to mainstay tavernas, Athens has upscale eateries (wear your most stylish togs at night). Eat streets include Mitropoleos, Adrianou and Navarchou Apostoli in Monastiraki, the area around Plateia Psyrri, and Gazi, near Keramikos metro.

The fruit and vegetable market (Varvakios Agora; Map p238; Athinas, btwn Sofokleous & Evripidou; ☺7am-3pm Mon-Sat; ⓂMonastiraki, Panepistimio, Omonia) is opposite the meat market.

Syntagma & Monastiraki

TOP CHOICE Café Avyssinia
MEZEDHES €

(Map p246; ☑210 321 7047; www.avissinia.gr; Kynetou 7, Monastiraki; mains €10-16; ☺11am-1am Tue-Sat, to 7pm Sun; ⓂMonastiraki) Hidden away on the edge of grungy Plateia Avyssinias in the middle of the flea market, this *mezedhopoleio* (*mezedhes* restaurant) gets top marks for atmosphere, and the food is not far behind. Often has live music on weekends.

TOP CHOICE Tzitzikas & Mermingas
MEZEDHES €

(Map p246; ☑210 324 7607; Mitropoleos 12-14, Syntagma; mezedhes €6-11; ⓂSyntagma) Greek merchandise lines the walls of this cheery, modern *mezedhopoleio*. The great range of delicious and creative *mezedhes* (appetisers) draws a bustling local crowd. Don't miss the decadent honey-coated fried cheese with ham...it's the kind of special dish that will haunt your future dreams.

Mama Roux
INTERNATIONAL €

(Map p238; ☑213 004 8382; Eoulou 48-50, Monastiraki; mains €5-10; ☺9am-midnight Tue-Sat, to 5pm Mon, noon-5pm Sun; ☎; MMonastiraki) Downtown's hottest cheap-eats restaurant fills up with locals digging into a fresh, delicious mix of dishes: from real burritos and Cajun specials to whopping American-style burgers.

Kalnterimi
TAVERNA €

(Map p238; ☑210 331 0049; www.kalnterimi.gr; Plateia Agion Theodoron, cnr Skouleniou; mains €5-8; ☺lunch & dinner; MPanepistimio) Find your way back behind the Church of Agii Theodori to this open-air taverna offering Greek food at its most authentic. Everything is fresh-cooked and delicious.

Thanasis
SOUVLAKI €

(Map p246; ☑210 324 4705; Mitropoleos 69, Monastiraki; gyros €2.50; ☺8.30am-2.30am; MMonastiraki) In the heart of Athens' souvlaki hub, Thanasis is known for its kebabs on pitta with grilled tomato and onions. Live music, grill aromas and crowds give the area an almost permanently festive air.

Plaka & Makrygianni

TOP CHOICE **Mani Mani**
REGIONAL CUISINE €

(Map p238; ☑210 921 8180; www.manimani.com.gr; Falirou 10, Makrygianni; mains €10-16; ☺3pm-12.30am Tue-Thu, from 1pm Fri & Sat, 1-5.30pm Sun, closed Jul & Aug; MAkropoli) Sample cuisine from Mani in the Peloponnese, such as tangy sausage with orange. Most dishes can be ordered as half-serves (at half-price), allowing you to try a wide range.

Paradosiako
TAVERNA €

(Map p246; ☑210 321 4121; Voulis 44a, Plaka; mains €5-11; ☎; MSyntagma) For great traditional fare, you can't beat this inconspicuous, no-frills taverna on the periphery of Plaka. Choose from daily specials such as delicious shrimp *saganaki* (fried Greek cheese).

Avocado
VEGETARIAN €

(Map p246; ☑210 323 7878; www.avocadoathens.com; Nikis 30, Plaka; mains €6.50-9.50; ☺11am-10pm Mon-Sat, to 7pm Sun; ☎☑; MSyntagma) A full array of vegan, gluten-free and organic treats (a rarity in Greece). Enjoy everything from fresh juices and sandwiches to quinoa with eggplant or mixed veg coconut curry.

Cucina Povera
MEDITERRANEAN €

(Map p238; ☑210 756 6008; www.cucinapovera.gr; Efforionos 13, Pangrati; mains €9-14; ☺dinner Tue-Sat, brunch Sun; MEvangelismos) Dishes can be occasionally incandescent, like the salad with avocado, pear and goat cheese. The dining room embodies relaxed hipness, and the wine list rocks.

Platanos
TAVERNA €

(Map p246; ☑210 322 0666; Diogenous 4, Plaka; mains €7-9; ☺lunch & dinner; MMonastiraki) Tasty, home-cooked-style Greek cuisine include delicious lamb dishes, and we love the leafy courtyard.

Palia Taverna Tou Psara
TAVERNA €€

(Map p246; ☑210 321 8734; www.psaras-taverna.gr; Erehtheos 16, Plaka; mains €12-24; ☺11am-12.30am Wed-Mon; MAkropoli) Situated on a path leading up towards the Acropolis, this gem of a taverna is one of Plaka's best, serving scrumptious *mezedhes* and excellent fish and meat classics on a tree-lined terrace.

Keramikos, Thisio & Gazi

Varoulko
SEAFOOD €€€

(Map p238; ☑210 522 8400; www.varoulko.gr; Pireos 80, Keramikos; mains €35-60; ☺from 8.30pm Mon-Sat; MThisio, Keramikos) For a magical Greek dining experience, you can't beat the winning combination of Acropolis views and delicious seafood by celebrated Michelin-starred chef Lefteris Lazarou. Athenian celebrities feast in an airy, glass-fronted dining room.

Kanella
TAVERNA €

(Map p238; ☑210 347 6320; Leoforos Konstantinoupoleos 70, Gazi; dishes €7-10; ☺1.30pm-late; MKeramikos) Home-made village-style bread, mismatched retro crockery and brown-paper tablecloths set the tone for this trendy, modern taverna serving regional Greek cuisine.

Filistron
MEZEDHES €€

(Map p246; ☑210 346 7554; Apostolou Pavlou 23, Thisio; mezedhes €8-14; ☺lunch & dinner Tue-Sun; MThisio) Book a prized table on the rooftop terrace of this excellent *mezedhopoleio*, which enjoys breathtaking Acropolis- and Lykavittos-views.

Sardelles
SEAFOOD €€

(Map p238; ☑210 347 8050; Persefonis 15, Gazi; fish dishes €10-17; MKeramikos) As the name suggests (Sardelles means 'sardines'), this modern fish taverna facing the illuminated gasworks specialises in seafood *mezedhes*.

Kolonaki & Pangrati

TOP CHOICE **Spondi** MEDITERRANEAN €€€
(Map p238; 210 752 0658; Pyrronos 5, Pangrati; mains €35-50; 8pm-late) Dining in this superb restaurant's gorgeous vaulted cellar or in its bougainvillea-draped courtyard in summer is quite an understatedly elegant affair. Chef Arnaud Bignon has won two Michelin stars, creating extravagant seasonal menus adhering to French technique but embodying vibrant Greek flavours.

TOP CHOICE **Oikeio** TAVERNA €
(Map p238; 210 725 9216; Ploutarhou 15, Kolonaki; mains €7-13; 1pm-2.30am Mon-Sat; Evangelismos) With excellent home-style cooking, this modern taverna lives up to its name ('Homey'). The intimate bistro atmosphere spills out to tables on the pavement for glitterati-watching without the usual high Kolonaki bill. Reservations recommended.

Filippou TAVERNA €
(Map p238; 210 721 6390; Xenokratous 19, Kolonaki; mains €8-12; lunch & dinner, closed Sat night & Sun; Evangelismos) Filippou has been dishing out yummy Greek dishes since 1923. Think soul cooking, with white linen, in the heart of chic Kolonaki.

Drinking

Athenians know how to party. Everyone has their favourite *steki* (hang-out), but expect people to show up after midnight. Head to Gazi (around Voutadon and the Keramikos metro station), Kolonaki (around Ploutarhou and Haritos, or Skoufa and Omirou) or Monastiraki (around Plateia Karytsi or Kolokotroni) and explore!

Omonia is best avoided late at night, and although Exarhia has a bohemian bar scene, the neighbourhood has been affected recently by street demonstrations.

Kolonaki has a mind-boggling array of cafes off Plateia Kolonakiou on Skoufa and Tsakalof. Another cafe-thick area is Adrianou, along the Ancient Agora.

Hoxton BAR
(Map p238; Voutadon 42, Gazi; Keramikos) Kick back on overstuffed leather couches under modern art in this industrial space that fills up late with bohemians, ruggers and the occasional pop star.

Mai Tai BAR
(Map p238; Ploutarhou 18, Kolonaki; Evangelismos) Jam-packed with well-heeled young

WHAT'S ON

For comprehensive events listings, with links to online ticket sales points, try: www.breathtakingathens.gr, www.el culture.gr, www.tickethour.com, www. tickethouse.gr, www.ticketservices.gr. The *Kathimerini* supplement inside the *International Herald Tribune* contains event listings and a cinema guide.

Athenians, this is just one in a group of happening spots in Kolonaki.

Seven Jokers BAR
(Map p238; Voulis 7, Syntagma; Syntagma) Lively and central Seven Jokers anchors the party block, also shared by spacious **42** (Kolokotroni 3, Syntagma) around the corner, for cocktails in wood-panelled splendour, with **Baba Au Rum** (Klitiou 6, Syntagma; Syntagma) and **Gin Joint** (Lada 1, Syntagma; Syntagma) nearby.

Gazarte BAR
(Map p238; 210 346 0347; www.gazarte.gr; Voutadon 32-34, Gazi; Keramikos) Trendy crowd takes in mainstream music and rooftop city views including the Acropolis.

Brettos BAR
(Map p246; Kydathineon 41, Plaka; Akropoli) This bar-distillery is back-lit by an eye-catching collection of coloured bottles.

Tailor Made CAFE, BAR
(Map p238; 213 004 9645; www.tailormade.gr; Plateia Agia Irini 2, Monastiraki; Monastiraki) Cheerful Athenians spill from the mod artfestooned micro-roastery to tables alongside the flower market. At night it turns into a happening cocktail and wine bar.

Entertainment

Nightclubs

Athenians go clubbing after midnight and dress up. In summer try beachfront venues.

Rock'n'Roll CLUB, BAR
(Map p238; 210 721 7127; Plateia Kolonakiou, Kolonaki; Evangelismos) Dependably fun, with a casual-cool Kolonaki crowd.

TOP CHOICE **Venue** CLUB
(210 341 1410; www.venue-club.com; Pireos 130, Rouf; Sep-May; Keramikos) Arguably the city's biggest dance club: three-stage dance floor and an energetic crowd.

GREECE ATHENS

WANT MORE?

For in-depth information, reviews and recommendations at your fingertips, head to the Apple App Store to purchase Lonely Planet's *Athens City Guide* iPhone app.

Alternatively, head to **Lonely Planet** (www.lonelyplanet.com/greece/athens) for planning advice, author recommendations, traveller reviews and insider tips.

Akrotiri CLUB
(210 985 9147; www.akrotirilounge.gr; Vasileos Georgiou B5, Agios Kosmas) Beach-side in summer with a capacity for 3000 people, bars and lounges cover multiple levels.

Gay & Lesbian Venues

Gay bars cluster in Gazi near the railway line on Leoforos Konstantinoupoleos and Megalou Alexandrou, as well as Makrygianni, Psyrri, Metaxourghio and Exarhia. Check out www.athensinfoguide.com, www.gay.gr or a copy of the *Greek Gay Guide* booklet at newspaper kiosks.

Sodade GAY
(Map p238; 210 346 8657; www.sodade.gr; Triptolemou 10, Gazi; Keramikos) Tiny, sleek and super-fun for dancing. It draws a great group.

Noiz Club LESBIAN
(Map p238; 210 342 4771; www.noizclub.gr; Evmolpidon 41, Gazi; Keramikos) In Gazi's gay triangle, for a female crowd.

Lamda Club GAY
(Map p238; 210 942 4202; Lembesi 15, cnr Leoforos Syngrou, Makrygianni; Akropoli) Busy, three levels and not for the faint of heart.

Magaze CAFE, BAR
(Map p238; 210 324 3740; Eolou 33, Monastiraki; Monastiraki) All-day hang-out with Acropolis views from pavement tables; lively bar after sunset.

Live Music

In summer, concerts rock plazas and parks; some clubs shut down. Most authentic *rembetika* venues close during summer, but you can see a popularised version at some tavernas in Psyrri.

TOP CHOICE **Half Note Jazz Club** JAZZ
(Map p238; 210 921 3310; www.halfnote.gr; Trivonianou 17, Mets; Akropoli) Dark, smoky venue for serious jazz.

Cafe Alavastron LIVE MUSIC
(210 756 0102; www.cafealavastron.gr; Damareos 78, Pangrati) Eclectic mix of modern jazz, ethnic and Greek music in a casual, intimate venue.

TOP CHOICE **Gagarin 205 Club** LIVE MUSIC
(www.gagarin205.gr; Liosion 205, Thymarakia; Agios Nikolaos) Interesting international and local rock acts.

TOP CHOICE **Stoa Athanaton** REMBETIKA
(Map p238; 210 321 4362; Sofokleous 19, Central Market; 3-6pm & midnight-6am Mon-Sat, closed Jun-Sep; Monastiraki, Panepistimio, Omonia) Located above the meat market, this is still *the* place to listen to *rembetika*, often referred to as Greek blues.

Classical Music, Theatre & Dance

In summer, the excellent Hellenic Festival (p10) swings into action.

Megaron Mousikis PERFORMING ARTS
(Athens Concert Hall; 210 728 2333; www.megaron.gr; Kokkali 1, cnr Leoforos Vasilissis Sofias, Ilissia; box office 10am-6pm Mon-Fri, to 2pm Sat; Megaro Mousikis) Superb concert venue hosting winter performances by local and international artists.

National Theatre THEATRE
(Map p238; 210 522 3243; www.n-t.gr; Agiou Konstantinou 22-24, Omonia; Omonia) Contemporary plays and ancient theatre on the main stage and other venues.

Olympia Theatre PERFORMING ARTS
(Map p238; 210 361 2461; Akadimias 59, Exarhia; Panepistimio) November to June: ballet, symphony and the **Greek National Opera** (Ethniki Lyriki Skini; Map p238; 210 360 0180; www.national opera.gr).

Dora Stratou Dance Theatre TRADITIONAL DANCE
(Map p238; 210 921 4650; www.grdance.org; Filopappou Hill; adult/child €15/5; performances 9.30pm Wed-Fri, 8.15pm Sat & Sun Jun-Sep; Petralona) Traditional folk-dancing shows feature more than 75 musicians and dancers in an open-air amphitheatre.

Cinema

Most cinemas, like **Astor** (Map p238; ☑210 323 1297; Stadiou 28, Syntagma; ⓂPanepistimio), show recent releases in their original language; tickets cost around €8. In summer, watch outdoors at **Aigli Cinema** (Map p238; ☑210 336 9369; Zappeio Gardens, Syntagma; ⓂSyntagma), **Dexameni** (Map p238; ☑210 362 3942; Plateia Dexameni, Kolonaki; ⓂEvangelismos) or **Cine Paris** (Map p246; ☑210 322 0721; Kydathineon 22, Plaka; ⓂSyntagma).

🛍 Shopping

Shop for cool jewellery, clothes, shoes and souvenirs such as backgammon sets, handwoven textiles, olive-oil beauty products, worry beads and ceramics. Find boutiques around Syntagma, from the Attica department store past Voukourestiou and on Ermou; designer brands and cool shops in Kolonaki; and souvenirs, folk art and leather in Plaka and Monastiraki.

Monastiraki Flea Market MARKET
(Map p246; Adrianou, Monastiraki; ⊘daily; ⓂMonastiraki) Enthralling; spreads daily from Plateia Monastirakiou.

To Pantopoleion FOOD, DRINK
(Map p238; ☑210 323 4612; Sofokleous 1, Omonia; ⓂPanepistimio) Expansive store selling traditional food products from all over Greece.

Ioanna Kourbela CLOTHING
(Map p246; ☑210 322 4591; www.ioannakourbela.com; Adrianou 109, Plaka; ⓂSytnatgma) Classic, cool fashion by a young Greek designer.

Eleftheroudakis BOOKS
Syntagma (Map p238; ☑210 331 4180; Panepistimiou 17, Syntagma; ⓂSyntagma); **Plaka** (Map p246; ☑210 322 9388; Nikis 20, Plaka; ⓂSyntagma) English-language books.

Public BOOKS, ELECTRONICS
(Map p246; ☑210 324 6210; Plateia Syntagmatos, Syntagma; ⓒ; ⓂSyntagma) English-language books on 3rd floor.

ℹ Information

Emergency
Visitor Emergency Assistance (☑112) Toll-free, 24 hours; in English.
Tourist Police (☑210 920 0724, 24hr 171; Veïkou 43-45, Koukaki; ⊘8am-10pm; ⓂSyngrou-Fix)
Police Station (☑210 725 7000; Plateia Syntagmatos; ⓂSyntagma) Phone ☑100 for the police.
SOS Doctors (☑1016, 210 821 1888; ⊘24hr) Pay service with English-speaking doctors.
Ambulance/First-aid Advice (☑166)

Internet Access
There are free wi-fi hot spots at Plateia Syntagmatos, Thisio, Gazi, the port of Piraeus, many cafes and on the 3rd floor of Public (see above).

GREECE ATHENS

ℹ DANGERS & ANNOYANCES

» Crime has heightened in Athens with the onset of the financial crisis. Though violent street crime remains relatively rare, travellers should be alert on the streets, especially at night, and beware the traps listed here.

» Streets surrounding Omonia have become markedly seedier, with an increase in prostitutes and junkies; avoid the area, especially at night.

» Watch for pickpockets on the metro and at the markets.

» When taking taxis, ask the driver to use the meter or negotiate a price in advance. Ignore stories that the hotel you've chosen is closed or full: they're angling for a commission from another hotel.

» Bar scams are commonplace, particularly in Plaka and Syntagma. They go something like this: friendly Greek approaches solo male traveller, discovers traveller is new to Athens, and reveals that he, too, is out of town. However, friendly Greek knows a great bar where they order drinks and equally friendly owner offers another drink. Women appear and more drinks are served; at the end of the night the traveller is hit with an exorbitant bill.

» The recent financial reforms in Greece have caused strikes in Athens. If there is a strike while you are here (check http://livingingreece.gr/strikes), confirm that the sights you wish to see will be open and the transport you are planning to use will be running. Picketers tend to march in Plateia Syntagmatos.

Internet Resources

Official visitor site (www.breathtakingathens.gr)

Media

Kathimerini (www.ekathimerini.com) and **Athens News** (www.athensnews.gr) have English-language coverage.

Money

Banks suround Plateia Syntagmatos.
Eurochange (📞210 331 2462; Karageorgi Servias 2, Syntagma; ⊘8am-9pm; ⓜSyntagma)

Telephone

Kiosks sell phonecards for public phones and prepaid SIM cards for mobiles.

Tourist Information

EOT (Greek National Tourist Organisation; 📞210 331 0716, 210 331 0347; www.visitgreece.gr; Dionysiou Areopagitou 18-20, Makrygianni; ⊘8am-8pm Mon-Fri, 10am-4pm Sat & Sun May-Sep, 9am-7pm Mon-Fri Oct-Apr; ⓜAkropoli)

Athens Information Kiosk Acropolis (Acropolis; ⊘9am-9pm Jun-Aug; ⓜAkropoli)

Athens Information Kiosk Airport (📞210 353 0390; www.breathtakingathens.com; Airport; ⊘8am-8pm; ⓜAirport) Maps, transport information and all Athens info.

🛈 Getting There & Away

Air

Modern **Eleftherios Venizelos International Airport** (ATH; 📞210 353 0000; www.aia.gr), 27km east of Athens.

Boat

Most ferries, hydrofoils and high-speed catamarans leave from the massive port at Piraeus. Some depart from smaller ports at Rafina and Lavrio.

Bus

KTEL (📞14505; www.ktel.org) Athens has two main intercity bus stations, one 5km and one 7km to the north of Omonia. Tourist offices have timetables.

Mavromateon Terminal (📞210 822 5148, 210 880 8000; cnr Leoforos Alexandras & 28 Oktovriou-Patision, Pedion Areos; ⓜViktoria) Buses for destinations in southern Attica leave from this terminal, about 250m north of the National Archaeological Museum.

Kifissos Terminal A (📞210 512 4910; Kifissou 100, Peristeri; ⓜAgios Antonios) Buses to the Peloponnese, Igoumenitsa, Ionian Islands, Florina, Ioannina, Kastoria, Edessa and Thessaloniki, among other destinations. Bus 051 goes to central Athens (junction of Zinonos and

Menandrou, near Omonia) every 15 minutes from 5am to midnight. Taxis to Syntagma cost about €8.

Liossion Terminal B (📞210 831 7153; Liossion 260, Thymarakia; ⓜAgios Nikolaos) Buses to Trikala (for Meteora), Delphi, Larissa, Thiva, Volos and other destinations. To get here, take bus 024 from outside the main gate of the National Gardens on Amalias and ask to get off at Praktoria KTEL. Get off the bus at Liossion 260, turn right onto Gousiou and you'll see the terminal.

Car & Motorcycle

The airport has car rental, and Syngrou, just south of the Temple of Olympian Zeus, is dotted with car-hire firms, though driving in Athens is treacherous.

Avis (📞210 322 4951; Leoforos Vasilissis Amalias 48, Makrygianni; ⓜAkropoli)

Budget (📞210 922 4200; Leoforos Syngrou Andrea 23, Makrygianni; ⓜAkropoli)

Europcar (📞210 921 1444; Leoforos Syngrou Andrea 25, Makrygianni; ⓜAkropoli)

Train

Intercity trains to central and northern Greece depart from the central **Larisis train station**, about 1km northwest of Plateia Omonias. For the Peloponnese, take the suburban rail to Kiato and change for other OSE services, or check for available lines at the Larisis station. International trains have been discontinued.

OSE Office (📞210 529 7005, in English 1110; www.ose.gr; Karolou 1, Omonia; ⊘8am-3pm Mon-Fri; ⓜMetaxourghio)

🛈 Getting Around

To/From the Airport

BUS Tickets cost €5. Twenty-four-hour services:
Plateia Syntagmatos (Bus X95, 60 to 90 minutes, every 15 minutes) The Syntagma stop is on Othonos.

Piraeus Port (Bus X96, 1½ hrs, every 20 minutes)

Terminal A (Kifissos) Bus Station (Bus X93, 35 minutes, every 30 minutes)

METRO Blue line 3 links the airport to the city centre in around 40 minutes; it operates from Monastiraki from 5.50am to midnight, and from the airport from 5.30am to 11.30pm. Tickets (€8) are valid for all public transport for 90 minutes. Fare for two or more passengers is €14 total.

TAXI Fares vary according to the time of day and level of traffic; expect at least €35 from the airport to the centre, and €50 to Piraeus. Both trips can take up to an hour, more in heavy traffic.

Public Transport

The metro, tram and bus system makes getting around central Athens and to Piraeus easy. Athens' road traffic can be horrendous. Get maps and timetables at the tourist offices or **Athens Urban Transport Organisation** (OASA; ☑185; www.oasa.gr; ☺6.30am-11.30pm Mon-Fri, 7.30am-10.30pm Sat & Sun).

BUS & TROLLEYBUS

Buses and electric trolleybuses operate every 15 minutes from 5am to midnight.

Piraeus From Syntagma and Filellinon to Akti Xaveriou catch Bus 040; from Omonia end of Athinas to Plateia Themistokleous, catch Bus 049.

METRO

Trains operate from 5am to midnight (Friday and Saturday to around 2am), every three to 10 minutes. Get timetables at www.ametro.gr.

TAXI

Flag fall is €1.16 with an additional surcharge of €1.05 from ports and train and bus stations, and €3.77 from the airport; then the day rate (tariff 1 on the meter) is €0.66 per kilometre. The night rate (tariff 2 on the meter, from midnight to 5am) is €1.16 per kilometre. Baggage costs €0.38 per item over 10kg. Minimum fare is €3.10. Booking a radio taxi costs €1.88 extra. Fixed rates are posted at the airport.

Taxibeat (https://taxibeat.gr) Mobile app for hailing available taxis by location and rating. Can book from abroad.

Athina 1 (☑210 921 2800)

Enotita (☑801 115 1000)

Ikaros (☑210 515 2800)

TRAIN

Fast **suburban rail** (☑1110; www.trainose.gr) links Athens with the airport, Piraeus, the outer regions and the northern Peloponnese. It connects to the metro at Larisis, Doukissis Plakentias and Nerantziotissa stations, and goes from the airport to Kiato.

AROUND ATHENS

Piraeus   Πειραιάς

TRANSPORT HUB
POP 179,500

The highlights of Greece's main port and ferry hub are the otherworldly rows of ferries, ships and hydrofoils filling its seemingly endless quays. It takes around 40 minutes to get here (10km) from Athens' centre by

metro, so there's no reason to stay in shabby Piraeus. The Mikrolimano (Small Harbour), with its cafes and fish restaurants, reveals the city's gentler side.

🛏 Sleeping

Piraeus Theoxenia   LUXURY HOTEL €€
(☑210 411 2550; www.theoxeniapalace.com; Karaoli Dimitriou 23; s/d/tr incl breakfast €99/110/150; ❄@☎; ⓂPiraeus) Pireaus' most upmarket, central hotel, with plump bathrobes and satellite TV; get the best deals online.

Hotel Triton   HOTEL €€
(☑210 417 3457; www.htriton.gr; Tsamadou 8; s/d/tr incl breakfast €45/70/80; ❄@; ⓂPiraeus) Refurbished hotel with simple executive-style rooms; a treat compared with Pireaus' usual run-down joints.

🍴 Eating

If you're killing time, take trolleybus 20 to Mikrolimano for harbourfront seafood.

Rakadiko   TAVERNA €
(☑210 417 8470; Stoa Kouvelou, Karaoli Dimitriou 5; mains €12-20; ☺lunch & dinner Tue-Sat) Under grapevines, dine quietly on *mezedhes* from all over Greece. Live *rembetika* on weekends.

Mandragoras   DELI €
(☑210 417 2961; Gounari 14; ☺7.30am-4pm Mon, Wed & Sat, to 8pm Tue, Thu & Fri) Fantastic array of fresh Greek products.

General Market   MARKET €
(Dimosthenous; ☺6am-4pm Mon-Fri)

Piraikon   SUPERMARKET
(Makras Stoas 1; ☺8am-8pm Mon-Fri, to 4pm Sat)

Piraeus

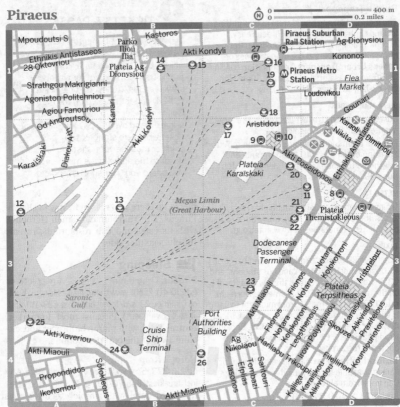

Piraeus

ℹ Information

Internet Access Free wi-fi around the port.
Left Luggage At the metro station (€3 per 24 hours).

ℹ Getting There & Away

Boat

All ferry companies have online timetables and booths on the quays. EOT (p252) in Athens has a weekly schedule, or check www.openseas.gr. Schedules are reduced in April, May and October, and are radically cut in winter, especially to smaller islands. When buying tickets, confirm the departure point. For more details contact the **Piraeus Port Authority** (☏1441; www.olp.gr).

Hellenic Seaways (☏210 419 9000; www.hellenicseaways.gr; cnr Akti Kondyli & Elotikou) operates high-speed hydrofoils and catamarans to the Cyclades from early April to the end of October, and year-round services to the Saronic Gulf Islands. Other high-speed services include **Aegean Speedlines** (☏210 969 0950; www.aegeanspeedlines.gr).

Bus

The **X96** Piraeus–Athens Airport Express (€5) leaves from the southwestern corner of Plateia Karaïskaki. **Bus 040** goes to Syntagma in downtown Athens.

Metro

The fastest and most convenient link to Athens is the metro (€1.40, 40 minutes, every 10 minutes, 5am to midnight), near the ferries.

Train

Piraeus has a station for Athens' suburban rail.

ℹ Getting Around

Local bus 904 runs between the metro station and Zea Marina.

THE PELOPONNESE
ΠΕΛΟΠΟΝΝΗΣΟΣ

The Peloponnese encompasses a breathtaking array of landscapes, villages and ruins, where much of Greek history has played out. It's home to Olympia, birthplace of the Olympic Games; the ancient archaeological sites of magical Epidavros, Mycenae and Corinth; the fairy-tale Byzantine city of Mystras; and ancient Sparta.

Two of Greece's most memorable towns grace its shores: Venetian-style Nafplio and romantic Monemvasia. The isolated Mani Peninsula, best known for its wild landscape and people, bristles with fortified tower settlements and is blanketed with a colourful collection of spectacular wildflowers in spring.

Patra   Πάτρα
POP 168,900

Greece's third-largest city, Patra is the principal ferry port for the Ionian Islands and Italy. Despite its 3000-year history, ancient sites and vibrant social life, few travellers linger here longer than necessary to transfer to their ferries.

◉ Sights

FREE Archaeological
Museum of Patras   MUSEUM
(☏261 042 0645; cnr Amerikis & Patras-Athens National Rd; ⊙8.30am-3pm Tue-Sun) The country's second-largest museum features objects from prehistoric to Roman times.

FREE **Kastro**   CASTLE
(⊙8.30am-3pm Tue-Sun) The Byzantine castle, originally Roman-built around AD 550, but rebuilt since, has excellent views to the Ionian Islands.

✦ Festivals

Patras Carnival   MARDI GRAS
(www.carnivalpatras.gr) Wild weekend of costume parades and floats in spring.

🛏 Sleeping

Pension Nikos   HOTEL €
(☏261 062 3757; cnr Patreos 3 & Agiou Andreou 121; s/d/tr €30/40/55, s/d without bathroom €25/35; ❄) Marble stairs lead to spotlessly clean rooms smack in the city centre.

Olympic Star Hotel   BUSINESS HOTEL €€
(☏261 062 2939; www.olympicstar.gr; Agiou Nikolau 46; s/d/tr incl breakfast €55/70/90; ❄🛜) Business-style rooms feature hydro showers.

✕ Eating & Drinking

Scores of stylish cafes and fast-food eateries lie between Kolokotroni and Ermou; drinking hot spots cluster on Agiou Nikolaou and near pedestrainised Riga Fereou. Pedestrianised Trion Navarhon is lined with tavernas.

Kouzina tis Kornilias   BISTRO €
(☏261 027 2987; Plateia Kapodistrio 4; mains €8-14; ⊙dinner, lunch Sat & Sun) Dig in to Turkish braised beef with aubergine puree (€14) and

other delicate specialities in this cool bistro tucked in the corner of a quiet square.

Mythos TAVERNA €
(261 032 9984; cnr Trion Navarhon 181 & Riga Fereou; mains €8-14; ⊙dinner) Friendly waiters serve excellent home-cooked Greek classics in a chandelier-strewn town house.

Dia Discount Supermarket SUPERMARKET €
(Agiou Andreou 29; ⊙Mon-Sat)

❶ Information

Tourist Office (261 046 1741; www.info centerpatras.gr; Agiou Andreou 12-14, btwn Zaimi & Aratou; ⊙7.30am-9pm; ☎) Friendly multilingual staff with information on transport. A kiosk in central Plateia Trion Symahon operates from 7.30am to 9pm in summer.

Tourist Police (261 069 5191; Gounari 52; ⊙7.30am-9pm)

❶ Getting There & Away

Boat

Schedules vary; the tourist office provides timetables. Ticket agencies line the waterfront.

Strintzis (261 024 0000; www.strintzis ferries.gr) sails to:

Ithaki (€18.60, four hours, one daily)
Kefallonia (€18.20, 2¾ hours, one to two daily)
Minoan Lines (261 042 6000; www.minoan. gr), **ANEK Lines** (261 022 6053; www.anek. gr) and others sail to:
Igoumenitsa (€25, seven hours, one daily)
Italy (from €65/70 to Venice/Ancona)

WORTH A TRIP

DIAKOFTO– KALAVRYTA RAILWAY
ΔΙΑΚΟΦΤΟ–ΚΑΛΑΒΡΥΤΑ

This spectacular rack-and-pinion **train** (26910 43206), built in the 1890s, crawls up the deep **Vouraïkos river gorge** from the small coastal town of Diakofto, one hour east of Patra, to the mountain resort of Kalavryta, 22km away. It's a thrilling one-hour journey, with dramatic scenery best viewed from any forward-facing seat. They book up, so buy tickets (€10, five daily) in advance at any train station or online at **Trainose** (www.trainose. gr). Visit www.odontotos.com for more information.

Bus

Services from **KTEL Achaia bus station** (261 062 3886; cnr Zaimi 2 & Othonos Amalias):
Athens (€20, three hours, half-hourly, via Corinth)
Ioannina (€24, 4½ hours, two daily)
Kalamata (€23, four hours, two daily)
Kalavryta (€7, two hours, two daily)
Pyrgos (for Olympia; €10, two hours, 10 daily)
Thessaloniki (€44, seven hours, four daily)

Buses to the Ionian Islands, via the port of Kyllini, leave from the **KTEL Lefkada & Zakynthos bus station** (261 022 0993; www.ktel -zakynthos.gr; Othonos Amalias 48) or nearby **KTEL Kefallonia bus station** (261 027 4938; Othonos Amalias 58).

Train

At the time of research, train lines from **Patra train station** (261 063 9108; Othonos Amalias 27) were under construction and may reopen in 2013. Replacement buses serve Athens' Kiato station (connects to suburban rail), Diakofto, Kalamata and Pyrgos (for Olympia).

Corinth Κόρινθος
POP 26,400

Drab, modern Corinth (ko-rin-thoss), 6km west of the Corinth Canal, is an uninspiring town; it's better to stay in the village near Ancient Corinth if visiting the ruins.

🛏 Sleeping

Hotel Ephira HOTEL €
(27410 22434; www.ephirahotel.gr; Ethnikis Andistasis 52; d €50; ❀☎) Corinth's smartest hotel is comfortably furnished, but hides a few blemishes. Suites are a notch more upmarket.

Blue Dolphin Camping CAMPGROUND €
(27410 25766; www.camping-blue-dolphin.gr; campsites per tent/adult €5/6.50; ⊙Apr-Oct; ☎) Has a beach, decent facilities and offers tours. It's at Lecheon, about 4km west of Corinth, just after the ancient Corinth turnoff. Offers pick-up from train or bus stations.

❶ Getting There & Away

BUS Buses to Athens (€8, 1½ hours, halfhourly) and Ancient Corinth (€1.70, 20 minutes, hourly) leave from the **KTEL Korinthos bus station** (27410 75425; www.ktel-korinthias. gr; Dimocratias 4). Buses to the rest of the Peloponnese leave from the **Corinth Isthmus (Peloponnese) KTEL bus station** (27410 73987, 27410 83000) on the Peloponnese side of the Corinth Canal. All buses from Athens to the Peloponnese stop here. To get there from Corinth, catch one of the frequent local buses to Loutraki.

TRAIN At the time of research, train lines to Patra and Athens were closed for construction; they may reopen in 2013. The *proastiako* suburban train at nearby Kiato goes to Athens airport (€12, one hour, eight daily). Buses to/from the *proastiako* station go to/from Corinth's Plateia Kentriki (€1.50, 20 minutes).

Ancient Corinth & Acrocorinth
Αρχαία Κόρινθος & Ακροκόρινθος

Seven kilometres southwest of Corinth's modern city, the ruins of Ancient Corinth (27410 31207; site & museum €6; 8.30am-8pm Apr-Oct, to 3pm Nov-Mar) and its lovely museum lie at the edge of a small village in the midst of fields sweeping to the sea. It was one of ancient Greece's wealthiest cities, but earthquakes and invasions have left only one Greek monument remaining: the imposing Temple of Apollo; the rest of the ruins are Roman. Acrocorinth (8am-3pm), the remains of a citadel built on a massive outcrop of limestone, looms majestically over the site.

The great-value digs at Tasos Taverna & Rooms (27410 31225; s/d/tr €30/45/55; ▒), 200m from the museum, are spotlessly clean and above an excellent eatery serving Greek classics.

Nafplio   Ναύπλιο
POP 14,000

Elegant Venetian houses and neoclassical mansions dripping with crimson bougainvillea cascade down Nafplio's hillside to the azure sea. Vibrant cafes, shops and restaurants fill winding pedestrian streets. Crenulated Palamidi Fortress perches above it all. What's not to love?

◉ Sights

Palamidi Fortress   FORTRESS
(27520 28036; admission €4; 8am-7.30pm May–mid-Oct, to 4.30pm mid-Oct–Apr) Enjoy spectacular views of the town and surrounding coast from the magnificent hilltop fortress built by the Venetians between 1711 and 1714.

WORTH A TRIP

THE WINE ROAD

The Nemea region, in the rolling hills southwest of Corinth, is one of Greece's premier wine-producing areas, famous for its full-bodied reds from the local *agiorgitiko* grape and a white from *roditis* grapes. Some wineries offer tastings:

Skouras (27510 23688; www.skouras wines.com) Northwest of Argos.

Ktima (27460 24190; www.palivos.gr; Ancient Nemea) Palivou

Lafkioti (27460 31000; www.lafkiotis. gr; Ancient Kleonai) Located 3km east of Ancient Nemea.

Gaia Wines (27460 22057; www.gaia -wines.gr; Koutsi) North of Nemea.

Archaeological Museum   MUSEUM
(27520 27502; Plateia Syntagmatos; admission €3; noon-4pm Mon, 9am-4pm Tue-Sun) Fine exhibits include fire middens from 32,000 BC and bronze armour from near Mycenae (12th to 13th centuries BC).

Peloponnese Folklore Foundation Museum   MUSEUM
(27520 28379; www.pli.gr; Vas Alexandrou 1; admission €2; 9am-2.30pm) One of Greece's best small museums, with displays of vibrant regional costumes and rotating exhibitions.

🛏 Sleeping

Exquisite hotels abound in Nafplio. The Old Town is *the* place to stay, but it has few budget options. Friday to Sunday the town fills and prices rise; book ahead. Cheaper spots dot the road to Argos and Tolo.

TOP CHOICE Amfitriti Pension   PENSION €€
(27520 96250; www.amfitriti-pension.gr; Kapodistriou 24; d incl breakfast from €60; ▒🐾) Quaint antiques fill these intimate rooms in a house in the Old Town. You can also enjoy stellar views at its nearby sister hotel, Amfitriti Belvedere, which is chock-full of brightly coloured tapestries and emits a feeling of cheery serenity.

Pension Marianna   PENSION €€
(27520 24256; www.pensionmarianna.gr; Potamianou 9; s/d/tr incl breakfast €50/65/85;

P❀🛜) Welcoming owners epitomise Greek *filoxenia* (hospitality) and serve delicious organic breakfasts. Up a steep set of stairs, and tucked under the fortress walls, a dizzying array of rooms intermix with sea-view terraces.

Adiandi BOUTIQUE HOTEL €€
(☑27520 22073; www.hotel-adiandi.com; Othonos 31; r incl breakfast €75-120; ❀🛜) Rooms in this fun and upmarket place are quirkily decorated with artistic bedheads fashioned from doors and contemporary decor. Fantastic farm-fresh breakfasts.

Hotel Byron PENSION €
(☑27520 22351; www.byronhotel.gr; Platonos 2; d incl breakfast from €45; ❀) Tucked into two fine Venetian buildings, iron bedsteads, rich carpets and period furniture fill immaculate rooms.

Hotel Grande Bretagne LUXURY HOTEL €€
(☑27520 96200; www.grandebretagne.com.gr; Plateia Filellinon; d incl breakfast from €115; ❀🛜) In the heart of Nafplio's cafe action and overlooking the sea, this splendidly restored hotel with high ceilings, antiques and chandeliers radiates plush opulence.

Kapodistrias PENSION €
(☑27520 29366; www.hotelkapodistrias.gr; Kokinou 20; d incl breakfast from €50; ⊘Mar–mid-Oct; ❀🛜) Beautiful rooms, many with elegant canopy beds, come with sea or old-town views.

Pension Dimitris Bekas PENSION €
(☑27520 24594; Efthimiopoulou 26; s/d/tr €25/30/45) The only good, central budget option. Clean, homey rooms (some with shared bath) have a top-value location on the slopes of the Akronafplia, and the owner has a killer baseball cap collection.

✘ Eating

Nafplio's Old Town streets are loaded with standard tavernas; those on Staïkopoulou or overlooking the port on Bouboulinas get jam-packed on weekends; Vasilissis Olgas is better, with tavernas like **Aeolos** (☑27520 26828; Vasilissis Olgas 30; mains €5-13) and **To Omorfo Tavernaki** (☑27520 25944; Vasilissis Olgas 1; mains €7-14).

TOP
CHOICE **Alaloum** GREEK €€
(☑27520 29883; Papanikolaou 10; mains €10-18) Heaping creative interpretations of traditional dishes like rooster, veal or homemade pasta can be shared. Everything is made from scratch and salads are a meal in their own right.

TOP
CHOICE **Antica Gelateria di Roma** ICE CREAM €
(☑27520 23520; cnr Farmakopoulou & Komninou) The best (yes, best) traditional gelati outside Italy.

To Kentrikon CAFE €
(☑27520 29933; Plateia Syntagmatos; mains €4-10) Relax under the shady trees on this pretty square during extensive breakfasts. Best coffees and teas.

Arapakos SEAFOOD €€
(☑27520 27675; www.arapakos.gr; Bouboulinas 81; mains €10-15) The best of the boardwalk catch for fresh seafood.

🛍 Shopping

Nafplio shopping is a delight, with jewellery workshops like **Metallagi** (☑27520 21267; Sofroni 3), boutiques and wonderful regional products, such as worry beads, honey, wine and handicrafts.

Odyssey BOOKS
(☑27520 23430; Plateia Syntagmatos) International papers, magazines and novels.

🍷 Drinking & Entertainment

Wander the Old Town to cafe- and bar-hop the lively scene. You could start at newcomer **O Mavros Gatos** (Sofroni 1), or creative stalwarts near Plateia Syntagmatos like **Cafe Rosso** (Komninou 5), where every table is different.

TOP
CHOICE **Fougaro** CULTURAL CENTRE
(☑27520 96005; www.fougaro.gr; Asklipiou 98) Nafplio's marquee arts and cultural centre opened with fanfare in 2012 in an impeccably renovated factory that now houses an art shop, library, cafe and exhibition spaces, and holds performing arts programs.

ℹ Information

Emergency
Tourist Police (☑27520 28131; Kountouridou 16)

Tourist Information
Staikos Tours (☑27520 27950; Bouboulinas 50) Helpful; Avis rental cars; full travel services like occasional day-long boat trips (www.pegasus-cruises.gr) to Spetses, Hydra and Monemvasia.

GORGE YOURSELF

The picturesque prefecture of **Arkadia** occupies much of the central Peloponnese and is synonymous with grassy meadows, forested mountains and gurgling streams. West of Tripoli, a tangle of medieval villages and narrow winding roads weave into valleys of dense vegetation beneath the **Menalon Mountains**. These areas are best accessed by car.

Wonderful walks along the **Lousios Gorge** leave from **Dimitsana** (population 230), a delightful medieval village built amphitheatrically on two hills at the beginning of the gorge. It sits 11km north of **Stemnitsa** (population 412), another gorge gateway and a striking village of stone houses and Byzantine churches.

Trekking Hellas (☑697 445 9753, 27910 25978; www.trekkinghellas.gr) offers rafting (from €50) on the nearby Lousios and Alfios Rivers, gorge hikes (from €20) and multi-day tours (€275).

Leonidio (population 3224), 90km east of Sparta, is dramatically set at the mouth of the **Badron Gorge**. Some older residents still speak Tsakonika, a distinctive dialect from the time of ancient Sparta.

❶ Getting There & Away

KTEL Argolis Bus Station (☑27520 27323; www.ktel-argolidas.gr; Syngrou 8) has the following services:

Argos (for Peloponnese connections; €1.60, 30 minutes, half-hourly)

Athens (via Corinth; €13.10, 2½ hours, hourly)

Epidavros (€2.90, 45 minutes, two Mon-Sat)

Mycenae (€2.90, one hour, three daily)

Epidavros   Επίδαυρος

Spectacular World Heritage–listed **Epidavros** (☑27530 22009; admission €6; ⊙8am-6pm Apr-Oct, to 5pm Nov-Mar) was the sanctuary of Asclepius, god of medicine. Amid pine-covered hills, the magnificent **theatre** is still a venue during the Hellenic Festival, but don't miss the peaceful **Sanctuary of Asclepius**, an ancient spa and healing centre.

Go as a day trip from Nafplio (€2.90, 45 minutes, two daily buses Monday to Saturday).

For an early-morning visit to the site, stay at the **Hotel Avaton** (☑27530 22178; s/d €40/50; ▣❄), 1km away, at the junction of the road to Kranidi.

Mycenae   Μυκήνες

Although settled as early as the 6th millennium BC, **Ancient Mycenae** (☑27510 76585; admission €8; ⊙8am-7pm Mon-Sat, to 4pm Sun Jun-Sep, 8am-6pm Mon-Sat, to 4pm Sun Oct-May), pronounced mih-*kee*-nes, was at its most powerful from 1600 to 1200 BC. Mycenae's grand entrance, the **Lion Gate**, is Europe's oldest monumental sculpture. Homer accurately described Mycenae as being 'rich in gold': excavations of **Grave Circle A** by Heinrich Schliemann in the 1870s uncovered magnificent gold treasures, such as the Mask of Agamemnon, now on display at Athens' National Archaeological Museum.

Most people visit on day trips from Nafplio, but the bare-bones **Belle Helene Hotel** (☑27510 76225; Christou Tsounta; d without bathroom, incl breakfast €35) is where Schliemann lived during excavations.

Three buses go daily to Mycenae from Argos (€1.60, 30 minutes) and Nafplio (€2.90, one hour).

Sparta   Σπάρτη
POP 14,200

Cheerful, unpretentious modern Sparta (*spar*-tee) is at odds with its ancient Spartan image of discipline and deprivation. Although there's little to see, the town makes a convenient base from which to visit Mystras.

Modern **Hotel Lakonia** (☑27310 28951; www.lakoniahotel.gr; Palaeologou 89; s/d from €40/55; ❄🛜) maintains comfy, welcoming rooms with spotless bathrooms. **Hotel Maniatis** (☑27310 22665; www.maniatishotel.gr; Paleologou 72-76; s/d incl breakfast €80/100; ❄🛜) offers the sleekest digs in town.

The sweet smell of spices inundates **Restaurant Elysse** (☑27310 29896; Palaeologou 113; mains €6-12), which is run by a friendly

Greek-Canadian family. Locals chill out next door at **Café Ouzeri** (mains €4-6).

Sparta's **KTEL Lakonia bus station** (☎27310 26441; cnr Lykourgou & Thivronos), on the east edge of town, services Athens (€20, 3½ hours, eight daily) via Corinth, Gythio (€4.50, one hour, five daily), Monemvasia (€11, two hours, three daily) and Mystras (€2, 30 minutes, 11 daily).

Mystras   Μυστράς

Magical **Mystras** (☎27310 83377; adult/child €5/3; ⊙8.30am-5.30pm Mon-Sat, to 3pm Sun, sometimes longer in summer) was once the effective capital of the Byzantine Empire. Ruins of palaces, monasteries and churches, most of them dating from between 1271 and 1460, nestle at the base of the Taÿgetos Mountains, and are surrounded by verdant olive and orange groves.

Allow half a day to explore the site. While only 7km from Sparta, staying in the village nearby allows you to get there early before it heats up. Enjoy exquisite views and a beautiful swimming pool at **Hotel Byzantion** (☎27310 83309; www.byzantionhotel.gr; s/d/tr €50/70/80; P❄@☀). Have a decadent escape at **Hotel Pyrgos Mystra** (☎27310 20870; www.pyrgosmystra.com; Manousaki 3; d incl breakfast €200; ❄), with its lovingly appointed rooms in a restored mansion.

Camp at **Castle View** (☎27310 83303; www.castleview.gr; campsites per adult/tent/car €6/4/4, 2-person bungalow €30; ⊙Apr-Oct; ❄), about 1km before Mystras village and set in olive trees, or **Camping Paleologio Mystras** (☎27310 22724; campsites per adult/tent/car €7/4/4; ⊙year-round; ❄), 2km west of Sparta and approximately 4km from Mystras. Buses will stop outside either if you ask.

Several tavernas serve traditional Greek meals.

Monemvasia & Gefyra
Μονεμβάσια & Γέφυρα

POP 1320

Slip out along a narrow causeway, up around the edge of a towering rock rising dramatically from the sea and arrive at the exquisite walled village of Monemvasia. Enter the *kastro* (castle), which was separated from mainland Gefyra by an earthquake in AD 375, through a narrow tunnel on foot, and emerge into a stunning (carless) warren of cobblestone streets and stone houses. Beat the throngs of day trippers by staying over.

Signposted steps lead up to the ruins of a **fortress** built by the Venetians in the 16th century, and the Byzantine **Church of Agia Sophia**, perched precariously on the edge of the cliff. Views are spectacular, and wildflowers grow shoulder-high in spring.

🛏 Sleeping & Eating

Staying in a hotel in the *kastro* could be one of the most romantic things you ever do (ask for discounts in low season), but if you're on a tight budget stay in Gefyra.

Three traditional Greek tavernas sit cheek to cheek in Monemvasia's old town: **Matoula** (☎27320 61660; mains €8-13), **Marianthi** (☎27320 61371; mains €8-13) and **To Kanoni** (☎27320 61387; mains €8-13). You can't really go wrong with any of them.

TOP CHOICE **Hotel Malvasia**   HISTORIC HOTEL €€
(☎27320 61160; malvasia@otenet.gr; d/apt from €60/100; ❄) A variety of cosy, traditionally decorated rooms and apartments (most with sea views) are scattered around the Old Town. Another branch, known as the **Malvasia Hotel** (http://malvasia-hotel.gr), has higher-end rooms.

Hotel Aktaion   HOTEL €
(☎27320 61234; www.aktaion-monemvasia.gr; s/d €40/50) This clean, sunny hotel, on the Gefyra end of the causeway, has balconies with views of the sea and 'the rock'.

Taverna O Botsalo   TAVERNA €
(☎27320 61486; mains €4-9) Just down the wharf on the mainland; serves savoury meals.

❶ Getting There & Away

Buses stop in Gefyra at the friendly **Malvasia Travel** (☎27320 61752), where you can buy tickets. Four daily buses travel to Athens (€32, six hours) via Corinth and Sparta (€11, 2½ hours).

Gythio   Γύθειο

POP 4490

Gythio (*yee*-thih-o) was once the port of ancient Sparta. Now it's an earthy fishing town on the Lakonian Gulf and gateway to the rugged, much more beautiful Mani Peninsula.

Peaceful **Marathonisi islet**, linked to the mainland by a causeway, is said to be ancient Cranae, where Paris (prince of Troy) and Helen (the wife of Menelaus of Sparta) consummated the love affair that sparked the Trojan War. You'll find the tiny **Museum of Mani History** (☑27330 24484; admission €2; ☺8am-2.30pm) here in an 18th-century tower.

🛏 Sleeping & Eating

The waterfront is packed with fish taverna, like **I Gonia** (Vassilis Pavlou; mains €6-15), and cafes.

Hotel La Boheme   BOUTIQUE HOTEL €
(☑27330 21992; www.labohemehotel.gr; Tzani Tzanitaki; s/d incl breakfast €45/60; [P][✱][@]) Sea views, upmarket rooms and a zippy downstairs bar-restaurant draw crowds.

Camping Meltemi   CAMPGROUND €
(☑27330 23260; www.campingmeltemi.gr; campsites per tent/adult €5.50/6, bungalows €30-60; ☺Apr-Oct; [🛜][🏊]) Birds chirp in these idyllic silver olive groves, 3km south of Gythio; private beach, swimming pool and summer beauty contests! The Areopoli bus stops here.

Xenia Karlaftis Rooms to Rent   PENSION €
(☑27330 22719; opp Marathonisi islet; s/d €25/40) Friendly owner Voula keeps clean (if worn) rooms and offers kitchen access. Several nearby places are of similar quality if you can't get in here.

❶ Getting There & Away

BUS The **KTEL Lakonia bus station** (☑27330 22228; http://ktel-lakonias.gr; cnr Vasileos Georgios & Evrikleos) is on the square near Hotel Aktion.

Areopoli (€2.80, 30 minutes, four daily)
Athens (€24, 4½ hours, six daily)
Geroliminas (€6, 1¼ hours, one daily)
Sparta (€4.50, one hour, four daily)

CAR & BOAT **LANE Lines** (www.lane.gr) has a weekly ferry to Crete (€23, seven hours) via Kythira (€11, 2½ hours) and Antikythira. Schedules change; check with **Rozakis Travel** (☑27330 22207; rosakigy@otenet.gr; Pavlou 5) which also rents cars.

The Mani   Η Μάνη

The exquisite Mani completely lives up to its reputation for rugged beauty, with abundant wildflowers in spring and dramatic juxtapositions of sea and the Taÿgetos Mountains (threaded with wonderful walking trails). The Mani occupies the central peninsula

of the southern Peloponnese and is divided into two regions: the arid Lakonian (inner) Mani in the south and the verdant Messinian (outer) Mani in the northwest near Kalamata. Explore the winding roads by car.

LAKONIAN MANI

For centuries the Maniots were a law unto themselves, renowned for their fierce independence and their spectacularly murderous internal feuds. To this day, bizarre tower settlements built as refuges during clan wars dot the rocky slopes of Lakonian Mani.

Areopoli (population 775), 30km southwest of Gythio and named after Ares, the god of war, is a warren of cobblestone and ancient towers. Stay in a tastefully decorated 200-year-old tower house at **Londas Pension** (☑27330 51360; www.londas.com; near Church of Taxiarhes; s/d/tr incl breakfast €65/75/103, s/d without bathroom €56/65). For a cushy boutique hotel experience, book in at **Areos Polis** (☑27330 51028; www.areospolis.gr; s/d/tr incl breakfast from €40/65/80; [✱][🛜]).

Step behind the counter to choose from the scrumptious specials at **Nicola's Corner Taverna** (☑27330 51366; Plateia Athanaton; mains €8-10), on the central square.

The **bus station** (☑27330 51229) services Athens (€28, four daily) via Gythio (€2.80, 30 minutes), Itilo (for the Messinian Mani, €2, 20 minutes, two daily Monday to Saturday), Gerolimenas (€3.40, 45 minutes, three daily) and the Diros Caves (€1.60, 15 minutes, one daily).

Eleven kilometres south, the extensive, though touristy **Diros Caves** (☑27330 52222; adult/child €12/7; ☺8.30am-5.30pm Jun-Sep, to 3pm Oct-May) contain a subterranean river. In neighbouring **Pyrgos Dirou**, stay over at chic **Vlyhada** (☑27330 52469; www.vlyhada.gr; d incl breakfast €70; [P][✱]).

Gerolimenas, a tranquil fishing village on a sheltered bay 20km further south, is home to the exceedingly popular boutique establishment **Kyrimai Hotel** (☑27330 54288; www.kyrimai.gr; d incl breakfast from €110; [P][✱][🏊]). Groovy music and mood lighting fill this exquisitely renovated castle with a seaside swimming pool and top-notch restaurant.

MESSINIAN MANI

Stone hamlets dot aquamarine swimming coves. Silver olive groves climb the foothills to the snow-capped Taÿgetos Mountains. Explore the splendid meandering roads and hiking trails from Itilo to Kalamata.

The people of the enchanting seaside village of Kardamyli, 37km south of Kalamata, know how good they've got it. Sir Patrick Leigh Fermor famously wrote about his rambles here in *Mani: Travels in the Southern Peloponnese*. Trekkers come for the magnificent Vyros Gorge. Walks are well organised and colour-coded.

Kardamyli has a good choice of small hotels and private rooms for all budgets; book ahead for summer.

Notos Hotel (☏27210 73730; www.notos hotel.gr; studio €110, apt €135-160; P❄) is really a boutique hamlet of individual stone houses with fully equipped kitchens, verandas and views overlooking the village, the mountains and the sea.

Olympia Koumounakou Rooms (☏27210 73623; s/d €30/40) is basic but clean and popular with backpackers, who like the communal kitchen and courtyard.

Beautiful Elies (☏27210 73140; mains €6-12; ◷lunch), right by the beach 1km north of town, is worth a lunchtime stop.

Kardamyli is on the main bus route from Itilo to Kalamata (€4, one hour) and two to four buses stop daily at the central square.

Olympia Ολυμπία

POP 1000

Tucked alongside the Kladeos River, in fertile delta country, the modern town of Olympia supports the extensive ruins of the same name. The first Olympics were staged here in 776 BC, and every four years thereafter until AD 394, when Emperor Theodosius I banned them. During the competition the city-states were bound by a sacred truce to stop fighting and take part in athletic events and cultural exhibitions.

Ancient Olympia (☏26240 22517; adult/child €6/3, site & museum €9/5; ◷8am-8pm Apr-Oct, 8.30am-3pm Nov-Mar) is dominated by the immense ruined Temple of Zeus, to whom the games were dedicated. Don't miss the statue of Hermes of Praxiteles, a classical sculpture masterpiece, at the exceptional Archaeological Museum (adult/child €6/3; ◷1.30-8pm Mon, 8am-8pm Tue-Sun Apr-Oct, to 3pm Nov-Mar).

Sparkling-clean Pension Posidon (☏26240 22567; www.pensionposidon.gr; Stefanopoulou 9; s/d/tr €35/40/50; ❄) and quiet, spacious Hotel Pelops (☏26240 22543; www.hotelpelops.gr; Varela 2; s/d/tr incl breakfast €40/50/70; ❄❄@❄) offer the best value

in the centre. Family-run Best Western Europa (☏26240 22650; www.hoteleuropa.gr; Drouva 1; s/d €80/100; P❄@❄❄) perches on a hill above town and has gorgeous sweeping vistas from room balconies and the wonderful swimming pool.

Pitch your tent in the leafy grove at Camping Diana (☏26240 22314; www.camping-diana.gr; campsites per tent/adult €6/8; ❄), 250m west of town.

There are no outstanding favourites among Olympia's ho-hum restaurants. Take your pick, or head to outer villages. O Thea (☏26240 23264; mains €6-11; ◷dinner year-round, lunch May-Oct), 1.5km north in Floka, offers hearty taverna fare and terrace views. Call to ensure it's open outside high season.

Olympia Municipal Tourist Office (☏26240 22262; Praxitelous Kondyli; ◷9am-3pm Mon-Fri May-Sep) has transport schedules.

Catch buses at the stop on the north end of town. Northbound buses go via Pyrgos (€2, 30 minutes), where you connect to buses for Athens, Corinth and Patra. Two buses go east from Olympia to Tripoli (€12, 2½ hours) – you must reserve ahead at KTEL Pyrgos (☏26210 20600; www.ktelileias.gr). Local trains run daily to Pyrgos (€1, 30 minutes).

CENTRAL GREECE
ΚΕΝΤΡΙΚΗ ΕΛΛΑΔΑ

This dramatic landscape of deep gorges, rugged mountains and fertile valleys is home to the magical stone pinnacle-topping monasteries of Meteora and the iconic ruins of ancient Delphi, where Alexander the Great sought advice from the Delphic oracle. Established in 1938, Parnassos National Park (www.routes.gr), to the north of Delphi, attracts naturalists, hikers (it's part of the E4 European long-distance path) and skiers.

Delphi Δελφοί

POP 2800

Modern Delphi and its adjoining ruins hang stunningly on the slopes of Mt Parnassos overlooking the shimmering Gulf of Corinth.

According to mythology, Zeus released two eagles at opposite ends of the world and they met here, thus making Delphi the centre of the world. By the 6th century BC, Ancient Delphi (☏22650 82312; www.culture.gr; site or museum €6, combined adult/concession

€9/5; ⊗8am-3pm; sometimes varies) had become the Sanctuary of Apollo. Thousands of pilgrims flocked here to consult the middle-aged female oracle who sat at the mouth of a fume-emitting chasm. After sacrificing a sheep or goat, pilgrims would ask a question, and a priest would translate the oracle's response into verse. Wars, voyages and business transactions were undertaken on the strength of these prophecies. From the entrance, take the Sacred Way up to the Temple of Apollo, where the oracle sat. From here the path continues to the well-preserved theatre and stadium.

Opposite the main site and down the hill some 100m, don't miss the Sanctuary of Athena and the much-photographed Tholos, a 4th-century-BC columned rotunda of Pentelic marble.

In the town centre, the welcoming Hotel Hermes (☑22650 82318; www.hermeshotel.com.gr; Vasileon Pavlou & Friderikis 27; s/d incl breakfast €40/50; ❄) has spacious rooms sporting balconies with excellent valley views. Hotel Apollonia (☑22650 82919; www.hotelapollonia.gr; Ifeigenias 37-39; s/d/tr incl breakfast €60/80/100; ❄@🛜) is a bit more upmarket.

Apollon Camping (☑22650 82762; www.apolloncamping.gr; campsites per person/tent €8.50/4; P@🛜❄), 2km west of town, has great facilities, including restaurant, pool and minimarket.

Specialities at Taverna Vakhos (☑22650 83186; Apollonos 31; mains €6-17) include stuffed zucchini flowers and rabbit stew. Locals pack Taverna Gargadouas (☑22650 82488; Vasileon Pavlou & Friderikis; mains €6-10) for grilled meats and slow-roasted lamb.

The bus station (☑22660 82317), post office and banks are all on modern Delphi's main street, Vasileon Pavlou. Six buses a day go to Athens (€15.50, three hours). Take a bus to Lamia (€9.20, two hours, two daily) or Trikala (€14, 4½ hours, two daily) to transfer for Meteora.

Meteora   Μετέωρα

Meteora (meh-*teh*-o-rah) should be a certified Wonder of the World with its magnificent late-14th-century monasteries perched dramatically atop enormous rocky pinnacles. Try not to miss it. The tranquil village of Kastraki, 2km from Kalambaka, is the best base for visiting.

While there were once monasteries on all 24 pinnacles, only six are still occupied:

PELION PENINSULA

The Pelion Peninsula, a dramatic mountain range whose highest peak is Pourianos Stavros (1624m), was inhabited, according to mythology, by half-man and half-horse *kentavri* (centaurs). Today it is a verdant destination for trekkers. The largely inaccessible eastern flank consists of high cliffs that plunge into the sea. The gentler western flank coils round the Pagasitikos Gulf.

Megalou Meteorou (Grand Meteoron; ☑24320 22278; ⊗9am-5pm Wed-Mon Apr-Oct, to 4pm Thu-Mon Nov-Mar), Varlaam (☑24320 22277; ⊗9am-4pm Sat-Thu Apr-Oct, to 3pm Sat-Wed Nov-Mar), Agiou Stefanou (☑24320 22279; ⊗9am-1.30pm & 3.30-5.30pm Tue-Sun Apr-Oct, 9.30am-1pm & 3-5pm Nov-Mar), Agias Triados (Holy Trinity; ☑24320 22220; ⊗9am-5pm Fri-Wed Apr-Oct, 10am-3pm Nov-Mar), Agiou Nikolaou Anapafsa (☑24320 22375; ⊗9am-3.30pm Sat-Thu) and Agias Varvaras Rousanou (⊗9am-6pm Thu-Tue Apr-Oct, to 4pm Nov-Mar). Admission is €2 for each monastery and strict dress codes apply (no bare shoulders or knees and women must wear skirts; borrow a long skirt at the door if you don't have one). Walk the footpaths between monasteries, drive the back asphalt road, or take the bus (€1.20, 20 minutes) that departs from Kalambaka and Kastraki at 9am, and returns at 1pm.

Meteora's stunning rocks are also a climbing paradise. Licensed mountain guide Lazaros Botelis (☑694 804 3655, 24320 79165; meteora.guide@gmail.gr; Kastraki) and mountaineering instructor Kostas Liolos (☑69725 67582; ksds_liolios@yahoo.com; Kalambaka) show the way.

🛏 Sleeping & Eating

TOP CHOICE Doupiani House   PENSION €

(☑24320 75326; www.doupianihouse.com; s/d/tr incl breakfast €40/50/60; P❄@🛜) Gregarious hosts Thanassis and Toula Nakis offer this comfy home from which to explore or simply enjoy the panoramic views. Request a balcony room.

Vrachos Camping   CAMPGROUND €

(☑24320 22293; www.campingmeteora.gr; campsites per tent/adult €9/free; ❄) Great views, excellent facilities and a good taverna; a short stroll from Kastraki.

GREECE METEORA

Taverna Paradisos TAVERNA €
(☎24320 22723; mains €6.50-9) Look for outstanding traditional meals with spectacular views.

Taverna Gardenia TAVERNA, PENSION €
(☎24320 22504; Kastrakiou St; mains €6-9; s/d/tr incl breakfast €35/45/55) Freshest Greek food served with aplomb and more splendid views. The owners also have good-value, spacious rooms.

Getting There & Around

Local buses shuttle between Kalambaka and Kastraki (€1.90). Hourly buses go from Kalambaka's **KTEL bus station** (☎24320 22432; Ikonomou) to the transport hub of Trikala (€2, 30 minutes), from where buses go to Ioannina (€13.10, three hours, two daily) and Athens (€27, 4½ hours, seven daily).

From Kalambaka **train station** (☎24320 22451), trains run to Athens (regular/IC €15/25, 5½/4½ hours, both twice daily) and Thessaloniki (€13, four hours, three daily).

NORTHERN GREECE
ΒΟΡΕΙΑ ΕΛΛΑΔΑ

Northern Greece is graced with magnificent mountains, thick forests, tranquil lakes and archaeological sites. It's easy to get off the beaten track and experience aspects of Greece noticeably different to other mainland areas and the islands.

Thessaloniki
Θεσσαλονίκη

POP 342,200

Dodge cherry sellers in the street, smell spices in the air and enjoy waterfront breezes in Thessaloniki (thess-ah-lo-*nee*-kih), also known as Salonica. The second city of Byzantium and of modern Greece boasts countless Byzantine churches, a smattering of Roman ruins, engaging museums, shopping to rival Athens, fine restaurants and a lively cafe scene and nightlife.

Sights & Activites

Check out the seafront **White Tower** (Lefkos Pyrgos; ☎231 026 7832; www.lpth.gr; ⌚8.30am-3pm Tue-Sun) and wander *hammams* (Turkish baths), Ottoman and Roman sites, and churches such as the enormous, 5th-century **Church of Agios Dimitrios** (☎231 027 0008; Agiou Dimitriou 97; ⌚8am-10pm).

The award-winning **Museum of Byzantine Culture** (☎231 330 6400; www.mbp.gr; Leoforos Stratou 2; admission €4; ⌚9am-4pm) beautifully displays splendid sculptures, mosaics, icons and other intriguing artefacts. The **Archaeological Museum** (☎231 083 0538; www.amth.gr; Manoli Andronikou 6; admission €6; ⌚10am-6pm Mon, 9am-6pm Tue-Sat, 9am-4pm Sun) showcases prehistoric, ancient Macedonian and Hellenistic finds.

The compelling **Thessaloniki Centre of Contemporary Art** (☎231 059 3270; www.cact.gr; Warehouse B1; ⌚10am-6pm Tue-Sat, 11am-3pm Sun) and hip **Thessaloniki Museum of Photography** (☎231 056 6716; www.thmphoto.gr; Warehouse A, Thessaloniki Port; admission €2; ⌚11am-7pm Tue-Sun), beside the port, are worth an hour.

Wonderfully seen on foot, Thessaloniki can also be zigzagged by **bus tour** (ticket €3; ⌚hourly 8am-9pm Jun-Sep, 9am-4pm Oct-May) leaving from the White Tower. Get information at the tourist office.

Sleeping

Steep discounts abound during summer; prices rise during conventions (listed at www.helexpo.gr).

Electra Palace Hotel LUXURY HOTEL €€€
(☎231 029 4000; www.electrahotels.gr; Plateia Aristotelous 9; d from €150; ❄@🛜🏊) Dive into five-star seafront pampering: impeccable service, plush rooms, a rooftop bar, indoor and outdoor swimming pools and a *hammam*.

Rent Rooms Thessaloniki HOSTEL €
(☎231 020 4080; www.rentrooms-thessaloniki.com; Konstantinou Melenikou 9, near Kamara; dm/s/d/tr/q incl breakfast €19/38/49/67/82; ❄🛜) Cheery, clean and modern, with a back-garden cafe looking onto the Rotunda. Communal breakfast-cafe nook and cheap bike hire add to the appeal. Some dorms/rooms have minikitchens, and all have bathrooms. Book ahead.

Hotel Orestias Kastorias HOTEL €
(☎231 027 6517; www.okhotel.gr; Agnostou Stratiotou 14; s/d/tr €37/46/58; ❄@🛜) A friendly favourite with cosy, clean rooms, renovated in 2011.

Thessaloniki

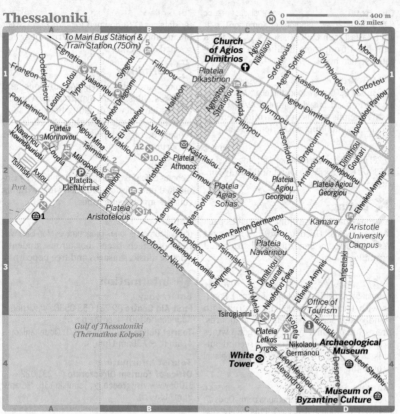

Thessaloniki

◎ Top Sights

Archaeological Museum	D4
Church of Agios Dimitrios	C1
Museum of Byzantine Culture	D4
White Tower	C4

◎ Sights

1	Thessaloniki Centre of Contemporary Art	A2

🛏 Sleeping

2	City Hotel	B2
3	Electra Palace Hotel	B2
4	Hotel Orestias Kastorias	C1
5	Hotel Pella	B1
6	Hotel Tourist	B2
7	Rent Rooms Thessaloniki	D2

🍴 Eating

8	Dore Zythos	C4
9	Kitchen Bar	A2
10	Modiano Market	B2
11	Myrsini	C4
12	O Arhontis	B2
13	Paparouna	A2
14	Turkenlis	B2
15	Zythos	A2

🍷 Drinking

16	Gambrinus	B1
17	Spiti Mou	A1

City Hotel
BUSINESS HOTEL €€

(☎2310269421; www.cityhotel.gr; Komninon 11; d/tr incl breakfast from €90/110; ❄@☎) Ask for a light-filled front room in this excellently located stylish hotel.

Hotel Tourist
BUSINESS HOTEL €

(☎231 027 0501; www.touristhotel.gr; Mitropoleos 21; s/d/tr/q incl breakfast from €50/58/68/85; ❄@) Spacious rooms in a charming, central, neoclassical building with friendly staff.

Hotel Pella
HOTEL €

(☎231 052 4221; www.pella-hotel.gr; Ionos Dragoumi 63; s/d €30/36; ❄☎) Quiet and family-run, with spotless rooms.

Eating

Tavernas dot Plateia Athonos and cafes pack Leoforos Nikis. Head to Modiano Market (Vassiliou Irakliou or Ermo) for fresh fruit and vegetables.

TOP CHOICE Zythos
TAVERNA €

(Katouni 5; mains €8-12; ☉lunch & dinner) Popular with locals, this excellent taverna with friendly staff serves up delicious standards, interesting regional specialities, good wines by the glass and beers on tap. Its second outlet is Dore Zythos (☎231 027 9010; Tsirogianni 7), near the White Tower.

Paparouna
GREEK €

(☎231 051 0852; www.paparouna.com; Doxis 7; mains €8-16; ☉lunch & dinner) This lively restaurant whips up inventive cuisine like chicken with peppermint and honey.

Myrsini
CRETAN €

(☎231 022 8300; Tsopela 2; mains €8-12; ☉Sep-Jun) Hearty portions of delicious Cretan dishes such as roast rabbit and *myzithropitakia* (flaky filo triangles with sweet sheep's-milk cheese).

Kitchen Bar
INTERNATIONAL €

(☎231 050 2241; www.kitchenbar.com.gr; Warehouse B, Thessaloniki Port; mains €8-13; ☉lunch & dinner) This perennial favourite offers both drinks and artfully prepared eclectic food, in a sumptuously decorated, renovated warehouse with waterfront tables.

O Arhontis
STREET FOOD €

(Ermou 26; mains €5; ☉11am-5pm) Eat delicious grilled sausages and potatoes off butcher's paper at this popular workers' eatery in Modiano Market.

Turkenlis
BAKERY €

(Aristotelous 4) Renowned for *tzoureki* (sweet bread) and a mind-boggling array of sweet-scented confections.

Drinking

Funky bars line Plateia Aristotelous and Leoforos Nikis, while Syngrou and Valaoritou Sts have newer drinking holes. In summer many city-centre nightclubs close and reopen in bigger spaces outdoors, on the airport road.

Spiti Mou
BAR

(Leontos Sofou 26, cnr Egnatia; ☉1pm-late; ☎) Unmarked entrance and relaxed vibe, with big couches and eclectic tunes.

Gambrinus
BAR

(cnr Valaoritou & Ionos Dragoumi; ☉Mon-Sat) Variety of Czech beers, boisterous students, eclectic music, sausages and free popcorn.

Information

Emergency
First-Aid Centre (☎231 053 0530; Navarhou Koundourioti 10) Near the port.

Tourist Police (☎231 055 4871; Dodekanisou 4, 5th fl; ☉7.30am-11pm)

Tourist Information
Office of Tourism Directorate (☎231 022 1100; www.visitgreece.gr; Tsimiski 136; ☉9am-3pm Mon-Fri)

Getting There & Away

Air

Makedonia Airport (SKG; ☎231 047 3212; www.thessalonikiairport.com) is 16km southeast of the centre and served by local bus 78 (www.oasth.gr; €0.80, one hour, from 5am to 10pm). Taxis cost €12 (20 minutes).

Olympic Air, Aegean Airlines and Astra Airlines (☎231 048 9392; www.astra-airlines.gr) fly throughout Greece.

Boat

Weekly ferries go to, among others, Limnos (€22, eight hours), Lesvos (€32, 14 hours) and Chios (€35, 19 hours). Karaharisis Travel & Shipping Agency (☎231 052 4544; Navarhou Koundourioti 8) handles tickets.

Bus

The main bus station (☎231 059 5408; www.ktel-thes.gr; Monastiriou 319) services Athens (€42, 6¼ hours, 10 daily), Ioannina (€30, 4¾ hours, six daily) and other destinations. Buses to

HALKIDIKI   ΧΑΛΚΙΔΙΚΗ

Beautiful pine-covered Halkidiki is a three-pronged peninsula that extends into the Aegean Sea, southeast of Thessaloniki. Splendid, if built-up, sandy beaches rim its 500km of coastline. The middle Sithonian Peninsula is most spectacular. With camping and rooms to rent, it is more suited to independent travellers than overdeveloped Kassandra Peninsula, although Kassandra has the summertime Sani Jazz Festival (www.sanifestival.gr). You'll need your own wheels to explore Halkidiki properly.

Halkidiki's third prong is occupied by the all-male Monastic Republic of Mt Athos (known in Greek as Agion Oros, the Holy Mountain), where 20 monasteries full of priceless treasures stand amid an impressive landscape of gorges, mountains and sea. Only men may visit, a permit is required and the summer waiting-list is long. Start months in advance by contacting the Thessaloniki-based Mt Athos Pilgrims' Bureau (☑231 025 2578; pilgrimsbureau@c-lab.gr; Egnatia 109; ☺9am-1pm Mon-Fri, 10am-noon Sat).

the Halkidiki Peninsula leave from the **Halkidiki bus terminal** (☑231 031 6555; www.ktel-chal kidikis.gr; Karakasi 68).

At the time of writing, small bus companies, mostly across from the courthouse (Dikastirion), provided the only services to international destinations like Skopje, Sofia and Bucharest. Try **Simeonidis Tours** (☑231 054 0970; www. simeonidistours.gr; 26 Oktovriou 14). Train company OSE has run buses to Sofia and Tirana but service was in flux at the time of writing. Check at the office on the eastern side of the train station.

Train

The **train station** (☑231 059 9421; www.train-ose.gr; Monastiriou) serves Athens (regular/ IC €28/36, 6¾/5½ hours, seven/10 daily) but other lines like Alexandroupolis have been reduced, and all international trains were discontinued at the time of writing. Check schedules at the **train ticket office** (OSE; ☑231 059 8120; Aristotelous 18) or the station.

Alexandroupolis
Αλεξανδρούπολη
POP 59,900

Alexandroupolis (ah-lex-an-*dhroo*-po-lih) and nearby Komotini (ko-mo-tih-*nee*) enjoy lively student atmospheres that make for a satisfying stopover on the way to Turkey or Samothraki.

Waterfront Hotel Bao Bab (☑25510 34823; Alexandroupoli–Komotini Hwy; s/d/tr incl breakfast €40/50/60; P✳@), 1km west of town, has large, comfortable rooms and an excellent restaurant. Downtown, Hotel Marianna (☑25510 81456; Malgaron 11; s/d €40/50) has small, clean rooms.

Tuck into today's fresh catch at Psarotav-erna tis Kyra Dimitras (☑25510 34434; cnr Kountourioti & Dikastirion; fish €6-11).

Alexandroupoli's cool nightspots change with the whims of its students. Leoforos Dimokratias has trendy bars; cafes line the waterfront.

The municipal tourist office (☑25510 64184; Leoforos Dimokratias 306; ☺7.30am-3pm) is helpful.

❶ Getting There & Away

AIR & BOAT Dimokritos Airport (☑25510 89300; www.alxd.gr), 7km east of town, is served by Olympic Air and Aegean Airlines. **Sever Travel** (☑25510 22555; sever1@otenet. gr; Megalou Alexandrou 24) handles ferry (to Samothraki and Limnos) and airline tickets. **BUS** The **bus station** (☑25510 26479; Eleftheriou Venizelou 36) has departures to the following:

Athens (€64, 10 hours, one daily)
Thessaloniki (€30, 3¾ hours, nine daily)
İstanbul (Turkey; OSE bus €15, six hours, one daily Tue-Sun)
TRAIN At the time of writing, international trains were cancelled. Other schedules change. Check ahead at the **train station** (☑25510 26395; www.trainose.gr).
Athens (€50, 14 hours, one daily)
Thessaloniki (€9, seven hours, four daily)

Mt Olympus
Όλυμπος Όρος

Just as it did for the ancients, Greece's highest mountain, the cloud-covered lair of the Greek pantheon, fires the visitor's imagination today. The highest of Olympus' eight peaks is **Mytikas** (2917m), popular with trekkers, who use **Litohoro** (305m), 5km inland from the Athens–Thessaloniki highway, as their base. The main route up takes two days, with a stay overnight at one of the **refuges** (⊘May-Oct). Good protective clothing is essential, even in summer. **EOS** (Greek Alpine Club; ☑23520 84544; Plateia Kentriki, Litohoro; ⊘Mon-Sat Jun-Sep) has information on treks.

From the **bus station** (☑23520 81271; Agiou Nikolaou, Litohoro) 13 buses daily go to Thessaloniki (€9, 1¼ hours) and three to Athens (€33, 5½ hours). Litohoro's **train station**, 9km away, gets 10 daily trains on the Athens–Volos–Thessaloniki line.

Xenonas Papanikolaou
GUESTHOUSE €

(☑23520 81236; www.xenonas-papanikolaou.gr; Nikolaou Episkopou Kitrous 1; s/d incl breakfast €45/55; P❋@) This romantic guesthouse sits in a flowery garden up in the backstreets, a world away from tourist crowds.

Olympos Beach Camping
CAMPGROUND €

(☑23520 22111; www.olympos-beach.gr; campsites per adult/tent €7/6, bungalows €45; ⊘Apr-Oct) Has a booming waterfront lounge and a pleasant beach.

TOP CHOICE Gastrodromio En Olympio
GREEK €

(☑23520 21300; Plateia Eleftherias; mains €7-13; ⊘lunch & dinner) One of Greece's best country restaurants serves up specialities such as *soutzoukakia* (minced meat with cumin and mint) and delicious wild mushrooms with an impressive regional wine list and gorgeous Olympus views.

Ioannina   Ιωάννινα

POP 64,500

Charming Ioannina (ih-o-*ah*-nih-nah) on the western shore of Lake Pamvotida at the foot of the Pindos Mountains, was a major intellectual centre during Ottoman rule. Today it's a thriving university town with a lively waterfront cafe scene.

◎ Sights

Kastro
NEIGHBOURHOOD

The narrow stone streets of the evocative old quarter sit on a small peninsula jutting into the lake. Within its impressive fortifications, **Its Kale**, an inner citadel with lovely grounds and lake views, is home to the splendid **Fetiye Cami** (Victory Mosque),

built in 1611, and the gemlike **Byzantine Museum** (☑26510 25989; admission €3; ⊘8am-5pm Tue-Sun).

Lake Pamvotida
LAKE

The lake's serene *nisi* (island) shelters four **monasteries** among its trees. Frequent ferries (€2) leave from near Plateia Mavili.

🛏 Sleeping

TOP CHOICE Filyra
BOUTIQUE HOTEL €

(☑26510 83560; http://hotelfilyra.gr; alley off Andronikou Paleologou 18; s/d €45/55; P❋) Five Old Town self-catering suites fill up fast. The affiliated **Traditional Hotel Dafni** (Ioustinianou 12; s/d/q €45/65/90) is built into the Kastro's outer walls.

Hotel Kastro
PENSION €€

(☑26510 22866; www.hotelkastro.gr; Andronikou Paleologou 57; s/d incl breakfast €50/65; P❋) Ask for a high-ceilinged upstairs room at this quaint hotel, across from Its Kale.

Limnopoula Camping
CAMPGROUND €

(☑26510 25265; Kanari 10; campsites per tent/adult €4/8; ⊘Apr-Oct) Tree-lined and splendidly set on the edge of the lake 2km northwest of town.

🍴 Eating & Drinking

Scores of cafes and restaurants line the waterfront. Enjoy a cold beer on a sunny day in Its Kale, at its exquisitely situated **cafe** (mains €4-8).

Sirios
GREEK €

(☑26510 77070; www.seirioskouzina.gr; Patriarhou Evangelidi 1; mains €8-12; ⊘noon-11pm) An imaginative menu of decidedly delicious dishes, ranging from braised rooster to pork cutlets.

Taverna To Manteio
TAVERNA €

(☑26510 25452; Plateia Georgiou 15; mains €7-8; ⊘lunch & dinner Tue-Sun) Join local families along the flower-filled Its Kale wall for deliciously simple *mezedhes,* salads and grills.

Ananta
BAR

(cnr Anexartisias & Stoa Labei) Rock out in the shadows of the long bar.

❶ Information

EOT (Tourist Office; ☑26510 41142; Dodonis 39; ⊘7.30am-2.30pm Mon-Fri)

EOS (Greek Alpine Club; ☑26510 22138; Despotatou Ipirou 2; ⊘7-9pm Mon-Fri)

ℹ️ Getting There & Away

AIR **Aegean Airlines** (📞26510 64444) and **Olympic Air** (📞26510 26518) fly to Athens. Slow buses ply the 2km road into town.

BUS The **station** (📞26510 26286; Georgiou Papandreou) is 300m north of Plateia Dimokratias.

Athens (€40, 6½ hours, nine daily)

Igoumenitsa (€9.80, 1¼ hours, eight daily)

Thessaloniki (€32, 4¾ hours, six daily)

Trikala (€15.50, 2¼ hours, two daily)

Zagorohoria & Vikos Gorge
Τα Ζαγοροχώρια & Χαράδρα του Βικού

Do not miss the spectacular Zagori region, with its deep gorges, abundant wildlife, dense forests and snowcapped mountains. Some 46 charming villages, famous for their grey-slate architecture, and known collectively as the Zagorohoria, are sprinkled across a large expanse of the Pindos Mountains north of Ioannina. These beautifully restored gems were once only connected by stone paths and arching footbridges, but paved roads now wind between them. Get information on walks from Ioannina's EOT and EOS offices. Book ahead during high season (Christmas, Greek Easter and August); prices plummet in low season.

Tiny, carless **Dilofo** makes for a peaceful sojourn, especially if you lodge at excellent **Gaia** (📞26530 22570; www.gaia-dilofo.gr; s/d/tr incl breakfast from €60/70/80; 🛜) or **Arhontiko Dilofo** (📞26530 22455; www.dilofo.com; d incl breakfast from €55; 🅿️) and sup on the square at **Sopotseli** (📞26530 22629; mains €5-7).

Delightful **Monodendri**, known for its special pitta bread, is a popular departure point for treks through dramatic 12km-long, 900m-deep **Vikos Gorge**, with its sheer limestone walls. Get cosy at quaint **Arhontiko Zarkada** (📞26530 71305; www.monodendri.com; s/d incl breakfast €40/60; 🅿️), one of Greece's best-value small hotels.

Exquisite inns with attached tavernas abound in remote (but popular) twin villages **Megalo Papingo** and **Mikro Papingo**. Visit the **WWF Information Centre** (www.wwf.gr; Mikro Papingo; ⏱11am-5.30pm Fri-Wed) to learn about the area.

In Megalo Papingo, simple **Lakis** (📞26530 41087; d incl breakfast €35) is a *domatia* (B&B), taverna and store. Spectacular views and family-friendly studios add to the charms of **Papaevangelou** (📞26530 41135; www.ho-

telpapaevangelou.gr; d/studio incl breakfast from €75/120). Stylish **Tsoumani** (📞26530 41893; www.tsoumanisnikos.gr; d incl breakfast from €70; 🛜) also serves some of the best food around. Two friendly brothers run charming **Xenonas tou Kouli** (📞26530 41115; d €60).

Hide away in Mikro Papingo's sweetly rustic **Xenonas Dias** (📞26530 41257; www.diaspapigo.gr; s/d incl breakfast €40/55) or fabulous, sumptuously minimalist **1700** (📞26530 41179; www.mikropapigo.gr; d from €80).

Infrequent buses run to Ioannina from Dilofo (€3.80, 40 minutes, three weekly), Monodendri (€3.60, one hour, three weekly) and the Papingos (€5.10, two hours, three weekly). It's best to explore by rental car from Ioannina; in a pinch take an (expensive) taxi.

Igoumenitsa
Ηγουμενίτσα

TRANSPORT HUB
POP 9160

Though tucked beneath verdant hills and lying on the sea, this characterless port is little more than a ferry hub: keep moving.

If you must stay over, look for *domatia* signs or opt for the most modern: **Angelika Pallas Hotel** (📞26650 26100; www.angelikapallas.gr; Agion Apostolon 145; s/d/tr incl breakfast from €60/70/90; 🅰️🛜) across from the Corfu ferry terminal. It also has a restaurant.

The **bus station** (📞26650 22309) services Ioannina (€9.80, 2½ hours, nine daily) and Athens (€45, eight hours, five daily).

Several companies operate 90-minute **ferries to Corfu** (📞26650 99460; person/car €10/40; ⏱hourly) and hydrofoils in summer. International ferries go to the Italian ports of Ancona, Bari, Brindisi and Venice. Ticket agencies line the port. Book ahead for car tickets or sleeping cabins.

SARONIC GULF ISLANDS
ΝΗΣΙΑ ΤΟΥ ΣΑΡΩΝΙΚΟΥ

Scattered about the Saronic Gulf, these islands are within easy reach of Athens. The Saronics are named after the mythical King Saron of Argos, a keen hunter who drowned while chasing a deer that had swum into the gulf to escape.

You can either island-hop through the group then return to Piraeus, or carry on to the Peloponnese from any of the islands mentioned.

HELLENIC WILDLIFE HOSPITAL

While some Greeks may not appear too environmentally minded, others are making a sterling effort to face the country's ecological problems head-on. The **Hellenic Wildlife Hospital** (✆22970 28367; www.ekpaz.gr; ⊙by appointment) on the Saronic Gulf island of Aegina is one such place. As the oldest and largest wildlife rehabilitation centre in southern Europe, it tackles damage caused to wild birds and animals from hunting and pollution, and runs projects such as the release of raptors into the wilds of Crete and Northern Greece. You can visit the centre for free, though donations are appreciated. Better yet, the centre welcomes volunteers and accommodation is supplied.

Aegina   Αίγινα

POP 14,500

Once a major player in the Hellenic world, thanks to its strategic position at the mouth of the gulf, Aegina (*eh-*yee-nah) now enjoys its position as Greece's premier producer of pistachios. Pick up a bag before you leave!

Bustling **Aegina Town**, on the west coast, is the island's capital and main port. There is no official tourist office, but information can be gleaned at www.aeginagreece.com.

The impressive **Temple of Aphaia** (adult/under 18yr €4/free; ⊙8am-6.30pm) is a well-preserved Doric temple 12km east of Aegina Town. It's said to have served as a model for the construction of the Parthenon. Standing on a pine-clad hill with imposing views out over the gulf, it is well worth a visit. Buses from Aegina Town to the small resort of Agia Marina can drop you at the site.

In Aegina Town, **Hotel Rastoni** (✆22970 27039; www.rastoni.gr; d/tr incl breakfast €90/120; P❈@🖝), a boutique hotel with excellent service, gets a big thumbs up for its quiet location, spacious rooms and lovely garden. **Electra Pension** (✆22970 26715; www.aegina-electra.gr; s/d €45/50; ❈🖝) is in a quiet corner of town with rooms that are impeccable and comfy.

A flotilla of ferries (€9.50, 70 minutes) and hydrofoils (€13.50, 40 minutes) ply the waters between Aegina and Piraeus with great regularity. You can head back to Pi-raeus, carry on through the Saronic Gulf Islands or take a boat to Methana (€5.70, 40 minutes) on the Peloponnese. There is a good public bus service on the island.

Poros   Πόρος

POP 5250

Only a few hundred metres from the village of Galatas on the shores of the mountainous Peloponnese, Poros is an attractive island with a friendly feel that is worth the effort. **Poros Town**, on the island's southern coast, is a haven for yachties, and with boats from all over tied up along the waterfront, there is a happy mood in the air.

Seven Brothers Hotel (✆22980 23412; www.7brothers.gr; s/d/tr €55/65/75; ❈🖝) is conveniently close to the hydrofoil dock. This modern hotel has bright, comfy rooms with balconies and impressive bathrooms.

There is no tourist office, but also no shortage of businesses hoping to sell you your onward ticket. Hit www.poros.gr for extensive information.

There are ferry (€12.80, 2½ hours) and hydrofoil (€22.20, one hour) services daily between Poros and Piraeus. The ferries go via Aegina (€8.30, 1¼ hours), while the hydrofoils go direct. Many of the outbound boats head on to Hydra and Spetses. Small boats shuttle back and forth between Poros and Galatas (€1, five minutes) on the Peloponnese.

Hydra   Ύδρα

POP 2900

The catwalk queen of the Saronics, Hydra (*ee*-drah) is a delight. On the northern side of this sparsely populated island, **Hydra Town** has a picturesque horseshoe-shaped harbour with gracious white and pastel stone mansions stacked up the rocky hillsides that surround it. The island is known as a retreat for artists, writers and celebrities, and wears its celebrity with panache.

A major attraction is Hydra's tranquillity. Forget noisy motorbikes keeping you awake half the night! There are no motorised vehicles – apart from sanitation trucks – and the main forms of transport are foot and donkey.

Pension Erofili (✆22980 54049; www.pensionerofili.gr; Tombazi; s/d/tr €45/55/65; ❈🖝), tucked away in the inner town, has clean, comfortable rooms, an attractive courtyard and breakfast features home-made preserves and jams. The owners add a friendly sparkle. **Hotel Miranda** (☎22980 52230; www.mirandahotel.gr; Miaouli; s/d incl breakfast €120/140; ❄) is worth a splurge. Originally built in 1810 as the mansion of a wealthy Hydriot sea captain, this stylish place retains much of its historical charac-ter and is a National Heritage building.

There is no tourist office, but check out www.hydra.com.gr for detailed information.

High-speed boat services (€25.50, 1½ hours) connect Hydra with Piraeus seven times daily. There are also services to Ermio-ni and Porto Heli on the Peloponnese main-land, inbound boats to Poros and outbound boats to Spetses.

Spetses Σπέτσες

POP 4400

Spetses is an appealing island that is packed with visitors in summer. Its attractiveness is largely thanks to Spetses-born philan-thropist Sotirios Anargyrios, who made a fortune in the US after emigrating in 1848. Anargyrios returned in 1914, bought two-thirds of the then-barren island, planted Aleppo pines, financed the island's road sys-tem and commissioned many of the town's grandest buildings.

Spetses Town, the main port, sprawls along half the northeast coast of the island.

Opposite the small town beach to the east of the ferry quay, **Villa Marina** (☎22980 72646; www.villamarinaspetses.com; s/d €55/65; ❄) is a convenient, welcoming place with tidy rooms. Ask for a sea view.

There is no tourist office. See the website www.spetsesdirect.com for more information.

High-speed boats head regularly to Pirae-us (€35, 2¼ hours). Another option is to car-ry on to the Peloponnese mainland on boats to Ermioni (€7.50, 30 minutes) or Porto Heli (€5.50, 15 minutes).

CYCLADES ΚΥΚΛΑΔΕΣ

The Cyclades (kih-*klah*-dez) are Greek is-lands to dream about. Named after the rough *kyklos* (circle) they form around the island of Delos, they are rugged outcrops of rock in the azure Aegean, speckled with white cubist buildings and blue-domed Byzantine churches. Throw in sun-blasted golden beaches, more than a dash of hedon-ism and a fascinating culture, and it's easy to see why many find the Cyclades irresistible.

Some of the islands, such as Mykonos, Ios and Santorini, have seized tourism with great enthusiasm. Prepare to battle the crowds if you turn up at the height of summer. Others are little more than clumps of rock, with a village, secluded coves and a few curious tourists. Ferry services rarely run in winter, while from July to September the Cyclades are vulnerable to the *meltemi,* a fierce northeasterly wind that can play havoc with ferry schedules.

History

Said to have been inhabited since at least 7000 BC, the Cyclades enjoyed a flourish-ing Bronze Age civilisation (3000–1100 BC), more or less concurrent with the Minoan civilisation. From the 4th century AD, the islands, like the rest of Greece, suffered a se-ries of invasions and occupations. The Turks turned up in 1537 but neglected the Cyclades to the extent that they became backwaters prone to raids by pirates – hence the laby-rinthine character of their towns, which was meant to confuse attackers. On some islands the whole population moved into the moun-tainous interior to escape the pirates, while on others they braved it out on the coast. Consequently, the *hora* (main town) is on the coast on some islands, while on others it is inland.

The Cyclades became part of independ-ent Greece in 1827. During WWII they were occupied by the Italians. Before the revival of the islands' fortunes by the tourist boom that began in the 1970s, many islanders lived in poverty and many more headed for the mainland or emigrated to America or Australia in search of work.

Mykonos Μύκονος

POP 8000

Sophisticated Mykonos glitters happily un-der the Aegean sun, shamelessly surviving on tourism. The island has something for everyone, with marvellous beaches, roman-tic sunsets, chic boutiques, excellent restau-rants and bars, and its long-held reputation as a mecca for gay travellers. The maze of white-walled streets in Mykonos Town was designed to confuse pirates, and it certain-ly manages to captivate and confuse the crowds that consume the island's capital in summer.

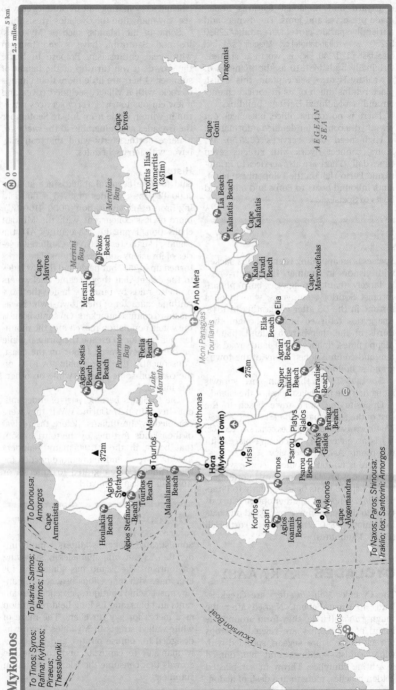

Mykonos

To Tinos; Syros;
Rafina; Kythnos;
Piraeus;
Thessaloniki

To Ikaria; Samos;
Patmos; Lipsi

To Donousa;
Amorgos

To Naxos; Paros; Shinousa;
Iraklio; Ios; Santorini; Amorgos

5 km

2.5 miles

N

AEGEAN
SEA

Dragonisi

Cape
Evros

Cape
Goni

Profitis Ilias
Anomeritis
(351m)

Merchias
Bay

Lia Beach

Kalafatis Beach
Cape
Kalafatis

Kalo
Livadi
Beach

Cape
Mavrokefalas

Mersini
Bay

Fokos
Beach

Cape
Mavros

Mersini
Beach

Ano Mera

Moni Panagias
Tourlianis

Elia
Beach

Elia

Agrari
Beach

Super
Paradise
Beach

Paradise
Beach

Agios Sostis
Beach

Panormos
Beach

Panormos
Bay

Frelia
Beach

Lake
Marathi

275m

Vothonas

Marathi

372m

Tourlos

Hora
(Mykonos Town)

Vrissi

Ornos

Platys
Gialos

Psarou

Paraga
Beach

Platys
Gialos

Psarou
Beach

Agios
Stefanos

Tourlos
Beach

Malaliamos
Beach

Houlakia
Beach

Agios Stefanos
Beach

Cape
Armenistis

Korfos

Kapari

Agios
Ioannis
Beach

Nea
Mykonos

Cape
Alogomandra

Excursion Boat

Delos

Sights & Activities

Mykonos Town
NEIGHBOURHOOD

A stroll around Mykonos Town, shuffling through snaking streets with blinding white walls and balconies of flowers is a must for any visitor. This is the centre of the action on the island. Little Venice, where the sea laps up to the edge of the restaurants and bars, and Mykonos' famous hilltop row of windmills should be included in the spots-to-see list. You're bound to run into one of Mykonos' famous resident pelicans on your walk.

Beaches

The island's most popular beaches are on the southern coast. Platys Gialos has wall-to-wall sun lounges, while nudity is not uncommon at Paradise Beach, Super Paradise, Agrari and gay-friendly Elia.

Sleeping

Rooms in Mykonos Town fill up quickly in high season; book ahead. Prices mentioned are for the peak season – they plummet further than on most islands outside of July and August.

Mykonos has two camping areas, both on the south coast. Minibuses from both meet the ferries, and buses go regularly into town.

Carbonaki Hotel
TOP CHOICE · BOUTIQUE HOTEL €€€

(www.carbonaki.gr; 23 Panahrantou; s/d/tr/q €140/168/210/240; ❄️📶) This family-run place on the edge of the old town has bright and comfortable rooms dotted around a sunny central courtyard. Throw in a Jacuzzi, sauna and delightful ambiance and this is a top place to stay.

Hotel Philippi
HOTEL €€

(☎22890 22294; www.philippihotel.com; 25 Kalogera, Mykonos Town; s €60-90, d €75-120; ❄️📶) In the heart of the *hora*, Philippi, one of Mykonos' few affordable options, has spacious and clean rooms that open onto a railed veranda overlooking a lush garden. An extremely peaceful, pleasant place to stay. Free wi-fi.

Hotel Lefteris
HOTEL €€

(☎22890 23128; www.lefterishotel.gr; 9 Apollonas, Mykonos Town; s/d €99/129, studios €239-279; ❄️@) Tucked away just up from Plateia Taxi (Taxi Sq), Lefteris has bright, comfy rooms, and a relaxing sun terrace with superb views over town. A good international meeting place.

CYCLADIC CONNECTIONS

For planning purposes, it's worth noting that once the season kicks in, a batch of companies run daily catamarans and ferries up and down the Cyclades. You can start from Piraeus (for Athens), Iraklio on Crete, or just about anywhere in-between.

One boat heads south daily from Piraeus to Paros, Naxos, Ios and Santorini, returning along the same route. There's also a daily run from Piraeus to Syros, Tinos and Mykonos.

Heading north from Iraklio, another catamaran runs to Santorini, Ios, Paros, Mykonos and return.

If it all get a bits much to comprehend (the schedules are constantly changing!), check the online guide Open Seas (www.openseas.gr).

Island-hopping through the Cyclades from Piraeus to Crete (or vice-versa) is getting easier and easier – though ease of travel means there are more people out there doing it!

Paradise Beach Camping
CAMPGROUND €

(☎22890 22852; www.paradisemykonos.com; campsites per tent/person €5/10; @🏊) There are lots of options here on the south coast of the island, including camping, beach cabins and apartments, as well as bars, a swimming pool, games etc. It is skin-to-skin mayhem in summer with a real party atmosphere. The website has it all.

Eating

There is no shortage of places to eat and drink in Mykonos Town. Cheap eateries are found around Plateia Taxi and the southern bus station. Restaurants offering abundant seafood abound in Little Venice and towards the Delos excursion boats. Mykonos' top touts are its two resident pelicans, who wander the restaurants looking for handouts, often with visitors following them.

Fato a Mano
MEDITERRANEAN €

(Plateia Meletopoulou; mains €8-15) In the middle of the maze, this place is worth taking the effort to find. It serves up tasty Mediterranean and traditional Greek dishes with pride.

DELOS ΔΗΛΟΣ

Southwest of Mykonos, the island of **Delos** (sites & museum €5; ⊙8.30am-3pm Tue-Sun) is the Cyclades' archaeological jewel. The opportunity to clamber among the ruins shouldn't be missed.

According to mythology, Delos was the birthplace of Apollo – the god of light, poetry, music, healing and prophecy. The island flourished as an important religious and commercial centre from the 3rd millennium BC, reaching its apex of power in the 5th century BC.

Ruins include the **Sanctuary of Apollo**, containing temples dedicated to him, and the **Terrace of the Lions**. These proud beasts were carved in the early 6th century BC using marble from Naxos to guard the sacred area. The original lions are in the island's **museum**, with replicas on the original site. The **Sacred Lake** (dry since 1926) is where Leto supposedly gave birth to Apollo, while the **Theatre Quarter** is where private houses were built around the **Theatre of Delos**.

The climb up **Mt Kynthos** (113m), the island's highest point, is a highlight. The view of Delos and the surrounding islands is spectacular, and it's easy to see how the Cyclades got their name.

Take a sunhat, sunscreen and sturdy footwear. The island's cafeteria sells food and drinks. Staying overnight on Delos is forbidden.

Numerous boat companies offer trips from Mykonos to Delos (€18 return, 30 minutes) between 9am and 1pm. The return boats leave Delos between noon and 3pm. There is also a €5 per person entry fee on arrival at Delos.

Katerina's　　　　　　GREEK €€
(Agion Anargyron; mains €11-25) Long a legendary bar in Little Venice with breath-taking views out over the water, Katerina's has added an excellent restaurant offering up Greek dishes. The seafood is superb.

🍷 Drinking & Entertainment

The waterfront is perfect for sitting with a drink and watching an interesting array of passers-by, while Little Venice has bars with dreamy views and water lapping below your feet.

Long feted as a gay travel destination, there are many gay-centric clubs and hangouts. The waterfront area, between the Old Harbour and the Church of Paraportiani, is popular for late night gay interaction.

Cavo Paradiso　　　　　　CLUB
(☑22890 27205; www.cavoparadiso.gr) For those who want to go the whole hog, this place 300m above Paradise Beach picks up around 2am and boasts a pool the shape of Mykonos. A bus transports clubbers from town in summer.

ℹ Information

Mykonos Accommodation Centre (☑22890 23408; www.mykonos-accommodation.com; Enoplon Dynameon 10) This helpful place can do it all, from arranging hotels to tours.

Hoteliers Association of Mykonos (☑22890 24540; www.mha.gr; ⊙9.30am-4pm Apr-Oct) At the old port; can book accommodation. They also have a desk at the airport.

Island Mykonos Travel (☑22890 22232; www.discovergreece.org) On Plateia Taxi, where the port road meets the town; helpful for travel information, hotels, transfers and tickets.

ℹ Getting There & Around

Mykonos Town has two ferry quays. The old quay, where the smaller ferries and catamarans dock, is 400m north of the town waterfront. The new quay, where the bigger boats dock, is 2.5km north of town. Buses meet arriving ferries. When leaving Mykonos, double-check which quay your boat leaves from.

Air

There are daily flights connecting Mykonos airport (JMK) to Athens, plus a growing number of international flights winging in directly from May to September. Don't just assume you'll have to fly through Athens to get to Mykonos. The airport is 3km southeast of the town centre; €1.60 by bus from the southern bus station.

Boat

Daily ferries (€32, five hours) and catamarans (€50, three hours) arrive from Piraeus. From Mykonos, there are daily ferries and hydrofoils to most major Cycladic islands, daily services to Crete, and less-frequent services to the northeastern Aegean Islands and the Dodecanese.

Bus

The northern bus station is near the old port. It serves Agios Stefanos, Elia, Kalafatis and Ano Mera. The southern bus station, a 300m walk up from the windmills, serves the airport, Agios Ioannis, Psarou, Platys Gialos and Paradise Beach.

Local Boats

In summer, *caiques* (small fishing boats) from Mykonos Town and Platys Gialos putter to Paradise, Super Paradise, Agrari and Elia beaches.

Paros   Πάρος
POP 13,000

Paros is an attractive, laid-back island with an enticing main town, good swimming beaches and terraced hills that build up to Mt Profitis Ilias (770m). It has long been prosperous, thanks to an abundance of pure white marble (from which the *Venus de Milo* and Napoleon's tomb were sculpted).

Paros' main town and port is **Parikia**, on the west coast. Opposite the ferry terminal, on the far side of Windmill roundabout, is Plateia Mavrogenous, the main square. Agora, also known as Market St, the main commercial thoroughfare, runs southwest from the far end of the square.

◉ Sights

Panagia Ekatondapyliani   CHURCH
(Parikia; ◉7.30am-9.30pm) Dating from AD 326 and known for its beautiful ornate interior, this is one of the most impressive churches in the Cyclades. Within the church compound, the **Byzantine Museum** (admission €1.50; ◉9.30am-2pm & 6-9pm) has an interesting collection of icons and artefacts.

🏃 Activities

A great option on Paros is to rent a scooter or car at one of the many outlets in Parikia and cruise around the island. There are sealed

Paros & Antiparos

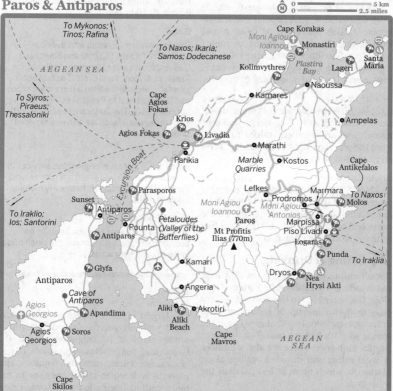

roads the whole way, and the opportunity to explore villages such as **Naoussa**, **Marpissa** and **Aliki**, and swim at beaches such as **Logaras**, **Punda** and **Golden Beach**. Naoussa is a cute little fishing village on the northeastern coast that is all geared up to welcome tourists.

Less than 2km from Paros, the small island of **Antiparos** has fantastic beaches, which have made it wildly popular. Another attraction is its **Cave of Antiparos** (admission €3.60; �10.45am-3.45pm summer), considered to be one of Europe's best.

🛏 Sleeping

TOP CHOICE Pension Sofia
PENSION €€

(☎22840 22085; www.sofiapension-paros.com; Parikia; d/tr €75/90; P❋@�) If you don't mind a stroll to town, this place, with a beautifully tended garden and immaculate rooms, is a great option that won't be regretted. It's run with pride and passion.

Rooms Mike
PENSION €

(☎22840 22856; www.roomsmike.com; Parikia; s/d/tr €25/40/60; ❋�) A popular and friendly place, Mike's offers a good location and local advice. There are options of rooms with shared facilities through to fully self-contained units with kitchens. Mike's sign is easy to spot from the quay, away to the left.

Rooms Rena
PENSION €

(☎22840 22220; www.cycladesnet.gr/rena; Parikia; s/d/tr €35/45/55; ❋�) The quiet, well-kept rooms here are excellent value. Turn left from the pier then right at the ancient cemetery and follow the signs.

Koula Camping
CAMPGROUND €

(☎22840 22801; www.campingkoula.gr; campsites per tent/person €4/8; ☻Apr-Oct; P�) A pleasant shaded spot behind the beach at the north end of the waterfront. They have free transfers to and from the port.

🍴 Eating & Drinking

Budget eating spots are easy to find near the Windmill roundabout in Parikia. Head along the waterfront to the west of the ferry quay to find a line-up of restaurants and drinking establishments that gaze out at the setting sun. It's hard to beat **Pebbles Jazz Bar** for ambience. There are also a number of good eating and drinking options along Market St, which more or less parallels the waterfront.

Happy Green Cows
VEGETARIAN €€

(dishes €12-18; ☻dinner; 🖉) Cheerful service goes with the quirky name of this little eatery, a vegetarian's delight at the back of the main square. It's a touch pricey, but worth it for the often saucily named dishes.

Levantis
GREEK €€

(Kastro; dishes €11-19) A courtyard garden setting enhances the experience at this long-established restaurant at the heart of Kastro that serves excellent house wine.

❶ Information

There is no tourist office. See www.parosweb.com for information.

Santorineos Travel (☎22840 24245; www.traveltoparos.gr) On the waterfront near the Windmill roundabout; good for ticketing, information and luggage storage.

❶ Getting There & Around

Air

Paros' airport (PAS) has daily flight connections with Athens. The airport is 8km south of Parikia; €1.50 by bus.

Boat

Parikia is a major ferry hub with daily connections to Piraeus (€32.50, five hours) and frequent ferries and catamarans to Naxos, Ios, Santorini, Mykonos and Crete. The fast boats generally take half the time but are more expensive (eg a fast boat to Piraeus takes 2½ hours but costs €40). The Dodecanese and the northeastern Aegean Islands are also well serviced from here.

Bus

From Parikia there are frequent bus services to the entire island. A free green bus runs around Parikia at regular intervals from early morning to late at night.

Local Boats

In summer there are excursion boats to Antiparos from Parikia port, or you can catch a bus to Pounta and ferry across.

Naxos
Νάξος

POP 12,000

The largest of the Cyclades islands, Naxos could probably survive without tourism – unlike many of its neighbouring islands. Green and fertile, Naxos produces olives, grapes, figs, citrus, corn and potatoes. The island is well worth taking the time to explore, with its fascinating main town, excel-

Naxos

lent beaches, remote villages and striking interior.

Naxos Town, on the west coast, is the island's capital and port. The ferry quay is at the northern end of the waterfront, with the bus terminal out front. The island of Paros seems surprisingly close, directly to the west.

Sights & Activities

Kastro CASTLE
Behind the waterfront in Naxos Town, narrow alleyways scramble up to the spectacular hilltop 13th-century *kastro,* where the Venetian Catholics lived. The *kastro* looks out over the town, and has a well-stocked **archaeological museum** (admission €3; ◷8.30am-3pm Tue-Sun).

Temple of Apollo ARCHAEOLOGICAL SITE
From the ferry quay it's a short stroll to the unfinished Temple of Apollo, Naxos' most fa-

mous landmark. Though there's not much to see other than two columns with a crowning lintel, people gather at sunset for views back to the whitewashed houses of town.

Beaches
The popular beach of **Agios Georgios** is just a 10-minute walk south from the main waterfront. Beyond it, wonderful sandy beaches stretch as far south as **Pyrgaki Beach**. **Agia Anna Beach**, 6km from town, and **Plaka Beach** are lined with accommodation and packed in summer.

Villages
A hire car or scooter will help reveal Naxos' dramatic and rugged landscape. The **Tragaea** region has tranquil villages, churches atop rocky crags and huge olive groves. **Filoti**, the largest inland settlement, perches on the slopes of **Mt Zeus** (1004m), the highest peak in the Cyclades. The historic village of

KITRON-TASTING IN HALKI

The historic village of Halki, which lies at the heart of the Tragaea region, is a top spot to try *kitron*, a liqueur unique to Naxos. Usually consumed cold after meals, *kitron* is made from the fruit of the citron (*Citrus medica*). The fruit may be barely edible in its raw state, but when it and its leaves are boiled with pure alcohol, the result is a tasty concoction that has been keeping Naxians happy since the 1870s. While the exact recipe is top secret, visitors can taste it and stock up on supplies at the **Vallindras Distillery** (☎22850 31220; ◷10am-11pm Jul-Aug, 10am-6pm May-Jun & Sep-Oct) in Halki's main square. There is a **Kitron Museum** (admission free), complimentary tastings, and a shop selling the distillery's products.

Halki, one-time centre of Naxian commerce, is well worth a visit.

Apollonas is a lovely spot near Naxos' northern tip. There's a **beach**, excellent taverna, and the mysterious 10.5m **kouros** (naked male statue), constructed in the 7th century BC, lying abandoned and unfinished in an ancient marble quarry.

🛏 Sleeping

TOP CHOICE Pension Sofi PENSION €
(☎22850 23077; www.pensionsofi.gr; r €30-90; ◷year-round; ❄❸) Run by members of the Koufopoulos family, Pension Sofi is in Naxos Town, while their **Studios Panos** (☎22850 26078; www.studiospanos.com; Agios Georgios Beach; r €30-75; ❄❸) is a 10-minute walk away near Agios Georgios Beach. Guests are met with family-made wine, and immaculate rooms come with bathroom and kitchen. Rates at both places halve out of the high season. Call ahead for pick-up at the port.

Hotel Grotta HOTEL €€
(☎22850 22215; www.hotelgrotta.gr; s/d incl breakfast €70/85; ℗❄@❸⛵) Overlooking Grotta Beach at the northern end of town, this modern hotel has comfortable and immaculate rooms, a Jacuzzi and minipool, and offers great sea views.

Camping Maragas CAMPGROUND €
(☎22850 42552; www.maragascamping.gr; campsites €9, d €45, studio €70) On Agia Anna Beach to the south of town, this place has all sorts of options, including camping, rooms and studios, and there is a restaurant and minimarket on-site.

🍴 Eating & Drinking

Naxos Town's waterfront is lined with eating and drinking establishments. Head into Market St in the Old Town, just down from the ferry quay, to find quality tavernas. South of the waterfront, but only a few minutes' walk away, Plateia Main is home to plenty of excellent eateries.

TOP CHOICE Picasso MEXICAN €
(www.picassoismexican.com; Agiou Arseniou; dishes €6-18; ◷all day Jun-Sep, dinner only Oct-May) Definitely the best Mexican fare in Greece (and possibly in Europe!). Just off Plateia Main, Picasso boasts that it serves 'extraordinary Mexican food' and it does. It also offers up exquisite frozen margaritas.

Metaximas TAVERNA €
(Market St; dishes €8-20) Tucked away in the little maze that is Market St, Metaximas serves Naxian seafood at its best. Try the grilled octopus.

ℹ Information

There's no official tourist information office. Try www.naxos-greece.net for more information.
Zas Travel (☎22850 23330; www.zastravel.com) Good for boat and air tickets, car rental, internet and luggage storage.

ℹ Getting There & Around

AIR Naxos airport (JNX) has daily flight connections with Athens. The airport is 3km south of town; no buses – a taxi costs €15.

BOAT There are daily ferries (€31, five hours) and catamarans (€48, 3¾ hours) from Naxos to Piraeus, and good ferry and hydrofoil connections to most Cycladic islands and Crete.

BUS Buses travel to most villages regularly from the bus terminal in front of the port.

CAR & MOTORCYCLE Having your own wheels is a good option on Naxos. Car and motorcycle rentals are readily available in Naxos Town.

Ios

Ιος

POP 1900

Ios has long held a reputation as 'Party Island'. There are wall-to-wall bars and nightclubs in 'the village' that thump all night, and fantastic fun facilities at Milopotas Beach that entertain all day. You won't leave disappointed if you're there to party.

But there's more to Ios than just hedonistic activities. British poet and novelist Lawrence Durrell thought highly of Ios as a place of poetry and beauty, and there is an enduring claim that Homer was buried here, with his alleged tomb in the north of the island.

Ios' three population centres are close together on the west coast. Ormos is the port, where ferries arrive. Two kilometres inland and up overlooking the port is 'the village', Hora, while 2km down from Hora to the southeast is Milopotas Beach.

◉ Sights & Activities

The village has an intrinsic charm with its labyrinth of white-walled streets, and it's very easy to get lost, even if you haven't had one too many. Milopotas has everything a resort beach could ask for and parties hard. A rental car or scooter is a good option for exploring Ios.

Skarkos
ARCHAEOLOGICAL SITE

('The Snail'; ⊙8.30am-3pm Tue-Sun) An award-winning archaeological triumph for Ios! This Bronze Age settlement crowns a low hill in the plain just to the north of Hora, and its excavations have been opened to the public. There are interpretation boards in Greek and English.

Manganari Beach
BEACH

This isolated beach on the south coast is reached by rental vehicle, or by excursion boat or bus in summer. It's a beautiful spot

Ios

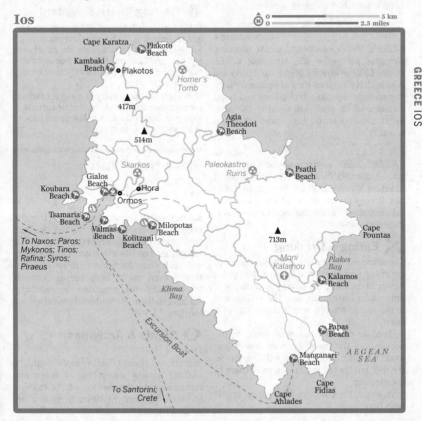

GREECE IOS

and the drive on Ios' newest sealed road is an experience in itself.

Homer's Tomb
TOMB

You'll need your own wheels to get here, 12km north of Hora.

Meltemi Water Sports
WATER SPORTS

(☎22860 91680; www.meltemiwatersports.com) This outfit at Milopotas Beach's far end has everything a beach could possibly provide, including rental windsurfers, sailboats and canoes.

🛏 Sleeping

TOP CHOICE Francesco's
HOSTEL €

(☎22860 91223; www.francescos.net; s €40-45, d €50-60 ; ❄@🛜🏊) A lively meeting place in the village with superlative views from its terrace bar, legendary Francesco's is convenient for party-going, and rates halve out of high season. The party spirit rules here. Long established and very well run.

Far Out Camping & Beach Club
CAMPGROUND €

(☎22860 91468; www.faroutclub.com; Milopotas; campsites per person €12, bungalows €15-22, studios €100; P@🛜🏊) Right on Milopotas Beach, this place has tons of options. Facilities include camping, bungalows and hotel rooms, and its pools are open to the public. It also has rental cars, quad bikes and scooters.

Hotel Nissos Ios
HOTEL €€

(☎22860 91610; www.nissosios-hotel.com; Milopotas; s/d/tr €60/75/90; ❄@🛜) This cheerful place on Milopotas Beach is great for families. Rooms feature huge colourful wall murals, and the excellent Bamboo Restaurant & Pizzeria is on-site.

🍴 Eating & Drinking

There are numerous places in the village to get cheap eats like gyros. Down at Milopotas Beach, there's a great bakery and stacks of options for during the day. The restaurants in the village are of a very high standard for later.

Another option is to head down to the port, where the tavernas serve superb seafood. The port may be filled with visitors in the day, but it's the locals who head there in the evening.

At night, the compact little village erupts with bars.

Ali Baba's
THAI €

(Hora; dishes €7-12) This great Ios favourite is the place for tasty Thai dishes. The service is very upbeat and there's a garden courtyard. It's on the same street as the Emporiki bank.

Pithari
GREEK €

(Hora; mains from €10) Behind the cathedral at the entrance to the Hora, Pithari offers an excellent array of tasty dishes; the seafood spaghetti is especially good.

Blue Note
BAR

(Hora) A perennial village favourite, where happy hour continues all night long!

ℹ Information

There's no tourist office. See www.iosgreece.com for more information.

Acteon Travel (☎22860 91343; www.acteon.gr) Has offices in Ormos, the village and Milopotas and is extremely helpful.

ℹ Getting There & Around

BOAT Ios has daily ferry (€32.50, seven hours) and catamaran (€55, 3½ hours) connections with Piraeus. Being strategically placed between Mykonos and Santorini, there are frequent catamarans and ferries to the major Cycladic islands and Crete.

BUS There are buses every 15 minutes between the port, the village and Milopotas Beach until early morning. Buses head to Manganari Beach in summer (€3.50 each way).

Santorini (Thira)
Σαντορίνη (Θήρα)

POP 13,500

Stunning Santorini is unique and should not be missed. The startling sight of the submerged caldera almost encircled by sheer lava-layered cliffs – topped off by clifftop towns that look like a dusting of icing sugar – will grab your attention and not let it go. If you turn up in high season, though, be prepared for relentless crowds and commercialism – Santorini survives on tourism.

👁 Sights & Activities

Fira

Santorini's vibrant main town with its snaking narrow streets full of shops and restaurants perches on top of the caldera; the stunning caldera views from Fira are unparalleled.

Santorini (Thira)

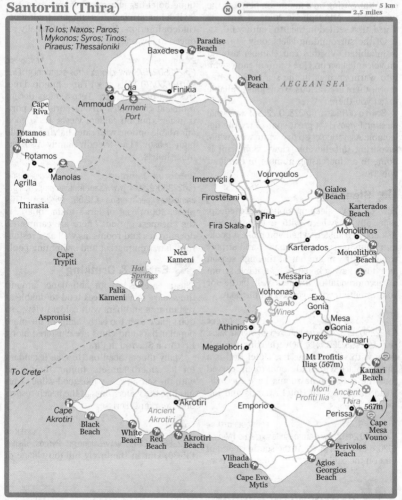

0 ____ 5 km
0 ____ 2.5 miles

MUSEUMS

The exceptional **Museum of Prehistoric Thira** (admission €3; ⊗8.30am-8pm Tue-Sun), which has wonderful displays of artefacts predominantly from ancient Akrotiri, is two blocks south of the main square. **Megaron Gyzi Museum** (admission €3.50; ⊗10.30am-1.30pm & 5-8pm Mon-Sat, 10.30am-4.30pm Sun), behind the Catholic cathedral, houses local memorabilia, including photographs of Fira before and after the 1956 earthquake.

Around the Island

At the north of the island, the intriguing village of **Oia** (ee-ah), famed for its postcard sunsets, is less hectic than Fira and a must-visit. Its caldera-facing tavernas are superb spots for brunch. There's a path from Fira to Oia along the top of the caldera that takes three to four hours to walk; otherwise take a taxi or bus.

Excavations in 1967 uncovered the remarkably well-preserved Minoan settlement of **Akrotiri** at the south of the island, with its remains of two- and three-storey buildings. Akrotiri has recently reopened to the public after a seven-year hiatus.

Santorini's black-sand **beaches** of **Perissa** and **Kamari** sizzle – beach mats are essential. Sitting on a mountain between the two are the atmospheric ruins of **Ancient Thira**, first settled in the 9th century BC.

Of the surrounding islets, only **Thirasia** is inhabited. Visitors can clamber around on volcanic lava on **Nea Kameni** then swim into warm springs in the sea at **Palia Kameni**; there are various excursions available to get you there.

Santo Wines (☎22860 22596; www.santowines.gr; Pyrgos) is a great spot to try the delectable Assyrtico crisp dry white wine while savouring unbelievable views. Santorini is home to an increasing number of excellent wineries.

🛏 Sleeping

Few of Fira's sleeping options are cheap, especially anywhere with a caldera view. Ask about transfers when you make a booking; many places offer free port and airport transfers. If you are out of the high season and don't have a booking, a veritable scrum of accommodation owners will battle for your attention when you get off the boat.

TOP CHOICE Hotel Keti HOTEL €€
(☎22860 22324; www.hotelketi.gr; Agiou Mina, Fira; d/tr €95/120; ❉☎) Overlooking the caldera, with views to die for, Hotel Keti is a smaller place with traditional rooms carved into the cliffs. Some rooms have Jacuzzis. Head down next to Hotel Atlantis and follow the signs.

Aroma Suites BOUTIQUE HOTEL €€
(☎22860 24112; www.aromasuites.gr; Agiou Mina; s €120, d €140-160; ❉☎) At the southern end of Fira on the caldera edge, this delightful boutique hotel has charming owners to match. Stylish modern facilities enhance traditional caldera interiors. Rates are substantially reduced in low season.

Pension Petros PENSION €€
(☎22860 22573; www.hotelpetros-santorini.gr; Fira; s/d/tr €60/70/85; ❉☎☎) Three hundred metres east of the square, Petros offers decent rooms at good rates, free airport- and port-transfers, but no caldera views. It's a good affordable option, with rates halving outside high season. The friendly family also has other hotels.

Santorini Camping CAMPGROUND €
(☎22860 22944; www.santorinicamping.gr; Fira; campsites per person €12.50; ℗@☎) This place, 500m east of Fira's main square, is the cheapest option. There are campsites, dormitories and rooms, as well as a restaurant, bar, minimarket and swimming pool.

🍴 Eating & Drinking

Cheap eateries are in abundance around the square in Fira. Prices tend to double at restaurants and bars with caldera views, so don't glaze over too early. Many of the more popular bars and clubs are clustered along Erythrou Stavrou in Fira.

Many diners head out to Oia, legendary for its superb sunsets, timing their meal with the setting sun, while good-value tavernas line the waterfronts at the beach resorts of Kamari and Perissa.

TOP CHOICE Selene GREEK €€
(☎22860 22249; www.selene.gr; Pyrgos; dishes €15-30) Out in the lovely hill-top village of

---

ℹ SANTORINI ON A BUDGET

Spectacular Santorini will take your breath away, and if you're on a tight budget, its prices might too. Expect to pay through the nose for caldera views at accommodation and eating establishments in and around Fira.

A budget alternative with the added bonus of a stunning black-sand beach is to head out to Perissa, on the southeast coast, and stay at **Stelios Place** (☎22860 81860; www.steliosplace.com; r €30-120; ℗❉☎☎). Stelios is an excellent option one block back from the beach. There's a refreshing pool, very friendly service and free port- and airport-transfers. Rates halve out of high season.

All of your needs will be catered for in Perissa, which has bars and restaurants lining the waterfront. **Taverna Lava** (☎22860 81776), at the southern end of the waterfront, is an island-wide favourite that features a mouth-watering menu. Or just head back into the kitchen, see what Yiannis has conjured up for the day's meals and pick whatever looks good.

Public buses run regularly into Fira.

Pyrgos, Selene is in the heart of Santorinian farming and culinary culture, and specialises in creative cuisine based on Cycladic produce and unique local ingredients, such as small tomatoes and fava beans. The wine cellar houses some of Santorini's best.

Fanari GREEK €
(☏22860 25107; www.fanari-restaurant.gr; Fira; dishes €7-20) On the street leading down to the old port, Fanari serves up both tasty traditional dishes and superlative views.

❶ Information

There is no tourist office. Try www.santorini.net for more information.

Dakoutros Travel (☏22860 22958; www. dakoutrostravel.gr; ⊗8.30am-10pm) Just down from the square and opposite the taxi station in Fira; extremely helpful and good for ticketing.

❶ Getting There & Around

The bus station and taxi station are just south of Fira's main square, Plateia Theotokopoulou. The new port of Athinios, where most ferries dock, is 10km south of Fira by road. The old port of Fira Skala, used by cruise ships and excursion boats, is directly below Fira and accessed by cable car (adult/child €4/2 one way), donkey (€5, up only) or by foot (588 steps).

Air

Santorini airport (JTR) has daily flight connections with Athens, plus a growing number of domestic destinations and direct international flights from all over Europe. The airport is 5km southeast of Fira; frequent buses (€1.50) and taxis (€12).

Boat

There are daily ferries (€33.50, nine hours) and fast boats (€60, 5¼ hours) to Piraeus; daily connections in summer to Mykonos, Ios, Naxos, Paros and Iraklio; and ferries to the smaller islands in the Cyclades. Large ferries use Athinios port, where they are met by buses and taxis.

Bus

Buses go frequently to Oia, Kamari, Perissa and Akrotiri from Fira. Port buses usually leave Fira, Kamari and Perissa one to 1½ hours before ferry departures.

Car & Motorcycle

A car or scooter is a great option on Santorini. There are plenty of places to rent them (from €30 per day).

CRETE KPHTH

POP 550,000

Crete is Greece's largest and most southerly island and its size and distance from the rest of Greece give it the feel of a different country. With its dramatic landscape and unique cultural identity, Crete is a delight to explore.

The island is split by a spectacular chain of mountains running east to west. Major towns are on the more hospitable northern coast, while most of the southern coast is too precipitous to support large settlements. The rugged mountainous interior, dotted with caves and sliced by dramatic gorges, offers rigorous hiking and climbing.

While Crete's proud, friendly and hospitable people have enthusiastically embraced tourism, they continue to fiercely protect their traditions and culture – and it is the people that remain a major part of the island's appeal.

For more detailed information, snap up a copy of Lonely Planet's *Crete*. Good websites on Crete include www.interkriti.org and www.explorecrete.com.

History

Crete was the birthplace of Minoan culture, Europe's first advanced civilisation, which flourished between 2800 and 1450 BC. Very little is known of Minoan civilisation, which came to an abrupt end, possibly destroyed by Santorini's volcanic eruption in around 1650 BC. Later, Crete passed from the warlike Dorians to the Romans, and then to the Genoese, who in turn sold it to the Venetians. Under the Venetians, Crete became a refuge for artists, writers and philosophers, who fled after it fell to the Turks. Their influence inspired the young Cretan painter Domenikos Theotokopoulos, who moved to Spain and there won immortality as the great El Greco.

The Turks conquered Crete in 1670. In 1898 Crete became a British protectorate after a series of insurrections and was united with independent Greece in 1913. There was fierce fighting during WWII when a German airborne invasion defeated Allied forces in the 10-day Battle of Crete. A fierce resistance movement drew heavy German reprisals, including the slaughter of whole villages.

Crete

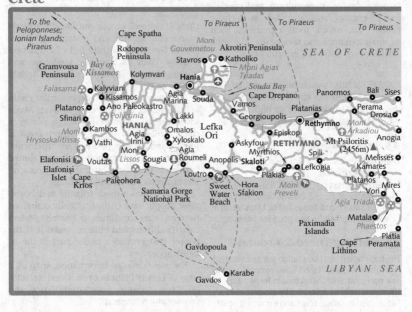

Iraklio   Ηράκλειο

POP 138,000

Iraklio (ee-*rah*-klee-oh; often spelt Heraklion), Crete's capital and economic hub, is a bustling modern city and the fifth-largest in Greece. It has a lively city centre, an excellent archaeological museum and is close to Knossos, Crete's major visitor attraction.

Iraklio's harbours face north into the Sea of Crete. The old harbour is instantly recognisable, as it is protected by the old Venetian fortress. The new harbour is 400m east. Plateia Venizelou, known for its Lion Fountain, is the heart of the city, 400m south of the old harbour up 25 Avgoustou.

◉ Sights & Activities

Archaeological Museum   MUSEUM

(www.odysseus.culture.gr; Xanthoudidou 2; adult/student €4/2; ⊗8.30am-3pm Nov-Mar) The outstanding Minoan collection here is second only to that of the national museum in Athens. The museum was under long-term reconstruction at the time of research, but its key exhibits are beautifully displayed in an annex.

Koules Venetian Fortress   FORTRESS

(admission €2; ⊗8.30am-7pm Tue-Sun May-Oct, to 3pm Nov-Apr) Protecting the old harbour, this impressive fortress is also known as Rocca al Mare, which, like the city walls, was built by the Venetians in the 16th century. It stopped the Turks for 21 years and later became a Turkish prison for Cretan rebels.

City Walls   FORTRESS

Iraklio burst out of its city walls long ago, but these massive Venetian fortifications, with seven bastions and four gates, are still very conspicuous, dwarfing the concrete structures of the 20th century.

Morosini Fountain   FOUNTAIN

(Plateia Venizelou) Iraklio's much loved 'lion fountain', built in 1628 by the Venetians, spurts water from four lions into eight ornate U-shaped marble troughs.

🏕 Cretan Adventures   OUTDOORS

(☑28103 32772; www.cretanadventures.gr; Evans 10, 3rd fl) Cretan Adventures is a well-regarded local company run by Fondas Spinthaikos that can organise hiking tours, mountain biking, and other specialist and extreme activities.

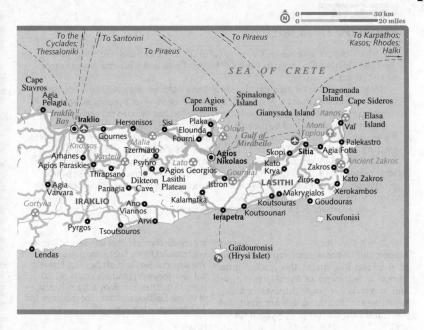

🛏 Sleeping

Lato Hotel ⌂TOP CHOICE   BOUTIQUE HOTEL €€
(☑28102 28103; www.lato.gr; Epimenidou 15; d incl breakfast €90-120; P❄@⑤) This stylish boutique hotel overlooking the waterfront is a top place to stay. Ask for a room with harbour views. The contemporary interior design extends to the bar, breakfast restaurant and **Brillant** (☑28102 28103; www.brillantrestaurant.gr; mains €10-25), the superb fine-dining restaurant on the ground floor. From May to October, the restaurant renames itself **Herb's Garden** and moves to the hotel rooftop for alfresco dining with harbour views.

Kronos Hotel   HOTEL €
(☑28102 82240; www.kronoshotel.gr; Sofokli Venizelou 2; s/d €44/50; ❄@⑤) After a thorough makeover, this waterfront hotel has polevaulted to the top of the budget hotel category. The comfortable rooms have double-glazed windows and balconies. Ask for one of the rooms with sea views.

Hotel Mirabello   HOTEL €
(☑28102 85052; www.mirabello-hotel.gr; Theotokopoulou 20; s/d €42/48; ❄@⑤) A pleasant, relaxed budget hotel on a quiet street in the centre of town, this place is run by an ex-sea captain who has travelled the world. A good-value option.

🍴 Eating & Drinking

There's a congregation of cheap eateries, bars and cafes in the Plateia Venizelou (Morosini Fountain) and El Greco Park area. The places around the park are packed at night. Head down towards the old harbour for plenty of seafood options.

DON'T MISS

MARKET ON 1866

Heading inland from Lion Fountain, cross the main street diagonally to the left and you'll be on Odos 1866 (1866 St). This bustling, colourful market street, perfect for people-watching, has everything on offer from fruit and vegetables to honey, herbs and succulent olives. Crete is known for its leather goods and this is a good spot to purchase them.

DON'T MISS

KNOSSOS ΚΝΩΣΣΟΣ

Five kilometres south of Iraklio, **Knossos** ([image]28102 31940; admission €6; [image]8am-7pm Jun-Oct, to 3pm Nov-May) was the capital of Minoan Crete, and is now the island's major tourist attraction.

Knossos (k-nos-os) is the most famous of Crete's Minoan sites and is the inspiration for the myth of the Minotaur. According to legend, King Minos of Knossos was given a magnificent white bull to sacrifice to the god Poseidon, but decided to keep it. This enraged Poseidon, who punished the king by causing his wife Pasiphae to fall in love with the animal. The result of this odd union was the Minotaur – half-man and half-bull – who lived in a labyrinth beneath the king's palace, munching on youths and maidens.

In 1900 Arthur Evans uncovered the ruins of Knossos. Although archaeologists tend to disparage Evans' reconstruction, the buildings – incorporating an immense palace, courtyards, private apartments, baths, lively frescos and more – give a fine idea of what a Minoan palace might have looked like.

Buses to Knossos (€1.50, 20 minutes, three per hour) leave from Bus Station A.

Giakoumis Taverna TAVERNA €

Among the tavernas clustered around the 1866 market side streets, this is a favourite. There's a full menu of Cretan specialities and vegetarian options. Turnover is heavy, which means that the dishes are fresh, and you can see the meat being prepared for the grill.

Ippokambos Ouzerie SEAFOOD €

Many locals come to this classic Iraklio haunt at the edge of the tourist-driven waterfront dining strip. Take a peek inside at the fresh trays and pots of *mayirefta* (ready-cooked meals) such as baked cuttlefish, and dine at one of the sidewalk tables or on the promenade across the road.

Veneto CAFE

([image]28102 23686; Epimenidou 9) This cafe has the best view of the harbour and fortress from its lovely terrace. It's in an historic building near Lato Hotel.

ℹ Information

Visit www.heraklion.gr for more information about the city.

Tourist Office ([image]28102 46299; Xanthoudidou 1; [image]8.30am-8.30pm Apr-Oct, to 3pm Nov-Mar)
Skoutelis Travel ([image]28102 80808; www.skoutelis rentacar.gr; 25 Avgoustou 20) Between Lion Fountain and the old harbour, handles airline and ferry bookings, runs tours and rents cars.

ℹ Getting There & Around

Air

Flights depart daily from Iraklio's Nikos Kazantzakis airport (HER) for Athens and there are regular flights to Thessaloniki and Rhodes. International flights buzz in from all over Europe. The airport is 5km east of town. Bus 1 travels between the airport and city centre (€1.20) every 15 minutes from 6am to 11pm. It stops at Plateia Eleftherias, across the road from the Archaeological Museum.

Boat

Daily ferries service Piraeus (€37, seven hours), and catamarans head daily to Santorini and continue on to other Cycladic islands. Ferries sail east to Rhodes (€28, 12 hours) via Agios Nikolaos, Sitia, Kasos, Karpathos and Halki.

Bus

KTEL (Koino Tamio Eispraxeon Leoforion; http://www.bus-service-crete-ktel.com/) runs the buses on Crete and has useful tourist information inside Bus Station A.

Iraklio has two bus stations. The main **Bus Station A** is just inland from the new harbour and serves eastern Crete (Agios Nikolaos, Ierapetra, Sitia, Malia and the Lasithi Plateau), as well as Hania and Rethymno. **Bus Station B**, 50m beyond the Hania Gate, serves the southern route (Phaestos, Matala and Anogia).

Phaestos & Other Minoan Sites Φαιστός

Phaestos ([image]29820 42315; admission €6; [image]8am-7pm May-Oct, to 5pm Nov-Apr), 63km southwest of Iraklio, is Crete's second-most important Minoan site. While not as impressive as Knossos, Phaestos (fes-*tos*) is still worth a visit for its stunning views of the surrounding Mesara plain and Mt Psiloritis (2456m; also known as Mt Ida). The layout is similar to Knossos, with rooms arranged around a central courtyard. Eight buses a day head to Phaestos from Iraklio's Bus Station B (€6.30, 1½ hours).

Other important Minoan sites can be found at Malia, 34km east of Iraklio, where there's a palace complex and adjoining town, and Zakros, 40km southeast of Sitia, the last Minoan palace to have been discovered, in 1962.

Rethymno   Ρέθυμνο
POP 28,000

Rethymno (*reth*-im-no) is Crete's third-largest town. It's also one of the island's architectural treasures, due to its stunning fortress and mix of Venetian and Turkish houses in the old quarter. Most spots of interest are within a small area around the old Venetian harbour.

The old quarter is on a peninsula that juts out into the Sea of Crete; the fortress sits at its head, while the Venetian harbour, ferry quay and beach are on its eastern side. El Venizelou is the main strip along the waterfront and beach.

Rethymno's 16th-century Venetian fortezza (Fortress; Paleokastro Hill; admission €4; ☺8am-8pm May-Oct) is the site of the city's ancient acropolis and affords great views across the town and mountains. The main gate is on the eastern side of the fortress, opposite the interesting archaeological museum (☏28310 54668; admission €3; ☺8.30am-3pm Tue-Sun), which was once a prison.

Happy Walker (☏28310 52920; www.happywalker.com; Tombazi 56) runs an excellent program of daily walks in the countryside and also longer walking tours.

Sea Front (☏28310 51981; www.rethymnoatcrete.com; Arkadiou 159; d €40-50; ❋☎) has all sorts of sleeping options and is ideally positioned with beach views and spacious rooms. Hotel Fortezza (☏28310 55551; www.fortezza.gr; Melissinou 16; s/d incl breakfast €75/88; ❑❋☎☀) is more upmarket; with a refreshing pool, it's in a refurbished old building in the heart of the Old Town. Rethymno Youth Hostel (☏28310 22848; www.yhrethymno.com; Tombazi 41; dm €11; ☎) is a well-run place with crowded dorms, free hot showers and no curfew.

The municipal tourist office (☏28310 29148; www.rethymno.gr; Eleftheriou Venizelou; ☺9am-8.30pm), on the beach side of El Ven-izelou, is convenient and helpful. Ellotia Tours (☏28310 24533; www.rethymnoatcrete.com; Arkadiou 155) will answer all transport, accommodation and tour enquiries.

There are regular ferries between Piraeus and Rethymno (€30, nine hours), and a high-speed service in summer. Buses depart regularly to Iraklio (€7.60, 1½ hours) and Hania (€6.20, one hour).

Hania   Χανιά
POP 54,000

Crete's most romantic, evocative and alluring town, Hania (hahn-*yah*; often spelt Chania) is the former capital and the island's second-largest city. There is a rich mosaic of Venetian and Ottoman architecture, particularly in the area of the old harbour, which lures tourists in droves. Modern Hania retains the exoticism of a city caught between East and West, and is an excellent base for exploring nearby idyllic beaches and a spectacular mountainous interior.

◉ Sights & Activities

Old Harbour   HISTORIC SITE
From Plateia 1866 in the middle of town, the old harbour is a short walk down Halidon. A stroll around here is a must for any visitor to Hania. It is worth the 1.5km walk around the sea wall to get to the Venetian lighthouse at the entrance to the harbour.

Venetian Fortifications   FORTRESS
Part of a defensive system built by the Venetians from 1538, Hania's massive fortifications remain impressive. Best preserved is the western wall, running from the Firkas Fortress at the western entrance to the Old Harbour.

Archaeological Museum   MUSEUM
(Halidon 30; admission €2; ☺8.30am-3pm Tue-Sun) The museum is housed in a 16th-century Venetian church that the Turks made into a mosque. The building, 200m up Halidon from the Old Harbour, became a movie theatre in 1913 and then was a munitions depot for the Germans during WWII.

Food Market   MARKET
Hania's covered food market, in a massive cross-shaped building 400m southeast of the Old Harbour, is definitely worth an inspection.

🛌 Sleeping

TOP CHOICE **Pension Lena** PENSION €

(☎28210 86860; www.lenachania.gr; Ritsou 5; s/d €35/55; ❋☎) For some real character in where you stay, Lena's pension (in an old Turkish building near the mouth of the old harbour) is the place to go. Help yourself to one of the appealing rooms if proprietor Lena isn't there – pick from the available ones on the list on the blackboard.

Amphora Hotel HOTEL €€

(☎28210 93224; www.amphora.gr; Parodos Theotokopoulou 20; s/d €95/120; ❋☎) Most easily found from the waterfront, this is Hania's most historically evocative hotel. Amphora is in an impressively restored Venetian mansion with elegantly decorated rooms around a courtyard. The hotel also runs the **waterfront restaurant**, which ranks as the best along that golden mile.

Vranas Studios APARTMENT €

(☎28210 58618; www.vranas.gr; Agion Deka 10; studio €40-70; ❋☎) This place is on a lively pedestrian street and has spacious, immaculately maintained studios with kitchenettes. All rooms have polished wooden floors, balconies, TVs and telephones.

Camping Hania CAMPGROUND €

(☎28210 31138; www.camping-chania.gr; Agii Apostoli; campsites per tent/person €4/7; ℗❋) Take the Kalamaki Beach bus from the east corner of Plateia 1866 (every 15 minutes) to get to this camping ground, which is 3km west of town on the beach. There is a restaurant, bar and minimarket.

🍴 Eating & Drinking

The entire waterfront of the old harbour is lined with restaurants and tavernas, many of which qualify as tourist traps. Watch out for touts trying to reel you in. There are a number of good options one street back.

TOP CHOICE **Michelas** GREEK €

(☎28210 90026; mains €4-12; ☺10am-4pm Mon-Sat) Serving up authentic Cretan specialities at reasonable prices for 75 years, this family-run place in the Food Market uses only local ingredients and cooks up a great selection each day that you can peruse, then choose from.

Taverna Tamam TAVERNA €€

(☎28210 58639; Zambeliou 49; mains €10-20; ☑) A taverna in an old converted *hammam* (Turkish bathhouse) one street back from the Old Harbour, Tamam has tables that spill out onto the street. This place has tasty soups and a superb selection of vegetarian specialities.

Café Kriti BAR

(Kalergon 22; ☺8pm-late) Near the eastern end of the Venetian harbour, Kriti is known for its down-to-earth atmosphere and live traditional Cretan music.

❶ Information

For more information visit the **Hania website** (www.chania.gr).

Tellus Travel (☎28210 91500; www.tellustravel.gr; Halidon 108; ☺8am-11pm) Has schedules and does ticketing, plus it rents out cars.

Tourist Information Office (☎28210 36155; Kydonias 29; ☺8am-2.30pm) Under the town hall; helpful and provides practical information and maps.

❶ Getting There & Away

Air

There are several flights a day between Hania airport (CHQ) and Athens, plus a number of flights to Thessaloniki each week. An increasing number of international flights are winging directly into Hania from around Europe. The airport is 14km east of town on the Akrotiri Peninsula. Taxis to town cost €20; buses cost €2.30.

Boat

Daily ferries sail between Piraeus (€35, nine hours) and the port of Souda, 9km southeast of Hania. Frequent buses (€1.65) and taxis (€10) connect town and Souda.

Bus

Frequent buses run along Crete's northern coast to Iraklio (€13.80, 2¾ hours, half-hourly) and Rethymno (€6.20, one hour, half hourly); buses run less frequently to Paleohora (€7.60, one hour 50 minutes, four daily), Omalos (€6.90, one hour, three daily) and Hora Sfakion (€7.60, 1½ hours, three daily) from the main bus station.

Hania's bus station is on Kydonias, two blocks southwest of Plateia 1866, one of the city's main squares. Buses for the beaches west of Hania leave from the eastern side of Plateia 1866.

Samaria Gorge
Φαράγγι της Σαμαριάς

The **Samaria Gorge** (☎28250 67179; admission €5; ☺6am-3pm May–mid-Oct) is one of Europe's most spectacular gorges and a superb hike. Walkers should take rugged footwear,

BEAT THE CROWDS AT SAMARIA

The Samaria Gorge walk is extremely popular and can get quite crowded, especially in summer. Most walkers have given the gorge a day and are on a rushed trip from Hania or other northern-coast cities.

If you've got a bit of time on your hands, and decide to do things on your own, there are a couple of excellent options.

One is to take the afternoon bus from Hania and spend the night in the Cretan mountains at 1200m above sea level in Omalos (population 30) at the very pleasant Neos Omalos Hotel (☎28210 67269; www.neos-omalos.gr; s/d €25/35; ✳@). The hotel's restaurant serves excellent Cretan cuisine and local wine by the litre (€6); there's a shuttle to the start of the gorge track the next morning. Keen hikers may want to stay here a couple of nights and tackle Mt Gingilos (2080m; five hours return from Xyloskalo) before hiking the gorge.

Another option is to leave from Hania in the morning, but let the sprinters go and take your time hiking through this stupendous gorge. When you hit the coast at Agia Roumeli (population 125), down a cool beer and take a dip in the refreshing Libyan Sea. There are a number of restaurants and Paralia Taverna & Rooms (☎28250 91408; www.taverna-paralia.com; d €30; ✳☎), right on the waterfront, is a good spot to stay the night. The next day you can take a ferry either west to Sougia or Paleohora, or east to Loutro or Hora Sfakion.

food, drinks and sun protection for this strenuous five- to six-hour trek.

You can do the walk as part of an excursion tour, or independently by taking the Omalos bus from the main bus station in Hania (€6.90, one hour) to the head of the gorge at Xyloskalo (1230m). It's a 16.7km walk (all downhill) to Agia Roumeli on the coast, from where you take a boat to Hora Sfakion (€10, 1¼ hours) and then a bus back to Hania (€7.60, 1½ hours). You are not allowed to spend the night in the gorge, so you need to complete the walk in a day.

Paleohora   Παλαιόχωρα

POP 2200

Paleohora (pal-ee-o-hor-a) has a sleepy end-of-the-line feel about it. Isolated and a bit hard to get to, the village is on a peninsula with a sandy beach to the west and a pebbly beach to the east. On summer evenings the main street is closed to traffic and the tavernas move onto the road. If you're after a relaxing few days, Paleohora is a great spot to chill out.

Heading south from the bus stop, you'll find the main street, which is called Eleftheriou Venizelou.

The ruins of the 13th-century Venetian castle are worth clambering over, although there's not much left after the fortress was destroyed by the Turks, the pirate Barbarossa in the 16th-century and then the Germans during WWII.

Homestay Anonymous (☎28230 41509; www.cityofpaleochora.gr/cp; s/d/tr €23/28/32; ✳) is a great option with its warm service and communal kitchen. Across the road from the sandy beach, the refurbished Poseidon Hotel (☎28230 41374; www.poseidon-paleohora.com; s/d/apt €35/40/50; ✳@) has a mix of tidy double rooms, studios and apartments. Camping Paleohora (☎28230 41120; campsites per tent/person €3/5) is 1.5km northeast of town, near the pebble beach. There's a taverna but no minimarket here.

There are plenty of eating options on the main street. Vegetarians rave about Third Eye (mains from €5; ☎), just inland from the sandy beach.

There's a welcoming tourist office (☎28230 41507; ⊙10am-1pm & 6-9pm Wed-Mon May-Oct) on the pebble beach road near the harbour and ferry quay. The opening hours listed here are indicative only! Back on the main street, Notos Rentals/Tsiskakis Travel (☎28230 42110; www.notoscar.com; ⊙8am-10pm) handles almost everything, including tickets, rental cars/scooters and internet access.

There are four to six buses daily between Hania and Paleohora (€7.60, two hours). In summer, a bus for those hiking Samaria Gorge leaves for Omalos (€5.50, two hours) each morning at 6.15am. It also drops off hikers at the head of the Agia Irini Gorge.

SOUTHWEST COAST VILLAGES

Crete's southern coastline at its western end is dotted with remote, attractive little villages that are brilliant spots to take it easy for a few days.

Heading east from Paleohora are Sougia, Agia Roumeli, Loutro and Hora Sfakion. No road links the coastal resorts, but a daily boat from Paleohora to Sougia (€8.50, one hour), Agia Roumeli (€12.50, 1½ hours), Loutro (€14, 2½ hours) and Hora Sfakion (€16, three hours) connects the villages in summer. The ferry leaves Paleohora at 9.45am and returns along the same route from Hora Sfakion at 1pm. See www.sfakia-crete.com/sfakia-crete/ferries.html for up-to-date information.

If you're a keen hiker, keep in mind that it's also possible to walk right along this southern coast.

Sougia

At the mouth of the Agia Irini gorge, Sougia (soo-yah) is a laid-back and refreshingly undeveloped spot with a wide curve of sand-and-pebble beach. The 14.5km (six hours) walk from Paleohora is popular, as is the Agia Irini gorge walk which ends (or starts!) in Sougia. It's possible to get here by ferry, by car or on foot. Stay at **Santa Irene Hotel** (☎28230 51342; www.santa-irene.gr; d/tr €55/70; ❄☎), a smart beachside complex of apartments and studios that has its own cafe and bar.

Agia Roumeli

At the mouth of the Samaria Gorge, Agia Roumeli bristles with gorge-walkers from mid-afternoon until the ferry comes to take them away. Once they are gone, this pleasant little town goes into quiet mode until the first walkers turn up early afternoon the following day. Take your time to enjoy the village. Right on the waterfront, Paralia Taverna & Rooms (p289) offers everything you need; excellent views, tasty Cretan cuisine, cold beer and simple, clean rooms.

Loutro

This tiny village is a particularly picturesque spot, curled around the only natural harbour on the southern coast of Crete. With no vehicle access, the only way in is by boat or on foot. If you decide to walk, the track from Hora Sfakion comes via the stunning Sweetwater Beach. **Hotel Porto Loutro** (☎28250 91433; www.hotelportoloutro.com; s/d incl breakfast €50/60; ❄@) has tasteful rooms with balconies overlooking the harbour. The village beach, excellent walks, rental kayaks and boat transfers to Sweetwater Beach will help to fill in a peaceful few days. Take a book and chill out.

Hora Sfakion

Renowned in Cretan history for its rebellious streak, Hora Sfakion is an amiable town. WWII history buffs know this as the place where thousands of Allied troops were evacuated by sea after the Battle of Crete. To the visitor with a bit of time, Hora Sfakion offers a row of seafront tavernas serving fresh seafood, some intriguing and eccentric locals, and an opportunity to see 'the real Crete'. Hotel Stavris (☎28250 91220; http://www.hotel-stavris-chora-sfakion.com; s/d/tr €31/36/41; ❄☎) has simple rooms and breakfast outside in its courtyard.

Start or finish your southwest coast villages sojourn in Hora Sfakion. There are four buses daily both to and from Hania (€7.60, two hours).

Lasithi Plateau
Οροπέδιο Λασιθίου

The mountain-fringed Lasithi Plateau in eastern Crete is laid out like an immense patchwork quilt. At 900m above sea level, it is a vast flat expanse of orchards and fields, once dotted with thousands of stone windmills with white canvas sails. There are still plenty of windmills, but most are now of the rusted metal variety and don't work.

There are 20 villages around the periphery of the plain, the largest being **Tzermiado** (population 750), **Agios Georgios** (population 550) and **Psyhro** (population 210).

The **Dikteon Cave** (☑28440 31316; admission €4; ☺8am-6pm Jun-Oct, to 2.30pm Nov-May) is where, according to mythology, Rhea hid the newborn Zeus from Cronos, his offspring-gobbling father. The cave, which covers 2200 sq metres and features numerous stalactites and stalagmites, is 1km from the village of Psyhro.

There are daily buses to the area from Iraklio and Agios Nikolaos, though having your own wheels would make life a lot easier.

Agios Nikolaos
Άγιος Νικόλαος

Agios Nikolaos (*ah*-yee-os nih-*ko*-laos) is an attractive former fishing village on Crete's northeast coast. The de facto town centre is around the picturesque **Voulismeni Lake**, which is ringed with cafes and tavernas, and is linked to the sea by a short canal. The ferry port is 150m past the canal.

The two nice little beaches in town, **Kytroplatia** and **Ammos**, get a bit crowded in summer. **Almyros Beach**, about 1km south, gets less so. Agios Nikolaos acts as a base for excursion tours to **Spinalonga Island**. The island's massive fortress was built by the Venetians in 1579 but taken by the Turks in 1715. It later became a leper colony. Nowadays it's a fascinating place to explore. Tours cost around €25.

Pergola Hotel (☑28410 28152; Sarolidi 20; s/d €35-40; ✻�) is a friendly family-run place out near the ferry port, with clean rooms, balconies and sea views. **Du Lac Hotel** (☑28410 22711; www.dulachotel.gr; Oktovriou 17; s/d €40/60; ✻�) is a refurbished hotel in a great location with views out over the lake.

Finding a place to eat will not be a problem; there are a lot of options around the lake. **Taverna Itanos** (☑28410 25340; Kyprou 1; mains €6-12), tucked away on a backstreet off the main square, is superb, has reasonable prices and offers the opportunity to wander into the kitchen and see what looks good.

The very helpful **municipal tourist office** (☑28410 22357; www.agiosnikolaos.gr; ☺8am-9pm Apr-Nov) is on the north side of the bridge over the canal and does a good job of finding sleeping options.

Buses to Iraklio run every 30 minutes (€7.10, 1½ hours).

Sitia
Σητεία

POP 9000

Sitia (si-*tee*-a) is a laid-back little town in the northeastern corner of Crete that has escaped much of the tourism frenzy along the north coast. It is on an attractive bay flanked by mountains, and is an easy place to unwind.

The main square, Plateia Iroon Plytehniou, is in the corner of the bay, and recognisable by its palm trees and statue of a dying soldier.

Porto Belis Travel (☑28430 22370; www.portobelis-crete.gr; Karamanli Aven 34), on the waterfront just before the start of the town beach, is a one-stop shop, handling ticketing, rental cars and scooters, and accommodation bookings in town. It also runs **Porto Belis House** (☑28430 22370; d/q €35/60; ✻�) above the travel agency. These rooms are immaculate, have kitchens and look straight out onto the beach.

Itanos Hotel (☑28430 22900; www.itanoshotel.com; Karamanli 4; s/d incl breakfast €50/68; ✻@) is an upmarket establishment next to the square with its own excellent **Itanos Taverna** on the waterfront outside the front door.

The waterfront is lined with tavernas. **Balcony** (☑28430 25084; www.balcony-restaurant.com; Foundalidou 19; mains €12-19), a couple of streets back, is the finest dining in Sitia. It's in a charmingly decorated neoclassical building.

The helpful **tourist office** (☑28430 28300; Karamanli; ☺9.30am-2.30pm & 5-8.30pm Mon-Fri, 9.30am-2pm Sat), on the waterfront, has town maps.

Sitia airport (JSH) has flights to Athens. There are buses daily to Iraklio (€14.70, 3½ hours) via Agios Nikolaos (€7.60, 1½ hours).

DODECANESE
ΔΩΔΕΚΑΝΗΣΑ

Strung out along the coast of western Turkey, the 12 main islands of the Dodecanese (*dodeca* means 12) have suffered a turbulent past of invasions and occupations that have endowed them with a fascinating diversity.

Conquered successively by the Romans, the Arabs, the Knights of St John, the Turks, the Italians, then liberated from the Germans by British and Greek commandos in

1944, the Dodecanese became part of Greece in 1947. These days, tourists rule.

The islands themselves range from the verdant and mountainous to the rocky and dry. While Rhodes and Kos host highly developed tourism, the more remote islands await those in search of traditional island life.

Rhodes   Ρόδος

POP 98,000

Rhodes (Rodos in Greek) is the largest island in the Dodecanese. According to mythology, the sun god Helios chose Rhodes as his bride and bestowed light, warmth and vegetation upon her. The blessing seems to have paid off, for Rhodes produces more flowers and sunny days than most Greek islands. Throw in an east coast of virtually uninterrupted sandy beaches and it's easy to understand why sun-starved northern Europeans flock here.

ⓘ Getting There & Away

Air

There are plenty of flights daily between Rhodes' **Diagoras airport** (RHO) and Athens, plus less-regular flights to Karpathos, Kastellorizo, Thessaloniki, Iraklio and Samos. Options are growing.

Rhodes

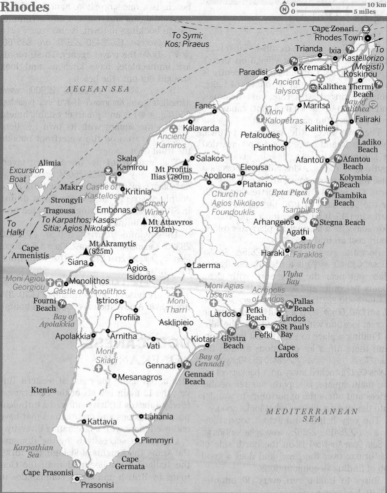

TALKING TURKEY

Turkey is so close that it looks like you could swim there from many of the Dodecanese and Northeastern Aegean islands. Here are the boat options:

Marmaris or Fethiye from Rhodes (p625)

Bodrum from Kos (p629)

Kuşadasi (near Ephesus) from Samos (p630)

Çeşme (near İzmir) from Chios (p633)

Dikili (near Ayvalık) from Lesvos (p633)

International charter flights swarm in summer, plus budget airlines fly in with scheduled flights. The airport is on the west coast, 16km southwest of Rhodes Town; 25 minutes and €2.20 by bus.

Boat

Rhodes is the main port of the Dodecanese and there is a complex array of departures. There are daily ferries from Rhodes to Piraeus (€59, 13 hours). Most sail via the Dodecanese north of Rhodes, but at least twice a week there is a service via Karpathos, Crete and the Cyclades.

In summer, catamaran services run up and down the Dodecanese daily from Rhodes to Symi, Kos, Kalymnos, Nisyros, Tilos, Patmos and Leros.

To Turkey

There are boats between Rhodes and Marmaris in Turkey (one-way/return including port taxes,

€50/75, 50 minutes). Check www.marmarisinfo.com for up-to-date details.

You can also travel between Rhodes and Fethiye, Turkey (one way/return including port taxes €50/75, 90 minutes). See www.alaturkaturkey.com.

RHODES TOWN
POP 56,000

Rhodes' capital is Rhodes Town, on the northern tip of the island. Its Old Town, the largest inhabited medieval town in Europe, is enclosed within massive walls and is a joy to explore. To the north is New Town, the commercial centre. The town beach, which looks out at Turkey runs around the peninsula at the northern end of New Town.

The main port, Commercial Harbour, is east of the Old Town, and is where the big interisland ferries dock. Northwest of here is Mandraki Harbour, lined with excursion boats and smaller ferries, hydrofoils and catamarans. It was the supposed site of the Colossus of Rhodes, a 32m-high bronze statue of Apollo built over 12 years (294–282 BC). The statue stood for a mere 65 years before being toppled by an earthquake.

🛏 Sleeping

TOP CHOICE Marco Polo Mansion   BOUTIQUE HOTEL €€
(☑22410 25562; www.marcopolomansion.gr; Agiou Fanouriou 40, Old Town; d incl breakfast from €90-180; ✱☑) In a 15th-century building in the Turkish quarter of the Old Town, this place is rich in Ottoman-era colours and features

DON'T MISS

OLD TOWN

A wander around Rhodes' World Heritage–listed Old Town is a must. It is reputedly the world's finest surviving example of medieval fortification, with 12m-thick walls. Throngs of visitors pack its busier streets and eating, sleeping and shopping options abound.

The Knights of St John lived in the Knights' Quarter in the northern end of the Old Town. The cobbled Odos Ippoton (Ave of the Knights) is lined with magnificent medieval buildings, the most imposing of which is the Palace of the Grand Masters (☑22410 23359; admission €6; ⊗8.30am-3pm Tue-Sun), which is restored, but never used, as a holiday home for Mussolini.

The 15th-century Knight's Hospital now houses the Archaeological Museum (☑22410 27657; Plateia Mousiou; admission €3; ⊗8am-4pm Tue-Sun). The splendid building was restored by the Italians and has an impressive collection that includes the ethereal marble statue *Aphrodite of Rhodes*.

The pink-domed Mosque of Süleyman, at the top of Sokratous, was built in 1522 to commemorate the Ottoman victory against the knights, then rebuilt in 1808.

You can take a pleasant walk around the imposing walls of the Old Town via the wide and pedestrianised moat walk.

MARCO POLO CAFÉ

A top spot to eat in Rhodes, Marco Polo Café (22410 25562; www.marco polomansion.gr; Agiou Fanouriou 40, Old Town) is worth finding in the backstreets of the Old Town. Owner Efi is as tastefully colourful as her mansion and garden restaurant. This place serves its guests with a rare passion – and the desserts are exquisite!

in glossy European magazines. In the secluded garden is the highly recommended Marco Polo Café.

TOP CHOICE Mango Rooms PENSION €
(22410 24877; www.mango.gr; Plateia Dorieos 3, Old Town; s/d/tr €44/58/66; ❄@🖧) A good-value, friendly one-stop shop near the back of the Old Town, Mango has an outdoor restaurant, bar and internet cafe down below, six well-kept rooms above, and a sunny terrace on top. Open year-round.

Hotel Andreas PENSION €€
(22410 34156; www.hotelandreas.com; Omirou 28d, Old Town; s/d/tr €45/70/85; ❄@🖧) Tasteful Hotel Andreas has individually decorated rooms and terrific views from its terrace. Rates differ by room; check it all out online, and choose your room before you go.

Hotel International HOTEL €€
(22410 24595; www.international-hotel.gr; 12 Kazouli St, New Town; s/d/tr €45/60/75; ❄🖧) In New Town, the International is a friendly family-run operation with immaculately clean and good-value rooms only a few minutes from Rhodes' main town beach. It's a 10-minute stroll to Old Town, and prices drop by a third out of high season.

✗ Eating & Drinking

There's food and drink everywhere you look in Rhodes. Outside the city walls are many cheap places in the New Market, at the southern end of Mandraki Harbour. Head further north into New Town for countless restaurants and bars.

Inside the walls, Old Town has it all in terms of touts and over-priced tavernas trying to separate less-savvy tourists from their euro. The back alleys tend to throw up better-quality eateries and prices. Delve into the maze and see what you can come up with.

To Meltemi TAVERNA €
(Kountourioti 8; mains €10-15) At the northern end of Mandraki Harbour, To Meltemi is one place worth heading to. Gaze out on Turkey from this beachside taverna where the seafood is superb. Try the grilled calamari stuffed with tomato and feta, and inspect the old photos of Rhodes.

ℹ Information

For more information, visit the Rodos website (www.rodos.gr).
Tourist Information Office (EOT; 22410 35226; cnr Makariou & Papagou; 8am-2.45pm Mon-Fri) Has brochures, maps and *Rodos News*, a free English-language newspaper.
Triton Holidays (22410 21690; www.triton dmc.gr; Plastira 9, Mandraki) In the New Town, this place is exceptionally helpful, handling accommodation bookings, ticketing and rental cars. The island-hopping experts, Triton can provide up-to-date advice in these times of constantly changing flight and boat schedules. Email ahead for advice.

ℹ Getting Around

BUS Rhodes Town has two bus stations a block apart next to the New Market. The west-side bus station serves the airport, Kamiros (€4.60, 55 minutes) and the west coast. The east-side bus station serves the east coast, Lindos (€5, 1½ hours) and the inland southern villages.

AROUND THE ISLAND

The **Acropolis of Lindos** (admission €6; 8.30am-6pm Tue-Sun Jun-Aug, to 2.30pm Sep-May), 47km south from Rhodes Town, is an ancient city spectacularly perched atop a 116m-high rocky outcrop. Below is the town of **Lindos**, a tangle of streets with elaborately decorated 17th-century houses.

The extensive ruins of **Kamiros**, an ancient Doric city on the west coast, are well preserved, with the remains of houses, baths, a cemetery and a temple, but the site should be visited as much for its lovely setting on a gentle hillside overlooking the sea.

Karpathos Κάρπαθος
POP 6000

The elongated, mountainous island of Karpathos (*kar*-pah-thos), midway between Crete and Rhodes, is a scenic, hype-free place with a cosy port, numerous beaches and unspoilt villages. It is a wealthy island, reputedly receiving more money from emigrants living abroad than any other Greek island.

The main port and capital is Pigadia, on the southeast coast. The northern village of Olymbos is like a living museum. Locals wear traditional outfits and the facades of houses are decorated with bright plaster reliefs.

A great option on Karpathos is to hire a car and tour this rugged island on its excellent roads. The 19km stretch from Spoa to Olymbos may finally be sealed by the time you read this. Check before you go though!

Elias Rooms (22450 22446; www.elias rooms.com; s/d €35/40; 🛜) is an excellent accommodation option. Owner Elias is a mine of information and his rooms have great views while being in a quiet part of town. Elias' website can tell you all you need to know about Karpathos and he is happy to provide information by email.

Possi Travel (22450 22235; www.possi -holidays.gr; 8am-1pm & 5.30-8.30pm), on pedestrianised Apodimon Karpathion, can suggest local tours and handles air and ferry tickets.

In summer, Karpathos airport (AOK), 13km southwest of Pigadia, has daily flights to Rhodes and Athens. With a huge new terminal, international charter flights also wing their way in. There are two ferries a week to Rhodes (€23, four hours) and two to Piraeus (€41, 17 hours) via Crete and the Cyclades.

There are also excursions from Pigadia to Diafani, at the north of the island, that include a bus trip to Olymbos.

Symi Σύμη

POP 2600

Simply superb, Symi is an inviting island to the north of Rhodes that should be on all island-hopper itineraries. The port town of Gialos is a Greek treasure, with pastel-coloured mansions heaped up the hills surrounding the protective little harbour. Symi is swamped by day trippers from Rhodes, and it's worth staying over to enjoy the island in cruise control. The town is divided into Gialos, the port and the tranquil *horio* (village) above it, accessible by taxi, bus or 360 steps from the harbour.

There is no tourist office. The best source of information is the free monthly English-language Symi Visitor (www.symivisitor.com), which includes maps of the town.

The Monastery of Panormitis (dawn-sunset) is a hugely popular complex at the

WORTH A TRIP

CRYSTAL CLEAR

If you like mind-bogglingly clear water when you go to the beach, head to Karpathos for some of the clearest turquoise wet stuff to be seen anywhere. Apella and Ahata beaches, both north of Pigadia, are stunning; Ammoöpi, 8km south of the capital, will make you drool. Karpathos' top beaches are best accessed with your own wheels.

southern end of the island. Its museum is impressive, but try to avoid the hordes of day trippers who arrive at around 10.30am on excursion boats from Rhodes.

Budget accommodation is scarce. Rooms Katerina (69451 30112, 22460 71813; www. symigreece.com/sg/villakaterina; d €30; 🌐🛜) is excellent, but get in quick as there are only three rooms. There is a communal kitchen with breathtaking views down over the port, and helpful Katerina is happy to answer all your questions.

On the waterfront next to the clock tower, Hotel Nireus (22460 72400; www.nireus-hotel.gr; s/d incl breakfast €80/115; 🌐🛜) is bright, friendly, has free wi-fi and the bonus of being able to swim right out front.

Kalodoukas Holidays (22460 71077; www.kalodoukas.gr) handles accommodation bookings, ticketing and has a book of walking trails on the island.

There are frequent boats between Rhodes and Kos that stop at Symi, as well as daily excursion boats from Rhodes. Symi Tours (www.symitours.com) runs excursions on Saturdays to Datça in Turkey for €40.

Small taxi boats visit inaccessible east-coast beaches daily in summer, including spectacular Agios Georgious, backed by a 150m sheer cliff.

Kos Κως

POP 17,900

Captivating Kos, only 5km from the Turkish peninsula of Bodrum, is popular with history buffs as the birthplace of Hippocrates (460–377 BC), the father of medicine. The island also attracts an entirely different crowd – sun-worshipping beach lovers from northern Europe who flock here during summer. Tourism rules the roost, and whether you are there to explore the Castle of the Knights or to party till you drop, Kos should keep you happy for at least a few days.

Kos Town is based around a circular harbour, protected by the imposing Castle of the Knights, at the eastern end of the island. The ferry quay is just to the north of the castle.

◉ Sights & Activities

Kos Town has recently developed a number of bicycle paths and renting a bike from one of the many places along the waterfront is a great option for getting around town and seeing the sights.

If the historical stuff is all too much, wander around and relax with the Scandinavians at the town beach past the northern end of the harbour.

Castle of the Knights   CASTLE
(☏22420 27927; admission €4; ⊙8am-2.30pm Tue-Sun) Built in the 14th century, this impressive castle protected the knights from the encroaching Ottomans, and was originally separated from town by a moat. That moat is now Finikon, a major street. Entrance to the castle is over the stone bridge behind the Hippocrates Plane Tree.

THE KNIGHTS OF ST JOHN

Do some island-hopping in the Dodecanese and you'll quickly realise that the Knights of St John left behind a whole lot of castles.

Originally formed as the Knights Hospitaller in Jerusalem in AD 1080 to provide care for poor and sick pilgrims, the knights relocated to Rhodes (via Cyprus) after the loss of Jerusalem in the First Crusade. They ousted the ruling Genoese in 1309, built a stack of castles in the Dodecanese to protect their new home, then set about irking the neighbours by committing acts of piracy against Ottoman shipping. Sultan Süleyman the Magnificent, not a man you'd want to irk, took offence and set about dislodging the knights from their strongholds. Rhodes finally capitulated in 1523 and the remaining knights relocated to Malta. They set up there as the Sovereign Military Hospitaller of Jerusalem, of Rhodes, and of Malta.

Asklipieion   ARCHAEOLOGICAL SITE
(☏22420 28763; adult/student €4/3; ⊙8am-7.30pm Tue-Sun) On a pine-clad hill 4km southwest of Kos Town stand the extensive ruins of the renowned healing centre where Hippocrates practised medicine. Groups of doctors come from all over the world to visit.

Ancient Agora   RUIN
The ancient agora, with the ruins of the Shrine of Aphrodite and Temple of Hercules, is just off Plateia Eleftherias. North of the agora is the Hippocrates Plane Tree, under which the man himself is said to have taught his pupils.

🛏 Sleeping

TOP CHOICE Hotel Afendoulis   HOTEL €
(☏22420 25321; www.afendoulishotel.com; Evripilou 1; s/d €30/50; ⊙Mar-Nov; ❋@🛜) In a pleasant, quiet area about 500m south of the ferry quay, this well-kept hotel won't disappoint. Run by the charismatic English-speaking Alexis, this is a great place to relax and enjoy Kos. Port- and bus-station transfers are complimentary, and you can get your laundry done here.

Hotel Sonia   HOTEL €
(☏22420 28798; www.hotelsonia.gr; Irodotou 9; s/d/tr €35/50/85; ❋🛜) Recently refurbished, Sonia's place has long been a popular spot to stay in Kos. It has large rooms and a relaxing veranda and garden. They'll pick you up at the port or bus station for free and there are laundry facilities on site. It's back behind the Dolphin roundabout.

🍴 Eating & Drinking

Restaurants line the central waterfront of the old harbour, but you might want to hit the backstreets for value. There are plenty of cheap places to eat on the beach to the north of the harbour, and a dozen discos and clubs around the streets of Diakon and Nafklirou, just north of the agora.

Stadium Restaurant   SEAFOOD €
(☏22420 27880; mains €10-18) On the long waterfront 500m southeast of the castle, Stadium serves succulent seafood at good prices, along with excellent views of Turkey.

ℹ Information

Visit www.kosinfo.gr for more information.
Exas Travel (☏22420 28545; www.exas.gr) Near the Archaeological Museum, in the heart

of town, to the southwest of the harbour; handles schedules, ticketing and excursions.

Municipal Tourist Office (☑22420 24460; www.kosinfo.gr; Vasileos Georgiou 1; ☺8am-2.30pm & 3-10pm Mon-Fri, 9am-2pm Sat May-Oct) On the waterfront directly south of the port; provides maps and accommodation information.

ℹ Getting There & Around

Air

There are daily flights to Athens from Kos' Ippokratis airport (KGS), which is 28km southwest of Kos Town. International charters and scheduled flights wing in throughout the summer from around Europe. Get to/from the airport by bus (€4) or taxi (€30).

Boat

There are frequent ferries from Rhodes to Kos that continue on to Piraeus (€53, 10 hours), as well as ferries heading the opposite way. Daily fast-boat connections head north to Patmos and Samos, and south to Symi and Rhodes.

To Turkey

In summer boats depart daily for Bodrum in Turkey (€20 return, one hour). Wander the waterfront and take your pick.

Bus

There is a good public bus system on Kos, with the bus station on Kleopatras, near the ruins at the back of town.

Mini-Train

Next to the tourist office is a blue mini-train for Asklipion (€5 return, hourly, Tuesday to Sunday) and a green mini-train that does city tours (€4, 20 minutes).

Patmos   Πάτμος

POP 3050

Patmos has a sense of 'spirit of place', and with its great beaches and relaxed atmosphere, it's a superb place to unwind.

The main town and port of Skala is about halfway down the east coast of Patmos, with a protected harbour. Towering above Skala to the south is the *hora*, crowned by the immense Monastery of St John the Theologian.

◉ Sights & Activities

Beaches   BEACHES

Patmos' coastline provides secluded coves, mostly with pebble beaches. The best is **Psili Ammos**, in the south, reached by excursion boat from Skala port. **Lambi Beach**, on the

ST JOHN & THE APOCALYPSE

For the religiously motivated, Patmos is not to be missed. Orthodox and Western Christians have long made pilgrimages to Patmos, for it was here that John the Divine ensconced himself in a cave and wrote the Book of Revelation.

The **Cave of the Apocalypse** (admission free, treasury €6; ☺8am-1.30pm daily & 4-6pm Tue, Thu & Sun) is halfway between the port and Hora. Take a bus from the port or hike up the Byzantine path, which starts from a signposted spot on the Skala–Hora road.

The **Monastery of St John the Theologian** (admission free; ☺8am-1.30pm daily & 4-6pm Tue, Thu & Sun) looks more like a castle than a monastery and tops Patmos like a crown. It exhibits all kinds of monastic treasures, and attending a service here is unforgettable.

---

north coast, is a pebble-beach-lover's dream come true.

🛏 Sleeping

Pension Maria Pascalidis   PENSION €

(☑22470 32152; s/d without bathroom €20/30) Maria has cosy rooms in a fragrant citrus-tree garden on the road heading up to the Hora and Monastery. A travellers' favourite, guests share a communal bathroom and kitchen.

Blue Bay Hotel   BOUTIQUE HOTEL €€

(☑22470 31165; www.bluebaypatmos.gr; s/d/tr incl breakfast €65/90/108; ✻@☞) South of the harbour in Skala, this recommended waterfront hotel has superb rooms, internet access, and breakfast included in its rates (which tumble outside of high season).

ℹ Information

See the websites www.patmosweb.gr, and www.patmos-island.com for more information.

Apollon Travel (☑22470 31324; apollontravel@stratas.gr) On the waterfront; handles schedules and ticketing.

Tourist Office (☑22470 31666; ☺8am-6pm Mon-Fri Jun-Sep) In the white building opposite the port in Skala, along with the post office and police station.

ℹ️ Getting There & Away

BOAT Patmos is well connected, with ferries to Piraeus (€37, seven hours) and south to Rhodes (€32, six hours). In summer, daily high-speed services head south to Kos and Rhodes, and north to Samos.

NORTHEASTERN AEGEAN ISLANDS
ΤΑ ΝΗΣΙΑ ΤΟΥ ΒΟΡΕΙΟ ΑΝΑΤΟΛΙΚΟ ΑΙΓΑΙΟΥ

One of Greece's best-kept secrets, these far-flung islands are strewn across the north-eastern corner of the Aegean Sea, closer to Turkey than mainland Greece. They harbour unspoilt scenery, welcoming locals, fascinating independent cultures and remain relatively calm even when other Greek islands are sagging with tourists at the height of summer.

Samos   Σάμος
POP 32,800

A lush mountainous island only 3km from Turkey, Samos has a glorious history as the legendary birthplace of Hera, wife and sister of god-of-all-gods Zeus. Samos was an important centre of Hellenic culture, and the mathematician Pythagoras and storyteller Aesop are among its sons. The island has beaches that bake in summer, and a hinterland that is superb for hiking. Spring brings with it pink flamingos, wildflowers and orchids that the island grows for export, while summer brings throngs of package tourists.

ℹ️ Getting There & Around
Air

There are daily flights to Athens from **Samos airport** (SMI), 4km west of Pythagorio, plus less-regular flights to Iraklio, Rhodes, Chios and Thessaloniki. Charter flights wing in from Europe in summer.

Boat

Samos has two main ports: Vathy (Samos Town) in the northeast and Pythagorio on the southeast coast. Those coming from the south by boat generally arrive in Pythagorio. Big ferries use Vathy. Once you're on Samos and have onward tickets, double-check where your boat is leaving from. Buses between the two take 25 minutes.

A maritime hub, Samos offers daily ferries to Piraeus (€48, 10 hours), plus ferries heading north to Chios and west to the Cyclades. Once the season is up and going, fast speed services head south to Patmos and continue to Kos.

Bus
You can get to most of the island's villages and beaches by bus.

Car & Motorcycle
Rental cars and scooters are readily available around the island (cars/scooters from €60/30 per day).

To Turkey
There are daily ferries to Kuşadası (for Ephesus) in Turkey (one-way/return €35/45, plus €10 port taxes). Day excursions are also available from April to October. Check with ITSA Travel in Vathy for up-to-date details.

VATHY (SAMOS TOWN)   ΒΑΘΥ ΣΑΜΟΣ
POP 2030
Busy Vathy is an attractive working port town. Most of the action is along Themis-

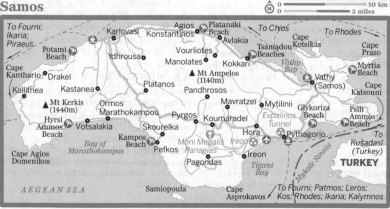

Samos

tokleous Sofouli, the main street that runs along the waterfront. The main square, Plateia Pythagorou, in the middle of the waterfront, is recognisable by its four palm trees and statue of a lion.

The **Archaeological Museum** (adult/student €3/2, free Sun; ⊙8.30am-3pm Tue-Sun) by the municipal gardens, is first-rate and one of the best in the islands.

Pythagoras Hotel (⌨22730 28601; www.pythagorashotel.com; Kallistratou 12; s/d/tr €20/35/45; ⊙Feb-Nov; ✽@⊙) is a friendly, great-value place with a convivial atmosphere, run by English-speaking Stelio. There is a restaurant serving tasty home-cooked meals, a bar, satellite TV and internet access. Facing inland, the hotel is 400m to the left of the quay. Call ahead for free pick-up on arrival.

Ino Village Hotel (⌨22730 23241; www.inovillagehotel.com; Kalami; s/d/tr incl breakfast €65/80/100; ᴘ✽⊙✽) is an impressive, elegant place in the hills north of the ferry quay. Its **Elea Restaurant** on the terrace serves up both invigorated Greek cuisine and views over town and the harbour.

ITSA Travel (⌨22730 23605; www.itsatravelsamos.gr), opposite the quay, is helpful with travel enquiries, excursions, accommodation and luggage storage.

To get to Vathy's bus station, follow the waterfront south and turn left onto Lekati, 250m south of Plateia Pythagorou (just before the police station).

PYTHAGORIO   ΠΥΘΑΓΟΡΕΙΟ
POP 1300
Pretty Pythagorio, 25 minutes south of Vathy by bus, is where you'll disembark if you've come by boat from Patmos. It is a small, enticing town with a yacht-lined harbour and a holiday atmosphere.

The 1034m-long **Evpalinos Tunnel** (adult/student €4/2; ⊙8am-8pm Tue-Sun), built in the 6th century BC, was dug by political prisoners and used as an aqueduct to bring water from Mt Ampelos (1140m). In the Middle Ages, locals hid out in it during pirate raids. It's a 20-minute walk north of town.

Polyxeni Hotel (⌨22730 61590; www.polyxenihotel.com; s/d/tr €40/45/55; ✽⊙) is a fun place to stay in the heart of the waterfront action. **Pension Despina** (⌨22730 61677; www.samosrooms.gr/despina; A Nikolaou; d €35; ✽⊙), a block back from the water, offers simple studios and rooms, some with balconies and kitchenettes.

Tavernas and bars line the waterfront. **Poseidon Restaurant** (⌨22730 62530; mains

from €7), on the small town beach, past the jetty with the Pythagoras statue on it, offers superb seafood.

The cordial **municipal tourist office** (⌨22730 61389; deap5@otenet.gr; ⊙8am-9.30pm) is two blocks from the waterfront on the main street, Lykourgou Logotheti. The bus stop is two blocks further inland on the same street.

Around Samos

Ireon (adult/student €4/2; ⊙8.30am-8pm Tue-Sun), the legendary birthplace of the goddess Hera, is 8km west of Pythagorio. The temple at this World Heritage site was enormous – four times the Parthenon – though only one column remains.

The captivating villages of **Vourliotes** and **Manolates**, on the slopes of imposing Mt Ampelos, northwest of Vathy, are excellent walking territory and have many marked pathways.

Choice beaches include **Tsamadou** on the north coast, **Votsalakia** in the southwest and **Psili Ammos** to the east of Pythagorio. The latter is sandy and stares straight out at Turkey, barely a couple of kilometres away.

Chios   Χίος
POP 54,000
Due to its thriving shipping and mastic industries (mastic produces the resin used in chewing gum), Chios (*hee*-os) has never really bothered much with tourism. If you are an off-the-beaten-track type of Greek Islands traveller, you'll find Chios all the more appealing.

Chios Town, on the island's eastern coast, is a working port and home to half the island's inhabitants. A main street runs in a semicircle

THE ORIGINAL CHEWING GUM

Chios is home to the world's only gum-producing mastic trees and the southern *masti-hohoria* (mastic villages) were wealthy for centuries. Not only were they wealthy, but the mastic trees are also said to have saved them when the Turks came and slaughtered the rest of the island's residents. The sultan's reputed fondness for mastic chewing gum – and the rumour that his harem girls used it for keeping their teeth clean and their breath fresh – meant that the *mastihohoria* were spared.

These days, **Masticulture Ecotourism Activities** (☎22710 76084; www.masticul-ture.com) in the southern village of Mesta, introduces visitors to the local history and culture, including mastic cultivation tours. In Chios Town, on the waterfront, **Mastihashop** (☎22710 81600; www.mastihashop.com; Leoforos Egeou 36) sells products such as mastic chewing gum, toothpaste and soaps, and **Mastic Spa** (☎22710 28643; www.masticspa.com; Leoforos Egeou 12) sells mastic-based cosmetics.

around the port, with most ferries docking at its northern end. The *kastro* (old Turkish quarter) is to the north of the ferry quay, and Plateia Vounakiou, the main square, is just south and inland from the quay.

◉ Sights & Activities

In Chios Town, **Philip Argenti Museum** (Korais; admission €1.50; ⊙8am-2pm Mon-Thu, to 2pm & 5-7.30pm Fri, 8am-12.30pm Sat) contains the treasures of the wealthy Argenti family.

World Heritage–listed **Nea Moni** (New Monastery; admission free; ⊙8am-1pm & 4-8pm) is 14km west of Chios Town and reveals some fine Byzantine art, with mosaics dating from the 11th century. The mosaics survived, but the resident monks were massacred by the Turks in 1822. You can see their dented skulls in the chapel at the monastery's entrance.

Those in the ghost village of **Anavatos**, 10km from Nea Moni and built on a precipitous cliff, preferred a different fate, hurling themselves off the cliff rather than being taken captive by the Turks.

Pyrgi, 24km southwest of Chios Town, is one of Greece's most unusual villages. The facades of the town's dwellings are decorated with intricate grey-and-white geometric patterns and motifs. The tiny medieval town of **Mesta**, 10km from Pyrgi and nestled within fortified walls, features cobbled streets, overhead arches and a labyrinth of streets designed to confuse pirates.

⌁ Sleeping

Chios Rooms — TOP CHOICE — PENSION €
(☎22710 20198; www.chiosrooms.gr; Leoforos Egeou 110; s/d/tr €30/35/45; ⏾) A top location to stay, this place is upstairs in a restored neoclassical house on the waterfront at the southern

end of the harbour. It has bright, airy rooms, some with en suite bathrooms, and is being restored lovingly by its Kiwi owner, Don, who is a mine of information on Chios.

Hotel Kyma — HOTEL €€
(☎22710 44500; kyma@chi.forthnet.gr; Evgenias Handris 1; s/d/tr incl breakfast €70/90/110; ✶⏾) Just past the southern end of the waterfront, this place occupies a charismatic century-old mansion and is run by the enthusiastic multilingual Theodoris. Ask for a room overlooking the sea.

✕ Eating

The waterfront has ample options in the way of eateries and bars, though for cheap eats, head one street back onto El Venizelou, which is lined with shops. The Plateia Vounakiou area, inland from where the ferries dock, also has up some good options.

Hotzas Taverna — TOP CHOICE — TAVERNA €
(☎22710 42787; Kondyli 3; mains from €6) Up the back of town, Hotzas is known by locals to provide the best Greek fare on the island. Get a local to mark it on a map, and enjoy the walk. It's worth the effort of finding.

❶ Information

Check out the **Chios website** (www.chios.gr) for more information.

Agean Travel (☎22710 41277; www.aegean spirit.gr; Leoforos Egeou 114)

Municipal Tourist Office (☎22710 44389; infochio@otenet.gr; Kanari 18; ⊙7am-3pm & 6.30-10pm Apr-Oct, to 3pm Nov-Mar) Information on accommodation, car rental, bus and boat schedules.

ℹ Getting There & Around

Air

There are daily flights from Chios airport (JKH) to Athens and some to Rhodes, Samos, Lesvos and Thessaloniki. The airport is 4km south of Chios Town; there's no bus, a taxi costs €8.

Boat

Ferries sail daily to Piraeus (€32.50, six hours) and Lesvos (€19.50, three hours). Boats also head out less regularly to Thessaloniki and Samos.

Bus

Chios Town has two bus stations. Blue buses go regularly to local villages and Karfas Beach, and leave from the local bus station at the main square. Buses to Pyrgi (€2.70) and Mesta (€3.90) and other distant points leave from the long-distance bus station on the waterfront near the ferry quay.

To Turkey

Boats to Turkey run all year from Chios, with daily sailings from July to September to Çeşme (one-way/return €25/30), near İzmir. For details, check out **Miniotis Lines** (☏22710 24670; www.miniotis.gr; Neorion 24).

Lesvos (Mytilini) Λέσβος (Μυτιλήνη)

POP 93,500

Lesvos, or Mytilini as it is often called, tends to do things in a big way. The third-largest of the Greek Islands after Crete and Evia, Lesvos produces half the world's ouzo and is home to over 11 million olive trees. Mountainous yet fertile, the island presents excellent hiking and birdwatching opportunities, but remains relatively untouched in terms of tourism development.

Lesvos has always been a centre of philosophy and artistic achievement, and to this day is a spawning ground for innovative ideas in the arts and politics. An excellent source of information on the island is www.greeknet.com.

The two main towns on the island are the capital, Mytilini, on the southeast coast, and attractive Mithymna on the north coast.

ℹ Getting There & Away

Air

Written up on flight schedules as Mytilene, Lesvos' Odysseas airport (MJT) has daily connections with Athens, plus flights to Thessaloniki,

Iraklio and a growing number of domestic destinations. The airport is 8km south of Mytilini town; a taxi costs €9 and a bus to town costs €1.50.

Boat

In summer there are daily fast/slow boats to Piraeus (€37/27, eight/13 hours) via Chios, and boats to Limnos, Thessaloniki and Samos.

To Turkey

There are regular ferries a week to Dikeli port (which serves Ayvalık) and to Fokias (which serves İzmir). Stop by Zoumboulis Tours in Mytilini for ticketing and schedules.

MYTILINI ΜΥΤΙΛΗΝΗ
POP 27,300

The capital and main port, Mytilini, is built between two harbours (north and south) with an imposing fortress on the promontory to the east. All ferries dock at the southern harbour, and most of the town's action is around this waterfront. With a large university campus, Mytilini is a lively place year-round.

⊙ Sights & Activities

Archaeological Museum MUSEUM
(8 Noemvriou; adult/child €3/2; ⊘8.30am-3pm Tue-Sun) Mytilini's excellent neoclassical Archaeological Museum has a fascinating collection from Neolithic to Roman times.

SAPPHO, LESBIANS & LESBOS

Sappho, one of Greece's great ancient poets, was born on Lesvos during the 7th century BC. Most of her work was devoted to love and desire, and the objects of her affection were often female. Because of this, Sappho's name and birthplace have come to be associated with female homosexuality.

These days, Lesvos is visited by many lesbians paying homage to Sappho. The whole island is very gay-friendly, in particular the southwestern beach resort of Skala Eresou, which is built over ancient Eresos, where Sappho was born. The village is well set up to cater to lesbian needs and has a 'Women Together' festival held annually in September. Check out www.sapphotravel.com for details.

There is an excellent statue of Sappho in the main square on the waterfront in Mytilini.

GREECE LESVOS (MYTILINI)

Teriade Museum
MUSEUM

(☎22510 23372; admission €2; ◷8.30am-2pm &
5-8pm Tue-Sun) Take a local bus 4km south of
Mytilini to the village of Varia, where an unexpected treasure awaits: the Teriade Museum,
with its astonishing collection of paintings
by world-renowned artists like Picasso, Cha-
gall, Miro, Le Corbusier and Matisse.

Theophilos Museum
MUSEUM

(admission €2; ◷9am-1pm & 5-8pm Tue-Sun) This
shrine to the prolific folk painter and Lesvos
native Theophilos is located 4km south of
Mytilini in Varia village, next to the Teriade
Museum.

Fortress
FORTRESS

(adult/student €2/1; ◷8am-2.30pm Tue-Sun) Mytilini's impressive fortress was built in early
Byzantine times and enlarged by the Turks.
The pine forest surrounding it is a superb
place for a stroll or to have a picnic.

🛌 Sleeping

Porto Lesvos 1 Hotel
HOTEL €€

(☎22510 41771; www.portolesvos.gr; Komninaki 21;
s/d/tr incl breakfast €50/60/70; ❊❄🛜) This hotel has attractive rooms and service – right
down to robes and slippers – in a restored
building one block back from the waterfront.

Pension Thalia
PENSION €

(☎22510 24640; Kinikiou 1; s/d €25/30) This
pension has clean, bright rooms in a large
house. It is about a five-minute walk north
of the main square, up Ermou, the road that
links the south and north harbours. Follow
the signs from the corner of Ermou and
Adramytiou.

🍴 Eating & Drinking

Mytilini's top spots are a road or two back at
the northern end of the harbour.

Stou Mihali
GREEK €

(☎22510 43311; Ikarias 7, Plateia Sapphou; mains
€4-10; ◷9am-9pm) It's getting hard to find a
free table at lunch at this tasty and inexpensive place. Everything is good; try the *soutzoukakia, imam baïldi* (roast eggplant) and
Greek salad.

Mousiko Kafenio
CAFE

(cnr Mitropoleos & Vernardaki; ◷7.30am-2am)
This relaxed, arty student cafe just in from
the waterfront is full of colour, with eclectic
paintings, mirrors and well-worn wooden
fixtures.

❶ Information

See www.lesvos.net for more information.

Tourist Office (EOT; ☎22510 42512; 6 Aristarhou; ◷9am-1pm Mon-Fri) Located 50m
up Aristarhou inland from the quay; offers
brochures and maps, but its opening hours are
limited.

Zoumboulis Tours (☎22510 37755; Kountourioti 69) On the waterfront; handles flights, boat
schedules, ticketing and excursions to Turkey.

❶ Getting Around

Mytilini has two bus stations. For local buses,
head along the waterfront to the main square.
For long-distance buses, walk 600m from
the ferry along the waterfront to El Venizelou
and turn right until you reach Agia Irinis park,
which is next to the station. There are regular
services in summer to Mithymna and Skala
Eresou.

MITHYMNA
ΜΗΘΥΜΝΑ

POP 1500

The gracious, preserved town of Mithymna
(known by locals as Molyvos) is 62km north
of Mytilini. Cobbled streets canopied by
flowering vines wind up the hill below the
impressive castle. The town is full of cosy
tavernas and genteel stone cottages.

The noble **Genoese castle** (admission €2;
◷8.30am-7pm Tue-Sun) perches above the town
like a crown and affords tremendous views
out to Turkey. Pebbly **Mithymna Beach** sits
below the town and is good for swimming.
Don't forget to stroll down to the harbour.

Eftalou hot springs (public/private bath per
person €4/5; ◷6am-9pm), 4km from town on
the beach, is a superb bathhouse complex
with a whitewashed dome and steaming,
pebbled pool.

Nassos Guest House (☎22530 71432;
www.nassosguesthouse.com; Arionis; d/tr without bathroom €20/35; 🛜) is an airy, friendly
place with shared facilities and a communal kitchen, in an old Turkish house oozing
character. With rapturous views, it's highly
recommended. It's the only blue house below the castle.

Betty's Restaurant (☎22530 71421; Agora;
mains €3-12) has superb home-style Greek
food, views and atmosphere in a building
that was once a notorious bordello. Betty
also has a couple of **cottages** (☎22530 71022;
www.bettyscottages.molivos.net; cottages €50)
with kitchens in her garden.

From the bus stop, walk straight ahead
towards the town for 100m to the helpful
municipal tourist office (www.mithymna.gr),

which has good maps. Some 50m further on, the cobbled main thoroughfare of 17 Noemvriou heads up to the right. Go straight to get to the colourful fishing port.

Buses to Mithymna (€6.90) take 1¾ hours from Mytilini, though a rental car is a good option.

AROUND THE ISLAND
Southern Lesvos is dominated by **Mt Olympus** (968m) and the very pretty village of **Agiasos**, which has good artisan workshops making everything from handcrafted furniture to pottery.

Western Lesvos is known for its petrified forest, with petrified wood at least 500,000 years old, and for the gay-friendly town of **Skala Eresou**, the birthplace of Sappho, see boxed text p301.

SPORADES ΣΠΟΡΑΔΕΣ

Scattered to the southeast of the Pelion Peninsula, to which they were joined in prehistoric times, the 11 islands that make up the Sporades group have mountainous terrain, dense vegetation and are surrounded by scintillatingly clear seas.

The main ports for the Sporades are Volos and Agios Konstantinos on the mainland.

Skiathos Σκιάθος
POP 6150
Lush and green, Skiathos has a beach resort feel about it. Charter flights bring loads of package tourists, but the island still oozes enjoyment. Skiathos Town and some excellent beaches are on the hospitable south coast, while the north coast is precipitous and less accessible.

Skiathos Town's main thoroughfare is Papadiamanti, named after the 19th-century novelist Alexandros Papadiamanti, who was born here. It runs inland opposite the quay.

● Sights & Activities
Beaches
Skiathos has superb beaches, particularly on the south coast. **Koukounaries** is popular with families. A stroll over the headland, **Big Banana Beach** is stunning, but if you want an all-over tan, head a tad further to **Little Banana Beach**, where bathing suits are a rarity.

MOVIES UNDER THE STARS
Greece has such great weather in summer that not only does it have a history of open-air theatre, there is also an open-air cinema culture. **Cinema Attikon** (☎24720 22352; ticket €7), on Skiathos Town's main street of Papadiamanti, is a great example. You can catch current English-language movies under the stars, sip a beer and practise speed-reading Greek subtitles at the same time! Films are usually shown in their original language in Greece (ie not dubbed).

A number of other islands have similar outdoor cinemas.

Boat Trips
At the Old Harbour in Skiathos Town, there are all sorts of offerings in terms of **boat excursions** – trips to nearby beaches (€10), trips around Skiathos Island (€25) and full-day trips that take in Skopelos, Alonnisos and the Marine Park (€35).

🛏 Sleeping
TOP CHOICE Hotel Bourtzi BOUTIQUE HOTEL €€
(☎24720 21304; www.hotelbourtzi.gr; s/d/tr incl breakfast €80/115/140; P❄🖵❄) On upper Papadiamanti, the swanky Bourtzi escapes much of the downtown noise and features lovely rooms, along with an inviting garden and pool.

Pension Pandora PENSION €
(☎694 413 7377, 24270 24357; www.skiathosinfo.com/accomm/pension-pandora; r €30-70; P❄🖵) Run by the effervescent Georgina, this family-run place is 10 minutes' walk north of the quay and a great budget option. The spotless rooms have TV, kitchens and balconies. Georgina also has two exceptional apartments just off Papadiamanti.

Camping Koukounaries CAMPGROUND €
(☎24270 49250; campsites per tent/person €4/10; P) This place, 30 minutes from town by bus and at the southwestern end of the island, is at beautiful Koukounaries Beach. There are good facilities, a minimarket and a taverna.

ECOTOURISM ON THE RISE

In a country not noted for its ecological long-sightedness, locals (especially the fishermen) initially struggled with the idea of the National Marine Park of Alonnisos when it was established in 1992 to protect the highly endangered Mediterranean monk seal and to promote the recovery of fish stocks.

These days, though, the people of the Sporades have caught on to the advantages of having such a park on their doorstep. Ecotourism is on the rise, with daily excursions on licensed boats into the park from Skiathos, Skopelos and Alonnisos. Though your odds of seeing the shy monk seal aren't great – it's on the list of the 20 most endangered species worldwide – the chances of cruising among pods of dolphins (striped, bottlenose and common) are high.

Eating & Drinking

Skiathos Town is brimming with eateries. There are seafood options around the Old Harbour, and some excellent places up the stairs from there behind the small church.

TOP CHOICE Piccolo ITALIAN €

(24270 22780; www.firponet.com/piccolo; mains from €8) This Italian place behind the church up from the Old Harbour does exquisite pizzas and pastas in a lovely setting.

1901 GREEK €€

(69485 26701; www.skiathos1901.gr; mains from €15) A superb fine-dining restaurant with a glowing reputation, 1901 is up Grigoriou, above the church up from the Old Harbour.

Kentavros BAR

(24270 22980) A popular drinking spot just off Plateia Papadiamanti. Expect a mellow ambience and mixture of rock, jazz and blues.

Information

See the website www.skiathosinfo,com for more information.

Heliotropio Travel (24270 22430; www.heliotropio.gr) Opposite the ferry quay; handles ticketing and rents cars and scooters.

Tourist Information Booth (24270 23172) At the port, but it opens irregularly.

Getting There & Around

AIR Along with numerous charter flights from northern Europe, in summer there is a daily flight from Athens and one from Thessaloniki. Skiathos airport (JSI) is 2km northeast of Skiathos Town.

BOAT There are frequent daily hydrofoils to/from the mainland ports of Volos (€34, 1¼ hours) and Agios Konstantinos (€36, two hours), as well as cheaper ferries. The hydrofoils head to/from Skopelos (€12, 45 minutes) and Alonnisos (€18, one hour). In summer there is also a hydrofoil to Thessaloniki (€47, 4½ hours).

BUS Crowded buses ply the south-coast road between Skiathos Town and Koukounaries every 30 minutes between 7.30am and 11pm year-round, stopping at all the beaches along the way. The bus stop is at the eastern end of the harbour.

Skopelos   Σκόπελος

POP 4700

A mountainous island, Skopelos is covered in pine forests, vineyards, olive groves and fruit orchards. While the northwest coast is exposed with high cliffs, the southeast is sheltered and harbours pleasant pebbled beaches. The island's main port and capital of Skopelos Town, on the east coast, skirts a semicircular bay and clambers in tiers up a hillside, culminating in a ruined fortress.

The island was used in the filming of *Mamma Mia*. The crew took over Skopelos Town's accommodation for a month and filmed at Agnontas and Kastani beaches on the western coast.

Pension Sotos (24240 22549; www.skopelos.net/sotos; s/d €30/45; ❄️📶), in the middle of the waterfront, has big rooms in an enchanting old Skopelete building. Check out individual rooms and its different prices online before you go. **Hotel Regina** (24240 22138; www.skopelosweb.gr/regina; s/d incl breakfast €45/60; ❄️📶) has bright and cheery rooms with balconies. The hotel's rooftop signage is easily spotted from the waterfront.

Top spot in town to chill out is under the huge plane tree at **Platanos Jazz Bar** (24240 23661) on the waterfront. It's open all day, plays wicked jazz and blues, and is the ideal place to recover from, or prepare for, a hangover.

In Skopelos Town, there is no tourist office, but **Thalpos Holidays** (24240 29036; www.holidayislands.com), on the waterfront, is

GREECE SKOPELOS

handy for accommodation and tours. The bus station is next to the port. Excursion boats along the waterfront offer trips into the marine park.

Hydrofoils dash daily to Skiathos (€12, 45 minutes), Alonnisos (€9, 20 minutes), Volos (€44, 2¼ hours) and Agios Konstantinos (€44, three hours). Most hydrofoils also call in at Loutraki, the port below Glossa on the northwest coast of the island. There is also a daily ferry along the same route that costs less but takes longer. There are frequent buses from Skopelos Town to Glossa (€4.80, one hour) stopping at all beaches along the way.

Alonnisos   Αλόννησος
POP 2700

Green, serene Alonnisos is at the end of the line and the least visited of the Sporades' main islands. The west coast is mostly precipitous cliffs, but the east coast is speckled with pebble-and-sand beaches. The island is well known as a walking destination.

The port village of Patitiri was slapped together in 1965 after an earthquake destroyed the hilltop capital of Alonnisos Town.

Pension Pleiades (☑24240 65235; www.pleiadeshotel.gr; s/d/tr from €25/35/50; ❋@) looks out over the harbour and is visible from the quay. The rooms are immaculate, balconied, bright and cheerful. There's also a good restaurant. Liadromia Hotel (☑24240 65521; www.liadromia.gr; d/tr/ste incl breakfast €50/70/95; P❋@☎) is an excellent-value place with tons of character, overlooking Patitiri's harbour. Follow the stairway opposite the National Bank. Camping Rocks (☑24240 65410; campsites per person €6) is a shady, basic camping ground. It is a steep hike about 1.5km from the port.

There is no tourist office, but on the waterfront, Alonnisos Travel (☑24240 66000; www.alonnisostravel.gr) handles boat scheduling and ticketing.

There are ferries with varying regularity connecting Alonnisos to Volos and Agios Konstantinos via Skopelos and Skiathos. Hydrofoils provide the most regular schedules between the islands. They travel several times a day to Skopelos Town (€9, 20 minutes), Skiathos (€16, 1½ hours), Volos (€44, three hours) and Agios Konstantinos (€44, four hours).

THE GREAT CHEESE PIE DEBATE

Tyropita (cheese pie), almost deified in its birthplace of the Sporades, is made with goat cheese rolled in delicate filo dough, coiled up, then fried quickly and served hot. The locals love it, but its origins are a source of hot debate.

Those from Alonnisos claim it evolved in the wood-fired oven kitchens of their island and was 'taken' to Skopelos in the 1950s, when farmers went to work on their neighbouring island. What smarts on Alonnisos is that the pie has become famous throughout Greece thanks to a popular TV host who credited Skopelos with its origin – and it is known as the 'Skopelos Cheese Pie'. Those on Alonnisos are cheesed off, to say the least!

IONIAN ISLANDS
ΤΑ ΕΠΤΑΝΗΣΑ

The idyllic cypress- and fir-covered Ionian Islands stretch down the western coast of Greece from Corfu in the north to Kythira, off the southern tip of the Peloponnese. Mountainous, with dramatic cliff-backed beaches, soft light and turquoise water, they're more Italian in feel, offering a contrasting experience to other Greek islands. Invest in a hire car to get to small villages tucked along quiet back roads. Prices drop in low season.

Corfu   Κέρκυρα
POP 122.700

Many consider Corfu, or Kerkyra (*ker*-kih-rah) in Greek, to be Greece's most beautiful island – the unfortunate consequence of which is that it's overbuilt and often overrun with crowds.

❶ Getting There & Away

Air

Ioannis Kapodistrias Airport (CFU; ☑26610 30180) is 3km from Corfu Town. **Olympic Air** (☑801 801 0101) and **Aegean Airlines** (☑26610 27100) fly daily to Athens and a few times a week to Thessaloniki.

Sky Express (www.skyexpress.gr) operates seasonal routes to Preveza, Kefallonia, Zakynthos, Kythira and Crete. Charter planes and

Corfu

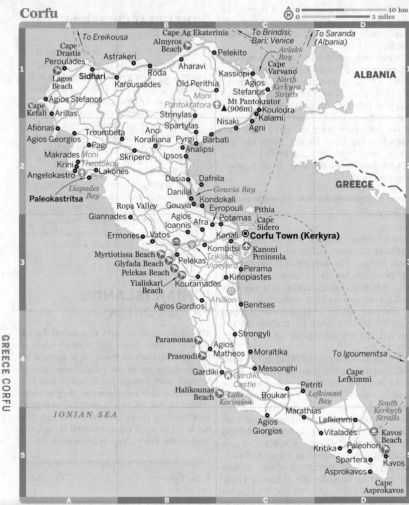

GREECE CORFU

easyJet fly internationally in summer. A taxi from the airport to the centre costs around €12. Buses 6 and 10 stop 800m from the airport.

Boat

Ferries go to Igoumenitsa (€10, 1½ hours, hourly). In summer, daily ferries and hydrofoils go to Paxi, and international ferries (Italy, Albania) also stop in Patra (€35, six hours).

Bus

Daily **buses** (☎26610 28898; www.ktelkerkyras. gr) to Athens (€50, 8½ hours) and Thessaloniki (€45, eight hours) leave from Corfu's **long-distance bus station** (☎26610 28927; Ioannou Theotoki).

CORFU TOWN
POP 28,800

Built on a promontory and wedged between two fortresses, Corfu's Old Town is a tangle of narrow walking streets through gorgeous Venetian buildings. Explore the winding alleys and surprising plazas in the early morning or late afternoon to avoid the hordes of day trippers seeking souvenirs.

⊙ Sights

TOP CHOICE Museum of Asian Art   MUSEUM

(☎26610 30443; adult/child €4/2; ⊗8.30am-8pm Tue-Sun Jun-Oct, 8.30am-2.30pm Tue-Sun Nov-May) Housed in the Palace of St Michael & St George this art collection is expertly curated with extensive English-language placards. Approximately 10,000 artefacts collected from China, Japan, India, Tibet and Thailand include priceless prehistoric bronzes, ceramics, jade figurines and coins.

TOP CHOICE Palaio Frourio   FORTRESS

(☎26610 48310; adult/concession €4/2; ⊗8am-8pm May-Oct, 8.30am-3pm Nov-Mar) Constructed by the Venetians in the 15th century on the remains of a Byzantine castle and further altered by the British, the Palaio Frourio stands on an eastern promontory; the Neo Frourio (New Fortress) lies to the northwest.

Antivouniotissa Museum   MUSEUM

(☎26610 38313; off Arseniou; admission €2; ⊗8am-2.30pm Tue-Sun) Exquisite basilica with an outstanding collection of Byzantine icons and artefacts dating from the 13th to the 17th centuries.

Mon Repos Estate   PARK

(Kanoni Peninsula; ⊗8am-7pm May-Oct, to 5pm Nov-Apr) Sprawling gardens boast two Doric temples.

Church of Agios Spiridon   CHURCH

(Agios Spiridonos) Richly decorated church displays the remains of St Spiridon.

Archaeological Museum   MUSEUM

(☎26610 30680; P Vraïla 5; admission €3; ⊗8.30am-3pm Tue-Sun) Houses a collection of finds from Mycenaean to classical times.

⊨ Sleeping

Accommodation prices fluctuate wildly depending on season; book ahead.

TOP CHOICE Bella Venezia   BOUTIQUE HOTEL €€

(☎26610 46500; www.bellaveneziahotel.com; N Zambeli 4; s/d incl breakfast from €100/120; ⊕❄🛜) Impeccable and understated; contemporary rooms are decked out in cream linens and marbles.

City Marina Hotel   HOTEL €€

(☎26610 39505; www.citymarina.gr; Donzelot 15, Old Port; s/d €75/80; ❄🛜) Recently renovated and with some sea views, light-filled rooms are managed by friendly staff.

Hermes Hotel   HOTEL €

(☎26610 39268; www.hermes-hotel.gr; Markora 12; s/d/tr €50/60/75; ❄🛜) Completely refurbished, pleasant, well-appointed rooms in the New Town.

✗ Eating & Drinking

Corfu has excellent restaurants. Cafes and bars line the arcaded Liston. Try Corfu Beer.

La Cucina   ITALIAN €€

(☎26610 45029; Guilford 17; mains €10-25) Every detail is cared for at this intimate bistro (and its annex down the street), from the hand-rolled tortelloni to the inventive pizzas and murals on the walls.

Rex   MEDITERRANEAN €€

(☎26610 39649; Kapodistriou 66; mains €8-21) Set back from the Liston, this elegant restaurant elevates Greek home cooking to fine dining.

Chrisomalis   TAVERNA €

(☎26610 30342; N Theotoki 6; mains €8-13) In the heart of the Old Town, this Ma and Pa operation dishes out the classics.

Rouvas   TAVERNA €

(☎26610 31182; S Desilla 13; mains €5-8; ⊗9am-5pm) A favourite lunch stop for locals.

To Dimarchio   ITALIAN, GREEK €€

(☎26610 39031; Plateia Dimarchio; mains €9-25) Relax in a luxuriant rose garden on a charming square.

ⓘ Information

Tourist Police (☎26610 30265; Samartzi 4, 3rd fl)

ⓘ Getting Around

Blue buses (€1.10 to €1.50) for villages near Corfu Town leave from Plateia San Rocco. Services to other destinations (around Corfu €1.60 to €4.40) leave from the long distance bus terminal.

GREECE CORFU

AROUND THE ISLAND

To explore fully all regions of the island your own transport is best. Much of the coast just north of Corfu Town is overwhelmed with beach resorts, the south is quieter, and the west has beautiful, if popular, coastline. The Corfu Trail (www.thecorfutrail.com) traverses the island north to south.

In Kassiopi, Manessis Apartments (☎26610 34990; http://manessiskassiopi.com; 4-person apt €100; ❄🛜) offers water-view apartments. In Sgombou, Casa Lucia

PAXI (ΠΑΞΟΙ)

Paxi lives up to its reputation as one of the Ionians' most idyllic and picturesque islands. At only 10km by 4km it's the smallest of the main holiday islands and makes a fine escape from Corfu's quicker-paced pleasures.

([☎]26610 91419; www.casa-lucia-corfu.com; studios & cottages €70-120; [P][⊠]) is a garden complex of lovely cottages with a strong alternative ethos. Don't miss a dinner at one of the island's best tavernas, **Klimataria** (Bellos; [☎]26610 71201; mains €8-14; ⊗dinner) in Benitses.

To gain an aerial view of the gorgeous cypress-backed bays around **Paleokastritsa**, the west coast's main resort, go to the quiet village of **Lakones**. Backpackers head to **Pelekas Beach** for low-key **Rolling Stone** ([☎]26610 94942; www.pelekasbeach.com; r/apt €35/98; [@][⊚]) or ramshackle **Sunrock** ([☎]26610 94637; www.sunrockcorfu.com; dm/r per person €18/24; [@][⊠]), a full-board hostel. Further south, good beaches surround tiny **Agios Gordios**.

Lefkada   Λευκάδα

POP 22,500

Joined to the mainland by a narrow isthmus, fertile Lefkada with its mountainous interior and pine forests also boasts truly splendid beaches and one of the hottest windsurfing spots in Europe.

❶ Getting There & Around

AIR Sky Express flies to Preveza-Aktio airport (PVK), 20km to the north.

BOAT West Ferry (www.westferry.gr) has an ever-changing schedule from Vasiliki to Kefallonia.

Ionian Pelagos ([☎]26450 31520) occasionally goes from Vasiliki via Piso Aetos (Ithaki) to Sami (Kefallonia).

Book with **Samba Tours** ([☎]26450 31520; www.sambatours.gr; Vasiliki) or **Borsalino Travel** ([☎]26450 92528; Nydri).

BUS & CAR KTEL Bus Station Lefkada Town ([☎]26450 22364; Ant Tzeveleki)

Athens (€32, 5½ hours, four daily)

Igoumenitsa (€12, two hours, daily)

Patra (€15, three hours, three weekly)

Preveza (€2.90, 30 minutes, six daily)

Thessaloniki (€41.50, eight hours, two weekly)

Rent cars in Lefkada Town, Nydri or Vasiliki.

LEFKADA TOWN

Most travellers' first port of call, Lefkada Town remains laid-back except for August high season. The town's unique earthquake-resistant corrugated-steel architecture somehow blends with its attractive marina, waterfront cafes and vibrant pedestrian thoroughfares.

🛏 Sleeping & Eating

Restaurants and cafes line the main street, **Dorpfeld**, central **Plateia Agiou Spyridonos** and the waterfront.

Boschetto Hotel   BOUTIQUE HOTEL €€
([☎]26450 24967; www.boschettohotel.com; Dorpfeld 1; d incl breakfast from €80; [❄][@][⊚]) Exquisite c 1900 building with four custom-designed rooms and one suite tricked out with all the chicest amenities.

Hotel Santa Maura   HOTEL €
([☎]26450 21308; Dorpfeld; s/d/tr incl breakfast €50/60/70; [❄][⊚]) Think tropical Bahamas with sky-blue and shell-pink interiors and breezy balconies; best rooms on the top floor.

Pension Pirofani   HOTEL €€
([☎]26450 25844; Dorpfeld; r €60-80; [❄][⊚]) Modern rooms have balconies for prime people-watching.

Ey Zhn   INTERNATIONAL €
([☎]69746 41160; Filarmonikis 8; mains €7-12; ⊗dinner Jan-Oct) Roadhouse meets artist's loft at this ambience-rich restaurant with excellent, eclectic food.

AROUND THE ISLAND

With its lovely bay, **Nydri** is unfortunately blighted by tacky souvenir shops and touristy tavernas. Lefkada's true gifts are its west-coast beaches. Cliffs drop to broad sweeps of white sand and turquoise waters. Explore! Tiny, bohemian **Agios Nikitas** village draws travellers, but gets very crowded in summer. Nearby, in Athani, get simple clean studios at **Aloni Studios** ([☎]26450 33604; www.aloni studios-lefkada.com; r €40; [P][❄]).

Southernmost eucalyptus-scented **Vasiliki** is popular with windsurfers. Organise lessons through **Club Vass** ([☎]26450 31588; www. clubvass.com). Overlooking the port, **Pension Holidays** ([☎]26450 31426; s/d €45/50; [❄][⊚]) has great-value rooms with kitchens.

Kefallonia Κεφαλλονιά

POP 37,800

Tranquil cypress- and fir-covered Kefallonia, the largest Ionian island, is breathtakingly beautiful with rugged mountain ranges, rich vineyards, soaring coastal cliffs and golden beaches. It has not succumbed to package tourism to the extent that some of the other Ionian Islands have and remains low-key outside resort areas. Due to the widespread destruction of an earthquake in 1953, much of the island's historic architecture was levelled; Assos and Fiskardo are exceptions.

ℹ️ Getting There & Around

Air

Olympic Air (☎26710 41511) flies to Athens, and **Sky Express** serves the Ionians and Crete, from **Kefallonia Airport** (☎26710 41511), 9km south of Argostoli.

Boat

Ionian Ferries (www.ionianferries.gr) connects Poros and Argostoli to Kyllini (Peloponnese).
Ionian Pelagos (☎26450 31520) links Sami with Astakos (Peloponnese; sometimes via Piso Aetos in Ithaki).
Strintzis Lines (www.strintzisferries.gr) connects Sami with Patra (Peloponnese) and Vathy or Piso Aetos (Ithaki).
West Ferry (www.westferry.gr) loops from Fiskardo, and sometimes Sami, to Frikes (Ithaki) and Vasiliki.

In high season some ferries connect Sami with Bari, Italy. **Nautilus Travel** (☎26740 41440; Fiskardo) has information and tickets.

Bus

Three daily buses connect **KTEL Bus Station Argostoli** (☎26710 22276; Antoni Tritsi 5) with Athens (€47, seven hours) via Patra (€26, four hours). Buses also go to Athens from Sami (two daily), Poros (one daily) and Lixouri (one daily). Local buses don't run on Sunday.

Car

A car is best for exploring. **Pama Travel** (☎26740 41033; www.pamatravel.com; Fiskardo) rents cars and boats. **Karavomilos** (☎26740 22779; Sami) delivers cars.

FISKARDO

Pretty Fiskardo, with its pastel-coloured Venetian buildings set around a picturesque bay, is popular with European yachties but it's still peaceful enough to appeal to independent travellers. Take lovely walks to sheltered coves for swimming.

🛏️ Sleeping

Archontiko   PENSION €€
(☎26740 41342; r from €70; ❄️) Overlooking the harbour, people-watch from the balconies of luxurious rooms in a restored stone mansion.

Regina's Rooms   PENSION €
(☎26740 41125; d/tr €40/50; ❄️) Some of its colourful, breezy rooms have bay views or kitchenettes.

🍴 Eating

Fiskardo has no shortage of excellent waterside restaurants.

TOP CHOICE **Tassia**   MEDITERRANEAN €€
(☎26740 41205; mains €7-25) This unassuming but famous Fiskardo institution run by Tassia Dendrinou, celebrated chef and writer, serves up excellent seafood and Greek dishes.

Café Tselenti   ITALIAN €€
(☎26740 41344; mains €10-23) Enjoy outstanding Italian classics served by friendly waiters; tucked back in a romantic plaza.

AROUND THE ISLAND

In Argostoli, the capital, stay over at **Vivian Villa** (☎26710 23396; www.kefalonia-vivianvilla.gr; Deladetsima 11; d/tr/apt €60/65/100; ❄️🌐) with its big, bright rooms and friendly owners. Sample inventive Mediterranean cooking at

GREECE KEFALLONIA

KEFALLONIA HIGH-SEASON FERRIES

FROM	TO	FARE (€)	DURATION (HR)
Argostoli	Kyllini (Peloponnese)	14	5
Pesada	Agios Nikolaos (Zakynthos)	8.50	1½
Poros	Kyllini	10	1½
Sami	Bari (Italy)	45	12
Sami	Patra (Peloponnese)	19	2¾
Sami	Piso Aetos & Vathy (Ithaki)	3/7	45min

Casa Grec (26710 24091; Metaxa 12; mains €12-22; dinner nightly, closed Sun & Mon Nov-Apr) or top Kefallonian cuisine at **Arhontiko** (26710 27213; 5 Risospaston; mains €7-17; breakfast, lunch & dinner).

Straddling a slender isthmus on the northwest coast, the petite pastel-coloured village of **Assos** watches over the ruins of a Venetian fortress perched upon a pine-covered peninsula. Eat at **Platanos** (69446 71804; mains €6-15; breakfast, lunch & dinner Easter-Oct) for home-cooked food at its best. Splendid **Myrtos Beach**, 13km south of Assos, is spellbinding from above, with post-card views from the precarious roadway.

Near **Sami**, eat at **Paradise Beach** (Dendrinos; 26740 61392; Agia Evfymia; mains €6-13; lunch & dinner mid-May–mid-Oct), a renowned Kefallonian taverna.

The interior **Omala Valley** is home to **Robola wines** (www.robola.gr). **Paliki Peninsula** is filled with under-explored beauty.

Ithaki   Ιθάκη

POP 1550

Odysseus' long-lost home in Homer's *Odyssey*, Ithaki (ancient Ithaca) remains a pristine island blessed with cypress-covered hills and beautiful turquoise coves.

ⓘ Getting There & Away

Strintzis Lines (www.strintzisferries.gr) has two ferries daily connecting Vathy or Piso Aetos with Patra (Peloponnese) via Sami (Kefalonia).
Ionian Pelagos (26450 31520) goes daily in high season between Piso Aetos, Sami and Astakos (mainland).

West Ferry (www.westferry.gr) has an ever-changing schedule from Frikes to Vasiliki (Lefkada); sometimes it goes to Fiskardo, but at the time of research was considering cutting the Frikes stop.

Check routes and schedules at **Delas Tours** (26740 32104; www.ithaca.com.gr) or **Polyctor Tours** (26740 33120; www.ithakiholidays.com) in Vathy.

KIONI

Tucked in a tiny, tranquil bay, Kioni is a wonderful place to chill for a few days.

Individuals rent rooms and **Captain's Apartments** (26740 31481; www.captains-apartments.gr; 2-/4-person apt €60/70;) has shipshape, spacious apartments with kitchens, satellite TV and balconies overlooking the valley and village. **Mythos** (mains €6-10) taverna on the harbour has excellent *pastit-*

ⓘ FERRY BETWEEN ZAKYNTHOS & KEFALLONIA

From the northern port of Agios Nikolaos a ferry serves Pesada in southern Kefallonia twice daily from May to October (€8, 1½ hours). Get tickets at **Chionis Tours** (26950 23894; Lomvardou 8, Zakynthos Town). *BUT*, in high season, there are only two buses a week from Zakynthos Town to Agios Nikolaos and two buses daily from Pesada to Argostoli (Kefallonia), making crossing without your own transport difficult. An alternative is to cross to Kyllini and catch another ferry to Kefallonia.

---

sio (a thick noodle and ground beef casserole). Comfy **Cafe Spavento** (per hr €2) has internet.

AROUND THE ISLAND

The dusty port of **Frikes**, where some ferries dock, is a funkier alternative to Kioni and has rooms to rent.

Vathy, Ithaki's small, bustling capital, is the spot for hiring cars and getting cash (no banks in Kioni). Elegant mansions rise from around its bay and **Hotel Perantzada** (26740 33496; www.arthotel.gr/perantzada; Odyssea Androutsou; s/d incl breakfast from €120/150; Easter–mid-Oct;) occupies two with sensational rooms. **Odyssey Apartments** (26740 33400; www.ithaki-odyssey.com; d €60-80, studio €100, 1-/2-bedroom apt €120/150;) overlooks town (500m up) and the sea with spotless studios and a pool.

Zakynthos   Ζάκυνθος

POP 41,000

The beautiful island of Zakynthos, or Zante, has stunning coves, dramatic cliffs and extensive beaches, but unfortunately is swamped by package-tour groups, so only a few special spots warrant your time.

ⓘ Getting There & Around

AIR The **airport** (ZTH; 26950 28322) is 6km from Zakynthos Town. **Olympic Air** flies to Athens; **Sky Express** flies to Corfu via Kefallonia and Preveza, or to Crete; **easyJet** flies occasionally to Gatwick and Milan; **Air Berlin** flies to German cities.

BOAT Ionian Ferries (26950 22083/49500; www.ionianferries.gr; Lomvardou 40 & 72,

Zakynthos Town) travels from Zakynthos Town to Kyllini (Peloponnese; €8.50, one hour, four to seven daily).

Occasional ferries go to Brindisi, Italy (€75, 15½ hours), some via Igoumenitsa and Corfu (€32, 8¾hr, two weekly).

BUS The **KTEL bus station** (☎26950 22255; www.ktel-zakynthos.gr) is west of Zakynthos town. Budget an additional €8.50 for the ferry to Kyllini.

Athens (€26, six hours, four daily)
Patra (€8.50, 3½ hours, four daily)
Thessaloniki (€50, 10 hours, three weekly)

Local buses serve major resort towns.

CAR **Europcar** (☎26950 41541; Plateia Agiou Louka, Zakynthos Town) Delivers to the airport.

ZAKYNTHOS TOWN

The island's attractive Venetian capital and port were painstakingly reconstructed after the 1953 earthquake. The pine-tree-filled **Kastro** (☎26950 48099; admission €3; ⊙8.30am-2.30pm Tue-Sun), a ruined Venetian fortress high above town, makes for a peaceful outing. The **Byzantine Museum** (☎26950 42714; Plateia Solomou; admission €3; ⊙8.30am-3pm Tue-Sun) houses fabulous ecclesiastical art rescued from churches razed in the earthquake.

Sleeping & Eating

Restaurants abound but, as in most of the island, they tend to be overpriced and not overly inspiring. In Zakynthos Town, try **Mesathes** (☎26950 49315; Ethnikis Antistaseos; mains €9-11) for an elegant meal.

TOP CHOICE **Hotel Strada Marina** HOTEL €€
(☎26950 42761; www.stradamarina.gr; Lombardou 14; s/d incl breakfast from €60/70; ❄📶🏊) Well-situated, portside rooms have balconies with sea views.

Hotel Diana HOTEL €€
(☎26950 28547; Plateia Agiou Markou; r incl breakfast from €60; ❄@📶) This comfortable and well-appointed hotel in a good, central location has a two-bedroom family suite (€100).

Camping Zante CAMPGROUND €
(☎26950 61710; www.zantecamping.gr; Ampula Beach; campsites per person/tent €6/5; @🏊) Decent beachside camping 5km north of Zakynthos Town.

TOP CHOICE **Malanos** TAVERNA €
(☎26950 45936; www.malanos.gr; Agiou Athanasiou, Kiri area; mains €5-10; ⊙noon-4pm & 8pm-late) Serves up Zakynthos specialities like rooster, rabbit and wild boar. South, in the countryside; ask a local for directions.

AROUND THE ISLAND

Transport of your own is really necessary to unlock the charms of Zakynthos. The **Vasilikos Peninsula** is the pretty green region southeast of Zakynthos Town and fringing **Laganas Bay** with its long, lovely **Gerakas Beach**. The area has been declared **National Marine Park of Zakynthos** (NMPZ; www.nmp-zak.org) in order to protect the endangered loggerhead turtles that come ashore to lay their eggs in August, the peak of the tourist invasion. Inform yourself before exploring so as not to accidentally disrupt buried eggs.

Cape Keri, near the island's southernmost point, has spectacular views of sheer cliffs and beaches. **Villa Christina** (☎26950 49208; viganelichristina@hotmail.com; Limni Keriou; studio €50-55, apt €60-80, maisonette €150; ⊙May-Oct; P❄@🏊) is tops for tidy apartments in lush gardens with a pool. **Tartaruga Camping** (☎26950 51967; www.tartaruga-camping.com; camp sites per adult/car/tent €5/3/3.60, r per person €15; ⊙Apr-Oct; P❄@📶), signed on the road from Laganas to Keri, sprawls through terraced olive groves and pines next to the sea.

Continue north and try to arrive early at remote **Limnionas** for swimming in crystal-clear turquoise coves, or explore lovely **Louha** tumbling down a central valley.

Many descend on famous **Shipwreck Beach**, magnificent photos of which grace every tourist brochure about Zakynthos. It is in Navagio Bay, at the northwest tip of the island. From above, a lookout platform gives

> WORTH A TRIP
>
> **KYTHIRA** ΚΥΘΗΡΑ
>
> Kythira, despite its proximity to the Peloponnese, is considered a part of the Ionian Island group. Genuinely unspoilt, the population (3330) is spread among more than 40 villages with a white-cube Cycladic feel. Mythology suggests that Aphrodite was born in Kythira, but Cypriots claim otherwise. Tourism remains low-key except in July and August, when the island goes mad. Easiest way to get there: fly or get a ferry in Diakofti or Neapoli in the Peloponnese. **LANE Lines** (www.lane.gr) sometimes links Piraeus.

great views. For a (crowded in high season) sea-level look, take a boat from Cape Skinari near Agios Nikolaos, Porto Vromi or Alykes. Cape Skinari's **Windmill** (☏26950 31132; www.potamitisbros.gr; d €60; ✳) has quaint rooms, impressive views, cooking facilities and sea access.

UNDERSTAND GREECE

History

With its strategic position at the crossroads of Europe and Asia, Greece has endured a long and turbulent history. During the Bronze Age (3000–1200 BC in Greece), the advanced Cycladic, Minoan and Mycenaean civilisations flourished. The Mycenaeans were swept aside in the 12th century BC by the warrior-like Dorians, who introduced Greece to the Iron Age. The next 400 years are often referred to as the dark ages, a period about which little is known.

By 800 BC, when Homer's *Odyssey* and *Iliad* were first written down, Greece was undergoing a cultural and military revival with the evolution of the city states, the most powerful of which were Athens and Sparta. Greater Greece (Magna Graecia) was created, with southern Italy as an important component. The unified Greeks repelled the Persians twice, at Marathon (490 BC) and Salamis (480 BC). Victory over Persia was followed by unparalleled growth and prosperity known as the classical (or golden) age.

The Golden Age

During this period, Pericles commissioned the Parthenon, Sophocles wrote *Oedipus the King* and Socrates taught young Athenians to think. The golden age ended with the Peloponnesian War (431–404 BC), when the militaristic Spartans defeated the Athenians. They failed to notice the expansion of Macedonia under King Philip II, who easily conquered the war-weary city states.

Philip's ambitions were surpassed by those of his son, Alexander the Great, who marched triumphantly into Asia Minor, Egypt, Persia and what are now parts of Afghanistan and India. In 323 BC he met an untimely death at the age of 33, and his generals divided his empire between themselves.

Roman Rule & the Byzantine Empire

Roman incursions into Greece began in 205 BC. By 146 BC Greece and Macedonia had become Roman provinces. After the subdivision of the Roman Empire into eastern and western empires in AD 395, Greece became part of the Eastern (Byzantine) Empire, based at Constantinople.

In the centuries that followed, Venetians, Franks, Normans, Slavs, Persians, Arabs and, finally, Turks, took turns chipping away at the Byzantine Empire.

The Ottoman Empire & Independence

After the end of the Byzantine Empire in 1453, when Constantinople fell to the Turks, most of Greece became part of the Ottoman Empire. Crete was not captured until 1670, leaving Corfu as the only island not occupied by the Turks. By the 19th century the Ottoman Empire was in decline. The Greeks, seeing nationalism sweep through Europe, fought the War of Independence (1821–22). Greek independence was proclaimed on 13 January 1822, only for arguments among the leaders who had been united against the Turks to escalate into civil war. The Turks, with the help of the Egyptians, tried to retake Greece, but the great powers – Britain, France and Russia – intervened in 1827, and Ioannis Kapodistrias was elected the first Greek president.

ORIGINAL OLYMPICS

The Olympic tradition emerged around the 11th century BC as a paean to the Greek gods, in the form of contests of athletic feats that were attended initially by notable men and women, who assembled before the sanctuary priests and swore to uphold solemn oaths. By the 8th century BC, the attendance had grown to include a wide confederacy of city states, and the festival morphed into a male-only major event lasting five days at the site of Olympia. A ceremonial truce was enforced for the duration of the games. Crowds of spectators lined the tracks, where competitors vied for victory in athletics, chariot races, wrestling and boxing. Three millennia later, while the scale and scope of the games may have expanded considerably, the basic format has remained essentially unchanged.

Kapodistrias was assassinated in 1831 and the European powers stepped in once again, declaring that Greece should become a monarchy. In January 1833 Otho of Bavaria was installed as king. His ambition, called the Great Idea, was to unite all the lands of the Greek people to the Greek motherland. In 1862 he was peacefully ousted and the Greeks chose George I, a Danish prince, as king.

During WWI Prime Minister Venizelos allied Greece with France and Britain. King Constantine (George's son), who was married to the kaiser's sister Sophia, disputed this and left the country.

Smyrna & WWII

After the war Venizelos resurrected the Great Idea. Underestimating the new-found power of Turkey under the leadership of Atatürk (Mustafa Kemal), he sent forces to occupy Smyrna (the present-day Turkish port of İzmir), with its large Greek population. The army was heavily defeated and this led to a brutal population exchange between the two countries in 1923.

In 1930 George II, Constantine's son, was reinstated as king; he appointed the dictator General Metaxas as prime minister. Metaxas' grandiose ambition was to combine aspects of Greece's ancient and Byzantine past to create a Third Greek Civilisation. However, his chief claim to fame is his celebrated *ohi* (no) to Mussolini's request to allow Italian troops into Greece in 1940.

Greece fell to Germany in 1941 and resistance movements, polarised into royalist and communist factions, staged a bloody civil war lasting until 1949. The civil war was the trigger for a mass exodus that saw almost one million Greeks head off to countries such as Australia, Canada and the USA. Entire villages were abandoned as people gambled on a new start in cities such as Melbourne, Toronto, Chicago and New York.

The Colonels' Coup

Continuing political instability led to the colonels' coup d'état in 1967. The colonels' junta distinguished itself with its appalling brutality, repression and political incompetence. In 1974 it attempted to assassinate Cyprus' leader, Archbishop Makarios, and when he escaped the junta replaced him with the extremist Nikos Samson, prompting Turkey to occupy North Cyprus. The continued Turkish occupation of Cyprus remains one of the most contentious issues in Greek politics. The junta had little choice but to hand back power to the people. In November 1974 a plebiscite voted against restoration of the monarchy. Greece became a republic with the right-wing New Democracy (ND) party taking power.

The 1980s & 1990s

In 1981 Greece entered the European Community (now the EU) as its 10th, smallest and poorest member. Andreas Papandreou's Panhellenic Socialist Movement (Pasok) won the next election, giving Greece its first socialist government. Pasok, which ruled for most of the next two decades, promised the removal of US air bases and withdrawal from NATO, but delivered only rising unemployment and spiralling debt.

Elections in 1990 brought the ND party back to power, but tough economic reforms made the government unpopular and in 1993, Greeks again turned to Pasok and the ailing Papandreou. He had little option but to continue with the austerity program and became equally unpopular until he stood down in 1996 due to ill health. Pasok then abandoned its leftist policies, elected economist and lawyer Costas Simitis as leader, and romped to victory later that year.

The New Millennium

Simitis' government focused strongly on further integration with Europe and in January 2001 admission to the euro club was approved; Greece duly adopted the currency in 2002 and prices have been on the rise ever since.

Greece tilted to the right and in March 2004 elected the ND party led by Costas Karamanlis. This new broom was fortuitous, as the Olympic preparations were running late and suffering budget problems. While the Olympics were successful, Greece is still counting the cost.

During the long hot summer of 2007, forest fires threatened Athens and caused untold damage in the western Peloponnese, Epiros and Evia. Later that year, Karamanlis' government was returned to power for a second term, but amid growing discontent that included massive general strikes and riots, was turfed out in elections in October 2009 in favour of Pasok and George Papandreou, son and grandson of former prime ministers.

GREECE HISTORY

RECOGNISE THAT TWANG?

Don't be surprised if your hotel receptionist or waiter speaks perfect English with an Australian twang. A growing stream of young second- and third-generation Greeks are repatriating from the USA, Australia, Canada and other reaches of the Greek diaspora. A huge number of Greeks emigrated during their country's tumultuous history and it is said that over five million people of Greek descent live in 140 countries around the world. Strong sentimental attractions endure and many expat Greeks are involved in the political and cultural life of their ancestral islands, and many retire in Greece.

Greece Today

Textbooks are being written on Greece's 2010 financial crisis. Simply put, Greece almost fell over from years of over-borrowing, over-spending and breaking eurozone rules on deficit management. Financially crippled and looking likely to drag other failing eurozone economies down with it, Greece was on the receiving end of a succession of bail-out packages to help right the ship. Needless to say, austerity measures to help balance the budget were not popular, with citizens angry about cuts in spending, pensions and salaries, along with higher taxes.

Strikes and riots made world news and in May 2012 elections, no party or coalition of parties was able to form a government. New elections were called for June and in what was seen worldwide as a vote that would determine if Greece remained in the eurozone, a coalition of three parties formed a government with New Democracy's Antonis Samaris as prime minister.

Samaris hopes to keep both Greece's creditors and its populace happy, but without doubt, tough times are ahead.

People

Greece's population has topped 11.2 million, with around one-third of the people living in the Greater Athens area and more than two-thirds living in cities – confirming that Greece is now a primarily urban society. Less than 15% live on the islands, the most populous being Crete, Evia and Corfu. Greece has an ageing population and declining birth rate, with big families a thing of the past. Population growth over the last couple of decades is due to a flood of migrants, both legal and illegal.

About 95% of the Greek population belongs to the Greek Orthodox Church. The remainder is split between the Roman Catholic, Protestant, Evangelist, Jewish and Muslim faiths. While older Greeks and those in rural areas tend to be deeply religious, most young people are decidedly more secular.

The Greek year is centred on the saints' days and festivals of the church calendar. Name days (celebrating your namesake saint) are celebrated more than birthdays. Most people are named after a saint, as are boats, suburbs and train stations.

Orthodox Easter is usually at a different time than Easter celebrated by Western churches, though generally in April/May.

Arts

The arts have been integral to Greek life since ancient times, with architecture having had the most profound influence. Greek temples, seen throughout history as symbolic of democracy, were the inspiration for architectural movements such as the Italian Renaissance. Today masses of cheap concrete apartment blocks built in the 20th century in Greece's major cities belie this architectural legacy.

Thankfully, the great works of Greek literature are not as easily besmirched. The first and greatest Ancient Greek writer was Homer, author of *Iliad* and *Odyssey,* telling the story of the Trojan War and the subsequent wanderings of Odysseus.

Pindar (c 518–438 BC) is regarded as the pre-eminent lyric poet of ancient Greece and was commissioned to recite his odes at the Olympic Games. The great writers of love poetry were Sappho (6th century BC) and Alcaeus (5th century BC), both of whom lived on Lesvos. Sappho's poetic descriptions of her affections for women gave rise to the term 'lesbian'.

The Alexandrian Constantine Cavafy (1863–1933) revolutionised Greek poetry by introducing a personal, conversational style. Later, poet George Seferis (1900–71) won the Nobel Prize for literature in 1963, as did Odysseus Elytis (1911–96) in 1979. Nikos Kazantzakis, author of *Zorba the Greek* and numerous novels, plays and poems, is the most famous of 20th-century Greek novelists.

Greece's most famous painter was a young Cretan called Domenikos Theotokopoulos, who moved to Spain in 1577 and became known as the great El Greco. Famous painters of the 20th century include Konstantinos Parthenis and, later, George Bouzianis, whose work can be viewed at the National Art Gallery in Athens.

Music has been a facet of Greek life since ancient times. When visiting Greece today, your trip will inevitably be accompanied by the plucked-string sound of the ubiquitous bouzouki. The bouzouki is one of the main instruments of *rembetika* music – which is in many ways the Greek equivalent of the American blues and has its roots in the sufferings of refugees from Asia Minor in the 1920s.

Dance is also an integral part of Greek life. Whether at a wedding, nightclub or village celebration, traditional dance is widely practised.

Drama continues to feature in domestic arts, particularly in Athens and Thessaloniki. In summer, Greek dramas are staged in the ancient theatres where they were originally performed.

Greek film has for many years been associated with the work of film-maker Theo Angelopoulos, who won Cannes' Palme d'Or in 1998 with *An Eternity and One Day*. Yorgos Lanthimos was nominated for an Academy Award for Best Foreign Language Film for *Dogtooth* (Kynodonta) in 2011. However, the most internationally acclaimed film remains to be the 1964 classic, *Zorba the Greek*.

Greek TV is dominated by chat shows, sport and foreign movies, only to be interrupted by localised versions of the latest American 'reality TV' hit.

Environment

The Land

Greece sits at the southern tip of the Balkan Peninsula. Of its 1400 islands, only 169 are inhabited. The land mass is 131,944 sq km and Greek territorial waters cover a further 400,000 sq km. Nowhere in Greece is much more than 100km from the sea.

Around 80% of the land is mountainous, with less than a quarter of the country suitable for agriculture.

Greece sits in one of the most seismically active regions in the world – the eastern

Mediterranean lies at the meeting point of three continental plates: the Eurasian, African and Arabian. Consequently, Greece has had more than 20,000 earthquakes in the last 40 years, most of them very minor.

Wildlife

The variety of flora in Greece is unrivalled in Europe, with a dazzling array of spectacular wildflowers best seen in the mountains of Crete and the southern Peloponnese.

You won't encounter many animals in the wild, mainly due to hunting. Wild boar, still found in the north, is a favourite target. Squirrels, rabbits, hares, foxes and weasels are all fairly common on the mainland. Reptiles are well represented by snakes, including several poisonous viper species.

Lake Mikri Prespa in Macedonia has the richest colony of fish-eating birds in Europe, while the Dadia Forest Reserve in Thrace counts such majestic birds as the golden eagle and the giant black vulture among its residents.

The brown bear, Europe's largest land mammal, still survives in very small numbers in the mountains of northern Greece, as does the grey wolf.

Europe's rarest mammal, the monk seal, once very common in the Mediterranean Sea, is now on the brink of extinction in Europe. There are about 400 left in Europe, half of which live in Greece. About 40 frequent the Ionian Sea and the rest are found in the Aegean.

The waters around Zakynthos are home to Europe's last large sea turtle colony, that of the loggerhead turtle *(Careta careta)*. The **Sea Turtle Protection Society of Greece** (21052 31342; www.archelon.gr) runs monitoring programs and is always on the look-out for volunteers.

National Parks

While facilities in Greek national parks aren't on par with many other countries, all have refuges and some have marked hiking trails. The most visited parks are Mt Parnitha, north of Athens, and the Samaria Gorge on Crete. The others are Vikos-Aoös and Prespa National Parks in Epiros; Mt Olympus on the border of Thessaly and Macedonia; and Parnassos and Iti National Parks in central Greece. There is also a national marine park off the coast of Alonnisos, and another around the Bay of Laganas area off Zakynthos.

Environmental Issues

Greece is belatedly becoming environmentally conscious but, regrettably, it's too late for some regions. Deforestation and soil erosion are problems that go back thousands of years, with olive cultivation and goats being the main culprits. Forest fires are also a major problem, with an estimated 250 sq km destroyed every year.

General environmental awareness remains at a depressingly low level, especially where litter is concerned. The problem is particularly bad in rural areas, where roadsides are strewn with aluminium cans and plastic packaging hurled from passing cars. It is somewhat surprising that the waters of the Aegean are as clear as they are considering how many cigarette butts are tossed off ferries.

Food & Drink

Snacks

Greece has a great range of fast-food options. Foremost among them are gyros and souvlaki. The gyros is a giant skewer laden with seasoned meat that grills slowly as it rotates, the meat being steadily trimmed from the outside. Souvlaki are small cubes of meat cooked on a skewer. Both are served wrapped in pitta bread with salad and lashings of tzatziki (a yogurt, cucumber and garlic dip). Other snacks are pretzel rings, spanakopita (spinach and cheese pie) and *tyropita* (cheese pie).

Starters

Greece is famous for its appetisers, known as *mezedhes* (literally, 'tastes'; meze for short). Standards include tzatziki, *melitzanosalata* (aubergine dip), taramasalata (fish-roe dip), dolmadhes (stuffed vine leaves; dolmas for short), *fasolia* (beans) and *oktapodi* (octopus). A selection of three or four starters represents a good meal and makes an excellent vegetarian option.

Mains

You'll find moussaka (layers of aubergine and mince, topped with béchamel sauce and baked) on every menu, alongside a number of other taverna staples. They include *moschari* (oven-baked veal and potatoes), *keftedes* (meatballs), *stifado* (meat stew), *pastitsio* (baked dish of macaroni with minced meat and béchamel sauce) and *yemista* (either tomatoes or green peppers stuffed with minced meat and rice).

Kalamaria (fried squid) is the most popular (and cheapest) seafood, while *barbouni* (red mullet) and *sifias* (swordfish) tend to be more expensive than meat dishes.

Fortunately for vegetarians, salad is a mainstay of the Greek diet. The most popular is *horiatiki salata,* normally listed on English-language menus as Greek salad. It's a delicious mixed salad comprising cucumbers, peppers, onions, olives, tomatoes and feta cheese. For the full scoop on Greece's legendary feta cheese, check out www.feta.gr.

Desserts

Most Greek desserts are Turkish in origin and are variations on pastry soaked in honey, such as baklava (thin layers of pastry filled with honey and nuts). Delicious Greek yogurt also makes a great dessert, especially with honey.

Drinks

Bottled mineral water is cheap and available everywhere, as are soft drinks and packaged juices.

Mythos, in its distinctive green bottle, and Alfa, are popular Greek beers.

Greece is traditionally a wine-drinking society. An increasingly good range of wines

THE ART OF OUZO

Ouzo is Greece's most famous but misunderstood tipple. While it can be drunk as an aperitif, for most Greeks ouzo has come to embody a way of socialising – best enjoyed during a lazy, extended summer afternoon of seafood *mezedhes* (appetisers) by the beach. Ouzo is sipped slowly and ritually to clean the palate between tastes. It is served in small bottles or *karafakia* (carafes) with water and a bowl of ice cubes – and is commonly drunk on the rocks, diluted with water (it turns a cloudy white). Mixing it with cola is a foreign abomination!

Made from distilled grapes, ouzo is also distilled with residuals from fruit, grains and potatoes, and flavoured with spices, primarily aniseed, giving it that liquorice flavour. The best ouzo is produced on Lesvos and there are more than 360 brands.

NO MORE SMOKE

Legislation that brought in anti-smoking laws similar to those throughout Europe in 2009 was not exactly popular with Greeks, the EU's biggest smokers. Smoking is now officially banned inside public places, with the penalty fines placed on the business owners.

---

made from traditional grape varieties is available. Wine enthusiasts should take a look at www.allaboutgreekwine.com. Retsina, wine flavoured with pine-tree resin, is a tasty alternative – though an acquired taste for some. Most tavernas will offer locally made house wines by the carafe.

Metaxa, Greece's dominant brandy, is sweet, while if you are offered some raki, make sure to take a small sip first!

'Greek' coffee should be tried at least once, but don't drink the mudlike grounds at the bottom!

Where to Eat & Drink

The most common variety of restaurant in Greece is the taverna, traditionally an extension of the Greek home table. *Estiatorio* is Greek for restaurant and often has the same dishes as a taverna but with higher prices. A *psistaria* specialises in charcoal-grilled dishes, while a *psarotaverna* specialises in fish. *Ouzeria* (ouzo bars) often have such a range of *mezedhes* that they can be regarded as eateries. Many restaurants are open for lunch and dinner daily during high season.

Kafeneia are the smoke-filled cafes where men gather to drink 'Greek' coffee, play backgammon and cards, and engage in heated political discussion. Every Greek town you'll visit now has at least one cafe-bar where Greece's youth while away hours over a frappé (frothy ice coffee).

Buying and preparing your own food is easy in Greece – every town of consequence has a supermarket, as well as fruit and vegetable shops.

To have a go at producing your own Greek culinary masterpieces, check out www.gourmed.gr. You'll also find information on the healthy Greek diet at www.mediterraneandiet.gr, while www.oliveoil.gr can tell you all about one of Greece's best-known products.

SURVIVAL GUIDE

Directory A–Z
Accommodation

Campgrounds Generally open from April to October; standard facilities include hot showers, kitchens, restaurants and minimarkets – and often a swimming pool; Panhellenic Camping Association (☎21036 21560; www.panhellenic-camping-union.gr).

Domatia Greek equivalent of a B&B, minus the breakfast; don't worry about finding them – owners will find you as they greet ferries and buses shouting 'room!'.

Hotels Classified as deluxe, or A, B, C, D or E class; ratings seldom seem to have much bearing on the price, which is determined more by season and location.

Mountain refuges Listed in *Greece Mountain Refuges & Ski Centres*, available free of charge at EOT and EOS (Ellinikos Orivatikos Syndesmos, the Greek Alpine Club) offices.

Youth hostels In most major towns and on some islands; Greek Youth Hostel Organisation (☎21075 19530; www.athens-yhostel.com).

ℹ SEASONAL PRICES

'High season' is usually in July and August. If you turn up in the 'middle' or 'shoulder seasons' (May and June; September and October) expect to pay significantly less. During 'low season' (late October to late April) prices can be up to 50% cheaper, but a lot of places, especially on the islands, virtually close their shutters for winter. Websites will usually display these differences in price.

Greek accommodation is subject to strict price controls, and by law a notice must be displayed in every room stating the category of the room and the seasonal price. It's usually on the back of the door. If you think there's something amiss, contact the Tourist Police.

PRICE RANGES

Prices quoted in listings are for high season (usually July and August) and include a private bathroom.

€€€ more than €150

€€ €60 to €150

€ less than €60

Business Hours

Banks 8am to 2.30pm Monday to Thursday, 8am to 2pm Friday (in cities, also: 3.30p 6.30pm Monday to Friday, 8am to 1.30pm Saturday)

Cafes 10am to midnight

Post offices 7.30am to 2pm Monday Friday (in cities 7.30am to 8pm Monday Friday, 7.30am- to 2pm Saturday)

Restaurants 11am to 3pm & 7pm to 1am (varies greatly)

Supermarkets 8am to 8pm Monday to Friday, 8am to 3pm Saturday

Street kiosks (*Periptera*) early to late Monday to Sunday

Children

It's safe and easy to travel with children in Greece, as Greeks tends to be very family-oriented. See www.greece4kids.com.

» Be very careful crossing roads with kids!
» Travel on ferries, buses and trains is free to age four; half-fare to age 10 (ferries) or 12 (buses and trains).
» Kids' menus abound.

HAPHAZARD OPENING HOURS

It's worth noting that with businesses associated with tourism, opening hours can be rather haphazard. In high season when there are plenty of visitors around, restaurants, cafes, nightclubs and souvenir shops are pretty much open whenever they think they can do good business. If there are few people around, some businesses will simply close early or won't bother opening at all. And in low season, some places, including some sleeping options, may close up for months at a time.

Customs Regulations

There are no longer duty-free restrictions within the EU.

It is strictly forbidden to export antiquities (anything over 100 years old) without an export permit.

Embassies & Consulates

Australian Embassy (☑210 870 4000; www.greece.embassy.gov.au; Ambelokipi, 6th fl, Thon Building, cnr Leoforos Alexandras & Leoforos Kifisias)

Canadian Embassy (☑210 727 3400; www.greece.gc.ca; Genadiou 4)

Japanese Embassy (☑210 670 9900; www.gr.emb-japan.go.jp; Ethnikís Antistáseos 46, Halandri)

New Zealand Embassy (☑210 687 4701; www.nzembassy.com; Kifisias 268, Halandri)

UK Embassy (☑210 723 6211; www.ukingreece.fco.gov.uk; Ploutarhou 1)

US Embassy (☑210 721 2951; http://athens.usembassy.gov; Leoforos Vasilissis Sofias 91)

Food

Price ranges for Eating are as follows:

€€€ more than €40

€€ €15 to €40

€ less than €15

Gay & Lesbian Travellers

The church plays a significant role in shaping society's views on issues such as sexuality, and homosexuality is generally frowned-upon.

It is wise to be discreet and to avoid open displays of togetherness. That said, Greece is a popular destination for gay travellers.

Athens has a busy gay scene that packs up and heads to the islands for summer, with Mykonos famous for its bars, beaches and hedonism, and Eresos on Lesvos something of a pilgrimage for lesbians.

Internet Access

Greece has embraced the internet big-time, but charges differ wildly (as does speed of access). Most midrange and top-end hotels will offer their guests some form of internet connection, and laptop-wielding visitors will often be able to connect to wi-fi at hotels and most internet cafes.

Language Courses

For intensive language courses check out the **Athens Centre** (Map p238; ☏210 701 2268; www.athenscentre.gr; Arhimidous 48, Mets; ⓂAkropoli).

Money

ATMs Everywhere except the smallest villages.

Bargaining While souvenir shops will generally bargain, prices in other shops are normally clearly marked and non-negotiable; accommodation is nearly always negotiable outside peak season, especially for longer stays.

Cash Currency is king at street kiosks and small shops, and especially in the countryside.

Changing currency Banks, post offices and currency exchange offices are all over the places; exchange all major currencies.

Credit cards Generally accepted, but may not be on smaller islands or in small villages.

Tipping The service charge is included on the bill in restaurants, but it is the custom to 'round up the bill'; same for taxis.

Post

Tahydromia (post offices) are easily identified by the yellow sign outside.

Regular postboxes are yellow; red postboxes are for express mail.

The postal rate for postcards and airmail letters within the EU is €0.60; to other destinations it's €0.80.

Public Holidays

New Year's Day 1 January

Epiphany 6 January

First Sunday in Lent February

Greek Independence Day 25 March

Good Friday/Easter Sunday March/April

May Day (Protomagia) 1 May

Feast of the Assumption 15 August

Ohi Day 28 October

Christmas Day 25 December

St Stephen's Day 26 December

Safe Travel

Crime is traditionally low in Greece, but on the rise. Watch out for bar scams and *bombes* (spiked drinks), and be wary of pickpockets on the Athens metro, around Omonia and at the flea market. Generally speaking, thefts from tourists are often committed by other tourists.

Telephone

Maintained by Organismos Tilepikoinonion Ellados, known as OTE (*o-teh*). Public phones are everywhere, take all phonecards and are easy to use; pressing the 'i' button brings up the operating instructions in English.

For directory inquiries within Greece, call ☏131 or ☏132; for international directory enquiries, it's ☏161 or ☏162.

MOBILE PHONES

Mobile phones are a must-have in Greece. If you have a compatible GSM phone from a country with a global roaming agreement with Greece, you'll be able to use your phone there.

There are several mobile service providers in Greece; **CosmOTE** (www.cosmote.gr) has the best coverage. You can purchase a Greek SIM card for around €20.

The use of a mobile phone while driving in Greece is prohibited.

PHONE CODES

Telephone codes are part of the 10-digit number within Greece.

The landline prefix is 2 and for mobiles it's 6.

PHONECARDS

All public phones use OTE phonecards; sold at OTE offices and street kiosks. Phonecards come in €3, €5 and €10 versions; local calls cost €0.30 for three minutes. Discount-card schemes are available, offering much better value for money.

Time

There's one time zone throughout Greece, which is two hours ahead of GMT/UTC and three hours ahead on daylight-savings time (from the last Sunday in March to the last Sunday in October).

Toilets

Public toilets are rare, except at airports and bus and train stations.

Most places have Western-style toilets, but some public toilets may be Asian-style squat toilets.

Greek plumbing can't handle toilet paper: anything larger than a postage stamp will cause a blockage. Put your used toilet paper, sanitary napkins and tampons in the small bin provided next to every toilet.

Tourist Information

There's an EOT office or local tourist office In almost every town of consequence and on many of the islands, plus **Tourist Police** in popular destinations; they can also provide information. Head here if you think you've been ripped off.

Greek National Tourist Organisation (GNTO; www.gnto.gr) Known as EOT within Greece.

Travellers with Disabilities

Most hotels, museums and ancient sites are not wheelchair accessible; the uneven terrain is an issue even for able-bodied people. Few facilities exist for the visually or hearing impaired. Check out www.greecetravel.com/handicapped.

Visas

Visitors from most countries don't need a visa for Greece. Countries whose nationals can stay in Greece for up to three months include Australia, Canada, all EU countries, Iceland, Israel, Japan, New Zealand and the USA.

Getting There & Away

Air

Most visitors arrive by air, mostly into Athens. There are 17 international airports in Greece; most handle only summer charter flights to the islands.

There's a growing number of direct scheduled services into Greece by European budget airlines – Olympic Air (www. olympicair. com) and Aegean Airlines (www.aegeanair. com) also fly internationally.

Land

BORDER CROSSINGS

You can drive or ride through the following border crossings.

From Albania:

Kakavia (60km northwest of Ioannina)

Sagiada (28km north of Igoumenitsa)

Mertziani (17km west of Konitsa)

Krystallopigi (14km west of Kotas)

From Bulgaria:

Promahonas (109km northeast of Thessaloniki)

Ormenio (41km from Serres)

Exohi (50km north of Drama)

INTERNATIONAL AIRPORTS

CITY	AIRPORT	DESIGNATION
Aktion (for Lefkada)	Aktion National Airport	PVK
Athens	Eleftherios Venizelos Airport	ATH
Corfu	Corfu Intl Airport	CFU
Hania (Crete)	Hania Intl Airport	CHQ
Iraklio	Nikos Kazantzakis Airport	HER
Kalamata	Kalamata Intl Airport	KLX
Karpathos	Karpathos National Airport	AOK
Kavala	Alexander the Great Airport	KVA
Kefallonia	Kefallonia Intl Airport	EFL
Kos	Hippocrates Intl Airport	KGS
Mykonos	Mykonos National Airport	JMK
Rhodes	Diagoras Airport	RHO
Samos	Samos Intl Airport	SMI
Santorini (Thira)	Santorini National Airport	JTR
Skiathos	Skiathos National Airport	JSI
Thessaloniki	Macedonia Airport	SKG
Zakynthos	Zakynthos Intl Airport	ZTH

LONDON TO ATHENS OVERLAND

For overland enthusiasts, a trip from London to Athens can be accomplished in two days, taking in some gorgeous scenery along the way. A sample itinerary from London would see you catching the Eurostar to Paris and then an overnight sleeper train to Bologna in Italy. From there, a coastal train takes you to Bari, where there's an overnight boat to Patra on the Peloponnese. From Patra, it's a 4½-hour train journey to Athens.

From Macedonia:

Evzoni (68km north of Thessaloniki)

Niki (16km north of Florina)

Doïrani (31km north of Kilkis)

From Turkey:

Kipi (43km east of Alexandroupolis)

Kastanies (139km northeast of Alexandroupolis)

BUS

The **Hellenic Railways Organisation** (OSE; www.ose.gr) has been operating the following routes, but international buses are somewhat in limbo due to Greece's financial problems. Check the current status well in advance.

Albania Athens–Tirana overnight bus (16 hours, daily) via Ioannina and Gjirokastra

Bulgaria Athens–Sofia bus (15 hours, six weekly); Thessaloniki–Sofia (7½ hours, four daily)

Turkey Athens–İstanbul (22 hours, six weekly); stops at Thessaloniki (seven hours) and Alexandroupolis (13 hours)

TRAIN

Both international and domestic train routes have been severely curtailed due to the financial problems. Be sure to check the current situation well in advance. The following routes may or may not be in operation.

Bulgaria Sofia–Athens (18 hours, daily) via Thessaloniki

Macedonia Thessaloniki–Skopje (five hours, twice daily)

Turkey İstanbul–Thessaloniki (12 hours, daily)

Russia Thessaloniki–Moscow (70 hours, weekly, summer only)

Sea

Check out ferry routes, schedules and services online at www.greekferries.gr.

If you are travelling on a rail pass, check to see if ferry travel between Italy and Greece is included. Some ferries are free, others give a discount. On some routes you will need to make reservations.

ALBANIA

Saranda Petrakis Lines (☏26610 38690; www.ionian-cruises.com) has daily hydrofoils to Corfu (25 minutes).

ITALY

Ancona Patra (20 hours, three daily, summer)

Bari Patra (14½ hours, daily) via Corfu (eight hours) and Keffalonia (14 hours); also to Igoumenitsa (11½ hours, daily)

Brindisi Patra (15 hours, Apr–early Oct) via Igoumenitsa

Venice Patra (30 hours, up to 12 weekly, summer) via Corfu (25 hours)

TURKEY

Boat services operate between Turkey's Aegean coast and the Greek Islands.

Marmaris and Fethiye Rhodes (daily in summer, twice weekly in winter)

Bodrum Kos (one hour, daily in summer)

Kuşadası Samos (one hour, daily in summer, weekly in winter)

Çeşme Chios (one hour, daily in summer)

Ayvalık Lesvos (one hour, four times weekly in summer)

MOVING ON?

For tips, recommendations and reviews beyond Greece, head to www.shop.lonelyplanet.com, where you can purchase downloadable PDFs of the Albania and Turkey chapters from Lonely Planet's *Mediterranean Europe* guide, or the Macedonia and Bulgaria chapters from *Eastern Europe*.

Getting Around

Greece has a comprehensive transport system and is easy to get around.

Air

Domestic air travel has been very price competitive of late, and it's sometimes cheaper to fly than take the ferry, especially if you book ahead online. A plan to merge Olympic Air and Aegean Airlines was prohibited by the European Commission in January 2011 due to its potential effect on competition and prices.

DOMESTIC AIRLINES

Aegean Airlines (A3; www.aegeanair.com) The big competition for Olympic Air offers newer aircraft and similar prices on popular routes.

Astra Airlines (A2; www.astra-airlines.gr) Based in Thessaloniki; a newcomer flying limited routes.

Athens Airways (☑210 669 6600, 801 801 4000; www.athensairways.com) New kid on the block, but growing steadily.

Olympic Air (OA; www.olympicair.com) Recently privatised; has the most extensive network.

Sky Express (☑281 022 3500; www.sky express.gr) Based in Iraklio, Crete; mainly flies routes that the big two don't.

Bicycle

Greece has very hilly terrain and the summer heat can be stifling. In addition, many drivers totally disregard the road rules.

See www.cyclegreece.gr for bicycle tour ideas. Bicycles are carried for free on ferries.

Rental bicycles are available at most tourist centres, but are generally for pedalling around town rather than for serious riding. Prices generally range from €10 to €20 per day.

Boat

FERRY

Ferries come in all shapes and sizes, from state-of-the-art 'superferries' that run on the major routes, to ageing open ferries that operate local services to outlying islands.

Newer high-speed ferries are slashing travel times, but cost much more.

'Classes' on ferries are largely a thing of the past; you have the option of 'deck class', which is the cheapest ticket, or 'cabin class' with air-con cabins and a decent lounge and restaurant.

When buying tickets you will automatically be given deck class.

Tickets can be bought at the last minute at the dock, but in high season, some boats may be full – plan ahead.

The Greek Ships app for smartphones can be used for real-time tracking to see if your ferry is going to turn up on time – seach for 'Greek Ships' in your app store.

ℹ️ ISLAND-HOPPING

For many, the idea of meandering from island to island by boat in the Greek Islands is the ultimate dream. It's still a lot of fun, but to some extent not what it used to be. Many of those slow, romantic old ferries you may have seen in the movies have disappeared, replaced by big modern people-movers. If you turn up in high season you might find it just as stressful as rush hour back home.

It's still possible to get away from it all, but it will require some thought – head to smaller islands off the beaten path before high season kicks in. Every island has a boat service of some sort!

Boat operations are highly seasonal and based on the tourist trade, so there's not a lot happening in winter. Services pick up from April, and during July and August Greece's seas are a mass of wake and wash.

Summer also brings the *meltemi*, a strong dry northerly wind that can blow for days and cause havoc to ferry schedules.

In any season, changes to schedules can take place at the last minute. Be prepared to be flexible. Boats seldom arrive early, but often arrive late! And some don't come at all. Think of it as part of the fun.

Check out www.openseas.gr for schedules, costs and links to individual boat company websites.

Main Ferry Routes

CATAMARAN

High-speed catamarans have become an important part of the island travel scene and are much less prone to cancellation in rough weather.

Catamaran fares are generally more expensive than ferries and about the same as hydrofoils.

HYDROFOIL

Hydrofoils are a faster alternative to ferries on some routes, take half the time, but cost twice as much. Most routes will operate only during the high season.

Tickets for hydrofoils must be bought in advance and they are often sold with seat allocation.

Bus

Long-distance buses are operated by **KTEL** (www.ktel.org). Fares are fixed by the government and service routes can be found on the company's website. Buses are comfortable, generally run on time, reasonably priced – eg Athens–Volos (€25, five hours) and Athens–Patra (€17, three hours) – and there are frequent services on all major routes. Tickets should be bought at least an hour in advance to ensure a seat. Buses don't have toilets and refreshments, but stop for a break every couple of hours.

Car & Motorcycle

Driving yourself is a great way to explore areas in Greece that are off the beaten track, but be careful – Greece has the highest road-fatality rate in Europe. The road network has improved dramatically in recent years, but freeway tolls are fairly hefty.

Almost all islands are served by car ferries, but they are expensive; costs vary by the size of the vehicle.

The Greek automobile club, ELPA (www.elpa.gr), generally offers reciprocal services to

ROAD RULES

» Drive on the right.

» Overtake on the left (not all Greeks do this!).

» Compulsory to wear seatbelts in the front seats, and in the back if they are fitted.

» Drink-driving laws are strict; a blood alcohol content of 0.05% incurs a fine of around €150 and over 0.08% is a criminal offence.

members of other national motoring associations. If your vehicle breaks down, dial ☎104.

EU-registered vehicles are allowed free entry into Greece for six months without road taxes being due; a green card (international third party insurance) is all that's required.

RENTAL CARS

Available just about anywhere in Greece, you'll get better rates with local rental-car companies than with the big multinational outfits. Check the insurance waivers closely; check how they can assist in case of a breakdown.

High-season weekly rates start at about €280 for the smallest models, dropping to €200 in winter – add tax and extras. Major companies will request a credit-card deposit.

Minimum driving age in Greece is 18, but most car-hire firms require a driver of 21 or over.

RENTAL MOPEDS & MOTORCYCLES

These are available for hire everywhere. Regulations stipulate that you need a valid motorcycle licence stating proficiency for the size of motorcycle you wish to rent – from 50cc upwards.

Mopeds and 50cc motorcycles range from €10 to €25 per day or from €25 per day for a 250cc motorcycle. Outside high season, rates drop considerably.

Ensure that the bike is in good working order and the brakes work well, and check that your travel insurance covers you for injury resulting from motorcycle accidents.

Public Transport

Bus All major towns have local bus systems.

Metro Athens is the only city with a metro system.

TAXI

Taxis are widely available and reasonably priced. Yellow city cabs are metered; rates double between midnight and 5am. Grey rural taxis do not have meters; settle on a price before you get in.

Athens taxi drivers are gifted in their ability to somehow make a little bit extra with every fare. If you have a complaint, note the cab number and contact the Tourist Police. Rural taxi drivers are generally honest, friendly and helpful.

Train

Greece's train services were in a precarious state at the time of research. Check the Greek Railways Organisation website (www.ose.gr) for the latest.

Greece has only two main lines: Athens north to Thessaloniki and Alexandroupolis, and Athens to the Peloponnese.

There are a number of branch lines, eg Pyrgos–Olympia line and the spectacular Diakofto–Kalavryta mountain railway.

InterRail and Eurail passes are valid; you still need to make a reservation.

In summer make reservations at least two days in advance.

Kosovo

Best Places to Eat

» Tiffany (p329)

» Home Bar & Restaurant (p329)

» De Rada Brasserie (p329)

Best Places to Stay

» Swiss Diamond Hotel (p328)

» Dukagjini Hotel (p332)

» Hotel Sara (p329)

» Hotel Prizreni (p333)

Why Go?

Kosovo may be Europe's newest country, but its long and dramatic history can be witnessed at every turn. Far from being the dangerous or depressing place most people imagine when they hear the name, Kosovo is a fascinating land at the heart of the Balkans and one of the last corners of Eastern Europe where tourism has yet to take off.

Barbs of its past are impossible to miss however: roads are dotted with memorials to those killed in 1999, when Serbia stripped Kosovo of its autonomy and initiated ethnic cleansing, while NATO forces still guard Serbian monasteries. But with independence has come stability, and Kosovo is now the latest word in getting off the beaten track in the Balkans. Visitors who make the journey here will be rewarded with welcoming smiles, charming mountain towns, incredible hiking opportunities and 13th-century domed Serbian monasteries just for starters.

When to Go
Pristina

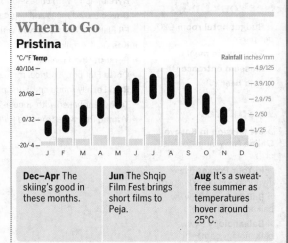

Dec–Apr The skiing's good in these months.

Jun The Shqip Film Fest brings short films to Peja.

Aug It's a sweat-free summer as temperatures hover around 25°C.

AT A GLANCE

» **Currency** Euro (€)

» **Language** Albanian, Serbian

» **Money** ATMs in larger towns; banks open Monday to Friday

» **Visas** Kosovo is visa-free for all nationalities. All passports are stamped on arrival for a 90-day stay.

Fast Facts

» **Area** 10,887 sq km

» **Capital** Pristina

» **Country code** ☑381

» **Emergency** Ambulance ☑94, fire ☑93, police ☑92

Exchange Rates

Australia	A$1	€0.82
Canada	C$1	€0.77
Japan	¥100	€0.83
New Zealand	NZ$1	€0.65
UK	UK£1	€1.18
USA	US$1	€0.78

Set Your Budget

» **Budget hotel room** €20 per person

» **Two-course meal** €12

» **Museum entrance** €1–3

» **Peja beer** €2

Resources

» **UN Mission in Kosovo Online** (www.unmikonline. org)

» **In Your Pocket** (www. inyourpocket.com/kosovo)

» **Balkan Insight** (www. balkaninsight.com)

» **Balkanology** (www. balkanology.com)

Connections

Kosovo has good bus connections between Albania, Montenegro and Macedonia, with regular services from Pristina, Peja and Prizren to Tirana (Albania), Skopje (Macedonia) and Podgorica (Montenegro). There's also a train line from Pristina to Macedonia's capital, Skopje.

Do note that Kosovo's independence is not recognised by Serbia, and so if you plan to continue to Serbia but entered Kosovo via Albania, Macedonia or Montenegro, officials at the Serbian border will deem that you entered Serbia illegally and you will not be let in. You'll need to exit Kosovo to a third country and then enter Serbia from there. If you entered Kosovo from Serbia, then there's no problem returning to Serbia.

ITINERARIES

Two to Three Days

Spend a day in cool little Pristina and get to know this burgeoning nation's charming capital. The next day, visit Gračanica Monastery and then curl through the mountains to Prizren's Ottoman sights, or make a beeline for mountainous Peja.

One Week

After a couple of days in the capital, and a visit to Gračanica Monastery, loop to Prizren for castle views and its Ethnological Museum, then Peja for monasteries and markets before taking a couple of days to hike in the beautiful Rugova Mountains.

Essential Food & Drink

» **Byrek** Pastry with cheese or meat.

» **Duvëc** Baked meat and vegetables.

» **Fli** Flaky pastry pie served with honey.

» **Kos** Goat's-milk yoghurt.

» **Pershut** Dried meat.

» **Qofta** Flat or cylindrical minced-meat rissoles.

» **Raki** Locally made spirit, usually made from grapes.

» **Tavë** Meat baked with cheese and egg.

» **Vranac** Red wine from the Rahovec region of Kosovo.

Kosovo Highlights

1 See the sights in Pristina's charming **bazaar area** (p328) and discover this bustling new capital.

2 Breathe deep at Peja's Saturday **Cheese Market** (p332).

3 Buy local wine and cheese at the serene 14th-century **Visoki Dečani Monastery** (p332).

4 Wander the picturesque streets of **Prizren's** (p333) charming old town.

5 Trek around the **Rugova mountains** (p332).

6 Visit the important hub of Serbian cultural that is the **Gračanica Monastery** (p329).

PRISTINA

☎038 / POP 198,000

Pristina (pronounced Prish-tEEna) is a city changing fast and one that feels full of the optimism and potential that you'd expect from Europe's newest capital city. Far more provincial town than great city, Pristina's vibe is laid back and frequently unpredictable: the UN and EU both have huge presences here and Pristina feels rich and more sophisticated as a result. But get out of the centre, with its international restaurants and smart cafes, and you'll find yourself in the quaint Turkic hillside neighbourhoods that have defined the city for centuries.

◉ Sights

BAZAAR AREA

To the north of the Vellusha district, around Rruga Agim Ramadani, are the narrow and twisting streets of the bazaar area, where you'll find many of Pristina's sights as well as the bustling market.

Ethnographic Museum HISTORIC BUILDING
(Rr Iliaz Agushi; admission €2.50; ◷10am-4pm) Follow the signs all around Pristina to locate this well-kept 'how we lived' Ottoman house.

Kosovo Museum MUSEUM
(Sheshi Adam Jashari; admission €3; ◷10am-4pm Tue-Sat) A written plea to have antiquities returned from Serbia greets visitors; while you're waiting, see modern exhibits upstairs (celebrating America's support for Kosovo when we visited) and delicate 6000-year-old statues on the ground floor. It was closed for a full renovation at the time of research.

Mosques MOSQUES
Fronting the Kosovo Museum is the 15th-century **Carshi Mosque** (Agim Ramadani). Nearby, the **Sultan Mehmet Fatih Mosque** (Big Mosque; Rr Ilir Konushevci) was built by its namesake around 1461, converted to a Catholic church during the Austro-Hungarian era and refurbished again during WWII. **Jashar Pasha Mosque** (Rr Ylfete Humolli) has vibrant interiors that exemplify Turkish baroque style.

Clock Tower LANDMARK
This 26m tower makes a good point of reference. The **Great Hamam** nearby is being renovated.

CENTRE

The centre of Pristina was being impressively spruced up in autumn 2012, based around the new Ibrahim Rugova Sq, the centrepiece of the city at the end of pedestrianised Bul Nenë Terezë.

National Library LIBRARY
(www.biblioteka-ks.org; Agim Ramadani; ◷7am-8pm Mon-Fri, 7am-2pm Sat) The National Library, completed in 1982 by Croatian Andrija Mutnjakovic, must be seen to be believed (think gelatinous eggs wearing armour).

FREE **Kosovo Art Gallery** ART GALLERY
(Agim Ramadani 60; ◷10am-6pm Tue & Fri-Sat) Behind the National Library, this gallery is a welcoming place featuring the works of local artists.

FREE **Independence House of Kosovo** HISTORIC BUILDING
(◷10am-5pm Mon-Sat) This small house opposite the stadium is devoted to former president Ibrahim Rugova and Kosovo's recent independence movement. English-speaking guides will show you around the small display, including video footage of Rugova's meetings with world leaders.

🛏 Sleeping

TOP CHOICE **Swiss Diamond Hotel** LUXURY HOTEL €€€
(☎220 000; www.swissdiamondhotelprishtina.com; Sheshi Nëna Terezë; s/d incl breakfast from €137/157; [P][⊖][✳][@][≈][❄]) This is the international standard five-star hotel that Pristina has been waiting for. Opened in 2012 right in the heart of the city, this place is all marble floors, obsequious staff and liveried bell boys. The rooms are lavish and the suites are immense, all decorated with expensive furnishings and many enjoying great city views. There's also a spa, restaurant, wine cellar and piano lounge.

TOP CHOICE **Velania Guesthouse** PENSION €
(☎044 167 455, 531 742; http://guesthouse-ks.net/eng/vlersimet.html; Velania 4/34; dm/s/d/apt €9/15/20/35; [@]) This bustling guesthouse is spread over two buildings in an affluent part of town. The jovial professor who runs it loves a chat and could double as your grandfather. The hike up to it is much more fun in a taxi (€1.50) – either way consult the website first and print out the map, as it's hard to find!

Hotel Begolli HOTEL €€
(☎244 277; www.hotelbegolli.com; Rr Maliq Pashë Gjinolli 8; s/d incl breakfast €40/50, ste €60; [✳][@][❄]) While it may have gone overboard with its '90s-style furniture, Begolli is a pleasant, rather sprawling place to stay. The suite

GRAČANICA MONASTERY & GADIMË CAVE

Explore beyond Pristina by heading southeast to Gračanica Monastery or south to Gadimë Cave. Dusty fingers of sunlight pierce the darkness of **Gračanica Monastery** (⏰6am-5pm), completed in 1321 by Serbian King Milutin. It's an oasis in a town that is the cultural centre of Serbs in central Kosovo. Take a Gjilan-bound bus (€0.50, 15 minutes, every 30 minutes); the monastery's on your left. Rumours abound that bus drivers won't let you on or off if you tell them where you're going, so be discreet.

Famed for helictites, **Gadimë Cave** (Shpella Mermerit; admission €2.50; ⏰9am-7pm) is visited with a guide who enthusiastically points out shapes like a hand, an elephant head and various body parts. Buses go to Gadimë (€1, 30 minutes, every half-hour) via Lipjan. Or take a Ferizaj-bound bus, get dropped at the Gadimë turn-off and walk the 3km to town.

has two bedrooms and is good value, while the normal rooms are a little on the small side, but comfy. Staff are friendly and a good breakfast is served in the ground-floor bar.

Hotel Sara
HOTEL €€

(☎236 203, 238 765; www.hotel-sara.com; Rr Maliq Pashë Gjinolli; s/d/tr/apt incl breakfast €30/40/50/70; ❄🖫) In a tiny street filled with hotels by the bazaar, this 33-room hotel is rather garishly furnished in a style that suggests aspiration to boutique quality, but sadly rather misses the mark. That said, the rooms are good value at this price, and room 603 has a small balcony with great city views if you can cope with the colour scheme.

Hotel Afa
HOTEL €€

(☎227 722, 225 226; www.hotelafa.com; Ali Kelmendi 15; s/d/ste €45/65/69; ❄@) There's a classy lobby here (and a thank-you note from one former guest, Joe Biden) but the rooms are rather less grand, all featuring fairly bizarre assemblages of furniture and art, although many have jacuzzis and other such vice-presidential trimmings. It's a solid midrange option though, and staff are super helpful.

Hotel Xhema
HOTEL €

(☎719 716; Rr Maliq Pashë Gjinolli; s/d/ste incl breakfast €25/30/60; 🅿❄🖫) Behind two other hotels on this tiny side street by the bazaar, this is the best budget deal in the city centre. The suites are hilariously furnished and feature jacuzzis, kitchens and plush beds, while the cheaper rooms all smell rather musty and could use a refit, though they're ok for the price. The welcome is friendly and it's central.

 Eating

TOP CHOICE
Tiffany
TRADITIONAL €€

(Fehmi Agani; mains €8; ⏰8am-11pm Mon-Sat, to 6pm Sun) The oral menu here can be a lit-

tle confusing (though the staff's English is not at fault), but other than that there's no problem to be found with this brilliant place, much prized by the foreign community in Pristina. Enjoy the day's grilled special (whatever's fresh that day), beautifully cooked seasonal vegetables and oven-baked bread on the sun-dappled terrace. The restaurant is unsigned, hidden behind a well-tended bush on Fehmi Agani.

De Rada Brasserie
INTERNATIONAL €€

(Rr UÇK 50; mains €5-8; ⏰7.30am-7pm) A smart and atmospheric place right in the heart of town that serves up breakfasts, lunches and early dinners to an international clientele. The menu leans towards Italian, but there's plenty of choice. Grab a table outside on the street when the weather's good.

Home Bar & Restaurant
INTERNATIONAL €

(Luan Haradinaj; mains €4-9; ⏰7am-11pm Mon-Sat, 11am-11pm Sun; 🖫) Having been here since the dark days of 2001, this is the closest Pristina has to an ex-pat institution, and it lives up to its name, being exceptionally cosy and friendly, with scattered curios and antiques. The menu is international and eclectic and offers exactly what most travellers will be dreaming of: spring rolls, hummus, curries, wraps, burgers and even fajitas.

Osteria Basilico
ITALIAN €€

(Fehmi Agani 29/1; mains €5-11) This smart place is Pristina's most reliable Italian restaurant. There's a lovely terrace and a stylish interior where you can enjoy the wide-ranging menu, including plenty of regional classics as well as some more inventive dishes.

NOMNOM
INTERNATIONAL €€

(Rr Rexhep Luci 5; mains €7-12; ⏰7am-midnight; 🖫) Just off the main drag, this modern

Pristina

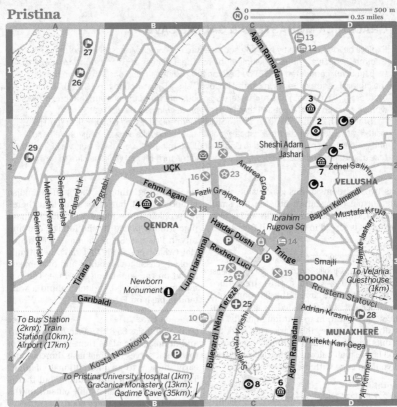

two-floor bar and restaurant caters to a smart local and foreign crowd. It has a huge summer terrace, and plenty of indoor seating too. The menu offers pizza, pasta, salad, grills and burgers. Sadly the place's overall style is compromised by terrible muzak.

Pishat TRADITIONAL €€
(Rr Qamil Hoxha 11; mains €4-11; ☉8am-11pm Mon-Sat, noon-11pm Sun) It's not only the cuisine that is typically Albanian here, but the fug of smoke hovering over the entire space. Despite that, this is a great spot to sample Albanian dishes with a largely local crowd.

🍷 Drinking

There's a slight madness to Pristina's drinking scene; places are hip one minute and empty the next. Try the bars along 2 Korriko, Haidar Dushi and Rehep Luci for 'spill-out-in-the-street' summer drinking.

Publicco BAR
(Rr Garibaldi 7) A suave option for coffee and cocktail seekers.

☆ Entertainment

Kino ABC CINEMA
(www.kinoabc.info; Rr Rexhep Luci 1; ☉8am-midnight) Two cinemas – the second is **ABC1** (www.kinoabc.info; R Luan Haradinaj) – usually show a couple of movies daily.

🛍 Shopping

Library Dukagjini BOOKS
(Bul Nëna Terezë 20; ☉8am-8pm Mon-Sat) Sells maps, language and history books and novels, including many titles in English.

ℹ Information

Barnatore Pharmacy (Bul Nëna Terezë; ☉8am-10pm)
Pristina University Hospital (Bul I Dëshmorët)

Pristina

◎ Sights
1	Carshi Mosque	D2
2	Clock Tower	D2
3	Ethnographic Museum	D1
4	Independence House of Kosovo	B2
5	Jashar Pasha Mosque	D2
6	Kosovo Art Gallery	C4
7	Kosovo Museum	D2
8	National Library	C4
9	Sultan Mehmet Fatih Mosque	D2

◎ Sleeping
10	Grand Hotel	C4
11	Hotel Afa	D4
12	Hotel Begolli	D1
13	Hotel Sara	C1
	Hotel Xhema	(see 13)
14	Swiss Diamond Hotel	C3

◎ Eating
15	De Rada Brasserie	C2
16	Home Bar & Restaurant	C2
17	NOMNOM	C3
18	Osteria Basilico	B2
19	Pishat	C3
20	Tiffany	B2

◎ Drinking
21	Publicco	B4

◎ Entertainment
22	Kino ABC	C3
23	Kino ABC1	C2

◎ Shopping
24	Library Dukagjini	C3

◎ Information
25	Barnatore Pharmacy	C3
26	French Embassy	A1
27	German Embassy	A1
28	Swiss Embassy	D4
29	UK Embassy	A2

PTK Post (Rr UÇK; ◎8am-10pm Mon-Sat) Post and phone services.

❶ Getting There & Around

AIR Taxis charge €25 for the 20-minute, 18km trip to **Pristina International Airport** (☑958 123; www.airportpristina.com). There is a bus service between the **Grand Hotel** (Bul Nëna Terezë) in Pristina and the airport every two hours 24 hours a day (€2).

BUS The **bus station** (Stacioni i Autobusëve; Rr Lidja e Pejes) is 2km southwest of the centre off Bul Bil Klinton. Taxis to the centre should cost €2. International buses from Pristina include Serbia's Belgrade (€20, six hours, 11pm) and Novi Pazar (€5, three hours, 10am); Sarajevo (Bosnia and Hercegovina) via Novi Pazar (€23, 4pm); Durres and Tirana, Albania (€10, five hours); Skopje, Macedonia (€5, 1½ hours, every 30 minutes 5.30am to 5pm); Podgorica, Montenegro (€15, seven hours, 5.45pm, 7pm and 7.30pm).

TAXI Local taxi trips cost a few euro; the meter starts at €1.50. A good operator is **Radio Taxi Victory** (☑044 111 222, 555 333). Fares for unofficial taxis must be negotiated beforehand.

TRAIN Trains run from Pristina to Peja (€3, two hours, 8.01am and 4.41pm) and, internationally, to Skopje in Macedonia (€4, three hours, 7.22am).

AROUND PRISTINA

Kosovo is a small country, which can be crossed by car in any direction in around an hour. Not far in distance, but worlds away from the chaotic capital, the smaller towns of Peja and Prizren both offer a different pace and a new perspective on Kosovar life. The attractive countryside is dotted with historic sites and heavily guarded Serbian monasteries, whose presence remains an extremely emotive subject for all ethnic groups.

Peja (Peć)

☑039 / POP 170,000

Peja (known as Peć in Serbian) is Kosovo's third-largest city and one flanked by sites vital to Orthodox Serbians. With a Turkish-style bazaar at its heart and the beautiful Rugova Mountains all around it, it's a diverse and progressive place that's ripe for tourism

Peja is also home to the Shqip Short Film Festival (www.shqipfilmfest.com), which takes place in the last week of June each year and attracts international film makers.

⊙ Sights

Patriarchate of Peć   MONASTERY
(☏044 15 07 55; ⊙9am-6pm) This church and monastery are a slice of Serbian Orthodoxy. Multilingual Mrs Dobrilla may be able to show you around. It's guarded by NATO's Kosovo Force (KFOR) and you will need to hand in your passport for the duration of your visit. From the food stands around the main square, walk along Lekë Dukagjini with the river on your left for 15 minutes until you reach the monastery walls.

Cheese Market   MARKET
(⊙8am-4pm Sat) The town's bustling bazaar makes you feel like you've turned left into İstanbul. Farmers gather here on Saturday with wooden barrels of goat's cheese, so follow your nose.

Ethnological Museum   MUSEUM
(Aquer Haxhi Zeka; admission €1; ⊙9am-noon & 3-7pm Tue-Sat, 9am-4pm Sun) This Ottoman house is filled with local traditional crafts and the various displays illustrate life in Peja under the Ottomans.

🏃 Activities

Rugova Experience   ADVENTURE TOUR
(☏044 137 734, 432 352; www.rugovaexperience. org; Mbretëreshë Teuta) This excellent, locally run company is championing the Rugova region for hikers and cultural tourists. It organises homestays in mountain villages, runs very good trekking tours, enjoys great local access and works with English-speaking guides. Its helpful office has maps and plenty of information about Peja's local trekking opportunities.

🛏 Sleeping & Eating

There are several good hotels in Peja, but by comparison a lack of decent places to eat. Both the Dukagjini and Cocktail hotels have recommended restaurants, and if you're looking for budget eats the pedestrianised Lekë Dukagjini, off the main square by the river, is lined with kebab shops and cafes.

TOP CHOICE › Dukagjini Hotel   HOTEL €€
(☏771 177; www.hoteldukagjini.com; Sheshi I Dëshmorëve 2; s/d incl breakfast €50/70; ❂❄☎🐾) What on earth is a hotel like this doing in Peja, you may well ask yourself as you step into the regal setting of the Dukagjini's lobby. The hotel has been totally remodelled and the entire place displays international standards you probably didn't expect in a small city in Kosovo. Rooms are large, grandly appointed and have supremely comfortable beds. Try for a 1st-floor room with access to an enormous balcony overlooking the town centre.

Cocktail Hotel   HOTEL €€
(☏039 428 735, 044 159 011; Mbretëresha Teuta; s/d incl breakfast €40/60; ☎) Opened in 2012, this new place contains both a pleasant hotel with spacious and clean rooms, and an expansive restaurant offering up a tasty menu of pizza, pasta, risotto, steak and other meat grills (mains €3-8).

Hotel Gold   HOTEL €€
(☏434 571; Rr Eliot Engl 122/2; s/d incl breakfast €40/50; ☎) 'Our experience, your relax' may

---

DON'T MISS

VISOKI DEČANI MONASTERY

This imposing whitewashed **monastery** (☏49-776 254; www.decani.org; ⊙11am-1pm & 4-6pm), 15km south of Peja, is one of Kosovo's absolute highlights. Located in an incredibly beautiful spot beneath the mountains and surrounded by a forest of pine and chestnut trees, the monastery has been here since 1327 and is today heavily guarded by KFOR. Despite frequent attacks from locals who'd like to see the Serbs leave – most recently a grenade attack in 2007 – the 25 Serbian monks living here in total isolation from the local community have stayed. Here they get on with the serious business of making delicious wines, cheeses and honey (on sale at the small shop) and of slowly restoring the monastery's fabulous icons and frescoes.

Buses go to the town of Dečani from Peja (€1, 30 minutes, every 15 minutes) on their way to Gjakovë. It's a pleasant 1km walk to the monastery from the bus stop. From the roundabout in the middle of town, take the second exit if you're coming from Peja. Keep to the roads – KFOR warns of UXO (unexploded ordnance) in the area. You'll need to surrender your passport while visiting.

be their somewhat garbled slogan, but all the basics are covered here at this admittedly rather sterile establishment. The rooms are on the small side for the price, and the furniture choices questionable, but at least it's unlikely to be booked up.

ⓘ Getting There & Away

BUS Frequent buses run to Pristina (€5, 90 minutes, every 20 minutes) and Prizren (€4, 80 minutes, hourly). International buses link Peja with Ulclinj (€15, 10am, 8.30pm) and Podgorica in Montenegro (€12, 10am).

TRAIN Trains depart Peja for Pristina at 5.30am and 11.10am (two hours) and depart Pristina for Peja at 7.22am and 4.41pm.

Prizren

🖉 029 / POP 178,000

Picturesque Prizren is Kosovo's second city and it shines with post-independence euphoria and enthusiasm that's infectious. If you're passing through between Albania and Pristina, the charming mosque-filled old town is well worth setting aside a few hours to wander about in.

◉ Sights

Prizren's 15th-century **Ottoman bridge** has been superbly restored. Nearby is **Sinan Pasha Mosque** (1561), which renovations are resurrecting as a central landmark in Prizren. Have a peek at the nonfunctioning **Gazi Mehmed Pasha Baths** nearby as well.

The **Orthodox Church of the Virgin of Leviša** is not exactly welcoming – it's heavily guarded, but at least it's no longer surrounded by barbed wire as it has been for the past decade.

The **Ethnological Museum** (admission €1; ⊙11am-7pm Tue-Sun) is where the Prizren League (for Albanian autonomy) organised itself in 1878.

There is not much of interest at the 11th-century **Kalaja** on top of the hill overlooking the old town, but the 180-degree views over Prizren from this fort are worth the walk. On the way, more barbed wire surrounds the heavily guarded **Saint Savior Church**, hinting at the fragility of Prizren's once-robust multiculturalism.

🛏 Sleeping & Eating

There are plenty of stylish new hotels in Prizren. There's also a vibrant strip of bars and eateries on the castle side of the river and around the old-town square.

TOP CHOICE Hotel Prizreni   HOTEL €€
(🖉225 200; www.hotelprizreni.com; Rr Shën Flori 2; r incl breakfast €40-50; ❄�⌂) With an unbeatable location just behind the Sinan Pasha Mosque (though you may well disagree at dawn), the Prizreni is a brand new place with 10 stylish and contemporary rooms, great views and enthusiastic staff. There's a good restaurant downstairs (open 8am to 11pm).

Hotel Centrum   HOTEL €€
(🖉230 530; www.centrumprizren.com; Rr Bujtinat 1; s/d €40/50; ❄�) A great choice is this sleekly designed 23-room place, which is a little tricky to find, but well worth the effort of doing so. Coming from the main square of the Old Town, turn right after the Orthodox Church and you'll find this stylish bolthole on a small side street. Some rooms have great balconies and below it there's a good restaurant.

Ambient   TRADITIONAL €
(Rr Vatrat Shqiptare; mains €3-7; ⊙8am-midnight) With by far the most charming location in Prizren by a waterfall cascading down the cliffside by the river, and views over the old town, this is a place to come for a romantic dinner or sundowner. The menu includes a Pasha burger, steaks, seafood and a catch of the day cooked to your specification.

Arasta   TRADITIONAL €
(Sheshi Shadërvan; mains €3-7; ⊙8am-midnight) On the riverside with a prime location and great outdoor seating, this traditional-style tavern also has a cosy interior perfect for an evening meal. The menu runs from meat grills to fresh fish, pizza and pasta.

ⓘ Getting There & Away

Prizren is well connected to Pristina (€4, 90 minutes, every 10 to 25 minutes), Peja (€4, 90 minutes, six daily) and Albania's Tirana (€12, four hours).

UNDERSTAND KOSOVO

History

Be aware that Kosovo's history is interpreted very differently depending on who you're talking to, with people of differing ethnic and religious backgrounds tending to be polarised along these lines.

In the 12th century Kosovo was the heart of the Orthodox Christian Serbian empire, until Turkish triumph at the pivotal 1389 Battle of Kosovo ushered in 500 years of Ottoman rule and Islam.

Serbia regained control in the 1912 Balkan War and the region became part of Yugoslavia upon its creation in 1918. In WWII the territory was incorporated into Italian-controlled Albania and was liberated and returned to Yugoslavia in October 1944 by Albanian partisans. Following decades of postwar neglect, Kosovo was granted de facto self-government status in 1974.

Kosovo War

In 1989 the autonomy Kosovo enjoyed under the 1974 constitution was suspended by Slobodan Milošević. Ethnic Albanian leaders declared independence from Serbia in 1990. War broke out in 1992 – that same year, Ibrahim Rugova was elected as the first president of the self-proclaimed Republic of Kosovo. Ethnic conflict heightened and the Kosovo Liberation Army (KLA) was formed in 1996.

In March 1999 a US-backed plan to return Kosovo's autonomy was rejected by Serbia, which moved to empty the province of its non-Serbian population. Nearly 850,000 Kosovo Albanians fled to Albania and Macedonia. After Serbia refused to desist, NATO unleashed a bombing campaign on 24 March 1999. In June, Milošević agreed to withdraw troops, air strikes ceased, the KLA disarmed and the NATO-led KFOR (Kosovo Force; the international force responsible for establishing security in Kosovo) took over. From June 1999, Kosovo was administered as a UN–NATO protectorate.

Kosovo caught the world's attention again in 2004 when violence broke out in Mitrovica between the ethnic Serbian and ethnic Albanian communities; 19 people were killed, 600 homes were burnt and 29 monasteries and churches were destroyed in the worst ethnic violence since 1999.

Independence

UN-sponsored talks on Kosovo's status began in February 2006 and Kosovo's parliament declared Kosovo independent on 17 February 2008. In June 2008 a new constitution transferred power from the UN to the government of Kosovo. Kosovo Serbs established their own assembly in Mitrovica.

In 2010 the International Court of Justice ruled that Kosovo's declaration of independence did not violate international law; however, Serbia's president reiterated that Serbia would 'never recognise the unilaterally proclaimed independence of Kosovo'. To date, Kosovo has been recognised as an independent country by 100 countries around the world, including most of the EU, the US and Canada.

New Leadership

Following a string of acting presidents after Ibrahim Rugova's death in 2006, Atifete Jahjaga became Kosovo's president in 2011. A non-partisan, female former police chief, Jahjaga has been a breath of fresh air for politics in Kosovo, even if controversy has never been far from Hashim Thaçi, the current prime minister and the position of real power in the country. Thaçi has been accused of everything from drug trafficking to selling the organs of Serbian prisoners during his time heading the KLA, although he denies all such charges.

People

The population was estimated at 1.8 million in 2010; 92% are Albanian and 8% are Serb (mostly living in enclaves), Bosniak, Gorani, Roma, Turks, Ashkali and Egyptians. The main religious groups are Muslims (mostly Albanians), Serbian Orthodox and Roman Catholic.

Arts

Former president Ibrahim Rugova was a significant figure in Kosovo's literary scene; his presidency of the Kosovo Writers' Association was a step towards presidency of the nation. Try Albanian writer Ismail Kadare's *Three Elegies for Kosovo* for a beautifully written taste of this land's sad history.

Kosovar music bears the imprint of five centuries of Turkish rule; high-whine flutes carry tunes above goat-skin drumbeats. Architecture also shows Islamic influence, mixed with Byzantine and vernacular styles.

The visual-arts scene is re-emerging after troubled times; visit Kosovo Art Gallery (p328) to check it out.

Environment

Kosovo is broadly flat but surrounded by impressive mountains, the highest being Đeravica (2656m). Most of Kosovo's protected area is in Šara National Park, created in 1986.

Among the estimated 46 species of mammal in Kosovo are bears, lynx, deer, weasels and the endangered river otter. Around 220 bird species live in or visit Kosovo, including eagles and falcons.

Pollutants emitted from infrastructure hit by NATO bombs have affected Kosovo's biodiversity. Industrial pollution, rapid urbanisation and overharvesting of wood threaten ecosystems.

Food & Drink

'Traditional' food is generally Albanian – most prominently, stewed and grilled meat and fish. *Kos* (goat's-cheese yoghurt) is eaten alone or with almost anything. Turkish kebabs and *đuveč* (baked meat and vegetables) are common. The local beer is Peja (from the town of the same name). The international presence has brought world cuisines to the capital. Outside Pristina, however, waiters respond to vegetarian requests with thigh-slapping laughter. Requests for nonsmoking areas will be met with the same reaction.

SURVIVAL GUIDE

Directory A–Z

Accommodation

Accommodation is booming in Kosovo, with most large towns now offering a good range of options.

Price ranges used in listings in this chapter are for a double room with bathroom.

€ less than €40

€€ €40 to €80

€€€ more than €80

Business Hours

Reviews include hours only if they differ significantly from these.

Banks 8am to 5pm Monday to Friday, until 2pm Saturday

Bars 8am to 11pm (on the dot if police are cracking down)

Shops 8am to 6pm Monday to Friday, until 3pm Saturday

Restaurants 8am to midnight

Embassies & Consulates

There are no embassies for Australia, Canada, New Zealand or Ireland in Kosovo, so consular issues are handled by the embassies in Belgrade. The following are all in Pristina:

French Embassy (☑2245 8800; www.ambafrance-kosovo.org; Ismail Qemali 67)

German Embassy (☑254 500; www.pristina.diplo.de; Azem Jashanica 17)

Netherlands Embassy (☑516 101; kosovo.nlembassy.org; Xhemajl Berisha 12)

Swiss Embassy (☑248 088; www.eda.admin.ch/pristina; Adrian Krasniqi 11)

UK Embassy (☑254 700; www.ukinkosovo.fco.gov.uk; Ismail Qemajli 6)

US Embassy (☑5959 3000; http://pristina.usembassy.gov; Nazim Hikmet 30)

Food

The following price categories for the average cost of a main course are used in this chapter.

€ less than €5

€€ €5 to €10

€€€ more than €10

Money

Kosovo's currency is the euro, despite not being part of the eurozone or the EU. It's best to arrive with small denominations and euro coins are particularly useful. ATMs are common and established businesses accept credit cards.

Post

PTK post and telecommunications offices operate in Kosovo's main towns.

Public Holidays

New Year's Day 1 January

Independence Day 17 February

Kosovo Constitution Day 9 April

Labour Day 1 May

Europe Holiday 9 May

Note that traditional Islamic holidays are also observed.

Safe Travel

Check government travel advisories before travelling to Kosovo. Sporadic violence occurs in North Mitrovica. Unexploded ordnance (UXO) has been cleared from roads and paths but you should seek KFOR (www.aco.nato.int/kfor.aspx) advice before venturing off beaten tracks.

Make sure your insurance covers you for travel in Kosovo. It's not a good idea to travel in Kosovo with Serbian plates on your car.

Telephone

Kosovo's country code is ☎381. Mobile phone numbers (starting with ☎044, ☎045, ☎043 or ☎049) are hosted by Monaco (☎377) and Slovenia (☎386). Various mobile phone operators have SIM cards that are effectively free; the €5 fee includes €5 worth of credit.

Visas

Visas are not required; check the Ministry of Foreign Affairs (www.mfa-ks.net) website for changes. Upon arrival, you get a 90-day entry stamp.

If you wish to travel between Serbia and Kosovo you'll need to enter Kosovo from Serbia first (see p326).

Getting There & Away

Air

Pristina International Airport (☎038-5958 123; www.airportpristina.com) is 18km from the centre of Pristina. The following airlines fly to Kosovo:

Adria Airways (www.adria.si)

Air Prishtina (☎038-222 099; info.airprishtina.com)

Austrian Airlines (☎038-548 435, 038-502 456; www.austrian.com)

Croatia Airways (☎038-233 833; www.croatiaairlines.com)

Germania Airlines (www.flygermania.de)

Germanwings (www.germanwings.com)

Kosova Airlines (☎038-220 220; www.kosovaairlines.com)

Swiss (☎038-243 446; www.swiss.com)

Turkish Airlines (☎038-247 696, 038-247 711; www.turkishairlines.com)

Land

You can take international bus trips to and from all neighbouring capital cities including Belgrade (the bus travels via Montenegro first) from Pristina. There's also a train to Skopje from Pristina (€4, three hours, 7.22am).

BORDER CROSSINGS

Albania To get to Albania's Koman Ferry use the Morina border crossing west of Gjakovë. A short distance further south is the Qafë Prush crossing, though the road continuing into Albania is bad here. The busiest border is at Vionica, where the excellent new motorway connects to Tirana.

Macedonia Blace from Pristina and Gllobocicë from Prizren.

Montenegro The main crossing is the Kulla/Rožaje crossing on the road between Rožaje and Peja.

Serbia Due to outbreaks of violence, travellers are advised to be extra vigilant if entering Kosovo at Jarinje or Bërnjak/Banja. There are a total of six border crossings between the countries in total. Note that it's not possible to leave Kosovo into Serbia unless you entered Kosovo from Serbia.

Getting Around

Bus

Buses stop at distinct blue signs, but can be flagged down anywhere. Bus journeys are generally cheap, but the going can be slow on Kosovo's single-lane roads.

Car

Serbian-plated cars have been attacked in Kosovo, and rental companies do not let cars hired in Kosovo travel to Serbia and vice versa. European Green Card vehicle insurance is not valid in the country. However, it's perfectly easy to hire cars here, and travel with them to neighbouring countries (with the exception of Serbia).

Train

The train system is something of a novelty, but routes inclue Pristina–Peja (€3, 1½ hours, 8.01am and 4.41pm) and Pristina–Skopje (€4, three hours, 7.22am). Locals generally catch buses.

Macedonia

Best Places to Eat

» Stara Gradska Kuča
(p343)

» La Bodeguito Del Medio
(p343)

» Letna Bavča Kaneo (p353)

» Restaurant Antiko (p353)

» El Greko (p356)

Best Places to Stay

» Hotel Radika (p349)

» Villa Dihovo (p357)

» Hi Skopje Hostel (p341)

» Vila Sveta Sofija (p352)

» Chola Guest House (p355)

» Hotel Pelister (p341)

Why Go?

Macedonia (Македонија) is hard to beat. Part Balkan and part Mediterranean, and offering impressive ancient sites and buzzing modern nightlife, the country packs in much more action, activities and natural beauty than would seem possible for a place its size.

Easygoing Skopje remains one of Europe's more unusual capitals, where constant urban renewal has made the city a continuous work in progress. With its hip cafes, restaurants, bars and clubs frequented by a large student population, Skopje is also emerging on the region's entertainment scene.

In summer try hiking, mountain biking and climbing in remote mountains, some concealing medieval monasteries. Visit Ohrid, noted for its summer festival, sublime Byzantine churches and a large lake. Winter offers skiing at resorts such as Mavrovo, and food-and-grog festivities in the villages. Meeting the locals and partaking in the country's living culture can be as memorable and rewarding as seeing the sights.

When to Go
Skopje

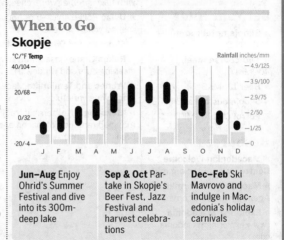

Jun–Aug Enjoy Ohrid's Summer Festival and dive into its 300m-deep lake

Sep & Oct Partake in Skopje's Beer Fest, Jazz Festival and harvest celebrations

Dec–Feb Ski Mavrovo and indulge in Macedonia's holiday carnivals

MACEDONIA

AT A GLANCE

» **Currency** Macedonian denar (MKD)

» **Language** Macedonian

» **Money** ATMs widespread in major towns

» **Visas** None for EU, US, Australian, Canadian or New Zealand citizens

Fast Facts

» **Area** 25,713 sq km

» **Capital** Skopje

» **Country code** ☑389

» **Emergency** Ambulance ☑194, fire ☑193, police ☑192

Exchange Rates

Australia	A$1	50.08MKD
Canada	C$1	47.18MKD
Euro Zone	€1	61.27MKD
Japan	¥100	50.81MKD
New Zealand	NZ$1	40.14MKD
UK	UK£1	72.54MKD
USA	US$1	47.94MKD

Set Your Budget

» **Skopje hotel room** 3000MKD

» **Two-course meal** 400MKD

» **Beer** 120MKD

» **Skopje bus ticket** 35MKD

» **Petrol (1L)** 100MKD

Resources

» **Macedonian Welcome Centre** (www.dmwc.org.mk)

» **Macedonian Information Agency** (www.mia.com.mk)

» **Exploring Macedonia** (www.exploringmacedonia.com)

Connections

Skopje's buses serve Sofia, Belgrade, Budapest, Pristina, Tirana, İstanbul, Thessaloniki and more. The train from Belgrade to Skopje reaches Gevgelija on the Greek border. The long-awaited arrival of budget airlines has improved Skopje's air connections.

ITINERARIES

One Week

Spend two nights in Skopje, marvelling at its bold new architecture on the square, and visiting its Čaršija (old quarter), with historic churches, mosques, museums and an Ottoman castle. Then travel southwest to Macedonia's most evocative and historic town, Ohrid, and its lake, via the lush forested mountains of Mavrovo and Bigorski Monastery, with its spectacular carved iconostasis. After two days, continue to cultured Bitola, the long-famed 'City of Consuls' known for its vibrant cafes and nearby ancient Heraclea and Pelister National Park.

Two Weeks

After Skopje, Ohrid and Bitola, visit Prilep, seeing its historic nearby monasteries. Before returning to Skopje, enjoy wines in the Tikveš wine region and see ancient Roman Stobi.

Essential Food & Drink

» **Ajvar** Sweet red-pepper sauce; accompanies meats and cheeses.

» **Šopska salata** Tomatoes, onions and cucumbers topped with flaky *sirenje* (white cheese).

» **Uviač** Rolled chicken or pork wrapped in bacon, filled with melted yellow cheese.

» **Skopsko** and **Dab lagers** Macedonia's favourite brews.

» **Rakija** Grape-based firewater, useful for toasts (and cleaning cuts and windows!).

» **Vranec** and **Temjanika** Macedonia's favourite red- and white-wine varietals.

» **'Bekonegs'** Not terribly traditional. but you will see this mangled rendition of 'bacon and eggs' on Macedonian breakfast menus.

SKOPJE

♪ 02 / POP 670,000

Skopje (Скопје) is among Europe's most entertaining and eclectic small capital cities. While a government construction spree has sparked controversy in recent years, Skopje's new abundance of statuary, bridges, museums and other structures has visitors' cameras snapping like never before and has defined the ever-changing city.

Yet plenty survives from earlier times – Skopje's Ottoman- and Byzantine-era wonders include the 15th-century Kameni Most (Stone Bridge), Čaršija (old Turkish bazaar), Sveti Spas Church, with its ornate, hand-carved iconostasis, and Tvrdina Kale Fortress, Skopje's guardian since the 5th century. And, with its bars, clubs and galleries, the city has modern culture too.

Macedonia Highlights

① Gaze out over Ohrid from the **Church of Sveti Jovan at Kaneo** (p351), immaculately set on a bluff above the lake.

② Dive into historic but still-changing **Skopje** (p339), a friendly, quintessentially Balkan capital.

③ Enjoy the old-world ambience of **Bitola** (p355) and hike nearby Pelister National Park.

④ Explore the **Tikveš wine region** (p358) and its ancient ruins and lake.

⑤ Soak up the serenity at clifftop **Zrze Monastery** (p358), with sweeping views of the Pelagonian Plain and priceless Byzantine artworks.

⑥ Ski **Mavrovo** (p348), Macedonia's premier winter resort.

SKOPJE IN...

One Day

After morning coffee on **Ploštad Makedonija**, cross this splendid, statue-studded square and the Vardar River via **Kameni Most** (Stone Bridge) into the **Čaršija**. Here peruse Turkish mosques, converted *hammams* (turkish baths) and churches, and the **Holocaust Memorial Center**, before ascending **Tvrdina Kale Fortress**; the ramparts offer impressive views. Then enjoy dinner and drinks in the centre, the Čaršija or the leafy **Debar Maalo neighbourhood**.

Three Days

After seeing the centre and **Čaršija** sights, get another perspective from the forested **Mt Vodno**, flanking Skopje, and visit the 12th-century **Sveti Pantelejmon Monastery**. Along cafe-lined ul Makedonija see the **Memorial House of Mother Teresa** and **Museum of the City of Skopje**.

West of Skopje, **Lake Matka** occupies a deep canyon and its forests offer hiking trails and monastic grottoes. Later, enjoy great beer, wine and live music at the Čaršija's stylish nightspots.

◉ Sights

The Čaršija houses Skopje's main historic sights. Other museums are on the Vardar's southern shore, where cafes line pedestrianised ul Makedonija. Buzzing Ploštad Makedonija (Macedonia Sq) stands smack by the Ottoman stone bridge (Kameni Most), which accesses Čaršija.

PLOŠTAD MAKEDONIJA & THE SOUTH BANK

Ploštad Makedonija   SQUARE
(Macedonia Sq) Fronted by a Triumphal Arch, this square has audacious statues dedicated to national heroes. The towering, central 'Warrior on a Horse' is bedecked by fountains that are illuminated at night. From here, stroll or cycle along the riverbank, or relax in a river-facing cafe.

FREE **Memorial House of Mother Teresa**   MUSEUM
(✆3290 674; www.memorialhouseofmotherteresa. org; ul Makedonija bb; ⊗9am-8pm Mon-Fri, to 2pm Sat & Sun) This retro-futuristic structure has memorabilia of the famed Catholic nun of Calcutta, born in Skopje in 1910.

FREE **Museum of the City of Skopje**   MUSEUM
(Mito Hadživasilev Jasmin bb; ⊗9am-3pm Tue-Sat, to 1pm Sun) Occupying the old train station, this museum specialises in local ancient and Byzantine finds. The stone fingers of its clock remain frozen in time at 5.17am – the moment Skopje's great earthquake struck on 27 July 1963.

NORTH BANK & ČARŠIJA

Čaršija   NEIGHBOURHOOD
Across Kameni Most, Čaršija evokes Skopje's Ottoman past – winding lanes filled with eateries, teahouses, craftsmen's stores and even good nightlife. It also boasts Skopje's best historic structures and museums. Čaršija runs from the Stone Bridge to Bit Pazar, a big, busy vegetable market purveying bric-a-brac, household goods and anything random.

Sveti Spas Church   CHURCH
(Makarie Frčkoski 8; admission 100MKD; ⊗8am-3pm Tue-Sun) Partially underground (the Turks banned churches from being taller than mosques), this church boasts a wood-carved iconostasis 10m wide and 6m high, built by early-19th-century master craftsmen Makarije Frčkovski and brothers Petar and Marko Filipovski.

Outside, the **Tomb and Museum of Goce Delčev** (Church of Sveti Spas) has the remains of Macedonia's foremost national hero. Leader of the VMRO (Internal Macedonian Revolutionary Organisation), Delčev was killed by Turks in 1903.

Museum of Macedonia   MUSEUM
(www.musmk.org.mk; Čurčiska bb; admission 50MKD; ⊗9am-5pm Tue-Sun) Documenting neolithic through communist times, this museum contains an ethnographic exhibition,

plus ancient jewellery and coins, icons and wood-carved iconostases.

Sultan Murat Mosque   MOSQUE
(bul K Misirkov) This 1436 mosque is among the Balkans' oldest and features a distinctive, red-tipped clock tower and Ottoman *madrasa* (Islamic school) remnants.

KALE & AROUND

Mustafa Paša Mosque   MOSQUE
(Samoilova bb) The 1492 Mustafa Paša Mosque exemplifies magnificent Ottoman architecture, with a lawn, garden and fountain.

FREE Tvrdina Kale Fortress   FORTRESS
(⊙daylight hours) This 6th-century AD Byzantine (and later, Ottoman) castle conceals archaeological finds from neolithic to Ottoman times. The ramparts offer great views over city and river.

Museum of Contemporary Art   MUSEUM
(✆3117 734; www.msuskopje.org.mk; Samoilova bb; ⊙10am-5pm Tue-Sat, 9am-1pm Sun) This elevated museum displays works by Macedonian and world-famous artists (there's even a Picasso).

MT VODNO & AROUND

Mt Vodno   MOUNTAIN
Framing Skopje to the south, Vodno's popular with hikers, though a gondola up the mountainside operates too. Two restaurants stand at Sredno (Middle) Vodno (taxis drive here for 200MKD). Hiking trails take you to the 66m-high Millenium Cross (2002), the world's largest and illuminated at night.

Sveti Pantelejmon Monastery   MONASTERY
(Gorno Nerezi village) Further west along Vodno, this 1164 monastery is among Macedonia's most significant churches. Its Byzantine frescos, such as the *Lamentation of Christ,* depict a pathos and realism predating the Renaissance by two centuries. It's 5km from the centre (by taxi, 300MKD) and offers great views.

☆ Festivals & Events

Skopsko Leto   ARTS
(www.dku.org.mk) Summer art exhibitions, performances and concerts.

Pivolend   BEER
(www.pivolend.com.mk) Held in September outside the Boris Trajkovski Sports Centre (p345), this event features rock acts and DJs, grilled meats and beer.

Skopje Jazz Festival   MUSIC
(✆3131 090; www.skopjejazzfest.com.mk) This October festival features artists from across the globe, and always a world-renowned player or group (Chick Corea, McCoy Tyner, Herbie Hancock and Tito Puente are some past headliners).

May Opera Evenings   OPERA
This event and Off-Fest (✆3131 090; www.offest.com.mk) combine world music and DJ events.

Taksirat Festival   MUSIC
(✆2775 430; www.taksirat.com.mk) Live rock music in November/December.

🛏 Sleeping

A few basic youth hostels lie between the bus/train stations and the Vardar River in the run-down (but safe enough) Madzar Maalo quarter. Better, but pricier, hotels are in the centre. The Debar Maalo neighbourhood (a 10-minute walk from centre towards the park) offers good midrange options amid cafes and restaurants.

TOP CHOICE Hotel Pelister   BOUTIQUE HOTEL €€
(✆3239 584; www.pelisterhotel.com.mk; Ploštad Makedonija; s/d/apt from €59/69/85; ❄@🛜) Located above Restaurant Pelister (p344; both formerly called 'Dal Met Fu'), this hotel enjoys an unbeatable location on the square, overlooking the city's new architectural wonders. The six rooms are spiffy, with somewhat standard decor though most come with a computer. The suites also have a spa, for the price of a smaller standard room elsewhere in the city.

TOP CHOICE Urban Hostel   HOSTEL €
(✆6142 785; www.urbanhostel.com.mk; Majka Teresa 22; dm/s/d/apt €13/24/34/75; ❄🛜) Skopje's best hostel is a short walk from the centre, opposite the leafy Debar Maalo neighbourhood, home to relaxed cafes and restaurants. Along with clean rooms, comfy beds and a fireplace, there's a piano, aquarium, computer room and friendly, helpful staff.

TOP CHOICE Hi Skopje Hostel   HOSTEL €
(✆6091-242; www.hiskopjehostel.com; Crniche 15; dm/s/d from 540/1200/2100MKD) In the cool shade of Mt Vodno, this cheerful new hostel offers dorms and two rooms (with a shared bathroom, however). There's a communal kitchen, and the relaxing back garden adds

Skopje

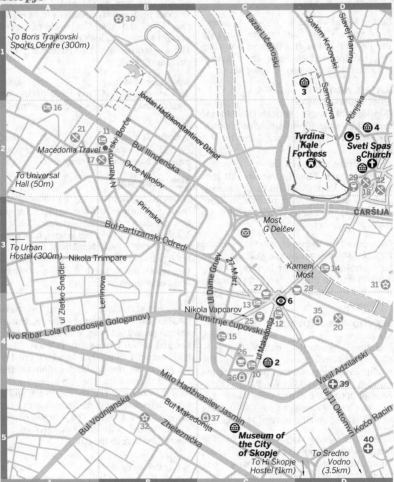

to the out-of-city vibe. The friendly young owners offer tons of info on city sights and events. It's located on a hilly street 2.5km from the bus/train stations (take a taxi for 150MKD).

Hotel City Park
HOTEL €€

(☑3290 860; www.hotelcitypark.com.mk; Mihail Cokov 8a, Gradski Park; s/d/ste from €75/90/105; ✳🛜) This sharp newcomer features bright, almost minimalist rooms with comfy beds and plenty of amenities. It's located opposite the park and its *fontana* (fountain) in the Debar Maalo neighbourhood, a 10-minute walk from centre.

Hotel Square
BUDGET HOTEL €€

(☑3225 090; www.hotelsquare.com.mk; 6th fl, Nikola Vapcarov 2; s/d/tr €45/60/75; ✳@) Well situated six floors above the action, the Square offers cosy, well-kept and modern rooms. The balcony cafe offers great views and an optional breakfast (€5) is in Café Trend (p345) nearby. Look for the sign-posted business/apartment block off Ploštad Makedonija.

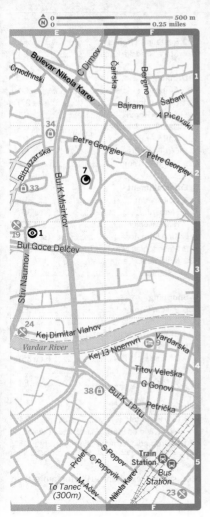

Best Western Hotel Turist
BUSINESS HOTEL €€€

(☎3289 111; www.bestwestern-ce.com/turist; ul Gjuro Strugar 11; s/d from €128/138; P✳🕸) The Turist lies on pedestrianised ul Makedonija, though it's not particularly conspicuous by chain hotel standards. Service is professional and the business rooms come with all the mod cons.

Hotel Stone Bridge
LUXURY HOTEL €€€

(☎3244 900; www.stonebridge-hotel.com; Kej Dimitar Vlahov 1; s/d/apt from €138/159/299; P✳@🕸) This Turkish-owned, five-star hotel sits across the Stone Bridge. The sophisticated rooms are graced with stylised Ottoman furnishings, and the restaurant is good. It's arguably overpriced (the grand 'Sultan Suite', certainly so, at a preposterous €549).

Art Hostel
HOSTEL €

(☎3223 789; www.art-hostel.com.mk; Ante Hadzimitkov 5; dm/s/d €12/25/40; ✳@🕸) Near the train station in the Madjir Maalo neighbourhood, by the River Vardar, Art Hostel is a passable backpacker fallback, though the six-bed dorms and private rooms (all with shared bathrooms) are cramped.

✕ Eating

Restaurants open until midnight; nonsmoking laws are strictly enforced. *Skara* (grilled meat) is popular, but international flavours are well represented too. For breakfast, try *burek* (white cheese, spinach or ground meat in filo pastry) with drinking yoghurt.

The old town has more *skara* places, and *kebapčilnici* (beef-kebab restaurants) and doner-kebab shops – avoid the less-visited, less-hygienic ones.

TOP CHOICE **Stara Gradska Kuča**
MACEDONIAN €€

(Pajko Maalo 14; mains 250-400MKD; ☺8am-midnight) This restored traditional house has warm ambience, an excellent assortment of traditional Macedonian dishes and, sometimes, live Macedonian music. It's a bit touristy, but still a snug and cosy spot with its wood furnishings and traditional decor.

TOP CHOICE **La Bodeguito Del Medio**
CUBAN €€

(Kej 13 Noemvri; mains 350-700MKD; ☺9am-2am) Known to locals as 'the Cuban', this gregarious riverfront place has sizzling Cuban specialities, Latin cocktails and music, and a long bar lined with carousers by night. Borrow a magic marker to scrawl your message among hundreds of others on the walls and ceilings.

Tim's Apartments
APARTMENT €€

(☎3237 650; www.tims.com.mk; Orce Nikolov 120; s/d/apt €69/89/110; ✳@🕸) Near the park, Tim's is a long-established and dependable option, with 10 classy rooms and seven en suite apartments.

Hotel TCC Plaza
LUXURY HOTEL €€€

(☎3111 807; www.tccplaza.com; Vasil Glavinov 12; s/d/ste from €84/110/145; P✳@🕸⛱) This five-star hotel offers spacious, well-lit rooms and suites, plus a spa centre with small swimming pool, and fitness and massage services. It lacks views or ambience, but it's very central.

Skopje

Restaurant Pelister INTERNATIONAL €€
(Dal Met Fu; Ploštad Makedonija; mains 280-350MKD; ⊙7.30am-midnight) This square-front place remains a local fixture – note the curious mix of pensioners debating politics over coffee, businessmen chatting up politicians, and random tourists. It does great pastas and offers a make-your-own-salad bar. The chocolate souffle with vanilla ice cream and spearmint sprig is worth the 10-minute wait.

Kebapčilnica Destan KEBAB €
(ul 104 6; 10 kebabs 120MKD) Skopje's best beef kebabs, accompanied by seasoned grilled bread, are served at this classic Čaršija place.

Idadija SKARA €€
(Rade Koncar 1; mains 180-250MKD) In Debar Maalo's *skara* corner, no-frills Idadija has

been serving excellent grills for more than 80 years.

Papu MACEDONIAN €€
(Djuro Djakovic 63; mains 250-400MKD) The tastes and decor of old Kruševo are preserved at this lovely place studded with stone arches and antiques, and filled with the sounds of cascading water.

Pivnica An MACEDONIAN, INTERNATIONAL €€
(mains 300-500MKD) You're paying for the ambience at this 'beerhouse' located in a restored Ottoman building's sumptuous courtyard as the tasty food is overpriced.

Restaurant Roulette SKARA €€
(Simeon Kavrakirov 9a; mains 150-350MKD) If you need a meal before a bus or train trip, this

local favourite on a residential street serves the best grills near the station.

K8
SWEETS €

(Gradište 7a; snacks 50-140 MKD; ⊘9am-7pm) Established by an American expat baker, this fun little place is unique for its typical American soccer-mum snacks such as lemon bars, choc-chip brownies and apple pie.

🍷 Drinking

Čaršija has a couple of fun nightspots. Good bars sit around the square, while clubbers find open-air venues in the park by summer and indoors under the bus station by winter. Cafes and bars open until 1am, though nightclubs continue until later. Supermarkets sell alcohol until 7pm in winter and 9pm in summer.

TOP CHOICE Bistro London
PUB

(pl Makedonija; ⊘8am-1am) Formerly 'London Pub,' this refurbished bar annex of neighbouring Café Trend (p345) has agreeable plaid-backed chairs, a decent pub ambience and friendly service. Along with a wide selection of beers, wines and cocktails it offers snacks and full meals. There's live music on weekends, including Sunday mid-morning jazz.

TOP CHOICE Vinoteka Temov
BAR

(Gradište 1a; ⊘9am-midnight Mon-Thu, to 1am Fri-Sun) Skopje's best wine bar, in a restored wood building near Sveti Spas, is refined and atmospheric. A vast (and pricey) wine list presents the manifold flavours of Macedonia's vineyards, while live traditional and classical guitarists often play.

Old Town Brewery
BEER HALL

(Gradište 1; ⊘10am-1am Sun-Thu, to 3am Fri & Sat) This beer bar above Vinoteka Temov is Skopje's only place for a yard of beer, and selection is good. In summer, the benches spill outside, where bands cover classic rock.

Café di Roma
CAFE

(ul Makedonija; ⊘8am-1am) This stylish place does Skopje's best espresso and other caffeinated drinks, hot and cold, plus cakes.

Caffé Firenze
CAFE

(pl Makedonija; ⊘8am-midnight) This sharp cafe on the square's southeastern edge is great for a relaxed espresso and also serves Italian fare (the pastas are more authentic than the desserts).

Arabesque
LOUNGE BAR

(📞072 304 304; www.arabesque.mk; Nikola Vapcarov 7) One of Skopje's newer nightspots, Arabesque has a long bar, big leather couches and eccentric orange lights but it aims for a swank, dressed-up clientele. Reservations suggested on weekends. Decent pastas are also served.

Café Trend
CAFE

(Ploštad Makedonija; ⊘8am-1am) Aspiring socialites mix with (and gossip about) local celebrities at this long-established, slick place on the square. It also has a good restaurant.

⭐ Entertainment

Skopje is a clubbing hot spot, hosting well-known international DJs; see www.skopjeclubbing.com.mk.

Colosseum
CLUB

(www.colosseum.com.mk; City Park in summer, under train station in winter) Skopje's biggest and most popular club, along with **Element** (www.element.com.mk; Gradski Park). When international DJs appear, tickets run from 250MKD to 500MKD.

Multimedia Center Mala Stanica
CAFE

(www.nationalgallery.mk; Zheleznička 18; ⊘9am-midnight) Featuring arty, ornate decor, the National Art Gallery's cafe hosts temporary exhibitions and live music.

Universal Hall
LIVE MUSIC

(Univerzalna Sala; 📞3224 158; bul Partizanski Odredi bb) Hosts classical, jazz, pop and kids' performances.

Boris Trajkovski Sports Centre
SPORTS CENTRE

(Sportski Centar Boris Trajkovski; 📞3089 661; www.salaboristrajkovski.gov.mk; bul Ilindenska; ⊘9am-11pm) Named for the late president, this big facility has everything from bowling, go-karts, ping pong and a kids' play land to cafes, an indoor pool and ice skating in winter. Sometimes international spectator sports (such as water polo) are held here.

Macedonian National Theatre
THEATRE

(📞3114 060; www.mnt.com.mk; Kej Dimitar Vlahov bb) Hosts opera, ballet and classical music in a communist-era building.

Kino Milenium
CINEMA

(📞3120 389; www.kinomilenium.mk; Gradski Trgovski Centar) Skopje's largest movie theatre.

Kino Ramstore CINEMA
(Ramstore Mall, Mito Hadživasilev Jasmin bb) This theatre gets second-rate Hollywood films but shows some popular kids' flicks.

🛍 Shopping

In Čaršija you can buy jewellery, traditional carpets, antiques, dresses and more but beware – most 'ancient' treasures on sale are fakes (and would be illegal to buy if they weren't). **Bit Pazar** sells fruit, vegetables, stolen phones and household items. The **Gradski Trgovski Centar** (11 Oktomvri), **Ramstore** (Mito Hadživasilev Jasmin bb) and

Vero Center (bul Jane Sandanski) are modern malls. Plenty of Macedonia-themed souvenir stalls are on or near the main square.

Balkan Corner JEWELLERY
(ul Bitpazarska; silver jewellery 600-4500MKD; ☺9.30am-7.30pm) This tiny shop halfway down the old town's central street specialises in all kinds of handmade silver jewellery (and other gifts). Friendly owner Adnan is happy to give details on individual pieces.

Ikona HANDICRAFTS
(Luj Paster 19; ☺9am-9pm Mon-Fri, to 4pm Sat) 'Traditional' souvenirs, including icons, ar-

TRANSPORT FROM SKOPJE

Domestic Bus

DESTINATION	PRICE (MKD)	DURATION (HR)	FREQUENCY
Bitola	480	3	12 daily
Gostivar	200	1	12 daily
Kavadarci	250	2	7 daily
Kruševo	380	3	3 daily
Makedonski Brod	330	3	5 daily
Mavrovo	330	2	7 Mon-Fri, 2 Sat-Sun
Negotino	210	2½	11 Mon-Fri, 9 Sat-Sun
Ohrid	520	3	11 daily
Prilep	390	2½	14 daily

International Bus

DESTINATION	PRICE (MKD)	DURATION (HR)	FREQUENCY
Belgrade	1400	10	12 daily
İstanbul	1900	12	5 daily
Ljubljana	3750	14	1 daily
Pristina	320	2	12 daily
Sofia	1040	5½	5 daily
Thessaloniki	1280	4	1 Mon, Wed & Fri
Zagreb	3150	12	1 daily

Domestic Train

DESTINATION	PRICE (MKD)	DURATION	FREQUENCY
Bitola	314	4hr	3 daily
Gevgelija	270	2½hr	3 daily
Kičevo	208	2hr	3 daily
Kumanovo	79	40min	4 daily
Negotino	198	2hr	3 daily
Prilep	250	3hr	3 daily

chaeological replicas, pottery, painted boxes and folk dolls.

Lithium
MUSIC
(www.lithiumrecords.com.mk; Gradski Trgovski Centar; ☺8.30am-8pm Mon-Sat) Buy Macedonian and international CDs, plus concert and festival tickets.

ℹ️ Information

Dangers & Annoyances

Pensioners on bicycles constitute the gravest threat to public safety, whether you're walking on the sidewalk or driving a car. In general, Skopje drivers are reckless, and sidewalks are pockmarked by unexpected cracks and holes. Roma children's begging can be an irritant, though violent crime is rare.

Skopje's wild dogs are less troublesome than before, though joggers and cyclists are still fair game.

Internet Access

Free wi-fi is widespread in cafes, restaurants, hotels and even buses – few internet cafes remain.

Medical Services

City Hospital (☑3130 111; 11 Oktomvri 53; ☺24hr)

Neuromedica Private Clinic (☑3133 313; 11 Oktomvri 25; ☺24hr) Good private specialists.

Money

ATMs and *menuvačnici* (exchange offices) abound.

Menuvačnica Euro (Gradski Trgovski Centar; ☺9am-8.30pm Mon-Sat) Dependable exchange office near the southern end of the Gradski Trgovski Centar on the ground floor.

Post & Telephone

The **main post office** (☑3141 141; Orce Nikolov 1; ☺7am-7.30pm Mon-Sat, 7.30am-2.30pm Sun) is 75m northwest of Ploštad Makedonija. Others are opposite the train station, in the Gradski Trgovski Centar and in Ramstore.

Some kiosks (newsagents) have private telephones.

Travel Agencies

Go Macedonia (☑3071 265; www.gomacedonia.com; Ankarska 29a) Arranges hiking, cycling, caving and winery tours.

Macedonia Travel (www.macedoniatravel.com; Orce Nikolov 109/1, lok 3) Does tours, including trips to Jasen Nature Reserve, and air tickets.

Websites

Lonely Planet (www.lonelyplanet.com/macedonia/skopje)

Skopje Official Website (www.skopje.gov.com)

Skopje Online (www.skopjeonline.com.mk)

Tourist Association of Skopje (www.skopje-tourism.org)

ℹ️ Getting There & Away

Air

Skopje Alexander the Great Airport (☑3148 333; www.airports.com.mk; Petrovec), 21km east of Skopje, has had a long-awaited upgrade thanks to the Turkish company TAV, which also operates it. New budget carriers connect Skopje with the UK, Central Europe, Italy, Turkey and the Gulf. Nevertheless, airlines come and go so check the airport website first.

Adria Airways (www.adria.si; Dame Gruev 7)

Austrian Airlines (www.austrian.com)

Croatia Airlines (www.croatiaairlines.hr)

Fly Dubai (www.flydubai.com) Connects Skopje with Dubai and further east.

JAT (Yugoslav Airlines; ☑3118 306; www.jat.com; bul Partizanski Odredi 17) Has an office near the centre.

Pegasus Airlines (www.flypgs.com) Turkish budget carrier offers great fares to Turkey and elsewhere.

Turkish Airlines (www.thy.com)

WizzAir (www.wizzair.com) Good budget rates to London-Luton, Central Europe and Italy.

Bus

Skopje's **bus station** (www.sas.com.mk; bul Jane Sandanski), with ATM, exchange office and English-language info, adjoins the train station.

Buses to Ohrid go via Kičevo (three hours, 167km) or Bitola (four to five hours, 261km) – book ahead in summer. Most intercity buses are air-conditioned and are generally faster than trains, though more expensive.

Train

The **train station** (Železnička Stanica; bul Jane Sandanski) serves local and international destinations. Northbound trains pass through Kumanovo for Serbia. The southbound service transits Veles; from here, one line continues south through Gevgelija for Greece, while the other forks southwest through Prilep for Bitola.

Another line serves eastern Macedonian towns, while a lesser-used western line terminates at Kičevo.

At time of research, the Greek government had suspended international train routes, but hopefully the Skopje–Thessaloniki run will return someday (4½ hours). A train serves Belgrade (1300MKD, eight to 10 hours, two daily), and another reaches Pristina in Kosovo.

ⓘ Getting Around

TO/FROM THE AIRPORT An airport shuttle bus, Vardar Express, runs between the airport and the city. Buy tickets (100MKD) from the marked arrivals terminal booth. The bus leaves half-hourly or hourly, depending on passengers, and stops at several places including the bus/train station and central square. It returns via the same stops, though allow extra time as it is somewhat irregular. Otherwise, arrange a taxi to the airport (800MKD to 1000MKD) in advance. From the airport to centre, taxis cost 1200MKD.

BUS Skopje's public city buses (including London-style red double-deckers) cost 35MKD. Private ones cost 25MKD. Both follow the same stops and numbered routes. You can buy and validate tickets on board. Both congregate under the bus/train station (officially, 'Transporten Centar'), behind the enclosed area where intercity buses depart. Bus 22 is useful, cutting through the centre and down bul Partizanski Odredi.

CAR Daily rental prices start at 26,000MKD. Try Budget Car Rental. Free parking is hard to find in Skopje – even if you think you're safe, check again. Large white placards around the city instruct how to pay for parking via text message (otherwise, you may have to pay a 1200MKD fine).

TAXI Skopje's taxis are cheaper than in Western Europe. The base rate is 40MKD for the first kilometre and 25MKD for subsequent kilometres, and drivers use their meters. Central destinations cost 60MKD to 150MKD. Lotus has spiffy, air-conditioned cars, and In-Taxi is also good. Legit companies usually have the five-digit ordering phone number (starting with 15). Although various dubious cabs hover near Bit Pazar, the city has largely removed the shadier operators from the bus and train stations.

WESTERN MACEDONIA

Western Macedonia gets most of Macedonia's visitors, and no wonder: its mountain ranges provide a stunning backdrop, running south from Šar Planina to the gentler Jablanica range, ending with the 34km-long Lake Ohrid.

Lying outstretched southward, and flanked by Galičica National Park, the lake is dotted with coastal and upland villages. Ohrid itself boasts manifold historic sites, a lovely old quarter and summer cultural events and nightlife.

Mavrovo National Park
Маврово Национален Парк

♪ 042

Mavrovo's ski resort is Macedonia's biggest, comprising 730 sq km of birch and pine forest, gorges, karst fields and waterfalls, plus Macedonia's highest peak, **Mt Korab** (2764m). The rarefied air and stunning vistas are great year-round. Located up a winding road southwest of Gostivar, Mavrovo lies near Sveti Jovan Bigorski Monastery and Galičnik, famous for its traditional village wedding.

◉ Sights & Activities

Sveti Jovan Bigorski Monastery   MONASTERY

This revered 1020 Byzantine monastery is off the Debar road. Legend attests an icon of Sveti Jovan Bigorski (St John the Forerunner, ie St John the Baptist) miraculously

---

AROUND SKOPJE

A half-hour drive, or slightly longer city bus trip, accesses tranquil **Lake Matka** (NW Macedonia; 🚍60 from Bulevar Partizanski in Skopje). Although crowded at weekends, this idyllic spot beneath steep **Treska Canyon** is excellent, offering hiking, rock climbing, caving (€10) and ancient churches in its forested environs. On-site restaurants provide nourishment and lake views. Matka's underwater caverns are as deep, or maybe deeper, than any in Europe, at almost 218m.

Matka's traditional link with the Virgin Mary (Matka means 'womb' in Macedonian) is accentuated by grotto shrines such as **Sveta Bogorodica**. From here a steep path reaches **Sveti Spas**, **Sveta Trojca** and **Sveta Nedela** – the last, a 4km walk (around 1½ hours). These caves once sheltered ascetics and anti-Ottoman revolutionaries.

After the **Church of Sveti Nikola**, beyond the dam and across the bridge, visit the frescoed **Church of Sveti Andrej** (1389). The adjoining mountaineering hut **Matka** (♪3052 655) offers guides, climbing gear and accommodation.

From Skopje come by car, taxi (450MKD) or bus 60 along bul Partizanski Odredi (50MKD, 40 minutes, hourly).

appeared, and since then it's been rebuilt often – the icon occasionally reappearing too. The impressive church also houses Jovan's alleged forearm.

Bigorski's awe-inspiring iconostasis was the final of just three carved by local craftsmen Makarije Frčkovski and the brothers Filipovski between 1829 and 1835. This colossal work depicting biblical scenes is enlivened with 700 tiny human and animal figures. Gazing up at this enormous, intricate masterpiece is breathtaking. Upon finishing, the carvers allegedly flung their tools into the nearby Radika River – ensuring that the secret of their artistic genius would be washed away forever.

Galičnik
VILLAGE

Up a winding, tree-lined road ending in a rocky moonscape 17km southwest of Mavrovo, almost depopulated Galičnik features traditional houses along the mountainside. It's placid except for 12 and 13 July, when the **Galičnik Wedding** sees one or two lucky couples wed here. Visit, along with 3000 happy Macedonians, and enjoy eating, drinking, traditional folk dancing and music.

Zare Lazarevski Ski Centre   SKIING
(☏489 065; www.zarelaz.com; ⏰8am-10pm) Macedonia's top ski resort, with average snow cover of 70cm and slopes from 1860m to 2255m. Zare Lazarevski offers ski rental (600MKD), lift tickets (800MKD/3500MKD per day/week) and ski school. Mavrovo's also good for summer hiking.

🍴 Sleeping & Eating

Go Macedonia (p347) arranges Galičnik Wedding trips including transport, guided activities, local accommodation and monastery tours. You will need to book ahead.

TOP CHOICE **Hotel Radika**   SPA HOTEL €€
(☏223 300; www.radika.com.mk; s/d/apt €43/60/69; P❄️🛜) Just 5km from Mavrovo, this ultraposh spa hotel is perfect for pampering, with numerous massage treatments and excellent rooms. Prices fall considerably in summer. Nondrivers should take a taxi from Gostivar (650MKD), on the Skopje–Ohrid road.

Sveti Jovan Bigorski   MONASTERY €
(☏478 675; www.bigorski.org.mk; per person €5) The self-catering dormitories here are under reconstruction – check ahead.

Hotel Srna   SKI LODGE €€
(☏388 083; www.hotelsrnamavrovo.com; s/d/apt €25/40/60; ❄️🛜) The small Srna, 400m from Mavrovo's chairlifts, has breezy, clean rooms.

Hotel Bistra   SKI LODGE €€
(☏489 002; www.bistra.com; s/d €45/70, d with spa €110; P❄️🛜🏊) The Bistra has comfortable, clean rooms and amenities (restaurant, bar, pool, fitness centre, sauna) for cultivating that ski-lodge glow, plus spas in the deluxe rooms. Prices fall in summer. It also runs the simpler **Hotel Ski Škola** (s/d €20/40) and **Hotel Mavrovski** (s/d €20/40); guests can use the Bistra's facilities.

ℹ️ Getting There & Away

Southbound buses reach Mavrovo Anovi (2km away) en route to Debar (120MKD, seven daily), or while travelling north to Tetovo (140MKD, five daily) and Skopje (180MKD, three daily).

For Sveti Jovan Bigorski Monastery, drive; alternatively, buses transiting Debar for Ohrid or Struga will drop you off.

Ohrid   Охрид
☏046 / POP 55,700

Sublime Ohrid is Macedonia's prime destination, with its atmospheric old quarter with beautiful churches along a graceful hill, topped by a medieval castle overlooking serene, 34km-long Lake Ohrid. Nearby, mountainous Galičica National Park offers pristine nature, while secluded beaches dot the lake's eastern shore.

Ohrid and its beaches are packed from 15 July to 15 August, during the popular summer festival. June or September are quieter (and cleaner).

Lake Ohrid, 300m deep and three million years old, shared by Macedonia (two-thirds) and Albania (one-third), is among Europe's deepest and oldest. Although usually calm, during storms Ohrid seethes with steely-grey whitecaps evoking the sea.

History

Lychnidos ('city of light' in Greek, evincing the lake's clarity) hugged the Via Egnatia connecting Constantinople with the Adriatic in the 4th century BC. It became a Byzantine trade, cultural and ecclesiastical centre.

Slavic migrations created the name Ohrid (from *vo rid*, or 'city on the hill'). Bulgarian Slavs arrived in 867, and the Ohrid literary school – the first Slavic university – was

Ohrid

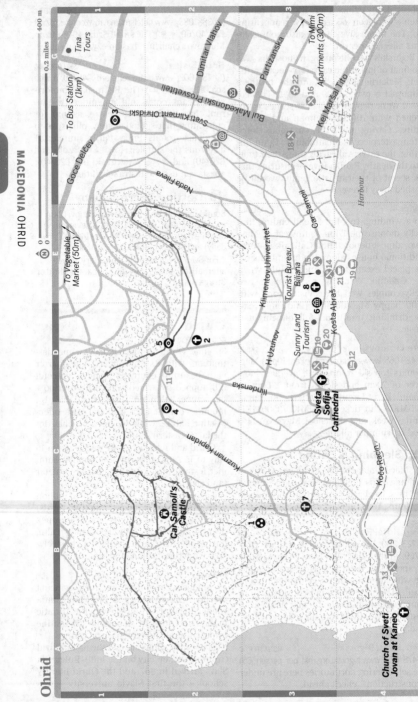

400 m

0.2 miles

Tina Tours

To Bus Station (1km)

Dimitar Vlahov

Partizanska

To Mimi Apartments (300m)

Goce Delcev

Sveti Kliment Ohridski

Bul Makedonski Prosvetitel

22

16

Kej Maršal Tito

To Vegetable Market (50m)

Nada Fileva

Klimentov Univerzitet

Tourist Bureau

Biljana

Car Samoil

Harbour

3

23

18

5

2

8

15

14

6

21

19

H Uzunov

Sunny Land Tourism

10

20

Ilindenska

11

4

17

12

Sveta Sofija Cathedral

Kuzman Kapidan

Koco Racin

Car Samoil's Castle

7

1

13

9

Church of Sveti Jovan at Kaneo

Ohrid

established by 9th-century Saints Kliment and Naum. Macedonia's Christianisation specifically and Slavic literacy in general were expedited when Kliment created the Cyrillic alphabet.

Bulgarian Cars Simeon (r 893–927) and Samoil (r 997–1014) ruled from here. When the Byzantines defeated Samoil, Ohrid was reclaimed. Ottoman Turks conquered Ohrid (and Macedonia), in the late 14th century. In 1767 Greek intrigue caused the abolition of Ohrid's archbishopric – a long-lasting grievance for both Macedonians and Bulgarians. Today, the restored archbishopric represents the Macedonian Orthodox Church's highest office.

⊙ Sights

Churches and museums are closed on Monday.

To see Ohrid's sights in the most efficient and least exhausting way, start at the Gorna Porta (Upper Gate), about 100MKD from centre by taxi, and walk down.

Church of Sveta
Bogorodica Perivlepta   CHURCH
(Gorna Porta; admission 100MKD; ⊙9am-1pm & 4-8pm) Just inside the Gorna Porta, this 13th-century Byzantine church has vivid biblical frescos and an icon gallery (Gorna Porta; ⊙9am-2pm & 5-8pm, closed Mon) highlighting the founders' artistic achievements.

FREE **Classical Amphitheatre**   AMPHITHEATRE
Ohrid's impressive amphitheatre was built for theatre; the Romans later removed 10 rows to accommodate gladiators. It hosts Summer Festival performances.

Car Samoil's Castle   CASTLE
(admission 30MKD; ⊙9am-6pm Tue-Sun) The massive, turreted walls of the 10th-century castle indicate the power of the medieval Bulgarian state. Ascend the narrow stone stairways to the ramparts for fantastic views.

FREE **Plaošnik**   CHURCH
(⊙9am-6pm) Down a wooded path, Plaošnik boasts the Church of Sveti Kliment i Pantelejmon. This 5th-century basilica was restored in 2002 according to its Byzantine design. The multidomed church has glass floor segments revealing original foundations. It houses St Kliment's relics, with intricate 5th-century mosaics outside. Nearby are 4th-century church foundations, replete with Early Christian flora and fauna mosaics.

Church of Sveti Jovan at
Kaneo   CHURCH
(admission 50MKD; ⊙9am-6pm) This stunning 13th-century church is set on a cliff over the lake, and is possibly Macedonia's most photographed structure. Peer down into the azure waters and you'll see why medieval monks found spiritual inspiration

here. The small church has original frescos behind the altar.

Sveta Sofija Cathedral   CHURCH
(Car Samoil bb; admission 100MKD; ⊙10am-8pm) Ohrid's grandest church, 11th-century Sveta Sofija is supported by columns and decorated with elaborate Byzantine frescoes. Its superb acoustics mean it's often used for concerts. Come by the road running down from Kaneo, past the Old Town's lovely houses, or along the new overwater walking bridge, beginning on the beach south of Kaneo.

National Museum   MUSEUM
(Car Samoil 62; admission 50MKD; ⊙9am-4pm & 7-11pm Tue-Sun) Near Sveta Sofija, the 1827 National Museum features distinctive white-and-brown architecture. The Robev Residence houses ancient epigraphy and the Urania Residence opposite has an ethnographic display.

Sveta Bogorodica Bolnička & Sveti Nikola Bolnički   CHURCHES
Ohrid's minor frescoed 14th-century churches are open infrequently (ask at the museum). Bolnica means 'hospital' in Macedonian; during plagues visitors faced 40-day quarantines here.

Činar   TREE
Stroll ul Sveti Kliment Ohridski, lined with cafes and shops, to reach this enormous, 900-year-old plane tree – a likeable Ohrid landmark.

🡒 Courses

Macedonian Language Course   LANGUAGE COURSE
(www.ukim.edu.mk/smjlk; per person €850) This three-week course, run each August by the SS Cyril & Methodius University, attracts international students. It includes language lessons, cultural excursions and accommodation, and is, by all accounts, great fun.

✻ Festivals & Events

Balkan Festival of Folk Dances & Songs   CULTURAL
This July festival draws regional folkloric groups.

Ohrid Summer Festival   ARTS
(☎262 304; www.ohridsummer.com.mk) Features classical and opera concerts, theatre and dance.

Sveti Naum–Ohrid Swimming Marathon   SWIMMING
This 30km event is usually in August, and gets dozens of international competitors.

🛏 Sleeping

Private rooms or apartments (per person €5 to €10) are advertised by the sign 'sobi' (rooms). Agencies also can book. Alternatively, good prices and central locations are offered by Apartmani Ohrid (www.apartmani -ohrid.com).

Avoid the touts waiting outside the bus station to pounce on arriving travellers.

TOP CHOICE Vila Sveta Sofija   HOTEL €€
(☎254 370; www.vilasofija.com.mk; Kosta Abraš 64; s/d €40/65, ste €80-125; ✳@) This opulent getaway combines traditional furnishings with chic modern bathrooms in an old Ohrid mansion near Sveta Sofija.

Villa Lucija   GUESTHOUSE €€
(☎265 608; www.vilalucija.com.mk; Kosta Abraš 29; s/d/apt €20/30/50; ✳@) Lucija has Old Town ambience and lovingly decorated, breezy rooms with lake views.

Stefan Kanevče Rooms   RENTED ROOMS €
(☎234 813; apostolanet@yahoo.co.uk; Kočo Racin 47; per person €10) Atmospheric 19th-century house near Kaneo beach boasting carved wooden ceilings and good hospitality.

Hotel Millenium   HOTEL €€€
(☎263 361; www.milleniumpalace.com.mk; Kej Maršal Tito bb; s/d/ste/apt €49/70/99/149; ✳🛜🏊) Odd on the outside but nice inside, this southern hotel has business-class rooms, gym, sauna and indoor swimming pool with cocktail bar. Suites have lake-view terraces.

Mimi Apartments   APARTMENT €
(☎250 103; mimioh@mail.com.mk; Strašo Pinđur 2; r incl breakfast 800MKD) Spacious, centrally located private rooms with fridge.

Villa Forum   HOTEL €€
(☎251 340; www.villaforumohrid.com.mk; Kuzman Kapidan 1; s/d/apt €30/65/75; ✳@) This luxurious Gorna Porta hotel has well-furnished, comfortable rooms with sparkling bathrooms.

✗ Eating

Self-caterers have Tinex supermarket (bul Makedonski Prosvetiteli) and the vegetable market (Kliment Ohridski).

Ohrid's endemic trout is endangered and (supposedly) protected from fishing – order the equally tasty *mavrovska* and *kaliforniska* varieties instead.

TOP CHOICE Letna Bavča

Kaneo SEAFOOD €€

(Kočo Racin 43; fish 150-300MKD; ☺9am-11pm) This simple 'summer terrace' on Kaneo beach is inexpensive and great. A fry-up of diminutive *plasnica* fish, plus salad, feeds two. Swim from the restaurant's dock and soak up the sun.

TOP CHOICE Restaurant Antiko

MACEDONIAN €€

(Car Samoil 30; mains 350-600MKD) In an old Ohrid mansion, the famous Antiko has great traditional ambience and pricey, but good, traditional dishes.

Restoran Belvedere SKARA €€

(Kej Maršal Tito 2; mains 300MKD) Try the excellent *skara* here, where outdoor tables extend under a leafy canopy.

Pizzeria Leonardo PIZZA €€

(Car Samoil 31; pizzas 200-350MKD) Ohrid's best pizza (it's popular with locals too).

Restoran Sveta Sofija MACEDONIAN €€€

(Car Samoil 88; mains 300-500MKD) This upscale restaurant opposite Sveta Sofija serves traditional fare and more than 100 Macedonian wines.

🍷 Drinking & Entertainment

TOP CHOICE Cuba Libre

BAR

(Kosta Abraš; ☺10pm-4am) Perennially popular Old Town bar and club. After midnight in summer it is a standing-room-only party spilling out on the courtyard.

Aquarius CAFE

(Kosta Abraš bb; ☺10am-1am) Ohrid's original lake-terrace cafe, Aquarius remains cool for a midday coffee and is lively at night.

Liquid CAFE

(Kosta Abraš 17; ☺9am-1am) Hip and relaxed chill-out place with a lake-front patio.

Arena CLUB

(cnr Jane Sandanski & Karpoš Vojvoda; ☺10pm-4am) Sweaty, packed pop-and-rock nightclub, 1.5km from town.

Dom na Kultura EVENTS, CINEMA

(Grigor Prličev; admission 50-100MKD) Holds cultural events and houses Ohrid's movie theatre.

🛍 Shopping

Bisera JEWELLERY

(Sveti Kliment Ohridski 60; ☺9am-1pm & 6-10pm) From his little shop, friendly Vane Talev continues a family tradition started in 1924: making the unique Ohrid pearls. Prices range from 1500MKD for a simple piece to 36,000MKD for an elaborate necklace.

ℹ Information

Internet Café Inside (Amam Trgovski Centar, bul Makedonski Prosveteli; per hour 60MKD; ☺9am-1am) Located in a mall near Ploštad Sveti Kliment Ohridski.

Ohrid.com (www.ohrid.com.mk) Municipal website.

Post Office (bul Makedonski Prosveteli; ☺7am-8pm Mon-Sat) Also changes money.

Sunny Land Tourism (www.sunnylandtourism. com; Car Samoil, by the National Museum; ☺9am-7pm) Local expert Zoran Grozdanovski can find accommodation and arrange tours and activities.

Telephone Centre (bul Makedonski Prosveteli; ☺7am-8pm Mon-Sat) Round the corner from the post office.

Tina Tours (bul Turisticka 66; ☺9am-6pm) Full-service central travel agency.

Tourist Bureau Biljana (www.beyondohrid. com; Car Samoil 38; ☺10am-midnight) Provides general info, accommodation and outdoor activities.

ℹ Getting There & Away

AIR Ohrid's **St Paul the Apostle Airport** (☎046 252 820; www.airports.com.mk), 10km north, handles summertime charter flights. Take a taxi (400MKD).

BUS From the **bus station** (7 Noemvri bb), 1.5km east of centre, buses serve Skopje, either via Kičevo (520MKD, three hours, 11 daily) or (the longer route) via Bitola; for Bitola itself, 10 daily buses run (200MKD, 1¼ hours). Buses to Struga (50MKD, 14km) leave every 30 minutes. In summer, reserve ahead for Skopje buses. Some *kombi* (minibuses) and taxis wait outside Tina Tours for intercity destinations.

International buses serve Belgrade (via Kičevo; 1800MKD, 15 hours, one daily). A 7pm bus serves Sofia (1450MKD, eight hours). For Albania, take a bus to Sveti Naum (110MKD, 29km). Cross the border and take a cab (€5, 6km) to Pogradeci. An Ohrid–Sveti Naum taxi costs 950MKD.

Around Ohrid

♪046

South of Ohrid, a long, wooded coast conceals pebble beaches, churches, villages and camping spots. In summer the big resort-style hotels and beaches are crowded and dirty (beyond them are better spots).

In summer, buses and *kombi* operate every 15 to 30 minutes until Gradište; further destinations such as Trpejca, Ljubaništa and Sveti Naum are served every hour or two.

◉ Sights & Activities

Beaches stretch down Ohrid's southern shore; unfortunately, in summer they're extremely overcrowded and unclean. Water clarity improves after overdeveloped **Peštani** (12km from Ohrid), which has an ATM and restaurants.

The wooded **Gradište camping ground**, 2km further, is popular with sunbathing students coming for beachside DJ parties at night. A fascinating **Neolithic Settlement Museum** here has artefacts from a 4000-year-old site where Ohrid's ancestors lived on stilt huts above the lake bed.

Trpejca   VILLAGE

(Трпејца) Cupped between a sloping hill and tranquil bay, Ohrid's last traditional fishing village features clustered houses with terracotta roofs and a white-pebble beach. At night, the sounds of crickets and frogs are omnipresent.

Trpejca has limited services, though in midsummer its small beach gets very crowded. The superb waters offer excellent swimming, and forested Mt Galičica's just opposite.

From Trpejca, boats visit **Sveta Bogorodica Zahumska Church** (simply called Sveti Zaum), 2.5km south, on a wooded beach near the lake's deepest part (294m). Its unusual frescos date from 1361. Fishermen or Ohrid travel agencies organise trips.

Sveti Naum Monastery   MONASTERY

(Свети Наум) Sveti Naum is 29km south of Ohrid, before the border, above a sandy beach. Naum was a contemporary of St Kliment, and their monastery was an educational centre. Naum's Church of the Holy Archangels (AD 900) became the 16th-century **Church of Sveti Naum**; this multidomed, Byzantine-style structure on a cliff, surrounded by roses and peacocks, boasts 16th- and 19th-century frescos.

Inside, drop an ear to the tomb of Sveti Naum to hear his muffled heartbeat. Outside, a wishing well collects spare denars. From the wall, lake views are excellent.

Sveti Naum has one of Ohrid's only sandy beaches, with good swimming and a hotel.

Galičica National Park   NATIONAL PARK

The rippling, rock-crested Mt Galičica, over 200m in points, separates Lake Ohrid from Lake Prespa – a winding mountain road starting near the village of Trpejca connects the two lakes (at one point at the peak, you can see both lakes simultaneously). This national park comprises 228 sq km and features endemic plants and trees.

Try hiking or paragliding, which can be arranged by Ohrid tour operators.

🛏 Sleeping & Eating

Coastal accommodation and restaurants mostly open in summer only; private accommodation (per person 300 to 600MKD) is generally plentiful.

Hotel Sveti Naum   HOTEL €€€

(📞283 080; www.hotel-stnaum.com.mk; Sveti Naum; s/d/ste from €37/74/116; ✳@) Fancy hotel with restaurant and luxurious, if dated, rooms. Lake-view rooms are €20 extra.

Vila De Niro   RENTED ROOMS €€

(📞070 212 518; d/apt €25/50; ✳@) Trpejca's only modern place, this yellow mansion is located where the walkway downhill diverges. It offers three doubles and an en suite apartment.

Camping Ljubaništa   CAMPGROUND €

(📞283 240; per tent 800MKD; ⊙May-Oct) On a sandy beach, 27km from Ohrid. Good place for families and solitude-seekers, though facilities are dated.

Restoran Ribar   SEAFOOD €€

(fish per person 300-750MKD; ⊙10am-midnight) Right on Trpejca's waterfront, Ribar serves local fish, meat and coffee.

❶ Getting There & Away

Frequent buses and *kombi* ply the Ohrid–Sveti Naum route in summer until Gradište. Services are less frequent to Trpejca, Ljubaništa and Sveti Naum. In Ohrid, wait for *kombi* by Tina Tours, opposite Ohridska Banka. These operate in summer until 2am.

Taxis are expensive; however, during summer some charge bus-ticket rates when filling up fast (check with the driver).

Boat tours from Ohrid to Sveti Naum (350MKD return) are regular in summer. Rates for village boat trips vary.

CENTRAL MACEDONIA

Macedonia's diverse central region is a wild, unexplored area flush with mountains, canyons, vineyards and caves. It also offers culture and significant historical sites.

Bitola Битола

047 / POP 95,400

With elegant buildings and beautiful people, elevated Bitola (660m) has a sophistication inherited from its Ottoman days as the 'City of Consuls'. Its 18th- and 19th-century colourful townhouses, Turkish mosques and cafe culture make it Macedonia's most intriguing and liveable major town. An essential experience is sipping a coffee and people-watching along the pedestrianised Širok Sokak ('Wide Street' in Turkish – still called ul Maršal Tito officially).

☉ Sights & Activities

Širok Sokak STREET
(ul Maršal Tito) Bitola's Širok Sokak is the city's most representative and stylish street, with its multicoloured facades and European honorary consulates attesting to the city's Ottoman-era sophistication. Enjoying the cafe life here as the beautiful people promenade past is an essential Bitola experience.

Church of Sveti Dimitrija CHURCH
(11 Oktomvri bb; ☉7am-6pm) This Orthodox church (1830) has rich frescos, ornate lamps and a huge iconostasis.

Mosques MOSQUES
Bitola's 16th-century Yeni, Isak and Yahdar-Kadi Mosques, all between the Dragor River and the Stara Čaršija (Old Bazaar), are Ottoman remnants, as is the enormous Clock Tower (Saat Kula).

Stara Čaršija BAZAAR
The Stara Čaršija boasted around 3000 clustered artisans' shops in Ottoman times; today, only about 70 different trades are conducted, but it's still worth a peek.

✺ Festivals & Events

The **Bit Fest** (☉Jun-Aug) features concerts, literary readings and art exhibits. The **Ilinden Festival** (☉2 Aug), honouring the Ilinden Uprising of 1903, is celebrated with food and music.

The **Manaki Brothers Film Festival** (www.manaki.com.mk; ☉late Sep–early Oct) screens independent foreign films. It honours Milton and Ianachia Manaki, the Balkans' first film-makers (1905). The Inter Fest features classical-music performances in the cultural centre and Bitola Museum.

🛏 Sleeping & Eating

TOP CHOICE Chola Guest House GUESTHOUSE €
(☏224 919; www.chola.mk; Stiv Naumov 80; s/d €12/20; ☎) Quiet place in an old mansion with clean, well-kept and pretty rooms and colourful modern bathrooms. Ask the taxi driver for Video Club Dju (opposite Chola).

Hotel De Niro HOTEL €€
(☏229 656; www.hotel-deniro.com; Kiril i Metodij 5; s/d/ste from €25/50/80; ✿☎) Central yet discreet with lovely old-Bitola-style rooms (more expensive suites also have waterbeds and spas). There's an excellent pizza-and-pasta restaurant (mains 200MKD to 450MKD) attached.

Via Apartments APARTMENTS €
(☏075 246 261; www.via.mk; Elpida Karamandi 4; s/d €12/24; ✿☎) These clean, well-designed central apartments share a kitchen, laundry, lounge and patio.

Hotel Rustiko HOTEL €
(☏227 712; www.hotelrustiko.com.mk; s/d/ste €17/28/33) Opened in 2012, the Rustiko has fresh and well-maintained rooms in a quiet location. Breakfast (€2) is served in the on-site restaurant – tasty, but not particularly rustic.

Hotel Milenium HOTEL €€
(☏241 001; h.milenium@t-home.mk; Marsal Tito 48; s/d/ste/apt €39/66/80/99; ✿☎) Atriums with stained glass, smooth marble opulence and historic relics channel old Bitola. The spacious rooms have sparkling bathrooms. Great value, and right on the Širok Sokak.

Hotel Epinal HOTEL €€
(☏224 777; www.hotelepinal.com; Maršal Tito bb; s/d €49/69; P✿☎☎) The big Epinal is old but quite nice – especially with its pool, spa and gym.

Premier Centar HOTEL €€
(☏202 070; www.centar.premier.com.mk; Stiv Naumov 12; s/d/tr incl breakfast 1540/2580/3420

MACEDONIA BITOLA

WORTH A TRIP

HERACLEA LYNCESTIS

Heraclea Lyncestis (admission 100MKD, photos 500MKD; ☉9am-3pm winter, to 5pm summer), 1km south of Bitola (70MKD by taxi), is among Macedonia's best archaeological sites. Founded by Philip II of Macedon, Heraclea became commercially significant before Romans conquered (168 BC) and its position on the Via Egnatia kept it prosperous. In the 4th century Heraclea became an episcopal seat, but it was sacked by Goths and then Slavs.

See the Roman baths, portico and amphitheatre, and the striking Early Christian basilica and episcopal palace ruins, with beautiful, well-preserved floor mosaics. They're unique in depicting endemic trees and animals. Excavations continue, so you may see newer discoveries.

MKD; ❄️☎️) Set in a renovated period house on a residential street, it has 19 modern rooms (and one apartment) and a banquet-hall restaurant that's good for groups.

TOP CHOICE **El Greko** PIZZA €
(☎071 279 848; cnr Maršal Tito & Elipda Karamandi; mains 180-350MKD; ☉10am-1am) This Sokak taverna and pizzeria has great beer-hall ambience and is popular with locals. At the time of research it was planning to also offer budget rooms.

🍷 Drinking & Entertainment

TOP CHOICE **Porta Jazz** BAR
(Kiril i Metodija; ☉8am-midnight) Popular, funky place that's packed when live jazz and blues bands play. It's located near the Centar na Kultura.

Basa BAR
(☉10pm-2am) This dark-lit bar on a side street off ul Leninova, behind Centar na Kultura, plays house music and local and Western pop.

Nightclub Rasčekor CLUB
(☉10pm-4am) The slick Rasčekor, near the train station, is probably the town's poshest option, with leading DJs and dressed-up local partiers.

City Club CLUB
(Pelagonka 2) Relaxed nightclub popular with students.

Positive Summer Club CLUB
(City Park; ☉9am-2am) Located by the city stadium and park, Positive is popular with locals for its swimming pool by day and open-air club by night.

ⓘ Information

Širok Sokak has free wi-fi.
Baloyannis Tours (☎075 207 273, 220 204; Solunska 118; ☉8am-6pm Mon-Sat) Provides city tours and outdoors trips (book ahead).
Tourist Information Centre (bitola-tourist-info@t-home.mk; Sterio Georgiev 1; ☉9am-6pm Mon-Sat) Friendly info centre.

ⓘ Getting There & Away

The **bus** and **train stations** (Nikola Tesla) are adjacent, 1km north of the centre. Buses serve Skopje (470MKD, 3½ hours, 12 daily) via Prilep (130MKD, one hour), Kavadarci (280MKD, two hours, five daily), Strumica (460MKD, four hours, two daily) and Ohrid (210MKD, 1¼ hours, 10 daily).

For Greece, go by taxi to the border (500MKD) and then find a cab to Florina. Some Bitola cab drivers will do the whole trip for about 3000MKD.

Three daily trains serve Skopje (210MKD) via Prilep (66MKD) and Veles (154MKD).

Pelister National Park

Macedonia's oldest national park (1948) covers 125 sq km on its third-highest mountain range, the quartz-filled Baba massif. Eight peaks top 2000m, crowned by Mt Pelister (2601m). Two glacial lakes, Pelisterski Oči (Pelister's Eyes), provide chilly refreshment.

Pelister's 88 tree species include the rare five-leafed Molika pine. It also hosts endemic Pelagonia trout, deer, wolves, chamois, wild boars, bears and eagles.

DIHOVO ДИХОВО
Only 5km from Bitola, the 830m-high mountainside hamlet of Dihovo is a base for Pelister hikes, with appealing stone houses and

the icon-rich **Church of Sveti Dimitrije** (1830). Dihovo's **outdoor swimming pool** is basically a very large basin containing ice-cold mountain-spring waters, rushing from the boulder-filled Sapungica River.

For summer hiking trips or winter skiing, see Petar Cvetkovski of Villa Dihovo. From Bitola, a taxi costs 150MKD.

🛏 Sleeping & Eating

TOP CHOICE **Villa Dihovo** GUESTHOUSE €€
(☑070 544 744; www.villadihovo.com; rates negotiable; P⊙) One of Macedonia's most remarkable guesthouses, Villa Dihovo comprises three traditionally decorated rooms in the 80-year-old home of Petar Cvetkovski and family, inside the first long driveway after Dihovo centre's restaurant. Its big flowering lawn is great for kids. The only fixed prices are for the homemade wine, beer and *rakija* (firewater); all else, room price included, is your choice.

Villa Patrice RENTED ROOMS €€
(☑075 466 878; s/d 900/1440MKD) Friendly family-run place with spacious, well-maintained rooms. A five-minute walk from the centre off the road towards the pool.

Restoran Idela SKARA €€
(mains 250-400MKD; ☺6am-midnight) Idela has a hunting-lodge feel and does great *skara*.

Prilep Прилеп

☑048 / POP 76,800

A hard-working, dusty, tobacco town, Prilep sits along the Pelagonian Plain, surrounded by weird, jagged-rock formations. It has some decent eating and drinking options along its smart new square, thronged by locals in the evening.

⊙ Sights & Activities

Prilep's marketplace, the **Čaršija**, houses artisans' shops and is, along with the nearby **Clock Tower**, a relic of Ottoman times. Prilep's well-kept centre – flush with squares, fountains, statues (and a duck pond) – has become a national example. There's a robust cafe and bar scene, with live bands playing outdoors in summer.

The **theatre festival** (☺Jun–Jul) has performances at the Dom na Kultura. The popular midsummer **Prilep beer festival** attracts thousands for prodigious consumption of beer and *skara* while being serenaded by well-known Balkan musical acts.

Some 2km from town, **King Marko's Towers** (Markovi Kuli) rise from a sharp cliff. Fortified since ancient times, this unique defensive position offers great views. It was famously commanded by King Marko (r 1371–95), a semiautonomous despot under the Turks, who ruled into today's northern Greece. Killed in battle while conscripted by Turks, King Marko is commemorated in Macedonian (and Serbian) folk songs, which celebrate his superhuman strength.

🛏 Sleeping

Hotel Sonce HOTEL €€
(☑401 800; www.makedonskosonce.com; Aleksandar Makedonski 4/3a; r incl breakfast 1240-2480MKD; P✳⊙≋) Decent rooms and restaurant, and a small outdoor swimming pool.

Hotel Crystal Palace HOTEL €€€
(☑418 000; www.kp.mk; Leninova 184; s/d/tr €35/59/83; P✳⊙) Near the train station, Prilep's four-star institution has well-appointed rooms.

✗ Eating & Drinking

Pizzeria Leone PIZZA €€
(Goce Delcev 30; pizza 200-350MKD; ☺11am-midnight) This central place does great pizzas.

Porta Club Restaurant RESTAURANT €€
(Republikanska 84; mains 300-450MKD; ☺10am-midnight) A spacious, well-lit bistro, Porta Club does fancy grills and fish.

Virus BAR
(Borka Taleski bb) With weathered wooden stairs, ornate print wallpaper, old paintings and little balcony tables, Virus has character and sometimes live rock bands.

ⓘ Getting There & Away

From Prilep's **bus station** (Sotka Gorgioski) buses serve Skopje (380MKD) via Negotino and Veles, and Kavadarci (190MKD, 1½ hours, two daily). Buses head south to Bitola (130MKD, 10 daily), and some continue to Ohrid (360MKD).

Prilep is on the Bitola–Skopje train line (three daily trains).

Around Prilep

About 10km from Prilep, 13th-century **Treskavec Monastery** (Манастир Тресквец) rises from Mt Zlato (1422m), a bare massif replete with twisted rock formations. Its frescos, including a rare depiction of Christ as a boy, line the 14th-century Church of Sveta Bogorodica, built over a 6th-century basilica. Earlier Roman remains are inside, along with graves, inscriptions and monks' skulls.

A paved road is being built, but a 4WD is best for the final rocky kilometres. Start from Prilep's cemetery and turn uphill at the sign marked 'Manastir Sveta Bogorodica, Treskavec'. Alternatively, to hike up, first drive or take a taxi to Dabnica, and then follow the cobbled track towards Mt Zlato; after the fountain, a path reaches Treskavec (two hours total; 4.5km).

Some 26km northwest of Prilep, towards Makedonski Brod, the 14th-century Zrze Monastery (Манастир Зрзе; ☑048 459 400; Manastir Sveto Preobrazhenije-Zrze; ⊗8am-5pm) of the Holy Transfiguration rises like a revelation from a clifftop. The monastery's tranquil position around a spacious lawn, with views over the outstretched Pelagonian Plain, is stunning. At dawn, a low-lying fog sometimes shrouds the plain in marble.

During Ottoman times, Zrze underwent periods of abandonment, rebuilding and plunder but remained an important spiritual centre. Its 17th-century Church of Saints Peter and Paul contains important frescoes and icons.

At time of research, Zrze was planning accommodation. Visitors can enjoy coffee with the kind monks and a tour of the church, with its priceless frescos and icons. While today the museum in Skopje houses Zrze's most famous icon, the Holy Mother of God Pelagonitsa (1422), a large copy remains in the church.

On the adjacent hillside, excavations continue on Zrze's precursor: a 5th-century basilica.

Take the road towards Makedonski Brod and turn at Ropotovo village; several villages lie between it and the monastery (take the left-hand turn at Kostinci). Zrze is infrequently signposted. The dirt roads are well built but worsen at nearly deserted Zrze village, beneath the mountain. From here, walk 2km uphill to the monastery, or drive it with a 4WD vehicle.

Tikveš Wine Region

Macedonia's winery heartland, Tikveš, has produced wine since the 4th century BC. It features rolling vineyards, lakes, caves and mountains, plus archaeological sites and churches. It's especially beautiful at dusk, when the fading sunlight suffuses soft hills laden with millions of grapes. Tikveš' local grapes generally retain an ideal sugar concentration (17% to 26%).

Travel agencies arrange tastings; alternatively, prearrange with the wineries.

KAVADARCI   КАВАДАРЦИ
☑043 / POP 38,700

West of the road and rail hub of Negotino, Kavadarci is fittingly dusty and agricultural, though it is improving its services. Attractions include wine tastings, monasteries, museums and Lake Tikveš, good for boating and birdwatching.

◉ Sights & Activities

FREE Kavadarci Museum   MUSEUM
(7 Septembri 58; ⊗8.30am-4.30pm Mon-Sat) Has ancient finds, some depicting wine bacchanalia.

Tikveš Winery   WINERY
(☑414 304; www.tikves.com.mk; 29 Noemvri 5; ⊗10am-5pm) Southeastern Europe's biggest winery (established 1885) offers tours and tastings of some of their 29 wines.

Vinoteka David   WINERY
(cnr Cano Pop Ristov & Ilindenska; ⊗8am-1pm & 5-7pm) This central winery offers regional wines.

✹ Festivals & Events

Kavadarci Wine Carnival   WINE FESTIVAL
Costumed parade, public wine tasting and merrymaking from 5 to 7 September.

⌷ Sleeping & Eating

Hotel Uni Palas   HOTEL €€
(☑419 600; Edvard Kardelj bb; s/d incl breakfast €36/56; ❉@) Comfortable, modern hotel by the bus station with well-appointed rooms, hydro-massage showers, and a popular cafe; a second location has similar rooms, but is less central.

Restoran Exclusive   MACEDONIAN €€
(bul Makedonija 66; mains 250-450MKD; ⊗9am-midnight) Kavadarci's best wine restaurant serves Macedonian and international dishes.

❶ Getting There & Away

From Kavadarci, buses serve Skopje (250MKD, seven daily), Prilep (190MKD, one hour, two daily) and Bitola (280MKD, five daily). For

OTHER WINERIES

Other wineries worth a visit include the following:

Bovin Winery (☎043 365 322; www.bovin.com.mk; Industriska bb; ☉10am-5pm) Award-winning winery in Negotino. Tours include extensive tastings.

Elenov Winery (☎043 367 232; vinarija_elenov@t-home.com.mk; Ivo Lola Ribar bb) Elenov is at the southeastern edge of the wine region, by the magnificent **Demir Kapija Gorge**. It's visible on the western side of the north–south E75 highway. Dating from 1928, it was Serbian king Aleksandar's official wine cellar, and it organises tastings.

Popova Kula Winery (☎023 228 781; d/ste €60/120) In Demir Kapija, up an 800m dirt road past the cemetery, is possibly Macedonia's most aesthetically pleasing winery, with great views over vineyards and the gorge from a traditionally decorated tasting room. For overnights, call ahead to book one of the modern rooms.

Disan Hills Winery (☎070 384 325, 043 362 520; ristov@mt.net.mk) In the village of Dolni Disan, 5km south of Negotino, Disan Hills is set amid vineyards and is run by people who put heart and soul into crafting limited quantities of high-quality wine. Tastings can be arranged.

Negotino, use local buses (30MKD, 15 minutes, six daily) or take a taxi (200MKD).

AROUND KAVADARCI

Three kilometres southwest of Kavadarci, past **Vataša**, the **Monastery of Sveti Nikola** sits alongside a forested river and displays rare 16th-century frescos.

Created in 1968 by damming the Crna River, nearby **Lake Tikveš** is surrounded by scrubland and stark cliffs, dotted with medieval hermitage frescos and circled by eagles and hawks. Being artificial, it has no endemic species, though it seems the monster catfish – weighing up to 200kg – has become pretty territorial since Comrade Tito first dispatched them into the 100m depths.

The 32km-long lake lies 11km southwest of Kavadarci; turn south at **Vozarci** to reach the small beach.

To arrange half-day **boat trips** with skippers and an English-speaking guide, check in Kavadarci at the Hotel Uni Palas (p358) or the local municipality building. Some Skopje travel agencies also arrange tours. Large groups use the 40-seater boat (4000MKD per group) while small groups use a regular fishermen's caique (1800MKD).

The tour navigates the lake's widest stretches for 20km, visiting the 14th-century **Pološki Monastery** (Polog Monastery), inhabited by a single nun. The monastery's **Church of Sveti Gjiorgji** was built by Serbian emperor Stefan Dušan (r 1331–55), and features expressive frescos of saints and the emperor.

Ringed by rugged cliffs, the lake offers **birdwatching** (look for the royal eagle, bearded vulture and white Egyptian vulture). Sometimes **fishing** is possible, though reeling in the obese catfish from the muddy depths might require a hydraulic lift. You can try **swimming**, but be mindful of the strong currents, steep drop-offs and rocks near the shore.

Stobi

The ruins of Roman **Stobi** (Стоби; www.stobi.mk; admission 100MKD; ☉9am-5pm) occupy a valley beside the E75 highway, 9km northwest of Negotino. Discovered in 1861, Stobi's major ruins are signposted. A gift shop by the snack bar sells replicas and wines.

Established in the 7th century BC, Stobi grew under the Macedonians and Romans. Its ancient Jewish population is indicated by synagogue foundations, beneath Christian basilica remains.

Although important as a Byzantine archbishopric, Stobi was sacked by Goths in 479 and further doomed by an earthquake in 518.

Start at the Roman amphitheatre (on the left) and clamber up further for Stobi's best mosaics. The path continues past well-marked ruins, including ancient sanctuaries to gods. At the end, turn right to the enormous city walls. Excavations continue.

UNDERSTAND MACEDONIA

History

Historical or geographical Macedonia is divided between the Republic of Macedonia (38%), Greek Macedonia (51%) and Bulgaria's Pirin Macedonia (11%). For its people, their history is a source of great pride but also a heavy burden. The post-Yugoslav experience has seen existential pressure from neighbours constantly challenging the Macedonian identity. Macedonia's history is too complex for simple answers, but many have strong opinions.

Ancient Macedonians & Romans

The powerful Macedonian dynasty of King Philip II (r 359–336 BC) dominated the Greek city-states. Philip's son, Alexander the Great, spread Macedonian might to India. After his death (323 BC), the empire dissolved amid infighting. In 168 BC, Rome conquered Macedonia; its position on the Via Egnatia, from Byzantium to the Adriatic, and the Axios (Vardar River) from Thessaloniki up the Vardar Valley, kept cities prosperous.

Christianity reached Macedonia with the Apostle Paul. The Roman Empire's 395 AD division brought Macedonia under Byzantine Constantinople and Greek-influenced Orthodox Christianity.

The Coming of the Slavs & the Macedonian Cars

The 7th-century Slavic migrations intermingled Macedonia's peoples. In 862, two Thessaloniki-born monks, St Cyril and St Methodius, were dispatched to spread orthodoxy and literacy among Moravia's Slavs (in modern-day Czech Republic). Their disciple, St Kliment of Ohrid, helped create the Cyrillic alphabet. With St Naum, he propagated literacy in Ohrid (the first Slavic university).

Byzantium and the Slavs could share a religion, but not political power. Chronic wars unfolded between Constantinople and the expansionist Bulgarian state of Car Simeon (r 893–927) and Car Samoil (r 997–1014). After being defeated in today's Bulgaria, Prespa and Ohrid in Macedonia became their strongholds. Finally, Byzantine Emperor Basil II defeated Samoil at the Battle of Belasica (near today's Strumica, in eastern Macedonia) in 1014, and Byzantium retook Macedonia.

Later, the Serbian Nemanjid dynasty expanded into Macedonia. After Emperor Stefan Dušan (r 1331–55) died, Serbian power waned. The Ottoman Turks soon arrived, ruling until 1913.

Ottoman Rule & the Macedonian Question

The Ottomans introduced Islam and Turkish settlers. Skopje became a trade centre, and beautiful mosques, hammams (Turkish baths) and castles were built. However, Greeks still wielded considerable power. In 1767, Greek intriguing caused the abolition of the 700-year-old Ohrid archbishopric. Greek priests opened schools and built churches, to the resentment of locals. Bulgaria and Serbia also sought Macedonia. The lines were drawn.

In Macedonia, Western European ethnic nationalism collided with the Ottomans' civil organisation by religion (not ethnicity). Europe's powers intervened after the 1877–78 Russo-Turkish War, when the Treaty of San Stefano awarded Macedonia to Bulgaria. Fearing Russia, Western powers reversed this with the Treaty of Berlin, fuelling 40 years of further conflict.

Although Macedonia remained Ottoman, the 'Macedonian Question' persisted. Various Balkan powers sponsored revolutionary groups. In 1893, the Internal Macedonian Revolutionary Organisation (Vnatrešna Makedonska Revolucionerna Organizacija, or VMRO) formed. VMRO was divided between 'Macedonia for the Macedonians' propagandists and a pro-Bulgarian wing.

In the St Elijah's Day (Ilinden) Uprising (2 August 1903), Macedonian revolutionaries declared the Balkans' first democratic republic, in Kruševo; the Turks swiftly crushed it. Although leader Goce Delčev had died months earlier, he's considered Macedonia's national hero.

In 1912 the Balkan League (Greece, Serbia, Bulgaria and Montenegro) fought Turkey (the First Balkan War), with Macedonia a prime battleground. The Turks were expelled, but a dissatisfied Bulgaria turned on its allies in 1913 (the Second Balkan War). Defeated, Bulgaria allied with Germany in WWI, reoccupying Macedonia and prolonging local suffering.

The Yugoslav Experience

When Bulgaria withdrew after WWI, Macedonia was divided between Greece and the new Kingdom of Serbs, Croats and Slovenes (Royalist Yugoslavia). Belgrade banned the Macedonian name and language, and disgruntled VMRO elements helped Croat nationalists assassinate Serbian King Aleksandar in 1934.

During WWII, Josip Broz Tito's Partisans resisted the Bulgarian–German occupation. Tito promised Macedonians republican status within communist Yugoslavia but was disinterested in their aspirations; Partisans seeking to fight for Greek-controlled Macedonia were shot as an example to the others. Nevertheless, in the 1946–49 Greek Civil War, some ethnic Macedonians joined the communists fighting Royalists. The communist defeat forced thousands, including many children (known as the *begalci*, meaning 'refugees'), to flee Greece.

Tito's nationalisation of property and industry ruined villages, with farmers deprived of flocks. Concrete communist monstrosities sheltered a newly urbanised population. Nevertheless, some nation-building overtures were made, such as a Macedonian grammar in 1952 and the Macedonian Orthodox Church's creation in 1967 – the 200th anniversary of the Ohrid archbishopric's abolition.

Macedonia after Independence

In a 1991 referendum, 74% of Macedonians voted to secede becoming the only Yugoslav republic to do so peacefully. However, the withdrawing Yugoslav army took everything, leaving the country defenceless. Greece's fears of an invasion from the north thus seemed farcical to everyone but them; nevertheless Macedonia changed its first flag (with the ancient Macedonian Vergina star) to appease Athens, after it had already accepted a 'provisional' name, the Former Yugoslav Republic of Macedonia (FYROM) to join the UN in 1993. When the USA (following six EU countries) recognised 'FYROM' in 1994, Greece defiantly announced an economic embargo.

This crippling embargo coincided with wars in other former Yugoslav states, creating ideal conditions for high-level schemes for smuggling fuel and other goods. This 1990s 'transition' period created a political/business oligarchy amid shady privatisations, deliberate bankrupting of state-owned firms and dubious pyramid schemes.

Worse, Macedonia's ethnic Albanians understood the Kosovo crisis as a template for addressing their own grievances. During the 1999 NATO bombing of Serbia, Macedonia sheltered more than 400,000 Kosovo Albanian refugees. Nevertheless, diaspora Albanians (using Kosovo as a staging ground) created the Ushtria Člirimtare Kombetare (UČK; National Liberation Army; NLA). In Macedonia's ensuing 2001 conflict, the NLA were first denounced as 'terrorists' by NATO and various world powers, but were turned into a political party with Western backing after the war. The conflict-ending Ohrid Framework Agreement granted minority language and national symbol rights, along with quota-based public-sector hiring.

Macedonians found the conflict a humiliating defeat. Albanians saw it as the first step to a full ethnic federation. Foreign powers have argued that this may well occur, if Macedonia cannot join NATO and the EU.

Towards Europe?

Despite four successive recommendations by the European Commission, Macedonia in December 2012 was still blocked by Greece from starting EU accession negotiations.

With ethnic Albanian nationalism rising and a Bulgarian government threatening to veto Macedonia's EU ambitions too, Macedonia has felt increasingly alienated. Well aware of this, Turkey has become Macedonia's best regional ally. The shared history, political goodwill and significant Turkish investments have greatly increased Ankara's prominence here in recent years. Macedonia's future will likely see a return to the past mixture of East and West – which may be best for everyone.

People

The 2011 census was delayed indefinitely over ethnic Albanian complaints of unfairness. A true population figure may never be achievable, considering that many Macedonian citizens live abroad.

In 2004, the population of 2,022,547 was divided thus: Macedonians (66.6%), Albanians (22.7%), Turks (4%), Roma (2.2%), Serbs (2.1%) and others (2.4%), including Vlachs – alleged descendants of Roman frontier soldiers.

MACEDONIA PEOPLE

Religion

Most Macedonians are Orthodox Christians, with some Macedonian-speaking Muslims (the Torbeši and Gorani). Turks are Muslim, like Albanians and (nominally, at least) the impoverished Roma. In recent years, social and ethnic complexities relating to religion have caused concern over Islamic fundamentalism, as seen in protests and violent attacks on Christians.

A 200-strong Jewish community descends from Sephardic Jews who fled Spain after 1492. Sadly, 98% of their ancestors (more than 7200 people) were deported to Treblinkal by Bulgarian occupiers in WWII. The community holds a Holocaust commemoration ceremony every 11 March.

The Macedonian Orthodox Church isn't recognised by some neighbouring Orthodox countries, but it's active in church-building and restoration work. Although Macedonians don't attend church services often, they do stop to light candles, kiss icons and pray.

Arts

Macedonian folk instruments include the *gajda* (a single-bag bagpipe) and *zurla* (a double-reed horn) often accompanied by the *tapan* drum. Other instruments include the *kaval* (flute) and *tambura* (small lute with two pairs of strings). The *Čalgija* music form, involving clarinet, violin, *darabuk* (hourglass-shaped drum) and *đoumbuš* (banjolike instrument) is representative. Macedonian music employs the 7/8 time signature.

Traditional dancing includes the *oro* circle dance, the male-only *Teškoto oro* ('difficult dance'), *Komitsko oro* (symbolising the anti-Turkish struggle), and the *Tresenica* for women.

The Ministry of Culture (www.culture.in.mk) lists performance dates and venues. Folk-dance ensemble Tanec (☑2461 021; www.tanec.com.mk; Vinjamin Macukovski 7) tours worldwide.

Many Macedonian musicians have won international acclaim, including pianist Simon Trpčevski, opera singer Boris Trajanov, jazz guitarist Vladimir Četkar and percussionists the Tavitjan Brothers. Especially beloved is Toše Proeski, a charismatic singer admired for both his music and his humanitarian work. Proeski died tragically in 2007, aged just 26.

Environment

The Continental and Mediterranean climate zones converge in Macedonia (25,713 sq km). Although mostly plateau (600m to 900m above sea level), it features more than 50 mountain peaks topping 2500m. The Vardar River starts in the west, passes Skopje and runs into Greece's Aegean Sea. Lakes Ohrid and Prespa are among Europe's oldest tectonic lakes (three million years old); at 300m, Ohrid is the Balkans' deepest. International borders are largely mountainous, including Šar Planina, near Kosovo in the northwest; Mt Belasica, in the southeast, bordering Greece; and the Osogovski and Maleševski ranges near Bulgaria. Macedonia's highest peak, Mt Korab (Golem Korab; 2764m), borders Albania in the Mavrovo National Park.

Wildlife

Macedonia's eastern Mediterranean and Euro-Siberian vegetation contains pine-clad slopes. Lower mountains feature beech and oak. Vineyards dominate the central plains. Endemic fauna includes the *molika* tree, a subalpine pine unique to Mt Pelister, and the rare *foja* tree on Lake Prespa's Golem Grad island.

Macedonia's alpine and low Mediterranean valley zones have bears, wild boars, wolves, foxes, chamois and deer. The rare lynx inhabits Šar Planina and Jasen Nature Reserve. Blackcaps, grouse, white Egyptian vultures, royal eagles and forest owls inhabit woodlands. Lake birds include Dalmatian pelicans, herons and cormorants. Storks (and their huge nests) are prominent. Macedonia's national dog, the *šar planinec*, is a 60cm-tall sheepdog that bravely fights bears and wolves.

Lakes Ohrid, Prespa and Dojran are separate fauna zones, due to territorial and temporal isolation. With 146 endemic species, Ohrid is a living fossil-age museum – its endemic trout predates the last Ice Age. Ohrid also has whitefish, gudgeon and roach, plus a 30-million-year-old snail genus, and the mysterious Ohrid eel, which arrives from the Sargasso Sea to live for 10 years before returning to breed and die.

National Parks

Pelister (near Bitola) and Galičica (between Lakes Ohrid and Prespa) national parks are in a tri-border protected area involving Albania and Greece. Mavrovo (between Debar and Tetovo) offers great hiking in summer and skiing in winter. All parks are accessible by road and free.

Environmental Issues

Lake Ohrid's endemic trout is an endangered species. Do the right thing and choose from three other tasty and cheaper varieties (*mavrovska, kaliforniska* or *rekna*) instead.

Food & Drink

Macedonia's specialities are part Ottoman, part Central European. *Lutenica* is a hot-pepper-and-tomato sauce. The national salad, *šopska salata*, features tomatoes and cucumbers topped with *sirenje* (white cheese). *Čorba* (soup) and *tavče gravče* (oven-cooked white beans) are other specialities. *Skara* (grilled meat) includes spare ribs, beef *kebapci* (kebabs) and *uviač* (rolled chicken or pork stuffed with yellow cheese). 'International' cuisine is also widespread.

For breakfast, try *burek* (cheese, spinach or minced meat in filo pastry) accompanied by drinking yoghurt or *kiselo mleko* ('sour milk', like yoghurt).

Bitter Skopsko Pivo is Macedonia's leading beer. The national firewater, *rakija,* is a strong grape spirit, delicious served hot with sugar in winter. *Mastika,* like ouzo, is also popular, as are homemade brandies made from cherries and plums.

SURVIVAL GUIDE

Directory A–Z

Accommodation

Skopje hotels are expensive; agencies find private rooms. Ohrid and villages have budget and midrange choices; book ahead for July and August, Orthodox Christmas (7 January), Orthodox Easter and during festivals or carnivals.

Prices quoted here are for rooms with a private bathroom unless otherwise stated.

The following price indicators apply (for a high-season double room):

€ less than 3000MKD/€50

€€ 3000MKD/€50 to 5000MKD/€80

€€€ more than 5000MKD/€80

Activities

Outdoor activities are endless. For skiing try Mavrovo's Zare Lazarevski. Mavrovo, Galičica and Pelister National Parks and Jasen Nature Reserve (www.jasen.com.mk) have great hiking and wildlife.

Enjoy wooded walks, boating and caving at Lake Matka, or swimming and boating at Lake Ohrid. Birdwatch on Lakes Prespa and Tikveš and paraglide on Mt Galičica.

Skopje, Ohrid and Bitola travel agencies run outdoors tours. Mountaineering association Korab Mountain Club (www.korab.org.mk/indexen.html) details mountain routes.

Macedonia is chronically affected by summer wildfires. Hikers should check conditions in advance – if you get stuck in the wrong patch of forest, not only could it be dangerous, it could also be illegal, if firemen or park wardens have closed the area.

Business Hours

Banks 7am to 5pm Monday to Friday

Businesses 8am to 8pm Monday to Friday, to 2pm Saturday

Cafes 10am to midnight

Post offices 6.30am to 8pm

Embassies & Consulates

All offices are in Skopje.

Australian Consulate (☑3061 114; www.serbia.embassy.gov.au/bgde/home.html; Londonska 11b)

Canadian Embassy (☑3225 630; www.canadianembassyinformation.com/embassy-in/republic-of-macedonia.html; bul Partizanski Odredi 17a)

French Embassy (☑3118 749; www.ambafrance-mk.org; Salvador Aljende 73)

German Embassy (☑3093 900; www.skopje.diplo.de/Vertretung/skopje/mk/Startseite.html; Lerinska 59)

Netherlands Embassy (☑023 129 319; www.nlembassy.org.mk; Leninova 69-71)

Russian Embassy (☑023 117 160; www.russia.org.mk; Pirinska 44)

UK Embassy (☎3299 299; www.ukinmacedo-nia.fco.gov.uk/en; Dimitrie Čupovski 26)

US Embassy (☎3102 000; http://macedonia.usembassy.gov; Samoilova bb)

Food

The following prices are for a main meal:

€ less than 150MKD

€€ 150MKD to 300MKD

€€€ more than 300MKD

Money

Macedonian denars (MKD) come in 10-, 50-, 100-, 500-, 1000- and 5000-denar notes, and one-, two-, five-, 10- and 50- denar coins. Taxi drivers hate it when you pay with a 1000-denar note, and may make you go into a shop to make change. Euros are generally accepted – some hotels quote euro rates, but denar payment is OK.

Macedonian *menuvačnici* (exchange offices) work commission-free. ATMs are widespread, except in villages, and using them is a good idea, considering that credit card fraud occasionally occurs. Avoid travellers cheques.

Post

Mail to Europe and North America takes seven to 10 days. *Preporačeno* (certified mail) is more expensive – fill out and keep the small green form. Letters to the USA cost 38MKD, to Australia 40MKD and to Europe 35MKD. Global-brand shipping companies operate.

Public Holidays

New Year's Day 1 January

Orthodox Christmas 7 January

Orthodox Easter Week March/April

Labour Day 1 May

Saints Cyril and Methodius Day 24 May

Ilinden Day 2 August

Republic Day 8 September

1941 Partisan Day 11 October

Safe Travel

The all-pervasive fear of a *promaja* (draft), which causes otherwise sane Macedonians to compulsively shut bus windows on swelteringly hot days, is undoubtedly the most

incomprehensible and aggravating thing foreigners complain about – fight for your rights, or suffer in silence.

Roma children's begging and pickpocketing attempts can irritate. Littering remains problematic. Selling alcohol in shops after 7pm (9pm in summer) is prohibited.

Telephone & Fax

Macedonia's country code is ☎389. Internet cafes offer cheap international phone service. Public telephone cards sold in kiosks or post offices for 100 (200MKD), 200 (300MKD), 500 (650MKD) or 1000 (1250MKD) units offer good value for domestic landline calls. Drop the initial zero in city codes and mobile prefixes (☎07) when calling from abroad.

Macedonia's largest mobile provider is T-Mobile, followed by One and VIP – buying a local SIM card is good for longer stays.

Major post offices do international faxing (about 400MKD).

Tourist Information

Travel agencies are best, though some towns have information offices.

Travellers with Disabilities

Historic sites and old quarters aren't wheelchair-friendly. Expensive hotels may provide wheelchair ramps. Buses and trains lack disabled access.

Visas

Citizens of former Yugoslav republics, Australia, Canada, the EU, Iceland, Israel, New Zealand, Norway, Switzerland, Turkey and the USA can stay for three months, visa-free. Otherwise, visa fees average from US$30 for a single-entry visa and US$60 for a multiple-entry visa. Check the Ministry of Foreign Affairs website (www.mfa.gov.mk) if unsure of your status.

Getting There & Away

Air

Alexander the Great Airport (☎3148 333; www.airports.com.mk; Petrovec), 21km from Skopje, is Macedonia's main airport, with Ohrid's **St Paul the Apostle Airport** (☎046 252 820; www.airports.com.mk) mostly used for summer charters. See the **Airports of Mac-**

edonia website (www.airports.com.mk) for information, including timetables, carriers and weather conditions. Skopje airport has exchange offices, ATMs and hotel-booking and car-rental services.

Land

Macedonia and Albania have four border crossings, the busiest Kafasan–Qafa e Thanës, 12km southwest of Struga, and Sveti Naum–Tushëmishti, 29km south of Ohrid. Blato, 5km northwest of Debar, and Stenje, on Lake Prespa's southwestern shore, are the least used.

For Bulgaria, Deve Bair (90km from Skopje, after Kriva Palanka) accesses Sofia. The Delcevo crossing (110km from Skopje) leads to Blagoevgrad, while the southeastern Novo Selo crossing, 160km from Skopje beyond Strumica, reaches Petrich.

Blace, 20 minutes north from Skopje, reaches Pristina in Kosovo, while Tetovo's Jazince crossing is closer to Prizren.

Tabanovce is the major road/rail crossing for Belgrade, Serbia.

BUS
Buses serve European, Balkan and Turkish cities.

CAR & MOTORCYCLE
You need a Green Card endorsed for Macedonia.

TRAIN
Macedonian Railway (www.mz.com.mk) serves Serbia and Kosovo. These antiquated trains offer the cheapest and most iconic way to go, passing through wild terrain. There are currently no services between Greece and Macedonia.

Getting Around
Bicycle
Cycling is popular in Skopje. Traffic is light in rural areas, though mountains and reckless drivers are common.

Bus
Skopje serves most domestic destinations. Larger buses are new and air-conditioned; *kombi* (minibuses) are usually not. During summer, pre-book for Ohrid.

Car & Motorcycle
There are occasional police checkpoints; make sure you have the correct documentation. Call ☑196 for roadside assistance.

AUTOMOBILE ASSOCIATIONS
AMSM (Avto Moto Soyuz na Makedonija; ☑3181 181; www.art.com.mk; Ivo Ribar Lola 51) offers road assistance, towing and information (in German, English and Macedonian), with branches nationwide.

DRIVER'S LICENCE
Your national driver's licence is fine, though an International Driving Permit is best.

FUEL & SPARE PARTS
Petrol stations are omnipresent except in rural areas. Unleaded and regular petrol cost about 100MKD per litre, while diesel is around 70MKD per litre.

HIRE
Skopje's rental agencies include international biggies and local companies. Ohrid has many, other cities have fewer. Sedans average €60 daily, including insurance. Bring your passport, driver's licence and credit card.

INSURANCE
Rental agencies provide insurance (€15 to €25 a day, depending on vehicle type; the nonwaivable excess is €1000 to €2500). Green Card insurance is accepted and third-party insurance is compulsory.

ROAD RULES
» Drive on the right.
» Speed limits are 120km/h (motorways), 80km/h (open road) and 50km/h to 60km/h (in towns).
» Speeding fines start from 1500MKD.
» Seatbelt and headlight use is compulsory.
» Cars must carry replacement bulbs, two warning triangles and a first-aid kit (available at big petrol stations).
» From 15 November to 15 March snow tyres must be used, otherwise you can be fined, and chains should be on-board too.
» Motorcyclists and passengers must wear helmets.
» Police also fine for drink driving (blood alcohol limit 0.05%). Fines are payable immediately.

Taxi
Taxis are relatively inexpensive. Skopje cabs cost 40MKD for the first kilometre, and

20MKD per subsequent kilometre. Smaller cities are cheaper. Although police crackdowns have reduced the practice, some drivers will still *vozi za bilet* (drive for the price of a bus ticket) when four passengers are gathered.

Intercity taxis are expensive if travelling alone (it's 4000MKD from Skopje to Ohrid), but can be preferable for international travel. Skopje to Pristina in Kosovo is only 3000MKD, and twice as fast as public transport.

Train

Major lines are Tabanovce (on the Serbian border) to Gevgelija (on the Greek border), via Kumanovo, Skopje, Veles, Negotino and Demir Kapija; and Skopje to Bitola, via Veles and Prilep. Smaller Skopje–Kičevo and Skopje–Kočani lines exist.

Montenegro

Why Go?

Imagine a place with sapphire beaches as spectacular as Croatia's, rugged peaks as dramatic as Switzerland's, canyons nearly as deep as Colorado's, *palazzi* as elegant as Venice's and towns as old as Greece's. Then wrap it up in a Mediterranean climate and squish it into an area two-thirds the size of Wales, and you start to get a picture of Montenegro (Црна Гора).

More adventurous travellers can easily sidestep the peak-season hordes on the coast by heading to the rugged mountains of the north. This is, after all, a country where wolves and bears still lurk in forgotten corners.

Montenegro, Crna Gora, Black Mountain: the name itself conjures up romance and drama. There are plenty of both on offer as you explore this perfumed land, bathed in the scent of wild herbs, conifers and Mediterranean blossoms. Yes, it really is as magical as it sounds.

Best Places to Eat

- » Konoba Ćatovića Mlini (p371)
- » Konoba kod Rada Vlahovića (p387)
- » Stari Most (p382)
- » Blanche (p377)
- » Miško (p380)

Best Places to Stay

- » Old Town Hostel (p373)
- » Palazzo Radomiri (p373)
- » Vila Drago (p377)
- » Eko-Oaza Suza Evrope (p388)

When to Go
Podgorica

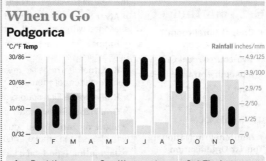

Jun Beat the peak-season rush and prices but enjoy the balmy weather.

Sep Warm water but fewer bods to share it with; not as scorching in Podgorica.

Oct The leaves turn golden, making a rich backdrop to walks in the national parks.

AT A GLANCE

» **Currency** Euro (€)

» **Language** Montenegrin

» **Money** ATMs in larger towns, banks open Monday to Friday and Saturday morning

» **Visas** None for citizens of EU, Canada, USA, Australia, New Zealand and many other countries

Fast Facts

» **Area** 13,812 sq km

» **Capital** Podgorica

» **Country code** ☑382

» **Emergency** Ambulance ☑124, fire ☑123, police ☑122

Exchange Rates

Australia	A$1	€0.82
Canada	C$1	€0.77
Japan	¥100	€0.83
New Zealand	NZ$1	€0.65
UK	UK£1	€1.18
USA	US$1	€0.78

Set Your Budget

» **Budget hotel room** €10–15 per person

» **Two-course meal** €10–30

» **Museum entrance** €1–5

» **Beer** €1.50

Resources

» **Montenegrin National Tourist Organisation** (www.montenegro.travel)

» **National Parks of Montenegro** (www.nparkovi.me)

» **Explore Montenegro** (www.exploremontenegro.com)

Connections

Many travellers make the most of the close proximity of Dubrovnik Airport to Herceg Novi to tie in a visit to Croatia with a Montenegrin sojourn. At the other end of the coast, Ulcinj is the perfect primer for exploring Albania and is connected by bus to Shkodra. Likewise, Rožaje captures elements of Kosovar culture and is well connected to Peja (Peć). A train line and frequent bus connections make a trip to Montenegro's closest cousins in Serbia a breeze. Montenegro shares a longer border with Bosnia and Hercegovina (BiH) than any of its neighbours. There are three main crossings for drivers, as well as regular bus services to Trebinje and Sarajevo. Ferries connect Bar to the Italian ports of Bari and Ancona.

ITINERARIES

One Week

Base yourself in the Bay of Kotor for two nights. Drive through Lovćen to Cetinje, then the next day continue to Šćepan Polje via Ostrog Monastery. Go rafting the following morning and spend the night in Podgorica. Head to Virpazar for a boat tour of Lake Skadar and then take the scenic lakeside road to Ulcinj. Finish in Sveti Stefan.

Two Weeks

Follow the itinerary above, but allow extra time in Kotor, Lake Skadar and Sveti Stefan. From Šćepan Polje, head instead to Žabljak and then to Biogradska Gora National Park before continuing to Podgorica.

Essential Food & Drink

» **Njeguški pršut i sir** Smoke-dried ham and cheese from the heartland village of Njeguši.

» **Ajvar** Spicy spread of fried red peppers and eggplant, seasoned with garlic, salt, vinegar and oil.

» **Kajmak** Soft cheese made from the salted cream from boiled milk.

» **Kačamak** Porridgelike mix of cream, cheese, potato and buckwheat or cornflour.

» **Riblja čorba** Fish soup, a staple of the coast.

» **Crni rižoto** Black risotto, coloured with squid ink.

» **Ligne na žaru** Grilled squid, sometimes stuffed (*punjene*) with cheese and smoke-dried ham.

» **Jagnjetina ispod sača** Lamb cooked (often with potatoes) under a metal lid covered with hot coals.

» **Rakija** Domestic brandy, made from nearly anything. The local favourite is grape-based *loza*.

» **Vranac** Local red wine varietal.

» **Krstač** Local white wine varietal.

Montenegro Highlights

1 Marvel at the majesty of the **Bay of Kotor** (p370) and exploring the historic towns hemmed in by the limestone cliffs.

2 Drive the vertiginous route from Kotor to the Njegoš Mausoleum at the top of **Lovćen National Park** (p380).

3 Enjoying the iconic island views while lazing on the sands of **Sveti Stefan** (p377).

4 Seeking the spiritual at peaceful **Ostrog Monastery** (p385).

5 Floating through paradise, rafting between the kilometre-plus walls of the **Tara Canyon** (p388).

6 Wandering through primeval forest mirrored in a tranquil alpine lake at **Biogradska Gora National Park** (p387).

7 Splashing through the floating meadows of water lilies garlanding vast **Lake Skadar** (p381).

BAY OF KOTOR

Coming from Croatia, the Bay of Kotor (Boka Kotorska) starts simply enough, but as you progress through fold upon fold of the bay and the surrounding mountains get steeper and steeper, the beauty meter gets close to bursting. It's often described as the Mediterranean's only fjord, and even though the geological label is not technically correct, the mental image that phrase conjures is spot on.

Herceg Novi   Херцег Нови

POP 12,700

It's easy to drive straight through Herceg Novi without noticing anything worth stopping for, especially if you've just come from Croatia with visions of Dubrovnik still dazzling your brain. However, just below the uninspiring roadside frontage hides an appealing Old Town with ancient walls, sunny squares and a lively atmosphere. The water's cleaner here, near the mouth of the bay, and while the town's pebbly coves and concrete swimming terraces aren't all that great, taxi boats do a brisk trade ferrying people to the secluded beaches on the Luština Peninsula.

◉ Sights

Stari Grad   NEIGHBOURHOOD

Herceg Novi's Old Town is at its most impressive when approached from the pedestrian-only section of ul Njegoševa, which is paved in the same shiny marble as Dubrovnik and lined in elegant, mainly 19th-century buildings. The street terminates in cafe-ringed Trg Nikole Đurkovića, where steps lead up

---

ADVENTURE RACE MONTENEGRO

Started by a bunch of British expats operating outdoor-adventure businesses out of Herceg Novi, the **Adventure Race** (www.adventureracemontenegro.com) should be high on the agenda for anyone who fancies themselves an action man or wonder woman. Held in late September/early October, the Coastal Challenge is a day of kayaking, mountain biking, hiking and orienteering amid the exceptional scenery of the Bay of Kotor.

---

to an elegant crenulated clock tower (1667) which was once the main city gate.

Just inside the walls is Trg Herceg Stjepana (commonly called Belavista Sq), a gleaming white piazza that's perfect for relaxing, drinking and chatting in the shade. At its centre is the Orthodox Archangel Michael's Church (Crkva Sv Arhanđela Mihaila; ⊙7am-midnight Jun-Aug, to 9pm Sep-May). Built between 1883 and 1905, its lovely proportions are capped by a dome and flanked by palm trees. Its Catholic counterpart, St Jerome's (Crkva Sv Jeronima), is further down the hill, dominating Trg Mića Pavlovića.

Kanli-Kula   FORTRESS

(Bloody Tower; admission €1; ⊙8am-midnight) The big fort visible from the main road was a notorious prison during Turkish rule (roughly 1482–1687). You can walk around its sturdy walls and enjoy views over the town. In the dungeon below the lower set of flagpoles, former inmates have carved crosses and ships into the walls.

Savina Monastery   MONASTERY

(Braće Grakalić bb; ⊙6am-8pm) From its hillside location in the town's eastern fringes, this peaceful Orthodox monastery enjoys wonderful coastal views. It's dominated by the elegant 18th-century Church of the Dormition, carved from pinkish stone. Inside there's a beautiful gilded iconostasis, but you'll need to be demurely dressed to enter (no shorts, singlets or bikinis). The smaller church beside it has the same name but is considerably older (possibly 14th century) and has the remains of frescos.

The monastery is well signposted from the large roundabout on the highway at Meljine.

Regional Museum   MUSEUM

(Zavičajni muzej; www.rastko.rs/rastko-bo/muzej; Mirka Komnenovića 9; admission €1.50; ⊙9am-6pm Mon-Sat) Apart from the building itself (which is a fab bougainvillea-shrouded baroque palace with absolute sea views), the highlight of this little museum is its impressive icon gallery.

Španjola Fortress   FORTRESS

Situated high above the town, this fortress was started and finished by the Turks but named after the Spanish (yep, in 1538 they had a brief stint here as well). If the graffiti and empty bottles are anything to go by, it's now regularly invaded by local teenagers.

🏃 Activities

🛶 Black Mountain
ADVENTURE TOURS
(☎067-640 869; www.montenegroholiday.com)
Can arrange pretty much anything, anywhere in the country, including mountain
biking, diving, rafting, hiking, paragliding,
canyoning, boat trips, wine tasting, accommodation, car hire and transfers.

🛶 Kayak Montenegro
KAYAKING
(☎067-382 472; www.kayakmontenegro.com; hire
per 1/4/8hr from €5/15/25) Offers paddling
day tours across the bay to Rose and Dobreč
or Mamula and Mirišta (€45 including
equipment), as well as day trips to explore
Lake Skadar.

Yachting Club 32
OUTDOORS
(www.yachtingclub32.com; Šetalište Pet Danica 32)
Hires jet skis (€50 per 20 minutes), pedal
boats (€8 per hour) and mountain bikes
(€3/6/15 per one hour/three hours/day).

🛏 Sleeping

Private rooms start at about €15 per person.
Either look for signs saying 'sobe' or book
through a local agency such as Trend Travel
(☎031-321 639; www.trendtravelmontenegro.com;
Bus Station, Jadranski Put).

🏕 Camp Full Monte
CAMPGROUND €
(☎067-899 208; www.full-monte.com; campsites
per person €10; ⊙May-Sep) Hidden in the
mountains near the Croatian border, this
small British-run camping ground offers
solar-generated hot water, odourless com-
posting toilets and a whole lot of seclusion.
If you hadn't guessed already, clothing is optional. Tents (with full bedding) can be hired
and meals can be arranged.

Hotel Perla
HOTEL €€€
(☎031-345 700; www.perla.me; Šetalište Pet Danica
98; s €84-112, d €104-140, apt €170-215; P❋☞)
It's a 15-minute stroll from the centre but if
it's beach you're after, Perla's position is perfect. The front rooms of this medium-sized
modern block have private terraces and sea
views.

Izvor
HOSTEL €
(☎069-397 957; www.izvor.me; Jadranski Put bb,
Igalo; dm €12; P☞) On the slopes above Igalo, this simple place consists of four basic
shared rooms which open on to a terrace
overlooking the bay. There's a traditional
restaurant downstairs (mains €4 to €9).

WORTH A TRIP

KONOBA ĆATOVIĆA MLINI

A crystalline stream flows around and
under this rustic former mill which
masquerades as a humble konoba (a
simple, family-run establishment) but in
reality is one of Montenegro's best restaurants (☎032-373 030; www.catovi-
camlini.me; mains €8-24; ⊙11am-11pm).
Watch the geese idle by as you sample
the magical bread and olive oil, which
appears unbidden at the table. Fish is
the focus but traditional specialities
from the heartland village of Njeguši are
also offered. You'll find it in the village
of Morinj, in the western corner of the
inner section of the Bay of Kotor.

Vila Aleksandar
HOTEL €€
(☎031-345 806; www.hotelvilaaleksandar.com;
Save Kovačevića 64; s/d €51/82; ❋☞☀) The
decor's a little dated but almost all of the
rooms have balconies with sea views, and
the blue-tiled pool on the sunny terrace is
extremely enticing. The restaurant opens
onto the waterfront promenade.

🍴 Eating

If you want to take on the local women in a
tussle for the best fresh fruit and vegetables,
get to the market (Trg Nikole Đurkovića; ⊙6am-
3pm Mon-Sat, to noon Sun) before 8am.

Konoba Feral
SEAFOOD €€
(Vasa Ćukovića 4; mains €7-17) A feral is a ship's
lantern, so it's seafood that takes pride
of place on the menu – not wild cat. The
grilled squid is excellent and comes with a
massive serving of seasonal vegetables and
salads.

ℹ️ Information

Tourist Information Kiosk (Šetalište Pet
Danica bb; ⊙9am-11pm May-Sep)

Tourist Office (☎031-350 820; www.herceg-
novi.travel; Jova Dabovića 12; ⊙9am-10pm
daily Jul & Aug, 9am-4pm Mon-Fri, 9am-2pm
Sat Sep-Jun)

ℹ️ Getting There & Around

BOAT Taxi boats ply the coast during summer,
charging about €10 to €15 to the beaches on the
Luštica Peninsula.

BUS Buses stop at the station just above the Old
Town. There are frequent buses to Kotor (€4,

one hour), Budva (€6, 1¾ hours), Cetinje (€7, 2½ hours) and Podgorica (€9, three hours). At least two buses head to Dubrovnik daily (€10, two hours).

CAR A tortuous, often gridlocked, one-way system runs through the town, so you're best to park in the parking building opposite the bus station. If you're driving to Tivat or Budva, it's usually quicker to take the **ferry** (car/motorcycle/passenger €4/1.50/free; ⊘24hr) from Kamenari (15km northeast of Herceg Novi) to Lepetane (north of Tivat). Queues can be long in summer.

Perast   Пераст

Looking like a chunk of Venice that has floated down the Adriatic and anchored itself onto the Bay of Kotor, Perast hums with melancholy memories of the days when it was rich and powerful. This tiny town boasts 16 churches and 17 formerly grand *palazzi*, one of which has been converted into **Perast Museum** (Muzej grada Perasta; ☑032-373 519; adult/child €2.50/1.50; ⊘9am-7pm) and showcases the town's proud seafaring history.

The 55m bell tower belongs to **St Nicholas' Church** (Crkva Sv Nikole; museum €1; ⊘museum 10am-6pm), which also has a museum containing relics and beautifully embroidered vestments.

Just offshore are two peculiarly picturesque islands. The smaller **St George's Island** (Sveti Đorđe) rises from a natural reef and houses a Benedictine monastery shaded by cypresses. Boats (€5 return) regularly head to its big sister, **Our-Lady-of-the-Rock Island** (Gospa od Škrpjela), which was artificially created in the 15th century. Every year on 22 July, the locals row over with stones to continue the task. Its magnificent church was erected in 1630.

Perast makes an atmospheric and peaceful base from which to explore the bay. Several houses rent rooms or you can try the **Hotel Conte** (☑032-373 687; www.hotel-conte.com; apt €100-160; P❄☎), where options range from deluxe studios to two-bedroom seaview apartments in historic buildings around St Nicholas' Church. Its wonderful restaurant (mains €9 to €20) serves fresh fish with lashings of romance on a waterside terrace.

Not far from Perast, **Risan** is the oldest town on the bay, dating to at least the 3rd century BC. Signposts point to some superb Roman **mosaics** (admission €2; ⊘9am-7pm mid-May–mid-Oct), discovered in 1930.

Kotor   Котор

POP 13,500

Wedged between brooding mountains and a moody corner of the bay, this dramatically beautiful town is perfectly at one with its setting. Its sturdy walls – started in the 9th century and tweaked until the 18th – arch steeply up the slopes behind it. From a distance they're barely discernible from the mountain's grey hide but at night they're spectacularly lit, reflecting in the water to give the town a golden halo. Within those walls lie labyrinthine marbled lanes where churches, shops, bars and restaurants surprise you on hidden piazzas.

Kotor's funnel-shaped **Stari Grad** (Old Town) sits between the bay and the lower slopes of Mt Lovćen. Newer suburbs surround the town, linking up to the old settlement of **Dobrota** to the north. Continuing around the bay towards Tivat, the coastal road narrows to a single lane and passes cute villages such as **Prčanj**, **Stoliv** and **Lastva**.

WORTH A TRIP

BACK ROAD TO MT LOVĆEN

The journey from Kotor to Mt Lovćen, the ancient core of the country, is one of Montenegro's great drives. Take the road heading towards the Tivat tunnel and turn right just past the graveyard. After 5km, follow the sign to Cetinje on your left opposite the fort. From here there's 17km of narrow road snaking up 25 hairpin turns, each one revealing a vista more spectacular than the last. Take your time and keep your wits about you; you'll need to pull over and be prepared to reverse if you meet oncoming traffic. From the top, the views stretch over the entire bay to the Adriatic. At the entrance to Lovćen National Park you can continue straight ahead through Njeguši for the shortest route to Cetinje or turn right and continue on the scenic route through the park.

LUŠTICA PENINSULA

Reaching out to form the southern headland of the Bay of Kotor, this gorgeous peninsula hides secluded beaches such as **Dobreč**, **Žanjic** and **Mirišta**, and the pretty fishing village **Rose**. They're all popular destinations for day trippers travelling from Herceg Novi by taxi boat

At **Bjelila**, a cluster of old stone houses, **Villa Kristina** (☏032-679 739; www.villakristina.me; Bjelila bb; apt €60-80; ❄🖧) has four apartments, each with its own little balcony gazing over the bay. It's terribly romantic, and there's a little private beach and a restaurant.

◉ Sights

The best thing to do in Kotor is to get lost and found again in the maze of streets. You'll soon know every corner, as the town is quite small, but there are plenty of churches to pop into and many coffees to be drunk in the shady squares.

Sea Gate
GATE
(Vrata od Mora) The main entrance to the town was constructed in 1555 when the town was under Venetian rule. Stepping through onto Trg od Oružja (Weapons Square), you'll see a strange stone pyramid in front of a **clock tower** (1602); it was once used as a pillory to shame wayward citizens.

St Tryphon's Cathedral
CHURCH
(Katedrala Sv Tripuna; Trg Sv Tripuna; admission €2; ⊙8am-7pm) Kotor's most impressive building is its Catholic Cathedral, which was originally built in the 12th century but reconstructed after several earthquakes. The gently hued interior is a masterpiece of Romanesque architecture, with slender Corinthian columns alternating with pillars of pink stone, thrusting upwards to support a series of vaulted roofs. Its gilded silver bas-relief altar screen is considered Kotor's most valuable treasure.

Town Walls
FORTRESS
(admission €2; ⊙24hr, fees apply 8am-8pm May-Sep) The energetic can make a 1200m-long ascent up the fortifications via 1350 steps to a height of 260m, for unforgettable views and a huge sense of achievement. There are entry points near the **River Gate** (North Gate) and Trg od Salate.

Maritime Museum of Montenegro
MUSEUM
(Pomorski muzej Crne Gore; www.museummaritimum.com; Trg Bokeljske Mornarice; adult/child €4/1; ⊙9am-6.30pm Mon-Sat, to 1pm Sun Apr-Oct, 9am-2pm daily Nov-Mar) Kotor's proud history as a naval power is celebrated in three storeys of displays housed in a wonderful early-18th-century palace.

⌂ Sleeping

Although the Stari Grad is a charming place to stay, you'd better pack earplugs. In summer the bars blast music onto the streets until 1am every night and rubbish collectors clank around at 6am. Some of the best options are just out of Kotor in quieter Dobrota. Enquire about private accommodation at the tourist information booth.

TOP CHOICE Old Town Hostel
HOSTEL €
(☏032-325 317; www.hostel-kotor.me; near Trg od Salata; dm €12-14, r without bathroom €30, apt €40) Sympathetic renovations have brought this 13th-century *palazzo* back to life, and the ancient stone walls now echo with the chatter of happy travellers. Comfortable, sociable, reasonable, historical... exceptional.

TOP CHOICE Palazzo Radomiri
HISTORIC HOTEL €€€
(☏032-333 172; www.palazzoradomiri.com; Dobrota; s €80-90, d €120-130, ste €150-220; ⊙Mar-Oct; 🅿❄🖧🏊) Exquisitely beautiful, this honey-coloured early-18th-century *palazzo* in Dobrota has been transformed into a first-rate boutique hotel. Some rooms are bigger and grander than others, but all 10 have sea views and luxurious furnishings.

Forza Mare
BOUTIQUE HOTEL €€€
(☏032-333 500; www.forzamare.com; Kriva bb, Dobrota; r €180-252; ⊙Apr-Oct; 🅿❄🖧🏊) A bridge arches over a small pool before you even reach the front door of this opulent Dobrota

Kotor

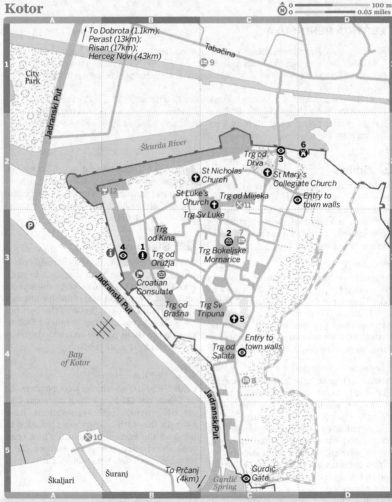

To Dobrota (1.1km);
Perast (13km);
Risan (17km);
Herceg Novi (43km)

Tabačina

City Park

Škurda River

Trg od Drva

St Nicholas' Church

St Mary's Collegiate Church

St Luke's Church

Trg od Mlijeka

Entry to town walls

Trg Sv Luke

Trg od Kina

Trg od Oružja

Croatian Consulate

Trg Bokeljske Mornarice

Trg od Brašna

Trg Sv Tripuna

Trg od Salata

Entry to town walls

Bay of Kotor

Jadranski Put

To Prčanj (4km)

Škaljari

Šuranj

Gurdić Spring

Gurdić Gate

hotel. Downstairs there's a tiny private beach, restaurant and spa centre.

Hotel Monte Cristo
HOTEL €€

(☏032-322 458; www.montecristo.co.me; near Trg Bokeljske Mornarice; r €75-90, apt €115-150; P❋🛜) It's not going to win any hip design awards but this old stone place offers a cheerful welcome and clean, brightly tiled rooms in a supremely central (but potentially noisy) location.

Tianis
APARTMENT €€

(☏032-302 178; www.tianis.net; Tabačina 569; apt €60-120; P❋🛜) Well located without being

in the midst of the melee, this friendly establishment has a clutch of reasonably priced apartments, some of which have magical views of the Old Town.

🍴 Eating & Drinking

There are dozens of cafe-bars, restaurants, bakeries and takeaway joints on Kotor's cobbled lanes.

TOP CHOICE Galion
SEAFOOD €€€

(☏032-325 054; Šuranj bb; meals €10-21) With an achingly romantic setting, upmarket Galion gazes directly at the Old Town across the

Kotor

yachts in the marina. Fresh fish is the focus, served as traditional grills. It usually closes in winter.

Restoran Stari Mlini　　SEAFOOD €€€
(☎032-333 555; www.starimlini.com; Jadranski Put; meals €12-20) It's well worth making the trip to Ljuta, just north of Dobrota, to this romantic restaurant set in an 18th-century mill by the edge of the bay. It's pricier than most and the service is variable, but the food is excellent.

Stari Grad　　SEAFOOD €€
(☎032-322 025; www.restoranstarigrad.com; Trg od Mlijeka; mains €8-18) Head straight through to the stone-walled courtyard, grab a seat under the vines and prepare to get absolutely stuffed full of fabulous food – the serves are huge.

☆ Entertainment

Maximus　　CLUB
(☎067-216 767; www.discomaximus.com; near Trg od Oružja; admission free–€5; ⊙11pm-5am Thu-Sat, nightly in summer) Montenegro's most pumping club comes into its own in summer, hosting big-name international DJs and local starlets.

ℹ Information

Tourist Information Booth (www.kotor.travel; ⊙8am-8pm)

ℹ Getting There & Away

The **bus station** (☎032-325 809; ⊙6am-9pm) is to the south of town, just off the road leading to the Tivat tunnel. Buses to Herceg Novi (€4, one hour), Budva (€3.50, 40 minutes), Tivat (€2.20, 20 minutes) and Podgorica (€7, two hours) are at least hourly. Further-flung destinations include Kolašin (€12, four daily).

A taxi to Tivat airport should cost around €10.

Tivat　　Тиват
POP 9,450

In the throes of a major makeover, courtesy of the multimillion-dollar redevelopment of its old naval base into the **Porto Montenegro** (www.portomontenegro.com; ⊙7am-1am) super-yacht marina, Tivat is becoming noticeably more schmick each year. While it will never rival Kotor for charm, it makes a pleasant stop on a trip around the bay, and a useful base for exploring the sweet villages of the Vrmac and Luštica Peninsulas.

🛏 Sleeping & Eating

Hotel Villa Royal　　HOTEL €€
(☎032-675 310; www.rotortivat.com; Kalimanjska 18; s/d €42/68; ❄@⊛) It's not a villa and it's certainly not fit for a king, but this minihotel near the old marina has clean, bright rooms and friendly staff, making it our pick of Tivat's extremely limited accommodation options...at least until the Regent opens in 2014.

One　　TOP CHOICE　ITALIAN €€€
(☎067-486 045; Porto Montenegro; mains €10-20; ⊙8am-1am) Murals and sail-like flourishes on the ceiling invoke the yachtie lifestyle in this smart but informal brasserie, while the menu sails clear across the Adriatic for an authentic take on Italian cuisine.

Prova　　MEDITERRANEAN €€
(www.prova.co.me; Šetalište Iva Vizina 1; mains €8-18; ⊙8am-1am) Shaped like a boat with chandeliers that look like mutant alien jellyfish, this upmarket eatery is the very epitome of the new, increasingly chic Tivat. The pasta is excellent.

ℹ Information

Tourist Office (☎032-671 324; www.tivat. travel; Palih Boraca 8; ⊙8am-8pm Mon-Fri,

8am-noon & 6-8pm Sat, 8am-noon Sun Jun-Aug, 8am-3pm Mon-Sat Sep-May)

ℹ️ Getting There & Away

AIR Tivat airport is 3km south of town and 8km through the tunnel from Kotor. Major local and international rental-car companies have counters here. Taxis charge around €5 to €7 for Tivat, €10 for Kotor and €25 to Budva.

BUS Buses to Kotor (€2.20, 20 minutes) stop outside a silver kiosk on Palih Boraca. The main stop for longer trips is inconveniently located halfway between Tivat and the airport.

ADRIATIC COAST

Much of Montenegro's determination to reinvent itself as a tourist mecca has focused firmly on its gorgeous Adriatic coastline. In July and August it seems that the entire Serbian world and a fair chunk of its northern Orthodox brethren can be found crammed onto this scant 100km stretch. Avoid these months and you'll find a charismatic set of fortified towns and fishing villages to explore, set against clear Adriatic waters and Montenegro's mountainous backdrop.

Budva   Будва

POP 13,400

The poster child of Montenegrin tourism, Budva – with its atmospheric Old Town and numerous beaches – certainly has a lot to offer. Yet the child has moved into a difficult adolescence, fuelled by rampant development that has leeched much of the charm from the place. In the height of the season the sands are blanketed with package holidaymakers from Russia and the Ukraine, while the nouveau riche park their multimillion-dollar yachts in the town's guarded marina. By night you'll run a gauntlet of scantily clad women attempting to cajole you into the beachside bars. It's the buzziest place on the coast so if you're in the mood to party, this is the place to be.

👁 Sights & Activities

Stari Grad   HISTORIC AREA

Budva's best feature and star attraction is the Old Town – a mini-Dubrovnik with marbled streets and Venetian walls rising from the clear waters below. Much of it was ruined by two earthquakes in 1979 but it has since been completely rebuilt and now

houses more shops, bars and restaurants than residences. At its seaward end, the **Citadela** (admission €2; ⊙9am-midnight May-Oct, to 5pm Nov-Apr) offers striking views, a small museum and a library full of rare tomes and maps. In the square in front of the citadel is a cluster of interesting churches. Nearby is the entry to the **town walls** (admission €1).

Archaeological Museum   MUSEUM

(Arheološki muzej; ☑033-453 308; Petra I Petrovića 11; adult/child €2/1; ⊙9am-9pm Tue-Fri, 2-9pm Sat & Sun) This museum shows off the town's ancient and complicated history – dating back to at least 500 BC – over three floors of exhibits.

FREE **Modern Gallery**   GALLERY

(Moderna galerija; Cara Dušana 19; ⊙8am-2pm & 6-9pm Mon-Fri, 6-9pm Sat) An attractive gallery displaying temporary exhibitions.

Montenegro Adventure Centre   PARAGLIDING

(☑067-580 664; www.montenegrofly.com) Rafting, hiking, mountain biking, diving and accommodation can all be arranged, as well as paragliding from launch sites around the country. An unforgettable tandem flight landing 750m below at Bečići beach costs €65.

🛏 Sleeping

TOP CHOICE **Hotel Astoria**   HOTEL €€€

(☑033-451 110; www.astoriamontenegro.com; Njegoševa 4; s €90-105, d €110-130, ste €130-210; ❄️@) Water shimmers down the corridor wall as you enter this chic boutique hotel hidden in the Old Town's fortifications. The rooms are on the small side but they're beautifully furnished.

Hotel Oliva   HOTEL €€

(☑033-459 429; olivai@t-com.me; Velji Vinogradi bb; s/d €30/58; P❄️🌐) Don't expect anything flashy, just a warm welcome, clean and comfortable rooms with balconies, and a nice garden studded with the olive trees that give this small hotel its name.

Saki Hostel & Apartmani   HOSTEL, APARTMENTS €

(☑067-368 065; www.saki-apartmani.com; IV Proleterska bb; dm €10, apt per person €25; P❄️🌐) Not quite a hostel and not quite an apartment hotel, this friendly family-run block on the outskirts of town offers elements of both. Individual beds are rented, hostel-style, in a rambling set of rooms.

✗ Eating

TOP CHOICE **Porto** SEAFOOD €€
(☎033-451 598; www.restoranporto.com; City Marina, Šetalište bb; mains €8-20; ⊙10am-1am) From the waterfront promenade, a little bridge arches over a fish pond and into this romantic restaurant where jocular bow-tie-wearing waiters flit about with plates laden with fresh seafood.

Pizza 10 Maradona PIZZERIA €
(Petra I Petrovića 10; pizza slice €2) A reader alerted us to this late-night hole-in-the-wall eatery selling pizza by the slice. We can confirm that after a hard night's hitting the city's night spots, Maradona's crispy-based pizza does indeed seem to come straight from the hand of God.

🍷 Drinking

Top Hill CLUB
(www.tophill.me; Topliški Put; events €10-25; ⊙11pm-5am Jul & Aug) The top cat of Montenegro's summer party scene attracts up to 5000 revellers to its open-air club atop Topliš hill, offering them top-notch sound and lighting, sea views, big-name touring DJs and performances by local pop stars.

ℹ Information

Tourist Office (☎033-452 750; www.budva. travel; Njegoševa 28; ⊙9am-9pm Mon-Sat, 5-9pm Sun)

ℹ Getting There & Away

The **bus station** (☎033-456 000; Popa Jola Zeca bb) has frequent services to Herceg Novi (€6), Kotor (€3.50), Bar (€4.50) and Podgorica (€6).

Pržno & Sveti Stefan
Пржно И Свети Стефан

Gazing down on impossibly picturesque Sveti Stefan, 5km south of Budva, provides the biggest 'wow' moment on the entire coast. And gazing on it is all most people will get to do, as this tiny island – connected to the shore by a narrow isthmus and crammed full of terracotta-roofed dwellings dating from the 15th century – was nationalised in the 1950s and the whole thing is now a luxurious resort.

Sveti Stefan is also the name of the settlement that's sprung up onshore. From its steep slopes you get to look down at that iconic view all day – which some might suggest is even better than staying in the surreally glamorous enclave below.

The general public can access the main Sveti Stefan beach, which faces the island. From the beach there's a very pleasant walk north to the cute village of Pržno where there are some excellent restaurants and another attractive, often crowded beach.

🛏 Sleeping & Eating

TOP CHOICE **Vila Drago** GUESTHOUSE €€
(☎030-468 477; www.viladrago.com; Slobode 32; r €45-60, apt €120-130; ❄🐾) The only problem with this family-run place is that you may never want to leave your terrace, as the views are so sublime. Watch the sunset over Sveti Stefan island from the grapevine-covered terrace restaurant (mains €5 to €17).

TOP CHOICE **Aman Sveti Stefan** RESORT €€€
(☎033-420 000; www.amanresorts.com; ste €750-3000; P❄🐾) Truly unique, this island resort offers 50 luxurious suites that showcase the stone walls and wooden beams of the ancient houses. Back on the shore, **Villa Miločer** has a further eight suites by the beach. Non-guests can avail themselves of three eateries: the **Olive Tree** at Sveti Stefan Beach, the **Beach Cafe** at Miločer and **Queen's Chair**, perched on a wooded hill facing Budva.

TOP CHOICE **Vila Levantin** APARTMENTS €
(☎033-468 206; www.villalevantin.com; Vukice Mitrović 3; r €30-50, apt €50-130; P❄🐾) Levantin has a variety of modern rooms and apartments at extremely reasonable prices. The block is modern and well finished, with red stone walls, blue-tiled bathrooms and an attractive plunge pool on the terrace.

Hotel Residence Miločer HOTEL €€
(☎033-427 100; www.residencemontenegro.com; Jadranski Put; s €69-99, d €79-119; P❄🐾) The decor's fresh and modern, there's secure parking, the breakfast buffets are excellent, and the staff aren't afraid to smile. It's worth paying the additional €10 for a spacious junior suite.

TOP CHOICE **Blanche** EUROPEAN €€
(☎062-504 272; www.blanche-restaurant.com; Obala 11; mains €8-24; ⊙10am-midnight) Higher than usual prices and upmarket decor don't necessary signal quality but in the case of this Pržno waterfront restaurant, you can

breathe easy. Sharing the menu with Dalmatian seafood classics are succulent steaks and a wide selection of Italian dishes.

ℹ Getting There & Away

Olimpia Express buses head to and from Budva (€1.50, 20 minutes) every 30 minutes in summer and hourly in winter.

Petrovac   Петровац

POP 1400

The Romans had the right idea, building their summer villas on this lovely bay. The pretty beachside promenade is perfumed with the scent of lush Mediterranean plants, and a picturesque 16th-century Venetian fortress guards a tiny stone harbour. This is one of the best places on the coast for families: the accommodation is reasonably priced, the water's clear and kids roam the esplanade at night with impunity.

In July and August you'll be lucky to find an inch of space on the town beach, but wander south and there's cypress- and oleander-lined Lučice Beach and, beyond it, the 2.5km-long sweep of Buljarica Beach.

🛏 Sleeping & Eating

Hotel Danica   HOTEL €€
(☑033-462 304; www.hoteldanica.net; s/d €55/60; P❈☀🌐☷) With a quiet location under the pine-covered hill immediately west of the town beach, this four-storey hotel is small enough to maintain a relaxed family ambience. There's a little pool on the terrace.

Camping Maslina   CAMPGROUND €
(☑033-461 215; akmaslina@t-com.me; Buljarica bb; per adult/child/tent/car/caravan €3/1.50/3/3/5; P🌐) Just off the road to Buljarica Beach, this well-kept campground has a tidy ablutions block with proper sit-down toilets and solar-powered hot water. As Montenegrin campsites go, this is one of the best.

Hotel Đurić   HOTEL €€
(☑033-462 005; www.hoteldjuric.com; Brežine bb; s/d €72/96; ☀May-Sep; ❈🌐☷) There's a vaguely Spanish Mission feel to this smart boutique hotel. All rooms have kitchen facilities and there's a restaurant at the back under a canopy of kiwifruit and grapevines.

Konoba Bonaca   MONTENEGRIN, SEAFOOD €€
(☑069-084 735; mains €8-15) Set back slightly from the main beach drag, this traditional restaurant focuses mainly on seafood but the local cheeses and olives are also excellent. Grab a table under the grapevines on the terrace.

ℹ Getting There & Away

Petrovac's bus station is near the top of town. Regular services head to Budva and Bar (both €2.50, 30 minutes).

Bar   Бар

POP 13,500

Dominated by Montenegro's main port and a large industrial area, Bar is unlikely to be anyone's highlight, but it is a handy transport hub welcoming trains from Belgrade and ferries from Italy. More interesting are the ruins of Stari Bar (Old Bar) in the mountains behind.

◉ Sights

TOP CHOICE Stari Bar   RUIN
(Old Bar; adult/child €2/1; ☀8am-10pm) Bar's original settlements stands on a bluff 4km northeast, off the Ulcinj road. A steep cobbled hill takes you past a cluster of old houses and shops to the fortified entrance, where a short, dark passage pops you out into a large expanse of vine-clad ruins and abandoned streets overgrown with grass and wild flowers. A small museum just inside the entrance explains the site and its history.

The Illyrians founded the city in around 800 BC. It passed in and out of Slavic and Byzantine rule until Venice took it in 1443 and held it until the Ottoman conquest in 1571. Nearly all the 240 buildings now lie in ruins, a result of Montenegrin shelling when the town was captured in 1878.

Buses marked Stari Bar depart from the centre of new Bar every hour (€1).

King Nikola's Palace   MUSEUM
(Dvorac Kralja Nikole; ☑030-314 079; Šetalište Kralje Nikole; adult/child €1/.50; ☀8am-2pm & 5-11pm) Presenting an elegant facade to the water, this former palace (1885) now houses a collection of antiquities, folk costumes and royal furniture. Its shady gardens contain plants cultivated from seeds and cuttings collected from around the world by Montenegro's sailors.

🛏 Sleeping & Eating

Hotel Princess   HOTEL €€€
(☑030-300 100; www.hotelprincess.me; Jovana Tomaševića 59; s €83-98, d €126-156, ste €205-275;

P✳@🖥🛜🛁) The standards aren't what you'd expect for the price but this resort-style hotel is the best option in Bar by far. Get your money's worth at the private beach, swimming pool and spa centre.

🍴 **Kaldrma** MONTENEGRIN €€
(📋030-341 744; kaldrmarestoran@t-com.me; mains €6-11; ⏰lunch & dinner; 🚗) Located on the steep road leading to Stari Bar's main gate, this wonderful little eatery manages to be simultaneously very traditional and slightly hippy-dippy. The focus is on the cuisine of Stari Bar itself, including tender lamb and seasonal vegetarian options. Accommodation is offered in a room upstairs with mattresses laid on woven rugs (€25).

ℹ Information

Tourist Information Centre (📋030-311 633; www.visitbar.org; Obala 13 Jula bb; ⏰8am-8pm Mon-Sat, to 2pm Sun Jul-Sep, 8am-4pm Mon-Fri Oct-Jun)

ℹ Getting There & Away

The bus station and adjacent train station are 1km southeast of the centre. Frequent buses head to Kotor (€6.50), Budva (€4.50), Ulcinj (€3) and Podgorica (€4.50). Trains head to Virpazar (€1.20, 23 minutes, seven daily), Podgorica (€2.40, one hour, nine daily) and Kolašin (€5.40, 2½ hours, four daily).

Montenegro Lines (📋030-311 164; www.montenegrolines.net) ferries to Italy (Bari and Ancona) leave from the ferry terminal near the centre of town.

Ulcinj Улцињ

POP 10,700

If you want a feel for Albania without actually crossing the border, buzzy Ulcinj's the place to go. The population is 61% Albanian and in summer it swells with Kosovar holidaymakers for the simple reason that it's nicer than any of the Albanian seaside towns. The elegant minarets of numerous mosques give Ulcinj a distinctly Eastern feel, as does the music echoing out of the kebab stands.

For centuries Ulcinj had a reputation as a pirate's lair. By the end of the 16th century as many as 400 pirates, mainly from Malta, Tunisia and Algeria, made Ulcinj their main port of call – wreaking havoc on passing vessels and then returning to party up large on Mala Plaža. Ulcinj became the centre of a thriving slave trade, with people – mainly from North Africa – paraded for sale on the town's main square.

👁 Sights & Activities

Beaches BEACHES

Mala Plaža may be a fine grin of a cove but it's a little hard to see the beach under all that suntanned flesh in July and August. You are better off strolling southeast where a succession of rocky bays offers clear water and a little more room to breathe. **Lady Beach 'Dada'** (admission €1.50) has a women-only policy, while a section of the **Hotel Albatros Beach** is clothing-optional.

The appropriately named **Velika Plaža** (Big Beach) starts 4km southeast of the town and stretches for 12 sandy kilometres. Sections of it sprout deckchairs but there's still plenty of relatively empty space. To be frank, this large flat expanse isn't as picturesque as it sounds and the water is painfully shallow – great for kids but you'll need to walk a fair way for a decent swim.

On your way to Velika Plaža you'll pass the murky Milena canal, where local fishermen use nets suspended from long willow rods attached to wooden stilt houses. The effect is remarkably redolent of Southeast Asia. There are more of these contraptions on the banks of the Bojana River at the other end of Veliki Plaža.

Stari Grad NEIGHBOURHOOD
The ancient Old Town is still largely residential and somewhat dilapidated – a legacy of the 1979 earthquake. A steep slope leads to the Upper Gate, where there's a small **museum** (admission €1; ⏰9am-8pm Tue-Sun) just inside the walls, containing Roman and Ottoman artefacts.

D'Olcinium Diving Club DIVING
(📋067-319 100; www.uldiving.com; Detarët e Ulqinit bb) Local dive sites include various wrecks (this is pirate territory, after all) and the remains of a submerged town. If you've got up-to-date qualifications you can rent gear (€20), take a guided shore dive (€15) or head out on a boat for a day's diving (€50).

🛏 Sleeping

🏆CHOICE **Haus Freiburg** HOTEL €€
(📋030-403 008; www.hotelhausfreiburg.me; Kosovska bb; s/d/apt €50/65/85; P✳🛜🛁) High on the slopes above the town, this family-run

hotel has well-kitted-out apartments and rooms, and a particularly attractive roof terrace with sea views, a swimming pool and small restaurant.

Dvori Balšića
HOTEL €€€

(☑030-421 609; www.hotel-dvoribalsica-montenegro.com; Stari Grad bb; s/d €65/100; ❀ 🛜) This stone *palazzo* and its equally grand sister, the **Palata Venecija**, are reached by the cobbled lanes and stairs of the Old Town. The sizeable rooms all have kitchenettes and sea views.

Real Estate Travel Agency
ACCOMMODATION SERVICES €

(☑030-421 609; www.realestate-travel.com; Hazif Ali Ulqinaku bb; per person from €15) Obliging English-speaking staff can help you find private rooms, apartments or hotel rooms. They also rent bikes (€10) and cars, run tours and sell maps of Ulcinj.

✖ Eating

TOP CHOICE Miško
SEAFOOD €€€

(Bojana River; mains €9-17) The most upmarket of the Bojana River restaurants (14km east of Ulcinj) is focused completely on seafood, including octopus, shrimps, shellfish, a big selection of fresh fish, and delicious *riblja čorba* (fish soup).

Restaurant Pizzeria Bazar
PIZZERIA, SEAFOOD €

(Hazif Ali Ulqinaku bb; mains €4-10; ⊘10am-1pm) An upstairs restaurant that's a great idling place when the streets below are heaving with tourists. People-watch in comfort as you enjoy a plate of *lignje na žaru* (grilled squid).

❶ Getting There & Away

The bus station is on the northeastern edge of town. Services head to Herceg Novi (€10, daily), Kotor (€9, daily), Budva (€7, eight daily), Podgorica (€6, 12 daily) and across the Albanian border to Shkodra (€6, two daily).

CENTRAL MONTENEGRO

The heart of Montenegro – physically, spiritually and politically – is easily accessed as a day trip from the coast but it's well deserving of a longer exploration. Two wonderful national parks separate it from the Adriatic and behind them lie the two capitals, the ancient current one and the newer former one.

Lovćen National Park
Ловћен

Directly behind Kotor is Mt Lovćen (1749m), the black mountain that gave *Crna Gora* (Montenegro) its name (*crna/negro* means 'black' and *gora/monte* means 'mountain' in Montenegrin and Italian respectively). This locale occupies a special place in the hearts of all Montenegrins. For most of its history it represented the entire nation – a rocky island of Slavic resistance in an Ottoman sea. The old capital of Cetinje nestles in its foothills.

Lovćen's star attraction is the magnificent **Njegoš Mausoleum** (Njegošev Mauzolej; admission €3; ⊘8am-6pm) at the top of its second-highest peak, Jezerski Vrh (1657m). Take the 461 steps up to the entry, where two granite giantesses guard the tomb. Inside, under a golden mosaic canopy, a 28-tonne Petar II Petrović Njegoš rests in the wings of an eagle, carved from a single block of black granite. The actual tomb lies below and a path at the rear leads to a dramatic circular viewing platform.

The national park's 6220 hectares are criss-crossed with well-marked hiking paths. The **National Park Visitor Centre** (www.nparkovi.me; ⊘9am-5pm) at Ivanova Korita offers accommodation in four-bedded bungalows (€40). If you're driving, the park can be approached from either Kotor or Cetinje (entry fee €2). Tour buses provide the only services into the park.

Cetinje
Цетиње

POP 14,000

Rising from a green vale surrounded by rough, grey mountains, Cetinje is an odd mix of former capital and overgrown village, where single-storey cottages and stately mansions share the same street. Pretty Njegoševa is a partly traffic-free thoroughfare lined with interesting buildings, including the **Blue Palace** (Plavi Dvorac), which houses the president, and various former embassies marked with plaques. Everything of significance is in the immediate vicinity.

◉ Sights

TOP CHOICE National Museum of Montenegro
MUSEUM

(www.mnmuseum.org; Narodni muzej Crne Gore; all museums adult/child €10/5; ⊘9am-4pm) The

National Museum is actually a collection of four museums and two galleries housed in a clump of important buildings. A joint ticket will get you into all of them or you can buy individual tickets.

Two are housed in the former parliament (1910), Cetinje's most imposing building. The fascinating **History Museum** (Istorijski muzej; ☑041-230 310; Novice Cerovića 7; adult/child €3/1.50) is very well laid out, following a timeline from the Stone Age to 1955. There are few English signs but the enthusiastic staff will walk you around and give you an overview before leaving you to your own devices.

Upstairs you'll find the equally excellent **Montenegrin Art Gallery** (Crnogorska galerija umjetnosti; adult/child €4/2). In 2012 an offshoot of the national gallery opened in a striking building on Cetinje's main street. The edgy **Miodrag Dado Đurić Gallery** (Galerija; Balšića Pazar; ☉10am-2pm & 6-9pm Tue-Sun) is devoted to 20th-century and contemporary Montenegrin art. The same ticket covers both galleries.

Entry to the **King Nikola Museum** (Muzej kralja Nikole; Dvorski Trg; adult/child €5/2.50) is by guided tour, which the staff will only give to a group, even if you've prepaid a ticket. Still, this 1871 palace of Nikola I, last sovereign of Montenegro, is worth the delay.

The castle-like **Njegoš Museum** (Njegošev muzej; Dvorski Trg; adult/child €3/1.50) was the residence of Montenegro's favourite son, prince-bishop and poet Petar II Petrović Njegoš. The palace was built in 1838 and housed the nation's first billiard table, hence the museum's alternative name, Biljarda. When you leave, turn right and follow the walls to the glass pavilion housing a fascinating large-scale **Relief Map** (admission €1) of Montenegro created by the Austrians in 1917.

Occupying the former Serbian Embassy, the **Ethnographic Museum** (Etnografski Muzej; Dvorski Trg; adult/child €2/1) is the least interesting of the six but if you've bought a joint ticket you may as well check it out. The collection of costumes and tools is well presented and has English notations.

Cetinje Monastery　　　　　MONASTERY
(Cetinjski Manastir; ☉8am-6pm) It's a case of four times lucky for the Cetinje Monastery, having been repeatedly destroyed during Ottoman attacks and rebuilt. This sturdy incarnation dates from 1786, with its only exterior ornamentation being the capitals of columns recycled from the original building, founded in 1484.

The chapel to the right of the courtyard holds what is said to be the mummified right hand of St John the Baptist. The casket's only occasionally opened for veneration, so if you miss out you can console yourself with the knowledge that it's not a very pleasant sight.

The monastery **treasury** (admission €2) is only open to groups but if you are persuasive enough and prepared to wait around, you may be able to get in (mornings are best). It holds a wealth of fascinating objects that form a blur as you're shunted around the rooms by one of the monks.

If your legs, shoulders or cleavage are on display you'll either be denied entry or given an unflattering smock to wear.

🛏 Sleeping & Eating

Pansion 22　　　　　GUESTHOUSE €€
(☑069-055 473; pansion22@mtel-cg.net; Ivana Crnojevića 22; s/d €22/40; 🛜) They may not be great at speaking English or answering emails, but the family that runs this central guesthouse offers a warm welcome nonetheless. The rooms are simply decorated yet clean and comfortable.

Kole　　　　MONTENEGRIN, EUROPEAN €
(☑041-231 620; www.restaurantkole.me; Bul Crnogorskih Junaka 12; mains €3-12; ☉7am-11pm) Omelettes and pasta are served at this snazzy modern eatery, but what are really great are the local specialities. Try the *Njeguški ražanj*, smoky spit-roasted meat stuffed with *pršut* and cheese.

ℹ Information

Tourist Information (☑078-108 788; www.cetinje.travel; Novice Cerovića bb; ☉8am-6pm)

ℹ Getting There & Away

Cetinje is on the main Budva–Podgorica highway and can also be reached by a glorious back road from Kotor via Lovćen National Park. Buses stop at Trg Golootočkih Žrtava, two blocks from the main street. There are regular services to Podgorica (€4) and Budva (€4).

Lake Skadar National Park Скадарско Језеро

The Balkans' largest lake, dolphin-shaped Lake Skadar has its tail and two-thirds of its body in Montenegro and its nose in Albania.

Covering between 370 and 550 sq km (depending on the time of year), it's one of the most important reserves for wetland birds in the whole of Europe. The endangered Dalmatian pelican nests here, along with 256 other species, while 48 species of fish lurk beneath its smooth surface. On the Montenegrin side, an area of 400 sq km is protected by a national park. It's a blissfully pretty area, encompassing steep mountains, hidden villages, island monasteries, clear waters and floating meadows of waterlilies.

Sights

Rijeka Crnojevića   VILLAGE
The northwestern end of the lake thins into the serpentine loops of the Crnojević River and terminates near the pretty village of the same name. It's a charming, tucked-away kind of place, accessed by side roads that lead off the Cetinje–Podgorica highway. Taxi boats dock at the marble riverside promenade, near the photogenic arched stone bridge (1854).

Žabljak Crnojevića   RUIN
For a brief time in the 15th century, this was the capital of Zetan ruler Ivan Crnojević. Now the enigmatic ruins stand forlornly on a hillside surrounded by green plains. The site's a little hard to find but well worth the effort. Heading towards Podgorica, turn left at the only set of traffic lights in Golubovci. After the railway bridge and the one-way bridge, turn left. Continue for about 4.5km until you see a bridge to your left. Cross the bridge and continue to the car park near the village. Take the stone stairs heading up from the path near the river and follow your nose along the overgrown path.

Virpazar   TOWN
This little town, gathered around a square and a river blanketed with water lilies, serves as the main gateway to the national park. Most of the boat tours of the lake depart from here.

Murići   BEACH
The southern edge of the lake is the most dramatic, with the Rumija Mountains rising precipitously from the water. From Virpazar there's a wonderful drive following the contours of the lake through the mountains towards the border before crossing the range and turning back towards Ulcinj. About halfway, a steep road descends to the village of Murići. This is one of the lake's best swimming spots. Local boatmen offer trips to the historic monasteries on the nearby islands for around €10 per hour.

Activities

Green Boats   BOAT TOUR
(Zeleni Brodovi; ☏069-998 737; greenboats.me@gmail.com; per hr from Virpazar/Vranjina €25/40) Lake cruises are offered every two hours by this association of small local operators. Two-hour cruises are the norm, although longer trips can be arranged. We've heard glowing reports about one particular boat, the Golden Frog (☏069-413 307; www.skadarlakecruise.blogspot.co.uk).

Undiscovered
Montenegro   ADVENTURE TOURS
(☏069-402 374; www.lake-skadar.com; ⊗Apr-Nov) Specialises in weeklong, all-inclusive, lake-based itineraries (per person €530 including accommodation at Villa Miela), but also offers an accommodation booking service and day tours. Options include guided hikes, kayaking, caving, boat tours, fishing, car safaris, wine tours and expert-led birdwatching.

Sleeping & Eating

Villa Miela   GUESTHOUSE €€
(☏020-3287 0015; www.undiscoveredmontenegro.com; r €80; ⊗Apr-Nov) Sitting pretty on the slopes near Virpazar, this lovingly renovated stone farmhouse has four rooms sharing a kitchen, BBQ area, orchard and lake views. In July and August it's reserved for Undiscovered Montenegro's seven-day activity holidays, but shorter stays are accepted at other times.

⌜TOP⌝ Stari Most   SEAFOOD €€
  ⌞CHOICE⌟
(☏041-239 505; mains €8-25) You wouldn't expect it, but sleepy Rijeka Crnojevića is home to one of Montenegro's best restaurants. Freshwater fish – particularly eel, trout and carp – is the speciality.

Konoba Badanj   MONTENEGRIN €€
(mains €6-12; ⊗8am-midnight) Near the bridge in Virpazar, a cool stone-walled interior with solid wooden beams makes this an atmo_spheric eating option. The fish soup comes with big chunks of fish and delicious scone-like homemade bread.

Information

National Park Visitor Centre (☏020-879 103; www.nparkovi.me; admission €2, free with national park entry ticket; ⊗8am-4pm, to 6pm summer) In Vranjina, this centre has excellent displays about all of Montenegro's national parks. A kiosk here and at Virpazar sells park entry tickets (per day €4) and fishing permits (per day summer/winter €10/5). In the busy months, tour operators have kiosks in the vicinity. Just across the busy highway and railway tracks are the remains of the 19th-century fortress Lesendro.

Virpazar Tourist Office (☑020-711 102; www.visitbar.org; ◷8am-5pm May-Sep, to 4pm Mon-Fri Oct-Apr; 🛜) This big new office on the main square can assist you with arranging anything in the area, including boat trips, wine tastings and private accommodation. Upstairs there are displays about the national park, and the office operates as a storefront for the region's small wine producers.

ℹ Getting There & Away

Buses on the Bar–Podgorica route stop on the highway. Virpazar's train station is off the main road, 800m south of town. There are seven trains to/from Bar (€1.20, 23 minutes) and Podgorica (€1.40, 30 minutes) every day.

Podgorica · Подгорица

POP 151,000

Podgorica's never going to be Europe's most happening capital, but if you can get past the sweltering summer temperatures and concrete apartment blocks, you'll find a pleasant little city with lots of green space and some excellent galleries and bars.

The city sits at the confluence of two rivers. West of the broad Morača is what passes for the business district. The smaller Ribnica River divides the eastern side in two. To the south is Stara Varoš, the heart of the former Ottoman town. North of the Ribnica is Nova Varoš, an attractive, mainly low-rise precinct of late-19th-century and early-20th-century buildings housing a lively mixture of shops and bars. At its centre is the main square, Trg Republika.

◉ Sights & Activities

FREE **Museums & Galleries of Podgorica** MUSEUM
(Muzeji i Galerije Podgorice; ☑020-242 543; Marka Miljanova 4; ◷9am-8pm) Despite Cetinje nabbing most of the national endowment, the new capital is well served by this collection of art and artefacts. There's an interesting section on Podgorica's history which includes antiquities exhumed from its Roman incarnation, Doclea.

FREE **Petrović Palace** PALACE, GALLERY
(Dvorac Petrovića; ☑020-243 513; www.csucg.co.me; Ljubljanska bb; ◷9am-2pm & 5-10pm Mon-Fri, 10am-2pm Sat) The Contemporary Art Centre operates two galleries in Podgorica. The bottom two floors of this former palace are given over to high-profile exhibitions, while the top floor has an oddball collection from its days as Yugoslavia's gallery devoted to art from Non-Aligned Movement countries.

Temporary exhibitions are also staged in the small **Galerija Centar** (☑020-665 409; Njegoševa 2; ◷10am-1pm & 6-pm Mon-Fri, 10am-1pm Sat).

Cathedral of Christ's Resurrection CHURCH
(Saborni Hram Hristovog Vaskrsenja; www.hramvaskrsenjapg.org; Bul Džordža Vašingtona) The large dome, white stone towers and gold crosses of this immense Serbian Orthodox cathedral are striking additions to Podgorica's skyline. Work commenced in 1993 and it's still a long way from completion, but you can usually enter and check out the glistening gold frescos inside.

Montenegro Adventures ADVENTURE TOURS
(☑020-208 000; www.montenegro-adventures.com; Jovana Tomaševića 35) This well-respected and long-standing agency creates tailor-made adventure tours, country-wide. It can organise mountain guides, cycling logistics, kitesurfing, hiking, cultural activities, accommodation, flights...you name it.

🛏 Sleeping

Most visitors to Podgorica are here for business, either commerce or government-related. Hotels set their prices accordingly and private accommodation isn't really an option.

Hotel Podgorica HOTEL €€€
(☑020-402 500; www.hotelpodgorica.co.me; Bul Sv Petra Cetinjskog 1; s €125-155, d €170-180, ste €190-200; P✳@🛜) A wonderful showcase of 1960s Yugoslav architecture, the Podgorica has been luxuriously modernised yet retains its riverstone cladding and period charm. The best rooms have terraces facing the river.

Aria HOTEL €€
(☑020-872 572; www.hotelaria.me; Mahala bb; s €56-76, d €93, apt €132-205; ✳🛜) An oasis of green lawns in the scorched field surrounding the airport, this new hotel offers better

Podgorica

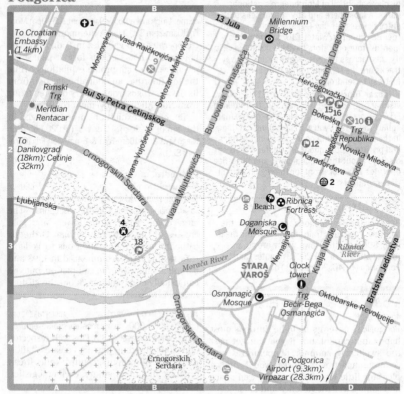

value than its city equivalents and is a great option if you've got a badly timed flight.

City Hotel　　　HOTEL €€€
(☑020-441 500; www.cityhotelmn.com; Crnogorskih serdara 5; s €75-95, d €100-120, apt €130-170; P✳@☎) A business-orientated makeover in 2008 has thankfully kept the 1970s exterior angularity of this city-fringe hotel, while the surrealist art of Dado Đurić has prevented a total beige-out inside.

Hotel Evropa　　　HOTEL €€
(☑020-623 444; www.hotelevropa.co.me; Orahovačka 16; s €40-55, d €70-90; P✳@☎) It's hardly a salubrious location, but Evropa is handy to the train and bus stations, and offers good clean rooms with comfortable beds, writing desks and decent showers.

✖ Eating & Drinking

Podgorica's nightlife is centred on Nova Varoš, particularly in the blocks west of ulica Slobode. The hippest strip right now is ulica Bokeška.

TOP CHOICE Lupo di Mare　　　SEAFOOD €€
(Trg Republika 22; mains €8-20; ☺8am-midnight) As you may have guessed from the name, there's a distinct Italian bent to this excellent seafood restaurant. Nautical knickknacks hang from the pale stone walls and there's an interesting wine list.

Leonardo　　　ITALIAN €€
(☑020-242 902; www.leonardo-restoran.com; Svetozara Markovića bb; mains €5-17; ☺8am-midnight; ☎✍) Leonardo's unlikely position at the centre of a residential block makes it a little tricky to find but the effort's well rewarded by accomplished Italian cuisine. The pasta dishes are delicious and reasonably priced.

Buda Bar　　　BAR
(☑067-344 944; www.facebook.com/Budabarpg; Stanka Dragojevića 26; ☺8am-2am) A golden

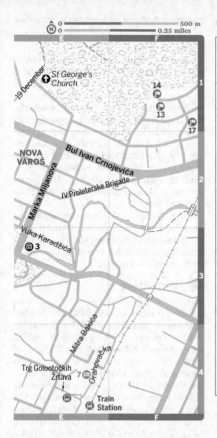

Podgorica

⊚ Sights
1 Cathedral of Christ's Resurrection A1
2 Galerija Centar.....................................D2
3 Museums & Galleries of Podgorica....E3
4 Petrović Palace..................................B3

Activities, Courses & Tours
5 Montenegro Adventures....................C1

Sleeping
6 City Hotel...C4
7 Hotel Evropa.......................................E4
8 Hotel Podgorica..................................C3

Eating
9 Leonardo.. B1
10 Lupo di Mare D2

Drinking
11 Buda Bar.. D1

Information
12 Albanian Embassy...............................D2
13 Bosnia & Hercegovinian Embassy F1
14 French Embassy..................................F1
15 German Embassy................................ D1
16 Serbian Embassy................................D2
17 UK Embassy..F1
18 USA Embassy.....................................B3

MONTENEGRO OSTROG MONASTERY

Buddha smiles serenely as you search for the eternal truth at the bottom of a cocktail glass. The semi-enclosed terrace is the place to be on balmy summer nights.

ⓘ Information

Tourist Organisation Podgorica (☑020-667 535; www.podgorica.travel; Slobode 47; ☺8am-8pm Mon-Fri)

ⓘ Getting There & Around

AIR Podgorica airport is 9km south of the city. Airport taxis have a standard €15 fare to the centre.

BUS Podgorica's **bus station** (☑020-620 430; Trg Goloatočkih Žrtava 1) has services to all major towns, including Herceg Novi (€9, three hours), Kotor (€7, 2¼ hours), Budva (€6, 1½ hours), Ulcinj (€6, one hour) and Cetinje (€3.50, 30 minutes)

TRAIN From Podgorica's **train station** (☑020-441 211; www.zpcg.me; Trg Goloatočkih Žrtava

13) there are services to Bar (€2.40, one hour, nine daily), Virpazar (€1.40, 30 minutes, seven daily), Kolašin (€5.90, 1½ hours, five daily) and Belgrade (€20, 10 hours, three daily).

Ostrog Monastery
Манастир Острог

Resting in a cliff face 900m above the Zeta valley, the gleaming white Ostrog Monastery (Manastir Ostrog) is the most important site in Montenegro for Orthodox Christians. Even with its numerous pilgrims, tourists and trashy souvenir stands, it's a strangely affecting place.

The **Lower Monastery** (Donji manastir) is 2km below the main shrine. Stop here to admire the vivid frescos in the **Holy Trinity Church** (Crkva Sv Trojice; 1824). Behind it is a natural spring where you can fill your bottles with deliciously fresh water and potentially benefit from an internal blessing as you sup it. From here the faithful, some of them barefoot, plod up the steep road to the top. Nonpilgrims and the pure of heart may drive directly to the main car park and limit their penitance to just the final 200m.

The Upper Monastery (Gornji manastir; the really impressive one) is dubbed 'Sv Vasilije's miracle', because no one seems to understand how it was built. Constructed in 1665 within two large caves, it gives the impression that it has grown out of the very rock. Sv Vasilije (St Basil) brought his monks here after the Ottomans destroyed Tvrdoš Monastery near Trebinje. Pilgrims queue to enter the shrine where the saint's fabric-wrapped bones are kept. To enter you'll need to be wearing a long skirt or trousers (jeans are fine) and cover your shoulders. At the very top of the monastery is another cave-like chapel with faded frescos dating from 1667.

A guesthouse (☎020-811 133; dm €5) near the Lower Monastery offers tidy single-sex dorm rooms, while in summer sleeping mats are provided for free to pilgrims in front of the Upper Monastery.

NORTHERN MOUNTAINS

This really is the full Monte: soaring peaks, hidden monasteries, secluded villages, steep river canyons and a whole heap of 'wild beauty', to quote the tourist slogan. It's well worth hiring a car for a couple of days to get off the beaten track – some of the roads are truly spectacular.

Morača Canyon

Heading north from Podgorica, it doesn't take long before the scenery becomes breathtaking. The highway gets progressively more precarious as it follows the Morača River into a nearly perpendicular canyon, 300m to 400m deep. If you're driving, pull over into one of the viewing areas to enjoy it properly, as this is an extremely busy and unforgiving stretch of road.

Near the canyon's northern end is Morača Monastery. As you enter the walled compound it's like stepping back into the 13th century, when the monastery was founded. The larger of its two churches has faded external frescos by the celebrated master Đorđe Mitrofanović and a wealth of religious art inside.

Kolašin   Колашин

POP 2800

Kolašin is Montenegro's main mountain resort. Although the skiing's not as reliable as Durmitor, Kolašin's much easier to get to (it's just off the main highway, 71km north of Podgorica) and has better accommodation. Like most ski towns, it looks prettier under a blanket of snow but even in summer it's a handy base for exploring Biogradska Gora National Park and other parts of the Bjelasica Mountains. A beautiful drive leads through the mountains to Andrijevica and on to Gusinje at the base of Prokletije National Park.

Most things of interest, including the banks and post office, are set around the two central squares (Trg Borca and Trg Vukmana Kruščića) and the short street that connects them (ul IV Proleterske).

🏃 Activities

Kolašin 1450 Ski Resort   SKIING

(☎020-717 845; www.kolasin1450.com; half-day/day/week ski pass €12/20/104) Located 10km east of Kolašin, at an elevation of 1450m, this ski centre offers 30km of runs (graded green, blue, red and black) reached by various ski lifts. You can hire a full ski or snowboard kit for €13 per day and there are shuttle buses from the Hotel Bianca; they're free if you're a hotel guest or if you purchase your ski pass from the hotel. The ski season lasts roughly from December to mid-April.

Hiking   HIKING

Three marked hiking paths start from Trg Borca and head into the Bjelasica mountains. From the ski centre there's a 16km, five-hour loop route through the forest to Mt Ključ (1973m) and back.

Explorer Tourist Agency   ADVENTURE TOURS

(☎020-864 200; www.montenegroexplorer.co.me; Mojkovačka bb) Located near the bus station, this agency specialises in action-packed holidays, including hiking, skiing, rafting, mountain biking, canyoning, caving, mountain climbing, jeep safaris, horse riding, paragliding and fishing expeditions. It also hires mountain bikes.

🛏 Sleeping & Eating

TOP CHOICE **Bianca Resort & Spa**   RESORT €€€

(☎020-863 000; www.biancaresort.com; Mirka Vešovića bb; s/d from €79/108; P🛜🏊) Take one large angular hotel with quirky hexagonal windows, completely gut it and give it a designer rustic look, and you end up with an atmospheric, idiosyncratic and first-rate ski resort.

Brile HOTEL, RESTAURANT €€

(☎020-865 021; www.montenegrohotelsonline.com/eng/hotel/46/brile.html; Buda Tomovića 2; s/d €35/70;) On the edge of the main square, this attractive family-run hotel has comfy rooms with polished wooden floors. There's a sauna for an après-ski defrost and a restaurant (mains €5 to €10) downstairs serving warming comfort food.

TOP CHOICE **Konoba kod Rada Vlahovića** MONTENEGRIN €€

(Trg Vukmana Kruščića; mains €6-8) Set on the square that was the heart of the old Turkish town, this rustic eatery is a standard-bearer for Montenegrin mountain cuisine, such as tender roast lamb which falls off the bone.

Vodenica MONTENEGRIN €€

(☎020-865 338; Dunje Dokić bb; mains €5-7) Set in a traditional watermill, Vodenica offers a taste of traditional stodgy mountain food designed to warm your belly on cold nights. Ease back and let your arteries clog.

Savardak MONTENEGRIN €€

(☎069-051 264; savardak@t-com.me; mains €8-9) Located 2.8km from Kolašin on the road to the ski centre, Savardak serves traditional food in what looks like a big haystack with a chimney attached. Four-person apartments (€40) are available in a thatch-roofed wooden chalet.

Information

Bjelasica & Komovi Regional Tourism Organisation (☎020-865 110; www.bjelasica-komovi.com; Trg Borca 2; ⊙9am-8pm Mon-Fri, 9am-noon & 4-8pm Sat & Sun)

Kolašin Tourist Office (☎020-864 254; www.kolasin.travel; Mirka Vešovića bb; ⊙8am-8pm Mon-Fri, 9am-3pm Sat)

Getting There & Away

BUS The **bus station** (☎020-864 033; Mojkovačka bb) is a shed set back from the road leading into town, about 200m from the centre. There are regular services to Podgorica (€5).

TRAIN Kolašin's train station is 1.5km from the centre. Trains head to Podgorica (€5, 90 minutes, five daily) and Bar (€5.48, 2½ hours, four daily). Buy your tickets onboard.

Biogradska Gora National Park Биоградска Гора

Nestled in the heart of the Bjelasica Mountain Range, this pretty national park has as its heart 16 sq km of virgin woodland – one of Europe's last primeval forests. The main entrance to the park is between Kolašin and Mojkovac on the Podgorica–Belgrade route. After paying a €2 entry fee you can drive the further 4km to the lake.

You can hire rowboats (per hour €8) and buy fishing permits (per day €20) from the **park office** (☎020-865 625; www.nparkovi.me; campsites per small tent/large tent/caravan €3/5/10, cabins €20; ⊙7.30am-8.30pm) by the car park. Nearby there's a camping ground and a cluster of 12 windowless log cabins. The ablutions block for the cabins is much nicer than the campsite's basic squat toilets. **Restoran Biogradsko Jezero** (mains €5.70-9) has a terrace where you can steal glimpses of the lake through the trees as you tuck into a traditional lamb or veal dish.

The nearest bus stop is an hour's walk away, at Kraljevo Kolo, and the nearest train station is a 90-minute walk, at Štitarička Rijeka.

Durmitor National Park Дурмитор

Magnificent scenery ratchets up to the stupendous in this national park (€2 entry fee per day), where ice and water have carved a dramatic landscape from the limestone. Eighteen glacial lakes known as *gorske oči* (mountain eyes) dot the Durmitor range, with the largest, **Black Lake** (Crno jezero), a pleasant 3km walk from Žabljak. The rounded mass of **Međed** (The Bear; 2287m) rears up behind the lake flanked by others of the park's 48 peaks over 2000m, including the highest, **Bobotov Kuk** (2523m). From late December to March, Durmitor is Montenegro's main ski resort; in summer it's a popular place for hiking, rafting and other active pursuits.

Žabljak, at the eastern edge of the range, is the park's principal gateway and the only town within its boundaries. It's not very big and neither is it attractive, but it has a supermarket, post office, bank, hotels and restaurants, all gathered around the parking lot that masquerades as the main square.

🏃 Activities

Rafting

Slicing through the mountains at the northern edge of the national park like they were made from the local soft cheese, the Tara River forms a canyon that at its peak is 1300m deep. The best views are from the water, which explains why rafting along the river is one of the country's most popular tourist activities.

There are a few rapids but don't expect an adrenaline-fuelled white-water experience. You'll get the most excitement in April and May, when the last of the melting snow revs up the flow. Various operators run trips between April and October.

The 82km section that is raftable starts from Splavište, south of the Tara Bridge, and ends at Šćepan Polje on the Bosnian border. The classic two-day trip heads through the deepest part of the canyon on the first day, stopping overnight at Radovan Luka. **Summit Travel Agency** (📞052-360 082; www.summit.co.me; Njegoševa 12, Žabljak) offers trips, including transfers from Žabljak (half-/one-/two-day tour €50/110/200).

Most of the day tours from the coast traverse only the last 18km from Brstanovica – this is outside the national park and hence avoids hefty fees. You'll miss out on the canyon's depths but it's still a beautiful stretch, including most of the rapids. The buses follow a spectacular road along the Piva River, giving you a double dose of canyon action.

If you've got your own wheels you can save a few bucks and avoid a lengthy coach tour by heading directly to Šćepan Polje. It's important to use a reputable operator; in 2010, two people died in one day on a trip with inexperienced guides. At a minimum, make sure you're given a helmet and lifejacket – wear them and do them up.

One good operator is **Kamp Grab** (📞040-200 598; www.tara-grab.com; half-day incl lunch €44, 2-day all-inclusive €180), with lodgings blissfully located 8km upstream from Šćepan Polje. To get there, you'll need to cross the Montenegrin side of the border crossing and hang a right (tell the guards you're heading to Grab); the last 3.5km is unsealed. Accommodation is available, and Grab also offers guided riverboarding (hydrospeed), where you direct yourself down the river on what looks like a kick board (€35).

Tara Tour (📞069-086 106; www.tara-tour.com) offers an excellent half-day trip (€40, including two meals) and has a cute set of wooden chalets in Šćepan Polje; accommodation, three meals and a half-day's rafting costs €55.

Hiking

Durmitor has dozens of hiking trails, some of which traverse seriously high-altitude paths which are prone to fog and summer thunderstorms. Ask the staff at the visitors centre about tracks that suit your level of experience and fitness.

Skiing

On the slopes of Savin Kuk (2313m), you'll find Durmitor's main ski centre. Its 3.5km run starts from a height of 2010m and is best suited to advanced skiers. On the outskirts of Žabljak, near the bus station, **Javorovača Ski Centar** (📞067-800 971) has a gentle 300m slope that's good for kids and beginners. One of the big attractions for skiing in Durmitor is the cost: day passes are around €15, weekly passes €70, and ski lessons cost between €10 and €20.

🛏 Sleeping & Eating

TOP CHOICE Eko-Oaza Suza

Evrope   CABINS, CAMPGROUND **€**
(📞069-444 590; ekooazatara@gmail.com; Dobrilovina; campsites per tent/person/campervan €5/1/10, cabins €50; ☺Apr-Oct) Consisting of four comfortable wooden cottages (each sleeping five people) and a fine stretch of lawn, this magical family-run 'eco oasis' offers a genuine experience of Montenegrin hospitality. Home-cooked meals are provided on request.

Hotel Soa   HOTEL **€€**
(📞052-360 110; www.hotelsoa.com; Njegoševa bb, Žabljak; s €55-82, d €75-110, ste €130-160; 🖥) Rooms are kitted out with monsoon shower heads, Etro toiletries, robes and slippers, and downstairs there's an appealing terrace restaurant. Best of all, the staff are genuinely friendly and the prices reasonable.

Zlatni Papagaj   PIZZERIA, CAFE **€**
(Vuka Karadžića 5, Žabljak; mains €4-13; 🖥) The 'Golden Parrot' has the feel of a pirate lair, with wine-barrel tables and a thick fug of cigarette smoke in the air. The menu offers a crowd-pleasing selection of pizza and steaks.

ℹ Information

Durmitor National Park Visitor Centre (www.nparkovi.co.me; Jovana Cvijića bb; ☺9am-5pm Mon-Fri)

PIVA CANYON

The highway to Šćepan Polje is a beautiful drive and quite a feat of engineering. It clings to the cliffs of the Piva Canyon and passes through 56 small tunnels carved out of the stone. The Piva River was blocked in 1975 by the building of a 220m-high hydroelectric dam at Plužine, flooding part of the canyon to create Lake Piva, which reaches depths of over 180m.

Great care was taken to move the **Piva Monastery** (Manastir Piva) to higher ground – a feat that took 12 years to complete. This Serbian Orthodox monastery has the distinction of being the only one to be built during the Turkish occupation.

Accommodation is available at the rafting camps around Šćepan Polje and in various *eko sela* (eco villages), scattered around Plužine and the back road to Žabljak. One excellent option is **Eko Selo Meadows** (☏069-718 078; www.meadows-eco.com; Donja Brezna bb; s/d/tr/q €20/30/42/50, mains €6-10; P), signposted from the highway, 17.5km south of Piva Monastery. Set on a flat plain edged by hills, the complex consists of a large restaurant serving local specialities and a collection of tidy wooden cabins.

ⓘ Getting There & Away

All of the approaches to Durmitor are spectacular. If you're coming from the coast, the quickest route is through Nikšić and Šavnik. There's a wonderful back road through the mountains leaving the highway near Plužine, but it's impassable as soon as the snows fall.

The bus station is at the southern edge of Žabljak, on the Šavnik road. Three buses head to Podgorica daily (€9.50).

UNDERSTAND MONTENEGRO

Montenegro Today

Going it alone was a brave move for a nation of this size but toughing it out is something this gutsy people have had plenty of experience in. Their national identity is built around resisting the Ottoman Empire for hundreds of years in a mountainous enclave much smaller than the nation's current borders.

The Never-Changing Government

In the 2012 general election, the Democratic Party of Socialists (DPS) fell two seats short of ruling in their own right but quickly formed a coalition with ethnic Bosniak, Albanian and Croat parties to form a government (ethnicity still plays a large role in political affiliation here). What's extraordinary about this is that the DPS has won every single vote since multiparty elections were established, marking the end of Communism in Yugoslavia.

Part of the party's continued popularity is the role they played in gaining Montenegro its independence. Several of the main opposition parties, especially the Serb-aligned parties, were strongly opposed to the break with Serbia, although most have publicly dropped their anti-independence stance.

The Đukanović Factor

Another factor in the DPS's success is the charismatic figure of returning Prime Minister Milo Đukanović. As a tall (198cm), handsome 26-year-old he was part of the 'antibureaucratic revolution' that took control of the Communist Party in 1989. At the age of 29 he became the first prime minister of post-Communist Montenegro and apart from a few years of 'retirement' he has been prime minister or president ever since.

However, Đukanović remains a controversial figure. While still president he was investigated by an Italian antimafia unit and charged for his alleged role in a multibillion-dollar cigarette-smuggling operation; the charges were dropped in 2009.

NATO and the EU

Shortly after independence, Montenegro applied to join both NATO and EU, and in June 2012 it opened formal EU accession negotiations. While most Montenegrins strongly favour EU membership, joining NATO is much more contentious. Memories of the NATO bombing of Serbia during the Kosovo conflict are still fresh. However, the

Montenegrin goverment has stood firm in its resolve, publicly stating that it expects to be invited to join the alliance in 2014.

History

Like all the modern states of the Balkan peninsula, Montenegro has a long, convoluted and eventful history. History is worn on the sleeve here and people discuss 600-year-old events (or their not-always-accurate versions of them) as if they happened yesterday. Events such as the split of the Roman Empire, the subsequent split in Christianity between Catholic and Orthodox, and the battles with the Ottoman Turks still have a direct bearing on the politics of today.

Before the Slavs

The Illyrians were the first known people to inhabit the region. By 1000 BC they had established a loose federation of tribes across much of the Balkans. By around 400 BC the Greeks had established some coastal colonies and by AD 10 the Romans had absorbed the entire region into their empire. In 395 the Roman Empire was split into two halves: the western half centred on Rome and the eastern half, which eventually became the Byzantine Empire, centred on Constantinople. Modern Montenegro lay on the fault line between the two entities.

In the early 7th century, the Slavs arrived from north of the Danube. Two main Slavic groups settled in the Balkans: the Croats along the Adriatic coast and the Serbs in the interior. With time most Serbs accepted the Orthodox faith, while the Croats accepted Catholicism.

First Serbian States

In the 9th century the first Serb kingdom, Raška, arose near Novi Pazar (in modern Serbia) followed shortly by another Serb state, Duklja, which sprang up on the site of present-day Podgorica. Raška eventually became known as Serbia and Duklja as Zeta. From the 12th century, Raška/Serbia became dominant over Zeta, which nonetheless remained a distinct area. At its greatest extent Serbia reached from the Adriatic to the Aegean and north to the Danube.

Expansion was halted in 1389 at the battle of Kosovo Polje, where the Serbs were defeated by the Ottoman Turks. By 1441 the Turks had rolled through Serbia and in the late 1470s they took on Zeta. The remnants of the Zetan nobility fled first to Žabljak Crnojevića, near Lake Skadar, and eventually into the mountains. In 1480 they established a stronghold at Cetinje on Mt Lovćen.

Montenegro & the Ottomans

This mountainous area became the last redoubt of Serbian Orthodox culture when all else fell to the Ottomans. It was during this time that the Venetians, who ruled Kotor, Budva and much of the Adriatic Coast, began calling Mt Lovćen the Monte Negro (Black Mountain). The Montenegrins, as they became known, built a reputation as fearsome warriors. The Ottomans opted for pragmatism, and largely left them to their own devices.

With the struggle against the Ottomans, the highly independent Montenegrin clans began to work collaboratively and the *vladika*, previously a metropolitan position within the Orthodox Church, began mediating between tribal chiefs. As such, the *vladika* assumed a political role, and *vladika* became a hereditary title: the prince-bishop.

In the late 18th century the Montenegrins under *vladika* Petar I Petrović began to expand their territory, doubling it within the space of a little over 50 years. Serbia achieved independence in 1835 and a similar rebellion against Ottoman control broke out in Bosnia in 1875. Montenegrins joined the insurgency and made significant territorial gains as a result. At the Congress of Berlin in 1878, Montenegro and Bosnia officially achieved independence.

In the early years of the 20th century there were increasing calls for union with Serbia and rising political opposition to Montenegro's autocratic Petrović dynasty. The Serbian king Petar Karadjordjević was suspected of involvement in an attempt to overthrow King Nikola Petrović, and Montenegrin–Serbian relations reached their historic low point.

The Balkan Wars of 1912–13 saw the Montenegrins joining the Serbs, Greeks and Bulgarians, and succeeding in throwing the Ottomans out of southeastern Europe. Now that Serbia and Montenegro were both independent and finally shared a border, the idea of a Serbian–Montenegrin union gained more currency. King Nikola pragmatically supported the idea on the stipulation that both the Serbian and Montenegrin royal houses be retained.

The Two Yugoslavias

Before the union could be realised WWI intervened. Serbia quickly entered the war and Montenegro followed in its footsteps. Austria-Hungary invaded Serbia shortly afterwards and swiftly captured Cetinje, with King Nikola escaping to France. In 1918 the Serbian army reclaimed Montenegro, and the French, keen to implement the Serbian–Montenegrin union, refused to allow Nikola to leave France. The following year Montenegro was incorporated in the Kingdom of the Serbs, Croats and Slovenes, the first Yugoslavia.

During WWII the Italians occupied Montenegro. Tito's Partisans and the Serbian Chetniks engaged the Italians, sometimes lapsing into fighting each other. Ultimately, the Partisans put up the best fight and with the support of the Allies, the Partisans entered Belgrade in October 1944 and Tito was made prime minister. Once the communist federation of Yugoslavia was established, Tito decreed that Montenegro have full republic status and the border of the modern Montenegrin state was set. Of all the Yugoslav states, Montenegro had the highest per-capita membership of the Communist Party and it was highly represented in the armed forces.

Union then Independence

In the decades following Tito's death in 1980, Slobodan Milošević used the issue of Kosovo to whip up a nationalist storm in Serbia and rode to power on a wave of nationalism. The Montenegrins largely supported their Orthodox coreligionists. In 1991 Montenegrin paramilitary groups were responsible for the shelling of Dubrovnik. In 1992, by which point Slovenia, Croatia and Bosnia and Hercegovina (BiH) had opted for independence, the Montenegrins voted overwhelmingly in support of a plebiscite to remain in Yugoslavia with Serbia.

In 1997 Montenegrin leader Milo Djukanović broke with an increasingly isolated Milošević and immediately became the darling of the West. As the Serbian regime became an international pariah, the Montenegrins increasingly wanted to re-establish their distinct identity.

In 2003 Yugoslavia was consigned to the dustbin of history, and Montenegro entered into a state union with Serbia. In theory this union was based on equality between the two republics; however, in practice Serbia was such a dominant partner that the union proved infeasible. In May 2006 the Montenegrins voted for independence.

People

In the last census (2011), 45% of the population identified as Montenegrin, 29% as Serb, 12% as Bosniak or Muslim, 5% as Albanian, 1% as Croat and 1% as Roma. Montenegrins are the majority along most of the coast and the centre of the country, while Albanians dominate in Ulcinj, Bosniaks in the far east (Rožaje and Plav), and Serbs in the north and Herceg Novi. Religion and ethnicity broadly go together in these parts. Over 72% of the population are Orthodox Christians (mainly Montenegrins and Serbs), 19% Muslim (mainly Bosniaks and Albanians) and 3% Roman Catholic (mainly Albanians and Croats).

Montenegrins traditionally considered themselves 'the best of the Serbs', and while most Montenegrins still feel a strong kinship to their closest siblings, this is coupled with a determination to maintain their distinct identity. After negotiating a reasonably amicable divorce from the unhappy state union in 2006, relations between the two countries took a turn for the worse. In 2008 Serbia expelled Montenegro's ambassador after Montenegro officially recognised the Serbian province of Kosovo as an independent country. Diplomatic relations have since resumed, but issues of ethnicity and identity remain thorny.

Food & Drink

Loosen your belt; you're in for a treat. Eating in Montenegro is generally an extremely pleasurable experience. By default, most of the food is local, fresh and organic, and hence very seasonal. The food on the coast is virtually indistinguishable from Dalmatian cuisine: lots of grilled seafood, garlic, olive oil and Italian dishes. Inland it's much more meaty and Serbian-influenced. The village of Njeguši in the Montenegrin heartland is famous for its *pršut* (dried ham) and cheese. Anything with Njeguški in its name is going to be a true Montenegrin dish and stuffed with these goodies.

Eating in Montenegro can be a trial for vegetarians and almost impossible for vegans. Pasta, pizza and salad are the best fallback options. Nonsmoking sections are a rumour from distant lands that have yet to trouble the citizens of Montenegro.

SURVIVAL GUIDE

Directory A–Z

Accommodation

Hotels and private accommodation (rooms and apartments for rent) form the bulk of the sleeping options, although hostels have been popping up in the more touristy areas in recent years. Camping grounds operate in summer and some of the mountainous areas have cabin accommodation in 'eco villages' or mountain huts.

In the peak summer season, some places require minimum stays (three days to a week). Many establishments on the coast, even some of the established hotels, close during winter.

An additional tourist tax (usually less than €1 per night) is added to the rate for all accommodation types. For private accommodation it's sometimes left up to the guest to pay it, but it can be nigh on impossible finding the right authority to pay it to (the procedure varies from area to area). Theoretically you could be asked to provide white accommodation receipt cards (or copies of invoices from hotels) when you leave the country, but in practice this is rarely required.

The following price categories for the cost of a room for a couple in the shoulder season (roughly June and September) are used in the listings in this chapter.

€ less than €20

€€ €30 to €90

€€€ more than €90

Business Hours

Business hours in Montenegro are a relative concept. Even if hours are posted on the doors of museums or shops, they may not be heeded.

Banks Usually 8am to 5pm Monday to Friday, 8am to noon Saturday

Cafes 10am to midnight (later in high season in busy areas)

Pubs 9pm to 2am

Restaurants 8am to midnight

Shops 8am to 7pm Monday to Friday, to 2pm Saturday; often closed in late afternoon

Supermarkets 8am to 8pm Monday to Friday, to 6pm Saturday, to 1pm Sunday

Embassies & Consulates

The following are all in Podgorica, unless otherwise stated. For a full list, see www.mip.gov.me.

Albanian Embassy (☏020-667 380; www.mfa.gov.al; Stanka Dragojevića 14)

Bosnia & Hercegovina Embassy (☏020-618 105; www.mvp.gov.ba; Atinska 58)

Croatian Embassy (☏020-269 760; Vladimira Ćetkovića 2)

Croatian Consulate (☏032-323 127; Trg od Oružja bb, Kotor)

French Embassy (☏020-655 348; Atinska 35)

German Embassy (☏020-441 000; www.auswaertiges-amt.de; Hercegovačka 10)

Serbian Embassy (☏020-667 305; www.podgorica.mfa.gov.rs; Hercegovačka 18)

Serbian Consulate (☏031-350 320; www.hercegnovi.mfa.gov.rs; Njegoševa 40, Herceg Novi)

UK Embassy (☏020-618 010; www.ukinmontenegro.fco.gov.uk; Ulcinjska 8)

US Embassy (☏020-410 500; http://podgorica.usembassy.gov; Ljubljanska bb)

Food

The following price categories for the cost of a main course are used in the listings in this chapter.

€ less than €5

€€ €5 to €10

€€€ more than €10

Gay & Lesbian Travellers

Although homosexuality was decriminalised in 1977 and discrimination outlawed in 2010, attitudes to homosexuality remain hostile and life for gay people is extremely difficult. Many gay men resort to online connections (try www.gayromeo.com) or take their chances at a handful of cruisy beaches. Lesbians will find it even harder to access the local community.

Money

» Montenegro uses the euro (€). You'll find banks with ATMs in all the main towns, most of which accept Visa, MasterCard, Maestro and Cirrus. Don't rely on restaurants, shops or smaller hotels accepting credit cards.

» Tipping isn't expected, although it's common to round up to the nearest euro.

Public Holidays

New Year's Day 1 and 2 January

Orthodox Christmas 6, 7 and 8 January

Orthodox Good Friday & Easter Monday Usually April/May

Labour Day 1 May

Independence Day 21 May

Statehood Day 13 July

Telephone

» The international access prefix is ☏00 or ☏+ from a mobile.

» Mobile numbers start with ☏06.

» Local SIM cards are easy to find. The main providers are T-Mobile, Telenor and M:tel.

Women Travellers

Other than a cursory interest shown by men towards solo women travellers, travelling is hassle-free and easy. In Muslim areas some women wear a headscarf but most don't.

Getting There & Away

Air

Montenegro has two international airports – Tivat (TIV; ☏032-670 930; www.montenegroairports.com) and Podgorica (TGD; ☏020-444 244; www.montenegroairports.com) – although many visitors use Croatia's Dubrovnik Airport, which is very near the border. While various airlines run summer charter flights, the following airlines have regular scheduled flights to/from Montenegro.

Adria Airlines (www.adria.si) Ljubljana to Podgorica.

Austrian Airlines (www.austrian.com) Vienna to Podgorica.

Croatia Airlines (www.croatiaairlines.com) Zagreb to Podgorica.

Jat Airways (www.jat.com) Belgrade to Podgorica and Tivat.

Montenegro Airlines (www.montenegroairlines.com) Tivat to Belgrade and Moscow. Podgorica to Belgrade, Frankfurt, Ljubljana, Moscow, Niš, Paris, Rome, Vienna and Zurich.

Moskovia Airlines (www.ak3r.ru) Moscow to Tivat.

Rossiya Airlines (FV; www.rossiya-airlines.ru) St Petersburg to Tivat.

S7 Airlines (S7; www.s7.ru) Moscow to Tivat.

Turkish Airlines (www.turkishairlines.com) Istanbul to Podgorica.

Land
BORDER CROSSINGS

Albania The main crossings link Shkodra to Ulcinj (Sukobin) and to Podgorica (Hani i Hotit).

BiH The main checkpoints are at Dolovi and Šćepan Polje.

Croatia There's a busy checkpoint on the Adriatic highway between Herceg Novi and Dubrovnik; expect delays in summer.

Kosovo The only crossing is Kulina, between Rožaje and Peć.

Serbia The busiest crossing is Dobrakovo (north of Bijelo Polje), followed by Dračenovac (northeast of Rožaje) and Ranče (east of Pljevlja).

BUS

There's a well-developed bus network linking Montenegro with the major cities of the region.

Belgrade (Serbia) To Podgorica (€27, frequent), Budva (€26, 15 daily), Ulcinj (€33, four daily), Kotor (€32, seven daily) and Herceg Novi (€33, seven daily).

Dubrovnik (Croatia) To Herceg Novi (€10, two daily), Kotor (€14, two daily), Petrovac (€18, daily) and Podgorica (€19, daily).

Priština (Kosovo) To Podgorica (€17, daily) and Ulcinj (€18, six daily).

Sarajevo (BiH) To Podgorica (€19, six daily), Budva (€22, four daily), Herceg Novi (€24, two daily) and Ulcinj (€26, daily).

Shkodra (Albania) To Ulcinj (€6, two daily).

Trebinje (BiH) To Nikšić (€6.50, three daily).

CAR & MOTORCYCLE

Drivers are recommended to carry an International Driving Permit (IDP) as well as their home country's driving licence. Vehicles need Green Card insurance or insurance must be bought at the border.

TRAIN

At least two trains head between Bar and Belgrade daily (€21, 11 hours), with one continuing on to Novi Sad and Subotica.

Sea

Montenegro Lines (☎030-303 469; www.montenegrolines.net) has boats to Bar from the Italian ports of Bari and Ancona.

Getting Around

Bicycle

Cyclists are a rare species, even in the cities. Don't expect drivers to be considerate. Wherever possible, try to get off the main roads.

Bus

The local bus network is extensive and reliable. Buses are usually comfortable and air-conditioned, and are rarely full. It's slightly cheaper to buy your ticket on the bus rather than at the station, but a station-bought ticket theoretically guarantees you a seat. Luggage carried below the bus is charged at €1 per piece.

Car & Motorcycle

Independent travel by car or motorcycle is an ideal way to gad about and discover the country; some of the drives are breathtakingly beautiful. Traffic police are everywhere, so stick to speed limits and carry an IDP. Allow more time than you'd expect for the distances involved, as the terrain will slow you down.

The major international car-hire companies have a presence in various centres. Meridian Rentacar (☎020-234 944; www.meridian-rentacar.com), which has offices in Budva, Bar, Podgorica and the airports, is a reliable local option; one-day hire starts from €30.

Train

Montenegro Railways (Željeznica Crne Gore; www.zpcg.me) runs the passenger train service, heading north from Bar. The trains are old and can be hot in summer but they're priced accordingly and the route through the mountains is spectacular. Useful stops include Virpazar, Podgorica and Kolašin.

Romania

Includes »

Why Go?

Beautiful and beguiling, Romania's rural landscape remains relatively untouched by the country's urban evolution. It's a land of aesthetically stirring hand-ploughed fields, sheep-instigated traffic jams, and lots and lots of homemade plum brandy. The Carpathian Mountains offer uncrowded hiking and skiing, while Transylvania's Saxon towns are time-warp strolling grounds for Gothic architecture, Austro-Hungarian legacies and, naturally, plenty of Vlad Ţepeş–inspired 'Dracula' shtick. Fish – and the birds that chomp them – thrive in the Danube Delta, bucolic Maramureş has the 'Merry Cemetery', and Unesco-listed painted monasteries dot southern Bucovina. And, for the record, the big cities are a blast too.

Best Places to Eat

- » Caru' cu Bere (p405)
- » Graf (p427)
- » Crama Sibiu Vechi (p419)
- » Chevalet (p446)
- » Bistro de l'Arte (p413)

Best Places to Stay

- » Doors (p404)
- » Hotel Elite (p427)
- » Hostel Costel (p425)
- » Felinarul Hostel (p418)
- » Casa Wagner (p413)

When to Go
Bucharest

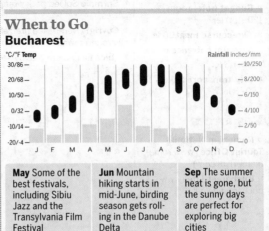

May Some of the best festivals, including Sibiu Jazz and the Transylvania Film Festival

Jun Mountain hiking starts in mid-June, birding season gets rolling in the Danube Delta

Sep The summer heat is gone, but the sunny days are perfect for exploring big cities

ROMANIA

Fast Facts

» **Area** 237,500 sq km

» **Capital** Bucharest

» **Country code** ☑40

» **Emergency** ☑112

Exchange Rates

Australia	A$1	3.59 lei
Canada	C$1	3.39 lei
Euro Zone	€1	4.41 lei
Japan	¥100	3.66 lei
New Zealand	NZ$1	2.88 lei
UK	UK£1	5.23 lei
USA	US$1	3.44 lei

Set Your Budget

» **Budget hotel room** 120–150 lei

» **Two-course meal** 30 lei

» **Museum entrance** 6 lei

» **Beer** 5 lei

» **City transport ticket** 1.50–3 lei

Resources

» **Romanian National Tourist Office** (www.romaniatourism.com)

» **Bucharest Life** (www.bucharestlife.net)

Connections

The main train corridor to Romania from Western Europe passes through Budapest, and at least one train daily makes the overnight slog from here down to Bucharest, via Braşov, and back. The western city of Timişoara has excellent train, bus and air connections throughout Europe. By road, the main entry points from the west are at Arad and Oradea. There are international border crossings to/from Hungary, Serbia, Bulgaria, Ukraine and Moldova, and four ferry crossings into Bulgaria.

ITINERARIES

One Week

Spend a day viewing the parts of Bucharest that survived the Nicolae Ceauşescu dictatorship, then take a train to Braşov – Transylvania's main event – for castles, activities and beer at streetside cafes. Spend a day in Sighişoara's medieval citadel, then catch a train back to Bucharest or on to Budapest.

Two Weeks

Arrive in Bucharest by plane or Timişoara by train, then head into Transylvania, devoting a day or two each to Braşov, Sighişoara and Sibiu. Tour southern Bucovina's painted monasteries, then continue on to Bucharest.

Essential Food & Drink

» **Mămăligă** Cornmeal mush that's boiled or fried, sometimes topped with sour cream or cheese.

» **Ciorbă** Sour soup that's a mainstay of the Romanian diet and a powerful hangover remedy.

» **Sarmale** Spiced pork wrapped in cabbage or grape leaves.

» **Covrigi** Oven-baked pretzels served warm from windows all around town.

» **Ţuică** Fiery plum brandy sold in water bottles at roadside rest stops.

BUCHAREST

♪021 / POP 2.1 MILLION

Romania's capital gets a bad rap, but in fact it's dynamic, energetic and more than a little bit funky. It's where still-unreconstructed communism meets unbridled capitalism; where the soporific forces of the EU meet the passions of the Balkans and Middle East. Many travellers give the city just a night or two before heading off to Transylvania, but we think that's not enough. Budget at least a few days to take in the good museums, stroll the parks and hang out at trendy cafes.

⊙ Sights

Bucharest teems with museums and attractions; all are fairly cheap and many are among the nation's best. The historic thoroughfare Calea Victoriei makes a nice walk, as it connects the two main squares of the city: Piaţa Victoriei in the north, and Piaţa Revoluţiei (Revolution Sq) in the centre. Continue south

ROMANIA BUCHAREST

Romania Highlights

❶ Ascend castles and mountains (and castles on top of mountains), using **Braşov** (p412) as a base.

❷ Follow the Unesco World Heritage line of painted monasteries in **southern Bucovina** (p436).

❸ Soak in **Sibiu** (p418), a beautifully restored Saxon town.

❹ Explore the medieval citadel of **Sighişoara** (p416), Dracula's birthplace.

❺ Rewind a few centuries in **Maramureş** (p427), Europe's last thriving peasant society.

❻ Row through the tributaries and the riot of nature in the **Danube Delta** (p439).

398

Bucharest

ROMANIA BUCHAREST

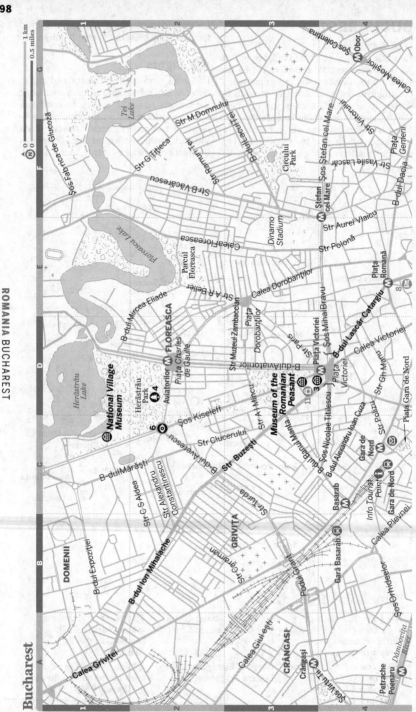

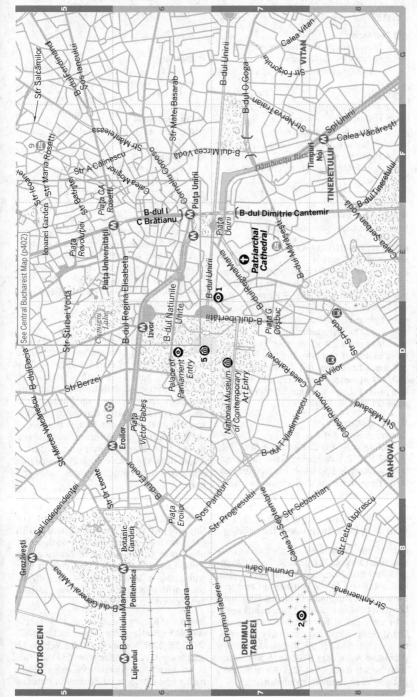

ROMANIA BUCHAREST

See Central Bucharest Map (p402)

COTROCENI

VITAN

TINERETULUI

RAHOVA

DRUMUL TABEREI

Patriarchal Cathedral

Palace of Parliament Entry

National Museum of Contemporary Art Entry

Botanic Garden

Cişmigiu Lake

Ioanei Garden

B-dul I C Brătianu

B-dul Dimitrie Cantemir

Piaţa Unirii

Piaţa Revoluţiei

Piaţa Universităţii

Piaţa CA Rosetti

Piaţa Victor Babeş

Piaţa Eroilor

Dâmboviţa River

Str Salcâmilor

B-dul Ferdinand

Şos Iancului

Str Iconei

Str Maria Rosetti

Str Mântuleasa

Str A Călinescu

Calea Moşilor

Str Batiştei

Corneliu Coposo

Str Matei Basarab

B-dul Mircea Vodă

Calea Vitan

Str Foişorului

B-dul Unirii

B-dul O Goga

Str Nerva Traian

Spl Unirii

Calea Văcăreşti

Timpuri Noi

B-dul Tineretului

Calea Şerban Vodă

Str Mitropoliei

Piaţa G Coşbuc

B-dul Unirii

B-dul Regina Elisabeta

B-dul Naţiunile Unite

B-dul Libertăţii

Izvor

Calea Rahovei

Calea Rahovei

Şos Vilor

Str Măgură

Str Preda

Str Petre Ispirescu

Str Antiaeriană

Str Sebastian

Calea 13 Septembrie

Drumul Sării

Şos Progresului

Şos Panduri

B-dul T Vladimirescu

Str Dr Leonte

B-dul Eroilor

Str Berzei

Str Ştirbei Vodă

B-dul Dacia

B-dul Mircea Vulcănescu

Spl Independenţei

B-dul General V Milea

B-dul Iuliului Maniu

B-dul Timişoara

Drumul Taberei

Eroilor

Politehnica

Grozăveşti

Lujerului

Str Şerban Vodă

Bucharest

and turn east to find the Old Town area, home to countless cafes, bars and clubs.

SOUTHERN BUCHAREST

Palace of Parliament HISTORIC BUILDING
(Palatul Parlamentului; Map p402; ✆tour bookings 021-414 1426; www.cdep.ro; B-dul Naţiunile Unite; tour adult/child from 25/13 lei; ◎10am-4pm; Mˈlzvor) Facing B-dul Unirii is the impossible-to-miss Palace of Parliament, the world's second-largest building (after the Pentagon near Washington DC) and dictator Ceauşescu's most infamous creation. Built in 1984, the building's 12 storeys and 3100 rooms cover 330,000 sq metres – an estimated €3.3 billion project. Entry is by guided tour. Bring a passport because they check ID.

**National Museum of
Contemporary Art** GALLERY
(Muzeul Naţionale Arta Contemporana; Map p398; ✆021-318 9137; www.mnac.ro; Calea 13 Septembrie 1; adult/student 5 lei/free; ◎10am-6pm Wed-Sun) The Palace of Parliament houses a superb art gallery that displays temporary exhibitions of eclectic installations and video art. There's also a top-floor cafe. Entry is from the southwestern side of the building.

Patriarchal Cathedral CHURCH
(Catedrala Patriahală; Map p398; Str Dealul Mitropoliei; ◎7am-8pm) From the centre of Piaţa Unirii, look southwest to the Patriarchal Cathedral, the centre of Romanian Orthodox faith, built between 1656 and 1658. It triumphantly peeks over once-grand housing blocks on B-dul Unirii designed to 'hide' the city's churches. One such fatality is the **Antim Monastery** (Mânăstirea Antim; Map p398; Str Antim; ◎7am-8pm), which dates from 1715. It's northwest, just one block before the boulevard ends.

FREE **Ghencea Civil Cemetery** CEMETERY
(Cimitirul Civil Ghencea; Map p398; Calea 13 Septembrie; ◎8am-8pm) A 45-minute walk west of the Palace of Parliament leads to this cemetery, where you can morbidly seek out the final resting spots of Nicolae Ceauşescu (row I-35) and his wife Elena (H-25), both executed on Christmas Day 1989.

OLD TOWN

The Old Town is home to Bucharest's **Old Princely Court** (Palatul Voievodal, Curtea Veche; Map p402; Str Franceză 21-23; ◎10am-5pm) dating back to the 15th century, when the city competed with former royal capitals like Curtea de Argeş and Târgovişte to lead the Wallachian principality. Bucharest eventually won out, though the core of the old court, on Str Franceza, was allowed to fall into disrepair over the centuries. These days, the area is rapidly gentrifying and is home to countless clubs, cafes and bars.

Stavropoleos Church CHURCH
(Map p402; Str Stavropoleos; ◎7am-8pm) The tiny and lovely Stavropoleos Church, which dates from 1724, perches a bit oddly just a block over from some of the craziest Old Town carousing, but it's one church that will make a lasting impression with its courtyard filled with tombstones and an ornate wooden interior.

National History Museum MUSEUM
(Muzeul National de Istorie a Romaniei; Map p402; ✆021-315 8207; www.mnir.ro; Calea Victoriei 12; adult/student 8/2 lei; ◎10am-6pm Wed-Sun) This is an excellent collection of maps, documents and artefacts on Romanian national

history. It's particularly strong on the country's Roman ties, including a replica of the 2nd-century Trajan's Column. Our favourite *piece*, though, is not inside the museum, but rather on the steps outside: a controversial **Statue of Emperor Trajan** (Map p402; Calea Victoriei 12) holding a Dacian wolf.

FREE **Jewish History Museum** MUSEUM
(Muzeul de Istorie al Comunitaţilor Evreieşti din România; Map p402; ☑021-311 0870; Str Mămulari 3; ☺9am-2pm Mon-Thu, to 1pm Fri & Sun) The Jewish History Museum is housed in a colourful synagogue that dates from 1836 (rebuilt in 1910). Exhibits (in English and Romanian) outline Jewish contributions to Romanian history, which not all Romanians know about. You need your passport to enter.

PIAŢA REVOLUŢIEI

National Art Museum MUSEUM
(Muzeul Naţional de Artă; Map p402; ☑021-313 3030; www.mnar.arts.ro; Calea Victoriei 49-53; admission 15 lei; ☺11am-7pm Wed-Sun) Housed in the 19th-century Royal Palace, this massive museum – signed in English – has three collections, including ancient and medieval Romanian art, modern Romanian painting, and European art. The ancient collection is strong on icons and religious art, while the Romanian painting section has an excellent survey of 19th-century masters.

Central Committee of the Communist Party Building HISTORIC BUILDING
(Map p402; www.mai.gov.ro; Piaţa Revoluţiei 1; ☺closed to the public) The scene of Ceauşescu's infamous last speech was on the balcony of the former Central Committee of the Communist Party building on 22 December 1989. Amid cries of 'Down with Ceauşescu!' he escaped (briefly) by helicopter from the roof. Meanwhile, the crowds were riddled with bullets, and many died.

Rebirth Memorial MONUMENT
(Memorialul Renaşterii; Map p402; Calea Victoriei) This striking memorial of a white obelisk piercing a basketlike crown stands on an island in Calea Victoriei. It's meant to mark the dramatic events of 1989, when many people died for their opposition to the Ceauşescu regime. Local wags have dubbed it the 'potato of the revolution' (because of its shape).

FREE **Cişmigiu Garden** PARK
(Map p402) West of Calea Victoriei is the locally loved Cişmigiu Garden, with shady walks, a lake, cafes and a ridiculous number of benches on which to sit and stare at Bucharestians going by.

NORTHERN BUCHAREST

Bucharest's most luxurious villas and parks line the grand avenue Şos Kiseleff, which begins at Piaţa Victoriei. The major landmark here is the **Triumphal Arch** (Arcul de Triumf; Map p398; Piaţa Arcul de Triumf; ☺occasionally open to the public), which stands halfway up Şos Kiseleff. The 27m arch was built in 1935 to commemorate the reunification of Romania in 1918. Heavy traffic makes it difficult to get close to the arch and the viewing platform is not always open to the public.

TOP CHOICE **Grigore Antipa Natural History Museum** MUSEUM
(Muzeul de Istorie Naturală Grigore Antipa; Map p398; ☑021-312 8826; www.antipa.ro; Şos Kiseleff 1; adult/student/child 20/10/5 lei ; ▣) One of the few attractions in Bucharest squarely aimed at kids, this natural history museum has been thoroughly renovated and features modern bells and whistles like video displays, games and interactive exhibits. Much of it is signed in English.

FREE THRILLS

Here are a few signature Bucharest activities that won't break the bank:

» Wander the Old Town (p400), admiring the jumble of recently renovated and still-crumbling buildings side by side.

» Take a break in the atmospheric courtyard at Stavropoleos Church (p400), central Bucharest's most serene spot.

» Escape the car-horn refrain of the centre in the exquisite grounds of Herăstrău Park (p404).

» Pay your disrespects to the final resting places of Nicolae and Elena Ceauşescu at Ghencea Civil Cemetery (p400).

» Enjoy a heat retreat in the heroically tended Cişmigiu Garden (p401).

ROMANIA BUCHAREST

Central Bucharest

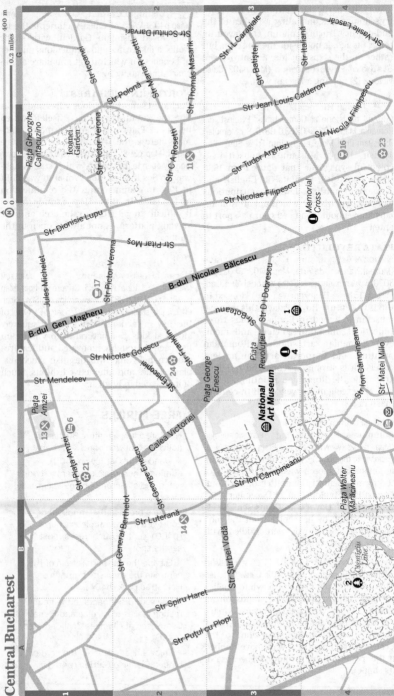

0 0 400 m
0 0.2 miles

Str Icoanei
Piața Gheorghe Cantacuzino
Icoanei Garden
Str Polonă
Str Maria Rosetti
Str Pictor Verona
Str Schitul Darvari
Str Thomas Masaryk
Str I L Caragiale
Str Batiștei
Str Italiană
Str Vasile Lascăr
Str Jean Louis Calderon
Str Nicolae Filipescu
Str C A Rosetti
11 ✗
Str Tudor Arghezi
16 ☕
23 ✿
Str Nicolae Filipescu
Str Dionisie Lupu
Str Pitar Moș
Memorial Cross 1 ⓘ
Jules Michelet
Str Pictor Verona
17 ⓘ
B-dul Nicolae Bălcescu
B-dul Gen Magheru
Str D I Dobrescu
Str Botеanu
1 ⓘ
Str Nicolae Golescu
Str Franklin
Piața Revoluţiei
1 ⓘ 4
Str Ion Câmpineanu
Str Matei Millo
24 ✿
Str Episcopiei
Piața George Enescu
Str Mendeleev
Piața Amzei
13 ✗
6 ⓘ
Calea Victoriei
National Art Museum 🏛
7 ⓘ
Str Piața Amzei
21 ✿
Str George Enescu
Str Ion Câmpineanu
Piața Walter Mărăcineanu
Str General Berthelot
Str Luterană
14 ✗
Str Știrbei Vodă
Str Spiru Haret
Cișmigiu Lake
2 ⓘ
Str Puțul cu Plopi

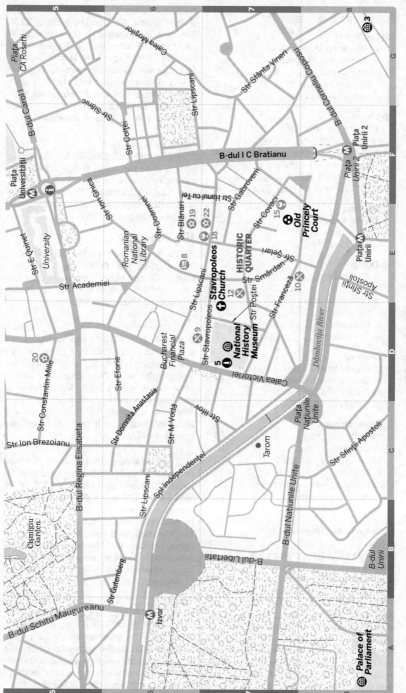

ROMANIA BUCHAREST

Central Bucharest

Museum of the Romanian Peasant
MUSEUM
(Muzeul Ţăranului Român; Map p398; ☑021-317 9661; www.muzeultaranuluiroman.ro; Şos Kiseleff 3; adult/child 8/2 lei; ⊙10am-6pm Tue-Sun) This collection of traditional peasant bric-a-brac, costumes, icons, artwork and partially restored houses and churches is one of the best museums in Bucharest. An 18th-century Transylvanian church is in the back lot, as is a gift shop. Don't miss the jarring communism exhibition downstairs, which focuses on the Ceauşescu-era program of land collectivisation.

National Village Museum
MUSEUM
(Muzeul Naţional al Satului; Map p398; ☑021-317 9103; www.muzeul-satului.ro; Şos Kiseleff 28-30; adult/child 10/5 lei; ⊙9am-7pm Tue-Sun, to 5pm Mon; 🖈) On the shores of Herăstrău Lake, this museum is a terrific open-air collection of several dozen homesteads, churches, mills and windmills, relocated from rural Romania. Built in 1936 by royal decree, it is one of Europe's oldest open-air museums.

FREE Herăstrău Park
PARK
(Parcul Herăstrău; Map p398; ⊙24hr) Facing the square from the north is this 200-hectare park which stretches along the wide namesake lake. It's (arguably) Bucharest's nicest park, with plenty of shaded strolls and open-air cafes, plus boats to hire.

⊟ Sleeping

Hotels in Bucharest are typically aimed at businessmen, and prices are higher here than in the rest of the country. Tips for getting discounts include booking in advance or using the hotel's website.

TOP CHOICE Doors
HOSTEL €
(Map p398; ☑021-336 2127; www.doorshostel.com; Str Olimpului 13; dm 45-60 lei, d 150 lei; ⊛@🛜) Our favourite hostel du jour is 15 minutes' walk southwest of Piaţa Unirii and all the better for it, with a quiet, residential location and a beautiful garden set up like a Moroccan tearoom. Dorms are in six- and eight-bed rooms, with one quad and one private double.

TOP CHOICE Rembrandt Hotel
HOTEL €€
(Map p402; ☑021-313 9315; www.rembrandt.ro; Str Smârdan 11; 'tourist class' s/d Mon-Fri 330/371 lei, Sat & Sun 294/334 lei; ⊛🟌@🛜) It's hard to say enough good things about this place. Stylish beyond its three-star rating, this 16-room, Dutch-owned hotel faces the landmark National Bank in the historic centre. Rooms feature polished wood floors, wall-sized timber headboards and DVD players. Book well in advance.

Vila Arte
BOUTIQUE HOTEL €€
(Map p398; ☑021-210 1035; www.vilaarte.ro; Str Vasile Lascăr 78; s/d 260/320 lei; ⊛🟌@🛜) A renovated villa transformed into a superb boutique hotel stuffed with original art that really pushes the envelope on design and colour. The services are top drawer and the helpful reception makes every guest feel special.

ROMANIA BUCHAREST

Hotel Amzei
HOTEL €€€

(Map p402; 021-313 9400; www.hotelamzei.ro; Piaţa Amzei 8; s/d 450/550 lei; ❄✳🖥) This tastefully reconstructed villa just off of Calea Victoriei has 22 rooms on four floors. The wrought-iron atrium in the lobby lends a refined feel. The rooms are in a more restrained contemporary style.

Midland Youth Hostel
HOSTEL €

(Map p398; 021-314 5323; www.themidlandhostel.com; Str Biserica Amzei 22; dm 35-60 lei; ❄✳@🖥) This is a bright, cheerful, well-run hostel, with an excellent central location not far from Piaţa Romană. Accommodation is in six-, 10- or 14-bed dorms.

Hotel Carpaţi
HOTEL €€

(Map p402; 021-315 0140; www.hotelcarpatibucuresti.ro; Str Matei Millo 16; s/d 160/220 lei; 🖥) This popular backpacker option in an old landmark hotel exudes a kind of communist-era charm; nevertheless, some of the 40 rooms have been renovated and offer good value. If you're on a strict budget, go for the cheaper rooms that don't have attached bath rooms.

✗ Eating

Self-caterers will want to head to the daily market (Map p402) on Piaţa Amzei, with a good selection of fresh fruit and veg.

TOP CHOICE Caru' cu Bere
ROMANIAN €€

(Map p402; 021-313 7560; www.carucubere.ro; Str Stavropoleos 3-5; mains 15-40 lei; ❄8am-midnight) Despite a decidedly touristy atmosphere, Bucharest's oldest beer house continues to draw a strong local crowd. The colourful belle époque interior and stained-glass windows dazzle, as does the classic Romanian food. Dinner reservations recommended.

Divan
MIDDLE EASTERN €€

(Map p402; 021-312 3034; www.thedivan.ro; Str Franceză 46-48; mains 20-30 lei; ❄10am-1am; 🖥) Deservedly popular Turkish and Middle Eastern place, where snagging a prized terrace table will take a mix of patience and good fortune.

Malagamba
ITALIAN €€

(Map p402; 021-313 3389; www.malagamba.ro; Str Sf Dumitru 2; mains 20-40 lei ; 🖥👶) Creative Italian cooking, with an inventive mix of pasta dishes and delicious salads. On weekends there are babysitters on hand and special kiddie shows so that parents can take a break.

Sale e Pepe
ITALIAN €€

(Map p402; 021-315 8989; www.saleepepe.ro; Str Luterană 3; pizzas 15-30 lei; ❄10am-midnight Mon-Fri, 3pm-midnight Sat & Sun) This tiny pizza/pasta place specialises in crunchy thin-crust pizzas – and for once in Romania, they don't undercook them. Pizza 'Pepperoni' comes topped with sliced red pepper and spicy sausage, and served with hot sauce on the side on request.

Lente & Cafea
INTERNATIONAL €€

(Map p402; 021-310 7424; www.lente.ro; Str Gen Praporgescu 31; mains 20-35 lei; ❄11.30am-1am; 🖥) Eclecticism is the theme at this trendy, in-the-know restaurant. The menu is an assortment of tempting fish and chicken concoctions (many with curry, wild rice, mushrooms etc) interspersed with pages of musical lyrics and musical '10 Best' lists, such as the best songs for a long road trip.

🍷 Drinking

Drinking options can be roughly broken down into cafes and bars, though there's little distinction in practice. Most of the popular places these days are in the Old Town.

TOP CHOICE Atelier Mecanic
CAFE

(Map p402; 0726-767 611; Str Covaci 12; ❄11am-4am; 🖥) The laid-back mood and the arty, mix-and-match junk-shop decor are a breath of fresh air compared with other Old Town cafes and pubs that are lined with corporate tat and tie-ins. They serve great coffee here, as well as wines and an impressive range of single-malt scotches.

Cafeneaua Actorilor
PUB

(Map p402; 0721-900 842; www.cafeneauaactorilor.ro; B-dul Nicolae Bălcescu 2; ❄9am-3am; 🖥) Located on the ground floor of the National Theatre (just behind the Inter-Continental Hotel). An oasis of good drink and good pizza in the middle of the centre. Drink (and breathe) on the open-air terrace in summer; in winter, the action shifts to the labyrinthine (and claustrophobic) rooms inside.

TOP CHOICE Grădina Verona
CAFE

(Map p402; 0732-003 061; Str Pictor Verona 13-15; ❄9am-1am; 🖥) A garden oasis hidden behind the Cărtureşti bookshop, serving standard-issue but excellent espresso drinks and some of the wackiest ice-tea infusions ever concocted in Romania, such as peony flower, mango and lime (it's not bad).

Old City
BAR

(Map p402; ☏0729-377 774; www.oldcity-lipscani.ro; Str Lipscani 45; ⊙10am-5am; 🛜) This remains one of our favourite go-to bars in the Old City, and most nights, especially weekends, bring big crowds and theme parties. There's a large, handsome bar area and a big garden out back.

⭐ Entertainment

Bucharest has a lively night scene of concerts, theatre, and rock and jazz. Check the weekly guide Şapte Seri (www.sapteseri.ro) for entertainment listings. To buy tickets online, visit the websites of the leading ticketing agencies: www.myticket.ro and www.eventim.ro.

Performing Arts

Bucharest National Opera House
OPERA

(Opera Naţională Bucureşti; Map p398; ☏021-314 6980, box office 021-313 1857; www.operanb.ro; B-dul Mihail Kogălniceanu 70-72; tickets 6-65 lei; ⊙box office 9am-1pm & 3-7pm) The city's premier venue for classical opera and ballet. Buy tickets online or at the venue box office.

National Theatre of Bucharest
THEATRE

(Teatrul Naţional Bucureşti; Map p402; ☏box office 021-314 7171, theatre 021-313 9175; www.tnb.ro; B-dul Nicolae Bălcescu 2; ⊙box office 10am-4pm Mon, to 7pm Tue-Sun) The National Theatre is the country's most prestigious dramatic stage. The building is a 1970s-era big box, but the facilities inside are excellent. Most dramatic works are performed in Romanian. Check the website for the program during your visit. Buy tickets at the box office.

Romanian Athenaeum
CLASSICAL MUSIC

(Ateneul Roman; Map p402; ☏box office 021-315 6875; www.fge.org.ro; Str Franklin 1-3; tickets 15-65 lei; ⊙box office noon-7pm Tue-Fri, 4-7pm Sat, 10-11am Sun) The Athenaeum is home to the respected George Enescu Philharmonic and offers a wide array of classical music concerts from September to May, as well as a number of one-off musical shows and spectacles throughout the year. Buy tickets at the venue box office.

Nightclubs & Live Music

Club A
CLUB

(Map p402; ☏021-316 1667; www.cluba.ro; Str Blănari 14; ⊙9pm-5am Thu-Sun) Run by students, this club is a classic and beloved by all who go there. Indie pop/rock tunes play until very late Friday and Saturday nights.

Control
CLUB

(Map p402; ☏0733-927 861; www.control-club.ro; Str Constantin Mille 4; ⊙ 6pm-4am; 🛜) This favourite among club-goers who like alternative, indie and garage sounds decamped to this new space not far from Calea Victoriei in 2012. Hosts both live acts and DJs, depending on the night.

Green Hours 22 Jazz Club
JAZZ

(Map p402; ☏0788-452 485; www.greenhours.ro; Calea Victoriei 120; ⊙24hr) This old-school basement jazz club runs a lively program of jazz nights through the week and hosts an international jazz fest in June. Check the website for the schedule during your trip. Book a seat in advance.

La Muse
CLUB

(Map p402; ☏0734-000 236; www.lamuse.ro; Str Lipscani 53; ⊙9am-3am Sun-Wed, to 6am Thu-Sat) Just about anything goes at this popular Old Town dance club. Try to arrive early, around 11pm, since it can get crowded later.

🛍 Shopping

For beautifully made woven rugs, table runners, national Romanian costumes, ceramics and other local crafts, don't miss the folk-art shop at the Museum of the Romanian Peasant. (Map p398; www.muzeultaranuluiroman.ro; Şos Kiseleff 3; ⊙10am-6pm Tue-Sun)

ℹ Information

Dangers & Annoyances

The biggest day-to-day nuisance are packs of feral dogs who wander the streets. While the number of dogs has fallen in the past few years, you'll still see them limping down the street or more likely passed out under a shady tree or car. The best advice is to ignore them and they will ignore you. Bites are rare but be sure to go to a hospital for antirabies injections within 36 hours if you get bitten.

Dishonest taxi drivers constitute another annoyance. The worst offenders are those who park outside the Gara de Nord, in front of the Hotel Inter-Continental or at the airport. By law, drivers are required to post their rates on taxi doors, so look for vehicles that charge from 1.39 to 1.79 lei per kilometre. Anything higher is a rip-off.

Internet Access

Best Cafe (B-dul Mihail Kogălniceanu 19; per hr 5 lei; ⊙24hr; 🛜)

Medical Services

Emergency Clinic Hospital (☏021-9622, 021-599 2300; www.urgentafloreasca.ro; Calea Floreasca 8; ⊙24hr)

Sensi-Blu (www.sensiblu.com; B-dul Nicolae Bălcescu 7; ☺8am-10pm Mon-Fri, 9am-9pm Sat & Sun) A highly recommended pharmacy chain with branches around town.

Money

You'll find hundreds of bank branches and ATMs in the centre. Most banks have a currency-exchange office and can provide cash advances against credit or debit cards. Always bring your passport, since you will have to show it to change money.

Outside of normal banking hours, you can change money at private *casa de schimb* (currency booths). There is a row of these along B-dul Gen Gheorghe Magheru, running north of Piața Universității. You'll have to show a passport here too.

Post

Central Post Office (Map p402; ☏021-315 9030; www.posta-romana.ro; Str Matei Millo 10; ☺7.30am-8pm Mon-Fri)

Tourist Information

Bucharest Tourist Information Center (Map p402; ☏021-305 5500, ext 1003; http://en.seebucharest.ro; Piața Universității; ☺10am-6pm Mon-Fri, to 2pm Sat & Sun) This small, poorly stocked tourist office is the best the city can offer for assisting visitors. Not much information on hand, but the English-speaking staff can field basic questions, make suggestions and help locate things on a map. It's in the underpass.

Info Tourist Point (Map p398; ☏0371-155 063; www.infotourist.ro; Gara de Nord; ☺10am-6pm Mon-Fri) This small booth, situated in the main terminal at the point where the rail tracks meet the station, can help with basic information and hotel booking.

Websites

Lonely Planet (www.lonelyplanet.com/romania/bucharest)

ⓘ Getting There & Away

Air

All international and domestic flights use **Henri Coandă International Airport** (OTP,Otopeni; ☏021-204 1000; www.otp-airport.ro; Şos Bucureşti-Ploieşti). Henri Coandă is 17km north of Bucharest on the road to Braşov. Arrivals and departures use separate terminals. The airport is a modern facility, with restaurants, newsagents, currency exchange offices and ATMs. There are 24-hour information desks at both terminals.

The airport is the hub for the national carrier **Tarom** (Map p402; ☏call centre 021-204 6464, office 021-316 0220; www.tarom.ro; Spl Independenței 17, City Centre; ☺8.30am-7.30pm Mon-Fri, 9am-1.30pm Sat). Tarom has a comprehensive network of internal flights to major Romanian cities as well to capitals and big cities around Europe and the Middle East.

Bus

It's possible to get just about anywhere in the country by bus from Bucharest, but figuring out where your bus or maxitaxi departs from can be tricky. Bucharest has several bus stations and they don't seem to follow any discernible logic. Even Bucharest residents have a hard time making sense of it.

The best bet is to consult the websites www.autogari.ro and www.cdy.ro. Both keep up-to-date timetables and are fairly easy to manage, though www.cdy.ro is only in Romanian. Be sure to follow up with a phone call just to make sure a particular bus is running on a particular day. Another option is to ask your hotel to help with arrangements or to book through a travel agency.

Car & Motorcycle

Driving in Bucharest is lunacy and you won't want to do it for more than a few minutes before you stow the car and use the metro. If you're travelling around the country by car and just want to visit Bucharest for the day, it's more sensible to park at a metro station on the outskirts and take the metro into the city.

In theory, hourly parking rates apply in the centre, particularly off Piața Victoriei and Piața Universității. Look for the wardens in yellow-and-blue uniforms or paid metered parking. In many places, though, you can just pull onto the sidewalk like everyone else. Petrol costs around 6 lei per litre.

Major rental agencies can be found at the Henri Coandă International Airport arrivals hall. Most large companies also have an in-town branch.

The cheapest rates available are from **Autonom** (☏airport branch 021-232 4325, call centre 0721-442 226; www.autonom.com; Henri Coandă International Airport), offering a Dacia Logan for around 140 lei per day (including unlimited mileage and insurance, minimum two days); rates drop if you rent for more than a week.

Train

Gara de Nord (☏021-319 9539, phone reservations 021-9522, phone reservations 021-9521; www.cfr.ro; Piața Gara de Nord 1) is the central station for most national and all international trains. The station is accessible by metro from the centre of the city.

Buy tickets at station ticket windows or in advance at **Agenția de Voiaj CFR** (☏021-313 2642; www.cfr.ro; Str Domnita Anastasia 10-14; ☺7.30am-7.30pm Mon-Fri, 8am-noon Sat).

DOMESTIC TRAINS FROM BUCHAREST

DESTINATION	COST (LEI)	DURATION (HR)	FREQUENCY
Braşov	70	2½	frequent
Cluj-Napoca	90	7½	4 daily
Constanţa	60	2-4	5 daily
Iaşi	80	6	3 daily
Sibiu	70	5	3 daily
Sighişoara	80	4½	3 daily
Suceava	80	8	3 daily
Timişoara	100	8	2 daily

A seat reservation is compulsory if you are travelling with an InterRail or Eurail pass. For international tickets, the private travel agency **Wasteels** (☑021-317 0370; www.wasteels.ro; Gara de Nord; ☺8am-7pm Mon-Fri, to 2pm Sat), located inside the train station, can help sort out complicated international connections.

Check the latest train schedules on either www.cfr.ro or the reliable German site www.bahn.de.

ℹ Getting Around

To/From the Airport

BUS Express bus 783 leaves every 15 minutes between 5.37am and 11.23pm (every half-hour at weekends) from Piaţas Unirii and Piaţas Victoriei and points in between. The Piaţa Unirii stop is on the south side. Buy a ticket, valid for one round trip or two people one way, for 7 lei at any RATB bus and ticket booth near a bus stop.

To get to the centre from the airport, catch bus 783 from the downstairs ramp outside the arrivals hall; you'll need to buy a ticket from the stand at the northern end of the waiting platform (to the right as you exit).

TAXI A reputable taxi from the centre to the airport should cost no more than 70 to 80 lei. Negotiate the fare in advance with the driver.

TRAIN There's a regular shuttle train service (8 lei, 35 minutes) from Gara de Nord to the airport. Trains leave hourly at 10 minutes past the hour, starting at 8.10am and continuing until 7.10pm.

Public Transport

Bucharest's public transport system of metros, buses, trams and trolleybuses is operated by the tranport authority **RATB** (Regia Autonomă de Transport Bucureşti ; ☑info 021-9391; www.ratb.ro). The system runs daily from about 5am to approximately 11.30pm.

For buses, trams and trolleybuses, buy tickets at any RATB street kiosk, marked 'casa de bilete', located at major stops and public squares. Tickets for standard buses cost 1.30 lei per trip and are sold in two-ticket increments for 2.60 lei. Tickets for a small number of express buses, such as bus 783 which goes to the airport, cost 7 lei (good for two journeys). Punch your ticket on board or risk a 50 lei on-the-spot fine.

Metro stations are identified by a large letter 'M'. To use the metro, buy a magnetic-strip ticket available at ticketing machines inside station entrances (have small bills handy). Tickets valid for two journeys cost 4 lei. A 10-trip ticket costs 15 lei. The metro is a speedy way of moving up and down the central north–south corridor from Piaţa Victoriei to Piaţa Unirii, passing through the convenient stations of Piaţa Romană and Universitate. The metro is also useful for travelling from Gara de Nord to the centre and back.

TRANSYLVANIA

Transylvania conjures a vivid landscape of mountains, castles, fortified churches and superstitious old crones. The Carpathian Mountains are truly spectacular and outdoor enthusiasts can choose from caving in the Apuseni range, rock climbing at Piatra Craiului National Park, biking atop the flat Bucegi plateau or hiking the Făgăraş. The skiing scene, particularly in the Bucegi Mountains, is a great draw, while well-beaten paths up to Bran and Peleş castles are also worth the crowds.

A melange of architecture and chic sidewalk cafes punctuate the towns of Braşov, Sighişoara and Sibiu, while the vibrant student town Cluj-Napoca has the country's most vigorous nightlife. Many of southern Transylvania's Saxon villages are dotted with fortified churches that date back half a millennium. An hour north, in Székely Land, ethnic Hungarian communities are the majority. Throughout, you're likely to spot many Roma villagers – look out for black cowboy hats and rich red dresses.

Sinaia

POP 14,600

Nestled in a slender fir-clad valley, this pretty town teems with hikers in summer and skiers in winter. Backed by the imposing crags of the Bucegi Mountains, it's a dramatic place for a day's hike or, using the network of cabanas (mountain huts) open to walkers, several days.

The town itself is a melange of crayon-coloured wooden houses contrasted with the 'wedding-cake' style of its grander 19th-century buildings. Once home to Romanian King Carol I, who created a summer retreat here, Peleş Castle is a dream of hidden passages, fairy-tale turrets, vertiginous galleries and classical statues; it's so beguilingly imaginative, it could raise a swoon from the most hardened cynic.

◉ Sights

Peleş Castle   CASTLE

(www.visit.peles.ro; tours adult/child from 20/5 lei, photots 3 lei; ⊗9am-5pm Tue-Sun;) The first European castle to have central heating, electricity and vacuuming(!), Peleş was intended as the summer residence of Romania's longest-serving monarch, King Carol I. Construction on the 3500-sq-metre edifice, built in neo-Renaissance style, began in 1875. Some 39 years later it was completed, just months before the king died in 1914.

The basic 40-minute tour takes in about 10 rooms, while two additional tours are available. In the first Armoury Hall (there's two), look for one of the 11 medieval knight suits with the long pointed boots. Rembrandt reproductions line the walls of the king's office, while real Gustav Klimt works are in the last stop, a theatre behind the entry.

Pelişor Palace   PALACE

(www.visit.peles.ro; compulsory tours adult/child 10/2.50 lei; ⊗noon-7pm Thu-Sun;) Heavily art nouveau in decor, and about 100m uphill from Peleş Castle, Pelişor Palace has a hard time competing with its neighbour. King Carol I planned this house for his nephew (and future king) Ferdinand (1865–1927) and wife Marie. Most of the furniture was imported from Vienna.

🏃 Activities

Skiing, hiking and biking are the main draws in the Bucegi Mountains, with a good range of basic, intermediate and advanced ski runs, and similarly challenging walking routes. A good source of ski equipment and information in town, **Snow** (Str Cuza Vodă 2a; ⊗9am-6pm), near the cable-car station, hires out skis (40 lei per day) and offers ski instruction services.

Bike, Ski and Rental Outlet (☎0745-015 241; Str O Goga 1; skis per day 40 lei; ⊗8am-7pm) next to the park, rents out skis, boards (40 lei per day) and bikes (20 lei per hour).

🛏 Sleeping

Travel agencies around town can find you a room in one of the countless pensions, which start at 100 lei.

BEARS!

Thanks to its megalomaniacal dictator (under Ceauşescu no one but he was allowed to hunt), 60% of Europe's brown bears are today found in Romania (an estimated 6000).

The chances of you seeing one of these sizeable Yogis are high if you're trekking or going to a bear hide (where you're more or less guaranteed a sighting). A cousin of the grizzly, Romanian bears are smaller but have the same powerful hump of muscle on their back, and they can also move at 50km/h.

Hikers have been mauled and even killed by bears in recent years, usually because they've been surprised, so here's a few tips to be mindful of. Try to pitch your tent in an open spot so they can see you, keeping your food at least 4m off the ground in the branches of a tree. Also, any used sanitary material or trash should be kept in a Ziploc bag. Should you find yourself in the presence of a mother and cub, stand still to signify you're not afraid, and make yourself bigger by waving your arms. Similarly, when walking through dense forest, talk loudly to announce your presence; the last thing a bear wants is to engage with you.

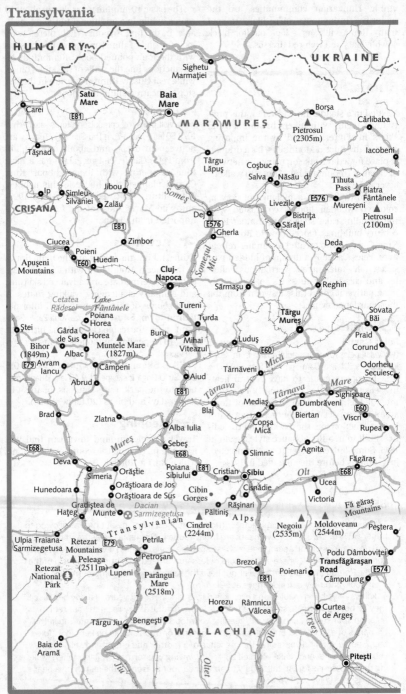

TOP CHOICE Hotel Caraiman
HOTEL €€

(☎0244-311 542; palace@rdslink.ro; B-dul Carol I nr 4; s/d/ste 145/200/240 lei; P🐕😷🏠) Built in 1880, this austere yet welcoming multi-gabled hotel has bags of atmosphere. Its stained-glass windows, chandeliers, sweeping stairways and wood-panelling hint at the affluent elite who used to patronise it. Fragrant rooms enjoy thick carpets, decent fittings, bathrooms and cable TV. Ask for one facing the park for the restful babble of the nearby fountain.

Hotel Economat
HOTEL €€

(☎0244-311 151; www.apps.ro; Aleea Peleşului 2; s/d/tr 90/150/180 lei; P) Like a slice of Hansel and Gretel, this gingerbread-roofed hotel is a delight. Rooms are cosy with clean bathrooms. Head to the excellent Vanatoresc, its sister restaurant across the courtyard and up the hill. Festooned in bear furs and stag antlers, this ex-hunter's lodge is a fun place to take your complimentary breakfast.

Casa Noastra
HOTEL €

(☎0244-314 556; www.casanoastra.sinaia.ro; B-dul Carol I; s/d/tr 70/100/120 lei; P🏠) Some 500m south of the roundabout in the centre of town, this four-floored traditional-style hotel has clean rooms with sparkling bathrooms and fine views of the mountains. Outside of August there are decent discounts.

✗ Eating

Irish House
INTERNATIONAL €€

(www.irishhouse.ro; B-dul Carol I nr 80; mains 15-25 lei; 🍴) Eat inside or out at this busy central watering hole, popular with families and après-skiers. Service is a little slow, but coffees are suitably frothy, and there's a menu spanning pizza, pasta and salads.

Bucegi Restaurant
ROMANIAN €€

(B-dul Carol I; mains 20 lei) Next to Irish House with an alpine ambience, this alfresco eatery dishes up specialities like venison, omelettes and pizza, as well as a range of salads.

ℹ Information

Central Post Office (Str Cuza Vodă; ⊗9am-7pm Mon-Fri, to noon Sat)

Salvamont (☎0244-313 131, 0-SALVAMONT; Primărie, B-dul Carol I) This 24-hour mountain-rescue service is located at the Cota 2000 chairlift station.

Sinaia Tourism Information Centre (☎0244-315 656; www.info-sinaia.ro; B-dul Carol I 47; ⊗8.30am-4.30pm Mon-Fri) This dinky office

DRACULA'S FINAL RESTING PLACE

Snagov Lake, 40km north of Bucharest, serves as the main weekend retreat for residents of the capital looking for a place to relax.

But the lake has an even bigger claim to fame: **Snagov Monastery** (Mănăstirea Snagov; ☎021-323 9905; www.snagov.ro; Snagov Island; adult/child 15/10 lei; ☺9am-6pm), on an island at the lake's northern end, just happens to be the reputed final resting place of none other than Vlad Ţepeş (aka 'Vlad the Impaler'), the legendarily brutal Wallachian prince who served as the inspiration for Bram Stoker's *Dracula*.

The monastery dates from the 15th century. Vlad Ţepeş' alleged grave is located inside towards the back.

As with many aspects of the 'Dracula' story, there's some debate as to whether the body buried here actually belongs to Ţepeş. The prince died in 1476 battling the Turks near Bucharest. His head was famously lopped off and carried back to İstanbul. What happened to the rest of the body was never clear.

The lake has a lovely rural setting, and there are plenty of opportunities for swimming, boating, fishing and sunbathing.

Though it's not far from Bucharest, it's not easy to get to Snagov without your own wheels. The best bet is to catch a maxitaxi (6 lei) from stands at Piaţa Presei Libera in the north of Bucharest. It will drop you at the centre of Snagov village, from where you can negotiate with a private boatsman to take you to the island (about 50 lei per person).

You can eat and stay the night at **Dolce Vita** (☎0723-580 780; www.dolcevitasnagov.ro; Snagov Parc; r 200 lei), across the lake from Snagov village. Once you arrive, give them a call and they will send a boatsman across the lake to fetch you.

packs a powerful punch, with free local maps, basic skiing and hiking maps, brochures, ideas for local activities and info on upcoming classical concerts.

ℹ Getting There & Away

BUS Buses and maxitaxis run every 45 minutes between 6am and 10pm from the train station to Azuga (4 lei) and Buşteni (3 lei, 10 minutes); some go all the way to Bucharest (25 lei, 1½ hours) or Braşov (16 lei, one hour).

TRAIN Sinaia is on the Bucharest–Braşov rail line – 126km from the former and 45km from the latter – so jumping on a train to Bucharest (38 lei, 1½ hours) or Braşov (13 lei, one hour) is a cinch.

Braşov

POP 274,400

Legend has it that the Pied Piper re-emerged from Hamelin in Braşov, and indeed there's something whimsically enchanting about the city, with its fairy-tale turrets and cobbled streets. Dramatically overlooked by Mt Tâmpa, her trees sporting a russet-gold coat (and cocky Hollywood-style sign), this is a remarkably relaxed city. Wander its maze of streets, stopping for caffeine injections at bohemian cafes, between losing yourself in a beguiling

coalescence of Austro-Hungarian gingerbread roofs, baroque gods, medieval spires and Soviet flat-tops. The city's centrepiece square is Piaţa Sfatului, a people-watcher's mecca. There are myriad things to see here, great restaurants and oodles of accommodation.

◎ Sights

Piaţa Sfatului   SQUARE
This wide square, chocka with cafes, was once the heart of medieval Braşov. In the centre stands the 1420 **council house** (Casa Sfatu-lui), topped by a Trumpeter's Tower in which town councillors, known as centurions, would meet.

Black Church   CHURCH
(Biserica Neagră; adult/child 6/3 lei; ☺10am-5pm Tue-Sat, to noon Sun, closed Mon) Braşov's main landmark, the Black Church is the largest Gothic church between Vienna and İstanbul, and still used by German Lutherans today. Built between 1383 and 1480, it was named for its appearance after a fire in 1689. The original statues on the exterior of the apse are now displayed inside.

The church's 4000-pipe organ, built by Buchholz of Berlin in 1839, is believed to be the only Buchholz preserved in its original form.

Mt Tâmpa
MOUNTAIN

Towering above town from the east is Mt Tâmpa, where Braşov's original defensive fortress was built. Vlad Ţepeş attacked it in 1458, finally dismantling it two years later and – out of habit – impaling some 40 merchants atop the peak. These days it's an easy trip up by cable car (telecabina; one way/return 9/15 lei; ☺9.30am-5pm Tue-Sun).

St Nicholas' Cathedral
CHURCH

(St Nicolae din Scheii; ☺6am-9pm) The black-spired Orthodox Church of St Nicholas' Cathedral, on Piaţa Unirii, was first built in wood in 1392, replaced by a Gothic stone church in 1495, and later embellished in Byzantine style. Inside are murals of Romania's last king and queen, covered by plaster to protect them from communist leaders and uncovered in 2004.

☞ Tours

Roving Romania
TOUR

(☎0724-348 272; www.roving-romania.co.uk) Run by an Englishman based near Braşov, this is an out-of-home agency for personalised, usually small-scale tours – great for birding and 4WD trips. Email for sample itineraries.

Dan Marin
TOUR

(☎0744-319 708; www.transylvanian.ro) Run by a local Romanian and winner of the coveted Wanderlust World Guide Award in 2007 for Best Guide, this tour company specialises in wildlife, historical and cultural treks. Dan knows the forests well and is an expert tracker. For a group of four, a one-day hike costs €70.

⌦ Sleeping

TOP CHOICE Casa Wagner
HOTEL €€

(☎0268-411 253; www.casa-wagner.com; Piaţa Sfatului; s/d incl breakfast 269/315 lei; @☎) This former 15th-century German bank is now a boutique hotel with 24 well-appointed rooms. Right in the heart of the city, its exposed brick walls, tasteful furnishings, modern bathrooms, welcoming breakfast area and pleasant management make this an excellent choice.

Bella Muzica
HOTEL €€

(☎0268-477 956; www.bellamuzica.ro; Piaţa Sfatului 19; s/d 220/270 lei; ☎) Within its wine-coloured corridors are 34 dark-wood and exposed-brick rooms. Very comfy beds, fans, bathrooms, friendly staff and cable TV all help make it a firm choice for aesthetes –

and we haven't even mentioned its dead central location or fabulous restaurant.

Rolling Stone Hostel
HOSTEL €

(☎0740-518 681, 0268-513 965; www.rolling-stone.ro; Str Piatra Mare 2a; dm 38 lei, r from 115 lei; ☺@☎) Run by helpful sisters with unlimited reserves of energy, superfriendly Stone attracts a cosmopolitan mix of travellers. Dorms are a little crowded but the private double room without bathroom has elegant couches and an armoire. You'll be given a map and bags of info on arrival, plus there are personal lockers and organised tours. Breakfast is basic and laundry is 15 lei.

Casa Rozelor
BOUTIQUE HOTEL €€€

(☎0268-475 212; www.casarozelor.ro; Str Michael Weiss 20; s/d incl breakfast 315/380 lei; @☎) This hidden courtyard oasis has five beautiful apartments, some with split-level floors adjoined by spiral staircases. Each is defiantly individual but all fuse contemporary chic with traditional Saxon; think antique furniture and modern art on brick walls.

✕ Eating

TOP CHOICE Bistro de l'Arte
BISTRO €€

(www.bistrodelarte.ro; Str Piaţa Enescu 11; mains 12-28 lei; ☎⌖) Tucked down a cobbled street straight out of a folk tale, this chi-chi joint

ROMANIA BRAŞOV

WORTH A TRIP

BUCEGI MOUNTAINS

These sandstone and limestone mountains rising 2505m are hugely popular. While some trails are poorly marked, there is a decent selection of cabanas and shelters, should your trek extend overnight or you get caught in inclement weather. Winter is severe and summer thunderstorms are common.

An added bonus is the hiker-friendly plateau above the horseshoe-shaped range that stands between Bran and Sinaia. The best walking map is Dimap's fold-out *Five Mountains from the Carpathian's Bend* (34 lei; www.dimap. hu) covering the Piatra Craiului, Bucegi, Postăvarul, Piatra Mare and Ciucaş ranges, plus a Braşov city map. A visit to the Sinaia Tourism Information Centre (p411) is essential before setting off on ambitious hikes.

Braşov

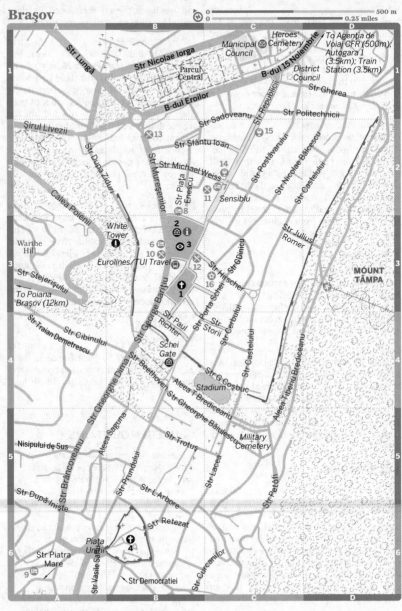

has decidedly boho genes, with sculpture and walls dotted with local artists' work. Gazpacho soup, shrimps and tomato gratin, snails...or just a croque monsieur. Perfect for nursing a cappucino and working on your laptop.

Bella Musica ROMANIAN, MEXICAN €€

(Str George Bariţiu 2; mains 20-30 lei; 🛜📱) In a vaulted grottolike cellar aflicker with candlelight, Musica offers intimate dining. Its menu spans Mexican fare like tasty fajitas, *ciorbă* (soup), pasta, foie gras, salads and

Braşov

schnitzel steak. Try the goulash beef stew with dumplings.

Sergiana ROMANIAN €€
(Str Mureşenilor 28; mains 30 lei; ⊙10am-11pm) Authentically Saxon, this subterranean carnivore's heaven has two sections: the white room for nonsmokers, and the exposed brick vaults for *fumeurs*. Choose from a menu of venison, stag, boar, pork ribs, sirloin steak, and Transylvanian sour soup with smoked gammon and tarragon (11.50 lei). A hunter's dream.

Keller Steak House STEAKHOUSE €€€
(www.kellersteakhouse.ro; Str Hirscher 2; mains 85 lei; 🖩🋠) One of Brasov's premier steakhouses, where you can eat inside its ochre interior or tackle your sirloin outside on the terrace. Steak and Roquefort cheese, salad and boar...one thing is for certain, you won't leave here with an empty stomach.

🍷 Drinking

Deane's Irish Pub & Grill PUB
(Str Republicii 19) As if transplanted from Donegal, this subterranean Irish pub, with its early-20th-century cloudy mirrored bar,

shadowy booths and old-world soundtracks, is a haven for Guinness-thirsty leprechauns. Live music some nights.

Festival 39 BAR
(Str Republicii 62; ⊙10am-1am) This romantic watering hole is an art deco dream of stained-glass ceilings, wrought-iron finery, candelabras and leather banquettes, and has a bar long enough to keep an army of barflies content.

☆ Entertainment

Gheorghe Dima State Philharmonic CLASSICAL MUSIC
(Str Hirscher 10) Performs mainly between September and May.

ⓘ Information

You'll find numerous ATMs, banks and currency exchange offices on and around Str Republicii and B-dul Eroilor.

County Hospital (📞0268-333 666; Calea Bucareşti 25-27; ⊙24hr)

Red Net Internet (Str George Bariţiu 8; per hr 2.50 lei; ⊙7.30am-10pm)

Sensiblu (📞0268-411 248; Str Republicii 15; ⊙9am-6pm Mon-Fri, 8am-3pm Sat)

Tourist Information Centre (📞0268-419 078; www.brasovcity.ro; Piaţa Sfatului 30) Easily spotted in the gold city council building in the centre of the square, the English-speaking staff offer free maps and brochures, and track down hotel vacancies and train and bus times. The centre shares space with the history museum.

ⓘ Getting There & Around

Bus

From 6am to 7.30pm, maxitaxis leave every half-hour for Bucharest (30 lei, 2½ hours), stopping in Buşteni and Sinaia. About four or five maxitaxis leave for Sibiu (35 lei, 2½ hours). Nine or 10 go daily to Sighişoara (30 lei). A handful of buses go to Constanţa (55 lei) and Iaşi (35 lei). The most accessible station is **Autogara 1** (Bus Station 1; 📞0268-427 267), next to the train station.

All European routes are handled by **Eurolines** (📞0268-475 219; www.eurolines.ro; Piaţa Sfatului 18; ⊙9am-8pm Mon-Fri, to 4pm Sat), which sells tickets for buses to Germany, Italy, Hungary and other European destinations.

Train

Advance tickets are sold at the **Agenţia de Voiaj CFR** (Str 15 de Noiembrie 43; ⊙8am-7.30pm Mon-Fri).

ROMANIA BRAŞOV

Daily domestic train services (prices are for 2nd-class seats on rapid trains) include at least hourly to Bucharest (42 lei, 3½ hours), a dozen to Sighişoara (36 lei, 2½ hours), two to Sibiu (50 lei, four hours) and 10 to Cluj-Napoca (65 lei, six hours). For Iaşi, transfer in Ploiesti or Bucharest (96 lei, nine hours).

Around Braşov

⊙ Sights

Bran Castle   CASTLE

(☑0268-237 700; www.bran-castle.com; adult/student 25/5 lei, camera/video 20 lei; ⊙9am-7pm Tue-Sun, noon-7pm Mon May-Sep, 9am-5pm Tue-Sun Oct-Apr) Facing the flatlands and backed by mountains, the 60m-tall Bran Castle is spectacular. If you can manage to avoid bottlenecks from tour groups that appear in waves, you may enjoy the largely renovated interiors and claustrophobic nooks and crannies.

Built by Saxons from Braşov in 1382 to defend the Bran Pass against Turks, the castle may have housed Vlad Ţepeş for a few nights on his flight from the Turks in 1462, following their attack on the Poienari fortress in the Argeş Valley. From 1920 Queen Marie lived in the castle, and it served as a summer royal residence until the forced abdication of King Michael in 1947.

Râsnov Fortress   FORTRESS

(Cetatea Râşnov; admission 10 lei; ⊙9am-8pm May-Oct, to 6pm Nov-Apr) Râşnov, 12km from Bran towards Braşov, doubles the castle action with the tempting ruins of the 13th-century fortress. From the central square, steps lead up the hill where inclined alleys and a museum await.

⊨ Sleeping

Guesthouse   PENSION €

(☑0744-306 062; Str Principala ; r from 120-140 lei, tr 150 lei) With terrific views of Bran Castle, this guesthouse sits almost opposite Hanul Bran. It's clean and family-friendly with a kids' adventure playground and communal lounge and dining room.

Hanul Bran   HOTEL €

(☑0268-236 556; www.hanulbran.ro; Str Principala 384; s/d 100/120 lei) Probably the plushest option dead central ('scuse the pun), this ochre-coloured hotel with a bubbly adjoining restaurant enjoys a dramatic view of the castle. Large genial rooms with comfy beds, TV and bathroom.

❶ Getting There & Away

Bran is an easy DIY day trip from Braşov. Buses marked 'Bran–Moieciu' (6 lei, one hour) depart every half-hour from Braşov's **Autogara 2** (Bus Station 2; ☑0268-426 332; Str Avram Iancu 114). Return buses to Braşov leave Bran every half-hour from roughly 7am to 6pm in winter, and 7am to 10pm in summer. All buses to Braşov stop each way at Râşnov.

Sighişoara

POP 26,400

So pretty it should be arrested, from the moment you enter Sighişoara's fortified walls, wending your way along cobblestones to its central square, the town burns itself into your memory. It's like stepping into a kid's fairy tale, the narrow streets aglow with lustrously coloured 16th-century houses, their gingerbread roofs tumbling down to pretty cafes. Horror fans won't be disappointed either, for this Unesco-protected citadel, the best preserved of its kind in Europe, was the birthplace of one of history's great monsters – Vlad Ţepeş (The Impaler).

⊙ Sights

Most of Sighişoara's sights are conveniently clustered in the compact old town, the magical medieval **citadel** perched on a hillock and fortified with a 14th-century wall (to which 14 towers and five artillery bastions were later added). Today the citadel, which is on the Unesco World Heritage list, retains just nine of its original towers (named for the guilds in charge of their upkeep) and two of its bastions.

Entering the citadel, you pass under the massive **clock tower** (Turnul cu Ceas; Piata Muzeului) with its peacock-coloured roof tiles; it dates from 1280 and once housed the town council. Formerly the main entrance to the fortified city, the tower is 64m tall, with 2.35m-thick walls. Inside, the 1648 clock is a pageant of slowly revolving 80cm-high wooden figurines, each representing a character from the Greek–Roman pantheon: Peace bears an olive branch, Justice has a set of scales and Law wields a sword. The executioner is also present and the drum-player strikes the hour. Above stand seven figures, each representing a day of the week.

The diminutive **Piaţa Cetăţii** is the heart of old Sighişoara. It was here that markets, craft fairs, public executions, impalings and witch trials were held.

From the square, turn left up Str Şcolii to the 172 steps of the covered stairway (scara acoperită; Str Şcolii), which has tunnelled its way up the hill since 1642, to the 1345 Gothic Church on the Hill (Biserica din Deal; Bergkirche; ☉mid-Apr–Oct), a 429m Lutheran church and the town's highest point. Facing its entry – behind the church when approaching from the steps – is an atmospheric, overgrown German cemetery.

Also behind the church are the remains of the Goldsmiths' Tower. The guilds of the goldsmiths, tailors, carpenters and tinsmiths existed until 1875.

From the church, head back down the hill, cross Piaţa Cetăţii, then head down Str Bastionul. At its northern end are the 1896 Roman Catholic church (Str Bastionul) and the Tailors' Tower (Turnul Cizmarilor; Str Bastionul).

🛏 Sleeping

TOP CHOICE Bed & Breakfast Kula PENSION €
(☎0265-777 907; Str Tâmplarilor 40; r/apt per person 65/150 lei; ❄) Spilling with antique furniture, wood floors and rugs, this pension in a 400-year-old house feels like you're staying at a friend's...which you are by the time you've sat chatting with the owners in the pretty garden, as they ply you with homemade wine.

Pensiune Cristina & Pavel PENSION €
(☎0744-159 667, 0744-119 211; www.pensiuneafaur.ro; Str Cojocarilor 1; dm/s/d 45/80/125 lei; ℗) The floors are so clean at this four-room, one-dorm guesthouse, you could eat your lunch off them. En suite rooms are spearmint white, plus there's an idyllic garden bursting with flowers.

Casa Wagner HOTEL €€
(☎0265-506 014; www.casa-wagner.com; Piaţa Cetăţii 7; s/d/ste €39/49/69; ℗❄☎) This ap-

pealing 16th-century hotel has 32 rooms spread across three buildings. Think peach walls, candelabras, dark-wood furniture and tasteful rugs. The rooms in the eaves are smaller but wood floored, cosy and very romantic for writing those *Harkeresque* diary entries.

Nathan's Villa HOSTEL €
(☎0265-772 546; www.nathansvilla.com; Str Libertăţii 8; dm 50 lei; @☎) Cramped dorms, but thoughtfully placed linen screens on bunks allow for a little more privacy. The purple dorm is cosy – check out the retro boiler. Another plus is a sofa and TV in dorms.

🍴 Eating

Café International & Family Centre CAFE €
(Piaţa Cetăţii 8; mains 13 lei; ☉8.30am-7.30pm Mon-Sat Jun-Sep, 9am-6pm Mon-Sat Oct-May; ☎🧒) This delightful family-run cafe dishes up delicious pies, cookies, quiche and cakes. Inside it's a Gustavian-meets-rustic chic interior, while outside chairs and tables spill onto the cobbles come summer.

Cositorarului Casa RESTAURANT €
(Str Cositorarilor 9; mains 15-25 lei; ☉9am-10pm) Refresh yourself with beautiful views of the old town and homemade lemonade. They also rustle up toasted sandwiches and breakfast. Inside is cosy, and outside there's a small terrace.

Casa Dracula ROMANIAN €€
(Str Cositorarilor 5; mains 28 lei; 🧒) Despite the ghoulish Dracula bust mounted on the wall, the house where Vlad was born could have been dealt a worse blow than this atmospheric, wood-panelled restaurant. The menu scuttles from tomato soup to salmon fillet – all with Dracula-related references.

ROMANIA SIGHIŞOARA

SAXON LAND

Sighişoara, Sibiu and Braşov – the 'Saxon Triangle', if you will – enclose an area loaded with undulating hills and cinematic villages. These yesteryear villages, some sitting at the ends of rather nasty dirt roads, frequently have outstanding fortified churches dating from the 12th century. Even just a kilometre or two off the Braşov–Sibiu highway you'll find a world where horse carriages and walking are generally the only ways anyone gets around, and where a car – any car – gets stares.

Popular destinations include Biertan (28km southwest of Sighişoara) and Viscri (about 40km east).

Bus services are infrequent, but several guided tours cruise this area from either Braşov or Sibiu. You can also arrange a taxi for the day.

ℹ️ Information

Cultural Heritage Info Centre (☑️0788-115 511; www.dordeduca.ro; Piaţa Muzeului; ⏱10am-6pm Tue-Sun) Rents out bikes (5 lei per hour) and offers guided tours of Sighişoara and the fortified churches.

Farmacia Genţiana (Piaţa Hermann Oberth 45; ⏱8am-8pm)

Post Office (☑️0265-774 854; Str O Goga 12; ⏱7.30am-7.30pm Mon-Fri)

Tourist Information (☑️0265-770 415; Str O Goga; ⏱10am-4pm Mon-Fri, 9am-1pm Sat) This useful English-speaking resource can book beds and check bus and train times, and has maps of the city.

ℹ️ Getting There & Away

BUS Next to the train station on Str Libertăţii, the **bus station** (☑️0265-771 260) sends buses of various sizes and colours to Sibiu (20 lei, 2½ hours, four daily), among other destinations. Buses to Braşov (38 lei, 2½ hours) stop at the bus station a couple of times per day and require a reservation (☑️0265-250 702).

TRAIN About a dozen trains connect Sighişoara with Braşov (21 lei, two hours), nine of which go on to Bucharest (65 lei, 4½ hours). Five daily trains go to Cluj-Napoca (59 lei, 3½ hours). You'll need to change trains in Mediaş to reach Sibiu (16 lei, 2½ hours), but the four daily trains are timed for easy transfers. Three daily trains go to Budapest (145 lei, nine hours), and the night train has a sleeper (from 200 lei). Buy tickets at the **train station** (☑️0265-771 886).

Sibiu

POP 154,500

Instantly charming with her maze of cobbled streets and baroque squares undulating downhill, Romania's cultural first lady has a magic all of her own. Composers Franz Liszt and Johann Strauss were drawn here in the 19th century, and in 2007 the city was named the European Union's Capital of Culture. In fact, the country's first hospital, school, library and pharmacy were all established here, so there must be a spirit of enterprise in the air. Most months have myriad things going on, from festivals (with more festivals here than any other city in Romania) and exhibitions to theatre and opera. There are also plenty of cafes for people-watching in the city's three main squares.

👁 Sights

TOWN CENTRE

At the centre of the old walled city, the expansive Piaţa Mare is a good start for exploring Sibiu. Climb to the top of the former **Council Tower** (Turnul Sfatului; admission 2 lei; ⏱10am-8pm), which links Piaţa Mare with its smaller sister square, Piaţa Mică.

Brukenthal Museum   MUSEUM

(www.brukenthalmuseum.ro; Piaţa Mare 5; adult/student 20/5 lei) The Brukenthal Museum is the oldest and possibly finest art gallery in Romania. Founded in 1817, the museum is in the baroque palace (1785) of former Austrian governor Baron Samuel Brukenthal (1721–1803), and hosts excellent collections of 16th- and 17th-century paintings.

History Museum   MUSEUM

(Str Mitropoliei 2; adult/child 20/5 lei) The History Museum displays Palaeolithic tools, ceramics, bronze, jewellery and life-sized home scenes, costumes and furniture. Other sections hold guild exhibits, an armoury, Roman artefacts and a treasury.

Biserica Evanghelică   CHURCH

(Evangelical Church; Piaţa Huet; church tower adult/child 3/2 lei) The Gothic Biserica Evanghelică, built from 1300 to 1520, is partially scaffolded due to renovation but you can still climb the church tower; ask for entry at Casa Luxemburg. Its 1772 organ features a staggering 6002 pipes (the largest in southeast Europe).

Pharmaceutical Museum   MUSEUM

(☑️0269-218 191; www.brukenthalmuseum.ro; Piaţa Mică 26; adult/child 10/2.50 lei; ⏱10am-6pm Tue-Sun Apr-Oct, 10am-6pm Wed-Sun Nov-Mar) Housed in the Piaţa Mică pharmacy (opened in 1600), the Pharmaceutical Museum is a three-room collection packed with pills and powders, old microscopes and scary medical instruments.

OUTSIDE THE CENTRE

Astra Museum of Traditional Folk Civilisation   MUSEUM

(Muzeul Civilizaţiei Populare Tradiţionale Astra; Calea Răşinarilor 14; adult/child 15/3.50 lei; ⏱museum 10am-6pm Tue-Sun, gift shop 9am-5pm Tue-Sun) Around 5km from the centre, this sprawling open-air museum has a dazzling 120 traditional dwellings, mills and churches brought from around the country and set among two small lakes and a tiny zoological garden. Many are signed in English, with maps showing where the structures came from.

🛏 Sleeping

TOP CHOICE Felinarul Hostel   HOSTEL €

(☑️0269-235 260; www.felinarulhostelsibiu.ro; Str Felinarul 8; dm/r 55/140 lei; ❄️@🌐) More *boutique* than hostel, this labour of love is a wood-accented, courtyard oasis with one eight-berth and two six-berth dorms. There are also two homely private rooms with bathrooms, a book exchange, wine-coloured cafe, antique-style kitchen, posh coffees from the bar and wi-fi. Prepare to stay a while.

Am Ring HOTEL €€
(☑0269-206 499; www.amringhotel.ro; Piaţa Mare 14; s/d/tr 250/290/420 lei; ❄🕸📶) This 26-roomed centrally placed diva is lavish, with marble busts of Hadrian and Achilles, and at every turn antique furniture, velvet curtains and wood-raftered ceilings. There's a nice bar too. Rooms have Gustavian-period furniture, thick carpets and huge beds.

Old Town Hostel HOSTEL €
(☑0728-184 959, 0269-216 445; www.hostelsibiu.ro; Piaţa Mică 26; dm/d 55/180 lei; 🕸) In a 450-year-old building with three dorms and two private rooms (one with bathroom), Old Town has sublime square views. It also has decidedly plush touches like parquet floors, fresh white walls, choice artwork, TV in dorms and considerably spaced beds (the antithesis of battery-hen mentality). It's a nice vibe too, from the communal kitchen room to the lounge.

Pensiunea Ela PENSION €
(☑0269-215 197; www.ela-hotels.ro; Str Nouă 43; s/d/tr 100/120/160 lei; 🕸) Down a quiet street in the Lower Town, you might have to knock on the door a few times to get an answer. Within its flowery courtyard there are eight basic rooms with a rustic signature. Owner Ella is a welcoming host.

✖ Eating & Drinking

TOP CHOICE **Crama Sibiu Vechi** ROMANIAN €€
(Str P Ilarian; mains 25 lei; 📵) Hidden in an old wine cellar with its staff dressed in trad garb, this is the most rustically evocative restaurant in Sibiu. It's certainly the most authentic place to explore Romanian fare like cheese croquettes, minced meatballs and peasant's stew with polenta.

Pardon Café and Bistro INTERNATIONAL, ITALIAN €€
(Str Cetatii 14; mains 20 lei; ⊘9am-10pm; 📵) Opposite the Philharmonic, this bijou treasure has walls stacked with old gramophones, clocks and antique telephones. Enjoy a pasta, steak, soup or salad in the cosy interior.

Zorba Greek Restaurant GREEK €€
(Piaţa Mică 8; mains 25 lei; ⊘11am-2am; 📵) Zorba dishes up Aegean-fresh fare: colossal Greek salads, souvlaki, calamari, pizza and pasta.

Imperium Club BAR
(Str Nicolae Bălcescu 24; ⊘9am-dawn) Cosy bar-fly joint with vampish vaulted ceilings, dimly lit booths for canoodling, great cocktails – try the mojito – and live jazz some nights.

☆ Entertainment

Philharmonic CLASSICAL MUSIC
(www.filarmonicasibiu.ro; Str Cetăţii 3-5; adult/child 10/7 lei) Founded in 1949, the Philharmonic has played a key role in maintaining Sibiu's prestige as a main cultural centre of Transylvania.

Radu Stancu State Theatre THEATRE
(B-dul Spitelor 2-4; tickets 20 lei) Plays here are usually in Romanian, with occasional productions in German on Wednesday. It hosts the International Theatre Festival in May/June.

Agenţia de Teatrală BOOKING SERVICE
(Str Nicolae Bălcescu 17; ⊘11am-6pm Mon-Fri, to 3pm Sat) Tickets for major events are sold here.

❶ Information

ATMs are located all over the centre.

Casa Luxemburg (☑0269-216 854; www.kultours.ro; Piaţa Mică 16) Travel agent offering loads of city tours (9 to 14 lei) and day trips (50 to 90 lei); has a useful free map of the centre too.

Farmasib (Str Nicolae Bălcescu 53; ⊘7am-11pm Mon-Fri, 8am-11pm Sat & Sun)

Hospital (☑0269-215 050; B-dul Corneliu Coposu 2-4)

Info Point (☑0269-244 442; www.kultours.ro; Piaţa Huet 1; ⊘9am-10pm) Info on local attractions, surrounding areas, booking bus tickets, car rental and bike hire (per day 35 lei). Also sells some decent souvenirs – books, bags and T-shirts.

Tourist Information Centre (☑0269-208 913; www.sibiu.ro; Piaţa Mare 2; ⊘9am-5pm Mon-Fri, to 1pm Sat & Sun) Based at the City Hall, staff here are fantastically helpful at guiding you to make the best of the city: cultural events, finding accommodation, and booking train and bus tickets.

❶ Getting There & Around

BUS The **bus station** (Piaţa 1 Decembrie 1918) is opposite the train station. Bus and maxitaxi services include Braşov (25 lei, 2½ hours, two daily), Bucharest (40 lei, 5½ hours, six daily),

Cluj-Napoca (30 lei, 3½ hours, 16 daily) and Timişoara (51 lei, six hours, three daily).

TRAIN There are seven daily direct trains to Braşov (35.60 lei, 2½ hours), three daily trains to Bucharest (67 lei, five hours) and Timişoara (67 lei, five hours), and one early-morning run to Arad (55 lei, five hours). To get to/from Sighişoara (13 lei) or Cluj-Napoca (55 lei), you'll have to change at Copşa Mică or Mediaş (about nine or 10 trains daily). The **Agenţia de Voiaj CFR office** (☎0269-212 085; Str Nicolae Bălcescu 6; ⊘7am-8pm Mon-Fri) sells advance tickets and serves as agents for Blue Air and Eurolines.

Cluj-Napoca

POP 294,800

It may not be flanked by mountains or as instantly arresting as Braşov or Sibiu, but Cluj is big on charm. Romania's largest student population make this city their home, and with its boulevards, baroque architecture, bohemian cafe society and backstreets animated with bon viveurs and subterranean bars, you can see why. It's also the country's film capital and the Transylvania International Film Festival (www.tiff.ro), held each year in May, attracts plenty of international talent.

◉ Sights

TOWN CENTRE

St Michael's Church   CHURCH

The vast 14th-century St Michael's Church dominates Piaţa Unirii. The neo-Gothic tower (1859) topping the Gothic hall church creates a great landmark, and the church is considered to be one of the finest examples of Gothic architecture in Romania.

Pharmaceutical Museum   MUSEUM

(Str Regele Ferdinand I; adult/child 5.20/3.10 lei; ⊘10am-4pm Mon-Wed & Fri, noon-6pm Thu) Tours are led by a hilarious pharmacist in a white lab coat, who points like a game-show model towards (seemingly ho-hum) glass cases of ground mummy dust, medieval alchemist symbols and painted 18th-century aphrodisiac bottles.

National Art Museum   MUSEUM

(Piaţa Unirii 30; adult/student 5/3 lei; ⊘10am-5pm Wed-Sun) On the eastern side of Piaţa Unirii is the National Art Museum, housed inside the baroque Banffy Palace (1791). The couple of dozen rooms are filled with paintings and artefacts, including a 16th-century church altar and many 20th-century paintings.

Ethnographic Museum of Transylvania   MUSEUM

(Muzeul Etnografic al Transilvaniei; www.muzeul-etnografic.ro; Str Memorandumului 21; adult/student 6/3 lei; ⊘9am-4pm Tue-Sat) The Ethnographic Museum of Transylvania has two floors of well-presented displays featuring tools, weapons, handcrafts, toys and household items with detailed descriptions in English.

OUTSIDE THE CENTRE

Museum of Zoology   MUSEUM

(Str Clinicilor 5-7; adult/student 3/1.50 lei; ⊘9am-3pm Mon-Fri, 10am-2pm Sat & Sun) In the 'student ghetto' west of the centre, inside the Biology and Geology Faculty you'll find the surprisingly rewarding Museum of Zoology, an L-shaped lab that looks like it hasn't changed in five decades. From Str Clinicilor, veer left through the brick gate.

Alexandru Borza Botanic Gardens   GARDENS

(Str Republicii 42; adult/student 5/3 lei) Through the campus housing, head past fast-food joints up Str Bogdan P Haşdeu to Str Pasteur to reach these fragrant 1930 gardens.

🏃 Activities

TOP CHOICE Green Mountain Holidays   HIKING

(☎0744-637 227; www.greenmountainholidays.ro) This terrific ecotourism organisation is recommended for its environmentally friendly, activity-filled week. Check the website for caving, hiking and biking tours in the Apuseni Mountains, with guides, transport, meals and accommodation, as well as self-guided trips.

🛌 Sleeping

TOP CHOICE Retro Hostel   HOSTEL €

(☎0264-450 452; www.retro.ro; Str Potaissa 13; dm/s/d/tr incl breakfast sandwich from 49/90/135/195 lei ; ⊜@☎) Well organised, central and with helpful staff, Retro has clean dorms and decent double rooms (all with TV and shared bathrooms). There's also a pleasant cafe downstairs. The private rooms face the narrow road in which sit two noisy bars, so bring earplugs. Retro rents out a car for €35 per day, and lends out bikes for free.

TOP CHOICE Fullton   HOTEL €€

(☎0264-597 898; www.fullton.ro; Str Sextil Puşcariu 10; s 170-210 lei; d 196-236 lei; ⊜❄☎) This boutique hotel with a pea-green facade has a great location in the old town and a couple of places to park. Rooms are fragrant and fresh, and have individual colour schemes (some, like room 101, have four-poster beds), bureaus and bathrooms. There's also a welcoming patio bar.

Piccola Italia
PENSION €

(☎0264-536 110; www.piccolaitalia.ro; Str Racoviţă 20; s/d/tr 115/130/150 lei; P❋) Immediately left after you pass north over the river, Piccolo is a short haul uphill on a quiet road. It has nine clean, whitewashed rooms with reading lights, TV and bathroom. Add to this a garden dripping in vines, hearty breakfast and friendly management, and it's a winner.

Transylvania Hostel
HOSTEL €€

(☎0264-443 266; www.transylvaniahostel.com; Str Iuliu Maniu 26; dm/d 50/150 lei; ❋@❋) Huddled around a leafy courtyard, this mercifully cool hostel has spacious dorms, private lockers and a lounge with comfy sofas that you may find hard to prise yourself off. There's also a games room, communal PC and flat-screen TV with plenty of DVDs.

✕ Eating

⬛TOP CHOICE Camino
CAFE €

(Piaţa Muzeului 4; mains 15 lei; ☺9am-midnight; ❋) With jazz piping through its peeling arched interior decked in candelabras and threadbare rugs, this boho restaurant is perfect for a solo book-reading jaunt or romantic alfresco dinner. The homemade pasta is delicious, and the salads and tapas are full of zing.

Magyar Vendeglo
HUNGARIAN €€

(Str Iuliu Maniu 6; mains 25 lei) Based at the Hotel Agape, rustically painted wooden walls

and finely carved furniture complement a menu spanning goulash, schnitzel, steak and, curiously, 'brain with egg'! Not sure whose brain.

Restaurant Matei Corvin
ROMANIAN €€

(Str Matei Corvin 3; mains 16-42 lei; 🍴) With its Romanesque arched ceilings and walls strung with oils, this old trusty delivers with a flavoursome menu of broths, soup, pork roulade and tortillas. Authentic.

🍷 Drinking

Many subterranean clubs and bars are spread throughout the centre: it pays to explore. The 'student ghetto', southwest of the centre (on and off Str Piezişă), teems with lively open-air bars.

Klausenberg Café
CAFE

(www.klausenburgcafe.ro; Str Universităţii 1; ☺9am-midnight; ❋) This swanky bar glitters with crystal.

Casa Tauffer Jazz Café
BAR, LIVE MUSIC

(Str Vasile Goldiş 2; ☺24hr) With its oxblood walls ornamented with Rat Pack prints and antique trumpets, and Armstrong and Gillespie jumping on the speakers, this smoky joint is a slice of New Orleans. There are piano evenings and exhibitions too.

☆ Entertainment

Şapte Seri (www.sapteseri.ro) and *24-Fun* are free biweekly booklets listing all the latest goings-on (in Romanian).

State Philharmonic
CLASSICAL MUSIC

(Filarmonica de Stat) The State had moved into the Student Culture House at research time. The improvised box office is just inside the front doors, on the right. Check with the

TRAINS FROM CLUJ

DESTINATION	PRICE (LEI)	DURATION (HR)	FREQUENCY (DAILY)
Braşov	67	5	8
Bucharest	82	9	5
Budapest (Hungary)	140	5	2
Iaşi	82	9	3
Oradea	39	2¼-4	12
Sibiu	48	5	2
Sighişoara	55	3½	5
Suceava	67	7	5
Timişoara	67	7	8

Cluj

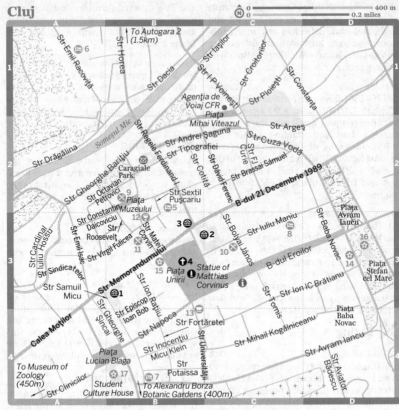

tourist information office to see where they are playing.

National Theatre Lucian Blaga　THEATRE
(Piaţa Ştefan cel Mare 2-4; tickets from 20 lei) National Theatre Lucian Blaga was designed by Viennese architects Fellner and Hellmer; performances are well attended. The **Opera** (☑0264-595 363; National Theatre Lucian Blaga) is in the same building. Tickets for both can be bought from the **Agenţia de Teatrală** (☑0264-595 363; Piaţa Ştefan cel Mare 14; ☺11am-5pm Tue-Fri), starting at 6.50 lei and 15 lei respectively.

Diesel　CLUB
(Piaţa Unirii 17; ☺6pm-dawn) Its outside terrace might look innocent enough but descend the stairway into the Sadean darkness and a dungeonlike interior awaits, complete with low-lit grotto bar, candelabras and a whole world of possibilities.

❶ Information

Clematis (Piaţa Unirii 11; ☺8am-10pm) Pharmacy.

Pan Travel (☑0264-420 516; www.pantravel.ro; Str Grozavescu 13; ☺9am-5pm Mon-Fri) Books accommodation, car rentals, self-drive tours and multiday tours to the Apuseni Mountains, Saxon villages or around Maramureş.

Tourist Information Office (☑0264-452 244; www.visitcluj.ro; B-dul Eroilor 6-8; ☺8.30am-8pm Mon-Fri, 10am-6pm Sat) This super-friendly office has bags of info on trekking, train and bus times, eating, accommodation and cultural unmissables.

Transylvania Ecological Club (Clubul Ecologic Transilvania; ☑0264-431 626; www.greenagenda. org) One of Romania's most active grassroots environmental groups, operating since the mid-1990s. Can provide trail maps and find guides.

❶ Getting There & Around

BUS Bus services from **Autogara 2** (Autogara Beta; ☑0264-455 249), 350m northwest of the

Cluj

◉ **Sights**

train station (take the overpass), include Braşov (50 lei, two daily), Bucharest (60 lei, 7½ hours, three daily), Budapest (75 lei, several daily) and Sibiu (28 lei, 3½ hours, eight daily).

TAXI Diesel Taxi (☎0264-946, 0264-953)

TRAIN The **Agenţia de Voiaj CFR** (☎0264-432 001; Piaţa Mihai Viteazul 20; ⊙8am-8pm Mon-Fri, 9am-1.30pm Sat) sells domestic and international train tickets in advance.

CRIŞANA & BANAT

Western Romania, with its geographic and cultural ties to neighbouring Hungary and Serbia, and historical links to the Austro-Hungarian Empire, enjoys an ethnic diversity that much of the rest of the country lacks. Timişoara, the regional hub, has a nationwide reputation as a beautiful and lively metropolis, and for a series of 'firsts'. It was the world's first city to adopt electric street lights (in 1884) and, more importantly, the first city to rise up against dictator Nicolae Ceauşescu in 1989. Outside the metropolitan areas, the remote and pristine Apuseni Mountains are littered with dozens of amazing caves that cry out for exploration, and miles and miles of isolated hiking trails.

Timişoara

POP 312,000

Romania's third- or fourth-largest city (depending on the source) is also one of the country's most attractive urban areas, built around a series of beautiful public squares and lavish parks and gardens. It's known as Primul Oraş Liber (First Free Town), for it was here that anti-Ceauşescu protests first exceeded the Securitate's capacity for violent suppression in 1989, eventually sending Ceauşescu and his wife to their demise. With western Romania's nicest hotels and restaurants, it makes a perfect base for exploring the Banat region.

◉ Sights

PIAŢA UNIRII

Piaţa Unirii is Timişoara's most picturesque square, featuring the imposing sight of the **Catholic cathedral** (Catedrală Episcopală Romano-Catolică; ☎0256-430 671; Piaţa Unirii 12; ⊙8am-6pm) and **Serbian church** (Biserica Ortodoxă Sârbă; Str Ungureanu 12) facing each other. A couple of blocks to the east, following Str Palanca, is the **Cetate** (Fortress), a classic 18th-century Austrian fortress that's been remodelled into a complex of shops and cafes.

TOP CHOICE **Permanent Exhibition of the 1989 Revolution** MUSEUM
(☎0256-294 936; www.memorialulrevolutiei.ro; Str Popa Sapcă 3-5; admission by donation; ⊙8am-4pm Mon-Fri, 9am-1pm Sat) This work in progress is an ideal venue to brush up on the December 1989 anticommunist revolution that began in Timişoara. Displays include documentation, posters and photography from those fateful days, capped by a graphic, 20-minute video (not suitable for young children), with English subtitles.

Art Museum MUSEUM
(Muzeul de Artă; ☎0256-491 592; www.muzeuldeartatm.ro; Old Prefecture Palace, Piaţa Unirii 1; admission 5 lei; ⊙10am-6pm Tue-Sun) The art museum displays a representative sample of paintings and visual arts over the centuries as well as regular, high-quality temporary exhibitions. It's housed in the baroque Old Prefecture Palace, built in 1754, and is worth a look inside for the graceful baroque interiors alone.

ROMANIA TIMIŞOARA

DON'T MESS WITH TIMIŞOARA

Even at the height of his power, Nicolea Ceauşescu never liked Romania's western-most metropolis. The dictator's visits to the city were few and brief, and required sur-reptitious, dread-fuelled travel and sleeping arrangements to allay his assassination concerns. So when the Romanian secret service, the Securitate, overplayed its hand in the already truculent city by trying to deport popular Hungarian pastor and outspo-ken Ceauşescu critic László Tőkés, the dictator should have sensed disaster looming. However, like most megalomaniacs, he didn't grasp the full scale of his folly until he was being shoved in front of a firing squad, looking genuinely stunned, a little more than a week later on Christmas Day 1989.

What started on 15 December 1989 as a human chain of Tőkés' parishioners protect-ing him from arrest mushroomed into a full-scale anticommunist revolt on 20 Decem-ber. Overconfident Ceauşescu actually left Romania during this time for a visit to Iran, leaving his wife Elena to cope with the escalating protests.

When Ceauşescu returned to Romania the next day, the situation was critical. Factory workers brought in by party officials to crush the demonstrations spontaneously joined the protesters in Piaţa Operei (today's Piaţa Victoriei), chanting antigovernment slogans and singing an old Romanian anthem ('Wake up, Romanians!') banned since the com-munists took power in 1947. The crowd, now over 100,000 strong, overpowered and then commandeered some of the tanks that had previously fired on demonstrators. Protests later ensued in Bucharest and around the country, and Ceauşescu's fate was sealed.

Learn more about the revolution and see video footage of the events at the excellent Permanent Exhibition of the 1989 Revolution.

PIAŢA VICTORIEI

Begging to be photographed with your widest lens is Piaţa Victoriei, a beautifully green pedestrian mall dotted with foun-tains in the middle and lined on both sides with shops and cafes. The square's northern end is marked by the 18th-century National Theatre & Opera House, where thousands of demonstrators gathered on 16 December 1989. A memorial on the front of the Opera House reads: 'So you, who pass by this build-ing, will dedicate a thought for free Rom-ania'. Towards the centre, there's a **statue of Romulus and Remus**.

Banat History Museum   MUSEUM
(Muzeul Banatului; Piaţa Huniades 1) The Ba-nat History Museum, housed in the his-toric Huniades Palace, was closed during our research for renovations expected to last until 2015. The exterior of the palace, though, is still worth a look. The origins of the building date to the 14th century and to Hungarian King Charles Robert, Prince of Anjou.

Metropolitan Cathedral   CHURCH
(Catedrala Ortodoxă; www.timisoara.org/catedrala; B-dul Regele Ferdinand I; ⊙10am-6pm) The Or-thodox Metropolitan Cathedral was built be-tween 1936 and 1946. Unique to the church

are its electric bells cast from iron imported from Indonesia.

OUTSIDE THE CENTRE

Tőkés Reformed Church   CHURCH
(Biserica Reformată Tőkés; Str Timotei Cipariu 1) The 1989 revolution began at the Tőkés Re-formed Church, where Father László Tőkés spoke out against the dictator. You can sometimes peek in at the church, but Tőkés' small apartment is privately inhabited.

Banat Village Museum   MUSEUM
(Muzeul Satului Banaţean; ☎0256-225 588; www.muzeulsatuluibanatean.ro; Str Avram Imbroane 1; admission 4.50 lei; ⊙10am-6pm Tue-Sat, noon-8pm Sun) The museum exhibits more than 30 traditional peasant houses dating from the 19th century. The open-air display was created in 1917. Take tram 1 (black number) from the northern train station.

🛏 Sleeping

Pension Casa Leone   PENSION €
(☎0256-292 621; www.casaleone.ro; B-dul Eroilor 67; s/d/tr 125/150/200 lei; P❄✿🕸🕾) This lovely seven-room pension offers exceptional serv-ice and individually decorated rooms. To find it, take tram 8 from the train station, alight at the 'Deliblata' station and walk

one block northeast to B-dul Eroilor (or call ahead to arrange transport).

Hostel Costel
HOSTEL €

(📞0726-240 223; www.hostel-costel.ro; Str Petru Sfetca 1; dm 40-45 lei, d 135 lei; 🖨@🛜) Run by an affable guy named Vlad, this charming 1920s art nouveau villa is arguably the city's only real youth hostel. With three dorm rooms and one private double, the vibe is relaxed and congenial. There are lots of little rooms to relax in and a big garden out back.

Hotel Central
HOTEL €€

(📞0256-490 091; www.hotel-central.ro; Str N Lenau 6; s/d 160/180 lei; P🅿️🛜) It's not exactly the Taj Mahal, but this communist-era hotel has had a decent facelift, leaving the rooms clean, modern and comfortable. There's ample guarded parking out front (per day 10 lei) if you're travelling by car, and you can't beat the price for the location.

Hotel Cina Banatul
HOTEL €

(📞0256-490 130; www.hotelcina.ro; B-dul Republicii 7; s/d 120/140 lei; P🅿️🛜) One of the best-value places in the centre, though not quite as appealing as the Hotel Central. The hotel has clean, ultramodern rooms and a good restaurant.

🍴 Eating

 Casa Bunicii
ROMANIAN €€

(📞0356-100 870; www.casa-bunicii.ro; Str Virgil Onitiu 3; mains 18-30 lei; 👶) The name translates to 'Granny's House' and indeed this casual, family-friendly restaurant specialises in home cooking and regional specialities from the Banat. We enjoyed the duck soup and the grilled chicken breast served in sour cherry sauce.

Casa cu Flori
ROMANIAN €€

(📞0256-435 080; www.casacuflori.ro; Str Alba Iulia 1; mains 18-28 lei) One of the best-known restaurants in the city and for good reason, serving excellent high-end Romanian cooking with refined service at moderate prices. In nice weather, climb three flights to the flower-lined rooftop terrace.

Intermezzo
ITALIAN €€

(📞0256-432 429; www.restaurant-intermezzo.ro; Piaţa Unirii 3; mains 22-36 lei, pizza 18-24 lei; 🕐noon-midnight) This place has great pizzas and even better pastas. Dine on the terrace on Piaţa Unirii or in the cellar restaurant.

Restaurant Lloyd
ROMANIAN €€

(📞0256-294 949; http://restaurantlloyd.ro; Piaţa Victoriei 2; mains 15-50 lei; 🕐9am-11pm; 🛜) A popular spot with visitors, located right on Piaţa Victoriei in front of the opera. The Romanian food is surprisingly good and the prices – given the terrace locale – are not as bad as you'd think.

🍷 Drinking

Aethernativ
CAFE

(📞0724-012 324; Str Mărăşeşti 14; 🕐10am-1am Mon-Fri, noon-1am Sat, 5pm-1am Sun; 🛜) This informal art club, cafe and bar occupies a courtyard of a rundown building two blocks west of Piaţa Unirii. It resembles a Budapest ruin pub, with its eclectic furnishings and alternative, student vibe. There are no signs to let you know you're here; simply find the address, push open the door and walk up a flight of stairs.

Scârţ loc lejer
CAFE

(📞0751-892 340; Str Zoe 1; 🕐10am-11pm Mon-Fri, 11am-11pm Sat, to 11pm Sun; 🛜) This is an old villa that's been retrofitted into a funky coffeehouse with albums pinned to the wall and chill tunes on the turntable. There are several cosy rooms in which to read, talk and relax, but our favourite is the lush garden out back.

☆ Entertainment

State Philharmonic Theatre
CLASSICAL MUSIC

(Filharmonica de Stat Banatul; 📞0256-492 521; www.filarmonicabanatul.ro; B-dul CD Loga 2; 🕐box office 2-7pm Wed, 9am-1pm Thu & Fri) Classical concerts are held most evenings here. Tickets (from 40 lei) can be bought at the box office inside the Philharmonic Theatre during limited opening hours or one hour before performances.

National Theatre & Opera House
THEATRE, OPERA

(Teatrul Naţional şi Opera Română; 📞opera 0256-201 286, theatre 0256-201 117; www.tntimisoara.com; Str Mărăşeşti 2) The National Theatre & Opera House features both dramatic works and classical opera, and is highly regarded. Buy tickets (from around 40 lei) in the nearby **Agenţia Teatrală** (📞0256-201 286; www.ort.ro; Str Mărăşeşti 2; 🕐10am-1pm & 5-7pm Tue-Sun).

Club 30
CLUB

(📞0256-247 878; www.club30.ro; Piaţa Victoriei 7; admission 10 lei; 🕐6pm-3am) This club has

ROMANIA TIMIŞOARA

been a staple on the dance scene for years and shows no signs of slowing down, particularly on retro '80s and '90s dance nights. There's live music on some evenings.

Cinema Timiş CINEMA
(☎0256-491 290; Piaţa Victoriei 7; tickets 6-8 lei) Centrally located cinema screens a mix of Hollywood blockbusters and popular European films. Movies are normally screened in their original language.

ⓘ Information

Online Centers (B-dul Mihai Eminescu 5; per hr 5.40 lei; ⊙24hr; 🐦)

Sensi Blu Pharmacy (☎0256-201 21; www.sensiblu.com; Piaţa Victoriei 7; ⊙8am-8pm Mon-Fri, 9am-8pm Sat & Sun) One of at least half a dozen similar, modern pharmacies on or around Piaţa Victoriei

Timişoara County Hospital (Spitalul Clinic Judeţean de Urgenţă Timişoara; ☎0356-433 111; www.hosptm.ro; B-dul Iosif Bulbuca 10) Modern hospital with high-quality medical care and 24-hour emergency service.

Tourist Information Centre (Info Centru Turistic; ☎0256-437 973; www.timisoara-info.ro; Str Alba Iulia 2) This great tourism office can assist with accommodation and trains, and provide maps and Banat regional info.

ⓘ Getting There & Away

BUS Timişoara lacks a centralised bus station for domestic services. Buses and minibuses are privately operated and depart from several points around the city, depending on the company. Consult the website www.autogari.ro for departure points. Bus service is extensive. Sample fares include Arad (15 lei), Cluj-Napoca (65 lei) and Sibiu (45 lei).

International buses leave from the **East bus station** (www.autogari.ro). The main international operators include **Atlassib** (☎0256-226 486; www.atlassib.ro; Calea Dorobantilor 59) and **Eurolines** (☎0256-288 132; www.eurolines.ro; Str M Kogălniceanu 20). Belgrade-based **Gea Tours** (www.geatours.rs) offers daily minibus service between Timişoara and Belgrade for one way/return 125/200 lei. Book over the website.

TRAIN Trains depart from **Gara Timişoara-Nord** (www.cfr.ro; Str Gării 2), the 'northern' station, though it's actually west of the centre. Daily express trains include two to Bucharest (100 lei, eight hours), two to Cluj-Napoca (127 lei, six hours) and five to Arad (20 lei, one hour). There's one daily train to Belgrade (70 lei, three hours), which leaves at 5.40am.

Oradea
POP 176,300

Fans of art nouveau and Secession architecture dating from the late 19th and early 20th centuries will want to make a special stopover in Oradea. While many of the once-elegant buildings here have been allowed to fall into disrepair, visitors with a sharp architectural eye will see Secession's signature lyric design elements and inlaid jewelwork on buildings up and down the main drag, Str Republicii, and across the Crişul Repede river at the Black Eagle Arcade (Pasajul Vulturul Negru; Str Independenţei 1).

⊙ Sights

The best way to see the city is to stroll Str Republicii, lined on both sides with architectural gems from the early 20th century. Don't miss the Moskovits Palace (Palatul Moskovits; Str Republicii 13), a Secession masterwork from 1905.

Moon Orthodox Church CHURCH
(Biserica cu Lună; www.bisericaculuna.ro; Piaţa Unirii; ⊙9am-5pm) The Orthodox Moon Church, built in 1784, has an unusual lunar mechanism on its tower that changes position in accordance with the moon's movement. Nearby, in the centre of Piaţa Unirii, stands an equestrian statue of Mihai Viteazul, the prince of Wallachia (r 1593–1601), who is said to have rested in Oradea in 1600.

Roman Catholic Cathedral CHURCH
(Sirul Canonicilor; ⊙9am-6pm) This cathedral, 2km north of the centre, was built between 1752 and 1780 and is the largest baroque church in Romania. Organ concerts are occasionally held here. The adjacent Bishop's Palace (⊙closed to the public) from 1770 boasts 100 fresco-adorned rooms and 365 windows.

The street Sirul Canonicilor that runs just east of the cathedral includes a series of 57 arches that form part of the original baroque design as laid out by Austrian master architect FA Hillebrandt.

Orthodox Synagogue SYNAGOGUE
(www.oradeajc.com; Str Mihai Viteazul 4; ⊙closed to the public) Oradea's Orthodox synagogue dates from 1890, and before WWII was the main house of worship for around a third of the city's residents. It survived the war intact but was badly neglected afterwards, and

is now undergoing a thorough multiyear renovation. Though it is closed to the public, phone the **Jewish Community Centre** (☑0359-191 021; www.fcer.jewishfed.ro; Str Mihai Viteazul 4) to take a look inside.

🛏 Sleeping

TOP CHOICE ▸ Hotel Elite
HOTEL €€

(☑0259-414 924; www.hotelelite.ro; Str IC Bratianu 26; s/d 250/280 lei; P❄🐾📶🏊👶) This beautiful hotel is worth the splurge, especially if you're travelling during the hot summer and have kids in tow. The rooms are spotless and well maintained, but the major drawcard is a gorgeous heated (and child-friendly) pool straight out of a Hollywood mansion.

Scorilo Hotel
HOTEL €€

(☑0259-470 910; www.hotelscorilo.ro; Str Parcul Petőfi 16; s/d/apt 180/220/300 lei; P❄📶) It's nearly impossible to book a room at this clean and way-too-popular family-run hotel, 10 minutes' walk from the train station. The rooms are small but tidy; some have balconies over the garden. The outdoor restaurant is the most festive place in town for an evening meal.

Hostel Felix
HOSTEL €

(☑0259-437 011; tineret_bh@yahoo.com; Mihai Eminescu 11; dm 40 lei) This 'sometimes open, sometimes not' hostel, run by the local department for youth affairs, has four-bed dorms with seatless toilets and zero ambience, yet it's undeniably central and cheap.

🍴 Eating

TOP CHOICE ▸ Graf
INTERNATIONAL €€€

(☑0259-421 421; www.restaurantgraf.ro; Str Barbu Stefanescu Delavrancea 3; mains 30-70 lei; ⏰11am-11pm; 📶) Graf is Oradea's nicest restaurant and a perfect splurge option. The menu features wood-grilled steaks, fish and pork; on our visit, the caramelised duck leg was one of our best meals in Romania. The wine list is top notch.

Lactobar
CAFE €

(www.lactobarretrobistro.ro; Calea Republicii 11; mains 8-15 lei; ⏰8am-11pm; 📶👶) Even if you're not hungry, stop by this charming, very kid-friendly 'retro bistro' on the main street. The colourful decor of period-piece found objects is remarkable, topped off with an orange, ultracool Dacia automobile.

Cyrano
ROMANIAN €€

(☑0740-163 943; Calea Republicii 7; mains 14-30 lei; ⏰8.30am-midnight Mon-Fri, 9.30am-midnight Sat, 11am-midnight Sun; 📶) Popular hang-out ideal for people-watching from the coveted terrace tables. Though the menu teems with Romanian favourites, the incredible *ciorbă de vițel cu tarhon in chiflă* (beef and vegie stew in a bread bowl, 12.80 lei) is all the food you need.

ℹ Information

Alpha Bank (☑0259-457 834; Piaţa Unirii 24; ⏰9am-4pm Mon-Fri)

Internet Cafe (☑0359-454 566; Str George Enescu 24; per hr 3 lei; ⏰8.30am-midnight Mon-Fri, noon-midnight Sat & Sun; 📶)

Post Office (☑0259-435 040; Str Roman Ciorogariu 12; ⏰8am-8pm Mon-Fri, to 2pm Sat)

ℹ Getting There & Away

BUS A small **bus station** (autogara; ☑0259-418 998; Str Râzboieni 81) is situated 2km south of the centre. From here you can catch frequent maxitaxis and regular buses to Băile Felix (4 lei, 10 minutes), Ştei (for access to Bear Cave; 13 lei, two hours) and Arieşeni (24 lei, three hours).

There's a small **maxitaxi** stand north of the train station for travelling to cities north of Oradea, such as Baia Mare (38 lei, three hours).

TRAIN Oradea's **train station** (☑0259-414 970; www.cfr.ro; Calea Republicii 114) is 2km north of the centre. Daily fast trains from Oradea include one to Budapest (150 lei, five hours), one slow overnight to Bucharest (about 105 lei, 12 hours), six to Cluj-Napoca (43 lei, three hours), two to Braşov (60 lei, nine hours) and five to Timişoara (47 lei, three hours).

MARAMUREŞ

This is widely regarded as Romania's most traditional region, scattered with steepled wooden churches and villagers' homes fronted by ornately carved gates. A visit to Maramureş is like climbing into a horse-drawn time machine and heading back 100 years. Smaller in scale and softer in contour than neighbouring Transylvania, Maramureş' tapestry of pastureland peopled by colourfully garbed peasants jumps straight from a Brothers Grimm story. But don't wait forever to visit – even here, the 21st century is making inroads.

Sighetu Marmaţiei

POP 44,200

Sleepy 'Sighet' (its shortened nickname) has a few sights for a morning's browsing, a pretty square bookended by a church, and the Ukrainian border crossing just a few minutes away; but your real reason for being in Maramureş is its rural charm, so you needn't linger long. For centuries Sighet formed a cultural and geographic border between Slav-dominated territories to the north and Hungary and Romania to the south. Its name is derived from the Thracian and Dacian word *seget* (fortress).

◉ Sights

On Piaţa Libertăţii stands the **Hungarian Reformed church**, built during the 15th century. Close by is the 16th-century **Roman Catholic church**.

Maramureş Museum   MUSEUM
(Piaţa Libertăţii 15; adult/student 4/2 lei; ⊘10am-6pm Tue-Sun) The Maramureş Museum displays colourful folk costumes, rugs and carnival masks.

Elie Wiesel's House   HISTORIC BUILDING
Elie Wiesel, the Jewish writer and 1986 Nobel Peace Prize winner, was born in (and later deported from) Sighet. His house, on the corner of Str Dragoş Vodă and Str Tudor Vladimirescu, is open to visitors. Along Str Gheorghe Doja there is a **monument** (Str Mureşan) to the victims of the Holocaust.

Synagogue   SYNAGOGUE
(Str Bessarabia 10) Sighet's only remaining synagogue is found near Piaţa Libertăţii. You can look around for free, but it's customary to leave a donation (10 lei). Before WWII the Jewish community was estimated at 50,000 – more than half of Sighet's pre-war population. Today the local Jewish community numbers around 200.

Most of the Jews perished at Auschwitz-Birkenau after being shipped there in 1944, when Hungary (which ruled over the area at the time) agreed to surrender its Jews to Nazi Germany.

Village Museum   MUSEUM
(Muzeul Satului; ☑0262-314 229; Str Dobăieş 40; adult/child/photo 4/2/4 lei) Allow two to three hours to wander through the incredible constructions at the open-air Village Museum, southeast of Sighet's centre. Children love the wooden dwellings, cobbled pathways and 'mini villages'. You can even stay overnight in tiny wooden cabins (20 lei) or pitch a tent (5 lei per person).

🛏 Sleeping

For homestays in the area, check out www.ruraltourism.ro and www.pensiuni.info.ro.

TOP CHOICE **Casa Iurca**   HOTEL €€
(☑0262-318 882; www.casaiurca.ro; Str Dragoş Vodă 14; r 150 lei, annexe s 92 lei, d 185-218 lei; ❂❄🛜) Rooms are elegant and cool in this fine wood-accented villa. Expect tasteful furniture, flat-screen TVs, tiled floors, leather chairs and spotless linen for your money. There's also in-room wi-fi, fridge, cable TV and fan. Hands down the best digs in town.

TOP CHOICE **Cobwobs Hostel**   PENSION €
(☑0745-635 673; www.cobwobs.com; Str 22 Decembrie 1989 nr; dm/d without bathroom 40/100 lei; ❂@🛜) Friendly Cobwobs sits down a grassy lane in a pleasant house whose garden is so crowded with apple and plum

---

SIGHET PRISON: A SUFFERING NATION

In May 1947 the communist regime slaughtered, imprisoned or tortured thousands of Romanians who might oppose the new leadership. While many leading prewar figures were sent to hard-labour camps, the regime's most feared intellectual opponents were held in Sighet's maximum-security prison. Between 1948 and 1952 about 180 members of Romania's academic and government elite were imprisoned here and some 51 died.

The prison, housed in the old courthouse, was closed in 1974. In the early '90s it reopened as the **Memorial to the Victims of Communism and to the Resistance** (☑0262-319 424; www.memorialsighet.ro; Str Corneliu Coposu 4; admission 6 lei; ⊘9.30am-6.30pm Mon-Sun, to 4pm winter). Photographs and objects with short descriptions are displayed in the torture chambers and cells on two levels. There's also a small bookstore and gift shop. The emotional bronze statues in the courtyard, shielding themselves and covering their mouths in horror, are dedicated to those who died.

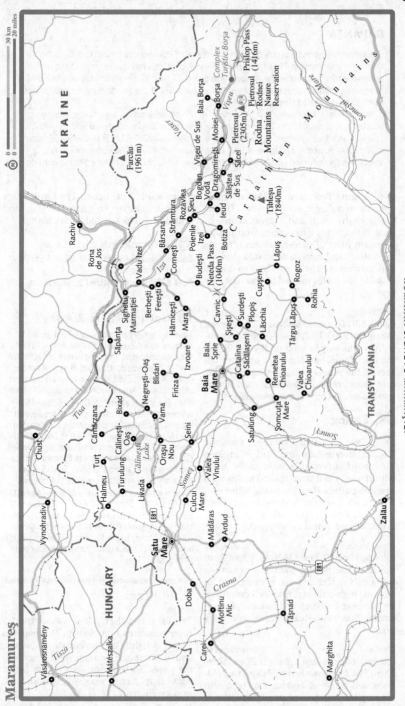

Maramureş

SĂPÂNŢA

Săpânţa village has a unique place in the hearts of Romanians. It boasts the Merry Cemetery (admission 4 lei), famous for the colourfully painted wooden crosses that adorn the tombstones in the village's graveyard. Shown in art exhibitions across Europe, the crosses attract coachloads of visitors who marvel at the gentle humour and human warmth that created them.

While most visitors stay just a couple of hours, there are a couple of nice pensions scattered around. With its traditional rooms nestled around a courtyard and its garden stacked with freshly shorn wool, Pensiunea Ileana (☏0262-372 137, 0745-491 756; sapantaileana@yahoo.com; d 80 lei) is old-school Maramureş. Ileana, the eponymous host, is lovely and has her own weaving workshop that she can show you. Opposite the cemetery.

trees, rioting flowers and talkative chickens, you may forget you're in town. Owner Lia is charm itself and a great source of local info (handy given there's no tourist office any more). Doubles and family rooms are homely and large, with shared showers and bathrooms. There are also two dorms. Outside are tables to read at and bikes for rent.

Motel Buţi   HOTEL €
(☏0262-311 035; www.hotelbuti.ro; Str Ştefan cel Mare 6; s/d/tr 100/120/180 lei; ⊕❄@❄) Admittedly rooms may be a bit on the small side, but considering how clean it is, and the high spec of the rooms with flat-screen TVs, decent furniture and crisp linen, this is very good value. There's a bar downstairs.

✕ Eating

TOP CHOICE **Restaurant Tineretului**   ROMANIAN €
(Str Ioan Mihaly de Apşa; mains 10 lei; ⊘7am-9pm) This rustic-accented restaurant is hung with cowbells and lanterns, and makes for a magic departure from the rest of Sighet's offerings. It's also lovely and cool in high summer, and serves gyros, cold meat platters, breakfast and grilled nape of pork.

Casa Veche   ROMANIAN €€
(Str Iuliu Maniu 27; mains 14-30 lei; ⊘8am-11pm) Probably the busiest joint in town, Casa has a bubbly terrace come evening, and an elegant, high-ceilinged interior besmirched by pumping Euro-pop and a stratosphere of smoke. Succulent steaks, salads and huge pizza.

David's   ROMANIAN €€
(Str Ioan Mihaly de Apşa 1; mains 11-25 lei; ⊘7am-10pm) With lime-washed walls sporting old-fashioned prints of London and booths to soak up the very smoky atmosphere, this is

an authentic local haunt. The menu offers up fresh salads with plenty of zing, and grilled pork, chicken and lamb dishes.

ℹ Information

Banca Română (Str Ioan Mihaly de Apşa 24; ⊘9am-5pm Mon-Fri)

Post & Telephone Office (Str Ioan Mihaly de Apşa 39)

ℹ Getting There & Away

There's a small car/footbridge from Sighet to Ukraine about 2km outside the centre. To find the crossing point, from the centre of Sighet follow Str Titelescu north about 2km. The border is open 24 hours. The Ukrainian town on the other side is called Slatina and has a number of hotels.

BUS The **bus station** (Str Gării; ⊘closed Sun) is opposite the train station. There are several local buses departing daily (except Sunday) to Baia Mare (12 lei, 65km) as well as Borşa (10 lei), Budeşti (7 lei), Călineşti (7 lei) and Vişeu de Sus (10 lei). There's also service to Bârsana, Botiza, Ieud and Mara (all around 6 lei). From Borşa, there are daily maxitaxi services to Moldavia.

TRAIN Advance tickets are sold at the **Agenţia de Voiaj CFR** (☏0262-312 666; Piaţa Libertăţii 25; ⊘7am-8pm Mon-Fri). There's one daily fast train to Timişoara (93 lei, 12 hours), Bucharest (90 lei, 12 hours), Cluj-Napoca (60 lei, six hours) and Braşov (77 lei, eight hours). A sleeper train here costs 121 lei.

Valea Izei

POP 3000

The Valea Izei (Izei Valley) follows the Iza River eastwards from Sighetu Marmaţiei to Moisei. A tightly knit procession of quintessential Maramureş peasant villages nestle in the valley, all featuring the region's famed elaborately carved wooden gates and tall wooden churches.

Gradually developing tourism in the region provides visitors with the opportunity to sample traditional cuisine or try their hand at woodcarving, wool weaving and glass painting.

In mid-July Vadu Izei, together with the neighbouring villages of Botiza and Ieud, hosts the Maramuzical Festival, a lively four-day international folk-music festival.

VADU IZEI

Vadu Izei lies at the confluence of the Iza and Mara Rivers, 6km south of Sighetu Marmaţiei. Its museum is in the oldest house in the village (1750).

Casa Muntean (☎0766-755 267; www.casa-muntean.ro; Str Dumbrava 505; s/d without bathroom 40/80 lei; ⊖@☎) offers colourful rooms enlivened by richly designed rugs, wood ceilings and wall hangings. The owner, Florin, can take you on a guided tour (60 lei) to local wooden churches or to the Merry Cemetery.

Nearby, the **Pensiunea Teodora Teleptean** (☎0742-492 240; Str Dumbrava 503; r 120 lei; P) has 10 rooms in a pretty wood-carved building (there are pots and pans hanging from a tree in the front garden – signifying there is a girl available for marriage in the house!). Rooms are spacious and fragrant with antique armoires, wood-raftered ceilings, TVs and bathrooms.

BÂRSANA

From Vadu Izei, continue for 12km through Onceşti to the village of Bârsana (formerly Bîrsana), dating from 1326. In 1720 it built its first church, the interior paintings of which were created by local artists Hodor Toador and Ion Plohod.

The famous Orthodox **Bârsana Monastery** (Mănăstirea Bârsana) is a popular pilgrimage spot in Maramureş; however, the church you see today was built in the 1990s. The 11am service is a magical experience among the rolling hills and wildflowers, and every 30 June the monastery celebrates the Twelve Apostles. Check out the beautiful church, shrine, museum and shop. Eleven nuns presently reside here.

ROZAVLEA

Continue south through Strâmtura to Rozavlea. Its fine church, dedicated to archangels Michael and Gabriel, was constructed between 1717 and 1720 in another village, then erected in Rozavlea on the site of an ancient church destroyed by the Tatars. The flower-strewn graveyard is a testament to the area's anarchic splendour.

BOTIZA

From Rozavlea, continue south to Şieu, then take the turn-off right for the sleepy village of Botiza, one of the prettiest in all of Maramureş and site of the some of the region's best homestays.

Botiza's old church, built in 1694, is overshadowed by the giant new church, constructed in 1974 to serve devout Orthodox families.

The 9am Sunday service is the major event of the week in Botiza. The *entire* village flocks to the church to partake in the religious activities, which continue well into the afternoon.

George Iurca (☎0722-942 140, 0262-334 110; botizavr@sintec.ro; Botiza 742; r per person 90 lei; @☎) is a friendly guide with a licence to conduct tours throughout Romania. He rents out clean, comfortable rooms as well as mountain bikes (25 lei per day) and vehicles with a driver/guide (300 lei per day for a group). You'll find his house four doors down from the new church.

Victoria Berbecaru (☎0262-334 107; r incl breakfast 80 lei) offers four rooms in her own home or, better yet, in the 19th-century wooden house just opposite. Downstairs there's a shop selling beautifully woven rugs.

IEUD

Packed with wooden houses and pensioners in traditional garb, the village of Ieud (6km off the road south from Şieu) has two beautiful churches, including what some consider to be the region's oldest wooden church.

Ieud was first documented in the 14th century, but evidence suggests the village was inhabited as early as the 11th century by Balc, Dragoş Vodă's grandson and later Prince of Moldavia.

Sometime in the 14th century, the town's fabulous Orthodox Church on the Hill (Biserica de Lemn din Deal) was built on castle ruins (though much of the current structure may date back only to the 17th century). Under its rooftop, the 'Ieud Codex' from 1391 was found, a document which is considered to be the oldest writing in Romanian language (today it is kept in the archives of the Romanian Academy in Bucharest).

Ieud's other church (Biserica de Lemn din Şes), today Greco-Catholic in denomination, was built in 1718. At the southern end of the village, it's unique to the region as it has no porch, and houses one of the largest collections of icons on glass found in Maramureş.

Cross the bridge to the modest **Eth-nographic Museum** (adult/child 5/3 lei; ☺8am-noon & 1pm-8pm Mon-Sun) to see an old lady spinning thread on a wheel like Rumplestiltskin.

Vasile Chindris (☎0262-336 197, 0743-811 077; leud 201; r per person 90 lei; ℗) offers rooms that are clean and homey, with shared bathrooms; meals cost 28 lei. The husband-and-wife team can drive you around.

MOISEI

About 9km southeast of the town of Vişeu de Sus, at the foot of the Rodna Massif (mountains), Moisei gained fame in 1944 when retreating Hungarian troops gunned down 31 people before setting fire to the entire village.

Only one house in Moisei survived the blaze – the one in which the prisoners were shot. Today, it houses a small **museum** (Expoziţia Documentar – Istorică Martirii de la Moisei 14 Octombrie 1944; admission 2 lei; ☺9.30am-4.30pm Tue-Sun), in tribute to those who died. Opposite the museum is a monument to the victims – 10 columns are decorated with a traditional carnival mask and two are decorated with human faces based on the features of the two survivors.

If the museum is locked, knock at the house next door and ask for the key.

Each year, on 15 August, the Feast of the Assumption shuts down the area. Villagers from around the county, walking in groups for two days or more, carry crosses and holy pictures to Moisei's monastery.

MOLDAVIA

Despite being among Romania's poorer regions, Moldavia is historically and culturally rich. Prince Ştefan cel Mare (r 1457–1504) defeated the Turks here, and built fortified painted monasteries which astonish with their kaleidoscopic ranges of colour and rich detail. Iaşi, a vibrant city dotted with impressive architecture, parks and buzzing bars, has been Moldavia's capital for five centuries.

Iaşi

POP 263,400

Exuberant, cultured Iaşi (pronounced 'yash') clearly enjoys being one of the country's biggest cities. Once dubbed the 'city of the hundred churches', Iaşi is indeed bursting with centuries of architectural creations. Yet besides the monasteries, theatres and other historic buildings, this eclectic place has botanical parks, big squares and (for better or for worse) communist-era concrete and gleaming modern shopping malls.

Sights

Union Museum   MUSEUM
(Muzeul Unirii; ☎0232-314 614; Str Alexandru Lăpuşneanu 14; adult/student 4/2 lei; ☺10am-5pm Tue-Sun) This small, neoclassical palace was Alexandru Cuza's home for three years (1859–62), and later housed King Ferdinand during his WWI retreat from Bucharest. It displays the Cuza family's opulent furniture, pictures and personal effects.

**Moldavian Metropolitan
Cathedral**   CHURCH
(Mitropolia Moldovei; B-dul Ştefan cel Mare) Southeast of Piaţa Unirii, B-dul Ştefan cel Mare leads to this cavernous cathedral (1833–39), designed by architect Alexandru Orascu and decorated by painter Gheorghe Tattarescu.

Church of the Three Hierarchs   CHURCH
(Biserica Sfinţilor Trei Ierarhi; B-dul Ştefan cel Mare; ☺9.30am-noon & 1-5.30pm) Built by Prince Vasile Lupu between 1637 and 1639, and restored between 1882 and 1904, this is one of Iaşi's most beautiful churches. Its exterior stone pattern-work is exquisite, and reveals Turkish, Georgian and Armenian influences.

Palace of Culture   MUSEUM
(Palatul Culturii; B-dul Ştefan cel Mare) At B-dul Ştefan cel Mare's southern end stands the giant neo-Gothic Palace of Culture, built between 1906 and 1925 over Prince Alexandru cel Bun's ruined 15th-century princely court. At time of research, renovations were ongoing but set to conclude by 2014.

FREE **Golia Monastery**   MONASTERY
(Str Cuza Voda 51) This fortified late-Renaissance-style monastery is guarded by thick walls and the 30m Golia tower. The 17th-century church is notable for its vibrant Byzantine frescos and intricately carved doorways, and features wall bastions from 1667.

Copou Park   PARK
(Parcol Copou; B-dul Carol I) Designed between 1834 and 1848 under Prince Mihail Sturza, this 10-hectare park is allegedly where poet Mihai Eminescu (1850–89) wrote beneath a

linden tree. It still stands, behind the 13m-high Obelisk of Lions, supposedly modern Romania's oldest monument. A bronze **bust of Eminescu** sits in front.

🛏 Sleeping

Pensiune Fiesta & Lavric   PENSION €
(☎0232-229 961; fiestalavric@yahoo.com; Str Horia 8; s/d 150/180 lei; ❄️🛜) Among Iași's better budget options, this popular place has six large and comfortable rooms, plus an on-site restaurant.

TOP CHOICE **Hotel Unirea**   HOTEL €€€
(☎0232-205 006; www.hotelunirea.ro; Piața Unirii 5; s/d/ste 225/295/395 lei; 🅿️❄️❄️🛜🏊) Although several contenders vie for Iași's best hotel around the main square, an indoor pool, spa centre and 13th-floor Panoramic Restaurant (with its expansive views) set the Unirea apart. Rooms are bright and businessy, with comfortable beds and all amenities.

Grand Hotel Traian   HOTEL €€€
(☎0232-266 666; www.grandhoteltraian.ro; Piața Unirii 1; s/d 315/360 lei; 🅿️❄️🛜) Right in the centre, the elegant Traian was designed by Gustave Eiffel himself. The rooms are appropriately outfitted with billowing curtains, high ceilings and big baths, and a general old-world ambience pervades.

Hotel Eden   HOTEL €€
(☎0332-144 486; www.hotels-eden.ro; Str S Sava 1; s/d 160/170 lei; ❄️🛜) An excellent new three-star option, the Eden is central and has a restaurant. The fresh-smelling rooms are spacious, and some have balconies. Breakfast's 15 lei extra.

🍴 Eating & Drinking

TOP CHOICE **La Castel**   INTERNATIONAL €€
(☎0232-225 225; www.lacastel.com; Str Aleea M Sadoveanu 54, Copou; mains 17-36 lei; 🛝) La Castel sprawls across breezy lawns on the Copou road (a 15-minute drive or cab ride from town). The varied cuisine, incorporating French and Bavarian flourishes, is complemented by a strong wine list and sinful desserts.

La Rustica   ITALIAN €€
(☎0735-522 405; www.larustica.ro; Str Anastasie Panu 30; mains 17-30 lei; ⏱8am-11pm) Run by an Italian chef and his Romanian wife, this classy subterranean restaurant is Iași's best Italian eatery. It's up Anastasie Panu, under a shopping and apartment complex.

Casa Lavric   ROMANIAN €€
(☎0232-229 960; Str Sf Atanasie 21; mains 10-40 lei) Good for Romanian cuisine, and decorated with classic musical instruments. Reserve ahead on weekends.

TOP CHOICE **Cafeneaua Acaju**   BAR
(☎0733-027 588; Str S Sava 15; ⏱9am-2am) Easy to miss and hard to forget, this hip but unpretentious bar is barely signposted on a street near the Armenian Church. Regulars include local artists, musicians and others of all ages.

La Baza   BAR
(B-dul Ștefan cel Mare, Cub; ⏱noon-3am) This festive indie fave has outlandish aquarium-green walls, saffron-curtain ceilings and what seem to be surrealist versions of Romanian monastic murals. But the beer is cheap.

Terasa Corso   PUB
(www.corsoterasa.ro; Str Alexandru Lăpușneanu 11; mains 15-30 lei; ⏱9am-2am; 🛜) Well-trimmed hedges and gardens adorn the centre of this expansive, amphitheatre-shaped pub with overlapping rows of long tables. It's good for coffee by day and drinks by night.

⭐ Entertainment

Vasile Alecsandri National Theatre   THEATRE, OPERA
(www.teatrulnationaliasi.ro; Str Agatha Bârsescu 18) Both the national theatre and opera are located in the same impressive neobaroque building. For advance bookings, go to the **Agenția de Teatrala** (B-dul Ștefan cel Mare 8; ⏱10am-5pm Mon-Sat). Tickets cost 18 to 22 lei, with 50% student discounts.

Filarmonica   CLASSICAL MUSIC
(www.filarmonicais.ro; Str Cuza Vodă 29; tickets 20 lei; ⏱box office 10am-1pm & 5-7pm Mon-Fri) The Iași State Philharmonic Orchestra's home hall is excellent for classical music. Tickets start at 20 lei, with 50% student discounts.

Underground   CLUB
(B-dul Ștefan cel Mare, Cub; DJ nights admission 15 lei; ⏱8pm-3am) Slightly posher than neighbouring student bars, Underground does good live alternative music and DJ dance parties.

Dublin   CLUB
(☎0729-802 765; www.dublinpub.ro; Str Vasile Conta 30; ⏱noon-4am) A cross between a bar and a club, the Dublin is known for its weekend disco parties.

Iaşi

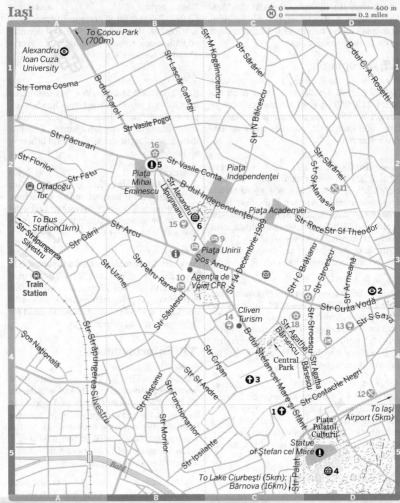

ROMANIA IAŞI

ⓘ Information

Cliven Turism (☎0232-258 326; www.cliven.
ro; B-dul Ştefan cel Mare 8-12; ⊙9am-6pm
Mon-Fri, to 2pm Sat)

Forte Cafe (B-dul Independenţei 27; per hr 4
lei; ⊙24hr)

Post Office (Str Cuza Vodă 10; ⊙9am-6pm
Mon-Fri, to 1pm Sat)

Sfântu Spiridon University Hospital (☎ext
193 0232-240 822; B-dul Independenţei 1)

Tourist Information Centre (☎0232-261 990;
www.turism-iasi.ro; Piaţa Unirii 12; ⊙9am-6pm
Mon-Fri, to 1pm Sat)

ⓘ Getting There & Around

BUS The **bus station** (Str Moara de Foc 15a) has
innumerable daily buses or maxitaxis, including for Suceava (30 lei, two hours, 12 daily),
Cluj-Napoca (70 lei, nine hours, one daily) and
Chişinău (30 lei, five hours, nine daily). Six daily
buses serve Bucharest (60 lei).

Buy tickets for the daily İstanbul bus (170 lei,
16 hours), departing from Billa, at **Ortadoğu
Tur** (☎0232-257 000; Str Bacinschi) across the
street.

TRAIN Most trains use the Gara Centrală **train
station** (Str Garii), also called Gara Mare and
Gara du Nord. The **Agenţia de Voiaj CFR** (Piaţa

Iaşi

Unirii 10; 8am-8pm Mon-Fri, 9am-12.30pm Sat) sells advance tickets. A *bagaje de mana* (left-luggage office) is by the car park (6/8 lei for hand bag/large bag per 24 hours).

Six daily trains serve Bucharest (86 to 110 lei, seven hours), nine go to Suceava (21 lei to 39 lei, 2¾ hours), one to Braşov (86 lei, 8½ hours) and four to Cluj-Napoca (86 lei, nine hours) and on to Timişoara (78 lei, 16 hours) via Oradea.

For Chişinău (55 lei, six hours), one train leaves at 3.13am on Thursdays, Fridays and Saturdays only, crossing at Ungheni.

Suceava

POP 86,300

Suceava, the capital of Moldavia from 1388 to 1565, was a thriving commercial centre on the Lviv–İstanbul trading route. Today it's the seat of Suceava county with a handful of interesting sights, and makes for a decent gateway for exploring the painted churches of Bucovina.

Sights

The unsightly **Casa de Cultură** (House of Culture) is at the western end of Piaţa 22 Decembrie, the city's main square. To the north is **St Dumitru's Church** (Biserica Sf Dumitru; Str Curtea Domnească) built by Petru Rareş in 1535.

Bucovina History Museum   MUSEUM
(Muzeul Naţional al Bucovinei; 0230-516 439; Str Ştefan cel Mare 33; adult/child 7/2 lei; 10am-6pm Tue-Sun) Displays here range from the Bronze Age to the present but highlight Moldavia's famous rulers, particularly Ştefan cel Mare. While the numismatics, medieval armour and tools are interesting, Ştefan's 'Hall of Thrones' court recreation seems rather contrived.

Monastery of St John the New   MONASTERY
(Mănăstirea Sfântu Ioan cel Nou; Str Ioan Voda Viteazul 2) This monastery off Str Mitropoliei (built 1514 to 1554) was an important pilgrimage destination: it houses, in a decorated silver casket, the relics of Saint John the New, which ruler Alexandru cel Bun had brought to Moldavia in 1415. The badly faded exterior paintings exemplify Bucovina style.

City of Residence Citadel   FORTRESS
(Cetatea de Scaun; adult/child 5/2 lei, photography 10 lei; 9am-6pm) Starting at McDonald's, follow the adjacent footpath along the stream, cross the little bridge and scale the 241 steps up to the equestrian statue of **Ştefan cel Mare** (1966). Follow the footpath to the left of the statue up to the City of Residence Citadel (p435), a fortress that held off Mehmed II, conqueror of Constantinople (İstanbul), in 1476. It's much more attractive from a distance than from the inside.

Ethnographic Museum   MUSEUM
(0230-516 439; Str Ciprian Porumbescu 5; adult/child 6/3 lei; 9am-5pm Tue-Sun) West of Piaţa 22 Decembrie, Hanul Domnesc is an 18th-century guesthouse housing the Ethnographic Museum. It displays Moldavian folk costumes and household items.

Sleeping

TOP CHOICE **Hotel Sonnenhof**   HOTEL €€
(0230-220 033; www.hotelsonnenhof.ro; B-dul Sofia Vicoveanca 68 ; s/d from 220/265 lei;) This fancy four-star place is good for drivers and those on a generous budget. It's 3km

ROMANIA SUCEAVA

from town on the Targu Neamt road (10 lei by taxi), but has excellent rooms loaded with amenities and is decorated in soothing tones (though the huge paintings above each bed are rather gauche).

Hotel Gloria HOTEL €
(☎0230-521 209; www.hotelgloria.ro; Str Vasile Bumbac 4-8; s/d/ste incl breakfast from 85/140/260 lei; ❋@) If Suceava is your base for local excursions, this three-star throwback is a good and central budget choice. It has fine, simple rooms with super-powered hot showers and cable internet. Although English is hit-or-miss, staff are unfailingly polite.

Union Apartment APARTMENT €
(☎0741-477 047; www.union-apartments.ro; B-dul Ana Ipatescu 7; apt from 135-410 lei; ❋☎) Run by local tour guide extraordinaire Gigi Traciu, this central apartment sleeping up to seven people provides an excellent budget option and flexibility for self-caterers. Free airport pick-up is offered for stays of over three days.

✖ Eating & Drinking

TOP
CHOICE **Latino** ITALIAN €€
(Str Curtea Domnească 9; mains 12-45 lei, pizza 18-30 lei) Suceava's best Italian restaurant, this long-standing favourite has subdued class and prompt service. There are numerous pizzas, and the varied pasta starters (15 lei to 30 lei) are all excellent.

Restaurant Mozaik INTERNATIONAL €€€
(B-dul Sofia Vicoveanca 68 , Hotel Sonnenhof; mains 25-45 lei) This upscale, gardened restaurant in the Hotel Sonnenhoff tries a bit too hard with its Romanian, French, Norwegian, German, Greek and Italian specialities, but, hey, the cooks were trained by a Michelin-starred French chef. Among the pricier dishes is beef in a doughy bread crust with mushrooms, pepper and cognac sauce.

Salzburg Cafe CAFE
(Str Ştefan cel Mare 28; ☺8am-10pm) This relaxing central cafe has a slightly Central European feel, and plays pop-rock and even live piano nights on Wednesdays. It's good for coffees, with a small desserts selection.

Oscar Wilde PUB
(Str Ştefan cel Mare 26; ☺8am-3am) Suceava's nearest thing to an Irish pub (look for the giant black Guinness canopies), Oscar Wilde's a big wood-floored bar with outdoor seating too.

❶ Information

There are several ATMs on Piaţa 22 Decembrie and along Str Ştefan cel Mare. Many restaurants, bars and cafes have free wi-fi.

AXA Travel (Str Sebastian Traciu; ☎0741-477 047; www.axatravel.ro) AXA is run by Sebastian 'Gigi' Traciu, an experienced local guide. One-day and multiday tours visit the Bucovina painted monasteries, Targu Neamt, Bicaz Gorge, Lacu Roşu and Maramureş. Rates depend on the number of participants.

Infoturism (☎0230-551 241; www.turism-suceava.ro; cnr B-dul Ana Ipătescu & Str Mitropoliei 4; ☺8am-4pm Mon-Fri) Provides maps and information on local sites. It's located beside the park, between Str Ştefan Cel Mare and Bdul Ana Ipatescu.

Post Office (Str Dimitrie Onciul)

❶ Getting There & Away

BUS The central **bus station** (☎0230-524 340) is on Str Armenească. Bus and maxitaxi services include 19 daily to Gura Humorului (9 lei, one hour) and four to Bucharest (70 lei, eight hours). Maxitaxis to Iaşi (30 lei, 2½ hours, 12 daily) leave from a parking lot behind the bus station, dubbed 'Autogara Intertrans'.

One daily bus theoretically serves Chernivtsi in Ukraine (35 lei, three hours), though if it doesn't have enough passengers, the bus may not even come from Chernivtsi.

One daily bus at 6.30am serves Chişinău (60 lei, seven to eight hours).

TRAIN Suceava's two train stations, Gara Suceava and Gara Nord, are both roughly 5km north of centre. The **Agenţia de Voiaj CFR** (Str Nicolae Bălcescu 8; ☺7.30am-8.30pm Mon-Fri) sells advance tickets. Most trains originate or terminate at Gara Suceava.

Train services include 10 to Gura Humorului (10 lei to 17 lei, 70 minutes), plus nine to Iaşi (39 lei, two hours), three to Timişoara (115 lei, 14 hours), four to Cluj-Napoca (71 lei, seven hours), one to Braşov (86 lei, 8½ hours) and six to Bucharest (86 lei to 107 lei, seven hours).

Southern Bucovina

Moldavian Prince Ştefan cel Mare and his successor Petru Rares endowed southern Bucovina with several spectacular monasteries, dating back to the 15th century. The best of these fortified structures, painted inside and out with exquisitely detailed frescos, are also Unesco World Heritage sites. Outside the monasteries, Bucovina is dotted with slant-roofed village houses and lovely groves of beech trees. As in

Southern Bucovina

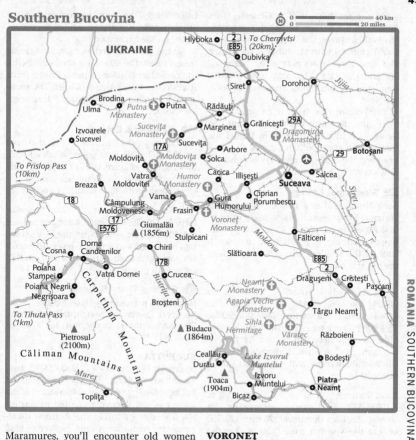

Maramureş, you'll encounter old women in traditional dress, fearless children riding bareback on horses and enterprising locals scouring the forest for truly massive mushrooms.

HUMOR

Of all the Bucovina monasteries, **Humor Monastery** (Mănăstirea Humorului; adult/student 5/2 lei; ☺8am-7pm summer, to 4pm winter) has the most impressive interior frescos.

On the southern exterior wall of the 1530 church, you can see the life of the Virgin Mary (on left), and St Nicholas and the parable of the prodigal son (on right). On the porch is the *Last Judgment* and, in the first chamber inside the church, scenes of martyrdom.

ⓘ Getting There & Away

Ten daily Suceava–Gura Humorului trains operate (10 lei to 17 lei, 50 minutes). Regular maxitaxis go the final 6km to the monastery,

VORONEŢ

Built in just three months and three weeks by Ştefan cel Mare following a key 1488 victory over the Turks, **Voroneţ Monastery** (adult/child 5/2 lei; ☺8am-7pm summer, to 4pm winter) is the only one to have a specific colour associated with it worldwide. 'Voroneţ Blue', a vibrant cerulean colour created from lapis lazuli and other ingredients, is prominent in its frescos. A 2011 restoration of frescos in the church's entryway revealed the incredible quality of these paintings even more clearly. Today Voroneţ is a nunnery.

The most famous Voroneţ painting, the *Last Judgment*, covers the western exterior wall. Angels at the top roll up the zodiac signs, indicating the end of time, while humanity is brought to judgment in the middle. On the left, St Paul escorts the believers, while a stern Moses takes the nonbelievers on the right.

On the northern wall is Genesis, from Adam and Eve to Cain and Abel. The southern wall features the Tree of Jesse (King David's father) with the biblical genealogy. The first three rows portray St Nicholas' life and miracles. The next two rows recount the martyrdom of Suceava's St John the New.

The bottom row, from left to right, features the monastery's patron saint, St George, fighting the dragon; St Daniel the Hermit with Metropolitan Grigorie; a Deisis icon; and the 1402 procession of St John the New's relics into Suceava.

🛏 Sleeping & Eating

Gura Humorului is a perfect base to visit Voroneţ. Every second house takes in tourists; expect to pay 50 to 75 lei per person. Rough camping is possible on the south bank of the Moldova River, 500m south of the bus station.

TOP CHOICE Hilde's Residence   GUESTHOUSE €€
(☑0744-386 698; www.lucy.ro; Str Şipotului 2, Gura Humorului; s/d/ste from 180/200/290 lei; P❄❀❁❂) The long-established Hilde's has nine uniquely designed rooms; it's just off the main road in Gura Humorului. The onsite Romanian restaurant is good too. Breakfast is 24 lei.

Casa Doamnei   GUESTHOUSE €€
(☑0735-530 753; www.casa-doamnei.ro; Str Voroneţ 255, Gura Humorului; s/d from 120/150 lei) On the Voroneţ road (500m after the train tracks, 3.5km before the monastery), this guesthouse has stylish wood furniture, balconies and nice bathrooms. Breakfast is 20 lei.

❶ Getting There & Away

Several buses and trains run daily from Suceava to Gura Humorului. A lovely option is to walk the 4km along a narrow village road to Voroneţ. The route is clearly marked and it's impossible to get lost.

MOLDOVIŢA

Moldoviţa Monastery (adult/student 5/2 lei; ⊘8am-7pm summer, to 4pm winter), built in 1532, occupies a fortified quadrangular enclosure with tower, gates and flowery lawns. The central painted church has been partly restored, and features impressive frescos from 1537. The southern exterior wall depicts the Siege of Constantinople in AD 626, under a combined Persian–Avar attack.

Interestingly, the besiegers are depicted in Turkish dress, keeping parishioners concentrated on the current enemy.

On the church's porch is *a Last Judgment* fresco. Inside the sanctuary, on a wall facing the carved iconostasis, a pious Prince Petru Rareş offers the church to Christ. The monastery's small museum displays Rareş' original throne.

🛏 Sleeping & Eating

Letitia Orsvischi Pension   GUESTHOUSE €€
(☑0745-869 529; letita_orsvischi@yahoo.fr; Str Gării 20; s/d half board 130/210 lei; ❄❁❂) This large guesthouse in Vama has simple but clean rooms with shared bathrooms.

Pensiunea Crizantema   PENSION €€
(☑0230-336 116; www.vilacrizantema.ro; s/d half board 140/180 lei; ❀❂) Near the monastery, this rustic eight-room place has cute, smallish rooms (though bathrooms are simple), some with monastery views.

❶ Getting There & Away

Moldoviţa is not easy to get to with public transport. Take one of the eight daily trains from Suceava to Vama (15 lei, one hour) and hitchhike the final 15km.

SUCEVIŢA

Suceviţa Monastery (☑0230 417-110; www.manastireasucevita.ro; Suceviţa; adult/student 5/2 lei; ⊘8am-7pm summer, to 4pm winter) is the largest of the Bucovina painted monasteries. The church inside the fortified quadrangular enclosure (built between 1582 and 1601) is almost completely covered in frescos. As you enter, you first see the *Ladder of Virtues* fresco covering most of the northern exterior wall, which depicts the 30 steps to paradise. On the southern exterior wall is Jesse's genealogical tree symbolising the continuity of the Old and New Testaments. The tree grows from the reclining figure of Jesse, who is flanked by a row of ancient Greek philosophers. To the left is the Virgin, with angels holding a red veil over her head. Mysteriously, the western wall remains blank. Legend has it that the artist fell off his scaffolding and died, leaving artists of the time too scared to follow in his footsteps.

🛏 Sleeping & Eating

It's worth spending a night here and doing a little hiking in the surrounding hills. The road from Marginea to Suceviţa is littered with *cazare* (room for rent) signs.

Pensiunea Emilia GUESTHOUSE €

(☎0743-117 827; Str Bercheza 173; r per person 80 lei) The most appealing local *pensiune* (pension), Emilia's has charming rooms and is 500m up the road opposite the monastery. Breakfast is 10 lei.

Ieremia Movilă GUESTHOUSE €

(☎0230-417 501; www.ieremiamovila.ro; Str Sucevita 459 ; r 110 lei; P⊖❀ 🕸 🛜) This modern place has nice rooms with great bathrooms, balconies and wi-fi. Some rooms have monastery views. Good on-site restaurant.

ⓘ Getting There & Away

Take one of the hourly maxitaxis from Suceava to Rădăuţi (8 lei, 45 minutes), then switch to one of the southbound maxitaxis leaving hourly from an unmarked intersection about 300m east (towards Piaţa Unirii) from the bus station. Ask the driver to stop at Suceviţa.

DANUBE DELTA & BLACK SEA COAST

Danube Delta

After passing through several countries and absorbing countless lesser waterways, the Danube empties into the Black Sea just south of the Ukrainian border. The Danube Delta (Delta Dunării), included on Unesco's World Heritage list, is one of Romania's leading tourist attractions.

At the inland port of Tulcea, the river splits into three separate channels: the Chilia, Sulina and Sfântu Gheorghe arms, creating a constantly evolving 4187-sq-km wetland of marshes, floating reed islets and sandbars, providing sanctuary for 300 species of birds and 160 species of fish. Reed marshes cover 156,300 hectares, constituting one of the largest single expanses of reed beds in the world.

The delta is a haven for wildlife lovers, birdwatchers, anglers and anyone wanting to get away from it all for a few days. There are beautiful, secluded beaches at both Sulina and Sfântu Gheorghe, and the fish and seafood, particularly the fish soup, is the best in Romania

Much of the the delta is under the protection of the administration of the Danube Delta Biosphere Reserve Authority (DDBRA), headquartered in Tulcea, with branch offices throughout the delta, including in Sulina and Sfântu Gheorghe. There are around 20 strictly

Black Sea Coast

Danube Delta

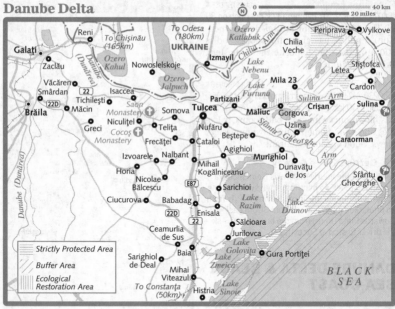

protected areas covering about 50,000 hectares that are off-limits to tourists, including the 500-year-old Leţea Forest and Europe's largest pelican colony. Visitation is limited in other areas. Note that visitors to the reserve are required to purchase an entry permit. Camping in the reserve is only allowed in official camping grounds.

ⓘ Getting Around

There is no rail service in the delta and few paved roads, meaning the primary mode of transport is by ferry. Regularly scheduled ferries, both traditional 'slow' ferries and faster (and more expensive) hydrofoils, leave from Tulcea's main port daily and access all major points in the delta. There are two main ferry operators and the ferry schedule can be bewildering on first glance. The helpful staff at the tourism information centre in Tulcea can help piece together a journey depending on your time and budget.

Ferries can get crowded in summer, so try to arrive at least an hour prior to departure to secure yourself a seat. Note that though the ferries run year-round, service is less reliable in winter.

PUBLIC FERRIES & HYDROFOILS

Two companies offer passenger-ferry service throughout the delta. State-run **Navrom** (☎0240-511 553; www.navromdelta.ro; Str Portului 26; ☺ticket office 11.30am-1.30pm)

operates both slower, traditional ferries (referred to as 'classic ships' on timetables) as well as faster hyrdrofoils (catamarans). A second company, **Nave Rapide** (☎0726-774 074, 0742-544 068; www.naverapide.ro), offers only hydrofoils.

For Navrom ferries, in Tulcea, buy tickets on the day of departure at the Navrom passenger ferry terminal (p442) daily from 11.30am to 1.30pm. Outside of Tulcea, buy tickets on departure at the entrance to the boat.

For Nave Rapide ferries, book at least a day in advance over the phone or turn to the tourism information centre for assistance

See p442 for details of ferries and hydrofoils from Tulcea.

TULCEA
POP 92,400

The Danube port of Tulcea (tool-*cha*) is the largest city in the delta and the main entry point for accessing the region. It has good bus and minibus connections to the rest of the country, and is home to the main passenger ferries. If you've only got a short amount of time (one to three days), base yourself here and explore the delta via boating day trips. If you have more time, you'll likely only transit through Tulcea on your way to deeper destinations like Sulina and Sfântu Gheorghe.

◉ Sights

Central Eco-Tourism Museum of the Danube Delta MUSEUM, AQUARIUM
(Centrul Muzeal Ecoturistic Delta Dunării; ✆0240-515 866; www.icemtl.ro; Str 14 Noiembrie 1; adult/student 15/5 lei; ⊙10am-6pm Tue-Sun; ⓐ) This combined museum and aquarium is a good primer on the delta's varied flora and fauna. There are stuffed animals on the main floor and a small but fascinating aquarium on the lower level, with ample signage in English.

Folk Art & Ethnographic Museum
MUSEUM
(✆0240-516 204; Str 9 Mai 4; adult/student 6/3 lei; ⊙10am-6pm Tue-Sun) This modest museum displays the ethnic and cultural diversity of the delta region over the centuries, and the interaction of Romanians with Turks, Russians, Ukrainians and Bulgarians.

Independence Monument
MONUMENT
As you stroll along the river you'll see the Independence Monument (1904) on Citadel Hill at the far eastern end of town. You can reach this by following Str Gloriei from behind the Egreta Hotel to its end.

History & Archaeology Museum
MUSEUM
(✆0240-513 626; Str Gloriei; admission 5 lei; ⊙10am-6pm Tue-Sun) Well worth visiting, this museum is presented on two levels, with the upper level given over to the extensive Roman findings and the lower level displaying even more fascinating artefacts of pre-Roman civilisations going back some 6000 years. The museum is situated at the Independence Monument.

🏃 Activities

Tulcea's main activities are boating, fishing and birdwatching. The port is lined with private boat operators offering a variety of excursions on slow boats, speedboats and pontoon boats; these can be tailored to accommodate special pursuits. Excursions are generally priced per person, assuming a minimum number. If the minimum is not reached, prices go higher.

Safca
TOUR
(✆0744-143 336; www.egretamica.ro) This small father-and-son company offers a variety of boat excursions for individuals or groups up to around eight persons. It offers a popular all-day 'hyper' trip to Sulina, including a visit to the beach, for 250 lei per person.

Ibis Tours
TRAVEL AGENCY
(✆0722-381 398, 0240-512 787; www.ibis-tours.ro; Str Dimitrie Sturza 6; ⊙9am-6pm Mon-Sat) Arranges wildlife and birdwatching tours in the delta and Dobrogea, led by professional ornithologists.

🛌 Sleeping

No camping is allowed within Tulcea's city limits. However, there are many areas where wild camping is permitted on the banks of the canal within a few kilometres of the city; ask at one of the tourist information offices for details.

Hotel Select HOTEL €€
(✆0240-506 180; www.calypsosrl.ro; Str Păcii 6; s/d 140/170 lei; P⊖✳@🛜) Though we normally shy away from these boxy high-rises, this is our favourite hotel in Tulcea. The rooms are plain but good value, with big and comfortable beds and light-blocking blinds on the windows. The restaurant is arguably the best in town.

Hotel Delta
HOTEL €€
(✆0240-514 720; www.deltahotelro.com; Str Isaccei 2; s/d 3-star 220/280 lei, 4-star 280/360 lei; ⊖✳🛜🏊) This landmark hotel towards the eastern end of the port offers both three- and four-star accommodation in adjoining separate buildings. The three-star rooms, with air-con and balcony views, are better value.

Insula Complex
HOTEL €
(✆0240-530 908; Lake Ciuperca; s/d 80/100 lei; 🛜) Minutes from the bus station on Lake Ciuperca, this two-star option has an on-site restaurant and large rooms. Turn right out of the train station and cross the small bridge to the island.

DELTA PERMITS

All visitors to the delta, including those on hiking or boating excursions from Tulcea, Sulina or Sfântu Gheorghe, are required to purchase an entry permit. Permits are available for one day (5 lei), one week (15 lei) or one year (30 lei) from Danube Delta Biosphere Reserve Authority offices in Tulcea (p442), Sulina (p443) or Sfântu Gheorghe (p443). Boats are subject to spot inspections and if you're caught without a permit you could be fined.

ROMANIA DANUBE DELTA

FERRIES & HYDROFOILS FROM TULCEA

DESTINATION	COMPANY	TYPE	PRICE (LEI)	DURATION (HR)	FREQUENCY
Sfântu Gheorghe (via Mahmudia)	Navrom	slow ferry	35	5-6	1.30pm Mon, Fri (return 7am Tue, Fri)
Sfântu Gheorghe (via Mahmudia)	Navrom	hydrofoil	46	3	1.30pm Wed, Thu (return 7am Thu, Fri)
Sfântu Gheorghe (via Mahmudia)	Nave Rapide	hydrofoil	60	1½	1.30pm (return 6.45am)
Sulina (via Crişan)	Navrom	slow ferry	34	4-5	1.30pm Mon, Wed, Fri (return 7am, Tue, Thu, Sun)
Sulina (via Crişan)	Navrom	hydrofoil	42	2-3	1.30pm Tue, Thu, Sat (return 7am Mon, Wed, Fri)
Sulina (via Crişan)	Nave Rapide	hydrofoil	60	1½	10am, 1pm (return 6.45am, noon)

✗ Eating & Drinking

Restaurant Select   ROMANIAN €€
(www.calypsosrl.ro; Str Păcii 6; mains 15-30 lei; ☏)
The multilingual, varied menu offers fresh
fish, pizza and the local speciality, *tochitu-
ra dobrogeana* (pan-fried meat with spicy
sauce).

Trident Pizzeria   PIZZA €
(Str Babadag; mains 13-20 lei; ☏) Excellent spot
for good thin-crust pizza and fast pasta.

Istru   PUB
(☏0740-075 330; Str Gării 12; ☺10am-midnight;
☏) This is the best watering hole in the immediate port area, with great coffee drinks
by day and Guinness and Skol wheat beer
during the evening. Draws a mostly local
student and arty (for Tulcea) crowd.

❶ Information

The central area is filled with ATMs, pharmacies,
and lots of shops and stores.

Danube Delta Biosphere Reserve Authority
(☏0240-518 945; www.ddbra.ro; Str Portului
34a; permits per day 5 lei; ☺8am-4pm Mon-
Fri) This office is run by the national group
charged with managing the delta. It's a good
source of information on what to see and do,
and publishes and distributes the helpful pamphlet *Guide of the Touristic Routes*, which lays
out 19 aquatic routes. Sells visitor permits.

Tourism Information Centre (☏0240-519
130; www.primariatulcea.ro; Str Gării 26;
☺8am-7pm Mon-Fri, to noon Sat May-Sep) The
helpful staff here can help sort through the
confusing ferry schedules as well as advise on
various travel agencies, hotels and restaurants.
It's hidden slightly back from the river promenade, halfway between the main port administration and the Hotel Delta.

❶ Getting There & Away

The **bus station** (☏0240-513 304; Str Portului
1) adjoins the **main ferry terminal** (Str Portului;
☺11.30am-1.30pm). As many as 10 buses and
maxitaxis head daily to Bucharest (55 lei, five
hours); there are two daily buses to Iaşi (65 lei,
four hours). Maxitaxis to Constanţa (30 lei, two
hours) leave every half-hour from 5.30am to
8pm.

SULINA

The sleepy fishing port of Sulina is Romania's easternmost point and the highlight
of any journey along the Danube's central
arm. There's a beautiful, tranquil (during
the day) beach here as well as a charming
canal-side promenade. It's also an excellent
base for forays deeper into the delta or onto
the Black Sea.

✗ Activities

Sulina is a quiet place. The main activities include strolling the main promenade
(Str I), soaking in the sun at **Sulina Beach**
(☺May-Oct) or hiring the services of a local
fisherman to take you around on the delta
by small **boat** (☏0744-821 365; Str I; per person
30-50 lei). You'll find the boats lines up along
Str I.

🛏 Sleeping & Eating

There are several *cazares* and pensions
here: you can accept an offer from those
who greet the boat, or ask around. Expect
to pay around 100 lei per room. Wild camping is possible on the beach, but there are

no services and two discos blast dance music into the night air in summer until 3am.

Pensiunea Ana
PENSION €

(☏0727-001 569, 0724-421 976; pensiuneana@ yahoo.com; Str IV 144; r 80 lei) This charming family-run affair has four rooms and a beautifully shaded garden. To find it, walk 200m west from the ferry port along the main promenade, bear left on Str Mihail Kogălniceanu, and walk four blocks inland.

Hotel Casa Coral
HOTEL €€

(☏0742-974 016; www.casacoralsulina.ro; Str I 195; r 150 lei; ✳🏿) This modern three-star property lacks character but is arguably the nicest hotel in Sulina centre. You'll have to book in advance in summer as it tends to fill up fast. You'll find it on the main promenade 100m west of the passenger ferry port.

Restaurant Marea Neagră
ROMANIAN €€

(☏0240-543 130; Str I 178; mains 17-30 lei) This large and popular open-air terrace offers more than a dozen fish specialities.

ℹ Information

All of Sulina's services for visitors, including a pharmacy, supermarket and ATM, lie along Str I that stretches for about 1km west of the passenger ferry port.

Danube Delta Biosphere Reserve Authority (www.ddbra.ro; Str I; ⊙8am-4pm Tue-Fri, noon-8pm Sat & Sun May-Oct) Sparsely furnished and funded information centre has basic information on the delta. Buy delta visitors' permits here. Located 20m east of the Casa Coral Hotel.

ℹ Getting There & Away

Access to Sulina is by boat only. See p442 for details of passenger ferries from Tulcea.

SFÂNTU GHEORGHE

First recorded in the mid-14th century by Visconti, a traveller from Genoa, the remote seaside village of Sfântu Gheorghe retains an ever-so-slight alternative vibe fed by the town's lovely, lonely beach and its sleepy, noncommercial core. It's also one of the best places in the delta to sample traditional cooking (including some fabulous fish soup). Each August, the village hosts what just might be the world's most remote film festival, the **Anonimul Fest** (www.festival-anonimul.ro).

🏃 Activities

The sandy beach is 3km east of the centre. Hop the tractor-pulled **transport plaja** (Tro-

carici; ☏0740-572 269; Str Principala; per person 2 lei) that departs regularly during the day from the centre of the village. Several private **boat owners** (☏0755-415 219; Portul; per person 50 lei) offer hour-long excursions into the delta or to the Black Sea for around 75 lei per person. The Delta Marina hotel organises boat trips too.

🛌 Sleeping & Eating

There are several *cazares* and pensions here: you can accept an offer from those who greet the boat, or ask around. Wild camping is possible on the beach, but it gets very windy and it's a long 3km hike in the dark. There's a handy **supermarket** (Complex Comercial, Str Principala; ⊙8am-2pm & 4-10pm Mon-Sat, 8am-1pm Sun) in the centre of the village.

Delta Marina
PENSION €€

(☏0240-546 946; www.deltamarina.ro; Str Principala (Str I); r 130 lei; ✳🏿) This modern hotel is situated on the water about 200m west of the ferry port. The popular terrace resraurant is one of the few places in town to grab a sit-down meal (mains 17 to 20 lei).

Vila Petru & Marcela Stefanov
PENSION €

(☏0763-088 859, 0240-546 811; near Str Principala; s/d half board 120/150 lei) This family-run pension offers clean and comfortable accommodation just a few metres' walk from the town centre. Rates include half board, often a delicious fish soup followed up with more grilled fish. The street is unmarked, but the pension is three houses north (on the left-hand side) of the Complex Comercial and supermarket, just beyond Str Principala (Str I).

Bar Terasa
CAFE

(Str Principala ; ⊙7am-3am May-Sep; 🏿) When it comes to evening drinking, this centrally located open-air terrace (one door down from the BRD bank branch) is the only game in town.

ℹ Information

There's an **ATM** (☏0240-546 721; Str Principala, Complex Comercial; ⊙9am-5pm Mon-Fri) machine in the centre of the village.

Danube Delta Biosphere Reserve Authority (☏0240-518 926; www.ddbra.ro; Str Ia 39; permits per day/week 5/15 lei; ⊙7am-noon & 4-7pm Tue-Fri, 9am-1pm Sat & Sun May-Oct) Sells visitors' permits for one day or one week. The office is located on the harbour, about 50m from the entrance to the passenger ferry port.

⏱ Getting There & Away

Access to Sfântu Gheorghe is by boat only. See p442 for details on passenger ferries from Tulcea.

Constanța

POP 260,000

Constanța is Romania's largest and most important port city on the Black Sea; in summer, it's also the gateway to the country's seaside resorts. Accommodation here is cheaper than Mamaia and maxitaxis cover the journey in about 15 minutes, so it may be worthwhile basing yourself here even if you're only coming for Mamaia's beaches and discos. While the city shows obvious signs of neglect, especially around the port area, there are some very good museums, and a pretty portside walk.

⊙ Sights

National History & Archaeological Museum   MUSEUM

(Muzeul de Istorie Nationala si Arheologie Constanța; ☑0241-618 763; www.minac.ro; Piața Ovidiu 12; adult/child 11/5 lei; ⊙9am-8pm Jun-Sep, to 5pm Tue-Sun Oct-May) The stunning ground-floor exhibits of vases, jewellery and statuary from the Greek and Roman periods, lasting until about AD 500, justify the admission price, but the upper floors on more recent times and Romanian national history are poorly lit and lack signage in English.

Art Museum   MUSEUM

(Muzeul de Artă; ☑0241-617 012; B-dul Tomis 82-84; adult/child 10/5 lei; ⊙9am-7pm Mon-Fri) This airy museum in an atrium is heavy on 19th-century realism and landscapes, including those by Nicolae Grigorescu, whose pointillist and impressionist paintings anticipated more modern movements.

Naval History Museum   MUSEUM

(Muzeul Marinei Române; ☑0241-619 035; Str Traian 53; adult/child 10/5 lei; ⊙9am-5pm Wed-Sun) Fascinating if slightly confusing stroll through 2000 years of maritime history on the Black Sea. The exhibit begins in the Greco-Roman period, with some intricate models of old Roman boats, but quickly moves to the 19th and 20th centuries.

Casino   HISTORIC BUILDING

(Faleza Casino Constanța; B-dul Elisabeta 1; admission free; ⊙10am-6pm Mon-Fri) Constanța's amazing art nouveau casino, dating from 1910, was awaiting a long overdue renovation at the time of research, but the city had opened the building to visitors to peek in and see some serious splendour.

Aquarium   AQUARIUM

(Acvariu; ☑0241-611 277; ww.delfinariu.ro; B-dul Elisabeta 1, Faleza Casino Constanța; adult/child 20/10 lei; ⊙9am-8pm Tue-Sun Jun–mid-Sep, 10am-6pm Tue-Sun mid-Sep–May; ⋓) This waterfront aquarium focuses on fish native to the Black Sea, including a large selection of endangered sturgeon, as well as local freshwater species. It's directly opposite the casino.

Dolphinarium   DOLPHIN SHOW

(Delfinariu; ☑0241-481 243; www.delfinariu.ro; B-dul Mamaia 255; adult/child 50/25 lei; ⊙shows at 11am, 3pm & 7pm Mon-Fri, 10am, 1pm, 4pm & 7pm Sat & Sun) The country's first Dolphinarium has been updated and modernised. Dolphin shows are held throughout the day in the large ampitheatre.

🛏 Sleeping

Hotel Ferdinand   HOTEL €€

(☑0241-617 974; www.hotelferdinand.ro; B-dul Ferdinand 12; s/d 220/260 lei; ⓟ✹⓯) This is our favourite three-star hotel in town. Nothing fancy, just a very well run hotel in a smart, nicely restored 1930s town house. Rooms have big comfy beds and fridges.

Hotel Maria   HOTEL €€

(☑0241-611 711; www.hotelmaria-ct.ro; B-dul 1 Decembrie 1918 2d; s/d 160/200 lei; ✹⓯) This modern, spotless option, across from the park facing the train station, has lots of glass, chrome and deep blues to soothe your sun-withered nerves.

Hotel Class   HOTEL €€

(☑0241-660 766; www.hotelclass.ro; Str Răscoala din 1907 1; s/d/ste 200/220/265 lei; ⓟ✹⓯) Well-managed three-star option, with clean rooms and comfortable beds with thick mattresses. Ask for a quiet room away from busy Str Răscoala.

🍴 Eating & Drinking

TOP CHOICE / **Irish Pub**   INTERNATIONAL €€

(☑0241-550 400; www.irishpub.ro; Str Ștefan cel Mare 1; mains 20-40 lei; ⊙8am-midnight; ⓯) There are a couple of pub staples like burgers and fish and chips, but the menu has higher aspirations, with steaks and grilled fish. It's equally good for beer or coffee. Booking at meal times is essential.

Pizzico INTERNATIONAL €€
(☎0241-615 555; www.newpizzico.ro; Piaţa Ovidiu 7; mains 15-40 lei; 🛜) Pizzico has expanded its range in the past couple of years, moving beyond wood-fired pizza to excellent grilled meats, seafood and chops. The location, on Ovid Sq, makes it easy to pair lunch here with a visit to a nearby museum.

On Plonge FISH €€
(☎0241-601 905; Portul Turistic Tomis; mains 15-40 lei; ⊙9am-10pm) Brawny portside eatery with an informal, everyman vibe that specialises in fresh fish hauled in off the boat. Gets packed on summer nights and service suffers accordingly.

Friends & Co CAFE
(Str Decebal 17; ⊙10am-midnight Mon-Thu, 11am-1am Fri & Sat, 2-11pm Sun; 🛜) Relaxed student cafe with an alternative, indie vibe and a pretty, secluded terrace.

☆ Entertainment

Oleg Danovski National Theatre OPERA, BALLET
(Teatrul Naţional de Operă şi Balet 'Oleg Danovski'; ☎0241-481 460; www.opera-balet-constanta.ro; Str Mircea cel Bătrân 97; tickets 30 lei; ⊙box office 10am-5pm Mon-Fri) The city's premier venue for opera and dance. Buy tickets at the theatre box office or the central **ticket office** (www.opera-balet-constanta.ro; B-dul Tomis 97; ⊙10am-3pm Mon-Fri, to 1pm Sat).

ℹ Information

Central Post Office (B-dul Tomis 79-81; ⊙7am-8pm Mon-Fri, 8am-1pm Sat)

Constanta Country Emergency Hospital (Spitalul Clinic Judeţean de Urgenţă Constanţa; ☎0241-662 222; www.spitalulconstanta.ro; B-dul Tomis 145)

Forte-Games (☎0241-551 251; www.forte-games.ro; B-dul Tomis 235; internet per hr 6 lei; ⊙24hr)

ℹ Getting There & Away

BUS Constanţa has several bus stations, depending on which bus line is operating the route. Buses to Bucharest (55 lei, three to four hours) depart from outside the train station. Many other buses, including some travelling to the Black Sea resorts, use the large **southern bus station** (Autogara Sud; ☎0241-665 289; B-dul Ferdinand), about 200m north of the train station. Buses to Tulcea (30 lei, two to three hours) and points north often leave from other parts of town. Your best bet is to check the website www.autogari.ro to see times and departure points.

TRAIN Constanţa's **train station** (☎0241-614 960; www.cfrcalatori.ro; B-dul Ferdinand 45) is near the southern bus station, 2km from the centre. There are two fast Inter-City trains a day to Bucharest (60 lei, three to four hours). There are also daily services to Suceava, Cluj-Napoca and Timişoara. In summer, several trains a day head from Constanţa south to Mangalia (7 lei, 1½ hours), with stops at resorts in between.

Mamaia

Mamaia, a thin strip of sand extending northwards from Constanţa, is Romania's most popular and expensive beach resort. In season, from early June to early September, the 8km-long beachfront is lined with sunbathers from around Romania who compete for that precious space of seaside real estate. By night, Mamaia morphs into party central, with dozens of high-adrenaline nightclubs and impromptu beach parties.

🏃 Activities

Mamaia's number-one attraction is its wide, golden beach, which stretches the length of the resort. The further north you go, the nicer it becomes.

Boats to Ovidiu Island BOATING
(Insula Ovidiu; B-dul Mamaia; per person return 20 lei; ⊙boats 9am-midnight) In summer, boats ferry tourists across Lake Siutghiol to Insula Ovidiu (Ovidiu Island), with a good restaurant and where Ovid's tomb is said to be located. They depart every 30 minutes from the Tic-Tac wharf on the lake (*not* the beach), at about the midpoint of the Mamaia resort.

Aqua Magic WATER PARK
(www.aqua-magic.ro; adult/child Jun & Sep 40/20 lei, Jul & Aug 60/30 lei; ⊙10am-6pm Jun & Sep, 9am-7pm Jul & Aug; 🛝) This amazing water park has pools and slides and inner-tube rides galore.

🛏 Sleeping

Mamaia is lined with resort complexes that are more attuned to dealing with package tours than walk-ins. If you know your dates in advance and plan to stay at least three to four days, you're better off arranging a package through a travel agency like Mistral Tours (p446). Note that Mamaia pretty much shuts down in the off-season (September to May) and only the biggest hotels stay open.

Hotel Splendid
HOTEL €€€

(☎0341-412 541; www.splendidhotel.ro; B-dul Mamaia , Mamaia Nord ; s/d 480/560 lei; P🅿➡❄@🖵) This five-storey modern hotel, built in 2007, is a quieter option since it's on the western side of main road (away from the beachfront, along Siutghiol Lake). You'll find it on the northern end of the resort.

Hotel Ovidiu
HOTEL €€

(☎0241-831 590; www.hotelovidiu.ro; d/tr 250/350 lei; ➡❄🖵) This simple two-star hotel offers basic, clean rooms at a good price and not much else. Request an upper-floor room to get a better sea view.

GPM Campground
CAMPGROUND €

(☎0241-831 001; www.gpm.ro; B-dul Mamaia Nord, Navodari; campsite per person 20 lei, bungalows 140-460 lei; ❄) Attractive camping ground at the far northern end of Mamaia. Call or arrive early to reserve a site near the beach. Excellent self-serve restaurant is open to campers and noncampers alike.

✖ Eating & Drinking

TOP CHOICE Chevalet
INTERNATIONAL €€€

(☎0721-421 501; www.restaurantchevalet.com; B-dul Mamaia; mains 50-80 lei; ⊙11am-11pm; 🖵) Head chef Nelu Păucă trained around the world before opening this romantic terrace restaurant on Lake Siutghiol, near the southern end of Mamaia. Specialities include steak tartare, frog legs and a mouth-watering array of beef, pork and seafood. Book in advance and try to time your booking for sunset.

Crazy Beach
CLUB

(☎0726-779 292; www.crazybeach.ro; B-dul Mamaia Nord; ⊙8am-1am) One of the hottest clubs in Mamaia is this open-air lounge and cocktail bar, situated in the extreme north of Mamaia, about 4km beyond the northern telegondola station. Take a taxi (about 10 lei from central Mamaia).

❶ Information

Asociatia de Promovare Litoral (☎0241-831 321; www.asociatia-litoral.ro; Telegondola base) Located inside the southern telegondola terminus, it can help with accommodation and tours of the region.

Mistral Tours (☎0241-557 007; www.mistraltours.ro; ⊙9am-5pm Mon-Fri, to 1pm Sat) Located at the southern end of Mamaia's telegondola line, Mistral Tours can help find accommodation and plan day trips and ex-

cursions, including to the Danube Delta and Bulgarian Black Sea coast.

❶ Getting There & Around

Frequent maxitaxis (2 lei, 15 minutes) ply the route between central Constanţa and Mamaia from June to September. Maxitaxis 301 and 303 depart regularly from Constanţa's train station. You can wave them down conveniently on B-dul Ferdinand, across the street from both the Hotel Class and Hotel Ferdinand.

Once in Mamaia, stroll the boardwalk or take the **telegondola** (cable car; one way 10 lei; ⊙9am-10pm Jun-Oct) that runs from the southern end of the resort to approximately the midway point.

Vama Veche

If you've got time for just one Romanian resort, make it Vama Veche, just north of the Bulgarian border. While it lacks the polish of Mamaia, it's smaller, more relaxed and more rustic. Under the communist regime, 'Vama' enjoyed a reputation as a haven for artists, hedonists and free-thinkers. While it's slowly moving towards the mainstream, there's still something of a counterculture vibe in the air.

🏃 Activities

The main activities are swimming, sunbathing, drinking and partying, and not necessarily in that order. There's a 5km bike path to an adjoining seaside village called Doi Mai (2 Mai), that starts from the northern end of Vama Veche. The BazArt Hostel rents **bikes** (☎0241-858 009; www.bazarthostel.ro; Str Ion Creangă, BazArt Hostel ; per 2hr/day 10/30 lei).

🛌 Sleeping

There's wild camping at both the far southern and northern ends of the beach. Club d'Or offers **camping** (☎0743-335 114; www.clubdor.ro; Plaja Vama Veche; per tent 10 lei) on a wide strip of beach towards the northern end and has showers and toilets.

TOP CHOICE Club d'Or
HOTEL €€

(☎0743-335 114; www.clubdor.ro; Str Ion Creangă; r 160 lei; P🅿🖵🖵) Clean, quiet and close enough to the beach to drift in and out when you want. The rooms resemble a motel and fan out around a gigantic, clean swimming pool. It's located 100m west of Hwy E87 at approximately the centre of the village.

Elga's Punk Rock Hotel
HOTEL €

(☑0722-366 711; www.punkrockhotel.com; Str Kogalniceanu, Hwy 87; r 80-100 lei; P🐾❄🢡) This welcoming family-run hotel offers small but ultraclean rooms with either double or twin beds in two price categories. 'A' level rooms are slightly larger and have air-conditioning, while category 'B' rooms are smaller and have fans.

BazArt
HOSTEL €

(☑0241-858 009; www.bazarthostel.ro; Str Ion Creangă; d 80-200 lei; q 150 lei; 🐾❄🢡) This popular student choice on Vama Veche's main drag offers a variety of rooms, including comfortable private doubles with bathrooms and air-conditioning, as well as budget twins and quads with shared facilities and no air-con.

✖ Eating & Drinking

TOP
CHOICE Cherhana
FISH €€

(mains 15-25 lei; ⏱10am-11pm) This informal beachfront place with grill and picnic tables draws big crowds, particularly campers from the nearby wild camping grounds The fresh fish is grilled on the spot. It's situated on the northern edge of Vama Veche, beyond the Club d'Or camping area.

Molotov
BAR

(molotov_bar@yahoo.com; Str Falezei, Plaja Vama Veche; ⏱10am-3am) This scruffily charming cocktail bar is one of the best places in town to sip your drink while you listen to the roar of the surf. It's located on the beach on the southern end of Vama Veche.

❶ Getting There & Away

There are no trains to Vama Veche; instead take a maxitaxi from Constanţa (about 10 lei) or take a train to Mangalia and a maxitaxi for 8km (5 lei).

UNDERSTAND ROMANIA

Romania Today

Romania today finds itself in a strange place. The big picture view is mainly positive. Since independence, Romania has made great strides in developing a free market economy and parliamentary democracy. Many Romanians, however, see the situation differently. Corruption remains a serious problem and the transition to democracy has been marked by a series of crippling political crises, the most recent coming in 2012 when president Traian Băsescu narrowly escaped dismissal in a public referendum. The ongoing crises have clouded Romania's aim to join the European Union's common border Schengen Zone, which was hoped to take place in 2013 or 2014.

History
Ancient Romania & 'Dracula'

Ancient Romania was inhabited by Thracian tribes, more commonly known as Dacians. The Greeks established trading colonies along the Black Sea from the 7th century BC, and the Romans conquered in AD 105–06. The slave-owning Romans brought with them their civilisation and the Latin language.

From the 10th century the Magyars (Hungarians) expanded into Transylvania, and by the 13th century all of Transylvania was under the Hungarian crown.

The Romanian-speaking principalities of Wallachia and Moldavia offered strong resistance to the Ottomans' northern expansion in the 14th and 15th centuries. Mircea the Old, Vlad Ţepeş and Ştefan cel Mare (Stephen the Great) were legendary figures in this struggle.

Vlad Drăculea, ruling prince of Wallachia from 1456 to 1462 and 1476 to 1477, posthumously gained the moniker 'Ţepeş' (Impaler) after his favoured form of punishing his enemies – impaling. A dull wooden stake was carefully inserted into the anus, driven slowly through the body avoiding vital organs, until it emerged from the mouth, resulting in hours, even days, of agony before death. He is perhaps more legendary as the inspiration for 19th-century novelist Bram Stoker's Count Dracula. (Vlad's surname, Drăculea, means 'son of the dragon', after his father, Vlad Dracul, a knight of the Order of the Dragon.)

When the Turks conquered Hungary in the 16th century, Transylvania became a vassal of the Ottoman Empire. In 1600 the three Romanian states – Transylvania, Wallachia and Moldavia – were briefly united under Mihai Viteazul (Michael the Brave). In 1687 Transylvania fell under Habsburg rule.

In 1859 Alexandru Ioan Cuza was elected to the thrones of Moldavia and Wallachia, creating a national state, which in 1862 took the name Romania. The reformist

Cuza was forced to abdicate in 1866, and his place was taken by Prussian prince Karl of Hohenzollern, who took the name Carol I. Romania declared independence from the Ottoman Empire in 1877, and, after the 1877–78 War of Independence, Dobrogea became part of Romania.

Romania in WWI & WWII

In 1916 Romania entered WWI on the side of the Triple Entente (Britain, France and Russia), with one of the objectives being to retake Transylvania from Austria-Hungary. With the defeat of Austria-Hungary in 1918, the regions of the Banat and Transylvania went to independent Romania.

In the years leading to WWII, Romania sought security in a French alliance. This broke down, and on 30 August 1940 Romania was forced to cede northern Transylvania to Hungary by order of Nazi Germany and fascist Italy.

This loss of territory threw the political situation into turmoil. The result was a fascist dictatorship led by General Ion Antonescu and alleed to Nazi Germany. Antonescu forced King Carol II to abdicate and imposed a harsh, dictatorial regime, which mimicked Germany's brutal anti-Semitism. Some 400,000 Romanian Jews and 36,000 Roma, including those on Hungarian-occupied territories, were eventually murdered at Auschwitz and camps in Ukraine and Moldova.

On 23 August 1944 Romania suddenly changed sides and joined the Allies. The army captured some 53,000 German soldiers and declared war on Nazi Germany. By this act, Romania salvaged its independence and shortened the war.

The Communist Period

After the war, the Soviet-engineered return of Transylvania enhanced the prestige of left-wing parties, which won the parliamentary elections of November 1946. A year later the monarchy was abolished and the Soviet-backed Romanian People's Republic was proclaimed.

Soviet troops formally withdrew in 1958, and after 1960 Romania adopted a quasi-independent foreign policy within the Soviet bloc under two leaders: Gheorghe Gheorghiu-Dej (from 1952 to 1965) and his protégé, Nicolae Ceaușescu (1965 to 1989).

Ceaușescu's reign will forever be seen as misguided, chaotic and megalomaniacal.

The early years of the regime were relatively successful. Ceaușescu managed to defy the Soviet Union and keep Romanian troops out of the Warsaw Pact invasion of Czechoslovakia in 1968. In the late 1960s and early '70s, he positioned Romania as a nonaligned state and curried favour with the USA and UK in their cold war with the Soviet Union.

But following a trip to North Korea in 1971, Ceaușescu steadily lost his grip on reality and established what became the most hardline regime within the Eastern Bloc states. He placed his wife Elena, son Nicu and three brothers in important political positions, and embarked on expensive follies like building the Danube Canal and tearing down large swaths of Bucharest to build his humungous 'House of the People' (today's Palace of Parliament). Meantime, much of the country experienced severe food shortages.

Ceaușescu's Downfall

Ceaușescu managed to survive throughout the fateful year of 1989, when communist regimes around Eastern Europe fell like dominoes, but his luck ran out in December – approximately a month after the fall of the Berlin Wall. On 15 December 1989, in the western city of Timișoara, a Hungarian priest named László Tőkés publicly condemned the dictator from his church in Timișoara. Police attempts to arrest demonstrating parishioners failed and civil unrest quickly spread.

On 21 December in Bucharest, Ceaușescu addressed a rally that was cut short by demonstrators. They booed him, then retreated to the streets between Piața Universității and Piața Romană, only to be crushed later by police gunfire and armoured cars. The next morning thousands more demonstrators took to the streets. At midday Ceaușescu reappeared on the balcony of the Central Committee building to speak, only to be forced to flee by helicopter. Ceaușescu and his wife were soon arrested near Târgoviște, taken to a military base and, on 25 December, executed by firing squad.

The toppling of the dictator provoked widespread jubilation, but this initial enthusiasm was quashed when a former Ceaușescu confidante, Ion Iliescu, won the country's first 'democratic' elections in May 1990. Many felt betrayed by Iliescu's win and students launched large-scale protests in

Bucharest in June of that year. Iliescu called in some 20,000 coal miners from the Jiu Valley to bash student heads and to end the protests. Dozens of people were killed in this hideous phalanx of violence known today as the *mineriadă*.

The years since independence have not all been positive. Over the past two decades, Romania has had its share of scandal, corruption, investment-fund collapses and unstable governments. Nevertheless, the overall trend has been positive, as the country has tried hard to make up for lost time after four decades of communist misrule.

People

Romanians make up 89% of the population; Hungarians are the next largest ethnic group (7%), followed by Roma (2%) and smaller populations of Ukrainians, Germans, Russians and Turks. Germans and Hungarians live almost exclusively in Transylvania, while Ukrainians and Russians live mainly near the Danube Delta, and Turks along the Black Sea coast.

The government estimates that only 400,000 Roma live in Romania, although other sources estimate between 1.5 and 2.5 million. A good site to learn more about the Roma is the Budapest-based **European Roma Rights Centre** (http://errc.org).

Religion

The majority of Romania's population is Eastern Orthodox Christian (87%). The rest is made up of Protestants (6.8%), Catholics (5.6%) and Muslims (0.4%), along with some 39,000 Jehovah's Witnesses and 10,000 Jews.

Arts
Folk Art

Painting on glass and wood remains a popular folk art today. Considered to be of Byzantine origin, this traditional peasant art was widespread in Romania from the 17th century onwards. Superstition and strong religious beliefs surrounded these icons, painted to protect the household from evil spirits. Well-known 19th-century icon painters include Dionisie Iuga, Maria Chifor and Tudor Tocariu. The glass icons of contemporary artist Georgeta Maria Uiga (from Baia Mare) are exhibited worldwide.

Sculpture

Sculpture has been an active art form in the territory of modern Romania since the days of the ancient Greeks along the Black Sea, and the history and archaeology museums in Tulcea and Constanţa are filled with the works of antiquity.

In the 19th and 20th centuries, sculpture often took the form of statues of national heroes as a way of honouring these (usually) men or of fostering a nascent national identity.

This rigid, didactic statue-making, however, was blown away in the early 20th century by the abstract works of master Constantin Brâncuşi (1876–1957). Brâncuşi turned the world of modern sculpture on its head with his dictum of using sculpture not to focus on form, but on inner essence. His works are featured at Craiova's Museum of Art and Bucharest's National Museum of Art, as well as in a series of open-air public works at Târgu Jiu, not far from where he was born.

Contemporary Romanian sculpture got a boost – or perhaps a setback (depending on your point of view) – by a controversial work unveiled in 2012 at Bucharest's Museum of National History. The bronze statue, by Vasile Gorduz (1931–2008), depicts a fully nude (and anatomically correct but not particularly well endowed) Roman Emperor Trajan holding a wolf to symbolise the synthesis of Roman and Dacian cultures. It's provoked derision on all sides, but tellingly has emerged as the city's most-photographed work of art.

Literature

Few modern Romanian writers have managed to break through to a wider international public, but one notable exception is German-speaking author Herta Müller (b 1953), who won the Nobel Prize for Literature in 2009. Müller grew up in a German-speaking village in the Banat during a time when the German minority was subject to harsh oppression and deportation.

Unsurprisingly, her work centres on the severity of life in communist Romania. She left Romania in 1987 and lives in Berlin. Her books are anything but easy reads, but several are available in English, including *The Land of Green Plums* (1998), *The Appointment* (2002) and *The Hunger Angel* (2012).

Any discussion of Romanian Nobel laureates would not be complete without mention of Holocaust survivor and acclaimed writer Elie Wiesel, who was born in the northern city of Sighetu Marmaţiei in 1928 and who was awarded the Nobel Peace Prize in 1986. Wiesel has written some 57 books, but he's best known for *Night*, a moving depiction of his experiences as a prisoner at the Auschwitz-Birkenau and Buchenwald concentration camps during WWII.

Music

The Romanian classical music world is nearly synonymous with George Enescu (1881–1955), whose *Romanian Rhapsodies Nos 1 & 2* and opera *Odeipe* are considered classics. He was as accomplished a violinist as a composer, studied under Fauré in Paris and was also a conductor, cellist and pianist. Other figures of note include composer Ciprian Porumbescu (1853–83) and Paul Constantinescu (1909–63).

FOLK MUSIC

You won't travel far without hearing Romanian folk music, which is still common at family celebrations, holidays and weddings.

Traditional Romanian folk instruments include the *bucium* (alphorn), the *cimpoi* (bagpipes), the *cobză* (a pear-shaped lute) and the *nai* (a pan pipe of about 20 cane tubes). Many kinds of flute are used, including the ocarina (a ceramic flute) and the *tilinca* (a flute without finger holes).

Folk music can take many forms. A *doină* is a solo, improvised love song, a sort of Romanian blues with a social or romantic theme that is sung in a number of contexts (at home, at work or during wakes). The *doină* was added to the Unesco World Heritage list of intangible cultural elements in 2009. Another common form, the *baladă* (ballad), is a collective narrative song steeped in feeling.

Cinema

The so-called 'Romanian Wave' in cinema is red hot and showing no signs of abating. Hits like Nae Caranfil's comedy *Filantropica* (2002) and Cristi Puiu's *The Death of Mr Lăzărescu* (2005) started things off, then in 2007 director Cristian Mungiu won the Cannes Film Festival's top prize with *4 Months, 3 Weeks and 2 Days,* a disturbing tale of illegal abortion in communist-era Romania, while the late Cristian Nemescu's film *California Dreamin'* also took honours.

More recent buzz-worthy films include rare Romanian comedy *Tales from the Golden Age* (2009) by Cristian Mungiu and *Police, Adjective* by Corneliu Porumboiu, which won the Jury Prize in the Un Certain Regard section at Cannes in 2009. The 'wave' at Cannes continues, with Cristi Puiu's *Aurora* and Radu Muntean's *Tuesday, After Christmas* both being selected for Un Certain Regard.

Environment

When the gods were doling out unspoilt wildernesses they seem to have been extra generous with Romania; covering 237,500 sq km, this oval-shaped country offers a panorama of mountains, pristine forests, lakes and rolling meadows unparalleled in the rest of Europe. And thanks to traditional methods of farming, incursions into the habitats of wild animals have been relatively low.

Increasingly, travellers on the hunt for isolated locations abundant with nature and wildlife are coming to Romania – be it for birdwatching in the Danube Delta, wolf tracking in Transylvania, or even crouching in a hide looking for brown bears.

Still, there are significant threats to the environment. Two of the biggest problems, and key EU criticisms of Romania, include the way the country processes factory waste and water pollution.

A disastrous cyanide spill by a mine into the Someş River near Baia Mare in 2000 was a bellwether event that heightened public concern over the waste issue and led to stiffer regulations on what companies can discharge. Environmental groups say the measures do not go far enough and have expressed fears another calamity occuring that is only a matter of time.

Food & Drink

Romanian dishes have a delightful, home-made character to them, incorporating the fertile land's fresh, organic produce into relatively uncomplicated but delicious concoctions. Many dishes, perhaps even the majority, use pork in some form, paired with a staple like polenta, potatoes or cooked cabbage. The recipes derive from peasant cooking going back hundreds of years, with a liberal dose of borrowings from neighbouring (and occasionally occupying) cultures like Turkish, Hungarian, German and Slav.

STREET EATS

Romanians love to eat on the go, and in most towns and cities there are plenty of decent street food options. Look out especially for the following:

Covrigi Hot pretzels sprinkled with salt or sesame or poppy seeds

Gogosi Doughnuts, either dusted with sugar or stuffed with fruit

Placinte Sweet or savoury pastries, served warm and stuffed with fruit, curd cheese or meat

Mici Grilled rolls of spiced minced pork or beef, always served with mustard

Shoarma Like a shawarma, though usually made from chicken or pork, with unorthodox toppings like cabbage and ketchup

Comfort Food

Romanian food wasn't bred so much to dazzle but to satisfy, and menus are rich in 'comfort foods'. *Mămăligă*, a cornmeal mush (often translated as 'polenta' on English menus), seemingly was designed to warm and fill the stomach. You'll find it at restaurants, inns and family homes around the country. It can be disappointingly bland or stodgy in restaurants, but when homemade and served with fresh *smântână* (sour cream), it certainly hits the spot.

Mămăligă pairs beautifully with *sarmale*, the country's de facto national dish (though it's actually an import from the days of Ottoman rule) and comfort food extraordinaire. *Sarmale* are cabbage or vine leaves that are stuffed with spiced meat and rice; the *mămăligă* here provides an excellent backstop for soaking up the juices.

Wine, Beer & Moonshine

Romania is the 9th-biggest winemaker in the world and produces many wines that are world class. Wineries turn out both reds (*negru* and *roşu*) and whites (*alb*). Look for bottles from one of the five traditional winemaking regions: Târnave plateau (outside Alba Iulia; whites), Cotnari (outside Iaşi; whites), Murfatlar (near the Black Sea coast; whites and reds), Dealu Mare (south of the Carpathians; reds) and Odobeşti (in southern Moldavia; whites and reds).

For day-to-day tippling, Romanians are beer drinkers at heart. The quality of the beer ranges from passable to pretty good. Most Romanian breweries are owned by big international brewers and it's sometimes easier to find a Tuborg or a Heineken than a Romanian label. The better local brands to look for include Ciuc, Ursus, Silva and Timişoara's local favourite, Timişoreana.

When it comes to serious drinking, the only real contender is *ţuică* (fruit brandy). Typically, *ţuică* is made from plums (three-quarters of the nation's plums end up in a bottle). The best batches are from the backyard still, and nearly everyone has an uncle or grandfather who makes the 'best in Romania'. Unless you're a seasoned drinker, though, hold the line at one or two shots. Batches can run as high as 50% to 60% alcohol (100–120 proof).

SURVIVAL GUIDE

Directory A–Z

Accommodation

Romania has a wide choice of accommodation options to suit most budgets, including hotels, pensions and private rooms, hostels and camping grounds. Prices across these categories have risen in recent years, but are still generally lower than in Western Europe.

This book divides accommodation options into three categories based on price: budget, midrange and top end. Budget properties normally include hostels, camping grounds and some cheaper guesthouses. Midrange accommodation includes three-star hotels and pensions. Top end usually means four- and five-star hotels, corporate chains and boutiques.

» Watch for seasonal fluctuations on rates. Summer resorts, particularly on the Black Sea, have much higher prices in July and August.

» We've usually quoted prices in this guide in lei, though many hotels quote rates in euro. You'll still have to pay in lei and your credit card will be debited at the current exchange rate.

The following price categories for the cost of a double room are used in the listings in this chapter.

€ less than 130 lei

€€ 130 lei to 280 lei

€€€ more than 280 lei

Business Hours

Banks 9am to noon and 1pm to 5pm Monday to Friday

Clubs 8pm to 2am

Restaurants 10am to 11pm

Shops 10am to 6pm Monday to Friday, 10am to 5pm Saturday

Customs Regulations

» You're allowed to import hard currency up to a maximum of €10,000 or the equivalent.

» For foreigners, duty-free allowances for items purchased *outside* of the EU are 4L of wine, 2L of spirits and 200 cigarettes. For more information, go to www.customs.ro.

Embassies & Consulates

Embassies are located in Bucharest, while several countries maintain consulates at other cities around the country. There is no New Zealand embassy in Romania, so citizens should turn to the country's embassy in Brussels for consular matters.

Australian Consulate (☑021-206 2200; www.dfat.gov.au; Str Praga 3)

Canadian Embassy (☑021-307 5000; www.canadainternational.gc.ca/romania-roumanie; Str Tuberozelor 1-3)

French Embassy (☑021-303 1000; www.ambafrance-ro.org; Str Biserica Amzei 13-15)

Irish Embassy (☑021-310 2131; www.embas-syofireland.ro; Str Buzeşti 50-52)

Netherlands Embassy (☑021-208 6030; http://romania.nlembassy.org; Aleea Alexandru 20)

UK Embassy (☑021-201 7200; www.ukinroma-nia.fco.gov.uk; Str Jules Michelet 24)

Ukrainian Embassy (☑021-230 3660; www.mfa.gov.ua/romania; B-dul Aviatorilor 24)

US Embassy (☑consulate 021-270-6000, embassy 021-200 3300; http://romania.usembassy.gov; B-dul Dr Liviu Librescu 4-6)

Food

The following price categories for the cost of a main course are used in the listings in this chapter.

€ less than 13 lei

€€ 15 lei to 30 lei

€€€ more than 30 lei

Gay & Lesbian Travellers

Public attitudes towards homosexuality remain relatively negative. In spite of this, Romania has made significant legal progress in decriminalising homosexual acts and adopting antidiscrimination laws.

» Bucharest remains the most tolerant city in the country, though gay couples should refrain from open displays of affection.

» Bucharest-based **Accept Association** (☑021-252 9000; www.accept-romania.ro) organises a six-day GayFest in the capital in early summer, with films, parties, conferences and a parade.

Money

CASH

The currency is the leu (plural: lei), noted in this guide as 'lei' but listed in banks as RON. One leu is divided into 100 bani. Banknotes come in denominations of 1 leu, 5 lei, 10 lei, 50 lei, 100 lei, 200 lei and 500 lei. The coins come in 50 and 10 bani.

Romania is a member of the European Union, but the euro does not circulate. There is no point in converting your money into euro prior to arrival, since you will have to convert it to lei anyway.

ATMS

ATMs are nearly everywhere and give 24-hour withdrawals in lei on a variety of international bank cards, including Visa and MasterCard. Romanian ATMs require a four-digit PIN.

CHANGING MONEY

The best place to exchange money is at a bank.You'll pay a small commission, but get a decent rate. You can also change money at a private *casa de schimb* (exchange booth), but be wary of commission charges.

You will need to show a passport to change money, so have it handy.

Never change money on the street with strangers; it's always a rip-off.

CREDIT CARDS & TRAVELLERS CHEQUES

International credit and debit cards, including Visa and MasterCard, are widely accepted at hotels, restaurants and shops in cities. In rural areas, you'll usually need to pay cash.

» Credit card transactions may also require a PIN number, so it's best to work that out with your bank prior to departure.

» You will need a valid credit card to hire a car.

» Travellers cheques are increasingly difficult to change in Romania.

Post

The Romanian Postal Service (www.posta-romana.ro) is slow but reliable. Buy stamps in post offices, as letters must be weighed to determine correct postage. Delivery time within Europe is one week; overseas will take seven to 10 days.

Public Holidays

New Year 1 and 2 January

Orthodox Easter Monday April/May

Labour Day 1 May

Pentecost May/June, 50 days after Easter Sunday

Assumption of Mary 15 August

Feast of St Andrew 30 November

Romanian National Day 1 December

Christmas 25 and 26 December

Telephone

Romania has a modern telephone network of landlines and mobile phones. Romania's country code is ☏40.

All Romanian landlines have 10 digits, consisting of a zero, plus a city code and the number. This formula differs depending on whether the number is in Bucharest or outside of Bucharest. Bucharest numbers take the form ☏0 plus a two-digit city code (☏21 or ☏31) plus the seven-digit number. Outside of Bucharest, numbers take the form ☏0 plus the three-digit city code plus the six-digit number.

Mobile phone numbers are identified by a three-digit prefix starting with ☏7. All mobile numbers have 10 digits: ☏0 plus the three-digit prefix (☏7xx) and six-digit number.

CALLING FROM WITHIN ROMANIA & ABROAD

If you're calling from within Romania, to reach a landline, dial ☏0 plus the city code and the six-digit number. A landline in Bucharest would take the form ☏0 plus ☏21 (or ☏31) and the seven-digit number. To reach a mobile number, dial ☏0 plus the three-digit mobile prefix and the six-digit number.

» To call abroad from Romania, dial ☏00 plus the country code you want to call, the local area code and the number.

» To call a Romanian number from outside the country, dial your country's international access code plus ☏40 (Romania's country code), the city code (minus the zero) and the six- (or seven-) digit local number.

» To call a mobile number, dial your international access code plus ☏40, then ☏7xx and the six-digit number.

MOBILE PHONES & SMARTPHONES

Romanian mobile (cell) phones use the GSM 900/1800 network, the standard throughout Europe as well as in Australia and New Zealand, but it's not compatible with mobile phones in North America or Japan (though some multiband phones do work across regions). Ask your provider if you're uncertain whether or not your phone will work.

» To reduce expensive roaming fees, buy a prepaid Romanian SIM card, which gives you a temporary local number and charges local (cheaper) rates for calls, texts and data transfers.

» Prepaid SIM plans start at about 20 lei per card and include bonus minutes. They are offered by all three of Romania's main carriers: Vodafone (www.vodafone.ro), Cosmote (www.cosmote.ro) and Orange (www.orange.ro).

» The situation is more complicated if you have a smartphone like an iPhone, Android or Blackberry that cannot easily be unlocked. With these phones, it's best to contact your home provider to consider short-term international calling and data plans.

PAY PHONES & PHONECARDS

Public phones require a magnetic-stripe phonecard, which you can buy from post offices and newspaper kiosks. Phonecard rates start at about 10 lei.

Tourist Information

» The Romanian National Tourist Office (www.romaniatourism.com) maintains a wonderful website with a trove of useful information.

» Romania's national network of tourist offices has made strides in recent years. Nearly all big cities have decent tourist offices.

Travellers with Disabilities

» Romania is not well equipped for people with disabilities, even though there has been some improvement in recent years.

» Wheelchair ramps are available only at some upmarket hotels and restaurants, and public transport will be a challenge.

Visas

Citizens of EU countries do not need visas to visit Romania and can stay indefinitely. Citizens of the USA, Canada, Australia, New Zealand, Israel, Japan and many other countries can stay for up to 90 days without a visa. Other nationalities should check with the Ministry of Foreign Affairs (www.mae.ro).

Getting There & Away

Travellers entering Romania should not experience any trouble at customs and immigration.

Air

Romania has good air connections to Europe and the Middle East. At the time of research there were no direct flights to Romania from North America or Southeast Asia.

AIRPORTS

The majority of international flights to Romania arrive at Bucharest's Henri Coandă International Airport (OTP, Otopeni; ☑021-204 1000; www.otp-airport.ro; Şos Bucureşti-Ploieşti). Several other cities have international airports:

Cluj Airport (☑0264-416 702; www.airportcluj.ro; Str Traian Vuia 149)

Iaşi Airport (☑info 0733-261 111; www.aeroport.ro; Str Moara de Vant 34)

Sibiu Airport (☑0269-253 135; www.sibiuairport.ro; Sos Alba Iulia 73)

Târgu Mureş Airport (☑0265-328 259; www.targumuresairport.ro; Str Ludus, km14.5)

Timişoara Airport (Traian Vuia Timişoara Airport; ☑0256-493 639; www.aerotim.ro; Str Aeroport 2, Ghiroda)

AIRLINES

Air France (☑021-206 9200; www.airfrance.com)

Austrian Airlines (☑021-204 4560; www.austrian.com)

Blue Air (☑1499; www.blueairweb.com)

British Airways (☑reservations 021-303 2222; www.britishairways.com)

Carpatair (☑0256-300 900; www.carpatair.com)

ČSA (Czech Airlines/OK; ☑021-223 3205; www.csa.cz)

EasyJet (U2; www.easyjet.com)

Germanwings (☑toll 0903-760 101; www.germanwings.com)

KLM (KL; ☑021-206 9222; www.klm.com)

Ryan Air (☑in the UK 0871 246 0002; www.ryanair.com)

Swiss Airlines (☑021-312 0238; www.swiss.com)

Tarom (☑021-204 6464; www.tarom.ro) National carrier with good connections to major European and Middle Eastern cities.

WizzAir (☑toll 0903-760 160; www.wizzair.com)

Land

Romania shares a border with five countries: Bulgaria, Hungary, Moldova, Serbia and Ukraine. It has four car-ferry crossings with Bulgaria.

Highway border posts are normally open 24 hours, though smaller crossings may only be open from 8am to 8pm.

BORDER CROSSINGS

Bulgaria Road crossings at Giurgiu, Vama Veche, Calafat (planned for 2013). Ferry crossings at Calafat, Bechet, Turnu Măgerele, Călăraşi

Hungary Road crossings at Nădlac, Borş, Cenad, Valea lui Mihai, Urziceni

Moldova Road crossings at Rădăuţi-Prut, Albiţa, Galaţi, Ştefăneşti, Sculeni

Serbia Road crossings at Moraviţa, Comloşu Mare, Jimbolia, Porţile de Fier I

Ukraine Road crossings at Siret, Sighetu Marmaţiei

BUS

Long-haul bus service remains a popular way of travelling from Romania to Western Europe, as well as to parts of southeastern Europe and Turkey. Bus travel is comparable in price to train travel, but can be faster.

Bus services to and from Western Europe are dominated by two companies: **Eurolines** (www.eurolines.ro) and **Atlassib** (www.atlassib. ro; Soseaua Alexandriei 164). Both maintain vast networks from cities throughout Europe to destinations all around Romania. Check the websites for latest schedules, prices and departure points.

Bucharest is the hub for coach travel to Bulgaria, Greece and Turkey. One bus departs daily from Bucharest's **Filaret** (☎021-335 3290, info 021-336 0692; www.acfilaret.ro; Piaţa Gării Filaret 1) bus station to Sofia (seven hours, €18), and Bucharest-based **Murat Turism & Transport** (☎021-316 5520; www.muratturism.ro; Soseaua Viilor 33;) offers a daily bus service from Bucharest to İstanbul (14 hours, €40) and to Athens (18 hours, €50).

CAR & MOTORCYCLE

Ensure your documents (personal ID, insurance, registration and visas, if required) are in order before crossing into Romania.

TRAIN

Romania is integrated into the European rail grid, and there are decent connections to Western Europe and neighbouring countries. Nearly all of these arrive at and depart from Bucharest's main station, **Gara de Nord** (☎021-319 9539, phone reservations 021-9522, 021-9521; www.cfr.ro; Piaţa Gara de Nord 1).

» Budapest is the main rail gateway in and out of Romania from Western Europe. There are two daily direct trains between Budapest and Bucharest, with regular onward direct connections from Budapest to Prague, Munich and Vienna.

» Buy international train tickets at train stations or at CFR (Romanian State Railways) in-town ticket offices (identified by an Agenţia de Voiaj CFR sign).

Getting Around

Air

Given the distances and poor state of the roads, flying between cities is a feasible option if time is a primary concern.

The Romanian national carrier **Tarom** (☎021-204 6464; www.tarom.ro) operates a comprehensive network of domestic routes. The airline flies regularly between Bucharest and Cluj-Napoca, Iaşi, Oradea, Sibiu, Suceava and Timişoara.

Timişoara-based **Carpatair** (☎0256-300 900; www.carpatair.com) also runs many domestic flights. The carrier flies from Timişoara to Iaşi, Craiova and Bacau.

Bicycle

It's possible to hire bicycles in many cities and towns. The group **i'velo** (☎021-310 6397; www.ivelo.ro) is trying to popularise cycling and has opened bike-hire outlets in several cities, including Bucharest, Timişoara, Braşov, Constanţa, Iaşi and Sibiu. Rates average about 5 lei per hour or 30 to 50 lei per day.

Bus

A mix of buses, minibuses and 'maxitaxis' form the backbone of the Romanian national transport system. If you understand how the system works, you can move around regions and even across the country easily and cheaply.

Unfortunately, buses and maxitaxi routes change frequently and towns and cities will sometimes have a half-dozen different bus stations, depending on the bus company and destination.

In this chapter, we've identified bus stations and routes for towns and cities where possible. In other areas, we've directed readers to the website www.autogari.ro, an up-to-date timetable that is easy to use and lists routes, times, fares and departure points.

Car & Motorcycle

Roads are generally crowded and in poor condition. The country has only a few short stretches of *autostrada* (motorway), meaning that most of your travel will be along two-lane *drum naţional* (national highways) or *drum judeţean* (secondary roads).

DRIVING RULES

» Blood-alcohol limit is zero.

» Seatbelts are compulsory.

» Headlights must be on day or night.

» Speed limits are 90km/h on major roads and 50km/h in villages and towns.

When calculating arrival times, figure on about 50km per hour.

Western-style petrol stations are plentiful. A litre of unleaded 95 octane costs about 6 lei. Most stations accept credit cards, but you'll need a PIN to use them.

Local Transport

Romanian cities generally have good public transportation systems comprising buses, trams, trolleybuses and, in some cases, maxitaxis. Bucharest is the only city with a metro. The method for accessing the systems is broadly similar. Purchase bus or tram tickets at newsagents or street kiosks marked *bilete* or *casă de bilete* before boarding, and validate the ticket once aboard. For maxitaxis, you usually buy a ticket directly from the driver.

TAXIS

Taxis are cheap and a useful supplement to the public transport systems. Drivers are required by law to post their rates on their doors or windscreens. The going rate varies from city to city, but runs anywhere from 1.39 to 1.89 lei per kilometre. Any driver posting a much higher fare is likely a rip-off.

While it's usually okay to use a taxi parked at a taxi rank (provided the taxi is not at Bucharest's airport or main train station) or to hail one from the street, we recommend ordering taxis by phone from reputable companies.

Train

The extensive network covers much of the country, including most of the main tourist sights.

» The national rail system is run by **Căile Ferate Române** (CFR, Romanian State Railways; www.cfr.ro). The CFR website has a handy online timetable (*mersul trenurilor*).

» Buy tickets at train station windows, specialised Agenţia de Voiaj CFR ticket offices, private travel agencies or online at www.cfrcalatori.ro.

» *Sosire* means arrivals and *plecare* is departures. On posted timetables, the number of the platform from which the train departs is listed under *linia*.

TYPES OF TRAINS

Romania has three different types of trains that travel at different speeds, offer varying levels of comfort and charge different fares for the same destination:

» InterCity are listed in blue or green as 'IC' on timetables; the most expensive and most comfortable but not always faster than 'IR' trains.

» InterRegional are listed in red as 'IR' on timetables; cheaper and nearly as fast as 'IC' trains, but may not be as modern.

» Regional are listed in black as 'R' on timetables; typically the oldest and slowest trains in the system, often sporting (pre-)historic rolling stock.

Serbia

Best Places to Eat

» Little Bay (p466)

» Dačo (p467)

» Šaran (p471)

» Hamam (p476)

Best Places to Stay

» Hotel Moskva (p465)

» Green Studio Hostel (p465)

» Hostel Sova (p472)

» Leopold I (p472)

Why Go?

Warm, welcoming and a hell of a lot of fun – everything you never heard about Serbia (Србија) is true. Exuding a feisty mix of élan and *inat* (Serbian trait of rebellious defiance), this country doesn't do 'mild': Belgrade is one of the world's wildest party destinations, the northern town of Novi Sad hosts the rocking EXIT festival, and even its hospitality is emphatic – expect to be greeted with *rakija* and a hearty three-kiss hello.

While political correctness is about as commonplace as a nonsmoking bar, Serbia is nevertheless a cultural crucible: the art nouveau town of Subotica revels in its proximity to Hungary, bohemian Niš echoes to the clip-clop of Roma horse carts, and minaret-studded Novi Pazar nudges some of the most sacred sites in Serbian Orthodoxy. And in the mountainous Kopaonik and Zlatibor regions, ancient traditions coexist with après-ski bling. Forget what you think you know: come and say *zdravo* (hello)...or better yet, *živeli* (cheers)!

When to Go

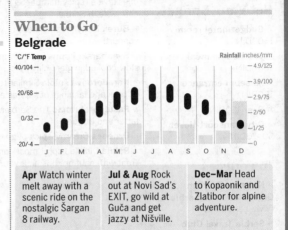

Belgrade

Apr Watch winter melt away with a scenic ride on the nostalgic Šargan 8 railway.

Jul & Aug Rock out at Novi Sad's EXIT, go wild at Guča and get jazzy at Nišville.

Dec–Mar Head to Kopaonik and Zlatibor for alpine adventure.

AT A GLANCE

» **Currency** Dinar (DIN)

» **Language** Serbian

» **Money** ATMs in all main and midsized towns

» **Visas** None for citizens of the EU, UK, Australia, New Zealand, Canada and the USA

Fast Facts

» **Area** 77,474 sq km

» **Capital** Belgrade

» **Country code** ☑381

» **Emergency** Ambulance ☑94, fire ☑93, police ☑92

Exchange Rates

Australia	A$1	91.56DIN
Canada	C$1	86.25DIN
Euro Zone	€1	112.03DIN
Japan	¥100	92.89DIN
New Zealand	NZ$1	73.38DIN
UK	UK£1	132.63DIN
USA	US$1	87.66DIN

Set Your Budget

» **Budget hotel room** 1500DIN

» **Two-course meal** 1000DIN

» **Museum entrance** 100DIN

» **Beer** 150DIN

» **City transport ticket** 50–70DIN

Resources

» **National Tourism Organisation of Serbia** (www.serbia.travel)

» **Serbia Travel Club** (www.serbiatravelers.org)

Connections

Serbia is landlocked by accessible neighbours. The northern town of Subotica is 10km from the Hungarian border, Vršac is the same distance from Romania, and Bulgaria is 45 minutes from Pirot. When things are calm on the Kosovo border, €5 and three hours get you from Novi Pazar to Priština. The Zlatibor region stretches to Bosnia and Hercegovina (BiH); travellers with wheels can take a day trip to the famous bridge on the Drina. All of Europe is accessible from Belgrade: Bucharest, Budapest, Ljubljana, Moscow, Sofia and Zagreb are a train ride away, and regular buses serve destinations including Vienna, Sarajevo and Podgorica.

ITINERARIES

One Week

Revel in three days of cultural and culinary exploration in Belgrade, allowing for at least one night of hitting the capital's legendary night spots. Carry on to Novi Sad for trips to the vineyards and monasteries of Fruška Gora and Sremski Karlovci.

Two Weeks

Follow the above itinerary then head north for the art nouveau architecture of Subotica, before slicing south to Zlatibor en route to Ottoman-influenced Novi Pazar and the lively city of Niš.

Essential Food & Drink

» **Kajmak** Along the lines of a salty clotted cream, this dairy delight is lashed on to everything from bread to burgers.

» **Ćevapčići** The ubiquitous skinless sausage and *pljeskavica* (spicy hamburger) make it very easy to be a carnivore in Serbia.

» **Burek** Flaky meat, cheese or vegetable pie eaten with yoghurt.

» **Svadbarski kupus** Sauerkraut and hunks of smoked pork slow-cooked in giant clay pots.

» **Karađorđeva šnicla** Similar to chicken Kiev, but with veal or pork and lashings of *kajmak* and tartar.

» **Pasulj prebranac** The Serbian take on baked beans, just fatter and porkier.

» **Urnebes** Creamy, spicy peppers-'n'-cheese spread.

» **Rakija** Distilled spirit most commonly made from plums. Treat with caution: this ain't your grandpa's brandy.

Serbia Highlights

① Marvel at Belgrade's mighty **Kalemegdan Citadel** (p460).

② Witness the laid-back town of **Novi Sad** (p472) as it morphs into the state of EXIT every July.

③ Ponder the exotic cultural fusions of Turkish-toned **Novi Pazar**(p477).

④ Steel your eardrums (and liver) at Guča's **Dragačevo Trumpet Assembly** (p476), one of the world's most frenetic music festivals.

⑤ Escape reality in the fantastic village of **Drvengrad** (p479), built by director Emir Kusturica for indie drama *Life is a Miracle.*

⑥ Goggle at splendid surprises bursting from the Vojvodinian plains, such as the art nouveau treasures of **Subotica** (p474).

⑦ Ski, hike or just take the mountain air in the magical villages of **Zlatibor** (p478).

BELGRADE

🎵 011 / POP 1.6 MILLION

Outspoken, adventurous, proud and audacious: Belgrade (Београд) is by no means a 'pretty' capital, but its gritty exuberance makes it one of the most happening cities in Europe. While it hurtles towards a brighter future, its chaotic past unfolds before your eyes: socialist blocks are squeezed between art nouveau masterpieces, and remnants of the Habsburg legacy contrast with Ottoman relics.

It is here where the Sava River meets the Danube (Dunav), contemplative parkland nudges hectic urban sprawl, and old-world culture gives way to new-world nightlife.

Grandiose coffee houses, quirky sidewalk ice-creameries and smoky dens all find rightful place along Knez Mihailova, a lively pedestrian boulevard flanked by historical buildings all the way to the ancient Kalemegdan Citadel, crown of the city. Deeper in Belgrade's bowels are museums guarding the cultural, religious and military heritage of the country. Josip Broz Tito and other ghosts of the past have been laid to rest here.

'Belgrade' literally translates as 'White City', but Serbia's colourful capital is red hot.

History

Belgrade has been destroyed and rebuilt countless times in its 2300-year history. Celts

first settled on the hill at the confluence of the Sava River and the Danube, the Romans came in the 1st century, and havoc was wreaked by Goths and Huns until the area was colonised by Slavic tribes in the 6th century.

In 1403 Hungary gave Belgrade to Despot Stefan Lazarević, making it the Serbian capital. The 1400s saw waves of Turkish attacks; it was conquered in 1521 and the city's population was shipped to İstanbul. The Karađorđević dynasty began in 1807 when Belgrade was liberated from the Turks, who finally relinquished control in 1867.

In 1914 the Austro-Hungarian empire captured Belgrade; they were soon driven out, only to return more triumphantly with German help in 1915, staying for three years. In 1918 Belgrade became the capital of Yugoslavia. The city was bombed by both Nazis and Allies during WWII.

In the 1990s Belgrade became the site of strong resistance against Slobodan Milošević. In 1999 NATO forces bombed Belgrade for three months after Milošević refused to end the repression of Albanians in Kosovo. The campaign killed dozens of Serbian civilians and destroyed not only military targets but also a hospital, residential buildings and, for still inexplicable reasons, the Chinese Embassy. In Belgrade's centre, the bombed building that housed the Yugoslavian Ministry of Defence has been left in ruins as a grim reminder of the city's darkest days.

⊙ Sights & Activities

KALEMGEDAN AREA

FREE **Kalemegdan Citadel** FORTRESS
(Kalemegdanska tvrđava) Some 115 battles have been fought over imposing, impressive Kalemegdan, and the citadel was destroyed more than 40 times throughout the centuries. Fortifications began in Celtic times, and the Romans extended it onto the flood plains during the settlement of 'Singidunum', Belgrade's Roman name. The fort's bloody history, discernible despite today's plethora of jolly cafes and funfairs, only makes Kalemegdan all the more fascinating.

Military Museum MUSEUM
(www.muzej.mod.gov.rs; adult/child 150/120DIN; ⊙10am-5pm Tue-Sun) Tucked away in Belgrade's sprawling Kalemegdan Citadel, this museum presents the complete military history of the former Yugoslavia. Gripping displays include captured Kosovo Liberation Army weapons, bombs and missiles (courtesy

---

BELGRADE IN TWO DAYS

Brunch at **Biblioteka** before exploring **Kalemegdan Citadel**. Take a stroll down **Knez Mihailova**, stopping at **Plato** for coffee and bookshelf browsing. People-watch at nearby **Trg Republike** and check whether the **National Museum** is open, or spend the afternoon in the **Ethnographic Museum**. When hunger sets in, drift down cobblestoned **Skadarska** to enjoy traditional Serbian fare and energetic Roma violins. Catch a live gig at the eclectic **Bitef Art Cafe** or join the retro revelry at **Kafana Pavle Korčagin**.

The next day, ponder the past at **Maršal Tito's Grave** before heading to **Zemun** for lunch. Back in the big smoke, hit a **Sava River barge-club** for a heady Belgrade nightlife experience. If clubbing's not for you, opt for a leisurely meal and live opera at **Little Bay**.

of NATO), rare guns and bits of the American stealth fighter that was shot down in 1999. You'll find the museum through the Stambol Gate, built by the Turks in the mid-1700s and used for public executions.

City Zoo
ZOO

(www.beozoovrt-izlog.org; Kalemegdan Citadel; adult/child 400/300DIN; ☻8am-8pm summer, to 4.30pm winter) The City Zoo is home to about 2000 animals, the ancestors of whom escaped en masse when Nazi bombs destroyed enclosures in WWII: the resulting mayhem is captured brilliantly in the opening scenes of Serbian indie drama *Underground*.

STARI GRAD

Architecture
NOTABLE BUILDINGS

South of Kalemegdan is **Stari Grad** (Old Town; www.starigrad.org.rs). This jumble of architecture covers two centuries, from when Belgrade was snatched from the Ottoman Empire and given a boost by the Habsburgs. People stroll along pedestrian strip Knez Mihailova, where cafes spill onto pavements. Fine buildings include the elegant pink and white **School of Fine Arts** (cnr Knez Mihailova & Rajićeva). Further down is the Serbian Academy of Arts & Sciences (p469), an art nouveau building with the goddess Nike at its helm.

National Museum
MUSEUM

(Narodni Muzej; www.narodnimuzej.rs; Trg Republike 1a) Trg Republike (Republic Sq), a meeting point and outdoor exhibition space, is home to the National Museum, which will hopefully reopen soon; lack of funding for renovations has kept it shuttered for the last decade.

Ethnographic Museum
MUSEUM

(Etnografski Muzej; www.etnografskimuzej.rs; Studentski Trg 13; adult/student 150/60DIN; ☻10am-5pm Tue-Sat, 9am-2pm Sun) This museum features traditional costumes, working utensils and folksy mountain-village interiors.

Palace of Princess Ljubica
PALACE

(Kneza Sime Markovića 8; adult/child 100/50DIN; ☻10am-6pm Tue, Wed, Fri & Sat, noon-8pm Thu, 10am-2pm Sun) This preserved Balkan-style palace was built in 1831 for the wife of Prince Miloš. Take coffee with 'the princess' (actually the museum custodian in period dress) each Saturday from noon (250DIN) as she leads you through privileged 19th-century life.

Museum of the Serbian
Orthodox Church
MUSEUM

(Kralja Petra 5; adult/child 50/20DIN; ☻8am-4pm Mon-Fri, 9am-noon Sat, 11am-1pm Sun) The

Patriarchate (Patrijaršija) building houses this collection of ecclesiastical items, many of which were collected by St Sava, founder of the independent Serbian Orthodox church.

DORĆOL

Named from the Turkish words for 'four roads' (*dört yol*), Dorćol stretches northeast from Stari Grad to the Danube. During the Ottoman occupation, Turks, Greeks, Jews, Germans, Armenians and Vlachs lived here side-by-side, bartering in a mix of languages. Today, Dorćol is a leafy, hip neighbourhood dotted with hidden *kafanas* (cafes) and cocktail bars.

Gallery of Frescos
GALLERY

(www.narodnimuzej.rs; Cara Uroša 20; admission 100DIN; ☻10am-5pm Tue, Wed, Fri & Sat, noon-8pm Thu, 10am-2pm Sun) The gallery features full-size replicas (and the odd original) of Byzantine Serbian church art, right down to the last scratch. Unlike the sensitive originals, these frescos can be photographed to your heart's content.

Bajrakli Mosque
MOSQUE

(cnr Kralja Petra & Gospodar Jevremova) The last remaining – and functioning – mosque (*džamija*) in Belgrade was built around 1575. Damage caused by riots in 2004 (a backlash against anti-Serb pogroms in Kosovo) has since been repaired.

St Aleksandar Nevski Church
CHURCH

(Cara Dušana 63) Built during the Serbian-Ottoman War (1877), this is the oldest Christian church in Dorćol.

SKADARSKA

Skadarska or 'Skadarlija' is Belgrade's Montmartre. This cobblestoned strip east of Trg Republike was the bohemian heartland at the

Central Belgrade

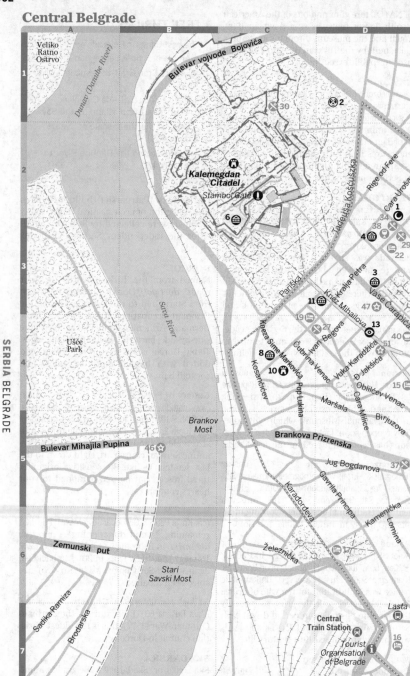

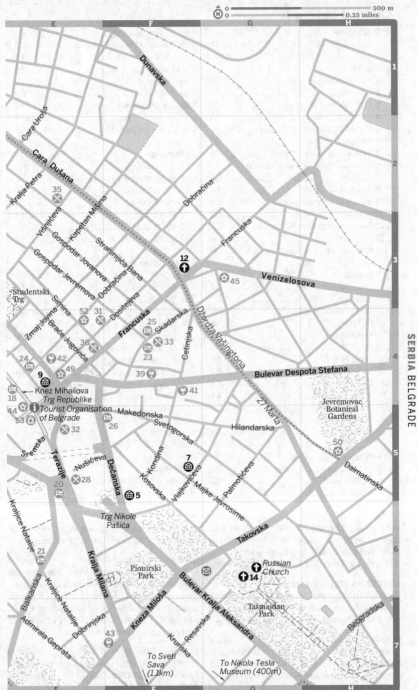

0 500 m
0 0.25 miles

SERBIA BELGRADE

E F G H

1

Dunavska

Cara Uroša

Cara Dušana

Kralja Petra

35

Višnjićeva

Kapetan Mišina

Gospodar Jovanova

Gospodar Jevremova

Dobračina

Francuska

Dobračina Bana

Strahinjića Bana

12

45

Venizelosova

3

Studentski Trg

Simina

Zmaj Jovina

Braće Jugovića

Dositejeva

Francuska

52 31

36

Skadarska

25

33

23

Cetinjska

Đorđa Vašingtona

Jevremovac Botanical Gardens

24

42

49

9

Knez Mihailova

18

Trg Republike

44

Tourist Organisation

53

of Belgrade

Makedonska

26

32

Svetogorska

Hilandarska

Bulevar Despota Stefana

27 Marta

50

Dalmatinska

39

41

4

5

Sremska

Terazije

Nušićeva

Dečanska

Kondina

7

Vlajkovićeva

Majke Jevrosime

Palmotićeva

20

28

Kosovska

5

Kraljice Natalije

Trg Nikole Pašića

Takovska

21

Balkanska

Kraljice Natalije

Kralja Milana

Pionirski Park

Bulevar Kralja Aleksandra

Russian Church

14

6

Kneza Miloša

Dobrinjska

Admirala Geprata

43

Krunska

Resavska

To Sveti Sava (1.1km)

To Nikola Tesla Museum (400m)

Tašmajdan Park

Beogradska

7

E F G H

Central Belgrade

turn of the 20th century; local artistes and dapper types still gather in its cute restaurants and cafes. Tuck into home-style cuisine while roving Roma bands provide ambience.

CENTRAL BELGRADE
Belgrade hustles and bustles along Terazije, crowned by the majestic Hotel Moskva, an art nouveau gem over a century old.

Nikola Tesla Museum   MUSEUM
(www.tesla-museum.org; Krunska 51; admission incl guided tour in English 300DIN; ☺10am-6pm Tue-Fri, to 3pm Sat & Sun) Meet the man on the 100DIN note at one of Belgrade's best mu-

seums. Release your inner nerd with some wondrously sci-fi-ish interactive elements.

Museum of Automobiles   MUSEUM
(www.automuseumbgd.com; Majke Jevrosime 30; adult/child 100/80DIN; ☺9am-9pm) This compelling collection of cars and motorcycles is located in Belgrade's first public garage. Check out the '57 Caddy convertible: only 25,000km and one careful owner – President Tito.

Historical Museum of Serbia   MUSEUM
(Istorijski Muzej Srbije; www.imus.org.rs; Trg Nikole Pašića 11; adult/child 100/50DIN; ☺noon-7pm Tue-Sun) Home to an absorbing wealth of ar-

chaeological, ethnographic and military collections. It's your best bet while the National Museum remains closed.

Sveti Marko Church   CHURCH
(Bul Kralja Aleksandra 17) This five-domed church, based on the design of Kosovo's Gračanica Monastery, houses priceless Serbian icons and the tomb of Emperor Dušan 'The Mighty' (1308–55). Behind is a tiny Russian Church erected by refugees who fled the October Revolution.

OUTER BELGRADE

Sveti Sava   CHURCH
(www.hramsvetogsave.com; Svetog Save) Sveti Sava is the world's biggest Orthodox church, a fact made entirely obvious when looking at the city skyline from a distance or standing under its dome. The church is built on the site where the Turks apparently burnt relics of St Sava. Work on the church interior (frequently interrupted by wars) continues today.

Maršal Tito's Grave   MONUMENT
(House of Flowers; www.mij.rs; Botićeva 6; incl entry to Museum of Yugoslav History 200DIN; ◷10am-4pm Tue-Sun) A visit to Tito's mausoleum is obligatory. Also on display are thousands of elaborate relay batons presented to him by young 'Pioneers', plus gifts from political leaders and the voguish set of the era. Take trolleybus 40 or 41 at the south end of Parliament on Kneza Miloša. It's the second stop after turning into Bul Mira: ask the driver for Kuća Cveća.

Ada Ciganlija   BEACH
(www.adaciganlija.rs) In summertime, join the hordes of sea-starved locals (up to 250,000 a day) for sun and fun at this artificial island on the Sava. Cool down with a swim, kayak or windsurf after a leap from the 55m bungee tower. Take bus 53 or 56 from Zeleni Venac.

Aviation Museum   MUSEUM
(www.muzejvazduhoplovstva.org.rs; Nikola Tesla airport; admission 500DIN; ◷8.30am-7pm Tue-Sun summer, 9am-3.30pm winter) This airport-based museum contains rare planes, a WWII collection and bits of the infamous American stealth fighter shot down in 1999.

☞ Tours

TOP CHOICE Belgrade
Underground   HISTORICAL TOUR
(www.go2serbia.net; per person from €12) Delve into Belgrade's tumultuous past – from Roman times until the Cold War – on this fascinating two-hour tour of subterranean caves, bunkers and secret passageways. Bookings are a must.

iBikeBelgrade   BIKE TOUR
(www.ibikebelgrade.com; ◷from 2pm May-Nov) Wheel around town on four-hour cycle tours that take in everywhere from Ada Ciganlija to Zemun.

Nightlife Academy   DRINKING TOUR
(☎669 008 386; www.nightlifeacademy.com; incl drinks & dinner €25) Take in Belgrade's (in)famous nightlife and learn how to party like a local during a 'kafana class'. Excellent value for money; reservations essential.

🛏 Sleeping

New hostels are popping up all the time, while some of the crumbling classics have had face (and price) lifts. Decent midrange options are few and far between. Private apartments (try www.bestbelgradeapartments.com) are a better bet for longer stays.

   The **Youth Hostel Association of Serbia** (Ferijalni Savez Beograd; ☎322 0762; www.serbia-hostels.org; Makedonska 22/2; ◷9am-5pm) does deals with local hotels. You need HI membership (under/over 26 years 500/800DIN) or an international student card.

Hotel Moskva   HISTORIC HOTEL €€€
(Hotel Moscow; ☎268 6255; www.hotelmoskva.rs; Balkanska 1; s €77-112, d €99-135, ste €130-330; ❉🛜) Art nouveau icon and proud symbol of the best of Belgrade, the majestic Moskva has been wowing guests – including Albert Einstein, Indira Gandhi and Alfred Hitchcock – since 1906. Laden with ye olde glamour, this is the place to write your memoirs at a big old desk.

TOP CHOICE Green Studio Hostel   HOSTEL €
(☎063-7562 357; www.greenstudiohostel.com; Karađorđeva 69, 6th floor; dm from €10, r €7-36, apt €40; ❉🛜) This sunny surprise goes down as one of the top budget options in Serbia. Clean, airy and staffed by your new best friends, it has a handy location near the bus and train stations, as well as Belgrade's main attractions. Free *rakija*!

Hostelche   HOSTEL €
(☎263 7793; www.hostelchehostel.com; Kralja Petra 8; dm from €14, s €25-27, tw €20-22; ❉🛜) A bend-over-backwards staff, homey atmosphere, free walking tours and a super location make this award-winner popular for all the right reasons.

Travelling Actor PENSION €€€
(☏323 4156; www.travellingactor.rs; Gospodar Jevremova 65; s €62-69, d €88-98, apt €188; ❉⚡) Trip down the cobblestones and back in time at this Skadarlija boutique pension. True to its name, the gilded apartments are almost melodramatically over the top, but this luxe-campness only adds to the fun.

Three Black Catz HOSTEL €
(☏262 9826; www.hostel.co.rs; Čika Ljubina 7; dm from €9, tw €16; @) Never mind the 'catz': it's the night owls that will adore this convivial spot. While the atmosphere can border on merry chaos, the hostel doesn't completely forgo business for pleasure, offering heaps of info and advice.

Hostel 360 HOSTEL €
(☏263 4957; www.threesixtyhostel.com; Knez Mihailova 21; dm/s/tw/d €15/29/44/50, apt from €40; ❉⚡) Super-tidy rooms and a garden terrace are surpassed only by spirited staff on a mission to immerse guests in local life.

Le Petit Piaf LUXURY HOTEL €€€
(☏303 5252; www.petitpiaf.com; Skadarska 34; s & d €84-92, ste €108; ❉⚡) Elegant loft rooms, refined decor and *soignée* service make this Skadarlija charmer a Parisian doppelgänger in all the right ways.

Arka Barka HOSTEL €
(☏064-925 3507; www.arkabarka.net; Bul Nikole Tesle bb; dm €13; ❉⚡) Bobbing off Ušće Park, a mere stagger from the Danube barges, this 'floating house' offers sparkling rooms in 'wake-up!' colours, party nights and fresh river breezes. It's a moderate walk, or a short ride on bus 15 or 84 from the centre. Cash only.

Belgrade Art Hotel BOUTIQUE HOTEL €€€
(☏331 2000; www.belgradearthotel.com; Knez Mihailova 27; s €115-135, d €130-150; ❉⚡) This Italian-designed hotel is everything its name suggests: stylish, refined and discerning. Soundproof windows are a godsend.

Hotel Royal HOTEL €€
(☏263 4222; www.hotelroyal.rs; Kralja Petra 56; s 3680-4370DIN, d 5175-7820DIN; ❉@) Rooms are basic and far from sparkling, but this (very) central spot disarms with character and buzz.

Belgrade City Hotel HOTEL €€
(☏360 0700; www.bgcityhotel.com; Savski Trg 7; s €49-65, d €65-95, tr €115, ste €89-109; ℗❉⚡) A convenient location (across the road from the train station), clean – if nondescript –

rooms and a decent continental breakfast make this a serviceable stopover.

Hotel Prag HOTEL €€€
(☏321 4444; www.hotelprag.rs; Kraljice Natalije 27; s €79-92, d €106, ste €157-192; ❉@) Totally refurbished business hotel.

✕ Eating

From Slavic staples to fusion cuisine, Belgrade offers a diverse bill of fare. The choice is particularly overwhelming along Knez Mihailova, Kralja Petra and Makedonska.

SKADARSKA

Šešir Moj SERBIAN €€
(My Hat; Skadarska 21; meals 400-1000DIN; ⊙9am-1am) Roma bands tug the heartstrings while traditional dishes like *punjena bela vešalica* (pork stuffed with *kajmak*) buoy up the belly.

Dva Jelena SERBIAN €€
(Two Deer; www.dvajelena.com; Skadarska 32; meals 400-900DIN; ⊙11am-1am) A local icon, Dva Jelena has been dishing up hearty fare for over 180 years. Rustic, homespun and with the obligatory violin serenades, it ticks all the Skadarlija boxes.

Writers' Club EUROPEAN €€€
(Klub Književnika; Francuska 7; meals 250-1500DIN; ⊙noon-1am Mon-Sat, to 6pm Sun) The former haunt of local literati and the visiting elite (think Simone de Beauvoir and Jean-Paul Sartre), this dignified spot is still a favourite for substantial steaks and stews.

CENTRAL BELGRADE

Indulge your post- or preclubbing munchies in cheap bakeries around Trg Republike. **Pekara Toma** (Kolarčeva 10; snacks 50-200DIN; ⊙24hr) is a favourite for fresh pizzas, sandwiches and salads. Forage through **Zeleni Venac Market** (cnr Brankova Prizrenska & Kraljice Natalije; ⊙6am-7pm) for DIY food – it's downhill from the Balkan Hotel towards the Sava River.

TOP CHOICE Little Bay EUROPEAN €€
(www.little-bay.co.uk; Dositejeva 9a; meals 495-1295DIN) Little wonder locals and visitors have long been singing the praises of this gem: it's one of the best dining experiences in Belgrade. Tuck yourself into a private opera box and let the salmon in beer and tarragon sauce (645DIN) or a traditional English roast lunch (695DIN, Sundays only) melt in your mouth as a live opera singer does wonderful things to your ears.

? EASTERN EUROPEAN €€

(Znak Pitanja; Kralja Petra 6; meals 450-800DIN) Belgrade's oldest *kafana* has been attracting the bohemian set since 1823 with dishes such as stuffed chicken and 'lamb under the iron pan'. Its quizzical name follows a dispute with the adjacent church, which objected to the boozy tavern – originally called 'By the Cathedral' – referring to a house of god.

Smokvica CAFE €€

(Kralja Petra 73; meals 200-1200DIN; ⊗9am-1am; ☏) With its courtyard terrace, arty crowd and gourmet menu, to stumble across Smokvica ('little fig') is to forget you're in hustling, bustling Belgrade. Graze on a blue cheese, rocket and fig salad, snarf down a sanga with homemade ciabatta or just sip good coffee in an atmosphere both rare and rarified.

Kafana Suvobor SERBIAN €€

(Kralja Petra 70; meals 500-1200DIN) Specialists in Serbian cuisine, offering dishes such as the to-die-for *rolovana pileća džigerica u slanini* (rolled chicken liver wrapped in bacon). Lip-smackingly good.

Kalemegdanska Terasa EUROPEAN €€€

(☏328 3011; www.kalemegdanskaterasa.com; Mali Kalemegdan bb; meals 870-1780DIN; ⊗noon-1am) By the fortress, this is a literal bastion of refined dining, featuring sumptuous dishes such as rolled steak and goose liver with truffle sauce. One for the romantics, and those who packed a tie.

Supermarket INTERNATIONAL €€

(www.supermarket.rs; cnr Višnjićeva & Strahinjića Bana; meals 575-1400DIN; ⊗9am-midnight Sun-Thu, to 1am Fri & Sat) The burgeoning breed of local hipsters descends on this slice of Brooklyn in Belgrade, a designer eatery for organic, oddball-on-purpose cuisine: ahem, pickle-stuffed cannelloni with marmalade sauce. Those with a plainer palate aren't left out: the cafe-style breakfasts here are sublime. It's part of the Supermarket 'concept store', with indie-label duds, cool trinkets and exhibitions all under one spiffy roof.

Biblioteka INTERNATIONAL €€

(Terazije 27; meals 300-900DIN; ⊗7am-1am; ☏) Buzzing outside and aptly library-ambient inside, Biblioteka is popular with locals for its extensive breakfast menu, served until 1pm.

OUTER BELGRADE

Dačo SERBIAN €€

(☏278 1009; www.kafanadaco.com; Patrisa Lumumbe 49; meals 500-1150DIN; ⊗noon-midnight Tue-Sun) Making the haul out here is like visiting the Serbian granny you never knew you had: the walls are cluttered with homey bits and bobs, chequered tablecloths adorn rickety tables and chooks strut around in the garden. And you won't have to be told twice to 'Eat! Eat!' either. Reservations recommended.

Maharaja INDIAN €€

(www.maharaja.rs; Ljubićka 1b; meals 380-1450DIN; ⊗noon-midnight Tue-Sun) Craving curry in a sea of *kajmak*? It's worth the trip out to one of Belgrade's only Indian restaurants, serving all the staples from tikka to tandoori. Vegetarians will find solace here.

🍷 Drinking

Quiet cafes morph into drinking dens at night and then thumping clubs in the early hours. In spring and summer, action spills onto terraces and pavements.

Coffee chains abound: look out for Costa Coffee, Greenet or Coffee Dream, or try your luck at any of the independents along Knez Mihailova.

TOP CHOICE Kafana Pavle Korčagin TAVERNA

(☏240 1980; Ćirila i Metodija 2a; ⊗8pm-1am) Raise a glass to Tito at this frantic, festive *kafana*. Lined with communist memorabilia and packed to the rafters with revellers and grinning accordionists, this table-thumping throwback fills up nightly; reserve a table in advance.

Federal Association of Globe Trotters BAR

(www.usp-aur.rs; Bul Despota Stefana 7/1; ⊗1pm-midnight Mon-Fri, 3pm-late Sat & Sun; ☏) Through the big black gate and down into the basement lies one of Belgrade's coolest hang-outs. Miscellaneous oddities clamour for wall space while an equally motley clientele yaks over cocktails.

Rakia Bar BAR

(www.rakiabar.com; Dobračina 5; ⊗9am-midnight Sun-Thu, to 1am Fri & Sat) An ideal spot for *rakija* rookies to get their first taste of the spirit of Serbia. English-speaking staff will gently guide you through the extensive drinks menu, but beware: this stuff is strong.

Pub Brod BAR

(Bul Despota Stefana 36; ⊗noon-4am) This congenial student hang-out thumbs its nose at dress codes, Top 40 and nouveau-Belgrade bling. Small and smoky inside, in summertime indie music pumps over a whooping sidewalk sprawl.

Bar Central
COCKTAIL BAR

(Kralja Petra 59; ☺9am-1am) This is the HQ of Serbia's Association of Bartenders, a fact made evident after one sip of any of the sublime cocktails on offer. With an interior as polished as a bottle flip-pour, this ain't the place for tacky tikis and those little drink umbrellas.

Plato Kafe
CAFE

(1 Akademski Plato; ☺9am-2am) Aptly located by 'Students' Square' off Knez Mihailova, Plato is a university bookshop-cafe offering fine coffees, booze, nibbles and smartypants live jazz and literary gigs.

Three Carrots
PUB

(Kneza Miloša 16; ☺9am-2am) Dimly lit like any Irish bar worth its quirky ceiling-hangings should be, this place pulls both pints and a cosmopolitan crowd.

☆ Entertainment

Nightclubs

Belgrade has a reputation as one of the world's top party cities, with a wild club scene limited only by imagination and hours in the day. Check out www.serbianightlife.com for more pointers.

Plastic
NIGHTCLUB

(www.clubplastic.rs; cnr Dalmatinska & Takovska; ☺Thu-Sat) A favourite among electro-heads and booty shakers, this slick venue is frequented by top local and international DJs. In summer, head to Plastic Light, the floating version of the club on the Sava River.

Bitef Art Cafe
LIVE MUSIC

(www.bitefartcafe.rs; Skver Mire Trailović 1; ☺7pm-4am) There's something for everyone at this delightful hotchpotch of a cafe-club. Funk, soul and jazz get a good airing, as do rock and classical. Karaoke competitions pack in the punters.

Tube
NIGHTCLUB

(www.thetube.rs; Simina 21; ☺Thu-Sat) Lovers of all music electronic will have a blast in this beautifully designed former nuclear bunker. Upmarket and oft-crowded, despite a whopping floor space, it's worth scrubbing up for.

Ona A Ne Neka Druga
NIGHTCLUB

(She and Not Some Other; ☎062-222 152; Grobljanska 9; ☺9pm-4am Tue-Sun) As its unusual name suggests, this cosy club caters entirely to women...but in true Serbia style, it steers far from any PC aspects one might expect of such a distinction. Instead, women (and brave male friends) are encouraged to smash glasses, table dance and pinch waiters on the bum. In the Gardoš part of Zemun; take a taxi. Reservations suggested.

Mr Stefan Braun
NIGHTCLUB

(www.mrstefanbraun.rs; Nemanjina 4) Those who want to party like (and with) Serbian superstars will find their bliss at this 9th-storey den of decadence. Get your finest threads – and most model-like pout – on and get there before 1am to beat the queues.

River Barges

According to Michael Palin, Belgrade has so many nightclubs 'they can't fit them all on land'. Indeed: adjacent to Hotel Jugoslavija in Novi Belgrade is a 1km strip of some 20 Danube River barges, known collectively as *splavovi*. Most are closed in winter. Get there with bus 15 or 84 from Zeleni Venac or 68, 603 or 701 from Trg Republike; get out at Hotel Jugoslavija.

On the western bank of the Sava River is a 1.5km strip of *splavovi*. Most are only open in summer. Walk over Brankov Most or catch tram 7, 9 or 11.

Blaywatch
BARGE

(Danube River; ☺midnight-late) This throbbing place gets crowded and dress codes may be enforced (scruffy bad on boys, skimpy good on girls). The crowd is a mix of local 'beautiful people' and foreigners, all occupied with each other and the turbo tunes.

Bahus
BARGE

(www.bahus.rs; Danube River; ☺10am-1pm) This chic alternative attracts a refined crowd who'd rather sip cocktails than spill them down someone else's back.

Acapulco
BARGE

(Danube River; ☺noon-late) Blinged-up boys come here to flaunt their (new) money and she-accessories. Got a low turbofolk threshold? Start swimming.

Freestyler
BARGE

(www.splavfree.rs; Brodarska bb, Sava River; ☺11pm-5am Tue-Sun) The gigantic Freestyler has been a symbol of *splav* saturnalia for years, not least for its infamous foam parties.

Exile
BARGE

(Savski kej bb, Sava River; ☺midnight-late) Exile pounds out techno.

Sound
BARGE

(Savski kej bb, Sava River; ☺midnight-3am) Sound plays house and disco to a slightly older following.

Povetarac BARGE
(Brodarska bb, Sava River; ☺midnight-late, 8pm-late winter) This rusting cargo ship attracts an indie crowd.

20/44 BARGE
(Savski kej bb, Sava River; ☺7pm-4am) Conga around a life-sized statue of John Cleese.

Performing Arts

For concert and theatre tickets, go to **Bilet Servis** (☎303 3311; www.biletservis.rs; Trg Republike 5; ☺9am-8pm Mon-Fri, 10am-8pm Sat). Large venues for visiting acts include **Sava Centar** (☎220 6060; www.savacentar.net; Milentija Popovića 9; ☺box office 10am-8pm Mon-Fri, to 3pm Sat) and **Belgrade Arena** (☎220 2222; www.arenabeograd.com; Bul Arsenija Čarnojevića 58; ☺box office 10am-8pm Mon-Fri, to 3pm Sat).

National Theatre THEATRE
(☎262 0946; www.narodnopozoriste.co.rs; Trg Republike; ☺box office 10am-2pm Tue-Sun) Stages operas, dramas and ballets during winter.

Kolarčev University Concert Hall LIVE MUSIC
(☎2630 550; www.kolarac.co.rs; Studentski Trg 5; ☺box office 10am-7.30pm) Home to the Belgrade Philharmonica.

Dom Omladine LIVE MUSIC, THEATRE
(www.domomladine.org; Makedonska 22; ☺box office 10am-8pm Mon-Fri, 3pm-8pm Sat) Hosts a range of mostly youth-based cultural events.

Serbian Academy of Arts & Sciences LIVE MUSIC
(☎202 7200; www.sanu.ac.rs; Knez Mihailova 35; ☺concerts from 6pm Mon & Thu Oct-Jun) Stages free concerts and exhibitions.

DAY TRIPS FROM BELGRADE

It's easy to get stuck in Belgrade, but catching a glimpse of the country around the capital is a cinch if you get an early start. Hop a bus and have a gander at the following.

Smederevo (one hour)

Smederevo Fortress (www.tvrdjava.com; admission 50DIN; ☺8am-8pm) is a huge, 25-tower fort constructed between 1427 and 1430. Once the temporary capital of Serbia, and one of the largest city-fortresses in Europe, it hosts a **theatre festival** (www.tvrdjavateatar.rs) each August and is home to the lovingly maintained **Smederevo Museum** (admission 70DIN; ☺10am-5pm Tue-Fri, to 3pm Sat & Sun). Regular buses (500DIN) leave from Belgrade's Lasta station.

Topola (2.5 hours)

This is where Karađorđe plotted the Serbian insurrection against the Turks in 1804. One ticket (300DIN) grants access to all the park's impressive attractions, open daily from 8am to 6pm.

The complex includes a **museum** (ul Kraljice Marije), the Winegrower's House gallery and the white-marble, five-domed **Church of St George** (Avenija Kralja Petra I), where vibrant mosaics are magnificently rendered with over 40 million pieces of coloured glass. Millions more adorn the **Karađorđe mausoleum** under the church.

Frequent buses run to and from Belgrade (570DIN).

Despotovac (2.5 hours)

This little town is a gateway to attractions ranging from the sacred to the subterraneous.

Manasija Monastery was a refuge for artists and writers fleeing the Turkish invasion of Kosovo in the early 1400s. Many consider Manasija's vivid frescos to be predecessors to the Serbian equivalent of Renaissance art.

A winding 20km beyond Despotovac, the eight-million-year-old **Resavska Pećina** (Resava Cave; www.resavska pecina.rs; adult/child 300/250DIN; ☺9am-5pm Apr-Nov) has guided tours through impressive underground halls, featuring natural formations with names like 'Hanged Sheep' and 'Thirst for Love'. Temperatures average just 7°C.

A taxi will take you to both sites from town; the return trip including waiting time should be around 2000DIN. Belgrade buses leave six times every weekday to Despotovac (1000DIN).

Shopping

Knez Mihailova is studded with global and luxury brands. Get souvenirs from Kalemegdan Park vendors or browse Zemun's Sunday-morning *buvljak* (flea market). Load up on Belgrade-themed art, clothes, books and fripperies at **Belgrade Window** (Knez Mihailova 6; ⊙9am-9pm Mon-Sat), or get your fashion fix at Dorćol's Supermarket (p467).

Information

Internet Access

Net cafes come and go in Belgrade faster than you can click a mouse. Wireless is free at venues throughout the city and available at almost every hostel/hotel.

Belgrade City Library (Knez Mihailova 56; per min 2DIN; ⊙8am-8pm Mon-Fri, to 2pm Sat)

Medical Services

Emergency Medical Assistance (⊘94; www.beograd94.rs; Bul Franše D'Eperea 5; ⊙24hr)

Klinički Centar (⊘361 7777; www.klinicki-centar.rs; Pasterova 2; ⊙24hr) Medical clinic.

Prima 1 (⊘361 099; www.primax.rs; Nemanjina 2; ⊙24hr) All-hours pharmacy.

Post

Central Post Office (⊙8am-7pm Mon-Fri, to 3pm Sat)

Tourist Information

Tourist Organisation of Belgrade (www.tob.rs) Trg Republike 5 (⊘328 1859; ⊙9am-9pm Mon-Sat, 10am-3pm Sun); Train Station (⊘361 2732; ⊙7am-1.30pm Mon-Sat); Nikola Tesla Airport (⊘209 7828; ⊙9am-9.30pm) Helpful folk with a raft of brochures, city maps and all the info you could need.

Websites

Belgrade in Your Pocket (www.inyourpocket.com/serbia/belgrade)

Belgraded (www.belgraded.com)

Lonely Planet (www.lonelyplanet.com/serbia/belgrade)

Getting There & Away

Bus

Belgrade has two adjacent bus stations, near the eastern banks of the Sava River: **BAS** (⊘263 6299; www.bas.rs; Železnička 4) serves the region, while **Lasta** (⊘334 8555; www.lasta.rs; Železnička 2) deals with destinations around Belgrade.

TRANSPORT FROM BELGRADE

International Bus

DESTINATION	PRICE (DIN)	DURATION (HR)	FREQUENCY
Banja Luka (Bosnia & Hercegovina)	2530	7½	daily
Bratislava (Slovakia)	4180	12	Wed & Sun
Ljubljana (Slovenia)	4170	7½	daily
Podgorica (Montenegro)	2500	9	daily
Sarajevo (Bosnia & Hercegovina)	2510	8	daily
Skopje (Macedonia)	2750	7	daily
Split (Croatia)	5570	12½	Mon-Sat
Vienna (Austria)	4330	9½	daily

International Train

DESTINATION	PRICE (€)	DURATION (HR)
Bucharest (Romania)	48	14
Budapest (Hungary)	15	7
Ljubljana (Slovenia)	25	10
Moscow (Russia)	122	50
Munich (Germany)	145	17
Sofia (Bulgaria)	30	11
Vienna (Austria)	70	11
Zagreb (Croatia)	32	7

Frequent domestic services include Subotica (1280DIN, three hours), Novi Sad (600DIN, one hour), Niš (1420DIN, three hours) and Novi Pazar (1520DIN, three hours).

Car & Motorcycle

Several car-hire companies have offices at Nikola Tesla Airport:

Avaco (☎228 6434; www.avaco.rs; ⊗8am-8pm)

Avis (☎209 7062; www.avis.rs; ⊗8am-8pm)

Budget (☎228 6361; www.budget.rs; ⊗8am-8pm Mon-Fri, 10am-6pm Sat, 10am-2pm Sun)

Train

The **central train station** (Savski Trg 2) has an information office on Platform 1, tourist information office, **exchange bureau** (⊗6am-10pm) and **sales counter** (⊗9am-4pm Mon-Sat).

Frequent trains go to Novi Sad (288DIN, 1½ hours), Subotica (480DIN, three hours) and Niš (784DIN, four hours).

🛈 Getting Around

TO/FROM THE AIRPORT Nikola Tesla airport is 18km from Belgrade. Local bus 72 connects the airport with Zeleni Venac (65DIN to 120DIN, half-hourly, 5.20am to midnight from airport, 4.40am to 11.40pm from town); the cheapest tickets must be purchased from news stands. A minibus also runs between the airport and the central Slavija Sq (250DIN, 5am to 3.50am from airport, 4.20am to 3.20am from the square).

Don't get swallowed up by the airport taxi shark pit: ask the tourist office in the arrivals hall to call one for you. A taxi from the airport to Knez Mihailova should be around 1250DIN.

CAR & MOTORCYCLE Parking in Belgrade is regulated by three parking zones – red (one hour, 56DIN), yellow (two hours, 38DIN per hour) and green (three hours, 31DIN per hour). Tickets must be bought from kiosks or via SMS (in Serbian).

PUBLIC TRANSPORT Trams and trolleybuses ply limited routes but buses chug all over town. Rechargeable BusPlus cards can be bought and topped up (70DIN per ticket) at kiosks across the city; they're 140DIN if you buy from the driver.

Tram 2 connects Kalemegdan Citadel with Trg Slavija, bus stations and the central train station.

TAXI Move away from obvious taxi traps and flag down a distinctly labelled cruising cab, or get a local to call you one. A 5km trip costs around 415DIN. Flagfall is 140DIN, and reputable cabs should charge between 55DIN and 70DIN per kilometre.

AROUND BELGRADE

Zemun   Земун

Some 6km northwest of central Belgrade, Zemun was the most southerly point of the Austro-Hungarian empire when the Turks ruled Belgrade. Today it's known for its fish restaurants and quaint, nonurban ambience.

Up the narrow cobbled street of Grobljan-ska, remnants of the old village lead towards the 9th-century Gardoš fortress. Walls from the 15th century remain, as does the Tower of Sibinjanin Janko, built in 1896 to celebrate the millennial anniversary of the Hungarian state and to keep an eye on the Turks. Today you can enjoy the spectacular view. Descending from the tower, stop in at the 1731 Nikolajevska Church (Njegoševa 43) to goggle at its astounding baroque iconostasis.

Zemun is a laid-back accommodation alternative to Belgrade. Floating between Zemun and Belgrade is the Arka Barka (p466) barge-hostel. The lobby of the more upmarket Hotel Skala (☎011-307 5032; www.hotelskala.rs; Bežanijska 3; s/d/apt 6300/8100/9000DIN; ❄🛜) has sunny, wi-fi-equipped rooms and a cavernous basement restaurant.

Among the many venues dishing up fish and fun along the Danube are Šaran (☎011-261 8235; www.saran.co.rs; Kej Oslobođenja 53; dishes from 1000DIN; ⊗noon-1am), renowned as one of Zemun's best fish restaurants, Reka (☎011-261 1625; www.reka.co.rs; Kej Oslobođenja 73b; dishes from 690DIN; ⊗noon-2am) and Malevilla (www.malevilla.rs; Kej Oslobođenja bb; dishes from 1000DIN; ⊗10am-midnight).

Zemun is a 45-minute walk from Belgrade (across Brankov Most, along Nikole Tesle and the Kej Oslobođenja waterside walkway). Alternatively, take bus 15 or 84 from Zeleni Venac market, or bus 83 or 78 from the main train station.

VOJVODINA

Home to more than 25 ethnic groups, six languages and the best of Hungarian and Serbian traditions, Vojvodina's (Војводина) pancake plains mask a diversity unheard of in the rest of the country. Affable capital Novi Sad hosts the eclectic EXIT festival – the largest in southeast Europe – while the hilly region of Fruška Gora keeps the noise down in hushed monasteries and ancestral vineyards. Charming Subotica, 10km from Hungary, is an oasis of art nouveau delights.

Novi Sad   Нови Сад

☑021 / POP 335.700

As convivial as a *rakija* toast – and at times just as carousing – Novi Sad is a chipper town with all the spoils and none of the stress of the big smoke. Locals sprawl in parks and outdoor cafes, and laneway bars pack out nightly. The looming Petrovaradin Citadel keeps a stern eye on proceedings, loosening its tie each July to host Serbia's largest music festival. You can walk to all of Novi Sad's attractions from the happening pedestrian thoroughfare, Zmaj Jovina, which stretches from the town square (Trg Slobode) to Dunavska street.

◎ Sights

Petrovaradin Citadel   FORTRESS

Towering over the river on a 40m-high volcanic slab, this mighty citadel (*tvrđava*) is aptly nicknamed 'Gibraltar on the Danube'. Constructed with slave labour between 1692 and 1780, its dungeons have held notable prisoners including Karađorđe (leader of the first uprising against the Turks and founder of a dynasty) and Tito. Have a good gawk at the iconic clock tower: the size of the minute and hour hands are reversed so far-flung fishermen can tell the time.

Within the citadel walls, a **museum** (☑433 155; admission 200DIN; ◎9am-5pm Tue-Sun) offers insight (sans English explanations) into the site's history. The museum can also arrange tours of Petrovaradin's creepy – but cool – underground passageways.

Museum of Vojvodina   MUSEUM

(Muzej Vojvodine; www.muzejvojvodine.org.rs; Dunavska 35-7; admission 100DIN; ◎9am-7pm Tue-Fri, 10am-6pm Sat & Sun) This museum houses historical, archaeological and ethnological exhibits. Building 35 covers Vojvodinian history from Palaeolithic times to the late 19th century. Building 37 takes the story to 1945 with harrowing emphasis on WWI and WWII.

Štrand   BEACH

One of Europe's best by-the-Danube beaches, this 700m-long stretch of sand morphs into a city of its own come summertime, with bars, stalls and all manner of recreational diversions attracting thousands of sun-'n'-fun seekers from across the globe. It's also the ultimate Novi Sad party venue, hosting everything from local punk gigs to EXIT raves.

✦ Festivals & Events

Some festivals are worth sculpting a trip around (and booking accommodation in advance for). The biggest is the EXIT festival with blockbusting line-ups performing at the Petrovaradin Fortress each July.

June's **Cinema City Festival** (www.cinemacity.org) is a weeklong, city-wide film extravaganza, while each September Novi Sad morphs into an open-air stage for the **International Festival of Street Musicians** (www.ulicnisviraci.com). The city toots its own horn at the **Novi Sad Jazz Festival** (http://jazzns.eunet.rs) every November.

⌘ Sleeping

While Novi Sad is loaded with hotels and hostels, it fills up fast during EXIT season: book far ahead. Try www.novisadproperty.com for house/flat rentals.

TOP CHOICE Hostel Sova   HOSTEL €

(☑066-152 30; www.hostelsova.com; Ilije Ognjanovića 26; dm from €10, d €15; ℙ🖛) This cute spot is akin to a mini Novi Sad: super-friendly, attractive and given to laid-back socialising (not to mention the odd *rakija* or two). It's perched above a deceptively quiet street that's just around the corner from buzzy Zmaj Jovina and a couple of minutes' stagger from the best bars in town.

Leopold I   LUXURY HOTEL €€€

(☑488 7878; www.leopoldns.com; Petrovaradin Citadel; s/d from 7000/8200DIN, ste 12,100-26,600DIN; ℙ🌢🖛) This rock-top indulgence offers rooms in Gothic, Renaissance or the (slightly) more economical modern style. Warning: the regal Leopold I apartment may induce delusions of grandeur.

ENTERING THE STATE OF EXIT

Home to the epic **EXIT Festival** (www.exitfest.org), the Petrovaradin Fortress is stormed by thousands of revellers each July. The first festival in 2000 lasted 100 days and galvanised a generation of young Serbs against the Milošević regime, who 'exited' himself just weeks after the event. The festival has been attended by the likes of Faith No More, Chemical Brothers, Gogol Bordello, Gossip and Patti Smith, not to mention an annual tally of about 200,000 merrymakers from around the world.

Downtown HOSTEL €
(☎69 139 7708; www.hostelnovisad.com; Njegoševa 2; dm from €10, s/d €25/30; @) Super-friendly staff and an 'in the thick of it' location off Trg Slobode make this rambunctious, slightly ramshackle hostel a Novi Sad experience in itself.

Hotel Vojvodina HISTORIC HOTEL €€
(☎622 122; www.hotelvojvodina.rs; Trg Slobode 2; s/d from 2800/4200DIN) Reeking of communist-era retro, Novi Sad's oldest hotel (1854) isn't as slick as others, but its location overlooking the town square is unbeatable, as is the semi-faded splendour of its restaurant.

Hotel Fontana HOTEL €€
(☎621 779; Pašićeva 27; s/d/tr incl breakfast 3200/4350/5700DIN; ✳) With its pink exterior and malapropos chandeliers, this hotel is peculiar but perky. Good-sized rooms overlook the leafy courtyard attached to the locally famous, eponymous restaurant.

✖ Eating

For dessert, lapse into a sugar coma at **Evropa** (Dunavska 6; cakes 100DIN) or **Poslastičarnica Šeherezada** (Zmaj Jovina 19; 2-scoop ice cream 80DIN).

TOP CHOICE **Kod Lipe** SERBIAN €
(Svetozara Miletića 7; meals from 400DIN; ⊙8am-11pm Mon-Fri, 7am-midnight Sat & Sun) This down-home eatery has been dishing up old-school ambience alongside traditional Vojvodinian fare since the 19th century.

Fish i Zeleniš MEDITERRANEAN €€
(Fish and Greens; ☎452 000; Skerlićeva 2; mains from 700DIN; ⊙noon-11pm Mon-Fri, to 1am Sat & Sun; ✎) This bright, snug little nook serves up the finest vegetarian/pescatarian meals in northern Serbia. Organic, locally sourced ingredients? Ambient? Ineffably delicious? Tick, tick, tick. A three-minute walk from Zmaj Jovina.

Lazina Bašta SERBIAN €
(Laze Telečkog 5; meals from 450DIN) Replete with hay bales and knick-knackery, Lazina Bašta serves up country-mouse cuisine on the most happening street in town.

🍷 Drinking

Laze Telečkog (a car-free sidestreet running off Zmaj Jovina) is lined with bars to suit every whim. Squeeze into the frenetic **London Underground Club** (Laze Telečkog 15; ⊙8am-3am) for good-timey tunes (and associated

NOVI SAD'S INDEX SANDWICH

New Orleans has the po'boy, England the chip butty, Philly the cheesesteak... and Novi Sad can proudly boast the *indeks sendvič* (index sandwich). Created in the early 1990s and named after a low-ranked local football team, the Index is an absurdly decadent take on the basic ham-'n'-cheese sanga: gooey cheese and mushrooms are melted between a thick fold of ham and shoved into a long toasted roll with *pavlaka* (sour cream), *urnebes*, tartar, mayonnaise, tomato slices and pickle, then dusted with chilli and curry powders. Too much? Trust us: it's never enough.

Sink your teeth into the local take on the sub sandwich at **Index House** (Bul Mihajla Pupina 5; sandwiches from 180DIN; ⊙24hr), and order yours *veliki* (large)!

drunken sing-a-longs) or sidle next door to **Cuba Libre** (Laze Telečkog 13) and stake your spot on the narrow dance floor. The infinitely more calm **Atrium** (Laze Telečkog 2) serves drinks in a civilised (faux) library. Hang with local eccentrics at **Crni Bik** (Trg Mladenaca 8; ⊙10am-late), a boisterous dive bar just a short stroll southeast from Laze Telečkog. During summer, check out any of the barefoot-bars along the Štrand (p472).

ℹ Information

The centre of town is awash with free wi-fi: both the username and password are 'gost'.

Apoteka Novi Sad (www.apotekanovisad.co.rs; Mihajla Pupina 7; ⊙24hr Mon-Sat) Art-deco pharmacy.

Main Post Office (Narodnih Heroja 2; ⊙9am-7pm Mon-Fri, to 2pm Sat)

Tourist Information Centre (☎661 7343; www.turizamns.rs; Ul Modene 1; ⊙7.30am-8pm Mon-Fri, 10am-3pm Sat) Ultra-helpful with maps and English info.

ℹ Getting There & Away

The **bus station** (Bul Jaše Tomića; ⊙information counter 6am-11pm) has regular departures to Belgrade (600DIN, one hour, every 10 minutes) and Subotica (600DIN, 1½ hours), plus services to Užice (1120DIN, five hours) and Zlatibor (1250DIN, six hours). From here, four stops on bus 4 will take you to the town centre: nip down the underpass and you'll see Trg Slobode on emerging.

Frequent trains leave the **train station** (Bul Jaše Tomića 4), next door to the bus station, for Belgrade (288DIN, 1½ hours) and Subotica (384DIN, 1½ hours).

Another option for roadtrippers is the Novi Sad–based **Rent-a-Yugo** (☑065-526 5256; Mileve Marić 64; per day from €11) car-hire firm.

Subotica   Суботица

☑024 / POP 140,400

Sugar-spun art nouveau marvels, a laid-back populace and a delicious sprinkling of Serbian and Hungarian flavours make this quaint town a worthy day trip or stopover.

◉ Sights

Even the least architecturally inclined will fall for Subotica's art nouveau charms. Most sights are along the pedestrian strip of Korzo or on the main square, Trg Republike.

Town Hall   HISTORIC BUILDING
(Trg Republike) Built in 1910, this behemoth is a curious mix of art nouveau and something Gaudí may have had a playful dab at. The council chambers – with exquisite stained-glass windows and elaborate decor – are not to be missed.

Modern Art Gallery   HISTORIC BUILDING
(www.likovnisusret.rs; Park Ferenca Rajhla 5; admission 50DIN; ⊙8am-2pm Mon, to 6pm Tue-Fri, 9am-noon Sat) This mansion was built in 1904 as an architect's design studio, and it shows. One of the most sumptuous buildings in Serbia, it's a vibrant flourish of mosaics, ceramic tiles, floral patterns and stained glass.

City Museum   MUSEUM
(www.gradskimuzej.subotica.rs; Trg Sinagoge 3; admission 100DIN; ⊙10am-8pm Tue-Sat) Eclectic exhibitions are the go in this art nouveau residence designed by Budapest's Vago brothers.

Synagogue   SYNAGOGUE
(Trg Sinagoge 2) Alas, Subotica's first art nouveau building, remains shuttered and dilapidated as long-awaited renovations have failed to materialise. Grasp its former glory from the footpath.

🛌 Sleeping

Hotel Patria   HOTEL €€
(☑554 500; www.hotelpatria.rs; Đure Đakovića bb; s 3800-4400DIN, d 6400-7000DIN, apt 9000-14,000DIN; ❀🛜) The Patria has well-groomed, well-appointed rooms (the presidential suite

rocks a jacuzzi), a wellness centre and a great location a few hundred metres from the train station.

Hostel Incognito   HOSTEL €
(☑062-666 674; www.hostel-subotica.com; Hugo Badalića 3; s/d/tr/apt 1000/1800/2400/7000DIN; 🛜) This basic but clean hostel is a couple of minutes' walk from all the Subotica sights. Reception is in the restaurant downstairs: call ahead before lobbing up.

Hotel Galleria   HOTEL €€
(☑647 111; www.galleria-center.com; Matije Korvina 17; r 5675-7670DIN, apt 9355-11,350DIN; presidential ste 20,850-27,910DIN; ❀🛜) These four-star rooms come over all 'gentleman's den', with warm mahogany-look fittings and beds lined with bookshelves. It's inside the Atrium shopping plaza.

Hostel Bosa Milićević   HOSTEL €
(☑548 290; Segedinski put 9-11; dm per person 1019DIN) Stay with the students at this cheapie tucked well away behind the Ekonomski Fakultet.

✖ Eating

Ravel   CAFE €
(Nušićeva 2; cakes 60-200DIN; ⊙9am-10pm Mon-Sat, 11am-10pm Sun) Dainty nibbles at *gateaux* and twee tea-taking is the name of the game at this adorable art nouveau classic.

Boss Caffe   INTERNATIONAL €
(www.bosscaffe.com; Matije Korvina 7-8) Boss' offerings include a variety of tacos (285DIN to 510DIN) and pizza with sour cream (465DN to 780DIN). It's directly behind the Modern Art Gallery.

① Information

Tourist Information Office (☑670 350; www.visitsubotica.rs; Town Hall; ⊙8am-6pm Mon-Fri, 9am-1pm Sat) Home to the Subotica Greeters, local volunteers only too thrilled to show you around their hometown (provided you book 10 working days before your arrival).

① Getting There & Away

From the **bus station** (www.sutrans.rs; Senćanski put 3) there are hourly services to Novi Sad (600DIN, two hours) and Belgrade (1280DIN, 3½ hours). See the website for updated prices and other destinations. Subotica's **train station** (Bose Milećević bb) has two trains to Szeged, Hungary (300DIN, 1¾ hours). Trains to Belgrade (480DIN, 3½ hours) stop at Novi Sad (384DIN, 1½ hours).

FRUŠKA GORA & SREMSKI KARLOVCI

Fruška Gora (Фрушка Гора) is an 80km stretch of rolling hills where monastic life has continued since 35 monasteries were built between the 15th and 18th centuries to safeguard Serbian culture and religion from the Turks. With your own vehicle you can flit freely between the 16 remaining monasteries; otherwise, ask about tours at tourist offices in Novi Sad and **Sremski Karlovci** (Сремски Карловци). Public transport gets you to villages within the park, from where you can walk between sights.

An easy outing is done with a bus from Novi Sad bound for Irig; ask to be let out at the **Novo Hopovo Monastery** (170DIN, 30 minutes). From here, walk or catch local buses to other points such as Vrdnik. Visit www.npfruskagora.co.rs for a rundown on the region; www.psdzeleznicarns.org.rs has detailed information on individual monasteries (click on 'manasija').

At the edge of Fruška Gora on the banks of the Danube is the photogenic village of **Sremski Karlovci**. Lined with stunning structures, including the Orthodox cathedral (1758–62), the baroque Four Lions fountain and the Chapel of Peace at the southern end of town (where the Turks and Austrians signed the 1699 Peace Treaty), Sremski Karlovci is also at the heart of a famed wine region. Visit the **Museum of Beekeeping & Wine Cellar** (www.muzejzivanovic.com; Mitropolita Stratimirovića 86) to try famous *bermet* wine, or drop in at any of the family-owned cellars around town. Buzzing during summer weekends with lively wedding parties, Sremski Karlovci also hosts a grape-harvesting festival every October.

Take frequent buses 61 or 62 from Novi Sad (140DIN, 30 minutes) and visit the **tourist organisation** (☑883 855; www.karlovci.org.rs; Patrijarha Rajačića 1; ◎8am-6pm Mon-Fri, 10am-6pm Sat) just off the main square.

SOUTHERN SERBIA

Great adventures await south of Belgrade. Zlatibor's rolling hills are a peaceful privilege to explore any time of the year. Dramatic Kopaonik is a popular ski destination for Europeans in the know. Pressed against Balkan neighbours are the melding cultural heritages of the Raška region (known interchangeably by the Turkish 'Sandžak'), the last to be liberated from Ottoman rule in 1912.

Novi Pazar feels more Turkish than some pockets of İstanbul, with winding streets and an Ottoman skyline spiked by minarets, yet some of Serbia's most revered Orthodox monasteries are but a cab ride away.

Niš   Ниш

☑018 / POP 202,200

Niš is a lively city of curious contrasts, where Roma in horse-drawn carriages trot alongside new cars, and posh cocktails are sipped in antiquated alleyways.

Niš was settled in pre-Roman times and flourished during the time of local-boy-made-good Emperor Constantine (AD 280–337). Turkish rule lasted from 1386 until 1877 despite several Serb revolts; the Tower of Skulls and Niš Fortress are reminders of Ottoman dominion. The Nazis built one of Serbia's most notorious concentration camps here, ironically named 'the Red Cross'.

◉ Sights

Niš Fortress   FORTRESS

(Niška tvrđava; Jadranska; ◎24hr) While its current incarnation was built by the Turks in the 18th century, there have been forts on this site since ancient Roman times. Today it's a sprawling recreational area with restaurants, cafes, market stalls and ample space for moseying. It hosts the **Nišville International Jazz Festival** (www.nisville.com) each August and **Nišomnia** (www.facebook.com/festivalnisomnia), featuring rock and electro acts, in September. The city's main pedestrian boulevard, Obrenoviceva, stretches before the citadel.

Tower of Skulls   MONUMENT

(Ćele Kula; Bul Zoran Đinđić; adult/child 120/100DIN; ◎8am-8pm Tue-Sun Apr-Oct, 9am-4pm Tue-Sat, 10am-4pm Sun Nov-Mar) With Serbian defeat imminent at the 1809 Battle of Čegar, the Duke of Resava kamikazeed towards the Turkish defences, firing at their gunpowder stores. In doing so, he killed himself, 4000 of his men, and 10,000 Turks. The Turks triumphed regardless, and to deter future acts of rebellion, they beheaded, scalped and

MADNESS, MADE IN SERBIA

On the surface, the **Dragačevo Trumpet Assembly** (an annual gathering of brass musicians) sounds harmless; nerdily endearing even. But band camp this ain't: it *is*, however, the most boisterous music festival in all of Europe, if not the world.

Known as 'Guča', after the western Serbian village that has hosted it each August since 1961, the six-day debauch is hedonism at its most rambunctious: tens of thousands of beer-and-brass-addled visitors dance wild *kola* through the streets, gorging on spit-meat and slapping dinar on the sweaty foreheads of the (mostly Roma) *trubači* performers. The music itself is relentless and frenzy-fast; even Miles Davis confessed, 'I didn't know you could play trumpet that way.' Sleep is a dubious proposition, but bring a tent or book ahead anyway: www.guca.rs has information on accommodation and transport.

embedded the skulls of the dead Serbs in this tower. Only 58 of the initial 952 skulls remain. Contrary to Turkish intention, the tower serves as a proud monument of Serbian resistance. Get there on any bus marked 'Niška Banja' from the stop opposite the Ambassador Hotel: ask to be let out at Ćele Kula.

Red Cross Concentration Camp   MUSEUM
(Crveni Krst; Bul 12 Februar; adult/child 120/100DIN; ⊙9am-4pm Tue-Sun Apr-Oct, 9am-4pm Tue-Fri, 10am-2pm Sat & Sun Nov-Mar) One of the best-preserved Nazi camps in Europe, the deceptively named Red Cross held about 30,000 Serbs, Roma, Jews and Partisans during the German occupation of Serbia (1941–45). Harrowing displays tell their stories, and those of the prisoners who attempted to flee in the biggest ever breakout from a concentration camp. A short walk north of the Niš bus station.

FREE Mediana   RUINS
(Bul Cara Konstantina; ⊙10am-6pm Tue-Sun) Mediana, on the eastern outskirts of Niš and a short walk from Ćele Kula, is what remains of Constantine's 4th-century Roman palace. Digging has revealed a palace, mosaics, forum and an expansive grain-storage area. There's an archaeology collection at the

small **museum** (Nikole Pašića 59; adult/child 120/100DIN; ⊙10am-6pm Tue-Sun).

🛏 Sleeping

Hostel Niš   HOSTEL €
(☑513 703; www.hostelnis.rs; Dobrička 3a; dm/d per person 1260/1780DIN; @) Perfectly central with outgoing, helpful staff, good-sized rooms and lockable storage? Winner. It's a five-minute walk (towards the river) from the bus station.

Hotel Niški Cvet   HOTEL €€
(☑297 700; www.niskicvet.com; Kej 29 Decembar 2; s/d €60/90, ste €78-120; P❋�) Top views over the Nišava River and fortress from slick surrounds. Prices drop on weekends.

Hostel Sponsor   HOSTEL €
(www.hostel-sponsor.rs; Generala Milojka Lešjanina 18b; dm/s/d €11/19/22; P❋�) Small, shiny and brand new, this amiable option is a mere 50m stroll from the centre of town. Prices are negotiable.

Hostel Sweet   HOSTEL €
(☑628-942 085; www.sweet-hostel.com; Milorad Veljkovića Špaje 11/4; dm/s/d/tr/q 1000/1500/2000/3000/4000DIN, apt 3000-10,000DIN; ❋�a) This clean, genial spot has lockable storage in each room and a laid-back vibe.

Hotel Ambassador   HOTEL €€
(☑501 800; www.srbijaturist.com; Trg Kralja Milana bb; s €39-46, d €47-55, ste from €60; ❋@) Elizabeth Taylor, a pal of Tito's, once stayed here... and not much has changed since. A communist relic, the rooms are stale but bearable.

🍴 Eating & Drinking

The cobblestoned Kopitareva (Tinkers' Alley) is chock-full of fast-paced eating and drinking options, including **Flo** (Kopitareva 11; ⊙7.30am-midnight Mon-Thu, to 2am Fri & Sat, 9am-midnight Sun) and **Tesla** (Kopitareva 8; ⊙8am-midnight; �a). Locals gather nightly to brown-bag it along the river.

Hamam   SERBIAN €€
(Tvrđava bb; meals 400-2200DIN; ⊙11am-midnight) A crumbling Turkish bath house outside, and an elegant multi-alcove dining space inside, the wonderful Hamam serves up mounds of meat worth salivating over (the Turkish-style grilled lamb is especially slobber-worthy).

Restoran Sindjelić   SERBIAN €
(Nikole Pasića 36; meals from 400DIN; ⊙8am-1am Sun-Fri, to 2am Sat) Hearty traditional fare.

Pekara Branković
BAKERY €
(Vožda Karađorđa 68; 24hr) Niš fancies itself the *burek* capital of Serbia (no arguments there), and this *pekara* (bakery) cooks up some of the tastiest slabs in town.

Crazy Horse
BAR
(Davidova 8; 8am-2am Sat-Thu, to 4am Fri;) Guinness, darts, live Irish music, Champions League on TV...in the birthplace of Constantine the Great? Crazy – like the name says – but somehow, this Irish bar works.

Lo-Co Tropic Open Bar
CAFE
(Kej Kola Srpskih Sestara bb; 8am-late Wed-Sat;) Kick back in a porch swing with coffees or cocktails and watch the Nišava River trickle past. Under the bridge across from the fortress.

❶ Information
Internet Cafe (Hotel Ambassador; per hr 50DIN; 7am-11pm)

Post Office (Voždova Karađorđa 13a; 8am-8pm) Internet access for 50DIN per hour.

Tourist Organisation of Niš (250 222; www.visitnis.com; Tvrđava; 7.30am-7pm Mon-Fri, 9am-1pm Sat) Within the citadel gates.

❶ Getting There & Away
The **bus station** (Bul 12 Februar) behind the fortress has frequent services to Belgrade (1420DIN, three hours) and Brus (714DIN, 1½ hours) for Kopaonik, and three daily to Novi Pazar (1120DIN, four hours).

From the **train station** (Dimitrija Tucovića), there are seven trains to Belgrade (784DIN, 4½ hours) and two to Sofia (702DIN, five hours).

Novi Pazar   Нови Пазар
020 / POP 60,600

Novi Pazar is the cultural centre of the Raška/Sandžak region, with a large Muslim population. Turkish coffee, cuisine and customs abound, yet some idyllic Orthodox sights are in the vicinity: this was the heartland of the Serbian medieval state.

◉ Sights
The Old Town is lined with cafes and shops peddling Turkish goods, while just across the Raška River, cafes and restaurants flank 28 Novembar. Attempts to restore the ruined *hammam* (Turkish bath; off Maj street) have failed dismally, leaving it at the mercy of coffee-drinking men and picnickers.

Sopoćani Monastery, the Church of St Peter and St George Monastery are accessible by taxi; a return trip to a single site should cost around 900DIN.

Sopoćani Monastery
MONASTERY
Built in the mid-13th century by King Uroš (who is buried here), this was destroyed by the Turks in the late 1600s and restored in the 1920s. Frescos inside the Romanesque church are prime examples of medieval art that miraculously survived over two centuries exposed to the elements. The *Assumption of the Virgin Mary* fresco is one of Serbia's most renowned.

Church of St Peter
CHURCH
(Petrova Crkva) Three kilometres from town, this small stone building is the oldest intact church in Serbia; it was founded in the 4th century, with additions made between 600 and 800. The cemetery holds the grave of a 5th-century Illyrian prince. If it's locked, ask at the nearby house to be let in.

St George Monastery
MONASTERY
(Đurđev Stupovi) Near the Church of St Peter, this 1170 cloister is the result of a promise to God by Stefan Nemanja that he would endow a monastery to St George if he was released from captivity (his brothers had imprisoned him in a cave). Ongoing efforts to restore the complex after extensive WWII damage are resurrecting monastic life.

⌷ Sleeping
Hotel Vrbak
HOTEL €
(314 548; www.hotelvrbak.com; Maršala Tita bb; s/d/apt 2500/4500/5500DIN;) The Vrbak is practically a destination in its own right: a motley mashup of architectural styles (think UFO-meets-magic-mushrooms, dolled up in nouveau-cement), it's an unmissable landmark in the centre of town. Though the lofty lobby atrium hints at Napoleonic delusions, the rooms are clean but basic. Still, it's worth staying just so you can say you did.

Hotel Tadž
HOTEL €€
(311 904; www.hoteltadz.rs; Rifata Burdževića 79; s/d/apt 4000/6000/8400DIN;) This modern, upmarket hotel has working wi-fi and a high-quality restaurant.

Hotel Atlas
HOTEL €€
(316 352; Jošanički Kej bb; s/d/tr from €30/50/60;) Modern, sprawling rooms that you'll be loathe to leave...though the

STUDENICA MONASTERY

One of the most sacred sites in Serbia, Studenica was established in the 1190s by founder of the Serbian empire (and future saint) Stefan Nemanja and developed by his sons Vukan, Stefan and Rastko (St Sava). Active monastic life was cultivated by Sava and continues today, though this thriving little community doesn't mind visitors.

Two well-preserved churches lie within impressive white-marble walls. **Bogorodičina Crkva** (Church of Our Lady), a royal funeral church, contains Stefan's tomb. Smaller **Kraljeva Crkva** (King's Church) houses the acclaimed *Birth of the Virgin* fresco and other masterpieces.

From Novi Pazar, catch a Kraljevo-bound bus to the village of Ušće (about one hour) and hop a local bus from there, or negotiate a return taxi journey.

free breakfast will lure you downstairs. Behind the marketplace *(pijaca)* near the river.

✖ Eating

Novi Pazar isn't a haven of haute cuisine, but there's plenty of local-style fast food to slaver over. The central 28 Novembar street is lined with no-frills eateries advertising *roštilj* (barbecue): you're in for a meaty treat at virtually any one of them. **Kod Jonuza** (28 Novembar 10; meals 100-300DIN; ⊘24hr) is a good choice.

ℹ Getting There & Away

Frequent buses leave the bus station (a five-minute walk to Hotel Vrbak) for Belgrade (1520DIN, four hours). An overnight bus goes to Sarajevo (€16, seven hours) and there's one to Priština (€5, three hours).

Kopaonik   Копаоник

☎036

Situated around Pančićev Peak (Pančićev Vrh, 2017m) overlooking Kosovo, Serbia's prime ski resort has 44km of ski slopes and 23 lifts, and is a pleasant hiking base. Prices plummet off season, though many places open arbitrarily or close completely.

🛏 Sleeping & Eating

Large-scale hotels with restaurants, gym facilities, pizzerias, discos and shops are the go.

Hotel Grand   LUXURY HOTEL €€
(☎471 977; www.grand-kopaonik.com; s €60-170, d €82-240; P❄☀🅿🌐) Grand indeed, with a swimming pool, fitness centre, tennis courts and ski slopes on your doorstep.

Hostel Montana   HOSTEL €
(☎062-563 657; www.montana.rs; dm €13-25; @) Log-cabiny good times on the cheap.

JAT Apartments   APARTMENT €€
(☎547 1044; www.jatapartmani.com; apt per 1/2/3/4/5 persons from €30/34/36/50/58; 🅿) Open year-round with spacious rooms and kitchenettes.

Komita Mountain House   SERBIAN €€
(Planinska kuća komita; ☎063-505 780; meals from 400DIN) A 3km cab ride from town, this endearing inn offers wholesome feasts (and blueberry pie!), plus a respite from Kop's relentlessly showy central choices.

ℹ Information

The resort centre is amply equipped with ATMs, shops, restaurants and a post office.
Ski Centre Kopaonik (www.skis.rs; ⊘9am-5pm) Ski passes at the base of Hotel Grand.
Skiline (www.skiline.co.uk) Books ski holidays in 'Kop'.
Tourist Centre Kopaonik (Turistički Centar Kopaonik; www.tckopaonik.com) For assistance with tours, packages and accommodation.

ℹ Getting There & Away

In season, there are three daily buses from Belgrade (1670DIN, five hours) and three from Niš to Brus (714DIN, 1½ hours). From Novi Pazar, pick up an infrequent connection in Raška; taxis cost around 2000DIN.

Zlatibor   Златибор

☎031 / POP 284,700

A romantic region of gentle mountains, traditions and hospitality, Zlatibor encompasses the Tara and Šargan mountains in the north and the Murtenica hills bordering BiH. The town centre *(tržni centar)* has everything you could need, but not far beyond are quaint villages where locals are oblivious to ski-bunny shenanigans.

🏃 Activities

Zlatibor's slopes are mild. Major skiing hills are Tornik (the highest peak in Zlatibor at 1496m) and Obudovica. The nordic skiing trail at the northern foothill of Šumatno Brdo is 1042m at its highest point.

Several walking trails start, end or pass the town centre. In easy reach is the monument in memory of local victims of German aggression in 1941; head south along Ul Sportova, cross the footbridge and follow the footpath to the monument and its wonderful views.

🛏 Sleeping & Eating

Private rooms and apartments offer more space and privacy for less money than resorts. In season they typically cost €25 to €80 for two to six people and €10 to €30 less out of season. Find them through Zlatibor Tours, travel agents or www.zlatibor.com. The best meals are found in local villages, but there are some decent options (and a trillion pizzerias) in the town centre.

Hotel Palisad   HOTEL €€
(☑841 151; www.palisad.rs; Naselje Jezero bb; s/d/apt from 3300/5600/5800DIN; P☀☎) With elegant, minimalistic room decor, modern art in the lobby and in-house bowling alley, this may seem like an unlikely hang-out for a communist honcho, but Tito adored this mountain retreat. You can even stay in his

favourite suite (ask for 'Titov apartman'). Overlooking the lake in the town centre.

Hotel Mona Zlatibor   HOTEL €€
(☑841 021; www.monazlatibor.com; Naselje Jezero 26; r 7700-9400DIN, apt from 8500DIN; ☎) This well-groomed hotel opposite the bus station does its best to keep you indoors, with a wellness centre, two restaurants and a bar.

Konoba   SERBIAN €€
(☑841 674; meals from 550DIN; �8am-midnight) Serbian for 'tavern', Konoba delivers on its promise, with an atmosphere as full-blooded as its substantial meals. Rousing live *tamburaši* music adds to the knees-up feel.

Vendome   NIGHTCLUB
(☀8am-2am) Innocuous cafe by day, contender for the most-strobe-lights-in-a-club-ever award by night. Ditzy fun.

ℹ Information

Banka Intesa (Tržni Centar; ☀8am-4pm Mon-Fri, to noon Sat) Has a 24-hour ATM inside.

Igraonica Internet Caffe (Tržni centar; per hr 200DIN; ☀9am-11pm)

Post Office (Tržni centar; ☀7am-7pm)

Zlatibor Tours (☑845 957; Tržni centar, bus station; ☀8am-9pm) The scarily efficient Danijela will have your homestay and tours booked before you know what hit you.

> **WORTH A TRIP**
>
> ## ZLATIBOR EXCURSIONS
>
> Tumble back in time to 19th-century Serbia at the **open-air museum** (www.sirogojno.org.rs; adult/child 150/100DIN; ☀9am-4pm Nov-Apr, to 7pm Apr-Nov) in the village of Sirogojno. High-roofed, fully furnished wooden houses are spread across a pleasant mountainside and are open for your exploration.
>
> Mokra Gora is home to the village of **Drvengrad** (Küstendorf; www.mecavnik.info; Mećavnik hill; adult/child 200/120DIN; ☀9am-9pm), built by enigmatic filmmaker Emir Kusturica in 2002 for his film *Life is a Miracle*. Quirky, colourful flourishes give the village a fantastical feel: the Stanley Kubrick cinema shows Kusturica's films, there's a life-size statue of Johnny Depp, and Bruce Lee St is home to a restaurant where you can sip 'Che Guevara biorevolution juice' and goggle at prime panoramas. Drvengrad hosts the international Küstendorf Film and Music Festival each January.
>
> The **Šargan 8 railway** (☑bookings 510 288; www.serbianrailways.com; adult/child 600/300DIN; ☀10.30am & 1.25pm daily Apr-Oct, also 8am & 4.10pm depending on demand) tourist train was once part of a narrow-gauge railway linking Belgrade with Sarajevo and Dubrovnik. The joy of the 2½-hour journey is in its disorienting twists, turns and tunnels (all 22 of them).
>
> Reach these sights via bus from Užice or on a tour with any of the agencies at Zlatibor bus station. Those with a smattering of Serbian should contact Toma of Mokra Gora's **Tomadija Tours** (☑060-0800 324; tomadija.tours@gmail.com). Born in a Šargan 8 tunnel, he's as local as it gets!

ⓘ Getting There & Around

Express buses leave the bus stand for Belgrade (1170DIN, four hours, hourly), Novi Sad (1250DIN, 6½ hours, four daily) and Užice (200DIN, 45 minutes, almost hourly 5.50am to 11.10pm), the nearest railhead.

Without your own wheels, the easiest way to go exploring is to join local tours. A return taxi to the edge of the region costs around 2400DIN.

UNDERSTAND SERBIA

Serbia Today

Serbia is a small but hugely misunderstood country. Artistic and passionate with a penchant for partying, it is also a fractious nation with many unresolved historical issues. Modern Serbs have an eye towards joining the EU; many others resist the changes such a move would bring to their fiercely independent country.

History

Events that took place centuries ago are as personal to many Serbs as if they happened last week. The country's history is extremely contentious and viewpoints differ between those of contrasting backgrounds.

Early Invasions

Serbian history has been punctuated by foreign invasions from the time the Celts supplanted the Illyrians in the 4th century BC through to the arrival of the Romans 100 years later, the Slavs in the 6th century AD, the Turks in the 14th century, the Austro-Hungarians in the late 19th and early 20th centuries, and the Germans briefly in WWII.

Enter the Ottomans

Independence briefly flowered from 1217 with a 'golden age' during Stefan Dušan's reign as emperor (1346–55). Serbia declined after his death, and the pivotal Battle of Kosovo in 1389, where the Turks defeated Serbia, ushered in 500 years of Islamic rule. Early revolts were crushed but an 1815 uprising led to de facto independence that became complete in 1878.

The Land of Southern Slavs

On 28 June 1914, Austria-Hungary used the assassination of Archduke Franz Ferdinand by a Bosnian Serb as cause to invade Serbia, sparking WWI: almost 60% of Serbia's male population perished. In 1918 Croatia, Slovenia, Bosnia & Hercegovina (BiH), Vojvodina, Serbia and its Kosovo province, Montenegro, and Macedonia were joined into the Kingdom of Serbs, Croats and Slovenes; these countries became Yugoslavia (Land of Southern Slavs) in 1929.

An anti-Axis coup in March 1941 led to the Nazi bombing of Belgrade. Royalist Četniks and communist Partisans fought the Germans, Croatia's pro-Nazi, genocidal Ustaše organisation and each other, with Josip Tito's Partisans finally gaining the upper hand. In 1945 they formed the government, abolished the monarchy and declared a federal republic including Serbia, Kosovo and Vojvodina.

Tito broke with former ally Stalin in 1948, and in 1961 founded the Non-Aligned Movement. Within Yugoslavia, growing regional inequalities and burgeoning Serbian expansionism fuelled demands for greater autonomy. Tito's death in1980 signalled the beginning of the rise of nationalism, stifled but long-simmering, within the republics.

A Turbulent Era

By 1986 Serbian nationalists were espousing a 'Greater Serbia', an ideology that would encompass Serbs from all republics into one state. Appropriated by Serbia's Communist Party leader Slobodan Milošević, the doctrine was fuelled by claims of the genocide of Serbs by Kosovo Albanians, leading to the abolishment of self-rule in Kosovo in 1990. Croatia, Slovenia, BiH and Macedonia seceded from the federation, sparking a series of violent conflicts known collectively as the Yugoslav Wars.

Bitter, bloody and monstrously complex, the wars – Slovenia's Ten-Day War, the Croatian War of Independence and the Bosnian War – were fought not just between breakaway forces and the majority-Serb Yugoslav Army, but along fractious ethnic and religious lines as well. Atrocities were committed on all sides: perhaps the most stunning display of savagery came with the Srebrenica massacre, in which 8000 Bosnian men and boys were allegedly killed under orders of Republika Srpska Army (RSA) commander Ratko Mladić and RS president Radovan Karadžić. Claims of rape camps, ethnic cleansing and other barbarisms saw Serbia assume the role of international pariah.

In April 1992 the remaining republics, Serbia and Montenegro, formed a 'third' Yugoslav federation without provision of autonomy for Kosovo, despite its Albanian majority. Violence erupted in January 1998.

In March 1999 peace talks failed when Serbia rejected the US-brokered Rambouillet Agreement. In response to organised resistance in Kosovo, Serbian forces attempted to empty the country of its Albanian population; hundreds of thousands fled into Macedonia and Albania, galvanising the US and NATO into a 78-day bombing campaign. On 12 June 1999 Serbian forces withdrew from Kosovo.

European Dawn

In the 2000 presidential elections, opposition parties led by Vojislav Koštunica declared victory, a claim denounced by Milošević. Opposition supporters from all over Serbia swarmed to Belgrade and stormed Parliament. When Russia recognised Koštunica's win, Milošević had to acknowledge defeat.

Koštunica restored ties with Europe, acknowledged Yugoslav atrocities in Kosovo and rejoined the UN. In April 2001 Milošević was arrested and extradited to the international war-crimes tribunal in The Hague.

In April 2002 a loose union of Serbia and Montenegro replaced Yugoslavia. In 2003 Serbia was shaken by the assassination of reformist Prime Minister Zoran Đinđić, who had been instrumental in handing Milošević to The Hague. In June 2004 Serbia gained a new president in pro-European Boris Tadić.

On 11 March 2006 Milošević was found dead in his cell. In May, 55% of Montenegrins voted for independence from Serbia. In February 2008 Kosovo declared its independence, a move that Serbia held to be illegal; later that year, Karadžić was arrested for war crimes after 12 years as a fugitive. Mladić was finally apprehended in 2011.

In the 2012 elections, Tadić lost to Tomislav Nikolić, a former member of the far-right Serbian Radical Party. Serbia is an official candidate for EU membership, but it remains unseen how Kosovo – and Nikolić – will affect these aspirations.

People

The population is estimated at 7.2 million people, made up of Serbs (83.3%), Hungarians (3.5%), Bosniaks (2%), Roma (2.1%) and others (5.1%). Around 85% of the population identify as Serbian Orthodox. The 5% Roman Catholic population are mostly Vojvodinian Hungarians. Muslims (Albanians and Slavic) comprise around 3% of the country's population.

Arts

The survival and active rebellion of artistic expression throughout dark periods in history is a source of pride. Today, creative juices flow thickly and freely, with films spawning idyllic villages, art sold in cocktail bars and eclectic music events.

Literature

Long-time Belgrade resident Ivo Andrić was awarded the Nobel prize for his epic (and very readable) *Bridge on the Drina*.

Internationally acclaimed word wizard Milorad Pavić writes in many dimensions: *The Inner Side of the Wind* can be read from the back or the front. Novelist Momo Kapor's *A Guide to the Serbian Mentality* is an amusing peek into the national psyche, while Vuk Drašković's *Knife* offers a harrowing introduction to inter-Balkan tensions.

Cinema

World-renowned director Emir Kusturica sets the bar on Serbian cinema with his raucous approach to storytelling. Check out *Underground* (1995), the surreal tale of seemingly never-ending Balkan conflicts, *Time of the Gypsies* (1989), *Black Cat, White Cat* (1998) and *Life is a Miracle* (2004), about an optimistic Serbian engineer working on the Mokra Gora railway. Serbian black humour gets a workout in Yugo-classics *Ko to Tamo Peva* (*Who's That Singing There?*, 1980) and *Balkanski Špijun* (*Balkan Spy*, 1984).

Music

Pleh muzika (wild, haunting brass sounds influenced by Turkish and Austrian military music), also called *trubači*, is the national music. Popular examples are the soundtrack to the film *Underground* and albums by trumpet player Boban Marković. *Trubači* gets an orgiastic outing at Guča's Dragačevo Trumpet Assembly each August.

Cross traditional folk with techno and you get 'turbofolk', controversial during the Milošević era for its nationalist overtones but now more mainstream fun.

'Ex-Yu' rock bands like Električni Orgazam and Partibrejkers offered a lively soundtrack to the fall of communism; these days, Novi

Sad punkers Athiest Rap serve up cheeky, if equally rebellious, ditties.

Architecture

Ottoman, Austro-Hungarian and Serbian-Byzantine styles have fought for dominance, often over the same buildings, which have been stripped, redressed and modified over the years depending on who was in charge. Layers of communist-era concrete aren't going anywhere in a hurry.

Environment

Serbia comprises 77,474 sq km. Midžor (2169m), on the Stara Planina range, is its highest peak. Zlatibor and Kopaonik are winter playgrounds.

Vojvodina is glass-flat agricultural land. South of the Danube (Dunav), the landscape rises through rolling green hills, which crest where the eastern outpost of the Dinaric Alps slices southeastwards across the country.

Major national parks are Kopaonik, Tara and Fruška Gora. Among Serbia's mammals are wild boars, wildcats, beavers, otters, susliks, lynx and mouflon. Around 40% of Serbia's 360 bird species are of European Conservation Concern.

Serbia faces air pollution around Belgrade and dumping of industrial waste into the Sava. Some remnants of the 1999 NATO bombings, such as factories outside Belgrade, are ecological hazards.

Food & Drink

The ubiquitous snack is *burek,* a filo-pastry pie made with *sir* (cheese), *meso* (meat), *krompir* (potato) or occasionally *pečurke* (mushrooms). Eat without yoghurt if you like the 'blasphemer' tag. Score *burek* and other snacks at shops labelled *pekara* (bakery).

Serbia is famous for grilled meats such as *ćevapčići* (rolled spicy mince), *pljeskavica* (spicy hamburger) and *ražnjići* (pork or veal shish kebabs).

Regional cuisines range from spicy Hungarian goulash in Vojvodina to Turkish kebabs in Novi Pazar, while the small central village of Ozrem takes extreme cuisine *do jaja* ('to the balls') at their annual Testicle Cooking Championships.

It's not an easy place for vegetarians. Try asking for *posna hrana* (meatless food); this is also suitable for vegans. Otherwise, there's always vegetarian pizza, *srpska salata* (raw peppers, onions and tomatoes, with oil, vinegar and occasionally chilli), *šopska salata* (tomatoes, cucumber and onion with grated white cheese), *gibanica* (cheese pie) or *zeljanica* (cheese pie with spinach).

Many people distil *rakija* (schnapps) from plums *(šljiva),* quince *(dunja)* or other fruits. The delicious – but deceptively potent – *medovača* is made from honey. Viscous Turkish coffee is omnipresent, but espresso is staging a takeover bid in larger towns.

SURVIVAL GUIDE

Directory A–Z

Accommodation

Private rooms and apartments offer superb value and can be organised through tourist offices. 'Wild' camping is possible outside national parks.

Tax is not always automatically included in hotel rates. If you depend on internet access, check that wireless actually works. Where a room is 'nonsmoking', it does not mean that the room has not been smoked in – only that you are free not to smoke in it.

The following price categories for the cost of a high-season double room are used in the listings in this chapter.

€ less than 3000DIN/€30

€€ 3000DIN/€30 to 70000DIN/€75

€€€ more than 7000DIN/€75

Activities

Serbia's national parks are havens for hikers looking for quiet paths; Tara National Park has almost 20 marked trails ranging from 2km to 18km. Climbers will enjoy the canyons of the Drina River.

It is possible to kayak and raft at Tara National Park along the Drina River; Serbia Rafting (www.serbiarafting.com/en) can organise rafting tours, as can the just-over-the-border, Bosnia-based Drina-Tara Rafting Club (www.raftingtara.com) and Bodo (www.tarabodo.com).

Several spots in Serbia have rich birdlife, including areas around Belgrade. Keen twitchers should contact the League for Ornithological Action of Serbia (www.ptica.org).

Business Hours

Banks 8am or 9am to 5pm Monday to Friday, 8am to 2pm Saturday

Bars 8am to 3am

Restaurants 8am to midnight or 1am

Shops 8am to 6pm Monday to Friday, some open Saturday evenings

Embassies & Consulates

A complete list of embassies and consulates in Serbia, as well as Serbian embassies around the world, is available at www.embassypages.com/serbia. New Zealand doesn't have an embassy in Serbia. It is represented through its embassy in The Hague. Countries represented in Belgrade (area code ☏011) include the following:

Australian Embassy (☏011-330 3400; www.serbia.embassy.gov.au; 7th fl, Vladimira Popovica 38-40)

Canadian Embassy (☏011-306 3000; bgrad@international.gc.ca; Kneza Miloša 75)

French Embassy (☏011-302 3500; www.ambafrance-srb.org; Pariska 11)

German Embassy (☏011-306 4300; www.belgrad.diplo.de; Neznanog Junaka 1)

Netherlands Embassy (☏011-2023 900; bel@minbuza.nl; Simina 29)

UK Embassy (☏011-264 5055; www.ukinserbia.fco.gov.uk; Resavska 46)

US Embassy (☏011-361 9344; http://serbia.usembassy.gov; Kneza Miloša 50)

Food

The following price categories for the cost of a main course are used in the listings in this chapter.

€ less than 600DIN/€6

€€ 600DIN/€6 to 1000DIN/€10

€€€ more than 1000DIN/€10

Money

Serbia retains the dinar (DIN), though payment in euros for services and accommodation is commonplace.

ATMs are widespread and cards are accepted by established businesses. Exchange offices *(menjačnica)* are on every street corner. Exchange machines accept euros, US dollars and British pounds. Commission is charged for travellers cheques.

Post

Parcels should be taken unsealed to the main post office for inspection. You can receive mail, addressed poste restante, for a small charge.

Public Holidays

New Year 1 January

Orthodox Christmas 7 January

St Sava's Day 27 January

Statehood Day 15 February

Orthodox Good Friday April/May

Orthodox Easter Monday April/May

International Labour Days 1 and 2 May

Victory Day 9 May

St Vitus's Day (Vidovdan) 28 June

Safe Travel

Travelling around Serbia is generally safe for travellers who exercise the usual caution. The exceptions can be border areas, particularly the southeast Kosovo border where Serb–Albanian tensions remain. Check the situation before attempting to cross overland, and think thrice about driving there in Serbian-plated cars.

As evidenced by the neverending furore over Belgrade's Pride Parades (chronicled in the brilliant 2011 film *Parada*), life is not all rainbows for homosexuals in this conservative country. Discretion is highly advised.

Telephone

The country code is ☏381. Press the *i* button on public phones for dialling commands in English. Calls to Europe/Australia/North America cost around 50/100/80DIN per minute. Long-distance calls can also be made from booths in post offices.

Phonecards can be bought in post offices and tobacco kiosks for 300DIN (local cards) and 600DIN (international cards). Halo Plus cards allow longer calls locally, in the former Yugoslav Republic region or internationally, depending on which category you buy. Calls to Europe/Australia/USA cost from 15/40/40DIN per minute.

Mobile-phone SIM cards (around 200DIN) and recharge cards can be purchased at supermarkets and kiosks. All mobile numbers in Serbia start with ☏06.

Tourist Information

Tourist offices in Novi Sad and Belgrade have plenty of English material and friendly fonts of knowledge behind the desk.

In addition to the **National Tourism Organisation of Serbia** (www.serbia.travel), the **Tourist Organisation of Belgrade** (www.tob.rs) is loaded with useful information.

SERBIA DIRECTORY A–Z

Visas

Tourist visas for stays of less than 90 days aren't required by citizens of EU countries, most other European countries, Australia, New Zealand, Canada and the USA. The Ministry of Foreign Affairs (www.mfa.gov. rs/Visas/Visas_en_how_to.htm) has full details.

Officially, all visitors must register with the police. Hotels and hostels will do this for you but if you're camping or staying in a private home, you are expected to register within 24 hours of arrival. Unofficially? This is rarely enforced, but being unable to produce registration documents upon leaving Serbia could result in a fine.

Getting There & Away

Air

Belgrade's Nikola Tesla Beograd Airport (☎011-209 4444; www.beg.aero) handles most international flights. The website has a full list of airlines.

Aeroflot (www.aeroflot.com)

Air France (www.airfrance.com)

Alitalia (www.alitalia.com)

Austrian Airlines (www.austrian.com)

JAT (www.jat.com)

Lufthansa (www.lufthansa.com)

Turkish Airlines (www.thy.com)

Land

Because Serbia does not acknowledge crossing points into Kosovo as international border crossings, it may not be possible to enter Serbia from Kosovo unless you first entered Kosovo from Serbia. Check with your embassy.

BUS

Bus services to both Western Europe and Turkey are well developed.

CAR & MOTORCYCLE

Drivers need International Driving Permits, and vehicles need either Green Card insurance or insurance purchased at the border (about €105 for a car, €66 for a motorbike).

Driving Serbian-plated cars into Kosovo isn't advised, and is often not permitted by rental agencies or insurers.

TRAIN

International rail connections leaving Serbia originate in Belgrade. Heading north and west, most call in at Novi Sad and Subotica. Heading east, they go via Niš.

Several trips from Serbia offer a nice slice of scenery, such as the route to Bar on the Montenegrin coast. For more information, visit Serbian Railways (www.serbianrailways. com).

Getting Around

Bicycle

Bicycle paths are improving in larger cities. Vojvodina is relatively flat, but main roads make for dull days. Mountainous regions such as Zlatibor offer mountain biking in summer months. Picturesque winding roads come with the downside of narrow shoulders.

Bus

Bus services are extensive, though outside major hubs sporadic connections may leave you in the lurch for a few hours. In southern Serbia particularly, you may have to double back to larger towns.

Reservations are only worthwhile for international buses and during festivals. Tickets can be purchased from the station before departure or on board.

Car & Motorcycle

The Automobile & Motorcycle Association of Serbia (Auto-Moto Savez Srbije; ☎011-333 1100, roadside assist 1987; www.amss.org.rs; Ruzveltova 18) provides roadside assistance and extensive information on its website.

Several car-hire companies (p471) have offices at Nikola Tesla Airport in Belgrade. Small-car hire typically costs €40 to €50 per day. Check where you are not able to take the car. In Belgrade and other large towns you may have to purchase parking tickets from machines, kiosks or via SMS (in Serbian only).

Traffic police are everywhere and accidents are workaday. The BAC limit is 0.03%.

Train

Serbian Railways (www.serbianrailways.com) serves Novi Sad, Subotica and Niš from Belgrade. Enthusiasts will enjoy the Šargan 8 railway in Mokra Gora.

Generally trains aren't as regular and reliable as buses, and can be murderously slow.

Slovenia

Best Places to Eat

» Gostilna na Gradu (p494)
» Gostilna Ribič (p518)
» Gril Ranca (p517)
» Hiša Franko (p509)
» Gostilna Lectar (p501)

Best Places to Stay

» Antiq Palace Hotel & Spa (p493)
» Max Piran (p513)
» Hostel Pekarna (p517)
» Camping Bled (p501)
» Penzion Gasperin (p504)

Why Go?

It's a pint-sized place, with a surface area of just more than 20,000 sq km and two million people. But 'good things come in small packages', and never was that old chestnut more appropriate than in describing Slovenia. The country has everything from beaches, snowcapped mountains, hills awash in grape vines and wide plains blanketed in sunflowers to Gothic churches, baroque palaces and art nouveau buildings. Its incredible mixture of climates brings warm Mediterranean breezes up to the foothills of the Alps, where it can snow in summer.

The capital, Ljubljana, is a culturally rich city that values livability and sustainability over unfettered growth. This sensitivity towards the environment extends to rural and lesser-developed parts of the country as well. With more than half of its total area covered in forest, Slovenia really is one of the 'greenest' countries in the world.

When to Go
Ljubljana

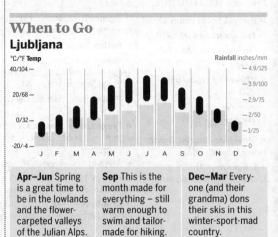

Apr–Jun Spring is a great time to be in the lowlands and the flower-carpeted valleys of the Julian Alps.

Sep This is the month made for everything – still warm enough to swim and tailor-made for hiking.

Dec–Mar Everyone (and their grandma) dons their skis in this winter-sport-mad country.

AT A GLANCE

» **Currency** Euro (€)

» **Language** Slovene

» **Money** ATMs are everywhere; banks open weekdays and Saturday morning

» **Visas** Not required for citizens of the EU, Australia, USA, Canada or New Zealand

Fast Facts

» **Area** 20,273 sq km

» **Capital** Ljubljana

» **Country code** ☑386

» **Emergency** Ambulance & fire ☑112, police ☑113

Exchange Rates

Australia	A$1	€0.82
Canada	C$1	€0.77
Japan	¥100	€0.83
New Zealand	NZ$1	€0.65
UK	UK£1	€1.18
USA	US$1	€0.78

Set Your Budget

» **Budget hotel room** €50

» **Two-course meal** €20

» **Museum entrance** €4

» **Beer** €3

» **100km by train/bus** €6/10

Resources

» **Slovenian Tourist Board** (www.slovenia.info)

» **E-uprava** (http://e-uprava.gov.si/e-unprava/en)

Connections

Border formalities with Slovenia's three European Union neighbours – Italy, Austria and Hungary – are nonexistent and all are accessible by train and bus. Venice can also be reached by boat from Piran. Expect a somewhat closer inspection of your documents when travelling to/from non-EU Croatia.

ITINERARIES

One Week

Spend a couple of days in Ljubljana, then head north to unwind in Bohinj or romantic Bled beside idyllic mountain lakes. Depending on the season, take a bus or drive over the hair-raising Vršič Pass into the valley of the vivid blue Soča River and take part in some adventure sports in Bovec or Kobarid before returning to Ljubljana.

Two Weeks

Another week will allow you to see just about everything: all of the above as well as the Karst caves at Škocjan and Postojna and the Venetian ports of Koper and Piran on the Adriatic. The country is small, so even the far eastern region, particularly the historically rich and picturesque city of Ptuj, is just a few hours away by car or train.

Essential Food & Drink

» **Pršut** Air-dried, thinly sliced ham from the Karst region not unlike Italian prosciutto.

» **Žlikrofi** Ravioli-like parcels filled with cheese, bacon and chives.

» **Žganci** The Slovenian stodge of choice – groats made from barley or corn but usually *ajda* (buckwheat).

» **Potica** A kind of nut roll eaten at teatime or as a dessert.

» **Wine** Distinctively Slovenian tipples include peppery red Teran from the Karst region and Malvazija, a straw-colour white wine from the coast.

» **Postrv** Trout, particularly the variety from the Soča River, is a real treat.

» **Prekmurska gibanica** A rich concoction of pastry filled with poppy seeds, walnuts, apples, and cheese and topped with cream.

» **Štruklji** Scrumptious dumplings made with curd cheese and served either savoury as a main course or sweet as a dessert.

» **Brinjevec** A very strong brandy made from fermented juniper berries (and a decidedly acquired taste).

LJUBLJANA

♪01 / POP 280,607

Slovenia's capital and largest city also happens to be one of Europe's greenest and most livable capitals. Car traffic is restricted in the centre, leaving the leafy banks of the emerald-green Ljubljanica River, which flows through the city's heart, free for pedestrians and cyclists. In summer, cafes set up terrace seating along the river, lending the feel of a perpetual street party. Slovenia's master of early-Modern, minimalist design,

Jože Plečnik, graced Ljubljana with beautiful alabaster bridges and baubles, pylons and pyramids that are both elegant and playful. The museums, hotels and restaurants are among the best in the country.

History

Legacies of the Roman city of Emona – remnants of walls, dwellings, early churches, even a gilded statuette – can be seen everywhere. Ljubljana took its present form in the mid-12th century as Laibach under the Habsburgs, but it gained regional prominence in 1809,

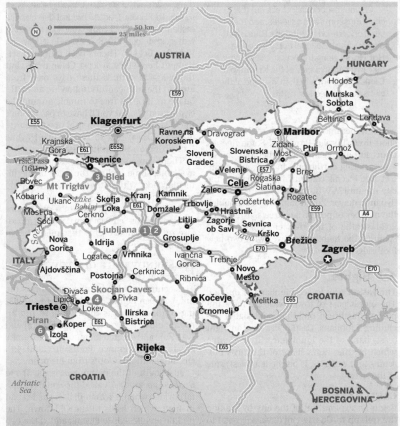

Slovenia Highlights

❶ Enjoy a flight up on the funicular to **Ljubljana Castle** (p488).

❷ Consider the genius of architect Jože Plečnik at Ljubljana's **National & University Library** (p489).

❸ Gaze at the natural perfection that is **Lake Bled** (p500).

❹ Gawk in awe at the 100m high walls of the incredible **Škocjan Caves** (p510).

❺ Climb to the top of the country's tallest mountain, **Mt Triglav** (p505).

❻ Get lost wandering the Venice-inspired, narrow alleyways of **Piran** (p512).

LJUBLJANA IN TWO DAYS

Take the funicular to Ljubljana Castle, then come down and explore the Central Market area. After a seafood lunch at Ribca, walk around the Old Town then cross the Ljubljanica River and walk north along Vegova ulica to Kongresni Trg and Prešernov Trg. Plan your evening over a fortifying libation at one of the many cafes along the Ljubljanica: low key at Jazz Club Gajo or alternative at Metelkova Mesto.

On your second day check out the city's museums and galleries, and then stroll or cycle on a Ljubljana Bike, stopping for an oh-so-local horse burger at Hot Horse along the way. In the evening, take in a performance at the Križanke or Cankarjev Dom and then visit one of the clubs you missed last night.

when it became the capital of Napoleon's short-lived 'Illyrian Provinces'. Some fine art nouveau buildings filled up the holes left by a devastating earthquake in 1895, and architect Jože Plečnik continued the remake of the city up until WWII. In recent years the city's dynamic mayor, Zoran Janković, has doubled the number of pedestrian streets, extended a great swathe of the river embankment and spanned the Ljubljanica River with two new footbridges.

◉ Sights

The easiest way to see Ljubljana is on foot. The oldest part of town, with the most important historical buildings and sights (including Ljubljana Castle) lies on the right (east) bank of the Ljubljanica River. Center, which has the lion's share of the city's museums and galleries, is on the left (west) side of the river.

CASTLE AREA

Begin an exploration of the city by making the trek up to Castle Hill (Grajska Planota) to poke around grand Ljubljana Castle. The castle area offers a couple of worthwhile exhibitions, and the castle watchtower affords amazing views out over the city. The prospect of lunch at one of the city's best restaurants, Gostilna na Gradu (p494), provides an added inducement.

There are several ways to access the castle, with the easiest (and for kids, the most

fun) being a 70m-long funicular (vzpenjača; ☑reservations 306 42 00; www.ljubljanskigrad.si; Krekov trg 3-7; return adult/child €4/3; ⊙9am-11pm Apr-Sep, 10am-9pm Oct-Mar) that leaves from Old Town not far from the market (p495) on Vodnikov trg. If you'd like to get some exercise, you can hike the hill in about 20 minutes. There are three main walking routes: Študentovska ulica, which runs south from Ciril Metodov trg; steep Reber ulica from Stari trg; and Ulica na Grad from Gornji trg.

TOP CHOICE Ljubljana Castle CASTLE
(Ljubljanski Grad; ☑306 42 93; www.ljubljanskigrad.si; Grajska Planota 1; adult/child incl funicular and castle attractions €8/5, castle attractions only €6/3; with guided tour €10/8; ⊙9am-11pm May-Sep, 10am-9pm Oct-Apr) There's been a human settlement here since at least Celtic times, but the oldest structures these days date from around the 16th-century, following an earthquake in 1511. It's free to ramble around the castle grounds, but you'll have to pay to enter the Watchtower, the Chapel of St George (Kapela Sv Jurija) and to see the worthwhile Exhibition on Slovenian History.

There are several admission options available; some include the price of the funicular ride, while others include a castle tour. Consult the castle website for details. The Ljubljana Castle Information Centre (⊙9am-9pm Apr-Sep, 9am-6pm Oct-Mar) can advise on tours and events that might be on during your visit.

PREŠERNOV TRG & OLD TOWN
Prešernov Trg SQUARE, PLAZA
This central and beautiful square forms the link between Center and the Old Town. Taking pride of place is the Prešeren monument (1905), designed by Maks Fabiani and Ivan Zajc and erected in honour of Slovenia's greatest poet, France Prešeren (1800–49). On the plinth are motifs from his poems.

Just south of the monument is the Triple Bridge (Tromostovje), called the Špital (Hospital) Bridge when it was built as a single span in 1842, which leads to the Old Town. The prolific architect Jože Plečnik added the two sides in 1931.

To the east of the monument at No 5 is the Italianate Central Pharmacy (Centralna Lekarna), an erstwhile cafe frequented by intellectuals in the 19th century. To the north, on the corner of Trubarjeva cesta and Miklošičeva cesta, is the delightful Secessionist Palača Urbanc (Urbanc Palace) building from 1903.

Mestni Trg · SQUARE

The first of the Old Town's three 'squares' (the other two – Stari trg and Gornji trg – are more like narrow cobbled streets), Mestni trg (Town Square) is dominated by the town hall, in front of which stands the **Robba Fountain** (the original is now in the National Gallery).

Town Hall · TOWN HALL

(Mestna Hiša; ☑306 30 00; Mestni trg; ☺7.30am-4pm Mon-Fri) The seat of the city government and sometimes referred to as the *Magistrat* or *Rotovž*. It was erected in the late 15th century and rebuilt in 1718. The Gothic courtyard inside, arcaded on three levels, is where theatrical performances once took place and contains some lovely sgraffiti.

If you look above the south portal leading to a second courtyard you'll see a relief map of Ljubljana as it appeared in the second half of the 17th century.

Stari Trg · SQUARE

The 'Old Square' is the true heart of the Old Town. It is lined with 19th-century wooden shopfronts, quiet courtyards and cobblestone passageways. From behind the medieval houses on the eastern side, paths once led to Castle Hill, which was a source of water. The buildings fronting the river had large passageways built to allow drainage in case of flooding.

Gornji Trg · SQUARE

Upper Square is the eastern extension of Stari trg. The five **medieval houses** at Nos 7 to 15 have narrow side passages (some with doors) where rubbish was once deposited so that it could be washed down into the river.

FREE Botanical Garden · PUBLIC GARDEN

(Botanični Vrt; ☑427 12 80; www.botanicni-vrt.si; Ižanska cesta 15; ☺7am-8pm Jul & Aug, 7am-7pm Apr-Jun, Sep & Oct, 7am-5pm Nov-Mar) About 800m southeast of the Old Town along Karlovška cesta and over the Ljubljanica River, this 2.5-hectare botanical garden was founded in 1810 as a sanctuary of native flora. It contains 4500 species of plants and trees, about a third of which are indigenous,

CENTER

This large district on the left bank of the Ljubljanica is the nerve centre of modern Ljubljana. It is filled with shops, commercial offices, government departments and embassies. The region is divided into several distinct neighbourhoods centred on town squares.

Trg Francoske Revolucije · SQUARE

'French Revolution Sq' was for centuries the headquarters of the Teutonic Knights of the Cross (Križniki). They built a commandery here in the early 13th century, which was transformed into the **Križanke** (☑241 60 00; Trg Francoske Revolucije 1-2) monastery complex in the early 18th century. Today it serves as the headquarters of the Ljubljana Festival (p493).

TOP CHOICE National & University Library · HISTORIC BUILDING

(☑200 11 09; Turjaška ulica 1; ☺9am-6pm Mon-Fri, 9am-2pm Sat) This library is Plečnik's masterpiece, completed in 1941. To appreciate this great man's philosophy, enter through the main door (note the horse-head doorknobs) on Turjaška ulica – you'll find yourself in near darkness, entombed in black marble. As you ascend the steps, you'll emerge into a colonnade suffused with light – the light of knowledge, according to the architect's plans.

The **Main Reading Room** (Velika Čitalnica), now open to nonstudents only by group tour in summer, has huge glass walls and some stunning lamps, also designed by Plečnik.

City Museum · MUSEUM

(Mestni Muzej; ☑241 25 00; www.mestnimuzej.si; Gosposka ulica 15; adult/child €4/2.50; ☺10am-6pm Tue & Wed, Fri-Sun, 10am-9pm Thu) The excellent city museum focuses on Ljubljana's history, culture and politics via imaginative multimedia and interactive displays. The reconstructed Roman street that linked the eastern gates of Emona to the Ljubljanica and the collection of well-preserved classical finds in the basement are worth a visit in themselves.

The permanent 'Faces of Ljubljana' exhibit of celebrated and lesser-known *žabarji* ('froggers', as natives of the capital are known) is memorable. They host some very good special exhibitions too.

National Museum of Slovenia · MUSEUM

(Narodni Muzej Slovenije; ☑241 44 00; www.nms.si; Prešernova cesta 20; adult/child €3/2.50, 1st Sun of month free; ☺10am-6pm Fri-Wed, 10am-8pm Thu) Highlights include a highly embossed *Vače situla*, a Celtic pail from the late 6th century BC unearthed in a town east of Ljubljana, and a Stone Age bone flute discovered near Cerkno in western Slovenia in 1995. There are also examples of Roman glass and jewellery found in 6th-century Slavic graves, along with many other historical finds.

Ljubljana

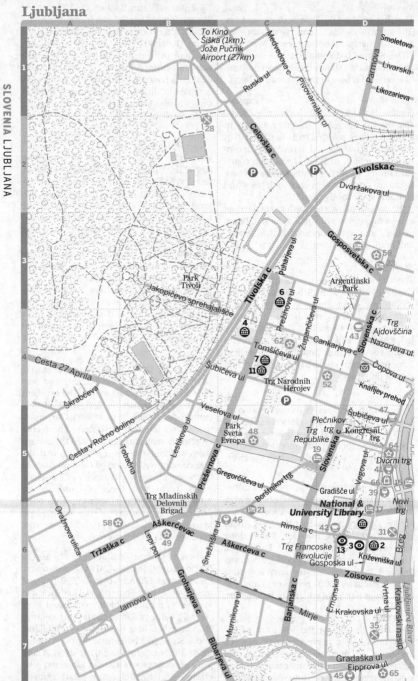

To Kino
Šiška (1km);
Jože Pučnik
Airport (27km)

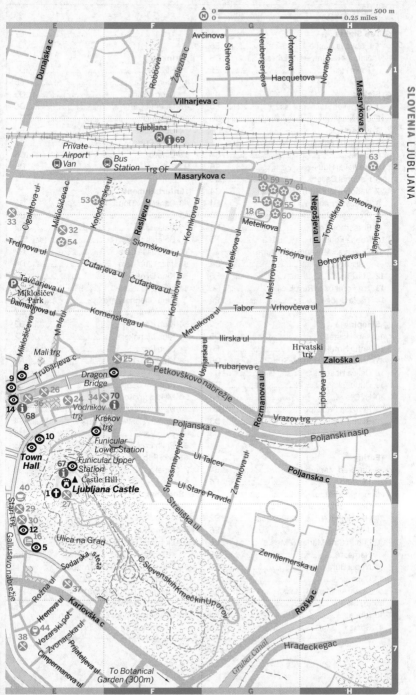

SLOVENIA LJUBLJANA

Ljubljana

Check out the ceiling fresco in the foyer, which features an allegorical Carniola surrounded by important Slovenes from the past and the statues of the Muses and Fates relaxing on the stairway banisters.

Slovenian Museum of Natural History   MUSEUM
(Prirodoslovni Muzej Slovenije; ☎241 09 40; www2. pms-lj.si; Prešernova cesta 20; adult/student €3/2.50, incl national museum €5/4; ☉10am-6pm Fri-Wed, 10am-8pm Thu; P) Housed in the same impressive building as the National Museum, the Natural History Museum contains the usual reassembled mammoth and whale skeletons, stuffed birds, reptiles and mammals. However, the mineral collections amassed by the philanthropic Baron Žiga Zois in the early 19th century and the display on Slovenia's unique salamander *Proteus anguinus* are worth a visit.

National Gallery   MUSEUM
(☎241 54 18; www.ng-slo.si; Prešernova cesta 24; adult/child €7/5, 1st Sun of month free; ☉10am-6pm Tue-Sun) Slovenia's foremost assembly of fine art is housed over two floors both in an old building dating to 1896 and an impressive modern wing.

Ljubljana Museum of Modern Art   MUSEUM
(☎241 68 00; www.mg-lj.si; Tomšičeva ulica 14; adult/student €5/2.50; ☉10am-6pm Tue-Sun) This museum houses the very best in Slovenian modern art. Keep an eye out for works by painters Tone Kralj *(Peasant Wedding)*, the expressionist France Mihelič *(The Quintet)* and the surrealist Štefan Planinc *(Primeval World series)* as well as sculptors such as Jakob Savinšek *(Protest)*.

The museum also owns works by the influential 1980s and 1990s multimedia group Neue Slowenische Kunst (NSK; *Suitcase for Spiritual Use: Baptism under Triglav*) and the artists' cooperative Irwin *(Kapital)*.

☞ Tours

Two-hour **walking tours** (adult/child €10/5; ☉10am, 2pm & 5pm Apr-Oct), combined with a ride on the funicular or the tourist train up to the castle or a cruise on the Ljubljanica, are organised by the TIC. They depart daily from the town hall on Mestni trg.

✺ Festivals & Events

Druga Godba   WORLD MUSIC
(http://festival.drugagodba.si; ☉May-Jun) This festival of alternative and world music, takes place in the Križanke from late May to early June.

Ljubljana Festival   MUSIC & THEATRE
(www.ljubljanafestival.si; ☉Jul & Aug) The number-one event on Ljubljana's social calendar is the Ljubljana Festival, a celebration from early July to late August of music, opera, theatre and dance held at venues throughout the city, but principally in the open-air theatre at the Križanke.

International Ljubljana Marathon   MARATHON
(www.ljubljanskimaraton.si; ☉Oct) Takes off on the last Saturday in October.

🛏 Sleeping

The TIC has comprehensive details of private rooms (from single/double €30/50) and apartments (from double/quad €55/80) though only a handful are central.

TOP CHOICE Antiq Palace
Hotel & Spa   BOUTIQUE HOTEL €€€
(☎051 364 124; www.antiqpalace.com; Gosposka ulica 10 & Vegova ul 5a; s/d €180/210; P🅿❄@🛜) Easily the city's most luxurious sleeping option, the Antiq Palace occupies a 16th-century townhouse, about a block from the river. Accommodation is in 13 individually designed suites, each with several rooms and some stretching to 250 sq m in size. The list of amenities is a mile long. The target market is upscale honeymooners and businessmen on expenses.

Cubo   BOUTIQUE HOTEL €€€
(☎425 60 00; www.hotelcubo.com; Slovenska cesta 15; s/d €120/140) This sleek boutique hotel in the centre of town boasts high-end, minimalist design that could have stepped out of the pages of *Wallpaper* magazine. The owners have placed great emphasis on using the best construction materials and high-quality bedding to ensure a good night's sleep. The in-house restaurant is very good.

Celica Hostel   HOSTEL €€
(☎230 97 00; www.hostelcelica.com; Metelkova ulica 8; dm €19-25, s/d/tr cell €53/60/70; P@🛜) This stylishly revamped former prison (1882) in Metelkova has 20 'cells', designed by different artists and architects and complete with original bars. There are nine rooms and apartments with three to seven beds and a packed, popular 12-bed dorm. The ground floor is home to a cafe and restaurant (set lunch €5 to €7, open 7.30am to midnight)

and the hostel boasts its own gallery where everyone can show their work.

Slamič B&B
PENSION €€

(☎433 82 33; www.slamic.si; Kersnikova ulica 1; s €65-75, d €95-100, ste from €135; P※@🛜) It's slightly away from the action but Slamič, a B&B above a famous cafe and teahouse, offers 11 bright rooms with antique(ish) furnishings and parquet floors. Choice rooms include the ones looking onto a back garden and the one just off an enormous terrace used by the cafe.

Penzion Pod Lipo
PENSION €€

(☎031 809 893; www.penzion-podlipo.com; Borštnikov trg 3; d/tr/q/ste €65/75/100/125; @) Sitting atop one of Ljubljana's oldest *gostilna* (inn-like restaurant) and a 400-year-old linden tree, this 10-room inn offers plain rooms, but excellent value in a part of the city that is filling up with bars and restaurants. We love the communal kitchen, the original hardwood floors and the east-facing terrace with deck chairs that catch the morning sun.

H2O
HOSTEL €

(☎041 662 266; www.h2ohostel.com; Petkovškovo nabrežje 47; dm €17-22, d €36-52, q €68-88; @🛜) One of our favourite hostels in Ljubljana, this six-room place wraps around a tiny courtyard bordering the Ljubljanica River and one room has views of the castle. Private doubles are available and guests have access to a common kitchen.

Antiq Hotel
BOUTIQUE HOTEL €€€

(☎421 35 60; www.antiqhotel.si; Gornji trg 3; s €75-120, d €85-150; ※@🛜) This attractive boutique has been cobbled together from several townhouses in the Old Town. There are 16 spacious rooms and a multitiered back garden. The decor is kitsch with a smirk and there are fabulous touches everywhere. Among our favourite rooms are enormous No 8, with views of the Hercules Fountain, and No 13, with glimpses of Ljubljana Castle.

Zeppelin Hostel
HOSTEL €

(☎059 191 427; www.zeppelinhostel.com; 2 fl, Slovenska cesta 47; dm €18-24, d €49-60; @🛜) Located in the historic Evropa building on the corner of Gosposvetska cesta, this hostel offers clean and bright dorm rooms (four to eight beds) and doubles and is run by a young team of international travellers who keep their guests informed on parties and happenings around town.

Alibi Hostel
HOSTEL €

(☎251 12 44; www.alibi.si; Cankarjevo nabrežje 27; dm €15-18, d €40-50; ※@) This very well-situated 106-bed hostel on the Ljubljanica has brightly painted, airy dorms with four to eight wooden bunks and a dozen doubles. There's a private suite at the top for six people.

✖ Eating

TOP CHOICE Gostilna na Gradu
SLOVENIAN €€

(☎031 523 760; www.nagradu.si; Grajska planota 1; mains €8-14; ⊙10am-midnight Mon-Sat, noon-6pm Sun) Be sure to plan a meal here at this marvelous traditional Slovenian restaurant during your visit to the castle. The chefs pride themselves on using only Slovenian-sourced breads, cheeses and meats, and age-old recipes to prepare a meal to remember. The castle setting is ideal. Book a table in advance to avoid disappointment.

Julija
MEDITERRANEAN €€

(☎425 64 63; http://julijarestaurant.com; Stari trg 9; €10.90-18.90; ⊙noon-10pm) This is arguably the best of a trio of restaurants standing side by side on touristy Stari trg. We love the three-course set lunches served on the sidewalk terrace for €9. The cuisine here revolves around risottos and pastas, though the chicken breast special served in a spicy peanut sauce was one of the best meals on our trip.

Ribca
SEAFOOD €

(☎425 15 44; www.ribca.si; Adamič-Lundrovo nabrežje 1; dishes €5-8; ⊙8am-4pm Mon-Fri, to 2pm Sat) One of the culinary joys of a visit to Ljubljana is the chance to sample inexpensive and well-prepared fish dishes. This basement seafood bar below the Plečnik Colonnade in Pogačarjev trg is one of the best for tasty fried squid, sardines and herrings. The setting is informal, though the cuisine is top notch. Set lunch on weekdays is €7.50.

Špajza
SLOVENIAN €€

(☎425 30 94; www.spajza-restaurant.si; Gornji trg 28; mains €15-25; ⊙noon-11pm) This popular Old Town restaurant is the perfect spot for a splurge or romantic meal for two. The interior is decorated with rough-hewn tables and chairs, wooden floors, frescoed ceilings and nostalgic bits and pieces. The terrace in summer is a delight. The cooking is traditional Slovenian, with an emphasis on less-common mains like rabbit and veal.

Pri Škofu
SLOVENIAN €€

(📞426 45 08; Rečna ulica 8; mains €8-22; ⏱7am-11pm; 📶) This wonderful little place in tranquil Krakovo, south of the centre, serves some of the best prepared local dishes and salads in Ljubljana, with an ever-changing menu. Weekday set lunches are good value at €8.

Lunch Café Marley & Me
INTERNATIONAL €€

(📞040 564 188; www.lunchcafe.si; Stari trg 9; mains from €7-20; ⏱11am-11pm; 📶) The name couldn't be more misleading. It's more than a lunch cafe…and the 'Marley' bit? We just don't get it. Still, it's a very popular spot for lunch or dinner over salads, pastas and a variety of meats and seafood. There's sidewalk dining in nice weather.

Trta
ITALIAN €

(📞426 50 66; www.trta.si; Grudnovo nabrežje 21; pizza €8-10; ⏱11am-10pm Mon-Fri, noon-10.30pm Sat; 📶) This award-winning pizzeria, with large pies cooked in a wood-fired oven, is slightly south of the centre, across the river opposite Trnovo.

Namasté
INDIAN €€

(📞425 01 59; www.restavracija-namaste.si; Breg 8; mains €10-20; ⏱11am-midnight Mon-Sat, to 10pm Sun; 🖋) Should you fancy a bit of Indian, head for this place on the left bank of the Ljubljanica. You won't get high-street-quality curry but the thalis and tandoori dishes are very good. The choice of vegetarian dishes is better than average and a set lunch costs between €6.50 €8.50. Eat along the river in nice weather.

Falafel
MIDDLE EASTERN €

(📞041 640 166; Trubarjeva cesta 40; sandwiches €4-6; ⏱11am-midnight Mon-Fri, noon-midnight Sat, 1-10pm Sun) Authentic Middle Eastern food, like falafel and hummus, served up to go or eat in at a few tables and chairs scattered about. Perfect choice for a quick meal on the run or the late-night munchies.

Hot Horse
BURGERS €

(📞521 14 27; www.hot-horse.si; Park Tivoli, Celovška cesta 25; snacks & burgers €3-6; ⏱9am-6pm Tue-Sun, 10am-6pm Mon) This little place in the city's biggest park supplies *Ljubljančani* (local people) with their favourite treat: horse burgers (€4). It's just down the hill from the Museum of Contemporary History.

Self-Catering

Self-caterers and those on a tight budget will want to head directly to Ljubljana's vast open-air market (Vodnikov trg; ⏱6am-6pm Mon-Fri, 6am-4pm Sat summer, 6am-4pm Mon-Sat winter) on Vodnikov trg, just across the Triple Bridge to the southeast of Prešernov trg. Here you'll find stalls selling everything from wild mushrooms and forest berries to honey and homemade cheeses. The covered market (Pogačarjev trg 1; ⏱7am-2pm Mon-Wed & Sat, 7am-4pm Thu & Fri) nearby sells meats and cheeses, and there's a fish market (Adamič-Lundrovo nabrežje 1; ⏱7am-4pm Mon-Fri, 7am-2pm Sat) too. You'll also find open-air fish stands selling plates of fried calamari for as low as €6. Another budget option is *burek*, pastry stuffed with cheese, meat or even apple. Reputedly the best places in town are Olimpije (Pražakova ulica 2; burek €2; ⏱24hr) southwest of the train and bus stations, and Nobel Burek (📞232 33 92; Miklošičeva cesta 30; burek €2, pizza slices €1.40; ⏱24hr).

🍷 Drinking

Few cities of this size have central Ljubljana's concentration of inviting cafes and bars, the vast majority with outdoor seating in the warmer months.

Bars & Pubs

Žmavc
TOP CHOICE

BAR

(📞251 03 24; Rimska cesta 21; ⏱7.30am-1am Mon-Fri, from 10am Sat, from 6pm Sun; 📶) A super-popular student hang-out west of Slovenska cesta, with *manga* comic-strip scenes and figures running halfway up the walls. There's a great garden terrace for summer-evening drinking, but try to arrive early to snag a table. Also excellent for morning coffee.

BiKoFe
BAR

(📞425 93 93; Židovska steza 2; ⏱7am-1am Mon-Fri, 10am-1pm Sat & Sun; 📶) A favourite with the hipster crowd, this cupboard of a bar has mosaic tables, studenty art on the walls, soul and jazz on the stereo, and a giant water pipe on the menu for that long, lingering smoke outside. The shady outdoor patio is a great place to enjoy a recent purchase from the Behemot (📞251 13 92; www.behemot.si; Židovska steza 3; ⏱10am-8pm Mon-Fri, 10am-3pm Sat) bookshop across the street.

Dvorni Bar
WINE BAR

(📞251 12 57; www.dvornibar.net; Dvorni trg 2; ⏱8am-1am Mon-Sat, 9am-midnight Sun; 📶) This wine bar is an excellent place to taste Slovenian vintages; it stocks more than 100 varieties and has wine tastings every month (usually the second Wednesday).

Šank Pub
PUB

(Eipprova ulica 19; ⊘7am-1am; 🛜) Down in studenty Trnovo, this raggedy little place with brick ceiling and wooden floor is a relaxed alternative to the nearby Sax. The Šank is one of a number of inviting bars and cafes along this stretch of Eipprova ulica.

Cafes & Teahouses

TOP CHOICE Nebotičnik
CAFE

(☑040 601 787; www.neboticnik.si; 12th fl, Štefanova ulica 1; ⊘9am-1am Sun-Wed, 9am-3am Thu-Sat; 🛜) After a decade-long hibernation this elegant cafe with its breathtaking terrace atop Ljubljana's famed art deco Skyscraper (1933) has reopened, and the 360-degree views are spectacular.

Le Petit Café
CAFE

(☑251 25 75; www.lepetit.si; Trg Francoske Revolucije 4; ⊘7.30am-1am; 🛜) Just opposite the Križanke, this pleasant, boho place offers great coffee and a wide range of breakfast goodies, lunches and light meals, plus a good restaurant on the 1st floor.

Čajna Hiša
TEAHOUSE

(☑421 24 40; Stari trg 3; ⊘9am-10.30pm Mon-Fri, 9am-3pm & 6-10pm Sat; 🛜) This elegant and centrally located teahouse takes its teas very seriously. They also serve light meals and there's a tea shop next door.

Open Cafe
GAY & LESBIAN

(☑041 391 371; www.open.si; Hrenova ulica 19; ⊘4pm-midnight; 🛜) This very stylish gay-owned-and-run cafe south of the Old Town has become the meeting point for Ljubljana's burgeoning queer culture. In June 2009 it was attacked by fascist homophobes who attempted to torch the place and some patrons fought back.

Zvezda
CAFE

(☑421 90 90; Wolfova ulica 14; ⊘7am-11pm Mon-Sat, 10am-8pm Sun; 🛜) The 'Star' has all the usual varieties of coffee and tea but is celebrated for its shop-made cakes, especially *skutina pečena* (€3), an eggy cheesecake.

☆ Entertainment

Ljubljana in Your Pocket (www.inyourpocket. com), which comes out every two months, is a good English source for what's on in the capital. Buy tickets for shows and events at the venue box office, online through **Eventim** (☑430 24 05; www.eventim.si), or at Ljubljana Tourist Information Centre (p498). Expect to pay around €10 to €20 for tickets to live acts, and less for club entry and DJ nights.

Nightclubs

Cirkus
CLUB

(Kinoklub Vič; ☑051 631 631; www.cirkusklub.si; Trg Mladinskih Delovnih Brigad 7; €5; ⊘8pm-5am Tue-Sat) This popular dance club, with DJs at the weekends, occupies the former Kinoklub Vič.

Klub K4
CLUB

(☑040 212 292; www.klubk4.org; Kersnikova ulica 4; ⊘10pm-2am Tue, 11pm-4am Wed & Thu, 11pm-6am Fri & Sat, 10pm-4am Sun) This evergreen venue in the basement of the Student Organisation of Ljubljana University (ŠOU) headquarters features rave-electronic music Friday and Saturday, with other styles of music on weeknights, and a popular gay and lesbian night on Sunday.

KMŠ
CLUB

(☑425 74 80; www.klubkms.si; Tržaška cesta 2; ⊘8am-10pm Mon-Fri, 9pm-5am Sat) Located in the deep recesses of a former tobacco factory complex, the Maribor Student Club stays comatose till Saturday when it turns into a raucous place with music and dancers all over the shop.

Live Music

Kino Šiška
INDIE & ROCK

(☑box office 030 310 110; www.kinosiska.si; Trg Prekomorskih brigad 3; ⊘5-8pm Mon-Fri, 10am-1pm Sat) This renovated old movie theatre has been reopened as an urban cultural centre, hosting mainly indie, rock and alternative bands from around Slovenia and the rest of Europe.

Orto Bar
ROCK

(☑232 16 74; www.orto-bar.com; Graboličeva ulica 1; ⊘9pm-4am Tue & Wed, to 5am Thu-Sat) A popular bar-club for late-night drinking and dancing with occasional live music, Orto is just five minutes' walk from Metelkova. Note the program takes a two-month hiatus in summer during July and August.

Jazz Club Gajo
JAZZ

(☑425 32 06; www.jazzclubgajo.com; Beethovnova ulica 8; ⊘7pm-2am Mon-Sat) Now in its 18th year, Gajo is the city's premier venue for live jazz and attracts both local and international talent. Jam sessions are at 8.30pm Monday.

Sax Pub
ROCK

(☑283 90 09; Eipprova ulica 7; ⊘noon-1am Mon, 10am-1am Tue-Sat, 4-10pm Sun) Two decades in

SOMETHING COMPLETELY DIFFERENT: METELKOVO MESTO

For a scruffy antidote to trendy clubs in Ljubljana, try **Metelkova Mesto** (Metelkova Town; www.metelkova.org; Masarykova cesta 24), an ex-army garrison taken over by squatters in the 1990s and converted into a free-living commune – a miniature version of Copenhagen's Christiania. In this two-courtyard block, a dozen idiosyncratic venues hide behind brightly tagged doorways, coming to life generally after midnight daily in summer and on Friday and Saturday the rest of the year. While it's certainly not for the genteel and the quality of the acts and performances varies with the night, there's usually a little of something for everyone on hand.

Entering the main 'city gate' from Masarykova cesta, the building to the right houses **Gala Hala** (☑431 70 63; www.galahala.com), with live bands and club nights, and **Klub Channel Zero** (www.ch0.org), with punk and hardcore. Above it on the 1st floor is **Galerija Mizzart** (www.mizzart.net) with a great exhibition space (the name is no comment on the quality of the creations – promise!).

Easy to miss in the first building to the left is the **Kulturni Center Q** (Q Cultural Centre) including **Tiffany** (www.kulturnicenterq.org/tiffany/klub) for gay men and **Klub Monokel** (www.klubmonokel.com) for lesbians. Due south is the ever-popular **Jalla Jalla Club** (www.metelkovamesto.org), a congenial pub with concerts. Beyond the first courtyard to the southwest, **Klub Gromka** (www.klubgromka.org) has folk concerts, theatre and lectures. Next door is **Menza pri Koritu** (☑434 03 45; www.menzaprikoritu.org), under the creepy ET-like figures, with performance and concerts. If you're staying at the Hostel Celica (p493), all of the action is just around the corner.

Trnovo and decorated with colourful murals and graffiti inside and out, the tiny Sax has live jazz at 9pm or 9.30pm on Thursday from late August to December and February to June. Canned stuff rules at other times.

Performing Arts

Cankarjev Dom　　　　　　　OPERA, DANCE
(☑241 71 00, box office 241 72 99; www.cd-cc.si; Prešernova cesta 10; ☺box office 11am-1pm & 3-8pm Mon-Fri, 11am-1pm Sat, 1hr before performance) Ljubljana's premier cultural and conference centre has two large auditoriums (the Gallus Hall is said to have perfect acoustics) and a dozen smaller performance spaces offering a remarkable smorgasbord of performance arts. Buy tickets at the box office.

Opera & Ballet Ljubljana　　　OPERA, DANCE
(☑box office 241 59 59; www.opera.si; Župančičeva ulica 1; ☺box office 10am-5pm Mon-Fri, 1hr before performance) Home to the Slovenian National Opera and Ballet companies, this historic neo-Renaissance theatre was fully renovated in 2011 and restored to its former luster.

Philharmonic Hall　　　　　　CLASSICAL
(Slovenska Filharmonija; ☑241 08 00; www.filharmonija.si; Kongresni trg 10; ☺7am-10pm) Home to the Slovenian Philharmonic Orchestra, this smaller but more atmospheric venue also stages concerts and hosts performances of the Slovenian Chamber Choir (Slovenski Komorni Zbor), which was founded in 1991.

Križanke　　　　　　　CLASSICAL, THEATRE
(☑241 60 00, box office 241 60 26; www.ljubljanafestival.si; Trg Francoske Revolucije 1-2; ☺box office 10am-8pm Mon-Fri, 10am-1pm Sat Apr-Sep) The open-air theatre at this sprawling 18th-century monastery hosts the events of the Ljubljana Summer Festival. The smaller Knights Hall (Viteška Dvorana) is the venue for chamber concerts.

Cinema

Kinoteka　　　　　　　　　　CINEMA
(☑547 15 80; www.kinoteka.si; Miklošičeva cesta 28) Shows archival art and classic films in their original language (not always English).

Kino Dvor　　　　　　　　　　CINEMA
(Court Cinema; ☑239 22 13; www.kinodvor.org; Kolodvorska ulica 13) The sister cinema to Kinoteka nearby screens more contemporary films from around the world.

❶ Information

Internet Access

Many cafes and restaurants offer free wi-fi for customers. Most hostels, and some hotels, maintain a public computer for guests to surf the internet. The Slovenia Tourist Information Centre has computers on-hand to check email (per 30 minutes €1).

Cyber Cafe Xplorer (☎430 19 91; Petkovškovo nabrežje 23; per 30min/1hr €2.50/4; ⏰10am-10pm Mon-Fri, 2-10pm Sat & Sun; 📶) Ljubljana's best internet cafe; also has wi-fi and offers discount international calling.

Medical Services

Central Pharmacy (Centralna Lekarna; ☎230 61 00; Prešernov trg 5; ⏰8am-7.30pm Mon-Fri, 8am-3pm Sat)

Health Centre Ljubljana (Zdravstveni Dom Ljubljana; ☎472 37 00; www.zd-lj.si; Metelkova ulica 9; ⏰7.30am-7pm) For non-emergencies.

University Medical Centre Ljubljana (Univerzitetni Klinični Center Ljubljana; ☎522 50 50, emergencies 522 84 08; www4.kclj.si; Zaloška cesta 2; ⏰24hr) University medical clinic with 24h accident and emergency service.

Money

There are ATMs at every turn, including a row of them outside the main Ljubljana Tourist Information Centre (TIC) office. At the train station you'll find a **bureau de change** (train station; ⏰7am-8pm) changing cash for no commission but not travellers cheques.

Abanka (☎300 15 00; www.abanka.si; Slovenska cesta 50; ⏰9am-1pm & 3pm-5pm Mon-Fri)

Nova Ljubljanska Banka (☎476 39 00; www.nlb.si; Trg Republike 2; ⏰8am-6pm Mon-Fri)

Post

Main Post Office (Slovenska cesta 32; ⏰8am-7pm Mon-Fri, to 1pm Sat) Holds poste restante for 30 days and changes money.

Tourist Information

Ljubljana Tourist Information Centre (TIC; ☎306 12 15; www.visitljubljana.si; Adamič-Lundrovo nabrežje 2; ⏰8am-9pm Jun-Sep, 8am-7pm Oct-May) Knowledgeable and enthusiastic staff dispense information, maps and useful literature and help with accommodation. Maintains an excellent website. Has a helpful **branch** (☎433 94 75; www.visitljubljana.si; Trg OF 6; ⏰8am-10pm Jun-Sep, 10am-7pm Mon-Fri, 8am-3pm Sat Oct-May) at the train station.

Slovenian Tourist Information Centre (STIC; ☎306 45 76; www.slovenia.info; Krekov trg 10; ⏰8am-9pm Jun-Sep, 8am-7pm Oct-May) Good source of information for the rest of Slovenia, with internet and bicycle rental also available.

Travel Agency

STA Ljubljana (☎439 16 90, 041 612 711; www.sta-lj.com; 1st fl, Trg Ajdovščina 1; ⏰10am-5pm Mon-Fri) Discount air fares for students and its cafe has internet access.

Trek Trek (☎425 13 92; www.trektrek.si; Bičevje ulica 5; ⏰10am-5pm Mon-Fri) Specialising in adventure travel in Slovenia, with emphasis on trekking and cycling holidays.

Websites

In addition to the websites of the Slovenian Tourist Information Centre and Ljubljana Tourist Information Centre the following sites might be useful:

City of Ljubljana (www.ljubljana.si) Comprehensive information portal on every aspect of life and tourism direct from city hall.

In Your Pocket (www.inyourpocket.com) Insider info on the capital updated regularly.

Lonely Planet (www.lonelyplanet.com/slovenia/ljubljana)

ℹ️ Getting There & Away

Bus

Buses to destinations both within Slovenia and abroad leave from the **bus station** (Avtobusna Postaja Ljubljana; ☎234 46 00; www.ap-ljubljana.si; Trg Osvobodilne Fronte 4; ⏰5.30am-10.30pm Sun-Fri, 5am-10pm Sat) just next to train station. Next to the ticket windows are multilingual information phones and a touch-screen computer. You do not usually have to buy a ticket in advance; just pay as you board the bus. But for long-distance trips on Friday, just before the school break and public holidays, book the day before to be safe. There's a **left luggage** (Trg OF 4; per day €2; ⏰5.30am-10.30pm Sun-Fri, 5am-10pm Sat) area at window 3.

You can reach virtually anywhere in the country by bus.

Train

Domestic and international trains arrive at and depart from central Ljubljana's **train station** (Železniška Postaja; ☎291 33 32; www.slo-zeleznice.si; Trg Osvobodilne Fronte 6; ⏰6am-10pm) where you'll find a separate Info Center next to the Ljubljana Tourist Information Centre branch. Buy domestic tickets from window nos 1 to 8 and international ones from either window no 9 or the Info Center. There are **coin lockers** (Trg OF 6; per day €2-3; ⏰24hr) for left luggage on platform 1.

There's a surcharge of €1.55 on domestic InterCity (IC) and EuroCity (EC) train tickets.

ℹ️ Getting Around

To/From the Airport

The cheapest way to Ljubljana's **Jože Pučnik Airport** (LJU/Aerodrom Ljubljana; ☎04-206 19 81; www.lju-airport.si/eng; Zgornji Brnik 130a, Brnik) is by public bus (€4.10, 45 minutes, 27km) from stop No 28 at the bus station. These run at 5.20am and hourly from 6.10am to 8.10pm

TRANSPORT FROM LJUBLJANA

Bus

DESTINATION	PRICE (€)	DURATION (HR)	DISTANCE (KM)	FREQUENCY
Bled	6.20	1½	57	hourly
Bohinj	9	2	91	hourly
Koper	12	2½	122	5 daily with more in season
Maribor	14	3	141	2-4 four daily
Piran	14	3	140	up to 7 daily
Postojna	7	1	53	up to 24 daily

Train

DESTINATION	PRICE (€)	DURATION	DISTANCE (KM)	FREQUENCY
Bled	6.20	55min	51	up to 21 daily
Koper	9	2½hr	153	up to 4 daily with more in summer
Maribor	15	1¾hr	156	up to 25 daily
Murska Sobota	14	3¼hr	216	up to 5 daily

Monday to Friday; at the weekend there's a bus at 6.10am and then one every two hours from 9.10am to 7.10pm. Buy tickets from the driver.

A **private airport van** (☑051 321 414; www.airport-shuttle.si) also links Trg OF, near the bus station, with the airport (€9) up to 11 times daily between 5.20am and 10.30pm, and is a 30-minute trip. It goes from the airport to Ljubljana 10 times a day between 5.45am and 11pm.

A taxi from the airport to Ljubljana will cost from €40 to €45.

Bicycle
Ljubljana is a pleasure for cyclists, and there are bike lanes and special traffic lights everywhere.

Ljubljana Bike (☑306 45 76; www.visitljubljana.si; Krekov trg 10; per 2hr/day €2/8; ☺8am-7pm or 9pm Apr-Oct) rents two-wheelers in two-hour or full-day increments from April through October from the Slovenia Tourist Information Centre.

For short rides, you can hire bikes as needed from **Bicike(lj)** (www.bicikelj.si; subscription weekly/yearly €1/€3 plus hourly rate; ☺24hr) bike stands located around the city. To rent a bike requires pre-registration and subscription over the company website plus a valid credit or debit card. After registration simply submit your card or an Urbana public-transport card plus a PIN number. The first hour of the rental is free, the second hour costs €1, the third hour €2, and each additional hour €4. Bikes must be returned within 24 hours.

Public Transport
Ljubljana's city buses operate every five to 15 minutes from 5am (6am on Sunday) to around 10.30pm. A flat fare of €1.20 (good for 90 minutes of unlimited travel, including transfers) is paid with a stored-value magnetic **Urbana** (☑430 51 74; www.jh-lj.si/urbana) card, which can be purchased at newsstands, tourist offices and the **LPP Information Centre** (☑430 51 75; www.jhl.si; Slovenska cesta 56; ☺7am-7pm Mon-Fri) for €2; credit can then be added (from €1 to €50).

JULIAN ALPS

Slovenia's Julian Alps, part of the wider European Alpine range, is the epicentre for all things outdoors. If you're into adventure sports, head to this area. Much of the region, including the country's highest mountain, Mt Triglav, is protected as part of the Triglav National Park. The park has hiking and biking trails galore. The beautiful alpine lakes at Bled and Bohinj offer boating and swimming amid shimmering mountain backdrops. The region is not just about nature pursuits; you'll also find some of the country's most attractive and important historical towns, like Radovljica. These are unexpected treasure troves of Gothic, Renaissance and baroque architecture.

Lake Bled

📞 04 / POP 10900

With its emerald-green lake, picture-postcard church on an islet, a medieval castle clinging to a rocky cliff and some of the highest peaks of the Julian Alps and the Karavanke as backdrops, Bled is Slovenia's most popular resort, drawing everyone from honeymooners lured by the over-the-top romantic setting to backpackers, who come for the hiking, biking, boating and canyoning possibilities. Bled can be overpriced and swarming with tourists in mid-summer. But as is the case with many popular destinations around the world, people come in droves – and will continue to do so – because the place is special.

◎ Sights

Lake Bled
LAKE

(Blejsko jezero) Bled's greatest attraction is its crystal blue-green lake, measuring just 2km by 1380m. The lake is lovely to behold from almost any vantage point, and makes a beautiful backdrop for the 6km walk along the shore. Mild thermal springs warm the water to a swimmable 26°C from June through August. You can rent boats, go diving or simply snap countless photos.

Bled Castle
CASTLE, MUSEUM

(Blejski Grad; www.blejski-grad.si; Grajska cesta 25; adult/child €8/3.50; ⊗8am-8pm Apr-Oct, 8am-6pm Nov-Mar) Perched atop a steep cliff more than 100m above the lake, Bled Castle is how most people imagine a medieval fortress to be, with towers, ramparts, moats and a terrace offering magnificent views. The castle houses a museum collection that traces the lake's history from earliest times to the development of Bled as a resort in the 19th century.

The castle, built on two levels, dates back to the early 11th century, although most of what stands here now is from the 16th century. For 800 years, it was the seat of the Bishops of Brixen. Among the museum holdings, there's a large collection of armour and weapons (swords, halberds and firearms from the 16th to 18th centuries).

Bled Island
ISLAND

(Blejski Otok; www.blejskiotok.si) Tiny, tear-shaped Bled Island beckons from the shore. There's a church and small museum, but the real thrill is the ride out by gondola (*pletna*). The boat sets you down on the south side at the monumental South Staircase (Južno Stopnišče), built in 1655.

Vintgar Gorge
NATURE PARK

(Soteska Vintgar; adult/child/student €4/2/3; ⊗8am-7pm late Apr-Oct) One of the easiest and most satisfying day trips from Bled is to Vintgar Gorge, some 4km to the northwest. The highlight is a 1600m wooden walkway, built in 1893 and continually rebuilt since. It criss-crosses the swirling Radovna River four times over rapids, waterfalls and pools before reaching 13m-high Šum Waterfall.

🏃 Activities

Several local outfits organise a wide range of outdoor activities in and around Bled, including trekking, mountaineering, rock climbing, ski touring, cross-country skiing, mountain biking, rafting, kayaking, canyoning, caving, horse riding and paragliding.

3glav Adventures
ADVENTURE SPORTS

(📞041 683 184; www.3glav-adventures.com; Ljubljanska cesta 1; ⊗9am-7pm Apr-Oct) The number-one adventure-sport specialists in Bled for warm-weather activities from 15 April to 15 October. The most popular trip is the Emerald River Adventure (€65), an 11-hour hiking and swimming foray into Triglav National Park. Also rents bikes (half-day/full day €8/15), conducts hot-air balloon flights (€150) and leads diving expeditions of Lake Bled (€70).

Gondola
BOATING

(Pletna; 📞041 427 155; per person return €12) Riding a piloted gondola out to Bled Island is the archetypal tourist experience. There is a convenient jetty just below the TIC and another in Mlino on the south shore. You get about half an hour to explore the island. In all, the trip to the island and back takes about 1¼ hours.

Horse-drawn Carriages
CARRIAGE

(Fijaker; 📞041 710 970; www.fijaker-bled.si) A romantic way to experience Bled is to take a horse-drawn carriage from the stand near the Festival Hall (Festivalna Dvorana; Cesta Svobode 11). A spin around the lake costs €40, and it's the same price to the castle; an extra 30 minutes inside costs €50. You can even get a carriage for four to Vintgar (adult/child €4/2; ⊗8am-7pm mid-May–Oct); the two-hour return trip costs €90.

🛏 Sleeping

Kompas has a list of private rooms and farmhouses, with singles/doubles starting at €24/38.

Hotel Triglav Bled HOTEL €€€
(☑575 26 10; www.hoteltriglavbled.si; Kolodvorska cesta 33; s €89-159, d €119-179, ste €139-209; P❋@⛱☎) This 22-room boutique hotel in a painstakingly restored caravanserai that opened in 1906 raises the bar of accommodation standards in Bled. The rooms have hardwood floors and oriental carpets and are furnished with antiques. There's an enormous sloped garden that grows the vegetables served in the terrace restaurants. The location is opposite Bled Jezero train station.

⌐TOP⌐ **Camping Bled** CAMPGROUND €
CHOICE
(☑575 20 00; www.camping-bled.com; Kidričeva cesta 10c; adult €10.90-12.90, child €7.60-9, glamping huts €60-80; ⊙Apr–mid-Oct; P@☎) Bled's upscale campground is one of the nicest in the country and one of the few places around to try 'glamping' – aka glamorous camping – in this case, ecofriendly, all-natural A-frame huts, some equipped with hot-tubs. The campground setting is a well-tended rural valley at the western end of the lake, about 2.5km from the bus station.

Garni Hotel Berc HOTEL €€
(☑576 56 58; www.berc-sp.si; Pod Stražo 13; s €45-50, d €70-80; P@☎) This purpose-built place, reminiscent of a Swiss chalet, has 15 rooms on two floors in a quiet location above the lake.

Penzion Mayer PENSION €€
(☑576 57 40; www.mayer-sp.si; Želeška cesta 7; s €57, d €77-82, apt €120-150; P@☎) This flower-bedecked 12-room inn in a renovated 19th-century house is in a quiet location above the lake. The larger apartment is in a delightful wooden cabin and the in-house restaurant is excellent.

Traveller's Haven HOSTEL €
(☑041 396 545; www.travellers-haven.si; Riklijeva cesta 1; dm/d €19/48; P@☎) This is arguably the nicest of several hostels clustered on a hillside on the eastern shore of the lake, about 500m north of the centre. The setting is a renovated villa, with six rooms (including one private double), a great kitchen and free laundry. Note the upstairs rooms get hot in mid-summer.

✕ Eating & Drinking

Vila Ajda SLOVENIAN €€
(☑576 83 20; www.vila-ajda.si; Cesta Svobode 27; mains €9-20; ⊙11am-11pm; ☎) Attractive destination restaurant with lovely views out over

---

WORTH A TRIP

RADOVLJICA

The town of Radovljica, an easy day trip from Bled, just 7km away, is filled with charming, historic buildings and blessed with stunning views of the Alps, including Mt Triglav. It was settled by the early Slavs and by the 14th century had grown into an important market town centred on a large rectangular square, today's **Linhartov trg**, and fortified with high stone walls. Much of the original architecture is still standing and looks remarkably unchanged from those early days.

Besides simply strolling historic Linhartov trg, don't miss the town's **Beekeeping Museum** (Čebelarski Muzej; www.muzeji-radovljica.si; Linhartov trg 1; adult/child €3/2; ⊙10am-6pm Tue-Sun May-Oct, 8am-3pm Tue, Thu & Fri, 10am-noon & 3-5pm Wed, Sat & Sun Mar, Apr, Nov & Dec, 8am-3pm Tue-Fri Jan & Feb), which is more interesting than it sounds. The museum's collection of illustrated beehive panels from the 18th and 19th centuries, a folk art unique to Slovenia, is the largest in the country. Ask to see a short, instructive video in English.

Radovljica's other claim to fame is food, and the town is blessed with several excellent restaurants. Our favourite is the traditional **Gostilna Lectar** (☑537 48 00; www.lectar. com; Linhartov trg 2; mains €9-15; ⊙noon-11pm; ☎), an inviting guesthouse on the main square. Everything from relatively common dishes like veal goulash to harder to find items like 'beef tongue served with kohlrabi' are given a gourmet touch.

Across the street, **Gostilna Augustin** (☑531 41 63; Linhartov trg 15; mains €10-17; ⊙10am-10pm) serves excellent Slovenian dishes to order. Don't miss the cellar dining room, which was once part of a prison (and may have seen an execution or two), and the wonderful back terrace with stunning views of Mt Triglav. Why not have lunch at one and dinner at the other?

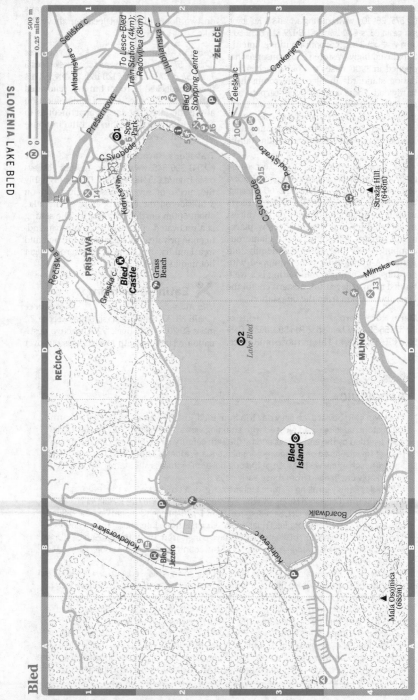

Bled

500 m
0.25 miles

ŽELEČE

Cankarjeva c

Seliška c

Mladinska c

To Lesce-Bled
Train Station (4km);
Radovljica (8km)

Ljubljanska c

Prešernova c

Bled
Shopping Centre

Želeška c

Spa
Park

C Svoboda

Pod Stražo

Kidričeva c

C Svoboda

Reciška c

PRISTAVA

Strāžza Hill
(646m)

Bled
Castle

Grajska c

Grass
Beach

Mlinska c

RECICA

Lake Bled

MLINO

Bled
Island

Boardwalk

Kolodvorska c

Bled
Jezero

Kidričeva c

Mala Osojnica
(685m)

the lake and a menu that features traditional Slovenian cooking made from locally sourced ingredients. Eat outdoors in the garden in nice weather, or in the upscale dining room. Book in advance on warm evenings in summer.

Ostarija Peglez'n SEAFOOD €€
(☎574 42 18; http://ostarija-peglezn.mestna-izlozba.com; Cesta Svobode 19a; mains €8-18; ⊙11am-11pm) One of the better restaurants in Bled, the Iron Inn is just opposite the landmark Grand Hotel Toplice. It has fascinating retro decor with lots of old household antiques and curios (including the eponymous iron) and serves some of the best fish dishes in town.

Penzion Mlino SLOVENIAN €€
(www.mlino.si; Cesta Svobode 45; mains €8-15; ⊙noon-11pm; 🕸) This is a wonderful choice for lunch along a quieter strip of the lake, about 3km outside the centre. The daily four-course set lunches (around €10) usually offer a fish choice, such as the unforgettable grilled trout we enjoyed on our stop.

Pizzeria Rustika PIZZA €
(☎576 89 00; www.pizzeria-rustika.com; Riklijeva cesta 13; pizza €6-10; ⊙noon-11pm; 🕸) Conveniently located on the same hill as many of Bled's hostels, so the best pizza in town is just a couple of minutes' walk away.

Pub Bled PUB
(Cesta Svobode 19a; ⊙9am-2am Sun-Thu, 9am-3am Fri & Sat) This friendly pub above the Oštarija Peglez'n restaurant has great cocktails and, on some nights, a DJ.

Slaščičarna Šmon CAFE
(http://slascicarna-smon.mestna-izlozba.com; Grajska cesta 3; ⊙7.30am-10pm; 🕸) Bled's culinary speciality is *kremna rezina* (€2.40), a layer of vanilla custard topped with whipped cream and sandwiched between two layers of flaky pastry, and while Šmon may not be its place of birth, it remains the best place in which to try it.

ⓘ Information

A Propos Bar (☎574 40 44; Bled Shopping Centre, Ljubljanska cesta 4; per 15/30/60min €1.25/2.10/4.20; ⊙8am-midnight Sun-Thu, to 1am Fri & Sat; 🕸) In Bled Shopping Centre, wireless connection as well.

Gorenjska Banka (Cesta Svobode 15) Just north of the Park Hotel.

Kompas (☎572 75 01; www.kompas-bled.si; Bled Shopping Centre, Ljubljanska cesta 4; ⊙8am-7pm Mon-Sat, 8am-noon & 4-7pm Sun) Full-service travel agency, organises excursions to Bohinj and Radovljica, airport transfers and transport, rents bikes and skis, sells fishing licenses and arranges accommodation in private homes and apartments.

Post Office (Ljubljanska cesta 10)

Tourist Information Centre Bled (☎574 11 22; www.bled.si; Cesta Svobode 10; ⊙8am-7pm Mon-Sat, 11am-5pm Sun) Occupies a small office behind the Casino at Cesta Svobode 10; sells maps and souvenirs, rents bikes (half day/full day €8/11); has a computer for checking email.

ⓘ Getting There & Around

BUS Bled is well connected by bus. There are buses every 30 minutes to Radovljica (€1.80, 15 minutes, 7km) and around 20 buses daily run from Bled to Lake Bohinj (€3.60, 45 minutes) via Bohinjska Bistrica, with the first bus leaving around 5am and the last about 9pm. Buses depart at least hourly for Ljubljana (€6.50, 1¼ hours, 57km).

TRAIN Bled has two train stations, though neither is close to the centre. Mainline trains for Ljubljana (€6.50, 55 minutes, 51km, up to 21 daily), via Škofja Loka and Radovljica, use

Lesce-Bled station, 4km to the east of town. Trains to Bohinjska Bistrica (€1.60, 20 minutes, 18km, eight daily), from where you can catch a bus to Lake Bohinj, use the smaller Bled Jezero station, which is 2km west of central Bled.

Lake Bohinj

♪ 04 / POP 5275

Many visitors to Slovenia say they've never seen a more beautiful lake than Bled...that is, until they've seen Lake Bohinj, just 26km to the southwest. We'll refrain from weighing in on the Bled vs Bohinj debate other than to say we see their point. Admittedly, Bohinj lacks Bled's glamour, but it's less crowded and in many ways more authentic. It's an ideal summer holiday destination. People come primarily to chill out or go for a swim in the crystal-clear, blue-green water. There are lots of outdoor pursuits like kayaking, cycling, climbing and horse riding if you've got the energy.

◎ Sights

Church of St John the Baptist CHURCH
(Cerkev Sv Janeza Krstnika; Ribčev Laz; ⊙10am-noon & 4-7pm summer, by appointment other times) This church, on the northern side of the Sava Bohinjka river across the stone bridge, is what every medieval church should be: small, on a reflecting body of water and full of exquisite frescos. The nave is Romanesque, but the Gothic presbytery dates from about 1440.

Alpine Dairy Museum MUSEUM
(Planšarski Muzej; www.bohinj.si; Stara Fužina 181; adult/child €3/2; ⊙11am-7pm Tue-Sun Jul & Aug, 10am-noon & 4-6pm Tue-Sun early Jan-Jun, Sep-late Oct) This museum in Stara Fužina, 1.5km north of Ribčev Laz, has a small collection related to Alpine dairy farming. The four rooms of the museum – once a cheese dairy itself – contain a mock-up of a mid-19th-century herder's cottage.

Savica Waterfall WATERFALL
(Slap Savica; Ukanc; adult/child €2.50/1.25; ⊙9am-6pm Jul & Aug, 9am-5pm Apr-Jun, Sep & Oct; P) The magnificent Savica Waterfall, which cuts deep into a gorge 60m below, is 4km from the Hotel Zlatorog in Ukanc and can be reached by footpath from there.

🏃 Activities

While most people come to Bohinj to relax, there are more exhilarating pursuits available, including canyoning, caving, and para-gliding from the top of Mt Vogel, among others. Two companies, Alpinsport and Perfect Adventure Choice (PAC) Sports, specialise in these activities.

Alpinsport ADVENTURE SPORTS
(♪572 34 86; www.alpinsport.si; Ribčev Laz 53; ⊙9am-8pm Jul-Sep, 9am-7pm Oct-Jun) Rents sporting equipment, canoes, kayaks and bikes; also operates guided rafting, canyoning and caving trips. Located in a kiosk at the stone bridge over the Sava Bohinjka river in Ribčev Laz.

Bohinj Cable Car HIKING, SKIING
(adult/child one way €9/7 return €13/9; ⊙every 30min 8am-6pm) The Bohinj cable car operates year-round, hauling skiiers in winter and hikers in summer. There are several day hikes and longer treks that set out from Mt Vogel (1922m).

Mrcina Ranč HORSE RIDING
(♪041 790 297; www.ranc-mrcina.com; Studor; per hr €20) Mrcina Ranč in Studor, 5km from Ribčev Laz, offers a range of guided tours on horseback, lasting one hour to three days on sturdy Icelandic ponies.

PAC Sports ADVENTURE SPORTS
(Perfect Adventure Choice; ♪572 34 61; www.pac-sports.com; Hostel Pod Voglom, Ribčev Laz; ⊙7am-11pm Jul & Aug, 10am-6pm Sep-Jun) Popular youth-oriented sports and adventure company, located in the Hostel pod Voglom, 3km west of Ribcev Laz on the road to Ukanc. Rents bikes, canoes and kayaks, and operates guided canyoning, rafting, paragliding and caving trips. In winter, they rent sleds and offer winter rafting near Vogel (per person €15).

Tourist Boat BOATING
(Turistična Ladja; ♪574 75 90; one way adult/child €9/6.50, return €10.50/7.50; ⊙half-hourly 9.30am-5.30pm Jun–mid-Sep, 10am, 11.30am, 1pm, 2.30pm, 4pm & 5.30pm early Apr-May, 11.30am, 1pm, 2.30pm & 4pm mid-Sep–Oct) An easy family-friendly sail from Ribčev Laz to Ukanc and back.

🛏 Sleeping

The tourist office can help arrange accommodation in private rooms and apartments. Expect to pay anywhere from €38 to €50 for a two-person apartment.

TOP CHOICE **Penzion Gasperin** PENSION €€
(♪041 540 805; www.bohinj.si/gasperin; Ribčev Laz 36a; r €48-60; P🐾❄@🛜) This spotless

chalet-style guesthouse with 23 rooms is just 350m southeast of the TIC and run by a friendly British/Slovenian couple. Most rooms have balconies. The buffet breakfast is fresh and includes a sampling of local meats and cheeses.

Hotel Stare
PENSION €€

(📱040 558 669; www.bohinj-hotel.com; Ukanc 128; per person €42-50; P@🛜) This beautifully appointed 10-room pension is situated on the Sava Bohinjka river in Ukanc and is surrounded by 3.5 hectares of lovely garden. If you really want to get away from it all without having to climb mountains, this is your place. Rates are half-board, including breakfast and dinner.

Hotel Jezero
HOTEL €€€

(📱572 91 00; www.bohinj.si/alpinum/jezero; Ribčev Laz 51; s €65-75, d €120-140; P@🛜🏊) Further renovations have raised the standards at this 76-room place just across from the lake. It has a lovely indoor swimming pool, two saunas and a fitness centre.

Hostel Pod Voglom
HOSTEL €

(📱572 34 61; www.hostel-podvoglom.com; Ribčev Laz 60; dm €18, r per person €23-26, without bathroom €20-22; P@) Bohinj's youth hostel, some 3km west of the centre of Ribčev Laz on the road to Ukanc, has 119 beds in 46 rooms in two buildings.

Autokamp Zlatorog
CAMPGROUND €

(📱577 80 00; www.hoteli-bohinj.si; Ukanc 2; per person €6-9; ☺May-Sep) This pleasant, pine-shaded 2.5-hectare camping ground accommodating 500 guests is at the lake's western end, 4.5km from Ribčev Laz. Prices vary according to site location, with the most expensive – and desirable – sites right on the lake.

✖ Eating

TOP CHOICE Gostilna Rupa
SLOVENIAN €€

(📱572 34 01; www.apartmajikatrnjek.com/rupa; Srednja Vas 87; mains €8-16; ☺10am-midnight Jul & Aug, Tue-Sun Sep-Jun) If you're under your own steam, head for this country-style restaurant in the next village over from Studor and about 5km from Ribčev Laz. Among the excellent home-cooked dishes are *ajdova krapi*, crescent-shaped dumplings made from buckwheat and cheese, various types of local *klobasa* (sausage) and Bohinj trout.

Gostilna Mihovc
SLOVENIAN €

(📱572 33 90; www.gostilna-mihovc.si; Stara Fužina 118; mains €7-10; ☺10am-midnight) This place in Stara Fužina is very popular – not least for its fiery homemade brandy. Try the *pasulj* (bean soup) with sausage (€6) or the beef *goláč* (goulash; €5.20). Live music on Friday and Saturday evenings. In

---

SUMMITING MT TRIGLAV

The 2864m limestone peak called Mt Triglav (Mt Three Heads) has been a source of inspiration and an object of devotion for Slovenes for more than a millennium. Under the Habsburgs in the 19th century, the 'pilgrimage' to Triglav became, in effect, a confirmation of one's ethnic identity, and this tradition continues to this day: a Slovene is expected to climb Triglav at least once in his or her life.

You can climb Slovenia's highest peak too, but Triglav is not for the unfit or faint-hearted. We strongly recommend hiring a guide for the ascent, even if you have some mountain-climbing experience under your belt. A local guide will know the trails and conditions, and can prove invaluable in helping to arrange sleeping space in mountain huts and providing transport. Guides can be hired through 3glav (p500) in Bled or Alpinsport in Bohinj, or book in advance through the **Alpine Association of Slovenia** (PZS; www.pzs.si/).

Triglav is inaccessible from middle to late October to late May. June and the first half of July are the rainiest times in the summer months, so late July, August and particularly September and early October are the best times to make the climb.

There are many ways to reach the top, with the most popular approaches coming from the south, either starting from **Pokljuka**, near Bled, or from the Savica Waterfall, near Lake Bohinj. You can also climb Triglav from the north and the east (Mojstrana and the Vrata Valley). All of the approaches offer varying degrees of difficulty and have their pluses and minuses. Note that treks normally require one or two overnight stays in the mountains.

summer book in advance to secure a garden table.

ⓘ Getting There & Away

Buses run regularly from Ljubljana (€9, two hours, 90km, hourly) to Bohinj Jezero and Ukanc – marked 'Bohinj Zlatorog' – via Bled and Bohinjska Bistrica. Around 20 buses daily run from Bled (€3.60, 45 minutes) to Bohinj Jezero (via Bohinjska Bistrica) and return, with the first bus leaving around 5am and the last about 9pm. From the end of June through August, **Alpetour** (☎532 04 45; www.alpetour.si) runs special tourist buses that leave from Ribčev Laz to Bohinjska Bistrica in one direction and to the Savica Waterfall (23 minutes) in the other.

Several trains daily make the run to Bohinjska Bistrica from Ljubljana (€6.70, two hours), though this route requires a change in Jesenice. There are also frequent trains between Bled's small Bled Jezero station (€1.60, 20 minutes, 18km, eight daily) and Bohinjska Bistrica.

Kranjska Gora

☑04 / POP 5510

Nestling in the Sava Dolinka Valley some 40km northwest of Bled, Kranjska Gora (Carniolan Mountain) is Slovenia's largest and best-equipped ski resort. It's at its most perfect under a blanket of snow, but its surroundings are wonderful to explore at other times as well. There are endless possibilities for hiking, cycling and mountaineering in Triglav National Park, which is right on the town's doorstep to the south, and few travellers will be unimpressed by a trip over Vršič Pass (1611m), the gateway to the Soča Valley.

⊙ Sights & Activities

Most of the sights are situated along the main street, Borovška cesta, 400m south of where the buses stop. The endearing **Liznjek House** (Liznjekova Domačija; www.gornjesav-skimuzej.si; Borovška 63; adult/child €2.50/1.70; ⊙10am-6pm Tue-Sat, 10am-5pm Sun), an 18th-century museum house, has a good collection of household objects and furnishings peculiar to the alpine region.

Kranjska Gora is best known as a winter resort, and chairlifts up to the **ski slopes** on Vitranc (1631m) are at the western end of town off Smerinje ulica. There are more ski slopes and a **ski-jumping facility** 6km to the west, near the villages of Rateče and Planica, which is home to the annual **Ski-Jumping World Cup Championships** (☎1 200 6241; www.planica.info; Planica; adult/child €20/3) in mid-March. There are lots of places offering ski tuition and hiring out equipment, including **ASK Kranjska Gora Ski School** (☎588 53 02; www.ask-kg.com; Borovška c 99a; ⊙9am-4pm Mon-Sat, 10am-6pm Sun mid-Dec–mid-Mar, 9am-3pm Mon-Fri mid-Mar–mid-Dec).

In summer, the town is quieter, but there are still plenty of things to do. Kranjska Gora makes an excellent base for hiking in the Triglav National Park, and Jasna Lake, the gateway to the park, is 2km to the south. The 1:30,000-scale *Kranjska Gora* hiking map is available at the **Tourist Information Centre** (TIC; ☎580 94 40; www.kranjska -gora.si; Tičarjeva cesta 2; ⊙8am-7pm Mon-Sat, 9am-6pm Sun Jun-Sep & mid-Dec–Mar, 8am-3pm Mon-Sat Apr, May & Oct–mid-Dec) for €9.

The hiking map also marks out 15 **cycling routes** of varying difficulty. Most ski-rental outfits hire out bikes in summer, including **Intersport** (www.intersport-bernik.com; Borovška cesta 88a; ⊙8am-8pm mid-Dec–mid-Mar, 8am-8pm Mon-Sat, 8am-1pm Sun mid-Mar–mid-Dec). Expect to pay €10 for a full-day rental and helmet.

🛏 Sleeping & Eating

Accommodation costs peak from December to March and in mid-summer. Private rooms and apartments can be arranged through the Tourist Information Centre.

Hotel Kotnik   HOTEL €€
(☎588 15 64; www.hotel-kotnik.si; Borovška cesta 75; s €50-60, d €72-80; ▣◉⊚) If you're not into big high-rise hotels with hundreds of rooms, choose this charming, bright-yellow, low-rise property. It has 15 cosy rooms, a great restaurant and pizzeria, and it couldn't be more central.

Natura Eco Camp Kranjska Gora   CAMPGROUND €
(☎064 121 966; www.naturacamp-kranjskagora.com; Borovška cesta 62; adult €8-10, child €5-7, cabin & tree tent €25-30) This wonderful site, some 300m from the main road on an isolated horse ranch in a forest clearing, is as close to paradise as we've been for awhile. Pitch a tent or stay in one of the little wooden cabins or the unique tree tents – great pouches with air mattresses suspended from the branches.

Hotel Miklič   HOTEL €€€
(☎588 16 35; www.hotelmiklic.com; Vitranška ulica 13; s €60-80, d €80-130; ▣◉⊚) This pristine 15-room small hotel south of the centre is

surrounded by luxurious lawns and flower beds and boasts an excellent restaurant and a small fitness room with sauna (€12 per hour). It's definitely a cut above most other accommodation in Kranjska Gora.

Hotel Kotnik   SLOVENIAN €€
(☑588 15 64; www.hotel-kotnik.si; Borovška c 75; mains €8-18; 🛜) One of Kranjska Gora's better eateries, the restaurant in this stylish inn, with bits of painted dowry chests on the walls, serves grilled meats – pepper steak is a speciality – that should keep you going for awhile. The adjoining pizzeria (pizza €6 to €9, open noon to 10.30pm) with the wood-burning stove is a great choice for something quicker.

Gostilna Pri Martinu   SLOVENIAN €
(☑582 03 00; Borovška c 61; mains €7-14; ⊘10am-11pm; 🛜) This atmospheric tavern-restaurant in an old house opposite the fire station is one of the best places in town to try local specialities, such as *ješprenj* (barley soup), *telečja obara* (veal stew) and *ričet* (barley stew with smoked pork ribs). One of the few places to offer a full three-course luncheon menu (€7).

❶ Getting There & Away

Buses run hourly to Ljubljana (€8.70, two hours, 91km) via Jesenice (€3.10, 30 minutes, 24km), where you should change for Bled (€2.70, 20 minutes, 19km). There's just one direct departure to Bled (€4.80, one hour, 40km) on weekdays at 9.15am and at 9.50am on weekends.

Alpetour (☑201 31 30; www.alpetour.si) runs regular buses to Trenta (€4.70, 70 minutes, 30km) and Bovec (€6.70, two hours, 46km) from June through September via the Vršič Pass. Check the website for a timetable. There are normally about four departures daily (more at the weekend). Buy tickets from the driver.

Soča Valley

The Soča Valley region (Posočje) stretches from Triglav National Park to Nova Gorica, including the outdoor activity centres of Bovec and Kobarid. Threading through it is the magically aquamarine Soča River. Most people come here for the rafting, hiking and skiing, though there are plenty of historical sights and locations, particularly relating to WWI, when millions of troops fought on the mountainous battle front here.

BOVEC
☑05 / POP 1810
Soča Valley's de facto capital, Bovec, offers plenty to adventure-sports enthusiasts. With

the Julian Alps above, the Soča River below and Triglav National Park all around, you could spend a week here hiking, kayaking, mountain biking and, in winter, skiing at Mt Kanin, Slovenia's highest ski station, without ever doing the same thing twice.

🏃 Activities

Rafting, kayaking and **canoeing** on the beautiful Soča River (10% to 40% gradient; Grades I to VI) are major draws. The season lasts from April to October.

Rafting trips of two to eight people over a distance of 8km to 10km (1½ hours) cost from €36 to €46 and for 21km (2½ hours) from €48 to €55, including neoprene long johns, windcheater, life jacket, helmet and paddle. Bring a swimsuit, T-shirt and towel. Canoes for two are €45 for the day; single kayaks €30. A number of beginners kayaking courses are also on offer (eg one-/two-days from €55/100). Longer guided kayak trips (up to 10km) are also available.

A 3km **canyoning** trip near the Soča, in which you descend through gorges and jump over falls attached to a rope, costs around €42.

Other popular activities include **cycling, hiking** and **fishing**. Visit the **Tourist Information Centre Bovec** (☑388 19 19; www.bovec.si; Trg Golobarskih Žrtev 8; ⊘8.30am-8.30pm summer, 9am-6pm winter) for specific information or check in with the following reputable agencies:

Soča Rafting   ADVENTURE SPORTS
(☑041-724 472, 389 62 00; www.socarafting.si; Trg Golobarskih Žrtev 14; ⊘9am-7pm year-round)

Top Extreme   ADVENTURE SPORTS
(☑041 620 636; www.top.si; Trg Golobarskih Žrtev 19; ⊘9am-7pm May-Sep)

Kanin Ski Centre   SKIING
(☑388 60 98; www.bovec.si; day pass adult/child/senior & student €22/16/18) The Kanin Ski Centre northwest of Bovec has skiing up to 2200m – the only real altitude alpine skiing in Slovenia. As a result, the season can be long, with good spring skiing in April and even May.

🛏 Sleeping & Eating

Private rooms are easy to come by in Bovec through the TIC.

TOP CHOICE Dobra Vila   BOUTIQUE HOTEL €€€
(☑389 64 00; www.dobra-vila-bovec.si; Mala Vas 112; d €120-145, tr €160-180; 🅿❄🛜) This stunner

of a 10-room boutique hotel is housed in an erstwhile telephone-exchange building dating to 1932. Peppered with interesting artefacts and objets d'art, it has its own library and wine cellar and a fabulous restaurant with a winter garden and outdoor terrace.

Martinov Hram GUESTHOUSE €€
(☎388 62 14; www.martinov-hram.si; Trg Golobarskih Žrtev 27; s/d €33/54; P🖥) This lovely and very friendly guesthouse just 100m east of the centre has 14 beautifully furnished rooms and an excellent restaurant with an emphasis on specialities from the Bovec region.

Kamp Palovnik CAMPGROUND €
(☎388 60 07; www.kamp-polovnik.com; Ledina 8; adult €6.50-7.50, child €5-5.75; ⏱Apr–mid-Oct; P) About 500m southeast of the Hotel Kanin, this is the closest camping ground to Bovec. It is small (just over a hectare with 70 sites) but located in an attractive setting.

Gostišče Stari Kovač PIZZA €
(☎388 66 99; Rupa 3; starters €6.50-7, mains €8-11, pizza €5-7.50; ⏱noon-10pm Tue-Sun) The 'Old Blacksmith' is a good choice for pizza cooked in a wood-burning stove.

❶ Getting There & Away

Buses to Kobarid (€3.10, 30 minutes) depart up to six times a day. There are also buses to Ljubljana (€13.60, 3½ hours) via Kobarid and Idrija. From late June to August a service to Kranjska Gora (€6.70, two hours) via the Vršič Pass departs four times daily, continuing to Ljubljana.

KOBARID
☎05 / POP 1250

The charming town of Kobarid is quainter than nearby Bovec, and despite being surrounded by mountain peaks, Kobarid feels more Mediterranean than Alpine. On the surface not a whole lot has changed since Ernest Hemingway described Kobarid (then Caporetto) in *A Farewell to Arms* (1929) as 'a little white town with a campanile in a valley' with 'a fine fountain in the square'. Kobarid was a military settlement during Roman times, was hotly contested in the Middle Ages and was hit by a devastating earthquake in 1976, but the world will remember Kobarid as the site of the decisive battle of 1917 in which the combined forces of the Central Powers defeated the Italian army.

❍ Sights

Kobarid Museum MUSEUM
(☎389 00 00; www.kobariski-muzej.si; Gregorčičeva ul 10; adult/child €5/2.50; ⏱9am-6pm Mon-Fri,

9am-7pm Sat & Sun summer, 10am-5pm Mon-Fri, 9am-6pm Sat & Sun winter) This museum is devoted almost entirely to the Soča Front and WWI. There are many photographs documenting the horrors of the front, military charts, diaries and maps, and two large relief displays showing the front lines and offensives through the Krn Mountains and the positions in the Upper Soča Valley. Don't miss the 20-minute multimedia presentation.

🏃 Activities

A free pamphlet and map titled *The Kobarid Historical Trail* outlines a 5km-long route that will take you past remnants of WWI troop emplacements to the impressive **Kozjak Stream Waterfalls** (Slapovi Potoka Kozjak) and **Napoleon Bridge** (Napoleonov Most) built in 1750. More ambitious is the hike outlined in the free *Pot Miru/Walk of Peace* brochure.

Kobarid gives Bovec a run for its money in adventure sports, and you'll find several outfits on or off the town's main square that can organise rafting (from €34), canyoning (from €45), kayaking (€40) and paragliding (€110) between April and October. Two recommended agencies are listed below:

X Point ADVENTURE SPORTS
(☎041 692 290, 388 53 08; www.xpoint.si; Trg Svobode 6)

Positive Sport ADVENTURE SPORTS
(☎040 654 475; www.positive-sport.com; Markova ulica 2)

🛌 Sleeping

TOP CHOICE **Hiša Franko** GUESTHOUSE €€€
(☎389 41 20; www.hisafranko.com; Staro Selo 1; r €80-135; P🖥) This guesthouse in an old farmhouse 3km west of Kobarid in Staro Selo, halfway to the Italian border, has 10 themed rooms – we love the Moja Afrika (My Africa) and Soba Zelenega Čaja (Green Tea Room) ones – some of which have terraces and jacuzzis. Eat in their excellent restaurant.

Hotel Hvala HOTEL €€€
(☎389 93 00; wwww.hotelhvala.si; Trg Svobode 1; s €72-76, d €104-112; P🖲🖥) The delightful 'Hotel Thanks' (actually it's the family's name), has 31 rooms. A snazzy lift takes you on a vertical tour of Kobarid (don't miss both the Soča trout and Papa Hemingway at work); there's a bar, a Mediterranean-style cafe in the garden and a superb restaurant.

Kamp Koren CAMPGROUND €
(☑389 13 11; www.kamp-koren.si; Drežniške Ravne 33; per person pitch €11.50, chalets d/tr from €55/60; P☎) The oldest camping ground in the valley, this 2-hectare site with 70 pitches is about 500m northeast of Kobarid on the left bank of the Soča River and just before the turn to Drežniške Ravne. In full view is the Napoleon Bridge.

✖ Eating

In the centre of Kobarid you'll find two of Slovenia's best restaurants.

TOP **Hiša Franko** SLOVENIAN €€
CHOICE
(☑389 41 20; www.hisafranko.com; Staro Selo 1; mains €22-24; ☉noon-3pm & 6-11pm Tue-Sun) Foodies will love this superb gourmet restaurant in the guesthouse of the same name in Staro Selo, just west of town. Impeccable tasting menus, strong on locally sourced ingredients and which change according to the season, cost €50/75 for five/eight courses. It closes on Tuesday in winter.

Topli Val SEAFOOD €€
(Trg Svobode 1; starters €8-10, mains €9.50-25; ☉noon-10pm) Seafood is the speciality here, and it's excellent – from the carpaccio of sea bass to the Soča trout and signature lobster with pasta. Expect to pay about €30 to €60 per person with a decent bottle of wine. There's a lovely front terrace and back garden open in warmer months.

❶ Information

Tourist Information Centre Kobarid (☑380 04 90; www.dolina-soce.com; Trg Svobode 16; ☉9am-1pm & 2-7pm Mon-Fri, 10am-1pm & 4-7pm Sat & Sun) Free internet.

❶ Getting There & Around

There are half a dozen buses a day to Bovec (€3.10, 30 minutes). Other destinations include Ljubljana (€11.40 three hours) via Most na Soči train station (good for Bled and Bohinj). Daily in July and August, buses cross the spectacular Vršič Pass to Kranjska Gora (€6.70, three hours).

KARST & COAST

Slovenia's short coast (47km) is an area for both history and recreation. The southernmost resort town of Portorož has some decent beaches, but towns like Koper and Piran, famed for their Venetian Gothic architecture, are the main drawcards here. En route from Ljubljana or the Soča Valley, you'll cross the Karst, a huge limestone plateau and a land of olives, ruby-red Teran wine, *pršut* (air-dried ham), old stone churches and deep subterranean caves, including Postojna and Škocjan.

Postojna

☑05 / POP 8910

The karst cave at Postojna is one of the largest in the world and its stalagmite and stalactite formations are unequalled anywhere. It's a busy destination (visited by as many as a third of all tourists coming to Slovenia). The amazing thing is how the large crowds at the entrance seem to get swallowed whole by the size of the caves.

The small town of Postojna lies in the Pivka Valley at the foot of Sovič Hill (677m) with Titov trg at its centre. Postojna's bus station is at Titova cesta 36, about 250m southwest of Titov trg. The train station is on Kolodvorska cesta about 600m southeast of the square.

◉ Sights

Postojna Cave CAVE
(☑700 01 00; www.postojnska-jama.si; Jamska c 30; adult/child/student €22.90/13.70/18.30; ☉tours hourly 9am-6pm summer, 3 or 4 times from 10am daily winter) Slovenia's single most-popular tourist attraction, Postojna Cave is about 1.5km northwest of Postojna. The 5.7km-long cavern is visited on a 1½-hour tour – 4km of it by electric train and the rest on foot. Inside, impressive stalagmites and stalactites in familiar shapes stretch almost endlessly in all directions.

Proteus Vivarium MUSEUM
(www.turizem-kras.si; adult/child €8/4.80, with cave €27/16.20; ☉9am-5.30pm May-Sep, 10.30am-3.30pm Oct-Apr) Just steps south of the Postojna Cave's entrance is Proteus Vivarium, a spelio-biological research station with a video introduction to underground zoology. A 45-minute tour then leads you into a small, darkened cave to peep at some of the endemic Proteus anguinus, a shy (and miniscule) salamander unique to Slovenia.

🛏 Sleeping & Eating

Hotel Kras HOTEL €€
(☑700 23 00; www.hotel-kras.si; Tržaška cesta 1; s €68-74, d €84-96, apt €100-120; P☎) This rather flash, modern hotel has risen, phoenix-like, from the ashes of a decrepit old caravanserai in the heart of town, and now boasts 27 comfortable rooms with all the mod cons. If you've got the dosh, choose one

PREDJAMA CASTLE

The tiny village of Predjama (population 85), 10km northwest of Postojna, is home to remarkable **Predjama Castle** (☑700 01 03; www.postojnska-jama.eu; Predjama 1; adult/child/student €9/5.40/7.20; ☺9am-7pm summer, 10am-4pm winter). The castle's lesson is clear: if you want to build an impregnable redoubt, put it in the gaping mouth of a cavern halfway up a 123m cliff. Its four storeys were built piece-meal over the years since 1202, but most of what you see today is 16th century. It looks simply unconquerable.

The castle holds great features for kids of any age – a drawbridge over a raging river, holes in the ceiling of the entrance tower for pouring boiling oil on intruders, a very dank dungeon, a 16th-century chest full of treasure (unearthed in the cellar in 1991), and a hiding place at the top called Erazem's Nook.

In mid-July, the castle hosts the **Erasmus Tournament**, a day of medieval duelling, jousting and archery.

The cave below Predjama Castle is a 6km network of galleries spread over four levels. Casual visitors can see about 900m of it; longer tours are available by prior arrangement only. **Gostilna Požar** (☑751 52 52; Predjama 2; meals from €11; ☺10am-10pm Thu-Tue, daily Aug) is a simple restaurant next to the ticket kiosk and in heart-stopping view of the castle.

of the apartments on the top (5th) floor with enormous terraces.

Hotel Sport   HOTEL, HOSTEL €€
(☑720 22 44; www.sport-hotel.si; Kolodvorska c 1; dm €25, s/d from €55/70; P@⊛) A hotel of some sort or another since 1880, the Sport offers reasonable value for money, with 37 spick-and-span and comfortable rooms, including five with nine dorm beds each. There's a kitchen with a small eating area. It's 300m north of the centre.

Jamski Dvorec   INTERNATIONAL €€
(☑700 01 81; starters €6.50-10, mains €13.50-22; ☺9am-6pm) Housed in a stunning 1920s-style building next to the entrance to the cave, the Cave Manor has fairly average international dishes but its set menus at €11 and €12 are a big attraction.

Čuk   PIZZA €
(☑720 13 00; Pot k Pivki 4; starters €5-7.50, pizza & pasta €6-9.50; ☺10am-11pm Mon-Fri, 11am-midnight Sat, noon-11pm Sun) Excellent restaurant southwest of Titov trg, just off Tržaška cesta, Čuk takes its pizza seriously but offers a wide range of Slovenian mains too.

ⓘ Getting There & Away

BUS Services from Ljubljana to the coast as well as Ajdovščina stop in Postojna (€6, one hour, 53km, hourly). Other destinations include Koper (€6.90, 1¼ hours, 68km, four to seven daily) and Piran (€8.30, 1½ hours, 86km, three or four a day).

TRAIN Postojna is on the main train line linking Ljubljana (€4.90, one hour, 67km) with Sežana and Trieste via Divača (€2.90 to €4.45, 40 minutes, 37km), and is an easy day trip from the capital. You can also reach here from Koper (€5.90 to €10.30, 1½ hours, 86km) on one of up to seven trains a day.

Škocjan Caves

☑05

The immense system of the **Škocjan Caves** (☑708 21 10; www.park-skocjanske-jame.si; Škocjan 2; adult/child €15/7; ☺10am-5pm), a Unesco World Heritage site, is more captivating than the larger one at Postojna, and for many travellers this will be the highlight of their trip to Slovenia.

Visitors walk in guided groups from the ticket office to the main entrance in the Globočak Valley. Through a tunnel built in 1933, you soon reach the head of the **Silent Cave**, a dry branch of the underground canyon that stretches for 500m. The first section, called **Paradise**, is filled with beautiful stalactites and stalagmites; the second part (called **Calvary**) was once the river bed. The Silent Cave ends at the **Great Hall**, a jungle of exotic dripstones and deposits; keep an eye out for the mighty stalagmites called the Giants and the Organ.

The sound of the Reka River heralds your entry into the **Murmuring Cave**, with walls 100m high. To get over the Reka and into Müller Hall, you must cross **Cerkevnik**

Bridge, some 45m high and surely the highlight of the trip.

Schmidl Hall, the final section, emerges into the Velika Dolina. From here you walk past Tominč Cave, where finds from a prehistoric settlement have been unearthed. A funicular takes you back to the entrance.

The temperature in the caves is constant at 12°C so bring along a light jacket or sweater. Good walking shoes, for the sometimes slippery paths, are recommended.

The nearest town with accommodation is Divača, 5km to the northwest. Gostilna Malovec (☑763 33 33; www.hotel-malovec.si; s/d €54/80; P@☎) has a half-dozen basic but renovated rooms in a building beside its traditional restaurant.The nearby Orient Express (☑763 30 10; pizza €4.60-14; ⊙11am-11pm Sun-Fri, 11am-2am Sat) is a popular pizzeria.

Buses from Ljubljana to Koper and the coast stop at Divača (€7.90, 1½ hours, half-hourly). Divača is also on the rail line to Ljubljana (€7.30, 1½ hours, hourly), with up to five trains a day to Koper (€4.05, 50 minutes) via Hrpelje-Kozina. The Škocjan Caves are about 5km by road southeast of the Divača train station – the route is signed. A courtesy van sometimes meets incoming Ljubljana trains.

Koper

☑05 / POP 24,725

Coastal Slovenia's largest town, Koper (Capodistria in Italian) at first glance appears to be a workaday city that scarcely gives tourism a second thought. Yet its central core is delightfully medieval and far less overrun than its ritzy cousin Piran, 18km down the coast. Known as Aegida to the ancient Greeks, Koper grew rich as a key port trading salt and was the capital of Istria under the Venetian republic during the 15th and 16th centuries. It remains Slovenia's most important port.

◉ Sights

The easiest way to see Koper's Old Town is to walk from the marina on Ukmarjev trg east along Kidričeva ulica to Titov trg and then south down Čevljarska ulica, taking various detours along the way.

Koper Regional Museum   MUSEUM
(☑663 35 70; www.pmk-kp.si; Kidričeva ul 19; adult/child €2/1.50; ⊙9am-7pm Tue-Fri, to 1pm Sat & Sun) The Belgramoni-Tacco Palace houses this museum with displays of old maps and

photos of the port and coast, Italianate sculpture, and paintings dating from the 16th to 18th centuries. Note the wonderful bronze knocker on the door of Venus arising from a seashell.

Cathedral of the Assumption   CATHEDRAL
(Stolnica Marijinega Vnebovzetja; ⊙7am-9pm) Opposite the Armoury in Titov trg is the Cathedral of the Assumption and its 36m-tall belfry, now called the City Tower. The cathedral, partly Romanesque and Gothic but mostly dating from the 18th century, has a white classical interior with a feeling of space and light that belies the sombre exterior.

FREE Beach   BEACH
(Kopališko nabrežje 1; ⊙8am-7pm May-Sep) Koper's tiny beach, on the northwest edge of the Old Town, has a small bathhouse with toilets and showers, grassy areas for lying in the sun and a bar and cafe.

🛏 Sleeping

Hotel Koper   HOTEL €€€
(☑610 05 00; www.terme-catez.si; Pristaniška ul 3; s €76-92, d €120-150; ✳@☒) This pleasant, 65-room property on the edge of the historic Old Town is the only really central hotel in town. Rates include entry to an aquapark. Choose a harbour-facing room.

Hotel Vodišek   HOTEL €€
(☑639 24 68; www.hotel-vodisek.com; Kolodvorska c 2; s €48-60, d €72-90; P✳@☎) This small hotel with 35 reasonably priced rooms is in a shopping centre halfway between the Old Town and the train and bus stations. Guests get to use the hotel's bicycles for free.

Museum Hostel   APARTMENTS €
(☑041 504 466, 626 18 70; bozic.doris@siol.net; Muzejski trg 6; per person €20-25; ☎) This place is more a series of apartments with kitchens and bathrooms than a hostel. Reception is at Museum Bife, a cafe-bar on Muzejski trg; the rooms are scattered nearby.

✕ Eating

Istrska Klet Slavček   ISTRIAN, SLOVENIAN €
(☑627 67 29; Župančičeva ul 39; dishes €3-12; ⊙7am-10pm Mon-Fri) The Istrian Cellar, situated below the 18th-century Carli Palace, is one of the most colourful places for a meal in Koper's Old Town. Filling set lunches go for less than €8, and there's local Malvazija and Teran wine from the barrel.

WORTH A TRIP

LIPICA'S LIPIZZANER HORSES

The impact of Lipica has been far greater than its tiny size would suggest. It's here where the famed snow-white 'Lipizzaner' horses, made famous at Vienna's Spanish Riding School, were first bred in the late 16th century.

The breed got its start by pairing Andalusian horses from Spain with the local Karst breed the Romans once used to pull chariots. The white colour came two centuries later, when white Arabian horses got into the act.

The breed has subsequently become scattered – moved to Hungary and Austria after WWI, to the Sudetenland in Bohemia by the Germans during WWII, and then shipped off to Italy by the American army in 1945. Only 11 horses returned when operations resumed at Lipica in 1947.

Today, some 400 Lipizzaners remain at the **Lipica Stud Farm** (☏739 15 80; www.lipica.org; Lipica 5; tour adult/child €11/5.50, training/classical performance €13/18; ☺training & classical performance Tue, Fri & Sun Apr-Oct), while Lipizzaners are also bred in various locations around the world, including Piber in Austria, which breeds the horses for the Spanish Riding School. The stud farm offers equestrian fans a large variety of tours and riding presentations as well as lessons and carriage rides. Tour times are complicated; see the website for details.

Most people visit Lipica as a day trip from Sežana, 4km to the north, or Divača, 13km to the northeast, both of which are on the Ljubljana–Koper rail line. There is no public transport from either train station; a taxi will cost between €10 and €20.

For overnights, try the 59-room **Hotel Maestoso** (☏739 15 80; s/d €80/120; P🕐🛈⌨), managed by the stud farm. It has many upscale amenities, including a restaurant, swimming pool, sauna and tennis courts.

La Storia   ITALIAN €€
(☏626 20 18; www.lastoria.si; Pristaniška ul 3; mains €8.50-25) This Italian-style trattoria with sky-view ceiling frescos focuses on salads, pasta and fish dishes and has outside seating in the warmer months.

ℹ Information

Banka Koper (Kidričeva ul 14)
Pina Internet Cafe (☏627 80 72; Kidričeva ul 43; per hr adult/student €4.20/1.20; ☺noon-10pm Mon-Fri, from 4pm Sat & Sun)
Post Office (Muzejski trg 3)
Tourist Information Centre Koper (☏664 64 03; www.koper.si; Praetorian Palace, Titov trg 3; ☺9am-8pm Jul & Aug, 9am-5pm Sep-Jun)

ℹ Getting There & Away

BUS Services run to Izola, Strunjan, Piran (€2.70, 30 minutes and Portorož every half-hour on weekdays. There's a handy bus stop at the corner of Piranška ulica. Some five daily buses make the run to Ljubljana (€11.10, 1¾ to 2½ hours). Buses to Trieste (€3, one hour) run along the coast via Ankaran and Muggia from Monday to Saturday. Destinations in Croatia include Rijeka (€11.20, two hours) and Rovinj (€12, three hours) via Poreč (€10, two hours).

TRAIN Half a dozen trains a day link Koper to Ljubljana (€10.70, 2½ hours, 153km) via Postojna and Divača.

Piran

☏05 / POP 4470

Picturesque Piran, sitting at the tip of a narrow peninsula, is everyone's favourite town on the coast. Its Old Town – one of the best preserved historical towns anywhere on the Adriatic – is a gem of Venetian architecture, but it can be a mob scene at the height of summer. In April or October, though, it's hard not to fall in love with the winding alleyways and tempting seafood restaurants.

◉ Sights

Tartinijev Trg   SQUARE
The **statue** of the nattily dressed gentleman in Tartinijev trg, an oval-shaped square that was the inner harbour until it was filled in 1894, is that of local boy-cum-composer Giuseppe Tartini (1692–1770). To the east is the **Church of St Peter** (Cerkev Sv Petra; Tartinijev trg), which contains the 14th-century **Piran Crucifix**. Across from the church is **Tartini House**, the composer's birthplace.

Sergej Mašera Maritime Museum
MUSEUM

(☎671 00 40; www.pommuz-pi.si; Cankarjevo nabrežje 3; adult/student & senior/child €3.50/2.50/2.10; ☺9am-noon & 5-9pm Tue-Sun summer, 9am-5pm Tue-Sun winter) Located in the lovely 19th-century Gabrielli Palace on the waterfront, this museum focuses on the sea, sailing and salt-making. There are some old photographs showing salt workers going about their duties, as well as a wind-powered salt pump and little wooden weights in the form of circles and diamonds that were used to weigh salt during the Venetian republic.

Cathedral of St George
CATHEDRAL

(Stolna Cerkev Sv Jurija; Adamičeva ul 2) Piran's hilltop cathedral was founded in 1344 and rebuilt in baroque style in 1637. It's undergoing a massive renovation, and visitors are allowed only into the choir to view the magnificent marble altar and star-vaulted ceiling. If time allows, visit the attached Parish Museum of St George (☎673 34 40; admission €1; ☺10am-1pm & 5-7pm Mon-Fri, 11am-7pm Sat & Sun), which contains paintings and a lapidary in the crypt.

Minorite Monastery
MONASTERY

(☎673 44 17; Bolniška ul 20) On your way up to Tartinijev trg are the Minorite Monastery with a wonderful cloister and the Church of St Francis Assisi, built originally in the early 14th century but enlarged and renovated over the centuries. Inside are ceiling frescos, a giant clam shell for donations and the Tartini family's burial plot.

🏃 Activities

The Maona Tourist Agency (☎673 45 20; www.maona.si; Cankarjevo nabrežje 7; ☺9am-8pm Mon-Sat, 10am-1pm & 5-7pm Sun) and several other agencies in Piran and Portorož can book you on any number of cruises – from a loop that takes in the towns along the coast to day-long excursions to Brioni National Park and Rovinj in Croatia, or Venice and Trieste in Italy.

For swimming, Piran has several 'beaches' – rocky areas along Prešernovo nabrežje – where you might get your feet wet. They are a little better on the north side near Punta, but as long as you've come this far keep walking eastward on the paved path for just under 1km to Fiesa, which has a small but clean beach.

🛌 Sleeping

TOP CHOICE ⟩ Max Piran
B&B €€

(☎041 692 928, 673 34 36; www.maxpiran.com; Ul IX Korpusa 26; d €60-70; ✳@🛜) Piran's most romantic accommodation has just six rooms, each bearing a woman's name rather than number, in a delightful coral-coloured 18th-century townhouse.

Miracolo di Mare
B&B €€

(☎051 445 511, 921 76 60; www.miracolodimare.si; Tomšičeva ul 23; s €50-55, d €60-70; @🛜) A lovely B&B on the coast, the Wonder of the Sea has a dozen charming (though smallish) rooms, some of which (like No 3 and the breakfast room) look on to the most charming raised back garden in Piran. Floors and stairs are wooden (and original).

Val Hostel
HOSTEL €

(☎673 25 55; www.hostel-val.com; Gregorčičeva ul 38a; per person €22-27; @🛜) This excellent central hostel on the corner of Vegova ulica has 22 rooms (including a few singles), with shared shower, kitchen and washing machine. It's a deserved favourite with backpackers, and prices include breakfast.

Kamp Fiesa
CAMPGROUND €

(☎674 62 30; autocamp.fiesa@siol.net; adult/child €12/4; ☺May-Sep; 🅿) The closest camping ground to Piran is at Fiesa, 4km by road but less than 1km if you follow the coastal path (obalna pešpot) east from the Cathedral of St George. It's tiny and gets crowded in summer, but it's in a quiet valley by two small ponds and right by the beach.

🍴 Eating

There's an outdoor fruit and vegetable market (Zelenjavni trg; ☺7am-2pm Mon-Sat) in the small square behind the town hall.

TOP CHOICE ⟩ Pri Mari
MEDITERRANEAN, SLOVENIAN €€

(☎041 616 488, 673 47 35; Dantejeva ul 17; mains €8.50-16; ☺noon-11pm Tue-Sun summer, noon-10pm Tue-Sat, noon-6pm Sun winter) This stylish and welcoming restaurant run by an Italian-Slovenian couple serves inventive Mediterranean and Slovenian dishes. Be sure to book ahead.

Riva Piran
SEAFOOD €€

(☎673 22 25; Gregorčičeva ul 46; mains €8-28; ☺11.30am-midnight) The best waterfront seafood restaurant, and worth patronising, is

Piran

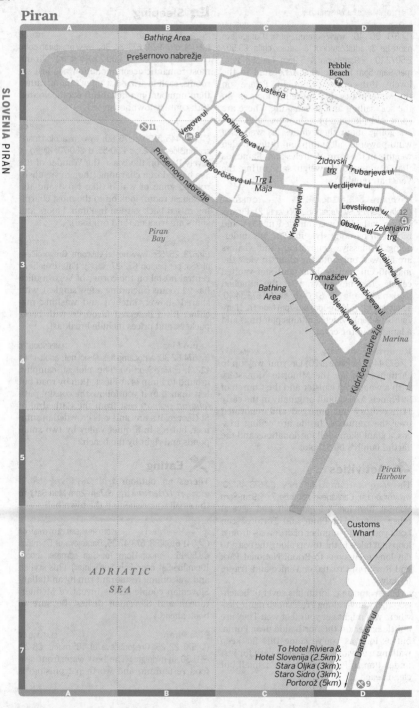

Bathing Area

Prešernovo nabrežje

Pebble Beach 🏖7

Pusterla

Prešernovo nabrežje

🍴11

Vegova ul 🏛8

Bonifacijeva ul

Gregorčičeva ul

Trg 1 Maja

Kosovelova ul

Piran Bay

Židovski trg

Trubarjeva ul

Verdijeva ul

Levstikova ul

Obzidna ul

Zelenjavni trg

12 🔒

Vidalijeva ul

Bathing Area

Tomažičev trg

Tomažičeva ul

Stjenkova ul

Marina

Piran Harbour

Kidričeva nabrežje

Customs Wharf

ADRIATIC SEA

Dantejeva ul

To Hotel Riviera & Hotel Slovenija (2.5km); Stara Oljka (3km); Staro Sidro (3km); Portorož (5km)

🍴9

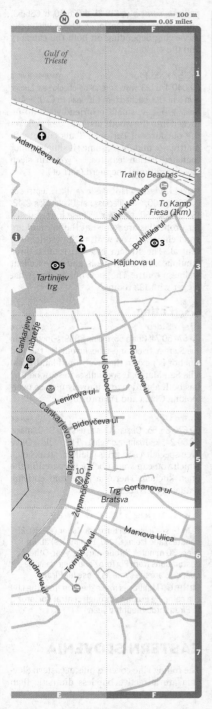

Piran

⊙ Sights

🛏 Sleeping

⊗ Eating

🛍 Shopping

this classy place with attractive decor and sea views.

Restaurant Neptune   SEAFOOD €
(☑673 41 11; Župančičeva 7; mains €6-12; ⊙noon-4pm, 6pm-midnight) It's no bad thing to be more popular with locals than tourists, and this family-run place hits all the buttons – a friendly welcome, big seafood platters (as well as meat dishes and salads), and a good-value, daily two-course set lunch.

❶ Information

Banka Koper (Tartinijev trg 12)

Caffe Neptun (☑041 724 237; www.caffeneptun.com; Dantejeva ul 4; per 20min €1; ⊙7am-1am; 🛜)

Post Office (Leninova ul 1)

Tourist Information Centre Piran (☑673 44 40, 673 02 20; www.portoroz.si; Tartinijev trg 2; ⊙9am-8pm summer, 9am-5pm winter)

❶ Getting There & Away

BUS Services run every 20 to 30 minutes to Koper (€2.70, 30 minutes). Other destinations include Ljubljana (€12, three hours) via Divača and Postojna, and Nova Gorica (€10.30, 2¾ hours).

Some five buses go daily to Trieste (€10, 1¾ hours) in Italy, except Sundays. One bus a day heads south for Croatian Istria from June to September, stopping at the coastal towns of Umag, Poreč and Rovinj (€10.30, 2¾ hours).

CATAMARAN There are catamarans from the harbour to Trieste (adult/child €8.30/4.75, 30 minutes) in Italy daily except Wednesday, departing around 7pm.

MINIBUS From Tartinijev trg, minibuses (€1 onboard, €0.40 in advance from newsagencies, €6 for 20 rides) shuttle to Portorož every half-hour from 5.40am to 11pm continuously year-round.

Portorož

🖉05 / POP 2900

Every country with a coast has got to have a honky-tonk beach resort and Portorož (Portorose in Italian) is Slovenia's. But the 'Port of Roses' is making a big effort to scrub itself up. Portorož's sandy beaches are relatively clean, and there are pleasant spas and wellness centres where you can take the waters or cover yourself in curative mud.

🏃 Activities

The **beaches** (⊘8am-8pm Apr-Sep) at Portorož, including the main one, which accommodates 6000 fried and bronzed bodies, have water slides and outside showers, and beach chairs (€4.10) and umbrellas (€4.10) are available for rent. Beaches are off-limits between 11pm and 6am, and camping is forbidden.

A couple of boats make the run between the main pier in Portorož and Izola in summer on trips lasting four hours. They include the **Meja** (🖉041 664 132; adult/child €10/7; ⊘9.15am Tue & Fri) and the **Svetko** (🖉041 623 191; adult/child €15/10.50; ⊘2.30pm daily). The **Solinarka** (🖉031 653 682; www.solinarka.com; adult/child €12.50/6.25; ⊘varies) tour boat sails from Portorož to Piran and Strunjan and back.

Terme & Wellness Centre Portorož SPA (🖉692 80 60; www.lifeclass.net; Obala 43; swimming pool 2/4hr pass Mon-Fri €8/12, Sat & Sun €10/15; ⊘8am-9pm Jun-Sep, 7am-7pm Oct-May, swimming pool 1-8pm Mon-Wed & Fri-Sun, 2-8pm Thu) This place is famous for treatments using sea water and by-products like mud, as well as a host of other therapies and beauty treatments. And there's a pool too.

🛌 Sleeping

Portorož counts upwards of two dozen hotels, and very few fit into the budget category. Many properties close for the winter in October and do not reopen until April or even May. The **Maona Tourist Agency** (🖉674 03 63; Obala 14/b; ⊘9am-8pm Mon-Sat, 10am-1pm & 5-8pm Sun Jul & Aug, 9am-7pm Mon-Fri, 10am-7pm Sat, 10am-1pm Sun Sep-Jun) has

private rooms (s €18-21, d €26-40, tr €36-52) and apartments (apt for 2 €40-50), with prices varying depending on both the category and the season.

🏆CHOICE **Kaki Plac** CAMPGROUND € (🖉040 476 123; www.adrenaline-check/sea; Lucija; own tent €13, pitched tent €15, lean-to €20; ⊘Apr-Nov; 🅿🐾) A small ecofriendly campsite tucked into the woods just outside Lucija on the outskirts of Portorož. Tents come with mattrasses and linen, some sit snugly under thatched Istrian lean-tos, so you can sleep like a traditional shepherd (sort of).

Hotel Riviera & Hotel Slovenija HOTEL €€€ (🖉692 00 00; www.lifeclass.net; Obala 33; s €142-185, d €184-250; 🅿❄@⊛) These four-star sister properties are joined at the hip and are good choices if you want to stay someplace central. The Riviera has 160 rooms, three fabulous swimming pools and an excellent wellness centre. The Slovenija is somewhat bigger with 183 rooms.

🍴 Eating

Staro Sidro SEAFOOD € (🖉674 50 74; Obala 55; mains €8-19; ⊘noon-11pm Tue-Sun) A tried-and-true favourite, the Old Anchor is next to the lovely (and landmark) Vila San Marco. It specialises in seafood and has both a garden and a lovely terrace overlooking Obala and Portorož Bay.

Stara Oljka BALKAN €€ (🖉674 85 55; Obala 20; starters €5-9.60, mains €8.60-24; ⊘10am-midnight) The Old Olive Tree specialises in grills (Balkan, steaks etc), which you can watch being prepared in the open kitchen. There's a large and enticing sea-facing terrace.

ℹ Getting There & Away

BUS Buses leave Portorož for Koper (€2.30, 25 minutes) and Izola (€1.80, 15 minutes) about every 30 minutes throughout the year. Other destinations from Portorož and their daily frequencies are the same as those for Piran.

MINIBUS Minibuses make the loop from the Lucija camping grounds through central Portorož to Piran throughout the year.

EASTERN SLOVENIA

The rolling vine-covered hills of eastern Slovenia are attractive but less dramatic than the Julian Alps or, indeed, the coast. Two cities worth a detour include lively Maribor, Slovenia's second-largest city, and postcard-perfect Ptuj, less than 30km down the road.

Maribor

02 / POP 88,350

Despite being the nation's second-largest city, Maribor has only about a third the population of Ljubljana and often feels more like an overgrown provincial town. It has no unmissable sights but oozes charm thanks to its delightfully patchy Old Town along the Drava River. Pedestrianised central streets buzz with cafes and student life and the riverside Lent district hosts major cultural events – indeed, Maribor was European Capital of Culture in 2012.

◉ Sights

Grajksi Trg
SQUARE

The centre of the Old Town, this square is graced with the 17th-century **Column of St Florian**, dedicated to the patron saint of fire fighters.

Maribor Castle
MUSEUM

(Grajski trg 2) On Grajski Trg, the centre of Maribor's Old Town, is Maribor's 15th-century castle. It contains a **Knights' Hall** (Viteška Dvorana) with a remarkable painted ceiling, the baroque **Loretska Chapel** and a magnificent **rococo staircase**.

Inside the castle, the **Maribor Regional Museum** (228 35 51; www.pmuzej-mb.si; Grajski trg; adult/child €3/2; ⊙9am-1pm & 4pm-7pm Mon-Fri, 9am-1pm Sat) has one of the richest collections in Slovenia. The building is undergoing renovation, so parts may be off-limits. On the ground floor there are archaeological, clothing and ethnographic exhibits, including florid, 19th-century bee-hive panels. Upstairs are rooms devoted to Maribor's history and guilds.

⌂ Sleeping

TOP CHOICE Hostel Pekarna
HOSTEL €

(059 180 880; www.mkc-hostelpekarna.si; Ob železnici 16; dm/s/d €17/21/42; 🖘🖷) This bright and welcoming hostel south of the river is a converted army bakery. Facilities, from the dorms to the cafe, are up to the minute, and there are several apartments with kitchens.

Hotel Lent
HOTEL €€

(250 67 69; www.hotel-lent.si; Dravska ulica 9; s/d €69/89; 🏵🖘) Shiny riverside hotel in Lent, with a café out front. Rooms are stylishly decorated and comfortable, though the suites are tricked out in unexpected gangster bling.

✖ Eating

TOP CHOICE Gril Ranca
BALKAN €

(252 55 50; Dravska ul 10; dishes €4.80-7.50; ⊙8am-11pm Mon-Sat, noon-9pm Sun) This place serves simple but scrumptious Balkan grills such as *pljeskavica* (spicy meat patties) and *čevapčiči* (spicy meatballs of beef or pork) in full view of the Drava. It's cool on a hot night.

Pri Florjanu
MEDITERRANEAN €€

(059 084 850; Grajski trg 6; starters €5.50-7, mains €9-18; ⊙11am-10pm Mon-Thu, 11am-11pm Fri & Sat; 🖉🖷) A great spot in full view of the Column of St Florian, this stylish place has both an open front and an enclosed back terrace and a huge minimalist restaurant in between. It serves inspired Mediterranean food, with a good supply of vegetarian options.

ⓘ Information

Tourist Information Centre Maribor (234 66 11; www.maribor-pohorje.si; Partinzanska c 6a; ⊙9am-7pm Mon-Fri, 9am-6pm Sat & Sun) Very helpful TIC in kiosk opposite the Franciscan church.

ⓘ Getting There & Away

BUS Services are frequent to Celje (€6.7, 1½ hours), Murska Sobota (€6.30, 1¼ hours), Ptuj (€3.60, 45 minutes) and Ljubljana (€12.40, three hours).

TRAIN From Ljubljana there is the ICS express service (€15.20, 1¾ hours), or more frequent slower trains (€9, 2½ hours). Both stop at Celje.

Ptuj

02 / POP 19,010

Rising gently above a wide valley, Ptuj forms a symphony of red-tile roofs best viewed from across the Drava River. One of the oldest towns in Slovenia, Ptuj equals Ljubljana in terms of historical importance but the compact medieval core, with its castle, museums, monasteries and churches, can easily be seen in a day.

◉ Sights

Ptuj's Gothic centre, with its Renaissance and baroque additions, can be viewed on a 'walking tour' taking in Minoritski trg and Mestni trg, Slovenski trg, Prešernova ulica, Muzejski trg and Ptuj Castle.

Ptuj Castle   CASTLE
(Grad Ptuj; ☑787 92 45, 748 03 60; Na Gradu 1)
Ptuj castle is an agglomeration of styles from
the 14th to the 18th centuries. It houses the
Ptuj Regional Museum (☑787 92 30; www.
pok-muzej-ptuj.si; adult/child €4/2.50; ☺9am-6pm
Mon-Fri, 9am-8pm Sat & Sun summer, 9am-5pm
daily winter) but is worth the trip for views
of Ptuj and the Drava. The shortest way to
the castle is to follow narrow Grajska ulica,
which leads to a covered wooden stairway
and the castle's Renaissance **Peruzzi Portal**
(1570).

✸✸ Festivals

Kurentovanje   CARNIVAL
(www.kurentovanje.net) Kurentovanje is a rite
of spring celebrated for 10 days in February
leading up to Shrove Tuesday; it's the most
popular and best-known folklore event in
Slovenia.

🛏 Sleeping

TOP
CHOICE **MuziKafe**   HOTEL €€
(☑787 88 60; www.muzikafe.si; Vrazov trg 1; 🛜)
This quirky cracker of a place is tucked away
off Jadranska ulica. Everything is bright,
with each room idiosyncratically decorated
by the hotel's artist owners. There's a terrace
café, plus a vaulted brick cellar for musical
and artistic events.

Hotel Mitra   HOTEL €€€
(☑051 603 069, 787 74 55; www.hotel-mitra.si;
Prešernova ul 6; s €62-88, d €106; P🅿✱@🛜) This
pleasant hotel has 25 generous-sized guest
rooms and four humongous suites, each
with its own name and story and specially
commissioned paintings on the wall. There
are lovely Oriental carpets on the original
wooden floors and a wellness centre in an
old courtyard cellar.

Hostel Eva   HOSTEL €
(☑040 226 522, 771 24 41; www.hostel-ptuj.si;
Jadranska ul 22; per person €12-20) This welcoming, up-to-date hostel connected to a
bike shop (per-day rental €10) has six rooms
containing two to six beds and a large light-
filled kitchen.

✕ Eating

TOP
CHOICE **Gostilna Ribič**   GOSTILNA €€
(☑749 06 35; Dravska ul 9; mains €9.50-20;
☺10am-11pm Sun-Thu, 10am-midnight Fri & Sat)
Arguably the best restaurant in Ptuj, the An-
gler Inn faces the river, with an enormous

terrace, and the speciality here is – not surprisingly – fish, especially herbed and baked
pike perch. The seafood soup served in a
bread loaf bowl is exceptional.

Amadeus   GOSTILNA €€
(☑771 70 51; Prešernova ul 36; mains €6.50-20;
☺noon-10pm Mon-Thu, noon-11pm Fri & Sat, noon-
4pm Sun) This pleasant *gostilna* (inn-like restaurant) above a pub and near the foot of the
road to the castle serves *štruklji* (dumplings
with herbs and cheese), steak, pork and fish.

ℹ Information

Tourist Information Centre Ptuj (☑779 60
11; www.ptuj.info; Slovenski trg 5; ☺8am-8pm
summer, 9am-6pm winter)

ℹ Getting There & Away

BUS Services to Maribor (€3.60, 45 minutes)
go every couple of hours, less frequently at
weekends.

TRAIN Connections are better for trains than
buses, with plentiful departures to Ljubljana
(€8 to €13.60) direct or via Pragersko. Up to a
dozen trains go to Maribor (€2.90 to €5.90, 50
minutes).

UNDERSTAND SLOVENIA

History
Early Years

Slovenes can make a credible claim to having invented democracy. By the early 7th
century, their Slavic ancestors had founded
the Duchy of Carantania (Karantanija),
based at Krn Castle (now Karnburg in Austria). Ruling dukes were elected by enobled
commoners and invested before ordinary
citizens.

This unique model was noted by the 16th-
century French political philosopher Jean
Bodin, whose work was a reference for Thomas Jefferson when he wrote the American
Declaration of Independence in 1776.

Carantania (later Carinthia) was fought
over by the Franks and Magyars from the 8th
to 10th centuries, and later divided up among
Austro-Germanic nobles and bishops.

The Habsburgs & Napoleon

Between the late 13th and early 16th centuries, almost all the lands inhabited by
Slovenes, with the exception of the Venetian-
controlled coastal towns, came under the

domination of the Habsburgs, ruled from Vienna.

Austrian rule continued until 1918, apart from a brief interlude between 1809 and 1813 when Napoleon created six so-called Illyrian Provinces from Slovenian and Croatian regions and made Ljubljana the capital.

Napoleon proved a popular conqueror as his relatively liberal regime de-Germanised the education system. Slovene was taught in schools for the first time, leading to an awakening of national consciousness. In tribute, Ljubljana still has a French Revolution Sq (Trg Francoske Revolucije) with a column bearing a likeness of the French emperor.

World Wars I & II

Fighting during WWI was particularly savage along the Soča Valley – the Isonzo Front– which was occupied by Italy then retaken by German-led Austro-Hungarian forces. The war ended with the collapse of Austria-Hungary, which handed western Slovenia to Italy as part of postwar reparations.

Northern Carinthia, including the towns of Beljak and Celovec (now Villach and Klagenfurt), voted to stay with Austria in a 1920 plebiscite. What remained of Slovenia joined fellow south (jug) Slavs in forming the Kingdom of Serbs, Croats and Slovenes, later Yugoslavia.

Nazi occupation in WWII was for the most part resisted by Slovenian partisans, though after Italy capitulated in 1943 the anti-partisan Slovenian Domobranci (Home Guards) were active in the west. To prevent their nemeses, the communists, from taking political control in liberated areas, the Domobranci threw their support behind the Germans.

The war ended with Slovenia regaining Italian-held areas from Piran to Bovec, but losing Trst (Trieste) and part of Gorica (Gorizia).

Tito's Yugoslavia

In Tito's Yugoslavia in the 1960s and '70s, Slovenia, with only 8% of the national population, was the economic powerhouse, creating up to 20% of the national GDP.

But by the 1980s the federation had become increasingly Serb-dominated, and Slovenes feared they would lose their political autonomy. In free elections, Slovenes voted overwhelmingly to break away from Yugoslavia and did so on 25 June 1991. A 10-day war that left 66 people dead followed; Yugoslavia swiftly signed a truce in order to concentrate on regaining control of coastal Croatia.

From Independence to Today

Shortly after the withdrawal of the federal army from Slovenian soil on 25 October 1991, Slovenia got a new constitution that provided for a bicameral parliamentary system of government.

The head of state, the president, is elected directly for a maximum of two five-year terms. Milan Kučan held that role from independence until 2002, when the late Janez Drnovšek (1950–2008), a former prime minister, was elected. Diplomat Danilo Türk has been president since 2007, having been re-elected in 2012.

Executive power is vested in the prime minister and his cabinet. The current premier is Janez Janša, who was returned to power in early 2012 after 3½ years in opposition.

Slovenia was admitted to the UN in 1992 as the 176th member-state. In May 2004, Slovenia entered the EU as a full member and less than three years later adopted the euro, replacing the tolar as the national currency.

People

The population of Slovenia is largely homogeneous. Just over 83% are ethnic Slovenes, with the remainder Serbs, Croats, Bosnians, Albanians and Roma; there are also small enclaves of Italians and Hungarians, who have special deputies looking after their interests in parliament.

Slovenes are ethnically Slavic, typically hardworking, multilingual and extrovert. Around 60% of Slovenes identify themselves as Catholics.

Arts

Slovenia's most cherished writer is the Romantic poet France Prešeren (1800–49). His patriotic yet humanistic verse was a driving force in raising Slovene national consciousness. Fittingly, a stanza of his poem 'Zdravljica' (A Toast) forms the lyrics of the national anthem.

Many of Ljubljana's most characteristic architectural features, including its recurring pyramid motif, were added by celebrated Slovenian architect Jože Plečnik (1872–1957), whose work fused classical building principles and folk-art traditions.

Postmodernist painting and sculpture were more or less dominated from the 1980s by the multimedia group NeueSlowenische Kunst (NSK) and the artists' cooperative Irwin. It also spawned the internationally known industrial-music group Laibach, whose leader, Tomaž Hostnik, died tragically in 1983 when he hanged himself from a *kozolec*, the traditional (and iconic) hayrack found only in Slovenia.

Slovenia's vibrant music scene embraces rave, techno, jazz, punk, thrash-metal and *chanson* (torch songs from the likes of Vita Mavrič); the most popular local rock group is Siddharta, formed in 1995 and still going strong. There's also been a folk-music revival: keep an ear out for the groups Katice and Katalena, who play traditional Slovenian music with a modern twist, and the vocalist Brina.

Films

Well-received Slovenian films in recent years include *Kruh in Mleko* (Bread & Milk, 2001), the tragic story by Jan Cvitkovič of a dysfunctional small-town family, and Damjan Kozole's *Rezerni Deli* (Spare Parts, 2003), about the trafficking of illegal immigrants through Slovenia from Croatia to Italy.

Much lighter fare is *Petelinji Zajtrk* (Rooster's Breakfast, 2007), a romance by Marko Naberšnik set on the Austrian border, and the bizarre US-made documentary *Big River Man* (John Maringouin, 2009) about an overweight marathon swimmer who takes on – wait for it – the Amazon and succeeds.

Environment

Slovenia is amazingly green; indeed, 58% of its total surface area is covered in forest and it's growing. Slovenia is home to almost 3200 plant species – some 70 of which are indigenous.

Triglav National Park is particularly rich in native flowering plants. Among the more peculiar endemic fauna in Slovenia is a blind salamander called *Proteus anguinus* that lives deep in Karst caves, can survive for years without eating and has been called a 'living fossil'.

Food & Drink

Slovenia boasts an incredibly diverse cuisine, but except for a few national favourites such as *žlikrofi* (pasta stuffed with cheese, bacon and chives) and *jota* (hearty bean soup) and incredibly rich desserts like *gibanica* (a layer cake stuffed with nuts, cheese and apple), you're not likely to encounter many of these regional specialities on menus.

Dishes like *brodet* (fish soup) from the coast, *ajdovi žganci z ocvirki* (buckwheat 'porridge' with savoury pork crackling) and salad greens doused in *bučno olje* (pumpkin-seed oil) are generally eaten at home.

A *gostilna* or *gostišče* (inn) or *restavracija* (restaurant) more frequently serves *rižota* (risotto), *klobasa* (sausage), *zrezek* (cutlet/steak), *golaž* (goulash) and *paprikaš* (piquant chicken or beef 'stew'). *Riba* (fish) is excellent and usually priced by the *dag* (100g). Common in Slovenia are such Balkan favourites as *cevapčiči* (spicy meatballs of beef or pork) and *pljeskavica* (spicy meat patties), often served with *kajmak* (a type of clotted cream).

You can snack cheaply on takeaway pizza slices or pieces of *burek* (€2), flaky pastry stuffed with meat, cheese or apple. Alternatives include *štruklji* (cottage-cheese dumplings) and *palačinke* (thin sweet pancakes).

Wine, Beer & Brandy

Distinctively Slovenian wines include peppery red Teran (made from Refošk grapes in the Karst region), Cviček (a dry light red – almost rosé – wine from eastern Slovenia) and Malvazija (a straw-colour white from the coast that is light and dry). Slovenes are justly proud of their top vintages, but cheaper bar-standard *odprto vino* (open wine) sold by the decilitre (100mL) is just so-so.

Pivo (beer), whether *svetlo* (lager) or *temno* (porter), is best on *točeno* (draught) but always available in cans and bottles too.

There are dozens of kinds of *žganje* (fruit brandy) available, including *češnjevec* (made with cherries), *sadjevec* (mixed fruit), *brinjevec* (juniper), *hruška* (pears, also called *viljamovka*) and *slivovka* (plums).

SURVIVAL GUIDE

Directory A–Z

Accommodation

Accommodation runs the gamut from riverside camping grounds, hostels, mountain huts, cosy *gostišča* (inns) and farmhouses, to elegant castle hotels and five-star hotels in Ljubljana, so you'll usually have little trouble finding accommodation to fit your budget, except perhaps at the height of the season (July and August) on the coast, at Bled or Bohinj, or in Ljubljana.

The following price ranges refer to a double room, with en suite toilet and bath or shower and breakfast, unless otherwise indicated. Virtually every municipality in the land levies a tourist tax of between €0.50 and €1 per person per night.

€ less than €50

€€ €50 to €100

€€€ more than €100

FARMSTAYS

Hundreds of working farms in Slovenia offer accommodation to paying guests, either in private rooms in the farmhouse itself or in Alpine-style guesthouses. Many farms offer outdoor sport activities and allow you to help out with the farm chores if you feel so inclined.

Expect to pay about €15 per person in a room with shared bathroom and breakfast (from €20 for half-board) in the low season (September to mid-December and mid-January to June), rising in the high season (July and August) to a minimum €17 per person (from €25 for half-board).

For more information, contact the Association of Tourist Farms of Slovenia (Združenje Turističnih Kmetij Slovenije; ☑041 435 528, 03-425 55 11; www.farmtourism.si; Trnoveljska cesta 1) or check with the Slovenian Tourist Board.

Business Hours

The *delovni čas* (opening times) are usually posted on the door. *Odprto* is 'open', *zaprto* is 'closed'. The following hours are standard and reviews won't list business hours unless they differ from these.

Banks 9am to 5pm weekdays, and (rarely) from 8am until noon on Saturday.

Grocery stores 8am to 7pm weekdays and 8am until 1pm on Saturday.

Museums 10am to 6pm Tuesday to Sunday. Winter hours may be shorter.

Post offices 8am to 6pm or 7pm weekdays and until noon on Saturday.

Restaurant Hours vary but count on 11am to 10pm daily. Bars usually open from 11am to midnight Sunday to Thursday and to 1am or 2am on Friday and Saturday.

Embassies & Consulates

All of the following are in Ljubljana:

Australian Consulate (☑01-234 86 75; Železna cesta 14; ☺9am-1pm Mon-Fri)

Canadian Consulate (☑01-252 44 44; 49a Linhartova cesta; ☺8am-noon Mon, Wed & Fri)

French Embassy (☑01-479 04 00; Barjanska cesta 1; ☺8.30am-12.30pm Mon-Fri)

German Embassy (☑01-479 03 00; Prešernova cesta 27; ☺9am-noon Mon-Thu, 9-11am Fri)

Irish Embassy (☑01-300 89 70; 1st fl, Palača Kapitelj, Poljanski nasip 6; ☺9.30am-12.30pm & 2.30-4pm Mon-Fri)

Netherlands Embassy (☑01-420 14 61; 1st fl, Palača Kapitelj, Poljanski nasip 6; ☺9am-noon Mon-Fri)

New Zealand Consulate (☑01-580 30 55; Verovškova ulica 57; ☺8am-3pm Mon-Fri)

UK Embassy (☑01-200 39 10; 4th fl, Trg Republike 3; ☺9am-noon Mon-Fri)

US Embassy (☑01-200 55 00; Prešernova cesta 31; ☺9-11.30am & 1-3pm Mon-Fri)

Festivals & Events

The official website of the Slovenian Tourist Board (www.slovenia.info), maintains a comprehensive list of major cultural events.

Food

The following price ranges are a rough approximation for a two-course sit-down meal for one person, with a drink. Many restaurants offer an excellent-value set menu of two or even three courses at lunch. These typically run from €5 to €9.

€ less than €15

€€ €16 to €30

€€€ over €30

Gay & Lesbian Travellers

National laws ban discrimination in employment and other areas on the basis of sexual preference. In recent years a highly visible campaign against homophobia has been put in place across the country. Outside Ljubljana, however, there is little evidence of a gay presence, much less a lifestyle.

Roza Klub (Klub K4 ; www.klubk4.org; Kersnikova ulica 4; ☺10pm-6am Sun Sep-Jun) in Ljubljana is made up of the gay and lesbian branches of KUC (www.skuc.org), which stands for Študentski Kulturni Center (Student Cultural

Centre) but is no longer student-orientated as such. It organises the gay and lesbian Ljubljana Pride (www.ljubljanapride.org) parade in late June and the Gay & Lesbian Film Festival (www.ljudmila.org/siqrd/fglf) in late November/early December. The gay male branch, Magnus (skucmagnus@hotmail.com), deals with AIDS prevention, networking and is behind the Kulturni Center Q (Q Cultural Centre) in Ljubljana's Metelkova Mesto, which includes Klub Tiffany for gay men and Klub Monokel for gay women.

A monthly publication called Narobe (Upside Down; www.narobe.si) is in Slovene only, though you might be able to at least glean some basic information from the listings.

Internet Access

Virtually every hotel and hostel now has internet access – a computer for guests' use (free or for a small fee), wi-fi – or both. Most of the country's tourist information centres offer free (or low-cost) access and many libraries in Slovenia have free terminals. Many cities and towns have at least one internet cafe (though they usually only have a handful of terminals), or even free wi-fi in town squares.

Money

The official currency is the euro. Exchanging cash is simple at banks, major post offices, travel agencies and *menjalnice* (bureaux de change), although many don't accept travellers cheques. Major credit and debit cards are accepted almost everywhere, and ATMs are ubiquitous.

Post

The Slovenian postal system (*Pošta Slovenije*), recognised by its bright yellow logo, offers a wide variety of services – from selling stamps and telephone cards to making photocopies and changing money. News stands also sell *znamke* (stamps). Post offices can sell you boxes.

Public Holidays

If a holiday falls on a Sunday, then the following Monday becomes the holiday.

New Year 1 and 2 January

Prešeren Day (Slovenian Culture Day) 8 February

Easter & Easter Monday March/April

Insurrection Day 27 April

Labour Day holidays 1 and 2 May

National Day 25 June

Assumption Day 15 August

Reformation Day 31 October

All Saints Day 1 November

Christmas Day 25 December

Independence Day 26 December

Telephone

Public telephones in Slovenia require a *telefonska kartica* or *telekartica* (telephone card) available at post offices and some newsstands. Phonecards cost €2.70/4/7.50/14.60 for 25/50/100/300 *impulzov* (impulses, or units).

To call Slovenia from abroad, dial the international access code, ☏386 (the country code for Slovenia), the area code (minus the initial zero) and the number. There are six area codes in Slovenia (☏01 to ☏05 and ☏07). To call abroad from Slovenia, dial ☏00 followed by the country and area codes and then the number. Numbers beginning with ☏80 in Slovenia are toll-free.

MOBILE PHONES

Network coverage amounts to more than 95% of the country. Mobile numbers carry the prefix ☏030 and ☏040 (SiMobil), ☏031, ☏041, ☏051 and ☏071 (Mobitel) and ☏070 (Tušmobil).

Slovenia uses GSM 900, which is compatible with the rest of Europe and Australia but not with the North American GSM 1900 or the totally different Japanese system. SIM cards with €5 credit are available for around €15 from SiMobil (www.simobil.si), Mobitel (www.mobitel.si) and Tušmobil (www.tusmobil.sil). Top-up scratch cards are available at post offices, news stands and petrol stations.

All three networks have outlets throughout Slovenia, including in Ljubljana.

Tourist Information

The Slovenian Tourist Board (Slovenska Turistična Organizacija, STO; ☏01-589 18 40; www.slovenia.info; Dunajska cesta 156), based in Ljubljana, is the umbrella organisation for tourist promotion in Slovenia, and produces a number of excellent brochures, pamphlets and booklets in English.

Walk-in visitors in Ljubljana can head to the Slovenian Tourist Information Centre (STIC; ☏306 45 76; www.slovenia.info; Krekov trg 10; ☉8am-9pm Jun-Sep, 8am-7pm Oct-May). In addition, the organisation oversees another five dozen or so local tourist offices and bureaus called 'tourist information centres' (TICs) across the country.

In the capital, the **Ljubljana Tourist Information Centre** (TIC; ☎306 12 15; www.visitljubljana.si; Adamič-Lundrovo nabrežje 2; ◷8am-9pm Jun-Sep, 8am-7pm Oct-May) knows just about everything there is to know about Ljubljana and almost as much about the rest of Slovenia. There's a branch at the train station.

Visas

Citizens of nearly all European countries, as well as Australia, Canada, Israel, Japan, New Zealand and the USA, do not require visas to visit Slovenia for stays of up to 90 days. Holders of EU and Swiss passports can enter using a national identity card.

Those who do require visas (including South Africans) can get them for up to 90 days at any Slovenian embassy or consulate – see the website of the **Ministry of Foreign Affairs** (www.mzz.gov.si) for a full listing. They cost €35 regardless of the type of visa or length of validity.

Getting There & Away

Border formalities with Slovenia's fellow European Union neighbours, Italy, Austria and Hungary, are virtually nonexistent. Croatia hopes to enter the EU in 2013 and plans to implement the Schengen border rules soon after. Until then expect a somewhat closer inspection of your documents – national ID (for EU citizens) or passport and, in some cases, visa when travelling to/from Croatia.

Air

Slovenia's only international airport is Ljubljana's **Jože Pučnik Airport** (LJU/Aerodrom Ljubljana; ☎04-206 19 81; www.lju-airport.si/eng; Zgornji Brnik 130a, Brnik) at Brnik, 27km north of Ljubljana. In the arrivals hall there's a **Slovenia Tourist Information Centre** (STIC; ◷11am-11pm Mon, Wed & Fri, 10am-10pm Tue & Thu, 10.30am-10.30pm Sat, 12.30pm-12.30am Sun) desk, a hotel-booking telephone and ATM. Car-rental agencies have outlets opposite the terminal.

From its base at Brnik, the Slovenian flag-carrier, **Adria Airways** (☎01-369 10 10, 080 13 00; www.adria-airways.com), serves some 20 European destinations on regularly scheduled flights.

Other airlines with regularly scheduled flights to and from Ljubljana include:

Air France (☎01-244 34 47; www.airfrance.com/si) Daily flights to Paris (CDG).

ČSA Czech Airlines (☎04-206 17 50; www.czechairlines.com) Flights to Prague.

EasyJet (☎04-206 16 77; www.easyjet.com) Low-cost daily flights to London Stansted.

JAT Airways (☎01-231 43 40; www.jat.com) Daily flights to Belgrade.

Lufthansa (☎01-434 72 46; www.lufthansa.com; Gosposvetska cesta 6) Code-shared flights with Adria.

Montenegro Airlines (☎04-259 42 52; www.montenegroairlines.com) Twice weekly flight to Podgorica.

Turkish Airlines (☎04-206 16 80; www.turkishairlines.com) Flights to Istanbul.

Land

BUS

International bus destinations from Ljubljana include Serbia, Germany, Croatia, Bosnia and Hercegovina, Macedonia, Italy and Scandinavia. You can also catch buses to Italy and Croatia from coastal towns, including Piran and Koper.

TRAIN

It is possible to travel to Italy, Austria, Germany, Croatia and Hungary by train; Ljubljana is the main hub, although you can, for example, hop on international trains in certain cities like Maribor and Ptuj). International train travel can be expensive. It is sometimes cheaper to travel as far as you can on domestic routes before crossing any borders.

Sea

Piran sends ferries to Trieste daily and catamarans to Venice at least once a week in season. There's also a catamaran between nearby Izola and Venice in summer months.

Getting Around

Bicycle

Cycling is a popular way of getting around. Bikes can be transported for €2.80 in the baggage compartments of some IC and regional trains. Larger buses can also carry bikes as luggage. Larger towns and cities have dedicated bicycle lanes and traffic lights.

ROAD RULES

» Drive on the right.

» Speed limits: 50km/h in town, 90km/h on secondary roads, 100km/h on highways; 130km/h on motorways.

» Seat belts are compulsory; motorcyclists must wear helmets.

» All motorists must illuminate their headlights throughout the day.

» Permitted blood-alcohol level for drivers is 0.05%.

Bus

Buy your ticket at the *avtobusna postaja* (bus station) or simply pay the driver as you board. In Ljubljana you should book your seat at least a day in advance if you're travelling on Friday, or to destinations in the mountains or on the coast on a public holiday. Bus services are restricted on Sunday and holidays.

A range of bus companies serve the country, but prices are uniform: €3.10/5.60/9.20/16.80 for 25/50/100/200km of travel.

Timetables in the bus station, or posted on a wall or column outside, list destinations and departure times. If you cannot find your bus listed or don't understand the schedule, get help from the *blagajna vozovnice* (information or ticket window), which are usually one and the same. *Odhodi* means 'departures' while *prihodi* is 'arrivals'.

Car & Motorcycle

Roads in Slovenia are generally good. There are two main motorway corridors – between Maribor and the coast (via the flyover at Črni Kal) and from the Karavanke Tunnel into Austria to Zagreb in Croatia – intersecting at the Ljubljana ring road, with a branch from Postojna to Nova Gorica. Motorways are numbered from A1 to A10 (for *avtocesta*).

Tolls are no longer paid separately on the motorways, instead all cars must display a *vinjeta* (road-toll sticker) on the windscreen. They cost €15/30/95 for a week/month/year for cars and €7.50/25/47.50 for motorbikes and are available at petrol stations, post offices and certain news stands and tourist information centres. These stickers will already be in place on a rental car; failure to display such a sticker risks a fine of up to €300.

Dial ☎1987 for roadside assistance.

HIRING A CAR

Renting a car in Slovenia allows access to cheaper out-of-centre hotels and farm or village homestays. Rentals from international firms such as Avis, Budget, Europcar and Hertz vary in price; expect to pay from €40/210 a day/week, including unlimited mileage, collision damage waiver (CDW), theft protection (TP), Personal Accident Insurance (PAI) and taxes. Some smaller agencies have somewhat more competitive rates; booking on the internet is always cheaper.

Train

Much of the country is accessible by rail, run by the national operator, Slovenian Railways (Slovenske Železnice, SŽ; ☎01-291 33 32; www.slo-zeleznice.si). The website has an easy-to-use timetable.

Figure on travelling at about 60km/h except on the fastest InterCity Slovenia (ICS) express trains that run between Ljubljana and Maribor (€13.60, 1¾ hours) at an average speed of 90km/h.

The provinces are served by *regionalni vlaki* (regional trains) and *primestni vlaki* (city trains), but the fastest are InterCity trains (IC).

An 'R' next to the train number on the timetable means seat reservations are available. If the 'R' is boxed, seat reservations are obligatory.

Purchase your ticket before travelling at the *železniška postaja* (train station); buying it from the conductor onboard costs an additional €2.50. Invalid tickets or fare dodging earn a €40 fine.

Turkey

Best Places to Eat

» Asmalı Cavit (p540)
» Köy Evi (p586)
» İkbal (p569)
» Reis (p566)

Best Places to Stay

» Hotel Ibrahim Pasha (p537)
» Esbelli Evi (p587)
» Hotel Villa Mahal (p567)
» Tuvana Hotel (p573)
» Assos Alarga (p550)

Why Go?

While many Turks see their country as European, Turkey packs in as many towering minarets and spice-trading bazaars as its Middle Eastern neighbours. This bridge between continents has absorbed the best of Europe and Asia. Travellers can enjoy historical hot spots, mountain outposts, expansive steppe and *caravanserai*-loads of the exotic, without forgoing comfy beds and buses.

Despite its reputation as a continental meeting point, Turkey can't be pigeonholed. Cappadocia, a dreamscape dotted with fairy chimneys (rock formations), is unlike anywhere else on the planet. Likewise, spots like Mt Nemrut (Nemrut Dağı), littered with giant stone heads, and Olympos, where Lycian ruins peek from the undergrowth, are quintessentially Turkish mixtures of natural splendour and ancient remains.

The beaches and mountains offer enough activities to impress the fussiest Ottoman sultan. Worldly pleasures include the many historic hotels, the meze to savour on panoramic terraces and, of course, Turkey's famous kebaps.

When to Go

Ankara

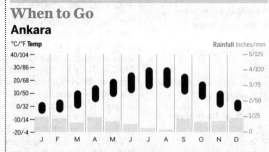

Apr–May Spring sunshine without summer crowds, apart from in İstanbul, where it is high season.

Jun–Aug İstanbul's shoulder season; music festivals and lazy summer days by the Bosphorus.

Sep–Oct Autumn walking and diving; outside of İstanbul crowds thin.

AT A GLANCE

» **Currency** Turkish lira (TL)

» **Languages** Turkish, Kurdish

» **Money** ATMs widespread; credit cards accepted in cities and tourist areas

» **Visas** On arrival

Fast Facts

» **Area** 783,562 sq km

» **Capital** Ankara

» **Country code** ☑90

» **Emergency** Police ☑155; Ambulance ☑112; Fire ☑110

Exchange Rates

Australia	A$1	TL1.88
Canada	C$1	TL1.77
Euro Zone	€1	TL2.32
Japan	¥100	TL1.94
New Zealand	NZ$1	TL1.51
UK	UK£1	TL2.75
USA	US$1	TL1.80

Set Your Budget

» **Budget hotel room** TL80

» **Midrange meal** TL9 to TL25

» **Museum entry** TL5

» **Beer** TL6

Resources

» **Hürriyet Daily News** (www.hurriyetdailynews.com)

» **Cornucopia** (www.cornucopia.net/blog)

» **tulumba.com** (www.tulumba.com)

Connections

İstanbul is well connected to Europe, with two international airports. Buses leave the *otogar* (bus station) for countries including Austria, Bulgaria, Germany, Greece, Italy, Macedonia, Romania and Slovenia.

Currently, the only daily train between İstanbul and Europe is the overnight Bosphorus/Balkan Express to Bucharest (Romania, 21 hours), Sofia (Bulgaria, 13 hours) and Belgrade (Serbia, 21½ hours). A suggested train route from London to İstanbul is the three-night journey via Paris, Munich, Vienna, Budapest and Bucharest; see www.seat61.com/turkey for more information and other routes.

Ferries connect Turkey's Aegean and Mediterranean coasts with Greek islands and Northern Cyprus; İstanbul with Ukraine; and Trabzon on the Black Sea coast with Russia.

ITINERARIES

One Week

Devote a few days to magical İstanbul, then cross the Sea of Marmara to Anatolia and head south to laid-back Selçuk or coastal Kuşadası, both convenient bases for visiting the marvellous ruins of Ephesus.

Two Weeks

From Ephesus, head inland to Pamukkale's shiny travertine formations, then return to the coast at the vibrant city of Antalya, with its Roman-Ottoman heritage quarter, and work your way around the glorious Teke Peninsula. Stop in Çıralı to see the eternal flame of the Chimaera, Kaş for activities and boat trips, and Patara for Turkey's longest beach. From Dalaman airport you can fly back to İstanbul and Europe.

Essential Food & Drink

Far from the uninspiring kebaps and stuffed vine leaves you may have seen at home, Turkish food is a celebration of community and life in its home country. Kebaps are swooningly succulent, *yaprak dolması* (stuffed vine leaves) are filled with subtly spiced rice and eating is social, slow and seasonal. Food is taken very seriously, with delicious results that vary between regions, meaning that travelling here will constantly surprise and seduce your taste buds.

Apart from kebaps, classic Turkish dishes and tipples include *köfte* (meatballs), meze, pide, *lahmacun* (Arabic pizza), *gözleme* (thin savoury crepes), *mantı* (Turkish ravioli), *börek* (filled pastries), baklava and *çay* (tea).

Rakı (a fiery, highly alcoholic aniseed drink) is best accompanied by meze, especially *beyaz peynir* (ewe's- or goat's-milk cheese) and melon, and *balık* (fish).

İSTANBUL

📞 0212 / POP 14 MILLION

Some ancient cities are the sum of their monuments. But others, such as İstanbul, factor a lot more into the equation. Here, you can visit Byzantine churches and Ottoman mosques in the morning, shop in chic boutiques during the afternoon and party at glamorous clubs through the night. In the space of a few minutes, you can hear the evocative strains of the call to prayer issuing from the Old City's minarets, the sonorous horn of a commuter ferry crossing between Europe and Asia, and the strident cries of a street hawker selling fresh seasonal produce. This marvellous metropolis is an exercise in sensory seduction like no other.

In terms of orientation, the Bosphorus strait, between the Black Sea and the Sea of Marmara, divides Europe from Asia. On its western shore, the European part of İstanbul is further divided by the Golden Horn (Haliç), an inlet of the Bosphorus, into the Old City in the southwest and Beyoğlu in the northeast.

Overlooked by the Galata Tower, the Galata Bridge (Galata Köprüsü) spans the Golden Horn between Eminönü, north of Sultanahmet in the Old City, and Karaköy. Ferries depart from Eminönü and Karaköy for the Asian shore.

Beyoğlu, uphill from Karaköy, was the city's 'European' quarter in the 19th century. The Tünel funicular railway links Karaköy up to the bottom of Beyoğlu's pedestrianised main street, İstiklal Caddesi. From here İstiklal Caddesi climbs to Taksim Sq, the heart of 'modern' İstanbul.

History

Late in the 2nd century AD, the Romans conquered the small city-state of Byzantium, which was renamed Constantinople in AD

İSTANBUL IN TWO DAYS

On day one, visit the **Blue Mosque**, **Aya Sofya** and **Basilica Cistern** in the morning and the **Grand Bazaar** in the afternoon. Cross the Golden Horn from Sultanahmet for dinner in **Beyoğlu**.

Spend your second morning in **Topkapı Palace**, then board a private excursion boat for a **Bosphorus cruise**. Afterwards, walk up through Galata (or catch the funicular) to **İstiklal Caddesi** to enjoy Beyoğlu's nightlife again.

ℹ️ **MUSEUM PASS**

The **Museum Pass İstanbul** (www.muze.gov.tr/museum_pass) offers a possible TL36 saving on entry to the Old City's major sights, and allows holders to skip admission queues.

---

330 after Emperor Constantine moved his capital there. Following the collapse of the Roman Empire, the city became the capital of the Christian, Greek-speaking Byzantine Empire.

In 1453, Mehmet the Conqueror (Mehmet Fatih) took Constantinople from the Byzantines and made it capital of the Ottoman Empire. During the glittering reign of Süleyman the Magnificent (1520–66), the great city was graced with many beautiful new buildings, and retained much of its charm even during the empire's long decline.

Occupied by Allied forces after WWI, the city came to be thought of as the decadent playpen of the sultans, notorious for its extravagant lifestyle, espionage and intrigue. As a result, when the Turkish Republic was proclaimed in 1923, Ankara became the new capital, in an attempt to wipe the slate clean. Nevertheless, İstanbul (Atatürk officially changed the city's name in the 1920s) remains a commercial, cultural and financial centre: Turkey's number-one city in all but title.

👁 Sights & Activities

SULTANAHMET & AROUND

The Sultanahmet area is the centre of the Old City, a World Heritage site packed with so many wonderful sights you could spend several weeks here.

Blue Mosque   MOSQUE
(Sultan Ahmet Camii; Map p532; Atmeydanı Caddesi; ⏱9am-12.15pm, 2-4.30pm & 5.30-6.30pm Sat-Thu, 9-11.15am, 2.30-4.30pm & 5.30-6.30pm Fri; 🚇Sultanahmet) In this 17th-century Ottoman mosque, Sultan Ahmet I attempted to rival the grandeur and beauty of the Byzantines' nearby Aya Sofya – with some success. Its exterior creates a visual wham-bam effect similar to the one achieved by Aya Sofya's interior, with voluptuous curves, six slender minarets and the biggest courtyard of all Ottoman mosques. Inside, the blue İznik tiles that give the building its unofficial name number in the tens of thousands, there are 260 windows and the central prayer space is huge.

TURKEY

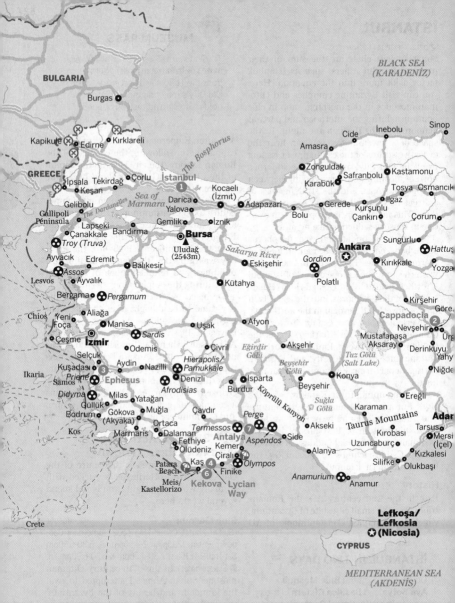

Turkey Highlights

1 Uncover **İstanbul** (p527), the glorious one-time Ottoman and Byzantine capital and one of the world's truly great cities.

2 Sleep in a fairy chimney in jaw-droppingly bizarre and beautiful **Cappadocia** (p583).

3 Imagine the tourists streaming down the Curetes Way are wearing togas in **Ephesus** (p556), one of the greatest surviving Graeco-Roman cities.

4 Hike through the Mediterranean countryside on

a section of the 500km **Lycian Way** (p565).

⑤ Explore Turkey's exotic east at **Nemrut Dağı** (p590), where decapitated stone heads litter a king's burial mound.

⑥ Cruise over a sunken city at **Kekova** (p569), one of many blue voyages offered at Aegean and Mediterranean harbours.

⑦ Wander the Roman-Ottoman old quarter of **Antalya** (p573), a stylish Mediterranean hub and gateway to the Turquoise Coast.

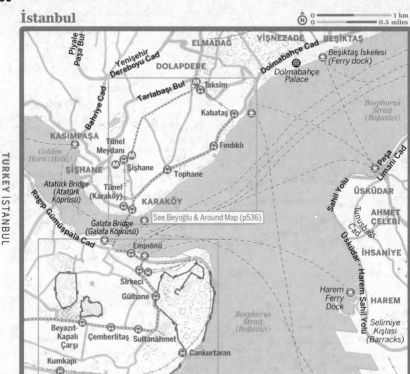

To the southeast, the **Arasta Bazaar** (Map p532; Sultanahmet), a great place for hassle-free shopping, specialises in carpets, jewellery, textiles and ceramics.

Topkapı Palace   PALACE
(Topkapı Sarayı; Map p532; www.topkapisarayi. gov.tr; Babıhümayun Caddesi; palace TL25, Harem TL15; ⊙9am-6pm Wed-Mon mid-Apr–Sep, to 4pm Oct–mid-Apr, Harem closes 4.30pm Apr-Oct, 3.30pm Nov-Mar; Sultanahmet) This great palace features in more colourful stories than most of the world's royal residences put together. Mehmet the Conqueror started work on the palace shortly after the Conquest in 1453, and Ottoman sultans lived in this rarefied environment until the 19th century. Visiting the palace's opulent **pavilions**, jewel-filled **Treasury** and sprawling **Harem**, once inhabited by libidinous sultans, ambitious courtiers, beautiful concubines and scheming eunuchs, gives a glimpse of life in the Ottoman court.

TOP CHOICE Grand Bazaar   MARKET
(Kapalı Çarşı, Covered Market; Map p532; www.kapali carsi.org.tr; ⊙9am-7pm Mon-Sat; ; Beyazıt-Kapalı Çarşı) This colourful and chaotic bazaar is the heart of the Old City and has been so for centuries. Starting as a small vaulted *bedesten* (warehouse) in 1461, it grew to cover a vast area as laneways between the *bedesten*, neighbouring shops and *hans* (caravanserais – trader's inns) were roofed and the market assumed the sprawling, labyrinthine form that it retains today.

Be sure to peep through doorways to discover hidden *hans*, veer down narrow laneways to watch artisans at work and wander the main thoroughfares to differentiate treasures from tourist tack.

Basilica Cistern   CISTERN
(Yerebatan Sarnıçı; Map p532; www.yerebatan.com; Yerebatan Caddesi 13; admission TL10; ⊙9am-6.30pm; Sultanahmet) Across the tram lines

from the Aya Sofya is the entrance to this majestic underground chamber, built by Justinian in AD 532 and visited by James Bond in *From Russia with Love*. The vast, atmospheric, column-filled cistern stored up to 80,000 cubic metres of water for the Great Palace and surrounding buildings. Its cavernous depths stay wonderfully cool in the summer.

İstanbul Archaeology Museums MUSEUM
(Map p532; www.istanbularkeologi.gov.tr; Osman Hamdi Bey Yokuşu, Gülhane; admission TL10; ⊙9am-6pm Tue-Sun mid-Apr–Sep, to 4pm Oct–mid-Apr; ☐Gülhane) Downhill from the Topkapı Palace's First Court, this superb museum complex houses ancient artefacts, artistic treasures and objects showcasing Anatolian history. The **Archaeology Museum** houses an outstanding collection of classical statuary, including the magnificent sarcophagi from the Royal Necropolis at Side in Lebanon. The 'İstanbul Through the Ages' exhibition traces the city's history through its neighbourhoods during different periods.

In a separate building, the **Museum of the Ancient Orient** houses Hittite and other pre-Islamic archaeological finds. Also in the complex is the **Tiled Pavilion** (1472), with a display of Seljuk, Anatolian and Ottoman tiles and ceramics.

Hippodrome PARK
(Atmeydanı; Map p532; ☐Sultanahmet) The Byzantine emperors loved nothing more than an afternoon at the chariot races, and this rectangular arena was their venue of choice. In its heyday, it was decorated by **obelisks** and **statues**, some of which remain in place today. Recently relandscaped, it is one of the city's most popular meeting places and promenades, and was the scene of many popular uprisings during the Byzantine and Ottoman eras.

Museum of Turkish & Islamic Arts MUSEUM
(Türk ve İslam Eserleri Müzesi; Map p532; www.tiem.gov.tr; Atmeydanı Caddesi 46; admission TL10; ⊙9am-6.30pm Tue-Sun Apr-Oct, to 4.30pm Nov-Mar; ☐Sultanahmet) This 16th-century Ottoman palace on the western edge of the Hippodrome houses a magnificent collection of artefacts, including exquisite examples of calligraphy and a collection of antique carpets that is generally held to be the best in the world. Don't miss the extraordinary collection of carpets in the *divanhane* (ceremonial hall), and stop for a Turkish coffee at **Müzenin Kahvesi** (⊙9am-6.30pm Tue-Sun Apr-Oct, to 4.30pm Nov-Mar) in the courtyard.

Süleymaniye Mosque MOSQUE
(Map p532; Prof Sıddık Sami Onar Caddesi; ☐Beyazıt-Kapalı Çarşı) One of the grandest Ottoman mosque complexes dominates the Golden Horn from atop one of the city's seven hills, providing a prominent landmark. It was commissioned by the greatest Ottoman sultan, Süleyman the Magnificent (r 1520–66), and designed by Mimar Sinan, the most famous imperial architect.

Spice Bazaar MARKET
(Mısır Çarşısı, Egyptian Market; Map p532; ⊙8am-6pm Mon-Sat, 9am-6pm Sun; ☐Eminönü) This bustling marketplace, constructed in the 1660s, was called the Egyptian Market because it was famous for selling goods shipped in from Cairo. As well as *baharat* (spices),

---

DON'T MISS

AYA SOFYA

No doubt you will gasp at the overblown splendour of the **Aya Sofya** (Hagia Sophia; Map p532; www.ayasofyamuzesi.gov.tr; Aya Sofya Meydanı 1; adult/under 12yr TL25/free; ⊙9am-6pm Tue-Sun mid-Apr–Sep, to 4pm Oct–mid-Apr; ☐Sultanahmet). Known as Sancta Sophia in Latin, Haghia Sofia in Greek and the Church of the Divine Wisdom in English, it is one of the world's most glorious buildings. Built as part of Emperor Justinian's effort to restore the greatness of the Roman Empire, it was completed in AD 537 and reigned as the grandest church in Christendom until the Ottomans took Constantinople in 1453. The victorious Mehmet the Conqueror converted the building to a mosque and it continued in that role until Atatürk declared it a museum in 1935. The basilica's interior, with its seemingly floating dome, frescos, and glittering mosaics of Byzantine emperors and empresses alongside Jesus and Mary, is truly a knockout.

Afterwards, visit the ornate **Aya Sofya Tombs** (Aya Sofya Müzesi Padişah Türbeleri; Map p532; Kabasakal Caddesi; ⊙9am-5pm; ☐Sultanahmet), the final resting place of five Ottoman sultans.

Sultanahmet & Around

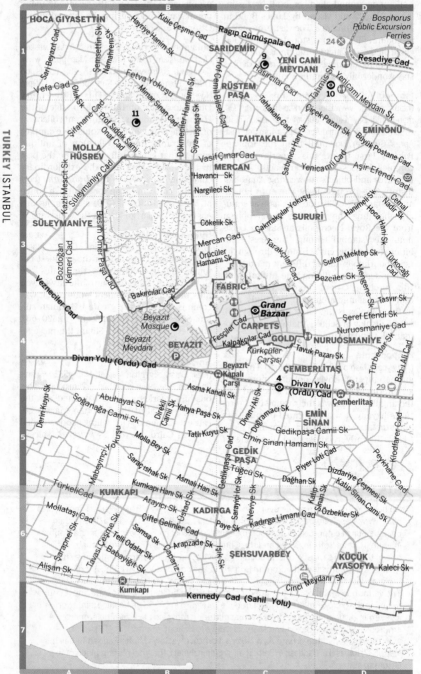

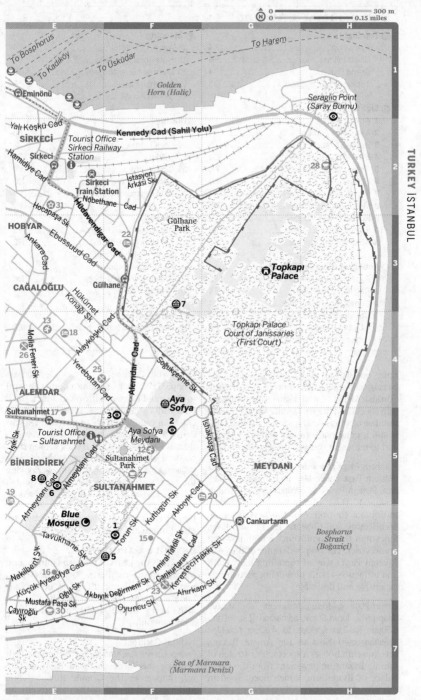

Sultanahmet & Around

nuts, honeycomb and olive-oil soaps, the bazaar sells truckloads of *incir* (figs), *lokum* (Turkish delight) and *pestil* (fruit pressed into sheets and dried). Despite the increasing number of shops selling tourist trinkets, this is still a great place to buy edible souvenirs and to marvel at the well-preserved building.

Rüstem Paşa Mosque   MOSQUE
(Rüstem Paşa Camii; Map p532; Hasırcılar Caddesi, Rüstem Paşa; 🚉Eminönü) Mimar Sinan designed this diminutive 16th-century mosque, a showpiece of the best Ottoman architecture and tilework, for Rüstem Paşa, Süleyman the Magnificent's son-in-law and grand vizier. The preponderance of tiles was Rüstem Paşa's way of signalling his wealth and influence – İznik tiles being particularly expensive and desirable.

Great Palace Mosaic Museum   MUSEUM
(Map p532; Torun Sokak; admission TL8; ⊙9am-6.30pm Tue-Sun Apr-Oct, to 4.30pm Nov-Mar; 🚉Sultanahmet) Next to the Arasta Bazaar, this museum houses a spectacular stretch of mosaic Byzantine pavement from the Great Palace of Byzantium, which once stood in this area.

Divan Yolu Caddesi   HISTORIC AREA
(Map p532) Walking or taking a tram westward to the Grand Bazaar from Sultanahmet, you'll pass various monuments, including a shady Ottoman cemetery with an attached tea garden, **Türk Ocaği Kültür ve Sanat Merkezi İktisadi İşletmesi Çay Bahçesi** (Map p532; cnr Divan Yolu & Bab-ı Ali Caddesi; ⊙8am-midnight; 🚉Çemberlitaş). Also on the right, overlooking the tram stop of the same name, is the tall column known as **Çemberlitaş**, erected by Emperor Constantine to celebrate the dedication of Constantinople as capital of the Roman Empire in AD 330.

BEYOĞLU & AROUND

Beyoğlu is the heart of modern İstanbul and *the* hot spot for galleries, boutiques, cafes, restaurants and nightlife. The neighbourhood is a showcase of cosmopolitan Turkey at its best – miss Beyoğlu and you haven't seen İstanbul.

İstiklal Caddesi   STREET
(Independence Ave; Map p536) In the late 19th century, this pedestrianised thoroughfare was known as the Grande Rue de Pera, and it carried the life of the modern city up

and down its lively promenade. It's still the centre of İstanbullu life, and a stroll along its length is a must. You can also catch the antique tram (see p542). Come between 4pm and 8pm daily – especially on Friday and Saturday – and you'll see İstiklal at its busy best.

Galata Tower
TOWER

(Galata Kulesi; Map p536; www.galatatower.net; Galata Meydanı, Galata; admission TL12; ⊙9am-8pm; ⊡Karaköy) Constructed in 1348, this cylindrical tower was the city's tallest structure for centuries, and it still dominates the skyline north of the Golden Horn. Its vertiginous upper balcony offers 360-degree views; the steep admission cost is just about worth it if you visit when it's quiet and don't have to queue.

Dolmabahçe Palace
PALACE

(Dolmabahçe Sarayı; www.millisaraylar.gov.tr; Dolmabahçe Caddesi, Beşiktaş; Selâmlık TL30, Harem TL20, joint ticket TL40; ⊙9am-6pm Tue-Wed & Fri-Sun Mar-Sep, to 4pm Oct-Feb; ⊡Kabataş) On the Bosphorus shore, northeast of Kabataş tram and funicular stops, this grandiose 19th-century royal pad housed some of the last Ottoman sultans. Its neobaroque and neoclassical flourishes reflect the decadence of the decaying empire. The palace was guaranteed a place in the Turkish history books when Atatürk died here on 10 November 1938 and all the palace clocks stopped.

Visitors are taken on separate guided tours of two sections: the over-the-top Selamlık (ceremonial suites) and slightly more restrained Harem. Afterwards, make sure you visit the Crystal Kiosk, with its fairy tale-like conservatory featuring a crystal piano.

BOSPHORUS

Don't leave İstanbul without exploring the Bosphorus on a cruise on one of the boats departing from Eminönü. Private excursion boats (TL10, 90 minutes) travel to Anadolu Hisarı and back, without stopping. İDO's Bosphorus Public Excursion Ferry (www. ido.com.tr; Boğaz İskelesi; long tour 1 way/return TL15/25, short tour TL10; ⊙long tour 10.35am, plus 1.35pm Apr–Oct & noon summer, short tour 2.30pm Apr-Oct) travels all the way to Anadolu Kavağı at the Black Sea (90 minutes one way), stopping en route on the European and Asian sides. Its two-hour 'short tour' travels to Fatih Bridge and back.

The shores are sprinkled with monuments and sights, including the Dolmabahçe Palace, the majestic Bosphorus Bridge, numerous mosques, lavish *yalı*s (waterfront wooden summer residences) and affluent suburbs on the hills above the strait.

For the thrill of crossing from Europe to Asia (and back), you can catch a commuter ferry across the Bosphorus (TL2) from Eminönü, Karaköy or Beşiktaş (near Dolmabahçe Palace) to Kadıköy.

🍴 Courses

Cooking Alaturka
COOKING

(Map p532; ☑0536 338 0896; www.cookingalaturka.com; Akbıyık Caddesi 72a, Cankurtaran; cooking class per person €60; ⊡Sultanahmet) Dutch-born Eveline Zoutendijk's hands-on classes offer a great introduction to Turkish cuisine, suitable for both novices and experienced cooks, and include a five-course meal in the school's restaurant (p539).

Turkish Flavours
COOKING

(☑0532 218 0653; www.turkishflavours.com; Apartment 3, Vali Konağı Caddesi 14; per person tours TL180-290, cooking classes TL180) As well as running excellent foodie tours of the Spice Bazaar and Kadıköy markets, which include a huge lunch (TL290 per person), Selin Rozanes conducts small-group cooking classes in her elegant Nişantaşı home (TL180 per person). The results are enjoyed over a four-course lunch with drinks.

👣 Tours

İstanbul Walks
WALKING TOUR

(Map p532; ☑212-516 6300; www.istanbulwalks. net; 2nd fl, Şifa Hamamı Sokak 1; walking tours €25-75, child under 6yr free; ⊡Sultanahmet) This small company, run by a group of history buffs, offers a range of guided walking tours, concentrating on İstanbul's various neighbourhoods or taking in major monuments including Topkapı Palace. Student discounts are available.

Culinary Backstreets
WALKING TOUR

(www.culinarybackstreets.com) Full-day walking tours of the Old City and Beyoğlu (with lunch), and a colourful evening tasting regional dishes from southeastern Anatolia in a progression of eateries. The guides produce the excellent foodie blog of the same name.

Urban Adventures
WALKING, CULTURAL TOURS

(Map p532; ☑212-512 7144; www.urbanadventures. com; 1st fl, Ticarethane Sokak 11; all tours TL50; ⊙8.30am-5.30pm; ⊡Sultanahmet) International

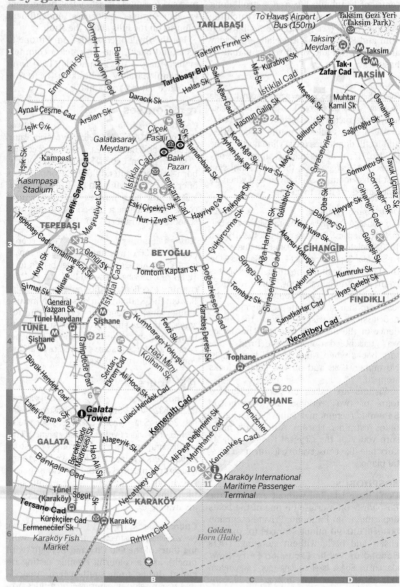

tour company Intrepid offers tours including a popular four-hour guided walk around Sultanahmet and the Bazaar District. The 'Home Cooked İstanbul' tour includes a no-frills dinner with a local family in their home.

🛏 Sleeping

During low season (October to April, but not around Christmas or Easter) you should be able to negotiate discounts of at least 20%. Before confirming bookings, ask if the hotel will give you a discount for cash payment

(usually 5% or 10%) and whether there are discounts for extended stays. A pick-up from the airport is often included if you stay more than three nights. Book ahead from May to September and for the Christmas–New Year period.

SULTANAHMET & AROUND
The Sultanahmet area has the most budget and midrange options, as well as some more luxurious accommodation. Most have stunning views from their roof terraces, and are close to the Old City's sights.

TOP CHOICE **Hotel Ibrahim Pasha** BOUTIQUE HOTEL €€
(Map p532; ☎212-518 0394; www.ibrahimpasha. com; Terzihane Sokak 7; r standard €99-195, deluxe €139-265; ❄@☎; 🚊Sultanahmet) Successfully combining Ottoman style with contemporary decor, the Ibrahim Pasha offers comfortable rooms, high levels of service, gorgeous ground-floor common areas and a terrace bar with Blue Mosque views.

HAMAMS

After a long day's sightseeing, few things could be better than relaxing in a *hamam* (Turkish bath). The ritual is invariably the same. First, you'll be shown to a cubicle where you can undress, store your clothes and wrap the provided *peştamal* (cloth) around you. Then an attendant will lead you through to the hot room, where you sit and sweat for a while.

It's cheapest to bring soap and a towel and wash yourself. The hot room is ringed with individual basins, which you can fill from the taps above, before sluicing the water over yourself with a plastic scoop. It's most enjoyable to let an attendant do it for you, dousing you with warm water and scrubbing you with a coarse cloth mitten. You'll be lathered with a sudsy swab, rinsed off and shampooed. When all this is complete, you'll likely be offered a massage.

Traditional *hamams* have separate sections for men and women or admit men and women at separate times. In tourist areas, many *hamams* are happy for foreign men and women to bathe together.

The Old City's pricey tourist *hamams*, including the following, are well worth a visit for the their gorgeous historic interiors, although their massages are generally short and not particularly good.

Ayasofya Hürrem Sultan Hamamı (Map p532; ☎212-517 3535; www.ayasofyahamami. com; Aya Sofya Meydanı; bath treatments €70-165, massages €40-75; ⊙8am-11pm; 🚇Sultanahmet) This restored 16th-century *hamam* offers the Old City's most luxurious traditional bath experience.

Cağaloğlu Hamamı (Map p532; ☎212-522 2424; www.cagalogluhamami.com.tr; Yerebatan Caddesi 34; bath, scrub & massage packages €50-110; ⊙8am-10pm; 🚇Sultanahmet) This 18th-century *hamam* is undoubtedly the city's most atmospheric. Bath services are overpriced; sign up for the self-service treatment (€30) only.

Çemberlitaş Hamamı (Map p532; ☎212-522 7974; Vezir Han Caddesi 8; bath, scrub & soap massage €29; ⊙6am-midnight; 🚇Çemberlitaş) Mimar Sinan designed this beautiful bathhouse dating back to 1584.

TOP CHOICE ⭐ Sirkeci Konak HOTEL €€
(Map p532; ☎212-528 4344; www.sirkecikonak. com; Taya Hatun Sokak 5, Sirkeci; standard d €155-185, superior & deluxe r €170-270; ❄@🛜🏊; 🚇Gülhane) Overlooking Gülhane Park, this terrific hotel's rooms are impeccably clean, well sized and loaded with amenities. It has a restaurant, a roof terrace, an indoor pool and a *hamam* (Turkish bath) and incredibly helpful staff. The complimentary entertainment program includes cooking classes, walking tours and afternoon teas.

Marmara Guesthouse PENSION €
(Map p532; ☎212-638 3638; www.marmaraguesthouse.com; Terbıyık Sokak 15, Cankurtaran; s €30-65, d €40-70, f €60-100; ❄@; 🚇Sultanahmet) Manager Elif Aytekin and her family go out of their way to make guests feel welcome, offering plenty of advice and serving a delicious breakfast on the vine-covered, seafacing roof terrace. Rooms have comfortable beds and double-glazed windows.

Saruhan Hotel HOTEL €
(Map p532; ☎212-458 7608; www.saruhanhotel. com; Cinci Meydanı Sokak 34, Kadırga; s €25-65, d €35-70, f €60-100; ❄@🛜; 🚇Çemberlitaş) In the quiet residential pocket of Kadırga, the impressive family-run Saruhan offers comfortable and well-equipped rooms plus a lovely terrace with a sea view. It's a 20-minute walk to Sultanahmet's sights and a shorter (but steep) walk to the Grand Bazaar.

Agora Life Hotel HOTEL €€
(Map p532; ☎212-526 1181; www.agoralifehotel.com; Cağoloğlu Hamamı Sokak 6, Cağoloğlu; s €69-129, d €79-209, ste €199-259; ❄@🛜) This hotel in a quiet cul-de-sac focuses on service and quiet elegance as its signatures. There are plenty of amenities in the rooms, and the rooftop terrace has a simply extraordinary view. Opt for a deluxe or suite room if possible.

BEYOĞLU & AROUND

Stay here to avoid the Old City touts, and because buzzing, bohemian Beyoğlu has

İstanbul's best wining, dining and shopping. It's also where most of the suite hotels and apartment rentals are located.

TOP CHOICE **Beş Oda**　　　BOUTIQUE HOTEL €€
(Map p536; ☑212-252 7501; www.5oda.com; Şahkulu Bostan Sokak 16, Galata; ste €85-150; ❄@☎; ☒Karaköy, then funicular to Tünel) The name means 'Five Rooms', and that's exactly what this stylish and friendly suite hotel in bohemian Galata is offering. Suites have equipped kitchenette, lounge area, custom-designed furniture, large bed and black-out curtains.

Witt Istanbul Hotel　　　BOUTIQUE HOTEL €€€
(Map p536; ☑212-293 1500; www.wittistanbul. com; Defterdar Yokuşu 26, Cihangir; ste €160-390; ❄@☎; ☒Tophane) Showcasing countless designer features, this stylish apartment hotel in trendy Cihangir has 18 suites with fully equipped kitchenette, seating area, CD/DVD player, iPod dock, Nespresso machine, king-sized bed and huge bathroom.

TomTom Suites　　　BOUTIQUE HOTEL €€€
(Map p536; ☑212-292 4949; www.tomtomsuites. com; Tomtom Kaptan Sokak 18; ste €185-720; ☒Karaköy, then funicular to Tünel) This suite hotel occupies a former Franciscan nunnery, with understated but elegant contemporary decor, impressive bathrooms and beautifully appointed suites. There's also a rooftop bar/ restaurant with fantastic views

Anemon Galata　　　HOTEL €€
(Map p536; ☑212-293 2343; www.anemonhotels. com; cnr Galata Kulesi Sokak & Büyük Hendek Sokak, Galata; s US$140-210, d US$160-230, ste US$225-270; ❄@; ☒Karaköy) Located on the attractive square surrounding Galata Tower, this 19th-century wooden building has been completely rebuilt inside. Rooms are elegantly decorated and well equipped; some have water views. There's a rooftop bar/ restaurant with great views and an atmospheric basement wine bar.

World House Hostel　　　HOSTEL €
(Map p536; ☑212-293 5520; www.worldhouseistanbul.com; Galipdede Caddesi 85, Galata; d €45-55; @☎; ☒Karaköy, then funicular to Tünel) Reasonably small and very friendly, World House is excellently located: close to Beyoğlu's entertainment strips but not too far from the sights in Sultanahmet. There are large and small dorms (one shower for every six beds), but none are female-only.

✖ Eating

İstanbul is a food-lover's paradise, but Sultanahmet has the least impressive range of eating options; we recommend crossing the Galata Bridge to join the locals.

If we've included a telephone number in the review, it means you should book ahead.

İstanbul Eats (www.culinarybackstreets.com /istanbul) is a good local foodie website.

SULTANAHMET & AROUND

İstanbul's favourite fast-food treat is the *balık ekmek* (fish kebap). On bobbing boats tied to the quay at the Eminönü end of Galata Bridge, fish fillets are grilled and crammed into fresh bread. You can buy the resulting snack at the adjoining stands (Map p532) on dry land for about TL5.

Avoid the rip-off eateries near the accommodation and bars on Akbıyık Caddesi.

TOP CHOICE **Ahırkapı Balıkçısı**　　　SEAFOOD €€
(Map p532; ☑212-518 4988; Keresteci Hakkı Sokak 46, Cankurtaran; meze TL5-25, fish TL15-70; ⊙4-11pm; ☒Sultanahmet) Tiny and relatively cheap, this neighbourhood fish restaurant's food is so good (and the nearby eating alternatives are so bad) that we're sharing the locals' secret.

Cihannüma　　　TURKISH €€€
(Map p532; ☑212-520 7676; www.cihannuma istanbul.com; And Hotel, Yerebatan Caddesi 18; meze TL5-19, mains TL27-47; ☒Sultanahmet) The view from the top-floor restaurant of this modest hotel is probably the best in the Old City. You can see as far as the Dolmabahçe Palace and Bosphorus Bridge, and it all provides a stunning backdrop for a menu showcasing good kebaps, Ottoman-influenced stews and a few vegetarian dishes.

Cooking Alaturka　　　TURKISH €€
(Map p532; ☑212-458 5919; www.cookingalaturka. com; Akbıyık Caddesi 72a, Cankurtaran; set lunch or dinner TL50; ⊙lunch Mon-Sat & dinner by reservation Mon-Sat; ☒; ☒Sultanahmet) This tranquil Dutch-Turkish restaurant serves a set four-course menu of simple Anatolian dishes. The menu can be tailored to suit vegetarians or those with food allergies (call ahead). No children under six at dinner and no credit cards.

Sefa Restaurant　　　TURKISH €
(Map p532; Nuruosmaniye Caddesi 17; portions TL7-12, kebaps TL12-18; ⊙7am-5pm; ☒; ☒Sultanahmet)

DON'T MISS

MEYHANES

A classic İstanbul night out involves carousing to live *fasıl*, a raucous local form of gypsy music, in Beyoğlu's *meyhanes* (Turkish taverns). A dizzying array of meze and fish dishes is on offer, washed down with *rakı*. On Friday and Saturday nights, the *meyhane* precinct **Nevizade Sokak** (Map p536) literally heaves with merrymakers.

Good, upmarket *meyhanes* include the following:

Asmalı Cavit (Asmalı Meyhane; Map p536; ☎212-292 4950; Asmalımescit Sokak 16, Asmalımescit; mezes TL6-20, mains TL18-24; ☒Karaköy, then funicular to Tünel)Quite possibly the city's best *meyhane*. Stand-out dishes include *yaprak ciğer* (liver fried with onions), *patlıcan salatası* (eggplant salad), *muska boreği* (filo stuffed with beef and onion) and *kalamar tava* (fried calamari).

Karaköy Lokantası (Map p536; ☎212-292 4455; Kemankeş Caddesi 37a, Karaköy; mezes TL6-10, portions TL7-12, grills TL11-16; ☺dinner daily, lunch Mon-Sat; ☒; ☒Karaköy) Known for its gorgeous tiled interior, genial owner and bustling vibe, the *lokanta* morphs into a *meyhane* at night.

Sofyalı 9 (Map p536; ☎212-245 0362; Sofyalı Sokak 9, Asmalımescit; mezes TL2.50-10, mains TL13-25; ☺closed Sun; ☒Karaköy, then funicular to Tünel) The food is fresh and tasty, and the atmosphere is convivial. Stick to meze rather than ordering mains.

Demeti (Map p536; ☎212-244 0628; www.demeti.com.tr; Şimşirci Sokak 6, Cihangir; mezes TL5-20, mains TL16-25; ☺4pm-2am Mon-Sat; ☒Kabataş, then funicular to Taksim) Bosphorus views from the terrace and occasional live music.

Jash (Map p536; ☎212-244 3042; www.jashistanbul.com; Cihangir Caddesi 9, Cihangir; mezes TL8-20, mains TL20-42; ☺lunch & dinner; ☒Kabataş, then funicular to Taksim) Armenian specialities and, at weekends, live accordion feature at Cihangir's bijou *meyhane*.

Locals rate this (unlicensed) place near the bazaar, which serves *hazır yemek* (ready-made) dishes and kebabs at reasonable prices. Order from an English menu or choose daily specials from the bain-marie, and arrive earlyish for lunch because many dishes run out by 1.30pm.

BEYOĞLU & AROUND

TOP CHOICE **Lokanta Maya**   MODERN TURKISH €€€
(Map p536; ☎212-252 6884; www.lokantamaya. com; Kemankeş Caddesi 35a, Karaköy; mezes TL11-28, mains TL26-35; ☺lunch Mon-Sat, dinner Tue-Sat, brunch Sun; ☒; ☒Karaköy) At her stylish restaurant near the Karaköy docks, chef Didem Şenol showcases her light, flavoursome, occasionally quirky and always assured food. Lunch is cheaper and more casual than dinner.

Zübeyir Ocakbaşı   KEBAP €€
(Map p536; ☎212-293 3951; www.zubeyirocakbasi. com; Bekar Sokak 28; meze TL4-6, kebaps TL10-20; ☺noon-1am; ☒Kabataş, then funicular to Taksim) At this popular *ocakbaşı* (grill house), top-quality meats are grilled on handsome copper-hooded barbecues: spicy chicken wings and Adana kebaps, flavoursome ribs,

pungent liver kebaps and well-marinated lamb *şiş* kebaps (small pieces of lamb grilled on a skewer).

Meze by Lemon Tree   MODERN TURKISH €€€
(Map p536; ☎212-252 8302; www.mezze.com.tr; Meşrutiyet Caddesi 83b, Tepebaşı; meze TL8-25, mains TL26-36; ☒Karaköy, then funicular to Tünel) Chef Gençay Üçok creates some of the most delicious, modern Turkish food in the city, including triumphs such as the monkfish casserole, and grilled lamb sirloin with baked potatoes and red beets.

Mikla   MODERN TURKISH €€€
(Map p536; ☎212-293 5656; www.miklarestaurant. com; Marmara Pera Hotel, Meşrutiyet Caddesi 15, Tepebaşı; appetisers TL25-38, mains TL51-79; ☺dinner; ☒Karaköy, then funicular to Tünel) Local celebrity chef Mehmet Gürs is a master of Mod Med, and the Turkish accents on the menu here make his food memorable. Extraordinary views, luxe surrounds and professional service complete the experience.

Zencefil   VEGETARIAN €
(Map p536; Kurabiye Sokak 8; soup TL7-9, mains TL9-17; ☺10am-11pm Mon-Sat, noon-10pm Sun; ☒; ☒Kabataş, then funicular to Taksim) Zencefil's

interior is comfortable and stylish, with a glassed courtyard and bright colour scheme, and its food is 100% homemade, fresh and varied. One chicken dish always features on the otherwise strictly vegetarian menu.

🍷 Drinking & Entertainment

For an overview of what's on, pick up *Time Out İstanbul*, check out its *Istanbul Beat* (www.istanbulbeatblog.com) blog and visit the *Biletix* (www.biletix.com), where you can buy tickets for major events.

SULTANAHMET & AROUND

Sultanahmet isn't as happening as Beyoğlu, but it has a few watering holes. The area's alcohol-free, atmosphere-rich *çay bahçesis* (tea gardens) and *kahvehanes* (coffee houses) are great for relaxing and sampling that great Turkish institution, the *nargile* (water pipe), along with a *Türk kahvesi* (Turkish coffee) or *çay*.

Set Üstü Çay Bahçesi   TEAHOUSE
(Map p532; Gülhane Park, Sultanahmet; ⊗9am-10.30pm; ⊠Gülhane) Come to this terraced tea garden to watch the ferries plying the route from Europe to Asia and enjoy an excellent pot of tea.

Yeni Marmara   TEAHOUSE
(Map p532; Çayıroğlu Sokak, Küçük Ayasofya; ⊗10am-1am; ⊠Sultanahmet) This is the genuine article: a neighbourhood teahouse frequented by backgammon-playing regulars who slurp tea and puff on *nargiles*. In winter a wood stove keeps the place cosy; in summer patrons sit on the rear terrace, overlooking the Sea of Marmara.

Derviş Aile Çay Bahçesi   TEAHOUSE
(Map p532; Mimar Mehmet Ağa Caddesi; ⊗9am-11pm Apr-Oct; ⊠Sultanahmet) Comfortable cane chairs, shady trees, efficient service, reasonable prices and peerless people-watching opportunities make this a great place for tea, *nargile* and backgammon.

Hocapaşa Culture Centre   PERFORMING ARTS
(Hodjapasha Culture Centre; Map p532; ☏212-511 4626; www.hodjapasha.com; Hocapaşa Hamamı Sokak 3b, Sirkeci; ⊠Sirkeci) Occupying a 550-year-old *hamam*, Hocapaşa stages one-hour whirling-dervish performances for tourists (adult/child under 12 years TL50/30; 7.30pm Monday, Wednesday, Friday, Saturday and Sunday; children under seven not admitted) and 1½-hour Turkish dance shows (adult/child under 12 years

TL60/40; 8pm Tuesday and Thursday and 9pm Saturday and Sunday).

BEYOĞLU & AROUND

CAFES & BARS

There's a thriving bar scene in Beyoğlu, which is almost permanently crowded with locals who patronise the atmosphere-laden side-street bars and *meyhanes* (Turkish taverns).

The city's bohemian and student set tends to gravitate to the bars in Beyoğlu's Cihangir, Asmalımescit and Nevizade enclaves.

Tophane Nargile Cafes   CAFE
(Map p536; off Necatibey Caddesi, Tophane; ⊗24hr; ⊠Tophane) This atmospheric row of *nargile* cafes is always packed with locals enjoying tea, *nargile* and snacks. Follow your nose to find it – the smell of apple tobacco is incredibly enticing.

Mikla   BAR
(Map p536; www.miklarestaurant.com; Marmara Pera Hotel, Meşrutiyet Caddesi 15, Tepebaşı; ⊗from 6pm Mon-Sat summer only; ⊠Karaköy, then funicular to Tünel) It's worth overlooking the occasional uppity service at this stylish rooftop bar to enjoy one of the best views in İstanbul.

Leb-i Derya   BAR
(Map p536; www.lebiderya.com; 6th fl, Kumbaracı Yokuşu 57, Galata; ⊗4pm-2am Mon-Thu, to 3am Fri, 10am-3am Sat, to 2am Sun; ⊠Karaköy, then funicular to Tünel) On the top floor of a dishevelled building off İstiklal, Leb-i Derya has wonderful views across to the Old City and down the Bosphorus.

Litera   BAR
(Map p536; www.literarestaurant.com; 5th fl, Yeni Çarşı Caddesi 32, Galatasaray; ⊗11am-4am; ⊠Karaköy, then funicular to Tünel) Occupying the 5th floor of the handsome Goethe Institute building, Litera revels in its views and hosts plenty of cultural events.

360   BAR
(Map p536; www.360istanbul.com; 8th fl, İstiklal Caddesi 163; ⊗noon-2am Mon-Thu & Sun, 3pm-4am Fri & Sat; ⊠Karaköy, then funicular to Tünel) İstanbul's most famous bar, with an extraordinary view from the bar stools on the terrace. It morphs into a club after midnight on Friday and Saturday, when a cover charge of around TL40 applies.

NIGHTCLUBS, MUSIC & PERFORMANCE

MiniMüzikHol   CLUB, LIVE MUSIC
(MMH; Map p536; www.minimuzikhol.com; Soğancı Sokak 7, Cihangir; ⊗Wed-Sat 10pm-late; ⊠Kabataş,

TURKEY İSTANBUL

then funicular to Taksim) This small, slightly grungy venue hosts live sets by local and international musicians midweek and the best dance party in town on weekends. It's best after 1am.

Munzur Cafe & Bar   LIVE MUSIC
(Map p536; www.munzurcafebar.com; Hasnun Galip Sokak, Galatasaray; ⊙1pm-4am Tue-Sun, music from 9pm; 🚇Kabataş, then funicular to Taksim) The best of this street's *Türkü evleri*, Kurdish-owned bars where musicians perform live, emotion-charged *halk meziği* (folk music). Nearby **Toprak** (Map p536; 📞212-293 4037; www.toprakturkubar.tr.gg/ana-sayfa.htm; Hasnun Galip Sokak, Galatasaray; ⊙4pm-4am, show from 10pm) offers more of the same.

Galata Mevlevi Museum   PERFORMING ARTS
(Galata Mevlevihanesi Müzesi; Map p536; Galipdede Caddesi 15, Tünel; TL40; ⊙performances 4pm Sun; 🚇Karaköy, then funicular to Tünel) The 15th-century *semahane* (whirling-dervish hall) at this *tekke* (dervish lodge) is the venue for a *sema* (ceremony) held most Sundays. Tickets are only available on the day of the performance; head to the museum as early as possible to purchase tickets (the ticket office opens at 9am).

ℹ️ Information

Emergency
Tourist Police (📞212-527 4503; Yerebatan Caddesi 6) Across the street from the Basilica Cistern.

Medical Services
Private hospitals, such as the following, charge around TL200 for a standard consultation (credit card accepted).
Universal Taksim Alman Hastanesi (Universal German Hospital; 📞212-293 2150; www.uhg.com.tr; Sıraselviler Caddesi 119; ⊙8.30am-6pm Mon-Fri, to 5pm Sat) Has a 24 hour emergency clinic and English-speaking staff.

Money
Banks, ATMs and exchange offices are widespread, including next to Sultanahmet's Aya Sofya Meydanı, in the Grand Bazaar and along İstiklal Caddesi (Beyoğlu). The exchange rates offered at Atatürk International Airport are usually as good as those offered in town.

Telephone
İstanbul has two area codes: 📞212 for the European side, 📞216 for the Asian zone.

Tourist Information
None of İstanbul's offices are particularly helpful.
Tourist office (📞212-465 3451; International Arrivals Hall, Atatürk International Airport; ⊙9am-10pm)

ℹ️ Getting There & Away

AIR Atatürk International Airport (IST, Atatürk Havalımanı; 📞212-463 3000; www.ataturkairport.com) Located 23km west of Sultanahmet.
Sabiha Gökçen International Airport (SAW, Sabiha Gökçen Havalımanı; 📞216-588 8888; www.sgairport.com) Located 50km east of Sultanahmet, and popular with low-cost European airlines.

BOAT Yenikapı is the main dock for **İDO** (İstanbul Deniz Otobüsleri; 📞212-444 4436; www.ido.com.tr) car and passenger ferries across the Sea of Marmara to Yalova, Bursa and Bandırma (from where you can catch a train to İzmir or a bus to Çanakkale).

BUS The aptly titled **Büyük İstanbul Otogarı** (Big İstanbul Bus Station; 📞212-658 0505; www.otogaristanbul.com), 10km west of Sultanahmet, is the city's main *otogar* for intercity and international routes. Regular services from here include Ankara (TL38 to TL43, six hours), Bursa (TL25 to TL30, four hours) and Çanakkale (TL45, six hours).

» Many bus companies offer a *servis* (free shuttle bus) to/from the *otogar*.

» The metro stops here en route between Atatürk International Airport and Aksaray, where you can pick up a tram to Sultanahmet.

» Bus 830/910 leaves for Taksim Sq/Eminönü (one hour) every 15 to 25 minutes from 6am and 8.45pm.

» A taxi to Sultanahmet/Taksim Sq costs around TL30/35 (30 minutes).

» If you're arriving from Anatolia, rather than travelling all the way to the Büyük İstanbul Otogarı, it's quicker to get out at the smaller **Harem Otogar** (📞216-333 3763) on the Asian shore, and take the ferry to Sirkeci/Eminönü.

TRAIN The daily Bosphorus/Balkan Express links İstanbul with Bucharest, Sofia and Belgrade (see p605).

Services to/from destinations in Anatolia have been severely curtailed by work on the line to/from Ankara. When this reopens in 2014 or 2015, it will feature high-speed trains that will depart from a new railway hub in Üsküdar, on the Asian shore.

ℹ️ Getting Around

Tickets on public transport in İstanbul generally cost TL2.

DANGERS & ANNOYANCES

İstanbul is no more nor less safe than any large metropolis, but are there some dangers worth highlighting. (See also p603.)

» Some İstanbullus drive like rally drivers, and there is no such thing as a generally acknowledged right of way for pedestrians.

» Bag-snatchings and muggings occasionally occur on Beyoğlu's side streets.

» In Sultanahmet, if a shoe cleaner drops his brush, don't pick it up. He will insist on giving you a 'free' clean in return, before demanding an extortionate fee.

» There has been a recent police crackdown on gay venues in the city, especially *hamams* (Turkish baths) and saunas.

» Males travelling alone or in pairs should be wary of being adopted by a friendly local who is keen to take them to a club for a few drinks – many such encounters end up at *pavyons*, sleazy nightclubs run by the mafia where a drink or two with a female hostess will end up costing hundreds – sometimes thousands – of euros. If you don't pay up, the consequences can be violent.

» The PKK (Kurdistan Workers Party) and other terrorist groups sporadically target İstanbul with bombings, normally aimed at affluent, touristy neighbourhoods. In October 2010 a Kurdish suicide bomber injured 32 people on Taksim Sq.

TO/FROM THE AIRPORT

Havataş (Havaş) Airport Bus (www.havas.net) Travels between the airports and Cumhuriyet Caddesi, just off Taksim Sq. Buses leave Atatürk (TL10, one hour) every 30 minutes between 4am and 1am, and Sabiha Gökçen (TL12, 1½ hours) between 5am and midnight, thereafter 30 minutes after flight arrivals.

Metro From Atatürk to Zeytinburnu, where you can connect with the tram to Sultanahmet (total TL4, one hour).

Shuttle Many hotels will provide a free pick-up service from Atatürk airport if you stay with them for three nights or more.

Taxi From Atatürk/Sabiha Gökçen to Sultanahmet should cost around TL40/120.

BUS İstanbul's efficient bus system runs between 6.30am and 11.30pm. You must have a ticket before boarding; buy tickets from the white booths at major stops or, for a small mark-up, from some nearby shops (look for 'İETT *otobüs bileti satılır*' signs).

FUNICULAR RAILWAY The 19th-century Tünel climbs the hill from Karaköy (near the tram stop) to the bottom of İstiklal Caddesi (every 10 minutes from 7.30am to 9pm). A funicular railway also climbs from the Bosphorus shore at Kabataş (near the tram stop) to the metro station at Taksim Sq.

METRO Connects Aksaray with the airport, stopping at 15 stations, including the *otogar*, along the way. Services depart every 10 minutes or so between 5.40am and 1.40am.

TAXI İstanbul is full of yellow taxis, all of them with meters; do not let drivers insist on a fixed rate. From Sultanahmet to Taksim Sq costs around TL15.

TRAM A *tramvay* (tramway) service runs between Zeytinburnu (where it connects with the metro to/from the airport) and Kabataş via Aksaray, Sultanahmet, Eminönü and Karaköy. Trams run every five minutes or so from 6am to midnight.

A quaint antique tram rattles up and down İstiklal Caddesi in Beyoğlu, from the Tünel station to Taksim Sq via Galatasaray Lycée.

AROUND İSTANBUL

Since İstanbul is such a vast city, few places are within easy reach on a day trip. If you make an early start, however, it's just possible to see the sights of Edirne in Thrace (Trakya), the only bit of Turkey that is geographically within Europe. Ferries cross the Sea of Marmara to Bursa, although it's better to overnight there.

Edirne

☎0284 / POP 144,531

European Turkey's largest settlement outside İstanbul, Edirne was the Ottoman capital before Constantinople (İstanbul), and many of its key buildings are in excellent shape. You can enjoy mosques as fine as almost any in İstanbul – without the crowds. With Greece and Bulgaria a half-hour's drive away, Edirne is also a bustling border town.

⊙ Sights

Selimiye Camii
MOSQUE

(Selimiye Mosque; Mimar Sinan Caddesi) Great Ottoman architect Mimar Sinan designed Edirne's grandest mosque (1569–75), and it is said that he considered it his finest work. Lit up at night, the complex is a spectacular sight, with four 71m-high minarets and a broad, lofty dome – marginally wider than that of İstanbul's Aya Sofya.

Eski Cami
MOSQUE

The 15th-century Old Mosque exemplifies one of the two classic mosque styles used by the Ottomans in their earlier capital, Bursa. Like Bursa's Ulu Cami, the Eski Cami has rows of arches and pillars supporting a series of small domes.

Üç Şerefeli Cami
MOSQUE

With its four strikingly different minarets, the 15th-century Üç Şerefeli Cami dominates Hürriyet Meydanı (Freedom Sq). Its name refers to the three balconies on the tallest minaret, and its design is halfway between Konya and Bursa's Seljuk Turkish-style mosques and the truly Ottoman style.

Museum of Health
MUSEUM

(Sağlık Müzesi; admission TL5; ⊙9am-5.30pm) Part of the Bayezid II mosque complex, north of the centre by the Tunca River, this museum illustrates the therapy and teaching that took place here. One of the most important Ottoman hospitals, it operated from 1488 to 1909, and music therapy was employed from 1652.

🛏 Sleeping & Eating

There's an assortment of eateries along Saraçlar and Maarif Caddesis. The riverside restaurants south of the centre are more atmospheric, but most open only in summer and are booked solid at weekends.

Efe Hotel
BOUTIQUE HOTEL €€

(☑213 6166; www.efehotel.com; Maarif Caddesi 13; s/d TL100/150; ❀@) The off-red Efe stands out for its atmospheric, archival lobby with tartan carpets and polished wood. There's an English pub open outside the summer months and a decent bar-restaurant called Patio.

Selimiye Taşodalar
BOUTIQUE HOTEL €€€

(☑212 3529; www.tasodalar.com.tr; Selimiye Arkası Hamam Sokak 3; s/d from TL160/210; ❀@) Next to Selimiye Camii and the 14th-century Sultan Selim Saray Hamam, the shared spaces

---

OIL WRESTLING

One of the world's oldest and most bizarre sporting events takes place annually in late June/early July at Sarayiçi in northern Edirne. At the 650-year-old **Tarihi Kırkpınar Yağlı Güreş Festivali** (Historic Kırpınar Oil Wrestling Festival), muscular men, naked bar a pair of heavy leather shorts, coat themselves with olive oil and throw each other around. For more information, visit **Kırpınar Evi** (Kırpınar House; ☑212 8622; www.kirkpinar.com; ⊙10am-noon & 2-6pm) in Edirne or www.turkish-wrestling.com.

---

of this 15th-century Ottoman house have an air of elegance, although the dusty kitsch in the rooms disappoints. The tea garden is pleasant and shady.

Grand Altunhan Hotel
HOTEL €€

(☑213 2200; www.altunhanhotel.com; Saraçalar Caddesi; s/d TL80/130) Located on a popular shopping strip, this friendly midrange hotel's rooms are modern, with flat-screen TVs, colourful furniture and brightly tiled bathrooms.

Melek Anne
CAFE €

('Angel' Anne's; ☑213 3263; Maarif Caddesi 18; mains TL7; ☑) Popular with students and foodies, 'Angel' Anne's occupies a 120-year-old house with a spacious courtyard. The rotating menu of homemade dishes includes unusual salads and hearty vegetarian choices.

ⓘ Getting There & Away

For the Bulgarian border crossing at Kapıkule, catch a *dolmuş* (minibus that follows a prescribed route; TL5, 25 minutes) from opposite the tourist office on Talat Paşa Caddesi. For the Greek border post at Pazarkule, catch a *dolmuş* (TL1, 20 minutes) from outside the tourist office on Maarif Caddesi.

Edirne's *otogar* is 9km southeast of the centre. There are regular buses to Çanakkale (TL30, four hours) and İstanbul (TL12, 2½ hours).

Bursa

☑0224 / POP 1.7 MILLION

The first capital of the Ottoman Empire, today Bursa mixes traditional Turkish flavour with modern vitality. Allow at least a day to take in the ancient mosques, tombs and market. The thermal springs in the villagelike suburb of Çekirge, 3km west of central Bursa, are the perfect salve after exploring the city.

The city centre is along Atatürk Caddesi, between the Ulu Camii and, to the east, the main square, Cumhuriyet Alanı, commonly called Heykel.

◉ Sights & Activities

Yeşil Camii
MOSQUE

(Green Mosque; Yeşil Caddesi) Built for Mehmet I, this 15th-century mosque represents a departure from the previous, Persian-influenced Seljuk architecture. Exemplifying Ottoman stylings, the mosque was named for the interior wall's greenish-blue tiles – fragments of a few original frescos remain.

Ulu Camii
MOSQUE

(Atatürk Caddesi) This enormous Seljuk-style shrine (1396) is Bursa's most dominant and durable mosque. Having pledged to build 20 mosques after defeating the Crusaders in the Battle of Nicopolis, Sultan Beyazıt I settled for one mosque, with 20 small domes. Behind Ulu Camii is the sprawling Kapalı Çarşı (Covered Market; Kapalı Çarşı Caddesi).

Bursa Citadel
CASTLE

(Osman Gazi ve Orhan Gazi Türbeleri; admission by donation) Some ramparts and walls still survive on the steep cliff, the site of Bursa's citadel and oldest neighbourhood. From Ulu Cami, walk west and up Orhan Gazi (Yiğitler) Caddesi. On the summit, a park contains the Tombs of Sultans Osman and Orhan (Osman Gazi ve Orhan Gazi Türbeleri; Timurtaş Paşa Park; admission by donation), the Ottoman Empire's founders. The six-storey clock tower adjoins a tea garden overlooking the valley.

Uludağ
NATURE RESERVE

Whether it's winter or summer, it's worth taking a cable-car ride up the Great Mountain (2543m) to take advantage of the views and the cool, clear air of Uludağ National Park. As well as one of Turkey's most popular ski resorts (the season runs from December to early April), the park offers pine forests and snowy peaks. Hiking to the summit of Uludağ takes three hours. To get to the teleferik (cable car; return TL8) from Bursa, take a city bus from stop 1 or a *dolmuş* from behind the City Museum (Kent Müzesi).

🛌 Sleeping

There are a few decent options in Bursa, mostly business hotels. Consider Çekirge, which has tranquil hotels for some R&R; prices can be higher, but generally include the use of the mineral baths.

Kitap Evi
BOUTIQUE HOTEL €€

(Book House; ☎225 4160; www.kitapevi.com.tr; cnr Kavaklı Mahallesi & Burç Üstü 21; s/d/ste €100/140/230; ❄@) 'The Book House', a former Ottoman house and bookstore, draws an artistically inclined clientele with its eclectic decor. The 12 rooms each have their own style, while well-polished wood fixtures and touches like artwork and stained glass complement the bookshelves and empty leather suitcases. The restaurant is excellent.

Hotel Gönlüferah
LUXURY HOTEL €€

(☎233 9210; www.gonluferah.com; Murat Caddesi; s/d €90/120; ❄@❄🏊) Dating from 1890 and a hotel since the early 20th century, Çekirge's hilltop Gönlüferah combines old-world charm with modern luxuries such as spa packages and an opulent bar. Day-use spa packages (TL30 per person) are available for nonguests too.

Safran Otel
PENSION €€

(☎224 7216; www.safranotel.com; Orta Pazar Caddesi; s/d TL90/150; ❄🏊) The Safran occupies an elegant restored Ottoman house near the Osman and Orhan tombs, in a historic district. Rooms are modern, spacious and well lit (with a hint of the Ottoman retained in the distinctive carpets).

Otel Güneş
HOSTEL €

(☎222 1404; İnebey Caddesi 75; s/d TL35/50) The Güneş has seen better days but remains the only true budget accommodation in Bursa's centre. Rooms are small but clean (choose between those with regular and 'Turkish traditional' toilets).

🍴 Eating & Drinking

Arap Şükrü
SEAFOOD €€

(Sakarya Caddesi; meze TL7-20; ⏰lunch & dinner) Situated in a cobblestoned lane in the former Jewish quarter, a 10-minute walk from Ulu Cami, this historic restaurant serves fresh seafood meze and mains. Similar restaurants line the same street, regaled by accordion-wielding Roma bands. After eating, have a drink at nearby 'photography cafe' Gren (☎223 6064; www.grencafe.com; Sakarya Caddesi 46), with exhibitions and antique-camera decor.

Kebapçı İskender
KEBAP €€

(Ünlü Caddesi 7; iskender kebap TL18; ⏰lunch & dinner) This famous refuge for serious carnivores is where the legendary *İskender kebap* – *döner* lamb on crumbled pide and yoghurt, topped with tomato and burnt butter sauces – was created in 1867. This is the main branch of the local chain.

Cafe My Kitchen   INTERNATIONAL €€
(234 6200; Çekirge Caddesi 114; pizzas TL11-18, mains TL17-24; ☺lunch & dinner; ☎) This 'international' restaurant, fashionable among up-and-coming young Bursans, is somewhat upscale, serving excellent pastas and salads. The wine bar's also good for a drink.

Mahfel Mado   RESTAURANT, BAR €
(Namazgah Caddesi 2; mains TL5-10; ☺breakfast, lunch & dinner) Bursa's oldest cafe is known for its *dondurma* (ice cream), and has a nice, shady ravine setting.

ℹ Information

Post office, payphones and ATMs are on Atatürk Caddesi; for exchange offices visit the Covered Market.

Tourist Office (☺9am-5pm Mon-Fri, to 6pm Sat) Beneath Atatürk Caddesi, in the shop row at the pedestrian subway Orhan Gazi Alt Geçidi's northern entrance.

ℹ Getting There & Around

Bursa's *otogar* is 10km north of the centre; take bus 38 (TL3, 45 minutes) from stop 4 on Atatürk Caddesi or a taxi (TL25 to TL30).

For İstanbul (TL24), *karayolu ile* (by road) buses drag you around the Bay of İzmit (four to five hours); better *feribot ile* (by ferry) buses go to Topçular, east of Yalova, and then by ferry to Eskihisar near İstanbul (three hours).

The fastest route to İstanbul is the metro-bus combo to Mudanya (take Bursa's metro to the final stop, then continue by public bus), then an İDO ferry (www.ido.com.tr) across the Sea of Marmara to Yenikapı. Alternatively, take a bus to Yalova (TL9, 1¼ hours, half hourly), then a ferry to Yenikapı (TL24). Catch a bus leaving Bursa's otogar at least 90 minutes before the scheduled boat departure. On both routes, to travel on a weekend or public holiday, purchase your ferry ticket in advance.

A *dolmuş* (in Bursa, these are cars as well as minibuses) to Çekirge from the terminal immediately south of Heykel costs TL2; a taxi is TL10.

THE AEGEAN COAST

Turkey's Aegean coast can convincingly claim more ancient ruins per square kilometre than any other region in the world.

Since time immemorial, conquerors, traders and travellers have beaten a path to the mighty monuments, and few leave disappointed.

Gallipoli (Gelibolu) Peninsula

☎0286

Antipodeans and many Brits won't need an introduction to Gallipoli; it's the backbone of the 'Anzac legend', in which an Allied campaign in 1915 to knock Turkey out of WWI and open a relief route to Russia turned into one of the war's greatest fiascos. Some 130,000 men died, roughly a third from Allied forces and the rest Turkish.

Today the Gallipoli battlefields are peaceful places, covered in brush and pine forests. But the battles fought here nearly a century ago are still alive in many memories, both Turkish and foreign, especially Australians and New Zealanders, who view the peninsula as a place of pilgrimage. The Turkish officer responsible for the defence of Gallipoli was Mustafa Kemal (the future Atatürk); his victory is commemorated in Turkey on 18 March. On Anzac Day (25 April), a dawn service marks the anniversary of the Allied landings.

The easiest way to see the battlefields is with your own transport or an afternoon minibus tour from nearby Eceabat/Çanakkale (typically TL60/90) with Crowded House Tours (☎814 1565; www.crowdedhousegallipoli.com; Eceabat) or Hassle Free Travel Agency (☎213 5969; www.anzachouse.com; Çanakkale). With a tour you get the benefit of a guide who can explain the battles as you go along.

Most people use Çanakkale or, on the Thracian (European) side of the strait, Eceabat as a base. From Eceabat, take a *dolmuş* (TL2.50) or taxi to the Kabatepe Information Centre & Museum, 750m from the bottom of the road up to the main battlefields.

Crowded House offers one- and two-day packages starting in İstanbul.

Eceabat (Maydos)

☎0286 / POP 5300

Eceabat is a small waterfront town with the best access to the main Gallipoli battlefields. Ferries dock by the main square, Cumhuriyet Meydanı, which has hotels, restaurants, ATMs, a post office,

Aegean Coast

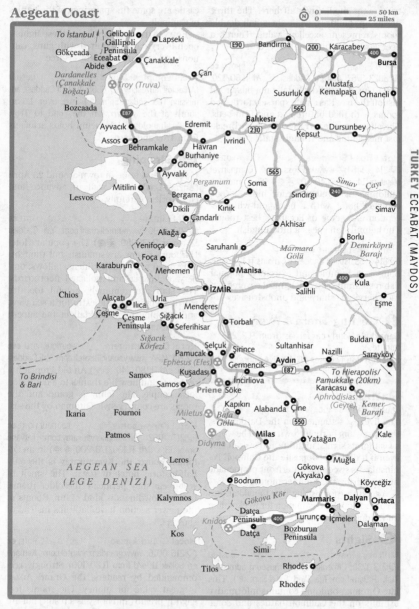

bus-company offices, *dolmuş* stands and taxis. Like most of the peninsula, Eceabat is swamped with students and tour groups at weekends from 18 March to mid-June and in late September.

🛏 Sleeping & Eating

TOP CHOICE **Hotel Crowded House** HOSTEL €
(📞814 1565; www.crowdedhousegallipoli.com; Hüseyin Avni Sokak 4; dm/s/d TL20/50/65; ❄@)
Guests of all budgets and persuasions will find real comfort, professionalism and a

truly accommodating staff here. The three dorms are faultless, while the small double rooms represent excellent value. There's a beer garden for summer barbecues.

Hotel Ejder   HOTEL €€

(☑8023 8757; Ataturk Caddesi 5; s/d TL60/120; ℗🐾) This new yellow hotel, on a busy road just off the bay, has small, sparsely furnished rooms with tiled bathrooms and firm beds. The pluses are the terrace views, huge breakfast mezzanine and friendly staff.

Hotel Boss Business   HOTEL €

(☑814 1464; www.heyboss.com; Cumhuriyet Meydanı 14; s/d TL40/70; ❄@) This narrow building's pale yellow facade hides a cool, compact hotel, with a black-and-white reception and some of Eceabat's best rooms. The helpful staff speak a little English.

Liman Restaurant   SEAFOOD €€

(☑814 2755; İstiklal Caddesi 67; mains TL12) 'Harbour' is a humble and extremely popular fish restaurant with a delightful covered terrace. Service is sharp and unobstrusive.

❶ Getting There & Away

Çanakkale Hourly car ferries (from TL2, 25 minutes).

İstanbul Hourly buses (TL40, five hours).

Çanakkale

☑0286 / POP 104,400

The liveliest settlement on the Dardanelles, this sprawling harbour town would be worth a visit for its sights, nightlife and overall vibe even if it didn't lie opposite the Gallipoli Peninsula. Its sweeping waterfront promenade heaves during the summer months.

A good base for visiting Troy, Çanakkale has become a popular destination for weekending Turks; during summer, try to visit midweek.

❍ Sights

Military Museum   MUSEUM

(☑213 1730; Çimenlik Sokak; museum admission TL4; ⊙9am-5pm Tue, Wed & Fri-Sun; ℗) This late-Ottoman building contains informative exhibits on the Gallipoli battles and some war relics, including fused bullets that hit each other in mid-air. Also here is a replica of the **Nusrat minelayer** (Nusrat Mayın Gemisi), which sank or crippled three Allied ships, and the impressive 15th-century **Çimenlik Kalesi** (Meadow Castle). Inside the

castle are some fine paintings of the battles of Gallipoli.

Entry to the park containing these sights – open every day and dotted with guns, cannons and military artefacts – is free.

Archaeological Museum   MUSEUM

(Arkeoloji Müzesi; ☑217 6565; 100 Yil Caddesi; admission TL5; ⊙8am-5pm; ℗) Just over 1.5km south of the *otogar,* on the road to Troy, the Archaeological Museum holds artefacts from Troy and Assos.

🛌 Sleeping

If you intend to be in town around 25 April (Anzac Day), book well in advance and check prices carefully.

Hotel Limani   HOTEL €€

(☑217 4090; www.hotellimani.com; Yalı Caddesi 12; rooms TL130-180; ❄@) The popular Hotel Harbour's rooms are smallish, but thoughtfully fitted with quality linens, pillows, drapery, wallpaper and polished floorboards. The staff are genuinely helpful too. It's worth spending a little extra for a sea view, and stopping for a cocktail in the superb lobby restaurant.

Hotel Des Etrangers   BOUTIQUE HOTEL €€€

(☑214 2424; www.yabancilaroteli.com; Yali Caddesi 25-27; s/d TL180/240; ❄🐾) An old French hotel has found new life thanks to a dedicated local couple. The lobby is grand and the rooms are country-style Ottoman by the sea.

Hotel Kervansaray   BOUTIQUE HOTEL €€

(☑217 8192; www.otelkervansaray.com; Fetvane Sokak 13; s/d/tr TL100/170/200; ❄@) In an Ottoman house, the Kervansaray is the only half-historic hotel in town. The smell of yesteryear may permeate the older rooms, but the dowdiness is kind of fun. Rooms in the newer section have bathtubs instead of showers.

Hotel Grand Anzac   HOTEL €€

(☑216 0016; www.grandanzachotel.com; Kemalyeri Sokak 11; s/d from TL80/100) Strongly recommended by readers, the Grand Anzac is great value for money. The rooms feel slightly prefab (and noisy as a result) but are bright and spacious. Service and location are both excellent.

Anzac House Hostel   HOSTEL €

(☑213 5969; www.anzachouse.com; Cumhuriyet Meydanı 59; dm/s/d without bathroom & excl breakfast TL20/30/45; @) The base of **Hassle Free Travel Agency** (☑213 5969; Cumhuriyet Meydanı

61) is Çanakkale's only genuine backpackers. The bright colours and friendly staff go some way to alleviate the cramped confines.

Eating & Drinking

Licensed restaurants line the waterfront, where stalls also offer corn on the cob, mussels and other simple items. Head to Fetvane and buzzing, pedestrianised Matbaa Sokaks for bars.

Yalova   SEAFOOD €€
(☏217 1045; www.yalovarestaurant.com; Gümrük Sokak 7; mains TL15-20) Yalova is a pure seafood restaurant that combines impeccable service with the best produce and preparation in Çanakkale. Ask for a tour of the 2nd floor, where you can select your own fish. Wine is matched to order.

Cafe du Port   RESTAURANT €€
(☏217 2908; Yalı Caddesi 12; ☻8am-11pm) Stylish and inviting, Hotel Limani's popular restaurant occupies a glass-fronted building on the *kordon* (seafront), with Çanakkale's most versatile chefs and good service. Specialities include steaks, salads, pastas and superb cocktails.

Benzin   BAR, CAFE
(Eski Balıkhane Sokak 11; ☏) This grungy waterfront bar-cafe, done out in 1960s decor, is a relaxing spot for a drink and a bite (pizzas TL8 to TL12.50). Heaves at weekends.

Time Out   LIVE MUSIC
(Kayserili Ahmet Paşa Caddesi; beer TL6) A rock club of the stylish (rather than dingy) variety, with pictures of Elvis et al, and outside tables.

ℹ Information

The **tourist office** (☏217 1187; Cumhuriyet Meydanı; ☻8.30am-5.30pm) is 150m from the ferry pier, and you can access the internet at **Araz Internet** (Fetvane Sokak 21; per hr TL1.50; ☻9am-midnight).

ℹ Getting There & Away

BUS Ayvalık TL25, 3½ hours, hourly
Bandırma TL20, 2½ hours, hourly
İstanbul TL35, six hours, frequent
İzmir TL35, 5½ hours, hourly
FERRY Eceabat Car ferries (from TL3, 15 minutes, several daily).

Behramkale & Assos

☏0286

Behramkale is an old hilltop Greek village spread out around the ruins of the 6th-century-BC Ionic **Temple of Athena** (☏217 6740; admission TL8; ☻8am-7.30pm), which has spectacular views of Lesvos and the dazzling Aegean. Next to the temple ticket booth, the 14th-century **Hüdavendigar Camii** is a simple, early-Ottoman mosque.

Just before the entrance to the village, a road winds down the steep hill to Assos, the ideal place to unwind over a glass of *çay*. Overlooking the picture-perfect harbour, the old stone buildings have been transformed into hotels and fish restaurants.

Try to avoid visiting on weekends and public holidays from the beginning of April to the end of August, when tourists pour in by the coachload.

WORTH A TRIP

TROY (TRUVA)

Of all the ancient centres in Turkey, the remains of the great city of Troy are in fact among the least impressive; you'll have to use your imagination. Still, for history buffs and fans of Homer's *Iliad*, it's an important site to tick off the list, and a new national archaeological and history museum is set to open here by 2015.

Approaching the ruins of Troy from the ticket booth, the first thing you see is a reconstruction of the Trojan Horse. The site is rather confusing for nonexpert eyes (guides are available), but the most conspicuous features include the **walls** from various periods; **megarons** (houses inhabited by the elite); and the Roman **Odeon**, where concerts were held.

The travel agencies offering Gallipoli tours also offer morning trips to Troy (around TL60 per person).

From Çanakkale, *dolmuşes* to Troy (TL4, 35 minutes, 9.30am to 4.30/7pm winter/ summer) leave on the half hour (less frequently at weekends) from a station at the northern end of the bridge over the Sarı River. Returning, *dolmuşes* leave on the hour (7am to 3pm/5pm winter/summer).

🛏 Sleeping

BEHRAMKALE

TOP CHOICE ⬦ Assos Alarga   BOUTIQUE HOTEL €€€
(☑721 7260; www.assosalarga.com; Berhamkale 88; r from TL200; P❄🍴📶🏊) Located in the quiet end of the village, just behind the temple ruins, Alarga may only have three rooms, but this ensures stellar service. All rooms have amazing views over the mountains and very cool bathrooms. There's a deluxe outdoor pool, garden, sauna and pool table.

Eris Pansiyon   PENSION €€
(☑721 7080; www.erispansiyon.com; s/d incl afternoon tea TL70/120) This guesthouse has three pleasant, peaceful rooms; those facing the sea are less impressive inside. Afternoon tea is served on a terrace with spectacular views over the hills. Call ahead out of season.

Dolunay Pansiyon   PENSION €€
(☑721 7172; s/d TL50/100; ❄) In the centre of the village on the main square, this basic, family-run place has six spotless rooms. You can have breakfast on the pretty terrace with sea views.

ASSOS

In high season most hotels here insist on *yarım pansiyon* (half board), though you could try negotiating.

Hotel Kervansaray   HOTEL €€€
(☑721 7093; www.assoskervansaray.com; s/d with sea view TL140/180; ❄🏊) A 19th-century acorn store, the Kervansaray is pretty good value in its newer 'Butik' section, although the restaurant's popularity can detract from the guest experience. The outdoor pool almost laps into the sea.

Yıldız Saray Hotel   PENSION €€
(☑721 7025; www.yildizsaray-hotels.com; s/d/f TL100/140/220; ❄) The Star Palace is drifting into postretro territory in its tired decor, but it's friendly, the upstairs terrace is sublime and the family apartment is good value. Breakfast is served on a floating platform.

Dr. No Antik Pansiyon   PENSION €
(☑721 7397; www.assosdrnoantikpansiyon.com; s/d TL40/80; ❄) This simple, friendly pension, with cramped rooms and a pleasant outdoor area, is the best budget option near the sea.

🍴 Eating

Proximity to the sea accounts for higher prices at the harbour. Be sure to check the cost of fish and bottles of wine before ordering.

Ehl-i Keyf   TURKISH €
(☑721 7106; www.assosehlikeyf.com.tr; gozleme TL5; 📶) This multilevel restaurant in Behramkale combines fresh food with attentive service and a pleasant outlook. Choose from a long menu of *izgara* (grills), *gozleme* (thin savoury crepes), cocktails, coffee and ice cream amid flowering plants.

Uzunev   SEAFOOD €€
(☑721 7007; mains TL15-20; ◷lunch & dinner) The pick of the nonhotel restaurants in Assos, Uzunev garners a lively crowd, especially on high-season weekends. Try the speciality, sea bass à l'Aristotle (steamed in a special stock), or the delicious seafood meze (TL10).

❶ Getting There & Away

Behramkale Regular buses run from Çanakkale to Ayvacık (TL12, 1½ hours), where you can pick up a *dolmuş* to Behramkale (TL3, 20 minutes). In low season the *dolmuşes* run less frequently; a taxi from Ayvacık costs around TL30.

Assos Some *dolmuşes* continue to Assos. In summer there's a half-hourly shuttle service between the villages (TL1). In winter *dolmuşes* occasionally link the two (TL8).

Ayvalık

🖉0266 / POP 37,200

Back from the palm trees and fish restaurants on Ayvalık's waterfront, the tumble-down old Greek village is a kind of outdoor museum. Horses and carts clatter down narrow streets, past headscarf-wearing women holding court outside picturesque shuttered houses.

Olive-oil production is the traditional business here, and the town is a gateway to local islands and the Greek isle of Lesvos.

Offshore is **Alibey Island** (known locally as Cunda), which is lined with open-air fish restaurants and linked to the mainland by ferries (June to early September) and a causeway. Summer **cruises** (TL50 per person including lunch) include it in their day tours of the bay's islands, leaving Ayvalık around 11am and stopping here and there for sunbathing and swimming.

🛏 Sleeping & Eating

Istanbul Pansiyon   PENSION €
(☑312 4001; www.istanbulpansiyonayvalik.com; Neşe Sokak Aralığı 4; s/d TL35/70; P❄📶) This lovely pension's blue and pink exterior gives way to six spacious rooms. Breakfast is a delight in the lush garden.

Kelebek Pension
PENSION €€

(☑312 3908; www.kelebek-pension.com; Mareşal Çakmak Caddesi 108; s/d/tr TL60/100/135; 🐾) In this colourful seven-room pension, you can see the sea from your bedroom. The white-and-blue building has a terrace for having breakfast in the fresh air.

Balıkçı
SEAFOOD €€

(☑312 9099; Balıkhane Sokak 7; mains TL17; ☉dinner) Run by a local fishing association, this is a fine place to sample seafood and settle into the tiled terrace, or sit inside for a better view of the Turkish troubadours.

Tarlakusu Gurmeko
CAFE €€

(☑312 3312; Cumhuriyet Caddesi 53; ☉8.30am-8.30pm; 🕾) This artsy coffee house serves top-notch brews. Nibbles include cookies, brownies, soup, salads, cheese plates and *börek* (TL4.50).

ℹ Information

In high season, an information **kiosk** (☉Jun-Sep) opens on the waterfront south of the main square.

ℹ Getting There & Away

BUS & DOLMUŞ The *otogar* is 1.7km northeast of the centre.

Alibey Island *Dolmuş* taxis (white with red stripes) run from the south side of Ayvalık main square (TL2, 20 minutes).

Bergama (TL7, 1¾ hours, hourly) Jump on a Bergama-bound bus at the main square.

Çanakkale (TL15, 3¼ hours, five a day) Smaller companies may drop you on the main highway outside Ayvalık. Larger companies, such as Ulusoy, provide a *servis* to the centre.

İzmir (TL16, three hours, hourly)

BOAT **Alibey Island** (TL4; 15 minutes; every 15 minutes) From a quay behind the tourist kiosk just off Ayvalık main square.

Lesvos (one way/return €60/70, 1½ hours) Daily except Sunday between May and September, with three boats a week from October to May. Advance reservations are essential; contact **Jale Tour** (☑331 3170; www.jaletour.com; Yeni Liman Karsisi).

Bergama (Pergamum)

☑0232 / POP 60,600

As Selçuk is to Ephesus, so Bergama is to Pergamum: the workaday market town has become a stop on the tourist trail because of its proximity to the remarkable ruins of Pergamum, site of ancient Rome's pre-eminent medical centre. During Pergamum's heyday (between Alexander the Great and the Roman domination of Asia Minor) it was one of the Middle East's richest and most powerful small kingdoms.

◉ Sights

A **cable car** (one way TL4) ascends to the Acropolis. A taxi from the centre to the Asclepion/Acropolis is TL8/15. A taxi tour, including waiting time at the Asclepion, Red Basilica and Acropolis, costs around TL50.

Asclepion
RUIN

(Temple of Asclepios; admission/parking TL15/3) Treatments at this anvient medical centre included mud baths, the use of herbs and ointments, enemas and sunbathing. Diagnosis was often by dream analysis. The centre came to the fore under the great early physician Galen (AD 131–210), whose work was the basis for Western medicine well into the 16th century.

The Asclepion is 2km uphill from the town centre as the crow flies (but it's a winding road), signposted from Cumhuriyet Caddesi just north of the tourist office. Walk down the Roman **bazaar street**, to ruins including the circular **Temple of Asclepios**, **library**, **Roman theatre**, **sacred well** and, accessed along a vaulted underground corridor, the **Temple of Telesphorus**.

Acropolis
RUIN

(Akropol; admission TL20) The road to the acropolis winds 5km uphill from the Red Basilica. At the top, the magnificent ruins include the **library**, the marble-columned **Temple of Trajan**, and the vertigo-inducing, 10,000-seat **theatre**. Impressive and unusual, the theatre is built into the hillside.

To escape the crowds and get a good view of the theatre and Temple of Trajan, walk downhill behind the **Altar of Zeus**, or turn left at the bottom of the theatre steps, and follow the sign to the *antik yol* (antique street). Ruins sprawl down the hill and you can follow this route to walk back to the Red Basilica.

Red Basilica
RUIN

(Kınık Caddesi; admission TL5) The cathedral-sized Red Basilica was originally a giant temple to the Egyptian gods Serapis, Isis and Harpocrates, built in the 2nd century AD. The building is so big that the Christians didn't convert it into a church but built a basilica inside it.

Sleeping

Hera Boutique Hotel
BOUTIQUE HOTEL €€€

(☏631 0634; www.hotelhera.com; Tabrak Körpü Caddesi 21; d from TL200; P☀☎) These two 200-year-old Greek houses have 10 rooms with timber ceilings, parquetry floors and curios handpicked by the erudite couple in charge. The breakfast spread is highly recommended.

Odyssey Guesthouse
PENSION €

(☏631 3501; www.odysseyguesthouse.com; Abacıhan Sokak 13; s/d from TL45/50, without bathroom from TL35/45) This grand old house has superb views of the Red Basilica from the upstairs terrace. The main building has some basic doubles, with excellent showers, and self-caterers can enjoy the small kitchenette.

Citi Hostel
HOSTEL €

(☏830 0668; Bankalar Caddesi 10; s/d/t TL35/60/80; ☀☎) Beside the *hamam,* this great new hostel run by the friendly Imdat, a Turkish-Australian chap. Basic, spotless rooms on two levels encircle a spacious courtyard.

Eating

Kervan
FAMILY RESTAURANT €€

(☏633 2632; İzmir Caddesi; mains TL12; ☀) Popular locally for its large outdoor terrace and excellent food, Kervan's menu features a good range of kebaps, pide and *çorba* (soup). It's cheap but prices are not listed.

Bergama Ticaret Odası
Sosyal Tesisleri
RESTAURANT €€

(☏632 9641; Ulucamii Mahallesi; mains TL15; ☺9am-midnight) This licensed restaurant's outdoor terrace and cafeteria-style interior offer panoramic views and reasonable food. It's in a park 300m up the hill behind the main street. Avoid walking in the area at night.

Information

The elongated main street (İzmir/Cumhuriyet/Bankalar Caddesi) is where you'll find banks, ATMs and the post office. The **tourist office** (☏631 2851; İzmir Caddesi 54; ☺8.30am-noon & 1-5.30pm) is north of the museum.

Getting There & Away

Between 6am and 7pm, a *servis* shuttles between Bergama's new *otogar* (7km from the centre, at the junction of the highway and the main road into town) and the central old *otogar*. A taxi costs about TL25.

Ayvalık TL8, 1¼ hours, hourly

İzmir TL10, two hours, every 45 minutes

İzmir

☏0232 / POP 2.8 MILLION

The grand port of İzmir, Turkey's third-largest city, is a proudly liberal, long-time centre of commerce that has emerged as a smart alternative base for travel in the west of the country. Formerly the famed Greek city of Smyrna, İzmir lives by its *kordon* and, especially around leafy Alsancak, is as fetching and lively as any large seaside city in the world.

Sights

Kordon & Alsancak
SEAFRONT, NEIGHBOURHOOD

A triumph of urban renewal, the pedestrianised *kordon* is home to a great selection of bars and restaurants for watching the picture-perfect sunsets.

Konak Meydanı
SQUARE

On a pedestrianised stretch of Cumhuriyet Bulvarı, this wide plaza, named after the Ottoman government mansion (*hükümet konağı*), pretty much marks the heart of the city. The ornate Oriental style of the late Ottoman clock tower (*saat kulesi*) may have been meant to atone for Smyrna's European ambience. Beside it is the lovely, tile-covered **Konak Camii** (1755).

Agora
RUIN

(Agora Caddesi; admission TL8; ☺8.30am-7pm, to 5.30pm Sat; P) The ancient Agora, built for Alexander the Great, was ruined in an earthquake in AD 178, but rebuilt soon after by the Romans. Colonnades of reconstructed Corinthian columns, vaulted chambers and arches give a good idea of what a Roman bazaar must have looked like.

Kemeraltı Bazaar
BAZAAR

(☺8am-5pm) A great place to get lost for a few hours, with bargains galore, especially leather goods, clothing and jewellery. Within the main bazaar, the glorious **Kızlarağası Han** is touristy, with many items from the far end of the Silk Road (China), but good for a wander.

Sleeping

İzmir's waterfront is dominated by large, high-end business hotels, while inland are more budget and midrange options, particularly around Kemeraltı Bazaar and Basmane train station. West of the station, 1368 Sokak is good for budget hotels.

TOP CHOICE **Key Hotel** BOUTIQUE HOTEL €€€
(☎482 1111; www.keyhotel.com; Mimar Kemalettin Caddesi 1; d TL270; P❄📶) This black, gold and brown masterpiece, located in a former bank building down by Konak Pier, has a glass-topped atrium, glass elevators, a superb ground-floor restaurant and concierge service. Rooms have hi-tech touches, rain showers and king-size beds.

İzmir Palas Oteli HOTEL €€
(☎465 0030; www.izmirpalas.com.tr; Atatürk Caddesi; s/d from TL120/165; P❄) Established in 1927 and rebuilt in 1972, the 138-room Palas is a storied beast, but it's popular, quite comfortable and overlooks the bay, with fine fish restaurants nearby.

Hotel Baylan Basmane HOTEL €€
(☎483 1426; www.hotelbaylan.com; 1299 Sokak 8; s/d TL80/140) Basmane's best option, the Baylan is a spacious and attractive hotel with a welcoming rear terrace. The rooms have polished floorboards and large bathrooms.

Güzel İzmir Oteli HOTEL €
(☎483 5069; www.guzelizmirhotel.com; 1368 Sokak 8; s/d TL40/70) One of Basmane's better choices, the Good İzmir is friendly, safe and convenient for bus and train access. Rooms are nothing special (avoid the small and damp few) but it's good value at the low end.

Eating & Drinking

For fresh fruit and veg, freshly baked bread and delicious savoury pastries, head for the **canopied market** just off Anafartalar Caddesi. The *kordon* restaurants have outside tables with views of the bay – some serve excellent food. On and around Kıbrıs Şehitleri Caddesi in Alsancak, you'll lose the sunset views but gain on atmosphere; in particular try 1453 Sokak.

Sakız MODERN TURKISH €€
(☎484 1103; Şehıt Nevresbey Bulvarı 9a; mains TL12-25; ⊙noon-2pm & 7.30-10pm Mon-Sat) With a wooden terrace and red-and-white tablecloths, Sakız is informal and fabulous. Its fresh meze and unusual mains include sardines, octopus, sea bass with asparagus, and stir-fried fish with artichoke.

Veli Usta Balık Pişiricisi SEAFOOD €€
(☎464 2705; Atatürk Caddesi 212; mains TL20; ⊙noon-10.30pm) This relaxed, quality seafood restaurant outstrips the strip thanks to dishes such as fresh, good-value *dil şiş* (grilled sole).

Aksak Lounge BAR
(1452 Sokak 10) In a typical İzmir mansion with high ceilings, balconies and a courtyard garden, Aksak attracts a cultured crowd to its jazz nights on Tuesday and Sunday.

Information

Banks, ATMs, internet cafes and wi-fi networks are found throughout the centre.

Tourist Office (☎483 5117; 1344 Sokak 2) Just off Atatürk Caddesi. Has English-, German- and French-speaking staff.

Getting There & Away

AIR There are many flights to İzmir's **Adnan Menderes Airport** (☎455 0000; www.adnanmenderesairport.com) from European destinations. Turkish Airlines flies to/from İstanbul (both airports), Ankara and 11 other Turkish locations. Onur Air, Atlasjet, Pegasus Airlines, Sun Express and Izair also serve İzmir.

BUS From the mammoth *otogar*, 6.5km northeast of the centre, frequent buses leave for nationwide destinations including the following:

Bergama TL10, two hours

Çeşme TL15, 1¾ hours. Buses also leave from a local bus terminal in Üçkuyular, 6.5km southwest of Konak.

Kuşadası TL15, 1¼ hours

Selçuk TL9, one hour

TRAIN Most intercity services arrive at Basmane station, although Alsancak is being vamped up.

Ankara TL27, 15 hours. Two a day in both directions; via Eskişehir (TL21, 11 hours).

Bandırma TL18, six hours. Every afternoon in both directions. Apart from on Tuesday, morning trains coordinate with the ferry to/from İstanbul.

Selçuk TL4.75, 1½ hours, six daily

Getting Around

TO/FROM THE AIRPORT Havaş buses (TL10, 30 minutes) leave from Gazi Osman Paşa Bulvarı near the Swissôtel on the half hour; and from domestic arrivals 25 minutes after flights arrive.

BUS Intercity bus companies operate *servises* to/from the *otogar*. *Dolmuşes* run to the centre; to the *otogar*, take the metro to Bornova and catch bus 505.

FERRY Roughly half-hourly services (TL3), with more at the beginning and end of the working day, link piers including Alsancak, Pasaport and Konak.

Çeşme Peninsula

☎0232

The Çeşme Peninsula is İzmir's summer playground, which means it fills with Turkish tourists over weekends and during school holidays, when prices rise accordingly. Çeşme itself is a transit point for the Greek island of Chios, and a pleasant base with a dramatic Genoese fortress. Alternatively, nearby Alaçatı is a boutique bolt-hole with old Greek stone houses and a windsurfing beach.

🛏 Sleeping

ÇEŞME

Levant Apart Otel   APARTMENT €€
(☎712 6553; www.cesmelevantaparts.com; 105 Sokak 23; 1/2-bedroom apt TL135/250; P❋🐾) Levant's slick designer apartments, one street back from the sea, are well ahead of Çeşme's otherwise humble digs. The 35-sq-metre studios are bright and cool, with plasmas, hairdryers, cute bathrooms and self-catering facilities.

Nese Hotel   HOTEL €
(☎712 6543; www.neseotel.net; Inkılap Caddesi, 3025 Sokak; s/d TL40/80; P❋🐾) A hit with readers, this charming white-and-blue hotel is a few streets from the sea. Rooms are tiled and pastel, cool and clean. The canopied restaurant is lovely in summer.

ALAÇATI

Prices plummet out of season, although most hotels open only from mid-May to mid-October and for Christmas and New Year. For more boutique hotels, visit www.charmingalacati.com.

Vintage Boutique Hotel   BOUTIQUE HOTEL €€€
(☎716 0716; www.vintagealacati.com; 3046 Sokak 2; TL250-400; P❋🐾) The Vintage's hip interior is aesthetically more modern than some may want in a historic neighbourhood, but its confidence and popularity are indicative of Alaçatı's maturing hotel scene. The all-white rooms feature high-end beauty products and linen.

Alaçatı Taş Otel   BOUTIQUE HOTEL €€€
(Stone Hotel; ☎716 7772; www.tasotel.com; s/d incl afternoon tea from TL150/200; ❋🐾) The Stone Hotel, Alaçatı oldest, continues to lead the boutique scene, with seven understated rooms overlooking a walled garden. The poolside afternoon teas are lavish, featuring freshly baked cakes. Open year-round.

🍴 Eating & Drinking

ÇEŞME

The most touristy restaurants are along the waterfront. For cheaper, more locally oriented places, head to İnkılap Caddesi.

Some of the restaurants along the marina morph into live-music venues during the summer.

Tiko's Cafe   TURKISH €
(2008 Sokak 8A; mains TL8-12; ⏰6am-3am winter, 24hr summer) This new, Ottoman-feeling establishment gets crammed with locals at lunchtime and with sailors and partygoers through summer. The regular menu includes seafood and grilled meat and a revolving display of fresh meze.

Pasifik Otel Restaurant   SEAFOOD €€
(☎712 1767; Tekke Plajı Mevkii 16; mains TL10-20; ⏰noon-midnight) If you fancy a walk and some fish, head to this hotel restaurant at the far northern end of the seafront, overlooking a small beach.

ALAÇATI

Restaurants here are mostly smart, gourmet affairs, with mains typically starting at around TL20. Many close for lunch, and open only at weekends (if at all) in low season. The cafes by the mosque serve cheaper fare.

Asma Yaprağı   AEGEAN €€
(☎716 0178; 1005 Sokak 50; meze TL10-15) Communal meals in this one-room restaurant are an Alaçatı experience for gastronomes and lucky stragglers. Expect plenty of fresh herbs, lashings of olive oil, Aegean vegetables and vine leaves.

❶ Information

Çeşme's **tourist office** (☎712 6653; fax 712 6653; İskele Meydanı 4; ⏰8.30am-noon & 1-5.30pm Mon-Fri), ferry and bus ticket offices, banks with ATMs, restaurants and hotels are all within two blocks of Cumhuriyet Meydanı, the main square near the waterfront.

❶ Getting There & Around

BOAT Between mid-May and mid-September, **Ertürk** (☎712 6768; www.erturk.com.tr; Beyazıt Caddesi 6; ⏰9am-7.30pm) sails once or twice daily to Chios (one way/return TL65/100, 1½ hours); outside that period, twice a week.

BUS Buses from Çeşme *otogar* run every 15 minutes to İzmir *otogar* (TL12, 1¾ hours) and the smaller, western Üçkuyular terminal (TL10, 1½ hours). *Dolmuşes* link Çeşme and Alaçatı (TL3.50).

Selçuk

📞 0232 / POP 28,200

The normal gateway to Ephesus, this provincial town has an impressive number of sights, including graceful Byzantine aqueduct ruins and one of the Seven Wonders of the Ancient World. The down-to-earth town acts more as a weigh station for the throngs of passers-through than a vibrant tourist hub.

◉ Sights

Temple of Artemis   RUIN
(Artemis Tapınağı; ⏰8.30am-5.30pm) Just beyond Selçuk's western extremities, in an empty field, stands a solitary reconstructed pillar: all that remains of the massive Temple of Artemis, one of the Seven Wonders of the Ancient World. At its height, the structure had 127 columns; Didyma's better-preserved Temple of Apollo (p559), which had 122 columns, gives a sense of this vanished grandeur.

Ephesus Museum   MUSEUM
(📞892 6010; Uğur Mumcu Sevgi Yolu Caddesi; admission TL5; ⏰8.30am-6.30pm summer, to 4.30pm winter) This museum holds artefacts from Ephesus' Terrace Houses, including scales, jewellery and cosmetic boxes, plus coins, funerary goods and ancient statuary. Look out for the famous effigy of phallic god Priapus, visible by pressing a button, and the multi-breasted, egg-holding marble Artemis statue. After midday, the museum gets crowded with cruise crowds being rushed through.

Basilica of St John   RUIN
(St Jean Caddesi; admission TL5; ⏰8.30am-6.30pm summer, to 4.30pm winter) This once-great basilica is a skeleton of its former self, but makes a pleasant stroll and warm-up to Ayasuluk Fortress, with excellent hilltop views. St John reportedly visited Ephesus twice and wrote his gospel on this hill. These legends, and the existence of a 4th-century tomb, supposedly housing John's relics, inspired the Byzantine Emperor Justinian to build the basilica.

Ayasuluk Fortress   CASTLE
(St Jean Caddesi; admission €8; ⏰8.30am-6.30pm summer, to 4.30pm winter) Selçuk's crowning achievement is accessed via the Basilica of St John – and on the same ticket. The partially restored fortress' remains date from Byzantine and Ottoman times.

🛏 Sleeping

Selçuk specialises in good-value, family-run pensions, though upscale hotels do exist. With all of the attentive service, free extras and bus-station pick-ups, there can be pressure to buy (carpets, tours etc). You should be OK at the following.

TOP CHOICE Atilla's Getaway   HOSTEL €
(📞892 3847; www.atillasgetaway.com; Acarlar Köyü; s/d incl breakfast & dinner €24/40; ❄@🎧🏊) This friendly 'backpacker's resort' is 2.5km south of town (linked to the *otogar* by regular free shuttles). Basic rooms and spacious dorms (no bunk beds) are spread around an outdoor pool, itself flanked by a billiards table, 'chill-out area', outdoor bar and dining area. Campers can use the lawn beside the sand volleyball court. Delicious home-cooked dinners are included (if eating out instead, deduct €5 from the given prices).

Akay Hotel   HOTEL €€
(📞892 3172; www.hotelakay.com; 1054 Sokak 7; s/d/tr from €30/50/80; ❄@🎧🏊) This smart, Swiss-run hotel near İsa Bey Camii offers impeccable service, attention to detail, and the quiet elegance of its stone foundations, white walls and green doors. The well-appointed rooms overlook a turquoise pool and patio. Dinners (mains TL12 to TL15) are on the roof terrace.

Homeros Pension   PENSION €€
(📞892 3995; www.homerospension.com; 1048 Sokak 3; s/d/tr TL50/80/110; ❄🎧) This long-time favourite has a dozen rooms with colourful hanging textiles and handcrafted furniture made by the friendly owner. Enjoy good views, coffee and dinners (TL15) from the roof terraces.

Wallabies Aquaduct Hotel   HOTEL €
(📞892 3204; www.wallabiesaquaducthotel.com; Cengiz Topel Caddesi 2; s/d/tr from TL50/70/105; ❄🎧) Right beside the aqueducts in Selçuk centre, Wallabies has clean, modern rooms, some overlooking the storks' nests atop the ruins. There's a great buffet breakfast, and the ground-floor restaurant is among the town's best.

Barım Pension   PENSION €
(📞892 6923; barim_pansiyon@hotmail.com; 1045 Sokak 34; s/d TL40/80; ❄🎧) Barım stands out for its unusual wire art, crafted by the owners, two friendly metalworking brothers. The pension occupies a 140-year-old stone house, with a leafy back garden for breakfasts and coffees.

Hotel Bella HOTEL €€€

(☎892 3944; www.hotelbella.com; St Jean Caddesi 7; s/d from €80/120; ❊@🛜) Well-situated near St John's Hill, this upmarket little hotel comes complete with a pricey carpet and jewellery shop. The well-designed rooms have Ottoman flourishes in the decor, and the roof terrace offers refined dinners (TL25).

✖ Eating

Most pensions offer good meals at reasonable prices. The Saturday market (Şahabettin Dede Caddesi; ⏰9am-5pm Sat winter, 8am-7pm Sat summer) and Wednesday market (respectively behind the bus and train stations) are great places to stock up for a picnic.

Ejder Restaurant ANATOLIAN €€

(Cengiz Topel Caddesi 9e; mains TL7-17) Roughly opposite the aqueduct, this tiny but time-tested local favourite serves delicious Turkish dishes – if you can't decide, take the whole sizzling Anatolian meat platter.

Wallabies Aquaduct Restaurant TURKISH €€

(☎892 3204; Cengiz Topel Caddesi 2; mains TL10-16) Beneath the hotel of the same name, Wallabies spills out onto the square beneath the aqueduct, guaranteeing atmospheric summer dining. The traditional Anatolian fare is complemented by more international offerings, including veggie dishes and fish. Try the house chicken dish, *krep tavuk sarması*.

Selçuk Köftecisi KÖFTE €

(Şahabettin Dede Caddesi; mains TL6-9) This classic *köfte* joint, family-run since 1959, offers great but small meat portions and tasty side salads.

Sişçi Yaşarın Yeri KÖFTE €

(Atatürk Caddesi; mains from TL6) A popular spot for *köfte* and kebaps, this stall has tables.

St John's Café MEDITERRANEAN €

(www.stjohn-cafe-ephesus.com; Uğur Mumcu Sevgi Yolu Caddesi 4c; mains TL8-13; 🛜) Selçuk's most touristy cafe-shop has the town's widest coffee selection, various toasts and other international snacks. There's a play area for restless youngsters, too.

❶ Information

Tourist Office (www.selcuk.gov.tr; Agora Caddesi 35; ⏰8am-noon & 1-5pm daily summer, Mon-Fri winter)

❶ Getting There & Away

Frequent *dolmuşes* run to Kuşadası (TL5, 30 minutes) and the beach at Pamucak (TL2.50, 10 minutes). There's a train to İzmir Adnan Menderes Airport (TL4.50, 55 minutes), which drops you a 20-minute stroll from the departures terminal. Buses include:

Bodrum TL25, 3¼ hours, three daily in summer

Denizli For Pamukkale and the Mediterranean, TL25, 4½ hours, two daily

İzmir TL9, one hour, every 40 minutes in summer

Ephesus (Efes)

Even if you're not an architecture buff, you can't help but be dazzled by the sheer beauty of the ruins of Ephesus (☎892 6010; admission/parking TL25/7.50; ⏰8am-6.30pm May-Oct, to 4.30pm Nov-Apr), the most complete classical metropolis in Europe. Once the capital of the Roman province of Asia Minor, with 250,000-plus inhabitants, today it's *the* place to get a feel for life in Greco-Roman times.

There's a couple of hours' worth of sights to explore, including the Great Theatre, reconstructed by the Romans between AD 41 and 117, and capable of holding 25,000 people; the 110-sq-metre Lower Agora, a textile and food market; and the Library of Celsus, adorned with niches holding statues of the classical Virtues. Going up Ephesus' Champs Élysées, the Curetes Way, you can't miss the impressive Corinthian-style Temple of Hadrian on the left, its arches decorated with deities; the magnificent Terraced Houses (Yamaç Evleri; admission TL15), which are well worth the extra outlay; and

Ephesus (Efes)

the **Trajan Fountain**. At the top of the Curetes Way, the **Pollio Fountain** and **Memius Monument** also hint at the lavish nature of the fountains that covered the ancient capital. Up the hill on the left are the ruined remains of the **Prytaneum** (Town Hall) and the **Temple of Hestia Boulaea**, where vestal virgins tended to a perpetually burning flame. Beyond, the **Odeon**, a 5000-seat theatre with marble seats and carved ornamentation, was used for municipal meetings.

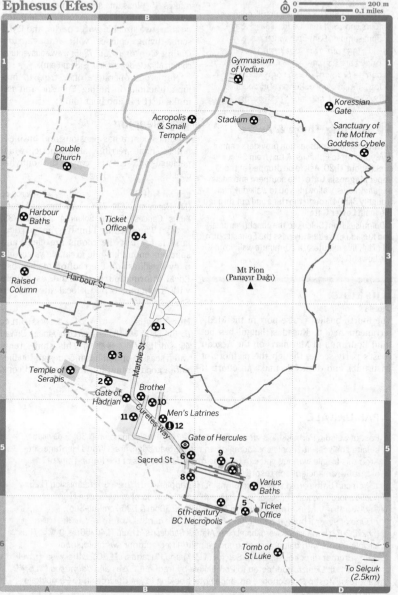

Ephesus (Efes)

0 — 200 m
0 — 0.1 miles

VISITING EPHESUS

The mediocre audioguide is not recommended, nor are the 'guides' loitering at the entrances. Organise a guide in advance through a company such as the Selçuk-based No-Frills Ephesus Tours (☑892 8838; www.nofrillsephesustours.com; Sen Jean Caddesi 3a ; ⊙8am-8pm summer, 9am-5pm winter).

Bring your own snacks and water, as prices are high here. Heat and crowds can be problematic so come early or late and avoid weekends and public holidays. The site lacks restrooms.

❶ Getting There & Away

Technically, accommodation providers cannot give you a lift to Ephesus. A taxi from Selçuk costs about TL20. Ask to be dropped at the upper **Magnesia Gate** (the southern entrance or *güney kapısı*), allowing you to walk downhill (roughly 3km) through the ruins and out through the main **Lower Gate**.

Dolmuşes from Selçuk to the coast (Pamucak and Kuşadası) frequently pass the Ephesus turn-off (TL4, five minutes), a 20-minute walk from the Lower Gate.

Kuşadası

☑0256 / POP 68,300

The fourth-busiest cruise port in the Mediterranean region, Kuşadası languishes behind Bodrum and Marmaris on the Aegean coast's party scene, though the plethora of Irish pubs and discos do make an effort. If you want nightlife, or simply like being near the sea, this is a good base.

◉ Sights & Activities

Kuşadası is short on specific sights, although the minor **stone fortress** on an island connected to the mainland by a causeway makes a pleasant stroll. There are also **beaches** south of town, a tourist-orientated **bazaar**, two sizeable **water parks**, and PADI scuba-diving courses with **Aquaventure Diving Center** (☑612 7845; www.aquaventure.com.tr; Miracle Beach Club; ⊙8am-6pm).

Numerous operators offer trips to major attractions including Ephesus and Pamukkale (€45), and boat tours.

⊨ Sleeping

Kuşadası centre has pensions and business hotels, none terribly atmospheric, while package-tour resorts cover the outlying coasts.

Liman Hotel   PENSION €€
(Mr Happy's; ☑614 7770; www.limanhotel.com; Kıbrıs Caddesi, Buyral Sokak 4; s/d €25/38; ✳@☎) The friendly Liman is not particularly fancy, but the rooms are clean and spacious enough, while great views accompany breakfast on the rooftop terrace/bar. Local information is on hand, as is help with arranging trips to local sites and to Samos.

Hotel Ilayda   BUSINESS HOTEL €€
(☑614 3807; www.hotelilayda.com; Atatürk Bulvarı 46; s/d TL80/140; ✳@☎) This shiny, renovated seaside option has nice design touches and a good restaurant. It has all mod cons,

---

WORTH A TRIP

PAMUKKALE

East of Selçuk, Pamukkale's gleaming white **travertines** (admission TL30; ⊙daylight), calcite shelves with pools cascading down the plateau edge, are a World Heritage site. Atop this fragile wonder, you can tour the magnificent ruins of the Roman city of **Hierapolis**, an ancient spa resort.

You can bathe amid sunken columns at Hierapolis' **Antique Pool** (admission TL25, public pool admission TL7.50; ⊙9am-7pm, public pool 9am-8pm) and visit the **Hierapolis Archaeology Museum** (admission TL3; ⊙9am-12.30pm & 1.30-7pm Tue-Sun).

One of several budget pensions in the village, the central **Artemis Yoruk Hotel** (☑272 2073; www.artemisyorukhotel.com; Atatürk Caddesi; s/d from TL40/50; ✳@☎≋) has simple rooms with balconies set around a palm-lined outdoor swimming pool.

In summer direct buses serve Selçuk (TL27) and Kuşadası (TL30). Otherwise, travel via local hub Denizli, connected to Pamukkale by frequent buses and *dolmuşes* (TL5, 40 minutes). Most people choose advance hotel booking to get the free lift to Pamukkale (and often back again).

and great views from the rooftop terrace and some rooms.

Club Caravanserail
HISTORIC HOTEL €€

(☎614 4115; www.kusadasihotelcaravanserail.com; Atatürk Bulvarı 2; s/d/ste €80/100/150; ❄🖗) A grand 17th-century stone *caravanserai*, this photogenic structure is spotlit at night. The rooms' Ottoman decor is authentic, the kitschy 'Turkish nights' less so.

✖ Eating & Drinking

Waterfront dining is atmospheric but can be expensive; verify seafood prices before ordering. Head inland for cheaper but tasty kebap shops. Kaleiçi, Kuşadası's old quarter, offers characterful backstreet eats and some fun, more Turkish, cafes.

Raucous Barlar Sokak (Bar St) is chock-a-block with Irish-theme pubs. Locals prefer Kaleiçi's laid-back old cafes, while Cape Yılancı on the southern coast has giant bar-club-concert complexes.

Ferah
SEAFOOD €€

(☎614 1281; İskele Yanı Güvercin Parkı İçi; mains TL15-25; ⊙lunch & dinner) This waterfront restaurant pairs great sunset sea views with good-quality meze and seafood.

Bebop
INTERNATIONAL €€

(☎618 0727; www.bebopjazzclub.com; mains from TL9; ⊙lunch & dinner) Located within the marina, Bebop offers breakfasts, a pool to laze by over drinks, generous portions of Turkish and international fare, and late-night live jazz.

Köftecı Ali
KÖFTE €

(Arslanlar Caddesi 14; mains TL5; ⊙24hr summer, 9am-midnight winter) This Bar St kebap booth caters to both well-mannered Turks and drunken foreign louts. The spicy wrapped pide kebap is nourishing.

❶ Information

There's a post office and several banks with ATMs on Barbaros Hayrettin Bulvarı. The **tourist office** (Liman Caddesi, İskele Meydanı; ⊙8am-noon & 1-5pm Mon-Fri) is near the cruise-ship dock, and under the walls.

❶ Getting There & Around

BOAT All Kuşadası travel agents sell tickets to the Greek island of **Samos**. Boats (one way/same-day return €35/40) depart daily between April and October.

BUS *Dolmuşes* run to/from the *otogar*, out on the bypass road, and along the coast. Heading

---

DON'T MISS

PRIENE, MILETUS & DIDYMA

Kuşadası makes a good base for visiting a trio of ancients sites to the south. Perched high on the craggy slopes of Mt Mykale, **Priene** has a beautiful, windswept setting; **Miletus**, another ruined Graeco-Roman port city, boasts a spectacular theatre and a **museum** (admission TL3; ⊙8.30am-4.30pm); and in **Didyma** is the stupendous **Temple of Apollo** (☎811 0035; admission TL3; ⊙9am-7.30pm mid-May–mid-Sep, to 5.30pm mid-Sep–mid-May), the ancient world's second-largest. *Dolmuşes* don't serve Miletus; the easiest way to visit the sites is on a 'PMD' tour from Kuşadası or Selçuk (€50).

---

out of Kuşadası, *dolmuşes* leave from the central Adnan Menderes Bulvarı and the *otogar*.

Bodrum In summer three daily buses (TL25, 2½ hours); in winter take a *dolmuş* to Söke (TL5).

Selçuk *Dolmuşes* (TL5, 30 minutes, every 30 minutes) via Pamucak and the Ephesus turn-off.

Bodrum

☎0252 / POP 34,900

The beating heart of a holiday-happy peninsula, Bodrum is a famously posh paradise where sun-kissed travellers dance the breezy summer nights away. With laws restricting the height of its buildings, the town has a nice architectural uniformity; the idyllic whitewashed houses with their bright-blue trim call out to tourists' cameras. Even when the clubs are bumpin' there's something rather refined about the town.

⊙ Sights & Activities

Castle of St Peter
MUSEUM

(☎316 2516; www.bodrum-museum.com; admission TL10; ⊙9am-noon & 1-7pm Tue-Sun summer, 8am-noon & 1-5pm winter) Tamerlane's Mongol invasion of Anatolia (1402) not only gave Byzantine Constantinople a reprieve from Turkish besiegers, it also allowed the Knights Hospitaller, based in Rhodes, to build a castle at ancient Halicarnassus, using marble and stones from the famed mausoleum. By 1437 they had finished the construction, adding defensive features right up until

Bodrum

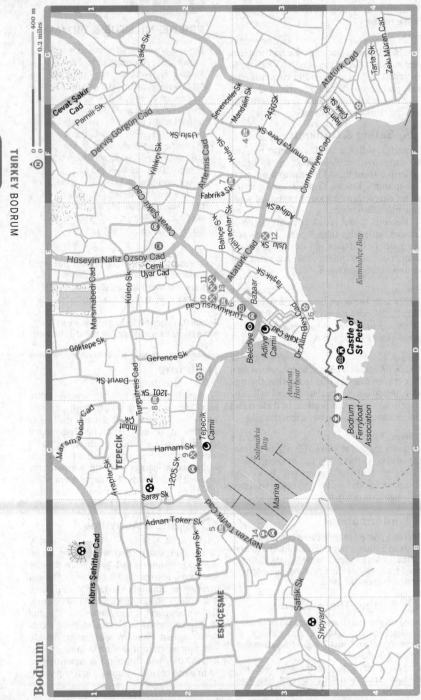

400 m
0.2 miles

Cevat Şakir Cad

Pamili Sk

Derviş Görgün Cad

Yaka Sk

Sevenceler Sk

Mandalin Sk

Atatürk Cad

Tarla Sk

Zeki Müren Cad

Onurca Dere Sk

2490 Sk

Işgın Sk

Çırak Sk

Uslu Sk

Yılıkçı Sk

Kilic Sk

Artemis Cad

Cumhuriyet Cad

Fabrika Sk

Cevat Şakir Cad

Bahçe Sk

Helvacılar Sk

Adliye Sk

Hüseyin Nafiz Özsoy Cad
Cemil
Uyar Cad

Uslu Sk

Kumbahçe Bay

Marsmabedi Cad

Külcü Sk

Atatürk Cad

Taşlık Sk

Bazaar

Göktepe Sk

Türkkuyusu Cad

Belediye

Adliye
Camii

Dr Alim Bey

Kale Cad

Castle of
St Peter

Davut Sk

Gerence Sk

Turgutreis Cad

1201 Sk

Ancient
Harbour

Bodrum
Ferryboat
Association

Marsmabedi Cad

İmbat Çık

Tepecik
Camii

Salmakis Bay

Hamam Sk

TEPECIK

1205 Sk

Araplar Sk

Saray Sk

Marina

Adnan Toker Sk

Nevzen Tevfik Cad

Kıbrıs Şehitler Cad

Fırkateyn Sk

ESKIÇEŞME

Şafak Sk

Shipyard

Bodrum

1522, when Süleyman the Magnificent captured Rhodes and this castle.

Renovations started in the 1960s, and the underwater archaeology treasures amassed therein became Bodrum's **Museum of Underwater Archaeology** (☏ 316 2516; Castle of St Peter; admission €5.55; ⊙ 9am-7pm Tue-Sun summer). The battalions offer splendid views and the castle contains numerous historic sights.

Mausoleum   RUIN
(Turgutreis Caddesi; admission TL8; ⊙ 8.30am-5.30pm Tue-Sun) One of the Seven Wonders of the Ancient World, the Mausoleum was the greatest achievement of Carian King Mausolus (r 376–353 BC). The king planned his own tomb and, following his death, his wife (and sister), Artemisia, oversaw the completion of an enormous, white-marble tomb topped by stepped pyramids.

The site includes relaxing gardens, a scale model of the Mausoleum and a few ancient fragments, among them the entry to Mausolus' tomb chamber.

Blue Cruises   BOAT TOUR
Countless excursion boats are moored along Neyzen Tevfik Caddesi; a 'blue cruise' on board one of these is a fun day trip. Like the ferry companies, some even access peninsula bays, saving you a sweaty minibus ride (check locally). **Karaada** (Black Island), with hot-spring waters gushing from a cave, is a popular destination where you can swim and loll in orange mud.

Book cruises at your hotel, or on the moored excursion boats, ideally a day ahead. Group tours start from €12.

🛏 Sleeping

With an efficient *dolmuş* shuttle system linking Bodrum to the rest of the peninsula, it's worth checking out hotels, apartments and villas on the other bays. Plan in advance: many hotels offer discounted rates for advance bookings, and places fill up fast in high summer. The marina-area hotels get the most noise from the clubs and bars.

Su Otel   BOUTIQUE HOTEL €€€
(☏ 316 6906; www.bodrumsuhotel.com; Turgutreis Caddesi, 1201 Sokak; s/d/ste from €70/95/115; ✱❄❅) Epitomising Bodrum's traditional white-and-bright-blue decor, the Su has sun-filled bedrooms, some with balconies overlooking the terraced gardens and inviting pool. The friendly management helps with all local activities; out of high season, it even runs a cooking class.

Kaya Pension   PENSION €€
(☏ 316 5745; www.kayapansiyon.com.tr; Eski Hükümet Sokak 14; s/d/tr TL100/120/140; ✱❅) Kaya has clean, simple rooms in town and a beautiful flowering courtyard for breakfast and drinks. Reception has a safe for valuables, and the helpful staff can arrange activities.

Otel Atrium   HOTEL €€
(☏ 316 2181; www.atriumbodrum.com; Fabrika Sokak 21; s/d incl half board from TL100/120; ℗✱❄❅) This midsize hotel amid tangerine trees has bright and fairly spacious rooms. It's good value for families and independent travellers. There's a pool (with separate kid's section), a poolside bar, two restaurants and free parking. It's a five- to 10-minute walk to both centre and beach.

Marmara Bodrum   LUXURY HOTEL €€€
(☎999 1010; www.themarmarahotels.com; Sulu-
hasan Caddesi 18; r/ste from €180/600; ❄@☒) High on a bluff, the Marmara has great views, elegant rooms, and facilities including tennis, spa, gym and two pools. A free shuttle accesses a private beach in Torba.

Bahçeli Ağar Aile Pansiyonu   PENSION €€
(☎316 1648; 1402 Sokak 4; s/d €50/65) This friendly little pension has small but spotless rooms with balconies, some overlooking a vine-draped courtyard, and a kitchen.

Anfora   PENSION €
(☎316 5530; www.anforapansiyon.com; Omurça Dere Sokak 23; s/d from TL45/70; ❄☎) Rooms are well kept and clean (though can be cramped) at this friendly pension. Although Bar St's a few blocks away, it's not too loud at night.

✖ Eating & Drinking

Bodrum's waterfront has pricey, big-menu restaurants (not all bad), while nearby are discreet backstreet contenders, fast-food stalls and a fruit and veg market (Cevat Şakir Caddesi).

Generally, Bodrum's western-bay eateries are more upscale, while the eastern bay has more informal, soak-up-the-Efes fare.

For drinking, follow the same rule of thumb: for cheap and cheerful head to the eastern bay; for expensive and classy, think western bay. Dr Alim Bey Caddesi and Cumhuriyet Caddesi function as Bodrum's water-
front 'Bar St'.

TOP CHOICE Fish Market   SEAFOOD €€
(Cevat Şakir Caddesi; meze from TL4; fish TL20; ☺dinner Mon-Sat) Bodrum's fish market offers a unique sort of direct dining: you choose between myriad fresh fish and seafood on ice at fishmongers' tables, and have them cooked (about TL6 extra) at any adjoining restaurant. The plain restaurants spill across the small streets; Meyhane Deniz Feneri (☎316 3534; Belediye Gıda Çarşısı 12; fish TL18-35) is the area's oldest, and many residents still consider it the best. Dinner for two with a few meze, drinks and fish will run at least TL100 here. In any fish-market restaurant, book ahead for evening dining.

TOP CHOICE La Pasión   SPANISH €€
(Restaurante Español; www.lapasion-bodrum.com; cnr Atatürk Caddesi & Uslu Sokak; set menus TL18-
35; ☺lunch & dinner) To see just how far Bod-
rum has come in its quest to join the ranks of international seaside sophistication, try this refined Spanish restaurant down a side street off Cumhuriyet Caddesi. The good-
value lunch menus (appetiser, mains, des-
sert and first drink are TL18 per person) change weekly.

Marina Köftecisi   KÖFTE €€
(☎313 5593; Neyzen Tevfik Caddesi 158; mains TL10-17) With a waterfront view, this is an excellent spot for various traditional *köfte* reci-
pes. Try *kaşarlı köfte* (meatballs with cheese from sheep's milk), served with pita bread drizzled with tomato sauce and yoghurt.

Döner Tepecik   KEBAP €
(Neyzen Tevfik Caddesi; kebaps from TL6; ☺break-
fast, lunch & dinner) Across from the epony-
mous mosque, this local favourite does tasty kebaps on homemade bread.

Marina Yacht Club   BAR
(☎316 1228; Neyzen Tevfik Caddesi 5; ☺8am-late) Marina serves meals (Italian and Turkish flavours, average TL22 per person), but its primary identity is as a big, breezy waterfront nightspot. Merrymakers congregrate around the extended, wrap-around bar or at the scattered tiny tables dotting the way to the water-facing deck, where cover bands liven things up.

☆ Entertainment

Nightclubs such as the floating Marine Club Catamaran (www.clubcatamaran.com; Dr Alim Bey Caddesi; admission weekday/weekend TL35/40; ☺10pm-4am mid-May–Sep) are famous party spots, and the likes of Helva (www.helvabod-
rum.com; Neyzen Tevfik Caddesi 54; ☺2pm-3am) are slicker clubs aimed at Turkish trendset-
ters. Mavi Bar (Cumhuriyet Caddesi 175; ☺6pm-
6am) hosts live music, as do the castle and ancient theatre (Kıbrıs Şehitler Caddesi); for upcoming events, visit www.biletix.com.

ⓘ Information

Head to Cevat Şakir Caddesi for ATMs.
Post office (Cevat Şakir Caddesi; ☺8.30am-
5pm, telephone exchange 8am-midnight)
Tourist Office (Kale Meydanı; ☺8am-6pm Mon-Fri, daily in summer)

ⓘ Getting There & Away

AIR Almost 50 airlines, including charter and budget operators, Turkish Airlines, AtlasJet and Pegasus Airlines, fly from Europe, İstanbul and elsewhere to Bodrum International Airport, 36km away. Havaş shuttle buses (TL19) tie in with Turkish Airlines, AnadoluJet, Onur Air, Sun Express and Pegasus Airlines flights; otherwise an expensive taxi (TL90 from the city centre; TL100 from the airport) is your only option.

BOAT For tickets and the latest times, contact the **Bodrum Ferryboat Association** (☑316 0882; www.bodrumferryboat.com; Kale Caddesi Cümrük Alanı 22; ☺8am-8pm).

Kos (one way or same-day return €32, one hour) Daily ferries to/from the Greek island.

Rhodes (one way or same-day return €60, 2¼ hours) From June to September there are two weekly hydrofoils to/from the Greek island.

Datça (single/return TL25/40, two hours) Daily ferries from mid-June to September; four weekly from April to mid-June and in October.

BUS There are services to more or less anywhere you could wish to go.

İstanbul TL68, 12 hours, 10 nightly
Kuşadası TL20, 2½ hours, four each afternoon
Marmaris TL15, three hours, hourly

Marmaris

☑0252 / POP 31,400

A popular resort town with a nonstop party atmosphere and good nearby beaches, in-your-face Marmaris is Mediterranean Turkey's version of Spain's Costa del Sol. Bar St offers unparalleled decadence, and charter boats will happily whisk you to Fethiye and beyond.

◉ Sights & Activities

Marmaris Castle & Museum
FORTRESS, MUSEUM

(Marmaris Kalesi ve Müzesi; ☑412 1459; admission TL3; ☺8am-noon & 1-5pm Tue-Sun) Marmaris' hilltop castle (1522) hosts **Marmaris Museum**, which exhibits amphorae, glassware, coins and other local finds. Saunter the castle's walls and gaze down on the bustling marina.

Boat Trips
BOAT TOUR

Marmaris Bay *dolmuş*-boat **day trips** (TL30 to TL35) offer eye-opening views and inviting swimming holes, and you can even hire a yacht, which offers the pleasure of a blue voyage down the coast (see p565). Cruises offered by the long-established **Yeşil Marmaris Travel & Yachting** (☑412 2290; www.yesilmarmaris.com; Barbaros Caddesi 13; 4 people from €300, incl all meals & soft drinks; ☺7am-11.30pm Mon-Sat high season, 8.30am-6.30pm low season) are recommended. As for the rest of the old salts advertising tours, compare prices, ask around, negotiate and, before signing up,

DATÇA & BOZBURUN PENINSULAS

Not far south, these deeply indented peninsulas hide azure bays backed by pine-covered mountains and gorgeous fishing villages. Reach them from Marmaris by *dolmuş*, boat or scooter (rentals average TL45 per day in high season).

confirm all details (exact boat, itinerary, lunch etc). Yachts sail from May to October.

From May to October, hourly water taxis, docked around the Atatürk statue, serve the beaches at **İçmeler** and **Turunç** (TL13, 45 minutes), respectively 10km and 20km southwest of Marmaris.

Diving
DIVING

Several harbourside companies along Yeni Kordon Caddesi offer scuba-diving excursions and courses (April through October), including **Marmaris Diving Center** (aytac.ozan@hotmail.com) and **Deep Blue Dive Center** (☑0541 374 5881, 0506 614 6408; www.sealung.com).

🛏 Sleeping

Marmaris is geared towards all-in package tour groups, so good independent sleeping options are rare.

Halıcı Hotel
HOTEL €€

(☑412 3626; www.halicihotel.com; Sokak 1; s/d TL80/130; P☀@☎☲) Despite being a big and somewhat dated package-tour hotel, this place is good value, with a big outdoor pool in a leafy tropical garden. It's a 10-minute walk west of the central waterfront.

Maltepe Pansiyon
PENSION €

(☑412 1629; www.maltepepansiyon.com; 66 Sokak 9; s/d/tr/q TL35/75/90/120; ☀@) A small pension in a shady garden, the Maltepe offers small but spotless rooms (most ensuite). You can use the kitchen.

Barış Motel & Pansiyon
PENSION €

(☑413 0652; www.barismotel.com; 66 Sokak 10; s/d TL50/70; ☀) Opposite the canal, this friendly little pension has spartan but clean rooms. Breakfast costs TL6. If coming by taxi, specify that you mean this Barış (and not the similarly named apartment complex).

✗ Eating & Drinking

Marmaris by night offers more neon than Vegas. Hedonistic crowds descend on the aptly named Bar St (39 Sokak) for foam parties, laser beams, dance music and tequilas by the half-dozen.

Ney   TURKISH €€
(☎412 0217; 26 Sokak 24; meze TL5-6, mains TL15-20) Up from the western marina, atmospheric little Ney occupies a 250-year-old Greek house. The home-cooked specialties include *tavuklu mantı böreği* (Turkish ravioli with chicken; TL14).

Liman Restaurant   SEAFOOD €€
(☎412 6336; 40 Sokak 38; mains TL10-20; ⊗8am-1am) This old favourite in the bazaar serves excellent meze and fish dishes (check prices in advance), including grilled sea bass, fish soup and calamari. Landlubbers will enjoy the *kavurma* (stir-fried lamb).

**Panorama Restaurant
& Bar**   INTERNATIONAL €€
(☎413 4835; Hacı İmam Sokağı 40; mains TL10-15; ⊗9am-1am) Panorama's marina-view terrace is more famous than the food, though it's still pleasant for pizza or pasta and sunset drinks.

Aquarium Restaurant   INTERNATIONAL €€
(☎413 1522; Barbaros Caddesi; mains TL15-30; ⊗9am-midnight) A portside restaurant with sublime views, this is a good spot for large grills and steaks.

Meryemana   TURKISH €
(☎412 7855; 35 Sokak 5b; mains TL5-6; 🛜) Meryemana's nourishing traditional tastes, including *mantı* (TL6), meze, spicy dips and homemade bread, attract Turks and foreigners alike.

ℹ Information

Tourist Office (☎412 1035; İskele Meydanı 2; ⊗8am-noon & 1-5pm Mon-Fri, daily Jun–mid-Sep) Below the castle; unhelpful.

ℹ Getting There & Away

AIR The nearest airports are at Dalaman, reached on the Havaş shuttle bus (TL25), and Bodrum.

BOAT Rhodes (Greece; one way/same-day return from €45/55, 50 minutes) Catamarans sail twice daily from April to October. In low season, cargo boats go two to three times weekly. Buy tickets from Marmaris agencies at least one day in advance.

BUS The *otogar* is 3km north of the centre, served by *dolmuşes*. Buses include:
Bodrum TL15, three hours, at least every two hours
Fethiye TL20, three hours, half-hourly
İzmir TL32, 4¼ hours, hourly

THE MEDITERRANEAN COAST

The western Mediterranean, known as the 'Turquoise Coast', is a region of endless azure sea lined with kilometres of sandy beaches and backed by mountains rising up to almost 3000m. It also has an embarrassment of ancient ruins strewn through the aromatic scrub and pine forests, and a broad menu of sports and activities.

The Med's seamless mix of history and holiday inspires and excites. The most dramatic way to see this stretch of coastline is aboard a *gület* (traditional wooden yacht) or by walking sections of the 500km-long Lycian Way, high above the crystal waters known locally as the Akdeniz (White Sea).

The eastern Mediterranean, meanwhile, has long lived in its more fashionable western neighbour's shadow. But the area facing Syria has Christian sites, Hittite settlements and Crusader castles between its timeless hillside villages, mountains and stunning coastline.

Fethiye

☎0252 / POP 81,500
In 1958 an earthquake levelled the harbour city of Fethiye, sparing only the ancient remains of Telmessos. Half a century on, Fethiye is once again a prosperous, growing hub of the western Mediterranean. Its natural harbour, tucked away in the southern reaches of a broad bay scattered with pretty islands, is perhaps the region's finest.

◎ Sights

Dolmuşes run southeast to the Lycian ruins dotting the countryside, including Tlos, Pınara, Letoön and Xanthos.

Telmessos   RUIN
The mammoth **Tomb of Amyntas** (admission TL8; ⊗8am-7pm May-Oct, to 5pm Nov-Apr), an Ionic temple facade, was carved into the sheer rock face in 350 BC. Located south of the centre, it is best visited at sunset.

BLUE CRUISE

Fethiye is the hub of Turkey's cruising scene, and the most popular route is the 'Blue Voyage' (Mavi Yolculuk) to Olympos: a four-day, three-night journey on a *gület* (traditional wooden sailing boat) that attracts young party animals. Boats usually call in at Ölüdeniz and Butterfly Valley and stop at Kaş, Kalkan and/or Kekova, with the final night at Gökkaya Bay opposite the eastern end of Kekova. A less-common (but some say prettier) route is between Marmaris and Fethiye.

Depending on the season, the price is typically €165 to €195 per person (food should be included, but you sometimes have to pay for water and soft drinks and always for alcohol). Make sure you shop around; many shoddy operators work the waters and wallets. Recommended operators include **Before Lunch Cruises** (☑0535 636 0076, 0532 623 4359; www.beforelunch.com), **Ocean Yachting Travel Agency** (☑612 4807; www.oceantravelagency.com; İskele Meydanı 1; ⊙9am-9pm Apr-Oct), **Olympos Yachting** (☑892 1145; www.olymposyachting.com) and **V-Go Yachting & Travel Agency** (☑612 2113; www.bluecruisesturkey.com).

Other, smaller rock tombs lie about 500m to the east.

Behind the harbour in the centre of town are the partly excavated remains of a 2nd-century BC Roman **theatre**. In town you'll also see curious **Lycian stone sarcophagi** dating from around 450 BC.

On the hillside south of town, and along the Kayaköy road, is the ruined tower of a 15th-century **Crusader fortress**.

Kayaköy   HISTORIC AREA
(admission TL5; ⊙8.30am-5pm) *Dolmuşes* (TL4) run to this nearby open-air museum, an evocative Ottoman Greek 'ghost town' that was abandoned during the population exchange of 1923.

🏃 Activities

Lycian Way   WALK
Acclaimed as one of the top 10 long-distance walks in the world, the Lycian Way follows signposted paths around the Teke peninsula to Antalya. The route leads through pine and cedar forests in the shadow of mountains rising almost 3000m, past villages, stunning coastal views and an embarrassment of ruins at ancient Lycian cities. Walk it in sections (unless you have plenty of time and stamina).

Fethiye is at the western end of this 500km walking trail, which leads south from here to Faralya and Butterfly Valley.

Fethiye offers numerous water-based activities and boat trips, including the **12-Island Tour** (per person TL30-50) and the **Butterfly Valley tour** (TL25) via Ölüdeniz. On dry land, the **Dalyan tour** (TL50)

includes Lake Köyceğiz, the Sultaniye mud baths, Kaunos ruins and İztuzu Beach, and the **Saklıkent Gorge tour** (TL45) includes Tlos and a trout lunch.

Seven Capes (☑0537 403 3779; www.sevencapes.com) offers sea kayaking, **European Diving Centre** (☑614 9771; www.europeandivingcentre.com; Fevzi Çakmak Caddesi 133) runs diving trips and courses, and **Ocean Yachting Travel Agency** (☑612 4807; www.oceantravelagency.com; İskele Meydanı 1) organises activities from rafting to horse riding.

🛏 Sleeping

Most accommodation is up the hill behind the marina in Karagözler or further west. Many pensions organise transport from the *otogar*.

Yildirim Guest House   PENSION, HOSTEL €
(☑614 4627, 0543 779 4732; www.yildirimguesthouse.com; Fevzi Çakmak Caddesi 21;, dm/d/tr TL25/80/120; ❄@🔊) Shipshape Yildirim, opposite the marina, features four- to six-bed dorms (two by gender and one mixed) and spotless rooms. The well-travelled host Omer offers excursions, pick-ups, laundry, evening meals (TL15), Saturday hikes on the Lycian Way (TL10) and free bikes.

Villa Daffodil   HOTEL €€
(☑614 9595; www.villadaffodil.com; Fevzi Çakmak Caddesi 115; s/d TL85/120; ❄🔊🏊) This large Ottoman-styled and flower-bedecked guesthouse, one of the few older buildings to survive the earthquake and development, has 41 rooms with stylish furnishings, a homely feel and, in some cases, balconies and sea views. The terrace and pool are centres of activity.

V-Go's Hotel & Guesthouse
PENSION, HOSTEL €€

(☎614 4004, 612 5409; www.v-gohotel.com; Fevzi Çakmak Caddesi 109; r per person €20, f €60; ✱@☎☎) This modern hostel/guesthouse at the western end of Karagözler has 28 rooms (four are four- to eight-bed dorms) across two buildings, most overlooking the sea or pool. There's a terrace with chill-out chairs and a bar with self-service music and DVDs.

✖ Eating & Drinking

Fethiye's enormous canalside Tuesday market takes place between Atatürk Caddesi and Pürşabey Caddesi next to the stadium. Bars and nightclubs are mostly on Hamam Sokak in the Old Town, and along Dispanser Caddesi south of the Martyrs' Monument.

TOP CHOICE Reis
SEAFOOD €€

(☎612 5368, 0532 472 5989; www.reisrestaurant.com; Hal ve Pazar Yeri 62; mains TL12-20; ⊘10am-midnight) To taste Fethiye's fabulous fish, buy your own (per kilo TL18 to TL25) from the fishmongers in the central covered market, then take it to one of the restaurants opposite. Reis charges TL5 per head for cooking the fish, plus a sauce, green salad, garlic bread and fruit. It also does meze and meat dishes. You should book.

İskele Ocakbaşı
BARBECUE €€

(☎614 9423; Şehit Feti Bey Parkı; meze TL6-19, grills TL12-26; ⊘9am-1am) This grill restaurant overlooks the water and a small park (outside seating), and serves excellent meat dishes from its central barbecue.

Meğri Lokantasi
TURKISH €€

(☎614 4047; www.megrirestaurant.com; Çarşı Caddesi 26; mains TL7-13, mixed plates TL17-25; ⊘8am-11.30pm low season, to 1am high season) Packed with locals who spill onto the streets, the Meğri offers hearty home-style cooking at palatable prices. Choose from the huge display of meze and savoury mains or try the güveç (casserole; TL20 to TL25).

Deniz Restaurant
SEAFOOD €€

(☎612 0212; Uğur Mumcu Parkı Yanı 10/1; mains TL15-30) The 'Sea' exhibits everything alive and swimming in tanks (the grouper is best) and excels in unusual meze. Try the semizotu (purslane) in yoghurt and the ceviche (fish preserved in lemon juice).

Kismet
BAR, CABARET

(☎0545 922 2301; Uğur Mumcu Parkı Yanı) This welcoming bar and cabaret venue (shows most Friday nights in season; phone for an update) off Dispanser Caddesi is open all day until the wee hours. Good for a sundowner or something cold much later.

❶ Information

Tourist Office (☎614 1527; İskele Meydanı; ⊘8am-7pm Mon-Fri, 10am-5pm Sat & Sun May-Sep, 8am-noon & 1-5pm Mon-Fri Oct-Apr) Helpful centre opposite the marina.

❶ Getting There & Away

BOAT Catamarans sail to Rhodes (Greece; one way/same-day return €50/60, 1½ hours) between late April and October.

BUS Fethiye's otogar is 2.5km east of the centre, connected to the centre and Karagözler by dolmuş (TL1.50).

Buses to Antalya either go via the quicker, inland (yayla) route (TL20, 3½ hours), or the the less-direct coastal (sahil) route (TL28, 6½ hours, hourly in summer), via Kalkan (TL11, 1½ hours), Kaş (TL13, two hours) and Olympos (TL35, 4¾ hours).

DOLMUŞ From the stops near the mosque, minibuses run to local destinations including Ölüdeniz (TL5) and Faralya (TL5.50).

Ölüdeniz

☎0252 / POP 4600

Ölüdeniz's many charms – a sheltered lagoon beside a lush national park, a long spit of sandy beach, and Baba Dağ (Mt Baba) casting its shadow across the sea – have been a curse as much as a blessing. Many people think package tourism has turned 'Dead Sea' into a Paradise Lost. But Ölüdeniz remains a good place to party between trips along the serene coastline.

The lagoon remains a lovely place to while away a few hours on the beach with mountains soaring above you. Ölüdeniz is also a hot spot for paragliding (and parasailing). Companies here offer tandem paragliding flights off Baba Dağ (1960m) for TL120 to TL150.

Day cruises (TL15 to TL25) explore the coast, and shuttle boats head south to the beautiful Butterfly Valley (TL20 return).

⌨ Sleeping & Eating

Ölüdeniz's camping grounds are almost like budget resorts, with comfortable and stylish bungalows. There are also laid-back accommodation options in the valley and nearby Faralya and Kabak.

Sugar Beach Club CAMPGROUND, RESORT €
(📞617 0048; www.thesugarbeachclub.com; Ölüdeniz Caddesi 20; camp site per person/car/caravan TL15/15/15, bungalows per person TL50-140; ❄@🛜) About 500m north of the entrance to the park, this ultrachilled spot is the pick of the crop for backpackers. The strip of beach is shaded by palms and lounging areas, with a waterfront bar-restaurant. There's free entry to the beach, canoes and pedalos to hire, and regular events such as barbecues. Nonguests can use the sun lounges, parasols and showers for TL7.

Oba Motel Restaurant INTERNATIONAL €€
(📞617 0158; www.obamotel.com.tr/Erestaurant. asp; Mimar Sinan Caddesi; mains TL15-25; ⊙8am-midnight) Partly housed in a wooden cabin, the Oba has a reputation for home-style food at good prices. It does great Turkish/European breakfasts (from TL12), snacks and full-on mains, including a half-dozen veggie options.

🛈 Getting There & Away

There are frequent minibuses to Fethiye (TL5, 25 minutes).

Patara

🎵 0242 / POP 950

With Turkey's longest uninterrupted beach, laid-back little Patara (Gelemiş) is the perfect spot to mix your ruin-rambling with some dedicated sand-shuffling. The extensive ruins (admission TL5; ⊙9am-7pm May-Oct, 8am-5pm Nov-Apr) include a 5000-seat theatre and the *bouleterion* (council chamber), ancient Patara's 'parliament' where it is believed the Lycian League met. All in all, the former hippy-trail stop offers a good combination of nature, culture and traditional village life.

🛏 Sleeping & Eating

TOP CHOICE **Patara View Point Hotel** HOTEL €€
(📞843 5184, 0533 350 0347; www.pataraviewpoint.com; s/d TL70/100; ❄@🛜🏊) Up the hill from the main road, the *très* stylish Patara View has a pleasant pool, an Ottoman-style cushioned terrace, 27 rooms with balconies, and killer views over the valley. You'll find old farm implements inside and out,

including a 2000-year-old olive press. There's a tractor-shuttle to and from the beach at 10am and 3pm.

Akay Pension PENSION €
(📞843 5055, 0532 410 2195; www.pataraakaypension.com; s/d/tr TL45/60/80; ❄@) Kazım and wife Ayşe's pension has 13 well-maintained rooms with comfortable beds and balconies overlooking citrus groves, and an Ottoman-style lounge. Sample at least one set meal (from TL18).

Flower Pension PENSION €
(📞843 5164, 0530 511 0206; www.pataraflowerpension.com; s/d TL45/60, 4-/6-person apt TL100/150; ❄@🛜) On the road before the turn-off to the centre, the Flower has simple and airy rooms with balconies overlooking the garden, plus kitchen-equipped studios and apartments. There's a free shuttle to the beach.

Tlos Restaurant TURKISH €€
(📞843 5135; meze TL3-6, pide TL6-15, mains TL12-20; ⊙8am-midnight) The BYO Tlos has an open kitchen by the centre under a large plane tree. Its *guveç* (TL15) is recommended.

🛈 Getting There & Away

Buses on the Fethiye–Kaş route drop you on the highway 4km from the village. From here *dolmuşes* run to the village every 30 to 40 minutes.

In high season minibuses run from the beach through the village to Fethiye (TL12, 1½ hours), Kalkan (TL7.50, 20 minutes) and Kaş (TL10, 45 minutes).

Kalkan

🎵 0242 / POP 3250

Kalkan is a stylish hillside harbour town overlooking a sparkling blue bay. It's as rightly famous for its restaurants as its small but central beach, and makes an upmarket alternative to neighbouring Kaş. Development continues on the hills, driven by the many tourists and expats, and the former Ottoman-Greek fishing village's charms are found in its compact Old Town.

🛏 Sleeping

TOP CHOICE **Hotel Villa Mahal** LUXURY HOTEL €€€
(📞844 3268, 0532 685 2136; www.villamahal.com; d €200-300, ste €550; ❄🛜🏊) One of Turkey's most elegant and stylish hotels lies atop a cliff on the western side of Kalkan Bay, about

2km by road from town. The 13 rooms, individually designed in whiter-than-white minimalist fashion, have private terraces and sea views. The sail-shaped infinity pool is spectacularly suspended on the edge of the void and steps descend to the sea and a bathing platform. There's a free water taxi into the centre and sailboats can be hired.

Caretta Boutique Hotel HOTEL €€
(☑844 3435, 0505 269 0753; www.carettaboutiquehotel.com; İskele Sokak 6; s €45-58, d €69-85; ✳@) A perennial favourite with isolated swimming platforms, excellent home-style cooking, a warm welcome, and 13 bright and sunny rooms. For an away-from-it-all experience, nab one of the two terrace rooms reached down steps along the cliff. There's a free boat service from below the lighthouse in the marina.

White House Pension PENSION €€
(☑844 3738, 0532 443 0012; www.kalkanwhitehouse.co.uk; Süleyman Yilmaz Caddesi 24-26; s/d/f TL100/150/175; ✳@) Situated on a quiet corner at the top of the hill, this attentively run pension has 10 compact, breezy rooms (four with balconies) in a spotless family home. The real winner here, though, is the view from the terrace. Sharing the garden is sister property the **Courtyard Hotel Kalkan** (☑844 3738, 0532 443 0012; www.courtyardkalkan.com; s & d TL350), cobbled out of a couple of 19th-century village houses.

Kelebek Hotel & Apartments HOTEL, APARTMENT €
(☑844 3770, 0543 375 7947; www.butterflyholidays.co.uk; Mantese Mah 4; s TL45-50, d TL70-85, 1-/2-bedroom apt TL75/125; ✳@☒) Though slightly away from the action to the north of the centre, and a couple of hundred metres off the D400, the family-run 'Butterfly' offers remarkably good value for Kalkan. Choose between rooms in the main building, with a pool table in the tiled lobby, and apartments with kitchens in a separate block.

✖ Eating & Drinking

Kalkan's main market day is Thursday, though there is a smaller one in the Akbel district to the northwest on Sunday. In high season, always book ahead.

Korsan Fish Terrace SEAFOOD €€€
(☑844 3076; www.korsankalkan.com; Atatürk Caddesi; mains TL26-40; ◷10am-midnight) On the roof of the 19th-century Patara Stone House, Korsan offers a fine seafood experience.

There's live jazz on Tuesday and Saturday from 8.30pm, and an alternative, fishless menu of modern Turkish and international dishes.

Guru's Place ANATOLIAN €€
(☑844 3848, 0536 331 1016; www.kalkanguru.com; Kaş Yolu; meze plate TL20, mains TL9-28; ◷8am-11pm) Affable Hüseyin and family have been running this seaside restaurant for 20 years. Food is authentic and fresh, coming from their own garden. The menu is often limited to daily specials such as the lamb shanks. It's a bit out of town on the road to Kaş, so a free transfer service is provided.

Hünkar Ocakbaşı TURKISH €€
(☑844 2077; Şehitler Caddesi 38e; mains TL9-17) This authentic grill house serves all the traditional favourites, as well as pide (TL6 to TL9), pizzas (TL8 to TL11) and güveç, including a vegetarian option.

The Lighthouse TEA GARDEN, CAFE
(☑844 3752; Yat Limanı; beer TL6; ◷8.30am-2.30am) The erstwhile Fener ('lighthouse' in Turkish – and no prizes for guessing its location) is popular with locals, expats and visitors.

❶ Getting There & Away

Minibuses go to Fethiye (TL11, 1½ hours), Kaş (TL5, 35 minutes) and Patara (TL5, 25 minutes).

Kaş

☑0242 / POP 7200
A more genuine destination than Kalkan, Kaş (pronounced 'cash') may not sport the region's finest beaches, but this yachties' haven has a wonderfully mellow atmosphere. The surrounding areas are ideal for day trips by sea or scooter, and a plethora of adventure sports are on offer, in particular some excellent wreck diving.

◎ Sights & Activities

Apart from enjoying the small pebble beaches, you can walk 500m west of the main square to the well-preserved Hellenistic theatre. Other ancient remnants from the Lycian port of Antiphellos include the rock tombs in the cliffs above town, which you can walk to. It's well worth climbing the hilly street to the east of the main square to reach the King's Tomb, a Lycian sarcophagus mounted on a high base. Overland excursions and *dolmuşes* go to Saklıkent Gorge.

Boat Trips
CRUISE

(TL40-TL50) The most popular trip is to Üçağız and Kekova, a three-hour bus-and-boat excursion that includes time to see several interesting ruins as well as swim. Off Kekova Island is the Batık Şehir (Sunken City), the submerged remains of Lycian Simena. Other standard tours go to the Mavi Mağara (Blue Cave), Patara and Kalkan, or to Longos and several small nearby islands.

Bougainville Travel
OUTDOOR

(☎836 3737; www.bougainville-turkey.com; İbrahim Serin Sokak 10, Kaş) This long-established English-Turkish tour operator organises a plethora of activities, including canyoning, mountain biking, paragliding, scuba diving and sea kayaking. They are also experts on Lycian Way trekking.

🛏 Sleeping

Hideaway Hotel
HOTEL €€

(☎836 1887, 0532 261 0170; www.hotelhideaway.com; Eski Kilise Arkası Sokak 7; s TL40-60, d TL60-120; ❄@🅿🏊) The aptly named Hideaway, located at the far end of town on a quiet street, has comfortable rooms with balcony, some facing the sea. There's also a roof terrace with terminals, DVD player, honour-system bar, and views over the water and amphitheatre. Full meals are available.

Hotel Hadrian
RESORT €€€

(☎836 2856; www.hotel-hadrian.de; Doğan Kaşaroğlu Sokak 10; s €80-100, d €125-140, ste from €160; ❄🏊) About halfway out on the peninsula, the German-owned Hadrian is a tropical, Teutonic oasis. The large seawater pool, private swimming platform and terrace bar with wow-factor views are all excellent.

White House Pension
PENSION €€

(☎836 1513, 0532 550 2663; www.orcholiday.com; Yeni Cami Caddesi 10; s TL60-85, d TL100-140; ❄🅿) Decked out in wood, wrought iron, marble and terracotta paint, this stylish little gem has attractive rooms and a pretty terrace. Very warm welcome.

Anı Pension & Guesthouse
PENSION €

(☎836 1791, 0533 326 4201; www.motelani.com; Süleyman Çavuş Caddesi 12; s TL30-50, d TL50-60; ❄@🅿) Host Ömer offers smallish but spotless rooms with balconies, a relaxing roof terrace with DVD player, lounge with

cushions and water pipes, and a bar. Guests can use the kitchen (occasional barbecues for TL15) and borrow a chaise longue and umbrella for the beach.

🍴 Eating

There are some excellent restaurants southeast of the main square, especially around Sandıkçı Sokak. A big outdoor Friday market takes place along the old road to Kalkan.

TOP CHOICE İkbal
MODERN TURKISH €€€

(☎836 3193; Sandıkçı Sokak 6; mains TL20-34; ⏰9am-midnight) This Turkish-German restaurant serves excellent prepared fish dishes and the house speciality – slow-cooked leg of lamb – from a small but well-chosen menu. There's also a good selection of Turkish wines from Mediterranean vineyards.

TOP CHOICE Şaraphane
TURKISH €€

(☎836 2715, 0532 520 3262; Yeni Cami Caddesi 3; mains TL12-25) In the old part of Kaş, the 'Wine House' emphasises the fruit of the vine amid cosy surrounds with an open kitchen, bleached wooden floors and a roaring fire in the cooler months. Nice touches include complimentary homemade meze.

Köşk
MEZE €€

(☎836 3857; Gürsoy Sokak 13; mains TL14-25) In a lovely little square off a cobbled street just up from the water, Köşk occupies a rustic, 150-year-old house with two terraces. It serves good grills and gorgeous meze (TL6 to TKL7).

Blue House
MEZE €€

(☎836 1320; Sandıkçı Sokak 8; mains TL20-34) This family-run restaurant, with its blue doorway and balcony, has a great ambience and lovely views. The ladies work from the kitchen of their home, which you have to pass through to reach the terrace.

Bi Lokma
MEZE €€

(☎836 3942; www.bilokma.com.tr; Hükümet Caddesi 2; mains TL13-21; ⏰9am-midnight) Also known as 'Mama's Kitchen', this place has tables meandering around a terraced garden overlooking the harbour. The great traditional dishes include *mantı* (TL13) and *börek* (TL13).

🍷 Drinking

Giorgio's Bar
BAR

(☎0544 608 8687; Cumhuriyet Meydanı) Facing the main square, Georgio's has great music

Kaş

TURKEY KAŞ

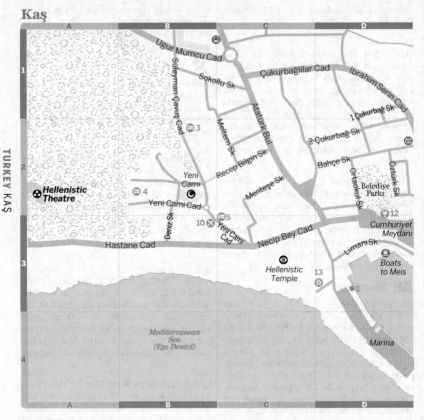

(played live several times a week). Cocktails from TL18.

Hideaway Bar & Cafe   BAR, CAFE
(☎836 3369; Cumhuriyet Meydanı 16/A; beer TL6-8; ☺4pm-3am) The enchanting Hideaway is tucked away in a garden accessed via a secret doorway. Turkish breakfast, Sunday brunch, snacks and cakes are offered.

Moon River   BAR
(☎836 4423; İbrahim Serin Caddesi 1d; beer TL5; ☺8am-3am; 🛜) This lounge offers live music throughout the week, good coffee, and reasonably priced drinks.

Echo Cafe & Bar   BAR, CLUB
(☎836 2047; www.echocafebar.com; Limanı Sokak; ☺8am-4am) Hip and stylish, this lounge near an ancient cistern on the harbour has Kaş high society sipping fruit daiquiris to both live and canned jazz.

🛈 Information

The **tourist office** (☎836 1238; Cumhuriyet Meydanı; ☺8am-5pm daily May-Oct, 8am-noon & 1-5pm Mon-Fri Nov-Apr) is on the main square.

🛈 Getting There & Away

BOAT The **Meis Express** (www.meisexpress.com; one way or same-day return TL40; 20 minutes) fast ferry sails daily throughout the year to the tiny Greek island of Meis (Kastellorizo). It's possible to spend the night there, or continue to Rhodes. Tickets can be bought from travel agencies or directly from Meis Express in the harbour.

BUS İstanbul TL65, 15 hours, 6.30am daily

İzmir TL40, 8½ hours, daily

DOLMUŞ There are regular *dolmuşes* to:

Antalya TL23, 3½ hours

Fethiye TL15; 2½ hours

Kalkan TL5, 35 minutes

Olympos TL18, 2½ hours

Patara TL7.50, 45 minutes.

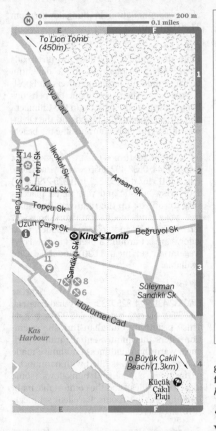

Kaş

⊙ Top Sights

Hellenistic Theatre	A2
King's Tomb	E3

Activities, Courses & Tours

1	Boat Trips	D3
2	Bougainville Travel	E2

Sleeping

3	Anı Pension & Guesthouse	B2
4	Hideaway Hotel	B2
5	White House Pension	C3

Eating

6	Bi Lokma	E3
7	Blue House	E3
8	İkbal	E3
9	Köşk	E3
10	Şaraphane	B3

Drinking

11	Giorgio's Bar	E3
12	Hideaway Bar & Cafe	D2

Entertainment

13	Echo Cafe & Bar	D3
14	Moon River	E2

Olympos & Çirali

☎0242

Olympos has long had ethereal appeal to travellers. It was an important Lycian city in the 2nd century BC, when the Olympians devoutly worshipped Hephaestus (Vulcan), the god of fire. No doubt this veneration sprang from reverence for the mysterious Chimaera, an eternal flame that still burns in the ground nearby. Along with the other Lycian coastal cities, Olympos went into decline in the 1st century BC, before its fortunes twisted and turned through Roman rule, 3rd-century AD pirate attacks, and fortress building during the Middle Ages by the Venetians and Genoese.

Neighbouring Çiralı, over the mountain and the narrow Ulupınar Stream, is another gem of a place. While Olympos has a well-established party reputation (though it has gentrified considerably), Çiralı is a family-friendly place to experience the fine art of *keyif* (quiet relaxation).

⊙ Sights & Activities

You can swim at the beach fronting the ruins of Olympos. Agencies and camps in Olympos offer activities including boat cruises, canyoning, mountain biking, rock climbing, diving, sea kayaking and hiking.

Ruins   RUIN
(admission TL3, 10 entry pass to ruins & beach TL7.50; ⊙9am-7.30pm May-Oct, 8am-6pm Nov-Apr) Set in a deep shaded valley running to the beach, the ruins of ancient Olympos appear undiscovered among the vines and flowered trees. Rambling along the trickling stream that runs through this rocky gorge is a treat.

Chimaera   HISTORIC SITE
(admission TL4, torch/flashlight rental TL3) This cluster of flames blazes from the crevices on the rocky slopes of Mt Olympos, near Çiralı and 7km from Olympos. Pensions and agencies offer lifts/evening tours (TL5/15).

🛏 Sleeping & Eating

OLYMPOS

Staying in an Olympos 'tree house' has long been the stuff of travel legend. The camps lining the valley have become overcrowded and institutionalised compared with their hippy-trail incarnations, and few huts are actually up in the trees. Still, they offer good value and an up-for-it party atmosphere in a lovely setting.

Unless specified otherwise, any prices listed here are for half board per person. Bathrooms are generally shared, but some bungalows have private facilities and even air-conditioning. Not all tree houses have reliable locks, so store valuables at reception.

Be extra attentive to personal hygiene while staying here; every year some travellers get ill. Especially in summer, the huge influx of visitors can overwhelm the camps' capacity for proper waste disposal. Be vigilant about where and what you eat.

Şaban Pansion   CAMPGROUND, PENSION €
(☑892 1265, 0532 457 3439; www.sabanpansion. com; tree house TL35-40, bungalow with bathroom TL45-50; ✳@) The place to come if you want to snooze in a hammock or on cushions in the shade of orange trees, Şaban sells itself on tranquillity, space and great home cooking. Room 7 really is a tree house.

Kadir's Tree Houses   CAMPGROUND, PENSION €
(☑892 1250, 0532 347 7242; www.kadirstree-houses.com; bungalow with bathroom TL40-65; ✳@) The place that put Olympos on the map looks like a Wild West boom town that just kept a-growin'. Kadir's has pillows in wooden bungalows, cabins and dorm rooms for 350 heads, the Bull and Hangar bars and travel agency **Adventure Centre** (☑892 1316; ⊘8.30am-10pm).

Bayrams   CAMPGROUND, PENSION €
(☑892 1243, 0532 494 7454; www.bayrams. com; dm TL30-35, tree house TL35-40, bungalow with air-con TL45-60, without air-con TL40-55; ✳@) Guests relax on cushioned platforms, play backgammon in the garden, puff on *nargiles* at the bar and socialise without necessarily partying.

Varuna Pansiyon   RESTAURANT €€
(☑892 1347, 0532 602 7839; www.olymposvaruna. com; mains TL10-15; ⊘8am-11pm) This popular restaurant serves snacks and mains including pide (TL7 to TL9), trout and *şiş* kebaps in an attractive open dining room. There's

also accommodation in bungalows (room TL30 to TL60).

ÇIRALI

Çıralı may initially look like two dirt roads lined with pensions, but it's a delightful beach community for nature lovers and post-backpackers. There are about 60 pensions here, some near the path up to the Chimaera and others close to the beach and the Olympos ruins. A dozen restaurants line the beach.

🌿 Myland Nature   PENSION €€€
(☑825 7044, 0532 407 9656; www.mylandnature. com; s TL113-167, d TL168-225, tr TL205-279; ✳@🖥) This artsy, holistic and very green place is sure to rub you up the right way (massage, free yoga and meditation workshops offered). Spotless and spacious wooden bungalows are set around a pretty garden. Food (vegetarian set meal TL20) and bikes are available.

⭐TOP CHOICE Hotel Canada   HOTEL €€
(☑0532 431 3414, 825 7233; www.canadahotel.net; d €55-60, 4-person bungalow €85-90; ✳@🖥) This beautiful Canadian-Turkish operation offers the quintessential Çıralı experience: warmth, friendliness and house-made honey. The garden is filled with hammocks, citrus trees, a pool and bungalows (some ideal for families), and the comfortable main building also has rooms. Excellent set meals (€10) are served.

Sima Peace Pension   PENSION €€
(☑825 7245, 0532 238 1177; www.simapeace.com; s/d/tr TL80/120/140; ✳@) A comfortable '60s throwback and Çıralı stalwart just down from the beach, Sima has five rooms and two bungalows hidden in an orange grove. Host Aynur cooks like a dream (evening buffet TL15-20).

❶ Getting There & Away

Buses and minibuses plying the Fethiye–Antalya coast road will halt at the stops near the Olympos and Çıralı junctions. From there, minibuses leave for both destinations (TL5). To Olympos (9km), they depart roughly hourly/half-hourly in winter/summer; to Çıralı (7km), roughly every two hours. Many accommodation options will pick you up from the highway (TL20 to TL25) if you book in advance.

The most pleasant way to travel between Olympos and Fethiye is on a cruise.

Antalya

☎0242 / POP 964,000

Once seen simply as the gateway to the 'Turkish Riviera', Antalya is is today very much a destination in its own right. Situated on the Gulf of Antalya (Antalya Körfezi), the largest city on Turkey's Mediterranean coast is both stylishly modern and classically beautiful. It boasts the wonderfully preserved Roman-Ottoman quarter of Kaleiçi, a splendid Roman harbour, plus superb ruins in the surrounding Beydağları (Bey Mountains). Kaleiçi's good-value boutique hotels are of an international standard, the museum is one of Turkey's finest, and there are excellent bars and clubs. The opera and ballet season at the Aspendos amphitheatre continues to draw attention.

◉ Sights & Activities

Antalya Museum   MUSEUM
(☎236 5688; www.antalya-ws.com/english/museum; Konyaaltı Caddesi 1; admission TL15; ⊙9am-7pm Tue-Sun mid-Apr–Oct, 8am-5pm Tue-Sun Nov–mid-Apr) This comprehensive museum is about 2km west of the centre and accessible on the old-fashioned *tramvay* (tram, TL1.25, Müze stop). Exhibitions in 14 big halls cover everything from the Stone and Bronze Ages to Byzantium, including finds from ancient Lycian cities (eg Patara and Xanthos) and sublime statues of Olympian gods.

KALEIÇI
Around the harbour is the lovely historic district Kaleiçi (literally 'within the castle'). It's a charming area full of twisting alleys, huge stone walls, atmosphere-laden courtyards, souvenir shops and lavishly restored mansions. Cliffside vantage points, including Karaalioğlu Parkı (Atatürk Caddesi), provide stunning views over the beautiful marina and soaring Beydağları. Kaleiçi is downhill from the main square, Kale Kapısı (Fortress Gate), with its old stone clock tower (*saat kalesi*).

Yivli Minare   LANDMARK
(Fluted Minaret) Antalya's symbol, this handsome and distinctive 'fluted' minaret was erected by the Seljuks in the early 13th century. The adjacent mosque (1373) is still in use. Within the complex is a restored Mevlevi Tekke (whirling-dervish monastery), and nearby to the west are two 14th- and 16th-century türbe (tombs). Cumhuriyet Meydanı to the west has an equestrian statue of Atatürk.

Hadriyanüs Kapısı   LANDMARK
(Hadrian's Gate) The monumental Hadrian's Gate was erected for the Roman emperor's visit to Antalya (130 BC).

Suna & İnan Kıraç
Kaleiçi Museum   MUSEUM
(☎243 4274; www.kaleicimuzesi.org; Kocatepe Sokak 25; admission TL2; ⊙9am-noon & 1-6pm Thu-Tue) This small but well-formed ethnography museum is housed in a lovingly restored Antalya mansion. Most impressive is the collection of ceramics in the exhibition hall behind the former Greek Orthodox church of Aya Yorgi (St George).

Balık Pazarı Hamamı   HAMAM
(Fish Market Bath; ☎243 6175; Balık Pazarı Sokak; bath TL15, package TL40; ⊙8am-11pm) Kaleiçi is a great place to experience a traditional Turkish *hamam*. At the 700-year-old Fish Market Bath, a bath, peeling, and soap and oil massage costs TL40 (TL15 for bath and scrub only). There are separate sections for men and women.

Boat Trips   CRUISE
(TL20 to TL80) Excursion yachts tie up in the marina, offering trips to the Gulf of Antalya islands and local beaches or further afield.

🛏 Sleeping

The best place to stay is Kaleiçi, where signs point the way to some excellent pensions.

TOP CHOICE Tuvana Hotel   BOUTIQUE HOTEL €€€
(☎247 6015; www.tuvanahotel.com; Karanlık Sokak 18; s & d €140-300; ❄❀🛜🍽) Among the most beautiful and intimate hotels on the Mediterranean coast, this discreet compound of six Ottoman houses has been converted into a refined city hotel. Rooms are suitably plush, with kilims, linen and brass light fittings as well as modcons. The main restaurant Seraser is world-class.

TOP CHOICE White Garden Pansiyon   PENSION €
(☎241 9115; www.whitegardenpansion.com; Hesapçı Geçidi 9; s/d TL40/60, 4-person apt TL120; @🍽) The 15-room White Garden offers tidiness, class beyond its price level and impeccable service. The building itself is a fine restoration with a charming courtyard. Guests can use the pool at the Secret Palace (☎244 1060; www.secretpalacepansion.

TURKEY ANTALYA

Kaleiçi

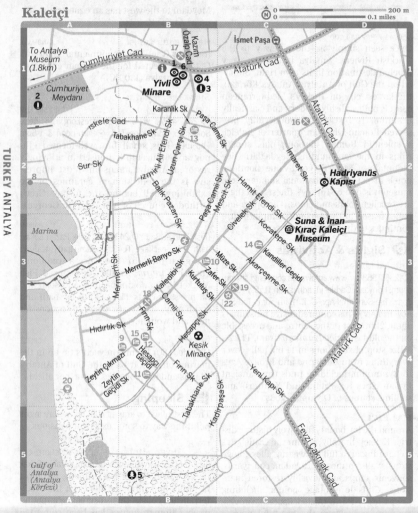

com; Fırın Sokak 10; s/d TL50/70; ✳@☎), an Ottoman conversion in the same stable behind the White Garden.

Hotel Hadrianus
HOTEL €€

(✆244 0030; www.hadrianushotel.com; Zeytin Çıkmazı 4; s TL65-80, d TL80-120; ✳☎) This 10-room hotel is set in a 750-sq-metre garden, a veritable oasis in Kaleiçi. Rooms at the top are larger and contain faux-antique and Ottoman-style furnishings.

Mediterra Art Hotel
BOUTIQUE HOTEL €€

(✆244 8624; www.mediterraart.com; Zafer Sokak 5; s €50-80, d €70-120; ✳@☎) This up-

scale masterpiece of wood and stone once housed a Greek tavern (see the 19th-century frescos and graffiti on the restaurant wall). The Mediterra offers sanctuary by a cutting-edge pool, a marvellous winter dining room, small, modestly luxurious rooms spread over four buildings, and an art gallery.

Sabah Pansiyon
PENSION €

(✆247 5345, 0555 365 8376; www.sabahpansiyon. com; Hesapçı Sokak 60; dm TL25, s/d with shower TL40/55, s/d without shower TL35/45, 2-bedroom apt TL200; ✳☎) The Sabah brothers run their place with aplomb while Mama takes

Kaleiçi

care of the kitchen. Attractions include the shaded courtyard and five new villas that can accommodate six people. Great for families. The 22 rooms vary greatly, so ask to see a couple.

Villa Perla　　　　　　　　PENSION €€
(📞248 4341; www.villaperla.com; Hesapçı Sokak 26; s/d €50/70; ❄️🛜🏊) At this authentic Ottoman place hidden in a courtyard (with pool and tortoises), the wooden ceilings are the real deal, and some rooms have four-poster beds and folk-painted cupboards. Mama Perla's in-house restaurant offers meze (plate TL19) and nine rabbit dishes (from TL19).

✖ Eating

A nearly endless assortment of cafes and eateries is tucked in and around the harbour area. For cheap eating, walk east to the **Dönerciler Çarşısı** (Market of Döner Makers; Atatürk Caddesi), or north to the rooftop kebap places around Kale Kapısı.

Vanilla　　　　　　INTERNATIONAL €€€
(📞247 6013; www.vanillaantalya.com; Zafer Sokak 13; mains TL22-40) At this outstanding, ultramodern restaurant led by a British chef and his Turkish wife, banquettes, glass surfaces and cheery orange bucket chairs provide a streamlined and unfussy setting for the Meditearranean-inspired international dishes. For dessert, retire next door to slick cafe-bar **The Lounge** (ice creams TL3.50, cakes TL10; ⊙9am-1am; 🛜) for Mövenpick ice cream and Lavazza coffee.

Seraser　　　　　　MEDITERRANEAN €€€
(📞247 6015; www.seraserrestaurant.com; Karanlık Sokak 18, Tuvana Hotel; mains TL29-50; ⊙1pm-midnight) The Tuvana Hotel's signature restaurant offers international dishes with a Mediterranean twist in fine Ottoman surrounds. The Turkish coffee *crème brûlée* is legendary.

Sim Restaurant　　　　　　MEZE €€
(📞248 0107; Kaledibi Sokak 7; mains TL12.50-20) This simple but charming restaurant offers a choice of seated areas: underneath the canopy in the narrow passageway at the front, wedged against ancient Byzantine walls; or inside, with global graffiti on the ground floor and, upstairs, eclectic antiques to complement *köfte* and glorious *çorbalar* (soups).

Parlak Restaurant　　　　ANATOLIAN €€
(📞241 6553; www.parlakrestaurant.com; Kazım Özlap Caddesi 7; mains TL10-24) Opposite the jewellery bazaar and just off pedestrian Kazım Özlap Caddesi, this sprawling open-air patio restaurant in an old *caravanserai* is famous for its charcoal-grilled chicken and meze, and favoured by locals.

🍷 Drinking

Kaleiçi offers buzzy beer gardens with million-dollar views, live-music venues, as well as raunchy clubs with outrageously expensive drinks.

It's worth seeking out the **Kale Bar** (📞248 6591; Mermerli Sokak 2; beer TL9, cocktails from TL21; ⊙11am-midnight), attached to the

TURKEY ANTALYA

TURKEY SIDE

AROUND ANTALYA

There are several magnificent Graeco-Roman ruins in the Mediterranean hinterland around Antalya. The ruins of Perge (admission TL15; ☉9am-7pm Apr-Oct, 8am-5.30pm Nov-Mar), one of the most important towns of ancient Pamphylia, are located 17km east of Antalya and 2km north of Aksu. On the access road you will see the stadium and theatre, which each sat 12,000 spectators.

At stunning Aspendos (admission TL15, parking TL5; ☉9am-7pm Apr-Oct, 8am-5pm Nov-Mar), 47km east of Antalya, you'll see the world's best-preserved Roman theatre, dating from the 2nd century AD and still used for performances during the Aspendos Opera & Ballet Festival (Aspendos Opera ve Bale Festivalı; www.aspendosfestival.gov.tr) every June and September.

The fierce Pisidians inhabited the ruined but still massive city of Termessos (admission TL5; ☉9am-7pm Apr-Oct, 8am-5pm Nov-Mar) for centuries, and repelled Alexander the Great from this rugged mountain valley. The ruins, 34km northwest of Antalya, have a spectacular setting, but demand some vigorous walking and climbing.

The Roman ruins continue at Köprülü Kanyon, about 100km northeast of Antalya and deservedly popular for hiking and white-water rafting. More than two-dozen companies offer rafting trips in the canyon, including Medraft (☎312 6296, in UK +44 20 8150 0687; www.medraft.com). An excursion on the intermediate rapids is about TL30, including a lesson, a two- to three-hour trip and lunch.

The easiest way to see these sights is with your own transport (Antalya has plenty of car-rental agencies) or on a tour with one of the many agencies based in Kaleiçi. A tour to Perge and Aspendos, with a side trip to Manavgat waterfall, should cost around TL115; an excursion/taxi tour to Termessos costs about TL100/150; and a tour to Köprülü Kanyon costs about TL100.

CH Hotels Türkevi and commanding some of Antalya's best harbour and sea views; the lively Castle Café (☎248 6594; Hıdırlık Sokak 48/1; beer TL7.50; ☉8am-11pm), filled with students; and Dem-Lik (☎247 1930; Zafer Sokak 6; beer TL5, coffee TL4; ☉noon-midnight), for jazz, reggae and blues (live at the weekend).

ℹ Information

Tourist Office (☎241 1747; Cumhuriyet Meydanı; ☉8am-6pm May-Oct, 8.30am-5.30pm Nov-Mar) Tiny but helpful office.

ℹ Getting There & Away

AIR Antalya's airport is 10km east of the city centre on the D400 highway. Turkish Airlines and budget AnadoluJet have several daily flights to/from İstanbul and Ankara year-round.

To reach the airport, catch bus 600 (TL2), which can be boarded along 100 Yıl. A taxi costs about TL35.

BUS From Kaleiçi, board the AntRay tram at the İsmet Paşa stop and travel for 20 minutes (TL1.50) to reach the otogar, 4km north of the centre on the D650 highway. A taxi costs TL25. Regular buses serve destinations including:

Göreme/Ürgüp TL40, nine hours
Kaş TL20, 3½ hours
Konya TL38, five hours
Olympos/Çıralı TL13, 1½ hours
Side/Manavgat TL13, 1½ hours

Side

☎0242 / POP 11,400

To some, the once-docile fishing town of Side (pronounced see-day) is mass tourism at its worst: endless rows of souvenirs, and matching restaurant menus in various European languages.

But move a couple of streets over and you'll find a different side to Side. Entering the town through the monumental Vespasian Gate is like walking onto a film set: Roman and Hellenistic ruins mark out the road, and a rebuilt agora could just as easily contain togas as T-shirts. The town is also blessed with sandy beaches.

◉ Sights

Side's impressive structures include the 2nd-century AD theatre (admission TL10; ☉9am-7.30pm mid-Apr-mid-Oct, 8am-5.30pm mid-Oct-mid-Apr) with 20,000 seats - one of the region's most dramatic; seaside temples to

Apollo and Athena (2nd century BC); and a 5th-century bathhouse, now Side Museum (admission TL10; ⊘9am-7.30pm Tue-Sun), with an excellent small collection of statues and sarcophagi.

🛏 Sleeping & Eating

Some accommodation has parking; otherwise you have to use the car park just beyond the theatre (TL3/15 per hour/day).

Beach House Hotel
HOTEL €€

(📞753 1607; www.beachhouse-hotel.com; Barbaros Caddesi; s/d TL50/100; ❋@⊚) Once the Pamphylia Hotel, a celebrity magnet in the 1960s, the Beach House's prime seafront location and welcoming staff lure a loyal band of regulars. Rooms have balconies and mostly face the sea. The roof terrace has a jacuzzi, and the garden boasts both a ruined Byzantine villa and rabbits.

Özden Pansiyon
PENSION €

(📞753 1337, 0534 552 3328; www.yoga-holidays-turkey.com; Gül Sokak 50; s/d TL30/60; ⊚) Simple but stylish wood-lined rooms frame a leafy courtyard that's a tranquil retreat from the souvenir-shop buzz outside. One-week yoga holidays here cost £395 per person.

Emir
TURKISH €€

(📞753 2224; Menekşe Caddesi; meze TL8-10, mains TL16-25; ✏) The Emir almost leans on the ruins of the Roman baths where Cleopatra is said to have dallied. The open kitchen produces excellent meze, grills and an array of vegetarian dishes.

ℹ Getting There & Away

In summer Side has daily buses to Ankara, İzmir and İstanbul. Otherwise, frequent minibuses connect Side with Manavgat otogar (TL2), 4km away, from where buses go to Antalya (TL10, 1½ hours), Alanya (TL10, 1½ hours) and Konya (TL25, four hours).

Alanya

📞0242 / POP 103,700

Alanya has mushroomed from a sparsely populated highway town with a sandy beach to a densely populated tourist haven. Aside from a quick boat cruise or waterfront stroll, many visitors to Alanya shuffle between their hotel's pool and all-inclusive buffet, venturing to the throbbing, laser-shooting nightclubs after dark. But Alanya

has something special up its ancient sleeve. Looming high above the promontory south of the modern centre is an impressive fortress complex, with the remains of a Seljuk castle, some atmospheric ruins and a small traditional village.

◉ Sights

Alanya Castle
FORTRESS

(Alanya Kalesı; admission TL10; ⊘9am-7pm Apr-Oct, 8am-5pm Nov-Mar) Alanya's awesome Seljuk-era castle overlooks the city, Pamphylian plain and Cilician mountains. Before reaching the entrance, the road passes a turn-off for the village of Ehmedek, which was the Turkish quarter during Ottoman and Seljuk times. Old wooden houses cluster around the 16th-century Süleymaniye Camii, Alanya's oldest; also here are an Ottoman bedesten and the Akşebe Türbesi, a 13th-century mausoleum.

In the castle's İç Kale (Inner Fortress), you'll mostly find poorly preserved ruins.

Catch a bus from opposite the tourist office (TL1.25). Taxis are around TL15 each way.

Kızılkule
HISTORIC BUILDING

(Red Tower; admission TL4; ⊘9am-7pm Apr-Oct, 8am-5pm Nov-Mar) Seljuk Sultan Alaeddin Keykubad I, who also built the fortress, constructed this five-storey octagonal tower by the harbour in 1226.

🏃 Activities

Every day at around 10.30am boats (per person incl lunch TL35) leave from near Rıhtım Caddesi for a six-hour voyage around the promontory, visiting several caves and Cleopatra's Beach.

Many local operators organise tours for landlubbers. A typical tour to Aspendos, Side and Manavgat waterfall costs around TL75 per person, while a 4WD safari in the Taurus Mountains costs about TL60.

🛏 Sleeping

Alanya has hundreds of hotels and pensions, almost all designed for groups and those in search of apart oteller (self-catering flats). The best alternatives are found along İskele Caddesi and in Tophane, the heritage district beneath the castle.

Centauera
BOUTIQUE HOTEL €€€

(📞519 0016; www.centauera.com; Andızlı Camii Sokak 4, Tophane; r €110-140; ℗❋⊚) A

TURKEY ANAMUR

10-minute stroll from the harbour, the romantic Centauera fills a restored Ottoman house. Views take in the elegant sweep of Alanya bay, and birdsong emanates from the surrounding Tophane neighbourhood. Dinner is available on request and for outside guests.

Seaport Hotel BUSINESS HOTEL €€
(☑513 6487; www.hotelseaport.com; İskele Caddesi 82; s/d TL120/200; ❄) The last hotel on the İskele strip, the Seaport offers efficient service and sea views from half of its rooms, which are not huge but are well appointed. Rates include a dinner buffet, but the food can be disappointing.

✖ Eating & Drinking

Many restaurants will pick you up from and bring you back to your accommodation.

İskele Sofrası SEAFOOD €€
(Tophane Caddesi 2b; meze TL6-8, mains TL15-30) This intimate, family-run place just off İskele Caddesi serves more than 70 meze. The terrace with harbour views is perfect for a cold beer and the shrimp *güveç*.

Ottoman House TURKISH €€€
(☑511 1421; www.ottomanhousealanya.com; Damlataş Caddesi 31; mains TL20-32) Alanya's most atmospheric eatery occupies a 100-year-old stone villa surrounded by lush gardens. Thursday and Sunday nights see an all-you-can-eat barbecue (€15); on Tuesdays there's a meze buffet (€15) and Turkish dancing.

Sofra ANATOLIAN €€
(İskele Caddesi 8a; mains TL8-16) Sofra delivers a modern spin on the traditional Turkish eatery with tasty kebaps, *mantı*, eastern Anatolian *içli köfte* (ground lamb and onion in a bulgur wheat shell) and a complimentary self-serve salad bar.

Cello BAR, LIVE MUSIC
(İskele Caddesi 36) This rustic wooden bar, showcasing 'protest and folk music', is a top spot for an acoustic-fuelled night. Friendly locals crowd in, and gigs kick off at 9.30pm most nights.

❶ Information

Tourist Office (☑513 1240; Damlataş Caddesi 1; ☉8am-5pm Mon-Fri) Opposite Alanya Museum, with a smaller branch (Damlataş Caddesi; ☉9am-6pm Mon-Fri) near the *belediye* (town hall).

❶ Getting There & Away

BOAT Fergün Denizcilik (☑511 5565, 511 5358; www.fergun.net; İskele Caddesi 84) runs ferries twice a week to **Girne/Kyrenia** (Northern Cyprus; one way/return TL77/127 plus harbour tax).

BUS The *otogar* is on the coastal highway (Atatürk Caddesi), 3km west of the centre (TL1.50/12 by *dolmuş*/taxi).

There are regular buses to Antalya (TL15, two hours), and to Adana (TL40, 10 hours) via Anamur.

Anamur

☑0324 / POP 35,100

Anamur has a pretty beach and waterfront at İskele, but the main reason to stop here is the ruined Byzantine city of **Anemurium** (Anemurium Ancient City; admission TL3; ☉8am-7pm Apr-Oct, to 5pm Nov-Mar), 8.5km west of the town. The sprawling site is eerily quiet, with ruins stretching 500m to the pebble beach, and city walls scaling the mountainside. About 7km east of town, the 13th-century **Mamure Castle** (Mamure Kalesi; admission TL3; ☉8am-7.30pm Apr-Oct, to 5pm Nov-Mar) is the biggest and best-preserved fortification on the Turkish Mediterranean coast, with 39 towers.

Good sleeping options are **Hotel Esya** (☑816 6595, 0532 491 0211; www.mersintatil.com/esyahotel.htm; İnönü Caddesi 55; s/d TL50/80; ❄❦) and **Hotel Luna Piena** (☑814 9045; www.hotellunapiena.com; Süleyman Bal Sokak; s TL60-80, d TL90-110; ❄❦).

Buses run to Alanya (TL25, three hours), Taşucu/Silifke (TL25, three hours) and Adana (TL35, six hours).

Kızkalesi

☑0324 / POP 1750

Wonderful 'Maiden's Castle', an easygoing and welcoming village with one of the region's loveliest beaches, is named after the astounding **Byzantine castle** (Maiden's Castle; admission TL3; ☉8am-5pm May-Oct) offshore, which looks from a distance as if it's suspended on top of the water. Unless you're up to swimming 300m, take a boat (TL5) or pedalo (TL10) to get there. The ruins of **Corycus Castle** (Korykos Kalesi; admission TL3; ☉8am-8pm Apr-Oct, to 5pm Nov-Mar) are on the beach; the two were once linked by a causeway.

Friendly **Rain Hotel** (☑523 2782; www.rainhotel.com; per person €40-70; ❄@) has spotless rooms and a long list of activities.

There are frequent buses to/from Silifke (TL4, 30 minutes).

From Taşucu, 11km southwest of Silifke, **Akgünler Denizcilik** (☏741 2303; www.akgunler.com.tr; İsmet İnönü Caddesi) *feribotlar* (car ferries; one way/return from TL59/99 plus harbour tax, four to 10 hours, Sunday to Thursday) and faster *ekspresler* (hydrofoils; one way/return TL69/114 plus harbour tax, two hours, daily) depart for Girne (Kyrenia) in Northern Cyprus.

Adana

TRANSPORT HUB

Turkey's fourth-largest city is a thoroughly modern affair, and its main use for travellers is as a transport hub. You may pass through en route along the Mediterranean coast or inland.

If you get stuck overnight, the boutique **Hotel Bosnalı** (☏359 8000; www.hotelbosnali.com; Seyhan Caddesi 29; s/d €75/85, ste €130-160; ❋ ?) occupies a 19th-century mansion, and the **Ibis Hotel** (☏355 9500; www.ibishotel.com; Turhan Cemal Beriker Bulvari 49; r TL100; ❋ ❋ ?) is a dependable chain choice.

Ova Ev Yemekleri (off Ataturk Caddesi; soups & rice TL3, mains TL6-11; ⊙Lunch) serves *yöresel yemekler* (hearty renditions of traditional homestyle recipes), and **Öz Asmaaltı** (☏351 4028; Pazarlar Caddesi 9; mains TL15-20) is another local favourite for its kebaps and meze.

ⓘ Getting There & Away

AIR Şakirpaşa airport is 4km west of the centre; a taxi costs about TL15.

BUS Adana's *otogar,* 2km beyond the airport, serves destinations throughout Turkey, including Antakya (TL20, 3½ hours), Konya (TL40, six hours), Ankara (TL40, seven hours) and İstanbul (TL60, 12 hours).

TRAIN Sleeper trains run nightly to/from Ankara (TL55, 12 hours).

Antakya (Hatay)

☏0326 / POP 213,300

Part of Syria until 1938, you might recognise Antakya by its biblical name, Antioch. Under the Romans, the city's important Christian community developed out of the already large Jewish population that was at one time led by St Paul. In today's prosperous, modern city, Arab influences permeate local life, food and language, and the ba-

zaars, back lanes and Orontes (Asi) River are well worth a wander.

At the time of writing, regions close to the Syrian border were offlimits due to the unrest in Syria and fighting between the Turkish army and PKK (Kurdistan Workers Party). Antakya is usually accessible and safe, but visitors should check on the current security situation before travel.

⊙ Sights

Hatay Archaeology Museum   MUSEUM
(Hatay Arkeoloji Müzesi; Gündüz Caddesi 1; admission TL8; ⊙9am-6.30pm Tue-Sun Apr-Oct, 8.30am-noon & 12.30-4.30pm Nov-Mar) This museum contains one of the world's finest collections of Roman and Byzantine mosaics, covering a period from the 1st century AD to the 5th century.

Church of St Peter   CHURCH
(St Pierre Kilisesi; admission TL8; ⊙9am-noon & 1-6pm Apr-Oct, 8am-noon & 1-5pm Nov-Mar) Both Peter and Paul almost certainly preached at this early Christian church, cut into the slopes of Mt Staurin (Mountain of the Cross) 2.5km northeast of town.

🛏 Sleeping

Belkis Konuk Evi ve Pansiyon   PENSION €€
(☏212 1511; www.belkisev.com; Gazipasa Caddesi, Güllübahçe Sokak; s/d TL60/120; ❋) Rooms in this cute family pension frame a whitewashed inner courtyard dotted with leafy trees. Expect decor merging rustic with chintzy, and a warm welcome.

Mozaik Otel   HOTEL €€
(☏215 5020; www.mozaikotel.com; İstiklal Caddesi 18; s/d TL85/130; ❋ ❋) Near the bazaar, rooms are decorated with folksy bedspreads and mosaic reproductions.

✗ Eating

For restaurants head south of Ulus Alanı on (or just off) Hürriyet Caddesi. Tea gardens are found in the park on the left bank of the Orontes, southwest of the museum.

Syrian influences permeate Antakya's cuisine. Handfuls of mint and wedges of lemon accompany many kebaps. Hummus is readily available and local specialities abound, including *künefe,* a cake of fine shredded wheat laid over a dollop of fresh, mild cheese, on a layer of sugar syrup, topped with chopped walnuts. You can try it at several places near the Ulu Camii, including **Kral Künefe** (Çarşı Caddesi 7).

Antakya Evi   TURKISH €€

(Silahlı Kuvvetler Caddesi 3; mains TL7-12) In this old villa decorated with photos and antique furniture, there are numerous spicy Hatay specialities, local meze (TL6 to TL8) and robust grills. Turkish folk music is played on Friday and Saturday night.

Hatay Sultan Sofrası   TURKISH €€

(www.sultansofrasi.com; İstiklal Caddesi 20a; mains TL10-16) A top spot for a diverse array of meze, spicy local kebaps, and (just maybe) Hatay's best *künefe*.

❶ Getting There & Away

Turkish Airlines and Pegasus Airlines serve İstanbul, İzmir and Ankara from Hatay aiport, 20km north of Antakya (TL10/30 by Havaş bus/taxi).

The *otogar* is 7km northwest of the centre. Destinations include Adana (TL20, 3½ hours).

CENTRAL ANATOLIA

On central Turkey's hazy plains, the sense of history is so pervasive that the average kebap chef can remind you that the Romans preceded the Seljuks. This is, after all, the region where the whirling dervishes first swirled, Atatürk began his revolution, Alexander the Great cut the Gordion knot and King Midas turned everything to gold. Julius Caesar came here to utter his famous line, '*Veni, vidi, vici*' ('I came, I saw, I conquered').

Ankara

📞 0312 / POP 4.5 MILLION

İstanbullus may quip that the best view in Ankara is the train home, but the Turkish capital has more substance than its reputation as a staid administrative centre suggests. The capital established by Atatürk offers a mellower, more manageable vignette of urban Turkey than İstanbul, and claims two of the country's most important sights: the Museum of Anatolian Civilisations and the Anıt Kabir. Ankara's flat, modest surroundings are hardly the stuff of national poetry, but a few neighbourhoods have some charm, notably the historic streets in the hilltop citadel and Kızılay, one of Turkey's hippest urban quarters.

◉ Sights

TOP CHOICE Museum of Anatolian Civilisations   MUSEUM

(Anadolu Medeniyetleri Müzesi; 📞324 3160; Gözcü Sokak 2, Ulus; admission TL15; ⊙Apr-Oct 8.30am-7pm, Nov-Mar to 5pm; Ⓜ Ulus) Displaying artefacts cherry-picked from just about every significant archaeological site in Anatolia, all housed in a beautifully restored 15th-century *bedesten*, the museum is the perfect introduction to the complex weave of Turkey's ancient past.

Citadel   NEIGHBOURHOOD

(Ankara Kalesi; Ⓜ Ulus) Just up the hill from the museum, the imposing *hisar* (citadel) is the most interesting part of Ankara to poke about in. This well-preserved quarter of thick walls and intriguing winding streets took its present shape in the 9th century AD, and locals still live here as if in a traditional Turkish village.

FREE Anıt Kabir   MONUMENT

(Atatürk Mausoleum and Museum; Gençlik Caddesi; audio guide TL5; ⊙9am-5pm May-Oct, to 4pm Nov-Apr; Ⓜ Tandoğan) The monumental mausoleum of Mustafa Kemal Atatürk (1881–1938), the beloved founder of modern Turkey, sits high above the city (2km west of Kızılay) with its abundance of marble and air of veneration.

FREE Vakıf Eserleri Müzesi   MUSEUM

(Ankara Museum of Religious Foundation Works; Atatürk Bulvarı, Ulus; ⊙9am-5pm Tue-Sun; Ⓜ Ulus) The tradition of carpets being gifted to mosques has helped preserve many of Turkey's finest specimens. This extensive collection once graced the floors of mosques throughout the country.

⮕ Sleeping

The Ulus area is most convenient for the Museum of Anatolian Civilisations and the citadel, but most of the restaurants and nightlife are in Kızılay and Kavaklıdere.

Angora House Hotel   HISTORIC HOTEL €€

(📞309 8380; www.angorahouse.com.tr; Kalekapısı Sokak 16; s/d/tr €50/69/75; 🛜; Ⓜ Ulus) This restored Ottoman house oozes subtle elegance at every turn. The six spacious rooms are infused with old-world atmosphere, while the walled courtyard garden is the perfect retreat from the citadel streets. Delightfully helpful staff add to the appeal.

Deeps Hostel
HOSTEL €

(☎213 6338; www.deepshostelankara.com; Ataç Sokak 46; dm/s/d without bathroom €10/18/32; ⓡ; ⓜKızılay) Ankara's best budget choice, friendly Deeps has colourful, light-filled rooms, a spacious dorm, and squeaky-clean, modern shared bathrooms. It's all topped off by a fully equipped kitchen (breakfast isn't included) and a cute communal area downstairs.

Divan Çukurhan
HISTORIC HOTEL €€€

(☎306 6400; www.divan.com.tr; Depo Sokak 3, Ankara Kalesi; s/d €130/150, ste €180-400; ❋ⓡ; ⓜUlus) This distinctive hotel offers a chance to stay in the 16th-century Çukurhan *caravanserai*. Set around a dramatic glass-ceilinged interior courtyard, each individually themed room blends ornate decadence with sassy contemporary style.

Hotel Eyüboğlu
HOTEL €€

(☎417 6400; www.eyubogluhotel.com; Karanfil Sokak 73; s/d €69/89; ❋ⓡ; ⓜKızılay) Although lacking in character, this great-value option is wonderfully efficient. Staff go out of their way to help (despite a shortage of English), and the no-nonsense rooms boast supremely comfy beds.

🍴 Eating & Drinking

Most Ulus options are basic. **Ulus Hali food market** sells provisions from oversized chilli peppers to jars of honey. In and around the citadel, inviting, atmospheric licensed restaurants occupy old wood-and-stone houses.

It's all about street stalls, hip bistros and cafe culture in Kızılay, where terraces line virtually every inch of space south of Ziya Gökalp Caddesi. Kızılay's tall, thin buildings also pack in up to five floors of studenty bars, cafes and *gazinos* (nightclubs).

Zenger Paşa Konağı
ANATOLIAN €€

(☎311 7070; www.zengerpasa.com; Doyran Sokak 13; mains TL12-17; ⓜUlus) Crammed with Ottoman ephemera, the Zenger Paşa at first looks like a deserted ethnographic museum, but climb up the rickety stairs and you'll find views of the city that are worth a visit alone. Wealthy Ankaralıs love the pide, meze and grills.

And Evi Cafe
MODERN TURKISH €€

(☎312 7978; İçkale Kapısı; mains TL12-24; ⓜUlus) This cafe, set into the citadel walls, is a winner for its cosy Ottoman-style interior and panoramic city views from the terrace. Tuck into a lunchtime crepe (TL11), sample the divine carrot cake (TL6) with a latte for afternoon tea, or choose a pasta dish for dinner.

Le Man Kültür
INTERNATIONAL €

(☎310 8617; Konur Sokak 8; mains TL6-16; ⓜKızılay) Named after a Turkish comic strip (and decorated accordingly), this is the pre-party pick for a substantial feed among Ankara's beautiful young educated things. Drinks are reasonably priced and the speakers crank everything from indie-electro to Türk pop.

Aylak Madam
CAFE

(☎419 7412; Karanfıl Sokak 2, Kızılay; ◷10am-late) A supercool French bistro/cafe with a mean weekend brunch (from 10am to 2.30pm), plus sandwiches, head-kicking cappuccinos, and a kick-backed jazz-fusion soundtrack.

ℹ Information

There are lots of banks with ATMs in Ulus, Kızılay and Kavaklıdere.

Main Post Office (Atatürk Bulvarı) In Ulus, with branches in Kızılay.

Tourist Office (☎310 8789; Gazi Mustafa Kemal Bulvarı; ◷9am-5pm Mon-Fri, 10am-5pm Sat) Also branches (usually unmanned) at the *otogar* and train station.

ℹ Getting There & Away

AIR Domestic and international carriers serve Esenboğa airport, 33km north of the city, but İstanbul's airports offer more choice and better deals. Lufthansa, Pegasus Airlines and Qatar Airways offer international connections, while AnadoluJet has direct flights to/from destinations nationwide.

BUS Ankara's huge AŞTİ (Ankara Şehirlerarası Terminali İşletmesi) *otogar*, 4.5km west of Kızılay, is the vehicular heart of the nation, with buses to/from every Turkish city or town of any size. Apart from over public holidays, you can often turn up, buy a ticket and be on your way in less than an hour. Services include İstanbul (TL40, six hours).

TRAIN A high-speed train serves Konya (economy/business class TL25/35, two hours, eight daily) and long-distance trains run overnight to eastern Anatolia. Services to/from İstanbul have been cancelled until at least 2014.

ℹ Getting Around

To/From the Airport

Havaş shuttle buses depart from Gate B at 19 May Stadium (Kazım Karabekir Caddesi, Ulus) every half hour between 2am and 10pm daily

SAFRANBOLU & AMASYA

Safranbolu and Amasya, respectively 145km north and 270km northeast of Ankara, are slightly off the beaten Anatolian track, but beckon savvy travellers with their ethereal settings and historic atmosphere.

Safranbolu is such an enchanting town that Unesco declared it a World Heritage site. It boasts a wonderful old Ottoman quarter bristling with 19th-century half-timbered houses; as part of the ongoing restoration, many have been turned into hotels or museums.

Blissfully located on riverbanks beneath cliffs carved with Pontic tombs, **Amasya** is one of Turkey's best-kept secrets, harbouring historic sites including a lofty castle, Seljuk mosques and enough picturesque Ottoman piles to satisfy the fussiest sultan.

Both towns boast excellent accommodation, with a profusion of delightful pensions set in skilfully restored Ottoman mansions. In Safranbolu, **Kahveciler Konağı** (☏725 5453; www.kahvecilerkonagi.com; Mescit Sokak 7; s/d TL60/TL120; ☏) was once the host's grandfather's house; Amasya's family-run **Gönül Sefası** (☏212 9461; Yalıboyu Sokak 24; s/d/tr TL60/100/120) has lots of local character.

There are buses from Ankara to Safranbolu (TL25, three hours) and Amasya (TL30, five hours), as well as from İstanbul.

(TL10, 35 minutes). After 10pm buses leave according to flight departure times. Havaş also links the airport and *otogar*. From the airport, buses leave 25 minutes after each flight arrival.

Don't pay more than TL60 for a taxi.

Public Transport

BUS Buses marked 'Ulus' and 'Çankaya' run the length of Atatürk Bulvarı. Those marked 'Gar' go to the train station, those marked 'AŞTİ' to the *otogar*. You can buy transport cards (TL3.50), valid for two journeys (bus or metro), from metro stations and major bus stops or anywhere displaying an EGO Bilet sign.

TAXI It costs about TL10 to cross the centre; charges rise at night.

METRO The network has two lines: the Ankaray line, running between AŞTİ *otogar* and Dikimevi via Kızılay; and the Metro line, runing from Kızılay northwest via Sıhhiye and Ulus to Batıkent. Trains run from 6.15am to 11.45pm daily. Tickets cost TL3.50/8.75 for two/five journeys.

Konya

☏0332 / POP 1.07 MILLION

Turkey's equivalent of the 'Bible Belt', conservative Konya treads a delicate path between its historical significance as the home town of the whirling-dervish orders and a bastion of Seljuk culture, and its modern importance as an economic boom town. The city derives considerable charm from this juxtaposition of old and new, and boasts one of Turkey's finest and most characteristic sights, the Mevlâna Museum.

The centre stretches from Alaaddin Tepesi, the hill topped by the Seljuk **Alaaddin Camii**, along Mevlâna Caddesi to the Mevlâna Museum.

The two-week **Mevlâna Festival** culminates on 17 December, the anniversary of Mevlâna's 'wedding night' with Allah. **Semas** (dervish ceremonies) also take place on Saturday evenings throughout the year; contact the tourist office about both.

⊙ Sights

TOP CHOICE **Mevlâna Museum** MUSEUM

(☏351 1215; admission TL3, audio guide TL5; ⊙9am-5pm Tue-Sun, 10am-5pm Mon) Join the pilgrims at this wonderful museum-cum-shrine, where embroidered velvet shrouds cover the turban-topped tombs of Mevlâna (Celaleddin Rumi) and other eminent dervishes. The former lodge of the whirling dervishes, it is topped by a brilliant turquoise-tiled dome. Although it's virtually under siege from devout crowds, there's a palpable mystique here.

Tile Museum MUSEUM

(Karatay Medresesi Çini Müzesi; ☏351 1914; Alaaddin Meydanı; admission TL3; ⊙9am-5pm) The interior central dome and walls of this former Seljuk theological school (1251) showcase some finely preserved blue-and-white Seljuk tilework. There is also an outstanding collection of ceramics on display.

Museum of Wooden Artefacts & Stone Carving
MUSEUM

(Tas ve Ahsap Eserler Müzesi; ☑351 3204; Adliye Bulvarı; admission TL3; ☺Tue-Sun 9am-5pm) The İnce Minare Medresesi (Seminary of the Slender Minaret), housing this museum, was built in 1264 for a Seljuk vizier. Inside, many of the carvings feature motifs similar to those used in tiles and ceramics.

🛏 Sleeping

Derviş Otel
BOUTIQUE HOTEL €€

(☑350 0842; www.dervishotel.com; Güngör Sokak 7; s/d/tr TL100/160/210; ❇☎) This airy, light-filled 200-year-old house has been converted into a rather wonderful boutique hotel, which has a taste of local character without scrimping on modern luxuries.

Ulusan Otel
HOTEL €

(☑351 5004; Çarşi PTT Arkasi 4; s/d without bathroom TL30/60; ☎) The pick of the Konya cheapies, with basic but bright and spotlessly clean rooms, both private and (immaculately kept) shared bathrooms, a communal area full of homely knick-knacks, and an enthusiastic and graceful host.

Hotel Rumi
HOTEL €€€

(☑353 1121; www.rumihotel.com; Durakfakih Sokak 5; s/d/tr/ste €60/90/110/130; ❇☎) Rooms are a tad on the small side, but are elegantly styled in soft mauves and sage green. Staff seem to delight in offering genuine service and the top-level breakfast room has killer views of the nearby Mevlâna Museum.

Mevlâna Sema Otel
HOTEL €€

(☑350 4623; www.semaotel.com; Mevlâna Caddesi 67; s/d TL60/90; ❇☎) Despite the strange plaster mouldings all over the room walls, this is a safe, solid choice with a great location and friendly staff. Ask for a rear-facing room to avoid the din of the main road.

🍴 Eating & Drinking

Restaurants around the Mevlâna Museum and tourist office have great views, but their food is not recommended – with the exception of **Gülbahçesi Konya Mutfağı** (☑351 0768; Gülbahçe Sokak 3; mains TL8-18; ☺8am-10pm). The fast-food restaurants on Adilye Bulvarı are lively places for a snack, but check the swift grub is thoroughly cooked. Head to Alaaddin Tepesi for tea gardens.

Konak Konya Mutfağı
ANATOLIAN €

(☑352 8547; Piriesat Caddesi 5; mains TL8-16; ☺11am-10pm) This excellent traditional restaurant is run by food writer Nevin Halıcı, who puts her personal twist on Turkish classics. Grab an outside table to rub shoulders with vine-draped pillars and a fragrant rose garden.

Osmanlı Çarşısı
CAFE

(☑353 3257; İnce Minare Sokak) An atmospheric, early-20th-century house with terraces, pavement seating and cushions galore where students talk politics while sucking on *nargiles*.

ℹ Information

Tourist Office (☑353 4020; Aslanı Kışla Caddesi; ☺8.30am-5.30pm Mon-Sat) Gives out a city map and a leaflet covering the nearby Mevlâna Museum; can also organise guides.

ℹ Getting There & Away

AIR Turkish Airlines and Pegasus Airlines both operate daily flights to/from İstanbul. The airport is 13km northeast of the centre; TL40 by taxi. Havaş runs shuttle buses (TL9).

BUS From the *otogar*, 7km north of the centre and accessible by tram from Alaaddin Tepesi, regular buses serve all major destinations.

Ankara TL18, 3½ hours

İstanbul TL45, 11½ hours

Kayseri TL30, four hours

TRAIN Eight high-speed trains run to/from Ankara daily (adult/child TL25/12.50, 1¾ hours). A taxi from the station to the centre should cost about TL15.

CAPPADOCIA (KAPADOKYA)

Cappadocia's surreal fairy chimneys – rock columns, pyramids, mushrooms and even a few shaped like camels – were formed, alongside the area's valleys of cascading white cliffs, when Erciyes Daği (Mt Erciyes) erupted. The intervening millennia added to the remarkable Cappadocian canvas, with Byzantines carving out cave churches and subterranean complexes large enough to house thousands. You could spend days hiking through the canyons and admiring the rock-cut churches and their frescos.

When the day's done, spots such as Göreme and Ürgüp have some of Anatolia's best restaurants and guesthouses, allowing guests to experience troglodyte living first hand.

☞ Tours

Most itineraries finish at a carpet shop, onyx factory or pottery workshop. It is interesting to see traditional Cappadocian craftsmen at work, but make it clear before the trip begins if you are not interested. Most tour companies offer full-day tours and guided day hikes.

Full-day tours To destinations such as the Ihlara Valley, the underground cities (which are best visited with a guide) and Soğanlı's valleys of rock-cut churches. The Ihlara Valley trip usually includes a short guided hike in the gorge, lunch and a trip to an underground city; most operators charge about TL90.

Guided day-hikes Usually in the Güllüdere (Rose), Kızılçuker (Red) or Meskendir Valleys. Costs vary according to the destination, degree of difficulty and length.

The following Göreme-based agencies offer good daily tours. There are also agencies in Avanos and Ürgüp. Do not book tours in Nevşehir, which has a reputation for unscrupulous operators; or in İstanbul, which will be more expensive than booking in Cappadocia.

Middle Earth Travel ADVENTURE TOUR
(☎271 2559; www.middleearthtravel.com; Cevizler Sokak 20) The adventure-travel specialist offers climbing and treks ranging from local, one-day expeditions to one-week missions, including the rugged Ala Dağlar National Park.

Heritage Travel GUIDED TOUR
(☎271 2687; www.turkishheritagetravel.com; Uzundere Caddesi) The knowledgeable Mustafa is recommended (group/private tours €45/100 per person).

Mehmet Güngör WALKING TOUR
(☎0532 382 2069; www.walkingmehmet.com; Noriyon Cafe, Müze Caddesi; four hours/full day €60/80) Recommended walking guide.

Yama Tours GUIDED TOUR
(☎271 2508; www.yamatours.com; Müze Caddesi 2) Also offers three-day trips to Nemrut Dağı (Mt Nemrut).

Neşe Tour GUIDED TOUR
(☎271 2525; www.nesetour.com; Avanos Yolu 54) Also organises two- to four-day trips to Nemrut Dağı.

Nomad Travel GUIDED TOUR
(☎271 2767; www.nomadtravel.com.tr; Belediye Caddesi) Offers an excellent Soğanlı tour.

New Göreme Tours GUIDED TOUR
(☎271 2166; www.newgoreme.com) Fun and friendly private tours.

ℹ️ Getting There & Away

AIR To travel between central Cappadocia and the two nearby airports, the easiest solution is to organise a transfer through your accommodation or **Cappadocia Express** (☎0384-271 3070; www.cappadociatransport.com; Iceridere Sokak 3, Göreme; per passenger TL20).

Kayseri airport Turkish Airlines and Pegasus Airlines have several daily flights to/from İstanbul.

Nevşehir airport Turkish Airlines has two daily flights to/from İstanbul.

BUS It's easy to get to Cappadocia by bus, although from İstanbul it will likely be an overnight journey. When you purchase your ticket, make sure it clearly states your final destination (Göreme, Ürgüp etc), not just 'Cappadocia'. There should be a *servis* from Nevşehir to the surrounding villages. If you get stuck, phone your accommodation for a pick-up and do *not*

ABOVE THE FAIRY CHIMNEYS

Cappadocia is one of the best places in the world to try hot-air ballooning, with favourable flight conditions and a wonderful network of valleys to explore. Flights take place at dawn (later-morning flights are also offered, but not recommended) and balloons operate most mornings throughout the year. The major drawback is that, with the activity's burgeoning popularity, dozens of balloons now fill the sky on typical mornings, and the numerous operators vary in expertise and safety standards. The following have good credentials:

Butterfly Balloons (☎271 3010; www.butterflyballoons.com; Uzundere Caddesi 29, Göreme) Standard flights (one hour, up to 16 passengers) cost €175.

Royal Balloon (☎271 3300; www.royalballoon.com; Dutlu Sokak 9) Standard flights (one hour, up to 20 passengers) cost €175.

Voyager Balloons (☎271 3030; www.voyagerballoons.com; Müze Caddesi 36/1, Göreme) Standard flights (one hour) cost €160.

book a tour in Nevşehir. A taxi to Göreme should cost around TL35.

Departing Cappadocia, Göreme and Ürgüp have *otogars*, as do Kayseri and Nevşehir. From Göreme buses go to:

Ankara TL30, 4½ hours

Antalya TL45, nine hours

İstanbul TL50, 12 hours

Konya TL20, three hours

❶ Getting Around

Travelling the quieter roads is a great way to cover the central sights and appreciate the landscape. Prices (in Göreme) for a day's rental:

Mountain bikes TL25

Mopeds and scooters TL45 to TL55

Small car TL90 to TL130

DOLMUŞ Belediye Bus Corp *dolmuşes* (TL2.50 to TL3) travel between Ürgüp and Avanos via Ortahisar, Göreme Open-Air Museum, Göreme village, Çavuşin and (on request) Paşabağı and Zelve. The services leave Ürgüp at 10am, noon, 4pm and 6pm; and Avanos at 9am, 11am, 1pm, 3pm and 5pm.

There's also an hourly *belediye* (municipal) bus between Avanos and Nevşehir (TL4) via Çavuşin (10 minutes), Göreme (15 minutes) and Uçhisar (30 minutes), leaving Avanos from 7am to 7pm.

Göreme

📞 0384 / POP 6350

Göreme is the archetypal travellers' utopia: a beatific village where the surreal surroundings spread a fat smile on everyone's face. Beneath the honeycomb cliffs, the locals live in fairy chimneys – or increasingly, run hotels in them. The encroaching maze of wavy white and pink valleys is dotted with hiking trails, panoramic viewpoints and rock-cut churches.

Tourism has inevitably changed this village, where you can start the day in a hot-air balloon before touring a valley of rock-cut Byzantine churches. Nonetheless, you can still see rural life continuing in a place where, once upon a time, if a man couldn't lay claim to one of the rock-hewn pigeon houses, he would struggle to woo a wife.

🏃 Activities

Hiking   HIKING

There are many hiking options around Göreme village. It's surrounded by a handful of gorgeous interconnected valleys that are easily explored on foot, allowing about one to

GÖREME OPEN-AIR MUSEUM

Cappadocia's top attraction and a World Heritage site, the **Göreme Open-Air Museum** (Göreme Açık Hava Müzesi; 📞271 2167; admission TL15, Karanlık Kilise admission TL8; ⊗8am-5pm) preserves a rock-hewn Byzantine monastic settlement, where some 20 monks lived. Frescos cover the 10th- to 13th-century cave churches – notably the stunning **Karanlık Kilise** (Dark Church), which is well worth the extra TL8. Across the road from the main entrance, the **Tokalı Kilise** (Buckle Church), with an underground chapel and fabulous frescos, is included in the museum entrance fee.

three hours for each. The valleys are remote in places and it's easy to get lost in them, so stick to the trails and walk with a companion if possible.

Recommended guides include Mehmet Güngör.

Horse Riding   HORSE RIDING

Cappadocia is excellent for horse riding, which allows you to access untrodden parts of the valleys. **Dalton Brothers** (📞0532 275 6869; Müze Caddesi; 1 hr TL45, 2 hr TL90), run by the Göreme-born 'horse whisperer' Ekrem Ilhan, uses sure-footed Anatolian horses from Erciyes Dağı.

🛏 Sleeping

If you're visiting between October and May, pack warm clothes as pension owners may delay putting the heating on, and ring ahead to check your choice is open. This is only a small sample of the huge number of rock-cut retreats.

TOP
CHOICE **Kelebek Hotel &**

Cave Pension   HOTEL €€

(📞271 2531; www.kelebekhotel.com; Yavuz Sokak 31; fairy chimney s/d €40/50, deluxe s/d €52/65, ste s €64-144, ste d 80-180; 🛜🏊) Spread over two gorgeous stone houses, each with fairy chimney protruding skyward, rooms here exude Anatolian inspiration. One of Göreme's original boutique hotels, Kelebek (Butterfly) continues to innovate, offering complimentary village garden breakfast visits.

TOP CHOICE Koza Cave Hotel
HOTEL €€

(☑271 2466; www.kozacavehotel.com; Cakmaklı Sokak 49; s/d €75/90, ste €115-140; ☎) Bringing eco-inspired chic to Göreme, Koza Cave is a masterclass in stylish sustainable tourism. Owner Derviş lived in Holland, and has incorporated Dutch ecosensibility into every cave crevice. Recycled materials and local handcrafted furniture are utilised to create sophisticated, elegant spaces.

Aydınlı Cave House
HOTEL €€

(☑271 2263; www.thecavehotel.com; Aydınlı Sokak 12; r €70-140; ☎) Proprietor Mustafa has converted his family home into a haven for honeymooners and those requiring a little rock-cut style with their solitude. Guests rave about the warm service and immaculate, spacious cave rooms, which include a family suite.

Dorm Cave
HOSTEL €

(☑271 2770; www.travellerscave.com; Hafız Abdullah Efendi Sokak 4; dm €10, d/tr €30/45; ☎) In this superb hostel, three spacious cave rooms are home to the dorm beds, and share small, modern bathrooms across a pretty courtyard. Upstairs a couple of snug private rooms also offer brilliant value.

Kismet Cave House
HOTEL €€

(☑271 2416; www.kismetcavehouse.com; Kağnı Yolu 9; d €75; ☎) Guests consistently hail the intimate experience created by the unobtrusive Faruk and his family at this cave house. The rooms host local antiques, colourful rugs and quirky artwork, while communal areas have cosy, cushion-scattered nooks.

Fairy Chimney Inn
HOTEL €€

(☑271 2655; www.fairychimney.com; Güvercinlik Sokak 5-7; r from €55-111; ☎) This highbrow retreat is run by Dr Andus Emge and his wife, who offer academic asides to their wonderful hospitality. The views from the garden and various peepholes are magnificent, while the rooms have simple furniture and traditional textiles.

Cappadocia Cave Suites
LUXURY HOTEL €€€

(☑271 2800; www.cappadociacavesuites.com; Ünlü Sokak 19; r €135-275; ❄☎) Uncomplicated service, spacious, modern-meets-megalithic suite rooms and cool, converted stables. Fairy Chimney 1 is our pick for its cosy living room, ideal for balloon-viewing.

✗ Eating

TOP CHOICE Köy Evi
ANATOLIAN €€€

(☑271 2008; Aydınkıragı Sokak 40; set menu TL25; ☑) The simple, wholesome, tasty flavours of village food are the main act at this brilliant set-menu restaurant, which offers a taste-bud tour of Göreme. The warren of cave rooms has been kept authentically basic, adding to the homespun appeal.

Seten Restaurant
MODERN TURKISH €€

(☑271 3025; www.setenrestaurant.com; Aydınlı Sokak; mains TL16-40) Brimming with an artful Anatolian aesthetic, Seten offers an education for newcomers to Turkish cuisine and a treat for well-travelled tongues. The classic dishes done right, and dazzling array of meze done differently, keep you coming back.

Topdeck Cave Restaurant
ANATOLIAN €€

(☑271 2474; Hafız Abdullah Efendi Sokak 15; mains TL15-20; ☾dinner only; ☑) Talented chef Mustafa and his gracious family have transformed an atmospheric cave room in their house into this cosy restaurant. Kids pitch in with the serving and diners dig into hearty helpings of Anatolian favourites with a spicy twist. Mustafa also offers reservation-only, morning cooking classes (€40; ☾classes 9-11am).

Nazar Börek
TURKISH €

(☑271 2441; Müze Caddesi; gözleme & börek TL6-9; ☎) Head here for supremely tasty traditional Turkish staples, including hearty plates of *gözleme* and *sosyete böregi* (stuffed spiral pastries served with yoghurt and tomato sauce).

Dibek
ANATOLIAN €€

(☑271 2209; Hakkı Paşa Meydanı 1; mains TL10-22; ☑) Diners sprawl on cushions and feast on traditional dishes and homemade wine at this family restaurant, set inside a 475-year-old building. Book ahead (at least three hours) for the slow-cooked *testi* kebap meal ('pottery kebap', with meat or mushrooms and vegetables cooked in a sealed terracotta pot, which is broken at the table; TL28).

Local Restaurant
MODERN TURKISH €€

(☑271 2629; Müze Caddesi 38; mains TL11-32) Local's steak dishes are scrumptious enough, but do order the *patlican* (aubergine) salad for gloriously smoky perfection on a plate.

ℹ️ Information

Services useful to travellers are mostly around the central *otogar*, including ATMs and a **tourist information booth** (☑271 2558; www.goreme. org). The **post office** (PTT; Posta Sokak), a good option for changing money, is nearby.

Uçhisar

☑0384 / POP 3800

Between Göreme and Nevşehir is picturesque, laid-back yet stylish Uçhisar, built around a **rock castle** (Uçhisar Kalesi; admission TL3; ⊙8am-8.15pm) that offers panoramic views from its summit. The local 'kilometre zero' for French holidaymakers, Uçhisar is nonetheless quieter than Göreme and worth considering as an alternative base.

There are some excellent places to stay, mostly with views across the rocky valleys.

Underground passageways, reading corners and shady terraces add magic to **Kale Konak** (☑219 2828; www.kalekonak.com; Kale Sokak 9; s/d/ste €90/110/140; 🖥), with a marble *hamam* and minimalist retreat-chic rooms in the shadow of Uçhisar castle.

Hospitable and spacious, **Kilim Pension** (☑219 2774; www.sisik.com; Tekelli Mahallesi; s/d/ tr TL70/130/170; 🖥) has smartly simple, light-filled rooms and a vine-draped terrace.

At cosy **Uçhisar Pension** (☑219 2662; www.uchisarpension.com; Göreme Caddesi; s/d/ tr €25/40/55; 🖥), Mustafa and Gül dispense lashings of old fashioned Turkish hospitality.

Eating options in the village range from **Elai** (☑219 3181; www.elairestaurant.com; Eski Göreme Yolu; mains TL24-45; ⊙10.30am-2.30pm & 6.30-11pm), which serves modern Anatolian dishes with international influences in sharp surrounds, to the humble **Center Café & Restaurant** (☑219 3117; Belediye Meydanı; mains TL10-25), offering crispy salads and *dondurma* (ice cream) in the town square.

Zelve Valley

Three valleys of abandoned rock-cut churches and homes converge at the excellent **Zelve Open-Air Museum** (admission TL8, parking TL2; ⊙8am-7pm Apr-Oct, to 5pm Nov-Mar), off the Göreme-Avanos road. Inhabited until 1952, its sinewy valley walls with rock antennae could have been made for poking around. In the same area, a three-headed formation and fine examples of mushroom-shaped

fairy chimneys can be seen at **Paşabağı**. You can climb inside one chimney to a monk's quarters. Near Zelve on the Ürgüp–Avanos road, **Devrent Valley** is also known as 'Imagination Valley' for its chimneys' anthropomorphic forms.

Ürgüp

☑0384 / POP 18,700

Ninety years after Ürgüp's Greek residents were evicted in the population exchange, international visitors are pained to leave their temporary boutique residences here. Like your favourite Turkish aunt, Ürgüp is elegant without even trying. With a few restaurants, the fabulous **Tarihi Şehir Hamamı** (☑341 2241; İstiklal Caddesi; soak, scrub & massage TL25; ⊙7am-11pm), the up-and-coming **Turasan Winery** (☑341 4961; Tevfik Fikret Caddesi; vineyard tour & wine tasting €5; ⊙8.30am-7pm) and valley views, the town is the connoisseurs' base for exploring the heart of Cappadocia.

🛏️ Sleeping

Most of Ürgüp's boutique hotels are on Esbelli hill.

TOP CHOICE **Esbelli Evi**   BOUTIQUE HOTEL €€€
(☑341 3395; www.esbelli.com; Esbelli Sokak 8; d €120, ste €150-235; ❋🖥) Jazz in the bathroom, whiskey by the tub, secret tunnels to secluded walled gardens covered in vines: Esbelli is the pick of Cappadocia's accommodation. Occupying 12 properties, the cultured yet unpretentious hotel has 14 rooms, which feel like first-class apartments for visiting dignitaries.

Serinn House   BOUTIQUE HOTEL €€€
(☑341 6076; www.serinnhouse.com; Esbelli Sokak 36; d €120-140; 🖥) Jetsetter hostess Eren Serpen has set a new standard for hotel design in Cappadocia with this contemporary effort, seamlessly merging İstanbul's European aesthetic with Turkish provincial life. The six minimally furnished rooms feature Archimedes lamps, signature chairs, hip floor rugs and tables too cool for coffee.

Melekler Evi   BOUTIQUE HOTEL €€
(☑341 7131; www.meleklerevi.com.tr; Dere Sokak 59; d €90-115, ste 145; 🖥) Architectural duo Muammer and Arzu have created a sweet little hideaway that brims with inspired artistic flourishes. Each room is an individual piece of interior-design heaven, where hi-fi

music and hi-tech shower systems merge with smatterings of winged sculpture, grand old stone fireplaces and homespun whimsy.

Cappadocia Palace
HOTEL €€

(☑341 2510; www.hotel-cappadocia.com; Mektep Sokak 2; s/d €30/44, cave €60/88; 🕾) An Ürgüp old-timer with helpful management and a choice of either enormous cave rooms hosting bathrooms big enough to boogie in, or plainer (and smaller) motel-style rooms.

✕ Eating & Drinking

The main square is the best place to grab an alcoholic or caffeinated beverage at an outside table and watch Cappadocia cruise by. The pedestrian walkway running northeast from Ehlikeyf restaurant is full of cafes, bars and old men playing backgammon. The most convivial and relaxed place for a drink is at the bar in Han Çirağan.

TOP CHOICE Ziggy's
MODERN TURKISH €€€

(☑341 7107; Yunak Mahallesi, Teyfik Fikret Caddesi 24; meze TL6-12, set menus TL45, mains TL25; ☑) With the finest meze menu in Cappadocia, and a terrace that fills day and night with humming tunes, strong cocktails and a hip clientele, Ziggy's backs up its glowing reputation with professional service and an innovative menu.

Han Çirağan Restaurant
RESTAURANT, BAR €€

(☑341 2566; Cumhuriyet Meydanı; mains TL15-25; ☑) Offering atmospheric yet casual dining, the Han's service is superfriendly and the menu meanders through Turkish favourites with a modern twist. After dinner, retire to the cool bar downstairs, under the vine trellis, for an excellent wine list and mean Martinis.

Cafe In
INTERNATIONAL €€

(Cumhuriyet Meydanı; mains TL13-17; ☑) For a pasta-orientated break from Turkish cuisine, this wee cafe should be your first port of call. Servings are on the generous side, service is swift and it does some excellent salads.

Develili Deringöller Pide ve Kebap Salonu
PIDE €

(Dumlupınar Caddesi; pide TL6-8; ☑) Shush. We're going to tell you a secret the locals have been trying to hide for years. This is, hands down, the best pide in Cappadocia.

Ailanpa Wine House
WINE BAR

(☑341 6927; İstiklal Caddesi; wine TL10) This trendy wine house mixes chatty staff, comfy red velvet seating and a decent soundtrack.

ℹ Information

Around Cumhuriyet Meydanı, the main square, you'll find banks with ATMs. The **tourist office** (☑341 4059; Kayseri Caddesi 37; ☉8am-5.30pm Mon-Fri) gives out a map and has a list of hotels.

Travel agencies **Argeus Tours** (☑341 4688; www.argeus.com.tr; İstiklal Caddesi 47) and **Peerless Travel Services** (☑341 6970; www.peerlessexcursions.com; İstiklal Caddesi 41) can arrange tours and transfers.

Mustafapaşa

☑0384 / POP 1600

Mustafapaşa is the sleeping beauty of Cappadocia – a peaceful village with pretty, old stone-carved houses, some minor rock-cut churches and a scattering of hotels. If you want to get away from it all, this is the place to base yourself. Until WWI it was called Sinasos and was a predominantly Ottoman-Greek settlement.

Ukabeyn Pansiyon (☑353 5533; www.ukabeyn.com; Gazi Sokak 62; s/d TL85/120; 🕾✕) is a well-presented, friendly cave hotel with light-filled, stone-vaulted rooms and, backing onto the downstairs terrace, more characterful cave rooms.

Old Greek House (☑353 5306; www.oldgreekhouse.com; Şahin Caddesi; s TL100, d TL150-200; 🕾) is well known for its Ottoman-flavoured set menus (TL35 to TL45), starring good versions of the usual suspects: *mantı, köfte*, lima beans, crispy salads and baklava. If the Turkish coffee hasn't kicked in, the large bedrooms have polished floorboards and an antique feel.

Dolmuşes to Mustafapaşa leave roughly every 30 minutes from Ürgüp's Mustafapaşa *otogar* (TL2, 10 minutes), next to the main bus station.

Kayseri

TRANSPORT HUB

Mixing Seljuk tombs, mosques and modern developments, Kayseri is both central Turkey's most devoutly Islamic city after Konya and one of the economic powerhouses nicknamed the 'Anatolian tigers'. You may well pass through en route to/from central Cappadocia.

🛏 Sleeping & Eating

If you get caught here overnight, the reasonable midrange options **Hotel Almer** (☑320 7970; www.almer.com.tr; Osman Kavuncu

IHLARA VALLEY

A beautiful canyon full of greenery and rock-cut churches dating back to Byzantine times, Ihlara Valley (TL8, parking TL2; ☉8am-6.30pm) is an excellent, if popular, spot for a walk. Footpaths follow the course of the river, Melendiz Suyu, which flows between the narrow gorge at Ihlara village and the wide valley around Selime Monastery (admission TL8; ☉dawn-dusk).

The easiest way to see the valley is on a day tour, which allows a few hours for a one-way walk through the stretch of the gorge with most churches. To get there by bus from Göreme, you must change in Nevşehir and Aksaray, making it a tricky day trip on public transport.

Midway along the gorge, below Belisırma village, four low-key riverside restaurants feed the hungry hikers. If you want to walk the whole valley, it takes about five to six hours, and there are modest pensions at both ends: Akar Pansion & Restaurant (☎453 7018; www.ihlara-akarmotel.com; Ihlara Village; s/d/tr TL40/70/90; ☎) in Ihlara village and Çatlak Hotel (☎454 5006; www.catlakturizm.com.tr; Selime; s/d TL45/90; ☎) in Selime. Note that most accommodation is closed out of season (December to March).

On weekdays six dolmuşes travel to/from Aksaray (TL4, 45 minutes), stopping in Selime, Belisırma and Ihlara village. In Belisırma, dolmuşes stop up on the plateau, and you have to hike a few hundred metres down into the valley. On the weekend there are fewer services.

Caddesi 1; s/d TL70/110; ❉☎), Bent Hotel (☎221 2400; www.benthotel.com; Atatürk Bulvarı 40; s/d/tr TL70/110/120; ❉☎) and Hotel Çapari (☎222 5278; Donanma Caddesi 12; s/d/tr/ste TL60/90/110/120; ❉☎) are all a few hundred metres east of main square Cumhuriyet Meydanı. Novotel (☎207 3000; www.novotel.com; Kocasinan Bulvarı; r from €60; ❉☎), 3km from the centre en route to the airport, is a very good version of the dependable international chain. Book accommodation in advance.

The western end of Sivas Caddesi has a strip of fast-food joints that still seem to be pumping when everything else in town is quiet, including the fish-loving İstanbul Balık Pazarı (☎231 8973; Sivas Caddesi; mains TL5-10; ☉8am-11pm). For an alcoholic tipple with your tucker, try Hotel Almer or, 500m northeast, Kale Rooftop Restaurant (☎207 5000; Hilton Hotel, Cumhuriyet Meydanı; İstasyon Caddesi 1; mains TL20-40; ☉noon-2am) at the Hilton.

❶ Getting There & Away

AIR Turkish Airlines and Pegasus Airlines have several daily flights to/from İstanbul.

A taxi between Kayseri city centre and the havaalanı (airport) costs TL15 and a dolmuş is TL1.25.

BUS The otogar is 9km west of the centre, reached by servis, taxi (TL15), local bus (TL1.25) or a tram to Selimiye (TL1), a 10-minute walk away.

On an important north–south and east–west crossroads, Kayseri has many services:

Göreme TL10, one hour

Malatya TL25, five hours

Van TL80, 13 hours

TRAIN There are daily long-distance trains to/from destinations including Adana, Ankara and Tatvan (Lake Van). The station is about 1.5km northwest of Cumhuriyet Meydanı.

EASTERN TURKEY

Like a challenge? Eastern Anatolia – vast, remote and culturally very Middle Eastern – is the toughest part of Turkey to travel in but definitely the most exotic, and certainly the least affected by mass tourism. Winter here can be bitterly cold and snowy.

Rugged southeastern Anatolia, bordering Syria, Iran and Iraq, makes a fascinating addition to an eastern Mediterranean or Cappadocian itinerary. A good selection of eastern Turkey's major sights are found among its expansive steppe and soaring mountains. Particularly near Iraq, a few places and roads are sometimes offlimits due to fighting between the military and the PKK. The same is also true of roads and regions close to the Syrian border owing to the unrest in Syria.

However, the southeast is mostly safe and accessible to independent travellers. What will linger longest in your memory is the incredibly warm-hearted welcome from the (predominantly Kurdish) locals. Expect a military presence, keep your passport handy for army checkpoints, and check the current security situation before you visit the area.

Mt Nemrut National Park

Nemrut Dağı Milli Parkı (admission TL8; ☺dawn-dusk) contains one of the country's most awe-inspiring sights. Two thousand years ago, right on top of Nemrut Dağı (Mt Nemrut; 2150m) and pretty much in the middle of nowhere, a meglomaniac Commagene king erected fabulous temples and a funerary mound. The fallen heads of the gigantic decorative statues of gods and kings, toppled by earthquakes, form one of the country's most enduring images.

☞ Tours

There are a few possible bases for visiting Mt Nemrut:

MALATYA

The Nemrut Dağı Information Booth (☎0535 760 5080; kemalmalatya@hotmail.com; Atatürk Caddesi; ☺8am-7pm May-Sep) organises all-inclusive daily minibus tours (TL100, early May–mid-Oct, min 2 people), with a night at the Güneş Hotel below the summit and visits to the heads at sunset and sunrise.

KAHTA

Hotels and guesthouses offer eight-hour sunrise and sunset 'long tours', as well as the less-interesting three-hour 'short tour'. This route is more scenic, and Kahta is slowly losing its reputation as a rip-off town. The Kommagene Hotel (www.nemrutguide.com; 'long tour' incl accommodation TL125 per person, daily Apr-Nov) and Zeus Hotel offer tours. Alternatively, hire a taxi at the otogar (short/long tour TL100/130); Kahta's 'tours' are usually just glorified taxi services anyway.

KARADUT

Near the park's southern entrance, hotels offer return trips to the summit for about TL50 per vehicle (Karadut Pension) or TL100 (Hotel Euphrat).

ŞANLIURFA

Several agencies run tours, including Harran-Nemrut Tours (☎215 1575, 0542 761 3065; www.aslankonukevi.com; Demokrasi Caddesi 12; per person €50, min two people), Mustafa

Çaycı (☎0532 685 2942, 313 1340; musma63@ yahoo.com; Hotel Uğur, Köprübaşı Caddesi 3; per person TL130, min 2 people) and Nomad Tours Turkey (☎0533 747 1850; www.nomadtoursturkey.com; per person €100).

CAPPADOCIA

Some people take a two-day tour (about TL350, mid-April to mid-November), but it's a tedious drive. If you have enough time, it's better to opt for a three-day tour, which usually also includes Harran and Şanlıurfa.

🛏 Sleeping

MALATYA

Grand W Aksaç Hotel   HOTEL €€
(☎0422-324 6565; www.aksachotel.com; Saray Mahallesi, Ömer Efendi Sokak 19; s/d TL100/140; ☀🛜) In a quiet central location, with flash services including a hamam, spacious bathrooms, flat-screen TVs, huge beds, and chocolate-covered apricots for sale in reception.

KAHTA

Kommagene Hotel   HOTEL €
(☎0416-725 9726, 0532 200 3856; ; Mustafa Kemal Caddesi 1; s/d TL45/70; ☀@🛜) The wood-lined rooms are cosy and colourful, and breakfast is served in a spacious top-floor salon with good views of Kahta's dusty main drag. A kitchen, laundry and free pickups from the Adıyaman and Kahta otogars are also offered.

Zeus Hotel   HOTEL €€
(☎0416-725 5694; www.zeushotel.com.tr; Mustafa Kemal Caddesi; camp sites per person TL20, s/d/ste €60/80/110; ☀🛜🏊) At this solid three-star option, with its pool and manicured garden, angle for the renovated rooms, which feature top-notch bathrooms and flat-screen TVs. Campers can pitch tents on the parking lot, and have access to their own ablutions block. Opposite, the recommended Papatya Restaurant (Mustafa Kemal Caddesi; mains TL8-10) whips up all the usual Turkish suspects.

KARADUT

Karadut Pension   PENSION €
(☎0416-737 2169, 0532 566 2857; www.karadutpansiyon.net; Karadut; d per person TL35; ☀@) This pension has neat, compact rooms (some with air-con), cleanish bathrooms and a shared kitchen. Meals are available with alcoholic drinks on the alfresco terrace bar. Campers can pitch their tent and they'll pick you up from Kahta for TL18.

Hotel Euphrat
HOTEL €€

(☎0416-737 2175; www.hoteleuphratnemrut.com; s/d/tr with half board €45/58/68; ❋❄) Popular with tour groups in peak season. Renovations have made the rooms larger and more comfortable, and the views from the restaurant terrace and pool are spectacular.

ŞANLIURFA

Aslan Konuk Evi
PENSION €€

(☎0414-215 1575, 0542 761 3065; www.aslankonukevi.com; Demokrasi Caddesi 12; r TL90-120; ❋@☎) Efficiently run by English teacher Özcan, with good food and cold beer available in this heritage building's rooftop terrace restaurant. Accommodation options range from shared dorm rooms to newer double rooms with private bathrooms. A good-value deal is TL120 for two people including breakfast and dinner.

Hotel Uğur
HOTEL €

(☎0414-313 1340, 0532 685 2942; musma63@yahoo.com; Köprübaşı Caddesi 3; per person with shared bathroom TL20; ❋☎) Rooms are sparsely decorated and relatively compact, but clean and spotless. There's a great travellers' vibe, enhanced by a few cold beers on the hotel's terrace. Rates exclude breakfast, but there's a good *kahvaltı salonu* (breakfast restaurant) downstairs.

❶ Getting There & Away

AIR Malatya and Şanlıurfa's airports both have daily Turkish Airlines and Pegasus Airlines flights to/from Ankara and İstanbul. Pegasus also links Urfa with İzmir, and Onur Air flies İstanbul–Malatya.

BUS Malatya, Kahta and Şanlıurfa are well connected, with regular buses to/from locations including Ankara, İstanbul and Kayseri.

DOLMUŞ During the summer season, there are minibuses (TL10) around every two hours between Kahta and the Çeşme Pansion, about 6km from the summit, via Karadut. Pension owners can pick you up at Kahta's *otogar* (set the price beforehand).

Mardin

☎0482 / POP 88,000

Pretty-as-a-picture Mardin is an addictive, unmissable spot. With its minarets poking out of a labyrinth of brown lanes, its castle dominating the Old City, and honey-coloured stone houses cascading down the hillside, Mardin emerges like a phoenix from the sun-roasted Mesopotamian plains. A mosaic of Kurdish, Yezidi, Christian and Syrian cultures, it also has a fascinating cultural mix.

The city has started to become popular with Turkish travellers – get here before it becomes too touristy.

Mardin is only 25km north of Turkey's border with Syria, and areas near this border are sometimes off limits due to the unrest in Syria and fighting between the Turkish army and the PKK. See p603 for advice on safe travel in the region.

◉ Sights & Activities

Sakıp Sabancı
Mardin City Museum
MUSEUM

(Sakıp Sabancı Mardin Kent Müzesi; www.sabancimuzesimardin.gov.tr; Eski Hükümet Caddesi; admission TL3; ☺8am-5pm Tue-Sun) Housed in a carefully restored former army barracks, this superb museum showcases Mardin's cosmopolitan and multicultural past. Downstairs is used as an art gallery.

Bazaar
MARKET

Mardin's rambling commercial hub parallels Cumhuriyet Caddesi one block down the hill. Donkeys are still a main form of transport, and saddle repairers ply their trade. Look for the secluded Ulu Camii, a 12th-century Iraqi Seljuk structure with delicate reliefs adorning its minaret.

Forty Martyrs Church
CHURCH

(Kırklar Kilisesi; Sağlık Sokak) This 4th-century church was renamed in the 15th century to commemorate Cappadocian martyrs, now remembered in the fine carvings above the entrance.

Cumhuriyet Caddesi
Mardin Museum
STREET

(Mardin Müzesi; admission TL5; ☺8am-5pm Tue-Sun) is housed in a restored late-19th-century mansion; east of there, the ornately carved old Mardin house, featuring a three-arched facade, is a fabulous example of the city's domestic architecture. Sultan İsa (Zinciriye) Medresesi (admission TL2) has an imposing recessed doorway, pretty courtyards and city views from the roof. Opposite the former post office, housed in a 17th-century *caravanserai*, rises the elegant, slender minaret of the 14th-century Şehidiye Camii. It's superbly carved, with colonnades all around and three small bulbs superimposed at the summit. Emir Hamamı (treatments from T20; ☺men 6.30am-noon & 6-10pm, women noon-5.30pm) dates back to Roman times and has views of the plains from its terrace.

TURKEY MARDIN

🛏 Sleeping & Eating

Mardin's popularity means that accommodation is expensive, and summer weekends are particularly busy. Rooms are often small and lack natural light; ask the right questions when you book.

Şahmeran Otanik Pansiyon PENSION €
(☏213 2300; www.sahmeranpansiyon.com; Cumhuriyet Caddesi, 246 Sokak 10; per person with/without bathroom TL35/40 ; 🛜) In Old Mardin, this good-value historic option is arrayed around a honey-coloured stone courtyard just a short uphill meander from Mardin's main thoroughfare. Breakfast is an additional TL5.

Reyhani Kasrı BOUTIQUE HOTEL €€€
(☏212 1333; www.reyhanikasri.com.tr; Cumhuriyet Caddesi; s/d TL150/190; ❀🛜) Sleek and modern rooms are concealed within a lovingly restored historic mansion, providing a contemporary spin on the boutique-hotel experience. Multiple floors cascade down the hillside, making it one of Mardin's more spectacular buildings, and the 'Sky Terrace' bar has unbeatable Mesopotamian views.

Antik Tatlıede Butik Hotel BOUTIQUE HOTEL €€
(☏213 2720; www.tatlidede.com.tr; Medrese Mahallesi; s/d/tr TL100/150/200; ❀🛜) In a quiet location near Mardin's bazaar, a labyrinthine heritage mansion is filled with rooms of varying sizes (mostly fairly spacious). Huge terraces have views across the plains.

Kamer Cafe Mutfak ANATOLIAN €€
(Cumhuriyet Caddesi; mains TL10-15) Operated by the Kamer Vakif (Moon Foundation), a support organisation for women who are victims of domestic violence, this terrific restaurant serves some of Mardin's best local cuisine. There's occasional live music amid the rustic and arty ambience.

ℹ Getting There & Away

AIR Any minibus to Kızıltepe can drop you at Mardin airport (TL3), 20km south of town. Turkish Airlines has daily flights to/from İstanbul and Ankara.

DOLMUŞ There are frequent minibuses to Diyarbakır (TL10, 1¼ hours), Midyat (TL9, 1¼ hours) and Şanlıurfa (TL25, three hours).

Van

☏0432 / POP 353,500
With young couples walking hand in hand on the main drag and live bands knocking out Kurdish tunes in pubs, Van is more urban, more casual and less rigorous than the rest of southeastern Anatolia. Its resilient population is rebuilding after the devastating earthquakes of 2011, and its satisfying urban buzz complements its brilliant location, near the eponymous lake.

⊙ Sights & Activities

Van Castle (Van Kalesi) RUIN
(Rock of Van; admission TL3; ⊙9am-dusk) Try to visit Van's imposing castle, about 4km west of the centre, at sunset for great views of the lake. On the southern side of the rock are the foundations of **Eski Van** (the old city).

Van Museum MUSEUM
(Van Müzesi; Kışla Caddesi; admission TL3; ⊙8am-noon & 1-5pm Tue-Sun) This compact museum was closed at the time of writing, and a potential move to near Van Castle was rumoured. It boasts an outstanding collection of Urartian exhibits, with gold jewellery, bronze belts, helmets, horse armour and terracotta figures.

Alkan Tours GUIDED TOURS
(☏215 2092, 0530 349 2793; www.easternturkeytour.org; Ordu Caddesi) Guided day trips (per person €20) taking in **Akdamar Island**, the photogenic 17th-century **Hoşap Castle** and the Urartian site at **Çavuştepe** are a time-efficient way to see the region's main sights.

🛏 Sleeping

Accommodation is often in high demand, and rates can be higher than elsewhere in eastern Turkey.

DON'T MISS

AKDAMAR KILISESI

This carefully restored island **church** (Church of the Holy Cross; admission TL3; ⊙8am-6pm) is one of the marvels of Armenian architecture. The wonderful relief carvings on its well-preserved walls are masterworks of Armenian art, and inside are frescos. Akdamar Island is 3km out in Lake Van, reached on boats from the south shore (TL8) and most easily on a day trip from Van.

Büyük Asur Oteli   HOTEL €€

(☎216 8792; www.buyukasur.com; Cumhuriyet Caddesi, Turizm Sokak; s/d TL100/150; ❄🖧) This reliable midrange venture's colourful rooms come complete with fresh linen, TV and well-scrubbed bathrooms. English is spoken and the hotel can organise tours to Akdamar Island, Hoşap Castle and other attractions.

Akdamar Otel   HOTEL €€

(☎214 9923; www.otelakdamar.com; Kazım Karabekir Caddesi; s/d TL120/160; ❄🖧) The Akdamar is centrally located, close to good restaurants and pastry shops, and has flat-screen TVs, and newly decorated, spacious bathrooms. The young, English-speaking staff have lots of recommendations.

✖ Eating & Drinking

Tamara Ocakbaşı   STEAKHOUSE €€

(Yüzbaşıoğlu Sokak; mains TL15-20; ⊙5pm-late) Dining at the Hotel Tamara's restaurant is dizzying, especially for carnivores: each table has its own grill. High-quality meat and fish dishes feature prominently, but the list of meze is equally impressive. Downstairs, you can get a cold beer at the North Shield pub.

Kervansaray   ANATOLIAN €€

(Cumhuriyet Caddesi; mains TL12-18) Van's go-to spot for an elegant and refined dining experience. Share plates of meze as you peruse a menu containing more than a few local specialities. Fans of incredibly tender lamb should definitely consider the *kağıt* kebap (paper kebab).

Halay Türkü Bar   LIVE MUSIC, BAR

(Kazım Karabekir Caddesi) At the multilevel Halay Türkü, enjoy tasty meze and grilled meat before graduating to draught beer, local spirits and regular live music.

❶ Information

Hotels, restaurants, ATMs, internet cafes, bus-company offices, the post office and the **tourist office** (☎216 2530; ⊙8.30am-noon & 1-5.30pm Mon-Fri) lie on and around Cumhuriyet Caddesi.

❶ Getting There & Away

AIR Turkish Airlines, AnadoluJet and Pegasus Airlines fly daily to/from İstanbul and Ankara. A taxi to the airport costs about TL30. Buses leave frequently from near the Akdamar Hotel (TL1.25).

BOAT A twice-daily ferry crosses Lake Van between Tatvan and Van (TL10, four hours), but there's no fixed schedule.

BREAKFAST OF CHAMPIONS

Van is famed for its tasty *kahvaltı* (breakfast), best tried on pedestrianised Eski Sümerbank Sokak, also called 'Kahvaltı Sokak' ('Breakfast St'). Here, a row of eateries offers complete Turkish breakfasts (around TL12 to TL15). Sample honey, olives, tomatoes, cucumbers, *sucuklu yumurta* (omelette with sausage) and dairy goodness including *otlu peynir* (cheese mixed with a tangy herb, Van's speciality) and *kaymak* (clotted cream).

BUS Daily buses connect Van with Ankara (TL90, 17 hours), Malatya (TL60, 12 hours) and Şanlıurfa (TL60, 11 hours).

TRAIN The twice-weekly *Vangölü Ekspresi* train from Ankara meets the ferry in Tatvan. The weekly *Trans Asya Ekspresi* connects Ankara to Tehran (Iran) via Van; a train also runs to Tabriz (Iran) on Tuesday.

UNDERSTAND TURKEY

History

The sheer weight and depth of history in Turkey is overwhelming. The Anatolian plateau features in various guises in both Homer's *Iliad* and the Bible; it has produced some of the world's longest-lasting dynasties, been the centre of ancient empires covering much of Europe and the Middle East, and still holds a strategic position at the meeting of two continents.

By about 6500 BC a Neolithic city, one of the oldest ever recorded, was established at Çatalhöyük, near Konya. The greatest of the early civilisations of Anatolia (Asian Turkey) was that of the Hittites, a force to be reckoned with from 2000 to 1200 BC, with their capital at Hattuşa, east of Ankara. Traces of their existence remain throughout central Turkey.

After the collapse of the Hittite empire, Anatolia splintered into several small states until the Graeco-Roman period, when parts of the country were reunited. Later, Christianity spread through Anatolia, carried by the apostle Paul, a native of Tarsus (near Adana).

Byzantine Empire & the Crusades

In AD 330 the Roman emperor Constantine founded a new imperial city at Byzantium (modern İstanbul). Renamed Constantinople, this strategic city became the capital of the Eastern Roman Empire and was the centre of the Byzantine Empire for 1000 years. During the European Dark Ages, the Byzantine Empire kept alive the flame of Western culture, despite threats from the empires of the East (Persians, Arabs and Turks) and the West (the Christian powers of Europe).

The Byzantine Empire's decline came with their defeat at the hands of the Seljuk Turks in 1071. Seljuks overran most of Anatolia, establishing a provincial capital at Konya, ruling domains that included today's Turkey, Iran and Iraq. The Byzantines endeavoured to protect their capital and reclaim Anatolia, but, during the Fourth Crusade (1202–04), a combined Venetian and crusader force took and plundered Constantinople. The Byzantines eventually regained the ravaged city in 1261.

Ottoman Empire

A Mongol invasion in the late 13th century ended Seljuk power, but new small Turkish states soon arose in western Anatolia. One, headed by Gazi Osman (1258–1326), grew into the Ottoman Empire. In 1453 Constantinople finally fell to the Ottoman sultan Mehmet II (the Conqueror), replacing Edirne as the capital of the dynasty.

A century later, under Süleyman the Magnificent, the Ottoman Empire reached its peak, spreading deep into Europe, Asia and North Africa. Ottoman success was based on military expansion; when their march westwards stalled at Vienna in 1683, the rot set in. İstanbul's Topkapı Palace became a centre of indolence and decadence for increasingly out-of-touch sultans.

Nationalist ideas swept through Europe after the French Revolution. In 1830 the Greeks won their independence, followed by Romania, Montenegro, Serbia and Bosnia in 1878. By the early 20th century, European diplomats were plotting how to cherry-pick the choicest parts of 'the sick man of Europe'.

Having sided with the Axis powers in 1914, the Turks emerged from WWI in disarray, with the French, Italians, Greeks, Armenians and Russians contolling much of Anatolia. The Treaty of Sèvres (1920) divvied out Anatolia among the European powers, leaving the Turks with a slither of steppe.

Mustafa Kemal Atatürk

At this low point, Mustafa Kemal, the father of modern Turkey, took over. Atatürk, as he was later called, had made his name by repelling the Anzacs in their heroic but futile attempt to capture the strategic Dardanelles strait at Gallipoli during WWI.

Rallying the remnants of the Turkish army during the Turkish War of Independence that followed WWI, Kemal pushed the last of the Ottoman rulers aside and out-manoeuvred the Allied forces. The Turks finally won in 1922 by repelling the invading Greeks at Smyrna (present-day İzmir). In the ensuing population exchange, whole communities were uprooted as Greek-speaking people from Anatolia were shipped to Greece, while Muslim residents of Greece were transferred to Turkey. One result of this upheaval was the 'ghost villages' that were vacated but never reoccupied.

After the Treaty of Lausanne (1923) undid the humiliations of Sèvres, a new Turkish republic, reduced to Anatolia and part of Thrace, was born. Atatürk embarked on a rapid modernisation program, establishing a secular democracy, introducing the Latin script and European dress, and adopting equal rights for women (at least in theory). The capital was moved from İstanbul to Ankara.

Relations with Greece improved in the 1930s (the Greek president even nominated Atatürk for the Nobel Peace Prize), but soured again after WWII due to the conflict over Cyprus, particularly after the Greek-led anti-Makarios coup and the subsequent Turkish invasion in 1974.

Modern Turkey

Atatürk died in 1938 and his successor, İsmet İnönü, stepped carefully to avoid involvement in WWII. The war over, Turkey found itself allied to the US, later becoming a NATO member. However, the second half of the 20th century was a tumultuous era. The political and economic turmoil included military coups in 1960, 1971 and 1980, and 1997's military memorandum (or 'postmodern coup'). The military considered themselves the guardians of Atatürk's vision – pro-Western and secular – and stepped in when they considered it necessary.

During the 1980s and '90s the country was wracked by the ongoing conflict with the PKK, led by Abdullah Öcalan, who wanted the creation of a Kurdish state in southeastern Anatolia. The conflict led to an estimated 35,000 deaths and huge population shifts. In 1999 Öcalan was captured, but Kurdish discontent and terrorist activities continue.

The current millennium has been a more positive era for Turkey, led by the Justice and Development (AKP) party, which began its third term in 2011. The next general election is due in 2015.

Turkey Today

The very heart of the world during the Ottoman and Byzantine empires, Turkey remains pivotal on the global stage. Its position at the meeting of Europe and Asia informs its political bent: the secular country has a moderate Islamic government and good relations with the West, for which Turkey is a key ally in the Middle East.

With eight neighbouring countries, cross-border tensions are a fact of life for the Turkish government. In 2012 its biggest concern was the unrest in Syria. Refugee camps sprung up along the border in southeastern Anatolia, and Turkey returned fire after stray Syrian shells hit the Turkish border town of Akçakale and killed five civilians.

Meanwhile, efforts to normalise Turkish–Armenian diplomatic relations, long strained over the alleged massacre of Ottoman Armenians during WWI, have faltered. The countries' border remains closed, but there are glimmers of hope in their increasing cultural and trade ties.

Turkey's bid to join the EU continues. Obstacles include Turkey's refusal to recognise EU member Cyprus, the marginalisation of its Kurdish minority, and freedom of speech. Turks resent the slow pace of the talks, especially given Turkey's economic boom and Eurozone woes. Turkey's economy was Europe's fastest growing in 2011.

Domestically, Turkey's most pressing problem is the Kurdish issue, which sparked a near civil war between the military and the PKK, classed as a terrorist group by organisations including the EU and the US government in the 1980s and '90s. Having simmered down, the situation worsened during the Syrian unrest, which made it easier for the PKK to move around and launch attacks. Clashes in the remote mountains of southeastern Anatolia claimed hundreds of lives during 2012, and 600 Kurdish prisoners went on hunger strike. Nonetheless, with relations seemingly thawing between Prime Minister Erdoğan and the Kurdish figurehead Abdullah Öcalan, there are hopes that peace talks may finally bring end the insurgency.

Despite the misgivings of groups from Kurds to secularist Kemalists, Erdoğan's AKP government has overseen a broadly positive era for Turkey. Decades of military coups have given way to stability, and the 2010 referendum on constitutional reform, in which Turkey voted for change, will lead to greater democracy.

People

Turkey's population (79.8 million) is predominantly made up of Turks, with a big Kurdish minority (about 15 million) and much smaller groups of Laz, Hemşin, Arabs, Jews, Greeks and Armenians. The Laz and Hemşin people are natives of the northeastern corner of Turkey, around the Black Sea coast and Kaçkar Mountains, while Arab influence is strongest in the Antakya (Hatay) area abutting Syria. Southeastern Turkey is pretty solidly Kurdish, although the problems of the last 30 years have led many to head west in search of a better life.

As a result of Atatürk's reforms, republican Turkey has largely adapted to a modern Westernised lifestyle, at least on the surface. In the big cities and coastal resorts, you will not feel much need to adapt to fit in. In smaller towns and villages, however, particularly in the east, you may find people warier and more conservative.

The gregarious, nationalistic Turks have an acute sense of pride and honour. They are fiercely proud of their history and heros, especially Atatürk, whose portrait and statues are ubiquitous. The extended family still plays a key role, and formality and politeness are important; if asked 'how is Turkey?', answer '*çok güzel*' (very beautiful).

Religion

Turkey is 99% Muslim – about 80% Sunni, with Shiites and Alevis mainly in the east. The religious practices of Sunnis and Alevis differ markedly, with the latter incorporating aspects of Anatolian folklore and less-strict segregation of the sexes.

The country espouses a more relaxed version of Islam than many Middle Eastern nations. Many men drink alcohol (although almost no one touches pork) and many women uncover their heads.

Today most of Turkey's Jews live in İstanbul, and some still speak Ladino, a Judaeo-Spanish language. The Christian minority includes some 70,000 Armenians, also mostly in İstanbul, Greeks and ancient southeastern Anatolian communities, such as Chaldean Catholics and Aramaic-speaking adherents of the Syriac Orthodox Church.

Arts

Turkey's artistic traditions are rich and diverse, displaying influences of the many cultures and civilisations that have waxed and waned in Anatolia over the centuries.

Carpets

Turkey is famous for its beautiful carpets and *kilims* (flat-weave rugs). It's thought that the Seljuk Turks introduced hand-woven carpet-making techniques to Anatolia in the 12th century. During the Ottoman era, textile production and trade contributed significantly to the economy.

Traditionally, village women wove carpets for their family's use, or for their dowry. Today, the dictates of the market rule, but carpets still incorporate traditional symbols and patterns. The Ministry of Culture has sponsored projects to revive aged weaving and dyeing methods in western Turkey; some shops stock these 'project carpets'.

Architecture

Turkey's architectural history encompasses everything from Hittite stonework and Graeco-Roman temples to modern tower blocks, but perhaps the most distinctively Turkish styles are Seljuk and Ottoman. The Seljuks left magnificent mosques, *madrasas* (Islamic schools) and *hans (caravanserais)*, distinguished by their elaborate entrances. The Ottomans also built grand religious structures, and fine wood-and-stone houses in towns such as Safranbolu and Amasya.

Literature

The most famous Turkish novelists are Yaşar Kemal, nominated for the Nobel Prize for Literature on numerous occasions, and Orhan Pamuk, the Nobel Prize laureate in 2006. Kemal's novels, which include *Memed, My Hawk, The Wind from the Plain* and *Salman the Solitary,* chronicle the desperate lives of villagers battling land-grabbing lords.

An inventive prose stylist, Pamuk's books include the Kars-set *Snow,* and the existential İstanbul whodunit *Black Book,* told through a series of newspaper columns. Other well-regarded contemporary writers include Elif Şafak *(The Flea Palace),* Latife

---

LOCAL KNOWLEDGE

CELAL COŞKUN: CARPET SELLER

Celal Coşkun learned to make carpets and weave *kilims* at his grandmother's knee in southeastern Anatolia, before apprenticing as a carpet repairer in İstanbul and opening **Old Orient Carpet & Kilim Bazaar** (✉0532 510 6108; c.c_since.1993@hotmail.com; Çarşı Caddesi 5) in Fethiye. We asked this veteran of the trade for his top carpet tips.

» Know the basics: a carpet is wool or silk pile with single (Persian) or double (Turkish) knots; a *kilim* is a flat weave and reversible; a *cicim* is a *kilim* with one side embroidered.

» Establish in advance your price range and what you want in terms of size, pattern and colour.

» Deal only with a seller who you feel you can trust, be it through reputation, recommendation or instinct.

» Counting knots is only important on silk-on-silk carpets, though a double-knotted wool carpet will wear better than a single-knotted one.

» Most reputable carpet shops can negotiate discounts of between 5% and 10%, depending on how you may pay; anything higher than that and the price has been inflated in the first place.

» To extend a carpet's life, always remove your shoes when walking on it and never beat it, as this breaks the knots and warp (vertical) and weft (horizontal) threads.

» If professional cleaning is too expensive and the traditional method – washing it with mild soap and water and drying it on wood blocks to allow air to circulate beneath it – is too much like hard work, lay the carpet face (pattern) side down for a few minutes in fresh snow (if available!).

» Anything made by hand – including a carpet – can be repaired by hand.

Tekin *(Dear Shameless Death)* and Ayşe Kulin *(Farewell)*.

Cinema

Several Turkish directors have won worldwide recognition, including the late Yılmaz Güney, whose *Yol* (The Road) explores the dilemmas of convicts on weekend-release. Cannes favourite Nuri Bilge Ceylan's films include *Uzak* (Distant), which probes the lives of village migrants in the big city, and *Once Upon a Time in Anatolia*, an intriguing all-night search for a corpse in the Turkish back woods.

Ferzan Özpetek's *Hamam* addresses the hitherto hidden issue of homosexuality in Turkish society. Golden Bear–winning Fatih Akın ponders the Turkish experience in Germany in *Duvara Karsi* (Head On) and *Edge of Heaven*. Yılmaz Erdoğan's *Vizontele* is a black comedy about the first family to get a TV in a southeastern Anatolian town.

Music

The big pop stars include pretty-boy Tarkan, and chanteuse Sezen Aksu. Burhan Öçal is one of Turkey's finest percussionists; his seminal *New Dream* is a funky take on classical Turkish music.

With an Arabic spin, Arabesk is also popular. The genre's stars are Orhan Gencebay and the Kurdish former construction worker İbrahim Tatlıses.

Two folk singers to listen out for are Kurdish chanteuses Aynur Doğan and the ululating Rojin.

For an excellent overview of Turkish music, watch Fatih Akın's documentary *Crossing the Bridge: the Sound of İstanbul,* which covers styles from rock and hip hop to *fasıl* (gypsy music), or listen to Baba Zulu's classic *Duble Oryantal*. Featuring *saz* (Turkish lute), electronic and pop, it's mixed by British dub master Mad Professor.

Sport

Turkish men are fanatical lovers of soccer, and will happily opine about English teams as well as domestic sides. Major teams include Bursaspor, Trabzonspor and İstanbul's Galatasaray, Fenerbahçe and Beşiktaş.

A major home-grown spectator sport is *yağlı güreş* (oil wrestling, p544), where burly men in leather shorts grease themselves up with olive oil and grapple – most famously in Edirne.

Environment

The Land

The Dardanelles, the Sea of Marmara and the Bosphorus divide Turkey into Asian and European parts. Eastern Thrace (European Turkey) comprises only 3% of the country's 769,632-sq-km land area; the remaining 97% is Anatolia, a vast plateau rising eastward towards the Caucasus mountains. With 7200km of coastline, snowcapped mountains, rolling steppe, vast lakes and broad rivers, Turkey is geographically diverse. Turkey's 33 national parks include Uludağ National Park near Bursa, Cappadocia's Ala Dağlar National Park and southeastern Anatolia's Mt Nemrut National Park.

Wildlife

Turkey's location at the junction between Asia and Europe and its varied geography has made it one of the most biodiverse temperate-zone countries, blessed with an exceptionally rich flora of more than 9000 species, 1200 of them endemic. In addition, some 400 bird species are found here, with about 250 of these passing through on migration from Africa to Europe.

In theory, you could see bears, deer, jackals, caracal, wild boars and wolves in Turkey, although you're unlikely to spot any wild animals unless you're hiking. Instead look out for Kangal dogs, originally bred to protect sheep from wolves and bears on mountain pastures. People wandering off the beaten track, especially in eastern Turkey, are often alarmed at the sight of these huge, yellow-coated, black-headed animals, especially as they often wear spiked collars to protect them against wolves.

Environmental Issues

Turkey's embryonic environmental movement is making slow progress; discarded litter and ugly concrete buildings (some half-finished) disfigure the west in particular.

Short of water and electricity, Turkey is one of the world's main builders of dams. The 22-dam Southeast Anatolia Project, known as GAP, is changing eastern Turkey's landscape as it generates hydroelectricity for industry. Parched valleys have become fish-filled lakes, causing an explosion of diseases such as malaria; communities have been uprooted; and archaeological sites are disappearing under dam water. Hasankeyf, which was a Silk Road commercial centre on the border of Anatolia and Mesopotamia, is slated to be submerged in 2015. There are also controversial plans to build three nuclear power plants, despite the risks posed by the country's seismic vulnerabilities.

Another major environmental challenge is the threat from maritime traffic along the Bosphorus. On the Mediterranean coast, the beach nesting grounds of the loggerhead turtle *(Caretta caretta)* – such as at İztuzu Beach at Dalyan, the Göksu Delta and Patara Beach – have long been endangered by tourism and development. Various schemes are underway to protect these areas during the breeding season – look out for signs telling you when to avoid certain stretches.

On the plus side, Turkey is slowly reclaiming its architectural heritage: central Anatolia's Ottoman towns Safranbolu and Amasya are masterpieces of restoration. The country is doing well when it comes to beach cleanliness, with 352 beaches qualifying for Blue Flag status (which recognises success in areas such as water quality and environmental management); go to www.blueflag.org for the complete list. Turkey's intended accession to the EU is also forcing it to lift its environmental standards.

İstanbul has a branch of Greenpeace Mediterranean (☏0212-292 7619; www.greenpeace.org/mediterranean).

Food & Drink

Afiyet olsun (bon appétit)! Not without reason is Turkish food regarded as one of the world's greatest cuisines. Kebaps are, of course, the mainstay of many restaurant meals; omnipresent *kebapçıs* (kebap restaurants) and *ocakbaşıs* (grill houses) sell a range of meat feasts. The ubiquitous *dürüm döner* kebap contains compressed meat (usually lamb) cooked on a revolving upright skewer over coals, then thinly sliced. When laid on crumbled pide bread and yoghurt, and topped with tomato sauce and browned butter, *döner* kebap becomes *İskender* kebap. Equally ubiquitous are *şiş* kebap (small pieces of lamb grilled on a skewer) and *köfte* (meatballs).

For a quick, cheap fill you could hardly do better than a freshly cooked pide, Turkey's version of pizza, topped with *peynir* (cheese), *yumurta* (egg) or *kıymalı* (minced meat). Alternatively, *lahmacun* is a paper-thin Arabic pizza topped with chopped onion, lamb and tomato. Other favourites are *gözleme* (thin savoury crepes) and *börek* (filled pastries – go for the white-cheese-and-parsley *su böreği*). *Mantı* (Turkish ravioli) is perfect in winter but can be overly rich and heavy in hot weather.

Balık (fish) dishes, although excellent, are often expensive; always check the price before ordering.

For vegetarians, a meal made up of meze can be an excellent way to ensure a varied diet. Most restaurants will be able to rustle up at least *beyaz peynir* (ewe's- or goat's-milk cheese), *sebze çorbası* (vegetable soup), *dolma* (stuffed vegetables), a *salata* (salad) such as the basic *çoban salatası* (shepherd's salad), *fasulye pilaki* (beans) and *patlıcan kızartması* (fried aubergine with tomato).

For dessert, try *fırın sütlaç* (rice pudding), baklava (honey-soaked flaky pastry stuffed with walnuts or pistachios), *kadayıf* (dough soaked in syrup and topped with clotted cream), *künefe* (*kadayıf* with sweet cheese, doused in syrup and served hot with a sprinkling of pistachio) and *dondurma* (ice cream). *Lokum* (Turkish delight) has been made here since the Ottoman sultans enjoyed it with their harems.

The national hot drink, *çay* (tea), is served in tiny tulip-shaped glasses with copious quantities of sugar. The wholly chemical *elma çay* (apple tea) is caffeine-free and only for tourists – locals wouldn't be seen dead drinking the stuff. If you're offered a tiny cup of traditional, industrial-strength Turkish *kahve* (coffee), you will be asked how sweet you like it: *çok şekerli* (very sweet), *orta şekerli* (middling), *az şekerli* (slightly sweet) or *sade* (not at all). Unfortunately, Nescafé is much more readily available than filter coffee or cappuccino. Don't miss the love-it-or-hate-it savoury dairy drink *ayran*, made by whipping up yoghurt with water and salt.

The Turks' meze accompaniment of choice is *rakı*, a fiery aniseed spirit like the Greek ouzo, Arab arrack or French pastis. Do as the Turks do and turn it milky white by adding water if you don't want to suffer ill effects. Turkish *şarap* (wine), both *kırmızı* (red) and *beyaz* (white), is improving in quality, particularly in Cappadocia and the Aegean island of Bozcaada. You can buy Tuborg or Efes Pilsen beers everywhere, although less Westernised towns may have only one licensed restaurant and/or liquor store. It's also worth remembering that licensed restaurants are generally more expensive than local eateries just serving *ayran* and *çay*.

SURVIVAL GUIDE

Directory A–Z

Accommodation

Rates quoted here are for high season (June to August; in İstanbul: April, May, September and October) and, unless otherwise mentioned, include tax (KDV), private bathroom and breakfast. Listings are ordered by preference.

In tourist-dependent areas, many accommodation options close from mid-October to late April. In those that remain open, rooms are discounted by about 20%, apart from around Christmas, Easter and major Islamic holidays.

Hotels quote tariffs in Turkish lira or euros, sometimes both, so we've used the currency quoted by the business being reviewed. Particularly in more-touristy locations, many places accept euros.

Virtually nowhere in Turkey is far from a mosque; light sleepers might want to bring earplugs for the early-morning call to prayer. In small tourist towns, touts or taxi drivers may try to persuade you to stay at a certain pension. Decide where you want to stay and stick to your guns; if you do view the pension in question, make it clear that you're only looking.

PRICE RANGES
The below prices indicators are based on the cost of a double room with private bathroom, and breakfast included.

İstanbul

€ less than €70

€€ €70 to €180

€€€ more than €180

Rest of Turkey

€ less than TL80

€€ TL80 to TL170

€€€ more than TL170

CAMPING
» Camping facilities dotted about Turkey, mostly along the coasts and in Cappadocia and Mt Nemrut National Park.
» Pensions and hostels often let you camp in their grounds and use their facilities for a fee.

HOSTELS
» Plenty of hostels with dormitories in popular destinations.

» Dorm beds usually cost about TL20 to TL45 per night.
» Hostelling International members in İstanbul, Cappadocia and the Aegean and western Mediterranean areas.

HOTELS
Budget In most cities and resort towns, good, inexpensive beds are readily available. Difficult places to find good, cheap rooms include İstanbul, Ankara, İzmir and package-holiday resort towns such as Alanya and Çeşme. The cheapest hotels, which charge around TL40/35 for a single with/without bathroom, are mostly used by working-class Turkish men, and are not suitable for solo women.

Midrange One- and two-star hotels vary from TL80 to TL125 for an ensuite double. They are generally less oppressively masculine in atmosphere, and three-star establishments are normally used to catering for female travellers.

Top End Turkey offers top-notch boutique accommodation in Ottoman mansions and other historic buildings, refurbished or completely rebuilt as hotels with all mod cons and bags of character.

PENSIONS
» Most tourist areas offer simple, family-run pensions where you can get a good, clean single/double from around TL40/70.
» Often cosy and represent good value, distinguished from cheap hotels by extras such as a choice of simple meals, laundry service and staff who speak a foreign language.

Activities
HIKING
The Lycian Way, which runs around the coast and mountains of Lycia from Fethiye to Antalya, and the St Paul Trail (Perge to Lake Eğirdir) are waymarked trails, each about 500km long. For more info on these and new trails in development, visit http://cultureroutesinturkey.com.

Popular hiking destinations include southern Cappadocia's Ala Dağlar National Park and northeastern Anatolia's Kaçkar Mountains. The spectacular valleys of central Cappadocia are excellent for day walks.

If you're a serious hiker, you could consider conquering Turkey's highest mountain, Mt Ararat (5137m), near Doğubayazıt, but you need a permit. **Tamzara Turizm**

(☎0544 555 3582; www.mtararattour.com; off Dr İsmail Beşikçi Caddesi) and **Mount Ararat Trek** (☎0537 502 6683; www.mountararattrek.com) in Doğubayazıt are good contacts.

WATER & WIND SPORTS

All sorts of activities, including windsurfing, rafting and kayaking, are available on the Aegean and Mediterranean coasts. The best diving spots are Ayvalık, Kuşadasi, Bodrum, Marmaris and Kaş. You can also try tandem paragliding in Ölüdeniz.

WINTER SPORTS

Most Turkish ski resorts are cheaper than their Western European counterparts and offer good facilities. The season lasts from December to April.

Palandöken, near Erzurum, has the best facilities, and pine-studded Sarıkamış, near Kars, has the most scenic runs. You can also ski on Uludağ, near Bursa, and Erciyes Dağı, above Kayseri.

RELAXING & REJUVENATING

Those of a lazier disposition may want to take a *gület* cruise along the coast, stopping off to swim in bays along the way.

Visiting one of the many *hamams*, some in historic Seljuk or Ottoman buildings, for a scrub and massage is a traditional Turkish activity.

Business Hours

Most museums close on Monday and, from April to October, close 1½ to two hours later. A bar is likely to open later in summer, when tourist offices in popular locations also open longer hours and at weekends.

The working day shortens during the holy month of Ramazan, which currently falls during summer. More-Islamic cities such as Konya and Kayseri virtually shut down during noon prayers on Friday (the Muslim sabbath); apart from that, Friday is a normal working day.

Bars 4pm to late

Government departments, offices and banks 8.30am to noon and 1.30pm to 5pm Monday to Friday

Nightclubs 11pm to late

Restaurants, cafes Breakfast 7.30am to 10am, lunch noon to 2.30pm, dinner 7.30pm to 10pm

Shops 9am to 6pm Monday to Friday (longer in tourist areas and big cities – including weekend opening)

Tourist information 8.30am to noon and 1.30pm to 5pm Monday to Friday

Children

Çocuklar (children) are the beloved centrepiece of family life and your children will be welcomed wherever they go.

However, Turkish safety consciousness rarely meets Western standards and children are not well catered for, although hotels and restaurants will often prepare special dishes for children.

Dangerous Turkish drivers and uneven surfaces can make using strollers, or just walking the streets with little ones, challenging. Other hazards include open power points and carelessly secured building sites.

Shops such as Migros supermarket sell baby food, although fresh milk is uncommon and formula is expensive.

Customs Regulations

IMPORT

Goods including the following can be imported duty-free:

» 600 cigarettes
» 200g of tobacco
» 1L of spirits (over 22%)
» 2L of wine and beer (under 22%)

EXPORT

» Buying and exporting antiquities is illegal.
» Carpet shops should be able to provide a form certifying that your purchase is not antique.
» Ask for advice from vendors and keep receipts and paperwork.

Discount Cards

The following offer discounts on accommodation, eating, entertainment, shopping and transport.

International Student Identity Card (ISIC; www.isic.org)

International Youth Travel Card (IYTC; http://tinyurl.com/25tlbv7)

International Teacher Identity Card (ITIC; http://tinyurl.com/25tlbv7)

Embassies & Consulates

Embassies are generally in Ankara. Many countries also have consulates in İstanbul and elsewhere. In general they open from 8am or 9am to noon Monday to Friday, then after lunch until 5pm or 6pm. For more information, visit http://tinyurl.com/6ywt8a.

Armenia (www.mfa.am/en) Contact Russian embassy.

Australian Embassy (☑0312-459 9500; www.embaustralia.org.tr; Uğur Mumcu Caddesi 88, MNG Bldg, Gaziosmanpaşa)

Azerbaijan Embassy (☑0312-491 1681; www.mfa.gov.az/eng; Baku Sokak 1, Diplomatik Site, Oran)

Bulgarian Embassy (☑0312-467 2071; www.bulgaria.bg/en/; Atatürk Bulvarı 124, Kavaklıdere)

Canadian Embassy (☑0312-409 2700; www.canadainternational.gc.ca; Cinnah Caddesi 58, Çankaya)

Georgian Embassy (☑0312-491 8030; www.turkey.mfa.gov.ge; Kılıç Ali Sokak 12, Diplomatik Site, Oran)

Greek Embassy (☑0312-448 0647; www.mfa.gr; Zia Ur Rahman Caddesi 9-11, Gaziosmanpaşa)

Iranian Embassy (☑0312-468 2820; www.mfa.gov.ir; Tahran Caddesi 10, Kavaklıdere)

Iraqi Embassy (☑0312-468 7421; http://iraqmissions.hostinguk.com; Turan Emeksiz Sokak 11, Gaziosmanpaşa)

New Zealand Embassy (☑0312-467 9054; www.nzembassy.com/turkey; İran Caddesi 13, Kavaklıdere)

Russian Embassy (☑0312-439 2122; www.turkey.mid.ru; Karyağdı Sokak 5, Çankaya)

Syrian Embassy (☑0312-440 9657; Sedat Simavi Sokak 40, Çankaya)

UK Embassy (☑0312-455 3344; http://ukinturkey.fco.gov.uk; Şehit Ersan Caddesi 46/A, Çankaya)

US Embassy (☑0312-455 5555; http://turkey.usembassy.gov; Atatürk Bulvarı 110, Kavaklıdere)

Food

Listings in this book are ordered by preference, and the following price indicators are used, based on the cost of a main course.

İstanbul

€ less than TL15

€€ TL15 to TL25

€€€ more than TL25

Rest of Turkey

€ less than TL9

€€ TL9 to TL17.50

€€€ more than TL17.50

Gay & Lesbian Travellers

Homosexuality is legal in Turkey and attitudes are changing, but prejudice remains strong – the message is discretion. İstanbul has a flourishing gay scene, as does Ankara.

Kaos GL (www.kaosgl.com) The lesbian, gay, bisexual, transgender (LGBT) rights organisation's website has content in English.

Lambda (www.lambdaistanbul.org) LGBT support group.

Pride Travel Agency (www.turkey-gay-travel.com) Gay-friendly travel agent.

Health

In addition to the routine vaccinations that all travellers should have, typhoid and hepatitis A and B are recommended for Turkey.

Rabies is endemic here, so if you will be travelling off the beaten track you might want to consider a vaccination.

Malaria is found in a few areas near the Syrian border.

Internet Access

» Most accommodation offers free wi-fi, as do many other businesses.

» Internet cafes are widespread.

» Fees typically about TL1.50 per hour (İstanbul TL3).

Language Courses

The most popular Turkish-language courses are offered by **Dilmer** (www.dilmer.com), near Taksim Sq in İstanbul, and the Ankara University–affiliated **Tömer** (www.tomer.com.tr), with branches throughout the country.

Legal Matters

» Technically, you should carry your passport at all times, but you may prefer to carry a photocopy.

» There are laws against treason, buying and smuggling antiques, and illegal drugs.

Money

» Turkey's currency, the Türk Lirası (Turkish Lira; TL), replaced the Yeni Türk Lirası (New Turkish Lira; YTL) in 2009.

» Lira come in notes of 5, 10, 20, 50, 100 and 200, and 1 lira coins.

» One lira is worth 100 kuruş, which are available in 1, 5, 10, 25 and 50 coins.

» Watch out for people dumping their old-currency coins on you.

» Prices in this book are quoted in lira or euros, depending on which currency is used by the business.

ATMS

ATMs dispense Turkish lira, and occasionally euros and US dollars, to Visa, MasterCard, Cirrus and Maestro card holders. Machines are found in most towns.

It's possible to get around Turkey using only ATMs, if you keep some cash in reserve to tide you through the villages, and for the inevitable day when the ATM throws a wobbly.

Some banks levy high charges for the conversion and/or withdrawal, so check your bank's fees before you leave home.

CASH

» Euros and US dollars the most readily accepted foreign currencies, and the easiest to change.
» Many exchange offices and banks change other major currencies such as UK pounds and Japanese yen.
» Foreign currencies accepted in shops, hotels and restaurants in many tourist areas, and by taxi drivers for big journeys.

CREDIT CARDS

» Visa and MasterCard widely accepted by hotels, shops and restaurants.
» Often not accepted by pensions and local restaurants outside main tourist areas.
» You can also get cash advances on these cards.
» Amex less commonly accepted outside top-end establishments.
» Inform your credit-card provider of your travel plans.

MONEY CHANGERS

» Turkish lira is weak against Western currencies; you will likely get a better exchange rate in Turkey than elsewhere.
» Exchange offices offer better rates than banks, and often don't charge commission. They offer the best rates in market areas.
» Offices also found at some post offices, shops and hotels.
» Banks more likely to change minor currencies, although will often make heavy weather of it.

TIPPING & BARGAINING

Turkey is fairly European in its approach to tipping and you won't be pestered with demands for baksheesh. Tipping is customary in restaurants, hotels and taxis; optional elsewhere.

» Round up metered taxi fares and leave waiters and masseurs around 10% to 15% of the bill. In more-expensive restaurants, check a *servis ücreti* (service charge) hasn't been automatically added to the bill.
» Hotel prices are sometimes negotiable, and you should always bargain for souvenirs.

TRAVELLERS CHEQUES

Banks, shops and hotels usually see it as a burden to change travellers cheques, and will either try to persuade you to go elsewhere or charge you a premium. If you do have to change them, try one of the major banks.

Photography

» People in Turkey are generally receptive to having their photo taken, apart from when they are praying or performing other religious activities.
» As in most countries, do not take photos of military sites, airfields, police stations and so on.

Post

Postanes (post offices) are indicated by blue-on-yellow 'PTT' signs.
» Postcards sent abroad cost about TL2.
» If you are shipping something from Turkey, don't close your parcel before it has been inspected by a customs official.
» Airmail tariffs are typically around TL40 for the first kilo, with an additional charge for every extra kilo (typically TL5 to Europe).

Public Holidays

New Year's Day 1 January

National Sovereignty & Children's Day 23 April

International Workers' Day 1 May

Youth & Sports Day 19 May

Victory Day 30 August

Republic Day 28–29 October

Turkey also celebrates the main Islamic holidays, the most important of which are Şeker Bayramı (Sweets Holiday; roughly 28 July 2014 and 17 July 2015), which marks the end of the holy month of Ramazan; and about two months later, Kurban Bayramı (Festival of the Sacrifice; roughly 4 October 2014 and 23 September 2015). Due to the fact that these holidays are celebrated according to the Muslim lunar calendar, they take place around 11 days earlier every year.

Safe Travel

Although Turkey is in no way a dangerous country to visit, it's always wise to be a little cautious, especially if you're travelling alone.

» As a pedestrian, note that there is no such thing as a generally acknowledged right of way, despite the little green man. İstanbullus in particular drive like rally drivers; give way to cars and trucks in all situations.

» Drugging is a risk, especially for lone men, and most commonly in İstanbul. It may involve so-called friends, a bar and perhaps a willowy temptress. Another İstanbul scam with these elements ends with the traveller buying a couple of drinks and receiving a bill for hundreds of euros. Be cautious about who you befriend, especially when you're new to the country.

» Sexual assaults have occurred against travellers of both sexes in hotels in central and eastern Anatolia. Make enquiries and do a little research if you are travelling alone or heading off the beaten track.

» Receiving the hard sell from carpet salesmen in places such as İstanbul's Grand Bazaar can drive you to distraction. Remember you're under no obligation to look or buy. 'Free' lifts and other suspiciously cheap services often lead to near-compulsory visits to carpet showrooms or hotel commission for touts.

» Do not buy coins or other artefacts offered to you by touts at ancient sites such as Ephesus and Perge.

» Fighting between the Turkish military and PKK continues in remote southeastern Anatolia. More of a risk are the bomb attacks, also linked to Kurdish separatist groups, that target affluent areas frequented by tourists, including attacks in İstanbul in 2008 and 2010. Check for travel warnings before visiting southeastern Anatolia, particularly areas near the Syrian and Iraqi borders.

» Nationalistic laws against insulting, defaming or making light of Atatürk, the Turkish flag and so on are taken seriously. Turks have been known to claim derogatory remarks were made in the heat of a quarrel, which is enough to get a foreigner carted off to jail.

Telephone

Türk Telekom (www.turktelekom.com.tr) has a monopoly on phone services, which are efficient if costly.

» Payphones are found in many major public buildings and facilities, public squares and transport terminals. International calls can be made from payphones, which require phonecards. Some accept credit cards.

» If you're only going to make one quick call, it's easier to look for a booth with a sign saying '*kontörlü telefon*', where the cost of your call is metered.

» Numbers starting with ☎444 don't require area codes and, wherever you call from, are charged at the local rate.

MOBILE PHONES

» Reception is generally excellent.

» Mobile phone numbers start with a four-figure number beginning with ☎05.

» If you set up a roaming facility with your home network, most mobiles can connect to Turkcell (the most comprehensive network), Vodafone and Avea.

» To buy a Turkcell SIM card (TL30 to TL40), you need to show your passport and ensure the seller phones through or inputs your details. If you plan to use a local SIM card in your phone for longer than two weeks, try to register the phone, or it will later be barred.

* *Kontör* (credit) is readily available at streetside booths, shops and mobile-phone outlets. You can pick up a basic mobile phone for about TL50.

PHONECARDS

» Phonecards can be bought at telephone centres or, for a small mark-up, from some shops.

» The cheapest option for international calls is phonecards such as IPC.

Toilets

» Most hotels have sit-down toilets, but hole-in-the-ground models are common.

» Toilet paper is often unavailable; keep some on you.

» In an emergency it's worth remembering that mosques have basic men's and women's toilets.

Tourist Information

Local tourist offices, run by the **Ministry of Culture and Tourism** (www.goturkey.com), can often do little more than hand out glossy brochures. Tour operators, pension owners and so on are often better sources of information.

Travellers with Disabilities

Turkey is challenging for disabled (engelli or özürlü) travellers, and not just because of the scarce facilities. Obstacles abound and crossing the dangerous roads is tough, although Selçuk, Bodrum and Fethiye are relatively user friendly.

Airlines, some trains and the top hotels and resorts have some provision for wheelchair access, with discounts offered by Turkish Airlines.

Hotel Rolli (www.hotel-rolli.de) Specially designed for wheelchair users.

Mephisto Voyage (☏532 7070; www.mephistovoyage.com) Tours of Cappadocia for mobility-impaired people, utilising the Joëlette system.

Visas

» Nationals of countries including Denmark, Finland, France, Germany, Israel, Italy, Japan, New Zealand, Sweden and Switzerland don't need a visa to visit Turkey for up to 90 days.
» Nationals of countries including Australia, Austria, Belgium, Canada, Ireland, the Netherlands, Norway, Portugal, Spain, the UK and the USA need a visa, but it is just a sticker bought on arrival at the airport or border post.
» The above nationals are given a 90-day multiple-entry visa. In many cases it stipulates 'per period 180 days'. This means you can spend three months in Turkey within a six-month period; when you leave after three months, you can't re-enter for three months.
» The cost of the visa varies. At the time of writing, Americans paid US$20 (or €15), Australians and Canadians US$60 (or €45) and British citizens UK£10 (or €15 or US$20).
» Some major entry points accept Visa and MasterCard, but it is generally worth having the fee ready in cash in one of the above currencies.
» Your passport must be valid for at least six months from the date you enter the country.
» See the **Ministry of Foreign Affairs** (www.mfa.gov.tr) for the latest information.

Volunteering

Alternative Camp (www.ayder.org.tr) Runs camps for people with disabilities.

Culture Routes in Turkey (tinyurl.com/d6fld8l) Help waymark and repair hiking trails.

Gençlik Servisleri Merkezi (Youth Services Centre; www.gsm-youth.org) Voluntary work camps.

Gençtur (genctur.com.tr) Voluntourism, including farmstays.

Women Travellers

Turkish society is still basically sexually segregated, especially once you get away from the big cities and tourist resorts. Although younger Turks are questioning the old ways and women hold positions of authority (there's even been a female prime minister), foreign women can find themselves being harassed. It's mostly just catcalls and dubious remarks, but assaults do occasionally occur.

» Travelling with companions usually helps. Dressing modestly will also reduce unwanted attention, and encourage most men to treat you with kindness and generosity.
» Tailor your behaviour and your clothing to your surrounds. Look at what local women are wearing. On the streets of Beyoğlu (İstanbul) you'll see skimpy tops and tight jeans, but cleavage and short skirts without leggings are a no-no everywhere except nightclubs in İstanbul and heavily touristed destinations along the coast.
» Bring a shawl to cover your head when visiting mosques.
» On the street, you don't need to don a headscarf, but keeping your legs, upper arms and neckline covered is often a good idea, particularly in eastern Anatolia. Here, long sleeves and baggy long pants should attract the least attention, and you should keep your dealings with men formal and polite, not friendly.
» When travelling by taxi and dolmuş, avoid getting into the seat beside the driver. Men and unrelated women are not supposed to sit together on long-distance buses, although the bus companies rarely enforce this in the case of foreigners. Lone women are often assigned seats at the front of the bus near the driver.
» Restaurants and tea gardens that aim to attract women often set aside a family room or section. Look for the term aile salonu (family dining room), or just aile.
» Stick to official camping grounds and camp where there are plenty of people around, especially out east.

Work

Travellers sometimes work illegally for room and board in pensions, bars and other businesses in tourist areas. These jobs are generally badly paid and only last a few months maximum, but they are a fun way to stay in a place and get to know the locals.

Job hunters may have luck with:
» http://istanbul.craigslist.org
» www.sahibinden.com/en/
» www.mymerhaba.com
» www.expatinturkey.com
» istanbul.angloinfo.com

NANNYING

One of the most lucrative nonspecialist jobs available to foreigners is nannying for the wealthy urban elite, with opportunities for English, French and German speakers.

TEACHING ENGLISH

There is lots of work available for qualified English teachers, although many employers are reluctant to deal with the bureaucratic headache of helping you get a work permit.

The best option is working for a university or a *dershane* (private school). Jobs are mostly advertised in May and June, then run from September until the following June.

Getting There & Away

Air

The cheapest flights are usually to İstanbul's Atatürk International Airport (Atatürk Havalimanı; ☑212-463 3000; www.ataturkairport.com), 23km west of Sultanahmet, and Sabiha Gökçen International Airport (Sabiha Gökçen Havalimanı; ☑216-588 8888; www.sgairport.com), 50km east of Sultanahmet on the Asian side of the city. To reach other Turkish airports you often have to transit in İstanbul.

Other international airports include Ankara, Antalya, Bodrum, Dalaman and İzmir.

It's a good idea to book at least two months in advance if you plan to arrive between April and August. If you plan to visit a resort, check with your local travel agents for flight and accommodation deals.

Turkey's national carrier, Turkish Airlines (☑0850-333 0849; www.thy.com), flies worldwide.

Asia and Middle East One of the cheapest ways to fly further afield is from İstanbul via Dubai.

Australia and New Zealand You can fly to İstanbul, normally via Dubai, Kuala Lumpur or Singapore. You can often get cheaper flights with European airlines, which involves a second flight change in Europe.

Europe İstanbul is connected to most major European cities by Turkish Airlines, with flights also available with its budget subsidiaries Sun Express (☑444 0797; www.sunexpress.com) and AnadoluJet (☑444 2538; www.anadolujet.com), its Turkish competitors including Pegasus Airlines (www.flypgs.com), and European carriers including easyJet (www.easyjet.com). Charter flights are a good option, particularly at the beginning and end of the peak summer holiday season.

North America Most flights connect with İstanbul-bound flights in the UK or Continental Europe, so it's worth looking at European airlines in addition to North American carriers. Another option is to cross the Atlantic to Europe and continue on a separate ticket with a budget carrier.

Land

Turkey shares borders with Armenia (closed), Azerbaijan, Bulgaria, Georgia, Greece, Iran, Iraq and Syria. There are many routes into and out of the country.

BUS

Austria, Bulgaria, Germany, Greece, Macedonia and Romania have the most direct buses to İstanbul.

The Turkish companies Varan Turizm (☑444 8999; www.varan.com.tr), Metro Turizm (☑444 3455; www.metroturizm.com.tr) and Ulusoy (☑444 1888; www.ulusoy.com.tr) operate on these routes. Ulusoy has weekly departures to/from Germany (about €200), with one line running through Slovenia and eastern Europe, and the other through Italy and Greece with a sea crossing.

If you're travelling from other European countries, you'll likely have to catch a connecting bus.

TRAIN

The daily Bosphorus/Balkan Express links İstanbul with Bucharest (Romania), Sofia (Bulgaria) and Belgrade (Serbia). Visit www.seat61.com/turkey2 and tinyurl.com/b3cx85s for more information.

Sea

Departure times and routes change between seasons, with less ferries running in winter. Ferrylines (www.ferrylines.com) is a good starting point for information.

FERRIES TO/FROM TURKEY

ROUTE	FREQUENCY	DURATION	FARE (ONE WAY/ RETURN)	COMPANY
Ayvalık–Lesvos, Greece	Mon-Sat May-Sep; 3 weekly Oct-Apr	1½hr	TL60/70, car TL120/130	Jale Tour (www.jaletour.com)
Alanya–Girne (Kyrenia), Northern Cyprus	2 weekly in summer	3½hr	TL77/127	Fergün Denizcilik (www.fergun.net)
Bodrum–Kos, Greece	daily	1hr	single or same-day return €32; open return €60	Bodrum Ferryboat Association (www.bodrumferryboat.com); Bodrum Express Lines (www.bodrumexpresslines.com)
Bodrum–Rhodes, Greece	2 weekly Jun-Sep	2¼hr	single or same-day return €60; open return €120	Bodrum Ferryboat Association (www.bodrumferryboat.com)
Çeşme–Chios, Greece	daily mid-May–mid-Sep; 2 weekly mid-Sep–mid-May	1½hr	TL65/100, car TL150/260	Ertürk (www.erturk.com.tr)
Datça–Rhodes, Greece	Sat May-Sep	45min	TL90/180	Knidos Yachting (www.knidosyachting.com)
Datça–Simi, Greece	hydrofoil Sat May-Sep, *gület* 2 weekly	hydrofoil 15min, *gület* 70min	hydrofoil TL60/120, *gület* TL140	Knidos Yachting (www.knidosyachting.com)
İstanbul–Illyichevsk (Odessa), Ukraine	2 weekly	28½hr	one way US$150, car US$325	Sea Lines (www.sea-lines.net)
Kaş–Meis (Kastellorizo), Greece	daily	20min	single or same-day return €20	Meis Express (www.meisexpress.com)
Kuşadası– Samos, Greece	daily Apr-Oct	1¼hr	€35/55	Meander Travel (www.meandertravel.com)
Marmaris–Rhodes, Greece	daily Apr-Oct	50min	from €45/65, car from €110/190	Yeşil Marmaris Travel & Yachting (www.yesil-marmaris.com)
Taşucu–Girne (Kyrenia), Northern Cyprus	daily	from 2hr	TL69/114	Akgünler Denizcilik (www.akgunler.com.tr)
Trabzon–Sochi, Russia	weekly	5-12hr	one way US$100 to US$200	Olympia Line (www.olympia-line.ru), Öz Star Denizcilik (Princess Victoria), Sarı Denizcilik (www.saridenizcilik.com/en); see also www.seaport-sochi.ru and www.al-port.com
Turgutreis–Kos, Greece	daily 25 May–31 Oct	30min	€12/20	Bodrum Ferryboat Association (www.bodrumferryboat.com)

Getting Around

Air

Turkey is well connected by air throughout the country, although many flights go via hubs İstanbul or Ankara. Internal flights are a good option in such a large country, and competition between the following Turkish airlines keeps tickets affordable.

AnadoluJet (☑444 2538; www.anadolujet.com)

Atlasjet (☑0850-222 0000; www.atlasjet.com)

Onur Air (☑0850-210 6687; www.onurair.com.tr)

Pegasus Airlines (☑0850-250 0737; www.pegasusairlines.com)

Sun Express (☑444 0797; www.sunexpress.com)

Turkish Airlines (☑0850-333 0849; www.thy.com)

Bicycle

Riding a bike is a great way of exploring the countryside, especially in touristy areas, where you can hire bikes from pensions and rental outfits. Road surfaces are generally acceptable, if a bit rough, though Turkey's notorious drivers are a hazard.

Bus

The Turkish bus network is excellent: coaches go just about everywhere, they're cheap and comfortable, smoking isn't permitted, drinks and snacks are often provided, and regular toilet stops are built into longer routes.

» The premium companies have nationwide networks offering greater speed and comfort for slightly higher fares. They also have the best safety records. Departures on popular routes can be as frequent as every 15 minutes, with hourly services the norm from major cities. Fares vary according to distance and the popularity of the route; typically, from İstanbul to Çanakkale costs TL45, İstanbul to Ankara TL38 to TL43, and İstanbul to Göreme (Cappadocia) TL65.

» Although you can usually walk into an *otogar* (bus station) and buy a ticket for the next bus, it's wise to plan ahead for public holidays, at weekends and during the school holidays from mid-June to early September. You can reserve seats online with the better companies.

» A town's *otogar* is often on the outskirts, but most bus companies provide a *servis* (free shuttle bus) to/from the centre.

Besides intercity buses, *otogars* often handle *dolmuşes* (minibuses) to outlying districts or villages. Larger bus stations have an *emanetçi* (left luggage) room, which you can use for a fee.

The best bus companies, with extensive route networks:

Kamil Koç (☑444 0562; www.kamilkoc.com.tr)

Metro Turizm (☑444 3455; www.metroturizm.com.tr)

Ulusoy (☑444 1888; www.ulusoy.com.tr)

Varan Turizm (☑444 8999; www.varan.com.tr)

Car & Motorcycle

Public transport is a much easier and less stressful way of getting around the traffic-clogged cities. Turkey's main motoring organisation is the **Türkiye Turing ve Otomobil Kurumu** (TTOK, Turkish Touring & Automobile Club; ☑212-513 3660; www.turing.org.tr; Soğukçeşme Sokağı, Sultanahmet, İstanbul).

BRINGING YOUR OWN VEHICLE

You can bring your vehicle into Turkey for six months without charge, but details of your car are marked in your passport to ensure it leaves the country with you.

DRIVING LICENCES

An international driving permit (IDP) is not obligatory, but may be handy if your driving licence is from a country likely to seem obscure to a Turkish police officer.

FUEL & SPARE PARTS

Turkey has the world's second most expensive petrol prices. Petrol/diesel costs about TL4/4.70 per litre.

» There are plenty of modern petrol stations in the west. In the east they are slightly less abundant and it's a good idea to have a full tank when you start out in the morning.

* *Yedek parçaları* (spare parts) are readily available in the big cities and *sanayi bölgesi* (industrial zones) on the outskirts, especially for European models such as Renaults, Fiats and Mercedes-Benz. Repairs are usually quick and cheap.

CAR HIRE

» Rental charges are similar to those in Continental Europe.

» You need to be at least 21 years old, with a year's driving experience, to hire a car.

» Most companies require a credit card.

» The big international companies (including Avis, Budget, Europcar, Hertz,

TOLLS

You must pay a toll to use the major motorways. You can buy green-and-orange toll cards and place *kontör* (credit) on them at the offices near motorway toll gates. The offices are not open 24 hours; most close on Sunday. There is a TL100 fine for nonpayment, which takes about two weeks to come through.

National and Sixt) are represented in the main cities, towns and airports. Particularly in eastern Anatolia, stick with these companies, as they have insurance and better emergency backup.

Economy Car Rentals (www.economycar-rentals.com) gets excellent rates with other companies, including Budget and National.

INSURANCE

You *must* have third-party insurance to drive in Turkey. Buying it at the border is a straightforward process (one month €80).

ROAD RULES & SAFETY

Turkey has one of the world's highest motor-vehicle accident rates.

Driving is hair-raising during the day because of fast, inappropriate driving and overladen trucks, and dangerous at night, when some drivers speed along with their headlights off. Always drive cautiously.

Unless otherwise posted, maximum speed limits are 50km/h in towns, 90km/h on highways and 120km/h on *otoyols* (motorways). Clamping is a fact of life in Turkey.

Hitching

Although we don't recommend hitching (*otostop*), short hitches are not uncommon in Turkey, for example to get from the highway to an archaeological site.

Offer to pay something towards the petrol, although most drivers pick up foreign hitchers for their curiosity value.

Instead of sticking out your thumb for a lift, you should face the traffic and wave your arm up and down as if bouncing a basketball.

Local Transport

Short-distance and local routes are usually served by medium-sized 'midibuses' or smaller *dolmuşes* (minibuses that follow prescribed routes).

A few cities, including Bursa, have old-fashioned *taksi dolmuşes* (shared taxis).

Most towns have a municipal bus network; this may be supplemented by underground, tram, train and ferries in the largest cities.

Taxis are plentiful; they have meters – just make sure they're switched on.

Tours

Areas where an organised tour makes sense, particularly with limited time, include the Gallipoli Peninsula, Troy and Cappadocia. There are unscrupulous operators, particularly in Sultanahmet (İstanbul) and Neveşehir (Cappadocia), but also plenty of good outfits.

Train

Although most people still opt for buses as train journey times are notoriously long, the system is being overhauled and a few fast lines (Ankara–Konya and Ankara–Eskişehir) are appearing. A growing number of fans appreciate the no-rush experience of a train journey, such as the stunning scenery rolling by and immersion with fellow passengers.

The occasional unannounced hold-up and public toilets gone feral by the end of the long journey are all part of the adventure. If you're on a budget, overnight train journeys are a great way to save accommodation costs. Don't try to attempt a trans-Turkey trip in one go, as the country is large and the trains slow.

InterRail, Balkan Flexipass and Eurodo-mino passes are valid on the Turkish railway network, but Eurail passes are not.

Turkish State Railways (444 8233; www.tcdd.gov.tr)

Man in Seat Sixty-One (www.seat61.com/turkey2) Information and inspiration on Turkish train travel.

ROUTES

The train network covers the country fairly well, with the notable exception of the coastlines. For the Aegean and Mediterranean coasts you can travel by train to either İzmir or Konya, and take the bus from there.

Trains are not currently running between İstanbul and destinations in Anatolia. From Ankara, long-distance destinations include Adana, Diyarbakır, İzmir, Kayseri, Kurtalan, Malatya and Tatvan (Lake Van).

Useful routes include the following:

» Ankara–Konya
» İstanbul–İzmir (including ferry to/from Bandırma)
» İzmir–Selcuk

Survival Guide

Directory A–Z

Directory A-Z answers questions about Southeastern Europe as a whole. For more detailed country-specific information, look in the Directory at the end of each individual country chapter.

Accommodation

Every budget is catered for in Southeastern Europe, from rural campsites and Soviet-era eyesores, to frilly-pillowed private rooms and five star palaces.

Throughout this book, we list reviews by author preference and give prices in local currency. The price indicators refer to the cost of a double room in high season, including private bathroom (any combination of toilet, bathtub, shower and washbasin), but excluding breakfast unless otherwise stated.

Prices

Individual price range breakdowns are listed in the respective country directories. In general:

Budget (€) Bare-bones hostels and hotels, or spare rooms at the back of someone's grandma's house. Often with shared bathrooms and limited amenities.

Midrange (€€) Hotels and guesthouses with private facilities, and more often than not with a television and wi-fi. Sometimes including breakfast.

Top end (€€€) The nicest places in town, which are generally well-appointed and have all the creature comforts you'd expect for the price you pay.

Reservations

Booking ahead is a good idea in high season and during key events. Reservations can usually be made by phone, and sometimes online. Where there are tourist offices they sometimes provide reservation services (some for a small fee), but don't expect the same efficiency of service here as you would in Western Europe. Otherwise, there are several websites (some of which we've provided below) that may help keep you off the streets, even at the last minute. In parts of Southeastern Europe, there is a shortage of good-value mid-range options, meaning that you may get stuck staying below or above the standard you are looking for.

Seasons

Rates often plummet outside of high season (typically July to August), sometimes by as much as 50%. In places that cater to business travellers, prices are more expensive during the week and cheaper over the weekend.

Camping

Camping is generally your cheapest option but the trade-off may be that you are far away from things you want to see. Before you commit, check out public transport connections to and from campsites and towns. Some camping grounds may be geared for motorists, though there's generally also room for backpackers with tents. Many offer on-site basic cabins, caravans or bungalows that may be cheaper than hostels, though not always. Don't count on these being free during high seasons.

The standard of camping grounds varies enormously throughout the region. They're unreliable in Romania, crowded in Slovenia, and variable in Bulgaria. In Turkey you may be able to camp on pension and hostel grounds. Croatia's coast is lined with nudist camping grounds (signposted with FKK, the German acronym for 'naturist'); these can offer delightful secluded locations for campers sans clothing.

BOOK YOUR STAY ONLINE

For more accommodation reviews by Lonely Planet authors, check out lonelyplanet.com/hotels. You'll find independent reviews, as well as recommendations on the best places to stay. Best of all, you can book online.

» Camping grounds may be open from April to October, May to September, or perhaps only June to August, depending on the category of the facility, the location and the demand.

» A few private camping grounds may be open all year.

» Camping in the wild is usually illegal; ask locals before you pitch your tent on a beach or in an open field.

» In some places you may be allowed to build a campfire. Always ask first.

Farmhouses

'Village tourism', which means staying at a farmhouse, is highly developed in Slovenia. It's like staying in a private room or pension, except the participating farms are in picturesque rural areas with outdoor activity options nearby. See **World Wide Opportunities on Organic Farms** (www.wwoof.org) for information about working on organic farms in exchange for room and board.

Guesthouses & Pensions

Small private pensions are common in parts of Southeastern Europe. Typically priced between hotels and private rooms, pensions sometimes offer basic breakfast at small on-site restaurants. Pensions are smaller and more personal than hotels, which can amount to a bit less privacy.

Homestays & Private Rooms

When you arrive in some towns, people will approach you offering private rooms or hostel beds. Some carry clipboards and pamphlets; others are little old ladies speaking halting English or German. Taking up these offers can be a good or bad experience; it's impossible to say until you do it. You may be lead to a pristine room in the centre of town, or to a cupboard in an outer suburb housing project. Obviously, don't commit until

PRACTICALITIES

» The emergency number 112 can be used throughout the region, though is still in its infancy in some parts. See individual country chapters for alternative country-specific numbers.

» The metric system is used for weights and measures.

» Smoking in parts of the region is ubiquitous; non-smoking tables and rooms won't always be available.

» Duty-free goods are not sold to those travelling from one EU country to another.

» Look for Global Blue Tax Free shopping signs in Croatia, Greece, Slovenia and Serbia; you may be able to claim tax back when you leave if you ask for a Tax Free Form when making your purchase (www.global-blue.com).

» This is a region rich with literature to read on the road. Rebecca West's *Black Lamb and Grey Falcon* is the quintessential classic to read during train journeys. Other recommended non-fiction reads include Misha Glenny's *The Balkans: Nationalism, War and the Great Powers, 1804–2011*, and Robert D Kaplan's *Balkan Ghosts: A Journey through History*. See individual country chapters for more recommendations.

» Try Freytag & Berndt for maps (www.freytagberndt.de/rtc-freytagberndt/de_DE/758).

» There are several print and online newspapers throughout the region, many of which have strong political leanings. Cross-check important information.

» International television networks (such as BBC World News, Al-Jazeera, Deutsche Welle and and TV5MONDE) are widely broadcast throughout the region.

you're comfortable with the place and clear on the price. It may be unwise to leave your valuables behind with strangers.

Agencies or intermediaries sometimes facilitate stays in private rooms and can offer some level of quality control. Alternatively, look for advertisements yourself; knock on the door or call when you see a *Zimmer Frei* (in German) sign advertising availability of private rooms. In Croatia, taxation has made private rooms less attractive than before, but it's still better value than a hotel.

Staying with friends in Southeastern Europe will be a wonderful experience given the famed hospitality of the region. Bring some

small gifts for your hosts – it's a deeply ingrained cultural tradition throughout the region.

Hostels

You don't have to be a 'youth' to be apart of the sociable hostel scene in Southeastern Europe. Hostels vary enormously in character and quality. Many are part of the **Youth Hostel Association** (YHA), which is affiliated with **Hostelling International** (HI).

» Hostel cards are rarely required, though may give you a small discount.

» Hostels give you a bed for the night, plus use of communal facilities.

» Facilities often include small kitchens where you can do your own cooking.

» Some hostels require that you have a sleeping sheet; if you don't have one, you may be able to rent one.

» Not all hostels are open all year round.

» Many hostels accept reservations, but not always during peak periods. They may be able to hold a bed for a couple of hours if you call from a bus or train station. You can also book hostels through national hostel offices.

HI offers listings online (and in print) for all countries of Southeastern Europe, with the exception of Kosovo.

Useful websites include:

» **Hostel World** (www. hostel-world.com)

» **Hostelling International** (HI; www.hihostels.com)

» **Hostelz** (www.hostelz.com)

Hotels

At the rock bottom end of the scale, cheap hotels may be no more expensive than private rooms or guesthouses, while at the other end you'll find unimaginable boutique luxury. In both cases, you get what you pay for.

» Often you pay for the room and not by the number of people staying in it, so singles may be pay almost as much as for a double.

» Particularly in older hotels, cheaper rooms may have washbasins but the toilet and shower may be down the corridor.

» Breakfast may or may not be included in the room price – ask at check-in.

» Cheap, basic hotels are often clustered around bus and train transport hubs. Useful websites for most countries in the region include:

» **Booking.com** (www.booking.com)

» **Direct Rooms** (www.directrooms.com)

» **Hotel Club** (www.hotelclub.net)

» **HRS** (www.hrs.com)

Rental Accommodation

In some cities, depending on how long you plan to stay, renting an apartment through a reputable website or local agency can be a good option. Renting an apartment can cost much less than you'd pay for an equivalent stay in a hotel, and allows you to cook for yourself.

» The quality and location of rental accommodation varies considerably, largely depending on their size and location and your budget.

» Generally, the longer you stay, the more you can negotiate.

» Some local agencies operate independently and sometimes only quasi-legally, meaning you may have no recourse in the event of a dispute; only go for those of good repute.

» When dealing with agencies online, never send money unless you are certain that the agency is genuine.

Useful websites for most countries in the region include:

» **Airbnb** (www.airbnb.com)

» **Vacations Abroad** (www.vacations-abroad.com)

» **Vacation Rentals by Owner** (www.vrbo.com)

University Accommodation

Some universities (notably in Croatia, Macedonia, Slovenia and Serbia) rent space in student halls during July and August.

» Accommodation will sometimes be in single rooms, but more commonly in doubles or triples with shared bathrooms.

» Basic cooking facilities may be available.

Ask at the college or university, at student information services or at tourist offices.

Activities

The varied landscape in Southeastern Europe makes it an ideal region in which to hike, ski, climb or parasail off mountains, paddle on lakes and rivers, kayak through canyons, or sail on or dive in seas. Some outdoor activity hubs draw big crowds, but some less known spots are only just emerging.

Cycling

There are some confronting hills and mountains to conquer in Southeastern Europe. Some inclines can be heavy going, but this is offset by the scenery. The Sinaia in Romania is a great place to mountain bike across the plateau atop the Bucegi Mountains.

Diving

The sparkling waters and varied marine life of the Adriatic support a vibrant diving industry. Explore caves and shipwrecks along the coast in Croatia, Montenegro and Slovenia, as well as Macedonia's Lake Ohrid. There are also some great dive sites near Sozopol and Varna in Bulgaria, and off the Aegean and Mediterranean coasts of Greece and Turkey.

Extreme Sports

Extreme sports are becoming increasingly popular in the region.

Bovec in Slovenia is a hotspot for hydrospeeding, canyoning and paragliding. For a quick adrenalin fix you can jump off the Old Bridge in Mostar, Bosnia and Hercegovina (BiH).

Hiking

Every country in the region offers excellent hiking, generally with public transport to trail heads and well-marked trails through forests, mountains and national parks. Chalets and mountain dot the paths in Bulgaria, Romania, and Slovenia, offering basic meals and dormitory accommodation.

The best months for hiking are from June to September, especially late August and early September, when the summer crowds will have largely disappeared.

Popular hiking destinations include:

» Rila Mountains, Bulgaria

» Julian Alps, Slovenia

» Uludağ National Park, Turkey

Less well-known spots include:

» Theth, Albania

» Tara National Park, Serbia

» Rugova Mountains, Kosovo

Kayaking, Canoeing & Rafting

Water sports are possible from March to October on a growing number of scenic spots, including:

» Slovenia's Soča River

» Croatia's Mljet island, Tragir, Rovinj, Pula and Hvar

» Montenegro's Tara Canyon in Durmitor National Park and the Bay of Kotor

» The Vrbas River and the River Una near Bihać in BiH

» The Drina from BiH or Serbia or the Ibar

» Rafting in Albania is also on the rise.

Skiing

Skiing is becoming big business in Southeastern Europe, but still remains among the most cost-effective you'll find in Europe. The season runs from early December to late March, give or take a month depending on altitude. January and February tend to be busiest from a snow reliability point of view.

Ski spots in Southeastern Europe include:

» Bucegi Mountains, Romania

» Bansko in the Rila Mountains, Bulgaria

» Julian Alps, Slovenia

» Sarajevo, the capital of BiH, which hosted the 1984 winter Olympics. Slopes are within an hour of the city.

» Bjelašnica, Jahorina and Vlašić in BiH

» Durmitor in Montenegro

Lesser-known but good value and well-equipped ski areas are to be found in Macedonia, Montenegro, Turkey, Serbia and Kosovo.

Sailing

Yachting tours, classes and rentals are available throughout the region including in Croatia, Montenegro, Greece and Turkey. The passage between the rugged islands off Croatia's Dalmatian coast is particularly popular. Sometimes crews are looking for another couple of members to join. Sailing trips generally are not for travellers on a budget.

Business Hours

Business hours vary across the region, changing by season and arbitrarily at will. As a rough guide:

» Saturday and Sunday are official days off (even in predominantly Muslim areas), although only banks and offices close; many shops and cafes open every day.

» Banks and offices are usually open from 9am to 5am, Monday to Friday with an hour or two off over lunch. Some may be open on Saturday mornings.

» Shops stay open until 7pm or later in busier areas.

» During the hot months, some businesses close for two or three hours over lunch, reopening at 3pm or 4pm and staying open into the evening.

» In Islamic areas, note that the working day is shorter during the holy month of Ramadan.

Children

Children are beloved in these parts, so having kids in tow can make for wonderful encounters with locals that you wouldn't have otherwise.

» The range of baby food, formulas, soy and cows' milk, disposable nappies and the

like is almost as extensive as in supermarkets as at home, though you may pay more than you would expect.

» Strollers can be hindrance to mobility in towns and cities with cobble stones or just messy pavements.

» If you need children's safety seats for rented cars, book them in advance.

» More restaurants provide high chairs, but don't expect cots in hotels.

» In Albania, praise won't be lavished on your child – and nor should you lavish praise on Albanian kids – as there are concerns about the all-observant 'evil eye'.

A good general resource for travelling parents is Lonely Planet's *Travel with Children*, written by a team of parent-authors.

Discount Cards

Discount cards may not work everywhere, but if used wisely can significantly cut the cost of your trip.

Camping Card International

The Camping Card International (CCI) is a camping ground ID valid for a year. It can be used instead of a passport when checking in to camping grounds and includes third-party insurance. Many camping grounds offer discounts of up to 25% to card-holders (though often not if you use credit card). CCIs are issued by automobile associations, camping federations and sometimes on the spot at camping grounds. See **Camping Card International** (www.campingcardinternational.org) for lists of participating camping grounds in Bulgaria, Croatia, Greece, Serbia, Slovenia and Romania.

Hostel Cards

You are not required to be a Hostelling International member to stay in hostels, but you sometimes will get a discount if you are. Some hostels issue cards on the spot or after a few days' stay, though this might cost more than getting one at home.

Senior Cards

After bemoaning your eligibility for a seniors card, embrace the benefits!

» Many attractions offer reduced-price admission for people over 60 or 65 (sometimes 55 for women).

» EU residents are eligible for discounts in many EU countries; bring proof of age.

» For a fee of around €20, European residents aged 60 and over can get a Railplus Card as an add-on to their national rail senior pass, entitling holders to fare reductions of about 25%. Before leaving home, check with an agency that caters to senior travel – such as **Road Scholar** (www.roadscholar. org) – for age-related travel packages and discounts.

Student, Youth & Teacher Cards

The International Student Identity Card (ISIC) provides discounts on many forms of transport (including planes and local transport), cheap or free admission to museums and other attractions, and even discounted meals in student cafeterias and restaurants. Full time students of any age are eligible.

If you aren't a student but are under 26, you are eligible to apply for an International Youth Travel Card (IYTC, formerly GO25) issued by the International Youth Travel Organisation, or the Euro26 card. Both cards go under different names in different countries, and give much the same discounts as an ISIC. The Euro26 card may not be recognised in Albania, Romania, Serbia and Montenegro. The International Teacher Identity Card (ITIC) does much the same thing for full-time teaching professionals. You will get more use from

your card in some countries than others.

For more information, see the **International Student Travel Confederation** (www. isic.org).

Electricity

Plugs in Southeastern Europe are the standard round two-pin variety, sometimes called the europlug.

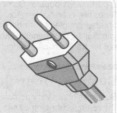

230V/50Hz

Embassies & Consulates

It is important to realise what your embassy can and cannot do to help if you get into trouble while travelling abroad.

» You are bound by the laws of the country in which you are travelling; your embassy cannot help much if your emergency is of your own making. Your embassy will not post bail or otherwise act to get you out of jail.

» Your embassy may refer you to a doctor or lawyer, but is unlikely to provide financial assistance, no matter what your emergency.

» Your embassy can assist you to replace lost or stolen

passports. This will be much simpler if you have a photocopy of your passport. Carry a copy of your passport (separately from your actual passport), and before you leave home email a copy to yourself along with travel insurance information so you can download it any time, anywhere.

Food

Experience as much of the diverse culinary culture of the region as you can while you are travelling in it. Vegetarians may get frustrated on occasion; it pays to learn some key food phrases in each country, so you can explain what you don't want to appear on your plate.

Gay & Lesbian Travellers

Though laws allow consensual homosexual sex, attitudes aren't necessarily as just. You are unlikely to raise an eyebrow by sharing a room (or bed) with your same-sex partner, but in many countries, societies still frown on overt displays of affection, particularly between members of the same gender.

» Many countries have hosted gay-pride events in recent years, but bad experiences with anti-gay protesters now means that heavy police presence is necessary.

» Despite the don't-ask-don't-tell situation prevalent in many parts of the region, there are some lively gay scenes in many capitals and cities, with notable exceptions of Pristina, Tirana, Skopje and Sarajevo where there are no gay- or lesbian-specific events or venues on offer for visitors.

» Notable gay-friendly hubs include the island oasis of Mykonos in Greece, and lesbians have long been making the pilgrimage to Eresos on Lesvos.

» Outside larger towns and specific hubs, gay and lesbian life is almost non-existent making the internet the only realistic way to make contact with other gay people in the region. Many countries in the region have online forums and advocacy groups.

Health

Southeastern Europe poses no notable health risks to travellers, though as with anywhere else in the world there are basic things you should be aware of.

Before You Go

Prevention is the key to staying healthy while abroad. A little planning, particularly for pre-existing illnesses, will save trouble later: see your dentist before a long trip, carry spare contact lenses or glasses, and take your optical prescription with you.

Bring medications in original, clearly labelled containers along with a signed and dated letter from your physician describing your medical conditions and medications, including generic names. If carrying syringes, have a physician's letter documenting their medical necessity.

Tap Water

Tap water may not be safe to drink, so it is best to stick to bottled water or boil for 10 minutes, use water purification tables or a filter. Do not drink water from rivers or lakes; it may contain bacteria or viruses that can cause diarrhoea or vomiting. Brushing your teeth with tap water is highly unlikely to lead to problems.

Availability & Cost of Healthcare

Good basic health care is readily available, and pharmacists can give valuable advice and sell over-the-counter medication for minor illnesses. They can also refer you to more specialised help when required. Outside major cities, medical care is not always readily available, but embassies, consulates and five star hotels can usually recommend doctors or clinics. Healthcare costs tend to be less expensive than in Western Europe, but given you may want to go to a private clinic for anything beyond a doctor's consultation, comprehensive health insurance is essential.

Potential Illnesses or Conditions

RABIES

Spread through bites or licks from an infected animal on broken skin, rabies is always fatal unless treated promptly and is present throughout Southeastern Europe. To be vaccinated, three injections are needed over a month. If you are bitten and have not been vaccinated, you will need a course of five injections starting within 24 hours or as soon as possible after the injury.

TICK-BORNE ENCEPHALITIS

Spread by tick bites, tick-borne encephalitis is a serious infection of the brain. Vaccination is advised for those in risk areas who are unable to avoid tick bites (such as campers, forestry workers and walkers). Two does of vaccine will provide protection for a year, while three doses provide up to three years' protection.

TRAVELLER'S DIARRHOEA

If you develop diarrhoea, drink plenty of fluids, preferably an oral rehydration solution (eg Dioralyte). A few loose stools don't require treatment, but if you start having more than four or five a day, you should start taking an antibiotic (usually a quinolone drug) and an antidiarrhoeal agent (such as loperamide). If diarrhoea is bloody, persists for more than 72 hours or is accompanied by fever or shaking, chills or severe abdominal pain, you should seek medical attention.

INSECT BITES & STINGS

Mosquitoes are found in most parts of Europe. They may not carry malaria but can cause irritation and infected bites. Use insect repellent, plug in anti-mosquito devices and cover your arms and legs in the evening.

Holidays

Throughout Southeastern Europe, children get the summer months (usually much of July and all of August) off school, making it one of the busiest times to go to the beach and other popular spots. There are also breaks for Easter and Christmas; keep in mind that dates for Orthodox Christmas and Easter are different to those of their Catholic and Protestant counterparts (though Easter sometimes falls on the same date by both calendars). Even in countries with a large Muslim population such as BiH, Albania and Turkey, school holidays generally follow these guidelines.

Insurance

If you can't afford insurance, you can't afford to travel (and Murphy's law dictates that if you don't have it, you will need it). You should get a travel-insurance policy to cover theft, loss and medical problems.

» Some insurance policies exclude specific 'dangerous activities' such as scuba diving, motorcycling and even hiking. Check that you are covered for all the things you might do.

» Some policies exclude certain countries; read the fine print.

» Some claims can only be made after you have made a police report or taken other steps; find out what you have to do to make a successful claim.

» Check that your policy covers ambulances and an emergency flight home.

» You may prefer a policy that pays doctors or hospitals directly rather than reimbursing your claims after the fact.

» Some policies ask you to call back (reverse charges) to a centre in your home country, where an immediate assessment of your problem is made.

» If you have to file a claim, make sure you keep all documentation.

» The policies issued by **STA Travel** and other student travel organisations are usually good value. Another option is **World Nomads** (www. worldnomads.com), which is easy to arrange online.

» Worldwide travel insurance is available at www.lonelyplanet.com/travel-insurance. You can buy, extend and claim online at anytime – even if you're already on the road.

Internet Access

With few exceptions, you will never be far from the world wide web. Any decent-sized town in Southeastern Europe has internet access even if you find yourself in a stinky room full of teenage gamers. In some places, internet cafes can be a great way of meeting locals and travellers, but elsewhere they are all but disappearing as handheld devices and ubiquitous wi-fi hotspots engulf the region. This is good news for BYO laptop, smart phone and i-everything users, who will enjoy hotspots in cafes, libraries, hotels, hostels and even some public places. It is now almost universal for high-standard or boutique hotels to have wi-fi in rooms, though some still charge. Paradoxically, the more you pay for the room the more

they tend to charge you for internet. If you are choosing accommodation based on the availability of internet, check that it is actually working before you commit.

Throughout this book, internet access is indicatied in reviews by an @ symbol.

Money
Currencies

The main irritation you'll face is switching between currencies. There is no longer any particular desire for 'hard' currency and most Southeastern European currencies are readily convertible. That said, the euro and the US dollar remain the easiest currency to change and can be used in Greece, Kosovo, Montenegro and Slovenia. In other countries, some businesses may accept euro for some transactions. It's not difficult to exchange other major currencies in big cities, but you will be at the mercy of exchange offices and their exploitative rates.

ATMs

ATMs are widespread, with some rural exceptions. Avoid situations where you leave big cities relying on being able to find one.

Cash and debit cards can be used at ATMs linked to international networks like Cirrus and Maestro. The major advantage of using ATMs is that you don't pay commission to exchange your money, although you may be hit by a bank fee (or two if you're charged by both your home bank and the one in the destination country). Still, the exchange rate is usually better than that offered for travellers cheques or cash exchanges.

If you rely on plastic, use two different cards so you have a backup if one is lost or not accepted. Even smarter is a combination of cards and back up cash.

Moneychangers

Unless you have no choice, never change your cash without first shopping around for a respectable rate. Rates are likely to be crappy in tourist areas, so try get away from them. Rates are never great at border crossings, airports and train stations.

Tipping

Tipping practices vary from country to country and sometimes from place to place within a given country. Tipping often means simply rounding up to the next whole figure; if this means giving a good waiter peanuts, add a couple of coins. As a rule of thumb, you can't go wrong if you add 10% onto your bill at a restaurant.

Porters at upmarket hotels will appreciate and expect a few euro for their efforts, as will wait staff in fashionable venues in urban centres, and taxi drivers. Meanwhile, tipping in rural areas may be met with astonishment.

Travellers Cheques

These days, travellers cheques are to the credit card what sextants are to the GPS. The advantage of travellers cheques is the protection they offer from theft, but most people prefer to withdraw cash from ATMs as they go.

Banks usually charge between 1% and 2% commission to change travellers cheques (or up to 5% in Bulgaria or Romania). Check the commission and rate before signing. Offices may be scarce and opening hours may be limited.

Travel Money Cards

Prepaid travel money cards let you load as much foreign currency as you like, then withdraw it at ATMs bearing the appropriate logo, or make direct purchases as you would with a Visa or MasterCard. They can be reloaded online or via telephone. Advantages are that you avoid foreign exchange fees, control of what you spend, and if it's stolen only results in the loss of whatever is on the card as it's not linked to your bank account. They also charge lower withdrawal fees. However, they cost you money to acquire and reload, and fees apply for unused currency. You'll lose what you don't spend upon an expiry date. As always, costs need to be weighed against benefits in the context of how you like to spend and travel.

Western Union

If everything goes horribly wrong – your money, credit cards and travellers cheques are all stolen – don't despair. A friend or relative back home will be able to wire money to you anywhere via Western Union. The sender is given a code that they communicate to you, and you take the code to the nearest office along with your passport to receive the cash. Western Union offices are everywhere; look for the yellow and black sign.

Photography & Video

Once upon a time, taking photos of bridges, official buildings or even train stations was frowned upon. These days, local officials are less likely to reproach you, but you still need to use common sense and courtesy; ask first.

» Photographing military facilities and border crossings anywhere in the world is never a brilliant idea.

» Museums often require payment for permission to photograph or film.

» Taking photographs of sacred things, including portrayals of deities, may be culturally inappropriate. Similarly, people may not be comfortable with you taking photos of them praying or otherwise participating in religious services.

» The larger the town, the larger the selection of digital memory, film and camera equipment. Anything purchased in tourist areas will be more expensive.

» Lonely Planet's *Travel Photography* covers all aspects of travel photography, and shows you how to develop your skills to capture the perfect picture.

» Remember to backup digital photos; if you lose all your stuff you'll discover that it's the photos that are irreplaceable.

Post

Reliability of postal services varies, but most things usually arrive in the end. In some countries your items will need to be taken unwrapped to the post office where they will be wrapped for you. Your passport and other information may be noted down, and you may be asked for a return address. If you don't have one, provide the address of any large hotel. If you really need something important to get to where it needs to, you may prefer to use a private delivery service like DHL.

Safe Travel

An accurate picture of what it's like to travel in Southeastern Europe can be found somewhere between overly-cautious government warnings at one end and claims that there is nothing to worry about at the other. If you can handle yourself in a big city of North America, Western Europe or Australia, you'll have little trouble here. You are unlikely to have any threatening encounters, but at all times, you should look purposeful, stay alert and use your judgment and instincts.

Some locals will regale you with tales of how dangerous their city is and recount various cases of muggings, break-ins and kidnappings, often involving Roma or other popular scapegoats (other Southeastern Europeans will tell you horror stories about the Romanians and Albanians). Most of these stories are overblown or exaggerated and you are unlikely to have any threatening encounters.

Corruption

Low-level corruption is largely disappearing. In all exchanges with people in official positions (such as police, border guards, train conductors, ticket inspectors or anyone else) be clear on what you are paying and why, so as to avoid ambiguous situations. Always insist on a receipt for any money you hand over.

If you do find yourself in a tangle with a gung-ho official testing the limits of his own power, consider the situation as a blog-worthy travel experience. Insist on calling your embassy, or suggest seeing their senior officer; assuming you have not committed a crime, more senior officers will likely let you go. The golden rule is keep your cool; if you've done nothing wrong, getting angry and potentially saying or doing something wrong is only going to make your situation worse.

Landmines

There are still some landmines in remote areas of BiH and Kosovo; stick to established roads and paths and pay heed to signs warning of unexploded ordinance (UXO). In areas too remote to have signs, ask locals for the latest advice.

Scams

There have been reports of credit cards being copied. Shopkeepers have been known to make several charge-slip imprints with your credit card when you're not looking and then copy your signature from the authorised slip. There have also been reports of people making quick hi-tech duplicates of credit or debit card information with a machine. If you think your credit card has been gone too long, consider cancelling it. As a rule, you should never let your credit card out of your sight.

The days of black market currency exchange are largely over, so ignore anyone offering a too good to be true rate. Whoever is offering is intending to scam or just steal your money.

It's not unheard of for solo male travellers to be approached by friendly blokes who quickly become their new best mate, or gorgeous women who become the evening flirt, only to be hit a few hours later with an outrageous bill and no way to not pay it.

Theft

» Be vigilant in looking after your passport, documents, tickets and money. These can be carried in a pouch on your belt or under your clothes.

» If you store luggage at train stations, don't leave valuables and be wary of anyone who offers to help you operate your locker.

» Be aware of snatch thieves who make a grab for cameras and bags from motorbikes or scooters. Simple precautions can be a deterrent, like wearing bags across your body, or using day packs instead of shoulder bags.

» Keep a tight grip on your bag in crowds, particularly on or around public transport. Be wary of gangs of kids; it's not unheard of to be distracted by some while one or the other deftly picks a pocket.

» Don't leave valuables lying around your hotel room or visible in your car. Parked cars containing luggage or visible valuables are prime targets, and foreign number plates and/or rental agency stickers may stand out. While driving in cities, beware of snatch thieves when you pull up at the lights; keep

doors locked and windows rolled up.

» Some thieving is done by fellow travellers. Carry your own padlock for hostel lockers and always use them.

» Always report theft to police and ask for a statement; some insurance companies won't pay up unless you do so.

Violence

The notorious criminal underworld in parts of the region will leave you alone if you leave it alone.

In areas that are racially and ethnically homogeneous, non-white travellers may attract more interest than their white counterparts, but this is generally curiosity rather than hostility. It is highly unlikely that you will encounter any violence in Southeastern Europe, but racism does exist in the region. Some countries in the region have thriving neo-Nazi movements, which tend to target local Roma populations and won't look favourably upon black and Asian migrants or travellers.

In Greece there have been incidents of non-white travellers detained and sometimes even assaulted by police upon being approached and requested to show their passports on suspicion of being migrants in the country irregularly.

Solo Travellers

Southeastern Europe offers the perfect mix of lesser-known sights that you can soak up in atmospheric isolation, and a developing tourism scene that lets you cross paths with some interesting people. In lonelier areas where this isn't the case (solo travellers are thin on the ground in Albania and Kosovo), there's generally an expat community (or at least an Irish pub) that may let you into the fold, albeit reluctantly.

Telephone

Telephone services are generally excellent. You will see numerous call centres in most cities, often with competitive rates catering to local migrant communities. Treat hotel telephones like you would any other thief. The cheapest way to make calls is with the winning combination of Skype and wi-fi.

Mobile Phones

» Mobile phones are ubiquitous throughout Southeastern Europe.

» If you plan to use your mobile on the road, check with your provider at home that it has been unlocked. If you are already on the road, you may be able to get it unlocked at a private call centre for a small fee.

» Consider buying a SIM card; they can cost as little as €5 or €10, and be topped up with credit purchased at supermarkets, kiosks, newsagents and phone dealers.

» If you are using roaming, your phone will switch automatically to local networks. Calls can be expensive, but this is useful if you frequently change countries and only use your phone on an ad hoc basis.

» Check data usage fees for email and web; smart phone users may be able to reduce costs by buying data packages.

Phone Codes

To call abroad from a landline, dial the international access code for the country you are calling from (most commonly 00). From a mobile phone, dial '+' followed by the country code, the city code and the local number.

To make a domestic call, you generally need to dial the area code (with the initial zero) and the number; however, in some countries the area code is always part of the phone number even if you're just calling next door.

Phonecards

Local and international phonecards – available from post offices, telephone centres, newsstands or retail outlets – are widely used in the region. For local calls you're usually better off with a local phonecard.

Time

Southeastern Europe spans two time zones: Central European Time (GMT+1) and Eastern European Time (GMT+2).

All countries employ daylight savings, usually on the last Sunday in March. They are set back one hour on the last Sunday in October.

Note that the 24-hour clock is widely used in Southeastern Europe, though not always conversationally.

Toilets

You aren't in for too many unpleasant surprises, other than the fact that you often have to pay for public toilets. Squat toilets are rare but not unheard of. When you can't find a toilet, your salvation lies in the nearest restaurant, hotel, cafe, mosque, library or other public building.

Keep some toilet paper on you in the event that none is available at the crucial moment.

Tourist Information

There has been a general improvement in the last few years with many countries upping efforts to attract and cater for foreign visitors. Greece and Turkey have been managing thriving tourist industries for years, and other countries that have realised their potential as holiday destinations have developed a network of

---

TIME ZONES

TIME ZONE	COUNTRY
Central European Time (GMT/UTC + 1hr)	Albania, BiH, Croatia, Kosovo, Macedonia, Montenegro, Serbia, Slovenia
Eastern European Time (GMT/UTC + 2hr)	Bulgaria, Greece, Romania, Turkey

---

tourist information centres. Slovenia, Croatia and Bulgaria are among them, and have tourist offices abroad as well. Montenegro, Romania, Albania, Macedonia and Kosovo are actively trying to encourage tourism, though campaigns remain obscure for the time being.

Ultimately, the usefulness of tourist information offices depends on their staff; some will bend over backwards to help, while others will do little more than shoo you away with a faded pamphlet for the local cement museum.

Travellers with Disabilities

Ensuring that public transport is accessible to people with disabilities hasn't been a high priority in the region. As a generalisation, wheelchair accessible rooms are only available at top-end hotels and are limited in number, so be sure to book in advance. Some museums and sites have disabled access, but many don't.

Get in touch with the travel officer (if there is one) at national support organisations and ask about countries you plan to visit. Some organisations often have libraries devoted to travel, including access guides, and staff can put you in touch with travel agencies who specialise in tours for the disabled.

In the UK, the **Royal Association for Disability & Rehabilitation** (www.radar.org.

uk) is a helpful association and sells useful publications.

Visas

Europe, the European Union and the Schengen area are not the same thing. All the countries of Southeastern Europe are in Europe, some are in the European Union, and only a couple of them are Schengen members. There are no border controls between Schengen countries, but border procedures between EU and non-EU countries can still be onerous.

The below table reflects the membership of countries in Southeastern Europe at the time of writing.

» Citizens of many countries do not require a visa for stays of up to 90 days in Schengen countries (Greece and Slovenia) as well as in Albania, BiH, Croatia, Kosovo, Macedonia, Montenegro, Romania and Serbia. Other nationals should contact embassies or consulates.

» Visas may sometimes be available in advance or upon arrival; generally visas on arrival are more expensive. Consider in advance if you want a tourist or transit visa; the latter can give you 48 or 72 hours and be issued more quickly and cheaply.

» Be aware that any visa you are issued has an expiry date you should stick to.

» In some countries you are required to register with local authorities within 48 hours of arrival, though your hotel will generally take care of this.

VISA REQUIREMENTS

COUNTRY	EUROPEAN UNION	SCHENGEN
Albania	Potential candidate	No
BiH	Potential Candidate	No
Bulgaria	Yes	No
Croatia	Acceding	No
Greece	Yes	Yes
Kosovo	Potential Candidate	No
Macedonia	Candidate	No
Montenegro	Candidate	No
Romania	Yes	No
Serbia	Candidate	No
Slovenia	Yes	Yes
Turkey	Candidate	No

Check the European Union website (http://europa.eu/about-eu/countries) for latest information and always check latest visa requirements before you travel.

Women Travellers

Generally, women travellers will find that Southeastern Europe is a safe and welcoming place to travel, whether you're in a group, with a mate, or on your own.

That is not to say that sexual harassment does not exist, however. It is not unusual for women to be propositioned by strangers on the street, which can be annoying and even feel threatening, but is rarely anything much more. As a rule, foreigners are still a little exotic and therefore attract more attention, but this attention is rarely dangerous and is easily deflected with a shake of the head and a firm 'no'. Do remember that in much of the Balkans a nod of the head means no, not yes, though! Use the local language if you can, but English usually works fine too.

In Muslim areas, women travelling solo will certainly be of interest or curiosity to both local men and women. In Albania, BiH, southern Serbia and Turkey, women may feel self-conscious in bars and cafes outside larger cities, which are usually populated only by men. Unmarried men rarely have contact with women outside their family unit and so may shower travelling women with too much attention. (In such areas, women travelling with a male companion will often experience the opposite and may need to pinch themselves as a reminder that yes, they actually exist.)

Unfortunately machismo still thrives in parts of the Mediterranean, where lewdness and harassment, though rarely dangerous, can become unsettling. If ignoring harassers, followed by progressively more forthright requests for them to bugger off, and truth or lies about your husband's imminent arrival don't work, then inform the police.

Whatever you do, don't let these sad realities of an imperfect world deter you from getting out into it. On the whole, this is a welcoming region populated by salt-of-the-earth, decent people.

Work

The working opportunities you'd likely take up to replenish your travelling funds aren't likely to be glamorous or well paid, but there are some options. Teaching English is one of them, but finding employers willing to help you get a work permit can be tough. Qualified English teachers have a better chance of finding work, so it might pay to take an accredited course. Your chances of picking up work increase in less popular places like Sofia and Bucharest.

Another non-specialist job possibility is nannying for middle to upper class families who may want to give their children exposure to English, French, German or some other language. Female nannies are generally preferred over males.

If you have some musical or other talent (or, say, can dress monochrome and stand really still), you could try busking. Permits may be required, so talk to other street artists before you start.

The following books give good practical advice:
» *Work Your Way around the World* by Susan Griffith
» *The Directory of Summer Jobs Abroad* by David Woodworth (ed)
» *Working Holidays* by Ben Jupp

Volunteering is a fantastic way to develop skills and experience as well as delve into local life and culture. Lonely Planet's *Volunteer: a Traveller's Guide* is filled with practical information about organising a volunteer-work placement. The following websites are also useful starting points:
» **The Coordinating Committee for International Voluntary Service** (www.ccivs.org)
» **Transitions Abroad** (www.transitionsabroad.com)
» **Serve Your World** (www.serveyourworld.com)

Transport

GETTING THERE & AWAY

Southeastern Europe is a piece of cake to get to from almost anywhere in the world: take a flight to a Western European hub, then get a cheap connection to wherever you want to start and you're there. Alternatively, you can jump on a train, bus or boat.

Flights, tours and rail tickets can be booked online at www.lonelyplanet.com/bookings.

Entering Southeastern Europe

Wherever you go you'll need a valid passport, valid for at least six months beyond the time you plan to leave.

Europeans should remember that while their national identify cards may be fine for travelling between European Union (EU) countries, they won't be of use outside the EU. At the time of writing, only four of the 12 countries covered in this book were members of the EU.

You will also need to consider whether or not you

need visas. Citizens of some countries will not require visas, while others will. See the section about visas (p619) and individual country chapters for more information.

Air

The region is well served by several major airlines. If you are coming from far away, it may be cheaper to fly to a key Western European hub, then pick up a cheap connecting flight (or even train or bus) from there.

The internet is crowded with cheap ticket search engines, and the airline websites themselves often offer deals of their own, sometimes including short break accommodation packages.

The earlier you book, the less you will pay. Don't forget to make use of any discount cards you're eligible for.

The following are some of the key international airlines that serve Southeastern Europe:

Air Berlin (www.airberlin. com)
Air France (www.airfrance. com)
Alitalia (www.alitalia.com)

Austrian Airlines (www. austrian.com)
Belle Air (www.belleair.it)
Blue Air (www.blueair-web. com)
British Airways (www. ba.com)
Carpatair (www.carpatair. com)
Delta Air (www.deltaair. com)
easyJet (www.easyjet.com)
El Al (www.elal.co.il)
Emirates (www.emirates. com)
Finnair (www.finnair.com)
Flybe (www.flybe.com)
Germanwings (www. germanwings.com)
Iberia (www.iberia.com)
Jet2.com (www.jet2.com)
KLM (www.klm.com)
Lufthansa (www.lufthansa. com)
Meridiana (www.meridiana. it)
Norwegian (www. norwegian.com)
Ryanair (www.ryanair.com)
SAS (www.flysas.com)
SmartWings (www.smart wings.com)
Swiss International Airlines (www.swiss.com)
TAP (www.flytap.com)
Vueling (www.vueling.com)
Wizz Air (www.wizzair.com)
For national carriers, see the table in Getting Around.

Tickets

Europe is now proliferated with budget airlines that may fly you in for much the same as you could pay for a train or bus. Sites like **flycheapo** (www.flycheapo.com) are invaluable for searching them, but keep in mind the following:

» Budget airlines may not take you to major airports, and the cost of getting to remote locations may offset the money you save.

» Check for connections; some super cheap tickets save you money but cost you a day of bouncing between airports for a trip that would be only an hour or two direct.

» Don't expect reclining seats and edible (or even any) food on budget airlines. Some also don't have much in the way of customer services.

» Check baggage allowances given that they are often lower, and can result in hefty excess baggage fees.

» Before you book, always check prices on non-budget airlines; they may not be so different and they may be more convenient.

Land

Bus

Buses are useful for getting to out of the way places, though long-haul bus rides can be a slog. There is an extensive network that can get you to the region from Western Europe, and prices are often significantly less than you'd pay by train or air. Advanced booking is advised in peak season and during holidays.

An overnight bus can save on a night's accommodation, and have you arriving at the crack of dawn. On the other hand, a bus journey during the day can be scenic but have you inconveniently arriving late at night.

You may be required to disembark buses at some border crossings for document and baggage checks.

The following websites are useful places to start:

Eurolines (www.eurolines. com) Has a vast network throughout the region and beyond.

Ecolines (www.ecolines.net) Runs between Western and Southeastern Europe.

See individual country chapters for more information.

Car & Motorcycle

Outside of Albania and Kosovo, most of the roads in the region are good, and taking your own wheels can give you freedom you wouldn't otherwise have. Keep in mind that some insurance packages won't cover you for all European countries and it's forbidden to take some rental cars into some countries; check specifically on the countries you will be visiting.

Road conditions may slow down motorcycles, but some of these thrilling winding roads were meant to be taken on two wheels.

Train

There are some epic routes into Southeastern Europe from Eastern and Western Europe. By and large, there is a dense web of railways across the region; Bucharest and Belgrade are notable hubs in the region. The exceptions are Albania, which has no international train service; Montenegro, with only a single line into Serbia; and Kosovo, with only a single line from Pristina to Skopje. Bus services are extensive to and from these places.

Sea

Travelling by sea into the region isn't as cheap or convenient as by air or land, but this may be besides the point. There are some decent ferry options. Albania, Croatia, Greece, Slovenia, Montenegro and Turkey are particularly well connected to Italy. Malta and Turkey are also connected.

See www.aferry.com for more information, and www.ferrysavers.com for information about discounts. Holders of Eurail passes are also entitled to discounted ferry tickets on some routes.

The following resources are useful:

Agoudimos (www.agoudimos-lines.com) Connects Italy and Greece.

Minoan Lines (www.minoan.gr) Connects Italy and Greece.

SNAV (www.snav.it) Connects Italy and Croatia.

Superfast Ferries (www.superfast.com) Connects Italy and Greece.

GETTING AROUND

Moving between countries of the region is relatively easy. The only border that can be a bit of trouble is that between Serbia and Kosovo; always check what the situation is before attempting to cross. Travelling into Turkey can be a time consuming process; passengers are generally required to disembark

---

CLIMATE CHANGE & TRAVEL

Every form of transport that relies on carbon-based fuel generates CO_2, the main cause of human-induced climate change. Modern travel is dependent on aeroplanes, which might use less fuel per kilometre per person than most cars but travel much greater distances. The altitude at which aircraft emit gases (including CO_2) and particles also contributes to their climate change impact. Many websites offer 'carbon calculators' that allow people to estimate the carbon emissions generated by their journey and, for those who wish to do so, to offset the impact of the greenhouse gases emitted with contributions to portfolios of climate-friendly initiatives throughout the world. Lonely Planet offsets the carbon footprint of all staff and author travel.

AIRPORTS & AIRLINES

Key national air carriers and key airports for countries in Southeastern Europe are below. Other airports may be more useful to reach specific sites; see country chapters for more information.

COUNTRY	NATIONAL AIRLINE	MAJOR AIRPORT
Albania	Belleair (www.belleair.eu)	Tirana International Airport (Nënë Tereza, TIA; www.tirana-airport.com.al)
Bosnia & Hercegovina	BH Airlines (www.bhairlines.ba)	Sarajevo International Airport (SJJ; www.sarajevo-airport.ba)
Bulgaria	Bulgaria Air (www.air.bg)	Sofia Airport (SOF; www.sofia-airport.bg)
Croatia	Croatia Airlines (www.croatiaairlines.hr)	Zagreb Airport (Zračna Luka Airport, ZAG; www.zagreb-airport.hr)
Greece	Olympic Air (www.olympicair.com)	Athens International Airport (Eleftherios Venizelos, ATH; www.aia.gr)
Kosovo	Kosova Airlines (www.kosovaairlines.com)	Pristina International Airport (Adem Jashari, PRN; www.airportpristina.com)
Macedonia	MAT Airways (www.matairways.mk)	Skopje Alexander the Great Airport (SKP; skp.airports.com.mk)
Montenegro	Montenegro Airlines (www.montenegroairlines.com)	Tivat International Airport (TIV) and Podgorica International Airport (TGD; www.montenegroairports.com)
Romania	Tarom Airlines (www.tarom.ro)	Bucharest International Airport (Henri Coandă airport, OTP; www.otp-airport.ro)
Serbia	Jat Airways (www.jat.com)	Nikola Tesla Beograd Airport (BEG; www.beg.aero)
Slovenia	Adria Airways (www.adria-airways.com)	Ljubljana Jože Pučnik Airport (LJU; www.lju-airport.si)
Turkey	Turkish Airlines (www.turkishairlines.com)	İstanbul Atatürk International Airport (IST; www.ataturkairport.com)

buses or trains for paperwork and baggage checks. If you need a visa you will buy it at the border.

Otherwise, remember which countries are Schengen, which are EU and which are neither. At the time of writing, only Greece and Slovenia are part of the Schengen region, but Bulgaria and Romania are both likely to get in in the near future. Check out the latest situation as some countries are set to sign up.

Expect delays crossing borders towards the coast in summer. Some crossings don't have ATMs or exchange facilities, so make sure you have cash on hand.

Air

Major Southeastern European cities are connected by regular flights to other cities in the region.

» Low cost airlines between some destinations compete with land options in terms of value, so consider all options.

» Which airports are the well-connected ones depends on where you are trying to go; sometimes it makes sense to fly to one country, then travel overland to the destination you want to reach in the country next door.

» Many countries in Southeastern Europe offer domestic flights, though there is

rarely a need to fly internally unless you are in a rush.

» Though air travel is efficient, there are the carbon emissions to consider as well as the opportunity costs of missed overland adventures. If you have the time, take a train or bus.

Bicycle

Some of the terrain in Southeastern Europe makes for interesting cycling, with enough mountains to keep it challenging. However, there are some drawbacks including less than courteous drivers, and the exhaust fumes farted from crumbling cars, buses and trucks notably in Albania, Bosnia and Hercegovina (BiH), Serbia, Macedonia, Montenegro and Turkey. Long-distance cycling certainly isn't as common in these parts as it is in Western Europe, so don't bank on meeting fellow cyclists en route. There's a tiny risk of landmines and unexploded ordnance in Kosovo and BiH, so don't be tempted to take back roads unless you've done your research first.

These issues aside, cycling around the more remote mountainous patches of Southeastern Europe will offer insight into a whole other world.

Keep in mind the following:

» Bike hire outside of tourist towns and specialised parts are hard to come by, so come prepared.

» Invest in a sturdy bike lock and use it. Secure your saddlebags well.

» Be equipped with sufficiently detailed maps and keep your eye on the contours; you don't want to unknowingly embark on a high-altitude pass as darkness descends.

» A seasoned cyclist can average about 80km a day, but this depends on the terrain and the weight they are carrying.

» For long tours, it's probably worth having a bike you are familiar with rather than buying one on arrival.

Transporting Bicycles

Transporting bikes is generally not a problem:

» On planes, if your bike doesn't exceed your weight allowance you should be able to check it on like normal luggage. If it does exceed the weigh allowance find out how much extra it will cost you so you can look for cheaper alternatives if need be.

» Different airlines have different rules; some require you to pack your bikes in bike boxes, others require that you remove pedals and deflate tires. Always check on airline baggage policies before you travel.

» On buses it's usually no problem to throw your bike underneath with all the other luggage; get to the station early to make sure it goes on without a hassle.

» Trains may have specific bike-storage sections, and may be subject to small supplementary fees.

Cycling Tours

There are plenty of companies offering cycling tours of Southeastern Europe. These specialised companies generally plan the itinerary, organise accommodation and transport luggage for you, making life a lot simpler for cyclists.

The following websites offer excellent advice and resources:

European Cyclists' Federation (www.ecf.com) Advocates bike-friendly policies, organises tours and manages the work-in-progress EuroVelo project to create bike routes across the continent.

Experience Plus (www.experienceplus.com) Offers cycling tours throughout the region.

Cyclists' Touring Club (www.ctc.org.uk) Offers maps and information services on cycling conditions and routes.

Boat

You will find that lakes and rivers are used more for pleasure than practicality in getting from A to B. But the hundreds of islands in Croatia, Greece and Turkey are well served by an intricate network of ferries. Between countries in Southeastern Europe, there are services between Corfu (Greece) and Albania. Turkey is also well connected by ferry to Greece.

» Some ferry crossings charge per car regardless of the number of passengers, others charge additionally per person.

» Discounts are given to Eurail pass holders on some routes.

» Ferry schedules vary by season with significantly fewer in winter months. Excellent online resources include www.ferrylines.com and www.ferrysavers.com.

Bus

In some parts of Southeastern Europe, buses are far more useful than trains. In Kosovo, Albania and Montenegro for instance, buses are regular, reliable, affordable and relatively comfortable over small distances – if you can endure the turbo-folk music that may be blaring on board in the Balkans. Long distance buses throughout the whole region are often surprisingly well equipped, well kept and comfortable.

» Buses tend to be a better option than trains for shorter trips, and they are often the only option in mountainous regions.

» Across the region, bus stations are generally more efficient and functional than they may appear at first glance; master saying the name of wherever you want to go and you'll eventually be pointed to the right counter or bus.

» As a general rule, the bigger the town the better the connections. This means that if you can't get to where you want to go from wherever you are, get the journey started by heading to the closest larger town.

» Advance reservations are rarely necessary on all but long-distance buses.

Eurolines (www.eurolines.com) is a well-organised consortium of bus companies operating under the same name. It offers reliable services across a lot of the region (with notable exceptions of Greece and Turkey) and can get you very far for decent money. Eurolines is used by Europeans visiting family on weekends, as well as travellers of all sorts.

Bus Tours

London-based **Busabout** (www.busabout.com) operates bus tours around Europe, covering many major cities in Southeastern Europe. With this system, you pay for travel on a specified route that allows you to hop off at any scheduled stop, then pick up another bus later. Tickets can be bought for single loops or for different stops. Busabout generally attracts the younger first-time travel crowd; if you want to mix with the party people, this is the place. If you'd rather mix with independent travellers and locals, use Eurolines or other companies or take the train.

Car & Motorcycle

Having your own wheels is an enormous asset in terms of freeing you to spontaneously take a road and discover what's off the beaten track. However, cars can also be a liability in cities that can have baffling one-ways systems, incomprehensible parking systems and narrow laneways that may be only fractionally wider than the curvature of your car. Theft from vehicles can also be a problem; don't leave things visibly lying around in your car. To the extent that you can choose the type of wheels you bring, pick something that blends in and isn't worth the collective annual earnings of a small sized town. Having said that, if you are hitting the coast roads in summer you'd better love your car, because you may be spending many hours in it during traffic jams.

The motorcycling scene is alive and well in Europe; two wheels may be your ticket into a very warm social scene. It is easy to spot the popular motorcycle rest stops that often serve hearty local fare. Some smaller guesthouses throughout the region may even offer small discounts to motorcyclists, and be able to advise you on safe places to park. There are many precarious roads in Southeastern Europe, but that, of course, is often their attraction. Be sure to know the rules that apply to you wherever you are going. In busy areas, particularly enjoy the moment where you wind your way to the front of the beach-bound queues of cars (and be careful of people opening doors to stretch their legs). If you don't want to venture too far off the beaten track on your own, consider joining a motorcycle tour.

In deciding whether or not you want to drive around the region, also remember to factor in the escalated costs not only for petrol but also entry fees, ferry fees, road tolls and taxes, and secured parking at some hotels.

Driving Licence & Documentation

Whatever driving licence you have will likely be recognised in most countries of the region. However, it is wise to obtain an International Driving Permit from your local motoring organisation. It doesn't cost much and minimises the risk of hassle.

Always have vehicle registration documents and identification for yourself with you when you drive.

Every vehicle crossing an international border should display a sticker showing the country of registration.

Fuel & Spare Parts

Fuel costs vary enormously from country to country and are fairly relative to the cost of living. Think about petrol prices when you are crossing borders to decide whether you want to fill up before or after you cross a border.

Unleaded petrol of 95 or 98 octane is widely available. Unleaded petrol is usually slightly cheaper than super premium grade.

Spare parts generally won't be a problem if you have time to track them down.

Hire

Car hire in Southeastern Europe is as straightforward as anywhere else.

» The big international companies offer reliable service and well-maintained vehicles. A key advantage of international companies is that they often allow you to collect a car in one place and return it in another.

» Local companies will usually offer lower prices than the blue-chip biggies, but ask around so as only to use those with a good reputation – see the local agencies listed in each country chapter of this book or try asking at your hotel.

» Pre-booked rates are generally lower than walk-in rates, but don't expect car hire to be cheaper than it is in Western Europe; it can actually cost 20% to 40% more.

» Always bear in mind that some companies won't let you take rental cars to some countries; discuss your intended route thoroughly before you take the keys.

» It is definitely not recommended to drive rental cards from Serbia into Kosovo or vice versa.

» If you are flying into Europe from afar, think ahead. Your airline may have affiliations with rental companies that can lead to some decent savings and the convenience of tumbling out of the plane into your own wheels. Key international hire companies include:

Avis (www.avis.com)
Budget (www.budget.com)
Europcar (www.europcar.com)
Hertz (www.hertz.com)
Sixt (www.sixt.com)

Insurance

Third-party motor insurance is compulsory in EU countries; check requirements for specific non-EU countries with your insurer.

In some countries you will need an International Insurance certificate, known as a Green Card. Get your insurer to issue you with one (which may cost extra). This is a certificate that confirms that your insurance policy meets the legal requirements of the countries in which it is required. Check whether it lists all the countries you plan to drive in, and in Turkey check that it covers both European and Asian parts of the country. If it doesn't cover everywhere you plan to go, you may need separate third-party cover at the border of the country in question.

Some insurers will need statements of accident. Do not sign an accident statement you cannot understand; insist on a translation and only sign it when you agree with it.

Significant stress will be alleviated if you take out breakdown-assistance policy, such as that offered by the **RAC** (www.rac.co.uk). Non-Europeans should check with their national motoring organisation before they leave home to find out about reciprocal services offered by affiliated organisations around Europe.

Road Rules & Safety

Make sure you brush up on road rules that apply wherever you are going. For instance, some countries require reflective vests and warning triangles to be carried in the car at all times, which you must use when parking on a highway or in an emergency. Others require a fire hydrant and first aid kit, or spare bulb kits to be on board as well. Some countries prohibit the use of radar detectors and fine you with unbridled glee if that function on your GPS has not been deactivated. Motorcycle lights may be required to be on even during the day. In short, do your research before you start your engine. A recommended place to start is the **AA** website (www.theaa.com/motoring_advice/overseas/countrybycountry.html), which provides useful country-specific information.

Standard international road rules apply, but you should also keep the following in mind:

» Traffic police generally issue fines on the spot. Always ask for a receipt.

» Drink-driving is a serious offence; most countries have a 0% limit which takes the guess work out of things.

» Children under 12 and drunk people aren't allowed in the front seat in most countries.

» Driving at night can be particularly hazardous in rural areas where unlit roads can wind into the darkness off a cliff, and where horse-drawn carts and livestock can appear suddenly in front of you.

» In the event of an accident, you are supposed to notify the police and file an insurance claim.

» If you are bringing in a vehicle that already has significant body damage, point it out to customs on arrival in the country and have it noted down somewhere. Damaged vehicles may only be able to leave with police permission.

» Remember that some minor roads may be closed in winter months. Make sure you have necessary equipment for extreme weather conditions, including snow chains.

Road Tolls

There are tolls on motorways in Croatia, Greece, Slovenia and Turkey. Some road tolls will be obvious, requiring that you queue up and pay a person or a machine. Machines often 'speak' various languages and accept cards. Keep some cash (and cards) handy in the car, so you don't hold people up and aren't limited to choosing lanes that accept only one type of payment only.

In other countries the system is a lot less obvious; you may be required to purchase a 'vignette' (road tax) sticker at the border or at service stations that grant you rights to use the roads for a period of time.

Hitching

Hitching is never entirely safe in any country and we don't recommend it. Travellers who decide to hitch should understand that they are taking a small but potentially serious risk.

Given the low price of public transport in many parts of Southeastern Europe, hitching is more about the adventure than the practicality. That said, in very remote rural areas it is not uncommon for local drivers to pick up pedestrians en route. In Albania and Romania, riders are expected to pay the equivalent of a bus fare.

If you do hitch remember the following:

» Hitching is safer in pairs.

» Hitching is often illegal of motorways, so stand on slip roads or approach drivers at petrol stations and truck stops.

» Ask drivers where they're going before you say where you are going.

» Only sit next to a door you can open, and don't let your luggage be put in the boot.

» Always let someone know where you are going before heading off.

Travellers considering hitching can find destination-based information and ride-share options at **Hitchhikers** (www.hitchhikers.org) and **Digihitch** (www.digihitch.com), which is a comprehensive site with forums, links and country-specific information.

Local Transport

In some ways, local public transport in Southeastern Europe makes the system in Western Europe look positively inefficient. Major cities offer lots of options – not only subways and buses, but also minibuses, which are cramped little vehicles that zip all over the place with an impressive lack of pomp. Some minibuses stick to inner city routes, but others will link to suburbs or even connect different towns. In some areas – like the mountain towns of Albania – this is the way you will likely travel.

Trolley buses are another phenomenon one doesn't see in Western Europe. These are slower beasts of burden, but to be praised for their eco-friendliness (being powered by electricity rather than guzzling something else).

Tours

Tours are not necessary for exploring Southeastern Europe, but are worth considering if you are short on time or keen on a specific theme that will be easier to realise with a company; for instance you may want to spend your time canoeing or sailing or cycling with a group of people who want to do likewise.

Some tours are expensive and luxuriant, some are intrepid and offer a means of accessing far-out places and having offbeat experiences. More and more local companies are emerging, so ask around and do your research; in some parts, opting to use local tour outfits can make a significant positive contribution to the development of the industry.

Some experienced operators include the following:

Regent Holidays (www. regent-holidays.co.uk) UK-based company offering comprehensive individual and group tours, which take in everything from easy beach tours to intrepid multi-country trips.

Eastern Europe Russian Travel Centre (www.eetb travel.com) Australia-based company offering dozens of upmarket tours to several countries in the region.

Road Scholar (www.road scholar.org) Offers educational tours throughout the region (and elsewhere) for people aged over 50.

Intrepid (www.intrepidtravel. com) Offers eponymous tours in several countries of the region of different durations.

Train

Travelling overland by train is a rite of passage in these parts; think of Rebecca West journeying through the Balkans. Overnight trains are a fun way of avoiding a night's accommodation and an interesting way of seeing the countryside and meeting the locals.

The audacious terrain that runs through much of the region has meant that while the networks aren't as prolific as the bus network (and generally cost more), the lines that do exist often traverse some of the most scenic parts of the region. With the exception of Albania, they are a reliable way of getting around almost all countries of Southeastern Europe.

Check individual country chapters for specific details. The following information is general:

» If travelling overnight, a bed reservation is included in the price of your ticket, though you may have to pay some extra euros on board for the actual bedding.

» Each carriage is administered by a steward, who punches your ticket and makes sure you get off where you want to. Particularly during the wee hours, make sure you get off at the correct stop.

» There are bathrooms with a toilet and washbasin at the end of each carriage; their cleanliness depends on who used it before you and the terrain they were passing through at the time.

» Be warned that toilets may be locked half an hour or so before arriving in big cities and while the train is at the platform.

» Check whether there is a dining car, snack bar or trolley on the train, and if not be sure to bring your own supply of food and drink. Consider doing so anyway, given inflated on-board prices.

» Be warned that some trains split en route to service two destinations, so make sure you are in the correct carriage.

If you plan to travel extensively by train, it might be worth checking out the following resources:

Thomas Cook European Rail Timetable (www. thomascookpublishing.com) A listing of train schedules; it's updated monthly and can be ordered online.

Rail Europe (www.raileurope. com) Provides information on fares and passes as well as schedules for the most popular routes in Europe.

Man in Seat 61 (www. seat61.com/railpass.htm) Provides excellent independent information and advice.

Classes

Short trips or trips that don't involve sleeping usually have benches on suburban trains and aeroplane-style seats on the inter-city services.

There are generally three classes of sleeping accommodation on trains – each country has a different name for them, but 3rd, 2nd and 1st is a relatively straight forward way of understanding them. The following information offers a general overview of them:

» **Third class** The cheapest option with six sleeping

berths in a closed compartment. Not particularly private given close confines with five other people, and uncomfortable as all hell in summer if the air conditioning doesn't work. Happily, this class is not widely available.

» **Second class** Four berths in a closed compartment. If there are two of you, you will share with two other people but if there are three of you, you will often have the compartment to yourselves.

» **First class** Two births in one cabin, perhaps with a washbasin and a bit of decoration, for approximately double the price of second class. If you really hit the jackpot, your compartment may even be adorned with plastic flowers.

Reservations

It is always advisable to book tickets in advance. Making seat reservations several days in advance is also recommended for busier routes and during peak summer periods, but this is only necessary if the timetable specifies that seat reservations are required.

You may be able to book tickets with travel agencies before you leave home, but at added cost. This is only worth considering if you are on a tight travel schedule that depends on a particular connection. Otherwise you can book most routes in the region from main train stations.

Safety

Trains are generally safe, but some petty crime does occur from time to time. Guarding against it requires the same common sense you apply normally.

» Keep your valuables on you at all times; sleep with your wallet and passport on your person and take them with you when you go to the bathroom. Keep bags closer to the window than the door.

» Some padlocks have a large enough loop to let you lock your bags to luggage racks.

» At night, make sure your door is locked from the inside.

» Most thieves strike when they can easily disembark from the train, so avoid leaving your compartment when the train is stationary.

» If you have a compartment to yourself, you can ask the steward to lock it while you go to the dining car or go for a wander outside when the train is stopped; however, be aware that most criminals strike when they can easily disembark the train, and on occasion the stewards are complicit.

» You will need to decide whether or not you trust the people who are sharing the compartment with you. If you feel particularly uncomfortable (notably if you are a woman), then arrange to move elsewhere.

Train Passes

Rail passes can certainly be worthwhile if you are concentrating on a particular part of the region. Rail passes are available online and through most travel agents. Make sure you shop around for the best prices. Not all the countries covered in this book are covered by rail passes; Kosovo and Albania are notable exceptions.

Keep in mind that all passes offer discounted 'youth' prices for travellers who are under 26 years of age on the first day of travel. Kids aged four to 11 are eligible for a child rate. Discounted fares are also available if you are travelling in a group of two to five people (although you must always travel together).

Useful resources include **Rail Europe** (www.raileurope.com) for general information and purchases in the USA, and **Rail Plus** (www.railplus.com.au) for information and purchases in Australia.

BALKAN FLEXIPASS

The Balkan Flexipass includes BiH, Bulgaria, Macedonia, Montenegro, Romania, Serbia and Turkey.

» You have a choice of five, 10 or 15 days of unlimited travel for one month in 1st class.

» The pass is not available to residents of BiH, Bulgaria, Croatia, Greece, Macedonia, Montenegro, Romania, Serbia, Slovenia or Turkey.

» Prices from the US are US$255/204/153/128 for adult/senior/youth/child.

» Check www.raileurope.com for the latest information.

EURAIL GLOBAL

The Eurail pass allows unlimited travel in 24 countries, including Bulgaria, Croatia, Greece, Slovenia and Turkey.

» The pass is available to non-European residents only.

» Prices start at €369, with a 35% discount for youth, 50% for children under 11, and 15% for groups of two to five people.

» Eurail passes also result in discounts for some ferry routes.

» Check www.eurail.com for the latest information.

EURAIL SELECT

The Eurail Select pass allows travel in three, four or five neighbouring countries, including Bulgaria, Croatia, Slovenia, Greece, Montenegro, Serbia, Romania and Turkey.

» The chosen countries must be connected by rail or ferry.

» The pass is available to non-European residents only.

» Prices start at €234/262/288 for three/four/five countries.

» Montenegro and Serbia are classified as one country for the purposes of this pass, as are Croatia and Slovenia.

» Check www.eurail.com for the latest information.

INTERRAIL GLOBAL

The InterRail Global pass is valid in 30 countries including BiH, Bulgaria, Croatia, Greece, Macedonia, Montenegro, Romania, Serbia, Slovenia and Turkey.

» The pass is only available to European residents who have been living in Europe for the last six months. Non-European residents should use the Eurail pass. Residents of Turkey and parts of North Africa can also buy the pass; terms and conditions vary from country to country, but essentially it is not valid for travel within your country of residence.

» Ticket options include: five days travel over 10 days; 10 days within 22 days; every day within 15 days; every day within 22 days; or, every day for a month.

» 2nd class prices for five days of travel within 10 days start at €276/249/181/138 for adult/senior/youth/child. 1st class tickets can also be purchased.

» Check www.interrail.eu for more information.

Language

This chapter offers basic vocabulary to help you get around Southeastern Europe. Read our coloured pronunciation guides as if they were English and you'll be understood. The stressed syllables are indicated with italics.

Some phrases in this chapter have both polite and informal forms (indicated by the abbreviations 'pol' and 'inf' respectively). The abbreviations 'm' and 'f' indicate masculine and feminine gender respectively.

ALBANIAN

There are two main varieties of Albanian – Tosk (spoken in southern Albania, Greece, Italy and Turkey) and Gheg (spoken in northern Albania, Kosovo, Serbia, Montenegro and Macedonia). Tosk is the official language of Albania and is also used in this chapter.

Note that ew is pronounced as 'ee' with rounded lips, uh as the 'a' in 'ago', dh as the 'th' in 'that', dz as the 'ds' in 'adds', and zh as the 's' in 'pleasure'. Also, ll and rr are pronounced stronger than when they are written as single letters.

Basics

Hello.	Tungjatjeta.	toon·dya·tye·ta
Goodbye.	Mirupafshim.	mee·roo·paf·sheem
Excuse me.	Më falni.	muh fal·nee
Sorry.	Më vjen keq.	muh vyen kech
Please.	Ju lutem.	yoo loo·tem
Thank you.	Faleminderit.	fa·le·meen·de·reet
Yes.	Po.	po
No.	Jo.	yo

WANT MORE?

For in-depth language information and handy phrases, check out Lonely Planet's *Eastern Europe Phrasebook* and *Mediterranean Europe Phrasebook*. You'll find them at **shop.lonelyplanet. com**, or you can buy Lonely Planet's iPhone phrasebooks at the Apple App Store.

What's your name?
Si quheni?   see *choo*·he·nee

My name is ...
Unë quhem ...   oo·nuh *choo*·hem ...

Do you speak English?
A flisni anglisht?   a *flees*·nee ang·*leesht*

I don't understand.
Unë nuk kuptoj.   oo·nuh nook koop·*toy*

Accommodation

campsite	vend kampimi	vend kam·*pee*·mee
guesthouse	bujtinë	booy·*tee*·nuh
hotel	hotel	ho·*tel*
youth hostel	fjetore për të rinj	fye·*to*·re puhr tuh reeny

Do you have a single/double room?
A keni një dhomë teke/dopjo?   a *ke*·nee nyuh *dho*·muh te·ke/*dop*·yo

How much is it per night/person?
Sa kushton për një natë/njeri?   sa koosh·*ton* puhr nyuh na·tuh/nye·ree

Numbers – Albanian		
1	një	nyuh
2	dy	dew
3	tre	tre
4	katër	ka·tuhr
5	pesë	pe·suh
6	gjashtë	dyash·tuh
7	shtatë	shta·tuh
8	tetë	te·tuh
9	nëntë	nuhn·tuh
10	dhjetë	dhye·tuh

Eating & Drinking

Is there a vegetarian restaurant near here?
A ka ndonjë restorant
vegjetarian
këtu afër?
a ka ndo·nyuh res·to·rant ve·dye·ta·ree·an kuh·too a·fuhr

What would you recommend?
Çfarë më
rekomandoni?
chfa·ruh muh re·ko·man·do·nee

I'd like the bill/menu, please.
Më sillni faturën/
menunë, ju lutem.
muh seell·nee fa·too·ruhn/ me·noo·nuh yoo loo·tem

I'll have ...	Dua ...	doo·a ...
Cheers!	Gëzuar!	guh·zoo·ar
breakfast	mëngjes	muhn·dyes
lunch	drekë	dre·kuh
dinner	darkë	dar·kuh

Emergencies

| Help! | Ndihmë! | ndeeh·muh |
| Go away! | Ik! | eek |

Call the doctor/police!
Thirrni doktorin/
policinë!
theerr·nee dok·to·reen/ po·lee·tsee·nuh

I'm lost.
Kam humbur rrugën. kam hoom·boor rroo·guhn

I'm ill.
Jam i/e sëmurë. (m/f) yam ee/e suh·moo·ruh

Where are the toilets?
Ku janë banjat? koo ya·nuh ba·nyat

Shopping & Services

I'm looking for ...
Po kërkoj për ... po kuhr·koy puhr ...

How much is it?
Sa kushton? sa koosh·ton

That's too expensive.
Është shumë
shtrenjtë.
uhsh·tuh shoo·muh shtreny·tuh

market	treg	treg
post office	posta	pos·ta
tourist office	zyrë	zew·ra
	turistike	too·rees·tee·ke

Transport & Directions

boat	anija	a·nee·ya
bus	autobusi	a·oo·to·boo·see
plane	aeroplani	a·e·ro·pla·nee
train	treni	tre·nee

One ... ticket (to Shkodër), please.	Një biletë ... (për në Shkodër), ju lutem.	nyuh bee·le·tuh ... (puhr nuh shko·duhr) yoo loo·tem
one-way	për vajtje	puhr vai·tye
return	kthimi	kthee·mee

Where's the ...?
Ku është ...? koo uhsh·tuh ...

What's the address?
Cila është adresa? tsee·la uhsh·tuh a·dre·sa

Can you show me (on the map)?
A mund të ma
tregoni (në hartë)?
a moond tuh ma tre·go·nee (nuh har·tuh)

BULGARIAN

In Bulgarian, vowels in unstressed syllables are generally pronounced shorter and weaker than they are in stressed syllables. Note that uh is pronounced as the 'a' in 'ago' and zh as the 's' in 'pleasure'.

Basics

Hello.	Здравейте.	zdra·vey·te
Goodbye.	Довиждане.	do·veezh·da·ne
Excuse me.	Извинете.	iz·vee·ne·te
Sorry.	Съжалявам .	suh·zhal·ya·vam
Please.	Моля .	mol·ya
Thank you.	Благодаря .	bla·go·dar·ya
Yes.	Да .	da
No.	Не.	ne

What's your name?
Как се казвате/
казваш? (pol/inf)
kak se kaz·va·te/ kaz·vash

My name is ...
Казвам се ... kaz·vam se ...

Do you speak English?
Говорите ли
английски?
go·*vo*·ree·te lee
ang·*lees*·kee

I don't understand.
Не разбирам.
ne raz·*bee*·ram

Accommodation

campsite	къмпинг	*kuhm*·peeng
guesthouse	пансион	pan·see·*on*
hotel	хотел	ho·*tel*
youth hostel	общежитие	ob·shte·*zhee*·tee·ye

Do you have a ... room?	Имате ли стая с ...?	ee·*ma*·te lee *sta*·ya s ...
single	едно легло	ed·*no* leg·*lo*
double	едно голямо легло	ed·*no* go·*lya*·mo leg·*lo*

How much is it per night/person?
Колко е на вечер/
човек?
kol·ko e na *ve*·cher/
cho·*vek*

Eating & Drinking

Do you have vegetarian food?
Имате ли
вегетерианска
храна?
ee·*ma*·te lee
ve·ge·te·ree·*an*·ska
hra·*na*

What would you recommend?
Какво ще
препоръчате?
kak·*vo* shte
pre·po·*ruh*·cha·te

I'd like the bill/menu, please.
Дайте ми сметката/
менюто, моля.
dai·te mee *smet*·ka·ta/
men·*yoo*·to *mol*·ya

I'll have ...	Ще взема ...	shte *vze*·ma ...
Cheers!	Наздраве!	na·*zdra*·ve

breakfast	закуска	za·*koos*·ka
lunch	обед	o·bed
dinner	вечеря	ve·*cher*·ya

Numbers – Bulgarian

1	един	ed·*een*
2	два	dva
3	три	tree
4	четири	che·tee·ree
5	пет	pet
6	шест	shest
7	седем	se·dem
8	осем	o·sem
9	девет	de·vet
10	десет	de·set

Emergencies

Help!	Помощ!	po·mosht
Go away!	Махайте се!	*ma*·hai·te se

Call the doctor/police!
Повикайте лекар/
полицията!
po·*vee*·kai·te le·*kar*/
po·*lee*·tsee·ya·ta

I'm lost.
Загубих се.
za·*goo*·beeh se

I'm ill.
Болен/Болна
съм. (m/f)
bo·len/*bol*·na
suhm

Where are the toilets?
Къде има тоалетни?
kuh·*de* ee·ma to·a·*let*·nee

Shopping & Services

I'm looking for ...
Търся ...
tuhr·sya ...

How much is it?
Колко струва?
kol·ko *stroo*·va

That's too expensive.
Скъпо е.
skuh·po e

bank	банка	*ban*·ka
post office	поща	*po*·shta
tourist office	бюро за туристическа информация	*byoo*·ro za too·*ree*·stee·ches·ka een·for·*ma*·tsee·ya

Transport & Directions

boat	корабът	ko·*ra*·buht
bus	автобусът	av·to·*boo*·suht
plane	самолетът	sa·mo·*le*·tuht
train	влакът	*vla*·kuht

One ... ticket (to Varna), please.	Един билет ... (за Варна), моля.	e-deen bee-let ... (za var-na), mol-ya
one-way	в едната посока	v ed-na-ta po-so-ka
return	за отиване и връщане	za o-tee-va-ne ee-vruhsh-ta-ne

Where's the ...?
Къде се намира ...?   kuh-de se na-mee-ra ...

What's the address?
Какъв е адресът?   ka-kuhv e ad-re-suht

Can you show me (on the map)?
Можете ли да ми   mo-zhe-te lee da mee
покажете (на картата)?   po-ka-zhe-te (na kar-ta-ta)

CROATIAN & SERBIAN

Croatian and Serbian are very similar and mutually intelligible. Using them, you will also be understood in Bosnia & Hercegovina and Montenegro.

In this section, significant vocabulary differences between Croatian and Serbian are indicated with (C) and (S) respectively. Note that Croatian is written in Roman script and Serbian in Cyrillic script. For the phrases below we've provided Roman script. Note also that the r sound is rolled and that zh is pronounced as the 's' in 'pleasure'.

Basics

Hello.	Zdravo.	zdra-vo
Goodbye.	Zbogom.	zbo-gom
Excuse me.	Oprostite.	o-pro-sti-te
Sorry.	Žao mi je.	zha-o mi ye
Please.	Molim.	mo-lim
Thank you.	Hvala.	hva-la
Yes.	Da.	da
No.	Ne.	ne

What's your name?
Kako se zovete/   ka-ko se zo-ve-te/
zoveš? (pol/inf)   zo-vesh

My name is ...
Zovem se ...   zo-vem se ...

Do you speak English?
Govorite/Govoriš li   go-vo-ri-te/go-vo-rish
engleski? (pol/inf)   li en-gle-ski

I don't understand.
Ja ne razumijem.   ya ne ra-zu-mi-yem

Accommodation

campsite	kamp	kamp
guesthouse	privatni smještaj	pri-vat-ni smyesh-tai

hotel	hotel	ho-tel
youth hostel	prenoćište za mladež	pre-no-chish-te za mla-dezh

Do you have a single/double room?
Imate li jednokrevetnu/   i-ma-te li yed-no-kre-vet-nu/
dvokrevetnu sobu?   dvo-kre-vet-nu so-bu

How much is it per night/person?
Koliko stoji po   ko-li-ko sto-yi po
noći/osobi?   no-chi/o-so-bi

Eating & Drinking

What would you recommend?
Što biste preporučili?   shto bi-ste pre-po-ru-chi-li

Do you have vegetarian food?
Da li imate   da li i-ma-te
vegetarijanski obrok?   ve-ge-ta-ri-yan-ski o-brok

I'd like the bill/menu, please.
Mogu li dobiti račun/   mo-gu li do-bi-ti ra-chun/
jelovnik, molim?   ye-lov-nik mo-lim

I'll have ...	Želim ...	zhe-lim ...
Cheers!	Živjeli!	zhi-vye-li
breakfast	doručak	do-ru-chak
lunch	ručak	ru-chak
dinner	večera	ve-che-ra

Emergencies

Help!	Upomoć!	u-po-moch
Go away!	Maknite se!	mak-ni-te se
Call the ...!	Zovite ...!	zo-vi-te ...
doctor	liječnika (C) lekara (S)	li-yech-ni-ka le-ka-ra
police	policiju	po-li-tsi-yu

I'm lost.
Izgubio/Izgubila   iz-gu-bi-o/iz-gu-bi-la
sam se. (m/f)   sam se

I'm ill.
Ja sam bolestan/   ya sam bo-le-stan/
bolesna. (m/f)   bo-le-sna

Signs – Croatian & Serbian	
Ulaz/Улаз	Entrance
Izlaz/Излаз	Exit
Otvoreno/Отворено	Open
Zatvoreno/Затворено	Closed
Zabranjeno/Забрањено	Prohibited
Zahodi/Тоалети	Toilets

Numbers – Croatian & Serbian		
1	jedan	ye·dan
2	dva	dva
3	tri	tri
4	četiri	che·ti·ri
5	pet	pet
6	šest	shest
7	sedam	se·dam
8	osam	o·sam
9	devet	de·vet
10	deset	de·set

Where are the toilets?
Gdje se nalaze   gdye se na·la·ze
zahodi/toaleti? (C/S)   za·ho·di/to·a·le·ti

Shopping & Services

I'm looking for ...
Tražim ...   tra·zhim

How much is it?
Koliko stoji/   ko·li·ko sto·yi/
košta? (C/S)   kosh·ta

That's too expensive.
To je preskupo.   to ye pre·sku·po

bank	banka	ban·ka
post office	poštanski ured	po·shtan·skee oo·red
tourist office	turistička agencija	tu·ris·tich·ka a·gen·tsi·ya

Transport & Directions

boat	brod	brod
bus	autobus	a·u·to·bus
plane	zrakoplov (C)	zra·ko·plov
	avion (S)	a·vi·on
train	vlak (C)	vlak
	voz (S)	voz

One ... ticket (to Sarajevo), please.	Jednu ... kartu (do Sarajeva), molim.	yed·nu ... kar·tu (do sa·ra·ye·va) mo·lim
one-way	jedno-smjernu	yed·no-smyer·nu
return	povratnu	po·vrat·nu

Where's the ...?
Gdje je ...?   gdye ye ...

What's the address?
Koja je adresa?   ko·ya ye a·dre·sa

Can you show me (on the map)?
Možete li mi to   mo·zhe·te li mi to
pokazati (na karti)?   po·ka·za·ti (na kar·ti)

GREEK
Note that dh is pronounced as the 'th' in 'that', dz as the 'ds' in 'lads', and gh and kh are both throaty sounds, similar to the 'ch' in the Scottish loch.

Basics

Hello.	Γεια σου.	yia su
Goodbye.	Αντίο.	a·di·o
Excuse me.	Με συγχωρείτε.	me sing·kho·ri·te
Sorry.	Συγνώμη.	si·ghno·mi
Please.	Παρακαλώ.	pa·ra·ka·lo
Thank you.	Ευχαριστώ.	ef·kha·ri·sto
Yes.	Ναι.	ne
No.	Οχι.	o·hi

What's your name?
Πως σε λένε;   pos se le·ne

My name is ...
Με λένε ...   me le·ne ...

Do you speak English?
Μιλάς Αγγλικά;   mi·las ang·gli·ka

I don't understand.
Δεν καταλαβαίνω.   dhen ka·ta·la·ve·no

Accommodation

campsite	χώρος για κάμπινγκ	kho·ros yia kam·ping
guesthouse	ξενώνας	kse·no·nas
hotel	ξενοδοχείο	kse·no·dho·hi·o
youth hostel	γιουθ χόστελ	yiuth kho·stel

Do you have a single/double room?
Εχετε ένα μονό/   e·he·te e·na mo·no/
διπλό δωμάτιο;   dhi·plo dho·ma·ti·o

How much is it per night/person?
Πόσο είναι για κάθε   po·so i·ne yia ka·the
νύχτα/άτομο;   nikh·ta/a·to·mo

Signs – Greek	
Είσοδος	Entrance
Εξοδος	Exit
Ανοικτός	Open
Κλειστός	Closed
Απαγορεύεται	Prohibited
Τουαλέτες	Toilets

Eating & Drinking

What would you recommend?
Τι θα συνιστούσες; ti tha si·ni·*stu*·ses

Do you have vegetarian food?
Εχετε φαγητό για e·he·te fa·yi·*to* yia
χορτοφάγους; khor·to·*fa*·ghus

I'll have ...	Θα πάρω ...	tha *pa*·ro ...
Cheers!	Εις υγείαν!	is i·*yi*·an

I'd like the ...,	Θα ήθελα το ...,	tha *i*·the·la to ...
please.	παρακαλώ.	pa·ra·ka·*lo*
bill	λογαριασμό	lo·gha·riaz·*mo*
menu	μενού	me·*nu*

breakfast	πρόγευμα	pro·*yev*·ma
lunch	γεύμα	*yev*·ma
dinner	δείπνο	*dhip*·no

Emergencies

Help!	Βοήθεια!	vo·*i*·thia
Go away!	Φύγε!	*fi*·ye

Call ...!	Κάλεσε ...!	*ka*·le·se ...
a doctor	ένα γιατρό	*e*·na yia·*tro*
the police	την αστυνομία	tin a·sti·no·*mi*·a

I'm lost.
Εχω χαθεί. e·kho kha·*thi*

I'm ill.
Είμαι άρρωστος/ i·me a·ro·stos/
άρρωστη. (m/f) a·ro·sti

Where are the toilets?
Που είναι η τουαλέτα; pu *i*·ne i tu·a·*le*·ta

Shopping & Services

I'd like to buy ...
Θα ήθελα να tha *i*·the·la na
αγοράσω ... a·gho·*ra*·so ...

How much is it?
Πόσο κάνει; *po*·so *ka*·ni

It's too expensive.
Είναι πολύ ακριβό. *i*·ne po·*li* a·kri·*vo*

bank	τράπεζα	*tra*·pe·za
post office	ταχυδρομείο	ta·hi·dhro·*mi*·o
tourist office	τουριστικό	tu·ri·sti·*ko*
	γραφείο	ghra·*fi*·o

Numbers – Greek

1	ένας	*e*·nas
2	δύο	*dhi*·o
3	τρεις	tris
4	τέσσερις	*te*·se·ris
5	πέντε	*pe*·de
6	έξι	*ek*·si
7	εφτά	ef·*ta*
8	οχτώ	okh·*to*
9	εννέα	e·*ne*·a
10	δέκα	*dhe*·ka

Transport & Directions

boat	πλοίο	*pli*·o
bus	λεωφορείο	le·o·fo·*ri*·o
plane	αεροπλάνο	a·e·ro·*pla*·no
train	τρένο	*tre*·no

One ... ticket Ένα εισιτήριο ... *e*·na i·si·*ti*·ri·o ...
to (Patras), για την (Πάτρα), yia tin (*pa*·tra)
please. παρακαλώ. pa·ra·ka·*lo*
  one-way απλό a·*plo*
  return με επιστροφή me e·pi·stro·*fi*

Where's ...?
Που είναι ...? pu *i*·ne ...

What's the address?
Ποια είναι η διεύθυνση; pia *i*·ne i dhi·*ef*·thin·si

Can you show me (on the map)?
Μπορείς να μου δείξεις bo·*ris* na mu *dhik*·sis
(στο χάρτη); (sto *khar*·ti)

MACEDONIAN

Note that dz is pronounced as the 'ds' in 'adds', zh as the 's' in 'pleasure' and r is rolled.

Basics

Hello.	Здраво.	*zdra*·vo
Goodbye.	До гледање.	do *gle*·da·nye
Excuse me.	Извинете.	iz·*vi*·ne·te
Sorry.	Простете.	*pros*·te·te
Please.	Молам.	*mo*·lam
Thank you.	Благодарам.	bla·*go*·da·ram
Yes.	Да.	da
No.	Не.	ne

What's your name?
Како се викате/ *ka*·ko se *vi*·ka·te/
викаш? (pol/inf) *vi*·kash

My name is ...
Јас се викам ...　　yas se *vi*·kam ...

Do you speak English?
Зборувате ли　　zbo·*ru*·va·te li
англиски?　　an·*glis*·ki

I don't understand.
Јас не разбирам.　　yas ne *raz*·bi·ram

Accommodation

campsite	камп	kamp
guesthouse	приватно сместување	*pri*·vat·no smes·*tu*·va·nye
hotel	хотел	*ho*·tel
youth hostel	младинско преноќиште	*mla*·din·sko pre·*no*·kyish·te

Do you have a single/double room?
Дали имате　　*da*·li i·ma·te
еднокреветна/　　ed·no·*kre*·vet·na/
двокреветна соба?　　dvo·*kre*·vet·na *so*·ba

How much is it per night/person?
Која е цената за　　*ko*·ya e *tse*·na·ta za
ноќ/еден?　　noky/*e*·den

Eating & Drinking

What would you recommend?
Што препорачувате　　shto pre·po·ra·*chu*·va·te
вие?　　*vi*·e

Do you have vegetarian food?
Дали имате　　*da*·li i·ma·te
вегетаријанска храна?　　ve·ge·ta·ri·*yan*·ska *hra*·na

I'd like the bill/menu, please.
Ве молам сметката/　　ve *mo*·lam *smet*·ka·ta/
мени.　　me·*ni*

I'll have ...
Јас ќе земам ...　　yas kye ze·mam ...

Cheers!
На здравје!　　na *zdrav*·ye

breakfast	појадок	*po*·ya·dok
lunch	ручек	*ru*·chek
dinner	вечера	ve·*che*·ra

Signs – Macedonian
Влез	Entrance
Излез	Exit
Отворено	Open
Затворено	Closed
Забането	Prohibited
Клозети	Toilets

Emergencies

| Help! | Помош! | *po*·mosh |
| Go away! | Одете си! | o·*de*·te si |

Call the doctor/police!
Викнете лекар/　　*vik*·ne·te le·*kar*/
полиција!　　po·*li*·tsi·ya

I'm lost.
Се загубив.　　se za·*gu*·biv

I'm ill.
Јас сум болен/　　yas sum *bo*·len/
болна. (m/f)　　*bol*·na

Where are the toilets?
Каде се тоалетите?　　*ka*·de se to·a·*le*·ti·te

Shopping & Services

I'm looking for ...
Барам ...　　*ba*·ram ...

How much is it?
Колку чини тоа?　　*kol*·ku *chi*·ni *to*·a

That's too expensive.
Тоа е многу скапо.　　*to*·a e *mno*·gu *ska*·po

market	пазар	*pa*·zar
post office	пошта	*posh*·ta
tourist office	туристичко биро	tu·ris·*tich*·ko·to bi·*ro*

Transport & Directions

boat	брод	brod
bus	автобус	*av*·to·bus
plane	авион	a·vi·*on*
train	воз	voz

One ... ticket (to Ohrid), please.
Еден ...　　*e*·den ...
(за Охрид),　　(za *oh*·rid)
ве молам.　　ve *mo*·lam

one-way　билет во еден правец　*bi*·let vo *e*·den *pra*·vets

return　повратен билет　*pov*·ra·ten *bi*·let

Where's the ...?
Каде е ...?　　*ka*·de e ...

What's the address?
Која е адресата?　　*ko*·ya e ad·*re*·sa·ta

Can you show me (on the map)?
Можете ли да ми　　*mo*·zhe·te li da mi
покажете　　po·*ka*·zhe·te
(на картава)?　　(na *kar*·ta·va)

Numbers – Macedonian

1	еден	e·den
2	два	dva
3	три	tri
4	четири	che·ti·ri
5	пет	pet
6	шест	shest
7	седум	se·dum
8	осум	o·sum
9	девет	de·vet
10	десет	de·set

ROMANIAN

Note that ew is pronounced as 'ee' with rounded lips, oh as the 'o' in 'note', ow as in 'how', uh as the 'a' in 'ago', and zh as the 's' in 'pleasure'. The apostrophe (') indicates a very short, unstressed i (almost silent). The sounds y and w generally act as semivowels.

Basics

Hello.	Bună ziua.	boo·nuh zee·wa
Goodbye.	La revedere.	la re·ve·de·re
Excuse me.	Scuzaţi-mă.	skoo·za·tsee·muh
Sorry.	Îmi pare rău.	ewm' pa·re ruh·oo
Please.	Vă rog.	vuh rog
Thank you.	Mulţumesc.	mool·tsoo·mesk
Yes.	Da.	da
No.	Nu.	noo

What's your name?
Cum vă numiţi? koom vuh noo·meets'

My name is ...
Numele meu este ... noo·me·le me·oo yes·te ...

Do you speak English?
Vorbiţi engleza? vor·beets' en·gle·za

I don't understand.
Eu nu înţeleg. ye·oo noo ewn·tse·leg

Accommodation

campsite	teren de camping	te·ren de kem·peeng
guesthouse	pensiune	pen·syoo·ne
hotel	hotel	ho·tel
youth hostel	hostel	hos·tel
Do you have a ... room?	Aveţi o cameră ...?	a·vets' o ka·me·ruh ...
single	de o persoană	de o per·so·a·nuh
double	dublă	doo·bluh

How much is it per ...?	Cît costă ...?	kewt kos·tuh ...
night	pe noapte	pe no·ap·te
person	de persoană	de per·so·a·nuh

Eating & Drinking

What would you recommend?
Ce recomandaţi? che re·ko·man·dats'

Do you have vegetarian food?
Aveţi mâncare vegetariană? a·ve·tsi mewn·ka·re ve·je·ta·rya·nuh

I'll have ...	Aş dori ...	ash do·ree ...
Cheers!	Noroc!	no·rok
I'd like the ..., please.	Vă rog, aş dori ...	vuh rog ash do·ree ...
bill	nota de plată	no·ta de pla·tuh
menu	meniul	me·nee·ool
breakfast	micul dejun	mee·kool de·zhoon
lunch	dejun	de·zhoon
dinner	cină	chee·nuh

Emergencies

Help!	Ajutor!	a·zhoo·tor
Go away!	Pleacă!	ple·a·kuh
Call the ...!	Chemaţi ...!	ke·mats' ...
doctor	un doctor	oon dok·tor
police	poliţia	po·lee·tsya

I'm lost.
M-am rătăcit. mam ruh·tuh·cheet

I'm ill.
Mă simt rău. muh seemt ruh·oo

Where are the toilets?
Unde este o toaletă? oon·de yes·te o to·a·le·tuh

Signs – Romanian

Intrare	Entrance
Ieşire	Exit
Deschis	Open
Închis	Closed
Interzis	Prohibited
Toalete	Toilets

Numbers – Romanian		
1	*unu*	oo·noo
2	*doi*	doy
3	*trei*	trey
4	*patru*	pa·troo
5	*cinci*	cheench'
6	*şase*	sha·se
7	*şapte*	shap·te
8	*opt*	opt
9	*nouă*	no·wuh
10	*zece*	ze·che

Shopping & Services

I'm looking for ...
Caut ...   kowt ...

How much is it?
Cât costă?   kewt kos·tuh

That's too expensive.
E prea scump.   ye pre·a skoomp

market	*piaţă*	pya·tsuh
post office	*poşta*	posh·ta
tourist office	*biroul de informaţii turistice*	bee·ro·ool de een·for·ma·tsee too·rees·tee·che

Transport & Directions

boat	*vapor*	va·por
bus	*autobuz*	ow·to·booz
plane	*avion*	a·vyon
train	*tren*	tren

One ... ticket (to Cluj), please.
Un bilet ... (până la Cluj),vă rog.   oon bee·let ... (pew·nuh la kloozh) vuh rog

  one-way   *dus*   doos

  return   *dus-întors*   doos ewn·tors

Where's the ...?
Unde este ...?   oon·de yes·te ...

What's the address?
Care este adresa?   ka·re yes·te a·dre·sa

Can you show me (on the map)?
Puteţi să-mi arătaţi (pe hartă)?   poo·te·tsi suh·mi a·ruh·tats' (pe har·tuh)

SLOVENE

We've used the symbols oh (as the 'o' in 'note') and ow (as in 'how') to help you pronounce vowels followed by the letters *l* and *v* in written Slovene – at the end of a syllable these combinations produce a sound similar to the 'w' in English.

Note also that uh is pronounced as the 'a' in 'ago', zh as the 's' in 'pleasure', r is rolled, and the apostrophe (') indicates a slight y sound.

Basics

Hello.	*Zdravo.*	zdra·vo
Goodbye.	*Na svidenje.*	na svee·den·ye
Excuse me.	*Dovolite.*	do·vo·lee·te
Sorry.	*Oprostite.*	op·ros·tee·te
Please.	*Prosim.*	pro·seem
Thank you.	*Hvala.*	hva·la
Yes.	*Da.*	da
No.	*Ne.*	ne

What's your name?
Kako vam/ti je ime? (pol/inf)   ka·ko vam/tee ye ee·me

My name is ...
Ime mi je ...   ee·me mee ye ...

Do you speak English?
Ali govorite angleško?   a·lee go·vo·ree·te, ang·lesh·ko

I don't understand.
Ne razumem.   ne ra·zoo·mem

Accommodation

campsite	*kamp*	kamp
guesthouse	*gostišče*	gos·teesh·che
hotel	*hotel*	ho·tel
youth hostel	*mladinski hotel*	mla·deen·skee ho·tel

Do you have a single/double room?
Ali imate enoposteljno/ dvoposteljno sobo?   a·lee ee·ma·te e·no·pos·tel'·no/ dvo·pos·tel'·no so·bo

How much is it per night/person?
Koliko stane na noč/osebo?   ko·lee·ko sta·ne na noch/o·se·bo

Signs – Slovene	
Vhod	Entrance
Izhod	Exit
Odprto	Open
Zaprto	Closed
Prepovedano	Prohibited
Stranišče	Toilets

Numbers – Slovene		
1	*en*	en
2	*dva*	dva
3	*trije*	tree·ye
4	*štirje*	shtee·rye
5	*pet*	pet
6	*šest*	shest
7	*sedem*	se·dem
8	*osem*	o·sem
9	*devet*	de·vet
10	*deset*	de·set

Eating & Drinking

What would you recommend?
Kaj priporočate?   kai pree·po·ro·cha·te

Do you have vegetarian food?
Ali imate   a·lee ee·ma·te
vegetarijansko   ve·ge·ta·ree·yan·sko
hrano?   hra·no

I'll have ...	*Jaz bom ...*	yaz bom ...
Cheers!	*Na zdravje!*	na zdrav·ye

I'd like the ..., please.	*Želim ..., prosim.*	zhe·leem ... pro·seem
bill	*račun*	ra·choon
menu	*jedilni list*	ye·deel·nee leest
breakfast	*zajtrk*	zai·tuhrk
lunch	*kosilo*	ko·see·lo
dinner	*večerja*	ve·cher·ya

Emergencies

Help!	*Na pomoč!*	na po·moch
Go away!	*Pojdite stran!*	poy·dee·te stran

Call the doctor/police!
Pokličite   pok·lee·chee·te
zdravnika/   zdrav·nee·ka
policijo!   po·lee·tsee·yo

I'm lost.
Izgubil/   eez·goo·beew/
Izgubila sem se. (m/f)   eez·goo·bee·la sem se

I'm ill.
Bolan/Bolna   bo·lan/boh·na
sem. (m/f)   sem

Where are the toilets?
Kje je stranišče?   kye ye stra·neesh·che

Shopping & Services

I'm looking for ...
Iščem ...   eesh·chem ...

How much is this?
Koliko stane?   ko·lee·ko sta·ne

That's too expensive.
To je predrago.   to ye pre·dra·go

market	*tržnica*	tuhrzh·nee·tsa
post office	*pošta*	posh·ta
tourist office	*turistični urad*	too·rees·teech·nee oo·rad

Transport & Directions

boat	*ladja*	lad·ya
bus	*avtobus*	av·to·boos
plane	*letalo*	le·ta·lo
train	*vlak*	vlak

One ... ticket to (Koper), please.	*... vozovnico do (Kopra), prosim.*	... vo·zov·nee·tso do (ko·pra), pro·seem
one-way	*Enosmerno*	e·no·smer·no
return	*Povratno*	pov·rat·no

Where's the ...?
Kje je ...?   kye ye ...

What's the address?
Na katerem naslovu je?   na ka·te·rem nas·lo·voo ye

Can you show me (on the map)?
Mi lahko pokažete   mee lah·ko po·ka·zhe·te
(na zemljevidu)?   (na zem·lye·vee·doo)

TURKISH

Turkish is the official language in Turkey and the northern part of Cyprus.

Double vowels are pronounced twice. Also note that eu is pronounced as the 'u' in 'nurse', ew as 'ee' with rounded lips, uh as the 'a' in 'ago', zh as the 's' in 'pleasure', r is always rolled and v is a little softer than in English.

Basics

Hello.	*Merhaba.*	mer·ha·ba
Goodbye.	*Hoşçakal.* (if leaving)	hosh·cha·kal
	Güle güle. (if staying)	gew·le gew·le
Excuse me.	*Bakar mısınız.*	ba·kar muh·suh·nuhz
Sorry.	*Özür dilerim.*	eu·zewr dee·le·reem

Please.	Lütfen.	lewt·fen
Thank you.	Teşekkür ederim.	te·shek·kewr e·de·reem
Yes.	Evet.	e·vet
No.	Hayır.	ha·yuhr

What's your name?
Adınız nedir? — a·duh·nuhz ne·deer

My name is ...
Benim adım ... — be·neem a·duhm ...

Do you speak English?
İngilizce konuşuyor musunuz? — een·gee·leez·je ko·noo·shoo·yor moo·soo·nooz

I don't understand.
Anlamıyorum. — an·la·muh·yo·room

Accommodation

campsite	kamp yeri	kamp ye·ree
guesthouse	misafirhane	mee·sa·feer·ha·ne
hotel	otel	o·tel
youth hostel	gençlik hosteli	gench·leek hos·te·lee

Do you have a single/double room?
Tek/İki kişilik odanız var mı? — tek/ee·kee kee·shee·leek o·da·nuz var muh

How much is it per night/person?
Geceliği/Kişi başına ne kadar? — ge·je·lee·ee/kee·shee ba·shuh·na ne ka·dar

Eating & Drinking

What would you recommend?
Ne tavsiye edersiniz? — ne tav·see·ye e·der·see·neez

Do you have vegetarian food?
Vejeteryan yiyecekleriniz var mı? — ve·zhe·ter·yan yee·ye·jek·le·ree·neez var muh

I'll have ...	... alayım.	... a·la·yuhm
Cheers!	Şerefe!	she·re·fe
I'd like the ...	... istiyorum.	... ees·tee·yo·room
bill	Hesabı	he·sa·buh
menu	Menüyü	me·new·yew
breakfast	kahvaltı	kah·val·tuh
lunch	öğle yemeği	eu·le ye·me·ee
dinner	akşam yemeği	ak·sham ye·me·ee

Emergencies

| Help! | İmdat! | eem·dat |
| Go away! | Git burdan! | geet boor·dan |

Call ...!	... çağırın!	... cha·uh·ruhn
a doctor	Doktor	dok·tor
the police	Polis	po·lees

I'm lost.
Kayboldum. — kai·bol·doom

I'm ill.
Hastayım. — has·ta·yuhm

Where are the toilets?
Tuvaletler nerede? — too·va·let·ler ne·re·de

Shopping & Services

I'd like to buy ...
... almak istiyorum. — ... al·mak ees·tee·yo·room

How much is it?
Ne kadar? — ne ka·dar

It's too expensive.
Bu çok pahalı. — boo chok pa·ha·luh

ATM	bankamatik	ban·ka·ma·teek
post office	postane	pos·ta·ne
tourist office	turizm bürosu	too·reezm bew·ro·soo

Transport & Directions

boat	vapur	va·poor
bus	otobüs	o·to·bews
plane	uçak	oo·chak
train	tren	tren

Numbers – Turkish		
1	bir	beer
2	iki	ee·kee
3	üç	ewch
4	dört	dert
5	beş	besh
6	altı	al·tuh
7	yedi	ye·dee
8	sekiz	se·keez
9	dokuz	do·kooz
10	on	on

I'd like a ...	*(Bostancı'ya)*	(bos·*tan*·juh·ya)
ticket to	*... bir bilet*	... beer bee·*let*
(Bostancı).	*lütfen.*	*lewt*·fen
one-way	*Gidiş*	gee·*deesh*
return	*Gidiş-*	gee·deesh·
	dönüş	deu·*newsh*

Where is ...?
... nerede? ... ne·re·de

Can you show me (on the map)?
Bana (haritada) ba·*na* (ha·ree·ta·*da*)
gösterebilir geus·te·re·bee·leer
misiniz? mee·seen·*neez*

Signs – Turkish	
Giriş	Entrance
Çıkışı	Exit
Açık	Open
Kapalı	Closed
Yasak	Prohibited
Tuvaletler	Toilets

What's the address?
Adresi nedir? ad·re·*see* ne·deer

LANGUAGE TURKISH

Behind the Scenes

SEND US YOUR FEEDBACK

We love to hear from travellers – your comments keep us on our toes and help make our books better. Our well-travelled team reads every word on what you loved or loathed about this book. Although we cannot reply individually to postal submissions, we always guarantee that your feedback goes straight to the appropriate authors, in time for the next edition. Each person who sends us information is thanked in the next edition – the most useful submissions are rewarded with a selection of digital PDF chapters.

Visit **lonelyplanet.com/contact** to submit your updates and suggestions or to ask for help. Our award-winning website also features inspirational travel stories, news and discussions.

Note: We may edit, reproduce and incorporate your comments in Lonely Planet products such as guidebooks, websites and digital products, so let us know if you don't want your comments reproduced or your name acknowledged. For a copy of our privacy policy visit lonelyplanet.com/privacy.

AUTHOR THANKS

Marika McAdam

Thanks as always to my fellow authors for turning hard work and on-the-road adventures into so many great chapters. Thank you to my handsome husband Jo for supporting me in every journey I've embarked on since our worlds first collided in Bangladesh. And eternal thanks to ever-inspiring Mum and Dad McAdam for taking me travelling throughout childhood, and always having the good sense to pack a Lonely Planet.

Alexis Averbuck

Hail Alexandra Stamopoulou for her spot-on recommendations. Marina Flenga was a superlative fairy godmother, connecting me to those in the know. Marilee Anargyrou Kyriazakou and Cali Doxiadis (in Kerkyra), Eleni Doxiadi (in Lefkada) and Manita Scocimara-Ponghis (in Kefallonia) shared their love and knowledge of their islands. In Athens, Lena Lambrinou decoded the Acropolis and Elina Lychoudi the nightlife. Anthy and Costas, as well as Margarita Kontzia and Kostas Karakatsanis, made it home.

James Bainbridge

A heartfelt çok teşekkürler, once again, to everyone who helped me find my way around the steppe on my last visit to northeastern Turkey. Celil in Kars and Necmettin in Akçaabat deserve special mention for your help on a few recent projects. Thanks, as ever, to everyone at Lonely Planet – Tom, Dora, Angela, James, Cliff et al – and to my wife Leigh-Robin.

Mark Baker

I met many helpful people all along the way in researching three countries for this guide and their names would too numerous to mention here. I've lived in Prague for two decades now and a very special thanks to my good friends here; in Slovenia, the staff of the Slovenia Tourist Board deserve special mention.

Chris Deliso

As always a number of kind and helpful Macedonians (and other folks too), provided good tips, advice and assistance in the course of my research. Among them I can mention Pece, Patrice, Stevche, Emilija, Biljana, Dane, Stojko. Ace and Julija – you know who you are! Of course, this book couldn't have been completed without the work of my patient and devoted Lonely Planet colleagues, including Katie O'Connell, the map-making and production teams.

Peter Dragicevich

Many thanks to all the wonderful people who helped me in Montenegro, especially Ivica Erdelja, Hayley Wright and Jack Delf, Emma and Ben Heywood, Krstinja Petranović, Danica

Ćeranić and Matthew Lane. Also, I owe a debt of gratitude to James and Lorraine Hedderman, Tim Benzie and Kerri Tyler for their contributions before and after the journey.

Mark Elliott

Many thanks to Wieland de Hoon, Hans Rossel, Guy Jacobs, Dani Systermans, Lesley Devos, Valerie de Kerpel, Sharon Taylor, Jan Beran, Mišo Marić and the helpful folks at Travellers Home and New Age hostels. As ever my greatest thanks go to my endlessly inspiring family for so much liberating love.

Tom Masters

An enormous debt of thanks to all my hardworking fellow authors on this book, and the teams in London and Melbourne who commissioned, edited and oversaw the project. Special thanks in Albania to Ardi Pulaj, Catherine Bohne, Tedi Sina and Bledi Strakosha; and in Kosovo to Hekuran Avdyli and the folks at Libertas in Pristina.

Craig McLachlan

A hearty thanks to all those who helped me out on the road, but most of all, to my exceptionally beautiful wife, Yuriko, who let me know when I'd had my daily quota of Mythos and gyros pitta.

Anja Mutić

Hvala mama, for your home cooking and contagious laughter. *Obrigada*, Hoji, for being there before, during and after. A huge *hvala* to my friends in Croatia who gave me endless recommendations – this book wouldn't be the same without you. Special thanks go to Lidija in Zagreb and Mila in Split, as well as the team at HTZ. Finally, to the inspiring memory of my father who travels with me still.

Tamara Sheward

To research here is to make a zillion friends, so in addition to thanking the population of Serbia, I'd like to offer clinks of the *rakija* glass and *mnogo hvala na*… the NS Kiosk Crew, Gagi of Niš, Toma of Mokra Gora, Zoran for saving us from snakes and wolves, all the helpful oddballs we met during our *medeni mesec*/research jaunt, Dragana Eremić, the Ljesević family, the Lučić clan, Pappa and Mumma, and as ever, to Dušan, *najbolje, najslađi čovek u svemiru*!

ACKNOWLEDGMENTS

Climate map data adapted from Peel MC, Finlayson BL & McMahon TA (2007) 'Updated World Map of the Köppen-Geiger Climate Classification', Hydrology and Earth System Sciences, 11, 1633-44.

Cover photograph: Stari Most, Mostar, Bosnia and Hercegovina, Richard l'Anson/ Getty Images.

THIS BOOK

Many people have helped to create this 1st edition of Lonely Planet's *Southeastern Europe* guidebook, which is part of Lonely Planet's Europe series. Other titles in this series include *Western Europe*, *Eastern Europe*, *Mediterranean Europe*, *Central Europe*, *Scandinavia* and *Europe on a Shoestring*. This guidebook was commissioned in Lonely Planet's London office, and produced by the following:

Commissioning Editors Erin Corrigan, Jo Cooke, Lucy Monie Hall, James Smart
Coordinating Editor Samantha Forge
Coordinating Cartographer Valentina Kremenchutskaya
Coordinating Layout Designer Lauren Egan
Managing Editors Annelies Mertens, Angela Tinson
Managing Cartographers Adrian Persoglia, Anthony Phelan, Amanda Sierp
Managing Layout Designer Chris Girdler
Assisting Editors Briohny Hooper, Anne Mason

Assisting Cartographers Xavier Di Toro
Assisting Layout Designer Frank Deim
Cover Research Kylie McLaughlin
Internal Image Research Aude Vauconsant
Language Content Branislava Vladisavljevic
Thanks to Elin Berglund, Laura Crawford, Ryan Evans, Larissa Frost, Genesys India, Jouve India, Andi Jones, Darren O'Connell, Trent Paton, Dianne Schallmeiner, Kerrianne Southway, Gerard Walker, Amanda Williamson

index

000 Map pages
000 Photo pages

how to use this book

These symbols will help you find the listings you want:

- ⊙ Sights
- 🏄 Beaches
- 🏃 Activities
- 🎓 Courses
- 👉 Tours
- 🎪 Festivals & Events
- 🛏 Sleeping
- 🍴 Eating
- 🍺 Drinking
- ⭐ Entertainment
- 🛍 Shopping
- ℹ Information/Transport

Look out for these icons:

- **TOP** CHOICE — Our author's recommendation
- **FREE** — No payment required
- 🌿 — A green or sustainable option

Our authors have nominated these places as demonstrating a strong commitment to sustainability – for example by supporting local communities and producers, operating in an environmentally friendly way, or supporting conservation projects.

These symbols give you the vital information for each listing:

- 📞 Telephone Numbers
- 🕐 Opening Hours
- P Parking
- ⊖ Nonsmoking
- ❄ Air-Conditioning
- @ Internet Access
- 🔊 Wi-Fi Access
- 🏊 Swimming Pool
- 🥗 Vegetarian Selection
- 🍴 English-Language Menu
- 👶 Family-Friendly
- 🐾 Pet-Friendly
- 🚌 Bus
- ⛴ Ferry
- Ⓜ Metro
- Ⓢ Subway
- 🚇 London Tube
- 🚊 Tram
- 🚆 Train

Reviews are organised by author preference.

Map Legend

Sights
- 🏄 Beach
- 🛕 Buddhist
- 🏰 Castle
- ✝ Christian
- 🕉 Hindu
- ☪ Islamic
- ✡ Jewish
- ◉ Monument
- 🏛 Museum/Gallery
- 🏚 Ruin
- 🍇 Winery/Vineyard
- 🐾 Zoo
- ⊙ Other Sight

Activities, Courses & Tours
- 🤿 Diving/Snorkelling
- 🛶 Canoeing/Kayaking
- ⛷ Skiing
- 🏄 Surfing
- 🏊 Swimming/Pool
- 🚶 Walking
- 🏄 Windsurfing
- ⊙ Other Activity/Course/Tour

Sleeping
- 🛏 Sleeping
- ⛺ Camping

Eating
- 🍴 Eating

Drinking
- ☕ Drinking
- ☕ Cafe

Entertainment
- 🎭 Entertainment

Shopping
- 🛍 Shopping

Information
- 💰 Bank
- 🏛 Embassy/Consulate
- ➕ Hospital/Medical
- @ Internet
- 👮 Police
- ✉ Post Office
- ☎ Telephone
- 🚻 Toilet
- ℹ Tourist Information
- ● Other Information

Transport
- ✈ Airport
- ⊗ Border Crossing
- 🚌 Bus
- 🚡 Cable Car/Funicular
- 🚲 Cycling
- ⛴ Ferry
- 🚝 Monorail
- P Parking
- ⛽ Petrol Station
- 🚕 Taxi
- 🚆 Train/Railway
- 🚊 Tram
- Ⓜ Underground Train Station
- ● Other Transport

Routes
- Tollway
- Freeway
- Primary
- Secondary
- Tertiary
- Lane
- Unsealed Road
- Plaza/Mall
- Steps
- Tunnel
- Pedestrian Overpass
- Walking Tour
- Walking Tour Detour
- Path

Geographic
- 🏠 Hut/Shelter
- 🗼 Lighthouse
- 👁 Lookout
- ▲ Mountain/Volcano
- 🌴 Oasis
- 🌳 Park
-)(Pass
- 🏕 Picnic Area
- 💧 Waterfall

Population
- ★ Capital (National)
- ◉ Capital (State/Province)
- ● City/Large Town
- ● Town/Village

Boundaries
- — — — International
- ———— State/Province
- — — Disputed
- – – Regional/Suburb
- Marine Park
- Cliff
- Wall

Hydrography
- River, Creek
- Intermittent River
- Swamp/Mangrove
- Reef
- Canal
- Water
- Dry/Salt/Intermittent Lake
- Glacier

Areas
- Beach/Desert
- +++ Cemetery (Christian)
- ××× Cemetery (Other)
- Park/Forest
- Sportsground
- Sight (Building)
- Top Sight (Building)

Chris Deliso

Macedonia Chris Deliso, an American travel writer and journalist, has been based in Macedonia for more than a decade and has written considerably about the country since then for a range of world media. In addition to covering Macedonia for this book, he has contributed to Lonely Planet guides to Greece, Crete, Turkey, Romania and Bulgaria. His original enthusiasm for the region and introduction to its cultures and history came with an MPhil in Byzantine Studies at Oxford University in 1999.

Peter Dragicevich

Montenegro After a dozen years working for newspapers and magazines in both his native New Zealand and Australia, Peter ditched the desk and hit the road. While it was family ties that first drew him to the Balkans, it's the history, natural beauty and the intriguing people that keep bringing him back. He wrote Lonely Planet's first guide to the newly independent Montenegro and has contributed to dozens of other Lonely Planet titles.

Mark Elliott

Bosnia & Hercegovina British-born travel writer Mark Elliott was only 11 when his family first dragged him to Sarajevo and stood him in the now defunct concrete footsteps of Gavrilo Princip. Fortunately no Austro-Hungarian emperors were passing at the time. He has since visited virtually every corner of Bosnia and Hercegovina, supping fine Hercegovinian wines with master vintners, talking philosophy with Serb monks and Sufi mystics, and drinking more Bosnian coffee than any healthy stomach should be subjected to.

Tom Masters

Albania, Kosovo Tom is a British writer and photographer whose work has taken him to some of the strangest and most challenging countries on earth. Having lived in Russia, travelled to all corners of eastern Europe in the decade that he's been working on the *Eastern Europe* guide and currently residing in East Berlin, he has a good understanding of what makes the former communist world tick. Tom wrote the Albania and Kosovo chapters of this book. You can find more of Tom's work at www.tommasters.net.

Craig McLachlan

Greece Craig has covered the Greek Islands for the last five editions of Lonely Planet's Europe guidebooks. He runs an outdoor activity company in Queenstown, New Zealand in the southern-hemisphere summer, then heads north for another summer, writing for Lonely Planet and leading tours all over the world, including Greece. A 'freelance anything', he has an MBA from the University of Hawaii and leads other lives as a pilot, karate instructor and Japanese interpreter. Check out www.craigmclachlan.com

Anja Mutić

Croatia It's been more than two decades since Anja left her native Croatia. The journey took her to several countries before she made New York City her base 13 years ago. But the roots are a'calling. She's been returning to Croatia frequently for work and play. She's happy that Croatia's beauties are appreciated worldwide but secretly longs for the time when you could head to Hvar and hear the sound of crickets instead of blasting music. Anja is online at www.everthenomad.com.

Tamara Sheward

Serbia After years of freelance travel writing, rock'n'roll journalism and insalubrious authordom, Tamara joined the Lonely Planet ranks as the presenter of LPTV's Roads Less Travelled: Cambodia documentary. Since then, she's stuck to covering decidedly less leech-infested destinations including arctic Russia and Serbia. She lives between northern Serbia, a mountain shack in Montenegro and Melbourne with her husband Dušan, whom she never would have met were it not for some late night "researching" for the last edition of *Eastern Europe*.

OUR STORY

A beat-up old car, a few dollars in the pocket and a sense of adventure. In 1972 that's all Tony and Maureen Wheeler needed for the trip of a lifetime – across Europe and Asia overland to Australia. It took several months, and at the end – broke but inspired – they sat at their kitchen table writing and stapling together their first travel guide, *Across Asia on the Cheap*. Within a week they'd sold 1500 copies. Lonely Planet was born.

Today, Lonely Planet has offices in Melbourne, London and Oakland, with more than 600 staff and writers. We share Tony's belief that 'a great guidebook should do three things: inform, educate and amuse'.

OUR WRITERS

Marika McAdam

Coordinating Author A lawyer by training and a traveller by conviction, Marika first started working at Lonely Planet's Melbourne office as a teenager, stuffing envelopes in the marketing department and packing books in the warehouse. Since becoming an author, she has written about places including Bangladesh, Goa, Poland and the Western Balkans. When she is not travel writing, she works as an independent consultant on human trafficking, migrant smuggling and other issues mostly for the United Nations. Marika is also a member of a research ethics review committee and is currently working towards a PhD in human rights law.

Alexis Averbuck

Greece Alexis Averbuck lives on Hydra, takes regular reverse R&R in Athens (she wrote *Pocket Athens*), and makes any excuse she can to travel the isolated back roads of her adopted land. She is committed to dispelling the stereotype that Greece is simply a string of sandy beaches. A travel writer for two decades, Alexis has lived in Antarctica for a year, crossed the Pacific by sailboat and written books on her journeys through Asia and the Americas. She's also a painter – visit www.alexisaverbuck.com.

James Bainbridge

Turkey Media assignments and extra-curricular wanderings have taken James to most of Turkey's far-flung regions, from Aegean islands to the eastern steppe via Cappadocia's surreal rock formations. He has coordinated three editions of Lonely Planet's Turkey guide, and deepened his local knowledge by living in İstanbul and grappling with suffixes on a Turkish course. For articles on Turkey, and a link to a blog with advice about travel writing, visit James's website at www.jamesbainbridge.net.

Read more about James at:
lonelyplanet.com/members/james_bains

Mark Baker

Bulgaria, Romania, Slovenia Based permanently in Prague, Mark has lived and worked in Central Europe for more than 20 years, first as a journalist for The Economist Group and then for Bloomberg News and Radio Free Europe/Radio Liberty. He travels frequently throughout the region and counts Bulgaria, Slovenia and Romania among his favourite countries in Europe. In addition to this book, Mark is co-author of the Lonely Planet guides to Prague, Slovenia, Romania and Bulgaria.

OVER PAGE — MORE WRITERS

Published by Lonely Planet Publications Pty Ltd
ABN 36 005 607 983
1st edition – Oct 2013
ISBN 978 1 74179 580 6
© Lonely Planet 2013 Photographs © as indicated 2013
10 9 8 7 6 5 4 3 2 1
Printed in China